A Complete History of Illinois from 1673 to 1873, etc.

Alexander Davidson, Bernard Stuvé

A Complete History of Illinois from 1673 to 1873, etc.
Davidson, Alexander
British Library, Historical Print Editions
British Library
Stuvé, Bernard
1874
x, 944 p. ; 8º.
9602.dd.7.

The BiblioLife Network

This project was made possible in part by the BiblioLife Network (BLN), a project aimed at addressing some of the huge challenges facing book preservationists around the world. The BLN includes libraries, library networks, archives, subject matter experts, online communities and library service providers. We believe every book ever published should be available as a high-quality print reproduction; printed on- demand anywhere in the world. This insures the ongoing accessibility of the content and helps generate sustainable revenue for the libraries and organizations that work to preserve these important materials.

The following book is in the "public domain" and represents an authentic reproduction of the text as printed by the original publisher. While we have attempted to accurately maintain the integrity of the original work, there are sometimes problems with the original book or micro-film from which the books were digitized. This can result in minor errors in reproduction. Possible imperfections include missing and blurred pages, poor pictures, markings and other reproduction issues beyond our control. Because this work is culturally important, we have made it available as part of our commitment to protecting, preserving, and promoting the world's literature.

GUIDE TO FOLD-OUTS, MAPS and OVERSIZED IMAGES

In an online database, page images do not need to conform to the size restrictions found in a printed book. When converting these images back into a printed bound book, the page sizes are standardized in ways that maintain the detail of the original. For large images, such as fold-out maps, the original page image is split into two or more pages.

Guidelines used to determine the split of oversize pages:

• Some images are split vertically; large images require vertical and horizontal splits.
• For horizontal splits, the content is split left to right.
• For vertical splits, the content is split from top to bottom.
• For both vertical and horizontal splits, the image is processed from top left to bottom right.

A

COMPLETE

HISTORY OF ILLINOIS

FROM

1673 TO 1873;

EMBRACING

THE PHYSICAL FEATURES OF THE COUNTRY; ITS
EARLY EXPLORATIONS; ABORIGINAL INHABITANTS;
FRENCH AND BRITISH OCCUPATION ; CONQUEST
BY VIRGINIA; TERRITORIAL CONDITION AND
THE SUBSEQUENT CIVIL, MILITARY AND
POLITICAL EVENTS OF THE STATE.

BY

ALEXANDER DAVIDSON AND BERNARD STUVÉ.

SPRINGFIELD:
ILLINOIS JOURNAL COMPANY,
1874.

STEREOTYPED BY THE
ILLINOIS STATE JOURNAL COMPANY.

TABLE OF CONTENTS.

Chapters 1, 2, 3, 4, 5, 6, 7, 8, 9, 10, 11, 12, 13, 14, 16, 17, 32, 33, 34, 35, 41, 42, 54, 55, 56, 57, 58, 59, 60, 61, 62, 63, 64; the Death of Lovejoy in 36, and "Note, Conspiracy of Chicago," in 65, have been written by Mr. DAVIDSON.

Chapters 15, 18, 19, 20, 21, 22, 23, 24, 25, 26, 27, 28, 29, 30, 31, 36, 37, 38, 39, 40, 43, 44, 45, 46, 47, 48, 49, 50, 51, 52, 53, 65, 66 and 67, have been written by Mr. STUVÉ.

PREFACE.

Although Illinois, whose grassy plains have been styled the Eden of the new world, contains the oldest permanent settlements in the Valley of the Mississippi, and in her strides to empire is destined to become the first State of the Union, her history has been strangely neglected. Fragments have been written at different times but only of detached periods and embracing but a small part of the two centuries, which have elapsed since the first explorations. To supply this deficiency and furnish a history commensurate with her present advancement in power and civilization is the object of the present work; whether it has been accomplished remains to be seen.

Not having taken any part in the shifting and instructive drama enacted by those who have directed the affairs of State, no rankling jealousies have been engendered to distort conclusions; no undue predelections to warp the judgement. Measures have been estimated by their results; men by their public acts. While no disposition has existed to assail any one, it must be remembered that none are faultless, and to speak well of all is the worst of detraction, for it places the good and the bad on a common level.

A principal aim has been to render the the work complete. A large amount of matter has been inserted never before published in connection with the history of the State; yet important facts, though familiar, have always been preferred to new ones of minor significance. The main consideration, however, has been to render it truthful. In the wide field which has been gleaned, every available source of information has been carefully consulted, and it is believed a degree of accuracy has been secured, which will compare favorably with that of other similar efforts. Still there will always be room for improvement, and any corrections which may be offered by parties who have witnessed, or been connected with events described, will be thankfully received and inserted in future editions of the work, the object being to make it a complete repository of reliable facts for the general reader, the politician, the lawyer, and all who may wish to become acquainted with the history of our noble State.

To the many in different parts of the State, who have furnished information, or aided us by valuable suggestions, we return our thanks, especially to Messrs. Rummel and Harlow, Secretaries of State, for the use of public documents, and to the proprietors of the *State Journal* and *State Register,* for access to their valuable files.

SPRINGFIELD, Dec. 19th, 1873.

CHAPTER I.

GEOLOGY OF ILLINOIS.

On the geological structure of a country depend the pursuits of
its inhabitants and the genius of its civilization. Agriculture is the
outgrowth of a fertile soil; mining results from mineral resources;
and from navigable waters spring navies and commerce. Every
great branch of industry requires, for its successful development,
the cultivation of kindred arts and sciences. Phases of life and
modes of thought are thus induced, which give to different communities and states characters as various as the diverse rocks
that underlie them. In like manner it may be shown that their
moral and intellectual qualities depend on material conditions.
Where the soil and subjacent rocks are profuse in the bestowal of
wealth, man is indolent and effeminate; where effort is required to
live, he becomes enlightened and virtuous; and where, on the sands
of the desert, labor is unable to procure the necessaries and comforts of life, he lives a savage. The civilization of states and
nations is, then, to a great extent, but the reflection of physical
conditions, and hence the propriety of introducing their civil, political and military history with a sketch of the geological substruc-
ture from which they originate.

GEOLOGY traces the history of the earth back through successive
stages of development to its rudimental condition in a state of
fusion. Speculative astronomy extends it beyond this to a gaseous
state, in which it and the other bodies of the solar system constituted a nebulous mass, without form and motion. When, in the
process of development, motion was communicated to the chaotic
matter, huge fragments were detached from its circumference,
which formed the primary planets. These retaining the rotary
motion of the sun, or central mass, in turn threw off other and
smaller fragments, thus forming the secondary planets, as in the
case of the moon which attends the earth. All these bodies are
similar in form, have a similar motion on their axes, move substantially in a common plain and in the same direction, the result of
the projectile force which detached them from the parent mass.
These facts are strong evidence that the sun, and the planetary
system that revolves around it, were originally a common mass,
and became separated in a gaseous state, as the want of cohesion
among the particles would then favor the dissevering force. From
the loss of heat they next passed into a fluid or plastic state, the
point in the history of the earth where it comes within the range
of geological investigation.

While in this condition it became flattened at the poles, a form
due to its diurnal rotation and the mobility of its particles. At a

further reduction of temperature its melted disk was transformed into a crust of igneous rock. A great many facts render it almost certain that the vast nucleus within this enveloping crust is still an incandescent mass. Compared with its enormous bulk, the external covering is of only filmy thickness, the ratio of the two being as the pulp and peel of an orange. In this world-crucible are held in solution the 61 elementary substances, which, variously combining, produce the great variety of forms, energies and modes of being, which diversify and enliven terrestrial nature. From the same source the precious metals have been forced into the fissures of the superincumbent rocks, whither the miner descends and brings them to the surface. Volcanoes are outlets for the tremendous forces generated in these deep-seated fires. As an evidence of their eruptive power, Vesuvius sometimes throws jets of lava, resembling columns of flame, 10,000 feet in hight. The amount of lava ejected at a single eruption from one of the volcanoes of Iceland, has been estimated at 40,000,000,000 tons, a quantity sufficient to cover a large city with a mountain as high as the tallest Alps. By the process of congelation, which has never ceased, the rocky crust which rests on this internal sea of fire, is now supposed to be from thirty to forty miles in thickness. The outer or upper portion of it was the most universal geological formation, and constituted the floors of the primitive oceans. The rocks composing it are designated unstratified, because they occur in irregular masses, and igneous from having originally been melted by intense heat. The vast cycle of time extending through their formation and reaching down to the introduction of life on the globe, constitutes the *Azoic age*. The earth's surface, consisting of arid wastes and boiling waters, and its atmosphere reeking with poisonous gases, were wholly incompatible with the existence of plants and animals. By the continued radiation of heat the nucleus within the hardened crust contracted, and the latter, to adapt itself to the diminished bulk, folded into huge corrugations, forming the primitive mountain chains and the first land that appeared above the face of the waters. The upheaval of these vast plications was attended with depressions in other parts of the surface constituting the valleys and basins of the original rivers and oceans. Through the agency of water the uplifted masses were disintegrated and the resulting sediment swept into the extended depressions. Here it settled in parallel layers and constitutes the stratified rocks. In some localities these are entirely wanting, in others many miles in depth, while their average thickness is supposed to be from six to eight miles.

The plain, separating the stratified from the unstratified rocks, runs parallel with the oldest part of the earth's crust. When solidification commenced it was the surface, and as induration advanced toward the centre the crust thickened by increments on the inside, and, therefore, the most recently formed igneous rocks are the farthest below the surface. Stratification commenced at the same plain and extended in an upward direction, and hence the most recent deposits are nearest the surface, when not displaced by disturbing causes.

In the silent depths of the stratified rocks are the former creations of plants and animals, which lived and died during the slow, dragging centuries of their formation. These fossil remains are fragments of history, which enable the geologist to extend his researches far back into the realms of the past, and not only determine their former modes of life, but study the contemporaneous history of their rocky beds, and group them into systems. The fossiliferous rocks are not only of great thickness but frequently their entire structure is an aggregation of cemented shells, so numerous that millions of them occur in a single cubic foot. Such has been the profusion of life that the great limestone formations of the globe consist mostly of animal remains, cemented by the infusion of mineral matter. A large part of the soil spread over the earth's surface has been elaborated in animal organisms. First, as nourishment, it enters the structure of plants and forms vegetable tissue. Passing thence as food into the animal, it becomes endowed with life, and when death occurs it returns to the soil and imparts to it additional elements of fertility. The different systems of stratified rocks, as determined by their organic remains, are usually denominated Ages or Systems.

The Laurentian System or *Age* is the lowest, and therefore the oldest, of the stratified series. From the effects of great heat it has assumed, to some extent, the character of the igneous rocks below, but still retains its original lines of stratification. A principal effect of the great heat to which its rocks were exposed is crystalization. Crystals are frequently formed by art, but the most beautiful specimens are the products of nature's laboratories, deep-seated in the crust of the earth. The Laurentian system was formerly supposed to be destitute of organic remains, but recent investigations have lead to the discovery of animals so low in the scale of organization as to be regarded as the first appearance of sentient existence. This discovery, as it extends the origin of life backward through 30,000 feet of strata, may be regarded as one of the most important advances made in American geology. Its supposed beginning, in a considerable degree of advancement in the Silurian system, was regarded by geologists as too abrupt to correspond with the gradual development of types in subsequent strata. The discovery, however, of these incipient forms in the Laurentian beds, renders the descending scale of life complete, and verifies the conjectures of physicists that in its earliest dawn it should commence with the most simple organisms.

The Huronian System, like the one that precedes it, and on which it rests, is highly crystalline. Although fossils have not been found in it, yet from its position the inference is they once existed, and if they do not now, the great transforming power of heat has caused their obliteration. This, and the subjacent system, extend from Labrador southwesterly to the great lakes, and thence northwesterly toward the Arctic Ocean. They derive their names from the St. Lawrence and Lake Huron, on the banks of which are found their principal outcrops. Their emergence from the ocean was the birth of the North American continent. One face of the uplift looked toward the Atlantic, and the other toward the Pacific, thus prefiguring the future shores of this great division of the globe, of which they are the germ. Eruptive forces have not operated with sufficient power to bring them to the surface in Illinois, and therefore the vast stores of mineral wealth, which they contain in other places, if they exist here, are too deep below the surface to be made available.

The Silurian Age, compared with the more stable formations of subsequent times, was one of commotion, in which fire and water played a conspicuous part. Earthquakes and volcanoes furrowed the yielding crust with ridges, and threw up islands whose craggy summits, here and there, stood like sentinels above the murky deep which dashed against their shores. The present diversities of climate did not exist, as the temperature was mostly due to the escape of internal heat, which was the same over every part of the surface. As the radiation of heat in future ages declined, the sun became the controlling power, and zones of climate appeared as the result of solar domination. Uniform thermal conditions imparted a corresponding character to vegetable and animal life, and one universal fauna and flora extended from the equator to the poles. These hardy marine types consisted of Radiates, Mollusks and Articulates, three of the four sub-kingdoms of animal life. Seaweed, which served as food for the animals, was the only plant of which any traces remain. During the Silurian age North America, like its inhabitants, was mostly submarine, as proved by wave-lines on the emerging lands. There lay along the eastern border of the continent an extended ridge, which served as a breakwater to the waves of the Atlantic. The region of the Alleghanies was subject to great elevations and depressions, and the latter largely preponderating, caused the deposit of some twelve thousand feet of strata. Although mostly under water, there was added to the original nucleus of the continent formations now found in New York, Michigan, Illinois, Wisconsin and Minnesota. Niagara limestone, a Silurian formation, is found over a large extent of country in northern Illinois, beyond the limits of the coal-fields. It is a compact grayish stone, susceptible of a high polish, and at Athens and Joliet is extensively quarried for building purposes, and shipped to different parts of the State. The new Capitol is being erected of this material. The Galena limestone, another Silurian deposit, is interesting, from the fact that it contains the lead and zinc ores of the State. St. Peters sandstone belongs also to the same system. Besides outcropping in a number of other localities, it appears in the bluffs of the Illinois, where it forms the island-like plateau known as Starved Rock. In some localities, being composed almost entirely of silica and nearly free from coloring matter, it is the best material in the West for the manufacture of glass.

The Devonian Age is distinguished for the introduction of Vertebrates, or the fourth sub-kingdom of animal life and the beginning of terrestrial vegetation. The latter appeared in two classes, the highest of the flowerless and the lowest of the flowering plants. The Lepidodendron, a noted instance of the former, was a majestic upland forest tree, which, during the coal period, grew to a light of 80 feet, and had a base of more than 3 feet in diameter. Beautiful spiral flutings, coiling in opposite directions and crossing each other at fixed angles, carved the trunks and branches into rhomboidal eminences, each of which was scarred with the mark of a falling leaf. At an altitude of 60 feet it sent off arms, each separating into branchlets covered with a needle-like foliage, destitute of flowers. It grew, not by internal or external accretions, as plants of the present day, but like the building of a monument, by additions to the top of its trunk. Mosses, rushes and other diminutive flowerless plants are now the only surviving representative of this cryptogamic vegetation, which so largely predominated in the early botany of the globe. Floral beauty and fragrance were not characteristic of the old Devonian woods. No bird existed to enliven their silent groves with song, no serpent to hiss in their fenny brakes, nor beast to pursue, with hideous yells, its panting prey.

The vertebrates consisted of fishes, of which the Ganoids and Placoids were the principal groups. The former were the forerunners of the reptile, which in many respects they closely resembled. They embraced a large number of species, many of which grew to a gigantic size; but with the exception of the gar and sturgeon, they have no living representatives. The Placoids, structurally formed for advancement, still remain among the highest types of the present seas. The shark, a noted instance, judging from its fossil remains, must have attained 100 feet in length. Both groups lived in the sea, and if any fresh water animals existed their remains have either perished or not been found. So numerous were the inhabitants of the ocean, that the Devonian has been styled the age of fishes. In their anatomical structure was foreshadowed the organization of man; reptiles, birds and mammals being the intermediate gradations. The continental sea of the preceding age still covered the larger part of North America, extending far northwest and opening south into the Gulf of Mexico. In its shallow basins were deposited sandstones, shales and limestones, which westerly attained a thickness of 500 feet, and in the region of the Alleghanies 1,500 feet. The great thickness of the latter deposits indicated oscillations, in which the downward movement exceeded the upward. Shallow waters, therefore, interspersed with reefs and islands, still occupied the sites of the Alleghanies and Rocky Mountains, which now look down from above the clouds on the finished continent. The St. Lawrence and the Hudson may have existed in miniature, but the area of land was too small for rivers and other bodies of fresh water of considerable extent. In the disturbances closing the Devonian age additions were made to the surface in Iowa, Wisconsin and Illinois. The two resulting formations in this State are the Devonian limestone and the Oriskany sandstone. There are outcrops of the former in the bluffs of the Mississippi, Rock and Illinois rivers. It contains a great variety of fossils, and is used for building material and the manufacture of quicklime. The latter appears in Union, Alexander and Jackson counties, and is used to some extent in the manufacture of glass.

The Carboniferous Age opened with the deposition of widely extended marine formations. Added to the strata previously deposited, the entire thickness in the region of the Alleghanies, now partially elevated, amounted to 7 miles. Wide areas of permanent elevation occurred between the 34th and 45th degrees of latitude, embracing most of the territory between the eastern continental border and the States of Kansas and Nebraska. Farther westward, and resulting from the gradual emergence of the Pacific coast, was an interior sea whose shallow waters still flowed over the site of the Rocky Mountains. The winter temperature near the poles was 66 degrees. A stagnant and stifling atmosphere rested upon the area now constituting the United States and British

America. The McKenzie river, now filled with icebergs, then
flowed through verdant banks to a coral sea, having the same temperature as the Gulf of Mexico at the present day. The most prominent feature of the age was the formation of coal. Being carbon-
ized vegetable tissue, the material furnished for this purpose was
the vast forest accumulations peculiar to the period. Vegetation,
commencing in the previous age, had now attained an expansion
which greatly exceeded the growth of prior or subsequent times.
Invigorated by a warm, moist and winterless climate, and an
atmosphere surcharged with carbonic acid gas, vast jungles spread
over the marshy plains, and impenetrable forests covered the
upland slopes and hights. The graceful lepidodendron, now fully
developed, was one of the principal coal producing plants; sub-
serving the same purpose and associated with it was the gigantic
conifer, a member of the pine family. The ancient fern, another
coal plant, grew to a hight of 80 feet. Its trunk, regularly fretted
with scars and destitute of branches, terminated in a crown of
foliage rivaling that of the palm in profuseness and beauty. The
sigillarid, however, as it contributed most largely to .the production of coal, was the characteristic plant of the period. The
trunk, which rose from 40 to 60 feet high from its alternate flutings
and ribs, appeared like a clustered column. At an altitude of 25
or 30 feet it separated into branches, covered with a grass-like
foliage intermingled with long catkins of obscure flowers or strings
of seed, arranged in whorls about a common stem. The structure
of the trunk was peculiar. One, 5 feet in diameter, was surrounded
with a bark 13 inches in thickness; within this was a cylinder of
wood 12 inches in thickness, and at the center a pith 10 inches in
diameter. Such a tree would be useless as timber, but the bark, of
which they largely consisted, was impervious to mineral solutions,
and valuable for the production of coal. The calamites, growing
with the sigillarids, covered with dense brakes the marshy flats.
Their hollow stems, marked vertically with flutings and horizontally with joints, grew in clumps to a hight of 20 feet. Some
species were branchless, while from the joints of other sprang
branches, subdividing into whorls of branchlets.

The vast accumulation of vegetable matter from these and other
carboniferous plants, either imbedded in the miry soil in which it
grew, or swept from adjacent elevations into shallow lakes, became
covered with sediment, and thus were transformed into coal. It
has been estimated that 8 perpendicular feet of wood were required to make 1 foot of bituminous coal, and 12 to make 1 of
anthracite. Some beds of the latter are 30 feet in thickness, and
hence 360 feet of timber must have been consumed in their production. The process of its formation was exactly the same as
practiced in the manufacture of charcoal, by burning wood under
a covering of earth. Vegetable tissue consists mostly of carbon
and oxygen, and decomposition must take place, either under
water or some other impervious covering, to prevent the elements
from forming carbonic acid gas, and thus escaping to the atmosphere. Conforming to these requirements, the immense vegetable
growths forming the coal-fields subsided with the surface on which
they grew, and were buried beneath the succeeding deposits.
Nova Scotia has 76 different beds, and Illinois 12; and consequently, in these localities there were as many different fields of

verdure overwhelmed in the dirt-beds of the sea. Thus, long before the starry cycles had measured half the history of the unfolding continent, and when first the expanding stream of life but dimly reflected the coming age of mind, this vast supply of fuel was stored away in the rocky frame-work of the globe. Here it slumbered till man made his appearance and dragged it from its rocky lairs. At his bidding it renders the factory animate with humming spindles, driving shuttles, whirling lathes, and clanking forges. Under his guidance the iron-horse, feeding upon its pitchy fragments, bounds with tireless tread over its far reaching track, dragging after him the products of distant marts and climes. By the skill of the one and the power of the other, the ocean steamer plows the deep in opposition to winds and waves, making its watery home a highway for the commerce of the world.

Prior to the formation of coal, so great was the volume of carbonic acid gas in the atmosphere that only slow breathing and cold-blooded animals could exist. Consequent upon its conversion into coal, all the preceding species of plants and animals perished, and new forms came upon the stage of being with organizations adapted to the improved conditions. In the new economy, as at the present time, stability is maintained in the atmosphere by the reciprocal relations subsisting between it and the incoming types. The animal inspires oxygen and expires carbonic acid gas; the vegetable inspires carbonic acid gas and expires oxygen, thus preserving the equilibrium of this breathing medium. The coal-fields of Europe are estimated at 18,000 square miles, those of the United States at 150,000. The Alleghany coal-field contains 60,000 square miles, with an aggregate thickness of 120 feet. The Illinois and Missouri 60,000 square miles, and an aggregate thickness in some localities of 70 feet. Other fields occur in different localities, of various thicknesses. In Illinois, three-fourths of the surface are underlaid by beds of coal, and the State consequently has a greater area than any other member of the Union. There are 12 different beds, the two most important of which are each from 6 to 8 feet in thickness. The entire carboniferous system, including the coal-beds and the intervening strata, in southern Illinois is 27,000 feet in thickness, and in the northern part only 500.

Next to the immense deposits of coal, the Burlington, Keokuk and St. Louis limestones are the most important formations. They receive their appellations from the cities whose names they bear—where their lithological characters were first studied—and in the vicinities of which they crop out in Illinois. The Burlington furnishes inexhaustible supplies of building stone and quicklime, but is mostly interesting on account of the immense number of interesting fossils which it contains. Along its northern outcrop Crinoids are found in a profusion unequalled by that of any locality of similar extent in the world. Though untold ages have elapsed since their incarceration in the rocks, so perfect has been their preservation, their structure can be determined with almost as much precision as if they had perished but yesterday. The Keokuk is extensively used for architectural purposes, and furnished the material for the celebrated Mormon Temple at Nauvoo, the new Post-office at Springfield, and the Custom Houses at Galena and Dubuque. It contains some of the most interesting crystals found in the State. These consist of hollow spheres of

quartz and chalcedony of various sizes, and lined on the inside
with crystalets of different minerals. Tons of specimens have
been taken from Hancock county and distributed over the United
States and Europe, to ornament the cabinets of mineralogists.
The St. Louis is almost pure carbonet of lime, and the best material in the State for the manufacture of quick-lime. It is largely
quarried at Alton.

The Age of Reptiles is distinguished for changes in the continental borders, which generally ran within their present limits.
The sub-marine outlines of the Bay of New York, and the course
of the Hudson, indicate that the adjacent shores during the early
part of this age were beyond their present limits. Southward the
sea line ran within the present shore, the distance increasing from
60 miles in Maryland to 100 in Georgia, and 200 in Alabama.
The Texan gulf-shore, and that of the peninsula and State of
California, were parallel, and mostly within their present positions.
These borders were fringed with deposits, while inland the trough
of the old continental sea was becoming more shallow. The altitude of the Alleghanies had nearly reached their present hight.
The Rocky Mountains, in the transition from the close of the
present to the beginning of the subsequent age, began slowly to
emerge from the waters under which they had hitherto slumbered.
The Gulf of Mexico formed a deep bay extending to the mouth of
the Ohio, and, protruding itself northwesterly, covered the region
of the Rocky Mountains. It may have connected with the Arctic
Ocean, but observations have been too limited to trace it with certainty beyond the head waters of the Missouri and Yellow Stone.
These are, therefore, among the more recently formed rivers, and
cannot be compared with the primeval St. Lawrence and Hudson.
The Mississippi was a stream of not more than one-half its present
length and volume, falling into the gulf not far from the site of
Cairo. The Ohio drained substantially the same region it does at
the present time. In the earlier part of the age the geographical
distribution of fossils indicates a common temperature, from Beh-
ring Strait in the Northern to that of Magellan in the Southern
Hemisphere. In the latter part, however, a difference is perceptible, indicating also a difference of temperature and the commencement of climatic zones. This change, caused by the partial
upheaval of mountain chains north of the Equator, and the decline of internal heat, marked a new era in the physical history
of the globe. As the result, currents commenced flowing in the
ocean; the constant monotony of previous ages was broken by
the pleasant diversities of changing seasons; life was imparted to
the atmosphere, and the breeze came forth laden with the breath
of spring; the tempest madly burst into being and began its work
of destruction, and the trade-winds commenced blowing, but it
was reserved for a future age to make them the common carriers
of the ocean's commerce.

The principal formations of the age, none of which exist in
Illinois, were sandstones, chalks and limestones, interstratified
with deposits of salt and gypsum. Their absence can be explained
either upon the supposition that the surface of the State was either
above the waters in which they were deposited, or, having originally
been deposited, they were subsequently swept away by denuding
agencies. The former was perhaps the case, as no aqueous action

could have operated with sufficient power to remove all traces of their former existence. The characteristic plants of the coal age, now declining, were replaced by cycads and many new forms of conifers and ferns. The cycad was intermediate in character, resembling the fern in the opening of its foliage, and the palm in its general habits. It was now in the full zenith of its expansion, while the fern was dying out and the conifer was yet to be developed. More than 100 angiosperms made their appearance, one-half of them closely allied to the trees of modern forests and the fruit trees of temperate regions. In the latter part of the age the palm, at present the most perfect type of the vegetable kingdom, was also introduced. New animal species made their appearance, attended by the extinction of all pre-existing forms. Reptiles now reached their culmination, the earth, sea and air, each having its peculiar kind. Their fossil remains indicate a large number of both herbiverous and carniverous species, which in many instances attained a length of 60 feet. The ichthyosaurus, a prominent example, united in its structure parts of several related animals, having the head of a lizard, the snout of a porpoise, the teeth of a crocodile, the spine of a fish and the paddles of a whale. Its eyes, enormously large, were arranged to act both like the telescope and the microscope, thus enabling it to see its prey both night and day, and at all distances. It subsisted on fish and the young of its own species, some of which must have been swallowed several feet in length. Associated with it was the Pleiosaurus, an animal resembling it in its general structure. A remarkable difference, however, was the great length of neck possessed by the latter, which contained 40 vertebræ, the largest number that has ever been found in animals living or fossil. These two reptiles for a long time ruled the seas and kept the increase of other animals within proper limits. But the most gigantic of reptile monsters was the Iguanodon. Some individuals were 60 feet long, 15 feet round the largest part of the body, had feet 12 feet in length, and thighs 7 feet in diameter. The most heteroclitic creature was the Pterodactyl. It had the neck of a bird, the mouth of a reptile, the wings of a bat, and the body and tail of a mammal. Its curious organization enabled it to walk on two feet, fly like a bat, and creep, climb or dive in pursuit of its food. The age is also remarkable as the era of the first mammels, the first birds, and the first common fishes.

The Mammalian Age witnessed the increase of the mass of the earth above the ocean's level three-fold. The world-constructing architect, the coral insect, built up Florida out of the sea, thus completing the southern expanse of the continent. Its eastern and western borders were substantially finished, and superficially its great plateaus, mountain chains and river systems, approximated their present geographical aspects. The Rocky Mountains were elevated to a hight of 7,000 feet, the Wind River chain 6,800, the Big Horn Mountains 6,000, Pike's Peak 4,500. The upheaval of the Rocky Mountain region greatly enlarged the Missouri, previously an inconsiderable stream, adding to it the Yellowstone, Platte, Kansas and other tributaries. The Lower Mississippi was formed and discharged its vast volume of accumulated waters near the present coast line of the Gulf. The elevation of mountain masses to snowy altitudes cooled down the temperature and introduced substantially the present climates. In Europe the change was gradual from tropical to subtropical and temperate; in North America abrupt. As a consequence the botany of the latter opened with the oak, poplar, dogwood, magnolia, fig, palm and other plants closely resembling those of the present day.

Of the animals the Mammoth was remarkable. Unlike the elephant of the present day, they were covered with a redish wool intermingled with hair and black bristles, the latter being more than a foot in length. Vast herds of these huge creatures, nearly three times as large as the present elephant, their living representative wandered over the northern part of both hemispheres. An individual in a perfect state of preservation was found in 1790, encased in ice, at the mouth of the river Lena. It still retained the wool on its hide, and otherwise was so free from decay, that its flesh was eaten by dogs. Their remains are abundantly distributed over the northern part of the United States, imbedded usually in marshes where the animals were perhaps mired while in search of food or water. A large fossil specimen was recently exhumed in Macon county, Illinois, 2 miles southeast of Illiopolis, in the edge of Long Point Slough, by the side of an oozy spring. The fossils have been found in other localities of the State, and the prairies may have been places of frequent resort. Contemporaneous with them were the Dinotherium and Megatherium, and other creatures of the most gigantic proportions. The magnitude of the Mammoth seems almost fabulous, but that of the Dinotherium probably surpassed it. One of its most remarkable features was its enormous tusks, projecting from the anterior extremity of the lower jaw, which curved down like those of the walrus. Like the rhinoceros, it lived in the water, and was well adapted to the lacustrine condition of the earth common at the time it flourished. The Megatherium, belonging to the sloth family, was also of colossal dimensions. Its body, in some instances 18 feet long, rested on legs resembling columns of support rather than organs of locomotion. Its spinal column contained a nerve a foot in diameter; its femur was three times the size of the elephant's, while its feet were a yard in length and more than a foot in width. The tail near the body was two feet in diameter, and used with its hind legs as a tripod on which the animal sat when it wielded its huge arms and hands.

Toward the close of the age oscillations occurred in the northern part of the continent, greatly modifying the condition of its surface. During the upward vibration vast glaciers spread over British America and the contiguous portion of the United States. These fields of ice, becoming filled with hard boulders, and moving southward by expansion, ground into fragments the underlying rocks. The sediment was gathered up by the moving mass, and when a latitude sufficiently warm to melt the ice was reached, it was spread over the surface. Accumulations of this kind constitute the drift which extends from New England westward beyond the Mississippi, and from the 39th parallel northward to an unknown limit. In Illinois, with the exception of small areas in the northwestern and southern parts of the State, it covers the entire surface with a varying stratum of from 10 to 200 feet in thickness. Here, and in other parts of the West, not only glaciers, but icebergs, were connected with its distribution. The waters of the lakes then extended southward perhaps to the highlands, crossing the State from Grand Tower east toward the Ohio. This barrier formed the southern limits of this sea, and also of the drift which was distributed over its bottom by floating bodies of ice filled with sediment previously detached from the glaciers farther north. The upward movement of the glacial epoch was followed by a depression of the surface below its present level. The subsidence in Connecticut was 50 feet; in Massachusetts, 170; in New Hampshire, 200; at Montreal, 450; and several hundred in the region of Illinois and the Pacific. Previously the adjacent Atlantic seaboard extended into the sea beyond its present limits; now it receded, and the St. Lawrence and Lake Champlain became gulfs extending far inland. As the result of the down-throw the temperature was elevated, causing the glaciers to melt, and a further dissemination of the drift. Regular outlines, due to the dinamic forces, ice and water, were thus imparted to the surface, which a subsequent emergence brought to its present level. Order, beauty, and utility sprang into being and harmony with man, the highest type of terrestrial life, now in the dawn of his existence.

The Age of Man commenced with the present geological conditions. The great mountain reliefs and diversities of climate attending the present and the close of the preceding age, largely augmented the variety of physical conditions which modify vegetable and animal life. Multiplying under these diverse influences, the present flora exceeds 100,000 species. The palm alone, culminating in the present era, and standing at the head of the vegetable kingdom, embraces 1,000. Commensurate with the variety of plants is the extent of their distribution. They are found universally, from Arctic snows to Tropical sands, growing in the air and water, covering the land with verdure, and ministering to the wants of their cousins, the different forms of animal life. In the jungle the wild beast makes his lair; the bird builds her nest in their sheltering leaves and branches, and subsists on their fruits; and man converts them into innumerable forms of food, ornaments and material for the construction of his dwellings. In the oak and towering cedar their forms are venerable and majestic; graceful and beautiful in the waving foliage and clinging vine, and profoundly interesting in their growth and structure; crowned with a floral magnificence greatly transcending their predecessors of previous ages, they give enchantment to the landscape, sweetness to the vernal breeze, and refinement and purity to all who come within their influence. As in the case of plants, a diversity of physical conditions has impressed a multiplicity and variety upon the animals. The approximate number of species at the present time is 350,000, each sub-kingdom numbering as follows: Radiates, 10,000; Mollusks, 20,000; Articulates, 300,000; Vertebrates, 21,000. Of the existing Vertebrates, Fishes embrace 10,000; Reptiles, 2,000; Birds, 7,000, and Mammals, 2,000. With the appearance of Man on the stage of being, in the latter part of the preceding age, many types of the lower animals, in which magnitude and brute ferocity were prominent characteristics, became extinct. Their successors, as if harmonizing with the higher life developing in their midst, were generally reduced in size, less brutal in their nature, and more active, beautiful and intelligent.

Recent discoveries have shown that the appearance of man, instead of being confined to the geological age which bears his name, must be extended back to an indefinite period. His remains and the relics of his art show that he was a contemporary of the mammoth; that he witnessed the inundation that buried the northern plains of the Old and New Worlds under the sea of ice; and that even before that time, when sub-tropical animals disported themselves in the forests of middle Europe, have traces of his existence been discovered. Though the absolute time of his advent cannot be determined, he doubtless was an inhabitant of the earth several hundred thousand years before he was sufficiently intelligent to .preserve the records of his own history. His appearance as the head of the animal kingdom marks a new stage in the unfoldment of terrestrial life. His claim to this preeminence is based on the superiority of his mental, moral and spiritual endowments. Having an understanding capable of endless progression in knowledge, he is able to study the laws of nature and make them subservient to his will and wants; to institute systems of government for his protection, and to hold in subjection the lower animals, however greatly they may exceed him in size or physical strength. He is the first of terrestrial beings capable of comprehending the nature of moral relations; of distinguishing right from wrong, and of deriving happiness from the practice of virtue and suffering in consequence of vice. In his reverence for the Deity and aspirations for immortality he is removed still further from the animal plain, and stands as a connecting link between the latter and spirit existance.

The present age still retains, in a diminished degree of activity, the geological forces of previous periods. Extensive flats at many points along the Atlantic coast, and the deltas and other alluvial formations of rivers, are slowly extending the present surface. The latter, in many places, is becoming modified by the production of peat-beds; in volcanic regions, by the ejection of lava, and in paroxysmal disturbances, extensive areas are still subject to elevations and depressions, evidently a continuation of previous oscillations. As observed by Moravian settlers, the western coast of Greenland, for a distance of 600 miles, has been slowly sinking during the last four centuries. The border of the continent, from Labrador southward to New Jersey, is supposed to be undergoing changes of level, but more accurate observations will be necessary to determine the extent of the movement.

Like the uninterrupted course of human history there are no strongly drawn lines between the ages and their corresponding system of rocks and organic remains. Culminent phases occur, giving distinctiveness to the center of each and distinguishing it from others. The germ of each was long working forward in the past before it attained its full development and peculiar character, and extended far into the future for its decline and final extinction. There is, hence, a blending of periods and their products, and, while centrally well defined, their beginnings and endings are without lines of demarkation. The ratios, representing the comparative length of each age as determined by the thickness of its rocks and the rate of their formation, are as follows: Salurian, including the Laurentian and Huronian, 49; Devonian, 15; Carboniferous, 15; Reptilian, 23; Mammalian, 18. In consequence of the constantly varying conditions attending the growth of rocks, these results are only approximations to the truth. They are, however, sufficiently correct to give the proportionate duration of these great geological eras, and will doubtless, by future research, be rendered more accurate. Could definite intervals of time be substituted for these ratios, the most ample evidence exists to prove that the results would be inconceivably great. Even within the period of existing causes, the mind is startled at the tremendous sweep of ages required to effect comparatively small results. The waters of Lake Erie originally extended below the present Falls of Niagara, and the cataract, in subsequently passing from the same point to its present position, excavated the intervening channel of the river. Allowing the rate of movement to be one inch per year, which is perhaps not too low an estimate, it would require 380,000 years to pass over the six miles of retrocession. Judging from this estimate, what time would be required to excavate the canon of the Colorado, which is 300 miles long, and has been worn a large part of the distance through granite from 3000 to 6000 feet in depth. Captain Hunt, who for many years was stationed at Key West, and whose opportunity for observations was good, estimates that the coral insects, which have built up the limestone formations of Florida, must have required more than 5,000,000 years to complete their labors.

CHAPTER II.

THE TOPOGRAPHY, RIVERS, SOIL AND CLIMATOLOGY.

The Rivers and Topography of the State are based upon and correspond with its geological formations. The surface, inclination and the direction of the interior drainage faces the southwest. Rock river, flowing southwesterly through one of the most beautiful and fertile regions, enters the Mississippi just below the Upper Rapids. The Desplaines, rising in Wisconsin west of Lake Michigan, and flowing southward, and the Kankakee, rising in Indiana, south of the lake, and flowing westward, form the Illinois. The latter stream, the largest in the State, courses across it in a southwesterly direction and falls into the Mississippi not far from the city of Alton. The Kaskaskia rises near the eastern boundary of the State and the 40th parallel of latitude, flows in a southwest direction, and forms a junction with the Mississippi not far from the town which bears its name. These and other smaller streams flow through valleys originally excavated in solid limestone by ancient rivers anterior to the formation of the drift. The latter material was subsequently deposited in these primitive water courses from 10 to more than 200 feet in thickness, and now forms the channel of the existing streams. For the formation of these ancient river beds of such great width and frequently excavated several hundred feet in hard carboniferous rocks, the diminished waters now flowing within their lining of drift are wholly inadequate. Furthermore, the alluvial valleys which the rivers now occupy are far too broad to correspond with the present volume and swiftness of the waters. The alluvial bottoms of the Illinois are nearly equal to those of the Mississippi, though the latter has a current twice as rapid and a quantity of water 6 times as large as the former stream. The smaller streams of the State occupy valleys filled with drift, through which the waters have been unable to cut their way to the ancient troughs below. Owing to this, the stratified rocks in many localities have never become exposed, and it is difficult for the geologist to determine the character of the underlying formations.

Though the surface of the State is generally level or slightly undulating, there are some portions of it considerably elevated. The highest summits are found along the northern border between Freeport and Galena, known as the mounds. The culminant points of altitude are 200 feet above the surrounding country, 575 above the waters of Lake Michigan, 900 above the junction of the Ohio and Mississippi, and 1,150 above the ocean. The tops of the mounds coincide with the original elevation of the surface, and their present condition as isolated hills is due to denuding forces which have carried away the surrounding strata. Mounds occur in other places, some of them having a hight of 50 feet, and frequently a crown of timber upon their summits, which gives them the appearance of islands in surrounding seas of prairie verdure. Besides the mounds there are in the State 5 principal axes of disturbance and elevation. The most northerly of these enters it in Stephenson county, crossing Rock river near Dixon, and the Illinois not far from LaSalle. On the former river it brings to the surface the St. Peters sandstone; on the latter, magnesian limestone, a Silurian formation. At LaSalle the coal strata are uplifted to the surface from a depth of 400 feet, which shows that the disturbance occurred after their formation. On the Mississippi, in Calhoun county, there occurred an upheaval of the strata, attended with a down-throw of more than 1,000 feet. On the south side of the axis the Burlington limestone of the subcarboniferous series had its strata tilted up almost perpendicular to the horizon. On the north side the St. Peters sandstone and magnesian limestone were elevated, and form the bluff known as Sandstone Cape. This bluff, at the time of its elevation, was doubtless a mountain mass of 1,500 feet in hight, and has since been reduced to its present altitude by the denuding effects of water. The same axes of disturbance, trending in a southeastern direction, crosses the Illinois 6 miles above its mouth, and farther southward again strikes the Mississippi and disappears in its channel. Farther down the river another uplift dislocates the strata near the southern line of St. Clair county. This disturbance extends by way of Columbia, in Monroe county, to the Mississippi, and brings to the surface the same limestone and the St. Peters sandstone. Again, farther southward, an uplifted mountain ridge extends from Grand Tower, on the Mississippi, to Shawneetown, on the Ohio; on the west of the Mississippi it brings the lower Silurian rocks to the surface; in Jackson county, Illinois, it tilts up the Devonian limestone at an angle of 25 degrees; and farther eastward the subcarboniferous limestone becomes the surface rock. The last important point of disturbance occurs in Alexander county, constituting the Grand Chain, a dangerous reef of rocks, extending across the Mississippi and forming a bluff on the Illinois shore 70 feet high. Passing thence in a southeastern direction, it crosses the Ohio a few miles above Caledonia, in Pulaski county.[*]

The Formation of the Soil is due to geological and other physical agencies. From long habit we are accustomed to look upon it without considering its wonderful properties and great importance in the economy of animal life. Not attractive itself, yet its productions far transcend the most elaborate works of art; and having but little diversity of appearance, the endless variety which pervades the vegetable and animal kingdoms springs from its prolific abundance. Its mysterious elements, incorporated in the structure of plants, clothes the earth with verdure and pleasant landscapes. They bloom in the flower, load the breeze with fragrant odors, blush in the clustering fruit, whiten the fields with harvests for the supply of food, furnish the tissues which, wrought into fabrics, decorate and protect the body, and yield the curative agents for healing the diseases to which it is subject. From the same source also proceed the elements which, entering the domain

---

[*]Geological Survey of Illinois, by A. H. Worthen.

of animal life, pulsate in the blood, suffuse the cheek with the glow of health, speak in the eye, in the nerve become the recipients of pleasure and pain, render the tongue vocal with music and eloquence, and fill the brain, the seat of reason and throne of the imagination, with its glowing imagery and brilliant fancies. But while the soil is the source of such munificent gifts, it is also the insatiable bourne to which they must all return. The lofty tree, spreading its vast canvass of leaves to the winds, and breasting the storms of a thousand years, finally dies, and undergoing decomposition, enriches the earth in which it grew. The king of beasts, whose loud roar can be heard for miles, and whose immense power enables him to prey upon the denizens of his native jungles, cannot resist the fate which at length consigns his sinewy frame to the mold. Even the lord of the lower world, notwithstanding his exalted position and grasp of intellect, must likewise suffer physical death and mingle with the sod that forms his grave.

The soil was originally formed by the decomposition of rocks. These, by long exposure to the air, water and frost, became disintegrated, and the comminuted material acted upon by vegetation, forms the fruitful mold of the surface. When of local origin, it varies in composition with the changing material from which it is derived. If sandstone prevails, it is too porous to retain fertilizing agents; if limestone is in excess, it is too hot and dry; and if slate predominates, the resulting clay is too wet and cold. Hence it is only a combination of these and other ingredients that can properly adapt the earth to the growth of vegetation. Happily for Illinois the origin of its surface formations precludes the possibility of sterile extremes arising from local causes. As we have stated before, almost the entire surface of the State is a stratum of drift, formed by the decomposition of every variety of rock, and commingled in a homogeneous mass by the agents employed in its distribution. This immense deposit, varying from 10 to 200 feet in thickness, required for its production physical conditions which do not now exist. We must go far back in the history of the planet, when the Polar world was a desolation of icy wastes. From these dreary realms of enduring frosts vast glaciers, reaching southward, dipped into the waters of an inland sea, extending over a large part of the upper Mississippi valley. These ponderous masses, moving southward with irresistible power, tore immense boulders from their parent ledges and incorporated them in their structure. By means of these, in their further progress, they grooved and planed down the subjacent rocks, gathering up and carrying with them part of the abraded material and strewing their track for hundreds of miles with the remainder. On reaching the shore of the interior sea huge icebergs were projected from their extremities into the waters, which, melting as they floated into warmer latitudes, distributed the detrital matter they contained over the bottom. Thus, long before the plains of Illinois clanked with the din of railroad trains, these ice-formed navies plowed the seas in which they were submerged, and distributed over them cargoes of soil-producing sediment. No mariner walked their crystal decks to direct their course, and no pennon attached to their glittering masts trailed in the winds that urged them forward; yet they might perhaps have sailed under the flags of a hundred succeeding empires, each as old as the present nationalities of the earth, during the performance of their labors. This splendid soil-forming deposit is destined to make Illinois the great centre of American wealth and population. Perhaps no other country of the same extent on the face of the globe can boast a soil so ubiquitous in its distribution and so universally productive. Enriched by all the minerals in the crust of the earth, it necessarily contains a great variety of constituents. Since plants differ so widely in the elements of which they are composed, this multiplicity of composition is the means of growing a great diversity of crops, and the amount produced is correspondingly large. So great is the fertility, that years of continued cultivation do not materially diminish the yield, and should sterility be induced by excessive working, the subsoil can be made available. This extends from 2 to 10 and even 20 and 30 feet in depth, and when mixed with the mold of the surface, gives it a greater producing capacity than it had at first. Other States have limited areas as productive, but nearly the entire surface of Illinois is arable land, and when brought under cultivation will become one continued scene of verdure and agricultural profusion. With not half of its area improved, the State has become the granary of the continent; far excels any other member of the Union in packing pork; fattens more than half of all the cattle shipped to the Eastern markets, and if prices were as remunerative, could furnish other products to a corresponding extent. Graded to a proper level, and free from obstructions, the State has become the principal theatre for the use and invention of agricultural implements. Owing to the cheapness attending the use of machinery, with a given amount of capital, a greater extent of lands can be cultivated. The severity of the labor expended is also proportionately diminished, and those engaged in husbandry have time to become acquainted with the theoretical as well as the practical part of their duties. The profound philosophy involved in the growth of plants furnishes a field for investigation and experiment requiring the highest order of talent and the most varied and extensive attainments. Agriculture, aided by chemistry, vegetable physiology and kindred branches of knowledge, will greatly enhance the productiveness of the land. Thus with the advantages of science, a superior soil, and the use of machinery, agriculture will always remain the most attractive, manly and profitable branch of industry in which the people of Illinois can engage, contributing more than any other pursuit to individual comfort, and proportionally adding to the prosperity of the State. The cultivation of the soil in all ages has furnished employment for the largest and best portion of mankind; yet the honor to which they are entitled has never been fully acknowledged. Though their occupation is the basis of national prosperity, and upon its progress more than any other branch of industry depends the march of civilization, yet its history remains to a great extent unwritten. Historians duly chronicle the feats of the warrior who ravages the earth and beggars its inhabitants, but leaves unnoticed the labors of him who causes the desolated country to bloom again, and heals with the balm of plenty the miseries of war. When true worth is duly recognized, instead of the mad ambition which subjugates nations to acquire power, the heroism which subdues the soil and feeds

2

the world, will be the theme of the poet's song and the orator's eloquence.

The Origin of the Prairies has been a source of speculation. One theory is that the soil resulted from the decomposition of vegetable matter under water, and that the attending conditions were incompatible with the growth of timber. According to this view, prairies are at present in process of formation along the shores of lakes and rivers. During river freshets the heaviest particles settle nearest the channel, and here by repeated deposits the banks first became elevated above the floods. These natural levees becoming sufficiently high, are overgrown with timber and inclose large areas of bottom lands back from the river, by which they are frequently inundated. The waters on these flats, when the flood subsides, are cut off from the river and form sloughs, frequently of great extent. Their shallow and stagnant waters are first invaded by mosses and other aquatic plants which grow under the surface and contain in their tissues lime, allumina, and silica, the constituents of clay. They also subsist immense numbers of small mollusks and other diminutive creatures, and the constant decomposition of both vegetables and animals forms a stratum of clay corresponding with that which underlies the finished prairies. As the marshy bottoms are by this means built up to the surface of the water, the mosses are then intermixed with coarse grasses, which become more and more abundant as the depth diminishes. These reedy plants, now rising above the surface, absorb and decompose the carbonic acid gas of the atmosphere, and convert it into woody matter, which at first forms a clayey mold and afterwards the black mold of the prairie. The same agencies, now operating in the ponds skirting the banks of rivers, originally formed all the prairies of the Mississippi Valley. We have already seen that the surface of the land was submerged during the dispersion of the drift, and in its slow emergence afterward, it was covered by vast sheets of shallow water, which first formed swamps and subsequently prairies. The present want of horizontality in some of them is due to the erosive action of water. The drainage, moving in the direction of the creeks and rivers, at length furrowed the surface with tortuous meanders, resulting finally in the present undulating prairies. The absence of trees, the most remarkable feature, is attributable first to the formation of ulmic acid, which favors the growth of herbacious plants and retards that of forests; secondly, trees absorb by their roots large quantities of air, which they cannot obtain when the surface is under water or covered by a compact sod; and thirdly, they require solid points of attachment which marshy flats are unable to furnish. When, however, the lands become dry and the sod is broken by the plow or otherwise destroyed, they produce all the varieties of arborescent vegetation common to their latitude. Indeed, since the settlement of Illinois, the woodland area of many localities extends far beyond its original limits.

The foregoing theory requires a large, unvarying quantity of water, while another, perhaps equally plausible, is based on aqueous conditions almost the reverse. It is well known that the different continental masses of the globe are in general surrounded by zones of timber, and have within them belts of grasses, and centrally large areas of inhospitable deserts. On the Atlantic side of North America there is a continuous wooded region, extending from Hudson Bay to the Gulf of Mexico, while on the Pacific a similar arborescent growth embraces some of the most gigantic specimens of the vegetable kingdom. Within these bands of timber, which approach each other in their northern and southern reaches, are the great prairies extending transversely across the Mississippi Valley, and having their greatest expansion in the valley of the Missouri. Farther westward, from increasing dryness, the grasses entirely disappear, and the great American Desert usurps their place. This alternation of forest, prairie, and desert, corresponds with the precipitation of moisture. The ocean is the great source of moisture, and the clouds are the vehicles employed for its distribution over the land. From actual measurement it has been ascertained that they discharge most of their water on the exterior rim of the continents; that farther toward the interior the amount precipitated is less, and finally it is almost entirely supplanted by the aridity of the desert. In a section extending across the continent from New York to San Francisco, the amount of rain-fall strikingly coincides with the alternations of wood-land, prairie, and desert. The region extending from New York, which has an annual rain-fall of 42 inches, to Ann Arbor, having 29 inches, is heavily covered with timber; thence to Galesburg, Ill., having 26 inches,* is mostly prairie interspersed with clumps of forest; thence to Fort Laramie, having 20 inches, it rapidly changes to a continuous prairie; thence to Fort Youma, having only 3 inches, it becomes an inhospitable desert; and thence to San Francisco, having 22 inches, it changes to luxuriant forests. Illinois is thus within the region of alternate wood and prairie, with the latter largely predominating. This wide belt, owing to a difference of capacity for retaining moisture, has its eastern and western borders thrown into irregular outlines, resembling deeply indented bays and projecting headlands. As the result of decreasing moisture, only 90 arborescent species are found in the wooded region which on the east extends a considerable distance into Illinois, and all of these, except 6, disappear farther westward. The diminished precipitation in Illinois, and the great valley east of the Mississippi, while it has an unfavorable effect on the growth of trees, seems rather to enhance the growth of crops. In further confirmation of this theory, the same physical laws which have diversified North America with forest, prairie, and desert, have produced similar effects upon other continents. Hence it is that South America has its Atacama, Africa its great Sahara, Europe its barren steppes, and Asia its rainless waste of sand and salt, extending through more than 100 degrees of longitude. All these desert places, where local causes do not interfere, are girt about by grassy plains and belts of forest.

* The subjoined table has been kindly furnished us by Prof. Livingstone, of Lombard University. It will be seen that the mean annual temperature of Galesburg is 48 degrees, and its mean annual precipitation of moisture 24 inches. The southern and western portions of the State slightly exceed the above figures:

Jan.		Feb.		Mar.		Apr.		May.		June.		July.		Aug.		Sep.		Oct.		Nov.		Dec.		Ann'l	
Tem.	Rain.	Tem.	Rain.	Tem.	Rain.	Tem.	Rain.	Tem.	Rain.	Tem.	Rain.	Tem.	Rain.	Tem.	Rain.	Tem.	Rain.	Tem.	Rain.	Tem.	Rain.	Tem.	Rain.	Tem.	Rain.
26°	11	24°	14	30°	25	49°	23	60°	29	70°	32	59°	40	71°	43	63°	33	50°	25	39°	11	26°	18	48°	26

Some eminent physicists refer the treeless character of the great
grassy plains to the mechanical and chemical character of the soil.
Perhaps, in the constantly varying physical conditions of different
localities, the forces alluded to in these theories advanced, may all
co-operate to produce these great grassy expanses, which constitute so large a part of the earth's surface. To Illinois they are
inexhaustible sources of wealth; and as intimately connected with
her destiny as the great coal fields which underlie them.   Both are
the expression of natural law, both destined to furnish the State
with the elements of future greatness and power, and both prophetic of labor, intelligence and the enjoyment of a noble manhood.*

The Climatology of the State, in common with other countries of
the same latitude, has four seasons. The melting snows of winter,
generally attended by rains, convert the rich soil of the prairie into
mud, and render early spring the most unpleasant part of the year.
The heat of summer, although more intense than in the same latitude on the Atlantic, is greatly relieved by the constant breezes
which fan the prairies. Autumn, with slowly diminishing heats,
terminates in the serene and beautiful season known as Indian
summer. Its mild and uniform temperature, soft and hazy atmosphere, and forests beautifully tinted with the hues of dying foliage,
all conspire to render it the pleasant part of the year. Next come
the boreal blasts of winter, with its social firesides, and tinkling
bells in the mystic light of the moon, as merry sleighs skim over
the level snow-clad prairies. The winter has its sudden changes
of temperature, causing colds and other diseases arising from
extreme vicissitudes of weather. This is the most unfavorable
feature of the climate, which in other respects is salubrious. The
general belief that Illinois is scourged by bilious diseases is substantially unfounded. It is well known that the pioneers of Ohio,
Indiana and Michigan suffered far worse from malarious diseases
than those who first subdued the soil of Illinois. The cause of
this is apparent. The malaria of marshes and unsubdued soils in
wooded districts, excluded from the light of the sun and a free
circulation of air, is far more malignant than that of the prairie
having the full benefit of these counteracting agents.†

The most distinguishing feature of the climate is its sub-tropical
summers and the arctic severities of its winters. The newly
arrived English immigrant is at first inclined to complain of these
climatic extremes, but a short residence in the country soon convinces him that many of the most kindly fruits and plants could
not be cultivated and matured without them. Owing to this tropical
element of the summer, the peach, grape, sweet potato, cotton,
corn and other plants readily mature in Illinois, though its mean
annual temperature is less than that of England, where their cultivation is impossible. These facts show that a high temperature
for a short season is more beneficial to some of the most valued
plants than a moderate temperature long continued. This is well
exemplified in the cultivation of our great staple, maize, or Indian
corn, which, wherever the conditions are favorable, yields a greater
amount of nutriment, with a given amount of labor, than any

---

*See Geographical Surveys of the State, and Foster's Physical Geography of the Missis-
sippi Valley.

†Foster's Physical Geography.

known cereal. It was originally a tropical grass, and when cultivated in regions of a high and protracted temperature, exhibits a
strong tendency to revert to its original condition. In the Gulf States
it grows to a greater hight than farther northward, but its yield of
seed is correspondingly less. In the valleys opening seaward along
the Pacific slope, it attains a medium size, but fails to mature for
the want of sufficient heat. Hence the districts of its maximum
production must be far north of its native latitudes, and have the
benefit of short but intense summer heats. In Illinois and adjacent parts of the great valley its greatest yield is about the 41st
parallel, and though far less imposing in its appearance than on
the Gulf, its productive capacity is said to be four-fold greater
than either there or on the Pacific. It is wonderful that a plant
should undergo such a great transformation in structure and natural habits, and that its greatest producing capacity should be
near the northern limits of its possible cultivation. These facts
suggest questions of great scientific value relative to the development of other plants by removing them from their native localities.

One of the causes which assist in imparting these extremes to
the climate may be thus explained. The different continental
masses during the summer become rapidly heated under the influence of the sun, while the surrounding oceans are less sensitive to
its effects. As the result, the lands bordering on the sea have a
comparatively mild temperature, while the interior is subject to
intense heat. During winter, for similar reasons, the interior
becomes severely cold, while the sea-girt shore still enjoys a much
milder temperature. But a greater modifying influence upon the
climate are the winds to which it is subject. The source of these
is at the equator, where the air, becoming rarified from the effects
of heat, rises and flows in vast masses toward the poles. On
reaching colder latitudes it descends to the earth, and as an under-
current returns to the equator and supplies the tropical vacuum
caused by its previous ascent. If the earth were at rest, the two
under and two upper currents would move at right angles to
the equator. But, owing to its daily revolution from west to east,
the under-currents, as they pass from the poles toward the equator
where the rotation is greatest, fall behind the earth, and that in
the northern hemisphere flows from the northeast, and that in the
southern from the southeast. In like manner the upper-currents,
flowing from the greater velocity of the equator toward the less at
the poles, get in advance of the earth; and the one in the north
flows from the southwest, and the other in the south from the
northwest. If the globe were a perfectly smooth sphere, the flow
of the winds as above described would be uniform, but the former
being crested with mountain chains, the latter are broken into a
great variety of local currents. In a belt of about 25 degrees on
each side of the equator, the under-currents blow with the greatest
regularity, and are called trade-winds, from their importance to navigation and commerce.

In making an application of these great primary currents to the
valley of the Mississippi, and consequently to Illinois, it will be
seen that the southwest winds, descending from their equato-
rial altitude, become the prevailing winds of the surface in our
latitude. Besides these, the northeast trade-winds, in their progress toward the equator, impinge against the lofty chain of the

Andes, and are deflected up the Mississippi Valley and mingle with the winds from the southwest. In their passage along the Andes Mountains, and across the Carribbean Sea and the Mexican Gulf, they become charged with tropical heat and moisture. On entering the great central valley of the continent, walled in on both sides by impassable mountain barriers, they are directed far northward, and, mingling with the southwest winds, dispense their waters, warmth and fertility, which are destined to make it the greatest theatre of human activities on the face of the globe. These winds, from local causes, frequently veer about to different points of the compass; and in Illinois and other prairies States, where there are no forest belts to break their force, frequently sweep over the country with the fury of tornadoes. Almost every year has recorded instances of the loss of life and property from this cause, and even in the great northern forests are tracks made by their passage, as well defined as the course of the reaper through a field of grain.

CHAPTER III.

ILLINOIS ANTIQUITIES—THE MOUND BUILDERS.

It is the opinion of antiquarians that three distinct races of people lived in North America prior to its occupation by the present population. Of these the builders of the magnificent cities whose remains are found in a number of localities of Central America were the most civilized. Judging from the ruins of broken columns, fallen arches and the crumbling walls of temples, palaces and pyramids, which in some places for miles bestrew the ground, these cities must have been of great extent and very populous. The mind is almost startled at the remoteness of their antiquity, when we consider the vast sweep of time necessary to erect such colossal structures of solid masonry, and afterwards convert them into the present utter wreck. Comparing their complete desolation with the ruins of Balbec, Palmyra, Thebes and Memphis, they must have been old when the latter were being built. May not America then be called the old world instead of the new; and may it not have contained, when these Central American cities were erected, a civilization equal if not superior to that which contemporaneously existed on the banks of the Nile, and made Egypt the cradle of eastern arts and science?

The second race, as determined by the character of their civilization, were the mound builders, the remains of whose works constitute the most interesting class of antiquities found within the limits of the United States. Like the ruins of Central America, they antedate the most ancient records; tradition can furnish no account of them, and their character can only be partially gleaned from the internal evidences which they themselves afford. They consist of the remains of what was apparently villages, altars, temples, idols, cemeteries, monuments, camps, fortifications, pleasure grounds, etc. The farthest relic of this kind, discovered in a northeastern direction, was near Black river on the south side of Lake Ontario. Thence they extend in a southwestern direction by way of the Ohio, the Mississippi, Mexican Gulf, Texas, New Mexico and Youcatan, into South America. Commencing in Cataraugus county, New York, there was a chain of forts extending more than 50 miles southwesterly, not more than 4 or 5 miles apart, and evidently built by a people rude in the arts and few in numbers. Further southward they increase in number and magnitude. In West Virginia, near the junction of Grave creek and the Ohio, is one of the most august monuments of remote antiquity found in the whole country. According to measurement it has an altitude of 90 feet, a diameter at the base of 100 feet, and at the summit of 45 feet, while a partial examination discloses within it the existence of many thousands of human skeletons. In Ohio, where the mounds have been carefully examined, are found some of the most extensive and interesting that occur in the United States. At the mouth of the Muskingum, among a number of curious works, was a rectangular fort containing 40 acres, encircled by a wall of earth 10 feet high, and perforated with openings resembling gateways. In the mound near the fort were found the remains of a sword, which appeared to have been buried with its owner. Resting on the forehead were found three large copper bosses, plated with silver and attached to a leather buckler. Near the side of the body was a plate of silver, which had perhaps been the upper part of a copper scabbard, portions of which were filled with iron rust, doubtless the remains of a sword. A fort of similar construction and dimensions was found on Licking river, near Newark. Eight gateways pierced the walls, and were guarded by mounds directly opposite each on the inside of the work. At Circleville, on the Scioto, there were two forts in juxtaposition; the one an exact circle 60 rods in diameter, and the other a perfect square, 55 rods on each side. The circular fortification was surrounded by two walls, with an intervening ditch 20 feet in depth. On Paint creek, 15 miles west of Chillicothe, besides other extensive works, was discovered the remains of a walled town. It was built on the summit of a hill about 300 feet in altitude, and encompassed by a wall 10 feet in hight, made of stone in their natural state. The area thus inclosed contained 130 acres. On the south side of it there were found the remains of what appeared originally to have been a row of furnaces or smith-shops, about which cinders were found several feet in depth. In the bed of the creek, which washes the foot of the hill, were found wells which had been cut through solid rock. They were more than 3 feet in diameter at the top, neatly walled with jointed stones, and, at the time of discovery, covered over by circular stones. So numerous were works of this kind in Ohio it would require a large volume to speak of them in detail.

Along the Mississippi they reach their maximum size and contain some of the most interesting relics. The number of mounds found here at an early day were estimated at more than 3,000, the smallest of which were not less than 20 feet in hight, and 100 feet in diameter at the base. A large number of them were found in Illinois, but, unfortunately, most of those who have examined them were little qualified to furnish correct information respecting their real character. It is greatly to be regretted that the State has never ordered a survey of these works by persons qualified to do the subject justice. Many of the most interesting have been ruthlessly destroyed, but it is believed a sufficient number still remain to justify an examination. It may, however, be safely assumed, from what is already known respecting them, that they were substantially the same as those found in other parts of the United States.

One of the most singular earthworks in this State was found in the lead region on the top of a ridge near the east bank of the Sinsinawa creek. It resembled some huge animal, the head, ears, nose, legs and tail and general outline of which being as perfect as if made by men versed in modern art. The ridge on which it was situated stands on the prairie, 300 yards wide, 100 feet in hight, and rounded on the top by a deep deposit of clay. Centrally, along the line of its summit and thrown up in the form of an embankment three feet high, extended the outline of a quadruped, measuring 250 feet from the tip of the nose to the end of the tail, and having a width of body at the center of 18 feet. The head was 35 feet in length, the ears 10, legs 60, and tail 75. The curvature in both the fore and hind legs was natural to an animal lying on its side. The general outline of the figure most nearly resembled the extinct animal known to geologists as the Megatherium. The question naturally arises, by whom and for what purpose was this earth figure raised. Some have conjectured that numbers of this now extinct animal lived and roamed over the prairies of Illinois when the mound builders first made their appearance in the upper part of the Mississippi Valley, and that their wonder and admiration, excited by the colossal dimensions of these huge creatures, found expression in the erection of this figure. The bones of some similar gigantic animals were exhumed on this stream about 3 miles from the same place.*

David Dale Owen, a celebrated western geologist, in his report to the land office in 1839, refers to a number of figures, similar to the one above described, as existing in Wisconsin. He thinks they were connected with the totemic system of the Indians who formerly dwelt in this part of the country. When, for example a distinguished chief died, he infers that his clansmen raised over his body a mound resembling the animal which had been used as a symbol to designate his family.

Mr. Breckenridge, who examined the antiquities of the western country in 1817, speaking of the mounds in the American Bottom, says: "The great number and the extremely large size of some of them may be regarded as furnishing, with other circumstances, evidence of their antiquity. I have sometimes been induced to think that at the period when they were constructed there was a population here as numerous as that which once animated the borders of the Nile or of the Euphrates or of Mexico. The most numerous as well as considerable of these remains are found in precisely those parts of the country where the traces of a numerous population might be looked for, namely, from the mouth of the Ohio, on the east side of the Mississippi, to the Illinois river, and on the west from the St. Francis to the Missouri. I am perfectly satisfied that cities similar to those of ancient Mexico, of several hundred thousand souls, have existed in this country."

Says Mr. C. Atwater, the author of an able work on the antiquities of Ohio: "Nearly opposite St. Louis there are traces of two such cities, in the distance of 5 miles. They were situated on the Cahokia, which crosses the American Bottom opposite St. Louis. One of the mounds is 800 yards in circumference at the base, and 100 feet in hight."

The following description of this mound, which is the largest in the United States, is condensed from an article in the Belleville *Eagle:* It is situated 6½ miles northeast of St. Louis, and is commonly known as the Monk's mound, from the Monks of La Trappe having settled on and around it. It is an irregular oblong, extending north and south, and its shortest sides east and west. The top contains about 3¼ acres, and about half way down the sides is a terrace, extending the whole width of the mound, and

*Galena Jeffersonian, 1853.

sufficiently broad to afford sites for a number of spacious buildings. The present want of regularity is due to the action of the
rains, which, during a long interval of time, has so changed its
surface that the original design of its builders has been lost. A
Mr. Hill, who lived on it, in making an excavation for an ice-house
on the northwest part, found human bones and white pottery in
large quantities. The bones, which crumbled to dust on being
exposed to the air, were larger than common, and the teeth were
double in front as well as behind. A well dug by Mr. Hill, whose
dwelling was on the summit, passed through several strata of
earth, and, it is said, the remains of weeds and grass were discovered between the layers, the color of which was still visible and
bright as when they were first inhumed. The writer thinks this
portion of the American Bottom might with propriety be called
the city of mounds, for in less than a mile square there are 60 or
80 of every size and form, none of which are more than one-third
as large as the Monk's mound. They extend in a westerly direction, five miles or more, along the Cahokia.

Notwithstanding the authorities referred to above, recent observations render it highly probable that these mounds are portions
of the original shore of the Mississippi, which, like islands, were
not wholly washed away by its waters. Professor Worthen, our
State Geologist, and others, think that the material of which they
are composed, and its stratification, correspond exactly in these
particulars with the opposite bluffs.

The greatest evidence of art which they exhibit is their form.
The base of the large mound, before denudation changed it, had
the form of a parallelogram, whose well defined right-angles could
not have resulted from the action of water. Its terrace, and the
same features which distinguished the mounds on the west side
of the river at St. Louis, at Marietta, Portsmouth, Paint Creek
and Circleville, Ohio, and large numbers of them in Mexico, are
remarkable coincidences, if they are not works of art. It is well
known that the ancients, instead of throwing up mounds, in
some instances selected natural elevations and shaped them with
terraces for sites of altars and temples, and this seems to have
been the character of the mounds in the American Bottom. Though
not originally intended for graves, they were subsequently used as
such by the Indians, that their dead might be above the floods of
the Mississippi.

But whatever may have been the nature of these, there is no
doubt as to the artificial character of others in many localities.
Pioneer evidence states that at an early date copper, and a great
variety of other implements, exceeding in their workmanship the
skill of the present Indians, were taken from the mounds of Southern Illinois. The existence of this metal in these earthworks refers them to the era of the mound builders, as the Indians are
ignorant of the process of working it, and never used it in the
manufacture of implements. The copper so frequently discovered
in mounds in the United States doubtless came from the region of
Lake Superior. Mines have been examined here extending over
large areas, the working of which antedates all existing records
or Indian traditions. Another of the many evidences of tribes,
who must have inhabited this country at a remote period, was
found a few years since at the Illinois Salines. Fragments of pot-

tery, from 4 to 5 feet in diameter, were exhumed some 30 feet below the surface, and had evidently been used in the manufacture of salt by the mound builders, or some other ancient people, different from the present Indians. The artificial character of these works not being a controverted point, the inquiry arises who were their builders? The hypothesis that they were the ancestors of the Algonquin and other tribes found living in their midst, when first visited by Europeans, but illy accords with the evidence furnished by an examination of the facts. These curious relics are fragments of a history which point to a people different in physical structure from the red men, and greatly in advance of them in art and civilization. The latter in general are a tall, rather slender, straight-limbed people, while the former were short and thick set, had low foreheads, high cheek bones, and were remarkable for their large eyes and broad chins. Their limbs were short and stout, while their whole physique more closely resembled that of the German than any existing race. The remains of their art also indicated a people wholly distinct. From these tumuli have been taken silver, iron and copper implements, exhibiting in their construction a degree of skill greatly exceeding Indian ingenuity and workmanship. The large number of medals, bracelets, pipes, and other instruments made of copper, show that its use among them was much more extensive than that of the other metals. They may have possessed the lost art of hardening it, for cut stone is occasionally found in some of their works. The manufacture of earthenware was one of their most advanced arts; vessels made from calcareous breccia have been taken from their tombs, equal in quality to any now made in Italy from the same material. A considerable number of these were urns, containing bones, which appear to have been burnt before they were deposited in them. Mirrors, made of isinglas, were of frequent occurrence in the mounds. Many of them were large and elegant, and must have answered well the purpose for which they were intended. Could they speak, they would doubtless tell us that the primitive belles, whose charms they reflected, had the same fondness for personal decoration that distinguishes their sisters of the present day.

Their habitations must have been tents, structures of wood, or some other perishable material; otherwise their remains would have been numerous. The remains, however, of fire-places, hearths and chimneys, imbedded in the alluvial banks of the Ohio and Muskingum rivers, are frequently brought to light by the action of their waters. The Indians of these localities never erected such works; while their great depth below the surface, and its heavy growth of trees, is evidence that they were not made by Europeans, hence must be referred to the mound builders. Evidence of this kind might be multiplied indefinitely, but what has been said is deemed sufficient.

Not only had the mound builders made considerable progress in the arts, but they were not wholly wanting in scientific attainments. The lines of nearly all their works, where the situation would admit of it, conform to the four cardinal points. Had their authors no knowledge of astronomy, they could never have determined the points of the compass with such exactness as their works indicate. This noble science, which in modern times has given us such extended views of the universe, was among the first in the earlier ages to arrest the attention of mankind. The pastoral life of primitive times, when men dwelt in tents, or the open air, with the heavenly bodies in full view, was very favorable to the study of astronomy.

If the mound builders were not the ancestors of our Indians, who were they? The oblivion which has closed over them is so complete that only conjectures can be given in answer to the question. Those who do not believe in the common parentage of mankind contend that they were an indigenous race of the western hemisphere. Others, with more plausibility, think they came from the east, and imagine that they can see coincidences in the religion of the Hindoos and Southern Tartars and the supposed theology of the mound builders. An idol was found in a tomb near Nashville, consisting of three busts, representing a man in a state of nudity. On the head of each were carved the sacred fillet and cake with which, in ancient Greece, during sacrifices, the heads of the idol, the victim, and priest were bound. The Greeks are supposed to have borrowed these sacred appliances from the Persians, with whom they had frequent wars and an intimate maritime intercourse. Another idol, consisting of three heads united at the back, was taken from a tomb on the headwaters of the Cumberland river. Their features, which were expressive, exhibited in a striking manner the lineaments of the Tartar countenance. It has been farther observed that wherever there was a group of mounds three of them were uniformly larger and more favorably situated than the rest. The triune character of these images and mounds are supposed to represent the three principal gods of the Hindoos, Brahmin, Vishnoo and Siva. This supposition has been farther strengthened by the discovery in many mounds of murex shells, which were sacred in the religion of the Hindoos, used as material in the construction of their idols, and as the musical instruments of their Tritons. In digging a well near Nashville, a clay vessel was found 20 feet below the surface. It was of a globose form, terminating at the top with a female head, the features of which were strongly marked and Asiatic. The crown of the head was covered with a cap of pyramidal form resembling the Asiatic head-dress. The vessel was found sitting on a rock from under which issued a stream of water, and may have been used at the fountain in performing the ablutions enjoined by some of the oriental religions. Indeed, for this purpose the temples and altars of the Hindoos are always erected on the banks of some river, as the Ganges and other sacred streams, and the same practice was observed by the authors of the American tumuli.

From evidence of this kind it is inferred that this people came from Asia, and that their migrations, like those from Europe at the present day, were made at different times and from different countries.

They were no doubt idolators, and it has been conjectured that the sun was an object of adoration. The mounds were generally built in a situation affording a view of the rising sun. When inclosed with walls their gateways were toward the east. The caves in which they were occasionally found buried always opened in the same direction. Whenever a mound was partially inclosed by a semicircular pavement, it was on the east side. When bodies were buried in graves, as was frequently the case, they lay in an eastern and western direction; and finally, medals have been found representing the sun and his rays of light.

At what period they came to this country is likewise a matter of speculation. From the comparatively rude state of the arts among them, it has been inferred that the time was very remote. Their axes were made of stone; their raiment, judging from the fragments which have been discovered, consisted of the barks of trees interwoven with feathers; and their military works were such as a people would erect who had just passed from the hunter to the pastoral state of society. The line of forts already referred to, in New York, were built on the brow of the hill which was originally the southern shore of Lake Erie. By the recession of the waters, they are now from 3 to 5 miles distant from their original limits. The surface, which became exposed by the retirement of the waters, is now covered with a vegetable mold from 6 to 10 inches deep, and it may reasonably be supposed that a long interval of time was required for the production of the forests by whose decomposition it was formed. But a much longer interval would be required for the Niagara to deepen its channel and thus cause the subsidence of the waters in the lake.

What finally became of this people is another query which has been extensively discussed. The fact that their works extend into Mexico and Peru has induced the belief that it was their posterity that dwelt in these countries when they were first visited by the Spaniards. The Mexican and Peruvian works, with the exception of their greater magnitude, are similar. Relics common to all of them have been occasionally found, and it is believed that the religious uses which they subserved were the same. One of the principal deities of the South Americans was the god of the shining mirror, so called because he was supposed to reflect, like a mirror, his divine perfections. The same god was also a Mexican divinity; and while other deities were symbolized by images, this one was represented by a mirror, and held in great veneration as the unknown god of the universe. Isinglas, common in the mounds in the United States, was the material generally employed for the construction of mirrors in Mexico; but in South America, obsidian, a volcanic product, which answered the same purpose, was more frequently used. If, indeed, the Mexicans and Peruvians were the progeny of the more ancient mound builders, then Spanish rapacity for gold was the cause of their overthrow and final extermination.

A thousand other interesting queries naturally arise respecting these nations which now repose under the ground, but the most searching investigation can only give us vague speculations for answers. No historian has preserved the names of their mighty chieftains nor given an account of their exploits, and even tradition is silent respecting them. If we knock at the tombs, no spirit comes back with a response, and only a sepulchral echo of forgetfulness and death reminds us how vain is the attempt to unlock the mysterious past upon which oblivion has fixed its seal. How forcibly their mouldering bones and perishing relics remind us of the transitory character of human existence. Generation after generation lives, moves and is no more; time has strewn the track of its ruthless march with the fragments of mighty empires; and at length not even their names nor works have an existence in the speculations of those who take their places.

CHAPTER IV.

THE INDIANS OF ILLINOIS.

The third distinct race which, according to ethnologists, has inhabited North America, is the present Indians. When visited by early European pioneers they were without cultivation, refinement or literature, and far behind their precursors, the mound builders, in a knowledge of the arts. The question of their origin has long interested archeologists, and is one of the most difficult they have been called on to answer. One hypothesis is that they are an original race indigenous to the Western Hemisphere. Those who entertain this view think their peculiarities of physical structure preclude the possibility of a common parentage with the rest of mankind. Prominent among these distinctive traits is the hair, which in the red man is round, in the white man oval, and in the black man flat. In the pile of the European the coloring matter is distributed by means of a central canal, but in that of the Indian it is incorporated in the fibrous structure. Brown, who has made an exhaustive examination of these varieties of hair, concludes that they are radically different, and belong to three distinct branches of the human family, which, instead of a common, have had a trinary origin. Since, therefore, these and other peculiar ethnological features are characteristic only of the aboriginal inhabitants of America, it is inferred that they are indigenous to this part of the globe.

A more common supposition, however, is that they are a derivative race, and sprang from one or more of the ancient peoples of Asia. In the absence of all authentic history, and when even tradition is wanting, any attempt to point out the particular theater of their origin must prove unsatisfactory. They are perhaps an offshoot of Shemitic parentage, and some imagine, from their tribal organization and some faint coincidences of language and religion, that they were the descendants of the ancient Hebrews. Others, with as much propriety, contend that their progenitors were the ancient Hindoos, and that the Brahmin idea, which uses the sun to symbolize the Creator of the Universe, has its counterpart in the sunworship of the Indians. They also see in the Hindoo polytheism, with its 30,000 divinities, a theology corresponding with the innumerable minor Indian deities, of which birds, quadrupeds, reptiles, and fishes are made the symbols. The Persians, and other primitive oriental stocks, and even the nations of Europe, if the testimony of different antiquarians could be accepted, might claim the honor of first peopling America.

Though the exact place of origin may never be known, yet the striking coincidences of physical organization between the oriental types of mankind and the Indians, point unmistakably to some part of Asia as the place whence they emigrated. Instead of 1800 years, the time of their roving in the wilds of America, as determined by Spanish interpretation of their pictographic records, the interval has perhaps been thrice that period. Their religions, superstitions and ceremonies, if of foreign origin, evidently belong to the crude theologies prevalent in the last centuries before the introduction of Mahometanism or Christianity. Scarcely 3000 years would suffice to blot out perhaps almost every trace of the language they brought with them from the Asiatic cradle of the race, and introduce the present diversity of aboriginal tongues. Like their oriental progenitors they have lived for centuries without progress, while the Caucassian variety of the race, under the transforming power of art, science, and improved systems of civil polity, have made the most rapid advancement. At the time of their departure eastward, a great current of emigration flowed westward to Europe, making it a great arena of human effort and improvement. Thence proceeding farther westward it met in America, the midway station in the circuit of the globe, the opposing current direct from Asia. The shock of the first contact was the beginning of the great conflict which has since been waged by the rival sons of Shem and Japheth. The first thought of the Indian, when hostilities commenced on the Atlantic border, was to retire westward. It was from beyond the Alleghanies, according to the traditions of their fathers, they had come, and in the same undefined region they located their paradise or happy hunting ground. To employ an aboriginal allegory, "The Indians had long discerned a dark cloud in the heavens, coming from the east, which threatened them with disaster and death. Slowly rising at first, it seemed shadow, but soon changed to substance. When it reached the summit of the Alleghanies it assumed a darker hue; deep murmurs, as of thunder, were heard; it was impelled westward by strong wind, and shot forth forked tongues of lightning."

The movement of the sombre cloud typified the advance of labor, science and civilization. Pontiac foresaw the coming storm when he beheld the French flag and French supremacy stricken down on the plains of Abraham. To the British officer sent westward to secure the fruits of victory, he said: "I stand in thy path." To the assembled chiefs of the nations in council, he unfolded his schemes of opposition, depicted the disasters which would attend the coming rush of the Anglo-Saxon, and climaxed his invective against the hated enemy with the exclamation, "Drive the dogs who wear red clothing into the sea." Fifty years after the defeat of Pontiac, Tecumseh, emulating his example, plotted the conspiracy of the Wabash. He brought to his aid the powerful influence of the Indian priest-hood; for years the forest haunts of his clansmen rang with his stirring appeals, and the valleys of the West ran with the blood of the white invaders. But Tecumseh fell a martyr to his cause, and the second attempt to turn back the tide of civilization was a failure. The Appalachian tribes, under the leadership of Tuscaloosa, next waged a continuous war of three years against the southern frontiers. The conflict terminated by the sublime act of its leader, who, after a reward had been offered for his head, voluntarily surrendered himself for the good of his

countrymen.   After this defeat, the southern tribes abandoned
their long cherished idea of re-establishing Indian supremacy.   A
last and fruitless effort of this kind, by the Sacs and Foxes of Illinois, placed the vast domain east of the Mississippi in the hands
of the ruthless conquerors.*

Algonquins and Iroquois.—Of the several great branches of
North American Indians, as determined by sameness of language
and mental and physical type, the only ones entitled to consideration in Illinois history, are the Algonquin, and incidentally the
Iroquois.   Before the encroachments of Europeans caused the retirement of the Algonquin tribes, they occupied most of the United
States between the 35th and 60th parallels of latitudes, and the
60th and 105th meridians of longitude.   They were Algonquins
whom Cartier found on the banks of the St. Lawrence, whom the
English discovered hunting and fishing on the Atlantic coast, from
Maine to the Carolinas.   They were tribes of this lineage whom
Jesuit missionaries taught to repeat prayers and sing *aris* on the
banks of the Mississippi and Illinois, and on the shores of the
great lakes and Hudson Bay.   The same great family waged war
with the Puritans of New England, entered into a covenant of
peace with Penn, and furnished a Pocahontas to intercede for the
life of the adventurous founder of Virginia.

The starting point in the wanderings of the Algonquin tribes on
the continent, as determined by tradition and the cultivation of the
maize, their favorite cereal, was in the southwest.   It is conjectured
as they passed up the western side of the Mississippi Valley, their
numbers were augmented by accessions from nomadic clans pass-
through the central and southern passes of the Rocky Mountains.
Then, turning eastward across the Mississippi, the southern margin of the broad track pursued toward the Atlantic was about the
35th parallel, the limits reached in this direction by these tribes.
This would place in the central line of march, Illinois, and the adjacent regions, where the first European explorers found corn
extensively cultivated and used as an article of food.   On reaching
the Atlantic they moved northeasterly along the seaboard to the
mouth of the St. Lawrence, introducing along their track the cultivation of maize, without which many of the early British colonists must have perished.   Next, ascending the St. Lawrence and
the great lakes, they spread northward and westward to Hudson's
Bay, the basin of Lake Winnepeg, and the valley of the Upper
Mississippi.   In this wide dispersion the original stock was broken
into minor tribes; each, in the course of time, deviating in speech
from the parent language, and forming a dialect of its own.   The
head of the migratory column, circling round the source of the
Mississippi, recrossed it in a southeasterly direction above the falls
of St. Anthony, and passed by way of Green Bay and Lake Michigan into the present limits of Illinois, Indiana and Ohio.   Thus,
after revolving in an irregular elipse of some 3000 miles in diameter, they fell into the original track eastward.

The territory of the Iroquois lay like an island in this vast area
of Algonquin population.   They had three conflicting traditions
of their origin: that they came from the west, from the north, and
sprung from the soil on which they lived.   Their confederacy at
first consisted of 5 tribes, the Mohawks, Oneidas, Onondagas,

*Schoolcraft's, Part 5; Spencer's History of the United States

Cayugas and Senecas, to which a 6th, the Tuscaroras was afterwards added. Each tribe had a separate political organization in which the sachems were the ruling spirits. When foreign tribes were to be consulted, or the general interests of the confederacy required deliberation, the sachems of the several tribes met in general council. Hasty writers, judging from their successes without carefully studying their character and history, have greatly overrated their virtues. There is no doubt as to their success in war, but it was rather the result of circumstances than inherent worth. Notwithstanding their much lauded eloquence, diplomacy and courage, there is little doubt that the Algonquin tribes of the same latitude were in these respects fully their equals. As it regards cranial indications, the Iroquois had an excessive development at the basillar region, and the Algonquins a larger intellectual lobe, and the conduct of the two races corresponds with their cerebral differences. It is well known that for the exhibition of brutish ferocity in battle, and the fiendish butchery of prisoners, the former were without rivals. Missionary evidence states that it was they who first taught the Illinois the cruel practice of burning prisoners at the stake. But admitting their natural superiority they must have lost it by amalgamation, for it was customary with them to repair their constant losses in war by adopting into their families the women and children captured from their Algonquin enemies. This infusion of blood, if in a few generations it did not give the foreign element the ascendancy, must have greatly modified the original stock. Indeed some of the adopted Algonquins became afterwards their prominent chiefs.

Their success in war was in a great measure the result of local and other advantages. Possessing a territory included in the present limits of New York, it gave them ready access to the nations living on the western lakes; while the Mohawk and the Hudson furnished them a highway to the tribes of the sea-coast. Having by savage barbarity converted all the surrounding nations into enemies, necessity taught them the advantage of union, fixity of habitation made them superior in agriculture, while a passion for war gave them a preeminence in the arts best suited to gratify their inordinate lust for blood. Deprived of these advantages it is doubtful whether they would have been long able to cope with the tribes which they outraged by incessant attacks.

The Algonquin tribes were too widely dispersed to admit of a general confederacy; the interposition of great lakes and rivers prevented concert of action, and hence each community had to contend single-handed with the united enemy. Even in these unequal contests they were sometimes the conquerors, as instanced in the triumph of the Illinois on the banks of the Iroquois, a stream in our State whose name still commemorates the victory.

It is not, however, in the petty broils of tribal warfare, but the fierce conflicts with the civilized intruders upon their soil, that a correct opinion is to be formed of these rival races. In these bloody struggles, which decided the fate of the entire aboriginal population, it was that the Algonquins evinced their great superiority. Unlike the Iroquois, who, in their haughty independence, disdained to go beyond their own narrow realms for assistance, and who, in their great thirst for carnage, even destroyed kindred nations, the Algonquins formed the most extensive alliance to

3

resist the encroachments of their English destroyers. Such was the
nature of King Philip's war, who, with his Algonquin braves,
spread terror and desolation throughout New England. Panic-
stricken at his audacity and success, the Puritans imagined they
saw dire portents of calamities in the air and sky, and shadowy
troops of careering horsemen imprinted on the face of the sun and
moon. This compactly formed confederacy of tribes was over-
thrown; but it cost the Colonists, with their superior numbers,
discipline and weapons, a bloody contest to accomplish it. Such,
too, was the character of the culminating struggle of the red race,
some 90 years later, for the dominion of the western wilderness.
Never before had the Indians exhibited such feats of courage,
such skill in diplomacy and such strategy in war; and never before,
nor afterwards, were their efforts attended with such terrible consequences. With an Algonquin chief and Algonquin warriors as
the controlling spirits, a confederacy of continental proportions
was the result, embracing in its alliance the tribes of every name
and lineage, from the northern lakes to the gulf on the south.
Pontiac, having breathed into them his implacable hate of the
English intruders, ordered the conflict to commence, and all the
British colonies trembled before the desolating fury of the onset.

Of the tribes of Algonquin lineage which formerly dwelt in
Illinois, those bearing the name of the State were the most numerous. Judging from the graves which were thickly planted over the
prairies, they must at an early date have been a prominent theater
of aboriginal activities. Long before the intrusion of the white
man, the stately warrior marshaled his swarthy clans to defend
the hunting grounds which embosomed the homes and graves of
his ancestors. Here, around the lodge fire, the young braves
listened to the exploits of their aged chiefs and marched forth to
perform the deeds which were to crown them with a chieftain's
honors. On the grass-cushioned lap of the prairie, when the
moon with mellow radiance flooded the valleys and silvered the
streams, the red swain went forth to woo his intended mate and
win her love. Where the game abounded which furnished him
with food and clothing he built the wigwam in which his faithful
partner dispensed the hospitalities of his frugal board. Nature
disclosed to his untutored mind the simple duties of life. The
opening flower revealed the time for planting corn, the falling leaf
when to provide for the frosts of winter, and from the lower
animals he learned industry, prudence and affection. His own
wondrous organization directed his thoughts to the Great Spirit,
and in the spacious temple, lighted by the sun and curtained with
clouds, where the tempest offers its loud anthem of praise, he
worshipped the God of Nature.

The Illinois Confederacy were composed of five tribes: the Tamaroas, Michigamies, Kaskaskias, Cahokias, and Peorias. Albert
Gallatin, who has prepared the most elaborate work on the structure of the Indian languages, gives the definition of Illinois as real
or superior men, and derives it from the Delaware word Leno,
Leni or Illini, as it is variously written by different authors. The
termination of the word as it is now, and applied to the State and
its principal river, is of French origin. The Illinois, Miamis and
Delawares are of the same stock, and, according to tradition, emigrated from the far west, the first stopping in their eastern round

of migration in the vicinity of Lake Michigan, the second in the territory of Indiana, and the third that of Pennsylvania.

As early as 1670 the Jesuit, Father Marquette, mentions frequent visits made by individuals of this confederacy to the missionary station of St. Esprit, near the western extremity of Lake Superior. At that time they lived west of the Mississippi in eight villages, whither the Iroquois had driven them from the shores of Lake Michigan, which received its name from one of the tribes. Shortly afterwards they commenced returning eastward, and finally settled mostly on the Illinois. Joliet and Marquette, in 1743, descending the Mississippi below the mouth of the Wisconsin, on their famous voyage of discovery, met with a band of them on the west bank of the river. The principal chief treated them with great hospitality, gave them a calumet as a pass down the river, and bid them a friendly farewell. The same explorers, in their return voyage up the Illinois, discovered and stopped at the principal town of the confederacy, situated on the banks of the river 7 miles below the present town of Ottawa. It was then called Kaskaskia, and according to Marquette, contained 74 lodges, each of which domiciled several families. Marquette returned to the village in the spring of 1675, and established the Mission of the Immaculate Conception, the oldest in Illinois, and subsequently transferred to the new town of Kaskaskia further southward.

When, in 1679, La Salle visited the town it had greatly increased, numbering, according to Hennepin, 460 lodges, and at the annual assembling of the different tribes from 6,000 to 8,000 souls. The lodges extended along the banks of the river a mile or more, according to the number of its fluctuating population, which extensively cultivated the adjacent meadows and raised crops of pumpkins, beans, and Indian corn. At this time the confederacy possessed the country from the present town of Ottawa and the lower rapids of the Mississippi to the mouth of the Ohio, and, according to the missionary Father Rasles, besides the principal town occupied some 10 or 12 other villages. In the irruption of the Iroquois, the following year, the principal town was burned and the several tribes pursued down the river to the Mississippi, where the Tamaroas were attacked and 700 of their women and children made prisoners. These were burned and butchered till the savage victors were sated with carnage, when the survivors were lead into captivity. With the withdrawal of the enemy the tribes returned, rebuilt their town, and in 1682 furnished 1,200 of the 3,800 warriors embraced in LaSalle's colony at Fort Saint Louis on the Illinois. After this they were forced further southward by northern nations, and Peoria, Cahokia and Kaskaskia became the centres of the tribes indicated by their names. The Tamaroas were associated with the Kaskaskias, and the Michigamies were located near Fort Chartres on the Mississippi. While here they were the centre of Jesuit missionary operations, and great efforts were made to convert them to Christianity, but with only partial success.

In 1729 they were summoned by M. Perrier, Governor-General of Louisiana, to assist in the reduction of the Natchez, who were disturbing the peace of the province. On the breaking out of the Chickasaw war they were again called to the assistance of their allies, the French, and under one of Illinois' most gallant generals,

the Chevalier D'Artagnette, they successively stormed and carried
two of the enemy's strongholds, and would have taken a third but
for the fall of their heroic leader.

In common with other western tribes they became involved in
the conspiracy of Pontiac, but from frequent defeats by surrounding tribes, and long contact with civilization, they had lost to a
great extent the warlike energy, for which, according to tradition, they were anciently distinguished. When, therefore, the
great chief visited them in the autumn of 1764, their zeal did not
meet his expectations, and he told them if they hesitated, he
would "consume their tribes as fire doth the dry grass on the
prairies." Finally, when Pontiac lost his life by the hand of an
Illinois, the nations which had followed him as a leader descended
from the north and the east to avenge his death, and almost annihilated the tribes of this lineage. Tradition states that a band
of fugitives, to escape the general slaughter, took refuge on the
high rock which had been the site of Fort St. Louis. There they
were besieged by a superior force of the Pottawatamies, whom the
great strength of this natural fortress enabled them easily to keep
at bay. Hunger and thirst, more formidable enemies, however,
soon accomplished what the foe was unable to effect. Their small
quantity of provisions quickly failed, and their supply water was
stopped by the enemy severing the cords attached to the vessels
by which they elevated it from the river below. Thus environed
by relentless foes, they took a last lingering look at their beautiful
hunting grounds, spread out like a panorama on the gently rolling
river, and, with true Indian fortitude, laid down and expired without a sigh or a tear. From their tragic fate the lofty citadel on
which they perished received the unpoetical name of "Starved
Rock," and years afterwards their bones were seen whitening on
its summit. The Tamaroas, although not entirely exterminated,
lost their identity as a tribe in a battle with the Shawnees, near
the eastern limits of Randolph county. At the commencement of
the present century the contracting circle of hostile tribes had
forced the remnants of this once powerful confederacy into a small
compass around Kaskaskia. When the country was first visited
by Europeans they numbered 12,000 souls; now they were reduced
to two tribes, the Kaskaskias and Peorias, and could only muster
150 warriors. Their chief at this time was a half-breed of considerable talent, named Du Quoin, who wore a medal presented to
him by Washington, whom he visited at Philadelphia. In the
early part of the present century the two tribes under his guidance
emigrated to the Southwest, and in 1850 they were in the Indian
Territory, and numbered 84 persons.

The Sacs and Foxes, who have figured extensively in the history of Illinois, dwelt in the northwest part of the State. The
word "Sau-Kee," now written "Sac," is derived from the compound word "A-sau-we-kee," of the Chippewa language, signifying
yellow earth, and "Mus-qua-kee," the original name of the Foxes,
means red earth. Though still retaining separate tribal names,
when living in Illinois they had, by long residence together and
intermarriage, become substantially one people. Both tribes originally lived on the St. Lawrence, in the neighborhood of Quebec
and Montreal. The Foxes first removed to the West and established themselves on the river which bears their name, empty-

ing into the head of Green Bay. Here they suffered a signal defeat from the combined forces of the French and their Indian allies, which caused them afterwards to unite with the Sacs, to prevent extermination.

The Sacs became involved in a long and bloody war with the Iroquois, who drove them from their habitation on the St. Lawrence toward the West. Retiring before these formidable enemies, they next encountered the Wyandots, by whom they were driven farther and farther along the shores of the great lakes till at length they found a temporary resting place on Green Bay, in the neighborhood of their relatives, the Foxes. For mutual protection against the surrounding nations a union was here instituted between the two tribes, which has remained unbroken to the present time. The time of their migration from the St. Lawrence to the region of the upper lakes cannot be definitely ascertained. Green Bay was visited in 1669 by Father Allouez, a Jesuit, who established a missionary station there, and in the winter of 1672 extended his labors to the Foxes, who at first treated him with the greatest contempt. Some of the tribe had recently been on a trading expedition to Montreal, where they had been foully dealt with by the French, and they now took occasion to show their resentment by deriding the utterances of the missionary. By the exercise of great patience, however, he at length obtained a hearing, and succeeded so well in impressing their minds with his religious instruction that when he exhibited a crucifix they threw tobacco on it as an offering. He soon afterwards taught the whole village to make the sign of the cross, and painting it on their shields, in one of their war expeditions, they obtained a great victory over their enemies. Thus, while they knew but little of its significance as a religious emblem, in war they regarded it as a talisman of more than ordinary power.

From Green Bay they moved southward, and shortly after the French pioneers visited the country they took possession of the fertile plains of Northwestern Illinois, driving out the Sauteaux, a branch of the Chippewas. In their southern migration, according to their traditions, a severe battle occurred between them and the Mascoutins, opposite the mouth of the Iowa, in which the latter were defeated, and only a few of them left to carry the news of their disaster to friends at home. Subsequently they formed alliances with the Potawatamies and other nations, forced the different tribes of the Illinois confederacy southward, and after years of strife almost exterminated them. In conjunction with the Menomonees, Winnebagoes, and other tribes living in the region of the lakes, they made an attempt, in 1779, to destroy the village of St. Louis, but were prevented by the timely arrival of George Rogers Clark with 500 men from Kaskaskia. Finally, in the Black Hawk war, waged by them against the troops of Illinois and the United States, they attracted the attention of the entire nation, and won a historical reputation.

Much labor has been expended to ascertain whether the celebrated Chief, Pontiac, was of Sac or Ottawa lineage. If a similarity in the traits of character, which distinguished him and the Sac tribe, could decide the question, the latter might, doubtless, claim the honor of his relationship. It is unnecessary to speak of the courage and fighting qualities of Pontiac. That of the Sacs and their relatives, the Foxes, is thus given by Drake, in

his " Life of Black Hawk :" "The Sacs and Foxes fought their
way from the waters of the St. Lawrence to Green Bay, and after
reaching that place not only sustained themselves against the hostile tribes, but were among the most active and courageous in the
subjugation, or rather extermination, of the numerous and powerful Illinois confederacy. They had many wars, offensive and defensive, with the Sioux, the Pawnees, the Osages and other tribes,
some of which are ranked among the most fierce and ferocious
warriors of the whole continent, and it does not appear that in
these conflicts, running through a long period of years, they were
found wanting in this the greatest of all savage virtues. In the
late war with Great Britain, a party of the Sacs and Foxes fought
under the British standard as a matter of choice, and in the recent
contest between a fragment of these tribes and the United States,
although defeated and literally cut to pieces by an overwhelming
force, it is very questionable whether their reputation as braves
would suffer by a comparison with that of their victors. It is believed that a careful review of their history, from the period when
they first established themselves on the waters of the Mississippi
down to the present time, will lead the inquirer to the conclusion
that the Sacs and Foxes are a truly courageous people, shrewd,
politic, and enterprising, with not more of ferocity and treachery
of character than is common among the tribes by whom they were
surrounded."

These tribes, at the time of the Black Hawk war, were divided into 20 families, 12 of which were Sacs and 8 Foxes. As marks of distinction, each family had its particular totemic symbol, represented
by some animal. There also existed a peculiar custom among
them of marking each male child at birth with black and white
paint, each mother being careful to apply the two colors alternately, so that each family and the entire nation might be divided into
two nearly equal classes, the whites and the blacks. The object of
these distinctive marks, which were retained during life, was to
keep alive a spirit of emulation in the tribes. In their games,
hunts, and public ceremonies, the blacks were the competitors of
the whites, and in war each party was ambitious to take more
scalps than the other.

Lieutenat Pike, in his travels to the source of the Mississippi,
in 1805, visited these tribes and found them residing in four principal villages. The first was at the head of the rapids of the river
DesMoines, the second farther up on the east shore of the same
stream, the third on the Iowa, and the fourth on Rock river near
its entrance into the Mississippi. The latter greatly exceeded the
others in political importance, and was among the largest and
most populous Indian villages on the continent. The country
around it, diversified with groves and prairies, was one of the most
beautiful regions in the valley of the Mississippi, and gave additional interest to this time-honored residence of the   nation.
According to Lieutenant Pike, the Sacs numbered 2,850 souls,
of whom 1400 were children, 750 women, and 700 warriors. The
total number of Foxes were 1750, of whom 850 were children, 500
women, and 400 warriors. In 1825, the Secretary of War estimated
the entire number of Sacs and Foxes at 4,600, showing in the intervening period of 20 years a considerable increase of population.
After the Black Hawk war, these tribes retired to their lands in

Iowa, whence they were finally transferred to the Indian Territory, and in 1850 numbered some 1600 souls.

The early traditions of the *Winnebagoes* fixes their ancient seat on the west shore of Lake Michigan, north of Green Bay. They believed that their ancestors were created by the Great Spirit, on the lands constituting their ancient territory, and that their title to it was a gift from their Creator. The Algonquins named them after the bay on which they lived, Ween-ni-ba-gogs, which subsequently became anglicized in the form of Winnebagoes. They were persons of good stature, manly bearing, had the charcteristic black circular hair of their race, and were generally more uncouth in their habits than the surrounding tribes. Their language was a deep gutteral, difficult to learn, and shows that they belonged to the great Dacotah stock of the West. Anciently, they were divided into clans distinguished by the bird, bear, fish, and other family totems.

How long they resided at Green Bay is not known. Father Allouez states that there was a tradition in his day, that they had been almost destroyed in 1640, by the Illinois. They had also, in this connection, a tradition that their ancestors built a fort, which Irwin and Hamilton, missionaries among them, think might have been identical with the archeological remains of an ancient work found on Rock river. Coming down to the era of authentic history, Carver, in 1766, found them on the Fox river, evidently wandering from their ancient place of habitation, and approaching southern Wisconsin and the northern part of Illinois and Iowa, where portions of the tribe subsequently settled. The Illinois portion occupied a section of country on Rock river, in the county which bears their name, and the country to the east of it. In Pontiac's war, they, with other lake tribes, hovered about the beleaguered fortress of Detroit, and made the surrounding forests dismal with midnight revelry and war-whoops. English agents, however, succeeded in molifying their resentment, and when the new American power arose, in 1776, they were subsequently arrayed on the side of the British authorities in regard to questions of local jurisdiction at Prairie du Chien, Green Bay and Mackinaw. In the war of 1812, they still remained the allies of England, and assisted in the defeat of Col. Croghan, at Mackinaw; Col. Dudley, at the rapids of the Maumee; and General Winchester, at the river Raisin. In the Winnebago war of 1827, they defiantly placed themselves in antagonism to the authority of the general government, by assaulting a steamboat on the Mississippi, engaged in furnishing supplies to the military post on the St. Peters.

The Kickapoos, in 1763, occupied the country southwest of the southern extremity of Lake Michigan. They subsequently moved southward, and at a more recent date dwelt in portions of the territory on the Mackinaw and Sangamon rivers, and had a village on Kickapoo creek, and at Elkhart Grove. They were more civilized, industrious, energetic and cleanly than the neighboring tribes, and it may also be added more implacable in their hatred of the Americans. They were among the first to commence battle, and the last to submit and enter into treaties. Unappeaseable enmity led them into the field against Generals Harmar, St. Clair and Wayne, and first in all the bloody charges at Tippecanoe. They were prominent among the northern nations, which, for more than a century, waged an exterminating war against the Illinois confederacy. Their last hostile act of this kind was perpetrated in 1805, against some poor Kaskaskia children, whom they found gathering strawberries on the prairie above the town which bears the name of their tribe. Seizing a considerable number of them, they fled to their villages before the enraged Kaskaskias could overtake them and rescue their offspring. During the years 1810 and 1811, in conjunction with the Chippewas, Potawatamies and Ottawas, they committed so many thefts and murders on the frontier settlements, that Governor Edwards was compelled to employ military force to suppress them. When removed from Illinois they still retained their old animosities against the Americans, and went to Texas, then a province of Mexico, to get beyond the jurisdiction of the United States. They claimed relationship with the Potawatamies, and perhaps the Sacs and Foxes, and Shawnees. The following tradition respecting the origin of this tribe was related in 1812, at the Indian Superintendency at St. Louis, by Louis Rodgers, a Shawnee:

"It is many years ago since the number of the Shawnees was very great. They were, on an important occasion, encamped together on the prairie. At night one-half of them fell asleep, the others remained awake. The latter abandoned the sleepers before morning, and betook themselves to the course where the sun rises. The others gradually pursued their route in the direction where the sun sets. This was the origin of the two nations, the first of which was called the Shawnees, and the other the Kickapoos. Prior to this separation these nations were considered one, and were blessed with bounties above any blessings which are now enjoyed by any portion of mankind; and they ascribe their present depressed condition, and the withdrawal of the favor of Providence, to the anger of the Great Spirit at their separation. Among the many tokens of divine favors which they formerly enjoyed was the art of walking on the surface of the ocean, by which they crossed from the East to America without vessels. Also the art of restoring life to the dead, by the use of medical art, continued for the space of six hours. Necromancy and prophecy were with them at their highest state, and were practiced without feigning; and, in fine, such were the gifts of heaven to them that nothing fell short of their inconceivable power to perform. And after the Shawnees have wandered to the remotest West, and returned East to the original place of separation, the world will have finished its career. It is believed by the Shawnees that the consummation of this prophecy is not far distant, because they have, in fulfillment of it, reached the extreme western point, and are now retrograding their steps."

A fragment of the Shawnee nation, in early times, dwelt in the southeastern part of Illinois, in the vicinity of Shawneetown, which bears their name. The nation, bold, roving and adventurous, originally inhabited the Atlantic seaboard, between the Altamaha and James rivers. Becoming embroiled in wars with the Iroquois, to save themselves some took refuge in the Carolinas and Florida. True to their native instincts, in their new location they soon came to blows with the owners of the soil, and about the year 1730 removed to the Sciota, in the present State of Ohio. About 1750, a discontented fraction broke off from the rest of the nation and went to East Tennessee, and thence to their location on the Ohio, at Shawneetown. Here, in common with neighboring tribes, they regarded Illinois as sacred ground, and during Pontiac's war assisted in repelling the attempts of their English enemies to get possession of the country in the present limits of the State. Here, too, both themselves and their brethren on the Sciota, obtained arms from the French, for whose supremacy they deluged the frontiers of Pennsylvania and Virginia with blood. Such had been the atrocity of their conduct, when the war was over they at first supposed they were excluded from the general amnesty extended to other western tribes, and even prepared to murder their prisoners and resume hostilities. After having, a short time before the conquest of Clark, destroyed the Tamaroas in battle, they rejoined their kindred on the Sciota.

The Mascoutins were a tribe holding friendly relations with the Illinois, and are supposed by some to have constituted a sixth tribe of their confederacy. The name, "Mascoutin," is synonymous with prairie, and was applied to this tribe from the circumstance of their dwelling on the great grassy plains east of the Mississippi. The first European who mentions them is Father Allouez, who found them, in 1669, on the Wisconsin river. Marquette saw them in 1673, near the portage of the Fox and Wisconsin rivers. Marest states that they had formed settlements in 1712 on the Wabash, and in subsequent times they ranged over the prairies between the Wabash and the Illinois. They were also intimately associated with the Foxes and Kickapoos, whom they resembled in deceit and treachery. Charlevoix states that the Mascoutins and the Kickapoos united with the Foxes in a plot of the latter against the French, but were surprised by the Ottawas and Potawatamies and 150 of them cut to pieces. After the cession of the French possessions to the English, Col. Croghan was sent to conciliate the western tribes. Having descended the Ohio to the site of Shawneetown, they, with the Kickapoos, attacked and made him and his men prisoners. Under the name of Meadow Indians they are mentioned by Gen. Clark, whom, in 1778, they endeavored to cut off by treachery. Subsequently they appear to have been absorbed by the Kickapoos and Foxes.

The Piankishaws occupied the lower Wabash country on both sides of that stream, and west into the Illinois territory as far as the dividing ridge between the sources of the streams flowing into the Wabash and those falling into the Kaskaskia. They were one member of the *Miami Confederacy*. This nation, in early times, resided on Fox river, Wisconsin, where they were visited, in 1670, by Fathers Allouez and Dablon. The latter is lavish in his praise of their chief, stating that he was honored by his subjects as a king, and that his bearing among his guests had all the courtly dignity of a civilized monarch. They were also visited the same year by St. Susson, who was received with the honors of a sham battle and entertained with a grand game of ball. He likewise speaks in glowing terms of the authority of the chief, who was attended night and day by a guard of warriors. The nation shortly afterward removed to the banks of the St. Joseph, and thence found their way to the Wabash and Maumee. They were more largely represented in La Salle's colony, at Fort St. Louis, than any other tribe, and were active participants in the conspiracy of Pontiac. The confederacy, like that of the Illinois, was reduced to the last extremity by repeated attacks from the Iroquois. But they fill a considerable space in western annals, and gave birth to Little Turtle, who commanded the Indians at St. Clair's defeat. The Piankishaws, after their removal from Illinois, were transferred to the Indian Territory, and in 1850 were reduced to 107 persons.

The Potawatamies are represented on early French maps as inhabiting the country east of the southern extremity of Lake Michigan. At the mouth of the St. Joseph, falling into this part of the lake, the Jesuits had a missionary station, which, according to Marest, was in a flourishing condition as early as 1712. Here, an immeasured distance from civilization, for more than half a century the devoted missionaries labored for their spiritual welfare. These years of toil and self-denial were, however, little appreciated, for in Pontiac's war they proved themselves to be among the most vindictive of his adherents. Disguising their object under the mask of friendship, they approached the small military post located on the same river, and having obtained ingress, in a few minutes butchered the whole of the garrison, except three men.

From this locality a portion of the tribe passed round the southern extremity of the lake, into northeastern Illinois. Time and a change of residence seems not to have modified their ferocious character. Partly as the result of British intrigue, and partly to gratify their thirst for blood, they perpetrated, in 1812, at Chicago, the most atrocious massacre in the annals of the northwest. After their removal from Illinois, they found their way to the Indian Territory, and in 1850 numbered 1,500 souls. The following legend of the tribe gives their theology and origin: "They believe in two great spirits, Kitchemonedo, the good or benevolent spirit, and Matchemonedo, the evil spirit. Some have doubts which is the most powerful, but the great part believe that the first is; that he made the world and called all things into being, and that the other ought to be despised. When Kitchemonedo first made the world he peopled it with a class of beings who only looked like men, but they were perverse, ungrateful, wicked dogs, who never raised their eyes from the ground to thank him for anything. Seeing this the Great Spirit plunged them, with the world itself, into a great lake and drowned them. He then withdrew it from the water and made a single man, a very handsome young man, who as he was lonesome, appeared sad. Kitchemonedo took pity on him and sent him a sister to cheer him in his loneliness. After many years the young man had a dream which he told to his sister. Five young men, said he, will come to your lodge door to-night to visit you. The Great Spirit forbids you to answer or even look up and smile at the first four; but when the fifth comes, you may speak and laugh and show that you are pleased. She acted accordingly. The first of the five strangers that called was Usama, or tobacco, and having been repulsed he fell down and died; the second, Wapako, or a pumpkin, shared the same fate; the third, Eshkossimin, or melon, and the fourth, Kokees, or the bean, met the same fate; but when Tamin or Montamin, which is maize, presented himself, she opened the skin tapestry door of her lodge, laughed very heartily, and gave him a friendly reception. They were immediately married, and from this union the Indians sprang. Tamin forthwith buried the four unsuccessful suitors, and from their graves there grew tobacco, melons of all sorts, and beans; and in this manner the Great Spirit provided that the race which he had made should have something to offer him as a gift in their feasts and ceremonies, and also something to put into their *akeeks* or kettles, along with their meat."*

Portions of the Chippewa and Ottawa tribes were associated with the Potawatamies in the northeastern part of the present limits of Illinois. They were among the most energetic and powerful nations of the northwest, and fought with great ferocity in most of the wars caused by the westward advance of civilization. In the conspiracy of Pontiac they were the immediate followers of the great war chief, and impelled by his imperious will, at Detroit, Mackinaw and other British posts, they were without rivals in the work of carnage and death. The *Sauteaux*, a branch of the Chippewas, dwelt on the eastern bank of the Mississippi, and had villages on the sites of Rock Island, Quincy and other adjacent places. They were driven west of the river by the Sacs and Foxes, after which their principal town was Davenport.

All these tribes have now passed beyond the limits of the State. Some long since were exterminated, while the degenerate offspring of others are found in the Indian Territory and other parts of the west. Inflexible as if hewn from a rock, they were unable to adapt themselves to the requirements of civilized life, and could but flee before it or perish. Their fast disappearing graves, and the relics occasionally turned up by the plow, are now the only melancholy vestiges of their former existence in Illinois.

In common with the whole Indian race, their most exalted conception of glory was success in war, and a knowledge of its arts the most valuable attainment. The aged chief looked back to his exploits in battle as the crowning acts of his life, while the growing youth looked forward to the time when he would be able to win distinction by like feats of prowess. Civilization offers to the votaries of ambition not only the sword but the pen, the forum, the paths of science, the painter's brush and the sculptor's chisel; the savage has only the triumphs of the war path. The war parties of the prairie tribes consisted of volunteers. The leader who attempted to raise one must have previously distinguished himself in order to be successful. He first appealed to the patriotism and courage of the warriors, and was careful to intimate that the Great Spirit had made known to him in dreams the success of his enterprise. Then, painted with vermillion to symbolize blood, he commenced the war dance. This performance expressed in pantomime the varied incidents of a successful campaign. The braves entering upon the war-path, the posting of sentinels to avoid surprise, the advance into the enemy's country, the formation of ambuscades to strike the unwary foe, the strife and carnage of battle, the writhing victim sinking under the blow of the war-club, the retreat of the enemy, the scalping of the slain, the feasting of vultures on the putrid bodies, the triumphant return of the war party to their village and the torturing of prisoners, were all portrayed with the vividness and vehemence of actual warfare. Warrior after warrior, wishing to volunteer for the expedition, rap-

*Schoolcraft.

idly fell into the dance with the leader. Each one, keeping time
with the beat of the drum, sped in mazy circles around a common
centre, until with increased numbers the whole, in movement and
uproar, resembled the whirlwind. The several actors taxed their
muscular energies to the utmost endurance, stamping the ground
with great fury, throwing their bodies into the different attitudes
of combat, distorting their faces with the frenzy of demons, and
uttering the war-cry with the frightful shriek of madmen. These
hideous orgies, waking up all the fire and energy of the Indian's
soul, were a fitting prelude to the premeditated carnage. If a
young man participated in the dance, it was tantamount to an enlistment, and he could not afterwards honorably withdraw.

The Art of Hunting not only supplied the Indian with food, but,
like that of war, was a means of gratifying his love of distinction.
The male children, as soon as they acquired sufficient age and
strength, were furnished with a bow and arrows and taught to
shoot birds and other small game. Success in killing large quadrupeds required years of careful study and practice, and the art
was as sedulously inculcated on the minds of the rising generation
as are the elements of reading, writing and arithmetic in the common schools of civilized communities. The mazes of the forest
and the dense tall grass of the prairies were the best fields for the
exercise of the hunter's skill. No feet could be impressed in the
yielding soil but they were objects of the most rigid scrutiny, and
revealed at a glance the animal that made them, the direction it
was pursuing, and the time that had elapsed since it had passed.
Even if the surface was too hard to admit of indentations, such
were his wonderful powers of observation, he discovered on it
evidences of a trail from which, with scarcely less certainty, he
derived the same information. In a forest country he selected for
his places of ambush valleys, because they are most frequently the
resort of game, and sallied forth at the first peep of day. In
ascending the valleys he was careful to take the side of the stream
which threw his shadow from it, thus leaving his view unobstructed in the opposite direction. The most easily taken, perhaps, of
all the animals of the chase was the deer. It is endowed with a
curiosity which prompts it to stop in its flight and look back at the
approaching hunter who always avails himself of this opportunity to
let fly his fatal arrow. An ingenious method of taking this animal,
practiced by the Indians on the small tributaries of the Mississippi,
was the use of the torch. For this purpose they constructed their
bark canoes with a place in front for the reception of a large flam-
beau, whose light was prevented from revealing the hunter by the
interposition of a screen. As he descended the narrow streams,
the deer, seeing only the light, was attracted by it to the banks
and easily shot.

But by far the noblest objects of the chase which the Indian encountered on the prairies, was the buffalo. It is an animal confined
to temperate latitudes, and was found in large numbers by the first
explorers, roaming over the grassy plains of Illinois, Indiana,
Southern Michigan and Western Ohio. It has a remarkably large
chest, a heavy mane covering the whole of its neck and breast, horns
turned slightly upward and large at the base, eyes red and fiery,
and the whole aspect furious. In its native haunts it is a furious
and formidable animal, worthy of the Indian's prowess. Like the

moose and other animals of the same family, nature has bestowed on it the most exquisite power of scent. The inexperienced hunter of the present day, unaware that the tainted breeze has revealed his presence to them, is often surprised to see them urging their rapid flight across the prairies, at a distance of two or three miles in advance, without any apparent cause of alarm. He is therefore necessitated to dismount and approach them on the leeward, under cover of the horse. When within a proper distance he vaults into the saddle and speeds forward in the direction of the prey, which commences its retreat, getting over the ground with great rapidity for animals so unwieldy. Intuitively it directs its course over the most broken and difficult ground, causing both horse and rider to frequently imperil their lives by falling. When wounded they sometimes turn with great fury upon their pursuer, and if he happens to be dismounted, nothing but the greatest coolness and dexterity can save his life.

The bow and arrow, in the hands of the tribes which formerly ranged the prairies, were said to be more formidable weapons in hunting the buffalo, than the guns subsequently introduced by Europeans. The arrows could be discharged with greater rapidity and with scarcely less precision. Such, too, was the force with which it was propelled, that the greater part of it was generally imbedded in the body of the buffalo, and sometimes protruded from the opposite side. Deep grooves cut in the side of the missile permitted the rapid effusion of blood, and animals, when pierced with it, survived only a short time.

One of the modes of killing the buffalo, practiced by the Illinois and other tribes of the West, was to drive them headlong over the precipitous banks of the rivers. Buffalo Rock, a large promontory rising fifty or sixty feet high, on the north side of the Illinois, six miles below Ottawa, is said to have derived its name from this practice. It was customary to select an active young man and disguise him in the skin of the buffalo, prepared for this purpose by preserving the ears, head and horns. Thus disguised, he took a position between a herd and a cliff of the river, while his companions, on the the rear and each side, put the animals in motion, following the decoy, who, on reaching the precipice, disappeared in a previously selected crevice, while the animals in front, pressed by the moving mass behind, were precipitated over the brink and crushed to death on the rocks below. The Indians also often captured large numbers of these buffalo, when the rivers were frozen over, by driving them on the ice. If the great weight of the animals broke the ice, they were usually killed in the water, but if too strong to break, its smoothness caused them to fall powerless on the surface, when they were remorselessly slaughtered, long after supplying the demands for food, merely to gratify a brutal love for the destruction of life.

Their General Councils were composed of the chiefs and old men. When in council they usually sat in concentric circles around the speaker, and each individual, notwithstanding the fiery passions that rankled within, preserved an exterior as immovable as if cast in bronze. Before commencing business, a person appeared with the sacred pipe and another with fire to kindle it. After being lighted, it was presented first to the heavens, secondly to the earth, thirdly to the presiding spirits, and lastly to the several councilors,

each of whom took a whiff. These formalities were observed with
as much scrupulous exactness as state etiquette in civilized courts.
After the speaker commenced and became animated in the discussion of his subject, his statue-like auditors signified their assent to
what he said by deep guttural ejaculations. These gatherings, in
dignity, gravity and decorum, were scarcely equalled by the deliberative bodies of the most enlightened centres. It is said that
the Indians were wont to express the greatest surprise on witnessing the levity exhibited by French officials, in their public assemblies at Fort Chartres.

The Indian council had no authority to give force and validity to
its enactments. If it decided to engage in war, it had no power
to enforce its enlistments, and therefore volunteers had to fight
the battles. If its decrees of peace were observed, it was not the
result of compulsion, but due to the confidence which the nation
placed in its wisdom and integrity. Where councils were convened
for negotiating treaties, or terms of peace, the presentation of gifts
was often a part of the proceedings. It was customary on these
occasions for the orator of the interceding party to rise and present them to those of the assemblage who were to be conciliated.
A particular object was assigned to each gift, which the speaker
explained as he proceeded in his discourse. Corresponding with
the various objects to be accomplished by negotiation, there were
gifts to propitiate the Great Spirit and cause him to look with favor
upon the council; to open the ears and minds of the contracting
parties, that they might hear what was said and understand their
duty; to inter the bones of the dead, and heal the wounds of their
living friends; to bury the tomahawk, that it might not again be
used in shedding blood, and to so brighten the chain of friendship
that the disaffected tribes might ever afterwards be as one people.

The thoughts uttered in these councils, and on other public occasions, were frequently of a high order. Deeply imbued with the
love of freedom and independence, their ideas on these subjects
were generally of a lofty, unselfish and heroic character. Patriotism, their most cherished virtue, furnished their orators with
themes for the most stirring appeals. Barrenness of language
necessitated the frequent employment of metaphors, many of which
were surprisingly beautiful, simple and appropriate. The frequent
use of imagery made it difficult for the interpreter to follow them
in their figurative vein of thought and do the orator justice. But
while this was true it was much more frequently the case that the
translator greatly improved the original. It may also be added that
some of the most sparkling gems of what purports to be Indian
eloquence are nothing but the fanciful creations of writers. Pontiac's
speeches are frequently referred to as among the best specimens
of aboriginal eloquence. The following retort was made by Keokuk,
in answer to charges preferred against his people by the Siouxs at
a convocation of chiefs in 1837, at the national capital:

" They say they would as soon make peace with a child as with
us. They know better, for when they made war on us they found
us men. They tell you that peace has often been made and we
have broken it. How happens it then that so many of their braves
have been slain in our country. I will tell you: They invaded us,
we never invaded them; none of our braves have been killed in

their land. We have their scalps and we can tell you where we took them."

Black Hawk's speech to Col. Eustice, in charge of Fortress Monroe, when he and his fellow prisoners were set at liberty, is not only eloquent, but shows that within his chest of steel there beat a heart keenly alive to the emotions of gratitude:

"Brother, I have come on my own part, and in behalf of my companions, to bid you farewell. Our great father has at length been pleased to permit us to return to our hunting grounds. We have buried the tomahawk, and the sound of the rifle will hereafter only bring death to the deer and the buffalo. Brother, you have treated the red men very kindly. Your squaws have made them presents, and you have given them plenty to eat and drink. The memory of your friendship will remain till the Great Spirit says it is time for Black Hawk to sing his death song. Brother, your houses are numerous as the leaves on the trees, and your young warriors like the sands upon the shore of the big lake that rolls before us. The red man has but few houses, and few warriors, but the red man has a heart which throbs as warmly as the heart of his white brother. The Great Spirit has given us our hunting grounds, and the skin of the deer which we kill there, is his favorite, for its color is white, and this is the emblem of peace. This hunting dress and these feathers of the eagle are white. Accept them, my brother; I have given one like this to the White Otter. Accept of it as a memorial of Black Hawk. When he is far away this will serve to remind you of him. May the Great Spirit bless you and your children. Farewell."

Constitution of the Indian Family.—The most important social feature of the prairie and other tribes, and that which disarmed their barbarism of much of its repulsiveness, was the family tie. The marital rite which precedes the family relations required only the consent of the parties and their parents, without any concurrent act of magistracy, to give it validity. The husband, with equal facility, might also dissolve this tie or increase the number of his wives without limit. Though the marriage compact was not very strong, the ties of consanguinity were rigidly preserved, and hereditary rights, generally traced through the female line, were handed down from the remotest ancestry. For this purpose they had the institution of the *Totem*, an emblem which served as a badge of distinction for different clans or families. This family surname was represented by some quadruped, bird, or other object of the animal world, as the wolf, deer, hawk, &c. Different degrees of rank and dignity were indicated by various totems, those of the bear, wolf, and turtle, being first in honor, secured the greatest respect for those who had the right to wear them. Each clansman was proud of his ensign, and if a member of the fraternity was killed, he felt called upon to avenge his death. As the different members of a clan were connected by ties of kindred, they were prohibited from intermarriage. A Bear could not marry a Bear, but might take a wife from the Wolf or Otter clan, whereby all the branches of a tribe or nation became united by bonds of consanguinity and friendship. By this simple institution, notwithstanding the wandering of tribes and their vicissitudes in war, family lineage was preserved and the hereditary rights of furnishing chiefs, accorded to certain clans, was transmitted from generation to generation.

Though in many of the most endearing relations of life the men, from immemorial custom, exhibited the most stolid indifference, yet instances were not wanting to show that in their family attachments they frequently manifested the greatest affection and sympathy. No calamity can cause more grief than the loss of a promising son, and the father has often given his life as a ransom to save him from the stake. A striking instance of this kind occurred in the war of the 17th century between the Foxes and Chippewas, near Montreal. In this war the Foxes captured the son of a celebrated and aged chief of the Chippewas, named Bi-ans-wah, while the father was absent from his wigwam. On reaching his home, the old man heard the heart-rending news, and knowing what the fate of his son would be, followed on the trail of the enemy, and, alone, reached the Fox village while they were in the act of kindling the fire to roast him alive. He stepped boldly into the arena and offered to take his son's place. " My son," said he "has seen but few winters, his feet have never trod the war path; but the hairs of my head are white; I have hung many scalps over the graves of my relations, which I have taken from the heads of your warriors. Kindle the fire about me and send my son to my lodge." The offer was accepted and the father, without deigning to utter a groan, was burned at the stake. Such are the severities of savage warfare, amidst which the family is maintained with a heroism which has no parallel in civilized life.

The Methods of Sepulture, among the Indians, varied in different localities. It was common, among the northern forest tribes of the United States, to choose elevated spots above the reach of floods, for places of burial. Not having suitable tools for making excavations, they interred their dead in shallow graves and placed over them trunks of trees to secure them from depredation by wild beasts. The bodies were sometimes extended at full length, in an eastern and western direction, but more frequently in a sitting posture. The Illinois and other prairie tribes frequently placed their dead on scaffolds erected on eminences commanding extensive and picturesque views. The corpse, after receiving its wrappings, was deposited in a rude coffin, fancifully painted with red colors. In this condition they were placed on scaffolds decorated with gifts of living relatives, and built sufficiently high to protect them from wolves and other animals of prey infesting the prairies. But judging from the remains of graves, by far the greater part of the ancient inhabitants of Illinois and the adjacent parts of the Mississippi Valley, deposited large numbers of their dead in a common tomb, and generally marked the place by the erection of a mound. The plains and alluviums of Southern Illinois, have in many places been literally sown with the dead, evincing a density of population greatly exceeding that found by the first European explorers of this region. The custom of raising heaps of earth over the graves, was perhaps practiced as a mark of distinction for the tombs of eminent personages, and for such as contained the bodies of warriors slain in battle, or were made common repositaries for the dead of whole clans and villages. It is sometimes difficult to distinguish between the places of sepulture raised by the ancient mound builders, and the more modern graves of the Indians. The tombs of the former were in general larger than the latter, were used as receptacles for a greater number of bodies, and contained relics of art evincing a higher degree of civilization than that attained by the present aboriginal tribes. The ancient tumuli of the mound builders have in some instances been appropriated as burial places by the Indians, but the skeletons of the latter may be distinguished from the osteological remains of the former by their greater stature.

The existence of a future state was regarded by the prairie tribes as an actuality, and upon this idea was predicated the custom of depositing in the graves of departed friends their favorite implements, and such as they thought would be useful to them in the land of spirits. When a warrior died they placed with him his war-club, gun and red paint, and some times his horse was slain upon his grave, that he might be ready to mount and proceed to to his appointed place of rest in the land of spirits. If a female was to be interred, they placed with her a kettle, canoe paddles, articles of apparel, and other objects of feminine use and interest. No trait of character was more commendable in the Indian than his scrupulous regard for the graves of his ancestors. Not even the invasion of his hunting grounds roused more quickly his patriotism and resentment, than the ruthless desecration of the graves of his fathers, by the unhallowed hands of strangers. So long as any part of their perishable bodies were supposed to remain, they were prompted by reverence to visit the sacred places where they slept, and pour out libations to their departed spirits.

Man is, by nature, a religious being. The exhibitions of his character, in this respect, are as universal as are the displays of his social, intellectual and moral nature No nations, tribes or individuals have been found, whatever may be their isolated condition or depth of degradation, but they are more or less governed by this inherent element. While the religious sentiment is universal, its manifestations are as various as the different degrees of advancement made by its subjects in knowledge. From the ignorant idolator who bows down before a lifeless image or some abject form of animal life, to the devotee of a more enlightened theology, the devotion is the same, but their theories and practices are infinitely diverse. The faculties which make man a worshipping being are unchangeable, and may not its manifestations become uniform, when the immutable attributes of the deity, and the invariable laws instituted by him for the government of the human family, are properly studied and understood.

The red man of the prairies and forests, like the rest of mankind, was also psychologically religious. Without speaking of the diversities of belief entertained by different tribes, only the general features of their faith can be given. Prominent among these was the idea that every natural phenomenon was the special manifestation of the Great Spirit. In the mutterings of the thunder cloud, in the angry roar of the cataract, or the sound of the billows which beat upon the shores of his lake-girt forests, he heard the voice of the Great Spirit. The lightning's flash, the mystic radiance of the stars, were to him familiar displays of a spirit essence which upheld and governed all things, even the minute destinies of men; while the Indian attributed to the Great Spirit the good he enjoyed in life, he recognized the existence of evil. To account for this, without attributing malevolence to the Great Spirit, an antagonistical deity was created in his theology, whom he regarded as the potent power of malignancy. By this duality of deities he was careful to guard his good and merciful God from all imputations of evil by attributing all the bad intentions and acts which afflict the human family to the Great Bad Spirit.

Doubtless, in part, as a result of missionary instructions, the Illinois and other branches of Algonquin stock, designated their

4

Great Spirit as the Author of Life, the Upholder of the Universe. They believed him all-wise, all-powerful, and all-good, and variously assigned him a dwelling place in the sun, moon or indefinite skies. They not only distinguished the principle of good and evil by two antagonistic gods, but supplied them with an innumerable number of minor divinities, whose office was to execute their will. These consisted of birds, reptiles, fairies, spirits, and a great variety of other objects, some being instrumentalities of good and others of evil. Under such a multiplicity of antagonistic powers, everything which the Indian saw or heard in the external world might be the cause of intense hope or fear, and keep him in perpetual doubt as to whether it foreboded good or evil. A prey to these mysterious fears, he readily fell into the belief of sorcery and other supposed magic influences. From this cause they were constantly victimized by their priests, jugglers, and prophets, a class who lived by these impositions instead of hunting.

The belief in a future state was common. According to their traditions, which had been modified by missionary teachings, the wicked, at death, sink into a dark retributive stream, while the good are rewarded with an abode in a delightful hunting ground. In their lively imagery, they spoke of this place as the land of the blest, or the country of souls, through which meandered gently flowing rivers. They supposed these streams replete with every kind of fish suitable for food, and that those who bathed in them were exempt from the ills which afflict life in the present state of being. Over the surface, agreeably diversified with hills and valleys, were prairies interspersed with noble forests, under whose sheltering branches disported the various creations of animal life. Birds warbled their sweetest music in waving groves, and noble animals grazed on the verdant plains so numerous and prolific that the demands of the hunter were always met without exhausting the supply. No tempest's destructive blast, no wasting pestilence nor desolating earthquake, emanating from the Spirit of Evil, occurred to mar the sweet and varied pleasures of life. Such was the Indian's future state of existence, the dwelling place of the Great Spirit, who welcomed home at death his wandering children. The belief in this terrene elysium, the Indian's most exalted idea of paradise, doubtless explains his stoical indifference of death. With him

> " Time comes unsighed for, unregretted flies;
> Pleased that he lives, happy that he dies."

As it regards the Indians in general, it is an adage among those whose observations have been the most extensive, that he who has seen one tribe has seen them all. This seems to be true, notwithstanding their wide geographical distribution, and the great extremes of climate to which they are exposed. Whether enjoying the great abundance and mild climate of the Mississippi Valley, or chilled and stinted by the bleak and barren regions of the extreme north and south of the hemisphere, over which they are scattered, they have the same general lineaments. "All possess, though in varied degrees, the same long, lank, black hair, the dull and sleepy eye, the full and compressed lips, and the salient but dilated nose."* The cheek bones are prominent, the nostril expanded, the orbit of the eye squared, and the whole max-

*Schoolcraft.

ilory region ponderous. The cranium is rounded, and the diametre, from front to back, less in some instances than between the sides. The posterior portion is flattened toward the crown, while the forehead is low and retreating. The hair, which, in the white man, is oval, and in the black man eccentrically eliptical, is invariably round. Not only its cylindrical form, but its great length and coarseness, are found in all the diversified climate in which this people is found. When contrasted with the European, they are found mentally and physically inferior. No measurement has been instituted to determine their average stature, whereby the difference between them and the races of Europe, in this respect, can be accurately determined. Shenandoah was 6 feet 3 inches high; Logan, 6 feet; Red Jacket, 5 feet 8 inches, and the distinguished Fox chief, Keokuk, 6 feet 2 inches. These celebrated instances doubtless exceeded the majority of their countrymen in hight, as all rude and uncultivated races admire superior physical development, and generally consult prominence of stature in the selection of their leaders. While their stature may average with that of the European, in muscular power and endurance they are surpassed. In feats of agility, connected with running and hunting, they are scarcely equal to their white competitors; while in all labors requiring compactness of muscle and protracted exertion, the latter are always the victors. In the severe labor of rowing, and the carrying of heavy burdens across the portages of the northwest, it was observed that the French boatmen of Illinois and Canada exhibited the greatest strength and endurance. The European also excels them in brain development and mental power. The facial angle, which indicated the volume of the intellectual lobe, has in the European an average of 80 degrees, while that of the Indian is only 75. The superiority of the former in this respect, and in the size and activity of his brain, is in keeping with their respective conditions. The history of the one is a history of human progress; that of the other details the struggles of a race perishing before the advance of civilization, which it is neither able to adopt nor successfully oppose.

Much has been said and written in regard to the unjust encroachments of white men upon the territory of the Indians. No doubt much hardship has grown out of the manner in which their lands have been taken, yet the right of civilized races to demand a part of their vast domain, even without their consent, when it could not be obtained otherwise, can hardly be questioned. The earth was designed by the Creator for the common habitation of man, and it is his destiny and duty to develop its resources. When, therefore, the occupants of any region fail to accomplish these objects, they must be regarded as unfaithful stewards, and give way to those who have the ability to make it yield the largest supplies and support the greatest number of inhabitants. Had the Indians, who refused to become tillers of the soil, been suffered to retain possession of the hemisphere over which they roamed, some of the most fertile portions of the globe must have remained a wilderness, thus defeating the object of the Creator, and doing great injustice to the rest of mankind. Failing to make a proper use of this heritage, they have lost it, but behold the gain! At the touch of civilization the wilderness has been made to blossom like the rose. Herds and harvests have followed the track of the pale-faced pioneer, and teeming millions of a higher life have taken the place of a few wandering hunters and fishermen. After Columbus made known to Europeans the existence of the new world, priority of discovery was considered as conferring upon the governments under whose patronage it was made, the right of extinguishing the Indian title. England, in the exercise of this right, treated the Indians substantially as she did her own subjects. She respected their claim to occupy and use the country for their own benefit, but did not permit them to alienate it except to her own people, in accordance with the principle of English law that all titles to lands are vested in the crown. The United States, by the acquisition of independence, succeeded to the right of the mother country, and has forced upon them similar restrictions, and accorded the same privileges. In every instance the government has extinguished their title by treaty or purchase. It must, however, be admitted that in many instances these treaties grew out of wars provoked by frontier settlers, for the sole purpose of demanding territory in the way of reprisal. It must also be added, that when lands have been obtained by purchase, the consideration was frequently of the most trivial character.

CHAPTER V.

OPERATION OF THE MISSIONARIES—EXTENT OF THEIR EXPLORATIONS UP TO 1673.

Although commercial enterprise is perhaps the principal agent for the dissemination of civilization in the undeveloped regions of the globe, its extension into the Mississippi valley was due to a different cause. Pioneers, actuated by a religious fervor and enthusiasm hitherto without a parallel in the history of the world, were the first to explore its trackless wilds, and attempt to teach its savage inhabitants the refinements of civilized life. These self-denying explorers belonged mostly to the Jesuits or the Society of Jesus, a famous religious order founded by Ignatius Loyola, a Spanish knight of the sixteenth century. He gave out that the constitution of his order was given him by immediate inspiration. Notwithstanding his high pretensions, he at first met with little encouragement, and the Pope, to whom he applied for the authority of his sanction, referred him to a committee of cardinals. The latter decided that his proposed establishment would not only be useless, but dangerous, and the Pope refused to give it his approval. To overcome the scruples of the Pope, in addition to the vows of other orders he required the members of his society to take a vow of obedience to the Pope, whereby they bound themselves to go whithersoever he should direct them in the service of religion, without requiring anything from him as a means of support. In other orders the primary object of the monk is to separate himself from the rest of the world, and in the solitude of the cloister to practice acts of self-mortification and purity. He is expected to eschew the pleasures and secular affairs of life, and can only benefit mankind by his example and prayers. Loyola, on the contrary, preferred that the members of his society should mingle in the affairs of men, and they were accordingly exempted from those austerities and ceremonies which consumed much of the time of other orders. Full of the idea of implicit obedience which he had learned from the profession of arms, he gave to his order a government wholly monarchical. To a general, who should be chosen for life from the several provinces, the members were compelled to yield not only an outward submission, but were required to make known to him even the thoughts and feelings of their inner life. At the time this offer was made, the papal power had received such a shock from the refusal of many nations to submit to its authority, that the Pope could not look upon it with indifference. He saw that it would place at his disposal a body of the most rigorously disciplined ecclesiastics, whose powerful influence would enable him to repel the violent

53

assaults with which the papal system was everywhere assailed. He therefore authorized the establishment of the order, and appointed Loyola its first general. The result proved the discernment of the Pope, for the enginery he thus put in motion at no distant day extended its influence to the uttermost limits of the earth. Before the termination of the 16th century, the society furnished the educators in most of the Catholic countries of Europe, a privilege which exerted a more controling influence in molding national character than that which emanates from all other sources combined. Although taking a vow of poverty, it managed to rapidly increase in wealth. Under the pretext of promoting the success of their missions, they obtained the privilege of trading with the nations they were endeavoring to convert, and thus frequently became the masters of extensive commercial enterprises.

Besides the Jesuits, the Recollet monks bore a conspicuous part in the history of the French-American possessions. They were a branch of the Franciscan order, founded in the early part of the 13th century by St. Francis of Assisi, a madman, saint or hero, according to the different views entertained respecting him. Like all other saints, he became the subject of supernatural visitations, consisting, in his case, largely of dreams revealing to him the nature of the work which providence had called him to perform. In entering upon the labors of his mission he dressed in the rags of a beggar, and at last presented himself in a state of nudity to the Bishop of Assisi, and begged the mantle of a peasant. He next robbed his father, to get means to build himself a chapel; crowds gathered to listen to his fanatical appeals, and Europe soon became dotted over with the convents of his order. In the course of time the Franciscans lost the vigor for which they were first distinguished, but the Recollets, a reformed branch of the order, at the time of the French explorations still retained much of its pristine spirit. These two orders, and incidentally that of St. Sulpice, played an important part in the exploration and colonization of the Mississippi valley.

The St. Lawrence and its chain of lakes entering the continent on the east, and the Mississippi from the south, are the two great avenues through which Europeans first made their way to Illinois. The former opening with a broad estuary into the Atlantic, directly opposite Europe, first diverted a portion of its Gallic emigration to the regions drained by its tributaries. Pioneers, led by the indefatigable Jesuits, soon reached Illinois, and made it an important centre in the vast schemes projected by the French court for the possession of the Mississippi valley.

The French on the St. Lawrence.—As early as 1535, four years before the discovery of the Mississippi by DeSoto, Jacques Cartier conducted an expedition to the St. Lawrence, which he ascended as far as the island of Orleans. Several attempts were shortly afterward made to plant colonies in the newly discovered region, but they failed in consequence of the inclemency of the climate and hostilities of the natives. France, at that time, was too much engaged in wars to further exhaust her resources in forming settlements, and it was not till 1608 that a permanent colony was established. During this year Champlain, a bold navigator, with a number of colonists, sailed up the St. Lawrence, and landed at the foot of the lofty promontory which rises in the angle formed by the confluence of the St. Charles. Carpenters were set to work, and within a few weeks a pile of buildings rose near the water's edge, the first representatives of the spacious churches, convents, dwellings and ramparts which now form the opulent and enterprising city of Quebec. These buildings constituted the headquarters of Champlain, and were surrounded by a wooden wall pierced with openings for a number of small cannon. To secure the friendship of the Hurons and neighboring Algonquin nations, Champlain was induced to assist them in a war against the Iroquois, inhabiting the country south of the St. Lawrence. Victory attended his superior arms, but it aroused the implacable hate of these tribes, and for a period of 90 years they continued to wreak their fury upon the Indian allies of France, and materially contributed to the final overthrow of her power.

In 1615 Champlain returned to France, and brought back with him four Recollet monks. Great was the astonishment of the Indians at first beholding these mendicants, clad in their rude gowns of coarse gray cloth. Their first care was to select a site and erect a convent, the completion of which was honored by the celebration of mass. All New France participated in the mysterious rite, while from the ships and ramparts of the fort cannon thundered forth an approving salute. Their great object was the salvation of the Indians, and unappalled by the perils that awaited them, they met in council and assigned to each his province in the vast field of labors. As the result of unwearied effort, they established missions from Nova Scotia to Lake Huron, but finding the task too great for their strength, they applied to the Jesuits for assistance. The followers of Loyola eagerly responded to the invitation, and Canada for the first time saw the order which, in after years, figured so extensively in her history. Though suffering must be their fate, and perhaps martyrdom their crown, they penetrated to the most remote regions and visited the most warlike tribes. Missions were established on the Straits of St. Mary, the northern shores of Lake Huron, the tributaries of Lake Michigan, and finally among their inveterate enemies, the Iroquois.

Champlain, after having acted as governor for a period of 27 years, died on the Christmas of 1635, a hundred years after the first visit of Cartier, and was buried in the city he had founded. Sharing with others of his time the illusion of finding a passage across the continent to the Pacific, he made voyages of discovery with a view of finding the long-sought commercial highway. In one of his excursions he discovered the lake which bears his name, and was among the first Europeans who set their feet on the lonely shores of Lake Huron. What indescribable thoughts must have thrilled his bosom as he looked out on its broad expanse, or perhaps awed by its majestic solitudes, he listened with strange delight to the loud refrain of its billow-lashed shores.

Discovery of the Ohio by LaSalle, 1669.—After the death of Champlain, the next actor in the field of exploration was Robert Cavalier, better known as LaSalle. His father's family was among the old and wealthy burghers of Rouen, France, and its several members were frequently entrusted with important positions by the government. Robert was born in 1643, and early exhibited the traits of character which distinguished him in his western career. Having a wealthy father, he enjoyed ample facilities for obtaining an education, and made rapid progress in the exact sciences. He was a Catholic, and it is said a Jesuit; but judging from his subsequent life, he was not a religious enthusiast. The order of Loyola, wielded at the centre by a single will so complicated and so harmonious, may have attracted his youthful imagination. It was, however, none the less likely that when he found himself not at the centre, but moving in a prescribed orbit at the circumference, he would leave it. Having an individuality which could not be molded by a shaping hand, he was better qualified for a different sphere of action. He therefore parted with the Jesuits on good terms, with an unblemished character, for his lofty ambition completely divested him of the petty animosities to which groveling minds are subject.

He had an older brother living in Canada—a priest of the order of St. Sulpice—and it was this circumstance which induced him to emigrate to America. His connection with the Jesuits deprived him, under the laws of France, from inheriting the property of his father, who died shortly before his departure. He, however, received a small allowance, and with this, in the spring of 1666, arrived at Montreal. Here he found a corporation of priests, known as the Seminary of St. Sulpice, who were disposing of lands on easy terms to settlers, hoping by this means to establish a barrier of settlements between themselves and the hostile Indians. The superior of the seminary, on hearing of LaSalle's arrival, gratuitously offered him a tract of land situated on the St. Lawrence, 8 miles above Montreal. The grant was accepted, and though the place was greatly exposed to the attacks of savages, it was favorably situated for the fur trade. Commencing at once to improve his new domain, he traced out the boundaries of a palisaded village, and disposed of his lands to settlers, who were to pay for them a rent in small annual installments.

While thus employed in developing his seignory, he commenced studying the Indian languages, and in three years is said to have made rapid progress in the Iroquois, and eight other tongues and dialects. From his home on the banks of the St. Lawrence, his thoughts often wandered over the "wild unknown world toward sunset," and like former explorers, dreamed of a direct westward passage to the commerce of China and Japan. While musing upon the subject, he was visited by a band of Senecas, and learned from them that a river called the Ohio, rising in their country, flowed into the sea, but at such a distance that it required eight months to reach its mouth. In this statement the Mississippi and its tributary were considered as one stream, and with the geographical views then prevalent, it was supposed to fall into the gulf of California.

Placing great confidence in this hypothesis, and determined to make an exploration to verify it, he repaired to Quebec, to obtain from Governor Courcelles his approval. His plausible statements soon won over to his plans both the Governor and Intendant Talon, and letters patent were issued authorizing the enterprise. No pecuniary aid being furnished by the government, and as LaSalle had expended all his means in improving his estate, he was compelled to sell it to procure funds. The superior of the Seminary, being favorably disposed toward him, bought the greater part of his improvement, and realizing 2800 livres, he purchased four canoes and the necessary supplies for the expedition.

The Seminary, at the same time, was preparing for a similar exploration. The priests of this organization, emulating the enterprise of the Jesuits, had established a mission on the northern shore of Lake Ontario. At this point, hearing of populous tribes further to the northwest, they resolved to essay their conversion, and an expedition, under two of their number, was fitted out for this purpose. On going to Quebec to procure the necessary outfit, they were advised by the Governor to so modify their plans as to act in concert with LaSalle in exploring the great river of the west. As the result, both expeditions were merged into one—an arrangement ill-suited to the genius of LaSalle, whom nature had formed for an undisputed chief, rather than a co-laborer in the enterprise. On the 6th of July, 1669, everything was in readiness, and the combined party, numbering 24 persons, embarked on the St. Lawrence in 7 canoes. Two additional canoes carried the Indians who had visited LaSalle, and who were now acting as guides. Threading the devious and romantic mazes of the river in opposition to its rapid current, after three days they appeared on the broad expanse of Lake Ontario. Their guides led them thence directly to their village, on the banks of the Genesee, where they expected to find guides to lead them to the Ohio. LaSalle, only partially understanding their language, was compelled to confer with them by means of a Jesuit priest, stationed at the village. The Indians refused to furnish a conductor, and even burned before their eyes a prisoner from one of the western tribes, the only person who could serve them as guide. This and other unfriendly treatment which they received, caused them to suspect that the Jesuit, jealous of their enterprise, had intentionally misrepresented their object, for the purpose of defeating it. With the hope of accomplishing their object, they lingered for a month, and at length had the good fortune to meet with an Indian from an Iroquois colony, situated near the head of the lake, who assured them that they could there find what they wanted, and offered to conduct them thither. With renewed hope they gladly accepted this proffered assistance, and left the Seneca village. Coursing along the southern shore of the lake, they passed the mouth of the Niagara, where they heard for the first time the distant thunder of the cataract, and soon arrived safely among the Iroquois. Here they met with a friendly reception, and were informed by a Shawnee prisoner that they could reach the Ohio in six weeks' time, and that he would guide them thither. Delighted with this unexpected good fortune, they prepared to commence the journey, when they unexpectedly heard of the arrival of two Frenchmen in a neighboring village. One of them proved to be Louis Joliet, a young man of about the age of LaSalle, and destined to acquire fame by his explorations in the west. He had been sent by Talon, the intendant of Canada, to explore the copper mines of Lake Superior, but had failed, and was now on his return. Giving the priests a map representing such parts of the upper lakes as he had visited, he informed them that the Indians of those regions were in great need of spiritual advisers. On receiving this information, the missionaries decided that the Indians must no longer sit in darkness, and thought that the discovery of the Mississippi might be effected as easily by a northern route, through these tribes, as by going farther southward. LaSalle, remonstrating against their determination, informed them that this direction was impracticable, and in case they should visit that region, they would perhaps find it already occupied by the Jesuits. He had, for some time, been afflicted with a violent fever, and finding his advice unheeded, he told the priests that his condition would not admit of following them further. The plea of sickness was doubtless a ruse to effect a separation; for the invincible determination of LaSalle never permitted an enterprise which he had undertaken to be defeated by other considerations. A friendly parting was arranged, and after the celebration of mass, LaSalle and his men fell back to Lake Ontario, while the Sulpitians descended Grand river to Lake Erie.

The latter prosecuted their journey up the lakes, and on arriving among the Indians of whom Joliet had spoken, they found, as LaSalle had surmised, Marquette and Dablon established among them. Learning, too, that they needed no assistance from St. Sulpice, nor from those who made him their patron saint, they retraced their steps, and arrived at Montreal the following June, without having made any discoveries or converted an Indian.

The course pursued by LaSalle and his party, after leaving the priests, is involved in doubt. The most reliable record of his movements is that contained in an anonymous paper, which purports to have been taken from the lips of LaSalle himself, during a visit subsequently made to Paris. According to this statement, he went to Onondaga, where he obtained guides, and passed thence to a tributary of the Ohio, south of Lake Erie, followed it to the principal river, and descended the latter as far as the falls at Louisville. It has also been maintained, that he reached the Mississippi and descended it some distance, when his men deserted, and he was compelled to return alone. It is stated in the same manuscript, that the following year he embarked on Lake Erie, ascended the Detroit to Lake Huron, and passed through the strait of Mackinaw to Lake Michigan. Passing to the southern shore, he proceeded by land to the Illinois, which he followed to its confluence with the Mississippi, and descended the latter to the 36th degree of latitude. Here, assured that the river did not fall into the gulf of California, but that of Mexico, he returned, with the intention of at some future day exploring it to the mouth.

The statement that he visited the falls of the Ohio, is doubtless correct. He himself affirms, in a letter to Count Frontenac, in 1677, that he discovered the Ohio, and descended it to the falls. Moreover, Joliet, his rival, subsequently made two maps representing. the region of the Mississippi and the lakes, on both of which he states that LaSalle discovered and explored the Ohio. It is, perhaps, also true that LaSalle discovered the Illinois, but that he descended either it or the Ohio to the Mississippi before the discovery of Joliet, is improbable. If such had been the case, he certainly would have left written evidence to that effect, as in the case of the Ohio especially, when the priority of Joliet's discovery had become a matter of great notoriety.

CHAPTER VI.

EXPLORATIONS BY JOLIET AND MARQUETTE—1673–'75.

———

LaSalle had explored one, and perhaps two, routes to the Mississippi, but as yet the upper portion of the great river had probably never been seen by any European. The honor of inaugurating the successful attempt to reach this stream is due to M. Talon, who wished to close the long and useful term of his services, as the Intendant of Canada, by removing the mystery which enshrouded it. For this purpose he selected Louis Joliet, a fur trader, to conduct the expedition, and Jacques Marquette, a Jesuit missionary, to assist him.

Talon, however, was not to remain in the country long enough to witness the completion of the enterprise. A misunderstanding arose between him and Governor Courcelles in regard to the jurisdiction of their respective offices, and both asked to be recalled. Their requests were granted, and early in the autumn of 1672, Count Frontenac arrived at Quebec, to take the place of the retiring governor. He belonged to the high nobility of France, was well advanced in life, and a man of prompt and decided action. Though intolerant to enemies, he partially atoned for this fault by his great magnanimity and devotion to friends, while his charm of manners and speech made him the favorite and ornament of the most polished circles. His career in Canada, at first, was beset with opposition and enmity, but its close was rewarded with admiration and gratitude for his broad views and unshaken firmness, when others despaired.

Before sailing for France, M. Talon recommended to Frotenac Joliet and Marquette, as suitable persons to execute his projected discoveries. The former was born at Quebec, in 1645, of humble parentage. He was educated by the Jesuits for the priesthood, but early abandoned his clerical vocation to engage in the fur trade. Though renouncing the priesthood, he still retained a partiality for the order which had educated him, and no doubt this was the principal reason which induced Talon to labor for his appointment. Possessing no very salient points of character, he yet had sufficient enterprise, boldness and determination properly to discharge the task before him.

His colleague, Marquette, greatly surpassed him in bold outlines of character. He was born in 1637, at Laon, France. Inheriting from his parents a mind of great religious susceptibility, he early united with the Jesuits, and was sent, in 1666, to America as a missionary, where he soon distinguished himself for devotion to his profession. To convert the Indians he penetrated a thousand miles in advance of civilization, and by his kind attentions in their afflictions, won their affections, and made them his lasting friends. Softening their savage asperities into smoothness and peace by the blended purity and humility of his own life, he was the most successful of all the missionaries in developing their higher and better feelings. His extensive acquaintance with the Indian languages, now enabled him to act in the threefold capacity of interpreter, explorer and missionary.

Joliet ascended the lakes and joined his companion at the Jesuit mission, on the strait of Mackinaw, where, for several years, he had been instructing the Ottawas and Hurons. With 5 other Frenchmen and a simple outfit, the daring explorers, on the 17th of May, 1673, set out on their perilous voyage. Coasting along the northern shore of Lake Michigan, they entered Green Bay, and passed thence up Fox river and Lake Winnebago to a village of the Mascoutins and Miamis. Marquette, who never suffered the beauties of nature to escape his attention, speaks in eloquent terms of the broad prairies and tall forests which he saw from the summit of the hill on which it was situated. His admiration of the scenery was, however, greatly exceeded by the joy which he experienced at beholding a cross planted in the midst of the place, and decorated with some of the most valued of Indian implements. With due ceremony they were introduced to a council of chiefs, when Marquette, pointing to Joliet, said : "My friend is an envoy of France, to discover new countries, and I am an embassador from God, to enlighten them with the truths of the gospel."* The speaker then made them some presents, and asked for guides to conduct them on their way. Though the Indians regarded their journey as extremely hazardous, these were granted, and the voyagers re-embarked in their canoes. All the village followed them down to the river, wondering that men could be found to undertake an enterprise so fraught with dangers. Their guides led them safely through the devious windings of the river, beset with lakes and marshes overgrown with wild rice. The seed of this plant largely furnished the Indians with food, and subsisted immense numbers of birds, which rose in clouds as the travelers advanced. Arriving at the portage, they soon carried their light canoes and scanty baggage to the Wisconsin, about three miles distant. France and papal christendom were now in the valley of the Mississippi, ready to commence the drama in which, for the next succeeding 90 years, they were the principal actors.

Their guides now refused to accompany them further, and endeavored to induce them to return, by reciting the dangers they must encounter in the further prosecution of the journey. They stated that huge demons dwelt in the great river, whose voices could be heard at a long distance, and who engulphed in the raging waters all who came within their reach. They also represented that, should any of them escape the dangers of the river, fierce and warring tribes dwelt on its banks, ready to complete the work of destruction. Marquette thanked them for the information, but could not think of trying to save his own perishable body, when the immortal souls of the Indians alluded to might be eternally lost. Embarking in their canoes, they slowly glided down the Wisconsin, passing shores and islands covered with forests, lawns, parks and pleasure grounds, greatly exceeding in

*Monette's Valley of the Mississippi, 124.

their natural beauty the most skillful training of cultured hands. The 17th of June brought them to the mouth of the river, and with great joy they pushed their frail barks out on the floods of the lordly Mississippi. Drifting rapidly with the current, the scenery of the two banks reminded them of the castled shores of their own beautiful rivers of France. For days of travel they passed a constant succession of headlands, separated by gracefully rounded valleys covered with verdure, and gently rising as they recede from the margin of the waters. The rocky summits of the headlands, rising high above their green bases, had been wrought by the corroding elements into a great variety of fantastic forms, which the lively imagination of Marquette shaped into towers, gigantic statues, and the crumbling ruins of fortifications. On going to the heads of the valleys, they could see a country of the greatest beauty and fertility, apparently destitute of inhabitants, yet presenting the appearance of extensive manors, under the fastidious cultivation of lordly proprietors. By and by great herds of buffalo appeared on the opposite banks, the more timid females keeping at a safe distance, while the old bulls approached, and through their tangled manes looked defiance at the strange invaders of their grassy realms.

Near a hundred miles below the mouth of the Wisconsin, the voyagers discovered an Indian trace, leading from the western shore. Joliet and Marquette, leaving their canoes in charge of their men, determined to follow it and make themselves acquainted with the tribes of this region. Moving cautiously through prairies and forests, rendered beautiful by the verdure and bloom of July, they discovered a village near the banks of the river and two others on a hill half a league distant. Commending themselves to the protection of Heaven, they approached and shouted to attract attention. When the commotion, excited by their unexpected salute, had partially subsided, four elders advanced with uplifted calumets to meet them. A friendly greeting ensued, and after informing the Frenchmen that they were Illinois, they conducted them to their village. Here they were presented to the chief, who, standing near the door of his wigwam in a state of complete nudity, delivered an address of welcome: "Frenchmen, how bright the sun shines when you come to visit us; all our village awaits you, and you shall enter our wigwams in peace." After entering and smoking a friendly pipe, they were invited to visit the great chief of the Illinois, at one of the other villages. Followed by a motley throng of warriors, squaws, and children, they proceeded thither and were received with great courtesy by the chief. On entering his wigwam, filled with the dignitaries of the tribe, Marquette announced the nature of their enterprise, asked for information concerning the Mississippi and alluded to their patron, the Governor of Canada, who had humbled the Iroquois and compelled them to sue for peace. This last item of information was good news to these remote tribes, and drew from their chief the compliment that the "presence of his guests added flavor to their tobacco, made the river more calm, the sky more serene and the earth more beautiful."* Next, followed a repast, consisting of hominy, fish, and buffalo and dog's meat. The Frenchmen partook sumptiously

Discov. of the Great West.

of all the dishes, except the last, which they failed to appreciate, although one of the greatest Indian delicacies. The generous hosts, with true forest courtesy, as they dished out the different articles, first blew their breath upon each morsel to cool it, and then, with their own hands, placed it in the mouths of their guests. They endeavored to persuade the explorers, by depicting the great dangers they would incur, to abandon their object. Finding that their efforts were unavailing, on the following day they hung on the neck of Marquette a sacred calumet, brilliantly decorated with feathers, as a protection among the tribes he was about to visit. The last mark of respect, which the chiefs could now offer their departing friends, was to escort them with 600 of their tribesmen to the river, where, after their stolid manner, they bade them a kindly adieu.

Again they were afloat on the broad bosom of the unknown stream. Passing the mouth of the Illinois they soon fell into the shadow of a tall promontory, and with great astonishment beheld the representation of two monsters painted on its lofty limestone front. According to Marquette, each of these frightful figures had the face of a man, the horns of a deer, the beard of a tiger, and the tail of a fish so long that it passed around the body over the head and between the legs. It was an object of Indian worship, and greatly impressed the mind of the pious missionary with the necessity of substituting for this monstrious idolatry, the worship of the true God.* Before these figures of the idols had faded from their minds, a new wonder arrested their attention. They ran into the current of the Missouri, sweeping directly across their track, and threatening to engulf them in its muddy waves. Fragments of trees were drifting in large numbers, which must have come from a vast unknown wilderness, judging from the magnitude of the stream which bore them along. Passing on, it was ascertained that for several miles the Mississippi refused to mingle with the turbid floods of the intruding stream.

Soon the forest covered site of St. Louis appeared on the right, but little did the voyagers dream of the emporium which now fills the river with its extended commerce. Farther on, their attention was attracted by the confluence of the Ohio, a stream which, in the purity of its waters, they found wholly different from that previously passed. Some distance below the mouth of this eastern tributary, the banks of the river became skirted with a dense growth of cane, whose feathery-like foliage formed a pleasing contrast with that which they had passed above. But a greater vegetable wonder was the Spanish moss which hung in long festoons from the branches of the trees, exquisitely beautiful, yet, like funeral drapery, exciting in the beholder feelings of sadness. Another change was the increasing heat, which, now rapidly dissipated the heavy fogs which previously, to a late hour, had hung over the river. Clouds of mosquitos also appeared in the relaxing atmosphere, to annoy them by day, and disturb their much needed rest at night.

---

*Near the mouth of the Piasa Creek, on the bluff, there is a smooth rock in a cavernous cleft, under an overhanging cliff, on whose face, 50 feet from the base, are painted some ancient pictures or hieroglyphics, of great interest to the curious. They are placed in a horizontal line from east to west, representing men, plants and animals. The paintings, though protected from dampness and storms, are in great part destroyed, marred by portions of the rock becoming detached and falling down. See *Prairie State*, 1859.

Without suspecting the presence of Indians, they suddenly discovered a number on the eastern banks of the river. Marquette held aloft the symbol of peace, furnished him by the Illinois, and the savages approached and invited him and his party ashore. Here they were feasted on buffalo meat and bear's oil, and after the repast was over, were informed that they could reach the mouth of the river in ten days. This statement was doubtless made with the best intention, but with little truth, for the distance was not far from 1,000 miles.

Taking leave of their hosts, and resuming the journey, they penetrated a long monotony of bluffs and forests, and again discovered Indians near the mouth of the Arkansas. Rushing from their wigwams to the river, some of them sallied forth in canoes to cut off their escape, while others plunged into the water to attack them. Marquette displayed the calumet, which was unheeded till the arrival of the chiefs, who ordered the warriors to desist, and conducted them ashore. A conference ensued, and as soon as the Indians understood the nature of the visit, they became reconciled. The day's proceedings closed with a feast, and the travelers spent the night in the wigwams of their entertainers. Early the next day, messengers were sent by the latter to the Arkansas tribe on the river below, to apprise them that Frenchmen were about to descend the stream. As announced, the explorers proceeded a distance of 24 miles, when they were met by a deputation of three Indians, who invited them to visit their town. Assent being given, they were conducted thither and seated on mats, which had been spread for their reception under a shed before the lodge of a principal chief. Soon they were surrounded by a semi-circle of the villagers—the warriors sitting nearest, next the elders, while a promiscuous crowd stared at them from the outside. The men were stark naked, and the women imperfectly clad in skins, wearing their hair in two masses, one of which was behind each ear. Fortunately, there was a young man in the village who could speak Illinois. By his aid, Marquette explained to the assemblage the mysteries of the Christian faith, and the object of the expedition, and learned in turn from them that the river below was infested with the most hostile tribes. During their stay at this place, they were forced to submit to the merciless demands of aboriginal hospitality, which imposed dish after dish upon their over-taxed organs of digestion, till repletion became intolerable.

It was now the middle of July and the voyagers debated the propriety of further lengthening out their journey. They had been on the river four weeks, and concluded they had descended sufficiently far to decide that its outlet was on the Atlantic side of the continent. Their provisions were nearly exhausted, and they also feared if they visited the river below they might be killed by the savages, and the benefit of their discovery would be lost.

Influenced by these considerations, they determined to retrace their steps. Leaving the Arkansas village, they commenced forcing their way in opposition to the swift current of the river, toiling by day under a July sun, and sleeping at night amidst the deadly exhalations of stagnant marshes. Several weeks of hard labor brought them to the mouth of the Illinois, but unfortunately, Marquette, enervated by the heat and the toils of the voyage, was suffering with an attack of dysentery. Here they were informed by the Indians that the Illinois furnished a much more direct route to the lakes than the Wisconsin. Acting upon this information, they entered the river, and found, besides being more direct, that its gentle current offered less resistance than that of the Mississippi. As they advanced into the country, a scene opened to their view which gave renewed strength to their wearied bodies, and awoke in their languid minds the greatest admiration and enthusiasm. Prairies spread out before them beyond the reach of vision, covered with tall grass, which undulated in the wind like waves of a sea. In further imitation of a watery expanse, the surface was studded with clumps of timber, resembling islands, in whose graceful outlines could be traced peninsulas, shores and headlands. Flowers, surpassing in the delicacy of their tints the pampered products of cultivation, were profusely sprinkled over the grassy landscape, and gave their wealth of fragrance to the passing breeze. Immense herds of buffalo and deer grazed on these rich pastures, so prolific that the continued destruction of them for ages by the Indians, had failed to diminish their numbers. For the further support of human life, the rivers swarmed with fish, great quantities of wild fruit grew in the forest and prairies, and so numerous were water-fowl and other birds, that the heavens were frequently obscured by their flight. This favorite land, with its profusion of vegetable and animal life, was the ideal of the Indian's Elysium. The explorers spoke of it as a terrestial paradise, in which earth, air and water, unbidden by labor, contributed the most copious supplies for the sustenance of life. In the early French explorations, desertions were of frequent occurrence, and is it strange that men, wearied by the toils and restraints of civilized life, should abandon their leaders for the abundance and wild independence of these prairies and woodlands?

Passing far up the river, they stopped at a town of the Illinois, called Kaskaskia, whose name, afterwards transferred to a different locality, has become famous in the history of the country. Here they secured a chief and his men to conduct them to Lake Michigan and proceeded thither by the way of the rivers Illinois, Desplaines and Chicago. Following the western shore of the lake, they entered Green Bay the latter part of September, having been absent about four months, and traveled a distance of 2,500 miles.

Marquette stopped at the mission on the head of the bay, to repair his shattered health, while Joliet hastened to Quebec, to report his discoveries. Hitherto fortune had greatly favored him, and it was only at the termination of his voyage that he met his first disaster. At the foot of the rapids, above Montreal, his canoe was capsized, and he lost the manuscript containing an account of his discoveries, and two of his men. He says, in a letter to Governor Frontenac: "I had escaped every peril from the Indians; I had passed 42 rapids, and was on the point of disembarking, full of joy at the success of so long and difficult an enterprise, when my canoe capsized after all the danger seemed over. I lost my two men and box of papers within sight of the first French settlements, which I had left almost two years before.

Nothing remains to me now but my life, and the ardent desire to employ it on any service you may please to direct."

When the successful issue of the voyage became known, a *Te Deum* was chanted in the cathedral of Quebec, and all Canada was filled with joy. The news crossed the Atlantic, and France saw, in the vista of coming years, a vast dependency springing up in the great valley partially explored, which was to enrich her merchant princes with the most lucrative commerce. Fearing that England, whose settlements were rapidly extending along the Atlantic, might attempt to grasp the rich prize before she could occupy it, she endeavored to prevent, as far as possible, the general publicity of the discovery. Joliet was rewarded by the gift of the island of Anticosti, in the gulf of St. Lawrence, while Marquette, who had rendered the most valuable services, was satisfied with the consciousness of having performed a noble duty.

Marquette suffered long from his malady, and it was not till the autumn of the following year that his superior permitted him to attempt the execution of a long cherished object. This was the establishment of a mission at the principal town of the Illinois, visited in his recent voyage of discovery. With this purpose in view, he set out on the 25th of October, 1674, accompanied by two Frenchmen and a number of Illinois and Potawatamie Indians. The rich and varied tints of autumn were now rapidly changing to a rusty brown, and entering Lake Michigan, they found it cold and stormy. Buffeted by adverse winds and waves, it was more than a month before they reached the mouth of the Chicago river. In the meantime Marquette's disease had returned in a more malignant form, attended by hemorrhage. On ascending the Chicago some distance, it was found that his condition was growing worse, compelling them to land. A hut was erected on the bank of the river, and here the invalid and the two Frenchmen prepared to spend the winter. As it wore away, the enfeebled missionary was unceasing in his spiritual devotions, while his companions obtained food by shooting deer, turkeys and other game in the surrounding forests. The Illinois furnished them with corn, and frequently, by their presence and other kindly attentions, greatly cheered their lonely exile.

Marquette, burning with the desire to establish his contemplated mission before he died, consecrated himself anew to the service of the Virgin, and soon began to regain his strength. By the 13th of March, being able to recommence his journey, the two men carried their canoes over the portage between the Chicago and Desplaines, and commenced to descend the latter stream. Amidst the incessant rains of opening spring, they were rapidly borne forward on the swollen river to its junction with the Illinois, and down the latter to the object of their destination. Here, it is said, he was viewed as a messenger from heaven, as he visited the wigwams of the villagers and discoursed of paradise, the Redeemer of the world, and his atonement for sinful men. The excitement at length drew together, on the plain between the river and the present town of Utica, some 500 chiefs, and a great unknown concourse of warriors, women and children. In the midst of this multitude he exhibited four large pictures of the Holy Virgin, and with great earnestness harangued them on the duties of christianity, and the necessity of making their conduct conform

5

to its precepts. The audience were deeply impressed with his gospel teachings, and eagerly besought him to remain with them, a request which his fast waning strength rendered it impossible to grant.

Finding he must leave, the Indians generously furnished him with an escort to the lake, on which he embarked with his two faithful attendants. They turned their canoes in the direction of the mission on the strait of Mackinaw, which the afflicted missionary hoped ro reach before he died. As they coasted along the eastern shore, advancing May began to deck the forest with her vernal beauties, but the eyes of the dying priest were now too dim to heed them. On the 19th of the month he could go no farther, when, at his request, his two friends landed and built a hut, into which he was carefully conveyed. Aware that he was rapidly approaching his end, he, with great composure, gave directions concerning his burial, and thanked God that he was permitted to die in the wilderness an unshaken believer in the faith which he had so devotedly preached. At night he told his weary attendants to rest, and when he found death approaching he would call them. At an early hour they were awakened by a feeble voice, and hastening to his side, in a few moments he breathed his last, grasping a crucifix, and murmuring the name of the Virgin Mary. Having buried his remains as directed, his trusted companions hastened to Mackinaw, to announce the sad news of his demise.

Three years afterward, a party of Ottawas, hunting in the vicinity of his grave, determined, in accordance with a custom of the tribe, to carry his bones with them to their home at the mission. Having opened the grave and carefully cleaned them, a funeral procession of 30 canoes bore them toward Mackinaw, the Indians singing the songs which he had taught them. At the shore, near the mission, the sacred relics were received by the priests, and, with the solemn ceremony of the church, deposited under the floor of the rude chapel.

CHAPTER VII.

EXPLORATIONS BY LaSALLE.

We must now turn from Marquette, whose great piety, energy and self-denial made him a model of the order to which he belonged, and again introduce LaSalle on the stage of action. The previous voyage had well nigh established the fact that the Mississippi discharged its waters into the Gulf of Mexico; yet he and others now entertained the opinion that some of its great tributaries might afford a direct passage to the Pacific. It was the great problem of the age to discover this passage, and LaSalle proposed not only to solve it by exploring the great river to its mouth, but to erect a fort on its outlet, and thus secure to France the possession of its valley. To further his object, he gained the influence and support of Frontenac, and induced some of the Canadian merchants to become partners in the adventure.

Fort Frontenac.—The new governor had no sooner been installed in office, than, with eagle eye, he surveyed the resources of Canada, and prepared to get them under his control. LaSalle had informed him that the English and Iroquois were intriguing with the Indians of the upper lakes to induce them to break their peace with the French, and transfer their trade in peltries from Montreal to New York. Partly to counteract this design, and in part to monopolize the fur trade for his own benefit, he determined to build a fort on Lake Ontario, near the site of the present city of Kingston. Lest he should excite the jealousy of the merchants, he gave out that he only intended to make a tour to the upper part of the colony, to look after the Indians. Being without sufficient means of his own, he required the merchants to furnish each a certain number of men and canoes for the expedition. When spring opened, he sent LaSalle in advance to summon the Iroquois sachems to meet at the site of the proposed fort, while he followed at his leisure. In obedience to his call, the chiefs arrived, and were much pleased with the attentions shown them by the governor. Flattered by his blandishments, and awed by his audacity, they suffered the erection of the fort, which was called Frontenac, after its founder. The governor writes: "With the aid of a vessel now building, we can command the lakes, keep peace with the Iroquois, and cut off the fur trade from the English. With another fort at Niagara, and a second vessel on the river above, we can control the entire chain of lakes." These far-reaching views accorded well with the schemes of LaSalle, who was shortly afterwards employed in reducing them to practice. The erection of the fort was in violation of the king's regulations, which required the fur traders of Canada to carry on their trade with the

Indians within the limits of the settlements. In view, however, of its great importance as a means of defence against the Iroquois, all legal objections were waived, and provision was made to maintain it. It also served as a stepping-stone for its subsequent owner to make other and greater westward strides in the cause of discovery.

In 1674, LaSalle visited France to petition the king for the rank of nobility, and to negotiate with him for a grant in seignory of the new fort and adjacent lands. As a consideration for the latter, he agreed to reimburse him for what it had already cost to maintain in it an adequate garrison, and provide for the spiritual wants of the settlements that might gather about it. His petition was granted, and he returned to Canada the proprietor of one of the most valuable estates in the province. His relatives, pleased with his flattering prospects, advanced him large sums of money, which enabled him to comply with his agreement. Besides furnishing the stipulated military and clerical forces, and providing a chapel for the latter, he built four small decked vessels to carry freight to the head of the lake, whither he next expected to advance. A period of more than three years now succeeded, in which all Canada was rent with civil feuds. Altercations sprang up between rival traders; Jesuits and Recollets were embittered by dissensions, and the civil authorities became corrupt, and engaged in intrigues, attended with the greatest acrimony. It was impossible for a person of LaSalle's prominence to avoid becoming a mark for the shafts of those who differed with him in opinion and interest. As soon, however, as he could extricate himself from the jarring factions, he again visited France, to obtain the recognition and support of the government in his contemplated undertaking. His object being regarded with favor by the minister, he was authorized to proceed with his discoveries, and occupy the new found countries by the erection of forts, while, in lieu of other support, he was granted a monopoly in buffalo skins, which, it was believed, would be a source of great wealth. His relatives made additional advances of money, and in July, 1678, he sailed with 30 men and a large supply of implements for the construction and outfit of vessels. After a prosperous voyage he arrived at Quebec, and proceeded thence up the river and lake to his seignory.

Among the employes he had brought with him was an Italian, named Henri Tonti, who had lost one of his hands by the explosion of a grenade in the Sicilian wars. Notwithstanding the loss of his hand, and a constitution naturally feeble, his indomitable will made him superior to most men in physical endurance. Besides these qualities, so valuable in the pioneer, he possessed a fidelity which neither adversity nor the intrigues of enemies could swerve from the interests of his employer.* On his way through Quebec, he also obtained the services of M. Lamotte, a person of much energy and integity of character, but not so efficient an assistant as Tonti.

Among the missionaries who became associated with LaSalle in his future explorations, may be mentioned Louis Hennepin, Gabriel Ribourde and Zenobe Membre. All of them were Flemings, all

---

*His father had been governor of Gaeta, but fled to France to escape the political convulsions of his native country. He was an able financier, and won distinction as the inventor of Tontine Life Insurance.

Recollets, but in other respects different. Hennepin, in early life, read with unwearied delight the adventures of travelers, and felt a burning desire to visit strange lands. Yielding to his ruling passion, he set out on a roving mission through Holland, where he exposed himself in trenches and seiges for the salvation of the soldier. Finding, at length, his old inclination to travel returning, he obtained permission of his superior to visit America, where, in accordance with his wandering proclivity, he became connected with the adventures of LaSalle. In this capacity he won distinction as an explorer, but afterwards tarnished his reputation with false pretensions. Ribourde was a hale and cheerful old man of 64 years, and though possessing fewer salient points of character than Hennepin, he greatly excelled him in purity of life. He renounced station and ease for the privations of a missionary, and at last was stricken down by the parricidal hand of those he fain would have benefited. Membre, like Hennepin, is accused of vanity and falsehood. He must, however, have possessed redeeming traits, for he long remained the faithful companion of LaSalle, and finally perished in his service.

On arriving at the fort, LaSalle sent 15 men with merchandise to Lake Michigan, to trade for furs. After disposing of the goods, they were instructed to proceed with the bartered commodities to Illinois, and there await his arrival. The next step he hoped to make in his westward progress was the erection of a fort at the mouth of the river Niagara. He thought if he could control this key to the chain of lakes above, he could also control the Indian trade of the interior. For this purpose, LaMotte and Henepin, with 16 men, on the 18th of November, embarked in one of the small vessels which lay at the fort, and started for the mouth of the river. Retarded by adverse winds, it was not till the 6th of December that they reached their destination and effected a landing. Here they met with a band of Senecas from a neighboring village, who gazed upon them with curious eyes, and listened with great wonderment to a song which they sung in honor of their safe arrival. When, however, the erection of a fort was commenced, their surprise gave way to jealousy, and it became necessary to obtain the consent of the chiefs before the work could be completed. With this object in view, LaMotte and Hennepin, loaded with presents, set out to visit the principal town, situated near the site of Rochester, New York. Arriving thither after a journey of 5 days, they were received by a committee of 32 chiefs, to whom they made known their object. LaMotte distributed gifts among the chiefs with a lavish hand, and by means of his interpreter, used all the tact and eloquence of which he was master to gain their consent to the erection of the fort. They readily received the gifts, but answered the interpreter with evasive generalities, and the embassy was compelled to return without a definite reply. In the meantime LaSalle and Tonti, who had been detained in procuring supplies for the new settlement, arrived. They had also encountered unfavorable winds, and LaSalle, anxious to hasten forward, entrusted one of his vessels to the pilot, who, disregarding his instructions, suffered her to become wrecked. The crew escaped, but with the exception of the cables and anchors intended to be used in building a ship above the cataract, the cargo was lost. LaSalle, who was more than an ordinary mas-

ter of Indian diplomacy, next visited the Senecas, and partially
obtained his request. In lieu of the fort, he was permitted to
erect a warehouse. This was completed, and used as a shelter for
the men during the ensuing winter, and a depository for merchandise in his subsequent transactions on the lakes.

The Griffin.—A more vital consideration, and that which next
engaged the attention of LaSalle, was the building of a vessel on
the river. The point selected for this purpose was on the east side
of the river, at the mouth of Cayuga creek, 6 miles above the
cataract. The men struggled up the steep hights above Lewiston
with the necessary equipments, and on the 22d of January, 1679,
commenced the laborious task of carrying them to the point
selected, some 12 miles distant. Arriving thither, Tonti immediately commenced the task of building the vessel, while LaSalle
returned to Frontenac, to replace the stores which had been lost
in the lake. Notwithstanding the attempt of the Senecas to burn
the vessel as she grew on the stocks, in due time she was finished
and ready to launch. The firing of cannon announced her completion, and as the men chanted a song in honor of their success,
and the Indians stared at the novel sight, she gracefully glided
out on the waters of the Niagara. During her construction, they
were greatly amazed at the ribs of the huge monster, but now
they looked with increased surprise at the grim muzzles of 5 cannon looking through her port holes, and a huge creature, part lion
and part eagle, carved on the prow. The figure was a griffin,
after which the vessel was named, in honor of the armorial bear-
ings of Frontenac. She was taken further up the river, where the
men supplied her with rigging, and Tonti anxiously awaited the
arrival of LaSalle. This did not occur till August, he having, in
the meantime, been detained by financial difficulties, growing out
of the attempt of enemies to injure his credit. He brought with
him Ribourde and Membre, to preach the faith among the tribes
of the west, which he now proposed to visit.

To defer the enterprise longer, would be to defeat it, and on the
7th of August, 1679, the voyagers embarked. The extended sails
of their little craft catching the breeze, bore her safely out on the
bosom of Lake Erie. Never before had been pictured in its
waters the image of fluttering canvas, and to the Griffin belongs
the honor of first coursing the highway which is now whitened
with the sails of such an extended commerce. After a prosperous
voyage up the lake, they entered the Detroit, and passed on each
bank a pleasant succession of prairies and forests, alive with
game. The men leaped ashore, and soon the decks of the Griffin
were strewn with the dead bodies of deer, turkeys and bears, upon
whose flesh the crew feasted with the greatest relish. Ascending
Lake St. Clair and the rest of the strait, they entered Lake Huron,
which appeared like a vast mirror set in a frame fantastic with
rocks and verdure. So pure and transparent were the waters,
the fish on the pebbled bottom below seemed the only inhabitants
of earth, while their little bark floated like a cloud in mid-air
above them. At first the voyage was prosperous, and islet after
islet loomed up before them, which the strange mirage of the
waters converted into huge Tritons stalking rapidly by, and disappearing in the distance behind. Soon, however, the breeze before
which they moved freshened into a gale, and at last became an

angry tempest, causing the greatest alarm. All fell to praying except the pilot, who was incensed at the idea of ignobly perishing in the lake, after having breasted the storms and won the honors of the ocean. LaSalle and the friars evoked the aid of St. Anthony of Padua, whom they declared the patron of the expedition, and promised a chapel if he would deliver them from the devouring waves. The saint, it is said, answered their prayers; the billow-tossed bosom of the lake became still, and the Griffin rode into the straits of Mackinaw uninjured. A salute of cannon announced their arrival at the Jesuit mission, where they effected a landing, and immediately repaired to the chapel to offer thanks for their recent deliverance.

Here, under the shadow of the cross, the votaries of mammon had erected a bazaar for the fur trade, which they carried on with or without a license, as best suited their interests. All of them looked with jealous eyes upon LaSalle, but openly extended a welcome to him, that they might allay suspicions respecting their secret designs against his enterprise. With motives little better, the Indians saluted him with a volley of musketry, and soon swarmed in canoes around the Griffin, which they called a floating fort, and evidently regarded it with greater curiosity than good will. Not only the residents were secretly hostile, but it soon appeared that his own men had proved treacherous. Most of those he had sent up the lakes with merchandise had sold it and kept the proceeds, instead of going with them, as directed, to Illinois. LaSalle arrested four of them at Mackinaw, and sent Tonti to the Straits of St. Mary after two others, whom he also succeeded in capturing.

As soon as Tonti returned, LaSalle weighed anchor and sailed through the Straits into Lake Michigan, and landed at an island near the entrance of Green Bay. Here he was received with great hospitality by a Potawatamie chief, and met with a number of his traders, who, unlike the others, had faithfully disposed of his goods and collected a large quantity of furs. He at once resolved to send them, with others he had collected on the way to Niagara, for the benefit of his creditors. Such a transaction was not authorized by his license of discovery, yet his will was law, and despite the protest of his followers, the furs were carried aboard the Griffin. The pilot, after disposing of the cargo, was instructed to return with her to the southern shore of the lake. Her cannons thundered forth a parting salute, and soon the little bark melted out of sight in the distance. LaSalle, with the remaining men, now embarked in canoes, laden with a forge, tools and arms, and started for the mouth of the St. Joseph. Unfortunately, they found the lake broken with constant storms, which frequently imperiled their own lives and made them tremble for the fate of the Griffin. After a long voyage, in which they suffered much from hardship and hunger, they arrived at their destination. Here they expected to meet with Tonti and twenty of the men who left Mackinaw simultaneously with the Griffin, expecting to make their way along the eastern shore of the lake. After waiting some time in vain for their arrival, those who had come with LaSalle urged upon him the necessity of pushing forward to obtain corn from the Illinois before they departed for their winter hunting grounds. He decided it unwise to grant their request, and, to divert their minds from the subject, commenced the erection of a fort. After laboring some twenty days, and the structure was far advanced, Tonti and ten of his companions arrived. At the instance of LaSalle he immediately went back with two men to hasten forward the others, who were without provisions, and hunting as a means of support. On their way a violent storm overset their canoes and destroyed their provisions, and they were compelled to return. Shortly after, of their own accord, the absent men made their way to the fort, and the entire party was again united. The only care which now oppressed LaSalle was the absence of the Griffin. Ample time had elapsed for her return, but nowhere on the wild solitude of waters was he cheered with the sight of a sail. Rueful forebodings saddened his breast when he thought of her fate, and two men were sent down the lake, with instructions to conduct her to the mouth of the St. Joseph, in case they were able to find her. The fort was finished and named Miami, after a neighboring tribe of Indians.

Without further delay, on the 3d of December, 1679, the party, numbering 33 persons, commenced ascending the St. Joseph. Already the margins of the stream were glassed with sheets of ice and the adjacent forests were gray and bare. Four days brought them to the site of South Bend, to look for the path leading across the portage to the Kankakee. A Mohegan hunter, who accompanied the expedition, and who was now expected to act as a guide, was absent in quest of game, and LaSalle sallied forth to find the way. In the blinding snow and tangled woods he soon became lost, and the day wore away without his return. Tonti, becoming alarmed for his safety, sent men to scour the forest and fire guns to direct his course to the camp. It was not, however, till the next afternoon that he made his appearance. Two opossums dangled in his girdle, which he had killed with a club, while suspended by their tails from overhanging boughs. After missing his way, he was compelled to make the circuit of a large swamp, and it was late at night before he got back to the river. Here he fired his gun as a signal, and soon after, discovering a light, made up to it, supposing it came from the camp of his men. To his surprise it proved to be the lonely bivouac of some Indian, who had fled at the report of his gun. He called aloud in several Indian tongues, but only the reverberations of his voice in the surrounding solitude met his ear. Looking around, he discovered under the trunk of a huge tree a couch made of dried grass, still warm and impressed with the form of its recent occupant. He took possession and slept unmolested till morning, when, without further difficulty, he found his way to camp. Meanwhile, the Mohegan hunter had arrived, and soon the whole party stood on the banks of the Kankakee, coursing its way in zig-zags among tufts of tall grass and clumps of alder. Into its current, which a tall man might easily bestride, they set their canoes, and slowly moved down its sluggish, slimy waters. So full was its channel that the voyagers seemed sailing on the surface of the ground, while their evening shadows, unobstructed by banks, fell far beyond their canoes, and trooped like huge phantoms along by their side. By and by it grew to a considerable stream, from the drainage of miry barrens and reedy marshes skirting its banks. Still farther on succeeded prairies and woodlands, recently scorched by the fires of Indian hunters, and here and there deeply scarred with the trails of buffalo. Occasionally, on the distant verge of the prairies, they could see Indians in pursuit of these animals, while at night the horizon blazed with camp fires where they were cooking and feasting upon their sweetly flavored meats. LaSalle's Mohegan hunter had been unsuccessful, and his half-starved men would gladly have shared with the Indians their rich repast. Their wants were however unexpectedly relieved by the happy discovery of a huge bull so deeply mired he was unable to escape. So ponderous was his huge body that when killed it required 12 men, with the aid of cables, to extricate him from the mud. Refreshed with a bountiful repast, they again betook themselves to their canoes, and soon entered the Illinois, meandering through plains of richest verdure. They were then the pasture grounds of innumerable deer and buffalo, but now wondrously transformed into scenes of agricultural thrift. On the right they passed the high plateau of Buffalo Rock, long the favorite resort of the Indians. Farther down, on the left, appeared a lofty promontory beautifully crested with trees, and soon destined to be crowned with the bulwarks of an impregnable fortress. Below, on the north shore, stood the principal town of the Illinois, in which Hennepin counted 461 lodges, each containing from 6 to 8 families. These structures were made of poles in the form of an oblong rectangle. Those composing the sides rose perpendicularly from the ground, and at the top were united in the form of an arch. Others crossing these at right angles completed the framework, which was afterward neatly inclosed in a covering of rushes. As had been feared by the voyagers, the Illinois were absent, and their village a voiceless solitude. The presence of savages is often a cause of alarm, but now the case was reversed, for LaSalle desired to obtain from them corn for his famishing companions. Soon some of his men discovered large quantities of it stored away in pits, but at first refrained from taking it, lest they might seriously offend its owners. Necessity, however, generally gets the better of prudence, and they took a quantity sufficient to supply their present wants, and departed down the river.

On the 1st of January, 1680, they again landed to hear mass, and wish each other a happy new year. Father Hennepin closed the exercises by haranguing the men on the importance of patience, faith and constancy. Two days afterward they entered the expansion of the river now called Peoria Lake, after the Indians who dwelt upon its banks. Columns of smoke, rising gracefully from the forest below, now announced the presence of Indians, who, LaSalle had reasons to suspect, were averse to his enterprise. Undismayed, they moved down the lake, which soon narrowed to the usual width of the river, when, just beyond, they discovered some 80 Illinois wigwams on the opposite banks. Dropping their paddles and seizing their weapons, they were rapidly borne toward the astounded savages. LaSalle, aware that the least hesitancy on his part would be construed as fear, leaped ashore with his little band of Frenchmen, each armed and ready for action. Such audacity was too much, even for Indian heroism. Women and children trembled with fear; brave warriors fled in the utmost terror, but a few of the more bold rallied and made overtures of peace. Two chiefs advanced and displayed a calumet, which La-

Salle recognized by exhibiting one of his own, and the hostile demonstrations terminated in friendship. Next succeeded a feast, and while some placed the food in the mouths of the Frenchmen, others, with great obsequiousness, greased their feet with bears' oil.

As soon as LaSalle could disengage himself from their caresses, he informed them that in descending the river he had visited their town and taken corn from their granaries. He stated that he had been forced to the commission of this unlawful act to save his men from hunger, and was now ready to make restitution. In explaining the object of his visit, he said he had come to erect a fort in their midst, to protect them against the Iroquois, and to build a large canoe in which to descend the Mississippi to the sea, and thence return with goods to exchange for their furs. If, however, they did not regard his plans with favor, he concluded by stating he would pass on to the Osages, in the present limits of Missouri, and give them the benefit of his trade and influence. The allusion to these Indians aroused their jealousy, which had long existed between the two tribes, and the Illinois readily assented to his wishes, and were loud in their professions of friendship.

Notwithstanding this auspicious reception, it soon became evident to LaSalle that secret enemies were intriguing to defeat his enterprise. Some of his men, dissatisfied and mutinous from the first, secretly endeavored to foment disaffection and ill-will in the better disposed of his followers. They represented to their comrades the folly of longer remaining the dupes and slaves of a leader whose wild schemes and imaginary hopes could never be realized. What could be expected, said they, after following him to the extreme confines of the earth and to remote and dangerous seas, but to either miserably perish or return the victims of disease and poverty. They urged that the only way to escape these evils was to return before distance and the waste of strength and means rendered it impossible. It was even hinted that it might be best to escape from their present calamities by the death of their author: then they might retrace their steps and share in the credit of what had already been accomplished, instead of further protracting their labors for another to monopolize the honors. Fortunately those who entertained these views were too few in numbers to reduce them to practice. Unable to effect anything with their own countrymen, they next turned to the savages. Having obtained a secret interview, they informed them that LaSalle had entered into a conspiracy with the Iroquois to effect their destruction, and that he was now in the country to ascertain their strength and build a fort in furtherance of this object. They also said that, while he was ostensibly preparing to visit Fort Frontenac, his real object was to invite the Iroquois to make an invasion into their country as soon as he was prepared to assist them. The Indians, ever suspicious and ready to listen to charges of this kind, became morose and reserved. LaSalle, noticing their altered demeanor, at once suspected his men, and soon obtained information establishing the truth of their perfidy. To remove the false impressions, he reminded the Indians that the smallness of his force indicated a mission of peace, and not of war; and that neither prudence nor humanity would ever permit him to form an alliance with the Iroquois, whose brutal and revengeful conduct he had always regarded with horror and detestation. His great self possession and frankness, together with the evident truthfulness of his remarks, completely divested the savages of suspicion and restored him to their confidence. Balked in their efforts to make enemies of the Indians, the conspirators, as a last resort, sought the life of their employer. Poison was secretly placed in his food, but fortune again came to his rescue. By the timely administration of an antidote the poison was neutralized, and his life was saved. This was an age of poisoners, and it had not been long since a similar attempt against the life of LaSalle had been made at Fort Frontenac.

Hardly had LaSalle escaped the machinations of his own men, before he became involved in the meshes of others, with whom he sustained not even the most remote connection. The new intrigues, LaSalle, in a letter to Count Frontenac, attributes to the Jesuit Priest, Allouez, then a missionary among the Miamis. Perhaps LaSalle on account of his partiality for the Recollets, or more likely fearing that the latter, through his influence, might become more potent than his own order, he sent a Mascoutin chief, called Monso, to excite the jealousy of the Illinois against him. They came equipped with presents, which drew together a nightly conclave of chiefs, to whom Monso unbosomed his object. Rising in their midst he said he had been sent by a certain Frenchman to warn them against the designs of LaSalle. He then denounced him as a spy of the Iroquois on his way to secure the co-operation of tribes beyond the Mississippi, with the hope that by a combined attack, to either destroy the Illinois or drive them from the country. In conclusion he added, the best way to avert these calamities was to stay his farther progress, by causing the desertion of his men. Having thus roused the suspicions of the Illinois, the envoys hurriedly departed, lest they might have to confront the object of their foul aspersions. The next morning the savages looked suspicious and sullen. A glance sufficed to convince LaSalle that new difficulties awaited him, nor was it long till he ascertained their character. A chief, to whom the day before he had given a liberal supply of presents, privately informed him of what had transpired at the council the preceding night. This information was confirmed by what occurred at a feast, given shortly afterward by a brother of the principal chief, to which LaSalle and his men were invited. While the repast was in preparation their host endeavored to persuade them to abandon their journey by magnifying the dangers which would attend it. He informed them that the object of his invitation was not only to refresh their bodies but to remove from their minds the infatuation of farther attempting an errand which could never be accomplished. If you endeavor to descend the Mississippi, said he, you will find its banks beset with tribes whom neither numbers nor courage can overcome, while all who enter its waters will be exposed to the devouring fangs of serpents and unnatural monsters. Should they avoid these, he added, the river at last becomes a succession of raging whirlpools, which plunge headlong into a storm smitten sea, from which, if they entered, escape would be impossible.

The most of LaSalle's men knew little of Indian artifice, and were greatly alarmed at the thought of having to encounter such formidable perils. Some of the older and more experienced endeavored to expose these misrepresentations, but as we shall presently see, with only partial success. LaSalle knew in a moment, from what had been told him, the object of the speaker was to deceive his men and seduce them from their allegiance. After expressing his thanks for the timely warning, he replied as follows:

"The greater the danger the greater the honor; and even if the danger were real, a Frenchman would never be afraid to meet it. But were not the Illinois jealous? Had they not been deluded by lies? We were not asleep, my brother, when Monso came to tell you, under cover of night, that we were spies of the Iroquois. The presents he gave you, that you might believe his falsehoods, are at this moment buried in the earth under this lodge. If he told the truth why did he skulk away in the dark? Why did he not show himself by day? Do you not see that when we first came among you, and your camp was all in confusion, we could have killed you without needing help from the Iroquois, and now while I am speaking, could we not put your old men to death, while your young warriors are all gone away to hunt. If we meant to make war on you, we should need no help from the Iroquois, who have so often felt the force of our arms. Look at what we have brought you. It is not weapons to disstroy you, but merchandise and tools for your good. If you still harbor evil thoughts of us, be frank as we are and speak them boldly. Go after the imposter, Monso, and bring him back that we may answer him face to face; for he never saw either us or the Iroquois and what can he know of the plots he pretends to reveal?"

The savage orator, too much astounded at these disclosures to attempt a reply, ordered the feast to proceed.

LaSalle, suspicious of danger, the night after the feast stationed sentinels near the lodges of the French to watch the movements of their recent entertainers. The night passed without disturbance, and at early dawn he salied forth to find, that instead of watching the enemy, 6 of his men had basely deserted. Doubtless, in part to escape the imaginary dangers already alluded to, but mostly on account of previous disaffection, they had abandoned their employer at the time when he had the greatest need of their services. LaSalle assembled the remainder, and spoke in severe terms of the baseness of those who had left him. "If any one yet remains," he continued, "who from cowardice desires to return, let him wait till spring, and he can then go without the stigma of desertion." One of the principal difficulties attending the early French enterprises of the West was to procure trusty men. The wilderness was full of vagabond hunters who had fled from the discipline of civilized life, and now exhibited an extreme of lawlessness proportioned to their previous restraints. Their freedom from care, and immunity from the consequences of crime, rendered them a perpetual lure to entice others from the duties of legitimate employment.

Fort Crevecœure.—LaSalle, wearied with these difficulties, now determined to erect a fort in which he and his men might pass the winter without molestation. A site was chosen on the east side of the river, a short distance below the outlet of the lake. This was the extremity of a ridge approaching within 200 yards of the shore, and protected on each side by deep ravines. To fortify the bluff thus formed, a ditch was dug behind to connect the two ravines. Embankments were thrown up to increase the altitude of the different sides, and the whole was surrounded with a palisade 25 feet in hight. The work was completed by erecting within the enclosure buildings for the accommodation of the men.

LaSalle bestowed on it the name Crevecœur,* an appellation which still perpetuates the misfortunes and disappointments of its founder. The Indians remained friendly, and the new fortification subserved more the purpose of a sanctuary than a place for the discharge of military duty. Hennepin preached twice on the Sabbath, chanted vespers, and regretted that the want of wine prevented the celebration of mass. Membre daily visited the Illinois and, despite their filth and disgusting manners, labored earnestly, but with little success, for their spiritual welfare. Such was the first French occupation of the territory now embraced in the present limits of Illinois. The place of this ancient fort may still be seen a short distance below the outlet of Peoria Lake. For years after its erection the country around the lake remained the home of savages, and rich pasture grounds for herds of deer and buffalo.

Hitherto, LaSalle had entertained some hope that the Griffin, which had on board anchors, rigging, and other necessary articles for the construction of another vessel, might still be safe. He proposed to build a vessel on the Illinois, freight her with buffalo hides, collected in the descent of the Mississippi, and thence sail to the West Indies or France, and dispose of the cargo. The Griffin, however, with her much needed stores, never made her appearance. It was variously believed at the time that she had foundered in a storm—that the Indians had boarded and burnt her—and that the Jesuits had contrived her destruction. LaSalle was of opinion that her own crew, after removing the cargo of furs and merchandise, sunk her and then ran away with their ill-gotten spoils. But the cause of the loss was of little moment; they were gone, and there was no alternative left LaSalle but to return to Frontenac and get others to supply their place. His great anxiety in connection with this step was the fear that others of his men might take advantage of his absence and desert.

While revolving this subject in his mind, an incident occurred which enabled him to disabuse their minds of the false statements they had heard in regard to the dangers of the Mississippi. During a hunt in the vicinity of the fort, he chanced to meet with a young Indian who had been absent some time on a distant war excursion. Finding him almost famished with hunger, he invited him to the fort, where he refreshed him with a generous meal, and questioned him with apparent indifference respecting the Mississippi. Owing to his long absence, he knew nothing of what had transpired between his countrymen and the French, and, with great ingenuousness, imparted all the information required. LaSalle now gave him presents not to mention the interview, and, with a number of his men, repaired to the camp of the Illinois to expose their misrepresentations. Having found the chiefs at a feast of bear's meat, he boldly accused them of falsehood, and at once proceeded to verify his charges. The Master of Life, he declared, was the friend of truth, and had revealed to him the actual character of the Mississippi. He then gave such an accurate account of it, that his astonished but credulous auditors believed his knowledge had been obtained in a supernatural manner, and at once confessed their guilt. It was their desire, they said, to have him remain with them, and they had resorted to artifice for this

*" Broken hearted."

purpose, and not to do him any injury. This confession removed a principal cause of desertion, and banished from the mind of La-Salle a fruitful source of anxiety. Lest idleness should breed new disturbances among his men during his absence, he set them at work on the new vessel. Some of his best carpenters had deserted, yet energy supplied the place of skill, and before his departure he saw the new craft on the stocks, rapidly approaching completion. He also thought that Hennepin might accomplish greater results by exploring the Upper Mississippi than by preaching sermons, and he was therefore requested to take charge of an expedition for this purpose. The friar, not wishing to incur the dangers of the undertaking, plead bodily infirmity, and endeavored to have one of his spiritual colleagues appointed in his stead. Ribourde was too old to endure the hardships, and Membre, though disgusted with his clerical duties among the Illinois, preferred an unpleasant field of labor to one beset with perils. Hennepin, finding no alternative but to accept, with rare modesty and great reliance upon providence, says: "Anybody but me would have been much much frightened with the dangers of such a journey, and in fact, if I had not placed all my trust in God, I should not have been the dupe of LaSalle, who exposed my life rashly.." A profusion of gifts was placed in his canoe, to conciliate the Indians, and on the last day of February, 1680, a party assembled on the banks of the Illinois to bid him him farewell. Father Ribourde invoked the blessing of heaven over the kneeling form of the clerical traveler; his two companions, Accau and DuGay, plied their paddles, and they were soon concealed from view in the meandering channel of the river.

CHAPTER VIII.

TONTI'S ENCOUNTER WITH THE IROQUOIS.

Only two days afterward, another parting occurred at the river. It was now LaSalle's time to bid adieu to the scenes where, during the winter, his motives had been so often misrepresented and impugned. Leaving Tonti in command of the fort, garrisoned with three or four honest men and a dozen knaves, he set out for Fort Frontenac with four men and his Mohegan hunter, whose faithfulness was a perpetual rebuke to French fickleness and treachery. The winter had been severe, and his progress up the river was greatly retarded by drifting sheets of ice. Reaching Peoria Lake, the ice was unbroken from shore to shore, and the party was compelled to land and make sledges on which to drag their canoes to a point in the river above, where the swiftness of the current kept the channel open. Little thought these lonely wanderers that the desolate spot where this incident transpired, was one day to resound with the tramp of the multitude which now throngs the streets of Peoria. A laborious march of four leagues, through melting snows, placed them above the icy barrier of the lake, and they launched their canoes. Thence, to the great town of the Illinois, they found the river at different points blocked with ice, and their journey was made alternately by land and water, in the drenching rains of opening spring. They found the village without inhabitants, and its lodges crested with snow. The adjacent meadows were still locked in the fetters of winter, and the more distant forests, bearded with crystals, flashed in the morning sun like a sea of diamonds. Yet the frozen landscape was not without life. The impress of moccasined feet could be traced in the snow, and occasionally a straggling buffalo could be seen, and one of them was shot. While his men were smoking the meat of the animal, LaSalle went out to reconnoitre the country, and soon fell in with 3 Indians, one of whom proved to be the principal chief of the Illinois. Inviting him and his associates to his camp, he made them presents, and refreshed them with the best food his scanty larder could furnish. He then informed the chief that he was on his way east to procure arms and ammunition for the defense of his tribes, and obtained from him a promise that he would send provisions to his men in the fort during his absence. While here, he visited Starved Rock, the remarkable cliff previously alluded to, a mile or more above the village, on the southern bank of the river. He afterwards sent word to Tonti to examine and fortify it, in case an outbreak of the Indians rendered it necessary.*

*Several years since, it was selected by some enterprising Yankees as a site for a town, which they very appropriately called Gibraltar; but now it remains houseless, as in the time of the great explorer.

On the 15th of March LaSalle left the village, and continued his journey as before, partly by land and in part by water, till within two miles of the site of Joliet. Here, in consequence of the ice, they found the further ascent of the river impossible, and, concealing their canoes, prepared to make a march directly across the country to Lake Michigan. Journeying lakeward, they found the country a dreary waste of mud and half-melted snow, intersected here and there by swollen streams, some of which they waded, and others they crossed on rafts. On the 23d they were gladdened by the distant surface of the lake glimmering through the openings of the forest, and at night stood on its bank, thankful that they were safe, and that their hardships had been no worse. The next day they followed its winding shores to the mouth of the St. Joseph, and rested at night in the fort. Here LaSalle found the two men whom he had sent to look for the Griffin, and learned from them that they had made the circuit of the lake without learning any tidings of her fate. Deeming it useless to further continue the search, he ordered the men to report themselves to Tonti, and started himself across the trackless wilds of Southern Michigan, to avoid the delay attending the indirect route by way of the lakes.

It was the worst of all seasons for such a journey, and almost every league traversed, brought with it some new hardship. Now they were lascerated by brambly thickets, now they plunged up to their waists in the mud of half-frozen marshes, and now they were chilled in wading swollen streams. Dogged by a pack of savages, they were compelled to pass the nights without fire, to escape their murderous attacks. At length, with two of their number sick, they arrived at the head of a stream supposed to be the Huron, which, after making a canoe, they descended to the Detroit. Thence, marching eastward to the lake, 30 miles distant, they embarked in a canoe and pushed across the lake for the falls of Niagara, whither they arrived on Easter Monday, 1680. Here he found the men left at the cataract the previous autumn, who not only confirmed the loss of the Griffin, but informed him that a cargo of merchandise belonging to him, valued at 2200 livres, had recently been swallowed up in the Gulf of St. Lawrence. Leaving the weary companions of his previous journey at Niagara, he set out with fresh men for Fort Frontenac, and on the 6th day of May discovered through the hazy atmosphere, the familiar outlines of his seigniory. He had now traveled within 65 days the distance of 1000 miles, which, considering the circumstances, was one of the most remarkable journeys ever made by the early French explorers. Possessing an invincible determination and a frame of iron, he surmounted obstacles from which a person less favorably endowed would have turned away in dispair. How changed has since become the wilderness through which he wandered. Its dark forests have become a region of harvests, and the traveler of to-day accomplishes in less than two days the journey which required of him more than two months.

At the fort he learned that his agents had treated him with bad faith; that his creditors had seized his property, and that several canoes belonging to him, loaded with valuables, had been lost in the rapids of the St. Lawrence. Without useless repining, he hastened to Montreal, where his presence excited the greatest surprise, and where, notwithstanding his great financial losses, his personal influence enabled him to obtain the necessary supplies.

Again he directed his course westward, to succor the forlorn hope under Tonti, isolated from the rest of mankind on the distant banks of the Illinois. At Frontenac he received intelligence of another of those crushing blows which both nature and man seemed to be aiming at the success of his enterprise. Two messengers came with a letter from Tonti, stating that soon after his departure, nearly all his men had deserted, and that, before leaving, they had destroyed the fort, and thrown away stores they were unable to carry. The news of this disaster had hardly been received, before two traders arrived from the upper lakes, and further stated that the deserters had destroyed the fort on the St. Joseph, seized a great quantity of furs belonging to him at Mackinaw, and then, with others, descending the lakes, had plundered his magazine at Niagara. And now, they added, some of them are coming down the northern shore of the lake to murder him, as a means of escaping punishment, while others are coasting the south shore, with a view of reaching Albany, and getting beyond his jurisdiction. On receipt of this information, LaSalle chose 9 of his trustiest men, and sallied forth to meet them. Coming upon them by surprise, he killed 2 of their number and captured 7, whom he imprisoned in the fort to await the sentence of a civil tribunal. It might be supposed that LaSalle had reached the utmost limits of human endurance, on seeing the hopes of his enterprise so frequently levelled to the ground. While, however, weaker men would have turned away in dispair, no eye could detect in his stern demeanor an altered purpose or a shaken resolve. His only hope now seemed to be in Tonti, and could that faithful officer preserve the vessel commenced on the Illinois, and the tools which had been conveyed thither with so much labor, it might constitute an anchor to which he could attach the drifting wreck of his fortunes.

Having procured supplies and everything needful for the outfit of a vessel, without further delay he set out, on the 10th of August, for Illinois, accompanied by his lieutenant, LaForest, and 25 men. He ascended the river Humber, crossed Simcoe Lake, and descended the Severn into Lake Huron, over which he passed to the Straits of Mackinaw. At the station he found it difficult to replenish his provisions, and, not to be delayed for this purpose, he pushed forward with 12 men, leaving LaForest and the remainder to follow as soon as they could procure supplies. November 24th he arrived at the St. Joseph, and, anxious to push forward more rapidly, he left the greater part of the stores, with 5 men, at the ruined fort, and with the remainder ascended the river, crossed the portage and commenced the descent of the Kankakee. Not meeting with any traces of Tonti and his men, he concluded they must still be at the fort on the river below, and hastened thither, greatly relieved of the anxiety he had felt for their safety. Rumors for some time had prevailed that the Iroquois were meditating a descent on the Illinois, and should it prove true, it might, after all his labors, involve his enterprise in ruin. On entering the Illinois, he found the great prairies, which he had left the previous spring sheeted in ice now alive with buffalo. Some were sleeping on the sward, many were cropping the tall grass, while groups, to slake their thirst, were moving toward the river, where they looked with strange bewilderment at the passing canoes. Wherever a squad appeared, it was guarded by bulls, whose formidable manes and unsightly forms might well have inspired an approaching foe with terror. But it was rather with domestic rivals than foreign enemies they performed the greatest feats of prowess. Battered heads and splintered horns told of many battles fought among themselves as the result of gallantry, or perhaps the more ambitious motive becoming the champions of their shaggy herds. The party wishing a supply of buffalo meat, landed and commenced a warfare on the tempting game. Some dragged themselves through the thick grass and with unerring aim brought down their favorite animals, while others, with less labor and greater success, concealed themselves behind the banks of the river and shot such as came to drink. Twelve huge carcasses rewarded the labors of the hunt, which the men cut into thin flakes and dried in the sun for future use.

With abundant supplies they again started down the river, pleased with the prospect of rejoining the men under Tonti and relieving their wants. Soon loomed up before them the rocky citadel to which LaSalle had directed the attention of Tonti, but they found on a near approach its lofty summit unfortified. At the great town of the Illinois they were appalled at the scene which opened to their view. No hunter appeared to break its death-like silence with a salutatory whoop of welcome. The plain on which the town had stood was now strewn with the charred fragments of lodges, which had so recently swarmed with savage life and hilarity. To render more hideous the picture of desolation, large numbers of skulls had been placed on the upper extremities of lodge poles, which had escaped the devouring flames. In the midst of the horrors was the rude fort of the spoilers, rendered frightful with the same ghastly relics. A near approach showed that the graves had been robbed of their bodies, and swarms of buzzards were discovered glutting their loathsome stomachs on their reeking corruption. To complete the work of destruction, the growing corn of the village had been cut down and burnt, while the pits containing the products of previous years had been rifled and their contents scattered with wanton waste. It was evident the suspected blow of the Iroquois had fallen with relentless fury. No other denizens of the wilderness were capable of perpetrating such acts of barbarity and unhallowed desecration. LaSalle carefully examined the scene of these hellish orgies, to ascertain whether Tonti and his men had become the victims of savage vengeance. Nightfall terminated his labors, and no certain traces of their presence were discovered. The nightly camp fire was kindled, and the men now listened with rueful faces at the discordant chorus of wolves, each striving to get his share of the putrid bodies which had been resurrected from the vilage graveyard. Sleep at length came to their relief, but LaSalle, perplexed with uncertainty and filled with anxiety, spent the whole night in pondering over the proper course to pursue in future. In his search the previous day he had discovered 6 posts near the river, on each of which was painted the figure of a man with bandaged eyes. Surmising that the figures might represent 6 French prisoners in the custody of the Iroquois, at daylight he made known his intention of further descending the river to unfold the mystery.

Before his departure he ordered 3 of his men to conceal themselves and baggage in the hollow of some rocks situated on a neighboring island, and keep a sharp lookout for further developments. They were instructed to refrain from the use of fires, whereby they might attract the attention of enemies; and should others of the men arrive they were to secrete themselves in the same place and await his return. He now set out with the 4 remaining men, each properly armed and furnished with merchandise to conciliate the Indians who might be met on the way. Several leagues below the town they landed on an island, near the western shore, where the fugitive Illinois had taken refuge. Directly opposite, on the main shore was the deserted camp of the Iroquois enemy. Each chief had carved on trees of the forest the totem of his clan, and signs indicating the strength of the forces he had led to the war and the number of the Illinois he had killed and captured. From these data LaSalle concluded that the entire strength of the invaders could not have been less than 580 warriors. Nothing was found to indicate the presence of Frenchmen, and LaSalle again fell down the river, and passed in one day 6 additional camps of the Illinois and as many more belonging to their enemy. Both parties seemed to have retreated in compact bodies toward the mouth of the river. Passing Peoria Lake they found the fort destroyed, as stated in the letter of Tonti, but the vessel was still on the stocks and only slightly injured. Further on they discovered 4 additional camps of the opposing armies, and near the mouth of the river met with the usual sequel of an Iroquois invasion. On the distant verge of a meadow they discovered the half-charred bodies of women and children still bound to the stakes, where they had suffered all the torments that hellish hate could devise. The men, regardless of their helpless charges, had evidently fled at the first approach of danger to save themselves. Their wives and children, unprotected, fell into the hands of the enemy, who, in addition to those who had been burnt, thickly covered the place with their mangled bodies, many of which bore marks of brutality too horrid for record. Helpless innocence, instead of exciting compassion in the hearts of these monsters, had only nerved them for the fiendish task of indiscriminate slaughter.

LaSalle, seeing no traces of his lost men, proceeded to the mouth of the river, where he saw the great highway which for years had been the object and hopes of his ambition. Its vast floods rolled mysteriously onward to an unknown bourne, for the discovery of which, with new resolves, he determined to devote his life. His men proposed, without further delay, to proceed on the long contemplated voyage, but LaSalle, hedged in by untoward complications, was compelled to await a more favorable time. Thinking that Tonti might still be in the neighborhood, he fastened to a tree a painting representing himself and party sitting in a canoe, and bearing the pipe of peace. To the painting he attached a letter, addressed to Tonti, the purport of which was that he should hasten up the river and join him at the great town of the Illinois. The party next commenced the ascent of the river to the same place, and vigorously plying their paddles night and day, arrived at their destination in 4 days. During the upward voyage, the great comet of 1680 nightly illumined the starry expanse above them, projecting its vast tail, with a terrible brilliancy, a distance of 60 degrees. LaSalle speaks of it as an object of scientific inquiry, while Increase Mather, a celebrated New England divine, with the superstition common to his time, said that "it was fraught with terrific portent to the nations of the world."

At the Indian town they found the men who had been left behind, unharmed, and anxiously awaiting their return. After getting some corn from the ravaged granaries of the burnt village, the whole party embarked, and commenced the ascent of the river. On the 6th of January, 1681, they arrived at the junction of the Desplaines and Kankakee, and passing up the latter a short distance, they discovered, not far from the shore, a rude hut. La-Salle landed, and entering it, found a block of wood which had recently been cut with a saw, thus indicating that Tonti must have passed up the river, This discovery kindled anew the hopes of the dispairing voyagers that their friends were still alive, and with lighter hearts they started directly overland to Fort Miami. On the way the snow fell in blinding storms, and not being sufficiently compact for the use of snow shoes, LaSalle led the way to open a track and urge on his followers. Such was the depth of the snow, his tall figure was frequently buried in drifts up to his waist, while the remainder of his person was showered with the crystal burdens of boughs overhead, whenever he chanced to touch them. On reaching their goal, LaSalle's first inquiry was for Tonti. No tidings, however, had been heard from him, and the hope he had entertained of meeting him here, was changed to disappointment. LaForest and the men whom he had left behind, with commendable industry had rebuilt the fort, prepared ground for raising a crop the ensuing year, and sawn material for building a new ship on the lake.

We must now endeavor to relate the adventures of Tonti. Meanwhile, we will leave LaSalle in the sheltering walls of the fort, pondering over the wasted energies of the past, and the gloomy prospects of the future. Yet his mind, so full of expedients, soon found means to evolve, from the fragments of his ruined fortunes, new resources for the furtherance of his daring schemes.

It will be remembered that Tonti had been left in command of Fort Crèvecœur with 15 men. Most of these disliking LaSalle, and having no interest in his enterprise, were ripe for revolt the first opportunity that promised success. LaSalle, stern, incomprehensible and cold, was much better qualified to command the respect of his men when present, than secure their good will and fidelity when absent. His departure eastward was, therefore, the commencement of unlawful acts among his men. A short time afterward, another event occurred which greatly increased the spirit of insubordination. The two men who had been sent to look for the Griffin, had, in pursuance of LaSalle's orders, arrived at the fort with disheartening intelligence. They informed the already disaffected garrison that the Griffin was lost; that Fort Frontenac was in the hands of LaSalle's creditors, and that he was now wholly without means to pay those in his employ. To prevent the desertion of his men, it was usual for LaSalle to withhold their wages till the term for which they were employed should expire. Now the belief that he would never pay them, gave rise to a spirit of mutiny, which soon found an opportunity for further developement. The two men alluded to were the bearers of a letter from LaSalle, directing Tonti to examine and fortify the Rock on the Illinois; and no sooner had he, with a few men, departed for this purpose, than the garrison of the fort refused longer to submit to authority. Their first act of lawlessness was the destruction of the fort; after which, they seized the ammunition, provisions, and other portables of value and fled. Only two of their number remained true, one of whom was the servant of LaSalle, who immediately hastened to apprise Tonti of what had occurred. He, thereupon, dispatched 4 of the men with him to carry the news to LaSalle; two of whom, as we have seen, successfully discharged their duty, while the others perhaps deserted.

Tonti, now in the midst of treacherous savages, had with him only 5 men, 2 of whom were the friars Ribourde and Membre. With these he immediately returned to the fort, collected the forge and tools which had not been destroyed by the mutineers, and conveyed them to the great town of the Illinois. By this voluntary display of confidence, he hoped to remove the jealousy with which the enemies of LaSalle had previously poisoned their minds. Here, awaiting the return of his leader, he was unmolested by the villagers, who, when the spring opened, amounted, according to the statement of Membre, to some 8,000 souls. Neither they nor their wild associates little suspected that hordes of Iroquois were then gathering in the fastnesses of the Alleghanies, to burst upon their country and reduce it to an uninhabitable waste. Already these hell-hounds of the wilderness had destroyed the Hurons, Eries, and other nations on the lakes, and were now directing their attention to the Illinois for new victims with which to flesh their rabid fangs. Not only homicidal fury, but commercial advantages now actuated the Iroquois, who expected, after reducing these vast regions of the west, to draw thence rich supplies of furs to barter with the English for merchandise. LaSalle had also enemies among the French, who, to defeat his enterprise, did not scruple to encourage the Iroquois in their rapacious designs. Under these circumstances a council was held by the latter. The ceremonies of inaugurating a campaign were duly celebrated, and 500 warriors, with a dispatch only equalled by their terrible earnestness, commenced traversing the wide waste of forest and prairie that lay between them and their intended prey. In the line of their march lay the Miamis, who by their crafty intrigues were induced to join in the movement against their neighbors and kindred. There had long existed a rankling jealousy between these tribes, and the Miamis were ready to enter into any alliance that promised revenge. It was the policy of the Iroquois to divide and conquer, and their new allies were marked as the next object of their vengeance, should the assault on the Illinois prove successful.

All was fancied security and idle repose in the great town of the Illinois, as the formidable war party stealthily approached. Suddenly, as a clap of thunder from a cloudless sky, the listless inhabitants were awakened from their lethargy. A Shawnee Indian, on his return home after a visit to the Illinois, first discovered the invaders. To save his friends from the impending danger, he hurriedly returned and apprised them of the coming enemy. This intelligence spread with lightning rapidity over the town, and each wigwam disgorged its boisterous and astounded inmates. Women snatched their children, and in a delirium of fright wandered aimlessly about, rending the air with their screams. The men, more self-possessed, seized their arms, and in a wild pantomime of battle, commenced nerving themselves for the coming fray. Tonti, long an object of suspicion, was soon surrounded by an angry crowd of warriors, who accused him of being an emissary of the enemy. His inability properly to defend himself, in consequence of not fully understanding their language, left them still inclined to believe him guilty, and they seized the forge and other effects brought from the fort, and threw them into the river. Doubting their ability to defend themselves without the assistance of their young men, who were absent on a war expedition, they embarked their women and children in canoes and sent them down to the island where LaSalle had seen their deserted huts. Sixty warriors remained with them for protection, and the remainder, not exceeding 400, returned late in the day to the village. Along the adjacent shore they kindled huge bonfires, which cast their glare for miles around, gilding the village, river and distant margins of the forest with the light of day. The entire night was spent in greasing their bodies, painting their faces and performing the war dance, to prepare themselves for the approaching conflict. At early dawn the scouts who had been sent out returned, closely followed by the Iroquois, most of whom were armed with guns, pistols and swords, obtained from the English. The scouts had seen a chief arrayed in French costume, and reported their suspicions that LaSalle was in the camp of the enemy, and Tonti again became an object of jealousy. A concourse of wildly gesticulating savages immediately gathered about him, demanding his life, and nothing saved him from their uplifted weapons but a promise that he and his men would go with them to meet the enemy. With their suspicions partially lulled, they hurriedly crossed the river and appeared on the plain beyond just as the enemy emerged in swarms from the woods skirting the banks of the Vermilion. The two foes were now face to face, and both commenced discharging their guns and simultaneously leaping from side to side, for the purpose of dodging each other's shots. Tonti, seeing the Illinois outnumbered and likely to sustain a defeat, determined, at the imminent risk of his life, to stay the fight by an attempt at mediation. Presuming on the treaty of peace then existing between the French and Iroquois, he exchanged his gun for a belt of wampum and advanced to meet the savage multitude, attended by three companions, who, being unnecessarily exposed to danger, he dismissed them and proceeded alone. A short walk brought him into the midst of a pack of yelping devils, writhing and distorted with fiendish rage, and impatient to shed his blood. As the result of his swarthy Italian complexion and half savage costume, he was at first taken for an Indian, and before the mistake was discovered a young warrior approached and stabbed at his heart. Fortunately the blade was turned aside by coming in contact with a rib, yet a large flesh wound was inflicted, which bled profusely. At this juncture a chief discovered his true character, and he was led to the rear and efforts made to staunch his wound. When sufficiently recovered, he declared the Illinois were under the protection of the French, and demanded, in consideration of the treaty between the latter and the Iroquois, that they should be suffered to remain without further molestation. During this conference, a young warrior snatched Tonti's hat, and, fleeing with it to the front, held it aloft on the end of his gun in view of the Illinois. The latter, judging from this circumstance that their envoy had been killed, caused the battle to "breeze up" with increased intensity. Simultaneously, intelligence was brought to the Iroquois that Frenchmen were assisting their enemies in the fight, when the contest over Tonti was renewed with redoubled fury. Some declared that he should be immediately put to death; while others, friendly to LaSalle, with equal earnestness demanded that he should be set at liberty. During their clamorous debate his hair was several times lifted by a huge savage who stood at his back with a scalping knife, ready for execution.

Tonti at length turned the current of the angry controversy in his favor, by stating that the Illinois were 1,200 strong, and that there were 60 Frenchmen at the village ready to assist them. This statement obtained at least a partial credence, and his tormentors now determined to use him as an instrument to delude the Illinois with a pretended truce. The old warriors therefore advanced to the front and ordered the firing to cease, while Tonti, dizzy from the loss of blood, was furnished with an emblem of peace and sent staggering across the plain to rejoin the Illinois. The two friars, who had just returned from a distant hut, whither they had retired for prayer and meditation, were the first to meet him and bless God for what they regarded as a miraculous deliverance.* With the assurance brought by Tonti, the Illinois recrossed the river to their lodges, followed by the enemy as far as the opposite bank. Not long after, large numbers of the latter, under the pretext of hunting, also crossed the river and hung in threatening groups about the town. These hostile indications, and the well known disregard which the Iroquois had always evinced for their pledges, soon convinced the Illinois that their only safety was in flight. With this conviction they set fire to their ancestral homes, and while the vast volume of flame and smoke diverted the attention of the enemy, they quietly dropped down the river to rejoin their women and children. Shortly after, the remainder of the Iroquois crossed the river, and as soon as the conflagration would permit, entrenched themselves on the site of the village. Tonti and his men, remaining at the village, were ordered by the suspicious savages to leave their hut and take up their abode in the fort.

At first their associates seemed much elated at the discomfiture of the Illinois, but two days after, when they discovered them reconnoitering on the low hills behind their intrenchments, their courage greatly subsided. With fear, they recalled the exaggerations of Tonti, respecting their numbers, and immediately concluded to send him with a hostage to make overtures of peace. He started on his mission, and he and the hostage were received with delight by the Illinois, who readily assented to this proposal which he brought, and in turn sent back with him a hostage to the Iroquois. On his return to the fort, his life was again placed in jeopardy, and

*Membre, perhaps prompted by vanity, claims that he accompanied Tonti in this interview. This is the only instance in which he is charged with a want of veracity, and doubtless in many respects was a good man.

the treaty was with great difficulty ratified. The young and inexperienced Illinois hostage betrayed to his crafty interviewers the
numerical weakness of his tribe, and the savages immediately
rushed upon Tonti, and charged him with having deprived them
of the spoils and honors of a victory. "Where," said they, "are
all your Illinois warriors, and where are the Frenchmen you said
were among them ?" It now required all the tact of which he was
master to escape the present difficulty, which he had brought on
himself by the artifice employed to escape the one previous. After
much opposition, the treaty was concluded, but the savages, to
show their contempt for it, immediately commenced the construction of canoes in which to descend the river and attack the Illinois.

Tonti managed to apprise the latter of their designs, and he and
Membre were soon after summoned to attend a council of the Iroquois. They still labored under a wholesome fear of Count Frontenac, and disliking to attack the Illinois in the presence of the
French, their object was to induce the latter to leave the country.
At the assembling of the council, 6 packages of beaver skins were
introduced, and the savage orator, presenting them separately to
Tonti, explained the nature of each. "The first two," said he,
"were to declare that the children of Count Frontenac, that is,
the Illinois, should not be eaten; the next was a plaster to heal
the wounds of Tonti; the next was oil wherewith to annoint him
and Membre, that they might not be fatigued in traveling; the
next proclaimed that the sun was bright; and the sixth, and
last, required them to decamp and go home."*

At the mention of going home, Tonti demanded of them when
they intended to set the example by leaving the Illinois in the
peaceable possession of their country, which they had so unjustly
invaded. The council grew boisterous and angry at the idea that
they should be demanded to do that which they required of the
French, and some of its members, forgetting their previous pledge,
declared that they would "eat Illinois flesh before they departed."
Tonti, in imitation of the Indian manner of expressing scorn, indignantly kicked away the presents of fur, saying, since they meant
to devour the children of Count Frontenac with cannibal ferocity,
he would not accept their gifts. This stern rebuke of perfidy resulted in the expulsion of Tonti and his companions from the
council, and the next day the enraged chiefs ordered them to leave
the country.

Tonti had now, at the great risk of his life, tried every expedient to avert from the unoffending Illinois the slaughter which the
unscrupulous invaders of their soil were seeking an opportunity
to effect. There was little to be accomplished by remaining in the
country, and as a longer delay might imperil the lives of his men,
he determined to depart, not knowing when or where he would be
able to rejoin LaSalle. With this object in view, the party, consisting of 6 persons, embarked in canoes, which soon proved leaky,
and they were compelled to land for the purpose of making repairs. While thus employed, Father Ribourde, attracted by the
beauty of the surrounding landscape, wandered forth among the
groves for meditation and prayer. Not returning in due time,
Tonti became alarmed, and started with a companion to ascertain

*Discoveries of the Great West.—Parkman.

the cause of the long delay. They soon discovered tracks of Indians, by whom it was supposed he had been seized, and guns were fired to direct his return, in case he was still alive. Seeing nothing of him during the day, at night they built fires along the bank of the river and retired to the opposite side, to see who might approach them. Near midnight, a number of Indians were seen flitting about the light, by whom, no doubt, had been made the tracks seen the previous evening. It was afterwards learned that they were a band of Kickapoos, who had, for several days, been hovering about the camp of the Iroquois in quest of scalps. Not being successful in obtaining the object of their desires from their enemies, they, by chance, fell in with the inoffensive old friar, and scalped him in their stead. " Thus, in the 65th year of his age, the only heir to a wealty Burgundian house perished under the war club of the savages, for whose salvation he had renounced ease and affluence."*

During the performance of this tragedy, a far more revolting one was being enacted at the great town of the Illinois. The Iroquois were tearing open the graves of the dead, and wreaking their vengeance upon the bodies made hideous by putrifaction. At this desecration, it is said, they even ate portions of the dead bodies, while subjecting them to every indignity that brutal hate could inflict. Still unsated by their hellish brutalities, and now unrestrained by the presence of the French, they started in pursuit of the retreating Illinois. Day after day they and the opposing forces moved in compact array down the river, neither being able to gain any advantage over the other. At length they obtained by falsehood that which numbers and prowess denied them. They gave out that their object was to possess the country, not by destroying, but by driving out its present inhabitants. Deceived by this mendacious statement, the Illinois separated, some descending the Mississippi, and others crossing to the western shore. Unfortunately, the Tamaroas, more credulous than the rest, remained near the mouth of the Illinois, and were suddenly attacked by an overwhelming force of the enemy. The men fled in dismay, and the women and children, to the number of 700, fell into the hands of the ferocious enemy. Then followed the tortures, butcheries and burnings which only the infuriated and imbruted Iroquois could perpetrate—the shocking evidence of which LaSalle saw only two weeks afterward. After the ravenous horde had sufficiently glutted their greed for carnage, they retired from the country, leading with them a number of women and children, whom they reserved either for adoption into their tribes, or as victims to grace the triumphs sometimes accorded them on their return home.

Their departure was the signal for the return of the Illinois, who rebuilt their town. The site of this celebrated village was on the northern bank of the river, where it flows by the modern town of Utica. Its immediate site was on the great meadow which, at this point, originally stretched up and down the stream. The large quantities of bones and rude implements of savage life which are annually turned up by the ploughshare, are the only sad traces of the populous tribes that once made this locality their

*Discovery of the Great West—Parkman.

principal home. Along the southern side of the river extends a range of hills, which terminate a mile and a half above in the natural abutment known as Starved Rock, on which the French, in 1682, built a fort. Several miles below, an opening occurs in the hills, through which the waters of the Big Vermilion unite with those of the Illinois. It was by means of these prominent landmarks Francis Parkman, Esq., a few years since, was enabled to identify the site of the Indian town, which, for many years previous, was entirely unknown.

After the death of Ribourde, the men under Tonti again resumed the ascent of the river, leaving no evidence of their passage at the junction of the two streams which form the Illinois. Their craft again becoming disabled, they abandoned it, and the party started on foot for Lake Michigan. Their supply of provisions soon became exhausted, and the travelers were compelled to subsist in a great measure on roots and acorns. One of their companions wandered off in search of game, lost his way, and several days elapsed before he had the good fortune of rejoining them. In his absence he was without flints and bullets, yet contrived to shoot some turkeys by using slugs cut from a pewter porringer and a firebrand to discharge his piece. It was their object to reach Green Bay and find an asylum for the winter among the Potawatamies. As the result of privation and exposure, Tonti fell sick of a fever and greatly retarded the progress of the march. Nearing Green Bay, the cold increased and the means of subsistence proportionately diminishing, the party would have perished had they not found a few ears of corn and some frozen squashes in the fields of a deserted village. Near the close of November they had the good fortune of reaching the Potawatamies, who greeted them with a warm reception, and supplied them with the necessaries of life. Their chief was an ardent admirer of the French, whom he had befriended the year previous, and was accustomed to say: "There were but three great captains in the world, himself, Tonti and LaSalle."

CHAPTER IX.

FURTHER EXPLORATIONS BY LASALLE.

We must now return to LaSalle, whose exploits stand out in such bold relief. In the previous discoveries he had observed that white enemies were using the Iroquois to circumvent his operations; that their incursions must be stopped, or his defeat was inevitable. After due consideration, he concluded the best way to prevent their inroads was to induce the western tribes to forget their animosities, and under a league against their inexorable enemies, colonize them around a fort in the valley of the Illinois, where, with the assistance of French arms and French generalship, the common enemy would be unable further to molest them. French colonists could teach them the arts of agriculture, Recollet monks instruct them in their religious duties, and the ships of France supply merchandise to traffic with them for the rich harvest of furs annually gathered from their vast interior wilds. Meanwhile he proposed to explore the Mississippi, and make it a highway for the commerce of the world. Thus, concluded LaSalle, the plains of Illinois, which for centuries have been a slaughter pen for warring savages, might be made the theatre of a civilization as famous as their past history had been rendered infamous by deeds of carnage. To the execution of this new expedient for advancing his plans, he now turned his attention.

After the terrible scourge of King Philip's war, a number of the conquered Indians left their eastern homes and took refuge in the vicinity of the fort, where LaSalle had spent the winter. These were mostly Abenakis and Mohegans—the latter having furnished the hunter who had so often, by his superior skill, provided LaSalle's hungry followers with food. He was also master of several Indian dialects, which, at this particular juncture of LaSalle's affairs, he could use with great advantage. To these exiles from the east LaSalle first directed his attention, and found them unanimously in favor of casting their lot with his, asking no recompense save the privilege of calling him chief. A new ally, in the person of a powerful chief from the valley of the Ohio, also appeared, and asked permission to enter the new confederation. LaSalle replied that his tribe was too distant, but let them come to me in the valley of the Illinois, and they shall be safe.. The chief, without stipulating further, agreed to join him with 150 warriors. To reconcile the Miamis and Illinois, and thus secure their co-operation, was now the principal obstacle. Although kindred tribes, they had long been estranged, and it was only after the recent depredations of the Iroquois, they began to see the advantage of opposing a united front to their outrages. Wish-

ing first to consult the Illinois, many of whom had returned after
the evacuation of the Iroquois, they found the prairies still encrusted
with snow, from the dazzling whiteness of which, LaSalle and
several of the men became snow-blind, and were compelled to en-
camp under the edge of a forest till they could recover. While
suffering from the loss of vision, they sent out a companion to
gather pine leaves, which were supposed to be a specific for their
malady. While on this errand he had the good fortune to fall in
with a band of the Foxes, from whom he learned that Tonti was
safe among the Potawatamies, and that Hennepin had passed
through their country, on his way to Canada. This was welcome
news to LaSalle, who had long been anxious in regard to his
safety. The afflicted soon after recovered, and the snow having
melted, they launched their canoes into the swollen tributary of
the Illinois. Following the river, they fell in with a band of the
Illinois, ranging the prairies in quest of game. LaSalle expressed
his regret at the great injury they had sustained from the Iroquois,and urged them to form an alliance with their kindred, the
Miamis, to prevent the recurrence of similar disasters in the future. He promised them that he and his companions would take
up their abode among them, furnish them with goods and arms,
and assist in defending them in the attacks of the common enemy
of the Algonquin race. Pleased with LaSalle's proposition, they
supplied him with corn, and promised to confer with others of
their countrymen on the subject, and let him know the result.

Having completed his negotiations with the Illinois, he sent La-
Forest to Mackinaw, whither Tonti was expected to go, and where
both of them were to remain till he could follow them. It now
remained for him to consult the Miamis, and he accordingly visited
one of their principal villages on the portage between the St.
Joseph and the Kankakee. Here he found a band of Iroquois,
who had for some time demeaned themselves with the greatest
insolence toward the villagers, and had spoken with the utmost
contempt of himself and men. He sternly rebuked them for their
arrogance and calumnies, which caused them to slink away, and
at night flee the country. The Miamis were astonished beyond
measure when they saw LaSalle, with only 10 Frenchmen, put
their haughty visitors to flight, while they, with hundreds of warriors, could not even secure respect. LaSalle now resolved to use
the prestige he had gained in furthering the object of his visit.
There were present in the village Indian refugees from recent
wars in Virginia, New York and Rhode Island, to whom LaSalle
communicated the nature of his errand, and promised homes and
protection in the valley of the Illinois. It is a goodly and beautiful land, said he, abounding in game, and well supplied with
goods, in which they should dwell, if they would only assist him
in restoring amicable relations between the Miamis and Illinois.
The co-operation of these friendless exiles, who now knew how to
value the blessings of peace and a settled habitation, was readily
enough secured.

The next day the Miamis were assembled in council, and La-
Salle made known to them he objects he wished to accomplish.
From long intercourse with the Indians, he had become an expert
in forest tact and eloquence. and on this occasion he had come
well provided with presents, to give additional efficacy to his pro-

ceedings. He began his address, which consisted of metaphorical allusions to the dead, by distributing gifts among the living. Presenting them with cloth, he told them it was to cover their dead; giving them hatchets, he informed them that they were to build a scaffold in their honor; distributing among them beads and bells, he stated they were to decorate their persons. The living, while appropriating these presents, were greatly pleased at the compliments paid, their departed friends, and thus placed in a suitable state of mind for that which was to follow. A chief, for whom they entertained the greatest respect, had recently been killed, and LaSalle told them he would raise him from the dead, meaning that he would assume his name and provide for his family. This generous offer was even more than Indian gravity could bear, and the whole assemblage became uproarious with excitement and applause. Lastly, to convince them of the sincerity of his intentions, he gave them 6 guns, a number of hatchets, and threw into their midst a huge pile of clothing, causing the entire multitude to explode with yells of the most extravagant delight. After this, LaSalle thus finished his harangue:

"He who is my master, and the master of all this country, is a mighty chief, feared by the whole world; but he loves peace, and his words are for good alone. He is called the king of France, and is the mightiest among the chiefs beyond the great water. His goodness extends even to your dead, and his subjects come among you to raise them to life. But it is his will to preserve the life he has given. It is his will that you should obey his laws, and make no war without the leave of Frontenac, who commands in his name at Quebec, and loves all the nations alike, because such is the will of the great king. You ought, then, to live in peace with your neighbors, and above all with the Illinois. You had cause of quarrel with them, but their defeat has avenged you. Though they are still strong, they wish to make peace with you. Be content with the glory of having compelled them to ask for it. You have an interest in preserving them, since, if the Iroquois destroy them, they will next destroy you. Let us all obey the great king, and live in peace under his protection. Be of my mind, and use these guns I have given you, not to make war, but only to hunt and defend yourselves."*

Having thus far been successful in uniting the western tribes, he was now ready to use the alliance formed in further extending his discoveries. First, it was necessary to return to Canada and collect his scattered resources, and satisfy his creditors. Toward the latter part of May, 1681, they left Fort Miami, and after a short and prosperous trip arrived at Mackinaw, where they had the happiness of meeting with Tonti. After the kindly greetings of the long absent friends were over, each recounted the story of his misfortunes. Such was LaSalle's equanimity and even cheerfulness, that Membre, in admiration of his conduct, exclaimed: "Any one else except him would have abandoned the enterprise, but he, with a firmness and constancy which never had its equal, was more resolved than ever to push forward his work." Having reviewed the past, and formed new resolves for the future, the party embarked for Frontenac. The watery track of 1000 miles intervening between them and their destination, was soon crossed, and LaSalle was again in consultation with his creditors. In addition to the cost incurred in building the fort, and maintaining in it a garrison, he was now further burdened with the debt of subsequent fruitless explorations. The fort and seigniory were mortgaged for a large sum, yet by parting with some of his mo-

* Discovery of the Great West—Parkman.

nopolies, and securing aid from a wealthy relative, he managed
to satisfy his creditors and secure means for another outfit.
Owing to unavoidable delays the season was far advanced when
his flotilla was pushed out on the waters of Lake Michigan.
Their canoes were headed for the mouth of the St.Joseph, and as
they slowly crept along the dreary shores of the lake, it is easy to
imagine the more dreary thought that harrassed the mind of
LaSalle. A past of unrequitted toil and sad disappointment, a
present embittered by the tongue of hate and slander, and the
future clouded with uncertainty, must have intruded themselves
into his mind, but could not for a moment divert him from the
accomplishment of the great object which for years had been the
guiding star of his destiny. The trees were bare of the beautiful
autumnal foliage when at length the walls of Fort Miami rose
above the waste of waters, and they drew up their canoes on the
adjacent shore. The columns of smoke that rose high in the still
November air, told LaSalle that his Mohegan and Abenaki allies
were awaiting his return. Notwithstanding these were the remnants of the tribes "whose midnight yells had startled the border hamlets of New England; who had danced around Puritan
scalps and whom Puritan imaginations painted as incarnate
fiends," LaSalle chose from them 18 men to accompany him.
These, added to the Frenchmen, made 41 men, who, on the 21st
of December, 1681, set out on this famous expedition. Tonti and
some of the men crossed in advance to the mouth of the Chicago,
where they were soon after joined by LaSalle and the remainder
of the men. The streams being now sheated over with ice, and
the land covered with snow, they were compelled to construct
sledges on which to drag their canoes and baggage to the western branch of the Illinois. Finding it also bridged over with ice
they filed down it in a long procession, passed the tenantless village of the Illinois and found the river open a short distance
below Peoria Lake. The season, and other unfavorable circumstances, rendered the building of a vessel, as originally contemplated, at this point wholy impossible. They were compelled
therefore to proceed in their canoes, and on the 6th of February
they reached the Great River which was to bear them onward to
the sea. Waiting a week for the floating ice to disappear, they
glided down the current toward the great unknown, which all
former attempts had failed to penetrate. The first night they encamped near the mouth of the Missouri, and witnessed its opaque
floods invade the purer waters of the Mississippi. Re-embarking
the next morning they passed several interesting localities, and
after several days, landed on the 24th of February, at Chickasaw
bluffs for the purpose of going out in quest of game to supply
their failing provisions. Here, one of the hunters named Prudhomme, lost himself in the dense forest, and it was only after a
search of more than a week he was found in a starving condition
and brought to camp. Meanwhile LaSalle caused a fort to be
erected which he named Prudhomme to evince his condolence for
the suffering of the hunter, who with a small party he left in
charge of it. Again embarking on the tortuous river, they were
soon apprised by the opening buds of semi-tropical vegetation, that
they were rapidly entering the realms of spring.

On the 13th of March, their attention was arrested by the booming of an Indian drum, and shouts proceeding from a war dance on the western side of the river. Being unable, in consequence of a fog, to see the authors of the demonstrations, they retired to the opposite shore and threw up breastworks as a means of protection. When the mist rolled away the astonished savages for the first time saw the strangers, who made signals for them to come over the river, Several of them, accepting the invitation, were met midway the stream by a Frenchman, who, in turn was invited in a friendly manner to visit their village. The whole party, thus assured, crossed the river, and LaSalle at their head marched to the open area of the town. Here in the midst of a vast concourse of admiring villagers, he erected a cross, bearing the arms of France, Membre sang a hymn in canonicals, and LaSalle, having obtained from the chiefs an acknowledgement of loyalty, took possession of the country in the name of the king. This lively and generous people, so different from the cold and taciturn Indians of the north, were a tribe or the Arkansas, and dwelt near the mouth of the river bearing their name. The travelers, on taking leave of them, were furnished with two guides, and next passed the sites of Vicksburg and Grand Gulf, where, 181 years afterward, were fought bloody struggles for the dominion of the river they were endeavoring to explore. Near 200 miles below the Arkansas, their guides pointed out the direction of the village of the Taensas. Tonti and Membre were directed to visit it, and were greatly surprised at the evidences of civilization which it exhibited. Its large square dwellings, built of sun-dried mortar and arched over with dome-shaped roofs, were situated in regular order around a square. The residence of the chief, made in the same manner, was a single hall 40 feet square and lighted by a single door, in which he sat in state, awaiting the arrival of the visitors. He was surrounded by a court of 60 old men clad in robes of mulbery bark, while near his person sat his three wives, who howled whenever he spoke, to do him honor. After making him a number of presents, which he graciously received, the visitors proceeded to examine the temple, similar in size to the building occupied by the king. Within were the bones of departed chiefs, and an altar kept perpetually burning by the two old men devoted to this sacred office. On the top of the temple were carved three eagles, looking toward the east; while around it was a wall studded with stakes, on the tops of which hung the skulls of enemies who had been sacrificed to the Sun. The chief, in response to a friendly call, visited the camp of LaSalle. A master of ceremonies was sent to announce his coming, after which he made his appearance, robed in white, and attended by three persons, two of them bearing white fans and the third a disk of burnished copper. The latter was doubtless intended to represent the Sun, which was not only an object of worship, but the source whence the chief claimed his ancestors were derived. His demeanor was grave and dignified in the presence of LaSalle, who treated him with becoming courtesy and friendship. After receiving a number of presents, the principal object of the visit, he returned to his village, and the travelers started down the river.

Shortly afterward, they fell in with another tribe, and LaSalle wishing to approach them in a friendly manner, encamped on the opposite shore. He then permitted Tonti, with a few companions, to make them a visit, who, finding them favorably disposed, La-Salle and Membre also joined the party. They next visited one of the Indian villages and were made the recipients of a hospitality limited only by the means of their generous entertainers. They were the Natchez, and LaSalle, learning that the principal town was not far distant, repaired thither to have an interview with the head chief of the tribe. As among the Taensas, he saw here a royal residence, a temple of the sun, with its perpetually burning fire, and other evidences of more than ordinary Indian progress. Before leaving, LaSalle erected a cross in the midst of the town, to which was attached the arms of France, an act which the inhabitants regarded with great satisfaction, but had they known its meaning their displeasure would have been equally intense.

Next, they discovered the mouth of Red River, and after passing a number of other villages, found themselves at the junction of the three channels of the river which branch off into the Gulf. A different party entered each passage, and as they moved southward the water rapidly changed to brine, and the land breeze became salty with the breath of the sea. On the 6th of April "The broad bosom of the great Gulf opened on their sight, tossing its restless billows, limitless, voiceless and lonely as when born of chaos, without a sign of life."*

The great mystery of the new world was now unveiled. LaSalle had at last triumphed over every opposing obstacle, and secured a fame which will live as long as the floods of the great river roll to the sea and impart fertility to the valley through which they flow.

After coasting for a short time the marshy shores of the Gulf and its inlets, the party ascended the river till its banks became sufficiently dry to afford a landing. Here LaSalle erected a column on which he inscribed the words: "Louis le Grand Roy de France et de Navarre, Regne; Le Neuvieme Avril, 1682."

In honor of his King, he called the country through which he had passed, Louisiana, and commenced the ceremony of taking formal possession by military display and the imposing pageantry of the Catholic church. Standing by the side of the column, he proclaimed in a loud voice:

"In the name of the most high, mighty, invincible, and victorious Prince Louis the Great, by the grace of God King of France and Navarre, fourteenth of that name, I, this 9th day of April, 1682, in virtue of the commission of his Majesty, which I hold in my hand, and which may be seen by all whom it may concern, have taken, and now do take, in the name of his majesty and of his successors to the crown, possession of this country of Louisiana, the seas, harbors, ports, bays, adjacent straits, and all the nations, peoples, provinces, cities, towns, villages, mines, minerals, fisheries, streams and rivers, comprised in the limits of the said Louisiana."

A song, with volleys of musketry, closed the ceremonies by which the realms of France received the stupendous accession of the great region drained by the Mississippi and its tributaries. †

The voyagers having now accomplished the great object of the expedition, started on their homeward journey. The tribes which had treated them with so much civility and generosity in the down-

*Discoveries of the Great West.
†Monette's Val. of the Miss

ward voyage, were now from some cause alienated, and indisposed to let him have food. On arriving among the Nachez, they found them hostile, and while they abundantly supplied them with corn, they at the same time surrounded them with a large force to cut them off. Fearing, however, to make an attack, the travelers departed, and, without further molestation, reached Fort Prudhomme, where LaSalle was seized with a dangerous illness. Unable to go himself, he sent Tonti and a few companions to announce the news of his discoveries at Mackinaw, whence it was to be dispatched to Canada. Although carefully attended by Membre, he lay sick in the fort till the latter part of July, when he, in a great measure, recovered, and reached Mackinaw on the 1st of September. Thence Membre was sent to France with dispatches making known the grandeur of LaSalle's discoveries; the vast region visited; the immensity of its mountain ranges, and its great plains, veined by mighty streams.

It was LaSalle's intention also to visit France, but hearing that the Iroquois were about to renew their attacks on the western tribes, he decided that his presence was necessary to the safety of his projected policy. He accordingly returned to the Illinois river, whither Tonti had already preceded him, and at once commenced preparations to meet the enemies. As a means of defence it was determined to fortify Starved Rock, whose military advantages had previously attracted the attention of LaSalle. From the waters which wash its base it rises to an altitude of 125 feet. Three of the sides it is impossible to scale, while the one next to the land may be climbed with difficulty. From its summit, almost as inaccessible as an eagle's nest, the valley of the Illinois spreads out in a landscape of exquisite beauty. The river, near by, struggles between a number of wooded islands, while further below, it quietly meanders through vast meadows, till it disappears like a thread of light in the dim distance. Here, on the summit of this rocky citadel, in the month of November he began to entrench himself. Storehouses were constructed from the trees that grew on the top, and when the supply was exhausted, at immense labor, timbers were dragged up the steep ascent to construct a palisaded inclosure. With the completion of this stronghold, which was called in honor of the French King the Fort of St. Louis, the Indians began to gather around it, regarding LaSalle as the great champion who was to protect them against the Iroquois. The country, which lay under the protection of the fort, recently strewn with the ghastly relics of an Iroquois victory, now became animated with a wild concourse of savage life. The great town of the Illinois, the Jerusalem of these tribes, Phœnix-like, had sprung from its ashes, and again echoed with the tramp of some 6,000 inhabitants. In addition to the Illinois, there were scattered along the valley of the river, among the neighboring hills and over the adjacent plains, the fragments of 10 or 12 other tribes, numbering some 14000 souls. Miamis, from the source of the Kankakee; Shawnees, from the Scioto, Abenakis and Mohegans, from the Atlantic seaboard, and other tribes whose rough names are too unpleasant for record, had buried their animosities, and now lounged here and there in lazy groups, while their wives performed the drudgery of their camps, and their children gamboled and whooped with the reckless abandon of mad-caps. LaSalle's nego-

7

tiations with the western Algonquins—aided by the universal hor
ror inspired by the brutal attacks of the Iroquois—had met with
unexampled success. In writing to the French Minister of Marine, he wrote that his colony had sprung up as if by magic, in a
single night, and contained 4,000 warriors and some 20,000 souls.
By the privileges which had been conferred on him as a discoverer
he ruled his wild domain as a seigniory, and granted portions of
land to his followers. Little profit, however, was realized in this
manner, for the greater part of his men were so reckless that
their traducers were wont to say of them that each married a new
squaw every day of the week.

To maintain his colony, he now found it necessary to furnish its
members with protection against the common enemy, and merchandise to barter for the immense quantities of furs annually
gathered in the interior of the continent. Previously, the avenue
of trade lay through Canada, but it was LaSalle's intention to
establish an entrepot at the mouth of the Mississippi, whereby his
colony would have the advantage of direct intercourse with the
West Indies and Europe. While he was thus maturing plans for
the benefit of his colony, his cotemporaries, either through envy or
too short-sighted to comprehend his objects, were striving to defeat
them. Unfortunately, Gov. Frontenac had been recalled, and De
La Barre, an avaricious old naval officer, had been sent out to
take his place. His conduct soon proved that he was wholly unfit
for the office he was called to fill. Like his predecessor, he was
guilty of violating the royal ordinances regulating the fur trade,
but the former partially atoned for this wrong by an energetic administration of public affairs, while the latter added inability to
his faults, whereby the best interests of the country became paral-
lized. He was the special champion of the enemies of LaSalle,
who, engrossed with the affairs of his colony, was ignorant of the
great jealousy with which his affairs were regarded. Not knowing the disposition of La Barre, he wrote to him from Fort St.
Louis in the spring of 1683, expressing the hope that he would
have the same counsel and support from him that he had received
from his predecessor. After cautioning the Governor that his enemies would endeavor to misrepresent his objects he proceeds to
give an account of his explorations:

With only 22 Frenchmen, he states, he had formed amicable
relations with the various tribes along the Mississippi, and that
his royal patent enabled him to establish forts in the newly discovered country, and to make grants around them as at Fort Frontenac. He adds:

"The losses in my enterprises have exceeded 40,000 crowns, I am now going 400 leagues southwest of this place to induce the Chickasaws to follow the
Shawnees and other tribes, and settle like them at Fort St. Louis. It remained
only to settle French colonists here, and this I have already done. I hope you
will not detain them as violators of the laws governing the fur trade when they
come down to Montreal to make necessary purchases. I am aware that I have
no right to trade with the tribes who descend to Montreal, and I shall not permit such trade to my men; nor have I ever issued licenses to that effect, as my
enemies say that I have done."

Notwithstanding this reasonable request, the men he sent on
important business were retained, and he a second time wrote to
the governor:

"The Iroquois are again invading the country. Last year the Miamis were so alarmed by them that they abandoned their town and fled, but on my return they came back, and have been induced to settle with the Illinois at my Fort of St. Louis. The Iroquois have lately murdered some families of their nation and they are all in terror again. I am afraid they will take flight and so prevent the Missouris and neighboring tribes from coming to settle at St. Louis, as they are about to do. Some of the Hurons and French tell the Miamis that I am keeping them here for the Iroquois to destroy. I pray that you will let me hear from you, that I may give these people some assurances of protection before they are destroyed in my sight. Do not suffer my men who have come down to the settlements to be longer prevented from returning. There is great need here of reinforcements. The Iroquois, as I have said, have lately entered the country, and a great terror prevails. I have postponed going to Mackinaw, because, if the Iroquois strike any blow in my absence, the Miamis will think that I am in league with them; whereas, if I and the French stay among them, they will regard us as protectors. But, Monsieur, it is in vain that we risk our lives here, and that I exhaust my means in order to fulfill the intentions of his majesty, if all my measures are crossed in the settlements below, and if those who go down to bring munitions, without which we cannot defend ourselves, are detained, under pretexts trumped up for the occasion. If I am prevented from bringing up men and supplies, as I am allowed to do by the permit of Count Frontenac, then my patent from the king is useless. It would be very hard for us, after having done what was required, even before the time prescribed, and after suffering severe losses, to have our efforts frustrated by obstacles got up designedly. I trust that, as it lies with you alone to prevent or to permit the return of the men whom I have sent down, you will not so act as to thwart my plans, as part of the goods which I have sent by them belong not not to me, but the Sieur de Tonti, and are a part of his pay. Others are to buy munitions indispensable for our defense. Do not let my creditors seize them. It is for their advantage that my fort, full as it is of goods, should be held against the enemy. I have only 20 men, with scarcely 100 pounds of powder, and I cannot long hold the country without more. The Illinois are very capricious and uncertain. . . If I had men enough to send out to reconnoitre the enemy, I would have done so before this; but I have not enough. I trust you will put it in my power to obtain more, that this important colony may be saved." *

While LaSalle was thus corresponding with the governor, the latter was writing letters to the French Colonial Minister, saying that he doubted the reality of LaSalle's discoveries; that with scarce a score of vagabonds he was about to set himself up as king, and was likely to involve Canada and the western tribes in a war with the Iroquois. The extent to which the enemies of La-Salle suffered their jealousies to lead them astray may be gathered from the posture of affairs at the time. The governor of New York, with the hope of diverting the fur trade from Montreal to Albany, was inciting the Iroquois to make another attack on the western tribes. Although this proceeding was fraught with the greatest danger to Canada, yet La Barre and his political menials were willing it might succeed, and the entire country be endangered, provided it resulted in the ruin of LaSalle. When, therefore, these pests of the forest, under the influence of British intrigue, were again making preparations to invade the country of the Illinois and Miamis, instead of an earnest effort to check their designs, they even encouraged them to kill LaSalle and cut off his supplies to aid them in their diabolical work. The continued calumnies uttered against LaSalle at length reached the ear of the king, who wrote to his Canadian governor, stating that he was convinced that LaSalle's discoveries were useless, and that such enterprises ought to be prevented in the future, as they tended to diminish the revenues derived from the fur trade.

*This letter is dated Portage de Chicagou, 4 Juni, 1863.—Discov. of the Great West.

Doubtless, emboldened by the king's letter, the governor now determined to seize Fort Frontenac, under the pretext that La Salle had not fulfilled the conditions of his contract by maintaining a sufficient garrison. Despite the remonstrance of LaSalle's creditors, he sent two of his political associates to take command of the fort. As soon as this was accomplished, they commenced living on LaSalle's provisions, and were afterward charged with selling those which had been furnished by the king for their own private benefit. The governor also sent an officer of the king's dragoons to Fort St. Louis, and made him the bearer of a letter to LaSalle, demanding his presence at Quebec. Meanwhile rumors were still rife at the Fort that the Iroquois were getting ready for an invasion, and the tribes comprising the colony flew to LaSalle and besought him to furnish the promised succor. Cut off from supplies, and robbed of the men whom he had sent to secure them, he was greatly mortified to find himself wholly unable to make good his pledge. Fortunately the rumors were premature, but as his relations with the governor were otherwise intolerable, he determined to visit France to obtain relief. With this object in view, he left Tonti in command of the fort, and on his way to Quebec met with the governor's officer, who made known to him the nature of his mission. LaSalle, submitting gracefully to an indignity he could not well avoid, wrote to Tonti to receive the officer with due courtesy, whereupon, without further business, they parted. In due time the dragoon arrived at the fort, and he and Tonti spent the winter harmoniously, the one commanding in the name of the governor, and the other in that of La-Salle. The threatened invasion of the Iroquois, though postponed, was not abandoned. During the latter part of the spring they made an incursion into the country and attacked the fort, but the rocky citadel proved too strong for the assault, and after a siege of 6 days they were compelled to retire.

LaSalle, on arriving at Quebec, sailed for France, taking a last leave of the great arena in which, for the last 16 years, he had been the principal actor; had suffered the most harrassing anxieties, and had won the proudest triumphs. From forest solitudes and squalid wigwams, a prosperous voyage introduced him to the busy throngs and sculptured magnificence of the French capital. Its venal court, bewildered by the pompous display of wealth and the trappings of power, regarded with little interest the sober habiliments of honest worth. · But the son of the burgher of Rouen, unmoved by regal vanities, and with a natural dignity far transcending the tinsel of titled rank, announced his discoveries to the giddy court. He asked for means to return to the new found lands, and to found a colony on the Mississippi, to protect them from the intrusion of foreigners. Two points on the Mississippi properly selected and fortified, he argued, would guard the whole interior of the continent, with its vast areas of fertile lands and boundless resources. Count Frontenac gave him the advantage of his influence, the minister of marine entered with vigor into the scheme, and recommended it to the king, who also became fascinated with the glittering project. As an act of justice, and to show his appreciation of LaSalle, he ordered LaBarre to restore to him the possession of Forts Frontenac and St. Louis, and make reparation for the damage he had sustained by their seizure. La-

Salle asked for two ships, but the king, in his zeal, gave him four —the Francais, the Belle, the Amiable, and the Jolly. Two hundred and eighty men embarked in the expedition, consisting of ecclesiastics, soldiers, sailors, mechanics, several families, and even a number of girls, lured by the prospects of marriage in the new land of promise. Such were the colonists who were to plant the standard of France and civilization in the wilderness of Louisiana. As in most of the early attempts at colonization, the men were illy qualified to grapple with the stern work it was proposed to accomplish. But, worst of all, was the naval commander, Beaujeu, who was envious, self-willed, deficient in judgment, and foolishly proud.

On the first of August, 1684, they sailed from Rochelle on their adventurous voyage. Frequent calms retarded their progress, and when at length they arrived at Hispaniola, the Francais, filled with munitions and other necessaries for the colony, was captured by a Spanish privateer. This disaster, for which Beaujeu was evidently to blame, was the first of the disasters which afterward attended the expedition. After obtaining supplies, and searching for information in regard to the direction in which he must sail to find the outlet of the Mississippi, the voyage was renewed. On entering the Gulf of Mexico, and sailing in a northwesterly direction, a sailor at the mast-head of the Amiable, on the 28th of December, discovered land. In coasting along the shore toward the west, searching for the mouth of the river, they incautiously passed it. Proceeding further, LaSalle discovered the mistake, but Beaujeu, refusing to return, they at length landed at Matagorda Bay. Entering this arm of the gulf, they discovered a considerable river falling into it, which LaSalle concluded might be the Lafourche, the most western outlet of the Mississippi. If his conjectures were true, he preferred to ascend it to the main stream, instead of returning on the gulf against contrary winds, and the still greater impediment of Beaujeu's obstinacy. He had differed with LaSalle from the commencement of the voyage, and in every instance proved to be in the wrong, and now, to get rid of him, he preferred to debark his followers on the lone shore of the bay.

For this purpose, the Amiable weighed anchor and entered the narrow passage leading into the bay, but was unfortunately careened over by the sand banks obstructing the channel. LaSalle, with a sad heart, beheld the disaster, yet with cool and patient energy set himself about the work of removing the cargo. A quantity of powder and flour was saved, but presently a storm arose, and the stranded vessel, rent assunder by the waves, scattered the remaining treasures upon the ravenous waters. After the landing was effected, the Indians became troublesome, and a fort was built, with great labor, two miles above the mouth of the La Vacca, a small stream falling into the Bay. LaSalle, as in previous instances, named the fortification St. Louis, in honor of his king. Here he planted the arms of France, opened a field for planting a crop, and thus founded the first French settlement made in Texas. The country, thus formally occupied, gave to France a claim which she never abandoned till Louisiana became a part of the United States, nearly 120 years afterward.

The scene around the fort was not uninteresting, and to some extent relieved the dejection arising from the recent misfortunes. The bay, bordered by marshes, stretched away in a southeastern direction, while the other points of the compass spread out in an expanse of prairie sprinkled with the bright flowers for which Texas is remarkable, and which still rank high among the floral beauties of southern gardens. At certain seasons of the year, the grassy area was dotted over with grazing buffalo, while the adjacent waters swarmed with fish and water fowl. Necessity soon taught the colonists the best methods of securing them, and the sports of the angler, the hunter and the fowler not only gave zest to their wilderness life, but furnished them with an abundance of food. It was customary for the women to mingle in the hunting parties and assist in cutting up the meat, and thus a hunter and fair huntress became enamored of each other, and were married. Their nuptials were solemnized with the usual expressions of merriment, for the genuine Frenchman, whatever may be his situation, always thinks it better to be merry, than to brood over the misfortunes he is unable to remedy.

LaSalle, having provided for the security of his people, next went 150 leagues along the coast, east and west, to search for the hidden river, but without success. He also determined to make a tour of observation toward the mines and settlements of Northern Mexico. After consuming four months in this expedition, and gathering such information from the Indians as convinced him that his previous conjectures respecting the situation of the Mississippi river were correct, the party retraced their steps, and arrived at the fort March 6th, 1686. travel-worn, weary, and their clothes in tatters. Soon after, it was ascertained that the Belle, the only remaining vessel, had been sunk, and her cargo, consisting of the personal effects of LaSalle and a great quantity of ammunition and tools, were scattered in the waters of the gulf. The loss was a fatal blow to all attempts in the future to move the colony to the Mississippi, and left little hope of the unhappy exiles ever again beholding the vine-clad homes of their sunny France.

LaSalle, forced by the necessities of his situation, now determined to make his way, eastward, to the Mississippi, and thence to Canada or France, to obtain relief. No sooner had he formed this resolve, the offspring of dire extremity, than preparations were completed for the journey. April 22d, 20 men issued from the fort and made their way across the prairie, followed by the anxious eyes of those who were left behind. Day after day they held a northeasterly direction, passing through a country of wild and pleasing landscapes, made up of prairies, woods and groves, green as an emerald with the beauty of May. After having made a distance of some 400 miles, their ammunition and provisions failed them, and they were compelled to return to the fort without having accomplished the object of their journey. Twenty men had gone out, but only 8 returned, some having deserted, and others perished in the attempt to reach the fort. The latter number would doubtless have been greatly increased, but for the assistance of horses purchased from the Cenis Indians, the most easterly tribe visited. The temporary elation produced by the return of the absent party, soon gave way to dejection, and LaSalle had a heavy task to prevent the ·latter from becoming dispair. He was naturally stern and unsympathizing, yet he could soften into compassion at the great extremes of danger and distress of those about him.

The audacity of hope with which he still clung to the accomplishment of his object, determined him to make a second and more persevering effort for this purpose. It was decided that the adventurers should consist of LaSalle, his brother, and two nephews, Cavalier and Moranget; DuHaut, a person of reputable birth; Leotot, a surgeon; Joutel, who afterwards became the historian of the expedition, and some 20 others. Among those left behind were the women and children, and Zenobe Membre, who had so long followed the fortunes of LaSalle. Everything being in readiness, the travelers for the last time entered the rude chapel of the fort, mass was solemnly celebrated, and, with the cloud of incense which rose from the altar, ascended the prayers of the colonists for the success of the journey. Next came the parting, of sighs, of tears, and of embraces—all seeming intuitively to know that they should see each other no more. January 12th, 1687, the chosen band filed out of the fort, placed their baggage on horses, and started off in the direction of the previous journey. Pushing forward across prairies and woodlands, among tribes some friendly and some hostile, they passed the Brazos, and encamped on the 15th of March near the western waters of the Trinity. They were now in the vicinity of some corn which La-Salle had concealed in his previous journey, and he sent DuHaut, Leotot and some others, to get it. The grain was found spoiled, but in returning they shot some large game, and sent for horses to convey it to camp. Moranget and two others were sent on this errand, and found, when they arrived, the meat cut up, and that, according to a woodland custom, the hunters had appropriated some of the best pieces to themselves. Moranget, whose violent temper had previously got him into difficulties, berated them in a violent manner for claiming this privilege, and ended by taking all the meat himself. This outburst of passion kindled to an avenging flame a grudge which had for some time existed between DuHaut and LaSalle, and the former conspired with Leotot to take the life of his nephew. Night came on, the evening meal was dispatched, and when the intended victim had fallen asleep, the assassins approached and shot him. The commission of one crime generally requires another, to save the perpetrator from merited punishment, and LaSalle was marked out as the next object of vengeance.

Two days passed by and the latter, hearing nothing of his nephew, began to entertain rueful forebodings in regard to his safety. At length, unable longer to endure his suspense, he left Joutel in command of the camp and started in search of his relative. Accompanied only by a friar and two Indians, he approached the camp of the assassins, and when near by fired a pistol to summon them to his presence. The conspirators, rightly judging who had caused the report, stealthily approached and shot their intended victim, Leotot exclaiming as he fell, " You are down now, Grand Bashaw, you are down now." * They then despoiled the body of its clothing, and left it to be devoured by the

Monette's Val. of the Miss.

wild beasts of the forest. Thus, at the age of 43, in his vigorous manhood's prime, perished one whose exploits have so greatly enriched
the history of the new world. His successes required for their accomplishment an undaunted will and invincible courage, which few
could bring to the aid of an enterprise. His failures were partly
caused by the vastness of his schemes, and in part because his
imperious nature would not permit him to conciliate the good will
of those he employed and was compelled to trust. While he
grasped one link in the chain of his extended enterprises, another,
through treachery, slipped from his hand.

"It is easy to reckon up his defects, but it is not easy to hide from sight the
Roman virtues that redeemed them. Beset by a throng of enemies, he stands,
like the King of Israel, head and shoulders above them all. He was a tower
of adamant, against whose impregnable front hardship and danger, the rage of
man and the elements, the southern sun, the northern blast, fatigue, famine
and disease, delay, disappointment and deferred hope, emptied their quivers
in vain. That very pride which, Coriolanus-like, declared itself most sternly
in the thickest press of foes, has in it something to challenge admiration. Never
under the impenetrable mail of paladin or crusader beat a heart of more intrepid mettle than within the stoic panoply that armed the breast of LaSalle.
To estimate aright the marvels of his patient fortitude, one must follow on his
track through the vast scene of his interminable journeyings, those thousands
of weary miles of forest, marsh and river, where, again and again, in the bitterness of baffled striving, the untiring pilgrim pushed onward toward the goal he
was never to attain. America owes him an enduring memory; for in this masculine figure, cast in iron, she sees the heroic pioneer who guided her to the
possession of her richest heritage." *

Those who were not in sympathy with the assassins concealed
their resentment, and on the 2d day after the murder the party
was again in motion. On the main stream of the Trinity they
were again compelled to halt for the purpose of buying provisions
of the Indians. Here the two murderers, who had arrogated to
themselves the command of the expedition, declared their intention of returning to the fort, and there building a ship in which to
escape to the West Indies. This impossible scheme, together with
their refusal to let their accomplices in the murder share in the
spoils obtained by it, soon led to dissensions. The breach rapidly
widened, and at last the aggrieved parties shot the murderers, an
act which was but the recoil of the crimes they were the first to introduce. Thus ended the bloody tragedy, enacted with such atrocity by these pioneers of Christianity and civilization, that even the
debased savage of the wildernesss looked on with the utmost
amazement and horror.

Joutel, with the brother and nephew of LaSalle and 4 others,
whose innocence would permit them to return to civilization, commenced anew their travels, leaving the guilty behind. Proceeding
in a northeastern direction, they encountered by day a monotony
of tangled forests, grassy plains, and miry fens; by night, chilly
rains alternating with starlit skies, in whose pale and mystic
radiance they soundly slept and dreamed of absent friends and
distant homes. At length, after a journey of two months, in
which they had been led by guides furnished by various tribes,
they stood on the banks of the Arkansas, opposite an Indian village. Gazing across the stream, their eyes fell on a hut, nestled
among the trees of the forest, while a cross near by showed it to
be the abode of Christians. Actuated by a common impulse, they

*Discov. of the Great West.—Parkman.

fell on their knees, and with emotions of gratitude thanked God for having directed them to this outpost of civilization. Two men issued from the cabin and fired a salute, which being answered by a volley from the travelers, a canoe put out from the shore and ferried them over the stream.

The long lost wanderers were cordially greeted in their mother tongue by the occupants of the dwelling, who proved to be 6 of Tonti's men, whom he had left here in his assent of the Mississippi.* This noble officer, who had been restored to the command of the fort on the Illinois by order of the King, had heard of La Salle's disaster, and immediately equipped an expedition with his own means to relieve him. With 25 Frenchmen and 5 Indians, he left the fort on the 13th of February, 1686, and soon descended the Illinois and Mississippi to the Gulf. Not finding any traces of him at the mouth of the river, he sent his canoes to scour the shores for a distance of 30 leagues on either side. Not seeing or hearing anything of LaSalle, who at the same time was wandering among the wilds of Texas, in a search equally fruitless, he retraced his course to the fort on the Illinois, leaving, as already mentioned, some of his men near the mouth of the Arkansas. The travelers, from motives of policy, carefully concealed the death of LaSalle from their hosts, and when sufficiently recruited recommenced their journey. Proceeding down the Arkansas, they soon found themselves on the great river which had so long been the object of their search. The 13th of September found them at the confluence of the Illinois, and 11 days more brought them to the fort-crowned rock, which, like a sentinel, stood watch over its peaceful waters. They landed and were soon met by parties from the fort, who, after the usual salutations, inquired for LaSalle. Substituting adroitness for a frank avowal of the truth, they replied that they had left him in Texas, and at the time of their departure he was in good health.

It is said the object of the evasion was to enable the old priest, Cavalier, as the representative of LaSalle, to derive some advantage for himself and companions in the settlement of his brother's estate. Tonti was absent, fighting the Iroquois, but his lieutenant received them with a salvo of musketry, and provided for them comfortable quarters in the fort. Tonti, not long after, returned from his martial expedition, and listened with profound interest and sympathy to the story of the disasters and sufferings of the travelers, as related by the elder Cavalier. He did not scruple to tell Tonti the same story by which he had deceived others in regard to the death of his brother. Moreover, after living for months on the hospitality of his generous host, he added fraud and meanness to deception. This flagrant outrage he perpetrated by forging an order on Tonti, in the name of LaSalle, for 4,000 livres, in furs and other goods, which his unsuspecting victim generously delivered to him at the time of his departure.

On leaving the fort, the travelers proceeded to Mackinaw, where they exchanged their ill-gotten furs for clothing and means to defray their expenses home. Without further delay, they made their way to Quebec, and thence to France, whither they arrived in October, 1688, having spent more than four years in their dis-

*This was the commencement of Arkansas Post, captured by Gen. McClernand during the Rebellion.

taut wanderings. They were men of only average ability and energy, yet, moved by the most pressing necessity, they performed one of the most remarkable voyages on record. They now, for the first time, divulged the secret of LaSalle's death, and the king issued orders for the arrest of all who were privy to his murder. It does not appear certain that any of them were ever subjected to a criminal prosecution; but rumor has it that part of them perished by their own hands, and part by the Indians, whom their misdeeds roused to vengeance.

In the mean time the news of LaSalle's death also reached Tonti's men on the Arkansas, and was thence carried to him in the fort on the Illinois. It is more easy to imagine than describe the feelings of this most devoted of all LaSalle's followers when he learned the tragical manner of his death. But without useless waste of time in grief for him whom he had so long and so faithfully served and who was now beyond reach of help, he determined to make an effort to rescue his perishing colonists. For this purpose he left the fort in December, 1688, with 5 Frenchmen and 3 Indians, and, after a toilsome journey, arrived at the mouth of Red River, where he learned that some of the accomplices of LaSalle's murderers were in a village some 80 leagues distant. On making known his intention to visit the town all his men refused to accompany him, except two, a Frenchman and an Indian. Not being able to enforce obedience, he resolutely set out with them, but unfortunately a few days afterwards, lost the greater part of his ammunition. Still undeterred, he pushed on to the town, but no trace of the criminals could be found. When, however, he questioned the villagers respecting them, he concluded from their suspicious demeanor, that they had previously been there, and that the Indians, incensed at their misdeeds, had probably put them to death. Having accomplished nothing thus far, and now almost without ammunition, with bitter disappointment he was compelled ·to return. In retracing their steps they met with more than the usual amount of hardships attending a march through an unexplored wilderness. On arriving at the Indian village on the Arkansas, Tonti, as the result of exhaustion and exposure, became sick of a fever, but recovered in time to reach the fort on the Illinois by the first of September.

This unsuccessful effort was the last attempt made to rescue the unfortunate colony from the savage immensity that shut them out from home and civilization. Their final destruction by the Indians was learned from the Spaniards of Mexico. Spain claimed the country bordering on the Gulf of Mexico, and from the capture of LaSalle's vessel in the West Indian Seas, his designs became known. After several attempts to find the location of his colony and destroy it, a Mexican expedition, guided by one of the French deserters, pushed across the wilderness to the fort. Seeing no evidences of life without, the Spaniards spurred their horses through the open gateway of the fort, and found only the ruins of what had once constituted the stores and furniture of the garrison. From French deserters domesticated among the Indians, it was learned that about 3 months before, a band of savages ambushed themselves under the banks of the river, while others drew the garrison out of the fort for the purpose of traffic. At a given signal, the concealed foe rushed from his covert, and immolated indiscriminately the men, women and children. Thus ends one of the most extensive explorations known to history. As a great geographical discovery, it is only second to that which made known to Europe the existence of the Western Hemisphere. The great valley thus thrown open has since been filled with a constellation of prosperous, happy states. The city which death deprived him of founding, and which his sagacity foresaw would become one of the great marts of the earth, is now the emporium of the South. America owes him a debt of gratitude which she will ever be unable to pay, and in like manner, as a type of incarnate energy, his deeds she will never forget.

HENNEPIN.—It will be remembered that LaSalle having concluded that Hennepin could do more good by exploring the Illinois and Upper Mississippi, than in preaching sermons, and that he with two companions were sent on that mission. Having descended the Illinois and commenced the ascent of the Mississippi, they were surprised, and taken by a band of Sioux, who conducted them up the river to the falls of St. Anthony, and thence to their villages in the vicinity of Mille Lac, Wisconsin Here Hennepin spent the Spring and Summer in hunting, acting as a physician, and studying the Sioux language. Autumn at lenght came, and with the consent of the chief they were permitted to depart. Proceeding by way of the Rum, Mississippi, Wisconsin, and Fox rivers to Green bay, they spent the Winter with the Jesuit Missionaries. With the opening of Spring they moved down the lakes and St Lawrence, to Quebec, where Hennepin was received by the governor, who listened with profound interest to the recital of his travels. From America he went to France, where an account of his travels were published in different languages, and read with great interest. Not meeting with the encouragement in France he expected, he went to England and was taken into the service of King William. This monarch wishing to set up a claim to Louisiana, induced him to modify the narrative of his discovery so as to favor his claim. Yielding to his request he wrote a new account, in which he falsely stated that before his voyage up the river he first descended it to the sea. Thus while he endeavored to rob LaSalle of his principal laurels, he tarnished his own fame and was afterwards stigmatized by his countrymen as the prince of liars.

CHAPTER X.

1700–1719—ILLINOIS A DEPENDENCY OF CANADA AND PART OF LOUISIANA—THE GOVERNMENT A THEOCRACY—OPERATIONS OF CROZAT.

A Dependency of Canada.—Twelve years elapsed after LaSalle's fruitless attempt to found a colony on the Mississippi, before the government of France made a second effort. At length, fearing that England might obtain precedence in the great valley, the king set on foot an enterprise for this purpose. M. d'Iberville, who had exhibited such mature judgment and prompt action in the wars of the French-American possessions, was chosen to command it. Having encountered the icebergs and snows of Hudson's Bay and the burning sands of Florida, he was now ready, at the command of his king, to encounter the malarious marshes of the Mississippi. The two preceding years he had established colonies on Ship Island and the head of Lake Borgne, and about the middle of February, 1700, sailed up the Mississippi, to found a third one on its banks. A site was selected for a fort and settlement, about 38 miles below New Orleans, and while he was engaged in its erection, Tonti descended from the fort on the Illinois, with a party of Canadians, to assist him. Tonti's intimate acquaintance with the Indian languages and the tribes living on the river, made him a valuable acquisition to the new colony. Availing himself of his assistance, D'Iberville resolved to further ascend the river, explore the country on its banks, and form alliances with its inhabitants. In company with Tonti, his brother Bienville, and other parties, he passed up the river to the Natchez tribe, which he found more powerful and civilized than others he had visited. The great beauty of the surrounding country induced him to select it as the seat of the future provincial government, and the bluff on which the city of Natchez is now built, he chose as the site of its capital. He named the prospective city Rosalie, in honor of the wife of his patron, the French minister of marine, and 15 years afterward a fort was erected on the site by his successor. D'Iberville now returned to his ships below and embarked for France, while Bienville explored the country about the mouth of Red river, and some of the party from Illinois were sent to ramble for 6 months in the remote west, in the vain search for gold.

With this expedition down the Mississippi, Tonti, the most trusted officer of LaSalle, disappears from the roll of authentic history. The following are some of the acts which distinguished his adventurous life during this period: His mediation in the attack of the Iroquois against the Illinois in 1680, whereby he greatly mitigated, but did not wholly prevent, the butchery of the latter; his government of the Illinois and the associated tribes at Fort St. Louis, during the absence of LaSalle, his effort to relieve LaSalle and his suffering colonists in Texas; the founding of Arkansas Post, made famous 177 years afterward by the reduction of the rebel fort located there, by McClernand and his brave Illinois and other western troops; and finally, the assistance he rendered DeNonville, the governor of Canada, with 170 Frenchmen and 300 Indians from the west, in his attack on the Senecas. Says De-Nonville: "God alone could have saved Canada in 1688. But for the assistance obtained from the posts of the west, Illinois must have been abandoned, the fort at Mackinaw lost, and a general uprising of the nations would have completed the destruction of New France."* Rumor states that, after the performance of these acts, he resided several years in Illinois, and then returned to France.

As the St. Lawrence had been made an avenue for the approach of settlers to Illinois, so, after the exploration of the Mississippi, it also became a highway for the in-flowing of population. Through these channels, communicating with the external world, came the pioneers who, between the years 1680'–90, founded the villages and settlements of Fort St. Louis, Kaskaskia, Cahokia, and others of more recent date. These settlements, in common with most of those established in the interior of the continent, were, to a great extent, the work of the Jesuit and Recollet missionaries. These hardy and enterprising embassadors of the cross, with a zeal which defied the opposition of the elements, heat, hunger and cold, fatigue, famine and pestilence, entered the prairies of Illinois 1000 miles in advance of its secular population. We justly admire the fortitude of Smith, the founder of Virginia, the courage of May-flower pilgrims, the fathers of New England; but all these had royal patrons; then what shall we say of the devoted missionaries, who laid the foundations of States in the remote wilderness, when their monastic vows denied them even the feeble aid of ecclesiastical support? Neither commercial gain nor secular fame, but religious fervor, could have nerved them to meet the toils and dangers incident to their wilderness life.

The first mission in Illinois, as we have already seen, was commenced by Marquette in April, 1675. It is said as he entered the rude dwellings of the inhabitants and preached of Christ and the Virgin, heaven and hell, demons and angels, and the life to come, he was received as a celestial visitor. The Indians besought him to remain among them and continue his instructions, but his life was fast ebbing away, and it behooved him to depart. He called the religious society which he had established the "Mission of the Immaculate Conception," and the town "Kaskaskia," after one of the Illinois tribes bearing the same name.

The first military occupation of the country was at Fort Creve-cœur, erected in February, 1680; but there is no evidence that a settlement was commenced there or at Peoria, on the lake above, at that early date.† The first settlement of which there is any authentic account, was commenced with the building of Fort St.

---

*Bancroft.
†Annals of the West.

HISTORY OF ILLINOIS.

Louis, on the Illinois river, in 1682. It remained in existence at least till 1700, when Tonti seems to have abandoned it and gone south, but how long after that date is not definitely known. The oldest permanent settlement, not only in Illinois but the valley of the Mississippi, is Kaskaskia, situated 6 miles above the mouth of the river of the same name.* There is no evidence to substantiate the statement that LaSalle left colonists here and at Cahokia on his return from the successful exploration of the Mississippi in 1682.

The mission here was originally established at the great town of the Illinois, but with the removal of the tribes farther southward, it was transferred to Kaskaskia. Father Gravier, who had previously been stationed at Mackinaw, effected the removal some time prior to 1690, the exact date being unknown. He was the first of the missionaries to ascertain the principles of the Illinois language and reduce them to rules. When recalled from Kaskaskia to Mackinaw, he was succeeded by Fathers Binneteau and Pinet, the latter of whom established the mission and village of Cahokia. So successful was Pinet in attracting the attention of the aborigines, his chapel was insufficient to hold the large number that attended his ministrations. The Indians under his charge were the Tamaroas and Cahokias, the latter tribe furnishing the village its name. Binneteau, to attend to his ministerial labors, followed the Kaskaskias in one of their hunts on the upland plains of the Mississippi, and died. Now stifled in the tall grass, now panting with thirst on the arid prairie, parched by day with heat, and by night exposed on the ground to chilling dues, he was seized with a mortal fever, and "left his bones on the wilderness range of the buffalo."† Shortly after his death, Pinet also died, and Father Marest, who had before explained the mysteries of the cross to the ice-bound denizens of Hudson's Bay, came to Kaskaskia and took charge of the missions of Illinois. In his correspondence, he says: "Our life is spent in roaming through thick woods, in clambering over hills, in paddling canoes across lakes and rivers, to catch a poor savage whom we can neither tame by teachings nor caresses." On Good Friday, 1711, he started for the Peorias, who desired a new mission, and thus speaks of his journey:

"I departed, having nothing about me but my crucifix and breviary, being accompanied by only two savages, who might abandon me from levity, or might fly through fear of enemies. The terror of these vast uninhabitable regions, in which for 12 days not a single soul was seen, almost took away my courage. This was a journey wherein there was no village, no bridge, no ferry-boat, no house, no beaten path; and over boundless prairies, intersected by rivulets and rivers, through forests and thickets filled with briars and thorns, through marshes, in which we sometimes plunged to the girdle. At night repose was sought on the grass or leaves, exposed to the winds and rains, happy if by the side of some rivulet whose waters might quench our thirst. Meals were prepared from such game as might be killed on the way, or by roasting ears of corn."

Early in the 18th century he was joined by Mermet, who had previously founded a mission on the Ohio.

"The gentle virtues and fervid eloquence of Mermet made him the soul of the Mission of Kaskaskia. At early dawn his pupils came to church, dressed neatly and modestly each in a deer-skin or a robe sewn together from several skins. After receiving lessons they chanted canticles; mass was then said in

*Bancroft.
†Bancroft.

presence of all the Christians, the French and the converts—the women on one side and the men on the other. From prayers and instructions the missionaries proceeded to visit the sick and administer medicine, and their skill as physicians did more than all the rest to win confidence. In the afternoon the catechism was taught in the presence of the young and the old, when every one without distinction of rank or age, answered the questions of the missionary. At evening all would assemble at the chapel for instruction, for prayer, and to chant the hymns of the church. On Sundays and festivals, even after vespers, a homily was pronounced; at the close of the day parties would meet in houses to recite the chaplets in alternate choirs, and sing psalms till late at night. These psalms were often homilies, with words set to familiar tunes. Saturday and Sunday were the days appointed for confession and communion, and every convert confessed once in a fortnight. The success of this mission was such that marriages of the French immigrants were sometimes solemnized with the daughters of the Illinois, according to the rites of the Catholic church. The occupation of the country was a cantonment among the native proprietors of the forests and prairies.*

Father Charlevoix, who visited Illinois in 1721, thus speaks of the Cahokia and Kaskaskia Missions :

"We lay last night in the village of the Cahokias and Tamaroas, two Illinois tribes which have been united, and compose no very numerous canton. This village is situated on a very small river which runs from the east, and has no water except in the Spring. On this account we had to walk half a league before we could get to our cabins. I was astonished that such a poor situation had been selected, when there are so many good ones. But I was told that the Mississippi washed the foot of the village when it was built; that in 3 years it had shifted its course half a league farther to the west, and that they were now thinking of changing their habitation, which is no great affair among these Indians. I passed the night with the missionaries, who are two ecclesiastics from the Seminary of Quebec, formerly my disciples, but they must now be my masters. One of them was absent, but I found the other such as he had been represented to me, rigid with himself, full of charity to others, and displaying in his own person an amiable pattern of virtues. Yesterday I arrived at Kaskaskia about 9 o'clock. The Jesuits here have a very flourishing mission, which has lately been divided into two, it being more convenient to have two cantons of Indians instead of one. The most numerous one is on the banks of the Mississippi, of which two Jesuits have the spiritual direction. Half a league below stands Fort Chartres, about the distance of a musket shot from the river. M. de Boisbrant commands here for the company to which the place belongs. The French are now beginning to settle the country between the fort and the first mission. Four leagues farther, and about a league from the river, is a large village, inhabited by the French, who are almost all Canadians, and have a Jesuit for their curate. The second village of the Illinois lies farther up the country, at the distance of two leagues from the last, and is under the charge of a fourth Jesuit.

"The Indians at this place live much at their ease. A Fleming, who was a domestic of the Jesuits, has taught them how to sow wheat, which succeeds well. They have swine and black cattle. The Illinois manure their ground after their fashion, and are very laborious. They likewise bring up poultry which they sell to the French. Their women are very neat handed and industrious. They spin the wool of the buffalo into threads as fine as can be made from that of the English sheep. Nay, sometimes it might be taken for silk. Of this they manufacture fabrics which are dyed black, yellow and red, after which they are made into robes, which they sew together with the sinews of the roebuck. They expose these to the sun for the space of three days, and when dry, beat them, and without difficulty draw out white threads of great fineness."

Besides the villages mentioned above, others sprang up in subsequent times, as Prairie du Roche, situated at the base of a rocky bluff of the Mississippi, 4 miles below Port Chartres, and Prairie du Pont, a mile south of Cahokia. Other missions were also established, and Romish clergy continued to visit the country, and in the absence of civil government, acted not only as spiritual

*Bancroft.

guides, but as temporal rulers of the people. In those days of
Jesuit enthusiasm, both the priests and their flocks, in addition to
their strong religious feelings, possessed in many instances an integrity which the most trying temptations were powerless to corrupt.
It is true much of this enthusiasm was fanaticism, which interpreted the results of natural law as special interpositions of providence; which regarded self-imposed physical pain an act of virtue,
and construed their trivial dreams as prophetic of future good or
evil. These superstitions were common to the age, and rather
added than detracted from their moral teachings. Under their
formative influence, the first French settlements of Illinois were
deeply imbued with a spirit of justice, honesty, charity, and other
virtues, which enabled them to exist nearly a century without a
court of law; without wars with their Indian neighbors, and up to
the time of Boisbriant, without a local government. The confidence inspired by the priests, as the ministers of a supposed infal-
lible church, gave them ample authority to settle, without the
tardy proceedings of courts and their attendant costs, all differences which occasionally disturbed the peace of the colonists.
Justice, under these circumstances, was dispensed as in Israel of
old, by the power of the mind to discriminate between right and
wrong, rather than by laws whose intricacies and technicalities
frequently suffer the guilty to go unpunished. Such was the respect for right, and the parental regard which animated the priestly
judges of this isolated theocracy of the wilderness, it might safely
challenge comparison with its Hebrew prototype for the religious
zeal and virtuous conduct manifested by its subjects.

A Part of Louisiana.—Hitherto the settlements of Illinois and
those subsequently founded on the Lower Mississippi by D'Iberville and his brother, Bienville, had been separate dependencies of
Canada. Now they were to be united as one province, under the
name of Louisiana, having its capital at Mobile, and in 1711
Dirou d'Artaguette became the Governor General.* It was believed that Louisiana presented a rich field for speculation and
enterprise, and it was determined to place its resources in the
hands of an individual who had the means and energy to develop
them. It was thought, too, that the colonists should become self-
supporting, by procuring from the soil products not only for their
own consumption, but to exchange with France for such articles
as they could not produce. In conformity with these views, in
1712, the commerce of the province was granted to Anthony Crozat, an officer of the royal household, and a merchant of great
wealth. The king, in his letters patent, after referring to the
orders he had given to LaSalle to explore the Mississippi, as a
means of developing the commerce of his American possessions,
enumerates the monopolies conferred on Crozat:

"From the information we have received concerning the situation and disposition of Louisiana, we are of opinion that there may be established therein a
considerable commerce, of great advantage to France. We can thus obtain
from the colonists the commodities which hitherto we have brought from other
countries, and give in exchange for them the manufactured and other products
of our own kingdom We have resolved, therefore, to grant the commerce of
Louisiana to the Sieur Anthony Crozat, our counselor and secretary of the
household and revenue, to whom we entrust the execution of this project. We

---

*Monette's Vel. of the Miss. and Dillon's Indiana.

permit him to search, open, and dig all mines, veins, minerals, precious stones, and pearls, throughout the whole extent of the country, and to transport the proceeds thereof into any port of France, during 15 years. And we grant, in perpetuity to him, his heirs, and all claiming under him, all the profits, except one-fifth, of the gold and silver which he or they shall cause to be exported to France We also will that the said Crozat, and those claiming under him, shall forfeit the monopolies herein granted should they fail to prosecute them for a period of three years, and that in such case they shall be fully restored to our dominion." *

The vast region thus farmed out, extended from Canada on the north, to the Gulf on the South; and from the Alleghanies on the east to the Rocky Mountains and the Bay of Matagorda on the west. "Not a fountain bubbled" along the summit of these great mountain barriers that made its way into the Mississippi, that was not included in French territory. Crozat entered the vast field of his labors with energy, and soon associated with him La Motte Cadilac, the royal governor of Louisiana. He expected to realize great profits from the fur trade, but the prospect of boundless wealth from the discovery of rich mines of gold and silver was the talisman that most enraptured his vision and induced him to make the most lavish expenditures of his money. To carry out his plans, expeditions were made to the most distant tribes, and posts were established on Red River, the Yazoo, high up the Washita at the present town of Monroe, on the Cumberland river near Nashville, and on the Coosa, 400 miles above the mouth of the Alabama, where fort Jackson was built 100 years afterward. The search for the precious metals has always been a mania affecting the pioneers of newly discovered countries, and whether discoveries are made or not, it generally retards their permanent growth and prosperity. To such an extent were Crozat and his partners influenced by this shining bubble that they frequently magnified the most trivial prospects into what they regarded as realities of the greatest value. An instance in which they suffered by their credulity, and which greatly resembles the impositions and deceptions of the present day, occurred at Kaskaskia. Two pieces of silver ore, left at this place by a traveler from Mexico, were exhibited to Cadilac as the produce of mines in Illinois, and so elated was he by this assurance of success that he hurried up the river, only to find it, like all previous prospects, vanish into empty air. But while silver and gold could not be found, large quantities of lead and iron ore were discovered in Missouri; but the great abundance of these metals in the civilized portions of the globe made their presence in the wilds of Louisiana of little consequence.

Crozat made an attempt to open trade with the Spaniards of Vera Cruz, but on sending a vessel with a rich cargo thither, it was not permitted either to land there or at any other harbor of the gulf. The occupation of Louisiana by the French was regarded as an encroachment upon Spanish territory, and Crozat, after three years of fruitless negotiations with the viceroy of Mexico, was compelled to abandon the scheme of commercial relations with the ports of the gulf. Another project was to establish trade by land with the interior Spanish provinces, but in this case he also failed, for, after a protracted effort of five years, his goods were seized and confiscated and his agents imprisoned. Nor had

*See Dillon's Indiana.
8

the fur trade with the Indians, another source of anticipated
wealth, met with success.   English emissaries from the Carolinas
had been active in their efforts to excite Indian hostilities against
the French, and wherever practicable, had controlled the fur trade,
by furnishing goods in exchange at reduced prices.   Agriculture,
the only resource of lasting prosperity to the country, had been
neglected, and Crozat, failing to realize any profits from his efforts
in other directions, was unable to meet his liabilities.   He had
expended 425,000 livres and realized only 300,000, and failing to
pay his men, dissatisfaction ensued.   Despairing also of being
more successful in the future, in 1717, he petitioned the king to
have his charter revoked, which was done, and the government
reverted solely to the officers of the crown.   During his connection
with the province, the growth of the settlements was slow, and
little was acomplished for their permanent benefit.   The greatest
prosperity they enjoyed grew out of the enterprise of humble individuals, who had succeeded in establishing a small trade between
themselves, the natives and some neighboring European settlements.
But even these small sources of prosperity were at length cut off by
the fatal monopolies of the Parisian merchant.   The white population of the country had slowly increased, and at the time of his
departure, that on the Lower Mississippi was estimated at 380, and
that of Illinois, which then included the settlements of the Wabash,
320 souls.

Crozat's partner had died the year previous, and was succeeded
in his official capacity by Bienville, the former governor.   Prior to
his installation some French hunters and stragglers had located
in the beautiful country of the Natchez, and difficulties arising between them and the Indians, two of the former had been murdered.
Bienville repaired to the tribe in question, and after punishing the
guilty parties, erected and garrisoned a fort, to prevent the recurrence of similar disturbances in the future.   It was built on the
site selected 16 years before by his brother, and was called Rosalie, the name of the capital he proposed to build at the same place.
This was the origin of the present city of Natchez, the oldest permanent settlement in the Mississippi Valley, south of Illinois.*
With the retirement of Crozat, Bienville was succeeded by L'Epi-
nai, who brought with him 50 emigrants and 3 companies of infantry, to reinforce the garrisons of the different posts.

_____

*It seems that Arkansas Post has never been abandoned since Tonti's men erected
their cabin there, after his fruitless search for LaSalle's colony, in the spring of 1686.

Chapter XI.

1717-1732—ILLINOIS AND LOUISIANA UNDER THE COMPANY OF THE WEST.

Louis XIV. had recently died, leaving a debt contracted by wars and extravagance amounting to 3,000,000,000 livres. He was succeeded by his grandson, Louis XV, who, being then only a child five years old, the Duke of Orleans was appointed regent. In the midst of the financial confusion growing out of the efforts of the regent to pay the interest on the overwhelming public debt, John Law presented himself at the French court with a scheme for affording relief. He was the son of an Edinburgh banker, and shortly after the death of his father, wasted his patrimony by gambling and extravagant living. For 3 years he wandered over Europe, supporting himself by gambling and studying the principles of finance. After perfecting his theory he returned to Edinburgh, and published the project of a land bank, which the wits of the day ridiculed by calling it a sand bank, which would wreck the ship of state. Several years afterward he presented his plan to the Duke of Savoy, who told him he was too poor a potentate and his dominion was too small, for so grand a project. He thought, however, that the French people would be delighted with a plan so new and plausible, and advised him to go to France.

According to his theory of banking, the currency of a country is the representative of its moving wealth, and need not, of itself, have an intrinsic value, as in the case of gold and silver, but may consist of paper or any substance that can be conveniently handled. He insisted that the financial embarrassment under which France labored, was not the fault of her rulers, but an insufficiency of currency, and gave England and Holland as examples. The regent, captivated by his views, published an edict in 1716, authorizing Law and his brother to establish a bank with a capital of 6,000,000 livres, the notes of which should be received for taxes, and made redeemable in the coin current at the time they were issued. Three-fourths of the capital consisted of government securities, and the remainder in specie, Law declaring that a banker deserved death who made issues without means of redemption. The government had already, by arbitrarily reducing the value of its coin, diminished the debt 1,000,000,000 livres; but Law's paper being based on the value of coin at the time he made his issues, was without fluctuations, and on this account soon commanded a premium of 15 per cent. The regent was astonished that paper money could thus aid specie and be at a premium, while state bonds were at 78 per cent. discount.

The banker's influence being now irresistible, he proposed his famous Mississippi scheme, which made him a prominent actor in the history of Louisiana and Illinois. The vast resources of Louisiana still filled the imaginations of French statesmen with visions of boundless wealth. The want of success which had hitherto attended the efforts of D'Iberville and Crozat, was still insufficient to produce in the public mind more sober views. The story of its vast mineral deposits was soon revived; ingots of gold, the products of its supposed mines, were exhibited in Paris. and the sanguine French court saw in the future of the province an empire, with its fruitful fields, growing cities, busy wharves, and exhaustless mines of gold and silver, pouring its precious freights into the avenues of French commerce. No sooner, therefore, had Crozat surrendered his charter, than others appeared, eager to enter this vast field of adventurous enterprise. Accordingly, in 1717, an organization was effected under the auspices of Law, known at first as the Western Company. Among the privileges conferred on it may be mentioned the right exclusively to control the commerce of the province for a period of 25 years; to make treaties with the Indians, and wage war against them in case of insult; to open and work all mines free of duty; to cast cannon; build ships of war, levy troops and nominate the governors and those who were to command them, after being duly commissioned by the king. To further encourage the company, he promised to give them the protection of his name against foreign powers, presented them the vessels, forts, munitions and merchandise surrendered by Crozat, and, during the continuance of the charter, exempted the inhabitants of the province from tax, and the company from duty.*

The stocks of the company consisted of 200,000 shares of 500 livres each, to be paid in certificates of state indebtedness. Thus nearly 1000,000,000 of the most depreciated of the public stocks were immediately absorbed, and the government became indebted to a company of its own creation, instead of individuals, for this amount. By means of Law's bank, the interest on this portion of the public debt was promptly paid, and, as the result, it immediately rose from a great depreciation to a high premium. Any person, therefore, who had invested 100 livres in state bonds, which he could have done at one-third of the value written on their face, could now realize their enhanced worth. Large fortunes were thus speedily acquired, though the union of the bank with the risks of a commercial company were ominous of its future destiny.

But humanity abounds in hope, and men, acting in large combinations, gather courage from the increase of their numbers. How far their anticipations were realized in the case under consideration, will appear in the sequel. All France was now infatuated with the glory of Louisiana, and imagined the opulence which it was to acquire in coming ages, already in their grasp. Law's bank wrought such wonders, that new privileges were conferred on it daily. It was permitted to monopolize the tobacco trade, was allowed the sole right to import negroes into the French colonies, and the exclusive right of refining gold and silver. Finally, in 1717, it was erected into the Royal Bank of France, and

*Martin's Louisiana.

shortly afterward the Western Company merged into the Company of the Indies, and new shares of its stocks were created and sold at immense profits. In addition to the exclusive privileges which it already held, it was now granted the trade of the Indian seas, the profits of the royal mint, and the proceeds of farming the royal revenue of France. The government, which was absolute, conspired to give the highest range to its credit, and Law, says a cotemporary, might have regulated at his pleasure the interest of money, the value of stocks, and the price of labor and produce. A speculating frenzy at once pervaded the whole nation. The maxim which Law had promulgated, that the "banker deserved death who made issues of paper without means of redemption," was overlooked or forgotten. While the affairs of the bank were under his control, its issues did not exceed 60,000,000 livres, but on becoming the Bank of France, they at once rose to 100,000,000. Whether this was the act of Law or the regent, we are not informed. That he lent his aid to inundate the whole country with paper money, is conceded, and perhaps dazzled by his former success, he was less guarded, and unconscious that an evil day was fast approaching. The chancellor, who opposed these extensive issues, was dismissed at the instance of Law, and a tool of the regent was appointed in his place. The French parliament foresaw the danger approaching, and remonstrated in vain with the regent. The latter annulled their decrees, and on their proposing that Law, whom they regarded as the cause of the whole evil, should be brought to trial, and, if found guilty, be hung at the gates of the Palace of Justice, some of the most prominent officers of the parliament were committed to prison. Law, alarmed for his safety, fled to the royal palace, threw himself on the protection of the regent, and for a time escaped the popular indignation.

He still devoted himself to the Mississippi scheme, the shares of which rose rapidly. In spite of parliament, 50,000 new shares were added, and its franchises extended. The stock was paid in state securities, with only 100 livres for 500 of stock. For these new shares 300,000 applications were made, and Law's house was beset from morning till night with eager applicants, and before the list of fortunate stockholders could be completed, the public impatience rose to a pitch of frenzy. Dukes, marquises and counts, with their wives and daughters, waited for hours in the streets before his door, to know the result; and to prevent being jostled by the plebeian crowd, took apartments in the adjacent houses, the rents of which rose from 100 to 1200, and, in some instances, to 1600 livres per annum. Induced by golden dreams, the demand for shares was so great it was thought best to increase them 300,000 more, at 500 livres each; and such was the eagerness of the people to subscribe, that, had the government ordered three times that number, they would all have been taken.

The first attempts of the company at colonization in Louisiana, were attended with careless prodigality. To entice emigrants thither, the rich prairies and the most inviting fields were granted to companies which sought principalities in the valley of the Mississippi. An extensive prairie in Arkansas, bounded on all sides by the sky, was granted to Law, where he designed to plant a colony, and he actually expended a half million of livres for that purpose. From the representations of the company, New Orleans

became famous in Paris as a beautiful city before the work of
cutting down the canebrakes, which covered its site, had been
commenced. Kaskaskia, then mostly a cantonment of savages,
was spoken of as an emporium of the most extensive traffic, and
as rivaling some of the cities of Europe in refinement, fashion and
religious culture. In fine, to doubt the wealth of Louisiana was
to provoke anger. Law was now in the zenith of his glory, and
the people in the zenith of their infatuation. The high and the
low, the rich and the poor, were at once filled with visions of untold weath, and every age, set, rank and condition were buying
and selling stocks.

The effect of this speculation on the public mind and manners
was overwhelming. The laxity of public morals, bad enough before, now became worse, and the pernicious love of gambling dif-
fused itself through society and bore down all public and nearly
all private virtue before it. While confidence lasted, an impulse
was given to trade never before known. Strangers flocked to the
capital from every part of the globe, and its population increased
305,000 souls. Beds were made in kitchens, garrets and even stables, for the accommodation of lodgers. Provisions shared the
general advance, and wages rose in the same proportion. An illu-
sory policy everywhere prevailed, and so dazzled the eye that none
could see in the horrizon the dark cloud that announced the approaching storm. Law, at the time, was by far, the most influential man in the realm, while his wife and daughters were courted
by the highest nobility and their alliance sought by ducal and
princely houses.

Suspicions, however, soon arose; specie was demanded and Law
became alarmed. The precious metals had all left the kingdom,
and coin for more than 500 livres was declared an illegal tender.

[NOTE.—A cobbler, whe had a stall near Law's office, gained near 200 livres per day by
letting it, and finding stationery for brokers and other clients. A humpbacked man,
who stood in the street, as the story goes, gained considerable sums by loaning his back
as a writing desk to the eager speculators. Law, finding his residence too small, exchanged it for the Place Vendome. whither the crowd followed him. and the spacious
square had the appearance of a public market. Booths were erected for the transaction of business and the sale of refreshments. The boulevards and public gardens
were forsaken, and the Place Vendome became the most fashionable lounge for parties
of pleasure. The Hotel d'Suson was taken. and its fine garden, ornamented with fountains and statuary, was covered over with tents and pavilions for the accommodation
of stock jobbers, and each tent being let at 500 livres per month, made a monthly revenue of 250,000 livres. Peers, judges and bishops thronged the Hotel de Suson, and
officers of the army and navy, ladies of title and fashion, were seen waiting in the
ante-chamber of Law, to beg a portion of his stock. He was unable to wait on one-
tenth part of the applicants, and every species of ingenuity was employed to gain an
audience. Peers, whose dignity would have been outraged if the regent had made
them wait half an hour for an interview, were content to wait 6 hours for the purpose
of seeing the wily adventurer. Enormous fees were paid to his servants to announce
their name, and ladies of rank employed the blandishments of their smiles. One lady
in particular, who had striven in vain many days to see Law, ordered her coachman to
keep a strict watch, and when he saw him coming. to drive against a post and upset her
carriage. This was successfully accomplished, and Law, who witnessed the apparent
accident, ran to her assistance. She was led to his house, and as soon as she thought it
advisable, recovered from her fright, apologized for the intrusion, and confessed the
stratagem. Law was a gallant, and could no longer refuse, and entered her name on
his book as the purchaser of some stock. Another lady of rank, knowing that Law
dined at a certain time, proceeded thither in her carriage and gave the alarm of fire,
and while everybody was scampering away, she made haste to meet him : but he, suspecting the trick, ran off in the opposite direction. A celebrated physician in Paris
had bought stock at an unfavorable time. and was anxious to sell out. While it was
rapidly falling, and while his mind was filled with the subject. he was called on to
attend a lady who thought herself unwell. Being shown up stairs. he felt the lady's
pulse, and. more intent upon his stocks than the patient, exclaimed : "It falls; good
God ! it falls continually." The lady started, and ringing the bell for assistance, said :
"O, doctor, I am dying. I am dying; it falls! "What falls?" inquired the doctor, in
amazement. "My pulse. my pulse," said the lady; "I am dying!" "Calm your
fears, my dear madam," said the doctor, "I was speaking of the stocks I have been
so great a loser, and my mind is so disturbed that I hardly know what I am saying."]

A council of state was held, and it was ascertained that 2,600,000,-000,000 in paper were in circulation, and the bank stopped payment. The people assaulted Law's carriage with stones, and but for the dexterity of his coachman, he would have been torn to pieces. On the following day his wife and daughter were attacked as they were returning in their carriage from the races. The regent being informed of these occurrences sent him a guard for his protection. Finding his house, even with a guard, insecure, he repaired to the palace and took apartments with the regent. Soon afterward, leaving the kingdom, his estate and library were confiscated, and he died at Vienna in extreme poverty.*

The lessons to be learned from these wild financial speculations, is, that the expansion of currency always gives an impetus to industry, but when it is based on credits, without means of redemption, it must meet with an overthrow attended with a prostration of business greatly overbalancing all temporary advantages.

We must now recount the operations of the company in Louisiana. On the 25th of August, 1718, its ships, after a pleasant voyage entered the port of Mobile, chanting the *Te Deum* for their safe arrival. On board the ships was the king's lieutenant, M. Boisbriant, bearing a commission authorizing Bienville to act as governor-general of the province, and 800 immigrants. The governor again commenced the duties of his office, still entertaining his previous convictions that the capital of the province should be removed from the sterile sands of the Gulf coast to the banks of the Mississippi. He reasoned that if established on the fertile alluvium or uplands of the great river, it would become the centre of a community devoted to agriculture, the only branch of industry that could give permanent growth and prosperity to the province. He therefore selected the site now occupied by New Orleans for a capital, and gave it the name it now bears, in honor of the Regent of France. Eight convicts were sent from the prisons of France to clear away the coppice which thickly studded the site. Two years afterward the royal engineer surveyed the outlets of the river and declared that it might be made a commercial port, and in 1783 it became the provincial and commercial capital of Louisiana. Although M. Hubert, who had charge of the company's affairs, reluctantly complied with the advice of Bienville in removing the depots to the new capital, time has proven the superior judgment of the former. From a depot for the commercial transactions of a single company, it has become the emporium of the noblest valley on the face of the globe.

The delusion that dreamed of silver and gold in Louisiana, and which had so largely contributed to the ruin of Crozat, still haunted the minds of his successors. Unwilling to profit by his experience, they concluded that his success was rather the result of his unskillful assayers than the absence of the precious metals, and accordingly Phillip Renault was made director-general of the mines. He left France in 1719, with 200 mechanics and laborers, and provided with all things necessary to prosecute the business of his office. On his way hither he bought 500 negro slaves at San Domingo, for working the mines, and on reaching the mouth of the Mississippi, sailed to Illinois, where it was supposed gold and silver existed in large quantities. He established himself a

*Condensed from Bancroft, Brown's Illinois, and M'Kay's Extraordinary Delusions.

few miles above Kaskaskia, in what is now the southwest corner of Monroe county, and called the village which he founded Saint Phillips. Great expectations prevailed in France at his prospective success, but they all ended in disappointment. From this point he sent out exploring parties into various parts of Illinois, which then constituted Upper Louisiana. Search was made for minerals along Drewry's creek, in Jackson county; about the St-Mary's, in Randolph county; in Monroe county, along Silver creek; in St. Clair county, and other parts of Illinois. Silver creek took its name from the explorations made on its banks, and tradition, very improbably, states that considerable quantities of silver were discoverd here and sent to France. The operations of Renault were at length brought to a close from a cause least expected. By the edict of the king the Western Company became the Company of the Indies, and the territory was retroceded to the crown. The efforts of the company had totally failed, and Renault was left to prosecute the business of mining without means.

In the meantime a fierce war had been raging between France and Spain, and their respective colonists in North America presented a continuous display of warlike preparations. Bienville, with his regulars and provincial troops, 400 Indians, and a few armed vessels, made a descent on Pensacola and laid it under siege before its garrison could be reinforced. After an assault of 5 hours, and a determined resistance on the part of the besieged, the Spanish commandant surrendered. The approach of a powerful Spanish armament shortly afterward, compelled Bienville to relinquish the fort and return to Mobile, where he, in turn, was besieged in the fort of Dauphin Island. The squadron endeavored, by a furious bombardment, to reduce the fort, but its commander, finding his efforts unavailing, after 13 days retired. The war continuing to harrass the coast of the gulf, Bienville the following year, with the whole available force of the province, again moved against the town of Pensacola. After a close investment by sea and land the town and fort were carried by storm, and, besides the munitions of the latter, 1,800 prisoners fell into the hands of the victors. Several Spanish vessels with rich cargoes, ignorant of the occupation of the town by the French, ran into port and were also captured. The occupation of the town, as before, was of short duration, for Bienville, anticipating the arrival of a Spanish force, blew up the fort, burned the town and returned to Mobile.

But the operations of the war were not confined to the lower part of the province. Traders and hunters had discovered a route across the western plains, and detachments of Spanish cavalry pushed across the great American desert, and were threatening Illinois. The Missouri Indians were at the time in alliance with the French, and the Spaniards planned an expedition for the extermination of this tribe, that they might afterward destroy the settlements of Illinois and replace them with colonists from Mexico. The expedition for this purpose was fitted out at Santa Fe, and directed to proceed by way of the Osages, to secure their co-operation in an attack on the Missouris. Consisting of soldiers, priests, families and domestic animals, it moved like an immense caravan across the desert, prepared both to overthrow the French colonies and to establish others in their stead. By mistake, their guides led them directly to the Missouris instead of the Osages, and as each spoke the same language they believed themselves in the presence of the latter tribe. The wily savages, on learning their business, encouraged the misunderstanding, and requested two days to assemble their warriors and prepare for the attack. More than 180 muskets were put into their hands, and before the Spaniards found out their mistake the Missouris fell upon them and put them indiscriminately to death. The priest alone was spared to tell the fate of his unfortunate countrymen. In anticipation of similar difficulties, Boisbriant was sent to Illinois in 1720 by the Western Company, to erect a fort on the Mississippi, for the protection of the surrounding regions. Thus originated Fort Chartres, which played such an important part in the subsequent history of Illinois. The fortification was built on the east side of the river, 22 miles northwest of Kaskaskia, and was at the time the most impregnable fortress in North America. Here the Western company finally built their warehouses, and when, in 1721 Louisiana was divided into districts. it became the headquarters of Boisbriant, the first local governor of Illinois. The 7 districts were New Orleans, Biloxi, Mobile, Alabama, Natchez, Natchitoches, and Illinois.

Soon after the erection of the fort, Cahokia, Prairie du Rocher, and some other villages, received large accessions to their populations. All the settlements between the rivers Mississippi and Kaskaskia became greatly extended and increased in number, and in 1721 the Jesuits established a monastery and college at Kaskaskia. Four years afterward it became an incorporated town, and Louis XV granted the inhabitants a commons, or pasture grounds, for their stock. Immigrants rapidly settled on the fertile lands of the American Bottom, and Port Chartres not only became the headquarters of the commandant of Upper Louisiana, but the centre of wealth and fashion in the West.*

In the Autumn of 1726, Bienville was succeeded by M. Perrier. The retiring governor had with much propriety, been called the Father of Louisiana, having, with the exception of two short intermissions, been its executive officer for 26 years. Not long after the arrival of the new governor, his attention was directed to the Chicasaw Indians. His predecessor had observed, in previous years, the insincerity of their friendship for the French, and had urged the directory of the company to institute some more effective protection for the adjacent settlement. M. Perrier now reiterated its importance, but his apprehensions were deemed groundless, and nothing was done. The Indians were now becoming jealous at the rapid encroachments of the whites, who sometimes punished them harshly for the most trivial offense. Under these circumstances the Chicasaws, Natchez, and other tribes conceived the design of destroying the French, and sent agents to the Illinois to induce them to cut off the settlements in their midst. The attack was to commence at different places at the same time, but from some unknown cause the Natchez were the first to carry the design into execution, although the Chicasaws were the first to propose the conspiracy. It is said that the number of days to elapse from the new moon to the time of the massacre, was indicated by a certain number of reeds, bundles of which were sent to the different tribes. One reed was to be drawn daily from each bundle, and the attack was to

---

* Monette's Val. of the Miss.

commence when the last one was drawn.* By design, or accident, the bundle sent to the Natchez was made smaller than the rest, and hence they struck the first blow. Indian tradition asserted that the plot was kept a profound secret till the fatal day arrived. This, according to Natchez computation, was on the 28th of November, 1729, at the dawn of which the Great Chief, or Sun, with a number of chosen warriors having concealed weapons, repaired to Fort Rosalie. At a preconcerted signal, the warriors drew their weapons, and at a single onset the little garrison slept the sleep of death. Other parties were distributed through the contiguous settlements, and when the ascending smoke of the burning fort was seen, these became the scenes of slaughter, till the entire white male population, numbering 700, were destroyed. While the massacre was raging, the Great Sun seated himself in the spacious warehouse of the company, and with the greatest apparent unconcern, smoked his pipe as his warriors piled up the heads of the garrison in the form of a pyramid near by, whose apex was the head of the commandant. When the warriors informed him that the last Frenchman ceased to live, he ordered the pillage to commence. The negro slaves were ordered to bring in the spoils for distribution, but the military stores were reserved for future use. As long as the ardent spirit lasted, day and night alike presented a continued scene of savage triumphs and drunken revelry. The settlements on the Yazoo and other places, met with a similar fate, but those within the present limits of Illinois, owing to the loyalty and friendship of the prairie tribes, remained unharmed.

As soon as the massacre became known, M. Perrier dispatched vessels to France for troops and military supplies, and couriers were sent to Port Chartres and other posts, urging upon the several commandants the necessity of preparation to co-operate with him against the common enemy. Agents were also sent to the Choctaws and other Indians in alliance with the French, for further assistance. The governor immediately got ready to march to the scene of disaster with the troops in the southern part of the province; but the negroes, numbering some 2,000, betrayed symptoms of revolt, and he was detained to watch the intended insurrection. In the meantime, the Choctaws, who had committed no overt act of hostility, had been visited by one of the company's agents, and induced to furnish 600 warriors. At Pearl river he received an accession of 600 more, and with this formidable body of warriors he moved forward and encamped near the enemy, to await the arrival of other forces. It was, however, soon ascertained that the Natchez, unsuspicious of danger, were spending their time in idle carousals, and the Choctaws rushed on them unexpectedly, and after a brief conflict, returned with 60 scalps. Not long afterward French troops arrived, completed the victory, and liberated the women and children. The larger part of the tribe, led by their Great Sun, fled across the Mississippi and fortified themselves on Black river. Thither they were followed by troops from France and the prinpcial settlements of the province, and in two successful battles were completely cut to pieces. The Great Sun and 400 warriors were captured and taken to New Orleans, and thence to San Domingo, and sold as slaves. Thus perished this powerful tribe, and with them their mysterious worship of the sun and bloody rites of sepulture. No tribe was, perhaps, more distinguished for refinement, intelligence, courage and contempt of death, in fighting for their rights and country.

The great expenditures in prosecuting the Natchez war, the consequent loss of trade with other tribes, and the financial embarrassments incident to Law's failure, induced the company to ask for a surrender of their charter. The king readily granted their petition, and on the 10th of April, 1732, issued a proclamation declaring Louisiana free to all his subjects, with equal privileges as to commerce and other interests. The 14 years the company had possession of the country, notwithstanding the many adverse circumstances, was a period of comparative prosperity. When it assumed control, the number of slaves was 20; now it was 2,000. Then the entire white population was 700; now 5,000, among which were many persons of worth, intelligence and enterprise. The extravagant hopes entertained respecting the precious metals, had not been realized, but the search for them had attracted population, which had now made such progress in agriculture as to be self-sustaining. Illinois, at this time, contained many flourishing settlements, more exclusively devoted to agriculture than those in other parts of the province. All industrial enterprises, however, were, to a great extent, paralyzed by the arbitrary exactions of the company. The agriculturists, the miners and the fur traders of Illinois were held in a sort of vassalage, which enabled those in power to dictate the price at which they should sell their products, and the amount they should pay them for imported merchandise. The interest of the company was always at variance with that of the producer, and it would have been difficult to devise a state of affairs so injurious to both parties, and so detrimental to the prosperity of Illinois and other parts of Louisiana.

CHAPTER XII.

1732-59—ILLINOIS AND LOUISIANA UNDER THE ROYAL GOVERNORS.

When the Company of the Indies gave up their charter, the government of France resumed the administration of public affairs. M. Perrier remained governor-general, and M. d'Artaguette became local governor of Illinois. The common law of Paris had previously been adopted as the code of Louisiana, but had never been formally extended over Illinois. The ecclesiastical affairs were under the superintendence of the vicar-general of New Orleans, as a part of the diocese of the bishop of Quebec. One of the principal objects of the governor was, to establish his authority over the different Indian tribes inhabiting the country under his command. The Chicasaws, instigated by English colonists, had made intercourse between Illinois and New Orleans so hazardous that commerce was virtually suspended, and the settlers kept in a constant state of alarm. Such was the animosity and activity of this tribe, it also sent secret envoys to the Illinois, for the purpose of debauching the time honored affection which had existed between them and their French neighbors, and inducing them to destroy the latter. These tawny sons of the prairies, however, refused to desert their friends, and sent an envoy to New Orleans to offer their services to the governor. Said this deputy to that functionary : "This is the pipe of peace or war; you have but to speak and our braves will strike the nations that are your foes."[*] It was now necessary to reduce the Chicasaws, to establish communication between the northern and southern portions of the province, and to save the eastern portion from the intrigues of emissaries, sent out among the Indians by the English colonies on the Atlantic. An officer was, therefore, dispatched to Fort Chartres, in 1736, directing D'Artaguette to get in readiness the French forces under his command, and such Indians of Illinois as he could induce to unite with him in the war. It was arranged that D'Artaguette should descend the Mississippi to some suitable point of debarkation, and then cross to the country on the head waters of the Talahatchee, where the enemy's stronghold was situated.

In the meantime Bienville, who had again been commissioned by the king as governor-general, with the forces of southern Louisiana, was to ascend the Tombigbee to the confluence of its two principal tributaries, and marching thence by land, effect a junction with the forces from the north. Early in the spring, Bienville moved with his forces from New Orleans to Mobile, and thence to

---

[*]Bancroft.

the point designated, where a fort had previously been erected to serve as a depot of supplies. Here, by offering rewards for scalps and making presents of merchandise, he drew together the large force of 1200 Choctaws. After disembarking the artillery and placing it in the fort, the solitude of the primitive forests and blooming prairies was broken by the tread of the forces moving in the direction of the enemy.* On the 25th of May, they arrived within 3 miles of the Chicasaw village, but several days behind the time fixed for meeting the northern forces; a delay, which, as the sequel will show, proved fatal. The village was 27 miles from the fort, and within a few miles of Pontotoc, Mississippi, which still perpetuates the name of the Indian stronghold, and became famous as a point in Grierson's great raid in the war of the rebellion. Before daylight, the next morning, the impatient and ungovernable Choctaws moved against the log citadel of the enemy, expecting to take its occupants by surprise. On the contrary, they found the garrison on the alert, and the fort a skillfully constructed fortification, erected under the supervison of English traders. Twice during the day, Bienville attempted to carry the works by vigorous attacks, but was repulsed with a loss of 65 wounded, and 32 killed; the latter embracing 4 officers of rank. The following day, some skirmishing occurred between the Choctaws and the enemy, without any decisive results, when Bienville, mortified at his defeat, and believing his own forces too inconsiderable for the reduction of such formidable works without the co-operation of the northern forces, of which he had heard nothing, concluded to abandon the enterprise. He accordingly dismissed his red auxiliaries, made a retrograde march to the fort on the Tombigbee, ingloriously threw his cannon into the river, and returned to New Orleans, covered with defeat and shame.

Prior to the inflicting of this disgrace upon the French arms, the gallant D'Artaguette, accompanied by De Vincennes and Father Lenat, had led his army of 50 Frenchmen and more than 1000 red warriors, from the prairies of the north to the Yalabusha. Here, at the appointed place of rendezvous, he waited for 10 days the arrival of the commander-in-chief, ready to co-operate with him in maintaining the jurisdiction and honor of France. The failure of the latter, however, to arrive in time, prevented the junction of the two armies, and thus defeated the campaign. On the 20th of May, his rash Indian confederates, who had the courage to strike a blow, but lacked the calculation and patience to wait the proper time, compelled him to commence offensive operations. Having skillfully arranged his forces, with great daring and impetuosity he drove the Chicasaws from two fortifications, and in the assault on the third was disabled in the moment of victory. Dismayed at the loss of their leader, the Indians fled precipitately, closely pursued a distance of 125 miles by the enemy in the flush of unexpected victory, while D'Artaguette and some of his brave comrades lay weltering in their gore, attended by Lenat, who, mindful only of the assistance he might render the suffering, refused to fly. Vincennes, too, whose name is perpetuated by the city of the Wabash, chose also to remain and share the captivity of his leader. The wounds of the prisoners were staunched, and at first they were treated with great kindness by their captors, who expected to get a large reward from Bien-

*Bancroft.

ville for their safe return. When, however, they heard of his discomfiture and withdrawal, they dispaired of receiving a ransom for the prisoners and proposed to make them victims of a savage triumph. For this purpose they were borne to a neighboring field, bound to stakes, and tortured before slow and intermitting fires till death mercifully released them from their sufferings. Thus perished the faithful Lenat, the young and intrepid D'Artaguette, and the heroic Vincennes, whose names will endure as long as the Illinois and Wabash shall flow by the dwellings of civilized men.

The Chickasaws, elated by victory, sent a deputation to announce their success and the torments inflicted on their captives to the English colonists, with whom they were now in sympathy. Bienville, on the other hand, chagrined at the result of the campaign, determined to retrieve his honor and the glory of France by a second invasion. The approbation of the Minister having been obtained, toward the close of the year 1739 he commenced putting in operation his plans for the reduction of the fierce antagonists who had before so successfully defied him. The signal for preparation was given to the commandants of the different posts, which resulted in efforts far transcending in military display anything before seen in the provinces. A fort was erected at the mouth of the St. Francis, which served as a place of rendezvous, and afterward of departure for the grand army eastward, to the country of the enemy. The force from Illinois. consisting of 200 French and 300 Indians, was commanded by La Buissoniere, who had succeeded the lamented D'Artaguette as commandant at Ft. Chartres. These, with the forces from other posts, amounted to 1200 Europeans and 500 Indians and negroes. The whole, under the command of Bienville, was soon moved to the mouth of Wolf river, where it was delayed in the erection of a second fort, in which to deposit their military stores, and care for the sick. Before the fort, which bore the name of Assumption, was completed, malarious fevers so fatal to European constitutions, had seriously disabled the army. Hardly had the early frosts of winter abated the disease, when famine, a more formidable enemy, threatened them with annihilation. Supplies could only be obtained at Ft. Chartres and New Orleans, and hence the consummation of the campaign was necessarily postponed till the following spring. Spring came, but such had been the debilitating effects of the winter and the want of wholesome food, that only 200 men were now fit for duty. Undeterred, however, by the want of numbers, M. Celeron, a lieutenant of La Buissoniere, boldly set out to meet the Chicasaws, who, supposing the whole French army was behind him, sued for peace. Celeron, taking advantage of the mistake, obtained from them a declaration that they would renounce the English and resume peaceable relations with the French. To confirm their statements, a deputation of chiefs accompanied them to Ft. Assumption and entered into a treaty of peace with Bienville, which was ratified with the customary Indian ceremonies and festivities. The army now returned to the fort on the St. Francis, where Bienville disbanded it, and "again ingloriously floated down the river to New Orleans."* This was the end of the second campaign against the Chicasaws, wherein Bienville not only failed to retrieve his tarnished military fame,

†Monette's Val. of the Miss.

but incurred the displeasure of his sovereign. Two armies had been sacrificed in an attempt to mete out to the Chicasaws the fate that had befallen the Natchez; but like their ancestors, who 200 years before had encountered the steel-clad chivalry of Deso- to, they still remained intact. With the close of these disastrous expeditions terminated the gubernatorial career of Bienville, which, with slight interruptions, had extended through a period of 40 years. Age had cooled down the ardor and energy of his manhood's prime, and the honors won in previous years were now obscured in a cloud of disapprobation and censure.

Retiring from office, he was succeeded by the Marquis de Van- dreuil, who subsequently became Governor of Canada. After the establishment of amicable relations with the Chicasaws, the na- tive tribes throughout the valley of the Mississippi submitted to the dominion of France and became her allies. A commercial in- tercourse with them succeeded, and agriculture, now freed from company monopolies, rapidly sprang into new life. Sugar cane was brought from San Domingo, and the first attempt at its culti- vation proving successful, it has since become the great staple of the present state of Louisiana. Cotton was introduced and suc- cessfully cultivated as far north as Illinois. A gin was subse- quently invented by M. Dubreuil, and though imperfect compared with Whitney's of the present day, it greatly facilitated the oper- ation of separating the fibre from the seed and thus gave a new impetus to the cultivation of the plant. The fig tree, the orange, and the lemon, began to bloom about the houses of the colonists on the Lower Mississippi and supply them with delicious fruit, while the sweet potato, extending over a broader range of latitude, contributed largely to the sustenance of both the northern and southern parts of the province. Every arrival from France aug- mented the population of the rapidly extending settlements. Many Canadians, retiring from the rigor of their winters, sought homes in the comparatively mild climate of Illinois and the region of the Wabash. Under the stimulus of individual enterprise the commerce between the northern and southern parts of the pro- vince, and between New Orleans and foreign countries, was great- ly extended. Regular cargoes of pork, flour, bacon, tallow, hides and leather were annually transported in barges from Illinois to New Orleans and Mobile, and thence shipped to France and the West Indies. In exchange were brought back rice, indigo, sugar and European fabrics. The two extremes of Louisiana were mu- tually dependent, and by means of the Mississippi and its hun- dred tributaries, naturally supplied each other's wants. The decade commencing with 1740 and closing with 1750 was one of unusual prosperity.

Manners and Customs of the French.—Unlike the English and other Europeans, who usually lived in sparse settlements, the French fixed their abode in compact villages. These were gen- erally built on the banks of some pure stream of water, contigu- ous to timber and prairie, the one furnishing them fuel and the other with ground for tillage. The construction of the dwellings was of a primitive character. The frame work consisted of posts planted in the earth three or four feet deep and strongly bound together by horizontal cross-ties. The interstices thus formed were filled with mortar, intermixed with straw or Spanish moss, to give it tenacity. The surface of the walls, both internal and external, were washed with white lime, which imparted to the buildings an air of cleanliness and domestic comfort. Most of the dwellings were surrounded by piazzas, on which the inmates found a pleasant retreat to while away in social converse the sultry summer evenings. Destitute of machinery for cutting their trees into boards, they split them into slabs, which were used for flooring, doors and other purposes, while as a substitute for shingles they thatched their buildings with straw. Although having the greatest amplitude for wide streets, they generally made them so narrow that the merry villagers living on opposite sides could carry on their sprightly conversations each from his own balcony. Even in detached settlements the social turn of the people induced them to group their dwellings as closely together as possible. Each settlement had its patriarchal homestead, which generally stood in a spacious enclosure, and was occupied by the oldest member of the family. Around this sprung up a cluster of cottages, the residence of each child and grand child as it married and became the head of a family. Not unfrequently the aged patriarch became the centre of a dozen growing families of his own lineage and embracing 3 or 4 generations.

Common Field.—A duty imposed upon the commandant of each village was to reserve a tract of land for a common field, in which all the inhabitants were interested. To each villager was assigned a portion of the field, the size of which was proportioned according to the extent of his family. Lands thus apportioned were subject to the regulations of the villages, and when the party in possession became negligent so as to endanger the common interest he forfeited his claim. The time of plowing, sowing and harvesting, and other agricultural operations, was subject to the enactment of the village senate. Even the form and arrangement of enclosures surrounding the dwellings and other buildings were the subject of special enactments, and were arranged with a view to protection against the Indians, should an exigency occur making it necessary.

Commons.—Besides the common field, which was designed for tillage, there was a common which was free to all the villagers for the pasture of their stock and the supply of fuel. As accessions were made to the families of the community, either by marriage or the arrival of strangers, portions of land were taken from the common and added to the common field for their benefit.

Intercourse with the Indians.—Owing to their amiable dispositions and the tact of ingratiating themselves with the tribes that surrounded them, the French almost entirely escaped the broils which weakened and destroyed other colonies less favored with this trait of character. Whether exploring remote rivers or traversing hunting grounds in pursuit of game; in the social circle or as participants in the religious exercises of the church, the red men became their associates and were treated with the kindness and consideration of brothers. Like the Quakers guided by the example of Penn, they kept up a mutual interchange of friendly offices with their red neighbors, and such was the community of interests, the feeling of dependence and social equality, that intermarriages frequently occurred. thus more closely uniting them in the bonds of peace. Penn and his followers for many years lived in unbroken peace with their brethren of the forest, but that established by these pioneers of Illinois was never interrupted and for more than a hundred years the country enjoyed the benign influence of peace; and when at length it terminated, it was not the conciliatory Frenchman, but the blunt and sturdy Anglo-Saxon who supplanted him that was made the victim of savage vengeance. *

The calm and quiet tenor of their lives, remote from the bustle and harrassing cares of civilization, imparted a serenity to their lives rarely witnessed in communities where the acquisition of wealth and honor are suffered to exclude the better feelings of human nature. Lands of unequaled fertility, and the still more prolific waters and the chase supplied almost unsolicited the wants of life and largely contributed to the light hearted gaiety of the people. With ample leisure and free from corroding cares, they engaged in their various amusements with more than ordinary pleasure. Prominent among their diversions was the light fantastic dance of the young. At this gay and innocent diversion could be seen the village priest and the aged patriarch and his companion, whose eyes beamed with delight at beholding the harmless mirth of their children. When parties assembled for this purpose it was customary to choose the older and more discreet persons to secure proper decorum during the entertainment and see that all had an opportunity to participate in its pleasure. Frequently, on these occasions, fathers and mothers whose youthful enthusiasm time had mellowed down to sober enjoyments again became young and participated in the mazy evolutions of the dance. Even the slave, imbibing the spirit of the gay assemblage, was delighted because his master was happy, and the latter in turn was pleased at the enjoyment of the slave. Whenever the old, who were authority in such cases, decided that the entertainment had been protracted sufficiently long, it was brought to a close; and thus the excesses which so frequently attend parties of this kind at the present day were avoided.

At the close of each year it was an unvarying and time-honored custom among them for the young men to disguise themselves in old clothes, visit the several houses of the village, and engage in friendly dances with the inmates. This was understood as an invitation for the members of the family to meet in a general ball, to dance the old year out and the new year in. Large crowds assembling on these occasions, and taking with them refreshments,

[*Says Hall in his Sketches of the West: "We have heard of an occasion on which this reciprocal kindness was very strongly shown. Many years ago a murder having been committed in some broil, three Indian young men were given up by the Kaskaskias to the civil authorities of the newly established American government. The population of Kaskaskia was still entirely French, who felt much sympathy for their Indian friends, and saw these hard proceedings of the law with great dissatisfaction. The ladies, particularly, took a warm interest in the fate of the young aborigines, and determined if they must die, they should at least be converted to christianity in the meanwhile, and be baptized in the true church. Accordingly, after due preparation, arrangements were made for a public baptism of the neophites in the old cathedral of the village. Each of the youths was adopted by a lady who gave him a name and was to stand godmother in the ceremony, and the lady patronesses with their respective friends were busily engaged for some time in preparing decorations for the festivities. There was quite a sensation in the village. Never were three young men brought into notoriety more suddenly or more decidedly. The ladies talked of nothing else and all the needles in the village were employed in the preparation of finery for the occasion. Previous to the evening of hanging, the aboriginals gave the jailer the slip and escaped, aided most probably by the ladies, who had planned the whole affair with a view to this end. The law is not vindictive in new communities. The danger soon blew over; the young men again appeared in public and evinced their gratitude to their benefactors.]

with good cheer and merry dance beguiled the flying hours till the clock on the mantle chimed the advent of the new born year. Another custom was, on the 6th of January, to choose by lot 4 kings, each of whom selected for himself a queen, after which the parties thus selected proceeded to make arrangements for an entertainment styled, in the parlance of the times, a king-ball. Toward the close of the first dance, the old queens selected new kings whom they kissed as the formality of introduction into office. In a similar manner, the newly selected kings chose new queens, and the lively and mirthful dance continued during the carnival, or the week preceding Lent. The numerous festivals of the Catholic church strongly. tended to awaken and develope the social and friendly intercourse of the people.

All were Catholics and revered the pope as the vice-gerent of God, and respected their priests as spiritual guides and friendly counselors in the secular affairs of life. Mostly without schools or learning, the priest was the oracle in science and religion, and their enunciations on these subjects were received with an unquestioning faith as true. Ignorant of creeds and logical disputations, their religion consisted, in the main, of gratitude to God and love for mankind—qualities by far more frequently found in the unpretending walks of life than in the glare of wealth and power.

As the result of these virtues, children were loving and obedient, husbands and wives kind and affectionate. The latter had the undivided control of domestic matters; and as a further tribute to her moral worth, she was the chief umpire in cases of social equity and propriety. None more than she, whose intuition could penetrate at a glance the most subtle casuistry, was better qualified to detect and enforce it in a gentle and impartial manner. The people attended church in the morning, after which they collected and spent the remainder of the day in social intercourse and innocent pastimes. To the more sedate Protestant, such amusements on the Sabbath, seem unreasonable; but the French inhabitants of the country, in these early times, regarded them as a part of their religion, and conducted them with the utmost propriety. If questioned as to their gaiety on the Sabbath, they replied, that man was made for happiness, and the more he enjoyed the innocent pleasures of life the more acceptable he rendered himself to his creator. They contended that those who, on the Sabbath, repressed the expression of joyous feelings under the guise of sanctity, were the persons ready to cheat their neighbors during the remainder of the week. Such, were the religious sentiments of a people prone to hospitality, urbanity of manners, and innocent recreation; who presented their daily orisons to the throne of grace with as much confidence of receiving a blessing, as that enjoyed by his most devout Puritan brother.

The *costume* of the Illinois French, like their manners and customs, was simple and peculiar. Too poor, and too remote to obtain finer fabrics, the men, during the summer, wore pantaloons made of coarse blue cloth, which, during winter, was supplanted by buckskin. Over their shirts and long vests, a flannel cloak was worn, to the collar of which a hood was attached, which, in cold weather, was drawn over the head, but in warm weather it fell back on the shoulders after the manner of a cape. Among voyagers and hunters, the head was more frequently covered with a blue handkerchief folded in the form of a turban. In the same manner, but tastefully trimmed with ribbons, was formed the fancy head dress which the women wore at balls and other festive occasions. The dress of the matron, though plain and of the antique short-waist, was frequently varied in its minor details to suit the diversities of taste. Both sexes wore moccasins which, on public occasions, were variously decorated with shells, beads, and ribbons, giving them a tasty and picturesque appearance.

No mechanical vocation as a means of earning a livelihood, was known. The principal occupation was agriculture, which, owing to the extreme fertility of the soil, produced the most munificent harvests. Young men of enterprise, anxious to see the world and to distinguish themselves, became voyagers, hunters, and agents of fur companies, and in discharging their duties, visited the remote sources of the Missouri, Mississippi, and their tributaries. After months of absence, spent in this adventurous employment among the most distant savage nations of the wilderness, they would return to their native villages, laden with furs and peltries. These articles for a long time constituted the only medium of exchange, and the means whereby they procured guns, ammunition, and other important requisites of their primitive life. The re-union with their friends was signalized by the dance, the most important requisite of hospitality, gaiety and happiness. The whole village would assemble on these occasions to see the renowed voyagers, and hear them recount the strange sights and the adventures which they had encountered.

No regular court was held in the country for more than a hundred years, or till its occupation by the English, evidencing that a virtuous and honest community can live in peace and harmony without the serious infraction of law. The governor, aided by the friendly advice of the commandants and priests of the villages, either prevented the existence of controversies, or settled them when they arose, without a resort to litigation. Although these civil functionaries were clothed with absolute power, such was the paternal manner in which it was exercised, it is said, that the "rod of domination fell on them so lightly as to hardly be felt." When, in 1765, the country passed into the possession of the English, many of them, rather than submit to a change in the institutions to which they were accustomed and attached, preferred to leave their fields and homes, and seek a new abode on the west side of the Mississippi, still supposed to be under the dominion of France. Upon the reception of assurances, however, from Great Britain, that they should be protected in their property and religion, many of them remained. Those who had removed to the west side of the river enjoyed but a brief interval of peace. Intelligence was received that France had ceded all western and southern Louisiana to Spain, and although Spanish authority was not extended over the territory for a period of five years, it was a period of uncertainty and anxiety. The Spanish government, like that of France, was mild and parental. Every indulgence was extended to her new subjects, and for thirty years they continued to enjoy their ancient customs and religion. The next inroads upon their antiquated habits was the advance of the Americans to the Mississippi, in the region of Illinois. The unwelcome news was received that all Louisiana was ceded to the United States and a new system of jurisprudence was to be extended over them. Previous to

this cession they had to a great extent become reconciled and
attached to Spanish rule, but when the new regime was extended
over them, totally at a loss to comprehend the workings of republicanism, they asked to be relieved of the intolerable burden of
self-government.

Thus, in the heart of the continent, more than a thousand miles
from either ocean, in a region styled by LaSalle a territorial paradise, flourished these interesting communities, in the enjoyment
of peace, contentment and happiness. It was, however, of a passive character, wanting in that intensity of enjoyment which flows
from fully developed powers and an energetic and progressive
mode of life. The faculties of both mind and body languish without labor, and that may be considered the normal condition of the
race which brings into healthy play all the diversified springs of
action and thought which make up the wonderful machinery of
man. Without effort and useful industry he is the creature of
languid enjoyments, and a stranger to the highly wrought sensibility and the exquisite delights resulting from cultured mental
and physical powers. Furthermore, without enterprise, the vast
material forces which slumber in the crust of the earth, and its
mantle of exhuberant soil, cannot be made available. While
there was peace and contentment on the banks of the Illinois, the
Wabash, and the Upper Mississippi, it was reserved for a different
race to develop the vast coal fields and exhaustless soil of this
favored region, and cause their life sustaining products to pulsate
through the great commercial arteries of the continent. While this
simple, virtuous and happy people, dwelt in the granary of North
America almost unconscious of its vast resources, there was clinging to the inhospitable shores of the Atlantic an intelligent and
sinewy race, which was destined to sweep over and occupy their
fruitful lands as the floods of the great river overwhelms and
imports fertility to its banks. Only a few remnants of them have
escaped the inflowing tide of American population, who still retain
to a great extent the ancient habits and customs of their fathers.
With their decline came the downfall of their tawny allies of the
forest, and a new direction was given to American history.
France, could she have remained supreme, with her far reaching
and adventurous genius, aided by Jesuit enterprise, would perhaps
have partially civilized the savages and thus have arrested their
destruction. Populations would have sprung up in the basins of
the Great Lakes, and in the Valley of the Mississippi, under the
impress of a feudal monarchy, and controlled by a hierarchy of
priests hostile to freedom of thought. The progress of civil and
religious liberty would have been temporarily but not permanently
suspended. The present free institutions of America would have
been delayed till the shifting phases of national life furnished new
opportunities for experiment and improvement.

[Many curious anecdotes might be still picked up in relation to these early settlers,
especially in Illinois and Missouri, where the Spanish, French, English and Americans,
have had sway in rapid succession. At one time the French had possession of one side
of the Mississippi river and the Spaniards the other; and a story is told of a Spaniard
living on one shore, who, having a creditor residing on the other, seized a child, the
daughter of the latter, and having borne her across the river which formed the national
boundary, held her a hostage for the payment of the debt. The civil authorities declined interfering, and the military did not think the matter of sufficient importance to
create a national war, and the Frenchman had to redeem the daughter by discharging
his creditor's demand. The lady who was thus abducted was still living a few years
ago near Cahokia, the mother of a numerous progeny of American French.]

In the year 1750 LaBuissonier, governor of Illinois, was succeeded by Chevalier Macarty. The peace which had given such unexampled prosperity to Louisiana, was soon to be broken by the clangor and discord of war. Already, in the controversy between France and England in regard to their respective possessions, could be heard the first throes of the revolution which gave a new master and new institutions not only to Illinois, but to the whole continent. France claimed the whole valley of the Mississippi, which her missionaries and pioneers had explored and partially settled, and England the right to extend her possessions on the Atlantic indefinitely west ward. The jealousies and animosities of the parent countries soon crossed the Atlantic, and colonial intrigues were the result. Traders from South Carolina and Georgia again commenced introducing large quantities of goods among the Chickasaws and other tribes of southern Louisiana, and again endeavored to alienate them from their treaty stipulations with the French. As the result, depredations were renewed by the Chicasaws, and a third expedition was sent to their forest fastnesses on the Tombigbee, to reduce them to submission, but like its predecessors, it was substantially a failure. Farther northward similar disturbances commenced. British merchants sent their agents to the Miamis and other western tribes, whose traffic had been previously monopolized by the French. A more grievous offense was the formation of a company to whom the king of England granted a large tract of land on the Ohio, and conferred on it the privilege of trading with the western Indians.

The operations of the Ohio company soon drew the French and English colonial authorities into a controversy, and the mother countries were ready to back any effort that either might make for the maintenence and extension of their respective possessions. As the traders, who were encouraged by the Ohio company, were mostly from Pennsylvania and New York, the governor of Canada informed the executives of these colonies that their traders had been trafficing with Indians dwelling on French territory, and unless they immediately desisted from this illicit commerce, he would cause them to be seized and punished. Notwithstanding this menace, the Ohio company employed an agent to survey their lands southwesterly to the Falls of the Ohio, and northwesterly some distance up the Miami and Scioto. Virginia, also seconding the efforts of the company, obtained from the Indians the privilege to form settlements on the southeast side of the Ohio, 18 miles below the junction of the Alleghany and Monongahela.

England and France now saw that their territorial contest could only be settled by a resort to arms, and each urged its colonial authorities to institute preparations for defending their respective boundaries. In the coming contest the result could not be doubtful, for the colonists of the former power numbered 1,051,000, while those of the latter were only 52,000. Beside this great disparity of numbers, France had transmitted to her possessions institutions which shackled their progress. The English colonists brought with them advanced ideas of government from their native land, and left behind them the monarch and the nobility. The French emigrant came with only the feudal ideas of the past, and cared little for the innovations of modern freedom. The former claiming the right of religious liberty, withdrew from the established church and had a self-appointed ministry. The latter was closed against every ray of theological light, and dominated by a foreign priesthood, from whose teachings there was not a single dissenter. The one were self-reliant, self-sustaining, and energetic; ever pressing their way against the receding forests; always advancing, but never retreating The other were accustomed to follow a leader, and depend upon the parent country for supplies, which they might have produced themselves. The inhabitants of British America had the press, local legislatures, municipal discipline, the benefit of free schools, and were accustomed to think and act for themselves. As the result, from the waters of the southern gulf to where civilization is stayed by barriers of perpetual frost, the continent is their heritage.

In response to the advice of the British government, Virginia raised a force for the protection of her frontier, and sent Major Washington with a letter to the French commandant on the Ohio, requesting him to withdraw his troops from the dominion of Great Britain. The officer courteously replied that "it was not his province to determine whether the land situated on the Ohio belonged to his sovereign, but he would transmit the letter to his superior officer, and act in accordance with his instructions. In the meantime, he did not think it incumbent upon him to obey the summons of the British government, and would defend his position with all the skill and force at his command." Washington, after encountering much hardship, returned safely, and reported the reply of the French officer. The following year he received orders from the governor of Virginia to proceed with 200 men and complete the erection of a fort at the junction of the Monongahela and the Alleghany, previously commenced by the Ohio company. The attempt to execute the order was defeated by the French officer, M. Contrecœur, who, anticipating the arrival of the Virginia forces, moved down to the mouth of the Monongahela in advance, with 18 pieces of cannon and a force of 1,000 French and Indians. He drove away the small detachment of Virginia militia and some employes in the Ohio company, and completing the fort they had commenced, they called it DuQuesne, in honor of the governor of New France. In the meantime, a small detachment under Jummonville, was sent to notify Washington to withdraw from French territory. The American officer, learning beforehand the approach of Jummonville, made arrangements to fall on him by surprise. At a place called the Little Meadows, the forces met, and Washington, ordering his men to fire, set the example by discharging his own musket. Its flash kindled the forests of America to a flame, and scattered its fires over the kingdom of Europe. It was the signal gun whose reverbrations followed the flight of years, announced the revolution which banished from the New World the institutions of the Middle Ages, and erected upon their ruins the fabric of free government. The tidings of the rencouter carried the fame of Washington across the Atlantic, and while his name was execrated by the advocates of feudal monarchy, they chanted in heroic verse the martyrdom of Jummonville, who had been slain in battle. "And at the very time Washington became known to France, the child was born who was one day to stretch out his hand for the relief of America. How many defeated interests bent over the grave of Jummonville, and how many hopes clustered about the cradle of the infant Louis. "*

Fort Chartres was at this time the depot of supplies and the place of rendezvous for the united forces of Illinois and other posts of Louisiana. Shortly after the affray at the Little Meadows, M. de Villiers, a brother of Jumonville, and at the time an officer at Fort Chartres, solicited Macarty, the commandant of the fortress, to go and avenge the death of his relative. Permission was granted, and with a force from the garrison and a large number of Indians, he passed down the Mississippi and up the Ohio to Fort DuQuesne, of which he subsequently became the commander. From the fort he proceeded to the ground of the recent battle. Washington, finding himself confronted with greatly superior forces, fell back to Fort Necessity, a rude stockade previously erected at the Great Meadows. Thither they were followed by De Villiers with a force of 600 French and a smaller number of Indians, who took possession of an adjacent eminence and commenced firing from behind trees on the men in the fort beneath them. Animated by the cool determination of their commander, the raw provincials, so unequal in numbers and position to their assailants, for nine hours maintained their position. At length the French commander, fearing the exhaustion of his ammunition, proposed terms of capitulation, which Washington in his critical situation was compelled to accept. The terms were magnanimous, the besieged being permitted to retire with the honors of war and all their munitions, except the artillery. Upon the defeat of the Virginia forces, England and France took up the gauntlet, and the contest between the colonists became further intensified. In 1755, General Braddock arrived in Virginia with two regiments of British regulars. Washington was made one of his aids-de-camp, and afterward his force was augmented by the addition of 1,000 provincials. Thus strengthened he started for Fort DuQuesne, and at the Little Meadows received intelligence of the expected arrival of 500 troops to strengthen the garrison of the fort. Leaving Col. Dunbar with 800 men to bring up his stores, he hastened forward with the remainder to reach the fort in advance of the reinforcements. Crossing the Monongahela he pushed forward with so much rapidity that he seldom took time to reconnoitre the woods and tangled thickets through which he was passing. In the meantime the commandant at Fort DuQuesne, apprised by the French and Indian scouts of the approach of the British force, sent M. Beaujeu with a force of 250 French and 600 Indians to check their advance. Seven miles from the fort they concealed themselves on the borders of a ravine through which Braddock must pass, and awaited his arrival. As soon as his men entered the hollow, the concealed enemy opened upon those in front, and the rear forces pushed rapidly forward to support them. Before this could be effected, the advanced columns fell back in a heap on the artillery, and the army became greatly confused. At this juncture the Virginia forces, contrary to orders, took positions behind trees and fought till all were killed except thirty men. The regulars, remaining in a compact body, were terribly cut to pieces. Braddock received a mortal wound and

*Bancroft.

died in the camp of Col. Dunbar, whither with the shattered remnants of his army he retreated. Never before had the Indians received such a harvest of scalps as that gathered from the fatal field. Dressed in the laced hats and scarlet coats of the dead, they celebrated the victory by exhibiting their personal decorations and firing guns, which were answered by the artillery of the fort.

When the news of the battle became known the two belligerents increased their forces, and in 1754 Fort Duquesne again became the objective point of an English army. Gen. Forbes, with a force of 7,000, approached it, and the garrison of Illinois and other troops being unable to cope with such a formidable army, dismantled the fort and retired to different parts of the West. A portion of the fugitives under M. Massac descended the Ohio river and built a fort on the Illinois side of the stream, forty miles from its mouth. The fort bore the name of its founder, and was furnished with a small garrison till the close of the war. Such was the origin of the last French fort built on the Ohio, divested of the romance which fable has thrown around its name.* In the course of the struggle Ticonderoga, Crown Point and Niagara, fell before the victorious arms of England, and finally it terminated in 1759 by the capture of Quebec. As the result of the contest on the Plains of Abraham, Illinois and its vast resources became the heritage of a different race. Anglo-Saxon energy and progress were now to gather from its prolific soil treasures far exceeding in value the exhaustless mines of gold, which had haunted the imagination of its Gallic inhabitants, even if their dreams had been realized. In this closing battle the colossal power of France in North America received a fatal blow. From her first permanent settlement on the St. Lawrence she held dominion over its waters for a period of 150 years. The Teutonic race, with its partiality for individual rights, for self-government and freedom, now obtained the dominion of a continent from the Gulf of Mexico to the Pole, and the English tongue, whose utterance 150 years before was confined to two small islands on the western verge of Europe, was now to become the language of a continent, and ultimately, perhaps, a universal vehicle for the expression of human thought.

*[NOTE.—Jas. Hall, in his Sketches of the West, says: "The French had also a fort on the Ohio, about 36 miles above the junction of that river with the Mississippi, of which the Indians obtained possession by a singular stratagem. A number of them appeared in the day time on the opposite side of the river, each covered with a bearskin, walking on all-fours, and imitating the motions of that animal. The French supposed them to be bears, and a party crossed the river in pursuit of them. The remainder of the troops left their quarters and resorted to the bank of the river, in front of the garrison, to observe the sport. In the meantime, a large body of warriors, who were concealed in the woods near by, came silently up behind the fort, entered it without opposition, and very few of the French escaped the carnage. They afterward built another fort on the same ground, which they called *Massacre*, in memory of this disastrous event, and which retained the name of Fort Massac after it passed into the hands of the American government." The Rev. J. M. Peck, in his "Annals of the West," thinks "the foregoing statement is a truthful one, according to all the traditional evidence we can collect." Dr. Lewis Beck's Gazeteer of Illinois and Missouri contains the same story, as also Reynold's Pioneer History of Illinois; and in his Life and Times, the latter says: "Fort Massacre was established by the French about the year 1711, and was also a missionary station It was only a small fortress until the war of 1755 between the English and French. In 1756 th fort was enlarged and made a respectable fortres, considering the wilderness it was in. It was at this place where the Christian missionaries instructed the Southern Indians in the gospel precepts, and it was here also that the French soldiers made a resolute stand against the enemy." The place is also referred to some times as the "old Cherokee Fort." The Letters Edifiantes indicate it to have been a mission and trading post about 1711 In 1800 two companies of U. S. troops were stationed at Fort Massac and a few families resided in the vicinity. In 1855, says Reynolds, he visted the site. The walls of the ruins were 135 feet square, pallisaded with earth between, and with strong bastions at each angle. Three or four acres were beautifully gravelled with pebbles from the river, on the north of the fort, as a parade ground. The site is a beautiful one.]

CHAPTER XIII.

1759–1763—THE CONSPIRACY OF PONTIAC—ATTACK UPON DETROIT—DESTRUCTION OF BRITISH POSTS AND SETTLEMENTS.

It has already been stated that the downfall of Quebec was the overthrow of French power in North America. It was not, however, until 1760, when the feeble and disheartened garrison of Montreal capitulated without resistance, that Canada and its dependencies were surrendered to the British. The overthrow of French supremacy was now assured, but the recoil of the blow which had smitten it down was the cause of another great struggle more desolating and widely extended than the first, but ended without accomplishing any political results. In the second contest the red man became the principal actor and exhibited a degree of sagacity and constancy of purpose never before witnessed in the history of his warfare. The English, to reap the fruits of their victory at Quebec, sent Major Robert Rogers to take possession of the outposts on the frontier. He was a native of New Hampshire, and his startling adventures in the recent colonial struggle had made him the model hero of New England firesides. As he coasted along the southern shore of Lake Erie in the early part of November, 1760, on his way to Detroit, it suddenly became cold and stormy, and he determined to put ashore and wait the return of pleasant weather. A camp was soon formed in the adjacent forest, then clothed in the fading hues of Autumn, when a number of chiefs made their appearance and announced themselves as an embassy from Pontiac. The day did not pass away before the daring chief himself came to the camp and demanded of Rogers his business in the country. The latter replied that he was on his way to Detroit to make peace with the white men and Indians. Pontiac listened with attention and said he would stand in his path till morning, and after inquiring if they needed anything which his country afforded withdrew. This was Rogers' first interview with the Napoleon of his race, whose great conspiracy forms the subject of this chapter.

According to tradition, he was of medium height, commanding appearance, and possessed a muscular frame of great symmetry and vigor. His complexion was darker than usual with individuals of his race; his features stern, bold, and irregular, and his bearing that of a person accustomed to surmount all opposition by the force of an imperious will. He was generally clad in a scanty cincture girt about his loins, with his long black hair flowing loosely behind, but on public occasions he plumed and painted

137

after the manner of his tribe. On the following morning, in company with his chiefs, he again visited the camp and told Rogers he was willing to be at peace with the English and suffer them to remain in his country as long as they treated him and his countrymen with due deference and justice. Hitherto he had been the devoted friend of the French, and the motive which now actuated him was apparent. Shrewd, politic, and ambitious, he sagaciously concluded that the power of France was declining, and it might be best to secure the good will of the English. He hoped by the aid of such powerful allies to extend his influence over the tribes of his own race, and flattered himself that they also would treat him with the deference which had previously been accorded him by the French. Rogers had several interviews with him, and was struck with the native vigor of his understanding and the wonderful power he exercised over those about him.

The storm abating, Rogers and his men resumed their voyage up the lake. A messenger had been sent in advance to notify Captain Beletre, the French Commandant at Detroit, that Canada had surrendered, and that an English force was on its way to relieve him. This officer was greatly incensed at the reception of the news; treated it as an informal communication, and stirred up the Indians to resist the advance of Rogers. When, therefore, the latter arrived at the mouth of the Detroit, and was about to ascend it, he found four hundred Indian warriors ready to dispute his further progress. Pontiac however, whose vigilance was ever on the alert, interposed in behalf of his new friends, and they were permitted to reach Detroit without further opposition. Rogers immediately took possession of the fort, and the French garrison defiled out on the plain and laid down their arms. As the French colors were lowered from the flagstaff, and those of England hoisted aloft, the spectacle was greeted by the yells of 700 Indian warriors. The Canadian militia were next disarmed, and the Indians, unable to comprehend why so many should submit to so few, regarded with astonishment what they considered as obsequious conduct on the part of their recent allies. Nothing is so effective in winning the respect of savages as an exhibition of power, and hence the Indians formed the most exalted conceptions of English prowess, but were greatly surprised at their sparing the lives of the vanquished.

Thus, on the 29th of November, 1760, Detroit passed into the hands of the English. The French garrison was sent prisoners down the lake, while the Canadian residents were suffered to retain their houses and lands on the condition of their swearing allegiance to the government. Officers were sent to the southwest to take possession of Forts Miami and Watannon,* the first situated on the head waters of the Maumee, and the latter on the Wabash not far from the site of the present town of Lafayette. Rogers next started to relieve the forts on the upper lakes, but was prevented by the gathering ice and storms of Lake Huron. The following season, however, the forts at the head of Green Bay and the mouth of the St. Joseph, and those on the straits of St. Mary and Mackinaw, were garrisoned by small detachments of English troops. The flag of France still waved over the plains of Illinois,

*Ouiatenon.

which was not included in the stipulations entered into at Montreal.

The country had not long been in the possession of England before a wide-spread feeling of dissatisfaction pervaded its inhabitants. The French element of the population, having their national hate of the English intensified by years of disastrous warfare, left their homes in Canada and settled in Illinois. Here they continued to cherish their animosity, and whenever an opportunity offered, were ever ready to embrace any scheme that might injure the objects of their ill will. In common with their brethren of Illinois, they still hoped that Canada might be restored to France, and no effort was spared by either to bring about this much desired result. Canada was powerless, yet Illinois, her intimate neighbor and sympathizer, was still an untrameled province of France, and now became the depot of supplies and the centre of French intrigues; all looking forward to the consummation of this object. The Indians, whose good will they had long since won by a conciliatory policy, they found ready instruments for the execution of their designs. Accordingly, swarms of French traders and Canadian refugees issued from the head-waters of the Illinois and other points of egress, and spreading over the conquered territory, held councils with the Indians in the secret places of the forests. At these secluded meetings they urged the excited savages to take up arms against the English, who they declared were endeavoring to compass their destruction by hedging them in with forts and settlements on one hand, and stirring up the Cherokees to attack them on the other. To give effect to these fabrications, they added more potent incentives of guns, ammunition and clothing, which the English had refused to grant them. These, long furnished by France, had now become a necessity, but England had incurred heavy expenses in the recent war, and it became necessary for her either to withhold or deal them out with scanty and reluctant hands. Want, suffering, and in some instances death, was the result which, without the aid of French machinations, was sufficient to make them dislike the English. Formerly, under the mild sway of France, when the chiefs visited the forts they were received with the greatest politeness and hospitality by the officers, and the petty annoyances of their men were disregarded. Now, when in their intrusive manner they came about the posts, they heard only words of reproach and abrupt orders to depart, frequently enforced by blows from ruffian soldiers. The intercourse of French traders had always been courteous and respectful, while those of the English treated them as inferiors, frequently outraged their families, and in various ways gave them an unfavorable opinion of the nation which now laid claim to their country.

Under these circumstances Pontiac, although he had wavered in his allegiance to the French so far as to permit Rogers to occupy the fort at Detroit, began to feel his partiality for his old friends returning. The Sacs, his native tribe,* under the immediate influence of the Illinois French, were among the first to espouse their cause, and it may safely be assumed that if he was not instrumen-

---

*In the Hist. Col. of Mass., 2nd series, the report of Morse, 1822, on the Sac and Fox wars against the Illinois, and the life of Tecumseh, he is spoken of as a Sac. Several tribes were ambitious to claim his lineage. His residence among the Ottawas may have been due to his partiality for their reputation as warriors.

tal in bringing about the result, he was not long in following their
example. By his own inherent powers and assistance obtained
from the French, he had become the acknowledged head of the
tribes of Illinois, and the nations dwelling in the region of the great
lakes and the Upper Mississippi. Says Captain Morris, who was
sent West by General Gage to conciliate the tribes of Illinois:
" This chief has a more extensive power than was ever known
among the Indians, for every chief used to command his own
tribe, but 18 nations by French intrigue have been brought to
unite and choose him as their commander." Thus the flame kindled in Illinois, and finding material in many other localities upon
the eve of ignition, as we shall see, spread farther and wider, until
all British America became involved in the fiery ordeal of war.
Operated upon by so many causes of irritation and apprehension, it
was impossible for a people so excitable as the Indians to long
remain quiet. Accordingly, as early as 1761, Maj. Campbell, then in
command of Detroit, received intimations that they meditated an
tack upon his fort, and upon further inquiry learned that there was
to be a general uprising of all the tribes from Illinois to Nova Scotia,
and that Forts Pitt and Niagara were also to be attacked. Intelligence of this discovery was immediately transmitted to the commanders of the threatened points, and the calamity averted. This
and another similar plot detected and suppressed the following summer, were only the precursors of the coming storm that swept the
whole country as with the besom of destruction. A plot was next
conceived in the scheming brain of Pontiac to attack all the English forts on the same day, and after having massacred their
unsuspecting garrisons, to turn upon the defenseless settlements
and continue the work of death until the entire English population, as the Indians fondly hoped and expected, should be driven
into the sea. For comprehensiveness of design and successful
execution, no similar conspiracy can be found in the annals of
Indian warfare.

Pontiac was now 50 years of age and brought to the contest a
judgment matured by the past experience of his adventurous life.
Before the breaking out of the French war, he had saved Detroit
from the overwhelming attack of some discontented tribes of the
North. During the war he fought valiantly for France, and is said
to have commanded the Ottawas at the defeat of Braddock and
materially contributed to his overthrow, For his devotion and
courage, he was presented with a full French uniform by the Marquis Montcalm, only a short time before the famous battle on the
Plains of Abraham. After the defeat of the French and the arrival
of Rogers, as previously intimated, he manifested a desire to cultivate the friendship of the conquerors, but was greatly disappointed
in the advantages he expected to derive from their influence. His
sagacious mind discovered in the altered posture of affairs the great
danger which threatened his race. The equilibrium hitherto
subsisting between the French and English, gave the Indians the
balance of power, and both parties were compelled to some extent
to respect their rights. Under English domination their importance as allies was gone and their doom already sealed, unless they
could re-establish the power of the French and use it as a check to
the encroachments of the English. Filled with this idea and fired
by patriotism and ambition, he now sent embassadors to the nations

of the upper lakes, to those on the Illinois, Mississippi and Ohio, and as far southward as the Gulf of Mexico. His emissaries, bearing the war belt and bloody hatchet as emblems of their mission, passed from tribe to tribe, and everywhere the dusky denizens of the forest eagerly assembled to hear the words of the great war chief. The principal of the embassy, holding aloft the emblems of war, with violent gesticulations delivered the fiery message previously prepared by Pontiac for this purpose. The attending chiefs and warriors, moved by these impassioned appeals, pledged themselves to assist in the war, and the fervor thus excited rapidly spread till the whole Algonquin race was aglow with enthusiasm.

The attack was to be made in May, 1763, only one month after the treaty of Paris, by which Illinois and all the vast possessions of France, east of the Mississippi, passed under the dominion of Great Britain. This event was one of the three important steps by which Illinois passed from a French province to its present position as a member of the American republic, the first being foreshadowed in the triumph of Wolfe on the Plains of Abraham, the second in the conquests of Clark, and the last in the battle of Yorktown. In accordance with the requirements of the cession, the posts of southern Louisiana were surrendered to British garrisons. In Illinois, owing to the impenetrable barrier of hostile savages, which surrounded it, this was impossible, and the French officers were empowered by Sir Jeffrey Amherst, the British Commander-in-chief, to retain their position till this difficulty could be overcome. In the exercise of this trust they betrayed the confidence reposed in them by furnishing the Indians with large supplies of guns and ammunition, and for a long time concealed the transfer which had been made, lest the knowledge of it might cause the Indians to relax their efforts in the prosecution of the war. But for this neglect of duty, the war which followed might have been either averted or its virulent character greatly modified. The king, in parceling out his newly acquired domain among the colonists, retained the valley of the Ohio and the region adjacent as a reservation for the Indians. The timely publication of his order in this respect would have prevented the intrusion of the settlers upon these lands, and thus have removed a principal cause of irritation among the Indians dwelling along the English frontiers. But while the benevolent intentions of the king slumbered in the breasts of unfaithful stewards, the forests were alive with preparations for strife and carnage. Indian maidens were chanting the war song; magicians were retiring to the gloom of rocky defiles and caverns to fast and learn the will of the Great Spirit in the coming struggle, while in the glare proceeding from hundreds of nightly camp fires, chiefs and warriors were enacting the savage pantomime of battle.

The warlike spirit of the Indians gave great satisfaction to the French inhabitants of Illinois, who had so unwillingly been made subjects of Britain. To impart additional life to their preparations, they declared that the King of France had of late years fallen asleep, and during his slumbers the English had taken possession of Canada, but that now he was awake again and his armies were advancing up the St. Lawrence and Mississippi, to drive out the intruders from the homes of his red children.

In accordance with the arrangement of Pontiac, the different posts were to be attacked on the same day by the adjacent Indians. The arch conspirator himself with some of his tribes lived in the vicinity of Detroit, and that point soon became the focus of the bloody struggle. To institute preliminary arrangements, a place of rendezvous was selected on the river below the town, and messengers sent to summon the tribes to meet him in council. In obedience to the call straggling bands of Ottawas, Wyandots, Chippewas, and Pottawatomies, of all ages, sexes and conditions, for several days were seen emerging from the forests. Squaws accompanied by swarms of naked children, came to attend to the domestic arrangements of the camps; youthful gallants attended by maidens, bedecked with feathers and ruddy with paint, were present looking love at each other and enjoying the social amusements of savage life. But the most important personages were stalwart warriors, who, while waiting the arrival of tardy delegagations, lounged the lazy hours away in feasting and gambling. At length, on the 27th of April, the last stragglers had arrived, when, variously costumed and armed after the manner of their respective tribes, they seated themselves in circles on the ground. Pontiac immediately appeared in their midst and with impassioned voice commenced his address. Contrasting the English with the French, he declared the former had treated himself with contempt and his countrymen with injustice and violence. Presenting a broad belt of wampum, he informed his wild auditors that he had received it from the great father, the King of France, who had heard the voice of his red children; had arisen from his sleep and was sending his great war canoes up the St. Lawrence and the Mississippi to wreak vengeance on his enemies, and that the French and their red brethren would again fight side by side as when many moons since they destroyed the army of their enemies on the banks of the Monongahela. Having awakened in his hearers their native passion for war and blood, he next appealed to their superstitions, by relating a legend composed by one of their magicians, which enjoined upon them as a duty to drive the "dogs that wear red clothing into the sea," and made known to them the best method of doing it. In conclusion he told them that the work must commence at Detroit; that he would gain admittance to the fort, and having thus learned the situation and strength of the garrison, at another council he would explain to them the plan of attack.

The object of the convocation was now consummated, and long before the morning sun broke through the mists that hung over the river, the savage multitude had disappeared in the gloomy recesses of the forest. Nothing remained to tell of the night's carousals and intrigues but the smouldering embers of camp fires and the slender frames of several hundred Indian lodges. Pontiac, impatient for the execution of his design as previously announced, advanced with 40 warriors, and presenting himself at the gate of the fort asked permission to dance before the officers of the garrison. After some hesitation permission was granted, and he and 30 of his men filed up to the residence of Major Gladwyn, then in command of the fort. The dance was commenced, and while the officers and men gathered round to witness the performance the remaining 10 Indians strolled about the premises to make observations. When the different parts of the fort had been examined the 40 retired, without causing the slightest suspicion as to the object which induced the visit. Messengers were again sent to summon the chiefs to meet in the village of the Pottawatomies. Here a hundred wily conspirators seated themselves in the council hall of the town to perfect in the darkness of night the black scheme they had concocted for the destruction of the fort. Fitful flashes from the fire in the centre of the room fell upon features stolid and immovable as if cast in iron, despite the fierce passions that rankled in the breasts beneath them. As Pontiac in an exciting harrangue reiterated the wrongs they had sustained at the hands of the English, and made known his plan of attack, deep guttural expressions of approval rose from his statue-like audience. Under pretense of holding a council he proposed to obtain admittance to the fort for himself and principal chiefs, and while in conference with the officers, with concealed weapons they would put them to death. Meanwhile the Indians loitering about the palisade were to rush on the unsuspecting garrison and inflict on them a similar fate.

Detroit, now threatened with destruction, was founded in 1701 by La Mott Cadilac, who subsequently became the Governor-General of Louisiana and the partner of Crozat. Rogers, who visited it at the close of the French war, estimated its population and that of the adjacent settlements at 2500 souls. The fort which surrounded the town was a palisade 25 feet high, furnished with bastions at the four angles and block-houses over the gate ways. On the same side of the river, and a little below the fort, was the village of the Pottawatomies; southeasterly, on the other side, was that of the Wyandots, while on the same bank, 5 miles above, was the town of the Ottawas. The river, about half a mile in width opposite the fort, flowed through a landscape of unrivaled beauty. In its pure waters were glassed the outlines of the noble forests that grew on its banks. Farther back white Canadian cottages looked cosily out of the dark green foliage, while in the distance Indian wigwams sent up wreathy columns of smoke high in the transparent northern atmosphere. Pontiac, the master spirit of this sylvan paradise, dwelt on an island at the outlet of Lake St. Clair, and like Satan of old revolved in his powerful mind schemes for marring its beauty and innocence. Though he was friendly to the French they seemed to apprehend some coming disaster. The October preceding the outbreak dark clouds gathered over the town and settlement, and drops of rain fell of a strong sulphurous odor, and so black the people are said to have collected and used them for ink. Many of the simple Canadians, refusing to accept a scientific explanation of the phenomenon, thought it was the precurser of some great calamity.

Although breathing out vengeance and slaughter against the English, the designs of the chief were to be defeated. According to local tradition, on the afternoon of the 6th of May, the day preceding the intended assault, intelligence of the conspiracy was communicated to Gladwyn by a beautiful Chippewa girl, who had formed for him an attachment and wished to save his life. Ostensibly she visited the fort to deliver a pair of ornamental moccasins which he had requested her to make. After delivering them, she was seen, late in the afternoon, lingering about the fort, with a dejected

countenance. Gladwyn himself at length noticed her altered manner, and asked the cause of her trouble. When assured that she
would not be betrayed, she stated that on the following day, Pontiac
and 60 chiefs, with guns concealed under their blankets, would visit
the fort to hold a council, and that after he had presented a peace
belt in a reversed position as a signal for attack, the chiefs were to
shoot down the officers, and their men in the streets were to murder
the garrison. Gladwyn immediately communicated what he had
heard to the garrison, and preparations were commenced to avert
the threatened calamity. Lest some wild impulse should precipitate an attack before morning, half the garrison was ordered
under arms, the number of sentinels doubled, and the officers
arranged to spend the night on the ramparts. In the immediate
vicinity of the fort there was quiet, but the winds that swept
across the river bore to the listening sentinels the distant boom
of Indian drums, and the wild yells of savages performing the war
dance. The following morning, when the mist had disappeared
a fleet of canoes was seen moving across the river, filled
with savages mostly in a recumbent position, lest if seen
their numbers might excite suspicions. Presently groups of tall
warriors wrapt in blankets up to their throats were seen stalking
across the common toward the fort. These were all admitted, for
not only the garrison but the whole population of fur traders were
armed, and Gladwyn defied their treachery. It said that as
Pontiac entered, he involuntarily uttered an exclamation of
surprise and disappointment. Recovering from his consternation,
he started in the direction of the council house, followed by his
chiefs, who, notwithstanding their usual stoicism, cast uneasy
glances at the ranks of glittering steel on each side of their path-
way. Passing into the hall they found the officers fully armed and
waiting to receive them. Pontiac, observing with suspicion their
swords and pistols, asked Gladwyn why so many of his young men
were in the attitude of war. The latter, with the dissimulation
which his adversary was practicing, replied that he had ordered
his soldiers under arms for the purpose of exercise and discipline.
With evident distrust the chiefs at length sat down on mats provided for their accommodation, while Pontiac commenced speaking,
holding in his hand the wampum which was to be the signal of
attack. Though it was thought he would hardly attempt to carry
out his design under present circumstances, yet during the
delivery of his speech he was subjected to the most rigid scrutiny
by the officers. Once, it is said, he was about to give the signal,
when Gladwyn by a slight movement of the hand made it known
to the attending soldiers, and instantly the drum beat a charge
and the clash of arms was heard in the passage leading to the
room. Pontiac, confounded at these demonstrations, and seeing
the stern eye of Gladwyn fastened upon him, in great perplexity
took his seat. Gladwyn, in a brief reply, assured him that the
friendly protection of the English would be extended to his people
as long as they deserved it, but threatened the most condign punishment for the first act of aggression. The council now broke up;
the gates were thrown open, and the Indians departed. It has
been a query why the chiefs were not detained as hostages, but
the full extent of their intrigues was unknown. The whole affair

was regarded as a paroxysmal outbreak which would soon terminate if an open rupture could be avoided.

Pontiac, foiled in his attempt against the fort, was enraged and mortified, but not discouraged. He considered his escape from the fort as evidence that his designs were not fully known, and on the following morning returned with three companions and endeavored to remove the suspicions which he had excited. Immediately after his interview with Gladwyn, however, he repaired to the village of the Pottawatomies and commenced consulting with their chiefs in regard to another attempt against the fort. As the result, on the 9th of May, the common behind the fort was crowded with savages, and their chief, advancing to the gate, asked that he and his warriors might be admitted and enjoy with the garrison the fragrance of the friendly calumet. Gladwyn concisely but uncourteously replied, that "he might enter, but his rabble must remain without." Thus circumvented, he became livid with hate and defiance, and stalked off in the direction of his warriors, large numbers of whom were prostrate on the ground, and suddenly rising up, the plain, as if by magic, seemed alive with yelping creatures part man, part wolf, and part devil, who rushed upon some English inhabitants outside of the fort and put them to death. Pontiac, taking no part in the brutal butcheries of his men, immediately leaped into a canoe, and with a speed commensurate with his rage and disappointment, forced his way up the river to the village of the Ottawas. Bounding ashore and pointing across the water, with imperious voice he ordered the entire population to move to the opposite side, that the river might no longer interpose a barrier between him and his enemy. At night-fall he leaped into the central area of the village, and brandishing his tomahawk, commenced the war dance. As warrior after warrior straggled in from the day's carnage, they fell into the ring, and circling round and round, made the night hideous with unearthly yells. Long however before morning the tribe was on the opposite side of the river and pitched their camp above the mouth of the small stream known as Bloody Run, from the tragedy which was shortly afterward enacted on its banks. In the early twilight of morning, with terrific yells, they bounded naked over the fields and commenced firing on the fort. Large numbers secured a position behind a low hill, and soon its summit became wreathed with puffs of white smoke from their rapidly discharging guns. Others gathered in the rear of some out-buildings, but a cannon, charged with red-hot missiles was immediately brought to bear on the dry material, which, becoming wrapt in flames, soon caused the concealed savages to retreat with precipitation. For six hours the attack was unabated, but as the day wore away the fire slackened, and at last only a gun could be heard now and then in the direction of the retiring foe.

After this discomfiture, Pontiac augmented his forces and, on the 12th of May, renewed the attack. Day after day the fighting was continued, till the rattle of bullets on the palisade and the discordant yells of savages became familiar sounds to the garrison within. Stealthy warriors wormed their way through the tall grass, and crouching behind some sheltering object, shot arrows tipped with burning tow upon the houses within the fort. These efforts, however, proved abortive. Cisterns were dug inside to

10

quench the flames and sorties outside were made from time to time till all the adjacent orchards, fences and buildings, were leveled to the ground, and no screen was left to conceal a lurking foe.

The Indians, expecting to take the fort at a single blow, had failed to provide for a protracted siege. Their numbers daily augmenting by the arrival of straggling bands of warriors from Illinois and other parts of the West and South, the question of food soon became an important consideration. To obtain it they had already irritated the Canadian farmers by committing depredations upon their stock, and a delegation of their head men called on Pontiac to remonstrate against these outrages. He admitted the truth of the allegations, expressed regret for the injuries they had sustained, and at once instituted means for obtaining supplies without their repetition in the future. He visited the different Canadian families, making a careful estimate of their provisions, levied upon each a proportionate amount for the sustenance of the assembled tribes, now numbering nearly 1,000 warriors and more than 2,000 women and children. The levies thus made were brought into camp, and a commissary appointed to prevent the excessive eating and waste which the savage always practices when unrestricted in his access to food. Pontiac, being unable to make immediate compensation, gave promissory notes, drawn on birch bark and signed with the figure of an otter, the totem of his family. To his credit it is said these were all afterward honorably paid. This approach to the usages of civilized life was doubtless suggested by some of his Canadian allies, yet his ready adoption of them indicates a sagacity which is without a parallel in the history of his race. In the prosecution of the siege he also endeavored to obtain from the Canadians the method of making approaches to a fort as practiced in civilized warfare. Likewise, to aid his undisciplined warriors, he sent embassadors to M. Neyon, the commandant of Fort Chartres, for regular soldiers. This officer had no soldiers at his disposal, but abundantly furnished munitions in their stead. Says Sir William Johnson, Superintendent of Indian affairs :

"It now appears from the very best authorities, and can be proven by the oath of several respectable persons, prisoners among the Indians of Illinois, and from the account of the Indians themselves, that not only many French traders, but also the French officers, went among the Indians, as they said, fully authorized to assure them that the French King was determined to support them to the utmost, and not only invited them to visit Illinois, where they were plentifully supplied with ammunition and other necessaries, but also sent several canoe loads at different times up the Illinois river to the Miamis, as well as up the Ohio to the Shawnees and Delawares."

Thus, while Detroit was the scene of the principal outbreak of the war, Illinois more largely than any other place furnished the means to put it in motion and keep it alive. But while other localities were bleeding and sore from the vengeful thrusts of the strife, the Illinois Frenchmen, caressed and protected by savage admirers, hunted and fished as usual in the peaceful forests and gentle rivers of his western paradise.

As the perils were thickening around Detroit, there came vague rumors from time to time of settlements destroyed, forts attacked and garrisons butchered. These flying reports were soon followed by definite information that, with the exception of Detroit, all the posts scattered at wide intervals throughout the vast forests west of Forts Pitt and Niagara, had fallen into the hands of the enemy. The first reliable evidence of this kind was the appearance of a party of warriors in the rear of Detroit, bearing aloft a number of scalps taken from victims they had slain in the capture of Fort Sandusky. Ensign Paully, in command of the fort at the time, and subsequently adopted by one of the tribes near Detroit, wrote to Gladwyn, giving an account of the capture. Seven Indians called at the fort, and being intimately acquainted with the garrison, were readily admitted. Two of the party seated themselves on each side of Paully, and after lighting their pipes, with feigned indifference commenced a conversation, during which they suddenly seized and disarmed him: Simultaneously a discordant din of yells and the clashing of arms was heard without, and when Paully afterward was taken from the room by his captors, he beheld the parade ground strewn with the mangled bodies of his men. At night he was conducted to the lake in the light of the burning fort and started over its still waters for Detroit.

On the 15th of June, a number of Pottawatomies with some prisoners, who proved to be Ensign Schlosser, the commander of Fort St. Joseph,* and three of his private soldiers. Their captors had come to exchange them for some of their own men, who for some time had been retained as prisoners in the fort. After this was effected, the Englishmen related the story of their capture. Early in the morning preceding the attack, the neighborhood of the fort was enlivened by the appearance of a large number of Pottawatomies, who stated that they had come to visit their relations residing on the river St. Joseph. Hardly had the commandant time to suspect danger when he was informed that the fort was surrounded by hundreds of Indians, evidently intending to make an assault. Schlosser hastened to get his men under arms, but before this could be effected an attack was made, and in a few minutes the fort was plundered and all its garrison slain, except himself and the prisoners mentioned.

Only three days later a Jesuit priest arrived at Detroit, bringing with him a letter from Captain Etherington detailing the capture of the fort at Mackinaw, of which he was commander. For several successive days the Chippewas had been assembling on a plain near the fort and playing games of ball. Finally, on the 14th of June, while engaged at this pastime, the ball was intentionally thrown near the fort, and the Indians, rushing up as if to get it, seized Captain Etherington and Lieut. Lesley standing near the gate, and hurried them off to the woods. At the same time, another party rushed into the fort, and with hatchets furnished by their squaws, who had previously entered with them, concealed under their blankets, slew 15 of the garrison, while the remainder and all the English fur traders were made prisoners.

The next disaster of this kind was the loss of Fort Watannon. A letter was received from Lieut. Jenkins, the commanding officer, informing Gladwyn that on the 1st of June he and several of his men were seized by strategy, and the rest of the garrison, being without a leader, surrendered. The Indians afterward apologized for their conduct by declaring the attack was not the result of their own inclinations but due to the pressure which had been brought

*Originally Miami.

to bear on them by surrounding tribes. This plea may have been true, for they were farther removed from English influence than most of the other tribes and hence more pacific.

Fort Miami, on the Maumee, in command of Ensign Holmes, added another to the list of captured forts. Though this officer had detected and circumvented a previous attempt against the fort, his cunning adversaries at length triumphed over his vigilance. On the 27th of May an Indian girl, who was living with him, told him that a squaw lay sick in a neighboring wigwam, and desired him to administer medical relief. Placing the utmost confidence in the girl, he followed her till they came in sight of a number of lodges, when she pointed out to him the one containing the invalid and withdrew. Holmes, unsuspicious of danger, continued on his errand of mercy till as he neared the wigwam two guns flashed from behind it, and his lifeless body fell prostrate on the ground. Exultant yells of savages followed the report of the guns, and a Canadian soon came to the fort and demanded its surrender, informing the garrison that their lives would be spared if they complied, but in case of refusal their claims to mercy would be forfeited. Taken by surprise, and without a commander to direct them, they threw open the gates and gave themselves up as prisoners.

With the previous disasters fresh in the minds of the beleaguered garrison at Detroit, on the 22d of June, their attention was attracted to the opposite side of the river where they saw the savages conducting Ensign Christie, the commandant of Presque Isle, and the prisoners to the camp of Pontiac. Christie afterward escaped and related the particulars of the seige and surrender of his post, situated near the present town of Erie on the southern shore of the lake after which it was named. On the 15th of June it was surrounded by 200 Indians, and the garrison immediately retired to the blockhouse, the most impregnable part of the fortifications. The savages, sheltered in a ravine, close by, sent volleys of bullets at the port holes and burning balls of pitch upon the roof and against the sides of the building. Repeatedly it took fire, and finally the barrels of water which had been provided for extinguishing the flames were all exhausted. There was a well in the parade ground, but it was instant death to approach it, and they were compelled to dig another in the blockhouse. Meanwhile the enemy had made a subterncan passage to the house of the commandant and set it on fire, and the walls of the blockhouse near by were soon wrapt in a sheet of flame. The well was now complete and the fire subdued, but the men were almost suffocated by heat and smoke. While in this condition they learned that another more effectual attempt would soon be made to burn them, and at the instance of the enemy they agreed to capitulate. Parties met for this purpose, and after stipulating that the garrison should march out and retire unmolested to the nearest post, the little fortress which had been defended with so much valor was surrendered. Notwithstanding the terms agreed upon, a part of the men were taken as prisoners to the camp of Pontiac, and part bedecked as warriors were adopted by the different tribes of the conquerers.

The destruction of Laboeuf and Venango, on the head waters of the Alleghany, closes the black catalogue of captured posts.

On the 18th of June, a large number of Indians surrounded the former, the only available defence of which was a block-house. Fire arrows were showered upon it, and by midnight, the upper story was wrapt in flames. The assailants gathered in front and eagerly watched for the inmates to rush out of the burning building, that they might shoot them. In the meantime, however, they hewed an opening through the rear wall, and passing out unperceived, left the savages exulting in the thought that they were perishing in the flames. But from Venango, destroyed about the same time, not a single person escaped or was left alive to tell of their fate. Not long afterward it was learned from Indians who witnessed its destruction, that a party of warriors entered it under the pretext of friendship, and closing the gates behind them, butchered all the garrison except the principal officer, whom they tortured over a slow fire several successive nights till life was extinct. Forts Pitt and Niagara were also attacked, but like that of Detroit, their garrisons proved too strong for the savage assailants who sought their destruction.

But the destruction of life and property in the forts was only a fraction of the losses. The storm of savage vengeance fell with appalling fury on the frontiers of Virginia, Maryland, and Pennsylvania, and for hundreds of miles north and south they became a continuous theatre of rapine, slaughters, and burnings, without a parallel in all past and succeeding years. Bands of infuriated savages skulking in the forests, suddenly bounded forth from their lurking places and surrounded the unprotected homes of settlers. The startled inmates where scarcely aware of danger before they became the victims of the most ferocious butcheries. Mothers were compelled to stand by and witness the brains of their helpless innocents dashed out against the walls of their dwellings; daughters were carried away into captivity to become the wives of their savage captors, while fathers and sons were bound to trees and roasted over slow-burning fires to protract and intensify their sufferings. Whole settlements in the valley retreats of the Alleghanies, where a prolific soil and industry were rapidly multiplying the necessaries of life, were entirely depopulated. Fields ripening for harvest were laid waste; herds of domestic animals, like their owners, were killed; dwellings were burnt to the ground, and where plenty and happiness had once lived together in peace, there was now only desolation and death. Thousands of fugitives fled to the interior towns and made known the fearful tragedies they had witnessed, and such had been the deep dissimulation of the savages, the story of their butcheries preceded even the faintest suspicions of danger.

CHAPTER XIV.

SIEGE OF DETROIT—PONTIAC RALLIES THE WESTERN TRIBES—HIS SUBMISSION AND DEATH.

———

Detroit was still the head of savage machinations and the home of the arch conspirator who, with the complacency of a Nero, looked round on the constantly widening circle of ruin and death. The garrison of which he had the immediate custody was confined, as if in a vice, to the narrow confines of the fort. The attempt of Cyler to reinforce it, terminated in the defeat and death of some 60 of his men. Most of the unfortunates taken alive were carried to the camp of Pontiac, where some were pierced with arrows, some had their hands and feet cut off, while others were fastened to trees and children employed to roast them alive. For several days after death had ended their sufferings, their bodies were seen floating down the river by the fort, still ghastly with the brutal atrocities which had caused their death. No expedient was left untried which might injure the besieged. Huge fire rafts were set afloat down the river to burn two small schooners opposite the fort. On one occasion a faint light was descried on the river above, which grew larger and brighter as it descended the stream. Presently it loomed up in a violent conflagration and, fortunately passing between the vessels and the fort, revealed with the light of day the tracery of cordage and spars on one side, and the long line of palisades on the other. The distant outlines of the forest and a dark multitude of savages were plainly visible on the opposite side of the stream, the latter watching the effects of their artifice as the crackling, glimmering mass floated down with the current of the waters, in which its fires were finally quenched. Though all the arts of savage warfare were employed to prevent the reinforcement of the fort, it was at length accomplished, and an assault made on the camp of Pontiac. In this fierce conflict, which rose to the dignity of a pitched battle, the English were defeated with a heavy loss, and compelled to retire to the fort for safety.

Attracted by this success, large numbers of warriors flocked to the standard of Pontiac, and the spirit of his men, previously beginning to flag, was revived and the siege prosecuted with unexampled vigor till the last of September. The Indian is naturally fickle and impulsive, and perhaps the history of his race does not furnish another instance of such protracted effort and constancy as this. Their remarkable perseverance must, no doubt, be attributed to their intense hatred of the English, the hope of assistance from France, and the controlling influence of Pontiac. Their ammunition, however, was now exhausted, and as intelligence had been received that Major Wilkins, with a large force, was on his way to

Detroit, many of them were inclined to sue for peace. They feared the immediate consequences of an attack, and proposed by lulling the English into security, to retire unmolested to their winter hunting ground and renew offensive operations in the spring. A chief of the Chippewas, therefore, visited the fort and informed Gladwyn that the Pottawatomies, Wyandots and his own people were sorry for what they had done, and desired thereafter to live in peace. The English officer well knew the emptiness of their pretentions, but granted their request that he might have an opportunity of replenishing the fort with provisions. The Ottawas, animated by the unconquerable spirit of Pontiac, continued a disultory warfare till the first of October, when an unexpected blow was dealt the imperious chief, and he, too, retired from the contest.

General Amherst, now aware that the occupation of the forts in Illinois by French garrisons greatly served to protract and intensify the war, would fain have removed them, but still found it impossible to break through the cordon of savage tribes which girt it about. Pontiac had derived thence not only moral support, but large supplies of guns and ammunition,* and the only remedy of the British general was to write to M. Neyon de Villiers, instructing him to make known to the Indians their altered relations under the treaty by which the country had been transferred to England. This officer, with evident reluctance and bad grace, was now compelled to make known what he had long concealed, and accordingly wrote to Pontiac that "he could not expect any assistance from the French; that they and the English were now at peace and regarded each other as brothers, and that the Indians should abandon their hostilities, which could lead to no good result." The chieftain, enraged and mortified at having his long cherished hope of assistance dashed to the ground, with a number of his countrymen immediately departed for the country of the Maumee, intending to stir up its inhabitants and renew the contest the ensuing spring. With his withdrawal, Detroit lost its significance in the war, and its leader was to return no more except as an interceder for peace.

The winter of 1763–4 passed away without the occurrence of any event of special interest. The ensuing summer two expeditions were fitted out by the English; one intended to operate against the savages residing on the great lakes, and the other for the reduction of those living in the valley of the Ohio. Bouquet having charge of the latter, advanced from Fort Pitt, and encountering the warlike Shawnees and Delawares on the banks of the Muskingum, soon reduced them to an unconditional peace. Among the demands made by this efficient officer, was the surrender of all their prisoners. Large numbers were brought in from Illinois and the region eastward, some of whom had been captured as far back as the French and English war, and had now almost forgotten their homes and friends of childhood.†

*Says Sir William Johnson: In an especial manner the French promote the interests of Pontiac, whose influence has now become so considerable, as General Gage observes in a letter to me, that it extends even to the mouth of the Mississippi, and has been the principal cause of our not gaining possession of Illinois, which the French, as well as the Indians, are interested in preventing."

†Of the scenes attending the reunion of broken families and long sundered friends, a few incidents have been preserved and are worthy of relation A young Virginian, who had been robbed of his wife and child, enlisted in the army of Bouquet for the purpose of recovering them. After suffering the most intense anxiety, he at length discovered her in a group of prisoners, bearing in her arms a child born in captivity; but

Bradstreet, who commanded the other force, wrested from the savages the military hosts, which cunning and treachery had placed in their power. As a part of his plan, while at Detroit, he sent Captain Morris, and a number of friendly Canadians and Indians, to induce the savages of Illinois to make peace with the English. Having effected arrangements for this purpose, they ascended the Maumee in a canoe, and soon fell in with a party of some 200 Indians who treated Morris with great violence. They had come directly from the camp of Pontiac, and soon led him into the presence of the great chief, who with a scrowling brow denounced the English as liars. He then displayed a letter written by some Frenchman, though purporting to be from the King of France, which Morris declares contained the greatest calumnies that ingenious malice could devise for prejudicing the minds of the Indians against the English. The party, after being stripped of everything except their clothing, arms, and canoe, were suffered to depart. Resuming the ascent of the river, in seven days they reached Fort Miami and effected a landing. This post not having been garrisoned since its capture the preceding year, the Canadians had built their houses within its palisades, and a few Indians made it a temporary abode. A Miami village was directly opposite on the other side of the stream, while the meadows immediately around it were dotted with lodges of the Kickapoos, who had recently arrived. After getting ashore they proceeded through the meadows toward the fort, but before reaching it they were suddenly surrounded by a mob of infuriated savages, bent on putting them to death. Fortunately the chiefs interposed, and before any serious violence was offered the sudden outburst of savage passion was checked. Threatened and insulted, however, Morris was conducted to the fort and there ordered to remain, while the Canadians were forbidden to shelter him in their houses. He had not long been in this situation before two warriors entered, and with uplifted tomahawks seized and conducted him to the river. Supposing it was their intention to drown him, he was agreeably disappointed when they drew him into the water and led him safe to the opposite shore. Here he was stripped, and with his hands bound behind him, led to the Miami village, where instantly a vast concourse of savages collected about him, the majority of whom were in favor of putting him to death. A tumultuous debate on the subject soon followed, during which two of his Canadian followers made their appearance to induce the chiefs to spare his life. The nephew of Pontiac, who possessed the bold spirit of his uncle, was also present and pointed out to the rabble the impro-

the pleasure of the meeting was alloyed by the absence of another child, which had been taken from the mother and carried she knew not wither. Anxious days and weeks passed away, but no tidings of its fate were received. At length the mother, almost frenzied with despair, discovered it in the arms of an Indian and seized it with irrepressible transports of joy.

Young women, now the wives of warriors and the mothers of a mongrel offspring, were reluctantly brought into the presence of their white relatives; and children whose long residence among their captors had obliterated the remembrance of former associations, struggled lustily to escape. With the returning army they were carried to the East, where they were visited by hundreds whose relatives had been abducted by the Indians. Among the fortunate seekers was a mother, who discovered in the swarthy features of one of the rescued captives the altered lineaments of her daughter. The latter had almost forgotten her native tongue; and making no response to the words of maternal endearment, the parent wept that the child she had so often sung to sleep on her knee had now forgotten her in old age. "The humanity of Bouquet suggested an expedient: 'Sing the songs you used to sing to her when a child.' The old lady obeyed, and a sudden start, a look of bewilderment, and a passionate flood of tears restored the long lost daughter to the mother's arms."—PARKMAN.]

priety of putting him to death, when so many of their kindred were in the hands of the English at Detroit. He was accordingly released, but soon afterward again seized by a maddened chief and bound to a post. Young Pontiac, now more determined than ever, rode up and severing the cords with his hatchet, exclaimed: "I give this man his life. If any of you want English meat go to Detroit, or the lakes, and you will have plenty of it. What business have you with the Englishman, who has come to speak with us?"*

The current of feeling now began to change in favor of sparing his life, and after having violently thrust him out of the village, they suffered him to return to the fort. Here the Canadians would have treated him with kindness, but were unable to do so without exposing themselves to the fierce resentments of the savages. Despite the inauspicious commencement of the journey, Morris was still desirous of completing it, but was notified by the Kickapoos if he attempted to pass them they would certainly put him to death. He was also informed that a delegation of Shawnee warriors was on its way to the post for the same purpose. The same party, with a number of Delawares, had visited the Miamis a short time before the arrival of the embassy, to urge upon them the necessity of renewing hostilities, and much of the bad treatment to which he had been subjected was due to the feeling which they had engendered. From the fort they proceeded westward, spreading the contagion of their hostile feelings among the tribes of Illinois, and other Indians, between the Ohio and Mississippi, declaring that they would fight the English as long as the sun furnished light for the continuance of the conflict. Thus it became evident that the Shawnees and Delawares had two sets of embassadors, and while one was sent to sue for peace with Bouquet, the other was urging the neighboring tribes to renew the atrocities of war. Under these circumstances the further prosecution of the journey was impracticable, and at the earnest solicitation of his Indian and Canadian attendants, Morris decided to return. Supposing that Bradstreet was still at Detroit, he made his way thither, but found that he had gone to Sandusky. Being too much exhausted to follow him, he sent a letter detailing his hardships among the Indians, and the unfavorable issue of the expedition.

Hardly had Morris escaped from the dark forests of the Maumee before Pontiac was again in motion. Preceding his advance, a wave of tumultuous excitement swept westward to the Mississippi. M. Neyon, commandant of Fort Chartres, in the meantime had retired, and St. Ange d'Bellrive had taken upon himself the arduous duties of the vacated situation. Mobs of Illinois, and embassies from the Delawares, Shawnees, and Miamis, daily importuned him for arms and ammunition, to be used against the English. The flag of France, which they had been taught to revere, still clung to the staff on the summit of the fort, and Illinois was now the only sanctuary which remained for them to defend. While thus actuated by feelings of patriotism there were other causes which gave intensity to their zeal. The whole region bordering the Mississippi was filled with French traders, who regarded the English as dangerous rivals and were ready to resort to any expedient which might be instrumental in their expulsion

*Parkman.

from the country. Using every calumny and falsehood that malice
could suggest, to excite opposition to the objects of their jealousy,
they now told the Indians that the English were endeavoring to
stir up civil feuds among them, whereby they might fight and
destroy each other. They still insisted that the long delayed
armies of France would soon be in the country, and to keep alive
this oft repeated falsehood the traders appeared frequently in
French uniforms, representing themselves as embassadors of the
King, and sent forged letters bearing the royal signature to
Pontiac, urging him to persist in his efforts against the common
enemy.

As intimated, Pontiac, with 400 warriors, in the Autumn of
1764 crossed the Wabash to visit these tribes and give direction to
their efforts. Unshaken amidst the ruin which threatened his
race, with tireless energy he entered the villages of the Miamis,
Kickapoos, and Piankishas, and breathed into them his own
unconquerable spirit. Receiving from them promises of co-operation, he next directed his course through trackless expanses of
prairie verdure, to the homes of the Illinois. These Indians, repeatedly subdued by surrounding nations, had lost their warlike
spirit, and were reprimanded by Pontiac for their want of zeal.
Hastily collecting an assemblage, he told the cowering multitude
that "he would consume them as the fire consumes the dry grass
on the prairies if they hesitated in offering assistance." This
summary method of dealing with the tardy savages drew from
them unanimous assent to his views, and promises of assistance
which the most warlike tribes would have been unable to perform.
Leaving the Illinois, he hastened to Fort Chartres, and entered
the council hall with a retinue of 400 warriors. Assuming the
gravity and dignity characteristic of his race on public occasions.
he addressed the commandant, as follows:

"Father, we have long desired to see you, and enjoy the pleasure of taking
you by the hand. While we refresh ourselves with the soothing incense of the
friendly calumet, we will recall the battles fought by our warriors against the
enemy which still seeks our overthrow. But while we speak of their valor
and victories, let us not forget our fallen heroes, and with renewed resolves and
more constant endeavors strive to avenge their death by the downfall of our
enemies. Father, I love the French, and have led hither my braves to maintain your authority and vindicate the insulted honor of France. But you must
not longer remain inactive and suffer your red brothers to contend alone against
the foe, who seek our common destruction. We demand of you arms and
warriors to assist us, and when the English dogs are driven into the sea, we
will again in peace and happiness enjoy with you these fruitful forests and
prairies, the noble heritage presented by the Great Spirit to our ancestors."

St. Ange', being unable to furnish him with men and munitions,
offered in their stead compliments and good will. But Pontiac,
regarding his mission too important to be thus rejected, complained bitterly that he should receive such poor encouragement
from those whose wrongs he was endeavoring to redress. His
warriors pitched their lodges about the fort, and such were the
manifestations of displeasure that the commandant apprehenced
an attack. Pontiac had previously caused his wives to prepare a
belt of wampum more than six feet in length, interwoven with the
totems of the different tribes and villages still associated with him
in the prosecution of the war. While at the fort this was assigned
to a chosen band of warriors who were instructed to descend the

Mississippi, and exhibiting it to the numerous nations living on its banks, exhort them to repel all attempts which the English might make to ascend the river. They were further required to call on the governor of New Orleans and obtain the assistance which St. Ange had refused. Pontiac, aware that the Mississippi on the south, and the Ohio on the east were the channels by which Illinois was most accessible to the English, wisely determined to interpose barriers to their approach by these great highways. Not long after the departure of his warriors, tidings were received at the fort which verified the sagacity and correctness of his anticipations.

The previous spring Major Loftus, with a force of 400 men, sailed from Pensacola to New Orleans, for the purpose of ascending the Mississippi and taking possession of Fort Chartres. Being embarked in unwieldy boats, his progress was slow, and when only a short distance above the town he was unexpectedly assailed by the warriors of Pontiac. They were fired upon from both sides of the river, which, swollen by a freshet, had inundated its banks and formed swampy labyrinths, from which it was impossible to dislodge the foe. Several soldiers were killed at the first discharge, and the terrified officers immediately deciding a farther advance impossible, fell back to New Orleans. Here they found the merriment of the French greatly excited at their discomfiture, which, it was alleged, had been caused by not more than 30 warriors. Loftus, smarting under the ridicule, boldly accused the governor of having been the author of his defeat, though there was not the slightest ground for such suspicion. As the result of fear, from which he had not yet recovered, he likewise conceived the idea that the Indians intended to attack him on his return on the river below, and petitioned the governor, whom he had just accused of collusion with the savages, to interpose and prevent it. The French officer, with a look of contempt, agreed to furnish him with an escort of French soldiers, but Loftus, rejecting this humiliating offer, declared he only wanted an interpreter to confer with the Indians whom he should meet on the way. One was granted, and he sailed from Pensacola, leaving the forts of Illinois still in the hands of the French, but virtually controlled and protected by the warriors of Pontiac. After this abortive effort to reach Fort Chartres, Captain Pitman sailed from Mobile to make a second attempt. Hearing in New Orleans the commotion excited among the savages by the messengers of Pontiac, he was deterred from proceeding openly without an escort. It however occurred to him that he might reach his destination in the guise of a Frenchman, by going with a company of creole traders, but owing to the great danger of detection, this also was abandoned.

In the meantime the ambassadors of Pontiac, true to the trust reposed in them, had traversed the immense forest solitudes, watered by the tortuous windings of the Mississippi, reeking with the deadly exhalations of poisonous marshes. Visiting the tribes scattered over this vast wilderness, even to the southern extreme of Louisiana, whither the fame of Pontiac had preceded them, they infused into them a spirit of resistance to British encroachments. Next repairing to New Orleans to demand military aid, they found the inhabitants excited over the transfer of their territory to the dominion of Spain. By a special provision New

Orleans had not been included in the cession made to England east of the Mississippi, and now they had just learned that their parent country had transferred all her remaining possessions to the crown of Spain. The inhabitants cordially hated the Spaniards, and their patriotic governor, mortified at the disgrace, became the victim of a disease that shortly afterward caused his death. Bowed with disease and shame, he received the messengers of Pontiac in the council hall of the town. Besides the French officials, a number of English officers were present at the interview. The orator of the Indian deputation was a Shawnee warrior, who, displaying the great belt of wampum and pointing to the English, said:

"These red* dogs have crowded upon us more and more, and when we ask why they do it, we are told that you, our French fathers, have given them our land. But we know they have lied. These lands are neither yours nor theirs, and no man shall give or sell them without our consent. Fathers, we have always been your faithful children, and we have come to obtain from you arms to aid us in this war."

After an ineffectual attempt by the governor to allay the animosity expressed in the speech, and a promise to furnish them with supplies for their immediate wants, the council adjourned till the next day. When, however, it again assembled, the dying governor had breathed out his life. M. Aubrey, his successor, presided in his place. After one of the Indian orators, according to the solemn custom of his people, had expressed his regret for the sudden death of the governor, a Miami chief arose and said:

"Since we last sat on these seats we have heard strange words. We have learned that you, whom we have loved and served so well, have given these lands on which we dwell to our common foe. We have also ascertained that the English have forbidden you to send traders to our villages, and that you, whom we thought so great and brave, have obeyed their commands like women, leaving us to die and starve in misery. We now tell you again that these lands are ours, and moreover that we can live without your aid and hunt and fish and fight as did our ancestors before us. All we ask is the guns, the knives, and the hatchets we have worn out in fighting your battles."

To these home-thrusts of Indian invective, M. Aubrey could make but a feeble reply. Presents were distributed among them, but produced no effect on the indignant warriors, and on the morrow they commenced their ascent of the great river.

The great influence of Pontiac in Illinois convinced General Gage, the successor of General Amherst, that as long as the posts of Illinois remained in the hands of French officers and the flag of France was recognized in any part of the ceded territory, it would be impossible to eradicate from the minds of the Indians the phantom of French assistance. He therefore determined to send a force westward of sufficient magnitude to overcome all opposition, and at once terminate the war, by removing the cause. After the repulse of Loftus the southern route to Illinois was regarded as impracticable, and it was decided to send the troops by way of the Ohio. George Croghan and Lieutenant Frazer, accompanied by a small escort, were sent in advance to prepare the Indians for the advent of the contemplated expedition. Croghan had for years been a trader among the western tribes, and by the aid of his manly character had won the respect of the savages, and was well fitted for the discharge of this important trust. The party set out

*Alluding to the red coats of the British soldiers

for Fort Pitt in February, 1765, and after having penetrated snow-bound forests and mountain defiles during the rigors of a severe winter, they arrived safely at the fort. Here Croghan was detained several weeks, for the purpose of having a consultation with the Shawnees and Delawares, along whose southern border the expedition was to pass. In the meantime, fearing that the delay attending his negotiations might have a prejudicial effect upon the tribes of Illinois, he sent Frazer immediately forward to enter upon the important duties with which they had been entrusted. The icy blockade which during the winter had obstructed the navigation of the Ohio, now disappeared, and the party embarking in a canoe, descended with the current of the river near 1,000 miles without encountering opposition. But when a landing was effected the followers of Pontiac were on hand, and he met with a reception similar to that accorded to Morris the previous autumn. Buffeted and threatened with death, he abandoned the object of his visit, and fled in disguise down the river to seek a refuge among the French. The universal overthrow which had attended the efforts of the Indians in all the surrounding regions, caused them to look upon Illinois as sacred ground, and hence their determined efforts to prevent its desecration by the intrusion of their hated foe.

The English, having thus far failed to effect an entrance into the country by force and negotiations, now determined to try their hand at conciliation. They had heard of the wonderful influence exerted over the savages in this way by the French, and concluded that their own efforts might be attended with similar results. For this purpose they secured the services of a Frenchman, and sent him up the river with a boat load of goods, which he was instructed to distribute among the Indians as presents from the English. Intelligence of this movement traveled far more rapidly than the supplies, and Pontiac determined that they should subserve his own interest and not that of his enemies. He, therefore, watched the arrival of the boat, and no sooner had a landing been effected than his men leaped aboard, and having flogged the Frenchman and his crew, distributed the goods among themselves. As was customary, these supplies were soon squandered with reckless prodigality, and the savages when pressed with want turned to the French for assistance. But the latter were now expecting the arrival of a British force to take possession of the country, and fearing that punishment might overtake them for past offences, concluded it best to withhold their assistance. St. Ange and other officers, also believing that their successors would soon arrive, informed them that henceforth they must look for supplies to the English, whose good will it was now their interest to cultivate.

Hunger itself is more powerful than an "army with banners," and when the savages saw other disasters equally appalling and imminent, the most resolute warriors began to hesitate in regard to the further prolongation of the struggle. Even Pontiac, whose masculine fibre and enduring fortitude the ordinary vicissitudes of war failed to affect, began to waver when he learned that the highest French dignitaries refused to grant him aid. The expectations which had so long nerved his arm were fast vanishing, and with a sorrowful heart he beheld the vast civil and military combinations he had formed, in a state of hopeless disintegration.

Deserted by allies on every hand, there was no place of refuge whither he might fly for safety. In the south and west were fierce tribes, the hereditary enemies of his people; from the east came an overwhelming foe to engulf him, while the north, the home of his children and the scenes of his youthful activities and aspirations, was under the guns of an impregnable fortress. At present, unable to extricate himself from the labyrinth of impending dangers, he was compelled to submit and wait a future day of vengeance.

Croghan, having completed his conference with the Indians at Fort Pitt, with his own men and a number of Delaware and Shawnee warriors, on the 15th of May, 1765, started down the Ohio. With little detention, he landed on the Illinois shore, a short distance below the mouth of the Wabash.* Soon after disembarking, he was unexpectedly greeted by a shower of bullets proceeding from tangled thickets on the banks of the river, whereby 5 of his men were killed and most of the remainder wounded. Immediately following the explosion of musketry, 80 yelping Kickapoos rushed from their coverts, and disarming the English, took possession of all their personal effects. When thus rendered powerless, the assailants began to apologize for the dastardly attack. They declared to Croghan that the French had told them that his escort consisted of Cherokees, their mortal enemies, and that under this false impression, they had made the assault. This pretext was, however, another instance of the deception for which that tribe was distinguished. Though endeavoring to excuse their conduct on the plea of ignorance, it was afterward ascertained that they had dogged Croghan for several days, and knew well the character of his escort. With less government over themselves than children, and filled with the instinct of devils, their real object was to wreak vengeance on the English and gratify a rabid desire for blood.

Carefully guarded as a prisoner, Croghan was conducted up the Wabash to Vincennes, where, fortunately, he met with a number of his former friends, who not only effected his release but sharply reprimanded his captors for their unjustifiable conduct. From Vincennes he was escorted farther up the river to Fort Watanon and entertained with much apparent cordiality by Indians with whom he had been previously acquainted. Here he spent several days in receiving and shaking hands with deputations of chiefs and warriors from the surrounding region, all of whom were apparently anxious to be on friendly terms with the English, and expressed a desire for the return of peace. In contrast with these evidences of good will, a Frenchman arrived with a message from a chief living in Illinois, urging the Indians in the vicinity of the fort to put the English ambassador to death. Despite this murderous request, he was assured by his savage friends that they would not only protect his person, but assist in taking possession of the country where the hostile chief resided. Unexpectedly a

---

*"On the 6th of June they arrived at the mouth of the Wabash. Here they found a breastwork, supposed to have been erected by Indians. Six miles further, they encamped at a place called the 'old Shawnee village,' upon or near the present site of Shawneetown, which perpetuates its name. At this place they remained 6 days for the purpose of opening a friendly intercourse and trade with the Wabash tribes; and while here, Col. Croghan sent messengers with dispatches for Lord (Lieut. ?) Frazer who had gone from Fort Pitt as commandant at Fort Chartres, and also to M. St. Ange, the former French commandant."—MONNET&, 1,346.

messenger next came from St. Ange, requesting him to visit Fort Chartres and adjust affairs preparatory to his withdrawal from the fort. As this was in accordance with his intentions, he immediately set out, but had not proceeded far before he was met by Pontiac and a numerous retinue of warriors. The chief had come to offer terms of peace, and Croghan returned with him to the fort for consultation. The chiefs and warriors of the surrounding nations also met in council, and Pontiac, in the presence of the multitude, introduced the pipe of peace and expressed his concurrence in the friendly sentiments which had been interchanged at the fort before his arrival. He declared that the French had misled him with the statement that the English proposed to stir up the Cherokees against his brethren of Illinois, and thus reduce them to servitude. The English, he agreed, might take possession of Fort Chartres and the other military posts, but sagaciously intimated that the French had never purchased the lands of the Illinois, and as they lived on them by sufferance only, their successors would have no legal right to their possession. The amicable feelings manifested by the Illinois chiefs who were present, obviated the necessity of his proceeding farther westward, and he next directed his attention to the tribes of the north-east.

Accompanied by Pontiac he crossed to Fort Miami, and descending the Maumee, held conferences with the different tribes dwelling in the immense forests which shelter the banks of the stream. Passing thence up the Detroit, he arrived at the fort on the 17th of August, where he found a vast concourse of neighboring tribes. The fear of punishment, and the long privations they had suffered from the suspension of the fur trade, had banished every thought of hostility, and all were anxious for peace and its attendant blessings. After numerous interviews with different tribes in the old town hall, where Pontiac first essayed the execution of his treachery, Croghan called a final meeting on the 27th of August. Imitating the forest eloquence with which he had long been familiar, he thus addressed the convocation:

"Children, we are very glad to see so many of you present at your ancient council fire, which has been neglected for some time past. Since then high winds have blown and raised heavy clouds over your country. I now, by this belt, re-kindle your ancient fires, and throw dry wood upon it, that the blaze may ascend to heaven, so that all nations may see it and know that you live in peace with your fathers, the English. By this belt I disperse all the black clouds from over your heads, that the sun may shine clear on your women and children, and that those unborn may enjoy the blessings of this general peace, now so happily settled between your fathers, the English, and you and all your younger brethren toward the sunsetting."

Pontiac replied:

"Father, we have all smoked together out of this peace pipe, and as the Great Spirit has brought us together for good, I declare to all the nations that I have made peace with the English. In the presence of all the tribes now assembled, I take the King of England for my father, and dedicate this pipe to his use, that thenceforth we may visit him and smoke together in peace."

The object of Croghan's visit was now consummated, but before he departed he exacted from Pontiac a promise that the following spring he would repair to Oswego and enter into a treaty with Sir William Johnson, in behalf of the western nations associated with him in the war.

"In the meantime a hundred Highlanders of the 42d regiment, those veterans whose battle cry had echoed over the bloodiest fields of America, had left Fort Pitt under command of Captain Stirling, and descending the Ohio undeterred by the rigor of the season, arrived at Chartres just as the snows of early winter began to whiten the naked forests. The flag of France descended from the rampart, and with the stern courtesies of war St. Ange yielded up his post, the citadel of Illinois, to its new masters. In that act was consummated the double triumph of British power in America. England had crushed her hereditary foe; France in her fall had left to irretrievable ruin the savage tribes to whom her policy and self-interest had lent a transient support."* The doomed nations were next to seal their submission to the power which had wrought their ruin, and British sway would be complete.

Reminded of his promise to Croghan by the leafy drapery of summer, Pontiac repaired to Oswego, and for the last time appeared before the representatives of English sovereignty. In the midst of a large concourse, which the importance of the occasion had drawn together, he arose and said: "Father, we thank the Great Spirit who has given us this day of bright skies and genial warmth to consider the great affairs now before us. In his presence, and in behalf of all the nations toward the sunsetting, of which I am the master, I now take you by the hand. I call upon him to witness, that I have spoken from my heart, and in the name of the tribes which I represent, I promise to keep this covenant as long as I live." Having now fulfilled his promise, he retired from the scene of his humiliation with a sad heart. Before his fierce glance the vail which hides the present from the future was withdrawn, and he saw his people, deceived by intruding strangers, driven from the home of their ancestors and fleeing westward to perish on the desert with hunger.

After the treaty he returned to the west, and for three years buried his disappointment in the seclusion of its dark forests, providing as a common hunter for his family. In the earlier part of the year 1769, some slight disturbance occurred between the Indians of Illinois and some French traders living in and around St. Louis. Simultaneously Pontiac appeared in the excited region, but whether he was connected with the disturbance is not known. The English evidently regarded him with distrust, and determined to take his life to prevent a repetition of the bloody drama he had formerly enacted. Soon after his arrival he went to St. Louis and called on his old friend St. Ange, then in command of the Spanish garrison. For this purpose he arrayed himself in the uniform which had been presented him by Montcalm, and which he had the good taste never to wear except on important occasions. St. Ange and the principal inhabitants of the place gave him a cordial welcome, and exerted themselves to render his visit agreeable. He had been there but a few days when he heard that there was a social gathering of the Indians at Cahokia, on the opposite side of the river, and informed his friend that he would cross over and see what they were doing. St. Ange, aware of the danger he would encounter, endeavored to dissuade him from his purpose, but the chief boasting that he was not afraid of the English, departed. At Cahokia he found the Indians engaged in a drunken carousal, and soon becoming intoxicated himself, started to the neighboring woods, and shortly afterward was heard singing magic songs, in

---

*Parkman.

the mystic influence of which he reposed the greatest confidence.

There was an English trader in the village at the time, who, in common with the rest of his countrymen, regarded him with the greatest distrust, and while the oportunity was favorable determined to effect his destruction. He approached a vagabond Indian of the Kaskaskia tribe, and bribed him with a barrel of whiskey to execute his murderous intent. The assassin approached the woods, and at a favorable moment glided up behind the chief and buried his tomahawk in his brain. Thus basely terminated the carreer of the warrior, whose great natural endowments made him the greatest hero of his race, and with him ended their last great struggle to resist the inroads of civilized men. The body was soon found, and the village became a pandemonium of howling savages. His friends, worse than brutalized by their fiery potations, seized their arms to wreak vengeance on the perpetrator of the murder, but the Illinois, interposing in behalf of their countryman, drove them from the town. Foiled in their attempt to obtain retribution, they fled to the neighboring nations, and making known the momentous intelligence, a war of extermination was declared against the abettors of this crime. Swarms of Sacs, Foxes, Pottawatomies, and other northern tribes who had been fired by the eloquence of the martyred chief, descended to the plains of Illinois, and whole villages were extirpated to appease his shade.* St. Ange procured the body of his guest, and mindful of his former friendship buried it with the honors of war near the fort under his command at St. Louis. His proud mausoleum is the great city which has since risen above his unknown grave, and his loud requiem the din of industry and the tramp of thousands descended from the race he hated with such remorseless rancor. The forest solitudes through which he loved to wander have been swept away, his warriors are no more, and the rusty relics of their former existence can only be found in the cabinet of the antiquary, while the great river which floated only their frail canoes is now beat into foam by the powerful enginery of the passing steamboat.

*It was at this time that the tragedy before described on the Rock of St. Louis was enacted, which has since been known as "Starved Rock."

CHAPTER XV.

1765-78—ILLINOIS AS A BRITISH PROVINCE—*Partial Exodus of the French — Their Dislike of English Law, and Restoration of their Own by the Quebec Bill — Land Grants by British Commandants—Curious Indian Deeds—Conditon of the Settlements in 1766, by Captain Pitman—Brady's and Meillette's Expeditions to the St. Joseph in 1777-78.*

It was on the 10th of October, 1765, that the ensign of France was replaced on the ramparts of Fort Chartres by the flag of Great Britain. At the time the colonies of the Atlantic seaboard were assembled in preliminary congress at New York, dreaming of liberty and independence for the continent, while the great valley east of the Mississippi, with its broad rivers rushing from the mountains and gathering in the plain, its vast prairies unsurpassed for their wealth of soil, its boundless primeval forests with their deep solitudes, into which were presently to be summoned the eager millions of many tongues to build their happy homes, passed finally from the dominion of France under the yoke of Great Britain.* Besides being constructively a part of Florida for over 100 years, during which time no Spaniard set foot upon her soil or rested his eye upon her beautiful plains, Illinois, for nearly 90 years, had been in the actual occupation of the French, their puny settlements slumbering quietly in colonial dependence on the far-off waters of the Kaskaskia, Illinois and Wabash. But the Anglo-Saxon had gained at last a permanent foot-hold on the banks of the great river, and a new life, instinct with energy and progress, was about to be infused into the country.

M. Neyon de Villiers, long the commandant of Fort Chartres, kept from the French, and particularly the Indians, so long as he could, a knowledge of the cession of the country to Great Britain by the treaty of Paris, and finally, when it had gained publicity and when the power and influence of the great Indian conspirator was broken, rather than dwell under the detested flag of the conqueror, he abandoned Illinois in the summer of 1764, followed by many of the inhabitants, to New Orleans. The command of the fort and country then devolved upon M. St. Ange de Bellerive, a veteran Canadian officer of rare tact and large experience, who, 40 years prior, had escorted Charlevoix through the West, the Jesuit traveler mentioning him with commendation. His position required

*Bancroft

162

skill and address to save his feeble colony from a renewed war
with the English, and from a general massacre by the incensed
hordes of savages under Pontiac surrounding him. By the home
government he had been advised of the cession to the British, and
ordered to surrender the country upon their arrival to claim it.
By repeated embassies from Pontiac and from various warlike
tribes toward the east, he was importuned for assistance against
the English, and unceasingly tormented by the Illinois demanding arms and ammunition. But in various dexterous ways, he put
off from time the importunate savages with fair speeches and occasional presents, while he anxiously awaited the coming of the British
garrison to take possession and relieve him of his dilemna.* After
the evacuation of Fort Chartres, he also retired from the country,
conducting his feeble garrison of 21 soldiers to the infant settlement of St. Louis, where, in the absence of any Spanish rule as
yet, he continued to exercise the functions of his office with great
satisfaction to the people until November, 1770, when his authority
was superceded by Piernas, commandant under the Spanish government. By a secret treaty, ratified November 3, 1762, the king
of France had ceded to the king of Spain all the territory west of the
Mississippi to its remotest tributaries, including New Orleans; but
the civil jurisdiction of Spain was not enforced in Upper Louisiana until 1769.† Prior to his departure, with a fatherly care and
benevolent intent, St. Ange instituted for those he left behind in
Illinois some wise and salutory regulations regarding titles to
their lands.‡

The exodus of the old Canadian French was large just prior and
during the British occupation. Unwilling to dwell under the flag
of their hereditary enemy, many, including some of the wealthiest families, removed with their slaves and other personal effects,
mostly to Upper Louisiana, just across the Mississippi, and settled
in the small hamlet of St. Genevieve. Others joined and aided
Laclede in founding the present great city of St. Louis, the site of
which had then but just been selected as a depot for the fur company of Louisiana. The number of inhabitants of foreign lineage
residing in the Illinois settlements were estimated as follows:
White men able to bear arms, 700; white women, 500; their children, 850; negroes of both sexes, 900; total, 2,950. By the hegira,
one-third of the whites and a greater proportion of the blacks
removed, leaving probably less than 2,000 souls at the commencement of the British occupation, during which the influx did not
more than keep pace with the efflux. Few English or Americans
even visited the country under the British rule, and less settled.
Scarcely an Anglo-Saxon (other than the British troops, traders,
officers and favored land speculators) was seen there during
this time, and until the conquest of Clark in 1778.

Captain Sterling, of the 42d Royal Highlanders, brought out
with him, and in taking possession of Fort Chartres, published
the following proclamation:

"By His Excellency, Thomas Gage, Major-General of the King's armies,
Colonel of the 22d regiment, General commanding in chief all the forces of His
Majesty in North America, etc., etc:

---

*See his letter to Governor D'Abbadie, Sept. 9th.
†Monette's Valley of the Mississippi.
‡Peck's Annals of the West.

"Whereas, by the peace concluded at Paris, on the 10th of February, 1763, the country of the Illinois has been ceded to His Britannic Majesty, and the taking possession of the said country of the Illinois by troops of His Majesty, though delayed, has been determined upon, we have found it good to make known to the inhabitants—

"That His Majesty grants to the inhabitants of the Illinois the liberty of the Catholic religion, as it has already been granted to his subjects in Canada; he has consequently given the most precise and effective orders, to the end that his new Roman Catholic subjects of the Illinois may exercise the worship of their religion according to the rights of the Roman Church, in the same manner as in Canada;

"That His Majesty, moreover, agrees that the French inhabitants, or others, who have been subjects of the Most Christian King, may retire in full safety and freedom, wherever they please, even to New Orleans, or any other part of Louisiana, although it should happen that the Spaniards take possession of it in the name of His Catholic Majesty; and they may sell their estate, provided it be to subjects of His Majesty, and transport their effects, as well as persons, without restraint upon their emigration, under any pretense whatever, except in consequence of debts or of criminal process;

"That those who choose to retain their lands and become subjects of His Majesty, shall enjoy the same rights and privileges, the same security for their persons and effects and liberty of trade, as the old subjects of the King;

"That they are commanded, by these presents, to take the oath of fidelity and obedience to His Majesty, in presence of Sieur Sterling, Captain of the Highland regiment, the bearer hereof, and furnished with our full powers for this purpose;

"That we recommend forcibly to the inhabitants, to conduct themselves like good and faithful subjects, avoiding by a wise and prudent demeanor all cause of complaint against them;

"That they act in concert with His Majesty's officers, so that his troops may take peaceable possession of all the posts, and order be kept in the country; by this means alone they will spare His Majesty the necessity of recurring to force of arms, and will find themselves saved from the scourge of a bloody war, and of all the evils which the march of an army into their country would draw after it."

"We direct that these presents be read, published, and posted up in the usual places.

"Done and given at Headquarters, New York. Signed with our hand, sealed with our seal at arms, and countersigned by our Secretary, this 30th of December, 1764.

                                      "THOMAS GAGE, [L. S.]
" By His Excellency:
      " G. MATURIN."

With such fair and liberal concessions, so well calculated to gain the favor and affection of the French, and stay their emigration, Captain Sterling began the government of this isolated colony. But it was destined to be of short duration. He died some three months after his arrival, leaving the office of commandant vacant. Under these circumstances their former beloved commandant, M. St. Ange, returned to Fort Chartres and discharged the duties of the office until a successor to Captain Sterling should be sent out. Major Frazer was next sent out from Fort Pitt. He exercised a brief but arbitrary power over the settlements, when he was relieved by a Colonel Reed, who proved for the colonists a bad exchange. For 18 months he enacted the petty tyrant by a series of military oppressions over these feeble settlements, which were, by reason of their isolation, entirely without redress. He was, however, at last removed and succeeded by Lieutenant Colonel Wilkins, who arrived September 5, 1768. He brought orders for the establishment of a court of justice in Illinois for the administration of the laws and the adjustment and trial of all controversies existing between the people relating to debts or property, either real or personal.

On the 21st of November, 1768, Col. Wilkins issued his proclamation for a civil administration of the laws of the country. For this purpose he appointed seven magistrates or judges, from among the people, as a civil tribunal, to hold monthly terms of court. The names of these first exponents of the principles of the common law of England upon the soil of Illinois, we are unable to transmit. A term of this court was held, commencing December 6, 1768, at Fort Chartres, which was the first common law jurisdiction ever exercised within the present limits of Illinois. Although we call this a common law court, it was in point of fact a very nondescript affair. It was a court of first and last resort—no appeal lay from it. It was the highest, as well as lowest—the only court in the country. It proved anything but popular, and it is just possible that the honorable judges, themselves taken from among the people, may not have been the most enlightened exponents of the law. The people were under the laws of England, but the trial by jury—that great bulwark of the subject's right, coeval with the common law and reiterated in the British Constitution — the French mind was unable to appreciate, particularly in civil trials. They thought it very inconsistent that the English should refer nice questions relating to the rights of property to a tribunal consisting of tailors, shoemakers or other artisans and tradespeople, for determination, rather than the judges learned in the law. While thus under the English administration civil jurisprudence was sought to be brought nearer to the people, where it should be, it failed, because, owing to the teachings and perhaps genius of the French mind, it could not be made of the people. For near 90 years had these settlements been ruled by the dicta and decisions of theocratic and military tribunals, absolute in both civil and criminal cases, but, as may well be imagined, in a post so remote, where there was neither wealth, culture nor fashion, all incentives tooppress the colony remained dormant, and the extraordinary powers of the priests and commandants were exercised in a patriarchal spirit which gained the love and implicit confidence of the people. Believing that their rulers were ever right, they gave themselves no trouble or pains to review their acts. Indeed, many years later, when Illinois had passed under the jurisdiction of the United States, the perplexed inhabitants, unable to comprehend the to them complicated machinery of republicanism, begged to be delivered from the intolerable burden of self-government and again subjected to the will of a military commandant.

In 1774 the English Parliament restored to the people their ancient laws in civil cases, without the trial by jury; guaranteed the free exercise of their religion, and rehabilitated the Roman Catholic clergy with the privileges stipulated in the articles of capitulation of Montreal in 1760. The act was known as the "Quebec bill," which extended the boundaries of the province of Quebec to the Mississippi, including all the French inhabitants at Detroit, Mackinaw, on the Wabash, and in the Illinois country. Its object was to firmly attach these remote French colonies, as well as all Canada, to the English government, and to thwart the rising opposition of the colonies on the Atlantic seaboard to its policy. The latter strongly disapprobated it, viewing it as but another stroke of ministerial policy to secure the aid of the French toward their subjugation. The colonists were then openly arrayed against the arbitrary acts of the home government. At a convention held at Falmouth, Mass., September 22, 1774, it was resolved that "As the very extraordinary and alarming act for establishing the Roman Catholic religion and French laws in Canada may introduce the French or Indians into our frontier towns, we recommend that every town and individual in this country should be provided with a proper stock of military stores," etc. The French colonists, apprised of the bitter opposition of the English colonists to the Quebec bill, and believing that Puritanism was inclined to deprive them of the religious privileges granted by it, were bound the closer to the support of the government during the first years of the revolutionary war. It is asserted that the French supplied Indian war parties with arms and ammunition to commit depredations upon the western frontiers of the English settlements.[*]

After the acquisition of New France by Great Britain, the king, by his proclamation of October 7th, 1763, forbade his subjects "making any purchases or settlements whatever, or taking possession of any of the lands beyond the sources of any of the rivers which fall into the Atlantic ocean from the west or northwest." The policy was to reserve this vast and fertile region as a hunting ground for the Indians, and by means of the lakes place within British control their enormous fur and peltry trade; to confine the English colonies to the seaboard within the reach of British shipping, which would be more promotive of trade and commerce, while the granting of large bodies of land in the remote interior, it was apprehended, would tend to separate and render independent the people, who would want to set up for themselves.[†]

Notwithstanding this policy of the home government, the most noticeable feature of Colonel Wilkins' administration was the wonderful liberality with which he parceled out the rich domain over which he ruled in large tracts to his favorites in Illinois, Philadelphia and elsewhere, without other consideration than the requiring of them to re-convey to him an interest. Under the proclamation of the king, dated October 7, 1763, the taking or purchasing of lands from the Indians in any of the American colonies was strictly forbidden, without special leave or license being first obtained. In view of this prohibition, Colonel Wilkins and some others of the commanders during the British occupation of Illinois, from 1765 to 1775, seem to have considered the property of the French absentees as actually forfeited, and granted it away. But this transaction never received the sanction of the king; by no official act was this property in any manner annexed to the British crown. True, under the laws of England, an alien could not hold land, yet to divest his title, and cause it to become escheated, a process in the nature of an inquisition was necessary. Did not the same rule apply in the case of a conquered country before the forfeiture of the lands of an absentee became complete?

Colonel Wilkins' grants amounted to many thousands of acres. One became afterwards somewhat notorious. This was made to

---

[*]Dillon's Ind. 90.
[†]See letter of the Royal Governor of Georgia to the British Lords of Trade, 1769.

John Baynton, Samuel Wharton and George Morgan, merchants of Philadelphia—who, " trading in this country, have greatly contributed to his majesty's service"—" for range of cattle and for tilling grain," said to contain 13,986 acres, but the metes and bounds disclosed it to cover some 30,000 acres.* It was a magnificent domain, lying between the villages of Kaskaskia and Prairie du Rocher, in the present county of Randolph. The conveyance opens and closes with the flourishes of the period: " John Wilkins, Esq., lieutenant colonel of his majesty's 18th, or royal regiment of Ireland, governor and commandant throughout the Illinois country, sends greeting," etc., etc., whereunto he " set his hand and seal-at-arms at Fort Chartres, this 12th day of April, in the ninth year of the reign of our sovereign, Lord George the Third, king of Great Britain, France and Ireland," etc., etc., 1769. A condition is annexed that " The foregoing be void if disapproved of by his majesty or the commander-in-chief."

On the 25th of June following, at Fort Chartres, George Morgan and J. Ramsey executed an instrument of writing, reciting a number of grants besides the foregoing, together with the names of the grantees, wherein in consideration of Colonel John Wilkins, "the better to promote the said service, has agreed to be interested one sixth part therein," they "engage that each of the before mentioned persons shall assign over to the whole, and to Colonel Wilkins, five-sixth parts thereof," etc. For the better carrying out of their plans, the British officers, and their grantees perhaps, committed a wanton outrage on the records of the ancient French grants at Kaskaskia, destroying to a great extent their regular chain of title and conveyances.†

By act of congress of 1788, the Governor of the Northwestern territory was authorized to confirm the possessions and titles of the French and Canadian inhabitants and other settlers on the public lands, who, on or before 1788, had professed themselves citizens of the United States, or any one of them. Governor St. Clair confirmed many of these grants in a very loose manner, sometimes by the bundle. But this British grant of 30,000 acres, which had been assigned to John Edgar, was patented by the Governor to Edgar and his (the Governor's) son, John Murray St. Clair, to whom Edgar, previous to the confirmation, had conveyed a moiety by deed. Much fault was found with this and many other transactions, and some grave charges were made by Michael Jones and E. Backus, U. S. land commissioners for the district of Kaskaskia, as to the manner of obtaining confirmation of innumerable old land grants. But the title to the claim in question was afterward confirmed by the U. S. Government to Edgar and St. Clair, notwithstanding the adverse report of the commissioners. Edgar was for many years the largest land holder and richest man in Illinois. He had deserted the British naval service, and in 1784 came to Kaskaskia with a stock of goods.

At an Indian council held at Kaskaskia, in 1773, an association of English traders and merchants, styling themselves "Illinois Land Company," obtained, July 5th, from ten chiefs and head men of the Kaskaskias, Cahokias, and Peorias, by a curiously signed deed, two immense tracts of land, the first

*American State Papers, vol. 11, Public Lands.
†Am. State papers.

"Beginning at the mouth of the Huron creek, called by the French the river of Mary, being about a league below the mouth of the Kaskaskia river; thence a northward of east course, in a direct line to the Hilly Plains, eight leagues or thereabouts, be the same more or less; thence the same course, in a direct line to the Crabtree Plains, seventeen leagues, or thereabouts, be the same more or less; thence the same course, in a direct line to a remarkable place known by the name of the Big Buffalo Hoofs, seventeen leagues, or thereabouts, be the same more or less; thence the same course, in a direct line to the Salt Lick creek, about seven leagues, be the same more or less; thence crossing the said creek, about one league below the ancient Shawneestown, in an easterly or a to the north of east course, in a direct line to the river Ohio, about four leagues, be the same more or less; thence down the Ohio, by the several courses thereof, until it empties itself into the Mississippi, about thirty-five leagues, be the same more or less; and then up the Mississippi, by the several courses thereof, to the place of beginning, thirty-three leagues, or thereabouts, be the same more or less."

This, it will be perceived by tracing the line, included ten or twelve of the most southerly counties in the State.

The other tract was bounded as follows:

"Beginning at a place or point in a direct line opposite to the mouth of the Missouri river; thence up the Mississippi, by the several courses thereof, to the mouth of the Illinois river, about six leagues, be the same more or less; and then up the Illinois river, by the several courses thereof, to Chicagou or Garlick creek, about ninety leagues or thereabouts, be the same more or less; then nearly a northerly course, in a direct line, to a certain place remarkable, being the ground on which an engagement or battle was fought, about forty or fifty years ago, between the Pewaria and Rinard Indians, about 50 leagues, be the same more or less; thence by the same course, in a direct line, to two remarkable hills, close together, in the middle of a large prairie or plain, about forty leagues, be the same more or less; thence a north-east course, in a direct line, to a remarkable spring, known by the Indians by the name of Foggy Spring, about fourteen leagues, be the same more or less; thence in the same course, in a direct line, to a great mountain to the northward of White Buffalo Plain, about fifteen leagues, be the same more or less; thence nearly a south-west course, in a direct line, to the place of beginning, about forty leagues, be the same more or less."

The consideration recited in the deed of conveyance was: 250 blankets, 260 stroudes, 350 shirts, 150 pairs of stroud and half thick stockings, 150 stroud breechcloths, 500 lbs. of gunpowder, 4,000 lbs. of lead, 1 gross of knives, 30 lbs. of vermilion, 2,000 gunflints, 200 lbs. of brass kettles, 200 lbs. of tobacco, 3 doz. gilt looking-glasses, 1 gross gun worms, 2 gross awls, 1 gross fire steels, 16 doz. of gartering, 10,000 lbs. of flour, 500 bus. of Indian corn, 12 horses, 12 horned cattle, 20 bus. of salt, 20 guns, and 5 shillings in money. This deed was duly signed by the Indian chiefs and attested by the names of ten persons, and was recorded in the office of a notary public at Kaskaskia, September 2d, 1773. The transaction was effected for the Illinois Land Company by a member named William Murray, then a trader in the Illinois country. There belonged to it two members in London, ten in Philadelphia, two in Lancaster, three in various counties of Pennsylvania, one in Pittsburg, and George Castler and James Rumsey, merchants of the Illinois country. The names indicate the members to have been mostly Jews.

In 1775, Louis Viviat, a merchant of the Illinois country, acting as the agent of an association denominated the Wabash Land Company,* obtained by a deed dated October 18th, from eleven Piaunkeshaw chiefs, immense tracts of land lying on both sides of

---

*We recognize in this company some of the same names as in the Illinois Company.

the Ouabach river, one commencing at Cat river 52 leagues above Vincennes, to Point Coupee, with 40 leagues in width on the east side and 30 leagues (90 miles) on the west side—Illinois. Another tract, also on both sides of the river, beginning at the mouth of White river, to the Ohio, 50 leagues, and extending 40 leagues into Indiana and 30 into Illinois. The number of acres contained in these grants was about 37,497,600. The consideration was much the same as recited in the other purchases. The deed was registered, as the other, at Kaskaskia.

The title thus acquired to enormous bodies of fertile lands, was contrary to the King's proclamation, and at best imperfect. But it was the revolt of the colonies and the establishment of their independence that frustrated the schemes of these powerful companies. Their grants might otherwise have been perfected by the King. In 1780 (April 29th), the two land companies effected a consolidation under the style of "The United Illinois and Wabash Land Companies." Through their agents they now applied to congress repeatedly for a recognition and confirmation of their Indian grants, in part at least, their efforts running through a period of 30 years—1787, 1791, 1797, 1804 and 1810; but that body was firm, and all their applications were rejected.

We here give some valuable extracts from an old English report of 108 pages, entitled, "The present state of the European Settlements on the Mississippi," by Captain Phillip Pitman, published at London in 1770. Captain Pitman was engineer in the British army and was sent out to make a survey of the forts and report the condition of the villages and improvements in these newly acquired territories of the British crown. This work is a document of rare value, filling up, as it does in a measure, a hiatus in Illinois history for which there are no other authentic sources of information. He visited Illinois in 1766. Of Kaskaskia, he gives the following description :

"The village of Notre Dame de Cascasquias is by far the most considerable settlement in the country of the Illinois, as well from its number of inhabitants as from its advantageous situation. * * * * *

"Mons. Paget was the first who introduced water-mills in this country, and he constructed a very fine one on the river Cascasquias, which was both for grinding corn and sawing boards. It lies about one mile from the village. The mill proved fatal to him, being killed as he was working it, with two negroes, by a party of the Cherokees, in the year 1764.

"The principal buildings are the church and Jesuits' House, which has a small chapel adjoining it; these, as well as some other houses in the village, are built of stone, and, considering this part of the world, make a very good appearance. The Jesuits' plantation consisted of 240 arpents (an arpent is 85-100 of an acre) of cultivated land, a very good stock of cattle, and a brewery ; which was sold by the French commandant, after the country was ceded to the English, for the crown, in consequence of the suppression of the order.

"Mons. Beauvais was the purchaser, who is the richest of the English subjects in this country ; he keeps 80 slaves; he furnishes 86,000 weight of flour to the King's magazine, which was only part of the harvest he reaped in one year. Sixty-five families reside in this village, beside merchants, other casual people, and slaves. The fort, which was burnt down in October, 1766, stood on the summit of a high rock opposite the village and on the opposite side of the river. It was an oblong quadrangle, of which the extreme polygon measured 290 by 251 feet. It was built of very thick square timber, and dove-tailed at the angles. An officer and twenty soldiers are quartered in the village. The officer governs the inhabitants, under the direction of the commandant at Fort Chartres. Here are also two companies of militia."

Prairie du Rocher—"La Prairie des Roches"—is described as being

"About 17 [14] miles from Cascasquias. It is a small village, consisting of 22 dwelling houses, all of which are inhabited by as many families. Here is a little chapel, formerly a chapel of ease to the church at Fort Chartres. The inhabitants are very industrious, and raise a great deal of corn and every kind of stock. The village is two miles from Fort Chartres. [This was *Little Village*, which was a mile or more nearer than the Fort.] It takes its name from its situation, being built under a rock that runs parallel with the river Mississsippi at a league distance, for 40 miles up. Here is a company of militia, the Captain of which regulates the police of the village.

"Saint Phillipe is a small village about five miles from Fort Chartres, on the road to Kaoquias. There are about sixteen houses and a small church standing; all of the inhabitants, except the Captain of the militia, deserted it in 1765, and went to the French side, (Missouri.) The Captain of the militia has about twenty slaves, a good stock of cattle, and a water-mill for corn and planks. This village stands on a very fine meadow, about one mile from the Mississippi."

"The village of Saint Famille de Kaoquias (Cahokia) is generally reckoned fifteen leagues from Fort Chartres and six leagues below the mouth of the Missouri. It stands near the side of the Mississippi, and is marked from the river by an island (Duncan's) two leagues long. The village is opposite the center of this island; it is long and straggling, being three-fourths of a mile from one end to the other. It contains forty-five dwelling houses, and a church near its center. The situation is not well chosen, as in the floods it is generally overflowed two or three feet deep. This was the first settlem·nt on the Mississippi. The land was purchased of the savages by a few Canadians, some of whom married women of the Kaoquias nation, and others brought wives from Canada, and then resided there, leaving their children to succeca them. The inhabitants of this place depend more on hunting and their Indian trade than on agriculture, as they scarcely raise corn enough for their own consumption; they have a great plenty of poultry and good stocks of horned cattle.

"The mission of St. Sulpice had a very fine plantation here, and an excellent house built on it. They sold this estate, and a very good mill for corn and planks, to a Frenchman who chose to remain under the English government. They also disposed of thirty negroes and a good stock of cattle to different people in the country, and returned to France in 1764. What is called the fort, is a small house standing in the center of the village. It differs nothing from the other houses, except in being one of the poorest. It was formerly inclosed with high palisades; but these were torn down and burnt. Indeed a fort at this place could be of but little use."

Regarding the soil, products and commerce, of the colony, Pittman says:

"The soil of this country, in general, is very rich and luxuriant; it produces all kinds of European grains, hops, hemp, flax, cotton and tobacco, and European fruits come to great perfection. The inhabitants make wine of the wild grapes, which is very inebriating, and is, in color and taste, very like the red wine of Provence.

In the late wars, New Orleans and the lower parts of Louisiana were supplied with flour, beef, wines, hams and other provisions, from this country. At present its commerce is mostly confined to the peltry and furs, which are got in traffic from the Indians; for which are received in return such European commodities as are necessary to carry on that commerce and the support of its inhabitants."

Of the Indians, he says:

"The principal Indian nations in this country are, the Cascasquias, Kahoquias, Mitchigamias, and Peoyas; these four tribes are generally called the Illinois Indians. Except in the hunting seasons, they reside near the English settlemen·s in this country. They are a poor, debauched, and detestable people. They count about 350 warriors. The Panquichas, Mascoutins, Miamies, Kickapous, and Pyatonons, though not very numerous, are a brave and warlike people."

Of old Fort Chartres, the strongest fortress in the Mississippi valley, which was re-built by the French government in 1756, during the French and English war in America, Captain Pitman furnishes the following description:

"Fort Chartres, when it belonged to France, was the seat of the government of the Illinois. The headquarters of the English commanding officer is now here, who, in fact, is the arbitrary governor of the country. The fort is an irregular quadrangle; the sides of the exterior polygon are 490 feet. It is built of stone, and plastered over, and is only designed as a defense against the Indians. The walls are two feet two inches thick, and are pierced with loop-holes at regular distances, and with two port-holes for cannon in the facies and two in the flanks of each bastion. The ditch has never been finished. The entrance to the fort is through a very handsome rustic gate. Within the walls is a banquette raised three feet, for the men to stand on when they fire through the loop-holes. The buildings within the fort are, a commandant's and a commissary's house, the magazine of stores, corps de garde, and two barracks; these occupy the square. Within the gorges of the bastion are a powder magazine, a bake house, and a prison, in the floor of which are four dungeons, and in the upper, two rooms, and an out-house belonging to the commandant. The commandant's house is thirty-two yards long and ten broad, and contains a kitchen, a dining-room, a bed-chamber, one small room, five closets for servants, and a cellar. The commissary's house (now occupied by officers) is built on the same line as this, and its proportion and the distribution of its apartments are the same. Opposite these are the store-house and the guard-house; they are each thirty yards long and eight broad. The former consists of two large store-rooms, (under which is a large vaulted cellar,) a large room, a bed-chamber, and a closet for the store-keeper; the latter of a soldiers' and officers' guard-room, a chapel, a bed-chamber, a closet for the chaplain, and an artillery store-room. The lines of barracks have never been finished; they at present consist of two rooms each for officers, and three for soldiers; they are each twenty feet square, and have betwixt a small passage. There are fine spacious lofts over each building which reach from end to end; these are made use of to lodge regimental stores, working and entrenching tools, &c. It is generally believed that this is the most convenient and best built fort in North America. * * * In the year 1764, there were about forty families in the village near the fort, and a parish church, served by a Franciscan friar, dedicated to St. Anne In the following year, when the English took possession of the country, they abandoned their houses. except three or four families, and settled in the villages on the west side of the Mississippi, choosing to continue under the French government."

In 1756, when the fort was rebuilt, the intervening distance to the bank of the Mississippi was some 900 yards. A sand bar was forming opposite, to which the river was fordable. At the time of Captain Pitman's visit, the current had cut the bank away to within 80 yards of the fort, the sand bar had become an island covered with a thick growth of cottonwoods, and the intervening channel was 40 feet deep. The great freshet of 1772, which inundated the American Bottom, produced such havoc upon the bank that the west walls and 2 bastions were precipitated into the raging current of the mighty river. The British garrison abandoned it and and took up their quarters at Fort Gage, on the bluff of the Kaskaskia, opposite the ancient village of that name, to which the seat of government was removed. Since then the great citadel of New France has been a ruin. Those of its walls which escaped destruction by the flood, were in great part hauled away by the neighboring villagers for building purposes. In 1820 the ruins were visited by Dr. Lewis C. Beck and Mr. Hanson of Illinois, who made an accurate drawing of the plan for the Illinois and Missouri Gazetter. Many of the rooms, cellars, parts of the walls, showing the opening for the large gate, port-holes, &c., were still found in a tolerable state of preservation. The exterior line of the walls measured 1447 feet. By 1850, a dense forest surrounded and covered the ruins, and trees, 3 feet in diameter, had grown up within the crumbling walls.*

Fort Gage, which continued to be the headquarters of the British while they occupied the country, was, in shape, an oblong parallelogram, 280 by 251 feet, built of large squared timbers. In 1772 the British garrison consisted of only 20 soldiers and an officer. In the village of Kaskaskia were organized 2 small companies of well disciplined French militia. When George Rogers Clark, in 1778, effected the bloodless conquest of Illinois, not a British soldier was on garrison duty in the country. M. Rocheblave, a Frenchman, was in command as the British governor. He occupied Fort Gage, and in Kaskaskia the French militia was kept in good order. We find no chronicle of how long Colonel Wilkins remained in command, or when the last remnant of the British garrison took up its line of departure. It is highly probable that these withdrawals were made with the breaking out of the war of the revolution.

The Illinois French were remote from the main theatre of the revolutionary war; and while they had perhaps little sympathy with the object for which the colonies struggled, their hatred of their hereditary foe was active. In 1777, Thomas Brady, whom they commonly called "Monsieur Tom," a courageous and enterprising Pennsylvanian who had wandered out to Cahokia, organized there and at Prairie du Pont a band of 16 volunteers, and in October, proceeding to the British post on the St. Joseph in Michigan, surprised and attacked the fort in the night time, defeating the garrison of 21 men. A negro slave who had escaped from the French in Illinois, was killed in his flight. A large quantity of goods for the Indian trade, fell into the hands of the victors, which doubtless had been one incentive to the expedition. With these, their homeward journey was retarded, and the British traders, having rallied the soldiers and stirred up the Indians, with a large force made pursuit and fell upon the camp of the marauders on the Calumet in the night time, killing 2, wounding 2 more (who were afterward dispatched with the tomahawk) and made prisoners of the rest. Brady, in being sent East, effected his escaped, and later returned to Cahokia, where he married the celebrated widow LeCompt.

The following year, while Colonel Clark was conducting his expedition against Kaskaskia, Paulette Meillet, the founder of Peoria, which was then called *Laville a Meillet*, who was a remarkable character for bravery, brutality and enterprise, burning to avenge the disaster of Brady's party, in which were many of his relatives, assembled about 300 warriors, red, white and mixed, and marched thence to St. Joseph. On the way, through the broad praries on foot under the rays of the summer's sun, M. Amlin, one of his men, exhausted with fatigue, gave out. Celerity and secrecy being essential to success, and unwilling to be encumbered with the sick, the soldier fell a sacrifice to the tomahawk, sunk in his brain by the brutal commander. Arriving at the post, the fort was surrounded, and, after an obstinate engagement, the garrison surrendered and was permitted to retire to Canada. The prisoners of Brady's party were released, and the stores of merchandise, said to have amounted to $50,000, were brought away to Peoria.†

---

*Reynold's Pioneer History.   †See Peck's Annals of the West.

CHAPTER XVI.

1778—CONQUEST OF ILLINOIS, BY GEORGE ROGERS CLARK.

While the colonists of the east were maintaining a fierce struggle with the armies of England, their western frontiers were ravaged by merciless butcheries of Indian warfare. The jealousy of the savage had been aroused to action by the rapid extension of American settlements westward and the improper influence exerted by a number of military posts garrisoned by British troops in different parts of the west. To prevent indiscriminate slaughters arising from these causes Illinois became the theatre of some of the most daring exploits connected with American history. The hero of these achievements by which this beautiful land was snatched as a gem from the British crown, was George Rogers Clark. He was born in Albemarle county, Virginia, November 19, 1752, and like his great cotemporary of the Revolution in his youth studied and practiced the art of surveying land. The manly exercise connected with the original surveys of the country seemed to create a partiality for the adventurous exposure of military life. Little is known in regard to Clark's early history. It is said he became a proficient in geography and devoted considerable time to the study of mathematics, but owing to the imperfect condition of the schools and the exciting times of his youth, the presumption is that his education was confined to the useful rather than ornamental branches of learning. Shortly after attaining his majority he enlisted as a staff officer in Governor Dunmore's war and with many other daring spirits of the times was present in the campaign of 1774 on the river Scioto. For meretorious conduct he was offered a commission in the royal service which, owing to the unfriendly feeling then existing between the colonists and the mother country and unsatisfactory termination of the war, he declined. Dunmore became apprehensive that the colonists would rebel, and it was believed by Washington and others that he was instructed to so treat with the Indians that he could use them as allies in case of revolt.

A spirit for adventure being awakened in the mind of young Clark by the war in 1775 he visited the wilds of Kentucky. Here he found the pioneers in a state of excitement as to whether the country on the south side of the Kentucky river was a part of the territory of Kentucky or Virginia. At the suggestion of Clark a meeting was called for considering the subject and devising the best means of remedying the perplexed state of affairs. The meeting was duly held and a paper prepared setting forth their grievances, and Clark and Gabriel Jones were appointed to lay it

173

before the legislature of Virginia. The envoys started on their journey, and after suffering the most distressing hardships arrived at the county of Bottetourt where they heard that the legislature had just adjourned. At the reception of this news Gabriel Jones returned to the settlement on the Holstein river and Clark proceeded on his way to Hanover county, where he found Governor Henry lying sick at his private residence. Clark made known to him the object of his visit, which the executive cordially approved, and to further his views gave him a letter to the council for further consideration. At the fall term of the Legislature of 1776, Clark and Jones presented their Kentucky petition to that body, and despite the efforts of Henderson and other North Carolina land speculators, the disputed territory was erected into the county of Kentucky, which embraced the limits of the present State of the same name. In addition to this political recognition, the parent State gave 500 lbs. of powder for the defense of the isolated settlement, a gift which now seems small, but then looked large, for the tremendous struggle of the revolution demanded all the energies of the donor to protect her own people and firesides from the ravages of the enemy.

Clark's great services for Kentucky and the good will inspired by his manly appearance and genial manners induced the pioneers to place him at the head of their irregular militia, and he soon instituted such effective means of defense that in all the fierce conflicts with the savages, which gave Kentucky the name of "Bloody Ground," his valor was more than equal to the emergency. Intimately acquainted with the progress of colonization west of the Alleghanies, he was the first to fully comprehend the advantages which would arise from the extension of American conquest to the banks of the Mississippi. While associated with the military operations in Kentucky, his sagacity enabled him to trace the Indian ravages to the instigations of British emissaries at Kaskaskia, Vincennes, Detroit and other places in their possession. These remote posts furnished the Indians with clothing and military stores, and Clark believing that their capture was the only possible way to abate the evils caused by their savage allies, sent two spies by the name of Moore and Dunn, to learn the nature of their defences. They having made observations returned and reported that their militia was well organized and active ; that the predatory excursions of the Indians were encouraged by the British authorities and that notwithstanding British agents had endeavored by misrepresentation to prejudice the minds of the French inhabitants against them colonists many of them were evidently in favor of their cause and interests. Clark, furnished with this information, again started to Virginia to make known to the government his plans respecting the subjugation of these British outposts. While on the road thither, fortunately for the enterprise which he had in view, the battle of Saratoga was fought, and resulting in victory to the Americans, prepared the public mind for a more spirited prosecution of the war. On reaching the capital, Clark's impressive representations captivated the mind of Governor Henry with the idea of subduing these British strongholds in the centre of their savage confederates. The enterprise, however, was regarded as extremely hazardous, and so great was secrecy indispensable to success that it was not deemed prudent to entrust the direction of it to the legislature. Being interrogated by Jefferson as to what he would do in case of defeat, he replied "cross the Mississippi and seek the protection of the Spaniards." The plan was so thoroughly digested that the approbation of the council was readily obtained, and to secure men, George Wythe, Thomas Jefferson and George Mason pledged themselves, if the enterprise was successful, to use their influence to secure a bounty of 300 acres of land for every one engaged in the service. Governor Henry gave him 1200 pounds in depreciated currency, and an order on the commandant of Ft. Pitt for ammunition boats, and other necessary equipments. He also furnished instructions, one set authorizing him to enlist 7 companies of 50 men each for the defense of Kentucky, and the other was drawn as follows :

" *Lieut. Colonel George Rogers Clark :*

"You are to proceed with all convenient speed to raise 7 companies of soldiers, to consist of 50 men each, officered in the usual manner, and armed most properly for the enterprise ; and with this force attack the British force at Kaskaskia. It is conjectured that there are many pieces of cannon, and military stores to a considerable amount at that place, the taking and preservation of which would be a valuable acquisition to the state. If you are so fortunate, therefore, as to succeed in your expedition, you will take every possible measure to secure the artillery and stores, and whatever may advantage the state. For the transportation of the troops, provisions, etc., down the Ohio, you are to apply to the commanding officer at Fort Pitt for boats, and during the whole transaction you are to take especial care to keep the true destination of your force secret ; its success depends upon this. Orders are, therefore, given to Captain Smith to secure the two men from Kaskaskia. It is earnestly desired that you show humanity to such British subjects and other persons as fall into your hands. If the white inhabitants of that post and neighborhood will give undoubted evidence of their attachment to this state, for it is certain they live within its limits, by taking the test prescribed by law, and by every other way and means in their power, let them be treated as fellow-citizens, and their persons and property be duly respected. Assistance and protection against all enemies, whatever, shall be afforded them, and the commonwealth of Virginia is pledged to accomplish it. But if these people will not accede to these reasonable demands, they must feel the consequences of war, under that direction of humanity that has hitherto distinguished Americans, and which it is expected you will ever consider as the rule of your conduct, and from which you are in no instance to depart. The corps you are to command are to receive the pay and allowance of militia, and to act under the laws and regulations of this state now in force as to militia. The inhabitants of this post will be informed by you that in case they accede to the offers of becoming citizens of this commonwealth, a proper garrison will be maintained among them, and every attention bestowed to render their commerce beneficial ; the fairest prospects being opened to the dominions of France and Spain. It is in contemplation to establish a post near the mouth of the Ohio. Cannon will be wanted to fortify it. Part of those at Kaskaskia will be easily brought thither, or otherwise secured as circumstances make necessary. You are to apply to General Hand, at Pittsburg, for powder and lead necessary for this expedition. If he cannot supply it, the person who has that which Captain Sims brought from New Orleans can. Lead was sent to Hampshire, by my orders, and that may be delivered to you. Wishing you success, I am your humble servant,

P. Henry. "

These instructions breathe a generosity and humanity in striking contrast with the spirit of the British government, whose minions were suffering our soldiers to perish by thousands in prison-ships for the want of food and offering bounties to encourage the merciless savages to murder and scalp our helpless women and children. It was thought best to raise the requisite number of troops west of the Alleghanies, as the colonies needed all the available forces of the east for the Atlantic defences. To enlist men Major William B. Smith went to the settlement of the Holstein, and for the same purpose Captains Leonard Helm and Joseph Bowman visited other localities. Clark proposed to get assistance at Pittsburg, but on account of jealousy arising from the rival claims of Pennsylvania and Virginia to the dominion of the Kentucky settlements, he was unsuccessful, and the latter colony furnished the troops. His real destination being unknown, many thought it would be better to remove the Kentuckians than to attempt their defence while their own citadels and the whole country round them was threatened by the savage confederates of England. Clark in the meantime being informed that Major Smith had raised 4 companies, and that Captains Helm and Bowman would join him with two others at Brownsville, on the Monongahela, made no further attempts to secure enlistments at Fort Pitt. Major Smith's men were to go by way of Cumberland Gap to Kentucky, and Clark, with the other troops, amounting to 300 men and a number of private adventurers, commenced the descent of the Ohio. At the mouth of the great Kanawa he was besought by Captain Arbuckle, commanding the fort at the junction of the two rivers, for assistance in capturing a band of Indians who had attacked him the preceding day. Thinking, however, his own enterprise was of greater moment, and wishing to strictly comply with his instructions, he continued on his course. He landed at the mouth of the Kentucky, with the intention of erecting a fortification at that point, but after mature consideration abandoned it for a more favorable position farther westward, at the falls of the Ohio. While here, learning that of the 4 companies promised by Major Smith, Captain Dillard's alone had arrived in Kentucky, he wrote to Captain Bowman, informing him of his intention to establish a fort at the falls, and having in view an enterprise of the greatest importance to the country, requested him to repair thither with Major Smith's men, and as many more as could be spared from the frontier stations. At this place he fortified Corn Island, opposite Louisville, not only as a base of operations, but as a means of protecting boatmen, who, in passing the rapids, were frequently attacked and plundered by the Indians. When joined by Captain Bowman's party from Kentucky, it was discovered that the withdrawal of his forces from the country left it to a great extent without protection, and therefore only a portion of them were engaged, with the understanding that when the remainder of Major Smith's men arrived the others should return for the defence of Kentucky. Clark now announced to his assembled forces the real destination of the expedition, and with the exception of Captain Dillard's company, the project met the enthusiastic approbation of the men. Lest desertions might occur in the disaffected company, the boats were secured and sentinels stationed at different points where the Ohio was supposed to be fordable. Notwithstanding these precautions, one of Captain Dillard's lieutenants and the most of the men, passing the sentinels unperceived, waded to the opposite shore and disappeared in the woods. A mounted party the next day was sent in pursuit of the fugitives, with orders to kill all who refused to return, and although overtaken 20 miles from the river, such was their vigilance that only 8 were caught and brought back. "The disappointment caused by the loss of the men," says Clark in his journal, "was cruel, and in its consequences alarming." The remainder of the deserters, dispersed in the woods to elude pursuit, suffered the most intense privations, and when finally they reached Harrodsburg, the brave Kentuckians were so exasperated at the baseness of their conduct that for a long time they refused to admit them into their stations. The forces were now about to separate, and in a day of rejoicing and mutual encouragement the heroes of the Kaskaskia expedition took leave of their friends who were to return for the defense of Kentucky. After the departure of the latter, Clark's little army, under the command of Captains Bowman, Helm, Harrod and Montgomery, only numbered 153 men. Everything being in readiness, on the 24th of June, 1778, while the sun was in a total eclipse, he left the position which he had fortified and fell down the river. This phenomenon fixes the time of Clark's embarkation, and by the same means other important events of history, the dates of which were wholly unknown, have been determined with perfect precision. Science in modern times has so far divested occurrences of this kind of the terrors which they excited in ancient armies, that among the men of the expedition but little importance was attached to the eclipse, as a harbinger for good or evil.

All unnecessary baggage was left behind that they might not be encumbered in the difficult march which they proposed to make across the country, in order to reach unperceived the post which they designed to capture. Clark was anxious to make an assault upon the post of Vincennes, but the greater extent of the French settlements in Illinois, the prospect of securing them as allies if they were conquered, and the facility of retreat to the Spanish possessions beyond the Mississippi, in case of defeat, inclined him to the original plan of the campaign. While descending the river a letter was fortunately received from Colonel Campbell, of Fort Pitt, stating that an alliance had been entered into between France and the United States, and that the army and navy of the former were coming to our assistance. This information was calculated to make a favorable impression upon the French and Indians of Illinois, and therefore of the greatest importance to the successful termination of the expedition. Landing on an island at the mouth of the Tennessee, the guard stopped a man by the name of John Duff and a number of other American hunters, from whom they also had the good fortune to obtain valuable information respecting the garrison at Kaskaskia. Duff and his party had recently been at that place, and he informed Clark that a French Canadian by the name of Rocheblave was in command; that he kept the militia well drilled; sentinels stationed on the Mississippi, and had ordered the hunters and Indians in their excursions through the country to watch for the rebels, or "Long Knives," as they designated the Virginians. They also stated the fort was kept in order as a place of retreat in case they were attacked; that its defence was attended to more for the purpose of military discipline than from any apprehensions of immediate danger, and that if any assault was anticipated, its great strength would enable the garrison to make a formidable resistance. The declaration of Moore and Dunn respecting the fearful apprehensions with which the inhabitants regarded the Virginians was likewise corrobora-

12

ted. Having obtained the hunters for guides, Clark dropped
down the stream, and landing near Fort Massac, concealed the
boats in a small creek emptying into the river. The distance from
this point to Kaskaskia is 120 miles, and at that time the intervening country was difficult to traverse, in consequence of streams,
swamps and other obstructions. The expedition started across
this tract in the direction of Kaskaskia, both leader and men
sharing the vicissitudes incident to travel in the wilds of an uncultivated region. Success depended entirely upon secrecy, and
to send out hunting parties in pursuit of game, upon which they
mostly depended for subsistence, it was feared might be the
means of discovery.

On the third day, John Saunders, the principal guide, becoming
bewildered and being unable to point out the course, suspicion was
immediately excited in regard to his fidelity, and a cry arose among
the men to put him to death. He, however, accompanied · by a
guard, was permitted to go to the adjoining prairie for further
search, and was told unless he directed them into the hunters'
path leading to Kaskaskia, a road in consequence of having so frequently traveled he could not easily forget, he should certainly be
hung. After spending some time in examining the features of the
country, he exclaimed : " I know that point of timber, " and pointing out the direction of Kaskaskia established his innocence. In
the afternoon of the 4th of July, 1778, the invading party, with
their garments worn and soiled, and beards of three weeks'
growth, approached the village where their long and wearisome
journey terminated, and concealed themselves among the hills east
of the Kaskaskia river. Clark sent out parties to reconnoitre, and
at night-fall, a detachment took possession of a house ¾ of a mile
above the town, and on the west side of the river. From the family
living in it, he learned that there were a great many men in town,
that but few of them were Indians, and that the militia had
recently been under arms, but no danger being discovered
they were dismissed. Boats having been procured for transporting the troops, the forces were divided into 3 parties; 2 of which
crossing to the west side of the river, were to proceed to different
parts of the town, while the other, under Colonel Clark, was to
capture the fort, on the east side. If Clark should be successful
in securing the fort, at a given signal the other detachments, with
a shout, were to take possession of the town and send heralds
who could speak the French language, to warn the inhabitants
that they would be shot down if they appeared in the street.

Kaskaskia, at that time, contained about 250 houses, and the
British officer, who had charge of the place after the revolt of the
Atlantic colonies, endeavored to create in the minds of the unsuspecting French the most dreadful apprehensions respecting the
ferocity and brutality of the " Long Knives; " telling them that
they not only plundered property but indiscriminately murdered
men, women and children when they fell into their hands. The
object of these falsehoods was to stimulate the people of these
remote outposts to make a determined resistance in case they were
attacked, and to induce them to supply the Indians with guns,
ammunition and scalping knives to aid them in their depredations
upon the Americans. Clark now wisely concluded if he could surprise them fear would cause them to submit without resistance,

and they would afterward become friendly from gratitude if treated with unexpected clemency. The plan of attack was successfully executed. Clark without resistance entered the fort through a postern gate on the side next to the river, and the others, passing into the village at both extremities with the most hideous outcries, alarmed the unsuspecting inhabitants, who commenced screaming "the Long Knives," "the Long Knives." In about two hours after the surprise, the townsmen, panic stricken, delivered up their arms, and though the victory was complete it had been obtained without shedding a drop of blood. The victors, in obedience orders, rendered the remainder of the night a pandemonium of tumult. This artifice as it prevented opposition and the effusion of blood, was the most innocent means that could have been resorted to to in order to be successful. M. Rocheblave, the British commadant, was not aware that he was a prisoner till an officer of the detachment which had entered the fort, penetrated to his bedroom and tapped him on the shoulder. The public papers were either concealed or destroyed. It was supposed that the governor's lady, presuming upon the deference which would be extended to her sex and rank, concealed them in her trunk, and such was the chivalry of these ancient Virginians that, although the papers were supposed to be valuable, they suffered her trunk to be removed without examination.

In seeking for information during the night, they learned that a considerable body of Indians was encamped near Cahokia, 50 miles higher up the Mississippi, and that M. Cerre, the principal merchant of Kaskaskia and an inveterate hater of the American cause, was at St. Louis on his way to Quebec. This information respecting the intensity of his hatred was, perhaps, a misrepresentation. None of the French inhabitants of Illinois were greatly attached to the British government, and it is probable that his unfriendly feeling was only the prejudice he, in common with the rest of his countrymen, entertained against the Virginians. His family and a large assortment of merchandise were then in Kaskaskia, and Clark thought that if these pledges were in his possession he could render the influence of this opulent merchant available in case an emergency should occur in which he might need it. A guard was accordingly placed about his house and seals put on his property, and also on all the merchandise belonging to other citizens of the place.

On the 5th day Clark withdrew his forces from the town to positions around it, and to augment the gloomy forebodings which had already unnerved the inhabitants, he sternly forbade all intercourse between them and his own men. After the removal of the troops the citizens were again permitted to appear in the streets, but when Clark perceived they assembled in groups and earnestly engaged in conversation, he caused some of the principal militia officers to be put in irons, without assigning any cause for the arrest or granting any opportunity for defense. This exhibition of arbitrary power did not spring from a despotic disposition or a disregard for the principles of liberty. No one excelled Clark in the respect which he entertained for the rights of others, and he keenly felt himself the hardships which the necessities of his situation compelled him to inflict upon those in his power. The terror hitherto intense now reached its climax, and when hope had nearly vanished Clark, who of all commanders had the clearest insight into human nature, granted an audience to the priest and five or six elderly men of the village. The shock which they received from the capture of their town, by an enemy which they regarded with so much horror, could only be equaled by their surprise when admitted to the presence of their captors. Their clothes were torn and soiled by the rough usage to which they had been exposed, and, as Clark says, they looked more frightful than savages. Their appearance, uncouth in the extreme, doubtless to the sensibility and refinement of the ancient French, seemed worse than the reality. After admission the deputatation remained sometime unable to speak and when at length their business was demanded they could not determine who should be addressed as commander so effectually had the hardships of the expedition obliterated the distinction between the chieftain and his men. Colonel Clark being pointed out, the priest in the most submissive tone and posture, said that "the people expected to be separated, perhaps never to meet again and they requested the privilege of meeting in the church to take leave of each other and commend their future lives to the protection of a merciful God." Clark, aware they suspected him of hostility to their religion, carelessly remarked that "the Americans did not interfere with the beliefs of others but let every one worship God according to his convictions of duty," that they might assemble in the church "but on no account must a single person venture outside of the village." Some farther conversation was attempted, but that the alarm might not abate it was roughly repelled, Clark abruptly informing them that he had not time for further intercourse. The entire population immediately convened in the church, and the houses being deserted orders were given that they should not under any pretext be entered by the soldiers, and that all private property should be honorably respected. After remaining in church a long time the priest and a few others again called upon Colonel Clark, and expressed their thanks for the great favor which he had granted them and also a desire that he would inform them what disposition he proposed to make of the people. They stated that, owing to the remoteness of their situation they did not fully comprehend the nature of the contest between England and her colonies; that their conduct had been influenced by British commanders whom they were constrained to obey, and that some of their citizens had expressed themselves in favor of the Americans, whenever the restraint to which they were subject would permit. They added, their present condition was the result of war and they were willing to submit to the loss of property, but begged that they might not be separated from their families, and that some food and clothing might be retained for their future support.

Clark having now sufficiently wrought upon their fear, resolved to try the effect of lenity. "What!" said he, abruptly addressing them, "do you mistake us for savages? Do you think Americans will strip women and children and take the bread out of their mouths?" "My countrymen," said the gallant colonel, "disdain to make war upon helpless innocence. It was to protect our own wives and children that we penetrated the wilderness and subjugated this stronghold of British and Indian barbarity, and not the despicable object of plunder. We do not war against Frenchmen

The King of France, your former ruler, is the ally of the colonies; his fleets and arms are fighting our battles, and the war must shortly terminate. Embrace which ever side you deem best, and enjoy your religion, for American law respects the believers of every creed and protects them in their rights. And now, to convince you of my sincerity, go and inform the inhabitants that they can dismiss their fears concerning their property, and families that they can conduct themselves as usual, and that their friends who are in confinement shall immediately be released." The revulsion of feeling which followed this speech can better be imagined than described. The village seniors endeavored to apologize for the suspicion they had entertained, upon the supposition that the property of a captured town belongs to the conquerers, but Clark gently dispensing with all explanations desired them immediately relieve the anxiety of their friends and strictly comply with the terms of a proclamation which he was about to issue. The good news soon spread throughout the village; the bell rang a merry peal and the people almost frantic with joy assembled in the church to thank God for their happy deliverance. Clark's anticipations were fully verified, the inhabitants were allowed all the liberty they could desire and all cheerfully submitted to him as the commandant of the village.

An expedition was now planned against Cahokia, and several influential Kaskaskians voluntarily offered to accompany it. They assured Clark that the Cahokians were their kindred and friends, and that when the situation of Kaskaskia was explained to them they would be willing to change their political relations. Their offer was accepted, and Major Bowman and his company were selected as one party for the new conquest, and the other the French militia commanded by their former officers, the entire detachment being but little inferior in numbers to that which invaded the country. Mounted on horseback the expedition reached Cahokia before the surrender of Kaskaskia was known to the inhabitants. On being perceived, the cry of "the Long Knives, the Long Knives," as at Kaskaskia, created the most intense consternation among the timid portion of the little community. As soon, however, as the new French allies could notify them of the change of government, this formidable appellation of the Virginians was changed to huzzas for freedom and the Americans. Major Bowman took possion of the fort without opposition; the Indian force in the vicinity was dispersed, and the inhabitants a few days afterward took the oath of allegiance.

The success which had hitherto attended the efforts of Clark greatly exceeded the means employed, but such were the complications of his position that he was compelled to use the greatest address in order to maintain it. He cultivated the most intimate relations with the Spanish on the west bank of the Mississippi, and instructed his men to create the impression that the headquarters of his army was at the Falls of the Ohio; that reinforcements were daily expected to arrive, and that when they came military operations would be resumed upon a more extended scale. This artifice enabled him to counteract the extensive influence of his adversaries, and ultimately triumph over their superior strength.

In the meantime M. Cerre, whose influence Clark had endeavored to obtain by securing his property and family, became anxious to return to Kaskaskia. Fearing to place himself in the hands of the American officer without some protection, he procured letters of recommendation from the Spanish governor of St. Louis, and the commandant of St. Genevieve, with a view to obtaining a passport. Clark, however, refused his application, and intimated that it need not be repeated, as he understood that M. Cerre was a man of sense, and if he had not been guilty of encouraging Indian barbarities, he need not apprehend any danger. These sentiments having been communicated to M. Cerre, he immediately repaired to Kaskaskia, and called upon Colonel Clark, who informed him that he was charged with inciting the Indians to plunder and murder the Americans, and that humanity required that such violators of honorable warfare should be punished according to the enormity of their crimes. The merchant, in reply to this accusation, said he challenged any man to prove that he had encouraged the depredations of the Indians, and that on the contrary, he could produce many witnesses who had heard him repeatedly condemn such cruelties in decided terms. He further remarked that he never interfered in matters of state, except when his business demanded it; that he was not well acquainted with the nature of the contest in which the colonists were engaged, and that these charges were perhaps preferred by some of his debtors, who sought by this means a release from their obligations. Being willing to submit to an examination in the presence of his accusers, Clark requested him to retire to another room, while he summoned them to appear. In a short time they came in, followed by a large part of the inhabitants, but when M. Cerre was brought into their midst they were confounded. Clark told them that he was unwilling to condemn any one without a trial; that M. Cerre was now in their presence, and if they found him guilty of the alleged crime he should be summarily punished. At the conclusion of these remarks, the witnesses commenced whispering with each other and retiring, till only 1 out of 7 was left. He being called on for his proof, replied that he had none, and M. Cerre was thus honorably acquitted. His friends and neighbors congratulated him upon the happy termination of the trial, and Clark informed him that although it was desirable he should become an American citizen, yet if he was not inclined to do so, he was at liberty to dispose of his property and remove from the village. M. Cerre was so pleased with the equitable and generous treatment which he had received at the hands of the American commander, he immediately took the oath of allegiance and thereafter remained the staunch friend of the new political power which he espoused.

Clark never resorted to artifice or punishment except when he could make it conducive to the public good. In the cases narrated he kept up the appearance of rigor with the view to enhancing the favors which policy and the magnanimity of his own disposition inclined him to grant. So adroit had been his management that he subdued without bloodshed all the French settlements within the present boundaries of Illinois. The captures, as we shall have occasion to show, were fraught with great consequences to the nation, and does it speak less honorably for him who, with great skill, had accomplished them with few instead of thousands, or because he had conquered without the shedding of blood instead of making the plains of Illinois gory with the blood of the enemy and that of his friends? The essence of true heroism is the same, whatever may be the scale of action, and although numbers are the standard by which military honors are usually awarded, they are in reality only one of the extrinsic circumstances. So important were Clark's achievements considered, that on the 23d of November, 1778, he and his brave officers and men were voted the thanks of the Virginia House of Delegates for their extraordinary resolution and perseverance in so hazardous an enterprise, and the important services thereby rendered the country. In this extraordinary conquest the Americans were doubtless assisted by the affection which the French inhabitants still retained for their ancient Fatherland, now allied with the colonies.

CHAPTER XVII.

CLARK OBTAINS POSSESSION OF VINCENNES—TREA-
TIES WITH THE INDIANS—VINCENNES FALLS INTO
THE HANDS OF THE ENGLISH, AND IS RE-CAPTURED
BY CLARK.

Clark now turned his attention to the British post of St. Vincents (Vincennes), the subjugation of which would not only extend
the dominion of his native State, but from its contiguity render his
own position and government more secure. He, therefore, sent for
M. Gibault, who, being the Catholic priest both of Vincennes and
Kaskaskia, could give him any information he desired. He
informed Clark that Governor Abbot had lately gone on business
to Detroit, and that a military expedition against the place was
wholly unnecessary. Desirous of having his parishioners free
from the violence of war, he offered to induce the people to transfer
their allegiance to the Americans without the assistance of troops.
This proposition was readily accepted, and DeLafont and a spy
were selected to accompany him. The embassy set off for Vincennes, and after a full explanation between the priest and his flock,
the inhabitants concluded to sever their relations with the British
government and take the oath of allegiance to the commonwealth
of Virginia. A temporary governor was appointed, and the American flag immediately displayed over the fort, to the great surprise of the Indians. The savages were told that their old father,
the king of France, had come to life and was angry with them
because they fought for the English, and that if they did not wish
the land to be bloody with war they must make peace with the
Americans. M. Gibault and party returned about the 1st of
August, with the joyful intelligence that everything was peaceably adjusted at Vincennes in favor of the Americans. This news
was both a source of astonishment and gratification, as such a
result was hardly to be expected.

The 3 months for which Clark's men had enlisted was now terminated, and his instructions being indefinite, he was at first at a
loss how to proceed. If the country was abandoned at this juncture, the immense advantages already gained would be sacrificed,
and, therefore, acting upon the discretion which necessity demanded,
he re-enlisted as many of his own men as were willing to continue
in the service, and commissioned French officers to raise a company of the inhabitants. He established a garrison at Kaskaskia,
under the command of Captain Williams, another at Cahokia
under Captain Bowman, and selected Captain Sims, who had
accompanied the expedition as a volunteer, to take charge of the
men who wished to return. The latter officer was also intrusted

184

with orders from Clark for the removal of the station from Corn Island, at the Falls of the Ohio, to the main land, and a stockade fort was erected where Louisville, the metropolis of Kentucky, has since been built. Captain John Montgomery, in charge of Rocheblave and the bearer of dispatches, was sent to Richmond, which had become the capital of Virginia. It had been the intention to restore to the British commander his slaves, which had been seized as public property, and he and some of his friends were invited to dine with Clark and his officers, when the restitution was to take place. M. Rocheblave, however, called them a set of rebels and exhibited such bitterness of feeling, that it was necessary to send him to the guard-house and finally a prisoner to Virginia. The generous idea of returning the slaves to their former owner having been frustated by this provocation, they were subsequently sold for 500 pounds, which was divided among the troops as prize money.

The government of Virginia in the meantime was informed of the reduction of the country and Clark desiring that a civil government might be instituted, an act was passed in October, 1778, organizing the county of Illinois which included all the territory of the commonwealth west of the Ohio river. This immense region, exceeding in superficial extent the whole of Great Britain and Ireland, was at that time the largest county in the world, and contained the best section of farming lands on the continent. A bill was also passed to raise 500 men for opening communication with New Orleans, for the benefit of the isolated settlements, and Col. John Todd was appointed the principal officer in the government of the new county, and justice was for the first time administered under the authority of Virginia.

About the middle of August, Clark appointed Capt. Helm commandant of Vincennes and Indian agent for the department of the Wabash. His great prudence and intimate knowledge of Indian character eminently qualified him for the duties of this important trust. It was also the intention of Col. Clark to place a strong detachment under his command as soon as reinforcements should arrive from Virginia.

At that time there lived in the vicinity of Vincennes a chief of the Piankashaw Indians, who possessed great influence over his people. He was complimented by his countrymen with the appellation of the Grand Door of the Wabash, in imitation of the title of Pontiac, who was styled the Grand Door of St. Joseph. Clark had exchanged messages with him through Gibault, the catholic priest, and he instructed Helm to secure his influence, as nothing could be done within the Indian confederacy of the Wabash without his approbation. The American agent arriving safe at Vincennes, and being received with acclamation by the inhabitants, he immediately invited the Grand Door to a conference. The proud and pompous chief was pleased with the courtesies of Capt. Helm, who, in a friendly talk, communicated to him an invitation from Clark to unite with the "Long Knives" and his old master, the King of France. In reply to this invitation, he said that he was glad to see a chief of the "Long Knives" in town, but with the caution peculiar to Indian character, declined giving a definite answer, until he could confer with the principal men of his tribe. In all their intercourse, the Grand Door observed the ceremonies of the most courtly dignity, and the American, to operate on his vanity, exhibited the same pomposity, till after several days the interview was concluded. Finally, Capt. Helm was invited to attend a council of chiefs, in which the Grand Door informed him, in a strain of Indian eloquence, that "the sky had been very dark in the war between the 'Long Knives' and English, but now the clouds were brushed away he could see the 'Long Knives' were in the right, and if the English conquered them, they might also treat the Indians in the same way." He then jumped up, struck his hands against his breast, and said, "he had always been a man and a warrior, and now he was a 'Long Knife' and would tell the red people to bloody the land no longer for the English." He and his red brethren then took Capt. Helm by the hand, and during the remainder of his life, he remained the staunch friend of the Americans. Dying two years afterward, at his request he was buried with the honors of war, near the Fort of Cahokia.

Many chiefs south of Lake Michigan followed the example of the Grand Door, and the British influence, which had caused great mischief to the frontier settlements, daily declined. Much of the success attending these negotiations was due to the influence of the French, for the Indians, relying implicitly upon their statements, became greatly alarmed at the growing power of the Americans. Clark's method of effecting treaties with them was attended with remarkable success. He had studied the French and Spanish methods of intercourse, and thought their plan of urging them to make treaties was founded upon a mistaken estimate of their character. He was of opinion that such overtures were construed by the savages as evidence of either fear or weakness, and therefore studiously avoided making the first advances. Unlike the English, who endeavored to win their good will by freely granting them presents, he either bestowed them reluctantly, or fought them until they were compelled to seek refuge in treaties as a means of self-preservation. The ceremonies attending his councils with these sons of the forest, as they illustrated their character, are worth recording. The first convocation of this kind in which Colonel Clark was present, met at Cahokia about the 1st of September. The various parties had assembled, and as the Indians were the solicitors, one of the chiefs approached the table where Colonel Clark was sitting, bearing three belts, one of which was emblematical of peace, another contained the sacred pipe, and a third the fire to light it. After the pipe was lighted, it was first presented to the heavens, then to the earth, next forming a circle, it was offered to all the spirits, invoking them to witness their proceedings, and finally to Colonel Clark and the other members of the council. At the conclusion of these formalities, a chief arose and spoke in favor of peace, after which he threw down the bloody belt and flag, which had been given to him by the English, and stamped on them, as evidence of their rejection. Clark coldly replied that he would consider what he had heard and give them an answer on the following day. He however intimated that their existence as a nation depended on the determination of the council, and as peace was not concluded, he cautioned the chief not to let any of his countrymen shake hands with the white people, saying it would be time to give the hand when the heart also could be given with it. When he had ceased speaking, one of the chiefs remarked that such sentiments were like men who had but one heart and who did not speak with a forked tongue. The council then adjourned till the next day, and when, at the appointed time the Indians reassembled, Clark thus addressed them:

" MEN AND WARRIORS : Pay attention to my words. You informed me yesterday that you hoped the Great Spirit had brought us together for good. I have the same hope, and trust each party will strictly adhere to whatever is agreed upon, whether it be peace or war. I am a man and warrior, not a councilor. I carry war in my right hand, peace in my left. I am sent by the.great council of the Long Knives and their friends, to take possession of all the towns occupied by the English in this country, and to watch the red people; to bloody the paths of those who attempt to stop the course of the rivers, and to clear the roads for those who desire to be in peace. I am ordered to call upon the Great Fire for warriors enough to darken the land, that the red people may hear no sound but of birds which live on blood. I know there is a mist before your eyes. I will dispel the clouds that you may clearly see the causes of the war between the Long Knives and the English ; then you may judge which party is in the right, and if you are warriors, as you profess, prove it by adhering faithfully to the party which you shall believe to be entitled to your friendship."

After Clark had explained in detail the cause and effect of the war existing beween the English and the colonies, he thus concluded :

" The whole land was dark ; the old men held down their heads for shame, because they could not see the sun ; and thus there was mourning for many years over the land. At last the Great Spirit took pity on us, and kindled a great council fire at Philadelphia, planted a post, put a tomahawk by it and went away. The sun immediately broke out, the sky was blue again, and the old men held up their heads and assembled at the fire. They took up the hatchet, sharpened it, and immediately put it in the hands of our young men, ordering them to strike the English as long as they could find one on this side of the Great Water. The young men immediately struck the war post and blood was shed. In this way the war began, and the English were driven from one place to another, until they got weak, and then hired the red people to fight for them. The Great Spirit got angry at this, and caused your old father, the French King, and other great nations to join the Long Knives, and fight with them against all their enemies. So the English have become like deer in the woods, and you can see that it was the Great Spirit that troubled your waters, because you have fought for the people with whom he was displeased. You can now judge who is in the right. I have already told you who I am. Here is a bloody belt, and a peace belt ; take which you please ; behave like men, and do not let your being surrounded by Long Knives cause you to take up one belt with your hands while your hearts take up the other. If you take the bloody path, you can go in safety and join your friends, the English. We will then try like warriors who can stain our clothes the longest with blood. If, on the other hand, you take the path of peace, and are received as brothers by the Long Knives, and then listen to bad birds that are flying through the land, you cannot longer be considered men, but creatures with two tongues, which ought to be destroyed. As I am convinced that you never heard the truth before, I do not wish you to answer me before you have taken time for consideration. We will therefore part this evening, and when the Great Spirit shall bring us together again, let us speak and think as men with but one heart and one tongue. "

On the following day, the council fire was kindled with more than ordinary ceremony, and one of the chiefs came forward and said :

" We have listened with great attention to what the chief of the Long Knives told us, and are thankful that the Great Spirit has opened our ears and hearts to receive the truth. We believe you tell us the truth, for you do not speak like other people, and that our old men are right, who always said the English spake with double tongues. We will take the belt of peace, and cast down the bloodly belt of war; our warriors shall be called home; the tomahawk shall be thrown into the river, where it can never be found; and we will carefully smooth the road for your brothers whenever they wish to come and see you. Our friends shall hear of the good talk you have given us, and we hope you will send chiefs among our countrymen, that they may see we are men, and adhere to all we have promised at this fire, which the Great Spirit has kindled for the good of all who attend."

The pipe was again lighted, the spirits were called on to witness the transactions, and the council concluded by shaking hands.

In this manner, alliances were formed with other tribes, and in a short time Clark's power was so well established that a single soldier could be sent in safety as far north as the head waters of the streams emptying into the lakes. In the vicinity of the lakes the British retained their influence, some of the tribes being divided between them and the Americans. This sudden and extensive change of sentiment among the Indians, was due to the stern and commanding influence of Colonel Clark, supported by the alliance of the French with the colonies, and the regard which the Indians still retained for their first Great Father. It required great skill on the part of Clark, while in command of such diminutive forces, to keep alive the impression which had originally been made respecting the arrival of forces from the Falls of the Ohio. To create a favorable impression, the fees connected with the administration of justice were abated. The maintenance of friendly intercourse with the Spanish authorities, and the permission of trade among the inhabitants on both sides of the Mississippi, was also productive of good will.

In his negotiation with the Indians, an incident occurred about this time which, from its romantic character, is worthy of mention. A large reward was offered the Meadow or Mascoutin Indians, who accompanied the other tribes to the council, to assassinate the American commander. For this purpose they pitched their camp on the same side of Cahokia creek occupied by Clark, distant 100 yards from the fort and the American headquarters. It was arranged that a part of their number should cross the creek, which could easily be waded, fire in the direction of the Indian encampment, and then flee to the quarters of Clark, where, under the pretense of fear, they were to obtain admission and put the garrison to death. The attempt was made about 1 o'clock in the morning. The flying party having discharged their guns in such a manner as to cast suspicion upon the Indians on the opposite side of the creek, started directly to the American encampment for protection. Clark was still awake with the multiplied cares of his situation, and the guards being stronger than had been anticipated, presented their pieces and compelled the fugitives to halt. The town and garrison were immediately under arms; the Mascoutins, whom the guard had recognized by moonlight, were sent for, and being interrogated respecting their conduct, declared that they had been fired upon by enemies on the opposite side of the creek, and that they had fled to the Americans for refuge. The French, however, understanding them better than their conquerors, called for a light, and on examination discovered that their leggings and moccasins were wet and muddy, which was evidence that they had crossed the creek and that the Indians they visited were friends instead of enemies. The intended assassins were dismayed at this discovery, and Clark, to convince the Indians of the confidence which he reposed in the French, handed over the culprits to them to be dealt with as they thought proper. Intimations were, however, made to them privately, that they ought to be confined, and they were accordingly manacled and sent to the guard-house. In this condition they were daily brought into the council, where he whom they had endeavored to kill, was forming friendly relations with their red brethren of other tribes. When all the other business of the council was transacted, Clark ordered the irons to be struck off, and said: "Justice requires that you die for your treacherous attempt upon my life during the sacred deliberations of a council. I had determined to inflict death upon you for your base designs, and you must be sensible that you have justly forfeited your lives; but on considering the meanness of watching a bear and catching him asleep, I have concluded that you are not warriors, but old women, and too mean to be killed by the Long Knives. Since, however, you must be punished for wearing the apparel of men, it shall be taken away from you, and you shall be furnished with plenty of provisions for your journey home, and while here you shall be treated in every respect as squaws." At the conclusion of these cutting remarks, Clark turned to converse with others. The offending Indians, expecting anger and punishment, instead of contempt and disgrace, were exceedingly agitated. After counseling with each other, one of the chiefs came forward, and laying a pipe and belt of peace on the table, made some explanatory remarks. The interpreter stood ready to translate these words of friendship, but Clark refused to hear them, and raising his sword and shattering the pipe, declared that the Long Knives never treated with women. Some of the other tribes with whom alliances had been formed, now interposing for the discomfitted Indians, besought Clark to pity their families and grant them pardon. To this entreaty he coldly replied, that "the Long Knives never made war upon these Indians; they are of a kind which we shoot like wolves when we meet them in the woods, lest they kill the deer." This rebuke wrought more and more upon the guilty parties, and, after again taking counsel, two of the young men came forward, covered their heads with blankets, and sat down at the feet of the inexorable Clark. Two chiefs also arose, and standing by the side of the victims who thus offered their lives as an atonement for the crime of their tribe, again presented the pipe of peace, saying, we hope this sacrifice will appease the anger of the Long Knife. The American commander, not replying immediately, as if still unsatisfied, the most profound silence reigned in the assembly, and nothing was heard but the deep breathing of the multitude, all turning their eyes upon Clark, as if to read in the expression of his countenance the fate of the devoted Indians. The sudden impulse caused by the heroism of this romantic incident, almost overcame the powerful nerve of Clark, who, from the first, had intended to grant these Indians peace, but with a reluctance, as he says, that should enhance its value. At length, to relieve the great suspense of the assembly, he advanced toward the young men and ordering them to uncover their heads and stand up, said: "I am rejoiced to find men

among all nations; these two young warriors who have offered
their lives a sacrifice, are at least proof for their own countrymen.
Such men only are worthy to be chiefs, and with such I like to
treat." He then took them by the hand, and in honor of their
magnanimity and courage, introduced them to the American officers
and other members of the assembly, after which all saluted them
as the chiefs of their tribe. "The Roman Curtius leaped into the
Gulf to save his countrymen, and Leonidas died in obedience to
the laws of Greece; but in neither of these instances was displayed
greater heroism than that exhibited by these unsophisticated
children of nature." They were ever after held in high esteem
among the braves of their own tribe, and the fame of the white
negotiator was correspondingly extended. A council was immediately convened for the benefit of the Meadow Indians; an alliance
was formed with their chiefs, and neither party ever afterward had
occasion to regret the reconciliation thus effected.

Although it was Clark's general aim not to ask favors of the
Indians, yet some of their chiefs were so intelligent and powerful
he occasionally invited them to visit him and explain the nature of
the contest between the English and the colonists. A noted instance
of this kind was his intercourse with Black Bird, a very distinguished chief whose lands bordered on Lake Michigan, and who
had obtained such a reputation among his people that a departure
from the usual policy was deemed advisable. Black Bird was in
St. Louis when the country was first invaded, but having little
confidence in Spanish protection, he wrote a letter to Clark apologizing for his absence, and returned to his tribe. A special messenger was sent requesting him to come to Kaskaskia, and complying with the invitation, he called upon Colonel Clark with only 8
attendants. Great preparations were immediately made for holding a council, but the sagacious chief, disliking the usual formalities of Indian negotiation, informed Clark that he came on business
of importance, and desired that no time might be wasted in useless
ceremonies. He stated that he wished to converse with him, and
proffered without ostentation to sit with him at the same table. A
room was accordingly furnished and both, provided with interpreters, took their seats at the same stand and commenced the conference. Black Bird said he had long wished to have an interview
with a chief of our nation; he had sought information from prisoners but could not confide in their statements, for they seemed
afraid to speak the truth. He admitted that he had fought against
us, although doubts of its justice occasionally crossed his mind;
some mystery hung over the matter which he desired to have
removed; he was anxious to hear both sides of the question, but
hitherto he had only been able to hear but one. Clark undertook
to impart the desired information, but owing to the difficulty of
rendering himself intelligent, several hours were spent in answering
his questions. At the conclusion, Black Bird, among other things,
said that he was glad that their old friends, the French, had united
their arms with ours, and that the Indians ought to do the same.
He affirmed that his sentiments were fixed in our favor; that he
would never again listen to the offers of the English, who must
certainly be afraid because they hire with merchandise the Indians to do their fighting. He closed by saying that he would call
in his young men, and thus put an end to the war, as soon as he

could get an opportunity of explaining to them the nature of the contest. This determination of the chief was very agreeable to Clark, who informed him that he would write to the government of Virginia and have them registered among the friends of the white people. A few days afterward, this intelligent Indian, supplied with presents and accompanied, at his request, by an agent of Clark, set off for his native forests. His conduct afterward exemplified the honesty of his professions, for he thereafter remained the faithful friend of the Americans.

Clark in his intercourse with the Indians, never blamed them for accepting the presents of the English, as the necessities of their condition and the inability of the Americans to supply their wants, rendered it unavoidable. Commerce had to some extent already introduced among them superior appliances of civilization. The rifle and its ammunition had long since superceded the bow and arrow, and blankets, cooking utensils, cutlery, and other implements manufactured in an advance state of arts, were as necessary to the savage as the civilized man. While, however, he forebore to reproach them for receiving presents from the English, he endeavored to impress upon their minds the degradation of fighting for hire. The "Long Knives," he said, "regarded the scalps taken while fighting in self-defence as the greatest of trophies, but those obtained in mercenary warfare, are thrown to the dogs or used as toys for the amusement of their children."

Another chief by the name of Lages, about this time, sent a letter to Clark. He was also known by the appellation of Big Gate, a title which he received from having shot a British soldier, standing at the fort when Pontiac, with whom he was then associated, besieged Detroit. Several marauding parties against our frontier settlements, had been successfully commanded by this warrior, who happened to fall in with a party of Piankeshaws going to Kaskaskia to make the Americans a visit. Gaudily decked in the full costume of war, and with the bloody belt, which the British had given him, suspended about his neck, he daily came to the council and occupied one of the most prominent seats. As a silent spectator he thus attended till all the public business was transacted, the American officer then accosted him with an apology for not having paid his respects during the deliberations of the assembly. Although we are enemies, said he, it is customary with the white people to treat celebrated warriors with respect, in proportion to the exploits which they have performed against each other in war. Being a distinguished warrior, Clark invited him to dinner. Surprised at this civility he at first endeavored to decline the invitation. The American officer, however, when he attempted to offer an excuse, repeated with greater warmth his solicitations, till the feelings of the chief were wrought up to the highest pitch of excitement. Roused in this manner he advanced to the center of the room, threw down the war belt, tore off the clothes and flag, which had been given him by his friends, the English. Despoiled of these presents, he struck himself violently on the breast, and said that he had been a warrior from his youth, and delighted in battles; that he had fought three times against the Americans and was preparing another war party, when he heard of Colonel Clark's arrival; that he had determined to visit the Americans, who he now thought were right, and that he was henceforth a "Long Knife" and would war no longer for the English. He then concluded by shaking hands with Clark and his officers and saluting them as brothers. The comical part of the affair was that the new brother was now naked, and since he must be clothed, a fine laced suit was provided and he appeared at the entertainment arrayed in all the trappings of military costume. After the repast was over, in a private interview, he disclosed to Clark the situation of Detroit, and offered to obtain a scalp or prisoner from its garri son. Clark not wishing to encourage the barbarities of the Indians, declined the former, but assured the warrior of his willingness to accept the latter, provided he treated the captive kindly when he got him in his power. This policy of appealing to the better feel- ings of humanity was little appreciated by the savages, and in some instances caused them to unite with the less scrupulous enemy who suffered them to plunder and murder without stint, provided British aggrandizement was the result. When the chief departed Clark gave him a captain's commission and a medal as evidence of the new relations and responsibilities which he had assumed.

While the American commander was thus negotiating with the Indians, Hamilton, the British governor of Detroit heard of Clark's invasion, and was incensed that the country which he had in charge should be wrested from him by a few ragged militia from Virginia. He therefore hurriedly collected a force consisting of 30 regulars, 50 French Canadians and 400 Indians, and marching by way of the Wabash appeared before the fort at Vincennes on the 15th of December, 1778. The inhabitants made no effort to defend the town, and when Hamilton's forces arrived Capt. Helm and a man by the name of Henry were the only Americans in the fort. The latter charging a cannon, placed it in the open gateway, and the captain standing by it with a lighted match cried out as Hamilton came in hailing distance, "halt." The British officer, not knowing the strength of the garrison stopped and demanded the surrender of the fort. Helm exclaimed "no man shall enter here till I know the terms." Hamilton responded, "you shall have the honors of war." The entire garrison, consisting of one officer and one private, then capitulated, and receiving the customary courtesies for their brave defense, marched out with the honors of war. Capt. Helm was retained a prisoner, the French inhabitants were disarmed, and a large portion of Hamilton's troops were detached against the settlements on the Ohio and Mississippi.

These movements transpired at Vincennes, 6 weeks before the intelligence reached Kaskaskia, thus verifying the serious appre- hensions which Clark, in the meantime, had entertained for the safety of the place. In consequence of these forebodings, he en- gaged Colonel Vigo to go and reconnoitre the situation of the post. No choice could have been more fortunate. Although Vigo was an Italian by birth, no one excelled him in devotion to the cause of freedom and sympathy for an oppressed people strug- gling for their rights. Associated as a merchant with the Spanish governor of St. Louis, he amassed a large fortune, which, with the greatest generosity, he expended during the revolution for the benefit of his adopted country. Having for a long time resided in Indiana, and died there, the State, in honor of his memory, called a county after his name, and Congress ultimately refunded a large part of the money which he had expended. After conferring with Clark, he started on his mission, and when within five miles of his destination, he was captured by the Indians and taken before Governor Hamilton. He was regarded as an American spy, but being a Spanish subject, and very popular with the inhabitants of the town, the British officer did not dare to proceed against him according to his suspicions. The citizens threatened to stop his supplies if he was not suffered to depart. Hamilton reluctantly proposed to let him go if, during the war, he would not do any act injurious to British interests. Colonel Vigo peremptorily refused to become a party to such a compact. Agreeing, however, not to do anything prejudicial in his homeward journey, he was permitted to return in a boat, down the Wabash and up the Mississippi, to St. Louis. He remained neutral just long enough to comply with his stipulations, for, on his arrival home, he immediately changed his clothes, and set off for Kaskaskia to communicate the information which he had obtained to Colonel Clark. After detailing the capitulation of Vincennes and the disposition of the British force, he made known Hamilton's intentions of re-conquering Illinois, and his meditated attack upon Kaskaskia, on the re-assembling of his forces in the spring, as the surest way of effecting this object. When this place was reduced, with his forces augmented by the addition of 700 warriors from Mackinaw, the Cherokees and Chickasaws, and other tribes, he proposed to penetrate as far as Fort Pitt, and subjugate in his march all the intervening settlements. So elated was the British commander with his hopes of conquest, he intended, in a short time, to be master of all the territory of Virginia between the Alleghanies and the Mississippi.

Clark, in view of the critical condition of the country, and the extreme peril of his own situation, wrote to Governor Henry, of Virginia, acquainting him of Hamilton's designs, and asking him for troops. Parties of hostile Indians, sent out by the British governor, began to appear, and as assistance could not be obtained from the State in time, with the promptness which the emergency demanded, he resolved to help himself. Anticipating his rival, he commenced preparations with his own limited means to carry the war into the enemy's country, for, as he says, "I knew if I did not take him, he would take me." Colonel Vigo had informed him that, owing to the dispersion of the British forces, the garrison at Vincennes was reduced to 80 men, three pieces of cannon and some swivels, and that if the town was attacked before the troops were recalled, it might, without difficulty, be recaptured. Without a moment's delay, a galley was fitted up, mounting two 4-pounders and 4 swivels, and placed in charge of Capt. John Rogers, and a company of 46 men, with orders after reaching the Wabash to force their way up the stream to the mouth of White River, and remain there for further instructions. Clark next ordered Captain Bowman to evacuate the fort at Cahokia for the purpose of organizing an expedition to proceed across by land, and co-operate with the force under Captain Rogers. The French inhabitants of Cahokia and Kaskaskia raised two companies, commanded by Captains McCarty and Charleville, which, with the Americans, amounted to 170 men. On the 7th of February, 1779, just 8 days after the reception of the news from

13

Vincennes, this forlorn hope commenced its march in a northeasterly direction, over the inundated flats of the country, in a wet,
but fortunately, not cold season.   To relieve the hardships of the
journey, which was perhaps the most dreary one performed during
the revolution, hunting, game feasts, and Indian war dances were
instituted for the amusement of the men.   After incredible hardships, on the 13th they reached the forks of the Little Wabash,
the low bottom lands of which were covered with water.   At this
part of the stream the opposite banks were ·5 miles apart
and the water so deep when Clark arrived as in many places
to be waded with the greatest difficulty.   Here, drenched in
the rains which fell almost daily, they managed to construct a
canoe, and ferry over their baggage to the opposite shore.   Hitherto they had borne their labors with great fortitude, but now
many became discouraged by the continued obstacles which beset
the way.   While wading the Wabash, and in some instances to
the shoulders in mud and water, an incident occurred which, by
its merriment, greatly relieved the desponding spirits of the men.
There was in the service an Irish drummer, who was of small stature, but possessed rare talent in singing comic songs.   On coming
to a depression beyond his depth, he put his drum into the water,
and mounting on the head, requested one of the tallest men to
pilot him across the stream, while he enlivened the company by
his wit and music.

On the morning of the 18th, 11 days after leaving Kaskaskia,
they heard the signal guns of the fort, and during the evening of
the same day, arrived at the Great Wabash, 9 miles below Vincennes.   The galley had not arrived with the supplies, and the
men being exhausted, destitute and almost in a starving con-
tion, it required all of Clark's address to keep them from giving up
in despair.   The river was out of its banks, all the low lands
were submerged, and before means of transportation could be procured they might be discovered by the British and the entire party
captured.   On the 20th, a boat from Vincennes was hailed and
brought to land, from the crew of which was received the cheering intelligence of the friendly disposition of the French inhabitants, and that no suspicion of Clark's movements was entertained
by the British garrison.   The last day of the march, the most
formidable difficulties were encountered.   Says Colonel Clark, in
his journal:

" The nearest land to us, in the direction of Vincennes, was a spot
called the 'Sugar Camp,' on the opposite side of a slough.   I sounded the
water, and finding it deep as my neck, returned with the design of having the men transported on board the canoes to the camp, though I knew
it would spend the whole day and the ensuing night, as the vessels would
pass slowly through the bushes.   The loss of so much time to men
half-starved, was a matter of serious consequence, and I would now
have given a great deal for a day's provisions or one of our horses.
When I returned, all ran to hear the report.   I unfortunately spoke in a
serious manner to one of the officers; the whole were alarmed without
knowing what I said.   I viewed their confusion for a minute, and whispered for those near me to do as I did.   I immediately put some water
in my hand, poured powder on it, blackened my face, gave the war-
whoop and marched into the water.   The party immediately followed,
one after another, without uttering a word of complaint.   I ordered those
near me to sing a favorite song, which soon passed through the line and
all went cheerfully.   I now intended to have them transported across

the deepest part of the water, but when about waist-deep, one of the men informed me that he thought he had discovered a path. We followed it, and finding that it kept on higher ground, without further difficulty arrived at the camp, where there was dry ground on which to pitch our lodges. The Frenchmen that we had taken on the river, appeared to be uneasy at our situation, and begged that they might be permitted, during the night, to visit the town in 2 canoes and bring, from their own houses, provisions. They said that some of our men could go with them as a surety for their conduct, and that it would be impossible to leave that place till the waters, which were too deep for marching, subsided. Some of the officers believed that this might be done, but I would not suffer it. I could never well account for my obstinacy on this occasion, or give satisfactory reasons to myself or anybody else why I denied a proposition apparently so easy to execute, and of so much advantage; but something seemed to tell me it should not be done.

"On the following morning, the finest we had experienced, I harangued the men. What I said I am not now able to recall; but it may be easily imagined by a person who possesses the regard which I, at that time, entertained for them, I concluded by informing them, that passing the sheet of water, which was then in full view and reaching the opposite woods, would put an end to their hardships; that in a few hours they would have a sight of their long-wished for object, and immediately stepped into the water without waiting for a reply. Before a third of the men had entered, I halted and called to Major Bowman, and ordered him to fall into the rear with 25 men and put to death any man who refused to march with us, as we did not wish to have any such among us. The whole gave a cry of approbation, and on we went. This was the most trying of all the difficulties we experienced. I generally kept 15 of the strongest men next myself, and judged from my own feelings, what must be that of the others. Getting near the middle of the inundated plain, I found myself sensibly failing, and as there were no trees for the men to support themselves, I feared that many of the weak would be drowned. I ordered the canoe to ply back and forth, and with all diligence to pick up the men; and to encourage the party, sent some of the strongest forward with orders that, when they had advanced a certain distance, to pass the word back that the water was getting shallow, and when near the woods, to cry out land. This stratagem had the desired effect. The men, encouraged by it, exerted themselves almost beyond their abilities; the weak holding on the stronger. On reaching the woods where the men expected land, the water was up to their shoulders; but gaining the timber was the greatest consequence, for the weakly hung to trees and floated on the drift till they were taken off by the canoes. The strong and tall got ashore and built fires; but many of the feeble, unable to support themselves on reaching land, would fall with their bodies half in the water. The latter were so benumbed with cold, we soon found that fires would not restore them, and the strong were compelled to exercise them with great severity to revive their circulation.

"Fortunately, a canoe in charge of some squaws was going to town, which our men captured, and which contained half a quarter of buffalo meat, some corn, tallow and kettles. Broth was made of this valuable prize and served out to the most weakly with great care. Most of the men got a small portion, but many of them gave part of theirs to the more famished, jocosely saying something cheering to their comrades. This little refreshment gave renewed life to the company. We next crossed a deep but narrow lake, in the canoes, and marching some distance, came to a copse of timber called Warrior's Island. We were now distant only two miles from town, which, without a single tree to obstruct the view, could be seen from the position we occupied.

"The lower portions of the land between us and the town were covered with water, which served at this season as a resort for ducks and other water fowl. We had observed several men out on horseback shooting them, half a mile distant, and sent out as many of our active young Frenchmen to decoy and take one of them prisoner, in such a manner as not to alarm the others. Being successful, in addition to the information which had been obtained from those taken on the river, the captive reported that the British had that evening completed the wall of the fort, and that there were a good many Indians in town. Our situation was truly critical. No possibility of retreat in case of defeat, and in full view of the town, which, at this time, had 600 men in it—troops, inhabitants and Indians. The crew of the galley, though not 50 men, would now have been a re-inforcement of immense magnitude to our little army, but we could not think of waiting for them. Each had forgotten his suffering, and was ready for the fray, saying what he had suffered was nothing but what a man should bear for the good of his country. The idea of being made a prisoner was foreign to every man, as each expected nothing but torture if they fell into the hands of the Indians. Our fate was to be determined in a few hours, and nothing but the most daring conduct would insure success. I knew that a number of the inhabitants wished us well; that many were lukewarm to the interests of either party. I also learned that the Grand Door had but a few days before openly declared, in council with the British, that he was a brother and friend of the Long Knives. These were favorable circumstances, and as there was little probability of our remaining until dark undiscovered, I determined to commence operations immediately, and wrote the following placard to the people of the town. ' To the inhabitants of Vincennes: Gentlemen, being now within two miles of your village with my army, determined to take your fort this night, and not being willing to surprise you, I take this opportunity to request such of you as are true citizens, and willing to enjoy the liberty which I bring you, to remain still in your houses, and those, if any there be, who are friends of the king, let them instantly repair to the fort and join the hair-buyer general*, and fight like men. And if any of the latter do not go to the fort, and shall be discovered afterward, they may depend upon severe punishment. On the contrary, those who are true friends to liberty, may depend upon being well treated, and I once more request them to keep out of the streets, for every one I find in arms on my arrival shall be treated as an enemy.' "

This forcible letter, which shows Clark's insight into human nature by inspiring confidence in the friendly, and filling the adverse party with dismay, was half the battle that followed. On the receipt of the letter, the people of the town supposed the invaders had come from Kentucky as no one imagined it possible that an expedition could come from Illinois, in consequence of the freshets which prevailed at that season of the year. To deepeen this impression, letters purporting to come from well known gentlemen in Kentucky, were written and sent to the inhabitants, and so well established was the conviction, that the presence of Clark could not be credited till his person was pointed out by one who knew him. The soldiers, as on previous occasions, were directed to greatly exaggerate the strength of the American forces.

About sunset on the 23d, they sallied forth to attack the fort. When in full view of it, they were divided into platoons, each dis. playing a different flag, and by marching and countermarching among some mounds between them and the town, their apparent numbers greatly exceeded their real strength. Nearing the village and encamping on the adjacent heights, some commotion was perceptible in the streets, but no hostile demonstration occurred at the fort, and it was afterward ascertained that even the friends of the British were afraid to give notice of Clark's presence. The utmost impatience prevailing in the American encampment, to know the cause of the silence, Lieut. Bailey, with 14 men was sent to make an attack upon the garrison. The fire of the party

*Thus named from having hired the Indians to murder the American prisoners, by paying so much per scalp.

was attributed to some drunken Indians, who had saluted the fort in that manner on previous occasions, and it was not till after one of the besciged was shot through a port hole that the real character of the assailants was ascertained, and the engagement commenced in earnest. Henry and Captain Helm were still retained as prisoners in the fort. Through the wife of the former, who lived in Vincennes, and was permitted to visit her husband daily, Clark obtained minute information respecting the garrison. Learning in this way where Capt. Helm lodged—knowing his fondness for apple-toddy, and believing he would have some on the hearth as usual, he suffered one of his men to fire on his quarters, with a view, as he said, to knock the mortar into the captain's favorite beverage. At the time he was playing cards with Hamilton, and when the bullets commenced rattling about the chimney, he jumped up and swore that it was Clark, that he would take all of them prisoners, and that the d—d rascal had ruined his toddy. While thus conversing, Helm observed some of the soldiers looking out of the port holes and cautioned them not to do so again as the Americans would certainly shoot out their eyes. It so happened that one of the men afterward attempting to look out was shot in the eye, which Capt. Helm observing exclaimed, "there, I told you so." These incidents, characteristic of the men and the times, doubtless had their effect upon the garrison.

The ammunition of the Americans, who had expected supplies from the galley, being now nearly exhausted, some of the inhabitants furnished them with powder and ball, which had been buried to keep it from falling into the hands of the British. Had the Americans also needed assistance, the Grand Door, with whom a treaty had previously been concluded, appeared with 100 warriors and offered his services to Clark, who, though declining his aid in the field, requested his presence and influence in council.

The Americans had advanced behind a bank to within 30 yards of the fort, whose guns in consequence of their elevation, were useless, and no sooner was a port hole darkened than a dozen rifles discharged their contents into the apperture, and the British soldiers could no longer be kept at their posts. Clark perceiving their difficulties, in the course of the morning demanded the surrender of the fort, which Hamilton refused, stating that he would not be awed into anything unbecoming a British officer. The men were urgent to take the fort by storm, but Clark knowing that he could get possession of it without the expenditure of life resulting from an assault, wisely opposed their desires. In the evening of the same day Hamilton, apprehensive that he would be compelled to surrender at discretion, sent a flag to the beseigers desiring a truce of three days. This Clark refused, although during the armistice the galley might arrive with its men and munitions, which would greatly facilitate his operations for the reduction of the fort. He proposed in return the unconditional surrender of the garrison, and informed the British commander if he wished to have an interview for that purpose, he might meet him at the church. In compliance with this offer, Gov. Hamilton, in company with Capt. Helm and Major Hay, waited on Col. Clark at the appointed place. At the conference which ensued, the American commander rejecting all the overtures of his antagonist, resolutely adhered to his first proposition, and when Capt. Helm attempted to moderate his demands, he informed him that a prisoner had no right to interfere. Hamilton thereupon replied, that he was free from that moment, but Clark unmoved, would not accept his release upon these terms, telling him he must return and abide his fate, and the British officers that the firing would recommence in 15 minutes. The gentlemen were about to retire to their respective quarters, when Hamilton called Clark aside, and politely asked his reasons for rejecting the liberal terms which had been offered. The latter sternly replied, "I am aware the principal Indian partisans from Detroit are in the fort, and I only want an honorable opportunity of putting such instigators of Indian barbarities to death. The cries of widows and orphans made by their butcheries, require such blood at my hands. I consider this claim upon me for punishment next to divine, and I would rather lose 50 men than not execute a vengeance demanded by so much innocent blood. If Gov. Hamilton is willing to risk his garrison for such miscreants, he is at perfect liberty to do so." Major Hay, who heard this statement inquired, "Pray, sir, who do you mean by 'Indian partisans?'" Clark promptly replied, "I consider Major Hay one of the principal ones." The latter, as if guilty of the charge, immediately turned deadly pale, trembled and could hardly stand. Gov. Hamilton blushed for this exhibition of cowardice in presence of the American officer, and Capt. Helm could hardly refrain from expressing contempt. Clark's feelings now relented, and secretly resolving to deal more leniently with the British officers, before separating he told them he would reconsider the matter and let them know the result. After retiring, a council of war was held and milder terms being submitted to Gov. Hamilton, he accepted them, and on the 24th of February, 1779, the garrison surrendered.[*]

The following day Clark took possession of the fort, hoisted the American flag, and fired 13 guns to celebrate the recovery of this important stronghold. Seventy prisoners were captured, and a considerable quantity of military stores became the property of the victors. Most of the prisoners were permitted to return to Detroit on parol of honor, but Hamilton and a few others were sent to Virginia, where the council ordered them into confinement as a punishment for their ultra barbariism, in offering rewards for the scalps of those who were captured by the Indians. Gen. Phillips protesting against this rigid treatment, Jefferson referred the matter to Washington, who considering it a violation of the agreement made at the surrender of the fort, they were released.

During the siege of the fort, a party of Indian warriors, bringing with them two white persons, whom they had captured in a raid on the frontier of Kentucky, arrived and camped in the vicinity of the village. Ignorant of Clark's presence, he sent against them a force which soon routed them, with a loss of nine warriors. The remainder precipitately fled, well pleased to escape with their lives from an enemy whose prowess on previous occasions they had learned to fear. A few days afterward, Capt. Helm and 60 men were detached to proceed up the Wabash and intercept valuable military stores then on the way from Detroit to Vincennes. The expedition was successful, securing the convoying party and property to the amount of $50,000. On the return of the detachment laden with their spoils, the galley hove in sight, and was

_____
*Butler's Kentucky.

preparing for an attack on the little river fleet, when the ensign of freedom was discovered waving over the fort. The crew, although rejoicing in the triumph of their brethren who had preceded them by land, regretted exceedingly the circumstances which had denied them the privilege of participating in the reduction of the fort.

After taking Vincennes under obstacles which, by any other commander except Clark, would have been deemed insurmountable, this brilliant achievement was only considered the stepping stone to other and richer conquests. Detroit was undoubtedly within the reach of the enterprising Virginian. "Fortune has thus twice placed this point in my power," he writes to Gov. Henry. "Had I been able to raise 500 men when I first arrived in the country, or 300 when at Vincennes, I should have attempted its subjugation." Intelligence was brought to him that the garrison at that time contained but 80 men, many of whom were invalids, and that the inhabitants of the town were so partial to the Americans as to rejoice exceedingly when they heard of Hamilton's capture. In view of these facts, Clark determined to make an attack upon the place, when receiving dispatches from the governor of Virginia promising a battalion of men, he deemed it most prudent to postpone operations till the reinforcements should arrive.

Leaving Capt. Helm in command at Vincennes, Clark embarked on board the galley and returned to Kaskaskia, where he found himself more embarrassed by the depreciated currency which had been advanced to him by the government of Virginia, than previously by the British and Indians. While adjusting these difficulties, the war with England and the colonies terminated in the independence of the latter, and with it followed a suspension of the hostilities which had so long devastated the western frontier. Clark's services being no longer needed, at the instance of Gen. Harrison he was relieved of his command, receiving the most hearty encomiums of Virginia's noblest statesmen for the valuable services he had rendered the country.

The advantages resulting from the capture of the military stations of Illinois cannot be over estimated. Hamilton, as intimated, had made arrangements to enlist all the southern and western Indians for his contemplated campaign the ensuing spring, and had he not been intercepted, the entire country between the Alleghanies and the Mississippi might have been overrun, and thus have changed the whole current of American history. Jefferson said, in a letter to Clark, "Much solicitude will be felt for the result of your expedition to the Wabash; if successful it will have an important bearing in determining our north-western boundary." Accordingly, as predicted by this great statesman, in the preliminary negotiations for peace and boundary of 1782 between the colonies and the three great rival powers of Europe, the conquest of Clark had a controlling influence in their deliberations. Spain claimed the entire region between the Ohio and Mississippi rivers, on the pretense, that in the winter of 1781, sixty-five Spaniards and an equal number of Indians captured St. Joseph, a small English fort near the source of the Illinois, and took possession of the adjacent country in the name of their sovereign. Dr. Franklin, one of the negotiators, referring to the claim of this power, said it was

the design of the Spanish court to restrict the United States to
the Alleghanies, and he hoped that Congress would insist on the
Mississippi as the western boundary. It was, however, found
impossible to connect the Spanish possessions on the Lower Mississippi with the disputed territory, for Clark had built Fort
Jefferson, below the mouth of the Ohio, and Virginia had actual
possession between the two rivers. France, at the treaty of Paris,
in 1763, had transferred all this vast region to England, and could
make no claim. She, however, objected to the right of the Americans, hoping by this stroke of policy in favor of her jealous rivals,
to gain some other point in the controversy where she was more
directly interested.

Nor had England the presumption to contend, that it did not
belong to the colonies, which had established themselves as the
United States. The patent of Virginia covered most of the disputed territory; the army of Clark had subdued and permanently
occupied it. Subsequently it had been organized as a county of
the State, and consequently the English envoy could not claim it,
with any more propriety than other parts of the commonwealth
after the battle of Yorktown. He was too accurate a jurist to
allow the claim of Spain, or to listen to the objections of France;
but what would have been his decision looking to British aggran-
disement, had it not been for the civil and military rule previously
established by the Americans?

In estimating the debt of gratitude we owe to Clark and his
sturdy Virginia veterans, let us consider whether the great country
of Louisiana, subsequently purchased by Jefferson from the First
Consul, could have been obtained but for the service which they
rendered. Nay, but for their valor, the magnificent national
domain now stretching away to the Pacific, and promising to
absorb the whole continent, might have been broken at the mountain's summit or the river's shore; and the Republic, now exerting
controlling influence among the great nationalities of the world,
would consequently have remained an inconsiderable power.

After his campaigns in Illinois, Clark engaged in a number of
expeditions against the Indians; fought under Baron Steuben in
the East against the traitor Arnold, and finally enlisted as a brigadier-general in the armies of France to operate against the
Spanish possessions on the lower Mississippi. Before anything
was effected, Genet, the French minister and leader of the enterprise, was recalled, Clark's commission was annulled, and he
retired to private life. During the latter years of his life he
became an invalid, suffering intensely from rheumatic affections
caused by exposure in his previous campaigns. With advancing
age the disease assumed the form of paralysis, and terminated
fatally, his death and burial occurring in 1818, at Locust Grove,
near Louisville.

The rippling waters of the beautiful Ohio still murmur a requiem
over the grave which contains his dust, and his tireless energy
still lives in the enterprise of the millions who dwell in the land
he loved and defended. In other respects the innovations of time
have ruthlessly effected a change.

Only the relics of the race which contended with him for the
empire of the wilderness, can be found in the cabinet of the
antiquary; forests, solitary and unproductive, have passed away,

and a new creation of fruitful fields and cultivated landscapes has taken their place ; the untrained energies and stationary condition of savage life have been superceded by a civilization whose onward march is heard in the turmoil of rising cities, the din of railroad trains, or the panting steamboat lashing into foam the watery highways which bear it on the errands of commerce.

CHAPTER XVIII.

1778-1787—ILLINOIS UNDER VIRGINIA.

The French Take the Oath of Allegiance—Illinois County—American Immigrants—La Balme's Expedition—The Cession of the Country, and Delays Incident Thereto—No Regular Courts of Law —Curious Land Speculation.

The respect shown by Clark and his followers for their property and religion, the news of an alliance between their mother country, France, and the United States, and perhaps their hereditary hatred to the British, readily reconciled the French inhabitants of Kaskaskia and neighboring towns to the change of government over them. In October, 1778, the Virginia Assembly erected the conquered country, embracing all the territory northwest of the Ohio, claimed under this conquest and otherwise, into the County of Illinois, a pretty extensive county, which has since been carved up into 5 large States, containing a population now exceeding 8,000,000 souls. A force of 500 men was ordered to be raised for its defence, an order which Clark had in part anticipated by enlistments made on his own reponsibility. Colonel Clark continued to be the military commander of all the western territory, both north and south of the Ohio, including Illinois.

Colonel John Todd, then residing in Fayette county, Kentucky, who, under Clark, had been the first man to enter Fort Gage, was appointed lieutenant-commandant of the County of Illinois. Patrick Henry, governor of Virginia, in his letter, dated Williamsburg, Virginia, December 12th, 1778, apprising Todd of his appointment, instructed him to cultivate and conciliate the affections of the French and Indians, and inculcate the value of liberty; that on account of his want of acquaintance with the usages and manners of the people, to advise with the intelligent and upright of the country; to give particular attention to Colonel Clark and his corps, and co-operate with him in any military undertaking; to tell his people that peace could not be expected so long as the British occupied Detroit and incited the savages to deeds of robbery and murder; that, in the military line, it would be expected of him to over-awe the Indians, that they might not war on the settlers southeast of the Ohio; to consider himself as the head of the civil department, and see that the inhabitants have justice done them for any injury received from the soldiery, and quell their licentiousness; to touch not upon the subject of boundaries and lands with the Indians and arouse their jealousy; to punish every tresspass upon the same, and preserve peace with them; to manifest a high regard toward His Catholic Majesty, and tender the friendship and services of his people to the Spanish commandant at St. Louis. A large discretion was given him in his administration of civil affairs, and monthly reports were asked.

In the spring of 1779, Colonel Todd visited Kaskaskia, and began at once to organize a temporary government for the colonies. On the 15th of June, he issued the following proclamation:

" *Illinois [County] to-wit*:

" Whereas, from the fertility and beautiful situation of the lands bordering upon the Mississippi, Ohio, Illinois and Wabash rivers, the taking up of the usual quantity of land heretofore allowed for a settlement by the government of Virginia, would injure both the strength and commerce of this country: I do, therefore, issue this proclamation, strictly enjoining all persons, whatsoever, from making any new settlements upon the flat lands of said rivers, or within one league of said lands, unless in manner and form of settlements heretofore made by French inhabitants, until further orders herein given. And, in order that all the claims to lands, in said county, may be fully known, and some method provided for perpetuating, by record, the just claims, every inhabitant is required, as soon as conveniently may be, to lay before the person, in each district appointed for that purpose, a memorandum of his or her land, with copies of all their vouchers; and where vouchers have been given, or are lost, such depositions or certificates as will tend to support their claims;—The memorandum to mention the quantity of land, to whom originally granted, and when, deducing the title through various occupants to the present possessor. The number of adventurers who will shortly overrun this country, renders the above method necessary. as well as to ascertain the vacant lands, as to guard against tresspasses which will probably be committed on lands not on record. Given under my hand and seal, at Kaskaskia, the 15th of June, in the 3rd year of the commonwealth, 1779.

" JOHN TODD, JR. "

Many of the French inhabitants at Kaskaskia, Cahokia and Vincennes, readily took the oath of allegiance to Virginia. Not only these, but many of the chief men of the Indian tribes expressed sentiments of friendship for the United States government.

At the period of which we write, with the exception of the French along the Mississippi, and a few families scattered along the Illinois and Wabash rivers, all within the present boundaries of Illinois was the abode of the nomadic savage. During the years 1779–80, the westward emigration from the Atlantic States, took a very considerable start. Among the circumstances which gave it impetus, were the brilliant achievements of Col. Clark at Kaskaskia and Vincennes, which were the occasion of publishing abroad the fertile plains of Illinois; the triumph of the British arms in the south, and a threatened advance upon Virginia; and the liberal manner of the latter State, in inviting families to take possession of the public lands claimed by her in the western country. Three hundred family boats arrived at the Falls of Ohio in the spring of 1780, mostly destined for Kentucky.* Among the immigrants to Illinois, we note the names of James Moore, Shadrach Bond, James Garrison, Robert Kidd and Larken Rutherford, the two latter having been with Clark. They were from Virginia and Maryland. With their families, they, without molestation in those perilous times, crossed the Alleghanies, descended the Ohio, stemmed the Mississippi, and landed safely at Kaskaskia. James

*Butler's Kentucky.

Moore, the leader, and a portion of his party, located on the hills near Bellefontaine, while Bond and the rest settled in the American Bottom (from which circumstance that name is derived), near Harrisonville, afterwards known as the blockhouse fort. James Piggot, John Doyle, Robert Whitehead and a Mr. Bowen, soldiers in Clark's expedition, also shortly after settled in Illinois. Doyle had a family and taught school. He was, perhaps, the first teacher to make that profession his business in Illinois. He also spoke French and Indian, and in the latter language was frequently employed as interpreter. Not until 1785 was this little band of American pioneers reinforced. Then came Joseph Ogle, Joseph Warley and James Andrews, all from Virginia and each with a large family. In the following year the American settlements were again augmented by the arrival of James Lemen, George Atcherson, and David Waddell with their families, besides several others.*

While the country was under the Virginia regime (but without the sanction of her authorities), La Balme, a native of France, in the fall of 1780 during the revolutionary war, made another attempt to lead an expedition from Kaskaskia against the British. It consisted of 30 men, and was ostensibly formed to capture the post of Detroit. At Vincennes it was reinforced by a few men. The party moved up the Wabash, and at the head of the Maumee attacked and destroyed a British trading post called Kekionga, on the site of the present Fort Wayne. After securing the booty, the party retired to the banks of the small river Aboite, where they encamped. Here a party of Indians attacked them in the night, the leader and a few of his followers were killed, the remainder dispersed, and the expedition against Detroit failed. Its object, like those of Brady and Meillet, was doubtless plunder.†

Col. Todd, the Virginia commandant, was but little of his time in our part of the Illinois county; he remained in command until the time of his death, which occurred at the battle of Blue Licks in Kentucky, August 18, 1782, where he was in command, not having resigned as commander of the militia of that district in Kentucky. This was the bloodiest Indian battle ever fought in Kentucky. Cols. Todd, Trig, Harlan, and a son of Daniel Boone, all fell. It was a sad day; the Kentuckians lost 67 men, more than a third of their force, mostly killed. Col. Todd had just returned from Virginia on business pertaining to the Illinois county. His government in Illinois was popular.

The successor of Col. Todd was a Frenchman, named Timothy de Montbrun, of whose administration, how long it lasted, or who was his successor, little or nothing is known. Montbrun's name appears to land grants and other documents among the archives at Kaskaskia.

The Cession of Illinois.—As we have seen, all of the Northwestern territory, by private conquest, passed under the dominion of Virginia at a time when all the States were engaged in a common war, defending against the power of the mother country to reduce them to subjection; and whatever was the right of a State to organize an individual war enterprise, and turn its success to

*See Annals of the West. .
†Reynold's Pioneer History.

private advantage, by extending her jurisdiction over a vast and fertile region for her separate benefit and aggrandizement, the congress of the States, probably for the sake of harmony, acquiesced in the validity of this. But Virginia and a number of other States asserted still another claim to these western lands, and during the revolutionary war these conflicting claims became quite a hindrance to the prompt adoption of the articles of confederation. Many of the original colonies had their boundaries exactly defined in their royal charters, but Virginia, Connecticut, Massachusetts, and the Carolinas, claimed to extend westward to the farther ocean, or to the Mississippi; since, under the treaty of Paris, 1763, that river had become the established western boundary of Great Britain. New York, too, under certain alleged concessions to her jurisdiction made by the Iroquois, or six nations, the conquerers of many Algonquin tribes including the Illinois, claimed almost the whole of the western country from beyond the lakes on the north to the Cumberland mountains on the south, and west to the great river.

Large ideas as to the pecuniary value of the western lands obtained at the time, from which vast revenues were anticipated. The prospective well-filled coffers of the States, as well as the broad expansion of their dominions, excited the envy of their landless sisters. The latter held, therefore, that as these lands, as well as their own independence, had to be wrested from the British crown by joint effort, they ought to become joint property. Still, the claimant States in congress had succeeded in getting a clause inserted into the proposed articles of confederation, that no State should be deprived of any territory for the joint benefit of all. But Maryland, a non-claimant State, refused her assent to the articles with that provision. The adoption of the articles, which would make of the colonies a union, was very much desired. New York now, whose claim was the most baseless, opened the way by allowing her delegates in congress, at discretion, to cede to the union all her interest west of a line drawn through the western extremity of Lake Ontario. Congress urged this example upon the other claimant states, guaranteeing that the ceded lands should be disposed of for the common benefit of all; and as the territories became populated they should be divided into States and admitted into the Union on an equal footing with the original States.

Connecticut next proposed a cession of her indefinite due western extension, retaining, however, a tract of some 3,000,000 acres in Northwestern Ohio, known since as the Western Reserve. This she also relinquished in the year 1800. The Virginia assembly, hoping to reanimate the flagging cause of the South by a more thorough union, just prior to its adjournment, December 31, 1780, on the approach of Arnold, who sacked and burned Richmond within a few days after, ceded to the United States all her claim to the territory north-west of the river Ohio, requiring from congress, however, a guarantee of her right to the remainder south of the Ohio and east of the Mississippi. The New York delegates soon after exercised the discretion confided to them by their State, and executed a deed of cession, reserving the right of retraction unless the same guarantees were extended to New York as to any other ceding States. On the same day the delegates of Maryland, being thereunto empowered by act of the State, signed the articles of confederation, which completed the ratification, and a nation was launched.

This was early in the sping of 1781; Virginia, however, did not execute her deed of cession till March 1, 1784. In the meantime peace had been made with Great Britain, by which nearly all this country passed to the ownership of the Nation, in common, and Virginia modified her act of cession by omitting her demand to the territory south-east of the Ohio. The deed of cession was executed by her delegates in Congress, Thomas Jefferson, Samuel Hardy, Arthur Lee and James Monroe. It stipulated that the territory should be cut into States not less than 100 nor more than 150 miles square; to be republican in form, and to be admitted into the union with "the same rights of sovereignty, freedom and independence as the other States;" that indemnity for the expenses of her expeditions incurred in subduing the British posts in the west be allowed her; that land, not exceeding 150,000 acres, promised by her, should be allowed to George Rogers Clark, his officers and soldiers; that the proceeds of the sales of the lands ceded shall be considered a common fund for all the States, present and future; and that "the French and Canadian inhabitants, and other settlers of the Kaskaskias, Post Vincennes, and the neighboring villages, who have professed themselves citizens of Virginia, shall have their possessions and titles confirmed to them, and be protcted in the enjoyment of their rights and liberties."

Immediately after the execution of the deed of cession by Virginia, Congress proposed by ordinance, (April 23, 1784,) to establish a form of government for the entire western region, from the Gulf to the Lakes, though it was not yet wholly acquired. The plan proposed to divide the whole into 17 States; a tier of 8 was to border on the Mississippi, whose eastern boundary was to be a north and south line through the falls of the Ohio, and each to contain two parallels of latitude, except the northernmost, which was to extend from the 45th parallel to the northern limits of the United States; to the east of these a corresponding tier of 8 more was to be laid off, whose eastern boundary was to be a north and south line running through the mouth of the Great Kanawha; the remaining tract, to the east of this and north of the Ohio, was to constitute the 17th State. In these territories, the settlers, either on their petition or by act of Congress, were to receive authority to create a temporary form of government; but when 20,000 free inhabitants had settled within any of them, they were authorized to call a convention, form a constitution, and establish for themselves a permanent government, subject to the following requirements: to remain forever a part of the confederacy of the United States; to be subject to the articles of confederation and the acts and ordinances of Congress like the original States; not to interfere with the disposal of the soil by Congress; to be liable to their proportion of the federal debt, present and prospective; not to tax the lands of the United States; their respective governments to be republican; not to tax lands belonging to non-residents higher than those of residents; and when any one got of free inhabitants as many as the least numerous of the original Thirteen States, to be admitted into the Union on an equal footing with them. The committee, of which Mr. Jefferson was chairman, reported also this remarkable provision, the adoption of which, and unalterable adherence to, would doubtless have prevented the late rebellion: "That after they car 1800, of the Christian era, there shall be neither slavery nor involuntary servitude in any of the said States, otherwise than in punishment of crimes, whereof the party shall have been duly convicted." But this proviso failed on account of not receiving a majority of the States. The four New England States, with New York and Pennsylvania, voted for it; New Jersey, Delaware and Georgia, were unrepresented; North Carolina was divided; Maryland, South Carolina and Virginia, (Mr. Jefferson being overborne by his colleagues,) voted against it. The anti-slavery clause was stricken out and the resolutions became an ordinance.

While such was the law for these territories, it never received application to any of them; no organization was ever effected under it. Nor had Massachusetts in the meantime relinquished her claim in the territories. In 1785, Rufus King renewed the anti-slavery proviso in congress, as a condition upon which she would make a cession of her claim. The question was referred to a committee of eight States, where it slept the sleep that knows no waking. Massachusetts, however, in accordance with the Virginia scheme of dividing the western territory into small States, ceded her claim, April 19, 1785; and with the consent of Congress to accept the cession of Connecticut, with the reservation of 3,000,000 acres, September 13th, 1786, the title of the confederated States to the lands north-west of the river Ohio became complete. In the meantime, by act of congress, surveys and explorations were going on in the territories which glaringly exposed the total disregard of natural boundaries, and the inconvenience resulting from cutting up the western country into fourteen small States. Virginia and Massachusetts were now called upon to modify the conditions of their deeds, so as to allow that portion of the territory northwest of the Ohio to be divided up into three or five States, at the option of Congress, which was accordingly done, and the following year Congress passed the ordinance of 1787.

This was a slow transition period, which was doubly experienced in the settlements of Illinois which were the fartherest removed from the seat of power, be it Virginia or the United States. During all this time, and for three years after the adoption of the ordinance of 1787, and until the organization of the county of St. Clair, by Governor St. Clair, in 1790, there was a very imperfect administration of the law, which consisted of a mixture of the civil or the French, the English, as resulting from the promulgations of the arbitrary acts of the British commandants at Fort Chartres, and such as had been instituted by the Virginia authorities. There were no regular courts of law in existence in the country, and no civil government worth mentioning. The people were a law unto themselves; their morals were simple and pure, and the grosser vices were kept dormant. Crimes against the peace of society were rare, misdemeanors infrequent, and fraud and dishonest dealings seldom practiced. During part of this time, too, the Indians were hostile, committing many brutal murders, which engaged the settlers in constant warfare and mutual protection against the savages; a state of affairs not con-

ducive to the civil administration of the law where even the most
perfect code exists. The following curious land speculation, on the
part of a territorial court instituted by Colonel Todd, as it relates
in part to Illinois, may not be amiss to transcribe, as it illustrates
also the fallibility of men in office, and the necessity of the people to ever hold a watchful eye over their official servants.

In June, 1779, Colonel Todd established a court of civil and
criminal jurisdiction at Post Vincennes, composed of several magistrates. Colonel J. M. P. Legras, having been appointed commandant of the post, acted as president of the court, and exercised
a controlling influence over its proceedings. Adopting in some
measure the usages and customs of the early French commandants, the court began to grant or concede tracts of land to the
French and American inhabitants, and to different civil and military officers of the country. Indeed, the court assumed the power
of granting lands to every applicant, mostly in tracts varying from
the size of a house lot to 400 acres, though some were several
leagues square. Before 1783, about 26,000 acres of land were thus
granted to different individuals; and from 1773 to 1787, when in
the latter year the practice was stopped by General Harmar, the
grants amounted to 22,000 acres, making a total, first and last,
of 48,000 acres. The commandant and magistrates, after having
exercised this power for some time, were easily led to believe that
they had the right to dispose of all that large tract of land which,
in 1742, had been granted by the Piankeshaw Indians, for the use
of the French inhabitants at Post Vincennes. Once convinced of
their supreme dominion over this entire tract, the court was not
long in arriving at the conclusion that they might make grants to
themselves with as much propriety as to others; and if they could
do this, with small tracts, they might with the whole; hoping,
doubtless, that, as the country passed under the government of the
United States, the grants would receive confirmation. Accordingly, all that tract of country extending on the Wabash 72 miles
from Pointe La Coupee to the mouth of White river, westward into
Illinois 120 miles and east from the Wabash 90 miles (excluding
lands already conceded), " to which the Indian title was supposed
to be extinguished, was divided between the members of the
court, and orders to that effect, entered on their journal; each
member [as a matter of delicacy] absenting himself from the
court on the day that the order was made in his favor, so as to give
it the appearance of being the [disinterested] act of his fellows
only."*

This shameful transaction being totally illegal, as no agent or
trustee can make sale to himself, failing to prove a source of profit
to the grantees in open market, was in a measure abandoned.
Still, as the grant was in due form, under the great seal and
authority of Virginia, land speculators, spying out the matter,
quietly purchased freely of the lands thus granted, which could
be readily done for a song, and then dispersed themselves over all
the United States, and for many years after, duped great numbers
of ignorant and credulous people, many of whom did not find out
the swindle until moving out to their lands so purchased, they discovered their titles to be a myth. These swindling practices

---

*Letter of Governor Harrison.

never wholly ceased until Governor Harrison, in 1802, at Vincennes, forbid prothonotaries from authenticating under the sanction of the official seal of the territory, and recorders from recording any of these fraudulent papers.*

*Annals of the West.

CHAPTER XIX.

1787—1800—ILLINOIS UNDER THE GOVERNMENT OF THE NORTH-WESTERN TERRITORY.

Ordinance of 1787—Organization of St. Clair County—Bar of Illinois in 1790—Impoverished Condition of the French—Indian Hostilities, 1783 to 1795—Randolph County—American Immigration—Sickness—Territorial Assembly at Cincinnati—Notable Women of the Olden Time—Witchcraft in Illinois.

———

The celebrated ordinance of 1787 was passed by the congress of the confederated States on the 13th of July of that year. By it, the whole of the country north-west of the river Ohio was constituted one district, for the purposes of temporary government. It provided for the descent of property in equal shares, substantially as under our present laws, (a just provision, not then generally recognized in the States,) "saving, however, to the French and Canadian inhabitants and other settlers of Kaskaskia, St. Vincents, and other neighboring villages, who have heretofore professed themselves citizens of Virginia, their laws and customs now in force among them, relative to the descent and conveyance of property." A governor was provided for, whose term of office was three years, who was to reside in the district and own a freehold of 1,000 acres of land; a secretary, whose commission was to run four years, subject to revocation: he was to reside in the district and own 500 acres of land. A court was provided for, to consist of three judges, two of them to constitute a court; they were to exercise common law jurisdiction, to reside in the district, own 500 acres of land, their commissions to last during good behavior. They, jointly with the governor, were to adopt such laws of the original States as were suitable to the conditions of the country, to remain in force until the organization of the general assembly, which might alter or re-adopt them; congress, also, might disapprove them. The governor was constituted commander-in-chief of the militia, with power to appoint all officers below the grade of general officers. Until the organization of the general assembly, the governor was to appoint all the civil officers in each county. He was to establish counties from time to time, to whose limits legal process was to run. With 5,000 free male inhabitants of full age, the territory was entitled to a general assembly, the time and place of election to be fixed by the governor; each 500 were entitled to one representative, till the number reached 25, after which the legislature was to regulate the number and proportion. The qualifications of a member were, either a residence in the territory three years, or citizenship in a State for three years and present residence in the territory, and a fee simple right to 200 acres of land within the same; qualification of an elector: freehold of 50 acres and citizenship in one of the States, or a like freehold and two years residence in the district. Representatives were elected for the term of two years. The assembly was to consist of the governor, council and house of representatives. The council was to consist of five members, three to constitute a quorum; time of service, five years. Congress was to select the council from ten men—residents of the territory, each having a freehold of 500 acres—nominated by the house of representatives. Bills, to become laws, must pass both houses by a majority and receive the signature of the governor, who possessed an absolute veto by simply withholding his approval. The two houses, by joint ballot, were to elect a delegate to congress, who was allowed to debate, but not to vote. An oath of office of office was to be taken by all the officers.

For extending the fundamental principles of civil and religious liberty, and to fix the basis of government of future States to be formed out of said territory, it was further provided, in six unalterable articles of perpetual compact between the people of the original states and the people of the territory:

I. No person, in peaceable demeanor, was to be molested on account of his mode of worship or religious sentiments.

II. The inhabitants were guaranteed the benefits of the writs of habeas corpus and trial by jury; a proportionate representation in the legislature and judicial proceedings according to the course of the common law. "All persons shall be bailable, unless for capital offenses, where the proof shall be evident or the presumption great. All fines shall be moderate; and no cruel or unusual punishments shall be inflicted. No man shall be deprived of his liberty or his property, but by the judgment of his peers, or the law of the land; and should the public exigencies make it necessary, for the common preservation, to take any person's property, or to demand his particular services, full compensation shall be made for the same." No law ought ever to be made or have force in said territory, that shall, in any manner, interfere with or affect private contracts or engagements made in good faith and without fraud.

III. Religion, morality and knowledge being necessary to good government and the happiness of mankind, schools and the means of education shall forever be encouraged. Good faith, justice and humanity toward the Indians, was to be observed; their lands and property not to be taken without consent, and peace and friendship to be cultivated.

IV. The territory, and States to be formed therein, were to remain forever a part of the United States, subject to her laws; the inhabitants to pay a just proportion of the public debt, contracted or to be contracted; not to tax the lands of the United States, nor those of non-residents higher than those of residents; the navigable waters of the lakes to remain forever free to all citizens of the United States.

V. The territory was not to be divided into less than three States, and, at its option, congress might "form one or two (more) States in that part which lies north of an east and west line drawn through the southerly bend or extreme of Lake Michigan." With 60,000 free inhabitants, such States were to be admitted into the union on an equal footing with the original States.

VI. " There shall be neither slavery nor involuntary servitude in the said territory, otherwise than in the punishment of crimes, whereof the party shall have been duly convicted;" this section providing also for the reclamation of fugitives from labor.

· Such was substantially the fundamental law of this vast territory, which has ever had a controlling influence upon the destiny of the States carved out of it, and saved some of them from the permanent blight of slavery. While the convention at Philadelphia was occupied with framing the constitution of the United States, congress, sitting in New York, disposed of this subject, which was fraught with an importance second only to the constitution itself. The anti-slavery clause, it will be observed, was substantially the same as that reported by Jefferson in 1784, for the organization of all the western territory, but which was then rejected. The ordinance was reported from committee by Mr. Dane, of Massachusetts, and unanimously adopted by the eight States then only represented in congress. On October 5, 1787, Major General Arthur St. Clair was, by congress, elected governor of the Northwestern territory. St. Clair was born in Scotland and emigrated to America in 1755. He served in the French and British war, under General Amherst, at the taking of Louisburg, in 1758, and at the storming of Quebec, under Wolfe, in 1759. After the peace of 1763, he settled in western Pennsylvania. In the war of the Revolution he was first commissioned a colonel, raised a regiment of 750 men and was afterward promoted to the rank of major general. In 1788 he was tried by court-martial for evacuating Ticonderoga and Mt. Independence, but was honorably acquitted. He remained in the service until the close of the war. In 1786 he was elected to congress, and was chosen president of that body. Owing to his losses in the war of the revolution, his friends pressed him for the governorship of the Northwestern Territory, that he might retrieve his fortune. But he "had neither taste nor genius for speculation in lands, nor did he think it consistent with the office."[*]

The instructions from congress were, in effect, to promote peace and harmony between the Indians and the United States, to defeat all combinations or confederations between them, and conciliate good feeling between them and the white settlers; to regulate trade with them; to ascertain as far as possible the several tribes, their head men and number of warriors, and by every means attach them to the government of the United States; and to neglect no opportunity to extinguish the Indian titles to lands westward as far as the Mississippi, and north to the 41st degree of north latitude.

In the summer of 1788, the governor and judges (Samuel Holden Parsons, James Mitchell Varnum, and John Cleves Symmes), met at Marietta, the seat of government, and adopted and promulgated a code of laws for the whole territory. The governor immediately established some counties, except in Illinois, appointed the civil officers for them, and thus, July 15th, the machinery of the territorial government under the U. S. was put into operation. These

---

[*] His letter to W. B. Giles, of Virginia.

steps by the judges and governor were commonly denominated the first grade of territorial government under the ordinance.

As characteristic of the period, we note that the punishment for crimes, owing to the want of prisons, were generally of a summary character: Death for murder, treason, and arson, (if loss of life ensued therefrom); whipping with 39 lashes, and fine, for larceny, burglary and robbery; for perjury, whipping, fine, or standing in the pillory; for forgery, fine, disfranchisement and standing in the pillory; drunkenness, fine, for non-payment of which to stand in the stocks; for non-payment of fines generally, the sheriff was empowered to bind out the convict for a term not exceeding 7 years; obscene conversation and profane swearing were admonished against, and threatened with the loss of the government's confidence; morality and piety were enjoyned, and the Sabbath pronounced sacred.

Under date of October 6th, 1789, president Washington wrote to Governor St. Clair: You will also proceed, as soon as you can, with safety, to execute the orders of the late congress respecting the inhabitants at Post Vincennes and at the Kaskaskias, and the other villages on the Mississippi. It is a circumstance of some importance, that the said inhabitants should, as soon as possible, possess the lands which they are entitled to, by some known and fixed principle. Accordingly in February, Gov. St. Clair and the Secretary, Winthrop Sargent, arrived at Kaskaskia. The country within the boundaries of our present State extending northward to the mouth of the Little Mackinaw creek on the Illinois was organized into a county, which was named after His Excellency, St. Clair, and may be called the mother of counties in Illinois. It was divided into three judicial districts, a court of common pleas established, 3 judges appointed, namely: John Edgar, of Kaskaskia; John Babtiste Barbeau, of Prairie du Rocher, and John D. Moulin, of Cahokia, each to hold the courts for and in the district of his residence. The terms were fixed to be held every three months, hence the name of quarter sessions, by which the courts were generally known. William St. Clair, brother of the governor, was appointed clerk and recorder of deeds, and William Biggs, sheriff. Cahokia became the county seat. While the clerk could issue process for the county, and the sheriff serve the same, suit had to be brought and entitled of the district where the defendant resided, and the writs to bear test of the judges of the respective districts, dated at the respective villages and run with the respective districts. Grand juries were to be quarterly organized in each district. The right of appeal was rendered practically nugatory, and in no case was it resorted to. The sessions of the U. S. judges for the territory were held in banc at either Cincinnati or Chillicothe, a distance so great from Illinois, by the then facilities of travel, as to render appeal impracticable. Of the judges, John de Moulin, a native of Switzerland, possessing a good education and fair knowledge of the civil law, was a large, fine looking man, a bachelor. He was also colonel of the militia, and showed well on parade days. He was very popular. Jean Babtiste Barbeau, was of the original Canadian French stock, long settled in Illinois; energetic, fair business talent, and extensive experience. John Edgar was an Englishman. Justices of the peace were also appointed throughout the county. Their jurisdiction was limited to

$20 in civil cases; in criminal, they possessed only examining power; juries before them were not countenanced. Appeal lay to the common pleas courts.* Thus was launched the first county of Illinois upon its career of usefulness, with all its political machinery duly organized under the laws of the United States. Down to this period, a mixture of the old French, English and Virginia laws had maintained a sort of obsolete existence and operation.

It may not be uninteresting to relate that the bar of Illinois, in 1790, was illuminated by but a single member, who was, however, a host himself. This was John Rice Jones, a Welchman, born 1750. He was an accomplished linguist, possessed of a classical education, and a thorough knowledge of the law. He was the earliest practitioner of law in Illinois and would have been conspicuous at any bar. His practice extended from Kaskaskia to Vincennes and Clarksville, (Louisville, Ky.) Contrary to the habits of frontier life, be was never idle. As a speaker, his capacity for invective under excitement was extraordinary. Removing to Vincennes, he became a member of the territorial legislature, and in 1807 rendered important services in revising the statute laws for the territory of Indiana.† In 1786, news found currency in the western country that congress, whose meetings were in great part secret, had by treaty agreed with Spain to a temporary relinquishment of the right to the free navigation of the Mississippi. The western people, who received these reports greatly magnified, were bitterly incensed thereat. At Vincennes a body of men were enlisted without authority, known as the Wabash regiment, to be subsisted by impressment or otherwise, of whom George Rogers Clark took command, and by his orders the Spanish traders there and in the Illinois, were plundered and despoiled of their goods and merchandise in retaliation of similar alleged offences by the Spaniards at Natchez. In these outrages John Rice Jones took a leading part. He became the commissary general of the marauders, to the support of whom Illinois merchants contributed. Such goods as were unsuited to the use of the garrison were sold by Jones. These acts tended to embroil us with Spain. Jones later removed to Missouri, became a member of the constitutional convention, and was a candidate for U. S. Senator in opposition to Mr. Benton. He held the office of judge of the Supreme Court of Missouri until his death, in 1824.

The second lawyer of Illinois, prior to 1800, was Isaac Darnielle. To a strong native intellect, classical education and a tolerable knowledge of the law, he added an engaging manner, free benevolent disposition, and a rather large, portly and attractive person. He was an agreeable speaker, conspicious at the bar, and popular with the people. He was said to have been educated for the ministry and had occupied the pulpit. But his great forte lay

---

*Brown, History of Ills. p. 273, (with a confused idea as to boundary), to show the inconvenient size of St. Clair County, relates the following:

Suit having been brought before a Justice of Cahokia to recover the value of a cow, and judgment having been rendered for $16, the case was appealed. The adverse party and witnesses resided at Prairie du Chien, Wisconsin, distance 400 miles. The Sheriff, who was also an Indian trader, having received a summons for the party and subpœnas for the witnesses, fitted out a boat with a suitable stock of goods for the Indian trade and proceeded thither with his papers. Having served the summons and subpœnaed the witnesses, which included the greater part of the inhabitants of Prairie du Chien, he made his return charging mileage and service for each, as he had a right to, his costs and the cost of the suit altogether, it is stated, exceeding $900. Whether the costs were ever paid or not, chroniclers have failed to transmit.

†See Reynold's Pioneer Hist. of Ills.

in the court of Venus, where he practiced with consummate art and with more studious assuidity than his books received. He never married and yet apparently was never without a wife. This course of life brought its inevitable consequences. While youth and vigor lasted all was well, but with advancing age, he was compelled to abandon his profession, and finally died in western Kentucky, at the age of 60, a poor and neglected school-teacher.*

As to the practice of those times, ex-governor Reynolds relates seeing the records of a proceeding in court at Prairie du Rocher, against a negro for the "murder" of a hog. The case was malicious mischief, for wantonly destroying a useful animal, which it was sought to bring before the court; but in the absence of a prosecuting attorney, officers disallowed at that time, the grand jury, groping about in the law books, met with a precedent of an indictment for murder and applied it to the case in hand. Perhaps justice was meted out as fully under this indictment as if drawn with the nicest precision as to the nature of the offence, and prosecuted by the ablest attorney in the country.

In the deed of cession from Virginia, it was stipulated that the French and Canadian inhabitants, and other settlers, who had professed allegiance to Virginia, should have their titles confirmed to them. By a law of congress of 1788, the governor of the territory was authorized to confirm the possessions and titles of the French to their lands (and those people in their rights,) who, on or before the year 1783, had professed themselves citizens of the United States, or any of them. But nothing had been done in this direction up to the arrival of Governor St. Clair at Kaskaskia. It was to this that Washington had called the governor's attention, in his letter of October 6, 1789. In March, 1790, to carry these instructions into effect, the governor issued his proclamation to the inhabitants, directing them to exhibit their titles and claims to the lands which they held, in order to be confirmed in their possessions. Numbers of these instruments were exhibited, and for those found to be authentic, orders of survey were issued, the expense whereof was to be paid by the owners. Such payment was anything but satisfactory to the people, as will be seen by the subjoined quotation from the governor's report to the secretary of state, in 1790; and from it may further be gleaned the deplorable condition of the French, at the time of the governor's visit in this oft-painted Eden of the Far West as if overflowing with abundance:

"Orders of survey were issued for all the claims at Kaskaskia, that appeared to be founded agreeably to the resolutions of congress; and surveys were made of the greater part of them. A part of these surveys, however, have only been returned, because the people objected to paying the surveyor, and it is too true that they are ill able to pay. The Illinois country, as well as that upon the Wabash, has been involved in great distress ever since it fell under the American dominion. With great cheerfulness, the people furnished the troops under Colonel Clark, and the Illinois regiment, with everything they could spare, and often with much more than they could spare with any convenience to themselves. Most of these certificates for these supplies are still in their hands,

---

* Reynold's Pioneer Hist.

unliquidated and unpaid; and in many instances, where application has been made for payment to the State of Virginia, under whose authority the certificates were granted, it has been refused. The Illinois regiment being disbanded, a set of men, pretending the authority of Virginia, embodied themselves, and a scene of general depredation ensued. To this, succeeded three successive and extraordinary inundations from the Mississippi, which either swept away their crops, or prevented their being planted. The loss of the greater part of their trade with the Indians, which was a great resource, came upon them at this juncture, as well as the hostile incursions of some of the tribes which had ever been in friendship with them; and to these was added the loss of their whole last crop of corn by an untimely frost. Extreme misery .could not fail to be the consequence of such accumulated misfortunes."

The impoverished condition of the French settlements is further portrayed, and doubtless truly, in a memorial addressed to Governor St. Clair, while in Illinois, which bears the date "June 9, 1790," and is signed by "P. Gibault, Priest," and 87 others. Gibault was the same ecclesiastic who, in 1788, conducted the successful embassy of Colonel Clark to Vincennes, severing the allegiance of that post from the British :

"The memorial humbly showeth, that by an act of congress of June 20, 1788, it was declared that the lands heretofore possessed by the said inhabitants, should be surveyed at their expense; and that this clause appears to them neither necessary nor adapted to quiet the minds of the people. It does not appear necessary, because from the establishment of the colony to this day, they have enjoyed their property and possessions without disputes or law suits on the subject of their limits; that the surveys of them were made at the time the concessions were obtained from their ancient kings, lords and commandants; and that each of them knew what belonged to him without attempting an encroachment on his neighbor, or fearing that his neighbor would encroach on him. It does not appear adapted to pacify them; because, instead of assuring to them the peaceable possessions of their ancient inheritances, as they have enjoyed it till now, that clause obliges them to bear expenses which, in their present situation, they are absolutely incapable of paying, and for the failure of which they must be deprived of their lands.

"Your Excellency is an eye-witness of the poverty to which the inhabitants are reduced, and of the total want of provisions to subsist on. Not knowing where to find a morsel of bread to nourish their families, by what means can they support the expenses of a survey which has not been sought for on their parts, and for which, it is conceived by them, there is no necessity? Loaded with misery, and groaning under the weight of misfortunes, accumulated since the Virginia troops entered the country, the unhappy inhabitants throw themselves under the protection of Your Excellency, and take the liberty to solicit you to lay their deplorable situation before congress; and as it may be interesting for the United States to know exactly the extent and limits of their ancient possesssion, in order to ascertain the lands which are yet at the disposal of congress, it appears to them, in their humble opinion, that the expenses of the survey ought more properly to be borne for whom alone it is useful, than by them who do not feel the necessity of it. Beside, this is no object for the United States; but it is great, too great, for a few unhappy beings, who, Your Excellency sees yourself, are scarcely able to support their pitiful existence."

The French settlements steadily declined and melted away in population from the time the country passed under Anglo-Saxon rule, 1765, until their exodus, many years later, became almost complete. After their first hegira, commencing with the English occupation, down to 1800, the immigration of the latter race scarcely counterbalanced the emigration of the former. Indeed, there was a time during the Indian troubles, that the balance fell much behind; but after the treaty of Greenville, in 1795, immigration was greatly increased. In 1800, the population was little, if any, greater than in 1765. In capacity for conquest or colonization, for energy of character, thrift, ingenious and labor-saving inventions, the Anglo-Saxon race surpasses all others. It was that race which established the British constitution; which permanently colonized the shores of America and gave to it municipal liberty, the gem of republicanism, and which furnished our unrivaled federative system, which may yet be the means of politically enfranchising the world. To have his secluded abode and remote quietude stirred up by such a race, with whom he felt himself incapable to enter the race of life, the Frenchman of these wilds lost his contentment, and he abandoned his ancient villages in Illinois, to the new life, instinct with the progress opening all around them, after an occupation of over a century.

INDIAN HOSTILITIES—1783 TO 1795.

After the tide of European immigration had forced back the red men of America from the Atlantic slopes, they found their best hunting grounds in the magnificient forests and grassy plains beyond the Alleghanies, north of the Ohio and east of the Mississippi. When, after the war of the Revolution, this empire region, wrested from the grasp of the British crown, was thrown open to settlement and the pioneers of the pale faces began to pour over the mountains and into the valley with a steadily augmenting stream, the red men determined not to give back farther. They resolved to wage a war of extermination for the retention of this vast and rich domain. Here had gathered the most warlike tribes of the Algonquin nations, who have given to known Indian history the ablest chieftains and greatest warriors, Pontiac, Little Turtle, Tecumseh, and his brother the one-eyed Prophet, Black Hawk, and Keokuk.

During the war of the Revolution all the most belligerent tribes residing within this region, and the fisheries along the great lakes of the north, had adhered to the side of Great Britain. But by the treaty of peace, 1783, the territory was transferred to the U. S. without any stipulations by England in favor of her savage allies. The British, during their twenty years rule, had not extinguished the Indian title to any part of the country. The French, during their long occupation, had made no considerable purchases of lands from the western Indians; and by the treaty of Paris, 1763, the English succeeded only to the small grants of the French about the various forts, Detroit, Kaskaskia, Vincennes, etc. True, in 1701, at Fort Stanwix, the Iroquois had ceded to Great Britain their shadowy claim over a part of the northwestern territory, acquired by their wars with the Hurons and Illinois, and in 1768 the six nations had conceded to her their rights to the lands south of the Ohio, but the conquered tribes residing upon them and making them their hunting grounds, abandoned them but temporarily, and returned and did not respect the transfers. An Indian conquest, unless followed by permanent occupation, was seldom more than a

mere raid, and could not be said to draw title after it. Therefore, by the treaty of peace of 1783, the U. S. received nothing
from England beyond the old small French grants, and the title of
the six nations by conquest, such as it was, to the western territory.
Indeed, the general government in the IVth article of the ordinance
of 1787, seems to acknowledge that it had yet to secure the title
to the lands from the Indians.

The general government, on account of the adherence of the
Indians to the side of the British during the war, if not deducing
actual title, was inclined to regard the lands of the hostile tribes
as conquered and forfeited. But while it attempted to obtain
treaties of cession from the several nations, it also immediately
threw open the country to settlers, made sales to citizens, and in
the exercise of supreme dominion, assigned reservations to some
of the natives, dictating terms and prescribing boundaries. This
at once produced a deep feeling of discontent among the Indians,
and led directly to the formation of an extensive confederation
among a great number of the northern tribes.

In October, 1784, the government Indian commissioners made a
second treaty at Fort Stanwix with a portion only of the Iroquois,
which, on account of its not being made at a general congress of
all the northern tribes, was refused to be acknowledged by their
leading chiefs, Brant, Red Jacket, and others. The following
year, at Fort McIntosh, the government again treated with a portion of the tribes—the Wyandot, Delaware, Chippewa, and
Ottawa nations—only partly represented; and in January, 1786,
at the mouth of the Great Miami (Fort Kinney,) with the Shawanese, the Wabash tribes refusing to attend.

We have seen that among the instructions issued to Gov. St.
Clair, he was to carefully examine into the real temper of the
Indians, and to use his best efforts to extinguish their titles to
lands, westward as far as the Mississippi, and north to the lakes.
In the fall of 1788, he invited the northern tribes to confirm the
late treaties of Fort Stanwix and Fort McIntosh, ceding lands;
but the Indians, in general council assembled, refused to do so and
informed the Governor "that no bargain or sale of any part of
these Indian lands would be considered as valid or binding." The
Governor, nevertheless, persisted in collecting a few chiefs of two
or three nations, at Fort Harmar, (mouth of the Muskingum), and
from them obtained acts of confirmation to the treaties of Forts
Stanwix and McIntosh, ceding an immense country, in which they
were interested only as a branch of the confederacy, and unauthorized to make any grant or cession whatever.* The nations, who
thus participated in the acts of confirmation, were the Wyandots,
Delawares, Ottawas, Chippewas, Potawattomies, and Sacs; but
the confederation of the north claimed that it was done without
authority, with the young men of the nation, alleged to have been
intimidated and over-reached.† But aside from the fact that the
government had treated with separate tribes, the grants obtained
from the Iroquois and their kindred, the Wyandots, and the Delawares and Shawanese, were open to scarcely any objections.‡ Those
most vehement in denouncing the validity of the concessions were

---

*Proceedings of Indian Council 1793—See American State papers, V. 357—7.
†Idem.
‡Stone, ii. 281.

the Miamis, Chippewas, Piankashaws, Eel River Indians, Weas (Quias Ouiatenons,) and Kaskaskias, the latter four making their residence in great part in Illinois.

The confederacy of Indians at all times strenuously insisted that the Ohio river should constitute a perpetual boundary between the red and white men; and to maintain this line the former organized a war against the latter, the ablest and most stupendous known to their annals, in the quelling of which the government was actively engaged for six years, and which was finally accomplished only by the prowess of "Mad Anthony" Wayne. In their determination, evidence is quite abundant that the Indians were inspired and supported by the advice and encouragement of British agents and officials, supplemented by the avarice of British traders. It was to their interest to have this splendid country remain the abode of the savages, with whom to exchange their gew-gaws for valuable pelts and furs; a lucrative trade which would cease with the advances of American civilization. The British continued to hold the northwestern posts from which to supply the Indians; and the home cabinet entertained hopes that circumstances might yet compel the U. S. to recognize the Ohio as its northwestern boundary.* Much of the dissatisfaction of the Indians was clearly traced to the influence and intrigues under the superintendence of Col. McKee, the British agent at Detroit and the Rapids of the Maumee.† The Indian discontent was openly encouraged, and their hostility fanned into a flame of war; the warrior bands obtained their outfit of arms and ammunition from the British traders; to trade with the Indians while at war with the U. S. they maintained as but fair and just.

As the main operations of this war occurred within the limits of the present States of Ohio and Indiana, we shall not treat of them in detail, notwithstanding Illinois was united with them under a common government. Indian depredations upon the settlements and murders of the whites became frequent, inspiring terror on every hand. In the fall of 1790, Gen. Harmar conducted a large, but fruitless, expedition of 1500 men, mostly Kentucky and Pennsylvania militia, poorly armed and without discipline, from Fort Washington, (Cincinnati) against the Miami villages on the Maumee and head waters of the Wabash. Caution had foolishly been taken so notify the British at Detroit, that the troops collected were to be used against the Indians alone.‡ The villages were found deserted. They were destroyed, together with 20,000 bushels of corn. Two detachments of from 300 to 400 men each, the first under Col. Trotter and the next under Col. Hardin, rival Kentuckians, engaged the Indians, but owing to wretched management and worse discipline, both met with defeat and very heavy losses.|| The defeated army marched back to Fort Washington, and the Indians were only encouraged in their dastardly work of murder upon the settlements.

In the spring of 1791, congress authorized Brig. Gen. Charles Scott, and others of Kentucky, to conduct an independent expedition against the Wabash Indians. It consisted of about 1,000

*See Burnett's Letters, p. 100.
†Am. State Papers—Wayne's Dispatches.
‡Ibid
|Am State Papers, Asheton's Statement, and Cists' Cin. Miscellany

mounted volunteers, who left the Ohio, May 23d. Early on the
morning of June 1st they reached the Wabash at the old Wea
towns, a few miles above the present Terre Haute. The villages
were discovered by the ascending smoke from the lodges. The army
was formed in order of battle and moved briskly forward; the inhabitants being in blissful ignorance of the stealthy approach of
the foe. Gen Scott reports that the town was situated on the low
ground bordering the Wabash below the plain across which they
marched. " On turning the point of woods, one house presented
in my front. Capt. Price was ordered to assault that with 40 men.
He executed the command with great gallantry, and killed two
warriors." This remarkably "gallant" exploit doubtless was the
means of saving many human lives, otherwise totally surprised on
this early June morning. Gen. Scott continues :

" When I gained the summit of the eminence which overlooks the
villages on the banks of the Wabash, I discovered the enemy in great
confusion, endeavoring to make their escape over the river in canoes. I
instantly ordered Lieutenant Colonel commanding Wilkinson to rush
forward with the first battalion. The order was executed with promptitude, and this detachment gained the bank of the river just as the rear
of the enemy had embarked ; and, regardless of a brisk fire kept up from
a Kickapoo town on the opposite bank, they, in a few minutes, by a well
directed fire from the rifles, destroyed all the savages with which five
canoes were crowded."*

How this attack differed from a regular murderous Indian raid,
is left to the discovery of the reader ; as also, how many of the enemy
were women and children. "Many of the inhabitants of the village
(Ouiatenon) were French and lived in a state of civilization. By
the books, letters, and other documents found there, it is evident
that the place was in close connection with and dependent on
Detroit. A large quantity of corn, a variety of household goods,
peltry, and other articles, were burned with this village, which
consisted of about 70 houses, many of them well finished."† Col.
John Hardin, "burning to retrieve his fame," was sent with a detachment to a village six miles down the river, where he killed six
warriors and took fifty-two prisoners. In the meantime another
force under Col. Wilkinson had crossed the swollen river at a
secluded place two miles above and proceeded on the opposite
bank to dislodge the refractory Kickapoos. On the following day
Col. W. was again detached with a force of 360, on foot, to destroy
the town of Kethtipenunk (Tippecanoe) which was done, no doubt
"gallantly." Gen. St. Clair in a letter to Washington dated Sept.
14, 1798, says the Kentuckians were "in the habit of retaliating,
perhaps, without attending precisely to the nations from which
the injuries are received."

In August, Col. Wilkinson, with an independent command, surprised the natives on Eel river. "The men," says Wilkinson,
"forcing their way over every obstacle, plunged through the river
with vast intrepidity. The enemy was unable to make the smallest
resistance. Six warriors, and (in the hurry and confusion of the
charge) two squaws and a child were killed, 34 prisoners (squaws
and children) were taken, and an unfortunate captive released,
with the loss of two men killed and one wounded." Four thousand

*Am. State Papers, V. 131.
†Scott's Report.

acres of corn were destroyed, and the cabins burned.* He was voted the thanks of congress.

On the early morning of November 4, 1791, occurred that most disastrous defeat of Gen. St. Clair, in western Ohio, on a small branch of the Wabash; by 9 o'clock a. m. his beaten and confused army, what little was left of it, was in a complete and precipitate rout toward Fort Jefferson, distance 29 miles. From the first onset, the troops were thrown into disorder and confusion by the murderous fire of the savages, and panic reigned supreme.† The loss was 890 out of a force of 1400 engaged in battle. "Six hundred skulls," writes George Mill from General Wayne's army which camped on the battle field three years later, "were gathered up and buried; when we went to lay down in our tents at night, we had to scrape the bones together and carry them out, to make our beds."‡ The Indians engaged were estimated at 1040. Little Turtle, Mechecunaqua, chief of the Miamis, was in command. The battle field was afterwards known as Fort Recovery.

The general government made repeated efforts, both before and during the war, to arrange a peace upon a fair equivalent for the lands of the aborigines. But the red men flushed with victories, and influenced by the artful whispers of the British emissaries, closed their ears to every appeal for peace, and rejected proposition after proposition; nothing but the boundary line of the Ohio would be entertained as a basis for peace. At the foot of the Maumee Rapids, August 13, 1793, 16 of the confederated nations being represented in council, replied to the American peace commissioners:

"Brothers: We shall be persuaded that you mean to do us justice, if you agree that the Ohio shall remain the boundary line between us. * * Money to us is of no value; and to most of us unknown; and, as no consideration whatever can induce us to sell the lands on which we get sustenance for our women and children, we hope we may be allowed to point out a mode by which your settlers may be easily removed, and peace thereby obtained.

"Brothers: We know that these settlers are poor, or they would never have ventured to live in a country which has been in continual trouble ever since they crossed the Ohio. Divide, therefore, this large sum of money, which you have offered to us, among these people. Give to each, also, a proportion of what you say you would give to us, annually, over and above this very large sum of money; and as we are persuaded, they would most readily accept of it in lieu of the land you sold them. If you add, also, the great sums you must expend in raising and paying armies, with a view to force us to yield you our country, you will certainly have more than sufficient for the purpose of repaying these settlers for all their labor and their improvements. * * We want peace. Restore to us our country, and we shall be enemies no longer."

It is a curious fact, illustrating our dealings with the Indians, that a treaty of peace and friendship was entered into at Vincennes, September 27, 1792, by Brig. Gen. Rufus Putnam, accompanied by John Heckvelder and 31 Indians of the Wabash and Illinois tribes, the 4th article of which contained the following language:

"Art. 4. The United States solemnly guaranty to the Wabash and Illinois nations or tribes of Indians, all the lands to which they have a just claim; and no part shall ever be taken from them

*Wilkinson's Report.
†Am. State Papers.
‡Am. Pioneer—Wayne's Statement.

but by a fair purchase, and to their satisfaction. That the lands originally belonged to the Indians; it is theirs, and theirs only. That they have a right to sell, and a right to refuse to sell. And that the United States will protect them in their said rights."

When the treaty, which contained 7 articles, was laid before the United States Senate, the 4th article was objectionable, and after much deliberation, it was, Jan. 9, 1794, rejected by a vote of 21 to 4.—Senate Jour. I. 128 to 146.

The Illinois settlements were fortunately beyond the main theatre of this savage war; still, owing to the general hostility of nearly all the tribes, their depredations were each year extended to them, and a comparatively great number of barbarous murders were committed by the Kickapoos. These we will give condensed from the "Annals of the West," pages 700 to 705:

In 1783, a single murder, that of James Flannory, was first committed while on a hunting excursion, but it was not accounted an act of war. In 1786 the Indians attacked the American settlements, killed James Andrews, his wife and daughter, James White and Samuel McClure, and two girls, daughters of Andrews were taken prisoners. One of these died with the Indians, and the other was ransomed by French traders. She is now (1850) alive, the mother of a large family, and resides in St. Clair county. The Indians had previously threatened the settlement, and the people had built and entered a blockhouse; but this family was out and defenceless.

1787. Early in this year, five families near Bellefountaine, united and built a blockhouse, surrounded it with palisades, in which these families resided. While laboring in the corn field they were obliged to carry their rifles, and often at night had to keep guard. Under these embarrassments, and in daily alarm, they cultivated their corn-fields.

1788. This year the war assumed a more threatening aspect. Early in the spring, William Biggs was taken prisoner. While himself, John Vallis, and Joseph and Benjamin Ogle, were passing from the station on the hills to the blockhouse fort in the bottom, they were attacked by the Indians. Biggs and Vallis were a few rods in advance of the party. Vallis was killed and Biggs taken prisoner. The others escaped unhurt. Biggs was taken through the prairies to the Kickapoo towns on the Wabash, from whence he was finally liberated by means of the French traders. The Indians treated him well, offered him the daughter of a brave for a wife, and proposed to adopt him into their tribe. He afterwards became a resident of St. Clair county, was a member of the territorial legislature, judge of the county court, and wrote and published a narrative of his captivity among the Indians.

On the 10th day of December, in the same year, James Garrison and Benjamin Ogle, while hauling hay from the bottom, were attacked by two Indians; Ogle was shot in the shoulder, where the ball remained; Garrison sprang from the load and escaped into the woods. The horses taking fright, carried Ogle safe to the settlement. In stacking the same hay, Samuel Garrison and Mr. Riddick were killed and scalped.

1789. This was a period of considerable mischief. Three boys were attacked by six Indians, a few yards from the blockhouse, one of which, David Waddel, was struck with a tomahawk in three places, scalped, and yet recovered; the others escaped unhurt. A short time previous, James Turner, a young man, was killed on the American bottom. Two men were afterwards killed and scalped while on their way to St. Louis. In another instant, two men were attacked on a load of hay, one was killed outright, the other was scalped, but recovered. The same year John Ferrel was killed, and John Demphsey was scalped and made his escape. The Indians frequently stole the horses and cattle of the settlers.

1790. The embarrassments of these frontier people greatly increased, and they lived in continual alarm. In the winter, a party of Osage Indians, who had not molested hitherto, came across the Mississippi, stole a number of horses and attempted to recross the river. The Americans followed and fired upon them. James Worley, an old settler, having got in advance of his party, was shot, scalped, and his head cut off and left on the sand-bar.

The same year, James Smith, a Baptist preacher from Kentucky, while on a visit to these frontiers, was taken prisoner by the Kickapoos. On the 19th of May. in company with Mrs. Huff and a Frenchman, he was proceeding from the blockhouse to a settlement then known by the name of Little Village. The Kickapoos fired upon them from an ambuscade near Bellefountaine, killed the Frenchman's horse, sprang upon the woman and her child, whom they despatched with a tomahawk, and took Smith prisoner. His horse being shot, he attempted to flee on foot; and having some valuable papers in his saddle bags, he threw them into a thicket, where they were found next day by his friend. Having retreated a few yards down the hill, he fell on his knees in prayer for the poor woman they were butchering, and who had been seriously impressed, for some days, about religion. The Frenchman escaped on foot in the thickets. The Indians soon had possession of Smith, loaded him with packs of plunder which they had collected, and took up their line of march through the prairies. Smith was a large, heavy man, and soon became tired under his heavy load, and with the hot sun. Several consultations were held by the Indians, how to dispose of their prisoner. Some were for despatching him outright, being fearful the whites would follow them from the settlement, and frequently pointing their guns at his breast. Knowing well the Indian character, he would bare his breast as if in defiance, and point upwards to signify the Great Spirit was his protector. Seeing him in the attitude of prayer, and hearing him singing hymns on his march, which he did to relieve his own mind of despondency, they came to the conclusion that he was a "great medicine," holding daily intercourse with the Good Spirit, and must not be put to death. After this, they took off his burdens and treated him kindly. They took him to the Kickapoo towns on the Wabash, where, in a few months, he obtained his deliverance, the inhabitants of New Design paying $170 for his ransom.

1791. In the spring of this year, the Indians again commenced their depredations by stealing horses. In May, John Dempsey was attacked, but made his escape. A party of eight men followed. The Indians were just double their number. A severe running fight was kept up for several hours, and conducted with great prudence and bravery on the part of the whites. Each party kept the trees for shelter, the Indians retreating, and the Americans pursuing, from tree to tree until night put an end to the conflict. Five Indians were killed without the loss of a man or a drop of blood on the other side. This party consisted of Capt. Hull, who commanded, Joseph Ogle, sen., Benjamin Ogle, James N. Semen, sen., J. Ryan, Wm. Bryson, John Porter, and D. Draper.

1792. This was a period of comparative quietness. No Indian fighting; and the only depredations committed, were in stealing a few horses.

1793. This was a period of contention and alarm. The little settlements were strengthened this year by the addition of a band of emigrants from Kentucky; among which was the family of Whiteside. In February, an Indian in ambuscade wounded Joel Whiteside, and was followed by John Moore, Andrew Kinney, Thos. Todd, and others, killed and scalped. Soon after, a party of Kickapoos, supposed to have been headed by the celebrated war chief, Old Pecan, made a predatary excursion into the American bottom, near the present residence of S. W. Miles, in Monroe county, and stole 9 horses from the citizens. A number of citizens rallied and commenced pursuit; but many having started without preparation for long absence, and being apprehensive that an expedition into the Indian country would be attended with much danger, all returned but 8 men. This little band consisted of Samuel Judy, John Whiteside, Wm. L. Whiteside, Uel Whiteside, William Harrington, John Dempsey and John Porter, with Wm. Whiteside, a man of great prudence and unquestionable bravery in Indian warfare, whom they chose commander.

They passed on the trail near the present site of Belleville, towards the Indian camps on Shoal Creek, where they found 3 of the stolen horses, which they secured, The party then, small as it was, divided into two parts of four men each, and approached the Indian camps from opposite sides. The signal for attack was the discharge of the captain's gun. One Indian, a son of Old Pecan, was killed, another mortally, and others slightly wounded, as the Indians fled, leaving their guns. Such a display of courage by the whites, and being attacked on two sides at once, made them believe there was a large force, and the old chief approached and begged for quarter. But when he discovered his foes to be an insignificant number, and his own party numerous, he called aloud to his braves to return and retrieve their honor. His own gun he surrendered to the whites, but now he seized the gun of the captain, and exerted all his force to wrest it from him. Captain Whiteside was a powerful man, and a stranger to fear, but he compelled the Indian to retire, deeming it dishonorable to destroy an unarmed man, who had previously surrendered. This intrepid band was now in the heart of the Indian country, where hundreds of warriors could be raised in a few hour's time. In this critical situation, Capt. Whiteside, not less distinguished for prudence than bravery, did not long hesitate. With the horses they had recovered, they immediately started for home without the loss of time in hunting the remainder. They traveled night and day, without eating or sleeping, till they reached in safety Whiteside's station, in Monroe county. On the same night, Old Pecan, with 70 warriors, arrived in the vicinity of Cahokia. From that time the very name of Whiteside struck terror among the Kickapoos. Hazardous and daring as this expedition was, it met with great disapprobation from many of the settlers. Some alleged that Old Pecan was decidedly friendly to the whites; that another party had stolen the horses; that the attack upon his camp was clandestine and wanton; and that it was the cause of much subsequent mischief. These nice points of casuistry are difficult to be settled at this period. It has long been known, that one portion of a nation or tribe will be on the war path, while another party will pretend to be peaceable. Hence it has been found necessary to hold the tribe responsible for the conduct of its party.

1794. The Indians, in revenge of the attack just narrated, shot Thos. Whiteside, a young man, near the 'station;' tomahawked a son of Wm. Whiteside, so that he died, all in revenge for the death of Old Pecan's son. In February of the same year, the Indians killed Mr. Huff, one of the early settlers, while on his way to Kaskaskia.

1795. Two men at one time, and some French negroes at another time were killed on the American bottom, and some prisoners taken. The same year the family of Mr. McMahon was killed and himself and daughters taken prisoners. This man lived in the outskirts of the settlement. Four Indians attacked his house in day-light, killed his wife and four children before his eyes, laid their bodies in a row on the floor of the cabin, took him and his daughters, and marched for their towns. On the second night, Mr. McMahon, finding the Indians asleep, put on their moccasins and made his escape. He arrived in the settlement just after his neighbors had buried his family. They had inclosed their bodies in rude coffins, and covered them with earth as he came in sight. He looked at the newly formed hillock, and raising his eyes to Heaven in pious resignation, said, "they were lovely and pleasant in their lives, and in their death are not divided."

His daughter, now Mrs. Catskill, of Ridge Prairie, was afterwards ransomed by the charitable contributions of the people. Not far from this period, the Whitesides and others to the number of 14 persons, made an attack upon an encampment of Indians of superior force, at the foot of the bluffs west of Belleville. Only one Indian ever returned to his nation to tell the story of their defeat. The graves of the rest were to be seen, a few years since, in the border of the thicket, near the battle ground. In this skirmish Capt. Wm. Whiteside was wounded, as thought, mortally, having received a shot in the side. As he fell, he exhorted his sons to fight valiantly, not yield an inch of ground, nor let the Indians touch his body. Uel Whiteside, who was shot in the arm, and disabled from using the rifle, examined the wound, and found the ball had glanced along the ribs and lodged against the spine. With that presence of mind which is sometimes characteristic of our backwoods hunters, he whipped out his knife, gashed the skin, extracted the ball, and holding it up, exultingly exclaimed, "Father, you are not dead!" The old man instantly jumped up on his feet, and renewed the fight, exclaiming, "Come on, boys, I can fight them yet!" Such instances of desperate intrepidity and martial energy of character, distinguished the men who defended the frontiers of Illinois in those days of peril.

After the defeat of St. Clair, the conduct of the war in the northwest was placed in the hands of Gen. Anthony Wayne. His campaign during the summer of 1794, which culminated in the victory of the 20th of August on the Maumee, proved a complete success. The confederated tribes, defeated and disheartened, now retired to wait the long promised support of the English. Brant, of the Iroquois, said: "A fort had been built in their country [by the English] under pretense of giving refuge in case of necessity, but when that time came, the gates were shut against them as enemies."* For several years difficulties had existed between Great Britain and the United States, which British Indian agents and traders had seduously taught to red men must speedily eventuate in war, when they would become their open and powerful ally. But on the 19th of November, 1794, after protracted negotiations, Jay, at London, concluded a treaty of amity, commerce, and navigation between the United States and Great Britain, in which the King pledged a firm peace and agreed to withdraw, by the 1st of June, 1796, all his troops and garrisons from the posts within the boundary lines of the United States, as fixed by the treaty of 1783. This took away from the Indians the last hope of British aid, so long promised them, and the vast confederation of savage tribes, bending to their inevitable fate, hastened to the headquarters of Gen. Wayne during the winter, and signed preliminary articles of peace, which resulted in the treaty of Greenville, and which, after a protracted council with all the sachems, chiefs, and principal men of the confederacy, lasting from June to August 3d, 1795, was finally signed. A vast body of land in Ohio and Indiana, large enough for a good sized State, was ceded by the confederate tribes, besides 16 tracts 6 miles square at various points in the northwest, among which we note, as being in Illinois, "one piece of land, 6 miles square, at the mouth of Chicago river, emptying into the south-west end of Lake Michigan, where a fort formerly stood;" one piece 12 miles square, at or near the mouth of the Illinois river, and "one piece 6 miles square, at the old Peorias fort and village, near the south end of the Illinois lake, on said Illinois river." The Indians also allowed free passage through their country, in Illinois from the mouth of the Chicago river and over the portage to the Illinois and down to the Mississippi, and down the Wabash. Under the treaty, of what may be considered Illinois tribes, the Pottawattomies were to receive an annual stipend of $1000 in goods (being as much as any tribes received,) and the Kickapoos, Piankeshaws, and Kaskaskias, $500 each.†

And now, as the news of this important treaty spead abroad, the retarded tide of emigration began to flow with a steadily augmenting stream into these territories; apprehension of danger from the Indians was banished, and friendly intercourse succeeded former enmity; forts, stations, and stockades were abandoned to decay; the hardy pioneer pushed ever forward and extended the

*Am. State Papers, V.
†Scott's Brant, II, 390.

frontier; and men of capital and enterprise, securing titles to extensive bodies of fertile lands, organized colonies for their occupation, and thus the wilderness under the tread of civilization was made to blossom as the rose.

By an act of congress, 1791, 400 acres of land were granted to all heads of families who made improvements in Illinois prior to 1788, except village improvements. These rights were commonly designated as "head-rights." A list of names of heads of families, who settled in Illinois previous to the year 1788, entitling them to these donations, which included also non-residents who should return in five year's time to occupy their claims, shows a total number of 244 claimants, 80 of whom were Americans. By allowing the usual number of 5 souls to the family, we have a population in that year of 1220. This excluded negroes. Before 1791, under the militia law of the governor and judges, the muster roll gives about 300 men capable of bearing arms, of which number 65 only were Americans.[*]

In 1797 a colony of 126 persons—the largest which had yet arrived—were most fatally stricken with disease. They were from Virginia, had descended the Ohio in the spring, and landed at Ft. Massac, from which they made their way across the land to the New Design. This place, in the present county of Monroe, was established in 1782. It was located on an elevated and beautiful plateau of ground, barren of timber, which commanded a view of both the Kaskaskia and Mississippi rivers. The season was exceedingly wet, the weather extremely warm, and the roads heavy and muddy. The colonists toiled through the woods and swamps of Southern Illinois for 26 days, distance about 135 miles. They were worn down, sick, and almost famished. Arrived at their destination, they found among the old settlers long harrassed by Indian warfare, from which they had not recovered, but poor accommodations. There was no lack of hospitality in feeling, but that did not enlarge the cabins, which usually contained but one room, into many of which 3 and 4 families were now crowded with their sick and all. Food was insufficient, salt was very scarce, and medical aid was almost out of the question. A putrid and malignant fever broke out among the new comers, attended by such fatality as to sweep half of them into the grave by the approach of winter. No such fatal disease ever appeared before or since in the country.[†] The old inhabitants were not affected. The intelligence of this unwonted mortality produced abroad the wrongful impression that Illinois was a sickly country, which tended no little to retard immigration. It is now well established that Illinois is far healthier than many of her western sisters.

Among the first Americans who formed settlements remote from the French, a great want was mills. The latter had had their wind mills and water mills since a very early date; but with their hegira the wind mills fell into decay, and for the others the water frequently failed, and the Americans were compelled to have recourse to other means. The simplest modes of trituration was by means of the grater and the mortar. The first consisted in the brisk rubbing of an ear of corn over a piece of tin closely pierced with orifices. The mortar was extemporized by excavating with

fire the butt of a good sized short log, up-ended, sufficiently deep
to hold a peck or more of corn. Over this was erected a sweep
to lift, by counter-traction, a piston with a firm, blunt end,
which served to pound the corn into meal. To these primitive and
laborious processes, succeeded, in the order of their simplicity and
in due time, hand mills, band mills, horse mills, and last water
mills.†

From 1788 to 1795, Gov. St. Clair and the Judges of the northwestern territory, in their legislative capacity, adopted 64 statutes, 38 at Cincinnati in the last named year. In April, 1798, 11
more were adopted.* Four-fifths of these laws were imported
from Pennslvania, and a few from Massachusetts and Virginia.
This gave to the country a complete system of statute law, which
was perhaps but little inferior to that of any of the States at that
early period. Among them was the common law of England and
statutes of Parliament in aid thereof, of a general nature and not local
to that Kingdom, down to the 4th year of the reign of James I; which
is the law in Illinois to this day, except as varied by statute. From
it we derive all those fundamental principles of the British Constitution which secure to the citizen personal liberty and protection
to life and property—the habeas corpus, trial by jury, &c. This
was imported from Virginia; but the bill of rights is also in the
ordinance of 1787. In 1795 the Governor also divided St. Clair
county in Illinois by running a line through the New Design settlement in the present Monroe county, due east to the Wabash—all
that country lying south of it being established into the county of
Randolph, named in honor of Edmund Randolph, of Virginia.

Before the close of the year 1796, the white population of Ohio
alone was ascertained to exceed 5,000. By the ordinance of 1787,
the country was entitled to the 2d grade of territorial government
so soon as it should contain 5,000 white inhabitants. There being
no longer any doubt regarding this, Gov. St. Clair, October 29,
1798, issued his proclamation directing the qualified voters to
hold elections for territorial representatives on the 3d Monday of
December, 1798. From Illinois, Shadrach Bond, subsequently the
first governor of this State, was elected. The representatives
elect were convened January 22d, 1799, at Cincinnati. In accordance with the provision of the ordinance of 1787, they nominated 10
men to the President of the U. S. (Adams) to select 5 from, who
were to constitute the legislative council. These were confirmed
by the Senate of the U. S., March 22, 1799. The assembly, after
making the nominations for the council, immediately adjourned to
September 16th following, at which time both houses met, though
they did not perfect their organization till the 24th. This was the
first time that the people of this country, through their representatives, enacted their own laws for their own local government. The
Legislature confirmed many of the laws enacted by the governor
and judges, and passed 48 new ones, the governor vetoing 11.
They were prorogued December 19, 1799.†

---

†Reynold's Pioneer History.
*Dillon's Ind. I. Chase's Statute 1790, 1795.
†See Dillons's Ind,, Vol. 11.

NOTABLE WOMEN OF THE OLDEN TIME.

Mrs. LeCompt.—Among the ladies of Illinois at the close of the
last and the beginning of the present century, presenting such
marked characteristics as to leave their impress upon the period
of their existence, we cannot in justice forbear to mention a few.
The first which we notice was the well known Mrs. LeCompt.
She was born in 1734, of French parents, on the eastern shore of
Lake Michigan, at the old station on the St. Joseph. This was the
country of the warlike Pottawatomie tribe of Indians. Throughout
her long life Mrs. LeCompt had ever the western savage for a
neighbor. She early became proficient in the dialect of the
Indians and gained a deep insight into their character. She was
married at Mackinaw, settled with her husband, whose name was
St. Ange, or Pelate, at Chicago, but subsequently removed to Cahokia, and, her husband dying, she here married Mr. LeCompt, a
Canadian. From this marriage sprung one of the largest French
families in Illinois. Later in life, after the death of LeCompt, she
married again, this time that Thomas Brady who conducted an unfortunate marauding expedition against the Fort St. Joseph in
1778. Of this union no issue resulted. This extraordinary woman
was possessed of an iron constitution, a strong mind and dauntless
courage. Her person was attractive and her manner winning.
She traveled much, took many long trips, and underwent much
exposure to the inclemencies of the weather, yet she was seldom
sick. She lived a hardy and frugal life. By her knowledge of the
Indian language, and a thorough appreciation of his character, she
acquired a wonderful influence over the tribes, with which she was
brought into contact. And this was turned to a blessed account
for the benefit of the settlement where she lived. From the conquest of Clark, the French, as we have seen, sided with the
Americans, while the Indians adhered to the British. From that
time down to the peace of Greenville, in 1795, the old kindly
feeling between the French and Indians was more or less interrupted, and many a meditated attack upon Cahokia did Mrs.
LeCompt frustrate by her rare sagacity and friendly counsel with
the savages. It is said, that such was the infatuated friendship of
the savages for her, that they would invariably advise her in
advance of their meditated attack upon the village. It was upon
such occasions that the heroine within her would become manifest.
In the dead hour of night she would go forth from the village to
meet the warrior hosts, often camped near the foot of the Quentin
mound, at the foot of the bluffs, or wherever they might be; in
their vicinity, dismiss her attendants, and solitary and alone proceed on foot amid the savage horde. Such devotion to her people
and such courage in a woman, joined by her ready wit, would
awaken a chord of sympathy in the warrior's breast. At times she
would remain among them for days, pleading for the delivery of
her village, counseling peace, and appeasing the anger of the
savages. Her efforts were not intermitted until she was well convinced that the storm was allayed and bloodshed averted. At
such times the young men of the village were mostly away on the
chase, or as boatmen down the river, while the remaining inhabitants, terror stricken, would arm themselves for such defence as

'hey were capable of. What would be their joy to see this extraordinary woman escorting a swarthy band of warriors to the village, changed from foes to friends! (The Indians, upon such occasion, would paint themselves black to manifest their sorrow for their infernal murderous intent upon their friends.) After a thorough feasting of the savages, sometimes for days, their reconciliation would usually last some time. Mrs. LeCompt, as she was still called after Brady's death, lived to the extreme age of 109 years. She died in 1843, at Cahokia. Ex-Gov. Reynolds, from whose pioneer history we are in great part indebted for the above account, says he knew her well for 30 years.

Mrs. John Edgar.—This accomplished woman, the center of fashion for remote Illinois in the olden time, presided for many years with equal grace and dignity over her husband's splendid mansion at Kaskaskia, the abode of hospitality and resort of the elite for near a half century. It was in the spacious and elegantly furnished parlors of this house that La Fayette, on his visit to Illinois in 1825, was sumptuously entertained, by a banquet and ball. Mrs. Edgar's name merits high rank on the scroll of revolutionary heroines. By birth, education, and sympathy, she was American, but her husband, John Edgar, was an officer in the British navy, fighting against the colonies in their struggle for liberty and independence. By her talent, shrewdness, and above all, her patriotic devotion to her country, she won over not only the heart of her husband to the American cause, but was the projector of many plans by which soldiers in the British army were induced to quit and join the ranks of the patriots. She had, upon one occasion, arranged a plan of escape for three soldiers and was to furnish them guns, American uniforms, etc., and all needful information to enable them to reach the patriot camp. When they came she was absent from home, but her husband, a *confidante* of all her operations, notwithstanding his position in the enemy's navy, supplied them with the outfit prepared for them by her. But the deserters were apprehended, returned to the British camp, and compelled to divulge the names of their abettors. This implicated Edgar and he fled; remaining a while in the American army he deemed it safer for his life to seek greater seclusion and came to Kaskaskia. His property was confiscated; but the rare sagacity of his patriotic and devoted wife, who remained back, enabled her to save from the wreck some $12,000, with which she joined her husband two years afterwards in his western home.[*] Their union was childless; but they were for many years the most wealthy family in Illinois. Edgar was a large, portly man. A county of the State perpetuates his name.

Mrs. Robert Morrison.—This talented lady was a rare acquisition to the society of Kaskaskia. Reared and educated in the monumental city, she, in 1805, accompanied her brother, Col. Donaldson, to St. Louis, in the far off wilds of the west, whither he was sent as a commissioner to investigate the land titles. But the west became her permanent home. She was married the following year to Robert Morrison, of Kaskaskia, which place became her residence thenceforth. Well educated, sprightly and energetic, her mind was gifted with originality and romance. "Her delight was

*See Hist. Sketch of Randolph & Co. and Reynold's Pioneer Hist.
†Reynold's Pioneer Hist. of Ills.

in the rosy fields of poetry."† Her pen was seldom idle. She composed with a ready facility and her writings possessed a high degree of merit. Her contributions to the scientific publications of W. Walsh, of Philadelphia, and other periodicals of the time, both verse and prose, were much admired. Nor did the political questions of the day escape her ready pen. The discussion of these topics in our newspapers were eagerly read by the politicians of Illinois. A feat of much ingenuity was her work of remoddling and converting into verse the Psalms of David. The volume was presented to the Philadelphia Presbytery and met with high commendation for many of its excellencies, though it was not adopted. Later in life, she gave a thorough investigation to the doctrines of religious sects, and after much reflection united with the Catholic church. Possessed of great force of character, and zealous and ardent in whatever she espoused, her example and precepts contributed greatly toward proselyting members to that faith. She became the mother of an interesting family. Some of her sons have been quite conspicious in the affairs of this State. Mrs. Morrison lived to an advanced age, and died at Belleville in 1843.

VOUDOUISM OR WITCHCRAFT IN ILLINOIS.

It is recorded‡ that at least two human lives have fallen a sacrifice to the miserable superstition of witchcraft in Illinois in early times. An African slave by the name of Moreau was, about the year 1790, hung on a tree a little ways southeast of Cahokia, charged with and convicted of this imaginary crime. He had acknowledged, it is said, that by his power of devilish incantation "he had poisoned his master, but that his mistress had proved too powerful for his necromancy," and this it seems was fully believed, and he was executed. The case was murder; but there was at this period a very imperfect administration of the laws in Illinois. In the same village, ignorantly inspired by a belief in the existence of this dread power of diabolism, another negro's life was offered up to the Moloch of superstition, by being shot down in the public streets. An old negress of that vicinity, named Janette, commonly reputed to possess the supernatural power of destroying life and property by the potency of her incantations, inspired such terror by her appearance that adults as well as children would flee at her approach. It was a very common feeling among the French to dread to incur in any way the displeasure of certain old colored people, under the vague belief and fear that they possessed a clandestine power by which to invoke the aid of the evil one to work mischief or injury to person or property. Nor was this belief solely confined to the French, or this power ascribed only to the colored people. An old woman living on Silver Creek was almost generally accredited with the power of witchcraft, which, it was believed, she exercised in taking milk from her neighbor's cows at pleasure, without the aid of any physical agency. The African's belief in fetishes, and the power of their divination, is well-known. Many superstitious blacks in this country have claimed the descent to them of fetish power; the infatuation regarding voudouism, formerly so wide spread, is not yet extinct among many ignorant

‡Reynold's Pioneer Hist.

blacks of Louisiana, as we read occasionally from New Orleans papers. Renault, agent of the "Company of the West," bought in 1720, at San Domingo, 500 slaves which he brought to Illinois, many of whom were direct from Africa, and thus was imported the claim to this occult power, which, perhaps, had no difficulty in finding lodgement in the minds of the superstitious French of Illinois. Mankind have ever been prone to superstitious beliefs; there are very many persons now who are daily governed in the multiplied affairs of life by some sign, omen, or augery.

Nor were the red children of the forest in American free from superstition. The brother of the Shawanee warrior, Tecumseh, named Lawlelueskaw, the loud voiced, better known as the one eyed Prophet, who commanded the Indians at the battle of Tippecanoe, seeking to reform his people, earnestly declaimed against the vice of witchcraft, as well as drunkenness, intermarrying with white men, etc. In obedience to the commands of the maniteau, the Great Spirit, he fulminated the penalty of death against those who practiced the black art of witchcraft and magic. His vehement harrangues evoked among his followers a paroxysm of superstitious infatuation. An old Delaware chief, named Tatebockoshe, was accused of witchcraft, tried, condemned, tomahawked and consumed on a pyre. This was enacted on the present site of Yorktown, Delaware county, Indiana.* The chief's wife, his nephew, Billy Patterson, and an aged Indian named Joshua, were next accused of witchcraft and the two latter convicted, sentenced and burned to the stake; but a brother of the chief's wife boldly stepped forward, seized his sister and led her from the council house, without opposition from those present, and immediately returned, and in a loud tone harangued the savages, exclaiming: "Maniteau, the evil spirit has come in our midst and we are murdering one another." This, together with the earnest letter of Gov. Harrison, sent by special messenger in the spring of 1806, exhorting the Indians to spurn the pretended prophet, checked the horrid delusion. See Drake's Tecumseh, 88.

---

*He had also offended by his influence in bringing about the treaty of Aug. 1804, by which the chiefs and head men of the Delawares ceded to the U. S. that large tract of land in southern Indiana, since known as the "pocket."

CHAPTER XX.

1800-1809—ILLINOIS AS PART OF THE INDIANA TERRITORY.

Its Organization—Extinguishing Indian Titles to Lands—Gov. Harrison's Facility in This—Land Speculations and Frauds in "Improvement-rights" and "Head-rights"—Meeting of the Legislaat Vincennes in 1805—Statutes of 1807.

———

By act of Congress, approved May 7, 1800, the large and unwieldy territory of the Northwest was divided; all that part of it lying westward of a line beginning on the Ohio river opposite the mouth of the Kentucky, running thence north via Fort Recovery to the British possessions, was constituted a separate territory and called Indiana. It enclosed the present States of Illinois, Wisconsin, Michigan, and Indiana except a little strip on the eastern side between the mouth of the Kentucky and Great Miami. The white population of the country was estimated at 4,875, and negro slaves 135, while the aggregate number of Indians within the extreme limits of the territory was fairly reckoned at 100,000. The seat of Government was fixed at Vincennes, and the ordinance of 1787 was applied to the territory in a modified form : that clause requiring 5,000 free white male inhabitants of the age of 21 years and upwards, before a general assembly could be organized, was changed to the wish of a simple majority of the freeholders. The law was to go into effect on the 4th of July following.

A chief reason for making this division was the large extent of the northwestern territory, which rendered the ordinary operations of government uncertain and the prompt and efficient administration of justice almost impossible. In the three western counties— Knox, St. Clair and Randolph, the latter two in Illinois, there had been but one term of court, having cognizance of crimes, held in five years. Such immunity to offenders offered a safe asylum to the vilest and most abandoned scoundrels. The law of 1791, confirming titles and granting lands to certain persons for military services, and the laying out thereof, remained unexecuted, causing great discontent;* and the unpopularity of Governor St. Clair was constantly on the increase. His unfortunate campaign against the Maumee towns, which had greatly shaken the confidence of the people, had but rendered his conduct of civil affairs more arbitrary and defiant. He vetoed nearly every act of the legislature establishing new counties, to the great inconvenience of the people

---

*See report of Committee in Congress—Am. State Pap. XX, 206.

in their transactions with clerks and recorders, and to the vexation of suitors at law.

The territorial legislature sitting at Cincinnati, elected, on the 3d of October, 1799, William Henry Harrison, then secretary of the territory, a delegate to congress, over Arthur St. Clair, jun., by a vote of 11 to 10. The contest elicited wide and unusual interest, and was not unattended by much acrimony and ill blood. The St. Clairs were federalists, and party feeling ran extremely high in those days. Harrison was largely instrumental in Congress in obtaining the passage of the act of division. Up to this time the smallest tract of public lands which could be entered was 400 acres, except fractional pieces cut by important streams. This was a great hindrance to settlement, and to the poor our land system was a curse rather than a blessing. Harrison, fully appreciating this grievance, urged through Congress a law authorizing the sale of the public lands in tracts of 320 acres, with a cash payment of only one-fourth and the balance in one, two and three years. The passage of this law was regarded in the west as a public service of the greatest importance, rendering Harrison extremely popular. He was, May 13, 1800, appointed Governor for the Indiana territory. John Gibson (he to whom in 1774, Logan, the great Indian chief had delivered his celebrated speech), was appointed secretary; and William Clark, John Griffin and Henry Vanderburgh, territorial judges. In the absence of the governor, secretary Gibson proceeded in July to put the machinery of territorial government in motion by appointing the necessary local officers for the administration of the laws, &c. In January, 1801, Governor Harrison, having arrived at his post of duty, immediately convened the judges with himself at the seat of government, for the adoption of "such laws as the exigency of the times" required, and to the discharge of such other duty for the government of the territory as congress had by law imposed upon them. They remained in session two weeks, passing several resolutions providing payment for various services, and adopted a number of laws, one providing for the establishment of courts of quarter sessions of the peace in the counties of St. Clair, Randolph and Knox. A term of the general court for the territory at large, was commenced by the three judges on the 3d of March, 1801. Thus the first grade of territorial government was put in full working order.

The purchase of Louisana from France having been consummated in 1803, that vast domain lying west of the Mississippi, was by act of Congress, March 26, 1804, annexed to the Indiana territory. Gov. Harrison and the judges, in October, 1804, adopted the necessary laws for the government of the district of Lousiana. The union was, however, of short duration; March 3, 1805, Louisiana was detached and erected into a separate territory. Shortly after this Aaron Burr entered upon his treasonable effort to wrest from the United States this large domain and to found his southwestern empire. To organize an expedition for his enterprise, he visited, among other places in the west, Vincennes and Kaskaskia, and induced a few men of the territory to enroll their names on the list of his followers; but the scheme came speedily to naught—his men abandoned it, and he was arrested in Mississippi in the spring of 1807. After the purchase of Louisiana, it became desirable to learn something respecting the vast region lying between the Mis-

sissippi and the Pacific. Congress therefore authorized an
overland exploring expedition, to the command of which the
President appointed Captains Merriweather Lewis and William
Clark, the latter a brother of Gen. George Rogers Clark. The
party, consisting of 34 men, encamped during the winter of
1803--4 in the American bottom, near the mouth of Wood river,
below Alton—then the ultama thule of the white settlements in Illinois—and started thence upon their toilsome and perilous journey,
May 14th, reaching the Pacific November 17, 1805. The explorers
returned in safety to St. Louis about a year the reafter. The
peninsula of Michigan was also, by act of Congress, January 11,
1805, detached from Indiana and erected into a separate territory,
the act to take effect June 30, 1805.

The main topics of interest during the 9 years that Illinois constituted a part of the Indiana territory, were : the acquisition of
land titles from the resident Indian tribes, land speculations, and
the adjustment of land titles; negro slavery; organizaiion of the
territorial legislature, extension of the right of suffrage and the
detachment of Illinois from the Indiana territory.* Captain William Henry Harrison, besides his appointment as governor, was
also constituted superintendent of Indian affairs, and vested
with plenary powers to negotiate treaties between the United
States and the several tribes of Indians residing within his official
jurisdiction, for the cession of lands. As the rapidly advancing
settlements of the whites penetrated farther daily, and crowded
upon the domain of the red man, it became desirable on the part
of the general government to enlarge the area of its landed acqui-
sitions beyond the stipulations of the treaty of Greenville, by
which 17,724,489 acres of land were obtained. By an active exercise of these powers, in which his Excellency discovered a
remarkable aptitude, no less than ten treaties were concluded with
various tribes by the close of the year 1805, extinguishing the Indian titles to about 30,000,000 acres more of land. We cite in
brief the treaties of that period, by which lands lying either wholly
or in part within Illinois, were relinquished :

Treaty of Fort Wayne, concluded June 7, 1803; with certain
chiefs and head men of the Delawares, Shawanese, Pottawatomies,
Eel River, Wea, Kickapoo, Piankeshaw, and Kaskaskia tribes—
ratified at Vincennes August 7, 1803, by three of the tribes and
the Wyandots, by which there were ceded to the United States,
1,634,000 acres of land, 336,128 of which were situated within
Illinois.

Treaty of Vincennes, concluded August 13, 1803, with certain
chiefs and warriors of the Kaskaskias, in consideration of the protecting care of the government, of $580 in cash, of an increase of
their annuity under the treaty of Greenville to $1000, of $300
toward building a church, and an annual payment for seven years
of $100 to a Catholic priest stationed among them, the tribe of
Kaskaskias, reduced to a few hundred individuals, but still representing the once powerful confederacy of the Illinois, ceded to the
United States, except a small reservation, all that tract included
within a line beginning below the mouth of the Illinois, descending the Mississippi to its junction with the Ohio, ascending the
latter to the Wabash, and from a point up the Wabash west to

---

*The subject of slavery is deferred to Gov. Cole's administration.

the Mississippi, embracing the greater part of southern Illinois, some 8,608,167 acres, a magnificient grant.

Treaty of St. Louis, concluded November 3d, 1804, by which the chiefs and head men of the united Sac and Fox nations ceded to the United States, a great tract on both sides of the Mississippi, extending on the east bank from the mouth of the Illinois to the head of that river and thence to the Wisconsin, and including on the west considerable portions of Iowa and Missouri, from the mouth of the Gasconade northward. (In 1816 the government granted back to the united tribes about 5,000,090 acres in Iowa). Out of this treaty, as we shall see, subsequently grew the Black Hawk war.

Treaty of Vincennes, concluded December 30th, 1805, by which the chiefs and warriors of the Piankeshaw tribe ceded to the United States their claim to a tract of country in Illinois, bordering on the Wabash river opposite Vincennes, extending north and south for a considerable distance, and comprising 2,616,924 acres.

Thus by successive treaties all the southern third of Illinois and a broad belt of land between the Illinois and Mississippi rivers, bordering on both streams and running northward to the Wisconsin, was divested of the Indian title as early as 1805; but while much of the country was thus lawfully thrown open to the advance of the enterprising pioneer, the children of the forest still lingered around their ancient hunting grounds, reluctant to abandon the scenes of their youth and the graves of their ancestors, notwithstanding the solemn cession of their native land to the powerful government of the pale faces, the receipt of payment, and their promises to retire. Nor did they abstain from occasional marauding excursions into the frontier settlements of the whites. The remoteness of Illinois from the Atlantic sea-board, its destitution of many of the comforts of civilized society, and exposure to the precarious amity of the savages, to a great extent deterred emigrants from coming hither. They found, aside from the quality of the soil, equal opportunities in Kentucky, Ohio, and southern Indiana, with greater security from danger and more convenience of access in their slow and toilsome mode of travel. Hence, at this time the settlements on the Wabash, the Illinois, and the Upper Mississippi, increased slowly, compared with the regions above mentioned.

Virginia, by her deed of cession, had stipulated that "the French and Canadian inhabitants, and all other settlers of the Kaskaskias, St. Vincents, and the neighboring villages, who professed themselves citizens of Virginia, shall have their possessions and titles confirmed to them, and be protected in the enjoyments of their rights and liberties." The congress of the old confederation, by resolutions of June 20th and August 29, 1788, ordained that steps be immediately taken for confirming in their possessions and titles to lands the French and Canadian inhabitants, and other settlers, who, on or before 1783, had professed themselves citizens of the United States, or of any State; and that a donation should be given each of the families then living at either of the villages of Kaskaskia, Prairie du Rocher, Cahokia, Fort Chartres, or St. Phillips. Out of this grew the old "head-right" claims, of which it seems there were only a total of 244 in all the country. We have seen that in 1790 the French, in their impoverished condition,

objected strenuously to paying the expense of surveys. Congress
passed a law March 3, 1791, providing further, that where lands had
been actually improved and cultivated, under a supposed grant of
the same by any commandant or court claiming authority to make
such grant, the Governor of the territory was empowered and
charged with the duty to confirm to the persons entitled thereto,
as above, their heirs or assigns, the land supposed to have been
granted to them, or such share of it as might be adjudged upon the
proof to be reasonable, not exceeding 400 acres to any one person
however. The benefits of this act were extended to persons entitled under it, but who had removed out of the country, provided
they or their heirs should return and occupy their lands within 5
years. By the 6th section of the same act, in the same manner, a
grant of land not exceeding 100 acres was provided to each person
who had not already obtained a donation as above from the United
States, and who, on the first day of August, 1790, had been enrolled in the militia and done militia duty.

Governor St Clair had made many confirmations of these grants,
but still a large number of claims remained unadjusted. The
abeyance of these confirmations was a great hindrance to the settlement of that portion of the country where they were located.
No one cared to invest a fair price in lands, the title whereof was
not established by survey and record. There was naturally much
anxiety on the part of claimants, and those who desired to see the
country fill up and prosper, to have these obstacles cleared away.
As a remedy, a law was passed by congress, March 15, 1804, establishing land offices at Kaskaskia, Vincennes and Detroit, for the
sale of the public lands, and constituting the registers and receivers
a board of commissioners, upon which was devolved, for the
respective districts at each place, the former powers and duties of
the governor to examine the validity of land claims, decide thereon
according to justice and equity, and not confirm, but report their
decisions to congress. The land office at Kaskaskia was authorized to sell such of the lands included in the cession of the Kaskaskia tribe of Indians, by treaty of August 13, 1803, as were not
claimed by any other tribes.

Michael Jones and E. Backus were appointed register and receiver, respectively, of the land office at Kaskaskia. These
gentlemen, in entering upon their duties as commissioners, soon
learned that it would be necessary to proceed with great circumspection, as many of the land claims presented discovered
evidences of fraud, and hence their labor of investigation became
immense, and they made but slow progress. They made an elaborate report in 1810, which may be seen in Vol. II, American State
Papers—Public Lands, to which we are indebted for our facts in
great part. See page 102.

From a very early time these land claims of ancient grants, both
French and English—of donations to heads of families, "head
rights," of improvement rights, and militia rights, became a rare
field for the operation of speculators. The French claims, owing
to the poverty of this people, were in great part unconfirmed,
and this circumstance, with others, contributed to force many of
them into market. We have seen, also, with what facility the
British commandant, Wilkins, made extensive grants to numerous
favorites in various portions of the country, and these being

apparently in contravention of the King's proclamation of October 7th, 1763, were purchased for a trifle; and as for the militia rights of 100 acre tracts, while valid, they sold freely at 30 cents per acre, in high priced and trifling merchandise. From the passage of the law of 1791 to the time that the commissioners took up the investigation of these claims, speculation in them was rife, and very few of them remained in the hands of original claimants. The greed of speculators caused numerous claims to pass current without close scrutiny as to the proofs upon which they rested, a circumstance which at the same time tended all the more to stimulate the production of fraudulent claims. The number of fraudulent claims was comparatively great, but by purchase and assignment they, more than the genuine, became concentrated in the hands of a few speculators. The official report of the commissioners for the district of Kaskaskia, made in 1810 to the secretary of the treasury, shows that they rejected 890 land claims as either illegal or fraudulent, 370 being supported by perjury, and a considerable number forged. The report further shows that the assignees were privy to both these attempted frauds; the perjured depositions appeared in the handwriting of claimant speculators not unfrequently without a word changed by the sworn signers. There are 14 names given, both English and French, who made it a regular business to furnish sworn certificates, professing an intimate knowledge, in every case, of the settlers who had made certain improvements, and when and where they were located, upon which claims were predicated. In some cases these names were assumed and the deponent would never appear; in some they were real and well known; while still in others, purporting to come from a distance, well known names would be forged. In one case several hundred depositions poured in upon the commissioners from St. Charles, Missouri, in the names of gentlemen formerly well known in Kaskaskia. The commissioners, having their suspicions aroused that they were forgeries, summoned them to appear before them, which they readily did, though they could not have been compelled to, and with tears in their eyes declared on oath that they lived in Upper Louisiana, that they had never been in St. Charles in their lives, and that the depositions were despicable forgeries. A Frenchman, clerk of the Parish of Prairie du Rocher, "without property and fond of liquor," after having given some 200 depositions in favor of three certain land claimant speculators, whose names would be familiarly recognized to-day, "was induced either by compensation, fear, or the impossibility of obtaining absolution on any other terms, to declare on oath that the said despositions were false, and that in giving them in, he had a regard to something beyond the truth."*

It is not pleasant for an Illinoisan to read in the public archives of our country, noted after the honored names of the first prominent settlers of our State, whose descendents have become conspicuous in its subsequent history, by sworn and intelligent officials the damaging words of "perjury," "deed forged," "fraud and perjury," time and again, in support of land claims; but such

---

[NOTE.—The forged and perjured depositions were mostly adduced to support claims presented by Robert Morrison, John Edgar, Robert Reynolds, Wm. Morrison. Richard Lord, Wm. Kelley, and others. Am. State Papers. vol. ii, 104—Pub. Lands, 2, ib. 115—130.]

is the fact. Well might a cotemporary, young at the time, subsequently exclaim, that "parties were branded with perjury and forgery to an alarming extent."† But when he further says that "the best citizens in the country were stigmatized with the above crimes, without cause," the facts appear against him. Much rancor and partisan feeling was engendered against the commissioners by the influential claimant speculators, who were thus thwarted to a great extent in their rascally schemes. The commissioners close their report with these words:

"We close this melancholy picture of human depravity, by rendering our devout acknowledgements that, in the awful alternative in which we have been placed, of either admitting perjured testimony in support of the claims before us, or having it turned against our characters and lives, it has, as yet, pleased Divine Providence which rules over the affairs of men, to preserve us both from legal murder and private assassination."

The claimants, particularly those who held by assignment, had met with little trouble in having their claims confirmed and patents issued to them by Gov. St. Clair, while Illinois was part of the northwestern territory. On the occasion of his visit to Illinois, in 1790, while the impoverished French were unable to bear the expense of the government surveys, the rich and influential speculators readily met this difficulty and obtained their patents. It seems that many of the governor's confirmations were made by the bundle. As but a single instance, out of many, we will cite his confirmation, in one bulk, of 90 donation rights to heads of families, of 400 acres each, amounting to 36,000 acres of land, in the hands of John Edgar as assignee. We have already noted his confirmation of an English grant described as containing 13,000, acres but which really contained 30,000, a moiety of which had been previously conveyed to his son. While this was the largest, there were many others in which his son shared, that readily received his confirmation. Evident fraud and imposition were also practiced upon Governor Harrison in procuring his confirmation to land claims.

As the report of the commissioners raised manifest doubts respecting the validity or propriety of a number of confirmations by the governors, and as there was much dissatisfaction on the part of the claimants, congress, Feb. 20, 1812, passed an act for the revision of these land claims in the district of Kaskaskia. The commissioners under this law were Michael Jones, John Caldwell, and Thomas Sloo. Their investigations resulted in unearthing more facts and confirming many previous ones, damaging to the good name of gentlemen high in official life. Regarding the English grant of 30,000 acres, which Governor St. Clair confirmed to his son, John Murray and John Edgar, they declared that the patent was issued after the governor's powers had ceased to exist and the Indiana Territory was stricken off, which rendered it a nullity, and that the claim was founded neither in law nor equity, and ought not to be confirmed. It was, however, confirmed by congress. Governor St. Clair was empowered to make absolute confirmations and issue patents for the lands; but the land commissioners under the act of 1804 were not vested with the power of confirmation—they were only an examining board for the in-

† Reynold's Pioneer History.

vestigation of the rights of claimants to ancient grants, head, improvement and militia rights.

A vote, taken September 11, 1804, showed a majority of 138 freeholders of the territory in favor of the second grade of territorial government, and in obedience to the will of the people, Governor Harrison ordered an election for representatives to the territorial general assembly, for January 3, 1805, which was to meet at Vincennes, February 7th following, and nominate ten men for the legislative council. The members elect from Illinois were Shadrach Bond and William Biggs, of St. Clair, and George Fisher, of Randolph. The names presented from Illinois for councilors, were Jean Francis Perrey and John Hay, of St. Clair, and Pierre Menard, of Randolph. President Jefferson waived his right of selection in favor of Governor Harrison, asking only that he reject "land jobbers, dishonest men, and those who, though honest, might suffer themselves to be warped by party prejudice." Perrey and Menard were selected for Illinois. On the 7th of June following, the governor issued his proclamation convening the legislature for the 29th of July, 1805. This was the second time that the people of this country, through their representatives, exercised the law making power for their own local government.

In his message, delivered the following day, the governor recommended the passage of laws to prevent the sale of intoxicating liquors to the Indians, saying: "You have seen our towns crowded with drunken savages; our streets flowing with blood; their arms and clothing bartered for the liquor that destroys them; and their miserable women and children enduring all the extremities of cold and hunger; whole villages have been swept away. A miserable remnant is all that remains to mark the situation of many warlike tribes." He recommended, also, a remodeling of the inferior courts, so as to insure a more efficient administration of justice; an improved militia system; more efficient punishment for horse stealing; and ways and means for raising a revenue, saying, that this latter would be their most difficult and delicate duty; that while few were the objects of taxation in a new country, it must still be a burthen, and the commencement of our financial operations must be expected to be attended by some trifling, though he trusted, temporary embarrassments. The legislature, by joint ballot, elected Benjamin Parke, of Indiana, territorial delegate to congress. The levying of taxes, as was anticipated, created considerable dissatisfaction among some of the people. The poll tax was particularly obnoxious to the French residents. Their indignation found vent at a public meeting, held at Vincennes, Sunday, August 16, 1807, where it was " resolved" that they would "withdraw their confidence and support forever from those men who advocated, or in any manner promoted, the second grade of government."*

The legislature re-enacted many of the general laws selected and adopted by the governors and judges of both the Northwestern and Indiana territorities, under the first grade of their respective governments. Provision was made for a collection and thorough revision of the laws, by a commission. Accordingly, a volume was, two years later, produced, bearing the following title: "Laws of the Indiana Territory, comprising those acts formerly in force, and as revised by Messrs. John Rice Jones and John Johnson, and

* Dillon's Indiana.

passed (after amendments) by the legislature; and the original
acts passed at the first session of the second general assembly of
the said territory—began and held at the borough of Vincennes,
on the 16th day of August, A. D. 1807." Messrs. Stout and
Smoot, "printers for the territory," were the publishers; the paper,
on which it was printed, was brought on horseback from Georgetown, Kentucky.

This collection of old statutes relates principally "to the organization of superior and inferior courts of justice, the appointment and duties of territorial and county officers, prison and
prison bounds, real estate, interest and money, marriages,
divorces, licenses, ferries, grist-mills, elections, militia, roads and
highways, estrays, trespassing, animals, inclosure and cultivation
of common fields, relief of poor, taverns, improving the breed of
horses, taxes and revenues, negroes and mulattoes under indentures as servants, fees of officers, sale of intoxicating liquors,
relief of persons imprisoned for debt, killing wolves, prohibiting
the sale of arms and ammunition to Indians and other persons,
the standard of weights and measures, vagrants, authorizing aliens
to purchase and hold real estate in the territory,"* etc. The penalties provided for crimes and misdemeanors, were, death for
treason, murder, arson and horse-stealing; manslaughter, punishable as provided at common law; burglary and robbery, each by
whipping, fine and, in some cases imprisonment not exceeding 40
years; riotous conduct, by fine and imprisonment; larceny, by
fine or whipping, and in certain cases, bound out to labor not
exceeding 7 years; forgery, by fine, disfranchisement and standing in the pillory; assault and battery, as a crime, by fine not
exceeding $100; hog-stealing, by fine and whipping; gambling,
profane swearing and Sabbath-breaking, each by fine; bigamy, by
fine, whipping and disfranchisement. The disobedience of servants and children, a justice of the peace was entitled to punish
by imprisonment in the jail until the culprit was "humbled," and
if the offense was accompanied by assault, he might be whipped,
not exceeding 10 stripes.

*Dillon's Indiana.
The laws, relating to indentured slaves, are treated under Governor Cole's administration.

CHAPTER XXI.

1809—ILLINOIS TERRITORY.

Opposition to Division—Jesse B. Thomas— Gov. Edwards—Nathaniel Pope—Territorial Federal Judges—The Governor avoids the meshes of the Separationists and Anti-Separationists—Condition and Population of the Territory.

By act of congress, approved February 3, 1809, all that part of the Indiana Territory lying "west of the Wabash river, and a direct line drawn from the said Wabash river and Post Vincennes, due north to the territorial line between the United States and Canada," should, after the first of March following, constitute a separate territory, and be called Illinois. This, it will be perceived, included the present State of Wisconsin. The population of the newly organized territory was estimated at about 9,000, leaving in Indiana about double that number.

There are many things which usually influence any American community in the desire to be independent. The main reasons advanced by Illinois in favor of a separation from Indiana were, the "wide extent of wilderness country" which intervened between the civilized settlements of the country on the Mississippi, about the only ones in Illinois, and the seat of government on the Wabash, rendering the ordinary protection of government to life and property almost nugatory; the inconvenience, expense and dangers of long journeys whose routes led through sections wholly inhabited by savages, which litigants in the superior courts of the territory were compelled to incur for themselves and witnesses; and the almost total obstruction to an efficient administration of the laws in counties so distant from the seat of government as those of Illinois. Notwithstanding the remoteness and isolation of this country from the centers of population in the United States at that early day, the tide of emigration pressed westward with a gradual but ever increasing flow. In 1805 Michigan was erected into a separate territory, and by this time Illinois contained a white population fully as great as that of the whole territory of Indiana when detached from Ohio five years before. The question of separation in Illinois grew apace from this time on; it was repeatedly pressed upon the attention of congress by legislative memorials in 1806, 1807 and 1808, until that body finally disposed of the subject as above stated. But while the people of Vincennes and neighboring villages east of the Wabash opposed the separation from interested motives, for a division would before many years elapsed take from them the seat of government and remove it to a more central locality, and would also increase the rates of taxation, what may appear difficult of solution was the fact that in Illinois there was anything but unanimity in favor of division and independence. A violent anti-separation party sprung up here, which, though greatly overborne by numbers, by its activity aroused a deep and angry feeling which ultimately resulted in bloodshed. By the machinations of the opposers to a division "one of the warmest friends and ablest advocates of the measure was assassinated at Kaskaskia in consequence."* The question of separation turned upon the ability of the Illinois members of the Legislature, in session at Vincennes in October 1808, to elect a delegate to congress in place of Benjamin Parke, resigned, who should be favorable to the division. The Illinoisans found a suitable candidate in an Indiana member of the House, who was also Speaker, by the name of Jesse B. Thomas, who, for the sake of going to congress, was ready to violate the sentiments of his constituents upon this question. But the Illinois members, with a due appreciation of the promises of politicians, even at that early day, required of this gentleman, before they would vote for him, to support his pledges by his bond, conditioned that he would procure from congress a division, whereupon he was triumphantly elected by a bare majority with the aid of his own vote.† He was hung in effigy at Vincennes by the anti-separationists; but he discharged his pledges and his bond, by procuring the division from congress; and, as it was doubtless desirable to change his residence, he came home with a commission for a federal judgeship of the new territory in his pocket and removed to Illinois.

By the act of separation, the people of Illinois were also entitled to all and singular the rights, privileges and advantages granted and secured to the people under the ordinance of 1787, which was applied to the territory—fair words enough, but the ordinance conferred little political power; the previous duties were imposed upon the new officers, and the President was empowered to make appointments during the recess of congress; provision was made for the organization of the second grade of territorial government, whenever the governor should at any time be satisfied that a majority of the freeholders of the territory desired the same, notwithstanding there were less than 5,000 inhabitants, fixing the number of representatives, in such case, at not less than seven nor more than nine, to be apportioned among the counties by the governor; the legislative council and delegates to congress were made elective by the people; the old officers were continued in the exercise of their duties in Indiana, but prohibited in Illinois; provision was made for the final disposition of all suits from Illinois pending in the court at Vincennes, for the collection of taxes levied and due; and the seat of government was fixed at Kaskaskia, until otherwise ordered by the legislature.

*See address of citizens to Gov. Edwards, at Kaskaskia, June, 1809,
†See Ford's Illinois, p. 30.

[NOTE.—A curious state of affairs obtained with regard to Indiana after the separation of Illinois. On the 26th of October, 1808, the governor had dissolved the legislature: by act of congress, February 3, 1809, Illinois was detached, taking with it five members, which would have dissolved the legislature had it not already been dissolved; later in the same month, on the 27th, congress passed a law extending the right of suffrage and prescribing the number of representatives for the territory, and further, directed the legislature to apportion the representatives; but there was no legislature in existence to make the apportionment. Indiana was in political chaos—something was required of a body that she did not possess, and which it was impossible for her to legally create. But Governor Harrison cut the gordean knot, and, legally or otherwise, apportioned the territory, issued writs of election for a new legislature, and in October

Ninian Edwards, at the time chief justice of the Court of Appeals in Kentucky, became governor of the newly organized territory of Illinois. John Boyle, of the same State, at first received the appointment of Governor, but declined the office and accepted that of associate justice of the same court whereof Edwards was Chief Justice. Edwards was desirous of filling the vacancy, and at the recommendation of Henry Clay, received the appointment from President Madison, his commission bearing date April 24, 1809.

In his letter to the president, Henry Clay spoke of Judge Edwards as follows: "The honorable appointments which this gentleman has held (first as a judge of our Superior Court, and then promoted to his present station), evince how highly he is estimated among us." And in a letter of the same date to the Hon. Robt. Smith, he said: "His political principles accord with those of the Republican party. His good understanding, weight of character and conciliatory manners, give him very fair pretentions to the office alluded to. * * * I have no doubt that the whole representation from the State, when consulted, would concur in ascribing to him every qualification for the office in question."

Ninian Edwards was born in Montgomery county, Md., in 1775, and at the time of his appointment as governor was about 34 years old. He obtained his early education in company with and partly under the tuition of William Wirt, his senior by two years, and life long friend. After a collegiate course at Carlyle, Pa., he commenced the study of law, but before finishing it was sent to Kentucky to select lands for his brothers and sisters and open a farm. He located in Nelson county, and being furnished with ample means in a new country where the character of society was as yet unformed, and surrounded by companions whose pleasures and pursuits were in sensual indulgences, he fell into indiscretions and excesses for two or three years.* But in the then standard of society, this did not prevent his election to the Kentucky Legislature. Subsequently he broke away from his dissolute companions and habits, removed to Russelville, and devoted himself to laborious study. He soon attained eminence in his profession. Before he was 32 years old he had filled in succession the offices of presiding judge of the general court, circuit judge, 4th judge of the court of appeals, and chief justice of the State, which last he held when his associate justice, Boyle, received the appointment of territorial governor for Illinois. The two, to suit their respective inclinations, exchanged offices, Edwards, through the patronage of Mr. Clay, becoming governor, and Boyle chief justice. Governor Edwards was a large, fine looking man, with a distinguished air and courtly manners, who wielded a ready pen and was fluent of speech.

The territorial judges appointed, besides Thomas, were Alexander Stuart and William Sprigg. The former was a Virginian, a man of fine education and polished manners, who,† however, re-

following convened it for business. But that body, entertaining doubts whether it was really a legislature or not, prepared a statement to congress, petitioning that power to constitue it a legal body, and adjourned temporarily to await action upon the case. Such are some of the inconveniences of government where original sovereignty does not reside in the people, but is derived from a power superior to them—an apparent anomoly in the theory of American government.—See Dillon's Ind.]

*Gov. Edward's Life, by his son.

†Judge Breese, in the address of laying the corner stone of the new State House by Judge Caton, says: "And withall a good liver, of whom it is said he esteemed the turkey the most inconvenient of the poultry tribe, as it was too large for one and not large enough for two."

mained on the bench in Illinois but a short time, being changed to Missouri. His successor was Stanley Griswold, a good lawyer and an honest man, who, as Gov. Reynolds says in his Pioneer History, "paid his debts and sung David's Psalms." He was afterwards transferred to Michigan, and Thomas Towles became his successor. William Sprigg was born and reared in Maryland, where his brother attained to the high office of governor. His education was classical and he was deeply read in the law. He was a man of singular purity of heart and simplicity of manner—lacking totally in all the arts of the politician.*

Nathaniel Pope, a relative of the governor, was appointed secretary of the territory. He was born in Kentucky, at the Falls of the Ohio, in 1784. His education was collegiate, being one of the early graduates of Transylvania University, at Lexington. His natural endowments of head and heart, were very superior. To a fine analytical mind, he added a genial and benevolent disposition, and great dignity of character. He selected the law for a profession, and soon mastered its intricacies. At the age of 21, he emigrated to St. Genevieve, then Upper Louisiana, where he learned to speak French quite fluently. Five years later, he was appointed secretary of the Illinois territory. As such, in the absence of the governor, he was empowered, under the ordinance of 1787, to discharge the duties of the latter's office. On the 25th of April, 1809, at St. Genevieve, before Judge Shrader, he took the oath of office, and coming to Illinois, inaugurated the new government on the 28th instant, by issuing his proclamation to that effect. The counties of St. Clair and Randolph were reinstated as the two counties of the Illinois territory. On the 3d of May, he appointed and commissioned Elias Rector attorney-general, John Hay sheriff, Enoch Moore coroner, and 17 justices of the peace.

On the 11th of Junefollowing, Governor Edwards assumed the duties of his office. He had taken the oath of office in Kentucky, before his departure. Upon his arrival at Kaskaskia, his Excellency was tendered a flattering public address by the citizens, in which he was asked to espouse the side of the "virtuous majority" by whose patriotic exertions the territory had been divided and his Excellency attained his high station, and to whom ought to be distributed the offices in his gift, rather than to those who never ceased to oppose the measure and heap calumnies and indignities upon its friends. The governor, unwilling to become a partisan on either side, made a felicitous but non-committal reply. He re-appointed John Hay clerk of St. Clair county, and, as a curious instance of official self-succession to office in this country, we will mention that he held that public trust from thence on, until his decease, in 1845. In place of Rector, Benjamin H. Doyle had been appointed attorney-general, and he resigning, John J. Crittenden, of Kentucky, was appointed; but the latter, after holding the office a few months, also resigned, when his brother, Thomas L., succeeded him.

On the 16th of June, 1809, the governor, joined by Judges Stuart and Sprigg (Thomas being still absent in Washington), constitut-

*Reynolds, in his Pioneer History, says that Sprigg accompanied Governor Edwards in his campaign against the Indians on Peoria Lake, in 1812, unencumbered by gun or other weapon indicating belligerency. "His pacific and sickly appearance, together with his perfect philosophic indifference as to war or peace, life or death made him the subject of much discussion among the troops. He was the only savant in the army."

ing a legislative body in the first grade of territorial government, under the 5th section of the ordinance of 1787, met and re-enacted such of the laws of the Indiana territory, with which the people, who for nine years had formed a part thereof, were familiar, and as were suitable and applicable to Illinois, and not local or special to Indiana. Many of these laws were those which, without change of phraseology, had either been originally imported or enacted by the authorities of the old Northwestern territory.

Thus was put into operation the machinery of civil government in the Territory of Illinois; but Governor Edwards, owing to the local political dissensions, growing out of the question of territorial division, which had degenerated into personal animosities, met with no inconsiderable difficulties in avoiding the meshes of these factions, struggling fiercely for respective ascendancy. He resolved not to be caught in the toils of either party, and for the interests and prosperity of the country, sought to ignore the entire question that it might pass into oblivion. At that day, the militia system, which had received the earnest recommendation of Governor Harrison, and which was also a necessity of the times, was in full and effective operation. With the dissolution of the Indiana territory, it became the duty of Governor Edwards to re-organize the militia for the new territory of Illinois. The separationists urged his Excellency to appoint none to office in the militia who had ever opposed the division of the territory; but this would have committed him contrary to his judgment. The anti-separationists pressed him to re-appoint all the old officers; but as a new commission would have voided all offenses for which any officer might have been tried and punished by dismissal, he refused to accede to that also. To steer clear of both Scylla and Charibdis, he referred the question to the people, by directing the militia companies to elect the company officers, and the latter to choose the field officers. With these orders, his Excellency retired from the field of contention to Kentucky, to wind up some unfinished court business, and upon his return, late in the fall, he issued an address to the people, explanatory of his course, and commissioned the militia officers returned to him as elected.

The population of the territory, at the time of its organization, was estimated at 9000; the census of 1810 returned it at a total of 12,282—11,501 whites, 168 slaves, 613 of all others, except Indians —being an increase of some 400 per cent during the preceding decade. The frontiers had been steadily advanced by the adventurous pioneers. To the north, the settlements had extended to the Wood river country, in the present Madison county; eastward, on Silver creek and up the Kaskaskia river; south and east, from Kaskaskia, some 15 miles out on the Fort Massac road; the Birds had located at the mouth of the Ohio; at old Massac and the Ohio salines, there had been nuclei of settlements for some time; Shawneetown,* the nearest point on the Ohio to the salt wells, 12 miles west, had contained a few straggling houses

---

*Shawneetown. which derives its name from a dissatisfied band of that tribe of Indians located there from 1735 to about 1760, was laid out by the direction of the United States goverment, in 1813-14, and for a quarter of a century was the principal town in the State. The site, chosen with reference to its contiguity to the United States salines, was an unfortunate one, being subject to repeated inundations. In 1813, a flood rose to the ridge poles on the roofs of many of the log houses, and swept 40 of them away, besides other damage to stock, fencing, etc. Petitions to change the location to the mouth of the Saline creek, 8 miles below, were disregarded.

since 1805; along the west side of the Wabash, opposite Vincennes, were scattered a few families, one McCawley having penetrated inland to the crossing of the Little Wabash by the Vincennes road, but the latter were mostly abandoned during the war of 1812. Indeed, the new settlements were very sparse and all feeble, and from 1810, until the close of the war, 4 years later, immigration was almost at a stand. Nine-tenths of the territory was a howling wilderness, over which red savages held dominion and roamed at will, outnumbering the whites at least three to one.

CHAPTER XXII.

INDIAN TROUBLES IN ILLINOIS PRECEDING THE WAR
OF 1812

*The Country put in a State of Defence by the Organization of Rang-
ing Companies and the Building of Block-house and Stockade
Forts—Governor Edwards Sends an Envoy to Gomo's Village—
Battle of Tippecanoe—Indian Council at Cahokia.*

————

The British, after the war of Independence, relinquished with
great reluctance, as we have seen, their hold upon the northwestern territory. The confederated tribes of the northwest only
ceased their warfare when they found their last hope of British
aid cut off by Jay's treaty at London, November, 1794; but this
treaty did not cover all the outrageous pretensions of Great Britain. In her desperatewar with France, later, she boldly boarded
American vessels on the high seas, searching for English-born
seamen, impressing them into her marine service upon the ground
of "once an Englishman, always an Englishman," and denying
expatriation and American citizenship by naturalization. Nor did
she scrutinize very closely as to the nationality of the seamen
impressed, as in the case of the Chesapeake, boarded off the
coast of Virginia, where, of four of the crew taken as deserters,
three were of American birth. In the retaliatory measures
between France and England, to prevent trade and commerce
with either power, our vessels, as neutrals, became the prey of both
hostile nations. The affair of the Chesapeake intensified the feeling already deep; Jefferson ordered all British ships-of-war out
of the waters of the United States, and congress laid an embargo
on American vessels, forbidding them to leave port, to the great
injury of American commerce.

In the West, British emissaries were busy arousing the northwestern savages to war against the United States. Harrison's
zeal and activity in divesting the Indian titles to western lands,
was no inconsiderable provocative. In September, 1809, he had
held a treaty at Fort Wayne with the Delawares, Potawattomies,
Miamis, Kickapoos, Weas and Eel River Indians, who, in consideration of $2,350 as annuities, and $8,200 of presents in hand,
ceded to the United States a large tract of country, comprising
near three million acres of land in Indiana, extending up the Wabash above Terre Haute, and interiorly to include the middle
waters of White river, and trenching upon the home and hunting
ground of the great Shawnee warrior, Tecumseh, whose nation

247

was not a party to the treaty, and who denounced it as unjust and
illegal.

At a council, invited by Governor Harrison and held at Vincennes, August 12, 1810, Tecumseh, followed by 400 warriors,
maintained that all the northwestern tribes were one nation, holding their lands in common, and that without the consent of all
the tribes concerned, no treaty of purchase and cession was valid;
that his purpose was to wrest power from the village chiefs
and put it in the hands of the war chiefs. Nor did he deny having
threatened to kill the chiefs who had treacherously signed the
treaty. An angry discussion arose between Harrison and Tecumseh, the latter boldly avowing his purpose to hold the lands conveyed by the treaty, and resist the further intrusion of the
whites. He made an impassioned and bitter recital of the wrongs
and aggressions of the whites upon the Indians, declaring they
had been driven back from the sea coast now to be pushed into
the lakes. Harrison ridiculed his pretensions and the wrongs of
his people, whereupon Tecumseh sprang to his feet, and excitedly
charged his Excellency with cheating and imposing upon the Indians. His red warriors, inflamed by his vehement manner, simultaneously siezed their tomahawks and brandished their war
clubs, as if ready for the work of massacre. A moment of silent
but awful suspense to the whites, who were unarmed, followed.
No further demonstration was however made, and Tecumseh,
spurned by Harrison, retired, determined to adhere to the old
boundary.

The ill-feeling, steadily on the increase, between the United
States and Great Britain, was early apprehended by the savages
through the machinations of British agents and traders on the northwestern frontier. Nicholas Jarrott, of Cahokia, having just
returned from a trip to Prairie du Chien, made affidavit, June 28,
1809, that British agents and traders at that post, and on the frontiers of Canada, were inciting the Indians to hostility, and fitting
them out with guns and ammunition for demonstrations against
the western settlers.* The savages were greatly emboldened by
these friendly offers to commit depredations upon the American
settlements. In July, 1810, a band of Potawattomies, from Illinois,
made a raid upon a settlement in Missouri, opposite the mouth of
the Gasconade, stealing horses and other property. The owners,
with their friends to the number of six, made pursuit. The Indians, who were discovered at the distance of a few miles, to baffle
their pursuers, changed their course. The whites, after a fatiguing
march, went into camp, and neglecting to post a guard, fell soundly
asleep. In the night, the Indians, with demoniac yells, pounced
upon the sleepers and tomahawked all but two. The survivors
speedily spread the dreadful tidings, which created great excitement at the time. The proof from various circumstances being
clear that the murderers were Potawattomies, the governor of
Missouri made a requisition upon the governor of Illinois for them.
During the same year, hostile demonstrations were made by the
Sac and Fox nations, from Illinois, against Fort Madison, situate
on the west bank of the Mississippi, above the DesMoines Rapids.
Hostilities also existed between the Iowas and Osages, both resid-

*Annals of the West.—Appendix. This was, however, denied by a communication
from Messrs. Bleakly and Portier, the parties implicated, of Prairie du Chien.

ing west of the Mississippi. In 1811, the Indians committed many murders upon the whites in Illinois. Near the forks of Shoal creek, on the 2d of June, the family of Mr. Cox being absent, except a young man and woman, a party of savages killed the former, mangling his body horribly, stole the horses, and carried off the girl a prisoner. The Coxes and neighbors, to the number of eight or ten, made pursuit, and some 50 miles north of the present Springfield, overtook the Indians, re-captured their property, and during the rambling fight, the girl, after being wounded by a tomahawk in the hip, made her escape and joined her friends. In the same month, at the lower part of the present city of Alton, where a Mr. Price and another named Ellis, were plowing corn, a party of Indians were observed approaching the spring in the vicinity, where there was a cabin. The whites unhitched their horses and seized their guns; but the Indians declared themselves friendly, and one of them, a tall, stout fellow, laid down his gun and gave Price his hand, but in so doing, held him fast while the others tomahawked him to death. At this, his companion bounded on his horse and made good his escape, with a wounded thigh.* But we will not further detail these horrid Indian butcheries. The people saw their imminence, and began to make preparations for defence. Forts and stockades began to be built, and in July of the same year, a company of "rangers," or mounted riflemen, was raised and organized in the Goshen settlement of Illinois.

Congress, in 1811, passed an act for the organization of 10 companies of mounted rangers, to protect the frontiers of the West. These companies constituted the 17th United States regiment, and Colonel William Russel, an old Indian fighter of Kentucky, was assigned to its command. The companies were generally made up of frontier citizens, who had the additional stimulus in their duties of immediately defending their homes, kindred and neighbors. Each ranger had to furnish his own horse, provisions and equipments all complete, and the recompense from the government was one dollar per day. They appointed their own company officers, and were enlisted for one year. Four companies were allotted to the defence of Illinois, whose respective captains were, Samuel and William B. Whitesides, James B. Moore, and Jacob Short. Independent cavalry companies were also organized for the protection of the remote settlements in the lower Wabash country, of which Willis Hargrave, William McHenry, Nathaniel Journey, Captain Craig, at Shawneetown, and William Boon, on the Big Muddy, were, respectively, commanders, ready on short notice of Indian outrages, to make pursuit of the depredators. These ranging companies performed most efficient service in the protection of the settlements in Illinois against the savage foe. The rangers and mounted militia, in times of supposed peril, constantly scoured the country a considerable distance in advance of the frontier settlers; and yet the savages would often prowl through the settlements, commit outrages, and elude successful pursuit.

Great numbers of block-house forts, or stations for the security of families, were built, extending from the Illinois river to the Kaskaskia, thence to the United States salines, near the present town of Equality, up the Ohio and Wabash, and nearly to all set-

* Reynold's Pioneer History.

tlements in Illinois. Some of these forts were situated as follows: One on the present site of the town of Carlyle; one a small distance above the present town of Aviston, known as Journey's fort; two on the east side of Shoal creek, known as Hill's and Jones' forts; one a few miles southeast of the present town of Lebanon, on the west side of Looking-glass prairie, known as Chambers' fort; on the Kaskaskia river were Middleton's and Going's forts; one on Doza creek, a few miles from its mouth, known as Nat. Hill's; two in the Jourdan settlement, eastern part of Franklin county, on the road to the salt works; one at the mouth of the Illinois river, and later, John Campbell, a United States officer, erected a small block-house on the west bank of the Illinois (Prairie Marcot), 19 miles above its mouth. More pretentious military stations were established on the Mississippi, opposite the mouth of the Missouri, to guard the river; and on Silver creek, near Troy. But the main military depot was established about a mile and a half northwest of the present town of Edwardsville, called Camp Russell, in honor of the colonel commanding the 10 ranging companies.

The simplest form of block-house forts consisted of a single house built of logs, compactly laid up a story and a half or two stories high, with the corners closely trimmed, to prevent scaling. The walls of the lower story were provided with port-holes; the door was made of thick puncheons, and was strongly barred on the inside. The upper story projected over the lower three or four feet, with port-holes through the floor of the projecting part, which commanded the walls and space below against any Indian attempts to force an entrance. They afforded entire security against the rude arts of savage war, but were only single family forts. A stockade fort consisted of four block-houses, as described above, or larger, placed one at each corner of a square piece of ground, of dimensions ample enough to accommodate the number of people seeking shelter therein. The intervening space was filled up with timbers or logs, firmly set on end in the ground, and extending upwards 12 or 15 feet. This was the stockade into whose sides port-holes were cut, high enough to be above the head, and to which platforms were raised, from which to fire upon the enemy. There were also port-holes in the projecting walls of the corner block-houses, which thus commanded the whole of the stockade walls on the outside. Within the stockade, cabins were built for the families to live in. Wells were dug for water, or, possibly, the site was selected over a spring. There were usually two heavy entrance gates in the stockade walls, securely barred on the inside, and large enough to admit teams. In times of extra peril, horses, and sometimes other valuable domestic animals, were taken into the stockade over night for safety. If the fort was not built out on the prairie, the woods was invariably cleared back some distance, so as to afford no place of concealment to the stealthy enemy. It was often hazardous to first open the gates of a morning. Milking parties, upon their errands, were not unfrequently attacked by the skulking red foe. At times, sentinels were often posted during the night, as in the case of regular garrisons.

The most notable, as also the largest, strongest, and best appointed in every respect of the stockade forts, was Fort Russell, established by Governor Edwards early in 1812, about 1½ miles northwest of the present Edwardsville, then on the extreme northern frontier. The cannon of Louis XIV, which had done service for many years in the ancient Fort Chartres, were removed thither and placed in position, where, if they served no other purpose, their thunder tones reverberated over the broad expanse of wilderness prairie, and upon days of festivity, dress parade, and other displays, added eclat to the occasions. This stockade was made the main depot for military stores, and became also the general rendezvous for the militia volunteers, rangers and regulars, as well as the great *point d'appui* for the organization of expeditions into the country of savages on the Peoria lake. The only United States regulars, however, which camped at this fort during the war, was a small company, under the command of Captain Ramsey, early in the spring of 1812.

When Governor Edwards, during the perilous times of 1812, with Indian hostilities threatening on every hand, assumed command of the Illinois forces, it was here that he established his headquarters. Here was gathered about him the beauty and chivalry of those days. Within the protecting walls of this stockade, defended without and within by brave, stout hearts, were attracted and found shelter, much of the talent, fashion and wealth of the country; and here, his Excellency, not devoid of a natural love for display and parade, presided with a courtly grace and stately dignity well befitting his fine personal appearance and his many accomplishments.

Early in the year 1811, numerous were the complaints of horses being stolen, houses plundered, and alleged murders committed by the savages. Governor Clark, of Missouri, after the murder of the four citizens near the mouth of the Gasconade, in August, 1810, made a requisition upon Governor Edwards for the authors of the crime. Governor Edwards also wanted the tribes on the Illinois to surrender the murderers of the Cox boy and Price, before noticed, and to deliver up the property stolen by the Indians for two years past. To effect these objects, he commissioned Captain Samuel Levering, an intelligent and discreet officer, who was fitted out with a boat by Governor Clark, duly provisioned, manned and equipped. Levering was accompanied by Captain Herbert Henry Swearingen, a Potawattomie named Wish-ha, and eight oarsmen, who signed articles to act as boatmen and soldiers, each armed with a gun. They started from Cahokia for Peoria, July 25, 1811. Before leaving the Mississippi, they met Captain Whitesides with his rangers from the block-house, near the mouth of the Illinois, who informed them of firing on a party of Sacs ascending the Illinois, but that their "summons" was disregarded. At Prairie Marcot, they found Lt. Campbell and his force of 17 men. On the 3d of August they arrived at Peoria, and met Mr. Forsythe, the government Indian agent, who, by his long residence among the Indians, was thoroughly versed in their tongue. The principal chief of the Potawattomies there was Masseno, better known as Gomo. To him Mr. Forsythe had previously delivered a letter from Governor Clark, demanding a surrender of the Gasconade murderers. Gomo was thought to be not unfavorable to the surrender, but claimed to not have power to enforce his sole will against so many. Here Captain Levering learned, from a Frenchman, named Jacques Mettie, the whereabouts of the murderers on Shoal creek, who were Potawattomies. A Frenchman, named Fournier, was sent forward to apprise Gomo of the arrival of Captain Levering with a letter for him from Governor Edwards; but an Indian had preceded him, and reported that Levering was accompanied by a force of 50 men, and Gomo was unwilling to meet him without an armed escort of 14 warriors. On the morning of the 5th, however, the chief raised the American flag, and in answer to a message, called and received the governor's letter from the hands of Levering. He immediately sent out his young men to call together in council all his chiefs, who were mostly absent on distant journeys. Gomo professed his readiness to do justice to the Americans, so far as his power extended. Levering gave Gomo tobacco to be sent as a present with a message to the chiefs, and retired. The murderers of Price were found to be five brothers, Polsawines.

In the meantime, Capt. Levering and Mr. Fournier made a visit to the Indian towns some 20 miles up the Illinois river. Gomo's town was still some 4 miles farther on and back of the river bottom, where they arrived late one night. They were hospitably entertained in the wigwam of the chief, which was built of bark and afforded lodging room for 30 or more persons. It was 25 by 50 feet on the inside; sleeping bunks, 6 by 7, and 5 feet high were arranged around the lodge, upon which the Indians slept or lounged, with their heads pointing toward the centre of the room and their feet toward the walls. Captain Levering and his companions were honored with one next to that of the chief and his family. Although it was late when the visitors arrived, a dish of new corn was set before them by the chief's squaw, and while they were partaking of it, the chief smoked his pipe, as also the men, who generally quitted their sleeping places and squatted around the lodge fires in the centre, "in all the solemnity of profound smoking," as a mark of etiquette due to strangers.*

In his frequent informal communications with the Indians, Captain Levering learned much of their internal polity and their feelings toward the Americans, whom they regarded as their enemies, notwithstanding their professions of peace and friendship for them. Their adroitness in diplomacy is well disclosed in the replies of the chiefs to Captain Levering; their most customary evasions to deliver up any of their braves, charged with crime, being, that they had departed with such and such chiefs on an expedition; that they had no control over them; that it was not their business, and did not concern them, etc. The ambition of the young braves to be able to exclaim, during their orgies, "I am a man: who can gainsay it? I have killed an Osage! I have killed a white!" stimulated them to the commission of outrages; while their frequent immunity from punishment, led them to infer inactivity, if not fear, on the part of the whites. Gomo was anxious the chiefs should attend at the delivery of the governor's address, and hear for themselves, so that they could not afterwards charge him with fear or treachery, and denounce him as "sugar mouth." In a conversation, Gomo spoke of seeing Washington at Philadelphia, in 1793, and his elder brother remembered the time when the British put the Indians in the front of battle.

*N. W. Edwards' Life of his Father.

A number of chiefs and warriors having arrived, in obedience to Gomo's summons, they indulged their contempt in a little act of offensiveness by displaying the American flag union down. Captain Levering, inclining to attribute this to their ignorance, attempted to explain its meaning, to which they replied that they knew it. But on the morning following, the flag was displayed union up. The Indians in council differed as to the policy to be adopted, regarding the demand of the Americans for the surrender of the murderers and the stolen property. The offenders were greatly scattered, receiving the protection of chiefs hundreds of miles away. Gomo favored the sending of an Indian commission for them, but foresaw that it would be said to him that he belonged on the Illinois, and that he better attend to his own tribe; and he disliked the cowardly appearance of having made the attempt and failed. Others opposed the surrender of anything but the stolen property. Meanwhile, the British inspired the policy of sending Little Chief, who was a "talkative fellow," to give the Americans any amount of assurance to answer present purposes, with which these, like many previous outrages, soon to be covered by passing events, would likewise directly blow over. Little Chief, in a preliminary conversation with Captain Levering, indicated his displeasure by saying that he hoped the letter of the governor would be fully told them as it was written, at which insinuation Mr. Forsythe, the interpreter, became not a little incensed.

On the morning of the 16th of August, 1811, Captain Levering being informed that the Indians were ready to proceed to the council chamber, promptly repaired thither, accompanied by his leading men and the inhabitants of Peoria whom he had invited. After a preliminary "talk" on the part of Captain Levering, and smoking the pipe, the address of Governor Edwards, dated Kaskaskia, July 21st, was slowly delivered to them and carefully interpreted. It was addressed "to the chiefs and warriors of the tribes of Potawattomies, residing on the Illinois river and its waters, in the territory of Illinois." The governor explained to them how faithfully the president had carried out all treaty obligations with the Indians, and that it was his great desire to have his red and white children live in peace and friendship; that the tomahawk and scalping-knife had been for a long time buried, but that a storm seemed now to be gathering; that the whites were being plundered and murdered; citing a number of acts of hostility and giving the names of Indians who had committed them; that the relatives and friends of these victims cried aloud to the Great Spirit, their hearts aflame with revenge, and who could only be repressed from instant war by showing them that these acts of barbarity were not approved by the nations of the authors of them, whom he demanded to be surrendered for trial. Allusion was also made to the British emissaries among them, who flattered, deceived and instigated them to the commission of these horrible acts; concluding with a full explanation of the power and resources of the American nation.

After the reading of the address the council dispersed, and on the following day Gomo made the subjoined reply, which was interpreted and written down on the spot, and is not only very interesting to peruse but shows this chief to have been the possessor of a high order of intellect. After inviting attention to his words, and expressing gladness for the opportunity, Gomo spoke as follows:

"You see the color of our skin. The Great Spirit, when he made and disposed of man, placed the red-skins in this land, and those who wore hats, on the other side of the big waters. When the Great Spirit placed us on this ground, we knew nothing but what was furnished to us by nature. We made use of our stone axes, stone knives and earthen vessels, and clothed ourselves from the skins of the beasts of the forest. Yet, we were contented! When the French first made large canoes, they crossed the wide waters to this country, and on first seeing the red people, they were rejoiced. They told us that we must consider ourselves as the children of the French, and they would be our father; the country was a good one, and they would change goods for skins.

"Formerly, we all lived in one large village. In that village there was only one chief, and all things went on well; but since our intercourse with the whites, there are almost as many chiefs as we have young men.

"At the the time of the taking of Canada, when the British and the French were fighting for the same country, the Indians were solicited to take part in that war—since which time there have been among us a number of foolish young men. The whites ought to have staid on the other side of the waters, and not have troubled us on this side. If we are fools, the whites are the cause of it. From the commencement of their wars, they used many persuasions with the Indians; they made them presents of merchandise in order to get them to join and assist in their battles—since which time there have always been fools among us, and the whites are blameable for it.

"The British asked the Indians to assist them in their wars with the Americans, telling them that if we allowed the Americans to remain upon our lands, they would in time take the whole country, and we would then have no place to go to. Some of the Indians did join the British, but all did not; some of this nation, in particular, did not join them. The British persisted in urging upon us that if we did not assist them in driving the Americans from our lands, our wives and children would be miserable for the remainder of our days. In the course of that war, the American general, Clark, came to Kaskaskia, and sent for the chiefs on this river to meet him there. We attended, and he desired us to remain still and quiet in our own villages, saying that the Americans were able of themselves to fight the British. You Americans generally speak sensibly and plainly. At the treaty of Greenville, General Wayne spoke to us in the same sensible and clear manner. I have listened with attention to you both. At the treaty of Greenville, General Wayne told us that the tomahawk must be buried, and even thrown into the great lake; and should any white man murder an Indian, he should be delivered up to the Indians; and we on our part, should deliver up the red men who murdered a white person to the Americans. [Mistake].

"A Potawattomie Indian, by the name of Turkey Foot, killed an American, for which he was demanded of us; and although he was a great warrior, we killed him ourselves in satisfaction for his murders. Some of the Kickapoos killed an American. They were demanded, were given up, and were tied up with ropes around their necks for the murders. This was not what the chief, who made the demand, promised, as they were put to death in another manner. Our custom is to tie up a dog that way when we make a sacrifice. Now, listen to me well in what I have to say to you.

"Some time ago, one of our young men was drunk at St. Louis, and was killed by an American. At another time, some person stole a horse near Cahokia. The citizens of the village followed the trail, met an innocent Kickapoo, on his way to Kaskaskia, and killed him. Last fall, on the other side, and not far from Fort Wayne, a Wyandot Indian set fire to the prairie; a settler came out and asked him how he came to set fire. The Indian answered that he was out hunting. The settler struck the Indian and continued to beat him till they were parted, when another settler shot the Indian. This summer, a Chippewa Indian, at Detroit, was looking at a gun, when it went off accidentally and shot an American. The Chippewa was demanded, delivered up and executed. Is this the way General Wayne exhibits his charity to the red-skins? Whenever an instance of this kind happens, it is usual for the red-skins to regard it as an accident. You Americans think that all the mischiefs that are committed are known to the chiefs, and immediately call on them for the surrender of the offenders. We know nothing of them ; our business is to hunt, in order to feed our women and children. It is generally supposed that we red-skins are always in the wrong. If we kill a hog, we are called fools or bad men ; the same, or worse, is said of us if we kill an horned animal; yet you do not take into consideration that, while the whites are hunting along our rivers, killing our deer and bears, we do not speak ill of them. When the French came to Niagara, Detroit, Mackinaw and Chicago, they built no forts or garrisons, nor did the English, who came after them ; but when the Americans came, all was changed. They build forts, and garrisons and blockades wherever they go. From these facts, we infer that they intend to make war upon us. Whenever the United States make the Indians presents, they afterwards say that we must give them such a tract of land ; and after a good many presents, they ask for a larger piece. This is the way we have been served. This is the way of extending to us charity. Formerly, when the French were here, they made us large presents ; so have the English; but the Americans, in giving their presents, have asked a piece of land in return. Such has been the treatment of the Americans.

" If the whites had kept on the other side of the waters, these accidents would not have happened ; we could not have crossed the wide waters to have killed them there; but they came here and turned the Indians into confusion. If an Indian goes into their village, like a dog he is hunted and threatened with death. The ideas of the Potawattomies, Ottawas and Chippewas are, that we wish to live peaceable with all mankind, and attend to our hunting and other pursuits, that we may be able to provide for the wants of our women and children. But there remains a lurking dissatisfaction in the breasts and minds of some of our young men. This has occasioned the late mischiefs which, at the time, were unknown to the chiefs and warriors of the nation. I am surprised at such threatenings to the chiefs and warriors (old people), who are inclined entirely for peace. The desires of the chiefs and warriors are to plant corn and pursue the deer. Do you think it possible for us to deliver the murderers here to-day? Think you, my friends, what would be the consequence of a war between the Americans and Indians. In times passed, when some of us were engaged in it, many women were left in a distressful condition. Should war now take place, the distress would be, in comparison, much more general. This is all I have to say on the part of myself and warriors of my village. I thank you for your patient attention to my words."*

Captain Levering replied to them, giving a resume of the history of the white settlers on this continent, and their contact with the red men. He denied that the forts at Chicago, Fort Wayne, or the one opposite the mouth of the Missouri, were established to threaten or make war on the Indians, but that they were built to afford protection to their friends; that the Americans, unlike the British, had never taught nor employed the red men to join in wars and outrages upon the whites; that even in the revolutionary struggle they had advised the Indians to lie on their skins at home, raise corn and kill deer, but not to engage on either side; he showed them their mistake regarding the treaty of Greenville, that all murderers, on either side, should be delivered up to the opposite party; that the government at Washington would not have

*See Edwards' Life of Edwards.

permitted Wayne to do this, but that all offenders against our laws must be tried under the laws by a jury of 12 men, and that justice would be meted out to Indians the same as the whites.

At the conclusion, Little Chief said: "I request you now to take the names of the chiefs and warriors, that you may show to your father in Kaskaskia, how ready we have been to attend his words." Gomo, the day following, upon the final adjournment of the council, said: "We have listened with patient attention, and I hope that the great Master of Light was noticing it. When the Master of Light made man, he endowed those who wear hats with every gift, art and knowledge. The red-skins, as you see, live in lodges and on the wilds of nature." This sentiment evinced a high appreciation of the relative status of the two races.

Two horses only were delivered up, Little Chief promising to return two more to Captain Heald, at Chicago, and Gomo promised to try and return all, as soon as they could be found. The murderers of the Coles party in Missouri, were revealed to be in a village about 20 miles west of the Prophet's town—Tippecanoe; that by inviting them to Fort Wayne with others they might there be seized in the fall. But it is said that some of them were, in point of fact, with them then. So ended Levering's mission. By the exposure incurred on the Illinois, this clear headed soldier contracted disease and died soon after his return to Kaskaskia.

A mission, in charge of Joseph Trotier, a sagacious French creole of Cahokia, was also sent to the Kickapoos, who inhabited the country along Sugar Creek in the northern part of the present county of Logan. The usual "talks," or speeches, with many fair promises from this rather shrewd but treacherous and implacable nation, were had, which were also written down as interpreted.

But throughout the west English emissaries kept up the dastardly work of "setting the red men like dogs upon the whites," in the energetic language of Tecumseh to Harrison. That great warrior, the fit successor of Pontiac, having conceived the plan of bringing the southern tribes, the Creeks, Choctaws, and Chicasaws, into a league with the tribes of the north, to make war against the United States till their lands were restored to them, started thither on his errand in the spring of 1811. The purposes of this chieftain and his brother, the one-eyed Prophet, being well understood by Gov. Harrison, he determined, during the former's absence, to strike and disperse the hostile forces collected under the latter at Tippecanoe. He started from Vincennes in the fall of 1811 and arrived in the vicinity of the Prophet's town on the 6th of Nov., with an effective force of something over 700 men. Here he was met by ambassadors from the Prophet, and a suspension of hostilities was arranged until an interview on the following day could be had. The governor, desiring a good piece of ground to camp upon, allowed the treacherous foe to point it out; but the site was not selected without examination and approval by his officers. Upon this spot, before the dawn of the following morning, the stealthy foe, with a superior force, attempted to re-enact the defeat of St. Clair 21 years before. Under cover of darkness he crept upon the American camp, and began a murderous attack with savage fury uncommon even to him, and maintained it with great obstinacy; but the surprise was not complete, and he was ultimately repulsed and put to flight, with a loss equaling that of the

Americans. The loss of the latter was, in killed, 37; mortally wounded, 25; wounded, 126. The loss in officers was particularly heavy. Of the Illinoisans who fell here we may mention Isaac White, for some years the government agent of the Ohio salines, who, having received the appointment of captain of a militia company from Gov. Edwards, in 1810, joined the expedition of Gov. Harrison. His death was much regretted, and the Territorial Legislature, in 1815, to perpetuate his memory, named the county of White in honor of him. Here, too, fell the gifted and brilliant young Major Joe Daviess, whose deeds of valor have also been commemorated in Illinois by naming a county after him. The intelligence of the battle of Tippecanoe was peculiarly alarming to the settlements of Illinois, so contiguous to these hordes of savages, and additional measures were concocted as speedily as circumstances permitted, to meet the exigency of the times.

During the winter of 1811-12, the Indians on the Upper Mississippi were very hostile and committed many murders. In anticipation of an early war with the United States, the British agent at Prairie du Chien, Col. Dixon, it was reported by Indian traders, had engaged all the warriors of that region to descend the Mississippi and exterminate the settlements on both sides of the river;* but upon the breaking out of actual hostilities in June of that year there was more pressing need for savage recruits in Canada, which doubtless saved the effusion of much blood in the denser settlements of Illinois; still many murders were committed. The *Louisiana Gazette*, March 21st, 1812, reports 9 murders in the district of St. Charles; 1 at Fort Madison; 2 at the lead mines in Illinois, and a party of men who left the Fort in February for the mines, not having been heard from, were supposed to have fallen into the hands of the savages. Two hundred Winnebagoes from Illinois made a plundering raid upon a "factory store" of the United States, situated on the west bank of the Mississippi, the present site of Bellevue. Lieutenants Hamilton and Vasques, with a small force of regulars, made a gallant defence and repulsed the savages.

A few marauding parties penetrated far down into Illinois. Andrew Moore and his son, on their way home from the Jourdan blockhouse, made camp near the middle fork of the Big Muddy, not far from the crossing of the old Massac road. Here they were attacked by the savages, and after a bloody encounter both father and son were killed and their horses stolen. Moore's Prairie in the present county of Jefferson, perpetuates their names. At Tom Jourdan's fort, on the road to Equality, three men ventured out after dark to gather firewood, when they were fired on by Indians concealed in the brush, killing Barbara, wounding James Jourdan, but missing Walker. A marauding band of Winnebagos attacked Lee's settlement at Hardscrabble, about 4 miles from Fort Dearbon, near the present junction of the canal with the Chicago river, and killed a Mr. White and a Canadian in his employ. Two other men escaped.

At Hill's Fort, later in the same year, a band of warriors appeared. They removed the mud from between the logs of a chimney of one of the blockhouses, inserted a gun, and shot a man sitting inside by the fire. A soldier by the name of Lindley, in

*Reynolds' Own Times.
17

carrying feed out to his horses, left the stockade gate open, for which the skulking foe made an instant rush, but the occupants quickly slammed the gate shut, leaving the soldier outside with the savages. He sheltered himself from their missiles among the cattle, which directly stampeding, he managed by feats of great dexterity to ride on and under an ox, thus escaping the savages and saving his life. The Indians were meanwhile engaged in a fight at the fort over the pickets, and were repulsed with loss, as indicated by the trails of blood, they, as usual, carrying away the wounded or dead.*

In March, 1812, Governor Edwards sent Capt. Edward Hebert with another friendly message to the Indians residing on the Illinois, inviting them to a council, and requesting traders of every description to withdraw till the Indian affairs became more settled, and if the latter did not instantly comply they need expect no further indulgence.

On the 16th of April, 1812, His Excellency met in protracted council at Cahokia, with the chiefs and warriors of the following nations: Of the Pottawatomies—Gomo, Pepper, White Hair, Little Sauk, Great Speaker, Yellow Son, Snake, Maukia, Bull, Ieman, Neckkeenesskeesheck, Ignance, Pottawatomie Prophet, Pamousa, Ishkeebee, Toad, Manwess, Pipe Bird, Cut Branch, The South Wind, and the Black Bird; of the Kickapoos—Little Deer, Blue Eyes (representative of Pamawattau), Sun Fish, Blind of an Eye, Otter, Makkak, Yellow Lips, Dog Bird, and Black Seed. Of the Ottawas—Mittitasse (representative of the Blackbird), Keeskagon, and Malshwashewii. Of the Chippewas—the White Dog.†

The Governor delivered in person a forcible address to them. He spoke of the ardent desire of the general government to maintain peace and harmony with all the Indian nations; defended the United States against the charge of rapacity for their lands; warned them against the arts and deceptions of the Shawanee Prophet and other "bad birds," or evil counselors, whom the British had sent among them; portrayed the power and resources of the American nation, which desired not war but peace; insisted that the murderers, whom they had harbored all the time, notwithstanding their denial to Levering, must be surrendered; that he understood well their unfriendly disposition and the efforts at combinations attempted to be formed among the tribes; warned them that their depredations could not be laid to the Winnebagos, who were at open hostility; that he was prepared with energetic measures to protect the whites and punish the Indians, &c.

The leading chiefs of the different tribes represented all deferred to Gomo as the one who was to answer the Governor's speech, which he did on the following day: He professed that the words of the Governor had sunk deep into his heart; that he spoke the sentiments of all the chiefs according to their instruction. He declared the Great Spirit to be angry with the red men for selling their lands, which he had given them to live upon, and denied the power of a chief to sell lands; they wanted to live in peace; if there was a chief among them of influence enough to deliver up a

---

*Reynolds' Own Times.
†Edwards' Life of his Father.

murderer he would like to see him; if he attempted to secure the murderers without the consent of all the chiefs he would be killed, and that the Missouri murderers were Kickapoos; he denied being himself a great chief, and said he could not control his young men who were so scattered that it would be impossible to bring them together; they had no laws among them like the whites to punish offenders; denied listening to evil birds or interfering between the British and Americans. They would not join the British, for in the last war they had left them in the lurch and would do so again. When he wanted a blanket he bought it. The British had invited them to aid them, but they had sent them word to fight their own battles, that they wanted to live in peace. He complained that the Americans did not live up to their promises in supplying their wants, and that they had been fired upon by whites in coming down to the council. Promised good behavior, which they hoped the Good Spirit would help them to perform, and professed great humility.*

The Indians had brought their women and children along to show his Excellency, as Gomo naively said, how ragged and needy they were. This, together with their fair promises of good behavior and peaceable intentions, had the desired effect. They came away loaded with substantial presents. An early writer says: "The wild men exercised the most diplomacy, and made the governor believe the Indians were for peace, and that the whites need dread nothing from them. They promised enough to obtain presents, and went off laughing at the credulity of the whites."† Some of them were in August following concerned in the horrible massacre at Chicago.

The savages of the northwest, however, were thoroughly stirred up and did not desire peace; in this the reports of travelers, traders, and spies all concurred; the red wampum was constantly, passing between the different tribes in all parts of the country, from the Sioux of the St. Peters to the tribes at the head of the Wabash, and a general combination was fast ripening. The British agents at Prairie du Chien, Fort Malden, and other points, in anticipation of a war with the United States, sought to enlist the favor of the savages by the distribution of large supplies of goods, arms and ammunition to them. The English continued their insults to our flag upon the high seas, and their government refusing to relinquish its offensive course, all hope of a peaceful issue was abandoned, and congress, on the 19th of June, 1812, formally declared war against Great Britain. In Illinois the threatened Indian troubles had already caused a more thorough organization of the militia along the frontiers, from the mouth of the Illinois down the Mississippi to the Ohio, thence up that stream and the Wabash above Vincennes. Additional forts were also built, one towards the mouth of the Little Wabash, and at the mouth of La Motte Creek.

*Edwards' Life of Edwards.
†Reynolds' Own Times.

Chapter XXIII.

THE MASSACRE AT CHICAGO—EARLY HISTORY OF THE PLACE.

The greatest, as well the most revolting, massacre of whites that ever occurred in Illinois, was perpetrated by the Potawattomie tribe of Indians, on the site of the present city of Chicago.

From early Indian tradition, it has been gathered that the mouth of the Chicago river was a favorite resort of the Illinois tribes in very remote times. Besides its fishing facilities, it was the only deep inlet from the lake on its southwesterly bend. The portage between the Chicago and the headwaters of the Illinois, offered but a narrow interruption to canoe travel from the great lakes on the north to the Gulf of Mexico. It is said, that the Tamaroas gave name to the river, derived from Checaqua, the title of a long succession of governing chiefs, which, by an easy transition, attached to the place. It was said also to mean thunder, the voice of Manitou, and "skunk," an appellation but too suggestive during a few years preceding the deepening of the canal, by which its current was reversed with the pure waters of the lake. But its most commonly accepted definition is "wild onion," from that rather odorous vegetable growing abundantly on its banks in early times.*

A small French trading post was established there in the period of the French explorations. For the better possession of their western empire, the French built forts at various points, from Canada, via Peoria, to New Orleans, including one at Chicago. On the earliest known map of this region, dated Quebec, 1688, a correct outline of the lake is given, and the river accurately located, with "Fort Chicago" marked at its mouth. Subsequently, the Americans found no vestige of the early French settlers there. By the treaty of Greenville, to which the Potawattomies from this region, with many others, were parties, "one piece of land 6 miles square, at the mouth of the Chekajo river, emptying into the south-west end of Lake Michigan, *where a fort formerly stood*," was relinquished. The tide of emigration setting into Indiana and Michigan after the treaty of Greenville, 1795, concentrated the Indians in greater numbers about this point, and largely increased the Indian trade, for which a number of traders were here located; John Kinzie being one whose descendants are residents of Chicago down to the present time. The general government, in 1804, built, on the south side of the river, Fort Dearborn,

---

* Chicago and its great conflagration.

named after a general of the army, and garrisoned it with 50 men and 3 pieces of artillery. The fort consisted of 2 block-houses, with a parade ground and sally-port, or subterranean passage to the river, the whole surrounded by a stockade. With this precarious protection, the number of traders increased and a few settlers gathered around the post.

For eight years, this isolated garrison and community furnished scarcely an incident worthy of record. Friendly intercourse between the garrison and neighboring Indians grew apace. The attachment of the Indians for the traders was particularly cordial. While nearly all the chiefs visited Fort Malden yearly, and received large amounts of presents, and many Potawattomies, Winnebagos and Ottawas were in the battle of Tippecanoe with the Shawanese, the principal chiefs of the neighborhood were yet on amicable terms here with the Americans. Then our trouble with Great Britain threatened an open rupture; but the Indians, long before the declaration of hostilities, took the war-path, as we have seen. We have already noticed their attack on an outpost of this place called Hardscrabble.

On the 7th of August, arrived the order of Governor Hull, commander-in-chief of the northwest, by the hand of a trusty chief of the Potawattomies, called Winnemeg, or Cat-fish, "to evacuate the post if practicable, and in that event, to distribute the property belonging to the United States, in the fort and in the factory or agency, to the Indians in the neighborhood." The dispatches further announced, that the British had taken Mackinaw, and that General Hull, with his army, was proceeding from Fort Wayne to Detroit.

The garrison, at the time, consisted of 75 men, few of whom were effective soldiers. The officers were, Captain Heald, the commander, Lieutenant Helm and Ensign Ronan (both very young men), and Doctor Voorhees, the surgeon. John Kinzie was the principal trader. He and the first two named officers had families there. So also some of the soldiers and other traders. Considerable coolness existed between Ensign Ronan, a brave and gallant soldier, but overbearing in his disposition, and Captain Heald.

Winnemeg, the bearer of the dispatches, well apprised of the hostile disposition of the treacherous savages, advised strongly against the evacuation, which was discretionary. The fort was well supplied with ammunition and provisions for six months, and in the meantime succor might come. He sought to learn the intention of the commander, and further urged, that if it should be decided to evacute, then let it be done immediately, and by forced marches elude the concentration of the savages before the news, of which they were yet ignorant, should circulate among them. To this most excellent advice, Captain Heald gave no heed; he decided not only to evacuate, but deemed it obedience to orders to collect the neighboring Indians and make an equitable distribution of the property among them. Again the sagacious Indian chief, strongly seconded by Mr. Kinzie, who had much at stake, suggested the expediency of promptly marching out, leaving all things standing, and while the Indians should be engaged in dividing the spoils, to effect an unmolested retreat. But the commander, not apprehending the murderous intent of the savages to the extent the advisers did, and impressed with the duty of obedience to orders, disregared this also, notwithstanding the discretion allowed him. On the following morning, without consultation with the subordinate officers—with whom he was estranged—he published on parade the order for evacuating the post. The officers whose council had been thus ignored in so important an emergency, remonstrated against this step, and pointed out the improbability of their party reaching Fort Wayne without molestation; how they would be retarded in their marches by the women and children, and invalid and superannuated soldiers; how the few friendly chiefs, who had from motives of private regard for the family of Mr. Kinzie, opposed successfully an attack upon the fort the preceding autumn, were now, when the country was at war with Great Britain, powerless to restrain their tribes. They advised remaining and fortifying themselves till succor came; at any rate, it was better to fall into the hands of the British, as prisoners, than a sacrifice to the brutal ferocity of the savages. Captain Heald, however, dreading censure, stood upon his idea of obedience to orders, and expressed confidence in the friendly professions of the Indians. With this, the officers, who regarded the project as little short of madness, held themselves aloof from their commander, and dissatisfaction and insubordination spread among the soldiers. The Indians, too, became daily more unruly. They entered the fort in defiance of the sentinels, and made their way without ceremony into the quarters of the officers. On one occasion, an Indian fired a rifle in the parlor of the commanding officer. This was by some construed as a signal to the young braves for an attack. The old chiefs were passing to and fro among the assembled groups with much agitation, while the squaws were rushing hither and hither, as if looking for a fearful scene. Still Captain Heald clung to his conviction of having created a feeling so amicable among them, as would ensure the safe passage of the party to Fort Wayne. In the meantime, a runner had arrived with a message from Tecumseh, who had joined the British with a large force, conveying the news to the Indians of the capture of Fort Mackinaw in July, the defeat of Major Van Horne at Brownstown, and the inglorious retreat of General Hull from Canada, saying further, that he had no doubt but that Hull would, in a short time, be compelled to surrender; and urged them to arm immediately.

The Indians from the neighboring villages having at length collected, a council was held on the 12th of August. Of the officers of the garrison, though requested, none attended beside the commander; the others, in anticipation of intended mischief, opened the port-holes of the blockhouses and with loaded cannons commanded the council. This action, it was supposed, prevented a massacre at the time. Capt. Heald promised the Indians to distribute among them all the goods in the United States factory, and the ammunition and provisions in the fort, desiring an escort of the Pottawatomies to Fort Wayne in return, and promising them a further liberal reward upon arrival there. The Indians, with many professions of friendship, assented to all he proposed and promised all he required.

No sooner had the commander made these indiscreet promises than he allowed himself to be persuaded to violate them. Mr. Kinzie, well knowing the treachery of the Indian character, represented to him the danger to their party of furnishing the savages with arms and ammunition, and liquor to fire their brains. This argument, true and excellent in itself, was now certainly inopportune, and, if acted upon could only incense the treacherous foe. But Capt. Heald, struck with the impolicy of his conduct and falling in with the advice, now resolved to break his indiscreet promise. Accordingly, on the 13th, all the goods in the factory store were duly distributed; but in the night time the arms were broken, the ammunition secretly thrown in a well, and the barrels of whisky, of which there was a large quantity, mostly belonging to traders, were rolled quietly through the sally-port, their heads knocked in and their contents emptied into the river. But the lurking redskins witnessed the breaking of the casks, and quickly apprehending how faith had been broken with them by the whites, were greatly exasperated at the loss of their fond "fire water," which they asserted was destroyed in such abundance as to make the river taste "groggy." At a second council held on the 14th, they expressed their indignation at this conduct, and their murmurs and threats were loud and deep. Black Hawk, who lived many years after, always maintained that this violation of promises on the part of the whites precipitated the massacre on the following day.

While nearly all the Indians in alliance with the British partook of the hostility of their people against the Americans, there were still several chiefs and braves who retained a personal regard for the inhabitants of this place. Among these was Black Partridge, a chief of some renown. He now entered the quarters of Capt. Heald and spoke as follows: "Father, I come to deliver up to you the medal I wear. It was given me by the Americans, and I have long worn it in token of our mutual friendship. But our young men are resolved to imbrue their hands in the blood of the whites. I cannot restrain them, and I will not wear a token of peace while I am compelled to act as an enemy."

On the same day, the 14th, the despondency of the garrison was for a time dispelled by the arrival of Capt. Wells from Ft. Wayne, with 15 friendly Miamis. Capt. Wells was the son of Gen. Wells, of Kentucky, and either a brother or uncle to Mrs. Capt. Heald. When a child, he was taken prisoner by the Miamis and reared and adopted in the family of Little Turtle, who commanded the Indians in the defeat of St. Clair, in 1790, Wells leading 300 of the warriors in the very front of that battle. He subsequently joined the army of Gen. Wayne, and by his knowledge of the country, proved a powerful auxiliary. Later he rejoined his foster father. He was a brave and fearless warrior. Having learned the order of evacuation, and knowing well the hostile disposition of the Pottawatomies, he made a rapid march through the wilderness to save, if possible, his sister and the garrison at Chicago, from their impending doom. But he came too late. The ammunition was destroyed and the savages were rioting on the provisions. Preparations were therefore made to march on the morrow. The reserved ammunition, 25 rounds to the man, was now distributed. The baggage wagons for the sick, the women and the children, containing also a box of cartridges, were got ready, and amid the pervading gloom, a fatiguing march through the wilderness in prospect, and the fears of disaster on the route, the whole party except the faithful sentinels retired for a little repose. The morning of the fatal 15th of August, 1812, arrived. The sun shone with its wonted splendor, and Lake Michigan "was a sheet of burnished gold." Early in the morning Mr. Kinzie received a message from Topeneebe, a friendly chief of the St. Joseph band of Pottawatomies, warning him that his people, notwithstanding their promise of safe conduct, designed mischief. Mr. Kinzie with his eldest son, who had agreed to accompany the garrison, was urged to go with his family, for which a boat had been fitted out to coast around the southerly end of the lake to the St. Joseph.

At 9 a. m. the party quitted the fort amidst martial music and in military array. Capt. Wells, at the head of his band of Miamis, led the van, his face blackened after the manner of the Indians. The troops with loaded arms came next, followed by the wagons containing the women and children, the sick and the lame and the baggage. A little distance in the rear followed the escort of about 500 Pottawatomies. The party took the beach road southward with the lake upon their left. On reaching the range of sand hills separating the beach from the prairie, the Indians defiled to the right, bringing these shore elevations between them and the whites down on the beach. They had marched about a mile and half from the fort, when Capt. Wells rode furiously back, shouting: "They are about to attack us; form instantly and charge upon them." The words were scarcely uttered when the savages poured a volley of musketry from behind the hills upon the party. The troops were hastily formed into line and they charged up the bank. One veteran of 70 years fell as they ascended. The action became general. The Miamis fled at the outset; their chief rode up to the Pottawatomies, charged them with treachery, and brandishing his tomahawk, declared "he would be the first to head a party to return and punish them." He then turned his horse and galloped after his cowardly companions. The troops behaved gallantly, but were overwhelmed by numbers. The savages flanked them, and "in about 15 minutes got possession of the horses, provisions, and baggage of every description."* Here the murderous work upon the helpless women and children was commenced.

Mrs. Helm, wife of Lieutenant Helm, was in the action, and furnished Mr. Kinzie, her step-father, many thrilling incidents.† Dr. Voorhees, who had been wounded at the first fire, was, while in a paroxysm of fear, cut down by her side. Ensign Ronan, a little ways off, though mortally wounded, was struggling with a powerful savage, but sank under his tomahawk. A young brave with uplifted tomahawk sought to cleave her skull; she sprang aside and the blow grazed her shoulder; she seized him around the neck and while grappling for his scalping knife, was forcibly borne away by another and plunged into the lake and held down in the water. She soon found, however, that her captor did not design to drown her, and now for the first time recognized, through his disguise of paint and feathers, the friendly chief, Black Partridge. When the firing had somewhat subsided her preserver bore her safely to the shore. A soldier's wife, under the conviction that prisoners taken by Indians were subjected to tortures worse than death, though assured of immunity, fought a party of savages, who attempted to take her, with such desperation that she was

*Heald's Report. †See J. H. Kinzie's Narative.

litterally cut to pieces and her mangled remains left on the field. "Mrs. Heald, too, fought life a perfect heroine and received several wounds. After she was in the boat, a savage assailed her with his tomahawk, when her life was saved by the interposition of a friendly chief."

The troops having fought gallantly till over half of their number were slain, the remainder, but 27 out of 66, surrendered. And now the most heart-rendering and sickening butchery. of this calamitous day was committed by a young brutal savage, who assailed one of the baggage wagons containing 12 children, every one of whom fell beneath his murderous tomahawk. When Capt. Wells, who with the others had become a prisoner, beheld this scene at a distance, he exclaimed in a tone loud enough to be heard by the savages around him: "If this be your game, I can kill too!" and turning his horse, started in full gallop for the Pottawatomie camp, located about what is now State street, near the crossing of Lake, where the squaws and pappooses had been left. The Indians pursued, and he avoided the deadly aim of their rifles for a time by laying flat on his horse's neck, but the animal was directly killed and he wounded. He again became a prisoner; Winnemeg and Wabansee, both friends of the whites, interceded to save him, but Peesotum, a Pottawatomie, while he was being supported along, gave him his death blow by a stab in the back. Thus fell Wm. Wayne Wells, a white man of excellent parentage and descent, reared among the Indians, and of as brave and generous a nature as man ever possessed, a sacrifice to his own rash impulse inspired by a deed of most savage ferocity. His remains were terribly multilated; the heart was cut in pieces and distributed among the tribes, as was their wont, for a token of bravery. Billy Caldwell, a half-breed Wyandot, long well-known in Chicago afterward, arriving next day, gathered up the several portions of the body and buried them in the sand. Wells street, in the present city of Chicago, perpetuates the memory of his name.

The following is copied from the official report of Captain Heald:

"We proceeded about a mile and a half, when it was discovered the Indians were prepared to attack us from behind the bank. I immediately marched the company up to the top of the bank, when the action commenced; after firing one round, recharged, and the Indians gave way in front and joined those on our flanks. In about 15 minutes, they got possession of all our horses, provision and baggage of every description, and finding the Miamis did not assist us, I drew off the few men I had left, and took possession of a small elevation in the open prairie out of shot of the bank or any other cover. The Indians did not follow me, but assembled in a body on the top of the bank, and, after some consultation among themselves, made signs for me to approach them. I advanced towards them alone, and was met by one of the Pottawatomie chiefs, called the Blackbird, with an interpreter. After shaking hands, he requested me to surrender, promising to spare the lives of all the prisoners. On a few moments consideration I concluded it would be the most prudent to comply with his request, although I did not put entire confidence in his promise. After delivering up our arms, we were taken back to their encampment near the fort and distributed among the different tribes. The next morning they set fire to the fort, and left the place, taking the prisoners with them. Their number of warriors was between 400 and 500, mostly of the Pottawatomie nation, and their loss, from the best information I could get, was about 15. Our strength was 54 regulars and 12 militia, out of which 26 regulars, and all the militia, were killed in the action, with two women and 12 children. Ensign George Ronan and Dr. Isaac V. Van Voorhees, of my company, with Captain Wells, of Fort Wayne, are to my great sorrow, numbered among the dead. Lieut. L. T. Helm, with 25 non-commissioned officers and privates, and 11 women and children, were prisoners, when we separated. Mrs. Heald and myself were taken to the mouth of the river St. Joseph, and being both badly wounded, were permitted to reside with Mr. Burnet, an Indian trader. In a few days after our arrival there, the Indians all went off to take Fort Wayne, and in their absence I engaged a Frenchman to take us to Mackinaw, by water, where I gave myself up as a prisoner of war, with one of my sergeants.

In the surrender, Captain Heald had stipulated for the safety of, the remnant of his force and the remaining women and children. The wounded prisoners, in the hurry of the moment, were unfortunately omitted, or rather, not particularly mentioned. These helpless sufferers, on reaching the Potawattomie camp, were therefore regarded as proper subjects upon to wreak their savage and cowardly brutality A distinguishing trait of civilized humanity is, protection for the helpless; with the savage, these become the objects of vengeance. Mrs. Helm writes: "An old squaw, infuriated by the loss of friends or excited by the sanguinary scenes around her, seemed possessed of demoniac fury. She seized a stable fork and assaulted one miserable victim, who lay groaning and writhing in the agony of his wounds, aggravated by the scorching beams of the sun. With a delicacy of feeling scarcely to have been expected under such circircumstances, Wanbee-nee-wau stretched a mat across two poles between me and this dreadful scene. I was thus spared, in some degree, a view of its horrors, although I could not entirely close my ears to the cries of the sufferer. The following night five more of the wounded prisoners were tomahawked."[*]

When the Indians about the fort first learned of the intended evacuation, they dispatched runners to all the villages of the nation, apprising them of the news and their purpose to overpower the garrison. Eager to share in the act of bloodshed and plunder, many warriors hastened forward, only to be too late.

A band of Potawattomies, from the Wabash, were met at the Aux Plains by a party from Chicago, bearing home a wounded chief. Being informed that the battle had been fought and won, the prisoners slain and scalped, and the spoils divided, their disappointment and rage knew no bounds. They accelerated their march, and reaching Chicago, determined to glut their taste for blood on new victims. They blackened their faces, and without ceremony entered the parlor of Mr. Kinzie and sullenly squatted upon the floor amidst the assembled family, who had been kindly restored to their home on the north side of the river by Black Patridge, Wabansee and others, and who now guarded them. Black Patridge, interpreting their looks and intent correctly, observed to Wabansee in an undertone, that their white friends were lost. But at this moment the whoop of another band of Indians was heard on the opposite shore. Black Patridge hastily advanced and met their chief in the darkness, on the river's bank. "Who," said he, "are you?" "A man," answered the chief, "who are you?" "A man, like yourself," replied Black Patridge; "but tell me, who are you for?" "I am," said the

*Brown, Hist. Ills., page 316, note 5. says: "Mrs. Heald and Mrs. Helm having eclipsed the most visionary taste of romance, with which modern literature abounds, lived for many years thereafter, highly respected."

chief, " the Sau-ga-nash" (that is, the Englishman). "Then make all speed to the house," was the reply; "your friends are in danger, and you alone can save them."

It was Billy Caldwell, the half-breed Wyandot, to whom we have referred as burying the remains of Captain Wells. He hurried forward, entered the house with a resolute step, deliberately removed his accoutrements, placed his rifle behind the door and saluted the Potawattomies : "How now, my friends, a good day to you. I was told there were enemies here; but I am glad to find only friends. Why have you blacked your faces? Are you mourning for friends lost in the battle? (adroitly mistaking the token of their evil intent), or, are you fasting? If so, ask our friend and he will give you food. He is the Indian's friend, and never refused them in their need."

Diverted by the coolness of his manner, they were ashamed to avow their murderous purpose, and simply asked for some cotton goods to wrap their dead, preparatory to burial. This, with other presents, was given them, and they quietly departed. Thus, by his presence of mind, Caldwell averted the murder of the Kinzie family.

The prisoners, with their wives and children, were dispersed among the Potawattomie tribes on the Illinois, Rock river, the Wabash, and some to Milwaukee. The most of them were ransomed at Detroit thefollowing spring. A part of them remained in captivity, however, another year, but were more kindly treated than they expected. Lieutenant Helm was taken to the AuSable, thence to St. Louis, where he was liberated through the intervention of Thomas Forsythe, long the government Indian agent at Peoria.*

*Brown's Hist. Ills.

CHAPTER XXIV.

ILLINOIS IN THE WAR OF 1812.—GOVERNOR EDWARDS' MILITARY CAMPAIGN TO PEORIA LAKE.

Gen. Hopkins with 2000 Mounted Kentucky Riflemen Marches over the Prairies of Illinois—His Force Mutinies and Marches back—Capt. Craig Burns Peoria and takes all its Inhabitants Prisoners.—Second Expedition to Peoria Lake—Indian Murders—Illinois and Missouri send two Expeditions up the Mississippi in 1814—Their Battles and Disasters.

————

After his ignominious retreat from Canada, Gen. Hull, in a most unaccountable manner, on the 16th of August, the day after the Chicago massacre, at Detroit surrendered his army all the military stores, and the whole of Michigan, without a struggle, while his men, it is said, wept at the disgrace. Thus by the middle of August the British and their red allies were in possession of the whole northwest, with the exception of Forts Wayne and Harrison. This activity and success of the enemy aroused the people of this region to a realization of their imminence. To the impulse of self-preservation was added the patriotic desire to wipe out the disgrace with which our arms were stained, stay the tide of savage desolation which menaced the frontiers, and retrieve our losses.

The savages grew bolder and penetrated deeper into the settlements. Early in September a large force from the Prophet's town made a night attack on Fort Harrison, located a few miles above the present city of Terre Haute, in command of Capt. Zachary Taylor, afterwards president. They ingeniously fired one of the blockhouses, killed during the engagement three men and wounded several more. By the coolness of the commander and the energy of the garrison, though greatly reduced by sickness, the buildings were mostly saved, and the Indians at daylight repulsed. They, however, shot, killed, or drove away, nearly all the hogs, cattle and work oxen belonging to the fort.

Gov. Harrison superseded Gen. Hull, and was also appointed major-general by brevet in the Kentucky militia. This young State, in the course of a few weeks, by the aid of Richard M. Johnson and others, had raised a force of 7,000 men, a portion of which was directed to the aid of Indiana and Illinois, Vincennes being designated as the rendezvous* The British had descended the Mississippi to Rock Island, and were distributing loads of goods as presents to the Indians, through one Girty.

In the meantime Governor Edwards was active in making preparations for an expedition against the Kickapoos and Potawattomies on the Illinois river. His excellency, "before congress had adopted any measures on the subject of volunteer rangers, organized companies, supplied them with arms, built stockade forts, and established a line of posts from the mouth of the Missouri to the Wabash." His commission had at this time expired and his appointment had not been renewed, rendering him legally liable for the expenses of the expedition, a responsibility which, relying upon the justice of hiscountry, he did not hesitate to assume.* Col. William Russell, of the 17th regiment, on the 11th of October, started from the neighborhood of Vincennes with two small companies of U. S. Rangers, commanded by Captains Perry and Modrell to join the expedition of Governor Edwards.† The place of rendezvous for these forces was Camp Russell, already described.

General Samuel Hopkins, a veteran officer of the Revolution, had been invested with the command of the Kentucky mounted volunteers, some 2,000 in number, at Vincennes. His instructions were to break up the villages and disperse the Indians residing on the Wabash and Illinois rivers.

The plan was now suggested that the expedition of Edwards, then in preparation, act in concert with that of Hopkins; that the latter, consisting of mounted Kentucky riflemen, should move up the Wabash to Fort Harrison, destroy the villages in its course, pass over into Illinois, march across the prairies via. the head waters of the Sangamon and Vermilion rivers to the Illinois, effect a junction with the Illinois forces under Edwards and Russell, and sweep all the villages along the Illinois river.‡ The plan thus arranged was sent by the hand of Col. Russell and readily acceded to by the Governor. But it was destined to meet with failure and disgrace on the part of the Kentuckians. In that ill-compacted and undisciplined crowd of horsemen there had already been discontent and murmurs against proceeding further, at Vincennes and Bosseron. At Fort Harrison a number of the men and one officer " broke off and returned." About the middle of October, however, the Wabash was crossed at this point, and great harmony prevailing the expedition bore promise of success. At the request of Gen. Hopkins, a council of the officers was now held, and the object and destination of the expedition considered, which were highly favored. In his letter to Gov. Shelby, of Kentucky, dated October 26, 1812, Gen. Hopkins writes:

" Thinking myself secure in the confidence of my brother officers and the army, we proceeded on our march early on the 15th, and continued it four days—our course lay north on the prairie—until we came to an Indian house where some corn, &c., had been cultivated. The last day of the march to this place I had been made acquainted with a return of that spirit of [discontent] that had, as I had hoped, subsided; and when I ordered a halt near sunset (for the first time that day), in a fine piece of grass in the prairie, to aid our horses, I was addressed in the most rude and dictatorial manner, requiring me immediately to resume my march, or his battalion would break from the army and return. This was a Major * * * I mention him in justice to the other officers of that grade; but, from every information, I began to fear that the army waited but for a pretext to return. This was afforded the next day by our guides, who thought they had discovered an Indian village at the site of a grove, about ten miles from where we had encamped on the fourth night of our march, and turned us six or eight miles out of our way. An almost

*Edwards' Life of of Edwards
†Dillon's Ind. 1.
‡Annals of the West.

universal discontent seemed to prevail, and we took our course in such a direction as we supposed would atone for the error in the morning. About or after sunset, we came to a thin grove affording water. Here we took our camp; and about this time arose one of the most violent gusts I ever remember to have seen, not proceeding from clouds. The Indians had set fire to the prairie, which drove on us so furiously that we were compelled to fire around our camp to protect ourselves. This seems to have decided the army to return. I was informed of it in so many ways, that, early the next morning, Oct. 20th, I requested the attendance of the general and field officers and stated to them my apprehensions—the expectations of our country—the disgrace attending the measure—the approbation of our own consciences. Against this I stated the weary situation of our horses and the want of provisions—which to me seemed only partial—six days only having passed since every part of the army was furnished with ten days' rations in bacon, beef, or breadstuff. The reasons given for returning, I requested the commandants of each regiment, with the whole of the officers belonging to it, to take fully the sense of the army on this measure * * * and to report to me in writing— adding that if 500 volunteers would turn out, I would put myself at their head, and proceed in quest of the towns; and the balance of the army might retreat, under the conduct of the officers, in safety, to Fort Harrison. In less than a hour the report was made, almost unanimously, to return. I then requested that I might dictate the course to be pursued that day only, which, I pledged, should not put them more than six miles out of their way—my object being to cover the reconnoitering parties I wished to send out for the discovery of the Indian towns. About this time—the troops being paraded—I put myself in front, took my course, and directed them to follow me. The columns moving off quite a contrary way, I sent Captain [Zachary] Taylor and Major Lee to apply to the officers to turn them. They were told that it was not in their power—the army had taken their own course, and would pursue it. Discovering great confusion and disorder in their march, I threw myself in the rear, fearing an attack on those who were there from necessity, and continued in that position the whole day. The exhausted state of the horses, nor the hunger of the men, retarded that day's march. * * * The generals—Ray, Ramsey and Allen—lent all their aid and authority in restoring our march to order; and so far succeeded as to bring on the whole with much less loss than I had feared." They were not followed or menaced by an enemy. They had "marched at least 80 or 90 miles into the heart of the enemy's country." A Major Dubois commanded the corps of spies and guides. Messrs. Barron, Lasselle and Laplante were the interpreters. Gen. Hopkins was certain they "were not 20 miles from the Indian village when [they] were *forced* to retire." The exact point at which they commenced their retrograde march is not known.

Governor Edwards had collected and was organizing all the disposable forces of Illinois, amounting to about 350 men, at Camp Russell, by the time Captain Russell arrived from Vincennes with a part of two companies, consisting of 50 privates. The volunteers were divided into two small regiments, commanded by Colonels Elias Rector and Benjamin Stephenson, respectively. Col. Russell commanded the U. S. Rangers. Col. Desha of the U. S. army, Major John Moredock and others, were the field officers. The companies were commanded respectively by Captains Samuel and William B. Whitesides, James B. Moore, Jacob Short, Willis Hargrave from the Ohio Salina, McHenry afterwards of White County, Janney, and Lieut. Roakson with a small independent company. Captain Samuel Judy had also organized an independent corps of spies, consisting of 21 men. The staff of Governor Edwards, who was in chief command, were Secretary Nathaniel Pope, Nelson Rector, and Lieut. Robert K. McLaughlin, of the U. S. Army. Col. Russell, an unpretending but very efficient officer, was next in command to his Excellency, but he neither had nor wanted aids. Baggage wagons for the army were not provided in this short campaign. The men were ordered to pack each on his horse 20 days' rations. The horses were to sustain themselves on prairie grass. Some of the officers employed extra pack-horses.

Captain Craig, of Shawneetown, was detached with a sufficient force to man two boats, one laden with provisions and the necessary tools to build a fort, and the other armed with blunderbusses and a swivel, both so fortified that the enemy's bullets could not penetrate their sides. He was dispatched in advance up the Illinois river, with orders to wait at Peoria until further word from the army. He was also to make offensive war upon the French inhabitants of Peoria, who were suspected of inciting the savages to their murderous raids, and he possessed besides large discretionary powers. On the 18th of October, the defenses of the frontiers having been duly provided for, this crude army of about 400 mounted men, took up its line of march from Camp Russell. The privates, it seems, looked upon the expedition as affording them rare sport, not caring whether they were "marched into danger or frolic." The route pursued was upon the west side of Cahokia creek, thence to the Magoupin, which was crossed near the present site of Carlinville; thence northeasterly, crossing the Sangamon below the junction of the north and south forks, east of the present capital of the State; passing thence east of Elkhart grove, crossing Salt creek not far from the present city of Lincoln, and thence in a northward direction striking an old deserted Kickapoo village on Sugar creek. These tenantless bark wigwams, which were painted up here and there with rude savage devices, mostly representing the red-skins scalping whites, provoked the warlike indignation of the army. The town was assaulted, set on fire and reduced to ashes! After this, fearing that their nightly camp-fires would reveal their approach to the Indians, the marches were mostly continued after dark till midnight. The course was now directed towards the upper end of Lake Peoria, where was located the Black Portridge village of the Potawattomies, on the eastern bluff of the river. A small party in charge of Lieut. Peyton was dispatched to Peoria on a direct west course, which, however, made no discoveries, and Capt. Craig had not yet arrived thither. The army moved rapidly but cautiously forward, and late in the night preceding the attack encamped within a few miles of the village. It was now desirable to reconnoitre the position of the enemy, or rather the Indian town. Four men, namely Thomas Carlin (subsequently governor), and three of the Whitesides— Robert, Stephen and Davis—volunteered for this perilous service, and were entrusted by the governor with its delicate execution. They proceeded to the village, explored it and the approaches to it, thoroughly, without starting an Indian or provoking the bark of a dog. The position of the town was ascertained to be about 5 miles distant, situated on a bluff separated in great part from the high lands by a swampy glade, through which meandered a miry branch or creek, whose low banks were covered by a rank growth of tall grass and clumps of brush, so high and dense as to readily conceal an Indian on horseback until within a few feet of him. The ground had become additionally yielding by recent rains, rendering it almost impassable to mounted men.

In the fireless and cheerless camp all was silent as the grave. A deep gloom, with many misgivings, had settled upon the men. The fatiguing marches had ceased to be frolicsome. The troops felt jaded and sulky, and they were within the enemy's country. They reposed upon their arms, with their horses tethered near at hand, ready saddled to be instantly mounted for action. During the night a gun in the hands of a trooper was carelessly discharged, which caused great consternation in the camp. The stealthy foe, with gleaming tomahawk raised over his victim, was momentarily expected. All the horrors of the night attack at Tippecanoe, then fresh in the minds of every one, presented themselves to the active imaginations of the men. Every white coated soldier at that battle, it was said, had been singled out in the dusky morning and killed by the savages. In a moment now not a white coat remained in sight. But directly the assuring voice of his Excellency cried out that the firing was an accident, and all became quiet again.

Early on the following morning, with a dense fog prevailing, the army took up its line of march for the Indian town, Captain Judy with his corps of spies in advance. On the route in the tall grass they came up with an Indian and his squaw, both mounted. The Indian wanted to surrender, but Capt. Judy observed that he "did not leave home to take prisoners," and instantly shot one of them. With the blood streaming from his mouth and nose, and in his agony "singing the death song," prompted by the instinctive emotion of self-defense which even a trodden worm will exercise, the dying Indian raised his gun, shot and mortally wounded in the groin a Mr. Wright, and in a few minutes expired. Wright was from the Wood river settlement, and died after he was brought home. The rest of those who had incautiously approached the wounded Indian, when they saw him seize his gun, quickly dismounted on the far sides of their horses, making of them, as it were, a breast-work. Many guns were immediately discharged at the other Indian, not then known to be a squaw, all of which, in the trepidation of the occasion, missed her. Badly scared, and her husband killed by her side, the agonizing wails of the squaw were heart-rending. She was taken prisoner, and subsequently restored to her nation.

Owing to the fog, the army was misled into the spongy bottom, some three-fourths of a mile below the town, with the miry creek to cross, which deranged the plan of attack. The village thus escaped a surprise; and while a halt was made, preparatory to crossing, the Indians were observed running from the town, bounding through the tall grass on their horses, almost hid from view. An attack was every moment expected while crossing the treacherous stream, and the advanced corps, under Judy, sat lightly in their saddles, expecting to draw the fire of the hidden foe. To their great satisfaction, no attack was made or meant; the Indians were fleeing from their village and impending death, pell-mell, women and children, some on horse-back and some on foot, into the swamp among the tall grass, and toward a point of timber, in which the governor, disappointed in his charge upon the town, judged they intended to make a stand for battle. "I immediately changed my course," he writes, "ordered and led on a general charge upon them," but "owing to the unsoundness of the ground," the pursuers, horses, riders, arms and baggage, from his Excellency so valiantly leading the charge to the shouting subaltern and private, all shared in the common catastrophe alike, and were unhorsed and overwhelmed in the morass. It was called a democratic overthrow, in which all were literally "swamped."

Upon this yielding ground, into which a horse would sink and plunge without avail, a mounted force could not be moved. A pursuit on foot was ordered, which was both difficult and extremely dangerous on account of the tall grass in which the Indians were lurking. Several parties on foot trailed in pursuit of the Indians, however, two or three miles across the saturated bottom to the river, killing some of the enemy while attempting to cross to the farther shore. To such a pitch of excitement were some of the men wrought, that Charles Kitchen, John Howard and Pierre St. Jean, finding some Indian canoes, in the fury of the chase, crossed the river alone in full view of the retreating foe, but without molestaion.

A Potawattomie town, called by the governor, Chequeneboc, after a chief, was here burned. The Indians fled toward the interior wilderness. Another party made pursuit of the fugitives in a different direction; but the Indians making a stand in considerable force, these were compelled to retreat. Reinforcements were sent, when the savages entirely dispersed. Some of the troops were wounded in this action it is reported, but none killed. In the meantime, the village was pillaged and burned by the main body of the troops. The Indians, in their precipitate flight, had left behind all of their winter's store of provisions, which was destroyed or taken away. Hiding about the burning embers of the ruins, were found some Indian children, left by the frightened fugitives; also, some disabled adults, one of whom was in a starving condition, and partook of the bread given him with a voracious appetite. He is said to have been killed by a cowardly trooper straggling behind, after the main army had resumed its retrograde march, who wanted to be able to assert or boast that he had killed an Indian. Governor Edwards reports that four prisoners were taken away, and some eighty head of horses; of the Indian losses, gathered from their own account, between 24 and 30 were killed; our loss being one wounded. The Indian losses, based entirely upon their own reports, made by the few prisoners taken, to please the vanity of the whites, were, doubtless, apochryphal. To show the reckless daring of the Indian character, it is mentioned that a warrior walked calmly down the bluff some 200 yards distant, deliberately raised his gun and fired upon the troops in the town, then turned and strode slowly away amid a shower of bullets.

Nothing having been heard from General Hopkins and his 2000 mounted Kentucky riflemen, and apprehensive that a large force of warriors would be speedily collected, it was deemed prudent not to protract their stay, and accordingly, the retrograde march of the army was commenced that very day. A heavy and continuous rain prevailed at the time, but the dread of pursuit caused them not to intermit their travels till darkness overtook them, when, greatly exhausted and wet, without fire to dry their clothes,

18

or food to nourish their bodies, they sank into sleep on the wet ground, their clothing covered with the mud of the morass. The dread warrior did not appear. "Our army returned home with all convenient speed," writes Governor Reynolds, who in the campaign earned the soubriquet of "Old Ranger," and to whose account we are largely indebted for this.

On the morrow, a detachment in charge of Lieutenant Peyton, was again sent over to Peoria with a message to Captain Craig in charge of the provision boats, to return as speedily as possible. This party on their way burnt a Miami village within a half-mile of Peoria.

The force of Captain Craig, in charge of the provision boats for the armies of Hopkins and Edwards, and under instruction from his Excellency to proceed to Peoria "and take prisoners those persons who were there for the purpose of assisting the savages to murder the frontier settlers," was not idle. His armed boat, by force of a gale having broken its cable and drifted ashore, it was in the night time fired upon by ten Indians, who immediately fled. Discovering at daylight their tracks leading up into the town, Captain Craig inquired of the French their whereabouts. These denying all knowledge of them, said "they had heard or seen nothing," but he took the whole of them prisoners, burned and destroyed Peoria, and bore the captured inhabitants away on his boats to a point below the present Alton, where he landed and left them in the woods—men women and children—in the inclement month of November, without shelter, and without food other than the slender stores they had themselves hurriedly gathered up before their departure. They found their way to St. Louis it is said, in almost a starving condition. They numbered perhaps 75, the names of the heads of families given exceeding a dozen.* Thomas Forsythe, the government Indian agent stationed at Peoria, was included among the number. This was owing to his true relation to the government not being disclosed to the Indians or others, that he might have more influence with them in releasing or ransoming the prisoners captured in the recent Chicago massacre. From his long residence among the Indians, he was very popular with them. The burning of Peoria and taking prisoners its inhabitants, upon the mere suspicion that they sympathized with the Indians, was generally regarded as a needless, if not wanton, act of military power.†

After an absence of 13 days the gallant army of Governor Edwards returned to Camp Russell without loss. It was received with the honors of war, amidst the booming of the old but royal cannon which had done duty for many years at Fort Chartres, and the rattle of small arms. The troops were mostly discharged ; the governor, in a letter to the secretary of war, bespeaks for them a speedy payment as "the reward due to their

*See life of Governor Edwards, by his son.
†After the building of Fort Crevecœur, in 1680, Peoria lake was ever familiar to western travel and history ; but there is no authentic account of a permanent European settlement there until 1778, when Laville de Meillet, named after its founder, was started. On account of the quality of the water and its greater salubrity, the location was changed further down the lake to the present site of Peoria, and by 1796, the old had been entirely abandoned for the new village. After its destruction, in 1812, it was not settled again until 1819, and then by American pioneers, though in 1813, Fort Clark was built there, which gave a name to the place for several years. In 1818, the fort was destroyed by fire. In 1825, the county of Peoria was established and the county seat located.

services." In his address, to the St. Clair county militia, the governor said: "Your bravery has enabled me to repel hostile invasion and to wage war upon the enemy in their own country. * * Your intrepidity and patriotism have been equally honorable to yourselves, and useful to your country." Not to be outdone in such flattering testimonials, the militia, through their officers, replied in as felicitous a vein, that his Excellency had "greatly increased his claims upon the gratitude of the country for his wise measures," and that they had "witnessed his coolness, deliberation and promptitude in the hour of peril." It seems, however, that his Excellency was not without rivals for the laurels of this campaign. With much concern, he writes, under date of December 25th, 1812: "I discover that some pitiful attempts are making to deprive me of the credit I am entitled to, by giving it to Colonel Russell, who happened to join me (about three days before I commenced my march) with 50 rangers. The injustice of this is known and attested by the whole of my little army," etc.*

1813.—Early in this year, the country was put in such state of defense against the hostile Indians as its sparse population admitted of. Block house stations and stockade forts were repaired and strengthened along the entire frontier, and the remote settlers and feeble garrisons were removed to the denser settlements. New ranging companies were formed and so stationed as to easily range through the settlements. From the present Alton to Kaskaskia, twenty-two family forts were scattered along. In spite of these precautions, the extent of the frontier was so great that no diligence in ranging afforded entire immunity from savage attacks. Numerous depredations and murders were committed by marauding bands of the red foe. Of these, only a few will be mentioned.

The savages fell upon the family of Mr. Lively, four miles southeast of Covington, in the present Washington county, and four were slain. The bodies of two women were shockingly mangled; a little boy of seven years was borne away from the house, his head severed from his body, his entrails torn out, and both carried away, it was thought, for purposes of cannibalism. Mr. Lively's body was indecently mutilated. A son and a stranger stopping there, were out in quest of their horses, and from a distance saw the house attacked. These in their retreat to the settlements, bivouaced in a grove 6 miles southeast of Fayetteville on the Kaskaskia river, which perpetuates the name of the murdered family. The Indians, supposed to be Kickapoos, were pursued by Captain Boon's company, but having 4 days the start, made good their escape. That a pursuing force should be 4 days behind, shows how incautiously remote from the denser settlements some families must have located. On the banks of Kaskaskia, near the present Carlyle, a Mr. Young and a minister by the name of McLean, had a desparate struggle with a party of savages. The former having been killed, as also both horses, a single but powerful savage pursued McLean, who was unarmed and on foot. McLean would come to a stand at times and in a menacing manner defy the savage to approach with his tomahawk. The Indian seeking the advantage, would hestitate. At such times, McLean would divest himself of a portion of his surplus

*Edwards' Life of Edwards.

clothing, and finally, the attention of the Indian having been arrested by his cast off garments, McLean plunged into the river, swam to the further shore, and effected his escape.* Some murders were also committed on Cache river in the present Alexander county. On the Wabash, 30 miles above Vincennes, near Fort Lamotte, the wife of a Mr. Houston and four children were killed. In a small prairie 2 or 3 miles from the present Albion, in Edwards county, a farmer by the name of Boltenhouse was killed, the prairie perpetuating his name.

Considering the frequent murders and the fact that the general government had made no provision to sustain the militia and volunteers, which caused those of Illinois to be discharged from the service on the 8th of June, by the governor, it may be said that the year 1813 presented but a gloomy prospect for the exposed settlements in the west.

Second Expedition to Peoria.—Large numbers of hostile Indians were known to have collected among the Potawattomies and Kickapoos on Lake Peoria, whence marauding parties, which harrassed the frontiers of both Illinois and Missouri, were sent out. It became again an object therefore to penetrate their country with a military force, disperse them from their convenient location, and drive them far into the interior. In the latter part of the summer a joint expedition from Illinois and Missouri, was projected for this purpose. An army of some 900 men was collected and Gen. Howard, who had resigned the office of Governor of Missouri to accept a Brigader General's commission in the United States Army, was placed in command. The Illinois troops were ordered to rendezvous at Camp Russell; one company was ordered to the Mississippi at a point called the Piasa, opposite the Portage des Sioux, where it remained several weeks and became quite sickly. The Illinois troops were formed into the second regiment, and Benjamin Stephenson, of Randolph county, was appointed colonel; W. B. Whitesides and John Moredock were majors; and Joseph Phillips, Samuel Judy, Nathaniel Journey, and Samuel Whitesides, captains. There was some delay on account of the Missourians, who were being collected at St. Louis.

Finally the order for a forward movement arrived, and the Illinoisans marched up the Mississippi by companies to the Illinois, which was crossed 2 or 3 miles above its mouth. The movement was slow; in Calhoun County, where the bee-trees were very numerous, a few rangers, who rambled from the main body, got into a skirmish with some Indians, but no loss was sustained except that a gun-stock was shivered by an Indian bullet. The Missourians marched 100 miles north, on the west side of the Mississippi to Fort Mason, where they swam the river mounted naked on their horses, while their garments were crossed on a platform, borne up by 2 canoes, and joined the Illinoisans. They were commanded by Col. McNair, afterward governor of Missouri. The whole force was re-organized into a brigade, of which General Howard was in chief command. The march was continued up the Mississippi. On the present site of Quincy they passed a recently deserted camp and village, supposed to have contained 1,000 Sac warriors. At a point called the "Two rivers," they struck out eastward and across the high prairies to the Illinois, which was reached

*Missouri Gazette, March 1813.

near the mouth of Spoon river.   Here their provision boats arrived and took on board the sick.   The march was continued up the Illinois to Peoria, where there was a small stockade in charge of Captain Nicholas of the U. S. Army.   Two days before, the Indians had made an attack on the fort, but were repulsed.   On the line of march from the Mississippi, numerous fresh trails indicated that the Indians, gaining knowledge of the invading force, were fleeing northward.

Being in the enemy's country, knowing his stealthy habits and the troops at no time observing a high degree of discipline, many unnecessary night alarms occurred; they were paraded, frequently ordered to arms, and under the general excitement incident to a constant dread of momentary attack, guns were incautiously fired, and one fine young Kentucky trooper, was shot dead by a fear smitten sentinel.   All this time the dread savages were far away.

The army was marched up the lake to Gomo's village, the present site of Chilicothe, and finding that the enemy had ascended the Illinois, two deserted villages were demolished under the shock of its onset, and burned, when it took up its retrograde march. At the outlet of the lake, the present site of Peoria, the troops remained in camp several weeks, building Fort Clark, named in memory of Gen. George Rogers Clark.   Major Christy, in the meantime, was dispatched with a force in charge of two fortified keel-boats up the river to the foot of the rapids, to chastise and rout such of the enemy as might have lodged in that region. Major Boone was sent with a force to scour the Spoon river country, towards Rock river.   Both expeditions returned without other discoveries than signs of alarm on the part of the enemy, and his retreat into the interior.   The army returned by a direct route to Camp Russell, where the volunteers and militia were disbanded, October 22d, 1813.

The campaign, though no battle was fought or enemy seen, was still fraught with great benefit in affording the frontiers immunity from the murderous incursions of the savages for the entire succeeding winter.   To the foe was unfolded the power and resources he had to contend with, and shaking his head he muttered, "pale faces like the leaves in the forest—like the grass on the prairies—they grow everywhere!"

1814.—The year 1814, was, however, also prolific with horrible deeds of savage butchery.   Those fiends, with a natural aptitude for such work, received additional incentives from their British allies.   Our naval victories on Lake Erie, the recovery of Detroit, and the defeat of the British at the battle of the Thames, where Tecumseh fell, which was fought before the close of 1813, had the effect to cause the savages to retreat from Canada, and concentrate in great numbers on the banks of the upper Mississippi; and marauding bands again visited the settlements of Illinois and Missouri, committing many depredations and murders.   We do not pretend to cite all.

In July, a band of Indians raiding in the Wood river settlement, 6 miles east of the present Alton, massacred a Mrs. Reagan and her 6 children.   The husband and father, absent at the time, was the first to discover the dreadful slaughter.   On arriving home after night-fall, and opening the door of his cabin, he

*Annals of the West—Appendix.

stepped into the gore of his loved family, and beheld their stark and mangled remains. Captain Samuel Whitesides with his company of rangers pursued the savages to the Sangamon, where, in a thicket, all escaped except the leader of the band, who was shot out of a tree-top. In his belt he had dangling the scalp of Mrs. Reagan.

In the western part of Clinton county, near the crossing of the present O. & M. R. R. over a stream, Jesse Bailes and wife were looking for their hogs on a Sunday evening in the creek bottom, and the dogs baying at a thicket, it was supposed they were found; but on approaching the thicket, the Indians, concealed within, fired upon both, the lady only being hit. She was taken to her father's house, Mr. Bradley, and died in a short time.

In August, while a company of Captain Short's rangers were encamped at the Lively cabins, a trail was discovered which led directly to the starting of 7 Indians with 14 stolen horses. When overtaken a skirmish ensued, in which the rangers were rather worsted; one was wounded, a horse killed, and another, Moses Short, received a bullet which lodged in a twist of tobacco in his pocket. William Stout, with great speed, went to camp for reinforcements. Captain Short with 30 men now followed the trail all night, and next morning overtook the marauders on a fork of the Little Wabash. A lagging Indian here shot a turkey, and the report of his gun apprised the pursuers of their proximity. On discovering the whites, the rear Indian ran in great haste forward, and all prepared for battle, in ignorance probably of the number of the pursuing force, and assured doubtless by their previous success, for they might have easily made their escape. They were directly surrounded, and when they realized their situation, sang the death song, shouted defiance, and fought bravely to the last. All were killed. The pursuers lost one man, William O'Neal, who, while taking deliberate aim, met an adversary quicker than himself, and was shot.

[NOTE.—The most desparate single-handed combat with Indians, ever fought on the soil of Illinois, was that of Tom Higgins, August 21, 1814. Higgins was 25 years old, of a muscular and compact build, not tall, but strong and active. In danger he possessed a quick and discerning judgment, and was without fear. He was a member of Journey's rangers, consisting of 11 men, stationed at Hills Fort, 8 miles southwest of the present Greenville. Discovering Indian signs near the fort, the company early the following morning started on the trail. They had not gone far before they were in an ambuscade of a larger party. At the first fire, their commander Journey and 3 men fell. Six retreated to the fort in flight, but Higgins stopped " to have another pull at the red skins," and taking deliberate aim at a straggling savage, shot him down. Higgin's horse had been wounded at the first fire, as he supposed, mortally, but coming to, he was about to effect his escape, when the familiar voice of Burgess hailed him from the long grass, "Tom don't leave me." Higgins told him to come along, but Burgess replied that his leg was smashed. Higgins attempted to raise him on his horse, but the animal took fright and ran away. Higgins then directed Burgess to limp off as best he could, and by crawling through the grass he reached the fort, while the former loaded his gun and remained behind to protect him against the pursuing enemy. When Burgess was well out of the way, to throw any wandering enemy off the trail, Higgins took another route which led by a small thicket. Here he was unexpectedly confronted by 3 savages approaching. He ran to a little ravine near at hand for shelter, but in the effort discovered for the first time that he was badly wounded in the leg. He was closely pressed by the largest, a powerful Indian, who lodged a ball in his thigh. He fell, but instantly rose again, only to draw the fire of the other two and again fell wounded. The Indians now advanced upon him with their tomahawks and scalping knives, but as he presented his gun first at one, then at another, from his place in the ravine, each wavered in his purpose. Neither party had time to load, and the large Indian, supposing finally that Higgins' gun was empty, rushed forward with uplifted tomahawk and a yell, but as he came near enough, was shot down. At this, the others raised the war-whoop and rushed upon the wounded Higgins, and now a hand to hand conflict ensued. They darted at him with their knifes time and again, inflicting many ghastly flesh wounds which bled profusely. One of the assailents threw his tomahawk at him with such precision as to sever his ear and lay bare his skull, knocking him down. They now rushed in on him, but he kicked them off, and grasping one of their spears thrust at

The military expeditions of 1814, in which Illinois participated, were by water on the Mississippi. The first projected in the west was that of Governor Clark (in the absence of General Howard), which left St. Louis about the 1st of May. It comprised a force of some 200 men in five armed barges, its destination being Prairie du Chien. The notorious Dickson, British agent and Indian trader, a man of pleasing manner and captivating address, had but a few days before recruited for the British army 300 Sioux, Winnebagoes and Folsavoisns, whom he was conducting to Canada. A small garrison of "Mackinac fencibles", in command of a British officer, was left in charge of the place, but being greatly outnumbered by Clark's forces, they joined the fleeing inhabitants. Clark's unopposed troops were quartered in the house of the Mackinaw Fur Company, and a fort, calledShelby, was built. In June Gov. Clark returned to St. Louis, where the people tendered him a public ovation in honor of his conquest. Thus easily did he win military glory. But in July a large force of British and Indians under Col. Mackey, came by water from Mackinaw, via Green Bay and the Wisconsin, and after a short seige, Gov. Clark's entire garrison capitulated and was paroled, leaving the British with the new fort in much better condition than two months before. Such are the fortunes of war.

In the meantime, Gen. Howard, having returned to his post, deemed it advisable to strengthen so remote a post as Prairie du Chien, and to that end sent reinforcements to the number of 108 men, in charge of Lieut. Campbell of the regular army, in three keel boats up the river. Of this force 66 men were Illinois Rangers, under Captains Stephen Rector, and Riggs, who occupied two boats. The remainder were with Campbell in the other boat. Rock Island, where they laid up for a night, was passed without molestation, but at the foot of the rapids great numbers of the Sacs and Fox Indians visited the boats with professions of friendship. Some of the French boatmen were known to the Indians, and very much liked by them. They would squeeze their hands with a pull down the river, indicating that it would be well for them to leave. It was rightly judged by them that the treacherous savages meditated an attack, of which Lieut. Campbell was duly informed. He, however, disregarded these hints. The sutler's and contractor's boats, and two barges with the Illinois rangers, had passed the rapids, and had got some two miles ahead, when Campbell's barge was struck by a gale from the west so strong as to force her against a small island, next to the Illinois shore. Thinking it advisable to lie to till the wind abated, sentinels were immediately stationed, while the men went ashore to cook break-

him, was raised up by it. He quickly seized his gun, and by a powerful blow crushed in the skull of one, but broke his rifle. His remaining antagonist still kept up the contest making thrusts with his knife at the bleeding and exhausted Higgins, which he parried with his broken gun as best he could. Most of this desperate engagement was in plain view of the Fort, but the rangers, having been in one ambuscade, saw in this fight only a ruse to draw out the balance of the garrison. But a Mrs. Pursely, residing at the Fort, no longer able to see so brave a man contend unaided for his life, seized a gun, and mounting a horse, started to his rescue. At this the men took courage and hastened along. The Indian seeing aid coming, fled. Higgins being nearly hacked to pieces, fainted from loss of blood. He was carried to the Fort. There being no surgeon, his comrades cut two balls from his flesh; others remained in For days his life was despaired of, but by tender nursing, he ultimately recovered his health, badly crippled. He resided in Fayette County for many years after, where he raised a large family, and died in 1829. He received a pension, pursued farming, and at one time was door-keeper of one of the houses of the General Assembly at Vandalia. Reynold's Pio. Hist.—p. 321.

fast. At this time a large force of Indians on the main shore,
under the command of Black Hawk, commenced an attack. The
savages, in canoes, passed rapidly to the island, and with a war
whoop rushed upon the men, who retreated and sought refuge in
the barge. A battle of brisk musketry now ensued between the
few regulars aboard the stranded barge and the hordes of Indians
under cover of trees on the island, with severe loss to the former.
Meanwhile, Captains Rector and Riggs, ahead with their barges,
seing the smoke of battle, essayed to return, but in the strong
gale Riggs' boat became unmanageable and was stranded on the
rapids. Rector, to avoid a similar disaster, let go his anchor. The
rangers, however, opened with good aim and telling effect on the
savages.

The unequal combat having raged for some time, the commander's barge, with many wounded and several dead on board, among
the former of whom, very badly, was Campbell himself, had almost
ceased fighting when she was discovered to be on fire. And now
Stephen Rector, and his brave crew of Illinois rangers, comprehending the horrid situation, performed, without delay, as cool
and heroic a deed, and did it well, as ever imperiled the life of
mortal man. In the howling gale, in full view of hundreds of the
infuriate savages, and within range of their rifles, they deliberately
raised anchor, lightened their barge by casting overboard quantities of provisions, and guided it with the utmost labor down the
swift current, to the windward of the burning barge, and, in the
galling fire of the enemy, rescued the survivors, removed the
wounded, the dying and all, to their vessel. This was as heroic a
deed of noble daring as was performed during the war in the
west. The island, in memory of the struggle, was named after
Campbell, but with Rector and his crew of Illinois rangers remains
the glory of the action.

The manner of effecting the rescue displays the resource of
courageous minds in the crisis of imminent peril. Rector's barge
was first quickly lightened by casting overboard the provisions,
the crew (mostly experienced French boatmen,) got into the water
on the windward side of the barge, which brought it between
them and the fire of the enemy. In this manner it was guided in
close proximity to the disabled barge, and held there till the removal was effected, when, after being hauled against the wind far
out into the stream, it glided safely away. The loss was 25; 9
killed—4 rangers, 3 regulars, 1 woman, 1 child ; wounded 16,
among whom were Lieut Campbell and Dr. Stewart, severely.*
Rector's barge was uncomfortably crowded for the wounded, but
as the force was large they rowed night and day until St. Louis was
reached. The Indians, after the abandonment of Campbell's
barge, feasted upon the contents of their prize.

It was now feared that Riggs and his company were captured
and sacrificed by the savages. His vessel, which was strong and well
armed, was for a time surrounded by the Indians, but the whites
on the inside were well sheltered. The wind becoming allayed in
the evening, the boat, under cover of the night, glided safely down
the river without the loss of a single man. At St. Louis there was
great rejoicing on the arrival of Riggs and crew, all safe. Many
fervent prayers had gone up, many anxious eyes had eagerly

*Mo. Gazette, July 30, 1814

watched the river, and many a patriot heart was made glad by the final tidings of their safety.

Still another expedition for the Upper Mississippi was projected this season after the two foregoing disasters. It was fitted out at Cape au Gris, and old French hamlet on the left bank of the Mississippi, a few miles above the mouth of the Illinois. It consisted of 334 effective men, 40 regulars and the rest rangers and volunteers, in command of Major Zackary Taylor (afterwards president.) Nelson Rector, and Samuel Whitesides, with the Illinoisans, were in command of boats. It was generally regarded as of material importance to have a strong fort with a garrison well up the Mississippi in the heart of the Indian country. The plan was to proceed above the rapids, and in descending sweep both banks of the river of the Indian villages, destroy their corn down to Rock Island, and there build the fort. The expedition departed its place of rendezvous, August 23, 1814, and passed Rock Island and the Rapids unmolested. It was now learned that the country was not only swarming with Indians, but that the English were there in command, with a detachment of regulars and artillery. The advanced boats in command of Rector, Whitesides, and Hempstead, turned about and began to descend the Rapids, fighting with great gallantry the hoardes of the enemy pouring their fire into them from the shore at every step. A little way above the mouth of Rock river, not far from some willow islands, Major Taylor anchored his fleet out in the Mississippi. During the night the English planted a battery of six pieces down at the water's edge to sink or disable the boats, and filled the islands with redskins to butcher our men, who might, unarmed, seek refuge there. But in this scheme they were frustrated. In the morning Taylor ordered all the force, except 20 boatmen on each vessel, to the upper island to dislodge the enemy. The order was executed with great gallantry, the island scoured and the savages, many of whom were killed, driven to the lower one. In the meantime the British cannon told with effect upon the fleet, piercing many of the boats. The men rushed back and the boats were dropped down the stream out of range of the cannon. Captain Rector was now ordered with his company to make a sortie on the lower island, which he did, driving the Indians back among the willows, but they being reinforced, in turn hurled Rector back upon the sand beach. A council of officers called by Taylor had by this time decided that their force was insufficient to contend with the enemy, who outnumbered them three to one, and the boats were in full retreat down the river. As Rector attempted to get under way, his boat grounded, and the savages, with demoniac yells, surrounded it, when a most desperate hand to hand engagement ensued. The gallant ranger, Samuel Whitesides, observing the imminent peril of his brave Illinois comrade, went immediately to his rescue, who, but for his timely aid, would undoubtedly have been overpowered with all his force and murdered. Taylor's loss was 11 men badly wounded, 3 of whom had died at the date of his report to Gen. Howard, Sept. 6, 1814.

Opposite the mouth of the Des Moines, on the site of the present town of Warsaw, a fort was built by Taylor's men, called Edwards, which consisted of a rough stockade and blockhouses of unhewn logs. Fort Madison, on the west side of the Mississippi and farther

up, after being repeatedly attacked by the enemy, was evacuted and
burnt. A few weeks later (in October) Fort Edwards shared a
similar fate; the troops got out of provisions, and unable to sustain
their position, retreated down the river to Cape au Gris. The
people of Illinois and Missouri were astonished at this extraordinary evacuation and destruction of the fort by our own troops.
The rangers and volunteers were discharged October 18th,
1814.*

Thus ended the last, like the two previous expeditions up the
Mississippi during the war of 1812, in defeat and disaster. The
enemy was in undisputed possession of all the country north of the
Illinois river, and the prospect respecting these territories boded
nothing but gloom. With the approach of winter, however,
Indian depredations ceased to be committed, and the peace of
Ghent, Dec. 24, 1814, closed the war.

---

*The account of these expeditions has been in great part gathered from Reynolds'
Own Times.

Chapter XXV.

CIVIL AFFAIRS OF THE ILLINOIS TERRITORY FROM 1812 TO 1818.

Meeting of the Legislature—The Members—Laws—Conflict between the Legislature and Judiciary—Curious Acts—Territorial Banks —Cairo Bank—Commerce—First Steamboats—Pursuits of the People.

For nearly four years after the organization of the territorial government no legislature existed in Illinois. The governor was both executive and, in great part, the law-making power. These extraordinary powers, authorized by the ordinance of 1787, viewed at this day, seem strangely inconsistent with our republican notions of the necessity of co-ordinate branches of government. Under that celebrated ordinance, the political privileges of the citizen were few or none. He could not exercise the elective franchise unless he was a freeholder of 50 acres, nor aspire to a seat in the territorial legislature unless he was a freeholder of from 200 to 500 acres. Those of the territorial officers whom the president did not appoint, were appointed by the governor. The people could not elect justices of the peace, county surveyors, treasurers, coroners, sheriffs, clerks, judges of the inferior courts, nor even choose the officers of the territorial militia; all this power and much more was vested in the governor. By the act establishing the Illinois territory, it was provided that whenever his Excellency was satisfied that a majority of the freeholders desired it, then he might authorize a legislature. While none of these extraordinary powers were perhaps ever arbitrarily exercised by any of the governors, unless it was St. Clair, the people were all the time clamorous for an extension of suffrage. Congress (not the governor) finally, by act of May 21, 1812, raised Illinois to the second grade of territorial government, and further extended the right of suffrage to any white male person 21 years old, who had paid a territorial tax and resided one year in the territory next preceding any election, authorizing such elector to vote for representative, member of the legislative council and delegate to congress. The property qualification, under the ordinance of 1787, was abolished. This was a very great concession to the people. The governor was required to apportion the territory. On the 14th of February, 1812, accordingly, he issued his proclamation, ordering an election to take the sense of the people for or against entering upon the second grade of territorial government. The election was to be held for three successive days in each county, commencing on the second Monday in April. The question was decided in the affirmative by a large

283

majority. On September 16th, following, the governor and judges
having organized the new counties of Madison, Gallatin and Johnson, making now, with the two old counties of St. Clair and Randolph, a total of five, a proclamation was issued, publishing their
establishment. By another proclamation of the same date, an
election for 5 members of the legislative council, 7 representatives
and a delegate to congress, was ordered to be held in each county
on the 8th, 9th and 10th days of October following. At this election, Shadrach Bond was elected to congress. The members elect
of the legislative council were, Pierre Menard, of Randolph—
chosen to preside; William Biggs, of St. Clair; Samuel Judy, of
Madison; Thomas Ferguson, of Johnson, and Benjamin Talbot,
of Gallatin.

The members elect of the house of representatives were, George
Fisher, of Randolph; Joshua Oglesby and Jacob Short, of St.
Clair; William Jones, of Madison; Phillip Trammel and Alexan-
der Wilson, of Gallatin, and John Grammar, of Johnson.

We subjoin brief sketches of the members constituting the first
general assembly of Illinois. *Pierre Menard*, a Canadian Frenchman, settled at Kaskaskia in 1790. He was a merchant and
enjoyed an extensive trade with the Indians, over whom he exerted a great influence and was for many years the government agent
for them. He was well informed, energetic, frank and honest,
and was very popular with all classes. *William Biggs* was an
intelligent and respectable member, who had been a soldier in
Clark's expedition, and ten years afterward had been a prisoner
for several years among the Kickapoos. He wrote and published a
complete narrative of his Indian captivity, and in 1826, congress
voted him three sections of land. He was for many years county
judge. *Samuel Judy*—the same who, in the fall preceding, commanded the corps of spies in Governor Edwards' military campaign to Peoria lake—was a man of "energy, fortitude and
enterprise." Some of his descendants now reside in Madison
county. *Joshua Oglesby* was a local Methodist preacher of ordinary
education, who lived on a farm and was greatly respected by his
neighbors. *Jacob Short*, the colleague of Oglesby, removed to
Illinois with his father, Moses, in 1796, and pursued farming. During the war of 1812, he distinguished himself as a ranger. *George
Fisher* possessed a fair education, and was by profession a physician. He removed from Virginia to Kaskaskia in 1800, and engaged in merchandizing, but at this time he resided on a farm. He
was afterward in public life. *Phillip Trammel* was a man of discriminating mind, inclined to the profession of arms. He was the
lessee of the United States saline in Gallatin county. His colleague, *Alexander Wilson*, was a popular tavern keeper at Shawneetown, of fair abilities. *William Jones* was a Baptist preacher,
grave in his deportment, and possessed of moderate abilities. He
was born in North Carolina, removed to Illinois in 1806, and settled in the Rattan prairie, east of Alton * This was the first
appearance in public life of *John Grammar*. He afterwards represented Union county frequently during a period of 20 years.
He had no education, yet was a man of shrewdness. After his
election, it is related that to procure the necessary apparel to
appear at the seat of government, he and the family gathered a

* Annals of the West.

large quantity of hickory nuts, which were taken to the Ohio saline and traded for blue strouding, such as the Indians wore for breech-cloth. When the neighboring women assembled to make up the garments, it was found that he had not invested quite enough nuts. The pattern was measured in every way possible, but was unmistakably scant. Whereupon it was decided to make a "bob-tailed coat and a long pair of leggings." Arrayed in these, he duly appeared at the seat of government, where he continued to wear his primitive suit for the greater part of the session. Notwithstanding his illiteracy, he had the honor of originating the practice much followed by public men since, of voting against all new measures—it being easier to conciliate public opinion for being remiss in voting for a good measure, than to suffer arraignment for aiding in the passage of an unpopular one.*

On the 10th of November, the governor, by proclamation, ordered the members elect to convene, on the 25th instant, at Kaskia, the seat of government. The two bodies met in a large, rough old building of uncut limestone, with steep roof and gables of unpainted boards, situated in the centre of a square, which, after the ruin and abandonment of Fort Chartres, had served the French as the headquarters of the military commandant. The first floor, a large, low, cheerless room, was fitted up for the house, and a small chamber above for the council chamber. The latter body chose John Thomas their secretary, and the former elected for clerk William C. Greenup. The two houses had a door-keeper in common. All the 12 members boarded with one family, and lodged, it is said, in one room. How unlike the present times! The members addressed themselves to the business in hand, without delay or circumlocution. Windy speeches or contention were unheard of, and parliamentary tacticians, if any there were, met with no indulgence. It has been naively remarked that not a lawyer appears on the roll of names.

The assembly effected a peaceful revolution of the civil polity of the territory, at a time when actual war was the all-absorbing public question. By act of December 13, 1812, all the laws passed by the Indiana legislature, and in force March 1, 1809, general in their nature and not local to Indiana, which stood unrepealed by the governor and judges of Illinois, and all laws originally adopted for Illinois under the first grade of territorial government, remaining unrepealed, were by them re-enacted. The idea manifestly was, that by the assembling of the legislature, the territory stood forth in utter nakedness, divested of all law until re-invested by them. The enacting clause of the territorial laws was: "Be it enacted by the legislative council and house of representatives, and it is hereby enacted by the authority of the same." To the courts of common pleas was given the same jurisdiction previously had under the Indiana territory. The general court, established at the seat of government, besides being a tribunal of oyer and terminer for jail delivery on indictments found by the grand juries of the common pleas court, was also constituted a court of original jurisdiction, of appeals, to correct errors of inferior courts, and to punish the contempts, neglects, favors or corruptions of the justices of the peace, clerks, sheriffs, etc., its process running to any county, to the great inconvenience of the

*Ford's Illinois.

people. Such other laws as it was deemed the country required, were passed, and after a brief session, the first legislature adjourned.

The laws of the territory were afterward revised and digested, under the authority of the legislatue, by Nathaniel Pope, and printed in one volume by Matthew Duncan, printer of the territory, which bears the date June 2, 1815. There are besides, two small volumes, by the same printer, of the session laws of 1815–16 and 181–718. While the laws are faithfully rendered, the mechanical appearance of these books, owing to the great coarseness of the paper and the use of clumsy type, illy compares with work of the present time. Many of the laws imported, revised and adopted by the governor and judges, were well drawn but the great body of those originated in the legislature present much crudity, both in composition and grasp of the subjects intended to be subserved. We will allude to some features of the territorial code, now happily obsolete, which give, by contrast with the present, an idea to the reader of the progress and amelioration attained in criminal jurisprudence and the punishment for debt. Thus, in the punishment of crimes, both felonies and misdemeanors, the barbarous practices of whipping on the bare back, confinement in stocks, standing in the pillory, and branding with hot irons, were the penalties frequently prescribed; besides fines, imprisonment, and loss of citizenship. These summary modes of chastisement grew, in part, out of the condition of the country. It was but sparsely settled, the people were poor, they had no general prison or penitentiary, and the few jails were so insecure as to present scarcely any barrier to the escape of prisoners. Whipping upon the bare back, besides other punishments at the option of the court, was prescribed in burglary or robbery, 39 stripes; in perjury, larceny, the receiving of stolen goods, and obtaining goods by fraudulent pretenses, 31 stripes; horse-stealing, first offence, from 50 to 100 lashes; hog-stealing, from 25 to 39 lashes; altering and defacing marks or brands on domestic animals at large, 40 lashes "well laid on;" bigamy, punished with from 100 to 500 stripes; for sodomy, from 100 to 500 lashes were prescribed; forcibly taking away a female to marry against her consent, was declared a felony and might be punished by whipping; children or servants for disobedience, might, upon complaint and conviction before a justice, be whipped not exceeding 10 stripes. In all these offences there were other penalties provided, alternatively or additionally, at the option of the court—such as fines, imprisonment, restitution, etc. Fines were collected from those unable to pay, by the sheriff hiring or selling them to any one who would pay the fine or costs, for such terms as the court might deem reasonable, and if the delinquent should abscond, the penalty was double the term of servitude and 39 stripes. Standing in pillory was prescribed, in addition to other penalties, in perjury, forgery, and the altering or defacing of brands or marks on domestic animals. For this last offence, on second conviction, the culprit was to have the letter T branded in the left hand with a red-hot iron. To prevent the common crime of killing stock running on the range, every one, including the owners, was required to exhibit the ears of hogs, or hides of cattle, killed, to a magistrate or two freeholders within three days, under a penalty of $10. For aiding the escape of a convict, the punishment was the same as that of the culprit, except in capital cases, when stripes, standing in pillory, or sitting on the gallows with the rope adjusted about the neck, at the option of the court, was the penalty. Besides in treason and murder, the penalty of death by hanging was denounced against arson and rape, and horse-stealing on second conviction. For selling intoxicating liquors to Indians, slaves, apprentices and minors, severe penalties were enacted. For reveling, quarreling, fighting, profanely cursing, disorderly behavior at divine worship, and hunting on the Sabbath, penalties by fines were prescribed. Cock-fighting, horse-racing on the highways, gambling, keeping E. O. tables, sending challenge to fight or box at fisticuffs, lotteries, etc., were punished by fines. In 1810, a law was adopted to suppress dueling, which made the fatal result of a duel murder, including the aiders, abettors or counselors as principals in the crime.

In regard to the collection of debts, the principles of the common law obtained, which wholly favored the creditor. All the property of the judgement debtor, both real and personal without any of the present humane features as to exemption, might be levied upon and sold under execution. The sale was absolute—no time of redemption, as at present, was allowed in the case of realty. If the land failed to sell for want of bidders, it was the judgment creditor's right, at his option, to take it absolutely at the appraised value made by 12 jurors. But this was not all. If the property was insufficient to pay the judgment, the body of the debtor might be seized and cast into prison. Here he would be allowed the prison bounds, extending 200 yards from the jail in any direction, on condition only of giving bonds in double the sum of the debt, not to depart therefrom.

The territorial revenue was raised by a tax upon lands. Those situated in the river bottoms of the Mississippi, Ohio and the Wabash were taxed at the rate of $1 on every 100 acres. The uplands were classed as second rate, and were taxed at the rate of 75 cents per 100 acres. Unlocated, but confirmed land claims, were taxed at the rate of 37½ cents per 100 acres. The county revenue was raised chiefly by a tax upon personal property, including slaves or indentured servants between the ages of 16 and 40, not to exceed $1 each. The only real property taxed was lots and houses in towns, and mansion houses in the country, worth $200 and upwards. There was levied also a capitation tax of $1 on every able-bodied single man, having attained his majority and owning $200 worth of taxable property. This ought to have induced marriage. Two men were appointed to appraise the property required to be assessed. Merchants and ferries were licensed at $15 and $10 respectively. Horses and cattle were taxed by the head, not exceeding 50 and 10 cents, respectively—not according to value, as at present.

The entire territorial revenue, between the 1st of November, 1811, and the 8th of November, 1814 (3 years), was reported by the legislative committee on finance, in 1814, to be $4,875 45. But of this amount, only $2,516 89 had actually been paid into the treasury; the balance—nearly half—$2, 378 47 remained in the hands of delinquent sheriffs. The delinquencies of sheriffs, in their capacity as collectors of the revenues, remained a curse to

Illinois not only during its territorial existence, but for many years after it became a State.

In 1814 the legislature attempted to reorganize the judiciary by establishing the supreme court of the territory. The United States judges for the territory were assigned to circuit duty, each having a circuit composed of two counties in each of which two terms of court were to be held annually. The courts possessed common law and chancery jurisdiction, and suits were to be tried in the counties in which they originated. Once a year the judges were to convene in banc at the seat of government, to hear appeals and revise erroneous decisions from the courts below. This arrangement was well calculated to give to the people in their counties a more thorough administration of the laws than the courts of common pleas afforded; but the idea of circuit duty was manifestly distasteful to the judges. In the legislature much discussion arose as to its power to prescribe the duties of the appointees of the general government. The judges were requested to give a written opinion upon the merits and legality of the proposed act. These gentlemen—Spriggs and Thomas, Griswold being absent—wanted no better opportunity to assail it, which they did in a very emphatic manner, arguing at length the invalidity of the act; that "the court established by the ordinance of 1787 cannot be subjected to the revision or control of any tribunal established by the Territorial Legislature; and that an appeal from the same court to the same was a solicism." The governor, at the instance of the legislature, in his message approving the bill, took up the question, elaborately argued the power of the legislature in the premises, and apparently demolished the position of the judges. The bill without finally becoming a law was by the legislature referred to congress, together with the objections of the judges and the reply of the governor, with an address "requesting the passage of a law declaring the aforesaid act valid, or to pass some law more explanatory of the relative duties and powers of the judges aforesaid and of this legislature." Congress, by act of March 3, 1815, passed "an act regulating and defining the duties 'of the United States judges for the Territory of Illinois," which substantially embodied the provisions required by the legislature. The judges were required to do circuit duties and reside in their respective circuits, and to meet in banc twice a year at the seat of government, as a court of appeals. They were also subjected to the regulations of the legislature as to the times of holding their terms. The governor appointed the clerks

In the meantime by a suplemental act the legislature at the same session had abolished the general court, whose jurisdiction was to be superseded by the supreme corut; and by another act the court of common pleas was abolished, and county courts (the germ of our present county system) which had no jurisdiction for the trial of ordinary cases, substituted. Until congress therefore acted, a period of some two months and a half, Illinois presented the anomalous condition of being without a judicial tribunal higher than that of a justice's court, whose civil jurisdiction, by another act of the same session, was enlarged to $20 in debt. Sitting as an examining tribunal, to what court could a justice of the peace have validly bound over a culprit during this period of partial judicial vacuum? However, we have nothing showing to the contrary, but that the people got along just as well as before and after. By act of Jan. 9, 1816, the duties of the judges of the court of appeals were more clearly defined, and a law relating to this court was amended in 1817 and the circuits reorganized; next by an act of June 12, 1818, a radical change was made. There being some obscurity in the county court act passed in 1814, its duties were more clearly defined by a supplemental act of the same session. The civil jurisdiction of the justice's court was in 1817 extended to $40..

Thus it will be observed that at a very early period the Legislature of Illinois fell into the habit, which became chronic, of changing and reorganizing the courts and modifying their jurisdiction at almost every session, down to the adoption of the constitution of 1848. Since then this species of legislation seems to have expended itself in the frequent changes of the terms of court in the various circuits. Next to changing and shifting the well settled principles of the law in its relation to the rights of property and the multifarious transactions of business, nothing is so pernicious as the varying of the means and modes of obtaining redress in our courts. Both ought to be permanent.

During the territorial existence of Illinois three general assemblies were elected by the people—the council holding over the second term. In 1814 Col. Benjamin Stephenson, father of the late gallant James W. Stephenson, of Gelena, was elected delegate to congress, and in 1816 Nathaniel Pope, who took his seat in congress December 1817. The legislature met every year at Kaskaskia, but the sessions were short. New counties were established from time to time; in 1815, the first formed by the legislature, was named Edwards, in honor of the governor. In 1815, White county was organized, named in honor of Capt. Isaac White, who fell at Tippecanoe; in 1816, Monroe, Crawford, Jackson, and Pope, the latter in honor of the newly elected delegate to congress; in 1816, Bond, in honor of Shadrack Bond, first Governor of the State afterward; and in 1818, Union, Franklin, and Washington counties were organized.

We subjoin a few specimens of curious legislation during territorial times. It will be observed that the Solons of that period thundered considerably in the preamble. By a law of September 17, 1809, to regulate the elections, all commissioned officers, either federal or territorial, except justices of the peace and militia officers, were made ineligible to a seat in either branch of the general assembly. The object of this law is not so clear, unless it was to avoid a monopoly of official dignity and importance; but such proscription could not be brooked, and accordingly it fell by act of December 14, 1814, the preamble of which, consisting of 3 whereases, is as huge a specimen of gaseous buncomb to conceal a true intent, and make it appear that the law of 1809 was immensely oppressive to the people, as can be reclaimed from the early annals of political demagoguery in Illinois:

"WHEREAS, The free people of this Territory are as competent as their public servants to decide on whom it is their interest to elect to represent them in the general a sembly; and are too enlightened and independent to recognize the odious and aristocratical doctrine that they are their own worst enemies, or to admit that it is the duty of their representatives to save the people from themselves; and

19

"WHEREAS, This legislature, being composed of the servants, not the masters of the people, cannot without an arbitrary assumption of power impose restrictions upon the latter as to the choice of their representatives, which are not warranted by the express words or necessary implications of the ordinance from which the legislature derives its powers; and

"WHEREAS, The duties of the judges of the county court established by law are such as have heretofore been performed in the territory by justices of the peace, by whom they are also usually performed in many of the States, and there being nothing in the ordinance, nor any reason to exclude from a seat in the legislature those judges of the county, or surveyors, or prosecuting attorneys, that do not apply with equal force to military officers and justices of the peace, and the duties of the former being no more incompatable with a seat in the legislature than those of the latter, therefore," &c. By one short section of two or three lines, laws inconsistent with the above sentiments were abolished.

Another specimen, whose object is disclosed in the preamble, we cannot forbear to give:

"WHEREAS, Voters have hitherto been obliged to vote by ballot, and the ignorant as well as those in embarassed circumstances are thereby subject to be imposed upon by electioneering zealots; and

"WHEREAS, It is consistent with the spirit of representative republican government, since the opening for bribery is so manifest which should ever be suppressed in such a government, for remedy whereof," &c., when follow the sections abolishing the ballot. These reasons would hardly be tenable at the present time, and were doubtless false then.

"By an act of December 24, 1814, "To promote retaliation upon hostile Indians," we find evidences of the extreme measures of defence to which the pioneers had to resort. This may be difficult for us at this time, with a population exceeding 2,500,000, and the Indians many hundreds of miles away, to appreciate. The preamble refers to the "hostile incursions of savages, their indiscriminate slaughter of men, women and children. Experience shows that nothing so much tends to check those blood-thirsty monsters as retaliation," and "to encourage the bravery and enterprises of our fellow citizens and other persons hereafter engaged in frontier defences," it is enacted: 1. That when in such incursions into the settlements, the commission of murder or other depredations by Indians, citizens, rangers, or other persons who shall make prisoners of, or kill such Indians, shall receive a reward for each Indian taken or killed, of $50—if done by rangers or others enlisted in the defence of the country, $25 only. 2. That any person, having obtained permission from a commanding officer on the frontier to go into the territory of hostile Indians, who shall kill a warrior, or take prisoner a squaw or child, is entitled to a reward of $100 for each warrior killed, or squaw or child taken prisoner. 3. That any party of rangers, not exceeding 15, who on leave granted make incursions into the country of hostile Indians, shall receive a reward of $50 for each warrior killed, or squaw or child taken prisoner.

In 1816 a retaliatory act was passed to prevent attorneys at law from Indiana practicing in any of the courts of Illinois, for the reason stated in the preamble, "Whereas, by a law now in force in the State of Indiana, persons who do not reside therein are not permitted to practice in the courts of the said State; and whereas, that restriction is illiberal, unjust, and contrary to those principles of liberality and reciprocity by which each and every State or territory should be governed, therefore," &c. The young Hoosier

State ought not to have put on such exalted airs; but, perhaps, she was right after all, as we find that by act of January 9, 1818, Illinois offered the following premiums for *sustained* indictments. In section 4, fixing the salary of prosecuting attorneys at $100, it is provided that in addition to his salary he shall receive " in each and every case of felony where his indictment is sustained the sum of $15;" and for other " presentments in cases less than felony, "if the indictment was sustained," he was to receive a perquisite of $5. But the most unaccountable feature of this law remains to be told. In section 6 it was provided that if the indictment was sustained, notwithstanding the accused should be acquitted by the traverse jury, the fee of the prosecuting attorney was to be paid by the prosecuting witness. What person, though never so good a citizen, in view of the quirks of the law, the finesse and the ability of counsel, and the notorious uncertainty of how any jury will decide, would, with the prospect of having such fee to pay, care to engage in an attempt to bring an offender to justice. A singular provision was contained in an act of Dec. 22, 1814, which did away with prosecution by an attorney, in cases of treason, murder, or other felony.

By an act of Dec. 31, 1817, the territory of Illinois was in a manner turned over to and parceled out between the medical doctors. It was divided into the east and west districts, the head quarters of the doctors being located at Carmi and Kaskaskia, respectively. The incorporators comprised about all the doctors in the territory, and they proposed and were empowered to hold these extensive fields of practice for their exclusive use and benefit, unless every new comer, proposing to practice the healing art, should first be examined by their board and procure from them permission to do so, for the sum of $10, failing to do which, he was disqualified from collecting his fees in any court or before any magistrate. The act was repealed by the first legislature under the State government.

With the close of the war of 1812, and the cessation of Indian hostilities, the tide of emigration set into Illinois with a volume unequaled and strength unabated. To this prosperity contributed, in no small degree, the act of congress passed in 1813, granting the right of pre-emption to settle upon the public domain. This was the first great lever to move Illinois forward in the path of empire. Prior to this, emigrants in four cases out of five "squatted" on the public lands, without right or title to what they were improving by their labor, and with the ever harrassing doubt that some speculator might spy out and buy their homes before they could do it themselves. Small and inferior improvements were of course the result, and prosperity lagged. To stimulate a man to industry and enterprise, let him be assured that his labor is not misapplied and his title is indisputable. Shadrach Bond, our delegate in congress at the time, contributed largely by his influence in procuring the passage of the act of pre-emption.

Prior to the close of the war of 1812, money was very scarce in the west. The pelts of the deer, raccoon, &c., for which there was a ready market, were to a certain extent a standard of exchange, and supplied in a manner the circulating medium. This condition of the country was greatly improved by the money distributed in the payment of the rangers and militia for their services during the war, and by the increased immigration after its close. Besides, the territorial legislature, emulating the financial aspirations of Ohio and Kentucky, which had each authorized a number of banks, incorporated at its session of 1816, the Bank of Illinois, located at Shawneetown, and at the succeeding session, the banks of Edwardsville and Kaskaskia. They were banks of issue. And the legislature, not satisfied with this, very unjustly lent its aid in forcing the issue of these banks upon the people; not only these, but the issues of the banks of Ohio, Kentucky, Tennessee and Missouri, by the enactment of laws postponing the collection of debts unless the creditor would receive the notes of these banks, were thus likewise forced upon the people. Both became banks of deposit for the United States funds, arising from the sales of public lands, which they used as their own. The government lost by the Edwardsville bank, $54,000, for which judgment was obtained, but never collected ; the Shawneetown bank eventually accounted to the government in full.

This made money, such as it was, abundant, times flush, and rendered a spirit of speculation rife, which was apparently a desirable state of affairs, if it had been all. The circulation of bank notes among a people largely ignorant and unused to them, afforded to the vicious a rare opportunity to set afloat quantities of counterfeit money. This evil became so great that, to restrain it, many of the best citizens of St. Clair county—did what no good citizen should ever do—organized themselves into "Regulating companies," as they designated themselves, to visit swift judgment and condign punishment in the forum of Judge Lynch, upon such offenders as were to their secret cabal proven guilty. A Dr. Estes, of Belleville, was chosen as their captain. Many makers or utterers of the base currency, and for other crimes, fell under their ban and were punished. It created great excitement in the country. Public opinion soon withdrew its countenance and condemned the order. After a few months time its organization ceased to exist.

The visionary schemes of banking operations during territorial times culminated in the Cairo City charter, granted at the session of 1817–18. The low tongue of land between the Ohio and Mississippi rivers at their confluence, was at a very early period regarded as the best position in the west for a great and important city, " as it respects commercial advantages and local supply," as the preamble had it. Such a city, it was argued, must become of vast consequence to the prosperity of the territory. But this low point of land was frequently inundated ; in answer to which it was further argued, that as the ordinary inundations of the two great rivers rarely happened simultaneously, an embankment might be constructed to effectually obviate the injurious consequences of floods. The proprietors and incorporators of the city and bank of Cairo were John G. Comyges, Thomas H. Harris, Charles Slade (afterwards member of Congress), Shadrach Bond (afterwards Governor), Michael Jones, Warren Brown, Edward Humphries, and Charles W. Hunter. These gentlemen proposed the following self-executing scheme to build up a large city there, pour wealth into their coffers, and at the same time render themselves public benefactors. The basis or capital of the banking institution was 2000 Cairo city lots, 66 by 120 feet, valued and limited at $150 each. The streets were to be 80 feet in width. As fast as the lots were sold $50 of the proceeds of each was to be devoted to the construction of a levee to secure them against the floods, and to the improvement of the city by the building of public edifices. The residue—being $100 per lot—was to constitute the capital of the bank, amounting to $200,000. Thus was a great city to be founded! Could Utopia go further? Of course the scheme proved a failure. Cairo languished for many years, but at the present, with actual capital, the power of nerve and muscle, and the concentration of railroads, she is making rapid strides toward the realization of her early dreams. During the internal improvement mania of 1837 this Cairo Bank was galvanized into life, but after flourishing a short period expired.

Another Utopia was the incorporation of a company, at the same session, for the cutting of a canal a few miles north of Cairo to unite the waters of the Mississippi with the Ohio, via the town of America, then in Johnson county, owned by the company. Tolls, wharfage charges, etc., under certain restrictions, were permitted to this company; but nothing came of it. The scheme was some 15 or 18 years since revived, in connection with the present Mound City.

Commerce throughout the early and territorial period of Illinois, and to no inconsiderable extent for some time afterward, was in its helpless infancy. All foreign products consumed here, either natural or manufactured, were brought to Illinois via New Orleans, in keel-boats, pushed at great labor, with long poles, and towed at points with long ropes, a process called "cordelling," against the strong current of the Mississippi, by the hardy boatmen of that day; or wagoned over the Alleghany mountains from Philadelphia to Pittsburg, or from Baltimore to Wheeling, thence in flat-boats floated down the Ohio and landed at convenient points, whence it was again taken by wagons to the final points of destination. A trip from St. Louis to New Orleans and back, with keel-boats, was a six months voyage. But a revolution in the carrying business of the world, was at hand. The power of steam had been utilized, and by Fulton successfully applied to the propulsion of vessels, which produced a wonderful effect upon the western country in contrast between steam as a motor for conveyance and the ordinary mode by keel or flat-boat, which inaugurated a new era.

The first steamboat to ascend the Upper Mississippi, reached St. Louis August 2, 1817. It was named the "General Pike," and was commanded by Captain Jacob Reed.

[Of the first steamboat on the Ohio, the "New Orleans," which was launched at Pittsburgh in the summer of 1811, it is related that, "The novel appearance of the vessel, and the fearful rapidity with which the passage was made over the broad reaches of the river, excited a mixture of terror and surprise among many of the settlers on the banks, whom the rumor of such an invention had never reached: and it is related that on the unexpected arrival of the boat before Louisville, in the course of a fine, still moonlight night, the extraordinary sound which filled the air as the pent up steam was allowed to escape from the valves, on rounding to, produced a general alarm, and multitudes in the town rose from their beds to ascertain the cause. * * The general impression among the good Kentuckians was, that the comet [of 1811, visible at the time with its immense fiery tail, and by the superstitious believed to be the harbinger of war and all sorts of dire evil], had fallen into the Ohio."

"She walked the waters like a thing of life,
And seemed to dare the elements of strife."

At Louisville, owing to the small depth of water on the falls, the boat was detained 3 weeks, during which time several trips were made by her between that place and Cincinnati. The waters finally rose, and the trip to New Orleans was resumed. On reaching the Lower Mississippi, the boat was nearly overwhelmed by the earthquakes which rocked the waters of the great river to and fro, and which continued for several days,

The pursuits of the people during territorial times, were mainly agricultural, varied by hunting and trapping. Few merchants were required to supply the ordinary articles of consumption not produced or manufactured at home. Coffee, tea, and sugar did not then generally enter into the daily meals of the family. Materials for personal wear were either grown, or taken in the chase, and manufactured into garments by wife or daughter, the merchant supplying only some of the dye stuff to color the wool, flax or cotton. Foreign manufactured boots and shoes, or hats and caps, were worn but by few—home-made moccasins and raccoon caps supplying the place. Mechanics in pursuit of their trades, are seldom pioneers, and every settler was his own carpenter. The houses, mostly log cabins, were built without glass, nails, hinges or locks; the furniture, too, modeled in the same rude fashion, was made by the same hand. Yokes for oxen, and harness for horses, the carts and wagons in daily use—without tires, boxes or iron—whose woeful creakings, for the want of tar, which was not imported, might be heard at a great distance, all were manufactured as occason required by self-taught artificers.*

commencing on the morning of the 16th of December, 1811. They were severest in the neighborhood of New Madrid, where, on the Tennessee side, a few miles back of the river, the earth sunk in many places 50 and 60 feet, carrying with it great trees left standing erect, producing what is known as the Reel-foot lake —Rambler in North America.

*As an instance of the ready ingenuity of the times, it is related of James Lemon, a well known pioneer of Monroe county, an old style Baptist preacher, and a farmer by occupation, who manufactured the harness for his teams as occasion required, that being employed plowing a piece of stubble ground one day, on turning out for dinner he left the harness on the beam of the plough, as was his wont. His son, not differing from the proverbial minister's boys perhaps, who had assisted him by removing the straw from the clogging plow with a pitchfork, remained behind long enough to conceal one of the collars, that he might have a playing spell while his father was occupied in making another. But his plot failed; on returning after dinner and missing the collar, his father, reflecting for a few minutes, promptly divested himself of his leather breeches, stuffed the legs with stubble, straddled them across the neck of the horse for a collar, and plowed the remainder of the day bare-legged requiring the assistance of the truantly inclined boy all the time. At this day, to provide for such a mishap, half-day would have been spent in going to town after another collar, and the boy would probaby have gained his point.—From Ford's History of Illinois.

CHAPTER XXVI.

ORGANIZATION OF THE STATE GOVERNMENT—ADMINISTRATION OF GOVERNOR BOND.

Our Northern Boundary—First Constitutional Convention and Something of the Instrument Framed—Governor Bond—Lieutenant-governor Menard—Meeting of the Legislature and Election of State Officers—First Supreme Court—Hard Times and First State Bank—Organization of Counties.

———

By the year 1818, owing to her rapid increase of population, Illinois aspired to a position among the sisterhood of sovereign States. Accordingly, the territorial legislature, in session at Kaskaskia in January of that year, prepared and sent to Nathaniel Pope, our delegate in congress, their petition praying for the admission of Illinois into the Union on an equal footing with the original States. The petition was promptly presented, and the committee on territories in due time reported a bill for the admission of Illinois with a population of 40,000. The ordinance of 1787 required 60,000. Mr. Pope, looking to the future of this State, succeeding in amending the bill as it came from the hands of the committee, in several essential features. One of these was to extend the northern boundary of the State to the parallel of 40 degrees 30 minutes north latitude. The 5th section of the ordinance of 1787, required that at least three States be formed out of the Northwest territory—defining the boundary of the western State by the Mississippi, the Ohio and the Wabash rivers, and a line running due north from Post Vincennes, on the last named stream, to Canada. This included the present States of Illinois and Wisconsin. But, by a proviso, it was reserved "that if congress shall hereafter find it expedient, they shall have authority to form one or two States in that part of said territory which lies north of an east and west line drawn through the southerly bend of Lake Michigan." The line of 40 deg. 30 min. extended the boundary 50 miles farther north. To the vigilance of Nathaniel Pope, therefore, are we indebted for a coast on Lake Michigan to this extent: for the site occupied by the present mighty city of Chicago; for the northern terminus of the Illinois and Michigan canal, and for the lead mines of Galena—all of which come within that extension. It was upon the above quoted language of the ordinance of 1787, which was declared a compact to remain forever unalterable, that Wisconsin subsequently based her claim to the 14 northern counties of this State.

While the foregoing were paramount considerations with the people of Illinois, others were urged with much force and entire effectiveness upon congress, acting for the nation at large. Even at that day statesmen had not failed to mark the inherent weakness, and consequent easy dissolution, of confederated republics. The late civil war had not then demonstrated the strength and unity of the American confederation through the loyalty of the people. European statesmen had entertained no other thought than that at the first internal hostile trouble, the bonds of the Union would be broken and scattered to the winds. It was easily shown that the geographical position of Illinois made her the key in the western arch of States. The southern extremity of Illinois penetrated far between the slaves States down to the main Mississippi, affording an outlet to the Gulf the year round, and skirted with hundreds of miles of navigable rivers on either side ; to give her, therefore, a fair coast on the lake would also unite her interests through the strong bonds of trade and commerce with the north and east. Linking thus the north and the south by her geographical position and the ties of intercourse, her interests must be conservative, and she would ever exert a controlling influence upon the perpetuity of the Union. This view has been amply verified in the late war by the prompt occupation of Cairo, and the rally of her near 200,000 sons to the national standard.

Another amendment was, that the three-fifths of the 5 per cent fund from the sale of public lands, applied to the construction of public works in other States carved out of the northwest territory, should instead be devoted by the legislature to the encouragement of education ; one-sixth of which to be exclusively bestowed on a college or university. These important amendments were suggested and urged by Mr. Pope without instruction, but they received the ready sanction of the people, and to-day we are realizing the full fruition of his foresight.* The bill became a law April 18, 1818.

*Nathaniel Pope was an able lawyer, and in his official relations was ever faithful to his trusts. His first appearance in Illinois, as we have seen, was as secretary of the territory. In 1816, he was elected delegate to congress and procured the enabling act for the admission of Illinois as a State. Subsequently he was appointed United States district judge, in which capacity he served for many years, residing in Springfield. He died in 1850,

[NOTE —The question of our northern boundary agitated the people of the section concerned for many years, entering into their political conflicts and exercising an important influence upon their local affairs. Many of the old settlers down to a late date, condemned this striking departure from the ordinance of 1787, which fixed the present line 50 miles further north. Boundary meetings at various places in the 14 northern counties continued to be held from time to time, showing the feeling to be deep and wide spread. We note the proceedings of a large meeting held at Oregon City, January 22, 1842, as showing the grounds of complaint, and the purpose of the people to either belong to Wisconsin or set up for themselves:

" *Resolved,* That in the opinion of this meeting, that part of the northwest territory, which lies north of an 'east and west line through the southerly bend or extreme of Lake Michigan,' belongs to and of right ought to be a part of the State or States which have been or may be formed north of said line."

Wisconsin was yet a territory. They resolved further that the ordinance of 1787 could not be altered or changed without the consent of the people of the original States and of the northwest territory ; that as part of the people of said territory, they would not so consent ; that the lines designated in the ordinance were better suited to the geographical situation and local interests of their region ; that they were decidedly opposed to place any of the territory north of said line within the jurisdiction of a State south of it ; that they recommended the legislature of Wisconsin to apply for admission into the Union, claiming the line of the ordinance as

In pursuance of the enabling act a convention was called to draft the first constitution of the State of Illinois, which assembled at Kaskaskia in July, 1818, and completed its labors by signing the constitution on the 26th of August following. We subjoin the names of the delegates, and the counties which they represented, in the order of their organization:

St. Clair county—Jesse B. Thomas, John Messinger, James Lemon, jr.

Randolph—George Fisher, Elias Kent Kane.

Madison—Benjamin Stephenson, Joseph Borough, Abraham Prickett.

Gallatin—Michael Jones, Leonard White, Adolphus Frederick Hubbard.

Johnson—Hezekiah West, Wm. McFatridge.

Edwards—Seth Gard, Levi Compton.

White—Willis Hargrave, Wm. McHenry.

Monroe—Caldwell Carns, Enoch Moore.

Pope—Samuel O'Melveny, Hamlet Ferguson.

Jackson—Conrad Will, James Hall, jr.

Crawford—Joseph Kitchell, Edward N. Cullom.

Bond—Thomas Kilpatrick, Samuel G. Morse.

Union—Wm. Echols, John Whitaker.

Washington—Andrew Bankson.*

Franklin—Isham Harrison, Thomas Roberts.

Jesse B. Thomas was chosen president, and Wm. C. Greenup secretary of the convention.

The constitution was not submitted to a vote of the people for their approval or rejection; nor did the people have much to do with the choice or election of officers generally under it, other than that of governors, the general assemblies, sheriffs and coroners. Notwithstanding the elective franchise was in a blazon manner extended to all white male inhabitants above the age of 21, having a residence in the State of 6 months next preceding any election, which it will be perceived included aliens and possibly invited immigration, there was scarcely an office left to be filled by its exercise.

The electors or people were not trusted with the choice of State officers, other than mentioned; nor of their judges, either supreme, circuit, or probate; nor of their prosecuting attorneys, county or circuit clerks, recorders, or justices of the peace; the appointment of nearly all these being vested in the general assembly, which body was not slow to avail itself of the powers thus conferred to their full extent. The language of the schedule was, "an auditor of public accounts, an attorney general, and such other officers of the State as may be necessary, may be appointed by the general assembly, whose duties may be regulated by law." It is said to have been a question for many years, in view of this language,

their southern boundary: that they disclaimed any intention to absolve themselves from any pecuniary responsibility created by the legislature of Illinois on account of the internal improvement system, etc. The resolutions were adopted unanimously. A committee of 9 was appointed to proceed to Madison, with full power to consult with the governor and the legislature of Wisconsin territory. Governor Doty and the legislature gave them their assurances of earnest co-operation in petitioning congress toward the end in view. But nothing ever came of all the clamor. The essential point was, whether the acts of the congress of the confederated States are of such binding force that a congress of the United States cannot annul or amend them —whether the former possessed a higher power than the latter.

*Bankson's colleague died during the session of the convention.

what was "an officer of the State." The governors were for a time allowed to appoint State's attorneys, recorders, State commissioners, bank directors, &c., but the legislatures afterward vested by law the appointment of all these and many more in themselves. Occasionally, when in full political accord, the governor would be allowed the appointing power pretty freely, to perhaps be shorn of by a succeeding legislature. In the administration of Duncan, who had forsaken Jackson and incurred the displeasure of the dominant party, the governor was finally stripped of all patronage, except the appointment of notaries public and public administrators. It was a bad feature of the constitution; it not only deprived the people of their just rights to elect the various officers as at present, but led hordes of place hunters to repair to the seat of government at every session of the legislature, to besiege and torment members for office. Indeed, this was the chief occupation of many an honorable member. Innumerable intrigues and corruptions for place and power were thus indulged.

To the governor was denied the veto power; but he, jointly with the four supreme judges, was constituted a council to revise all bills passed, before they should become laws. For this purpose the judges were required to attend at the seat of government during the sessions of the legislature, without compensation. The validity of all laws was thus decided in advance. If the council of revision, or a majority, deemed it improper for any bill to become a law, their objections were to be noted in writing; but the bill might, notwithstanding, be passed over their objections by a majority and become a law. While the executive is commonly a co-ordinate branch of the law-making power, here he was entirely stripped; and while the judicial department is never thus vested, here it was clothed with a *quasi* legislative prerogative.

The constitution was about the first organic law of any State in the Union to abolish imprisonment for debt. It did not prohibit the legislature from granting divorces; and this was a fruitful source of legislation, as the old statutes abundantly testify. But its worst feature, perhaps, was the want of a limitation against the legislature loaning or pledging the faith and credit of the State in aid of, or to the undertaking of, any public or private enterprise; or to the aid of any individuals, associations, or corporations. The absence of such most necessary limitations, caused her repeated connections afterward with banking schemes, and her undertaking the vast system of internal improvement in 1837, all of which proved detrimental to her credit, harrassing and expensive to her finances, and came near bankrupting and completing her ruin. Of the members of the convention, Elias Kent Kane, afterward a senator in congress, is mentioned with commendation as a leading spirit, and as largely stamping the constitution with its many excellencies.

["During the sitting of the convention the Rev. Mr. Wiley and congregation, of a sect called Covenanters, in Randolph county, sent in their petition asking that body to declare in the constitution, that "Jesus Christ was the head of the government, and that the Holy Scriptures were the only rule of faith and practice." The petition was not treated with any attention, wherefore the Covenanters have never fully recognized the State government. They have looked upon it as "an heathen and unbaptized government," which denies Christ; for which reason they have constantly refused to work the roads, serve on juries, hold any office, or do any other act showing that they recognized the government. For a long time they refused to vote, and never did until the election of 1824, when the question was, whether Illinois should be made a slave State, when they voted for the first time, and unanimously against slavery."—Governor Ford's History.]

The first election under the constitution, for governor, lieut. governor, and members of the general assembly, was, according to the appointment of the convention, held on the third Thursday, and the two succeeding days, in September, 1818. All white male inhabitants 21 years old, residing in the State at the adoption of the constitution were permitted to vote. The general assembly was to meet at Kaskaskia on the first Monday (being the 5th) of Oct. following, to set the machinery of the new government in motion. After that, regular sessions were to commence on the first Mondays of December. Shadrach Bond was elected governor and Pierre Menard lieutenant governor, as had been expected even before the formation of the constitution; they had no opposition. Their terms of service were till 1822, four years.

Governor Bond was born in Frederick county, Maryland, in 1773, and was raised a farmer on his father's plantation, and agriculture was his pursuit in Illinois, whither he emigrated in 1794. He had received but a plain English education. To a convivial, benevolent disposition, he joined a naturally shrewd observation of men and a clear appreciation of events. His person was erect, standing 6 feet in hight, and after middle life he became portly, weighing 200 pounds. His features were strongly masculine, complexion dark, hair jet, and eyes hazel. He was a favorite with the ladies.† His jovial disposition, thorough honesty and unostentatious intercourse with the people, made him the most popular man of his day. He had been a member of the general assembly under the Indiana Territory, a delegate to congress in 1812, and in the latter capacity he procured the right of pre-emption on the public domain; in 1814 he was appointed receiver of the public moneys at Kaskaskia. After his gubernatorial term expired he ran in 1824, for congress against Daniel P. Cook, but was beaten. Subsequently he was appointed register of the land office at Kaskaskia; where he died, in peace and contentment, April 11, 1830. The county of Bond was named in honor of his memory.

Pierre Menard was born at Quebec in 1767. At the age of 19, inspired by adventure, he came to Vincennes and entered the employ of Col. Vigo, a merchant. In 1790 he removed to Kaskaskia and engaged in merchandising with DuBois, of Vincennes. By his trade with the Indians, and in various public capacities, he soon became well known. Nature made him frank, kind and honest; his mind, with but an ordinary education, was strong, and his judgment quick and unerring. His industry was wonderful, being never idle. For many years he was government agent for the Indians, and that race had the most implicit confidence in his integrity. As a merchant, it is said, he could buy their peltries at half the price a "Long-Knife" would have to pay. He had been a member of the lower house of the legislature while Illinois was under the Indiana regime, and a member of the Illinois legislative council from 1812 to 1818, being the president of that body. In the framing of the constitution the qualifications for lieutenant governor were first fixed the same as those of the governor—one of which was citizenship of the United States for 30 years; but as that would exclude Col. Menard, who had been naturalized only some two years, the convention changed this provision in the shedule as a special favor to him, he being generally looked

† Reynold's Pioneer History.

forward to for that position. After the expiration of his term of office he declined all further tenders of office, accepting only that of United States Commissioner to treat with the Indians, whose character he knew so well. He accumulated quite a fortune, but it was greatly impaired by that kindness of heart which allowed him to become security for his friends. In 1839 the legislature honored his name by establishing the county of Menard. He died in 1844 at the ripe age of 77 years.

The State legislature met at the appointed time, October 5th, 1818. Ninian Edwards, the retiring executive of the defunct territorial government, and Jesse B. Thomas, one of the federal judges for the territory, who had also been president of the constitutional convention, both looked forward to the United States senatorship, and were not disappointed in their aspirations. Our member to the lower house of congress at the time, was John McLean, elected in the September previous, in one of the most memorable political campaigns ever had in Illinois, Daniel P. Cook being his opponent. Elijah C. Berry was elected auditor of public accounts, John Thomas, State treasurer, Daniel P. Cook, attorney general, and Messrs. Blackwell & Berry State printers. Elias Kent Kane was appointed Secretary of State. The supreme court, the judges whereof were required also to do circuit duty, was to consist of one chief justice and three associate justices. Both houses again met in joint session on the 8th, and on the first ballot Joseph Phillips was elected chief justice by 34 out of 40 votes cast; Thomas C. Brown receiving 4, and Henry S. Dodge 3. For associate justices, Wm. P. Foster and Thomas C. Brown were chosen on the first ballot, Henry S. Dodge receiving at the same time 18 votes, William Wilson 15, C. R. Matheny 9, John Warnock 1, James W. Whiting 1, and Joseph Kitchell 7. On balloting again, a new candidate, John Reynolds, afterwards governor, was brought forward and on the second ballot elected by 22 out of the 40 votes cast. Phillips was a lawyer of fine intellectual endowment. He had been a captain in the regular army, and during the war of 1812 had seen service in Illinois; afterward he was appointed secretary of the territory in place of Nathaniel Pope. Being ambitious, he aspired above the dull routine of the court at that day, and in 1822, becoming a candidate for governor against Coles, resigning his place upon the bench on the 4th of July, but was defeated. This was more than his high-strung nature would brook, and with feelings of disgust at the ingratitude of the people, afterward quitted the State and removed to Tennessee. On the 31st of August, 1822, Thomas Reynolds was appointed in his place. Brown was a large, somewhat stately looking, affable man, yielding in his disposition, with little industry for study, and few of the higher qualities for a judge. He remained on the bench till the constitution of 1848 went into effect, a period exceeding thirty years.

Reynolds, in his "Own Times," written many years later, tells how he came to be chosen a member of that exalted tribunal, the supreme court. At the time he resided at Cahokia and had no intention of visiting the session of the legislature, which was dispensing so many fat things on the first organization of the State government. He cared little who obtained office, and certainly wanted none for himself. But being urged by his friends, he joined them in a visit to Kaskaskia. Upon arrival they found much excitement and commotion at the capital, incident to the selection of State officers. In a few days he was urged to give his assent to become a candidate for supreme judge. This request, he says, broke upon him like a clap of thunder. His consent was yielded, he was elected. His experience in the law was four years practice of "commerce in land." * "I speculated, sold land and bought two stores of dry goods, amounting to $10,000." His first term of court was to him a "strange and novel business." This was at Covington, Washington county, among his former comrades of Indian rangers, who now failed to draw the line of distinction due him as a supreme judge. The sheriff, unmindful of the exalted position of his old comrade in arms, on opening court, made proclamation of the fact, without rising from the rude bench in the court room which he occupied astride, saying, in a familiar tone, "Boys, the court is now open, John is on the bench." These omissions of ceremony were not distasteful to his honor, for he utterly detested any kind of mock dignity, though he says he was not regardless of the "solemn, serious dignity and decorum" proper in the proceedings of court.*

Foster, another of the supreme judges, resigned within a year—June 22, 1819. He "was almost a total stanger in the country. He was a great rascal, but no one knew it then, he having been a citizen of the State only for about three weeks before he was elected. He was no lawyer, never having either studied or practiced law; but a man of winning, polished manners, and withal a gentlemanly swindler, from some part of Virginia. * * He was believed to be a clever fellow, in the American sense of that phrase, and a good hearted soul. He was assigned to hold courts in the circuit on the Wabash; but being fearful of exposing his utter incompetency, he never went near any of them. In the course of one year he resigned his high office, but took care first to pocket his salary, and then removed out of the State. He

*Gov. Ford in his history, writes: "This same judge presided at a court in which a man named Green was convicted of murder; and it became his unpleasant duty to pronounce sentence of death upon the culprit. He called the prisoner before him, and said to him: 'Mr. Green, the jury in their verdict say you are guilty of murder, and the law says you are to be hung. Now I want you and all your friends down on Indian Creek, to know that it is not I who condemns you, but it is the jury and the law. Mr. Green, the law allows you time for preparation, and so the court wants to know what time you would like to be hung.' To this the prisoner replied, 'May it please the court, I am ready at any time; those who kill the body have no power to kill the soul; my preparation is made, and I am ready to suffer at any time the court may appoint.' The judge then said, 'Mr. Green, you must know that it is a very serious matter to be hung; it can't happen to a man more than once in his life, and you had better take all the time you can get; the court will give you until this day four weeks. Mr. Clerk, look at the almanac, and see whether this day four weeks comes on Sunday.' The clerk looked at the almanac, as directed, and reported that 'that day four weeks came on Thursday.' The judge then said, 'Mr. Green, the court gives you until this day four weeks, at which time you are to be hung.' The case was prosecuted by James Turney, Esq., the attorney general of the State, who here interposed and said: 'May it please the court, on solemn occasions like the present, when the life of a human being is to be sentenced away for crime, by an earthly tribunal, it is usual and proper for courts to pronounce a formal sentence, in which the leading features of the crime shall be brought to the recollection of the prisoner, a sense of his guilt impressed upon his conscience, and in which the prisoner should be duly exhorted to repentance, and warned against the judgment in the world to come.' To this the judge replied, 'O! Mr. Turney, Mr Green understands the whole matter as well as if I had preached to him a month. He knows he has got to be hung this day four weeks. You understand it in that way, Mr. Green, don't you?' 'Yes,' said the prisoner; upon which the judge remanded him to jail, and the court then adjourned."
Reynolds, in his work entitled "My Own Times," takes pains to deny the "silly fabrication recorded in history," and says: "I may not have acted in that frigid, unfeeling and mechanical manner that would please heartless and superficial men, who generally write and detail these tea-pot slanders. * * I considered them both [alluding to the case of one Bennet also] guilty, and the judgment of the court was so understood, that they were both to be executed."

afterwards became a noted swindler, moving from city to city, and living by swindling strangers, and prostituting his daughters, who were very beautiful."[*]

On the 7th of August, 1819, William Wilson was appointed to fill the vacancy created by the resignation of Foster. Wilson was a young man, scarcely 25 years old, of spotless character, good education (though not collegiate), and fair attainments as a lawyer. He was social in his disposition, candid and artless by nature, with a manner pleasant and winning. He proved a sound judge, and presided with a dignity which inspired the utmost respect in the bar and attendants. Thus organized, and with these men to guide her helm of State, was Illinois launched on her career of independence among the sisterhood of sovereign States. The men who, a little over a half century ago, assisted at the political birth of this now great State, were, many of them, the equals in sturdy virtues of the heroes of the Revolution, and the peers in commanding intellect of the founders of any the States; but, without exception, they have passed to the land of shadows, and many of them lie buried in obscure graves, their deeds of greatness unknown to the great majority of the busy throng of to-day.

But Illinois had not yet been declared admitted into the Union; congress was not in session. At the October meeting of the assembly therefore, no legislation or business other than the election of officers, was attempted, for obvious reasons. After a session of eight days a recess was taken till the first Monday in January, 1819. In the meantime congress met, and by resolution of December 3d, 1818, declared Illinois to be "one of the United States of America, and admitted into the Union on an equal footing with the original States in all respects."

Of the 15 counties organized at the adoption of the constitution, the farthest north was Bond. Only about one-fourth of the territory of the State was embraced in these 15 counties. The settled portions of the State were all south of a line drawn from Alton, via Carlyle, to Palestine on the Wabash; but within this area were large tracts of wilderness country of several days journey in extent; the settlements being mostly scattered along the borders of the great rivers. All the vast prairies north of this line, comprising the most fertile lands of the State, and nearly every acre of which was susceptible of cultivation, ready cleared and prepared, as it were, for the hand of the husbandman, was a howling wilderness, uninhabited save by the red savage and the prairie wolf.

The population of the new State for admission into the Union was required to be 40,000; the census of 1820 showed 55,211. This was a remarkable ratio of increase—exceeding 300 per centum within the preceding decade—the greater part of which had come hither since the close of the war of 1812. Of this population, scarcely a twentieth part were the descendants of the old French or Canadian settlers, whose blood, by their long isolation, had become freely intermingled with that of the Indians. Nineteen-twentieths of the residue were Americans, and with the exception of some from Pennsylvania, were almost wholly from the southern States. The latter stamped their peculiar characteristics of manners and

[*] Ford's History Illinois,

customs, in business and social relations, upon all of southern Illinois, which are in great part retained to this day. The means of education were extremely limited, and with the exception of one school for surveying and book-keeping, the only branches of learning taught at that time were spelling, reading, writing and arithmetic. Nor were the latter generally taught, or without price. Professional men came almost invariably from abroad, unless they were ministers of the gospel, who, at that day, more than perhaps at the present, in obedience to the voice of the Lord, entered at once upon their sacred calling without other preparations than a diligent reading of the scriptures—the free quotation of which, often without point or application, and their vehement exhortations being about all that was expected of them by the people.

In his message to the general assembly, January, 1819, Governor Bond reported the treasury of the new State in an embarrassed condition, and advised a temporary loan. The total revenue of the State, due December 1st, 1818, was reported by the auditor at $7,510 44, part of which was in the hands of delinquent collectors, while for still another part, the sheriffs of St. Clair and Gallatin counties had refused to receive the warrants. A temporary loan of $25,000 was therefore authorized by the legislature. The governor also advised a revision and modification of the territorial laws for the punishment of crimes, the penalties whereof were unnecessarily severe. But this the legislature did not view in the same light, and no amelioration in the barbarous penalties of the territorial code was made. They were re-enacted verbatim (the enacting clause alone being changed to conform to the new government), with all the whippings, the stocks and pillory, and death by hanging for rape, arson, horse-stealing, etc., left intact. They were, however, modified at the session of 1821; and not only the criminal code, but all the standard laws were regularly altered at every session down to the revision of 1827.*

The building of jails and a penitentiary was also recommended by the governor; so also the leasing of the school sections—the proceeds to be expended for education, and those from the township of seminary lands, to be reserved for subsequent use. The governor also recommended at that early day, the taking of some steps toward the construction of the Illinois and Michigan canal, a work which was not accomplished, however, for thirty years after, but through which, at this writing, by the enterprise of Chicago, the limpid waters of Lake Michigan course their way to the Gulf of Mexico.

The legislature fixed the salaries of the State officers as follows: Governor and supreme judges, $1000 each; auditor, $700; secretary of State, $600; treasurer, $500; payable quarterly out of the State treasury. The per diem compensation allowed to members of the legislature, and also to the delegates who framed the constitution, was $4, and to each of the presiding officers $5.

The State revenue was chiefly raised by a tax upon lands owned by non-residents, which at an early day fell almost wholly upon the military tract between the Illinois and Mississippi rivers, while

*"For a long time the rage for amending and altering was so great, that it was said to be a good thing that the Holy Scriptures did not have to come before the legislature, for that body would be certain to alter or amend them, so that no one could tell what was or was not the word of God, any more than could be told what was or was not the law of the State."—Ford's History Ill.

the county revenues were raised by a tax on personal property, including slaves or indentured servants, and by a resident land tax. Unlike as at present, the valuation of lands were then fixed by law, in three classes, of $2, $3 and $4 per acre, respectively. The levies of taxes were made according to the estimates of the sums required to defray accruing expenses, either State or county. Non-residents were required to enter their lands for taxation directly with the auditor, under oath as to class; and the taxes on their lands were payable directly to this officer. The collection of the State revenue on delinquent lands was enforced by sending lists thereof to the sheriffs of counties where situated to be exposed at public sale. The penalty for failure of payment was three times the tax imposed and costs.

A peculiar feature in the legislation of the times was the making of important public improvements by means of private lottery schemes. Thus, the navigation of the Big Wabash at the Grand Rapids, near Palmyra, by the digging of a canal, was to be accomplished by a lottery. Perhaps a superfluous provision in the law was, that the overplus of any moneys arising from the scheme, should, at the discretion of the managers, be laid out in further improvements. Other like schemes had for their object the drainage of ponds in the American Bottom, the building of levees, and the reclamation of lands; all of them most worthy objects, but, as might have been expected, the means provided were very inadequate to the accomplishment of the ends. The session of 1819, was the last ever held at the ancient village of Kaskaskia.

We have noted the fact that the legislature, during the latter years of territorial existence, granted charters to several banks. Prior to that, Ohio and Kentucky had each a large number in operation. Missouri also authorized two at St. Louis. The result was that paper money became very abundant, times flush, credit unlimited, the throng of immigrants, all with more or less means to invest large, and property rose rapidly in value. A spirit of speculation became rife. Towns were numerously platted, lots purchased on credit, houses built on promises, government lands entered in large quantities—the price at the time being $2 per acre, one-fourth cash (the paper money of the banks being received at the land offices, which also deposited with the bank), and three-fourths on 5 years time, under penalty of forfeiture for non-payment at maturity of contracts. Everybody invested to the utmost limit of his credit, with the confident expectation of realizing a handsome advance before the expiration of his credit, from the coming immigrant. The merchants, ever enterprising, bought vast quantities of goods on time, transported hither by the increased facilities of steam navigation, while the ready credit obtained at the stores, begot extravagance among the people. Everybody was inextricably in debt to everybody.

By 1819, it became apparent that a day of reckoning would approach before their dreams of fortune could be realized. Banks everywhere began to waver, paper money became depreciated, while gold and silver were driven out of circulation by the irredeemable currency. The legislature, at its session of 1819, sought to bolster up the times, or stem the tide of approaching disaster, by incorporating a new Bank of Illinois, a monster concern, with a capital of $2,000,000; stock was divided into shares of $100, which might be subscribed by corporations or individuals, the State reserving the right to take part or all that should remain, as the condition of the treasury might warrant, whenever the legislature should deem it proper to do so. The charter was to run 27 years. When 15 per cent of the stock was paid in, it was to go into operation. The total amount of its debts was never to exceed twice the amount of paid up stock, beyond which officers were to become liable individually. It might deal in specie, exchange, or paper pledged by goods sold, or goods which might be the proceeds of its lands. This last was a very objectionable feature. Books were opened for subscription in divers towns, but not a dollar of stock was ever taken, and it utterly failed to meet the exigency of the times.

By 1820, the banks of neighboring States were broken, and those of Illinois suspended; specie had fled the country; immigrants came as moneyless as were those who had looked forward to their well filled purses; paper towns failed to grow into flourishing villages; trade flagged; there was no commerce to bring money into the country; real estate was unsaleable; while contracts wildly entered into, matured. As the folly of the people became apparent, ruin stared them in the face. Enormous sacrifices of property under prospective executions must ensue, unless some scheme for relief could be devised. In August, 1820, a new legislature was elected. The genius of this body was invoked on the behalf of the embarassed people. At its session of 1820–21, it willingly addressed itself to this work, and evolved the "Illinois State Bank" with a capital of half a million dollars, based entirely upon the credit of the State.

The bills of this bank, issued in from $1 to $20 notes, were, by section 12, directed to be loaned to the people in sums of $100 on personal security, deemed to be, in the opinion of the board, good and sufficient; and all sums over $100—not to exceed $1,000 to any one borrower—on real estate security of double value. Interest was six per cent. To bring the bank nearer to the people, a mother bank was located at Vandalia with branches well distributed—at Edwardsville, Brownsville, Shawneetown and the county seat of Edwards county—the State, for the convenience of the public, being apportioned into 4 bank districts. Each county was entitled to a director, who with the bank officers, were all elected by the legislature. The notes were made receivable in payment of all State and county taxes, costs and fees, and the salaries of the public officers were payable in them. They were also made a species of legal tender, for unless an execution creditor endorsed his execution "The bills of the State Bank of Illinois, or either of the branches, will be received in discharge of this execution," the defendant was entitled to three years stay by replevy and personal security, a most unjust feature. Three hundred thousand dollars were ordered to be issued immediately, to be distributed among the respective districts in proportion to the inhabitants thereof. When the banks commenced operation, every one who was able to furnish security, borrowed his $100, and those with lands unencumbered, took their $1000 on mortgages; and as both officers and directors were mostly politicians looking forward to place or political advancement, few applicants, it has been inferred, were denied or had their endorsers closely scrutinized; thus the $300,000 were soon absorbed by the people, and little of it was ever paid back. Many of those who received accommodations, regarded it from the start as " so much clear gain," and neither did nor intended to pay, although at the subsequent depreciation of the currency it was not difficult to do so.

The issues bore 2 per cent annual interest, and were redeemable by the State in 10 years time, which constituted them in fact bills of credit, whose emission is inimical to the constitution of the United States.* About this point, no trouble was made however, other than that the council of revision pointed out this among other objections to the bill; but it was promptly passed notwith- standing. Although no provision was made for the conversion of the notes into specie at any time, it was, nevertheless, confidently believed that the bills would keep at par with gold and silver, and our delegation in congress was gravely instructed to use their utmost exertion to procure them to be made receivable at the land offices in this State. "When this resolution was put to a vote in the senate, the old French lieutenant-governor, Colonel Menard, presiding over that body, did up the business as follows: Gentle- men of *de* senate, it is moved and seconded *dat de* notes of *dis* bank be made land office money. All in favor of *dat* motion say aye; all against it, say no. It is decided in *de* affirmative. And now, gentlemen, *I bet you $100 he never be made land office money.*† Such proved to be the fact.

The legislature were not unadvised of their infatuation. John McLean, subsequently a senator in congress, was speaker of the house. He was opposed to the measure, and his power as a forcible debater was justly dreaded by the bank men. It is rulable to debate all important bills in committee of the whole, that the speaker may participate. To avoid an arraignment of their bantling by him, the bank majority resorted to the trick of refusing to go into committee of the whole. Burning with indig- nation at such treatment, he promptly resigned the speakership, and taking the floor, denounced in scathing terms the expensive folly of the scheme, presaging the injurious results which must inevitably flow from its passage, involving creditors in ruin and the State in bankruptcy. But it was pre-determined to pass the bill, which was done over the veto by the requisite majority. The issues of the bank did not long remain at par; as their worthless- ness became apparent, good money was driven out of circulation. This was particularly so with small coins, and it became so diffi- cult to make change that bills had to be cut in two. By various steps, they depreciated to 25 cents on the dollar; and with this worthless State currency were the people cursed for a period ex- ceeding four years. By the year 1824, their depreciation had the effect to almost impede the wheels of government. The ordinary revenue for State purposes, amounting to some $30,000 annually, was raised by a tax on lands belonging to non-residents; the expen- ditures in good money equaled the revenue. As taxes might be paid in bills of the State bank, non-residents, as well as residents, availed themselves of the depreciated currency for this purpose. Taxes from non-residents were collected biennially—an unfair ad-

*Craig vs. the State of Missouri.—Supreme court of the U. S.
†Ford's Illinois.

vantage over residents whose tax went into the county treasuries. But the latter, in many instances, resorted to the artifice of listing their lands in the names of unknown or fictitious persons supposed to be non-residents, gaining thus the same advantages, which was a prolific source of injury to many counties. While the State thus nominally received its full revenue, it was in point of fact worth only one-fourth, or one-third, as much as good money. Under these circumstances, the legislature, the department of the government that had made the bills a quasi legal-tender which an execution creditor was compelled to take or wait three years for his pay—than which nothing could be more unjust—hesitated not to commit the enormity of voting themselves, the State officials, judges, and for other expenses, their per diem compensation, salaries, etc., in treble the amount of auditor's warrants, rated with the depreciated stuff to equal in value good money. Thus while the ordinary expenses of the State government were $30,000 annually, by these practices they were swollen to $90,000, which the tax-payers had ultimately to foot. Never was law more dishonorable. With such examples from their law makers, what would have been the moral effect upon the people had they been influenced by them. A crumb was, however, thrown to the latter. It was enacted for the accommodation of the debtors—the larger class, but again most unjustly to the creditors—authorizing the rendering of judgments against them for only one-third of their debts, and exempting, by another act, all real property, other than mortgaged lands, "from liability to satisfy judgments for said debts."

This banking folly, not to characterize it worse, is said to have cost the State, first and last, during the ten years for which its charter was to run, the full amount of the authorized issue, $500,000, though $300,000 was all that was ever actually issued. Its pernicious influence on the general prosperity of the State, and its damaging effects upon the revenue, became speedily so palpable that no legislature possessed hardihood enough to encounter the public resentment by proposing that the State issue the remaining $2000,000 provided for in the charter. Still issuing auditor's warrants and paying them out at $3 for $1 to defray State expenses generally, as authorized by the legislature, was infinitely worse. In 1825, the State thus paid out $107,000 in auditor's warrants when its ordinary annual expenses in good money would not at the uttermost have exceeded $35,000. This was equivalent to borrowing money at 200 per centum interest—a most ruinous policy if well followed.

The current expenses of the principal bank for the year 1824, exceeded the discounts by $2,403 90. Without ever meeting the fond expectations of its friends—unless it was in the contrivance of robbing the creditor class for the benefit and relief of the debtor class—without observing any of its promises, the old bank, a frightful source of legislation all its life, lingered out the allotted time of charter, and was finally wound up by the State in 1831. This was done by means of the "Wiggins loan" of $100,000, which gave to the State the requisite funds. This loan was for a long time, unpopular in many sections of the State, where it was currently believed, it is said, that the State was sold to Wiggins. It has been asserted that if the State had originally assumed directly and gratuitously the obligations of the clamorous debtors, it would have proved less expensive to the treasury; certainly less injurious to its credit.

At the session of 1821, the counties of Greene, Fayette, Montgomery, Lawrence, Hamilton, Sangamon and Pike, the latter including all the State north and west of the Illinois river and what is now Cook, were established. Applications for the authority to form new counties poured in so rapidly that the legislature provided for 12 weeks publication of their intentions before the petitions of parties would in future be entertained. A joint resolution was passed requesting of Kentucky concurrent jurisdiction on the Ohio river, so far as the same forms a common boundary to both States, which has been conceded by that State.

CHAPTER XXVII.

1822–1826—ADMINISTRATION OF GOVERNOR COLES.

A resume of Slavery in Illinois from its earliest date—Indentured Slaves—Black Laws—Kidnapping—Life and Character of Gov. Coles—The effort to make Illinois a Slave State in 1824.

The general election of August, 1822, resulted in the choice of Edward Coles as governor, by a plurality of votes over his principal opponent, Joseph Phillips, then chief justice of the State. There were two other candidates in the field, Thomas C. Brown, associate justice of the supreme court, and Major General James B. Moore, of the State militia. Adolphus Frederick Hubbard was elected lieutenant governor. The other candidates for lieutenant governor were James Lemon, jr., John G. Loften, Wm. Pine, and James A. Peacock.

Into this election the question of slavery entered to a very considerable extent, Coles and Moore being anti, and Phillips and Brown pro-slavery. The country had but just emerged from the angry contest over that subject as connected with the admission of Missouri into the Union, in which our senators in congress, Messrs. Edwards and Thomas, had taken a leading part, being the originators of the compromise line of 30 degress and 30 minutes, while our member of the House, Daniel P. Cook, with much vigor had opposed the admission of Missouri as a slave State. Thomas' term as senator would expire with the existing congress, and he looked forward to an approval of his course in congress and a re-election. Of the legislature chosen at the same election, a majority was against the governor in his anti-slavery views. But the subject of principal interest during his administration was the convention struggling to make Illinois a slave State. To give the reader a more connected idea, we have heretofore purposely omitted to present in chronological order the kindred subjects constituting the heading of this chapter, and now group them together.

African slaves were first brought to Illinois in 1720 by Renault, agent and business manager of the "Company of St. Phillips." The belief obtained in France at that time that the wealth of the western world consisted in its pearl fisheries, its mines of gold and silver, and the wool of its wild cattle.* A monopoly of these resources with many others, was first granted by the King to Crozat in 1812, and upon his resignation in 1717, to the great "Company of the West," of which the St. Phillips was a branch. Renault left France in 1719 with a cargo of mechanics, miners and laborers

---

*Charlevoix, iii, 389.

numbering some 200, and on his way hither touched with his vessels
at San Domingo, where he purchased 500 slaves, and thus prepared to prosecute the objects of the company, he arrived in
Illinois. He founded the village of "St. Phillips," in what is now
the southeast corner of Monroe county, whence he sent out exploring parties to various sections in Illinois and Missouri, to prospect
for the precious metals. In 1744, before his return to France,
Renault sold these slaves to the French colonists of Illinois.
Vivier, a missionary among the Illinois, six leagues from Fort
Chartres, under date of June 8, 1750, writes: "We have here,
whites, negroes, and Indians, to say nothing of the cross breeds.
There are five French villages, and three of the natives, within a
space of 21 leagues, situated between the Mississippi and another
river called the Kaskaskia. In the five French villages are,
perhaps, 1,100 whites, 300 blacks, and some 60 red slaves or
savages. The three Illinois [Indian] towns do not contain more
than 800 souls, all told." These San Domingo slaves thus introduced became the progenitors of the French slaves in
Illinois.

The edict of Louis the XIII, dated April 23, 1615, first recognized
slavery in the French possessions of America, and the French
settlers of Illinois brought with them from Canada the French
laws and customs, among them the law which tolerated slavery.
In March, 1724, Louis XV published an ordinance reenacting the
edict of XIII, and for the "regulation of the government and
administration of justice, police, disciple, and traffic in negro slaves
in the province of Louisiana," which included Illinois. It provides
that the slaves be baptized and instructed in the Roman Catholic
religion and that they observe the Sabbath; prohibits the intermarriage of whites and blacks, under penalties, and the priests
from solemnizing such marriages; provides that the children of
slaves shall be bondsmen, or if one parent is free the children shall
follow the condition of the mother; that slaves enfeebled by age or
infirmity shall be maintained by the master; allows the master to
pursue and recapture fugitives; prohibits their severe treatment,
and the separate sale of husband or wife, or children under age,
of a family, either by bill or execution; provides that no slave
over forty years old attached to lands, shall be sold from the land,
unless for the debt of his purchase; enjoins their parental treatment upon the masters, &c. The edict contains 55 articles, and
may be found at large in Dillon's History of Indiana, i, 31. It
was more just, and tempered with greater mercy, than most laws
of that character.

Thus was slavery originally established in Illinois. By the peace
concluded at Paris, Feb. 10, 1763, this country, as a dependency of
Canada, was ceded to Great Britain, and when General Gage took
possession of Illinois, he promised in his proclamation of Dec. 30,
1764, to the late subjects of France, "that those who choose to
retain their lands and become subjects of his [Britanic] majesty,
shall enjoy the same rights and privileges, the same security for
their persons and effects, and liberty of trade, as the old subjects
of the king." At this period England recognized slavery in all
her American colonies, and the acquisition of Canada and its
dependencies operated to extend her colonial laws and customs to
these.

Next, Virginia, 1778, through her expedition under the command of George Rogers Clark, made the conquest of Illinois, and as soon as the news was received, her house of burgesses further declared as within her chartered limits the whole of the northwest territory, and proceeded by act to erect it into a county which was called Illinois, and extended over this country her laws and jurisdiction. The preamble of the act recites, "that the inhabitants had acknowledged themselves citizens of the commonwealth of Virginia, and had taken the oath of fidelity to the State," wherefore it was declared "that they should enjoy their own religion, with all their civil rights and property." Other States came forward with charter claims, but that of Virginia was as broad as these; added to which was her title by conquest, going back to the first principles by which all titles are originally deduced, and her actual occupation constituting the best of tenures; and while it was urged that the latter could not operate against her confederate claimant sister States, engaged in a common war jointly with her, congress did not deny the right of her separate conquest. After some hesitation, Virginia finally authorized her delegates in congress to convey all of the northwestern territory to the United States. The deed of cession was executed March 1st, 1784, the same day accepted and by congress ordered to be enrolled among the public archives. In the meantime, by the treaty of peace with Great Britain, in 1783, the whole of this country was ceded to the United States.

The following stipulation in the deed of cession has given rise to much controversy in the history of slavery in Illinois: "That the French and Canadian inhabitants and other settlers of the Kaskaskias, St. Vincents, and the neighboring villages, who have professed themselves citizens of the State of Virginia, shall have their possessions and titles confirmed to them, and be protected in the enjoyment of their rights and liberties."

The first effort made by congress to organize the northwestern territory was as early as 1784. The bill contained the provision, "that after the year 1800 there shall be neither slavery nor involuntary servitude in any of the said States," to be formed out of the territory. When the bill came up for action, the proviso, on a separate vote, failed, although 6 States voted for it to 3 against; but under the articles of confederation the vote of 9 States was required to carry a measure.

On the 13th of July, 1787, congress adopted the ordinance for the government of the territories northwest of the river Ohio, the 6th article whereof reads as follows: "There shall be neither slavery nor involuntary servitude in the said territory, otherwise than in punishment of crimes whereof the party shall have been duly convicted." The ordinance was subsequently approved under the constitution, when the latter went into operation. The acts of congress dividing the territory, both in the case of Indiana and Illinois, extended to the inhabitants of each, all and singular the rights, privileges, and advantages granted by the ordinance originally, as we have seen. The census of 1800 gave the number of slaves in the Indiana territory, which then included Illinois, as 133. In 1810 Illinois separately had 168 slaves; in 1820, 917, which probably included indentured and registered servants, and in 1830, 746.

The 6th article of the ordinance of 1787, prohibiting slavery, became at an early period a subject of repeated complaints. In 1796 four persons in Kaskaskia, doubtless picturing to themselves in golden colors the ease and affluence incident to slave labor, petitioned congress to suspend the restriction of the ordinance. November 22, 1802, Gov. Harrison, in compliance with the wishes of a number of inhabitants, but with what legal right it is difficult to conceive, issued his proclamation directing the people to hold an election in the several counties of the territory on the 11th of December and choose delegates, who were to meet in convention at Vincennes on the 20th instant, to deliberate on "territorial interests." From Illinois, for the county of St. Clair, Shadrach Bond, John Moredock, and Jean F. Perry were returned, and for Randolph, Robert Morrison, Pierre Menard, and Robert Reynolds; Gov. Harrison presided. The object was to obtain from congress a repeal or modification of the 6th article of the organic act, prohibiting the introduction of slaves into this territory.

A memorial was prepared and transmitted to congress, declaring the consent of the people to a suspension of the prohibitory clause; that such suspension would be highly advantageous to the territory and would meet the approbation of nine-tenths of the good citizens" thereof; that "inasmuch as the number of slaves in the United States would not be augmented by the measure," the abstract question of liberty and slavery was not involved; that the introduction of slaves into the territory where labor was scarce, from the States where it was abundant, would prove equally advantageous to both sections; that slavery was prohibited in the territory by congress when "they were not represented in that body—without their being consulted and without their knowledge or approbation;" that the number of slaves could never bear such a ratio to the white population "as to endanger the internal peace or prosperity of the country; that slaves were tolerated in other territories; that among their small farmers they would be "better fed and clothed than where they were crowded on large plantations by hundreds," etc.*

In March, 1803, Mr. Randolph, of Virginia, as chairman of the special committee, reported that "the rapidly increasing population of the State of Ohio sufficiently evinces, in the opinion of your committee, that the labor of slaves is not necessary to promote the growth and settlement of colonies in that region. That this labor, demonstrably the dearest of any, can only be employed to advantage in the cultivation of products more valuable than any known to that quarter of the United States; that the committee deem it highly dangerous and inexpedient to impair a provision wisely calculated to promote the happiness and prosperity of the northwestern country, and to give strength and security to that extensive frontier. In the salutary operation of this sagacious and benevolent restraint, it is believed that the inhabitants will, at no very distant day, find ample renumeration for a temporary privation of labor and immigration." How prophetically true! A resolution embodying these views was also reported.

This report, made just before the close of the session, was not acted upon, and at the next session was referred to a new committee, with Mr. Rodney, of Delaware, as chairman, who reported

*See Annals of Congress, House, Nov. 1807.

Feb. 4, 1804, favorably to the memorialists, suspending the 6th article for ten years, allowing the importation of slaves from States only, and that the male descendents should be free at 25 and the females at 21; but no action was had on the report. Again, at the legislative session of 1805-6, additional memorials of similar import were prepared and submitted to congress, and in the House referred to a select committee, with Mr. Garnett, of Virginia, as chairman; and again a favorable report to the prayer of the memorialists was made, Feb. 14, concluding with a resolution substantially like the one of Mr. Rodney. The report was made the special order for a certain day, but it was never called up. With the opening of the next congress, more resolutions from the Indiana legislature transmitted by Gov. Harrison, were presented, urging in a long preamble a suspension of the 6th article of the ordinance. The subject was finally referred to a special committee, this time with Mr. Parke, the territorial delegate, as chairman, and for the third time a favorable report was made, together with a resolution suspending the obnoxious article; but no action was had and the report slept with its predecessors. Simultaneously with these importunities upon the House, copies of memorials and resolutions were also transmitted to the president and by him sent to the senate.

But while those favorable to throwing open the territory to the influx of slaves were active, the opponents were not idle. In October, 1807, a large and enthusiastic meeting of the citizens was held in Clark county, Indiana, and a remonstrance drafted expressive of the impropriety of the suspension, and soliciting congress to defer action until their population should entitle them to form a constitution, etc. They also charged that the slave party, by some "legerdemain," obtained the name of the president of the legislative council to the last resolutions sent to congress, which he denies signing. In the senate a committee, consisting of Franklin, of North Carolina; Kitchell, of New Jersey, and Tiffin, of Ohio, was appointed, to which the whole subject was referred. After duly considering the matter, they reported adversely to the prayer of the legislative memorialists. Thus ended the very persistent, but happily abortive, efforts to throw open the doors of this vast and fertile region to the blighting influences of slavery. Not the people at home, but congress sitting at Washington, saved us from this curse.

Notwithstanding the words of the ordinance, "there shall be neither slavery or involuntary servitude in said territory," it was very early contended that the words in the deed of cession from Virginia—"shall have their possessions and titles confirmed"—guaranteed to the holders of these slaves a right of property in them; that this provision in the deed overrode the ordinance and secured them a vested right for all time in that species of property; that slavery in the territories was not abolished, but its further introduction simply prohibited; that these slaves were the property of citizens of Virginia, or were then the descendants of such slaves, and remained slaves by the compact entered into between the State of Virginia and the general government. And although others contended that the words "titles," "possessions," "rights" and "liberty," in the deed of cession, "were never intended by Virginia to guarantee the possessions of slaves," still all that class

of persons were held as slaves, and the rightfulness of their tenure was not brought before the proper tribunal in this State until
the year 1845.

The first decision sustaining the sixth article of the ordinance of
1787, was made by the supreme court of Indiana. Next, by that
of Missouri.* In the former, the mother of plaintiff had been a
slave in Virginia, was taken to Illinois before the ordinance of
1787, held in slavery there before and after its passage, and there
the plaintiff was born after its passage. It was held that she was
free. In the case of Menard vs. Aspasia,† the mother of Aspasia
was born in Illinois before the ordinance, and held as a slave from
birth. Aspasia was born after the ordinance, at Kaskaskia, and
held as a slave. The supreme court of Missouri held that she
was entitled to her freedom, and upon a writ of error to the supreme court of the United States, that court declined jurisdiction,
which affirmed the judgment below. In 1845, for the first and
only time, was the question brought squarely before the supreme
court of this State, and it was decided that the descendants of
the slaves of the old French settlers, born since the adoption
of the ordinance of 1787, or before, or since the constitution, could
not be held in slavery in Illinois.‡

Indentured and Registered Slaves.—Failing in their effort with
congress to modify the restriction of the organic law with regard
to slavery, the next step to compass the same result, was by the
law-making powers of the territory, both of the 1st and 2d grades,
and in defiance of the prohibition, a law was adopted entitled " an
act concerning the introduction of negroes and mulattoes into this
territory." The act bears date September 17, 1807, but this simply means that it was reported among the revised laws by Jones
and Johnson, the whole batch of which was re-adopted on that
day at Vincennes. It was a law adopted by the first grade of territorial government. The first general assembly met at Vincennes
July 29, 1805, yet more than a year previous, April 6, 1804, Governor Harrison, learning that certain persons were about to remove
a number of indentured persons from the territory for the purpose of selling them as slaves, issued a proclamation forbidding
their removal and calling upon the civil authorities to interpose.
We quote from the law of 1807:

"SECTION 1. It shall and may be lawful for any person, being the
owner of any negroes or mulattoes of and above the age of 15 years, and
owing service and labor as slaves in any of the States or territories of the
United States, or for any citizen of the United States or territories,
purchasing the same, to bring the said negroes or mulattoes into this
territory."

Section 2 provided, that within 30 days after bringing the slaves into
the territory, the owner or master should take them before the clerk of the
court and have an indenture between the slave and his owner entered
upon record, specifying the time which the slave was compelled to serve
his master; [the term being generally fixed at 99 years, a period beyond
the ordinary term of human life].

Section 3 guarded the property of the master against loss by allowing
him, in the event of the slave refusing to enter into such agreement or
indenture, to have the lawful right, within 60 days, to remove such slave
to any State or territory where such property could be legally held.

*John Murry vs. Tiffin and Menard, 1 Mo. R. 725.
†5th Peters, 510.
‡See 2d Gilman, p. 1—Jarrot vs. Jarrot.

The 4th section prescribed the manner of correcting the servant for laziness, misbehaviour, or disorderly conduct, the punishment being chastisement with "stripes."

"SEC. 5. Any person removing into this territory, and being the owner of any negro or mulatto under the age of 15 years, it shall and may be lawful for such person, owner or possessor to hold the said negro or mulatto to service or labor, the males until they arrive at the age of 35 and the females until they arrive at the age of 32 years.

"SEC. 13. The children born in this territory of a parent of color, owing service of labor by indenture, according to the law, shall serve the master or mistress, the males until the age of 30, and females until the age of 28 years."

The other sections of the act were all in harmony with the purpose to introduce, maintain and protect slavery in Illinois in defiance of the ordinance of 1787. Slavery was thus not only introduced, but made hereditary, by imposing upon the children born under it the obligation to serve the owners of their parents until 28 and 30 years. It also pointed out the mode in which the master might sell his servants by an assignment of the indenture by which these people were made commerce, as completely as if in a condition of absolute slavery.

After the organization of the Illinois territory in 1809, the governor and judges adopted the same act as the law of Illinois, and upon the assembling of the first legislature at Kaskaskia, it was, December 13, 1812, re-adopted. The law was, to all intents and purposes, void under the ordinance of 1787. In the case of Phœbe vs. Jarrot,* of the supreme court, Lockwood, judge, decided that the act of September 17, 1807, respecting the introduction of negroes and mulattoes into the territory, was void, as being repugnant to the sixth article of the ordinance of 1787. But it was further held that the contracts of indenture under that law were rendered valid by the third section of the sixth article of the State constitution:

"Each and every person who has been bound to service by contract or indenture in virtue of the laws of Illinois territory heretofore existing, and in conformity to the provisions of the same, without fraud or collusion, shall be held to a specific performance of their contracts or indentures; and such negroes and mulattoes as have registered in conformity with the aforesaid laws, shall serve out the time appointed by said laws; provided, however, that the children hereafter born of such persons, negroes or mulattoes, shall become free, the males at the age of 21 years, the females at the age of 18 years."

The court say: A constitution can do what a legislative act cannot do, because it is the supreme, fixed and permanent will of the people in their original, sovereign and unlimited capacity; that the act of accepting that constitution and admitting it into the Union by congress, abrogated so much of the ordinance of 1787 as was repugnant to it. In Boone vs. Juliet,* the court held that "the children of negroes and mulattoes, registered under the laws of the territory of Indiana and Illinois, are unquestionably free— because of an absence in the law of 1807 providing for the children of registered slaves, notwithstanding the constitution of Illinois says that the children born of such registered persons shall render service until 18 and 21 years old."

The question of the validity of the indenture and registration act, under the sixth article of the ordinance of 1787, it seems, was not raised before the territorial courts, and indeed, not for some time afterwards. The convention, therefore, which enacted the constitution, gave that law the only legal vitality it ever had, but it is presumable that they were under the impression that it was valid and had been all the time; and it was only in require-ment of the enabling act of congress that they enacted article VI, section I: "Neither slavery nor involuntary servitude shall here-after be introduced into this State."

At the session of the territorial legislature, in 1817, a bill was passed to repeal so much of "an act concerning the introduction of negroes and mulattoes into this territory," as authorized the bringing of negroes and mulattoes into the territory and inden-turing them as slaves. The preamble declares the law to "intend to introduce and tolerate slavery under the pretense of voluntary servitude in contravention of the permanent law of the land," and "contrary to the ordinance of 1787." But the veto power of the territorial governor was absolute, and his Excellency Gover-nor Edwards hesitated not to exercise it, assigning reasons at considerable length, as was his wont: "I conscientiously believe that the legislature was competent to pass the law—of which opinion were also the judges with whom I was associated" in the adoption of the law, "previous to the organization of our general assembly." He held that congress could not violate the stipula-tions in the deed of cession from Virginia, "there was and still is slavery in the territory, notwithstanding the article in the ordi-nance;" but "waiving the question whether congress ever had any right to·impose the sixth article of the ordinance, or any more restrain the people from purchasing additional slaves to clear and cultivate their lands, than horses to plow them," he proceeded to argue the abstract right of "involuntary servitude." After finally stating that "such indentures would be and ought to be supported upon principles of law as well as common honesty," and that he "can see no evil in allowing them to be made," he concluded: "I am no advocate for slavery ; and if it depended upon my vote alone, it should never be admitted into any State or territory not already cursed with so great an evil ;" and that his objection to the repeal was, that there was no such law of Illinois as that of September 17, 1807, described in the bill. In this he was tech-nically right, because in 1807 Illinois was Indiana.* This veto message was now (1823–4) made use of by the convention party, seeking to graft slavery upon the constitution, as an electioneering document.†

The convention which framed the first constitution of the State, evaded the full requirement of the ordinance of 1787. In article VI, section I of that instrument, the further introduction of slaves into the State was prohibited ; but it did not only not abolish slavery, or liberate those in the State, but in section 3 of the same article, provided that the "indentured servants"—slaves for 99 years in most cases—should be held for the whole term specified in their contracts of indenture, and even their children were to owe ser-vice, the males till 21 and the females till 18 years of age ; and this provision, as we have seen, the supreme court held as valid. Thus slavery in Illinois, while it was steadily decreasing, was not

*Governor Edwards was himself the owner of quite a number of indentured slaves.
Ill. Intelligencer, Sept. 6, 1823.

wholly abolished until the adoption of the constitution of 1848, which contained the following provision : "There shall be neither slavery nor involuntary servitude in this State, except as a punishment for crime," etc.

The " Black Laws."—After the adoption of the constitution of 1818 and the admission of the State into the Union, the first general assembly, notwithstanding the small number of negroes as compared with the white inhabitants, re-enacted, March 30, 1819, the old stringent, not to say barbarous law "respecting free negroes, mulattoes, servants and slaves," with only such slight revision as became necessary by the transition from the territorial to the State government. Of course the territorial law which authorized the introduction of slaves from slaveholding States and territories was omitted, in obedience to article VI section I of the constitution. Perhaps no severer law was to be found in any slave State, even where the blacks outnumbered the whites. There was no adequate cause for this : it doubtless resulted from the early associations of our law makers, who at that time were men not only mostly born and bred in the midst of slaves, but who looked forward to the making of Illinois a slave State. •

No negro or mulatto, by himself or with his family, was permitted to reside or settle in the State, until he had first produced a certificate of freedom under seal of a court of record, which, together with a description of the person producing it, and his family, if any, was to be entered of record in the county he proposed settling in and so duly endorsed ; but the overseers of the poor were notwithstanding empowered to expel such family in their discretion. Any person coming to theState to emancipate his slaves, was required to execute to the county a bond in $1000 as guaranty that the emancipated person should not become a public charge ; for neglect or refusal of which he was liable to a fine of $200 ; all resident negroes or mulattoes, except slaves, before the 1st of June ensuing, were to enter their names and every member of their families, with the circuit clerk, together with their evidences of freedom to be certified by the clerk, but which should not bar the owners to reclaim them. No person was to employ any negro or mulatto without such certificate, under a penalty of $1.50 for each day employed, recoverable before a justice, one third going to the informer, the rest to the owner or the county. To harbor any slave or servant, or hinder the owner in retaking a slave, was declared a felony, punishable by restitution, or a fine of two-fold value and whipping not to exceed 30 stripes. Every black or mulatto not having a proper certificate was deemed a runaway slave, subject to arrest and commitment by a justice, then to be described and advertised for 6 weeks by the sheriff, when, if not reclaimed or his freedom established, he was to be sold for one year, at the end of which time he was entitled to a certificate, except as against his owner. No person was to sell to, buy of or trade with any servant or slave, without the consent of his master, under penalty of forfeiting to the master 4 times in value the amount of such transaction. Any slave or servant found ten miles from home without permit was liable to arrest and 35 stripes on the order of a justice ; or if he appeared at any dwelling or plantation without leave of his master, the owner of the place was entitled to administer, or have it done, 10 lashes on the bare back ; for being lazy, disorderly or misbehaving to his master or family, on the order of a justice, he was to be corrected with stripes, and for every day he refused to work he was to serve two.

Riots, routs, unlawful assemblies, trespass, seditious speeches by slaves or servants, were punishable with stripes not exceeding 39; persons suffering 3 or more slaves or servants to assemble on their premises for dancing, reveling, &c., were liable to a fine of $20, recoverable by *qui tam* action. It was made the duty of all coroners, sheriffs, judges, and justices of the peace, on view or knowledge of such assemblages, to have the offenders committed to jail, and upon judgment to order 39 stripes. In all cases where free persons were punishable by fine, slaves or servants, were to be chastised by whipping, at the rate of 20 lashes for every $8 of fine, not to exceed 40 stripes at any one time. Thus was the free State of Illinois provided with a complete slave code.

In 1847, the convention which revised the constitution, in article XIV, required of the general assembly at its first session under the amended constitution, to pass such laws as would effectually prohibit free persons of color from immigrating to or settling in this State and prevent the owners of slaves from bringing them into the State for the purpose of setting them free.

In pursuance of this provision, the legislature passed an act of Feb. 12, 1853, which provided that if any negro or mulatto, bond or free, came into this State and remained ten days, with the evident intention of residing therein, he should be deemed guilty of a high misdemeanor, and for the first offence should be fined $50, and if the fine was not forthwith paid he was to be committed to the custody of the sheriff, to be advertised ten days and then sold to any person who would pay the fine and costs for the shortest period, the purchaser being empowered to hold and work the culprit during the time. One case under this act was taken up to the supreme court from Hancock county, and decided* in 1864* The court held the law to be valid; that the punishment was not slavery, because the person was sold only for a limited period; it was only a species of apprenticeship; and that the State might define offences and prescribe the punishment, and the exercise of such powers could not be inquired into by the court.

The "black laws," as they were for a long time known, were continued, with slight modification, in all the revisions of the laws from 1819 down to 1865, when by act of Feb. 7th, they were repealed. During that time, however, efforts were repeatedly made to abolish them. But they had ceased to be enforced for many years previously, and, except the act of 1853, were regarded as a dead letter. The obstinacy with which they were retained was owing in great part to the Abolition excitement of modern times, which in a manner constituted them tests of party fealty.

Kidnapping.—But the most odious feature of the act of March 30, 1819, "respecting free negroes, mulattoes, servants and slaves," was one of omission, or the inadequate provision made for the punishment of the crime of kidnapping. It provided, "section 9, *and be it further enacted*, that any person or persons, who shall forcibly take and carry out of this State any negro or mulatto (slaves excepted by their owners), owing service or labor to any person in this State, or who shall forcibly take out of this State

---

*See Nelson vs. The People, &c.

any free negro or mulatto having gained a legal settlement in this State, shall forfeit and pay for every such offence the sum of $1000 to the party injured, to be recovered in the name of the people of the State of Illinois, by action of debt in any court having cognizance of the same." By a proviso it was added, that this should not apply to the recapture of fugitive slaves.

The fine, it will be observed, was for the party injured, who might have been successfully carried to so remote a section in the south and there sold into bondage, as to preclude the possibility of his return. No share of it was to go to a prosecutor. It in effect provided a premium for the successful kidnapper who would steal the remedy with the person. The remedy was civil; no provision occurs in the law for any other punishment if the culprit was worthless in visible worldly effects upon which to levy an execution, and this doubtless was the condition of the kidnapping scoundrels in 99 cases out of every 100. The law reads: who "shall forcibly take and carry out of this State" &c; but in the majority of cases the poor ignorant blacks, by fraud and deceit, were inveigled into a trip south on a flat boat, or other errand, and at some pre-arranged point on the river they would be turned over to confederates, forcibly and rapidly taken to the interior and there sold into slavery, the original parties often leaving the impression upon their black dupes that they had no hand in the outrage. Against such enticements the law cited made no provision, and they were perpetrated with impunity. Another mode was to seize a black and forcibly convey him to a rendezvous either on the Ohio or Mississippi, but not out of the State, where a confederate would appear and carry him beyond. Nor were the blacks allowed their oaths against whites, and hence it was generally impossible to convict.

The crime of seizing free blacks, running them south and selling them into slavery from this State, for a long time was quite common. The poor ignorant colored creatures, against whom was not only the law but apparently every man's hand, were hampered in the south by all the contrivances of ingenious slave codes to prevent their escape, while the weary years of unrequited toil rolled slowly around, ever embittered by heart longings to return to home and kindred. The same may be said of the affectionate ones left at home. No crime can be greater than this. Portions of southern Illinois for many years afforded a safe retreat to these kidnapping outlaws. We cannot cite the numerous cases of kidnapping. An early conviction for this crime was that of Jeptha Lambkins, at the term of the Madison county circuit court, November, 1822. We have not the particulars. On the night of May 25, 1823, a free colored man named Jackson Butler, his wife and 6 children, residing in Illinois a few miles from Vincennes, were kidnapped by a band of villians from Lawrence county in this State. Butler had been purchased by Gov. Harrison in Kentucky, brought to Indiana, indentured, and had served out his term faithfully. His wife was born free, which rendered the children also free. They were taken down the Wabash to the Ohio, thence south. Harrison learning of the outrage, offered a reward of $300 for the apprehension of the kidnappers. The name of Harrison gave it wide circulation, and in September following, news came

that the Butler family had been rescued at New Orleans, just as
they were about to be shipped to Cuba.*

In the first message to the general assembly, December, 5,
1822, Gov. Coles called special attention to the subject of kidnapping; that crime, he was sorry to say, was too often committed in
the State with impunity; urged that the duty of society as well as
every benevolent feeling demanded better protection for the free
blacks, while they remained in the State; that the peculiar situation of the State, bordering on three rivers communicating with
the country where there was always a demand for slaves, afforded a
great temptation and facility to the lawless and inhuman to engage
in this crime, and that more efficient laws were required to prevent
the kidnapping of free blacks.

This part of the message, with the subject of slavery, was referred to a special committee consisting of Messrs. Will, Emmit and
Moore, who reported Dec. 12, 1822, as follows : "Your committee
have carefully examined the laws upon the subject, and with deep
regret announce their incapability of devising a more effectual plan
than the one already prescribed by law for the suppression of such
infamous crimes. It is believed that the benevolent views of the
executive and the benign purposes of the statutes can only be
realized by the redoubled diligence of our grand juries and our
magistrates, aided by the well directed support of all just and
good men."

The legislature was politically opposed to the governor, and the
language of the committee, "benign statute," was the baldest of
irony. These gentlemen however were quite capable of devising
a scheme how to introduce slavery into the State, which they
reported at the same time, and to which we will now direct our
inquiry.

[In 1851 an attempted murder, growing out of the business of kidnapping, was curiously developed. It shows also the modus operandi and the desperate characters connected with this crime. A Mrs. Prather, deceased, of Weakley county, Tennessee, had
some years before emancipated her slaves, and they removed to Gallatin county,
Illinois. Here they were followed by parties from their former home, who conspired
to arrest them as fugitive slaves. The U. S. district court, Judge Pope presiding, decided upon full proof that they had not a shadow of claim to them. With the conspirators was connected a shrewd bad man by the name of Newton E. Wright, residing
in Kentucky, back of Wolf Island, who had long been engaged in kidnapping. While
here attempting to reclaim the Prather negroes as slaves, he formed the acquaintance
of a notorious kidnapper of Hamilton county, named Joe O'Neal, with whom was
associated a disreputable character by the name of Abe Thomas. Subsequently
O'Neal stole three likely children from an old negro named Scott, in Hamilton county,
Illinois, and ran them off and sold them partly on credit to Wright, who resold them at
New Madrid to one Phillips. When O'Neal's note matured he sent Thomas to collect
it, telling him further that Wright had business of a particular nature for him, for
which he would be well paid. Thomas proceeded by steamer to Wright's. There he
undertook for $150 to kill a Dr Swayne, at Hicco, Tennessee, who had sued Wright on a
note of $8000. If the doctor could be killed, Wright, by means of nicely forged receipts,
could successfully defend the suit.

In May, 1850, a man calling himself Stewart, rode up to the house of Dr. Swayne, desiring him to visit his father, a little way off, alleged to have been taken suddenly ill
on his return from Texas. The doctor invited the stranger to dinner, just ready ;
that attended to, the two rode away to see the sick man After proceeding some distance, Stewart, falling a little behind, drew a pistol and shot the do tor, the ball lodging in his arm, fracturing it badly. The cry of murder was raised, but Stewart made
his escape. Pursuit was made, and every effort to ferret out the assassin ; suspected
parties were followed even to Texas ; much money was expended, but without avail.
Dr. Swayne recovered.

But now unexpectedly a clue was gained. Two citizens of White county, Illinois.
John Eubanks and son, Shannon, took a lot of horses to Tennessee for sale, and while
in the neighborhood of Dr. Swayne's, heard him relate the particulars of the attempt
to assassinate him, giving also a minute description of his assailant, whose nose was
flat at the base, projecting forward like a hawk's bill. Shannon knew the description
fitted Abe Thomas, and no other living man, who was then stopping at Joe O.Neal's,
in Hamilton county, Illinois. Further description as too size, complexion, &c., tallied
exactly. A short time after, Thomas was seized by same Tennesseans, and carried
to that State for trial. (Shawneetown Mercury 1851.]

*Ill. Intelligencer, 1823.

The Convention question of 1824—The Effort to make Illinois a Slave State.—It has doubtless been noted that the voice of the people of the territory, as it found expression from time to time, was strongly in favor of slavery. By canvassing the names of leading convention advocates in 1823-4, and from other circumstances, it may be asserted with entire safety that the constitutional convention of 1818, left unrestrained by the ordinance of 1787, or the enabling act to form a constitution, would have established slavery. As it was, that convention in a manner evaded the full requirement of the acts of congress by declaring (article VI. sec. I.). "Neither slavery nor involuntary servitude shall *hereafter* be introduced into this State;" and by the 3d section of the same article they gave to indentured slavery the only validity it ever had. The feeling in favor of slavery was still strong after the admission of the State. The financial embarrassments of the people, to which we have adverted in the preceding chapter, coupled with the golden pictures of prosperity which that institution would bring to the country, as they were wont to regard it, did not abate their longings. The subject was further kept astir by the frenzied agitation of the slavery question as connected with the admission of Missouri, which convulsed the entire nation and threatened a dissolution of the Union.

It had also the effect to extensively advertise that new State, and stimulate emigration thither, as the crowds of immigrants from the southern States to Missouri, consisting in great part of the wealthiest and best educated classes, passed through southern Illinois, where immigration had been for some time stagnant, and the want of which was seriously felt. "Many of our people who had land and farms to sell, looked upon the good fortune of Missouri with envy; whilst the lordly immigrant, as he passed along with his money and droves of negroes, took a malicious pleasure in increasing it, by pretending to regret the short-sighted policy of Illinois, which excluded him from settling with his slaves among us, and from purchasing the lands of our people."[*]

Into the election of August, 1822, as we have noted, the question of slavery entered to a large extent, and while it was not generally sharply defined, it was well known that Coles was a zealous opponent of the institution of human chattels; so also was Gen. Moore; and for these reasons the partisans of freedom rallied with little division for Coles. His aggregate vote was 2810, that of Moore 522, total 3332. The vote of Phillips was 2760 and that of Brown 2543, total 5303—being a majority, so far as this expression was a criterion, of about 2000 in favor of the introduction of slavery. But personal considerations at that day entered more largely into election contests than principles.

Edward Coles, the governor elect of Illinois, was born in Virginia, Dec. 15, 1786, and was among the youngest of ten children. His father was a planter, owning many slaves. During college life the question of property in man first presented itself to Edward's mind, and he returned home impressed with its moral wrongfulness and political impolicy, and the resolution that when he should become the owner of his portion of his father's slaves he would emancipate them. Apprehending that these sentiments

[*]Ford's History.

21

would meet with no countenance at home he kept them sacred to himself. Upon the death of his father in 1808, he became entitled to 25 negroes and 1,000 acres of land. His father had taken no share in public life, but his home had been the resort of nearly all the great statesmen of the day. Edward became the private secretary of President Madison. In person Coles was tall and graceful, with face of the Grecian style. To a benevolent disposition he added a wide fund of information, social tact and conversational powers. By the judicious exercise of these he is said to have brought into new bonds of friendship Mr. Madison and Mr. Monroe, and Mr. Adams and Mr. Jefferson, who had respectively been somewhat estranged. In 1816 he was sent in the sloop of war "Promethious" on a special mission to Russia, as the bearer of important dispatches to the American embassadors at St. Petersburg. Before his return he made the tour of Europe. After his arrival home he shortly determined to go west. He spent the summer of 1818 in Illinois, and witnessed the labors of the convention at Kaskaskia to enact the first constitution. In the following spring, 1819, he removed with his slaves to Illinois. On the trip hither, made mostly on flat boats down the Ohio, the negroes, being ignorant of their destination, were one clear moonlight evening in June, while calmly floating down the placid stream, called together, and by their master addressed in a plain, short speech in which he pronounced them all free. Their gratitude was so profound that they tendered him one year's service at their new home. But being much touched at this manifestation of their attachment, he refused their offer. He gave, besides, to each head of a family 160 acres of land in Illinois, in the neighborhood of Edwardsville, aided them with money, and for many years exercised paternal care over them.*

In 1833, at the age of 47, he removed to Philadelphia, and was married to Miss Sallie Logan Roberts, by whom he had one daughter and two sons. He died July 7, 1868, in the 82d year of his age. On coming to Illinois, Coles received the appointment of register of the land office at Edwardsville, from Mr. Crawford, secretary of the treasury, who was an aspirant to the presidency. Coles, it was supposed, was sent out to counteract the influence of Gov. Edwards, who favored Calhoun.†

The partisans of slavery, although beaten for governor in 1822, by a schism in their own ranks, had carried both houses of the general assembly, and the lieutenant-governor, and throughout the first half of his term, the governor experienced a want of accord

---

*The law of 1819 respecting free negroes required the emancipator to give bond that they should not become a county charge. Having provided them amply with lands, Coles neglected to do this, whereby he incurred a liability to a fine of $200 for each negro, which might be sued for by the county in which they were settled. During the heat of the convention struggle the county commissioners of Madison were instigated to bring suit against the Governor for this penalty, resulting, in September, 1824, in a verdict of $2,000 for setting at liberty negroes without giving bond Pending a motion for a new trial, in January 1825, the legislature released all penalties incurred under the act, including those of Coles. At the next term of court he plead this release in bar of judgment against him. But Judge McRoberts decided that the legislature had no power to take from a municipal corporation its vested right in a fine, any more than from an individual, and rendered judgment on the verdict. This decision, believed to have been influenced by the feelings growing out of the slavery contest the year before, caused no little popular excitement. The case was taken to the supreme court and reversed, the power of the legislature being held to be ample in the premises. The opinion of the court, by Wilson, chief justice, says: "It is said the king cannot remit an informer's interest in a popular action after suit brought; this is no doubt true, but it is equally true that the Parliament can. It is not pretended that the executive could remit the penalty in this case, but that the legislature may."
†Ford's History of Illinois.

with that body. Governor Coles directed attention to the subject of slavery, and in clear and forcible language urged the emancipation of the French slaves, recommended a revision of the black laws in accordance with the dictates of humanity, and the enactment of more adequate laws to repress the frequent crime of kidnapping, as we have noticed. This was enough to immediately fan into flame the smouldering embers of the slavery question. The purpose was now to make a strong effort to introduce slavery into Illinois, which could only be done by amending the constitution, which required a two-thirds vote in each house to pass the proposition submitting the question to a vote of the people. So much of the message as related to the abrogation of slavery, was referred to a select committee, consisting of Messrs. Beaird, Boon, Ladd, Kinney and White, who in a few days reported as follows: After giving a historical resume of the establishment of slavery in Illinois, demonstrating its legal existence and claiming that the provision in the deed of cession from Virginia, viz: that the inhabitants of the territory who professed themselves to have been citizens of Virginia previous to the cession, should "have their possessions and titles confirmed to them, and be protected in the enjoyment of their rights and liberties," could not be overridden and set aside by the subsequent act of congress, which provided that "there shall be neither slavery nor involuntary servitude in the said territory;" that the language in the deed of cession was too plain and forcible to be misunderstood or evaded; that the constitution, in obedience to the behests of congress, for the purpose of having the State admitted, was careful to avoid any interference with this species of property, and left it in the same state of security that the ordinance had placed it; that thus the constitution of Illinois was ratified, no doubt upon the ground that no condition of the ordinance had been violated, and that the constitution left the right to property acquired under the compact with Virginia, entire.

They concluded their report by saying: "Your committee have now arrived at the period when Illinois was admitted into the Union upon an equal footing with the original States in all respects whatever; and whatever causes of regret were experienced by the restrictions imposed upon the first convention, your committee are clearly of the opinion that the people of Illinois have now the same right to alter their constitution as the people of the State of Virginia, or any other of the original States, and may make any disposition of negro slaves they choose, without any breach of faith or violation of compact, ordinances or acts of congress; and if the reasoning employed be correct, there is no other course left by which to accomplish the object of this portion of the governor's message, than to call a convention to alter the constitution."

And they recommended the adoption of the following resolution: "*Resolved*, That the general assembly of the State of Illinois (two-thirds thereof concurring therein), do recommend to the electors, at the next election for members to the general assembly, to vote for or against a convention, agreeably to the 7th article of the constitution."

*See Ill. Intelligencer, Dec. 14, 1822.

On motion of Michael Jones, the report was concurred in. A minorty report was made by Risden Moore and John Emmett, strongly and ably urging the abolition of slavery, the amelioration of the black laws, and greater stringency regarding the punish-. ment of kidnapping. Mr. Will made a separate report, of a milk and water character.

In the senate, it was speedily ascertained that the requisite two-thirds vote to pass the resolution for the call of a convention to amend the constitution, could be obtained, and to spare; but in the house the case stood otherwise—they needed one vote. At first it was strenuously argued that the two-thirds vote required by the constitution to pass the convention resolution, meant two-thirds of the two houses in joint session. But the opponents were too powerful in argument upon this point. The majority was not to be foiled in their purpose, however. Another mode presented itself—all that was required was courage to perpetrate a gross outrage upon a recalcitrant member.

There had been a contested election case from Pike county, which then included all the country between the Illinois and Mississippi rivers, north to the boundary of the State. The sitting member, decided by the house to be entitled to the seat, was Nicholas Hanson, and the contestant, John Shaw. Hanson's vote had been obtained for the re-election of Jesse B. Thomas, strongly pro-slavery, to the United States senate, but farther than this he would not go. Shaw, who favored the convention project, was now discovered to be justly entitled to the seat! A motion was thereupon made to reconsider the admission of Hanson, which prevailed. It was next further moved to strike out the name of Hanson and insert that of Shaw. During the pendency of the resolution, a tumultuous crowd assembled in the evening at the state house, and after the delivery of a number of incendiary speeches, inflaming the minds of the people against Hanson, they proceeded through the town with his effigy in a blaze, accompanied by the beating of drums, the sounds of bugles, and shouts of "Convention or death."

The motion to expel Hanson and admit Shaw was adopted, and the latter rewarded the majority by voting for the convention resolution, which thus barely passed by his aid on the night following. A number of the members of both houses entered their solemn protest against this glaring outrage of unseating Hanson, both as to the object intended and the manner of perpetrating it. Many reflecting men, earnest in their support of the convention question, condemned it; and it proved a powerful lever before the people in the defeat of the slavery scheme.

The passage of the convention resolution was regarded as tantamount to its carriage at the polls. The pro-slavery party celebrated their triumph by an illumination of the town and a procession, accompanied by all the horrid paraphernalia and discordant music of a chivarai, marched to the residence of Governor Coles and the quarters of the chief opponents of the measure, where they performed their demoniac music to annoy and insult them. The procession is said to have been headed by such dignataries as ex-judge and late gubernatorial canidate, Joseph Phillips; the newly chosen chief-justice, Thomas Reynolds, afterwards governor of Missouri; associate supreme judge, Smith; prospective lieutenant-governor Kinney, etc., followed by many of the honorable members of the legislature, the lobbyists—some of them strangers from adjoining slave States—the rabble, etc. The rejoicings of the convention party also found expression in public dinners, and of the toasts there given we subjoin a few: The convention: The means of introducing and spreading the African family—three cheers. The enemies of the convention: May they ride a porcupine saddle on a hard trotting horse, a long journey without money or friends. May those individuals who are opposed to our cause, before the next election, abandon the State of Illinois. The State of Illinois: the ground is good—prairies in abundance; give us plenty of negroes, a little industry and she will distribute her treasure

But these brutal proceedings, intended to intimidate, only recoiled upon the perpetrators. The anti-convention party was inspired with renewed courage and determination to defeat the call before the people. That indeed was the only hope for the liberty of *all* men in Illinois. At this period, the apportionment of the State into representative and senatorial districts was peculiarly unequal, the strongholds of the convention advocates being in the counties near the Ohio and the old French settlements, while the rapid progress of population northward was numerically far in advance of its just ratio of representation. If the convention should be ordered by the people, it was demonstrated that by reason of this unequal representation, one-fourth of the voters could, in a certain contingency, (that of the delegates being made to correspond to the number of representatives), elect a majority of the members, who might fasten slavery upon the State. It became, therefore, the paramount object of the friends of freedom to defeat the convention call before the people.

The canvass now opened and for nearly 18 months raged with unequaled violence throughout the State. Never was such canvass made in the State before. The young and old, without regard to sex entered the arena of party strife; families and neighborhoods became divided and surrendered themselves up to the bitter warfare. Detraction and personal abuse reigned supreme, while combats were not infrequent. The whole country seemed on the verge of a resort to physical force to settle the angry question.* The press, both for and against, teemed with incendiary publications on the subject. Both anti and pro-convention newspapers were established: of the former *"The Spectator,"* at Edwardsville, edited by Hooper Warren; one at Shawneetown, edited by Henry Eddy; the *Illinois Intelligencer*, located at Vandalia, which, at first pro-convention, was subsequently purchased by David Blackwell, secretary of State, and then ably conducted in opposition to the convention scheme. To these papers there were also a number of able and steady contributors, principal among whom may be mentioned, his excellency the governor; Morris Birbeck, the able English colonist, in Edwards county; Judge Lockwood, Thomas Lippincott, George Churchill, &c. Pamphlets were published and extensively circulated, containing statistics and observations regarding the working of slavery in other countries. Gov. Coles freely resigned the salary of his entire term, $4000, as a contribution to the cause. Through the efforts mainly of the Rev. Dr. J. M.

*Reynold's "Own Times."

Peck, anti-slavery societies were organized by the "friends of freedom," which ramified more or less throughout the State, to the number of 14, with headquarters in St. Clair county, and which were active during the canvass. The ministers of the gospel were enlisted in the cause, and they met together in large numbers to devise ways to avert the impending evil. Denominational questions, ordinarily much more bitter in those times than at the present, were laid aside for the time, and the pulpit now thundered its anathemas against spreading the great sin. All the means known to civilization to impart ideas of the enormity of slavery were made available. To the distribution of pamphlets and newspaper writings, were added tracts and handbills of a most incendiary tone. The Rev. Dr. Peck, who, in his vocation of distributing bibles, had the opportunity to observe the management of the campaign on the part of the opposition, shaped his ends with the tact and skill of a general, to meet them at every hand. Political meetings were called, and almost every stump resounded with the declamations of indignant orators, both pro and con. The rank and file of the people, no less excited, wrangled and argued with each other wherever they met. Much time was consumed, and industry was at a stand.

In the meantime, the pro-slavery party was not idle, and adopted the same means to reach the public mind. Elias Kent Kane; Thomas Reynolds, the chief justice; Judge Theophilus W. Smith, of the supreme court; Judge Samuel McRoberts, Emanuel J. West, A. P. Field, Joseph A. Baird, George Forquer and others, were their prominent writers; while among their chief orators, besides some of these, may be mentioned R. M. Young, John McLean, Jesse B. Thomas, ex Gov. Bond, (running for congress against D. P. Cook, at this time), Judge Phillips, and many others. The members of the legislature in favor of the convention, before they dispersed in the spring of 1823, levied a contribution upon each other by which they raised about $1000 for their side of the cause. William Kinney, afterward lieutenant governor, to his vocation as a pro-slavery politician added that of a baptist preacher, mingling the two with much freedom, traveled constantly over the State, acting with zeal and energy in arousing the people to the blessings of the institution of slavery. Emissaries of both parties ranged the State in every direction during the canvass, with bitter partisan tracts, and all manner of inflamatory appeals, to arouse the passions of the people, and awakened them to the duty of the hour. The principal newspapers of the pro-slavery party were located at Kaskaskia and Edwardsville.

In looking over the array of prominent names, it has been thought the most talented and influential public men were on the side of the convention party,* but in energy and zeal, which grew with the progress of the campaign, the opposition were better organized. Their attacks were, besides, direct upon the subject involving the merits of slavery; while the other side showed signs of avoiding the direct issue. The latter argued that the constitution needed amendment in many particulars; that the convention would not probably interfere in behalf of slavery, and if it did, it would establish it only for a limited period, or provide for indenturing and gradual emancipation. But the opponents were not to

*Ford's History.

be hoodwinked in this manner; indeed as the people took a very absorbing interest in the subject, and as the canvass was extended for a period of 18 months, they came to thoroughly appreciate all there was in it by the day of election. The contest was not devoid of extraneous pro-slavery influences from beyond the borders of the State, as might well be expected, but such impertenence was promptly met as it deserved.

When the day of election finally arrived, the utmost exertions at the polls throughout the State were used by both sides to bring out a full vote. The aged, the crippled, the chronic invalids, all that could be conveyed with their bodily infirmities, were brought out and cast their votes, either for against the call. The result was that the convention scheme was defeated by some 1800 majority. This was a wonderful victory to achieve, showing a gain for the anti-slavery cause, exceeding 3500 votes since the gubernatorial contest of two years before. The aggregate vote was 11,612; 4,972 for, and 6,640 against. This was a large vote; at the presidential election in November following, the aggregate vote of the State was 4,707.

And thus ended the most important, excited, and angry election that took place at that early day in Illinois. All feeling, however, speedily subsided, and in 6 months after, is it said, a politician who favored the introduction of slavery was a rara avis. The victory was decisive of the question for all time.

CHAPTER XXVIII.

1824–6—MISCELLANEOUS MATTERS.

Legislation—Re-organization of the Judiciary—Chief Justice Wilson—Hubbard as Governor ad interim—Population of 1825—Visit of LaFayette.

The convention struggle over, other affairs claim our attention. And first as to the legislature, which was anti-convention in its political sentiments. The members chosen simultaneously with the defeat of the convention call, constituted in a sense the first ever elected in Illinois upon other than personal considerations. Permanent party principles and organizations had been, as yet, foreign to the virgin soil of Illinois. To laud one and defame the other candidate was, up to that time, the only recognized mode of conducting a political canvass, and the campaigns were usually short. Governor Coles, in his message, congratulated the people upon the result over the slavery question, and again recommended the abolition of the remnant of African slavery still existing, as an anomaly in this free State. But the legislature, notwithstanding its anti-convention majority, was not abolition, and it paid little heed to his recommendation. Two United States senators, four supreme judges, and five circuit judges, besides a crowd of other officials, were to be elected at this session; but the majority proved itself of quite a forgiving disposition toward its recent bitter opponents, and the convention question was not made a test in the choice of the numerous officers during the session. John McLean, a leading pro-convention orator, was elected United States senator over Governor Edwards, who was not closely identified with the angry contest, being absent in Washington. It was at this time that he became involved in his unfortunate quarrel with Mr. Crawford, secretary of the treasury, which caused him to give up the Mexican mission to which he had been appointed. One week later, Elias Kent Kane was also elected to the United States senate. He defeated for the position such prominent anti-convention men as Governor Coles and Samuel D. Lockwood. Kane was perhaps the ablest writer that the convention party had during the contest, although a northern man by birth and education. Two leading pro-convention men were thus honored by an anti-convention legislature with the two highest offices in their gift.

By the constitution, the terms of office of supreme judges were to expire with the close of the year 1824. The legislature re-organized the judiciary by creating both circuit and supreme courts. The State was divided into five judicial circuits, providing two terms of court annually in each county. The salaries of the circuit judges were fixed at $600. The following circuit judges were chosen: John Y. Sawyer, Samuel McRoberts, Richard M. Young, James Hall and John O. Wattles, named in the order of their respective circuits. The supreme court was relieved of circuit duties and made a court of appellate jurisdiction. It was to be held twice a year at the seat of government, and as before, composed of four judges, but now commissioned during good behavior. Their salaries were cut down from $1000 to $800. December 30, 1824, the two houses met in joint session to elect one chief justice and three associate justices. On the first ballot, William Wilson received 35 votes, Thomas Reynolds, chief justice up to that time, 19. Wilson having received a majority of the whole number of votes cast, was duly declared chief justice of the State of Illinois.

For associate justices there were six candidates: Thomas C. Brown, Samuel D. Lockwood, Theophilus W. Smith, David Blackwell, Thomas Reynolds and John Reynolds. In the course of five ballotings, the first three named were chosen. James Turney was elected attorney-general. The two Reynolds, Thomas and John, uncle and nephew, who were rejected, had been on the supreme bench up to that time, and the former had been a conspicuous convention man.

William Wilson, at the time of his elevation to the high and honorable position of chief justice of Illinois, was but 29 years old, and had been already five years on the supreme bench as associate justice. He was born in Loudon county, Virginia, in 1795. When quite young his father died, leaving his widow with two sons and an embarrassed estate. At an early age, his mother obtained for him a situation in a store. But the young man discovered no aptitude for the business of merchandizing, and young as he was, developed an unusual greed for books, reading every one attainable, to the almost total neglect of his duties in the store. At the age of 18 he was placed in a law office under the tuition of the Hon. John Cook, who ranked high as a lawyer at the bar of Virginia, and who also served his country with honor and distinction abroad as minister to the court of France. In 1817, young Wilson came to Illinois to look for a home, and such was his personal bearing and prepossessing appearance, that one year later, at the inauguration of the State government, his name was brought before the legislature for associate supreme judge, and he came within 6 votes of an election. Within a year, as we have seen, he was chosen in the place of Foster. For five years he served the people so acceptably upon the bench as to be at this time chosen to the first position by a large majority over the former chief justice, Reynolds. This was the more a mark of approbation, because Judge Wilson was totally devoid of, and never in his life could wield, any of the arts of the politician or party schemer. As regards political intrigue, he was as innocent as a child. He was singularly pure in all his convictions of duty, and in his long public career of nearly 30 years as a supreme judge of Illinois, he commanded the full respect, confidence and esteem of the people for the probity of his official acts and his upright conduct as a citizen and a man. His education was such as he had acquired by diligent reading and self culture. As a writer his diction was pure, clear and elegant, as may be seen by reference to his published opinions in the supreme court reports. With a mind of rare analytical power, his judgment as a lawyer was discriminating and sound, and upon the bench his learning and impartiality commanded respect, while his own dignified deportment inspired decorum in others. By the members of the bar he was greatly esteemed; no new beginner was ever without the protection of almost a fatherly hand in his court, against the arts and powers of an older opponent. In politics, upon the formation of the Whig and Democratic parties, he associated himself with the former. He was an amiable and accomplished gentleman in private life, with manners most engaging and friendships strong. His hospitality was of the old Virginia style. Seldom did a summer season pass at his pleasant country seat, about two miles from Carmi, on the banks of the Little Wabash, that troops of friends, relatives and distinguished official visitors did not sojourn with him. His official career was terminated with the going into effect of the new constitution, December 4, 1848, when he retired to private life. He died at his home, in the ripeness of age and the consciousness of a life well spent, April 29, 1857, in his 63d year.

The legislature of 1824 was an important and able body. Throughout its session, harmony and cordiality obtained among the members. The men who were promoted or elevated to office, and charged with important responsibilities, were generally well known to the people for their character, merit and ability, and failed not to give satisfaction. Seventy thousand dollars of the State bank currency were committed to the flames in the presence of the governor, supreme judges and directors of the principal bank, according to the requirements of the law.

In the summer of 1825, immigration revived considerably. A great tide set in toward the central parts of the State. Through Vandalia alone, 250 wagons were counted in three weeks time, all going northward. Destined for Sangamon county alone, 80 wagons and 400 people were counted in two weeks time. Sangamon county was, at that time, without doubt the most populous county in the State. All the northern counties were most dispro-proportionately represented in the general assembly. While such counties as Randolph and White had each a senator and three representatives, Sangamon had one representative and one senator only.

It happened at this time, that Governor Coles was temporarily absent on a visit to Virginia, and Lieutenant-governor Hubbard was the acting governer. His Excellency *ad interim*, struck with the injustice of this unequal representation, issued his proclamation for an extra session of the legislature, to convene at the seat of government on the first Monday in January, 1826, for the purpose of apportioning the State, and for business generally. He was not loth to claim power. Governor Coles returned on the last day of October and resumed his office, but the acting governor was not inclined to yeild it up, claiming he had superseded the former and to be governor *de jure* under section 18, article III of the constitution, which read:

" In case of an impeachment of the governor, his removal from office, death, refusal to qualify, resignation or absence from the State, the lieutenant-governor shall exercise all the power and authority appertaining to the office of governor, until the time pointed out by the constitution for the election of a governor, shall arrive, unless the general assembly shall otherwise provide by law for the election of a governor to fill such vacancy."

After the arrival of Coles, Hubbard, as a test, issued a commission to W. L. D. Ewing as paymaster general of the State militia, which was presented to the secretary of State, George Forquer, for his signature, who refused to sign and affix the official seal thereto. In December following, the supreme court being in session, Ewing applied for a rule on the secretary to show cause why a mandamus should not be awarded requiring him to countersign and affix the seal of the State to his commission issued and signed by Adolphus Frederick Hubbard, governor of Illinois. The rule being granted, the secretary answered, stating the facts, whereby the whole question was brought before the court and argued at length with much ability by talented counsel for both sides. The judges, after much deliberation, delivered separate opinions of great learning and research, but all agreed in the judgment pronounced, that the rule must be discharged. Hubbard was still irrepressible, and next memorialized the legislature in reference to his grievance. But the senate decided that the subject was a judicial one, inexpedient to legislate upon, and the house laid his memorial upon the table.

The census of 1825 returned a population of 72,817, being considerably less than the sanguine expectations of many led them to hope for. The State was duly apportioned anew at the special session in January, 1826, with reference to the distribution of population. The question was also mooted at this session of repealing the circuit court system, not that the court did not subserve a great public need, but that politicians in their disappointment in obtaining office the winter preceding, sought to redress their grievances first by depriving the circuit judges altogether of office, and next by loading the supreme judges with additional labor by remanding them to circuit duty. The latter, being life members, could not be otherwise reached as objects of their vengeance, wherefore they were charged with having too easy a life as a court of appeals for a State so embarrassed as Illinois. The house, however, struck out of the bill to repeal all after the enacting clause and as a piece of pleasantry, inserted a section to repeal the wolf-scalp law, in which the senate did not concur.*

"THE NATION'S GUEST."

Visit of the Marquis de LaFayette to Illinois.—A pleasant episode in the spring of 1825, to vary the monotony of western life, and per adventure the pages of this book, was the visit to Illinois of General LaFayette, our able and opportune ally in the war of the Revolution, and now after the lapse of near a half century the honored guest of the nation. Having learned of his arrival in America, the general assembly of this State, early in its session of 1824-5, adopted an eloquent address of welcome to him, conched in terms of glowing admiration for his patriotic services, and

* In March succeeding, within 5 miles of where the legislature had sat, a five year old child of Daniel Hufman, which had wandered from home into the woods a mile or so, was attacked and killed by a wolf The animal was seen leaving its mangled and partly consumed body by the neighbors in search of it on the following day.

earnestly inviting him to extend his western visit to Illinois. On the 9th of December the address, with an affectionately written letter from Gov. Coles, who had formed his personal acquaintance in France in 1817, were transmitted to Gen. LaFayette. Under date of Washington, Jan. 16, 1825, he expressed his gratification for the honor done him by Illinois, adding: "It has ever been my eager desire, and it is now my earnest intention, to visit the western States and particularly the State of Illinois. The feelings which your distant welcome could not fail to excite, have increased that patriotic eagerness to admire on that blessed spot, the happy and rapid results of republican institutions, public and domestic virtues. I shall, after the celebration of the 22d of February anniversary day, leave this place for a journey to the southern, and from New Orleans to the western states, so as to return to Boston on the 14th of June, when the corner stone of the Bunker's Hill monument is to be laid; a ceremony sacred to the whole Union, and in which I have been engaged to act a peculiar and honorable part."

On the 28th of April, 1825, the steamboat Nachez, with General LaFayette and suit on board, anchored below St. Louis at the old French village of Caroudolet. On the following morning governors Clark of Missouri, and Coles of Illinois, Col. Benton, and others, repaired thither to escort the distinguished visitor up to the city. During the forenoon the boat with the entire party steamed up to St. Louis, where, upon the wharf, an immense concourse of people had assembled to greet and honor the patriot hero. He landed amidst the booming of cannon and the animated cheers of the vast multitude. He was accompanied by his son, named George Washington LaFayette, and his secretary, Col. LeVassear; by a deputation from Louisiana consisting of Col. Morse, aid to the governor, Mr. LeClair, his private secretary, and Mr. Prier, recorder of New Orleans, and Col. Ducros; by Col. Scott from the State of Mississippi, and by Maj. Gen. Gibbs, Maj. Rutledge, Mr. Bolch and Mr. Stewart, of Tenn. Addresses of welcome and responses were made, when the entire concourse moved to the elegant mansion of Pierre Choteau, where a reception was held. Supper was had, followed by a number of toasts and appropriate speeches, and in the evening a splendid ball at Massic's hotel, attended by General LaFayette, his suit, and all the dignitaries.

In person LaFayette was about six feet tall, inclining to corpulency, and a florid complexion. He limped upon his left leg, the result of a wound. He spoke the English language fluently and had a ready command of appropriate expression.

On Saturday, April 30, 1825, Gen. LaFayette and suit, attended by a large delegation of prominent citizens of Missouri, made a visit by the steamer Natchez to the ancient town of Kaskaskia. No military parade was attempted, but a great multitude of patriotic citizens bade him welcome. A reception was held at the elegant residence of Mr. Edgar. Gov. Coles, on behalf of the people of Illinois, delivered a glowing address of welcome to the illustrious guest, to which LaFayette replied in a most feeling and happy vein, expressive of his exquisite gratification for the honor done him upon that occasion.

After this a general introduction of the citizens and hand-shaking followed, when a most touching scene was presented. A few old revoluntionary soldiers collected around the General, who had fought under his eye at Brandywine and Yorktown, and who all recollected him and now greeted him most heartily. Although the géneral did not personally recollect them, the occasion was to him and all present most affecting. This meeting in the winter of their lives seemed to awaken youthful feeling and carry back these old soldier patriots to the eventful period when they were associated in arms and fighting the battles of liberty.

The entire company of distinguished guests, visitors, and citizens next proceeded to the tavern kept by Col. Sweet, where an ample dinner had been prepared. The patriotic ladies had decorated the dining hall with laurel wreaths in a most tasteful and appropriate manner, and over the table where the hero and honored guests were seated a beautiful rainbow of roses and flowers was spanned.

We can only give a very few of the after dinner toasts that were drank:

By LaFayette—Kaskaskia and Illinois; may their joint prosperity more and more evince the blessings of congenial industry and freedom.

By Gov. Coles —The inmates of LaGranges [LaFayette's home]: let them not be anxious; for though their father is 1,000 miles in the interior of America, he is yet in the midst of his affectionate children. [Very good].

By G. W. LaFayette—The grateful confidence of my father's children and grand-children, in the kindness of his American family towards him.

By Gov. Bond—General LaFayette; may he live to see that liberty established in his native country which he helped to establish in his adopted country. When this toast was given the general arose and observed that he would drink the latter part of the toast—the liberty of his adopted country—standing.

After dinner the distinguished party repaired to the large and commodious house of Wm. Morrison, Sr., Esq., where a grand ball was given for their delectation. Here during the night quite an interesting interview took place between the renowned General and an Indian squaw whose father had served under him in the Revolutionary war. The squaw, learning that the great White Chief was to be at Kaskaskia on that night, had ridden all day from early dawn till some time in the night, from her distant home, to see the man whose name had been so often upon her father's tongue and with which she was so familiar. In identification of her claim to his distinguished acquaintance, she brought with her an old worn letter which the general had written to her father, and which the Indian chief had preserved with great care, and finally bequeathed on his death bed to his daughter as the most precious legacy he had to leave her.

By 12 o'clock at night, Gen. LaFayette returned to the steamboat, and started on his route to Nashville, Gov. Coles accompanying him, the boat being chartered by the State.

He returned from Nashville on the steamboat Mechanic. On the 14th of May, 1825, when the boat appeared in sight at Shawneetown, a deputation of the citizens waited on the general, and apprised him of the reception in waiting for him. As the boat approached the landing, a salute of 24 rounds was fired. The people of the town and surrounding country had turned out en masse to greet the loved hero. Two lines were formed, extending from Rawling's hotel to the river. Down this passed the committees of reception, town officials, and other dignitaries, and received the nation's guest, who with the distinguished party accompanying him, passed up the line, the citizens standing uncovered in perfect silence, until his arrival at the door of the hotel, where a large number of ladies were assembled. Here an address of affectionate welcome was delivered by Judge James Hall. LaFayette replied without preparation, in a voice tremulous with emotion, thanking the people for this evidence of their love and gratitude. A collation was then partaken of, followed by a number of toasts suitable to the occasion. After spending a few hours in pleasant converse, the general was conducted back to the steamer, when he took a most affectionate leave. A salute was fired at the departure. The general appeared much worn with the fatigue of his trip. Governor Coles quitted him at Shawneetown, and proceeded by land to Vandalia.

CHAPTER XXIX.

1826–30—ADMINISTRATION OF GOVERNOR EDWARDS.

Campaign of 1826—The Gubernatorial Candidates—Contest between Daniel P. Cook and Joseph Duncan for Congress—Character of Gov. Edwards' speeches—His charges against the State Bank officers and result of the inquiry into their conduct—Repeal of the Circuit Court system—Gov. Edwards claims for the State title to all public lands within her limits.

At the general election of August, 1826, there were three gubernatorial candidates in the field: Ninian Edwards, Thomas C. Sloe, and Adolphus Frederick Hubbard. The latter was at the time lieutenant-governor. That he was ambitious to become governor, we have seen in his attempt to supercede Gov. Coles, failing in which he now sought that distinction, as was more becoming, directly from the hands of the people. "As a picture of the times," Gov. Coles gives the following morceau, from Hubbard's speeches to his constituents: "Fellow citizens, I offer myself as a candidate before you, for the office of governor. I do not pretend to be a man of extraordinary talents; nor do I claim to be equal to Julius Cæsar or Napoleon Bonaparte, nor yet to be as great a man as my opponent, Gov. Edwards. Nevertheless, I think I can govern you pretty well. I do not think it will require a very extraordinary smart man to govern you; for to tell you the truth, fellow-citizens, I do not think you will be very hard to govern, no how." He was an oddity.

The contest lay between Sloe and Edwards. Sloe was a gentleman of good sense and capacity, whose business was merchandising. He had been much in public life, and as a member of the legislature, time and again had wielded a large influence as a practical worker in that body. In deportment, he was dignified and urbane, but had not cultivated the art of public speaking, in which Edwards, an Apollo Belvedere in form and Titan in intellect, had quite the advantage of him.

"Edwards," says Gov. Ford, "was a large, well made man, with a noble, princely appearance," who "never condescended to the common low arts of electioneering. Whenever he went out among the people he arrayed himself in the style of a gentleman of the olden time, dressed in fine broadcloth, with short breeches, long stockings, and high, fair-topped boots; was drawn in a fine carriage driven by a negro; and for success he relied upon his speeches, which were delivered with great pomp and in a style of diffuse and florid eloquence. When he was inaugurated in

335.

1826, he appeared before the general assembly wearing a golden laced cloak, and with great pomp he pronounced his first message to the houses of the legislature."

For the office of lieutenant-governor there were but two candidates—Hubbard being without an associate. They were William Kinney and Samuel H. Thompson, and what may appear a little singular at this day, both were ministers of the gospel, the former a Baptist, the latter a Methodist. Kinney was one of the old pioneers, having emigrated to Illinois with his father in 1797.

He possessed naturally a good mind, but had recieved no education, until after marriage, when his wife taught him its rudiments. He had been much in public life, and was an efficient and untiring canvasser. In the convention contest, he had been unceasing in his efforts to render it a success. He was wealthy, and in a political canvass the duties of his holy calling were not a stumbling block in his way. The Rev. Mr. Thompson, his opponent, while he was his superior in scholastic attainments, had not his knowledge of men, nor his political art. This was his virgin effort to attain honors which perish. His character was irreproachable and forbade him to engage in any electioneering conduct to sully it. His candidacy was distasteful to him. The result of the secular contest between these two of the sacred cloth, was the reverse of that for governor. The Rev. Mr. Kinney, although running on the Sloe ticket, which failed, was elected by a small majority.

There was however, a more important contest connected with the election of 1826, in a political point of view, than that for the office of governor. We allude to the race for congress between Daniel P. Cook and Joseph Duncan, which marked the beginning of party principles, instead of mere local, personal scrambles for office. To help our understanding we must take a short view of national affairs.

Out of the presidential contest of 1824, grew the parties known afterwards as the whig and democratic. The election had failed before the people, and the house of representatives, in disregard of the will of the people, chose the one who had received next to the highest number of electoral votes, Mr. Adams. Mr. Clay accepted the highest position in the cabinet, but Mr. Crawford refused office under the new administration. Some bitterness of feeling sprang up between Mr. Clay and Gen. Jackson, the former having written a letter in which he deprecated the election of a "military chieftian" to the high office of president, which was thought to reflect upon the latter. A coalition of the Clay and Adams men followed, and as Jackson had received a plurality of electoral votes, more than double those of Crawford, and as he further, through the nomination of the legislature of Tennessee, directly became a candidate again for the same position, it became evident at an early day, that the next contest would lie between him and Mr. Adams. The friends of Mr. Crawford, therefore gave in their adhesion to the Jackson party, as by so doing, was there any hope of defeating Adams. Party principles did not as yet obtain; indeed Jackson had voted, while in the senate, with Adams and Clay, and supported affirmatively 8 different bills providing for internal improvements by the general government, and also the tariff of 1824, founded on the principle of protection.

Party divisions involved personal considerations only which were very acrimonious.

Daniel P. Cook, in the election of 1824, ran against Gov. Bond for congress, and was elected. During the campaign, the probability of the presidential election going into the house was not unforseen, and he had pledged himself in such contingency, "to vote, as a representative, in accordance with the clearly expressed sense of a majority of those whose will he should be called upon to express." The total popular vote of Illinois, which voted by districts, was 4,707, of which 1541 were cast for the electors of Adams, 1273 for Jackson, 1046 for Clay, 218 for Crawford, and 629 for James Turney, elector for Clay and Jackson jointly. If half of these latter votes had been added to Jackson's, it would have given him a pluraliy but not a majority. The electoral college of Illinois, in December following, dropping Clay and Crawford, gave to Jackson two votes, and to Adams one; but when the election of president came before the house of representatives in congress, Mr. Cook cast the vote of Illinois for Mr. Adams, as it was supposed by the people (who probably made no distinction between the highest popular vote and majority) in violation of his expressed pledges; and they believed that Gen. Jackson had been grossly cheated, by their representative. *

And now Mr. Cook was again a candidate for congress. Prior to his voting for Adams, he was the most popular man in the State. This was attributable in great part to his social qualities, being gifted with a natural charm of manner almost irresistible, and a ready adaptability to surroundings, which were to him a great aid in his electioneering intercourse with the people, and which enabled him to accommodate himself with acceptability to every circumstance and condition of western life. † Thus, with nothing against him but his vote for Adams, did he start into the campaign of 1826. His former opponents, John McLean, Elias Kent Kane, and ex-Gov. Bond had been beaten so badly and not appreciating the public resentment, they even now feared to again essay the race, and Joseph Duncan, afterward governor, then but little known in the State, had the temerity to come out against him. At that time Duncan was an original Jack-

*Reynold's Life and Times, page 254.

[†During the convention campaign, in 1824, when Mr. Cook running for congress, was opposed by ex-Gov. Bond, he had occasion to stop over night with a farmer in the southern part of the State. In conversation Cook inquired the news, to which the farmer replied "there was none, except they were afraid that that d—d little Yankee, Cook, would be re-elected to congress." The conversation continued during the evening on various topics; in the morning when Mr. Cook was about to take his departure, the farmer, pleased with his agreeable and intelligent guest, inquired his name. Mr. Cook replied, that he was "that d—d little Yankee Cook," he had alluded to the evening previous! The farmer became his devoted supporter. (Edwards' life of Edwards.) In stature Mr. Cook was below the medium hight, slender and erect, weighing not exceeding 120 pounds; his voice was soft and melodious, and his speech ready and fluent. He was born in Scott county, Kentucky, and was a self made man, having few educational advantages in his youth. In official life he exhibited an extensive and varied knowledge of public affairs. He settled in Illinois in 1815, was the first attorney general of the State, and the second congressman, beating John McLean in 1819, and was bi-ennially thereafter re-elected up to 1826. In congress he stood high; in 1825-6 he was transferred from the committee on public lands, to that of ways and means, and, owing to the absence of the chairman, acted in that laborious and responsible capacity most of the time. During his last term in congress he procured the very important grant of near 300,000 acres of land in this State for the construction, of the Illinois and Michigan canal. Mr. Cook's health having been feeble for some time, at the close of the session in the Spring of 1827, he made a visit to Cuba, but soon returned. He died of consumption, at the home of his nativity, October 16, 1827, at the early age of 34. He was the son-in-law of Gov. Edwards, and left one child, Gen. John Cook, now of Springfield. The county of Cook, was named appropriately in his honor.]

22

son man, attached to his political fortune in admiration of the
glory of his military achievements. He had been an ensign under
the dauntless Croghan at Lower Sandusky and acquitted himself
with credit. In the Illinois legislature he had served as a senator
from Jackson county. His chances of success against Cook were
regarded as hopeless; but he entered upon the campaign undaunted; his speeches, devoid of ornament, though short, were full
of good sense. He made a diligent canvass of the State, Mr.
Cook being much hindered by the state of his health. The most
that was expected of Duncan, however, was that he would get a
respectable vote—not the defeat of Cook. Both friends and foes
were struck with surprise and amazement at the result. The violence of party feeling smouldering in the breasts of the people on
account of the defeat of Jackson, was not duly appreciated until
the defeat of Cook and the election of Duncan by a majority of
641—the vote standing 6,321 for Duncan to 5,680 for Cook. Aside
from the convention struggle in 1824, none other than mere local and
personal considerations had ever before controlled the result of an
election in Illinois.

In the gubernatorial contest the party lines were not so closely
drawn. Sloe was the undoubted Jackson candidate, but Edwards,
too, professed adherence to the political fortunes of the "military
chieftain." But the burden of his speeches related to State affairs and
particularly the wasteful administration of the State finances, and
other abuses. He characterized in fitting terms the wretched legislation which had first saddled the State with the bank whose worthless issues it was bound to redeem in gold and silver by 1831; whose
notes it was bound to receive at par for taxes and other indebtedness, and which were paid out again, or auditor's warrants as their
equivalent, at $3 for $1; showed the loss from this policy must necessarily be $2 for $1 received; that a debt of $150,000 had been
imposed upon the State yearly when the ordinary current expenses
should have been but about $25,000; that these losses must event-
ually be wrung out of the people by treble taxation; that no
State, however great its energies or resources, could long withstand
so enormous a draft upon them; that it tended to check immigration; emigrants as a class were "neither the most able nor the most
willing to pay high taxes;" that while the annual State revenue
amounted to between $40,000 and $50,000, being nearly double the
current expenses of the government, these deplorable deficits and
depreciation of currency were taking place, humiliating to our pride
and disreputable to our character abroad. He inveighed against
the unjust discrimination whereby residents were compelled to pay
taxes yearly and non-residents semi-annually; that as the State
revenue was chiefly derived from the latter, human ingenuity
could not have devised a more effectual scheme to produce an annual
deficit in the State treasury. This it was that created the demand
for new issues of floods of auditor's warrants which depreciated
the currency and afforded the opportunity for speculators to riot on
the necessities of the people; but for this unfair advantage the
further emission of these warrants would cease. "But then," he
exclaimed to his auditory, "this would have withered, if not annihilated, that speculation which has so long been luxuriating upon
the resources of the State and the honest earnings of the sweat
of your brows. Such impositions as these, upon a free, highminded

and independent people, I boldly assert, have no parallel in the annals of free government, and they are only to be borne by that charity which hopeth all things, believeth all things, and endureth all things."*

Edwards fought his campaign battles single-handed, and solely upon the grounds of fiscal reform as affecting the welfare of the State, irrespective of party affiliations. This brought him in array against nearly every public man of any prominence in the State, while many of his friends stood aloof, deeming it hazardous to be identified with him. But from his triumph it may well be deduced that his forcible and instructive addresses gained the ear of the people. The legislature was, however, largely against him. His campaign speeches having produced a good effect upon the people, as evinced by their sustaining him, and encouraged by his remarkable triumph, he now attempted to go further. In his inaugural message he alluded to the delinquencies of the Shawneetown branch of the State bank, as reported by the committee of investigation, stating that "its concerns had been loosely and irregularly conducted;" that the deranged state of its accounts did not exhibit the amount of debts due, and that money had been loaned without security, contrary to the requirements of the law, sworn by all its officers to execute faithfully the injunction, "I will not permit money to be loaned to any individual without security." From which he deduced not only fraud and imposition, but the clearest moral perjury, voluntarily and deliberately committed.†

And now followed in short order several messages from him to the house, charging specific acts of corruption, particularly upon the officers of the Edwardsville branch of the State bank. A loan of $2,050 had been obtained by a mortgage upon real estate, which on execution was valued at $737.75 and which actually sold for only $491.83; another loan of $6,625 was effected upon realty valued at $3,140.71, when the sworn duty of the officers was to exact real estate security in double value of the loan, and to loan but $1,000 on such security at one time to one man. Three days later, in another message, he charged that these loans were to Thos. J. McGuire, Emanuel J. West, and Theophilus W. Smith, to establish a press at Edwardsville, intended to promote the introduction of slavery into the State; that lieutenant-governor Kinney president of the bank, advanced the money to buy the press, that McGuire was the printer who obtained the loan with West as security, and that Smith the cashier, became the editor; that no entries on the minute book showed when the loan was made, &c. These details were perhaps indiscrete, as they gave color to the charge that his excellency was actuated by something more than feelings purely of reform.

Having obtained further information, the governor, on the 25th of January, submitted to the house of representatives, as the grand inquest of the State, charges of grave and serious import against the officers and board of directors of the branch bank at Edwardsville, alleged to be predicated upon the books, accounts, and papers, delivered by the late cashier, T. W. Smith, to his successor, Mr. Miller: 1st, for making loans of more than $1000 upon real estate security to various individuals; 2d, making loans of

*Edward's Life, by his son N. W.
†See House Journal, session of 1826-7.

more than $100 upon personal security—that the president himself had two several loans of $1000 each on personal security, made, too, out of the 10 per cent fund which was never to be put into circulation; 3d, loaning on real estate not free from incumbrances; 4th, loaning on insufficient security; 5th, culpable neglect of duty in not protesting overdue paper and proceeding to the collection thereof; all in violation of the positive requirements of the law; stating that among the batch of promissory notes due and unrenewed, running back for three years, and handed over by T. W. Smith (late cashier) to his successor, there were eleven forgeries detected as early as 1822, yet no effort had been made to bring the offender to punishment; that in 1824, Thomas J. McGuire had obtained a loan of $100 on a mortgage improperly executed and without relinquishing dower (he being married), on a piece of property not worth $300; the same to Emanuel J. West on land valued on execution at $301 18; that by the law, all loans, before made, were to be passed upon by two-thirds of the board, yet T. W. Smith had obtained a loan without being so sanctioned, because at the time the president was absent from the State, two of the four directors were attending the legislature as senators, and Smith himself, one of the supreme judges, was also there in attendance. The governor further adroitly declared that he fully appreciated the formidable combinations that had grown out of the banking interest in the State, but as the crisis had arrived he proposed meeting it, notwithstanding menaces to intimidate him had been made. He would shrink from no danger, but fearlessly discharge the high trust reposed in him by the people. The message and accompanying documents were referred to a select committee of seven, composed of Henry J. Mills, George Churchill, Thomas Reynolds, William Sim, W. Cavarly and Conrad Will, with power to send for persons and papers.

Four days later, the governor, having embarked in the undertaking of ferreting out fiscal corruptions, boldly and circumstantially brought forward nine distinctive charges against the cashier of the principal bank at Vandalia, J. M. Duncan, mostly relating to withholding the required information as to the condition of the bank, failing to make out descriptive lists of the burnt notes, and failing to lay before the legislature his half yearly report as to the condition of the branches, all of which the law required, and in all which particulars the law had been violated. This message, too, was referred to a committee. Still again he charged that Theophilus W. Smith did, when acting as cashier, misapply and appropriate to his own use a large amount of funds of the bank, which he still withheld, and as he presided over the circuit court in the county of his residence, he asked that provision be made for instituting suit against him outside of his own circuit.

And now there was intense excitement at the capital. The governor had, single handed, to deal with adroit and sagacious politicians of the dominant party, some high in office, before a legislature with whom he was in a party minority. The cry was raised that the charges "emanated from a base and malignant determination, on the part of the governor, to prostrate every individual who had dared to oppose his election."[*]   Governor Ford

_____
[*]See J. M. Duncan's letter, House Journal, January 29, 1827.

says: "A powerful combination of influential men was thus formed to thwart the investigation. The governor was openly and boldly charged with base motives; and that kind of stigma was attempted to be cast on him which is apt to fix itself upon a common informer. His charges against Mr. Crawford were remembered, and he was now charged with being influenced by hostility towards Judge Smith, who had been a friend to Mr. Crawford's election."

The charges against J. M. Duncan were speedily disposed of. The committee, February 8th, reported, "exculpating the cashier of the principal bank from all censure," and that there was " not the least semblance of the violation of his duty," in any of the charges preferred by his Excellency; and as to the misapplication of the bank funds by Judge Smith, while cashier, they reported that it was not the province of the general assembly to decide upon the validity of the claims between the bank and its officers; the question was a judicial one; that a law already existed providing for a change of venue, where the judge of a court was interested in a suit.*

The committee of 7, which Governor Ford says was " packed" against the governor, gave the subject a long and apparently careful investigation, their proceedings being taken down in writing and fully reported to the house.† Many of the charges, apparently hastily made, were satisfactorily explained, yet much irregularity in the conduct and management of the bank also appeared, chief of which was in connection with the insufficiency of the real estate security required. But this was partly explained in that valuations were made after the depreciation of the bank notes, in accordance with the real value of the money received, while the hard times incident to that period also caused a very great depreciation of property generally. The loans exceeding $1000, made to directors and officers, it appeared, were authorized by section 18 of the law, which allowed them to borrow $750 " in addition to the amount which as individuals they might be entitled to." The law was further construed that they were entitled to borrow on personal security beyond the $100 allowed to individuals, which had been sanctioned by the governor himself in the case of Daniel Parkinson, a director from Sangamon, who had borrowed $850, August 9, 1821, on a note, with N. Edwards as personal security. It appeared further that this same Parkinson had presented and drawn the money on the eleven $100 notes alleged by the governor to be forged. The notes purported to be from a number of parties, but "appeared to have been signed in the handwriting of" the director from Sangamon. On inquiry, Parkinson said he was not personally acquainted with the makers of the notes, but he had heard that they were good, and lived down on Indian creek. T. W. Smith made affidavit that he had been informed by the sheriff and clerk of Sangamon county, who had made diligent search for them in order to serve them with process at the suit of the bank, that no such persons ever resided in the county to their knowledge and belief. The charge that money had been re-loaned out of the 10 per cent fund, the governor took occasion to retract.‡ The house of representatives, in committee of the whole, after

*See House Journal' 1826-7, 416-466,
†Ibid, 504 to 595
‡See House Journal, p. 454,

considering the report of the special committee, reported for adoption: "*Resolved*, That nothing has been proved against the late president, directors and cashier of the branch bank at Edwardsville, to-wit: William Kinney, Joseph A. Beaird, Thomas Carlin, Abraham Prickett, Elijah Iles and Theophilus W. Smith, which would justify the belief that they had acted corruptly and in bad faith in the management of the affairs of said bank;" which was adopted by the house. Thus did the attempt of the governor to impeach the managers of the old State Bank prove a complete failure.

As illustrative both of the cordiality existing between two of the co-ordinate branches of government and the relative dignity of the same, we give the following: Some joint resolutions, addressed to congress, were passed by the legislature in favor of amending the constitution according to Mr. Benton's idea, to allow the people to vote directly for president and vice president. The governor was *required* to transmit a copy of the resolutions to the executives of the several States, with the request that they be laid before the legislatures thereof, and also to our senators and representatives in congress. But he returned them to the house with an indignant letter, protesting against the "unprecedented language of the resolutions *requiring* him to transmit" them; that it implied an authority over a co-ordinate branch of the government, and was an assumption of power not granted to the two houses under the constitution; that such "language was violative of their relative independence," and that he "declined obedience to a command so unwarranted;" he would, however, comply with a "request" to that effect.* The offensive word was changed!

One of the most exciting measures passed at this session, was the repeal of the circuit court system, established 2 years before. During that time demagogues, well knowing how to create political capital by inference in the absence of facts, charged extravagance and a prodigal waste of the people's money in sustaining a judiciary, and virtually pensioning the supreme court, which might well perform all the circuit duty. A good deal of opposition had been stirred up among the people by the governor during his canvass, and he also urged the repeal in his inaugural message. Upon the other hand, all the nine judges, circuit and supreme, opposed it. But in this measure the governor was aided by some of his worst enemies, who had failed in their judicial aspirations two years before when the court was re-organized, and the bill prevailed. The State was divided into five circuits, assigning one of the supreme judges to each of four, to hold two terms of court in each county yearly. One of the circuit judges, the Hon. R. M. Young, was retained on a circuit in the military district. But one yearly term of the supreme court was provided. The salaries of the judges were increased from $800 to $1000. The salaries of the five circuit judges were $600 each. Thus was saved to the State treasury annually a total of $2400 from this source, at an incalculable delay and vexation to suitors in both the supreme and circuit courts. But the mere question of expense, and the petty revenge of sore aspirants, were not the only things which conspired to this repeal. One of the circuit judges was to be punished for "proscription," it was said. The circuit judges had power to appoint

*See House Journal, p. 454.

circuit clerks, but that from this as a corollary followed the power of removal, was not so clear. Judge McRoberts so viewed it, and had exercised both powers, proscriptively, it was thought. He had removed from that office, in Madison county, Joseph Conway, a political opponent, and appointed in his stead, Emanuel J. West, his friend. Conway, being well known and popular, was elected to the State senate, and after riding into office on his grievance before the people, in the legislature he brought it to bear against the entire system, and completed his revenge against McRoberts by repealing all the judges but one out of office. Judge McRoberts, intellectualy one of the first men of the State, was also unpopular on account of arbitrarily entering up judgment against Governor Coles, after he had been released by an act of the legislature from fine in emancipating his negroes without giving bond that they should not become a charge upon the county.

The supreme judges appointed at the session of 1824–5 to revise the statutes, submitted the result of their labor so far as completed. Appreciating the magnitude of such a work, fraught with such great interests, to the perfection of which great and uninterrupted re-search should be brought, they had not completed many chapters. A joint committee from both houses was appointed, which went earnestly at work to finish up the revision, employing as assistants the circuit judges in attendance at the seat of government. The revision embraced all the various laws relating to the right of property, contracts and civil actions, and the rights of persons and society, and the modes of redress. Justices of the peace were at this session made elective by the people.

1828-9—Early in the session of 1826-7, the legislature had under consideration some resolutions memorializing congress to reduce the price of public lands, and for a grant to the State of all the public lands lying therein, upon such principles as might be deemed just and equitable. Mr. Blackwell offered an amendment—"on condition that the State at all times grant to actual settlers each not less than a quarter section, to be occupied and improved." In a communication to the house, the governor recommended that our delegates in congress be instructed "to contract with the government for a surrender of the public lands within the State, on the following terms: the State to be at all the expenses of selling them at a price not exceeding 25 cents per acre; to keep an office constantly open for that purpose, and to pay to the general government annually 25 cents per acre for all that shall have been sold." Later, the committee to which the governor's communication had been referred, reported, and taking a step in advance, required from congress a surrender of the public lands "unconditionally, subject to such disposition as the people of the State, by their representatives, may deem most conducive to their prosperity and happiness."

This proposition threw the governor's effectually in the shade, and he was not heard from again during the session upon the subject. But by the meeting of the legislature in 1828, he had had ample time to work this subject up to its largest proportions. He now eclipsed the bold demand of the committee, by broadly claiming in his message of extraordinary length, evincing unusual legal research and acumen, that the public lands within the limits of Illinois belonged already to the State. He showed that the articles of confederation not only affirmed the right of every State to all the lands within its limits, but expressly declared that "no State shall be deprived of territory for the benefit of the United States." He argued that the United States, by the terms of the constitution, could not acquire or hold any land, in any original State, even with its own consent, except what may be necessary "for the erection of forts, magazines, arsenals, dock yards, and other needful buildings;" that as this State had been admitted on an equal footing with the original States, the United States could hold no more land than for these purposes within its limits, and for anything more the general government had to obtain "the consent of the legislature of the State;" that till the admission of the State into the Union, it had no rights as a State under the constitution, and consequently no competency to act in that character; it was like a minor, not within the age of consent; that the State could not therefore be bound by the acts of the territory, in consenting for the United States to hold lands within her limits; that if the federal government enjoyed this privilege of dominion over the public lands during "its political minority, it ceased on the admission of the State into the Union, having thence forward the same rights of sovereignty, freedom, and independence as the other States; that the sovereignty of a State includes the right to exercise supreme and exclusive control over all lands within it; that the freedom of a State is the right to do whatever may be done by any nation, and includes the right to dispose of all the public lands within its limits, according to its own will and pleasure; that the independence of a State includes an exemption from all control by any other State or nation over its will or action, within its own territory. The governor seems to have been deeply in earnest.

Beyond this broad claim it was impossible for the legislature to go. They did therefore the next best thing, which was, to divide the credit and honors of the grand discovery with his excellency. The committee who had considered the subject, reported: That from a careful examination of the governor's argument and aided by the best lights they could get, they believed the position assumed in the message to be correct. They close recommending the adoption of resolutions by the Senate and House of Representatives of the State of Illinois; that this State possesses the exclusive sovereignty over all lands within its limits; that the United States possesses no right of jurisdiction over any lands within the limits of Illinois; that the United States cannot hold any right of soil within the limits of the State but for the erection of forts, magazines, arsenals, dock-yards and other needful buildings, and that this State possesses the right of soil of all the public lands within its limits. The resolutions were passed, and it was further provided, that they be signed by the speakers of both houses and copies thereof sent to our senators and representatives in congress, with instructions to lay them before that body. Copies were also to be transmitted to the governors of the several States of the Union. "Having thus laid a broad foundation to enrich the State with the public lands, the members returned to their constituents swelling with importance and high expectations of future favor. But the people were not such big fools as was thought, for many laughed at their representatives in very scorn of their pretensions."* The splendid bantling fell still-born upon the public, and nothing more was heard of it afterward.

*Ford's History.

CHAPTER XXX.

1830—A RETROSPECT.

Advance of the Settlements—Note: Galena, its Early History; Origin of the term "Sucker;" Douglas' Humorous Account of it—Trials and Troubles of Pioneers in New Counties—European Colonies—Financial Condition of the State—Trade and Commerce—Early Mail Routes, Newspapers, and Literati—Politics of the People—Militia System.

The population of the State in 1820 was 157,447, having nearly trebled itself during the preceding decade. There were at this time 56 counties organized, but those in the northern portion of the State were mere skeletons and unwieldly in size. A third of the State, or more, lying between Galena and Chicago, extending southward to the Kaskaskia, the headwaters of the Vermilion, along the Rock River and far down into the military tract, constituting at present the most densely settled and best improved portions, was a trackless prairie waste, overrun by the Sac and Fox, Winnebago, and Potawattomie Indians. Much of the interior of the south part, and the country bordering the Embarrass, the Sangamon and their tributaries, had ceased to be a wilderness. Into the country of the Sangamon immigration had for some time thronged. Along the Illinois to Chicago, then just beginning to attract attention, there were scattered a few settlements long distances apart. For some years after, the settlers, either in clusters or separately, continued to hug the outskirts of the timber bordering the rivers and creeks, or the edge of groves, scarcely any venturing out on the open prairies. Along the Mississippi, settlements were scattered at distant intervals, culminating at the lead mines on Fever river, where had gathered a heterogenous population from many parts of the world, numbering about 1,000 souls, nine-tenths being men engaged in mining.*

---

*In 1804, Governor Harrison bought from the Sac and Fox tribes a tract of land at the mouth of the Fever river (Mecapiasipo) 15 miles square. Lead had been mined for many years on the Iowa side and was known to exist on the Illinois side. The first white settler at the mines on Fever river, was a Frenchman named Boutiller, in 1819. Shortly after, Jesse Shull, a trader, occupied an island there in the river, and being informed that the Indians had discovered lead near where Galena now stands, moved thither. This proved to be the noted "buck lead." A. P. Van Metre soon joined, and "all took to themselves wives of the daughters of the land, and were traders for their brethren." Later, Dr Samuel Mure also married to a squaw, and was associate of the well known Indian trader, Davenport, of Rock Island, located there. He gave to Galena its name (from the Greek, Galanas, a species of lead ore) In 1820, Colonel J. Johnson, authorized by the war department, arrived and assumed almost exclusive control of the mining. He was followed by a few others the same year, and more in 1823-4. Float or gravel mineral was extensively sown, some prospects sold, and thus by fraud, parties went further out, and some splendid "leads" were discovered.

In 1825, the 15 mile boundary was overleaped, and the country of the Winnebagos first trenched upon. The "Shullsburg," "East Fork" and "New Diggings" were found

346

As there was doubtless much sameness in the early settlement of new counties, particularly in the central and northern portions of the State, the details of which would probably prove both dull and improfitable to the general reader; and as such early data have, except in a few cases, generally been so unconspicuous as to cause them not to be preserved, and are now either lost or become traditional, we subjoin the following account by Nathan Dillon, picturing the condition of two counties after their first organization, which gives perhaps the fair average experience of many an old settler, and conveys to us their trials, privations and difficulties:

"As early as 1821, a few log cabins were already built in Sangamon county, which at that date embraced all the northern part of the State.

and developed, and the number of miners had increased to 1600. In 1826, a one horse mail was established from Vandalia to Galena, once every 2 weeks.

In 1827, the government first surveyed the town, permitting parties to occupy and improve lots, on condition that they vacate them on 30 days notice. This was all the title any occupant had up to 1838. The next neighbors of the Galenians, south, were the Peorians; and between the two places lay a vast wilderness of uninhabited territory. In 1825, Mr. Kellog started his "trail" from Peoria to Galena, crossing Rock river a few miles above the present Dixon, thence by the West Grove to Galena. The Winnebagos assisted in ferrying Rock river. Two canoes placed side by side formed the ferry boat, the wheels of one side of a wagon in one, and those of the opposite in the other canoe. The hores swam. The next year, "Bolles Trail" was established. The river was ferried at Dixon, where the Illinois Central railroad bridge now crosses. This was more direct, and became shortly the main route of travel to the lead mines. In the spring of 1827, the travel was so great that in a very few days 200 teams passed at this point. There were also other "trails" farther to the west. The "Lewiston trail" crossed Rock river a little above Prophetstown, Whiteside county. (From the History of Ogle county.)

The low cognomen of "sucker," as applied to Illinoisans, is said to have had its origin at the lead mines. Says George Brunk, of Sangamon: Late in the fall of 1826, I was stanning on the levee of what is now Galena, watching a number of our Illinois boys go on board of a steamboat bound down the river, when a man from Missouri stepped up and asked—"Boys, where are you going?" The answer was, "home." "Well," he replied, "you put me in mind of suckers; up in the spring, spawn, and all return in the fall." The appellation stuck to the Illinoisans; and when Judge Sawyer came up to the mines on his circuit duty, he was styled "King of the Suckers." These who stayed over winter, mostly from Wisconsin, were called Badgers. The following spring the Missourians poured into the mining region in such numbers that the State was said to have taken a puke, and the offensive appellation of "Pukes" was thenceforward applied to all Missourians. But the following is a more tasteful origin of the appellation of "Sucker":

On occasion of a pleasant entertainment at Petersburg, Virginia, Judge Douglas gave the following humorous account of the origin of the term "Suckers" as applied to Illinoisans; the account is valuable further, and confers a proud distinction upon Illinois, in that it clears up all doubt regarding the discovery of that important and inspiring beverage called "mint julep," a momentous question heretofore covered with obscurity and beset with many doubts, but now in the light of these facts, happily placed at rest. It is not improbable that a glass of the animating beverage served to quicken the memory of the honorable senator on the occasion.

"About the year 1777, George Rogers Clark applied to the governor of Virginia, and suggested to him that as peace might be declared at any time between Great Britain and the colonies, it would be well for us to be in possession of the northwest territory, so that when the commissioners came to negotiate a treaty, we might act on the well known principle of uti possidetis, each party holding all they had in possession. He suggested to the governor to permit him to go out to the northwest, conquer the country, and hold it until the treaty of peace, when we would become possessed of it. The governor consented and sent him across the mountains to Pittsburgh. From there he and his companions floated down the Ohio on rafts to the falls, where Louisville now is. After remaining there a short time, they again took to their rafts and floated down to the salines, just below the present Shawneetown in Illinois. Here they took up their march across the country to Kaskaskia, where the French had an old settlement, and by the aid of a guide they reached the Oquaw river, and encamped near Peter Menard's house, some little distance from the town. You see, I am well acquainted with the locality. [Laughter.] Next morning, Clark got his little army of ragamuffins together (for they had no army wagons with supplies, no sutler, and no stores, and by this time looked ragged enough), and took up his line of march for the little French town of Kaskaskia. It was summer and a very hot day, and as he entered the town he saw the Frenchmen sitting quietly on their little verandahs, in front of their houses, sucking their juleps through straws. He rushed upon them, crying, "surrender, you suckers, you!" [Great laughter.] The Frenchmen surrendered, and from that day to this, Illinoisans have been known as "Suckers." [Applause.]

"That was the origin of our cognomen, and when George Rogers Clarke returned to Virginia he introduced the juleps here. [Laughter.] Now, I want to give Virginians fair notice, that when they claim the honor of a Jefferson, of a Madison, of a Marshall, and of as many other distinguished sages and patriots as the world ever saw, we yield; when you claim the glory you achieved on the field of battle, we yield; when you claim credit for the cession of the northwestern territory, that out of it sovereign States might be created, we yield; when you claim the glory of never having polled a vote against the Democratic party, we yield; but when you claim the glory of the mint julep, hands off; Illinois wants that. [Shouts of laughter and applause.]—Ill. Reg. Sept. 19, 1860.

The cabins were filled to overflowing with the families, the pioneers of the county, my family being among the number. I was present at the election, August 1822, held at Springfield (the election precinct extending many miles east and west, and north to the State line), and saw all the voters who could come to vote in that wide scope of uninhabited country. Most of the voters residing in the precinct attended the election, though many of them had miles of wild country to travel in order to do so.

The voters were mostly immigrants from the east and south, though a large portion of the men present were Indians and darkies, they of course not being allowed the right of suffrage. The voting portion of the community were then called the Yankees and white men. Three men named Kinney, Parkinson, and Edwards, had a long bench ranged along side of the court house, on which they set their liquors. The polls were held in the interior. We all got plenty to drink. The white men sang songs, the Indians and darkeys danced, and a general frolic occurred; but what has surprised me as I have reflected upon these early days, we had no fighting. The great evil was, that every candidate had to fill his portmanteau with whiskey, and go around and see and treat every voter and his wife and family with the poisonous stuff, or stand a chance of being defeated. John Reynolds was our circuit judge. He held his court at Springfield, in a cabin built of round logs, the walls of which were only 6 feet high; it was also destitute of a floor; yet we continued to get along very well. The jury had to retire to the jail, another such building as I have described. Such is the outline of those happy days.

In the winter of 1823, I emigrated to what is now called Dillon settlement, in this county, 10 miles from Pekin, and 17 from Peoria, where I spent the season in quietude; my nearest neighbors living in Peoria, except one by the name of Avery, who had raised his cabin at Funk's hill. But things did not remain in this condition long; for during the same winter the legislature made a new county, with Peoria for the county seat, embracing all the country north of Sangamon county. Phelps, Stephen French and myself were appointed justices of the peace for the new county, which extended east as far as Bloomington, and north and west to the State line. We sent our summonses to Chicago and Galena, and they were promptly returned by our constable.

March, 1824, we held an election at Avery's, Wm. Holland, Joseph Smith and myself were elected county commissioners. The whole county was embraced in one election district. The number of votes polled was 20; had some whiskey on the occasion, but it was well tempered, having been imported a long way by water; and we did not succeed in getting on as great a spree as we did at Springfield.

In those days when we could not get the store room of Hamlin or Allen, or the dwelling house of John Dixon, we held our courts on the river bank; not being as wealthy or strong handed as in Sangamon, we had to do without a court house; Judge Sawyer was our circuit judge, and it was some time before we could scare up a jury. At that date there was not a cabin on the site of the city of Pekin, and perogues were the only crafts we had to freight our whiskey, salt, and iron from the State to Peoria.

Now let me tell you how we got along about mills. There were 3 or 4 horse mills in Sangamon, at 40 or 45 miles distance. Sometimes we went to them; sometimes to Southwick's, situated at a distance of 60 miles; we did not mind the journey much, unless the streams were swollen with rains, in which case the task of going to mill was severe, as there were no bridges and ferries in those days. By and by, to remedy our wants, Samuel Tutter erected a small horse mill in the neighborhood of Peoria; and a few years after, William Eds put up one at Elm Grove; a public improvement which made us feel quite rich. In those early times, we only took corn to mill, paying one-sixth and one bit per bushel, for grinding. The meal obtained was of an inferior quality when compared with what we now have. Our millers were good, honest fellows, and the somewhat heavy tariffs they laid on their customers not at all wrong, for their income was small.

Times are changed. The reader who now looks at the fertile prairies of Illinois, what does he behold. Large cities and flourishing towns! Behold the prairies, then wild and untrodden, now covered with fine farms and dwellings, behold the travel of our railroads and rivers, visit our county fairs and become acquainted with our intelligent farmers, and the vast and valuable amount of products derived from the soil they till; behold on every hand our numerous churches and school houses, our court houses and seats of justice, spread all over the wide territory which French, Philips and myself early governed as humble justices; and tell me, has not the changed improvement been great and remarkable."*

European Colonists.—It has been stated that the early settlers were mostly from the southern states. There were also some foreign colonists located in Illinois at an early date. The first were a few Irish families, under the leadership of Samuel O'Melvany, a popular pioneer, who located on the Ohio river about 1805.

Shortly after the war of 1812, Morris Birbeck, an Englishman imbued with republican principles, visited Illinois with a view to locating a colony of his countrymen. Being a man of fine scholarly attainments, he wrote home for publication a number of letters faithfully representing the advantages of this country, which received a wide circulation and proved of great benefit to Illinois abroad. In a short time after, he and George Flower, both men of wealth brought out from England a large colony consisting of several hundred families, representing almost every industrial pursuit. They located in Edwards county. The town of Albion, the present county seat, was started by Mr. Flower, and about a mile west of it another by Mr. Birbeck, called Wannock, which proved a failure. There was some rivalry. There was much wealth and refinement in the colony, aside from that in the possession of the founders. A few of the first settlers are still living, their descendents are quite numerous in and about Albion.†

About 1815, two German families, by the name of Markee and Germain, first settled in a gorge of the Mississippi bluff in St. Clair county, known from that circumstance as Dutch Hollow. These families became the nucleus of the present large German population of St. Clair and adjacent counties. Another English colony, Roman Catholic in belief, composed of 15 or 20 families from Lancashier, settled in Prairie du Long Creek, Monroe county, in 1817. Thomas Winstanly, Bamber, Threlfall and Newsham were the founders. They became a thrifty settlement. Numerous English immigrants also settled in Green county in 1820.

In 1819 Ferdinand Ernst, a gentlemen of wealth, education and literary taste, from the kingdom of Hanover, came to Vandalia, then just selected as the seat of government, and located a German colony consisting of 25 or 30 families. In 1822 Bernard Steiner settled a small Swiss colony of 8 or 10 families in the southeastern part of St. Clair county. Their location was on a beautiful and

---

*See Illinois State Journal June 30 1854.

†Mr. Flower lost his fortune by the breaking of the United States bank, and afterwards removed to Mt. Vernon, Indiana, but some of his descendents still live in the Boltenhouse prairie. Mr. Birbeck was secretary of State under Gov. Coles. In the convention contest of 1824, he contributed more by his writings than perhaps any one else to defeat the schemes of the cohorts of slavery. He was unfortunately drowned in a bayou of the great Wabash, called Fox river, swollen by heavy rains. He, accompanied by his son was on his way home from New Harmony, Indiana, then in charge of the Robert Owen communists, whither they had made a visit. In attempting to cross the stream, the rapid current swept their horses out of their course, and Mr. Birbeck and both horses perished. His son barely escaped the same fate. His untimely death was a great loss to the State.

commanding eminence called Dutch Hill. It was added to by subsequent immigrants until it formed a large settlement.*

Financial Condition of the State.—When the State government went into operation, in 1818, the total revenue reported in the treasury, and to become due on the 1st of December, was $7,310.40; it now amounted for the years 1829-30 to $78,938, of which $70,237 was derived solely from taxes on non-residents' lands, $2,787 from the Ohio salines, $2,866 from the sale of Vandalia lots, and $3,084 collected by sheriffs. The biennial State expenses were estimated by the treasurer, for salaries and to support the contingent fund, at $25000, and for a session of the general assembly at $15,000, total $40,000, or $20,000 annually, leaving at the lowest estimate a surplus revenue of $30,000 every two years. That was a good healthy condition of the State's fiscal affairs. Gov. Edwards was greatly instrumental in bringing about this highly creditable condition of the State treasury, which he found 4 years before empty, and auditor's warrants at a discount of 50 per cent. At the present writing we have a population 16 times as large, to-wit, 2,553,000; we have no public debt of consequence, and our gain of property is proportionately larger than our ratio of increase in population, yet our State expenses are 50 times greater, as every tax payer yearly feels.

During the period over which we are now casting a retrospect, the treasuries of the State and counties, and suitors at law individually, were subjected to serious losses by defaulting sheriffs, for taxes collected and moneys received on execution. If the sheriff was an aspirant for re-election, the State or county would not suffer much the first term, because he could not be commissioned for a second term without a certificate of settlement for all public funds placed in his hands; but to exhibit such a clearance, the money collected on executions and belonging to individuals would be used; while with the people generally, who felt little concern in these private affairs, and among whom his official duties constantly called him, he was in the condition to contradict rumors, and in the face of his dereliction enabled to make friends and secure a renewed lease of power.† No official who handles large sums of the people's money, or is so closely identified with all our property rights, either corporate or individual, as a sheriff or treasurer, ought by law to be allowed to become his own successor in office. We can but regard this as a bad feature in the constitution of 1870.

Trade and Commerce.—Internal improvements to facilitate trade and commercial intercourse, consisted, up to that time, mostly in acts of the legislature declaring certain streams navigable. In these declarations that honorable body was not the least parsimonious, but dealt them out to almost every rivulet with a prodigal hand; and a stranger, in looking over the old statutes, ante-dating, say, 1840, would inevitably conclude that the State of Illinois was intersected by navigable streams in every direction as abundantly as could possibly be desired by the most commercial people. To the Illinois and Michigan canal there was as yet nothing done

*Reynold's Life and Times
†Ford's History.

except some very imperfect surveys, though it had been the theme of recommendation by every governor, and its grant of land was procured from congress.

The progress of commerce from 1818 to 1830 was jostled but little from its beaten track by the improved facilities of quick conveyance offered by the introduction of steam. Steamboats upon the Ohio and Mississippi had become frequent, but the older settlers were not stirred from their drowsy condition of making simply enough to live on by the new life, and the recent settlers, if they desired, were not in a condition to raise anything beyond their present needs—the condition of all new comers. The Illinois river was not visited by the newly propelled craft, except small ones which ascended to Beardstown and occasionally to Peoria and above, as required. Gen. Joseph Street, writing from Peoria under date of March 30, 1827, says: "There is nothing doing on land and less on water. * * The harbor and town site are the best, I presume, in all the western country; but not one sail enlivens the monotonous prospect or one oar dips in the dark blue waves of the fairy lake from one years' end to another—if you will except the ferry boat, with now and then the canoe of a few miserable savages in quest of a dram." Keel-boat transportation had been superseded, it is true, but the scanty commerce and feeble trade made no demands for more extensive carrying facilities than we have mentioned. In development and wealth the State was in its merest infancy.

Merchandizing during this period consisted in the bare retailing of a few dry goods and groceries. None of the products of the country were taken in exchange, except peltries, beeswax* and tallow. The peoples' chief supply of money came from immigrants who bought of their grain, stock or produce, and often employed their labor besides. The money went out again into the hands of the merchants who sent it abroad in payment for goods, and thus the country was kept drained of anything like a sufficient currency. When credit was obtained at the stores, in default of payment and to gain time, mortgages would often be given, these foreclosed, the merchant would in time find himself the possessor of perhaps a number of farms, retire from business on a competency and dream away his life in village idleness, without ever benefiting the country in the least, but ruining perhaps a number of its citizens. For a long time there was no class of merchants who did a barter business. They were unwilling to exchange goods for produce and incur the responsibility of ownership until shipments to distant markets and sales could be effected. There was the risk of a fluctuating market in the interim; their capital as a rule was small, and a loss on produce might render them

---

*"Fifty years ago, or in the summer of 1821," writes Chas. Robertson of Arnzville, under date of Feb. 8, 1872, to the Chicago *Journal*, "there was not a bushel of corn to be had in Central Illinois. My father settled in that year 23 miles west of Springfield. We had to live for a time on venison, blackberries and milk, while the men were gone to Egypt to harvest and procure breadstuffs. The land we improved was surveyed that summer, and afterward bought of the government by sending beeswax down the Illinois river to St. Louis in an Indian canoe. Dressed deer skins and tanned hides were then in use, and we made one piece of cloth out of nettles instead of flax. Cotton matured well for a decade, until the deep snow," in 1830.

The southern part of the State, known as Egypt, received this appellation, as here indicated, because being older, better settled and cultivated, it "gathered corn as the sand of the sea," and the immigrants of the central part of the State, after the manner of the children of Israel, in their wants went "thither to buy and bring from thence that they might live and not die.

insolvent; no business connections with commission houses had been established; added to these was often a limited capacity. A few years later, it seems, merchants were forced into barter by the refusal of the United States bank at St. Louis to extend accommodations to them, in meeting their matured contracts for goods bought in the east. Then the grain, beef, and pork of the country were purchased and shipped forward in payment thereof, and not unfrequently, it was found, a double profit was realized, one on the goods sold at retail and another on the produce forwarded.*

It was no uncommon practice in early times for farmers to become their own carriers and merchants; the practice obtained to within quite a recent period in many parts of southern Illinois. A flat-boat would be built on the banks of a suitable stream, launched, loaded with the produce of the year—the flour, bacon, corn, etc., of perhaps a neighborhood—manned, and with the first rise of the waters, cut loose and floated down to New Orleans. After a tedious and often hazardous voyage, on arrival at the distant market a total stranger, it was not unfrequently the case that the farmer-merchant would fall into the clutches of sharpers who took advantage of his want of acquaintance with commercial transactions and fleeced him of his cargo. But these ventures proved at times exceedingly profitable. Before the day of steam the journey home was long, toilsome and weary, either on foot through the country inhabited by savages, or by keel-boats, laboriously pushed with poles, or *cordelled*—towed with long ropes—against the strong currents of the rivers. An entire season would thus often be wasted, a crop lost, and the farm abandoned to neglect, on account of the long absence of the proprietor.†

Early Mail Facilities.—The first mail route crossing the Alleghany mountains, was opened from Philadelphia to Pittsburgh in 1788, and, at intervals of six years, was extended, in 1794, to Louisville, and in 1800 to Vincennes. From the latter place, routes were extended, in 1805, to Cahokia, and in 1806, to Shawneetown. In 1810, mail routes were established by act of congress from Vincennes to St. Louis, via Kaskaskia, Prairie du Rocher and Cahokia, and from the former place to Cape Girardeau, via St. Genevieve, and also from Louisville to Shawneetown; in 1814, to Johnson Court-house (Johnson county, Illinois), and in 1818, to Belleville. In 1822, Edwardsville, Springfield and Peoria were connected by a mail route; and in 1823, Carrollton, Ross Settlement and New Atlas, in Pike county. In 1824, there was a direct mail route from Vandalia to Springfield. The first route from the central part of the State to Chicago, was established in 1832, from Shelbyville, via Decatur and Fox river; and in the same year, a route from Chicago to Danville, and to Green Bay. Direct routes from Chicago to Galena, and to Springfield, were opened in 1826. In 1827–8, four-horse coaches were put on the line from Vincennes to St. Louis. The difficulties and dangers encountered by the early mail carriers, in time of Indian troubles, were very serious. The bravery and ingenious devices of Harry Wilton (subsequently United States marshal), who, when a boy, in 1812, conveyed the

*Ford's History.
†Ford's History,

mail on a wild French pony, over swollen streams, and through the "enemy's country," from Shawneetown to St. Louis, are mentioned with special commendation. Stacy McDonald, of Randolph county, an old pioneer, who was at St. Clair's Defeat, and under Wayne in 1794, was the government mail contractor on that line. So infrequent and irregular were the communications by mail a great part of the time, that to-day, the remotest part of the United States is unable to appreciate it by example.*

Early Newspapers.—The first newspaper published north of the Ohio, and west of Cincinnati, was the Vincennes *Sun*, in 1803, edited by Elihu Stout. The next in the west was the Missouri *Gazette*, established at St. Louis, in 1808, by Joseph Charless, and continued ever since, but subsequently merged in the *Republican*. The next in the west, and the first within the limits of the State, was the *Illinois Herald*, established at Kaskaskia, by Matthew Duncan, brother of the subsequent governor. There is some variance as to the exact time of its establishment. Wm. H. Brown, afterward editor of the same paper at Vandalia, under the name of *Intelligencer*, and in after years president of the Chicago historical society, says, "at or before 1814." Gov. Reynolds says, 1809. Hooper Warren explains the latter statement by saying, "the press brought by Mr. Duncan was for years only used for the public printing." Matthew Duncan sold out to Robert Blackwell and Daniel P. Cook in 1815. The former succeeded Mr. Duncan, as public printer, and was, moreover, the territorial auditor of public accounts. In the latter office he was succeeded, in the fall of 1817, by Elijah C. Berry, who also succeeded to the same office under the State government in 1818, and who became a co-editor of the *Herald*. In the hands of Blackwell and Berry the name of the paper was changed to *Illinois Intelligencer*, and upon the removal of the seat of government to Vandalia in 1820, the *Intelligencer* establishment followed it. Mr. Berry relinquished his interest in the concern, and his place was taken by a brother and Wm. H. Brown. In the convention contest of 1824, differing with his associates, Mr. Brown withdrew. The *Intelligencer* was long an ably conducted paper, Mr. Blackwell, a well known lawyer, being for many years its editor.

The Illinois *Emigrant*, the second newspaper printed in Illinois, was established at Shawneetown by Henry Eddy and Singleton H. Kimmel, in the fall of 1818, when the State was admitted to the Union. James Hall succeeded Mr. Kimmel. Through this paper Mr. Eddy, a clear and vigorous writer, in the convention struggle of 1824, dealt herculean blows in opposition to slavery. The name had been changed to *Illinois Gazette*.

The third newspaper established in Illinois, was founded by Hooper Warren, at Edwardsville, in 1819, called the *Spectator*. The first year he had the assistance of the afterward Hon. George Churchill, a practical printer and experienced writer, whom he met at St. Louis. Mr. Churchill retired at the end of a year to his farm near Edwardsville, where he lived until quite recently. Hooper Warren was a bold, able, and vigorous writer, and did much to defeat the slavery schemes in 1824. In 1825, he

_____

*Paper read before the Chicago Hist. Society, by W. H. Brown in 1860

23

sold out to the Rev. Thomas Lippincott and Jerremiah Abbot. Mr. Warren afterward started newspapers in various places in the State, but never with the success that his ability promised.

In September, 1822, the "*Star of the West*" was started by a Mr. Miller and sons, also at Edwardsville. They had just come from Pennsylvania with a press and material, seeking a location. At Edwardsville, while stopping over night, they were persuaded by the opponents of Mr. Warren, to unload and set up their press. He remarks, "we had a lively time for a few months, when the "*Star*" went down." They sold in April, 1823, to Thomas J. McGuire & Co., who changed the name to *Illinois Republican*. Judge Theophilus W. Smith and Emanuel J. West were the leading editors during the convention contest, in counteracting the influence of the *Spectator*. It was discontinued with the close of that campaign, the last number being issued Saturday preceding the election in August, 1824

In January, 1823, R. K. Fleming commenced to publish the *Republican Advocate*, at Kaskaskia, which was the organ of the pro-convention party during the contest.

In 1826, at Galena, on the 4th of July, was issued the first number of the *Miners' Journal*, by James Jones. In 1832, he sold to Dr. Phillio, when its name was changed to *Galenian*.

In the winter of 1826-7, Hooper Warren established the *Sangamo Spectator* at Springfield. Mr. Warren says (letter to the old settlers' meeting of Sangamon county, October, 1859), "it was but a small affair, a medium sheet, worked by myself alone most of the time." It was transferred to S. C. Merredith in 1828. In the latter year was started at Edwardsville, the *Illinois Corrector*, and at Kaskaskia, the *Republican*. In 1829 was established the *Galena Advertiser*, by Newhall, Phillio & Co. The *Alton Spectator* was established about 1830, by Edward Breath. The *Telegraph* was established by Parks and Treadway, the latter transferring his interest in a short time to Mr. Bailhache, who was its principal editor for many years. In 1831, Simeon Francis established at Springfield, the *Sangamo Journal*, which he continued to edit until 1855, when he sold to Bailhache and Baker. In Chicago, on the 26th of November, 1833, was issued the first number of the *Democrat*, published by John Calhoun, which was the first newspaper there.

Literature and Literati.—The literature of Illinois, prior to 1830, aside from mere political articles in the newspapers, often well and forcibly written, was confined to few hands. We will here mention the prominent early literati of Illinois. *Morris Birbeck*, an Englishman, whom we have noted as settling a colony in Edwards county, in 1855, wrote home sketches of considerable merit regarding the advantages of Illinois, which received a wide publication and were afterwards collected in book form. He acquired considerable celebrity as an author. *Dr. Lewis C. Beck* wrote the valuable and well known Gazetteer of Missouri and Illinois, which in 1823, was published in book form. *Judge James Hall* was a Philadelphian, born 1793. He settled in Illinois about 1818. He had been a soldier in the war of 1812, having participated under Scott in the battles of Chippewa, Niagara and Fort Erie, and been with Commodore Decatur to Algiers. At Pittsburgh, in 1817, he completed his law studies, resigned his commission in the regular army, floated down the Ohio and settled at Shawneetown. He had already devoted much time to literary composition. Here he became a co-editor with Henry Eddy on the *Gazttee*. He also soon attained office at the hands of the legislature, being successively prosecuting attorney, circuit judge and State treasurer. In the first named position he became well acquainted with the operations of the gangs of villians, counterfeiters and freebooters, which then infested the shores of the Ohio and Mississippi, in southern Illinois, and which doubtless furnished him many an incident out of which to weave his "Border Tales." At Vandalia he started the *Illinois Magazine.* He also at that time edited the *Western Souvenir*, published at Cincinnati, whither he removed in 1833, and became connected with banking, but he pursued his literary labors until his death in 1868. Throughout life his pen was constantly active. He wrote with great facility, and his voluminous works evince a high degree of literary merit. He early became distinguished as a scholar and author throughout the United States. As a poet, too, he was rarely gifted. Among his works best known are perhaps, "Legends of the West." "Harpe's Head," "Border Tales," "Life of Gen. Harrison," "Tales of the Wigwam and War path," &c. He has also left an elaborate " History of the North American Indians."

Rev. John M. Peck, D. D. This distinguished Baptist divine, pioneer and historian of Illinois, resided for near 40 years on his farm at Belleville, known as "Rock Spring." He came to Illinois about 1820. There was no man in all the west who traveled, lectured or wrote so much as he, during his long life, throughout which he was also a constant, faithful and able preacher of the gospel. He was the founder in 1827, of the "Rock Spring theological seminary and high school," and became its professor of christian theology. John Messinger was professor of mathematics and natural philosophy, and Rev. Joshua Bradly principal. It opened with 100 students. In 1831 it was transferred to Alton, and became the foundation for Shurtleff college. Dr. Peck wielded a prolific pen. Among his voluminous works we mention, without order, The Emigrants Guide, Illinois Gazetteer, maps &c., Life of Rev. John Clark, The Indian Captive, Life of Rev. John Tanner, Moral Progress of the Mississippi Valley, Life of Rev. Jeremiah Vordeman, &c.; but the work which will transmit his name to posterity the longest is his revision and enlargement of the "Annals of the West," by Jas. H. Perkins. It evinces much research and contains a very accurate history of the northwest. We are considerably indebted to it in the preparation of this work.

John Russell, a native of Vermont, after marriage in 1819, removed west, and a few years later settled in Green county, at Bluff Dale, a beautiful and romantic site not far from the Illinois river. Much of his life was spent as a professor in various colleges in the west. He was a professor at an early day in Shurtleff college, a profound scholar and chaste and elegant writer, but his productions were not voluminous. Like many authors before him, he was unobtrusive with his talents. He led a quiet and retired life in his western home, but was ever an inde-

fatigable student. His literary morceaus were often set afloat
without the author's name.

Dr. Peck sold a manuscript for him in the east, a magazine
article called "The Legend of the Piasa," representing a terrible
bird of prey, which feasted on the Indians, under an injunction
not to disclose the writer's name. It attracted considerable attention, and was afterwards translated into French, as original. Dr.
Peck exposed the plagiarism, to the great mortification of the
Frenchman, who resided in America. One of Prof. Russel's
fugitive pieces, called the "Venomous Worm," gained a wide celebrity, being transalated into many languages. It conveys a deep
moral lesson in allegory on intemperance, and became a standard
piece in our earlier school books.*

[NOTE]—To anticipate a few years, we find Pegasus also bestrode upon the level plains
of Illinois, several regions having their local poets. Kane county had one apparently
enamored of the solid advantages which the State of his adoption afforded. He sang
as follows:

> "The timber here is very good—
> The forest dense of sturdy wood:
> The maple tree its sweets affords
> And walnut it is sawn to boards;
> The giant oak the axman hails
> Its massive trunk is torn to rails,
> And game is plenty in the State,
> Which makes the hunter's chances great—
> The prairie wolf infests the land,
> And the wild cats all bristling stand.'

To show the comparative excellence of our rivers, he sang further:

> "I've gazed upon the wild Scioto,
> And wondered where its waters go to;'

But the Illinois,

> "Rattling onward in its course,
> Doth seek the Mississippi's source"—

afforded him no such misgivings, for it will be perceived that by a poetic license, perhaps, but in defiance of natural law, he runs its waters up the Mississippi.

*Politics of the People—Manner of conducting Campaigns—In-
trigues of Politicians.*—Regarding the political sentiments of the
people, it is not flattering to our republican pride to read from an
accurate observer of the period: "Up to the year 1840, I can say
with perfect truth, that considerations of mere party, men's con-
descensions, agreeable carriage and professions of friendship, had
more influence with the great body of the people, than the most
important public services."† But it is more humiliating to confess
that these considerations play to-day no less a part than they did
40 and 50 years ago; and they probably always will be formidable
agencies in politics, however we may boast the intelligence of the
masses.

The masses did not expect that, nor did the public servants
think or study how, government might be made conducive to the
elevation of the people. To advance the civil condition and happiness of society was an object foreign to the purposes of legislation. Government was tolerated, and its forms and requirements
acquiesced in, by the masses, from a feeling of habit, so long as its
administration did not clash with or encroach upon their interests, enjoyments, or personal freedom too much.‡

*Reynolds Life and Times.   †Ford's Hist
‡An anecdote, related by Robert S. Blackwell Esq., at a New England supper on
Pilgrim's day in Chicago, December 21, 1853, may serve to illustrate this characteristic of the old pioneers: "They were great bee-hunters and had a custom of appropriating to the finder all bee trees, on whose land soever they happened to be growing.
When they discovered a bee tree without leave or license, they entered upon the
land and cut it down, and made themselves masters of the honey. The owner seldom

Among the pioneers were also many adventurers; and nearly all immigrants sought the new country for an easier life or the accumulation of property. Upon governmental affairs but little thought was bestowed. When aroused to the exercise of the great privilege of the citizen—the elective franchise—by interested demagogues, no other consideration entered into the act than to either favor a friend or punish an enemy. This indifference, so unworthy of the citizen, redounded to the advantage of the active and diligent place hunters, in that it permitted them, without molestation or exposure, to perfect their "pipe laying" for the partition of governmental patronage. There were no great political questions to divide the people prior to 1832–3. Politics were personal, and suffrage was bestowed, not with regard to public welfare, but as a matter of personal favor. In such elections, the ballot system, which in denser populations affords the greatest independence to the voter in eliciting his true intent, was here prostituted to double-dealing and dissimulation. Out of it grew what was known as the "keep dark Boon" system, in which were sacrificed on the part of both office seekers and, to a certain extent, the people, all principles of honor and sincerity, by mutual deceptions of every grade and character, from which the most adroit intriguer emerged with the greatest success. Promises of support would be violated as freely as they were made. To cure the evil, the legislature repealed the mode of voting by ballot at the session of 1828–9

The use of ardent spirits was almost a universal custom with the people, and "treating," as it was called, during a political canvass, was a *sine qua non* to success. Not unfrequently candidates for office would give orders to liquor saloons to treat freely whosoever would drink at their expense, on certain days, usually every Saturday and other days of public occasion, for weeks before the day of election. At such places the voters would congregate from all parts of the surrounding neighborhoods on "treating days" during the campaign, riding in to gather the news, and not unfrequently get drunk and engage in rough and tumble fights. The candidates, too, would often make it a point to be there on these days, either themselves or by proxy, and harangue the "sovereigns" upon the issues of the campaign, in a convenient shady grove, the auditors, not unfrequently interspersed with ladies, seated about on the green sward. The orators would thunder forth their claims to office, mounted on convenient wagons, logs, or stumps of trees, hence the phrase of "stump speech." The "vital questions of the day," discussed at these meetings, were not measures but men, and consisted in bitter personal arraignments of opponents, often of little general concern. Toward evening the crowd would disperse, mounted on their diminutive

ventured to complain, and when he did, the juries were sure to punish his presumption with the costs of the suit.

"Well, one of the old settlers, to whom I allude, came to my office one day, stated that he had felled a bee tree upon his neighbor's land, alluded to the old custom of conferring title by discovery, and that a suit was threatened, and requested my advice in the premises. I replied that he had committed a trespass and advised him to compromise the affair. He left the office in high dudgeon, saying as he was departing, "this country is getting too d—d civilized for me; I'll make tracks for Oregon, or some other country, where the old pioneer can get justice." Mr. Blackwell was, with other works, the author of "Blackwell on Tax Titles," an excellent standard treatise, held in high esteem throughout the United States. He was a native Illinoisan and self made man, endowed with fine intellectual powers. He died at Chicago, in 1863, at the early age of 38 years. His early life was an example to the young and aspiring—his middle age a monument to self made glory, and his early death a warning to all.—Chicago *Journal.*]

horses, galloping through the town, perhaps reeling from the influence of liquor, huzzahing and yelling for their favorite candidates, and groaning, cursing and berating the opposition.*

The pioneers in all parts of the State exercised a great influence at the elections. They were here first, claimed superior privilege on that account, which was mostly accorded to them, and knew well every subsequent comer. They were unfortunately in some instances not only extremely ignorant, but governed besides by passionate prejudices, and opposed every public policy which looked to the elevation of society; and their descendants in many cases at an early day, were no improvement on their prototypes. They were, as a rule, brave in personal combats and brawls, and had a propensity to indulge in them. They arrayed themselves in buckskin breeches, leather moccasins, raccoon caps and red hunting shirts belted at the waist, in which they carried a large knife, whence they were denominated "Butcher Boys." When proclaiming their bravery, a proceeding of which they were not chary, they would swear that they were "half horse and half alligator," meaning that it was impossible to overcome them in combat. The influence of this class was much courted by candidates, and with these and their peculiar characteristics thrown in the scale, success was no doubtful result.†

"Like people, like priest"—public servants under any form of government ultimately reflect the character of the people, for they are of the people. In the legislature, while the general interests of the people received but little attention, all manner of combinations for the parceling out and creation of offices were formed. Fat jobs were engineered for the benefit of friends; to "ring legislation," so rife in modern times, they were not strangers; the "good things" were apportioned by disreputable bargains made in advance—indeed, it was very much as it is at present—"the cohesive power of public plunder" was most potent; and the possessor of the greatest capacity for tact, blandishments, and intrigue generally carried off the lion's share. Governor Ford relates of Samuel Crozier, senator from Randolph, "a remarkable example of pure, kind and single-hearted honesty, after serving two sessions, and after he had been bought and sold a hundred times without knowing it, said he 'really did believe that some intrigue had been going on.' So little are honest men aware of the necessity of keeping their eyes open, in sleepless watchfulness, or otherwise, a few will monopolize all the advantages of government, and it will be done in the most unfair and corrupt manner." Good laws badly administered with the tacit acquiescence of the people, cannot reform any government. The virtue of the people should both demand and enforce them.

Militia.—The militia system was an important feature of the early times in Illinois, both during its territorial and State organizations. Militia duties, viewed from a modern stand point, doubtless appear droll, if not uninteresting, yet at the time when the system was fully in vogue, they were important and onerous. During the long peace which the country enjoyed between the war of 1812 and that with Mexico in 1846, it is not to be won-

*Ford's Hist.
†Ford's Hist.

dered, as the system also became the common target of much witticism and ridicule, that it fell under reproach and ultimately into disuse. Yet it is not unreasonable to assert, that if a vigorous militia system had all the time been maintained up to the breaking out of the late rebellion, perhaps many of the headlong fiascos of the Union forces in the early part of that war would have been avoided, and probably a year of the war—expended in perfecting and drilling the soldiery—saved besides. The military system of Prussia, which in the late war with France has brought that country forward as the very first military power of the world, is nothing but the militia system in its perfection. While the system of that country has demonstrated it to be the best, it is also by far the cheapest mode of maintaining a standing army, for which it becomes to a great extent a substitute. But notwithstanding its perfection in that country, Americans could never be brought fully to submit to its dependent and onerous duties, and it will, perhaps, never obtain any considerable foothold where the government is not strongly centralized.

During the territorial existence of Illinois the militia proved a valuable auxiliary to the defence of the country, in repelling hostile savages and affording protection to the frontier settlements. The law was substantially the same as that of 1819, from which we subjoin a synopsis. It contained equitable provisions for drafting or conscription—a drafted militia-man was known as a "forced volunteer." From the militia sprung, it may be said, the mounted rangers of that period. An early law passed at Vincennes, imported for Illinois by the governor and judges, and subsequently adopted by the territorial legislature, prohibited all commisioned officers, except justices of the peace and militia officers, from serving in either house of the legislature. This placed the road to political preferment in a manner in the hands of the militia, rendering it very obnoxious to other office-holding aspirants.

All free white inhabitants resident in the State, of the age of 18 years and under 45, except as hereinafter excepted, shall be enrolled in the militia by the commanding officer of the company within whose bounds such person shall reside, within ten days next after he shall be informed of such residence; and at all times thereafter in like manner, shall be enrolled those who may from time to time arrive at the age of 18, or come to reside in the district, being of that age and under 45. Such enrolled person was to be notified of his enrollment by an officer of the company, and within six months thereafter he was to provide himself with a good musket and bayonet, fusee or rifle, knapsack, blanket, canteen, two spare flints, cartridge-box to contain not less than 24 cartridges with powder and ball suited to the bore of his musket or fusee, or pouch and powder-horn with 1-4 lb. powder, and 24 balls suited to the bore of his rifle; and every enrolled person when called on shall so appear armed, accoutered and provided, except when called to exercise by companies, battalion or regiment, when he may appear without knapsack or blanket. Field and staff officers, ranking as commissioned officers, shall be armed with sword or hanger and a pair of pistols. Company officers with sufficient sword or hanger. Officers were to furnish their respective commands as follows: The colonel to each battalion a stand of colors, with the number of the battalion, regiment, brigade and division inscribed thereon. The captain was to furnish his company with drum and fife; regimental drum and fife-majors to furnish themselves, with instruments of music. The officers were to be re-imbursed for these articles out of the regimental fund (fines and penalties) upon the order of the regimental board—a slender chance. The entire militia of the State was apportioned into divisions, brigades, regiments, battalions and companies; all to take rank when in the field, agreeably to the date of the commissions of the officers in command. Each division was entitled to its major-general, with division inspector and aids; each brigade to a brigadier-general, major, and aid-de-camp who was also judge advocate and quartermaster; each regiment to a colonel, lieutenant-colonel, major, surgeon, surgeon's mate, adjutant (ex-officio clerk), quartermaster, sergeant, drum-major and fife-major. The superior officers appointed their subordinates, and their ranks were defined according to the U. S. army regulations. The companies elected their captains and lieutenants, and these appointed their subalterns.

The officers must be citizens of the U. S. and this State, and take an oath to support the constitutions of both. The regiments, battalions and companies elected their respective superior officers, who were commissioned by the governor. The governor, by virtue of his office, was commander-in-chief. Provision was made for one company of artillery and one of cavalry or troop of horse to each regiment, by voluntary enrollment. In the same manner a company of riflemen, grenadiers or light infantry, might be raised in the battalions; all of which were to equip and uniform themselves in manner fully pointed out. They were to appoint their officers in a manner similar to the first-mentioned. Companies were required to muster four times yearly, on the first Saturdays of April, June, August and October; and also the first battalions of each first regiment, on the first Mondays in April; the 2d on the succeeding Wednesdays; the 1st battalion of the 2d regiments on the succeeding Fridays; and the 2d battalion of the 2d regiments on the succeeding Mondays in each and every year. Regimental musters were provided for similarly to the above, in September of each year. The evolutions and exercises were to be conducted agreeably to the military discipline of the armies of the U. S. In addition to these times the commanders of regiments, battalions or companies, were empowered to call their respective commands out to muster, as " in their opinions the exigency of the case may require." The brigadier-generals were required to call together for drill or exercise all the commissioned officers in April and September of each year.

These repeated musters, it will be perceived, were no light duties. Every officer and soldier must appear at the places of muster, armed and equipped as the law directed, at the proper time. The roll was to be called and delinquents, either as to absence or improper equipments, were to be duly noted, for which fines and forfeitures were to be assessed by courts-martial, ranging as follows: privates from 50 cents to $1 50; commanders of divisions for neglect of any duties enjoined, from $20 to $200; commanders of brigades, for disobedience of orders or any duties enjoined by law, from $15 to $150; of regiments from $10 to $100; of battalions from $8 to $80; of companies from $5 to $50. Fathers were liable for the fines of their minor sons, guardians for their wards, and masters for their apprentices. Execution was to issue upon the findings of the courts-martial, directed to the hands of constables to be levied as in other cases.

The lieutenant-governor, judges of the supreme and circuit courts, attorney-general, licensed ministers of the Gospel, and jailors, were, in addition to those by the laws of the U. S. exempted from militia duty. From time to time acts were also passed for the relief of Dunkards, Quakers, and other religious persons conscientiously scrupulous against bearing arms. By act of Jan. 21, 1821, such persons were relieved by paying $3 each to the sheriff, and the entry of their names with a statement of their scruples, with the assessor of the county. But when detachments of militia for actual service were required, they like others, were not exempt from the tours of duty, but might respond by substitute like others.

The militia was liable to be called into actual service at any time for the space of three months on the requisition of the Executive of the U. S. in actual or threatened invasion of this or neighboring States or territories; for which purpose the number required were to be distributed among the classes (into which companies were to be formed), one man to be furnished by volunteering or draft out of each class; classes might furnish substitutes. The governor could exempt the militia from a call into actual service, in such frontier settlements as in his opinion their safety required defence, and make such further provision as the emergency demanded. While in actual service the militia was to be subject to the same rules and regulations as the armies of the U. S., and to receive the same pay, rations and forage; but their transgressions were to be tried and determined by a court-martial of militia officers only.

This is but a very brief outline of some of the main features of the militia system of Illinois. The law contains many sections and is a very long one.

While the requirements of the militia system in times of profound peace, without the stimulant of a common danger to aid in the discharge of its onerous duties, were perhaps dull and irksome, it nevertheless afforded to many a budding ambition for the "bubble reputation at the cannon's mouth," "that swelling of the heart you ne'er can feel again, while with fearless hearts though tired limbs, [they] fought the mimic fray." The military titles of general, colonel, &c., of many of our public men of the period, from 1812 to 1846, were mostly of militia origin, and had little other significance.

The militia system was much the same in all the States; and to come down to a later period the people abhorred it. But legislatures were unwilling to disturb the time honored law, which in many instances had been the means to originally bring them perhaps into prominence. But the shafts of wit and ridicule were hurled at it with such effect as to make it eventually succumb. The memorable attack of Tom Corwin in the Ohio legislature, by his celebrated "water mellon speech," is familiar to every schoolboy. How it fell into disuse all over Illinois, we do not pretend to recount, but we glean the following account of the means used to bring it into contempt in one place, from a speech of Mr. Lincoln :

"A number of years ago the militia laws of this state required that the militia should train at stated intervals. These trainings became a great bore to the people, and every person nearly was for putting them down; but the law required them to train and they could not get it repealed. So they tried another way, and that was to burlesque them. And hence they elected old Tim Langwell, the greatest drunkard and blackguard, for colonel over the best men of the country. But this did not succeed altogether. So they raised a company and elected Gordon Abrams commander. He was dressed in peculiar style, one part of his pants were of one collor and material, and the other different. He wore a pasteboard cap about 6 feet long, resembling an inverted ox-yoke. The shanks of his spurs were about 8 inches long, with rowels about the circumference of common saucers. He carried a sword made of pine wood, 9 feet long. They also had 'rules and regulations,' one of which was, 'That no officer should wear more than 20 lbs. of codfish for epaulets, nor more than 30 yards of Bologna sausage for a sash ; and on the banner was born aloft these words: 'We'll fight till we run and run till we die.' This succeeded to a demonstration. They were the last company that trained in Springfield."

CHAPTER XXXI.

1830-1—ADMINISTRATION OF GOVERNOR REYNOLDS.

The Gubernatorial Candidates, their Lives and Characters—The Campaign—The Wiggins Loan—Impeachment of Supreme Judge Smith—W. L. D. Ewing Governor for 15 days.

In August, 1830, another gubernatorial election was to take place. The candidates were William Kinney, then lieutenant governor, and John Reynolds, formerly one of the associate justices of the supreme court, both of the dominant party. Since 1826, the Jackson party had been regnant in both houses of the general assembly. The opposition, or anti-Jackson men, brought forward no candidate for governor at this election; they were in a hopeless minority. In Illinois party principles had not taken deep root, nor were they as yet well defined anywhere by the position of president Jackson. Those who were ardently and uncompromisingly attached to the fortunes of Gen. Jackson, were denominated, in the political slang of the period, "whole hog men." Mr. Kinney was a strong example of the thorough-going Jackson men. Of those who nominally espoused the cause of Jackson, not unmixed with policy perhaps, as that party was so largely in the majority, while at the same time, the support of the anti-Jackson men was not unacceptable, was Mr. Reynolds, who, it should be added, however, had always consistently acted with the Jackson party. The opposition, influenced not so much by any clearly defined party principles, as a dislike to the strong, arbitrary and personal characteristics of Gen. Jackson, came to the support of Reynolds, not on account of love for the latter, but of their hatred toward the former. Kinney had been to Washington and witnessed the inauguration of president Jackson, and was thought to have much agency in directing removals from federal offices in Illinois. It was reported he said, in his peculiar graphic manner, that the whigs ought to be whipped out of office "like dogs out of a meat house."*

Mr. Kinney was born 1781, in Kentucky, and emigrated to Illinois, in 1793. As has before been stated, he acquired his education after marriage, being taught its rudiments by his wife. By unwearied application he became remarkable for intelligence and business capacity. Shortly after his early marriage, contracted with a most estimable lady, he removed to a farm a short distance northeast of Belleville, and before long Mr. VonPhul, of St. Louis, induced him to engage in merchandizing. He brought his first

---

*Reynolds' Life and Times.

stock of goods from St. Louis, at one load on horse-back. He pros- pered as a merchant, became an extensive trader, and accumula- ted a fortune. Firmly impressed with religious convictions, he early became a member of the baptist church, and afterward forcibly preached the faith of that denomination of christians. He frequently had the honor of a seat in the legislature where he was noted for close attention to business. He was of a social dis- position, and had gathered a wonderful store of pithy anecdotes, which served him a good purpose in electioneering. He was regarded as one of the best political canvassers in the State, pos- sessing unbounded energy and great ambition. With his strong partisan bias he associated a rare jovial and witty pleasantry, which made him very acceptable in his intercourse with the peo- ple. Notwithstanding his clerical calling, which he did not lay aside while in quest of office, he availed himself fully of the worldly practice of those days in elections, by "treating" with intoxicating liquors, as did all other candidates. It was wittily remarked of him that he was invincible, because he went forth to the contest "armed with the sword of the Lord and the spirit." Yet with all these favorable traits, he was not sufficiently guarded during the canvass in his sarcastic utterances, which were caught up and distorted by his enemies, to his disadvantage. His strong denominational prejudices and clerical calling, induced him oc- casionally to berate other churches, which he discovered from the drift of things to be arrayed against him, often from no other than sectarian motives. He also arrayed himself in opposition to the canal, then much before the public, not on account of its intrinsic or public value, but because that great improvement would send a tide of "Yankee" emigrants to the State, which he and his ultra partisans affected to despise ever since the defeat of the proposi- tion to introduce slavery into the State six years before. These sentiments, inconsiderately expressed, did him much injury in the campaign.

His opponent, John Reynolds, was born in Pennsylvania, in 1788, of Irish parents, who removed to Tennessee while he was an infant, and to Illinois in 1800. In early manhood young Reynolds returned to Tennessee, where he received a "classical education," as he asserts in his "Life and Times," but for this assertion no one would ever have suspected it, either from his conversation, public addresses, or writings. He was reared among a frontier people, and imbibed their characteristics of manners, customs, and speech—disliked polish, contemned fashion, and was addicted to inordinate profanity, all of which attached to him through life, of none of which he took any pains to divest himself, and much of which is said to have been affected, which we doubt. These, garnished by his varied reading, a native shrewdness, and a won- derful faculty of garrulity, make him, considering the high offices to which he attained, one of the public oddities in the annals of Illinois. His imagination was fertile, but his ideas were poured forth regardless of logical sequence, evidencing his Milesian blood. He had an extraordinary, disconnected sort of memory, and possessed a large fund of detached facts relative to the early settlement of St. Clair and Randolph counties, which are embod- ied by him in a work entitled the " Pioneer History of Illinois," and are in the main correct and valuable, though badly arranged.* He was tall of stature; his face long, bony and deeply furrowed, and under his high, narrow forehead rolled his eyes, large and liquid, expressive of volubility. His nose projected well downward to his ample mouth. He was kindly by nature, treasured few resentments, and was ever ready to do a favor. His thoroughly democratic manners, social disposition and talkative habit caused him to mingle readily with the people and enjoy their confidence. He was much in public life. We have noted him as a judge; he served three terms in congress, was afterward commissioned (most unwisely) one of the State financial agents to negotiate large loans to carry on the State internal improvements, visiting Europe in this capacity; still again we find him in the legislature. He always claimed the staunchest adhesion to the democratic party. In 1858, however, he refused to follow the lead of Douglas, but sided with President Buchanan in his effort to fasten slavery upon Kansas by the Lecompton constitution, and his hatred of Douglas was such that he preferred Mr. Lincoln for the senate. In 1860, old and infirm, he attended the Charleston convention as an anti-Douglas delegate. Owing to his age, his extreme pro-slavery views and loquaciousness, no man from the north received more attention from the southern delegates than he. He supported Breckinridge for the presidency. After the elections of October, in Ohio, Indiana and Pennsylvania, had foreshadowed the success of Mr. Lincoln, he however published an address urging democrats to rally to the support of Douglas, that the election might be thrown into congress, where Breckinridge would succeed. Immediately preceding, and during the war of the rebellion, his correspondence with extra-Billy Smith of Virginia, and his letter to his brother-in-law, J. L. Wilson of Alabama, which was widely circulated, evinced a clear sympathy for the treason of the south. About the 1st of March, 1861, he urged upon Buchanan officials the seizure of the treasure and arms in the custom-house and arsenal at St. Louis. He died at Belleville, May, 1865. He left no will, and his fine property descended to his wife, who survived him but a few months. He had no children by either of his wives.

During the political campaign, Reynolds professed great admiration for the character of Jackson, though he was not accounted ultra enough by the real Jackson men who denounced him as an "outsider." He and his competitor made a thorough canvass of the State, and party excitement ran exceedingly high. Much personality entered into it, and bitter reproaches were indulged by the partisans of the respective candidates. The press was loaded with abusive articles on both sides, and hand-bills were scattered broadcast, containing distorted reports of the speeches of the candidates, and all sorts of scandalous charges. After a wearisome campaign of near 18 months, Reynolds was elected governor.

But with regard to the election for lieutenant governor, the same result did not obtain; it was the same as four years before. Rigdon B. Slocumb was on the ticket with Reynolds, and Zadock Casey with Mr. Kinney. Both candidates for lieutenant governor

*He writes: "In the year 1794, the Morrison family emigrated to Illinois. They were talented, industrious, and became very wealthy. In the same year the horse flies were very bad, and of these the green headed fly was the worst."

were gentlemen of sterling worth, character and ability. Slocumb was unused to the not uncommon accomplishment of the American politician, public speaking; nor did he electioneer much, it is said, in any other manner. Not so however with Casey; he was gifted with the power of charming oratory. Although lacking in thorough early education, by comprehensive reading he had stored his mind, naturally strong, with varied knowledge. He had frequently been a member of the legislature, and his fine personal appearance and large public experience gave him distinction throughout the State. Like his colleague, he, too, occupied the pulpit occasionally. The clerical ticket was somewhat injured by the fact that the people could not brook the worldly aspirations of men engaged in a calling so militant to honors that perish; but this objection did not extend to both gentlemen, for Casey was elected. Governor Casey possessed in an eminent degree the commanding tact of presiding over a deliberative body.

In his message, Governor Reynolds invited attention to the subject of education, internal improvement and the canal; urged that congress be memorialized to improve Chicago harbor; recommended three public highways, commencing respectively at Cairo, Shawneetown, and on the lower Wabash, all to terminate at the lead mines; the completion of the penitentiary; winding up of the old State bank; and, inoculated with his predecessor's theory, stated he was "satisfied that this State, in right of its sovereignty and independence, [was] the rightful owner of the soil within its limits." But His Excellency advocated no hobby, and his administration was not strongly personal.

The governor was not in political accord with a majority of the senate, and the usual conflicts between that body and the executive obtained. The senate desired the removal of A. P. Field, secretary of State, and with that view passed a resolution requesting his renomination—that they might reject him.* But the governor refused compliance, and would neither remove nor renominate him. He renominated Henry Eddy, Sidney Breese, Thomas Ford, and Alfred Cowles, who had been efficient and acceptable prosecuting attorneys, but as they had opposed the election of Kinney, the senate rejected them and turned all out of office, except Thomas Ford. They were again nominated and again rejected; but after the adjournment of the legislature, the governor reappointed them. He succeeded in having his choice of treasurer, John Dement, confirmed by the senate. Dement was an ultra Jackson man, but had supported Reynolds. The incumbent Judge James Hall, desired to be retained in the office; and although an anti-Jackson man, he had, as editor of the *Illinois Intelligencer*, with much power, supported Kinney; but this failed to avail him. That curious political posture would indicate both aspirants to the treasurership to have been governed in their course more by the hope of office than by party principles. But that is a weakness not peculiar to those days alone.†

Among the measures passed at the first legislative session of Reynolds' administration may be noted the adaptation of the criminal code to the penitentiary system. But the most notable measure of this session was the passage of the act providing for the

---

*Reynolds' Life and Times.
†Hall, as Treasurer, was in arrears with ₁0 State.

redemption of the notes of the old State bank, which would mature during the current year. The notorious "Wiggins loan" of $100,000 was authorized, and if that proved insufficient to redeem the out-standing notes, the residue was to be refunded by issuing State stocks bearing 6 per centum annual interest. This speedily raised the credit of the State and advanced its currency to par. But while the financial standing of the State was thus preserved, the honorable members who actively authorized it, it is said, sunk beneath the waves of popular indignation, never to rise again as politicians. The value of a financial character for the young State, or the disgrace of repudiation, was not duly appreciated by the people. Demogogues availed themselves of this and proclaimed to the people that their representatives had corruptly betrayed their interests, and sold out them and the State to Wiggins for generations to come. The members quailed before the first onset of public indignation as if stricken with the enormity of their wrong. Truth was crushed to earth never to rise again, in the case of these politicians. A blight swept over the State and laid low many promising buds of incipient statesmen. It is left for us at this day, who look back with swelling pride to the fact that our State has emerged from every impending financial crisis with her garments unsullied, to appreciate the merits of their act, only regretting that they did not boldly defend their course and hold up to public scorn the unprincipled demagogues who inflamed the people to the contrary.*

The United States census returns of 1830 showed a population for Illinois of 157,445, and in accordance therewith the State was apportioned into three congressional districts. Up to this time the State had had but one representative in the lower house of congress. A special election for one congressman was ordered for August 1831, at which Joseph Duncan was elected; but for the general election of August 1832, and every two years thereafter—it being provided that congressmen should be elected one year and over prior to taking their seats—three members were to be elected. Joseph Duncan, Zadock Casey (the lieutenant governor,) and Charles Slade were elected.

In his message to the session of the general assembly of 1832-3, governor Reynolds stated the ordinary receipts into the treasury for the two years ending November 30th, 1832, to be in round numbers, $102,000; the current expenses of the State government for the same period, were, in round numbers, $90,000. This indicated a healthy condition of the State finances, when it is considered that the Black Hawk war occurred during this period. The expenses of that war amounting to some two million dollars,† were however assumed by the general government. At this session the first earnest efforts were made to build railroads; several charters were granted incorporating railroad companies, but no stock, it is said, was ever subscribed to any of them. It was proposed to build a railroad from Lake Michigan to the Illinois river in place of the canal; surveys for the Northern Cross road (now the T. W. & W.,) and for the Central, from Peru to Cairo, were also proposed.

*Ford's History.
†Brown's Illinois, 355.

But the most absorbing topic of this session was the impeachment trial of Theophilus W. Smith, one of the associate judges of the supreme court. Petitions numerously signed were received by the house charging him with misdemeanors in office. The house voted seven articles of impeachment, which were transmitted to the senate for trial. The first three related to the corrupt sales of circuit clerkships; he had authorized his son, a minor, to bargain off the office in Madison county, by hiring one George Kelly at $25 per month, reserving the fees and emoluments to himself; he did the same—reserving the fees and emoluments—till his son became of age; and to subject said office to his will, he had made appointments three several times without requiring bonds from the appointees. He was also charged with being a co-plaintiff in several vexatious suits for an alleged trespass, commenced by affidavit in a court where he himself presided, holding the defendants illegally to excessive bail upon a trifling pretext, to oppress and injure them, and continuing the suits from term to term to harrass and persecute them. The 5th article charged him with arbitrarily suspending John S. Greathouse, a lawyer, from practice for advising his client to apply for a change of venue to a circuit where his honor did not preside; 6th, for tyranically committing to jail, in Montgomery county, a Quaker who entertained conscientious scruples against removing his hat in open court; 7th, for deciding an agreed case between the sheriff and treasurer of Madison county without process or pleading, to the prejudice of the county; rendering appeal to the supreme court necessary. The senate resolved itself into a high court of impeachment and a solemn trial was had, which lasted from January 9th to February 7th, 1833. The prosecution was conducted by a committee of managers from the house, consisting of Benjamin Mills, Murray McConnel, John T. Stuart, James Semple, and John Dougherty. The defendant was represented by Sidney Breese, R. M. Young, and Thomas Ford, subsequently governor. The array of talent on both sides, the exalted position of the accused, and the excitement thereby caused in political circles, gave to the trial unusual public attraction throughout the State, and during its protracted pendency little else was transacted by the legislature.

The trial was conducted throughout by marked ability and learning. A great number of witnesses were examined and much documentary evidence introduced. The arguments of counsel were of the highest order; and in the final summing up for the prosecution, the chairman of the house committee, Mr. Mills, one of the most brilliant orators of the time, spoke for three days in a strain of unsurpassed eloquence. Pending the trial, the defendant, after each adjournment, had the desks of senators carefully searched for scraps of paper containing scribbling concerning their status upon the respective charges. Being thus advised, his counsel enjoyed peculiar advantages in the management of the defence. The constitution required that "no person shall be convicted without the concurrence of two-thirds of all the senators present." When the vote was finally taken upon each article separately, 22 senators were present, 4 absent or excused. It required 15 to convict, 12 voted "guilty" on some of the charges, 10 were in favor of acquittal, and 15 "voted him guilty of one or other of the specifications, but as 12 was the highest vote on any one of them, he was acquitted."* Thereupon the house of representatives, well convinced of his guilt, immediately passed a resolution by a two-thirds vote under the constitution to remove him from office by address; but this, too, when reported to the senate, failed in that body, and Judge Smith retained his seat upon the supreme bench of Illinois until he died about ten years afterward.†

When Lieutenant Governor Zadock Casey was elected to congress in 1832 he resigned his office and Gen. W. Lee D. Ewing, a senator, was chosen to preside over the senate. At the August election of 1834, governor Reynolds was also elected to congress, more than a year ahead, as was then the law, to succeed Mr. Slade; but shortly after, the incumbent died, when Reynolds was also chosen to serve out his unexpired term. Accordingly he set out for Washington in November of that year to take his seat in congress, and Gen. Ewing, by virtue of his office as president of the senate, became governor of this State for just 15 days, when, upon the meeting of the legislature, to which he sent his message as acting governor, he was relieved of his exalted station by the governor elect, Duncan, being sworn into office. This is the only time that such a conjuncture has happened in the history of the State.

---

*Ford's History·
†See Senate Journals 1833, appendix, for full proceedings of this trial.

CHAPTER XXXII.

1827–1831—BLACK HAWK WAR.

1.• *Winnebago Hostilities—Indians unable to Resist the Encroachments of the Miners—Coalition with the Sioux—Attack on a Steamboat—Compelled to sue for Peace.*

2. *Sacs and Foxes—Black Hawk—Keokuk—Sac Villages—Invasion of the State—Militia and Regulars brought into Requisition—March to the Scene of Danger—Black Hawk compelled to enter into a Treaty of Peace.*

———

The most frequent cause of the difficulties which from time to time have disturbed the peaceful relations of the white and red men, has resulted from a desire of the former to possess the hunting grounds of the latter. Intrusions upon Indian territory, led to the war with Pontiac and that of King Phillip, 11 years afterward, and at a later date, and farther westward, to the sanguinary contest with Tecumseh. The original emigrants from Europe and their descendants, requiring lands for cultivation, purchased large tracts from the Indians. As fast as these became populated others were required, till the savages, seeing their forests and hunting grounds rapidly disappearing, endeavored to re-possess them. The Europeans met them in arms, and as the result, they have been driven from river to river and from forest to forest till scarcely an abiding place is left them. The last effort to resist encroachments of this kind, was made by the Winnebagoes and the Sacs and Foxes, within the limits of Illinois.

Winnebago War.—During the latter part of Governor Edwards' administration, the Indians on the northwestern frontier manifested symptoms of discontent. The dissatisfaction increased, and in the summer of 1827, culminated in what the writers of the time style the Winnebago war, an affray of no great magnitude but the precursor of the hostilities under Black Hawk, which filled the nation with alarm. This sudden ebulition of savage animosity, was the unjust occupation of their lands by the miners of Galena. At this period large number of adventurers from different States, were hastening to the lead mines, and in passing through the country of the Winnebagoes, purposely exasperated them with the intention of provoking hostilities and securing their lands by way of reprisal. The right of this tribe to the lands in question, was, however, involved in doubt. By the treaty of 1804, the Sacs and Foxes ceded to the United States all the land between the mouths of the Illinois and Wisconsin rivers. In 1816, that portion of the territority lying north of a line drawn west from the southern extremity of Lake Michigan, was retroceded by the government to the Ottawas, Chippewas and Potawattomies, the Winnebagoes not being included in the grant. Subsequently, however, a war broke out among these tribes in regard to their respective boundaries, and in 1825 the commissioners of the United States interposed as mediators to re-adjust them and terminate hostilities. In the new arrangement, the right of the Winnebagoes to the land in the vicinity of the lead mines, seems to have been admitted, although they were not recognized in the preceding treaty.

But waiving the question of title, they had been in possession of the country for years, and believing it belonged to them, regarded the intrusion of the whites with the same intense jealousy and ill-will manifested by civilized men on similar occasions. Rich deposits of lead ore had been found in their territory, and Mr. Thomas, the agent at Galena, gave permission to the miners to procure large quantities of mineral, despite the remonstrances of the Winnebagoes. The savages at length, finding their complaints unheeded, attempted to eject the trespassers by force, but were themselves repelled and greatly exasperated at being unable to protect their property. Assistance from others was now their only alternative, and for this purpose they sent a delegation to ask the advice of their principal chiefs north of Prairie du Chien. Another object of their visit was to secure the co-operation of the Sioux, who had also become offended at the Americans and only waited an opportunity to wreak their vengeance upon the objects of their ill-will. Some of their countrymen had not long before surprised and murdered a number of the Chippewas in the vicinity of Fort Snelling, and the commandant immediately caused their arrest and had them delivered up to the injured tribe for merited punishment. The interposition of the American officer was prompted only by a sense of justice, yet Red Bird, the chief of the tribe, became greatly offended and secretly resolved to form a coalition with the Winnebagoes. Both tribes, therefore, had grievances to redress, and each found the other ready to strike a united blow against the common enemy.

. Accordingly, while the Winnebagoes were in consultation with their chiefs, they were visited by a messenger of the Sioux, who after detailing the wrongs of his own tribe, resorted to falsehood to further exasperate his auditors against the Americans. He informed them that two Winnebago prisoners confined at Fort Snelling, had recently been cruelly murdered by the whites, under circumstances which demanded immediate and bloody retaliation. Notwithstanding the utter mendacity of this statement, the Winnebagoes, smarting under their treatment at the hands of the miners, were easily persuaded it was true, and resolved upon revenge, while the visitor assured them that as soon as they struck the first blow, his own tribe would assist them. They accordingly killed 2 white men, and a more justifiable pretext was not long wanting for them to strike another blow. On the 30th of July 1827, 2 keel boats, laden with supplies for Fort Snelling, landed at a large Winnebago encampment a short distance above Prairie du Chien. While here the Indians collected about the boats, doubtless for the purpose of plunder but were foiled in their designs. In the absence of other weapons the whites made them drunk, and taking advantage of their helpless condition, captured several squaws, and took them aboard for a purpose too base to mention. Before their intoxicated husbands became aware of the injury they had sustained, the boats and their squaws were too far up the river for pursuit, yet several hundred infuriate warriors now assembled with the determination of meeting out to the aggressors the most severe punishment when they returned. In due time, the boats were seen descending the river, but the crews aware that their misdeeds deserved castigation, had made preparation for defence. One of the boats passed by unobserved during the night, but the other, less fortunate, was assailed by an overwhelming force of savages, who fought with a determination only equalled by their passion for vengeance. The boat became grounded, and for a time the men on board seemed doomed. Directly in the face of a galling fire, the savages succeeded in lashing some of their canoes to the unmanageable craft, but when they attempted to board her, they were beaten back into the river, and finally retired from the contest. During the engagement the squaws escaped, and no doubt with the hearty consent of the boatmen, provided it might be the means of drawing after them their infuriate lords. Two of the Americans were killed, and so many others wounded, it was with difficulty that Captain Lindsey, who had charge of the boat, ran down to Galena, and made known the hostile attack. Dire alarm at the reception of the news spread among the miners, and in a short time not less than 3000 men, women and children fled to Galena for protection. Exaggerated reports spread rapidly over the country, and most of the settlements in the northern part of the State partook of the fear and excitement incident to an actual invasion. At Galena a committee of safety was formed, temporary defenses were erected, and in pursuance of an order from Gov. Edwards, the miners were formed into companies and equipped for action. A regiment was also raised in Sangamon and Morgan counties, and under the command of T. M. Neale, marched to the scene of danger. On his arrival, however, he found the war virtually at an end. Gen. Atkinson with 600 regulars and the Galena militia, under Gen. Dodge, had penetrated the enemy's country, as far as the portage of the Fox and Wisconsin, and compelled the hostile savages to sue for peace. The army returned from Prairie du Chien, with 7 of their principal men, among whom were Red Bird the chief of the Sioux, and Black Hawk who shortly afterward became the instigator of other and greater disturbances. They were all thrown into prison as abettors of the murderous attack on the boat, and suffered a long confinement before they were tried. As the result of the tardy trial, some were acquitted, and others convicted, and more than a year after their incarceration executed on the gallows.

In the meantime, Red Bird whose proud spirit could not endure the humiliation of confinement, sickened and died in prison. There was associated with the latter days of his life a romantic and melancholy interest, different from the usual phases of Indian character. He had always been the favorite of his own people and up to this illicit connection with the Winnebagoes the ardent and unalterable friend of the whites. Unlike other savage leaders, when his allies were pressed with a victorious force, he refused to desert them, and voluntarily gave himself up to suffer not only for his own misdeeds, but for the common offense of the tribe. Clad in a robe of skins, and bearing a white flag, he rode into camp, and with dauntless courage and an unclouded brow, placed himself in the hands of his enemy. Not even the restraints of prison life, although they impaired his health, could obscure the native vigor of his mind, and when called on by white men all the nobility of a great savage lit up his manly features. Incensed at the Americans because they had delivered his countrymen into the hands of their enemy, he was doubtless the secret instigator and ruling spirit of the war, although the Winnebagoes committed the overt acts. This tribe now completely humbled, in a subsequent talk with the federal authorities abandoned all their lands south of the Wisconsin river, to the insatiate grasp of the conquerors.

Hardly had the disturbances of the vanquished tribe ceased before the frontier inhabitants became embroiled in difficulties with the Sacs and Foxes. The first recognition of these Indians by the United States, was in a treaty concluded at Fort Harmer, in 1787, by Gov. St. Clair, wherein the government guaranteed them its protection. In 1804, Gov. W. H. Harrison was instructed by president Jefferson to institute negotiations with them for the purchase of lands, and shortly afterward a treaty was ratified with them, by which their beautiful country on Rock river was divested of the Indian title. Again in 1830, a third treaty was entered into, by the terms of which they were to remove from the lands which they had sold to the United States, east of the Mississippi, and peaceably retire across the river.

At this time, Keokuk and Black Hawk were the two principal chiefs of the nation. The latter was born at the principal village of his tribe, on Rock river, in 1767. Possessing no hereditary rank, his chieftainship was due to the native vigor of his character, and great success in war. In early youth he distinguished himself as a brave; and in the many fierce conflicts of his subsequent life with the Osages and Cherokees, he never lost a battle. When the war of 1812, broke out between the United States and England, he offered his services to the Americans, which from motives of humanity they declined. He however, soon found patrons among the British, who regardless of the brutal attrocities of savage warfare, furnished his men with arms. At the instance of their mercenary agents, he succeeded in collecting 200 braves, and repaired to Green Bay, where he met Col. Dixon and a large body of Indians assembled from the adjacent tribes. Of the interview which followed between him and the British officer, he says: "He received me with a hearty shake of the hand, and presented me to the other officers who shook my hand cordially, and seemed much pleased with my men. After I was seated, Col. Dixon said: 'Gen. Black Hawk, I sent for you to explain what we are going to do, and the reasons that have brought us here. Your English father has found out that the Americans want to take your country from you, and has sent me and his braves to drive them back. He has likewise sent a large quantity of arms and ammunition, and we want your warriors to

join us.' He then placed a medal around my neck, and gave me a
paper and a silk flag, saying, 'You are to command all the braves
which are to leave here day after tomorrow, to join our braves
at Detroit.' Black Hawk fought in 2 engagements with his new
allies, and annually received payment for his services up to the
time of his own war against the Americans. From this circumstance his force was designated the British band.

Keokuk, his rival, unlike him, remained the friend of the Americans. Notwithstanding the insatiate passion of the Sacs and
Foxes for war, and the belief that they had been injured by the
people of the United States, he drew after him a majority of the
nation, and thus weakened the efforts of Black Hawk. In diplomacy and judgment he was more than a match for his brother
chieftain, and as we shall see, through the influence of the United
States whose cause he had espoused, he became the sole chief of
his people.

In accordance with the treaty stipulations, Keokuk and his followers remained on the west side of the river. Black Hawk, however, actuated no doubt partly by patriotism, but mostly by the
ill will he entertained toward the Americans declared all the
previous treaties void, and in the Spring of 1831 recrossed the Mississippi with his women and children and 300 warriors. Every
argument had been used by his most prudent advisers, to deter
him from embarking in this hazardous enterprise, and even the
authorities of Canada, with whom he had consulted, counseled
him to leave his village if he had sold it. The government of the
United States, desirous of preventing bloodshed, bore with him a
long time, hoping after due reflection he would abandon his rash
design. This, however, being construed as weakness, he was
induced to believe that the government either could not or would
not attempt his removal. He also affected to believe it was an act
of cowardice to abandon his village, and thus leave the graves of
his fathers, to be ruthlessly plowed up by strangers, whose rights
to the soil was of doubtful authority.

This celebrated Indian town was romantically situated on a promontory formed by the junction of the Mississippi and Rock rivers, and
the great beauty and fertility of the adjacent country made it the
centre of attraction for emigrants from all parts of the country.
The village was capable of sheltering a population 6,000 or 7,000
inhabitants. The houses consisted of poles wrought into frames
and covered with bark, previously prepared by drying to adapt it
to the walls of these structures. Seven hundred such lodges of
various dimensions, the largest of which did not perhaps exceed
100 feet in length and 50 in breadth, constituted the dwellings of
the villagers. About 700 acres of the adjacent prairie was surrounded by a fence, and the enclosed soil cultivated by the Indian
women in corn, beans, peas and squashes. The place was said to
be 150 years old, and had for 60 or 70 years been the principal village of the Sac Nation. On the one hand flashed the broad waters of the Mississippi in the rays of the evening sun, on the other
the rippling stream of Rock river struggled between the dark
forest-clad islands which obstructed its channel. Hardly an individual could be found who did not have friends and relations
whose ashes were reposing in the adjacent grave yards. Hither,
in accordance with an immemorial custom of the nation, bereaved

mothers, wives and sisters performed annual pilgrimages to pay a tribute of respects to their departed relatives. On these melancholy occasions they carefully removed the growing vegetation from the mounds and addressed words of endearment to the dead, inquiring how they fared in the land of spirits and who performed the kindly office of mother, sister or wife. The depositing of food on the grave concluded these time-honored religious services.

As is usually the case with rival factions brought in contact, the conduct of both whites and Indians admitted of censure. The 7th article of the treaty of 1804 provided that as long as the lands which are now ceded to the U. S. shall remain their property the said Indians shall enjoy the privilege of living and hunting on them. These lands were not brought into market till the year 1829, and consequently all who had previously settled on them were trespassers, having violated the laws of congress and the pre-existing treaties. The most advanced settlements at that time did not approach nearer than 50 or 60 miles of Rock river, and the lands for even a greater distance had not been offered for sale, yet the government disposed of a few quarter sections at the mouth of this stream, embracing the site of the village and fields cultivated by the inhabitants. The manifest object of this advanced movement upon the Indian settlements was to evade the provisions of the treaty, by having the governmental title to the lands pass into the hands of individuals and thus obtain a pretext for removing its owners west of the Mississippi. The white inhabitants thus introduced, commenced depredations by destroying the corn of the Indians, killing their domestic animals, and in some instances whipping their women and children. They carried with them as articles of traffic intoxicating liquors, and by frequently selling them in violation of law, introduced scenes of drunkenness and disorder. Some of the chiefs remonstrated against these outrages and even visited the house of a white settler and emptied the contents of his whiskey barrels on the ground, to prevent their people from becoming intoxicated and murdering the white inhabitants. The Americans, on the other hand, preferred grave charges against the Indians, many of which were true. Notwithstanding, in 1816 Black Hawk had recognized the treaty of 1804, and to use his own expression, he touched the goose quill to this paper in its confirmation, he endeavored to deceive his tribe with statements that their lands were inalienable and that the previous cessions and treaties were fraudulent and void. Again, when the government surveyed and sold the site of their village, although the object which induced the purchasers to pass over such large scope of unoccupied territory was hardly justifiable, yet, when the title of the government became vested in individuals the right of the Indians ceased and they should have peaceably retired. Furthermore, Black Hawk and his band, when they crossed the river, notified the whites that they must depart from the village, and the latter refusing to comply with their demand, their property was destroyed and they suffered in person various indignities at the hands of the savages. A petition signed by 40 persons, was sent on the 30th of April, 1831, to the executive of Illinois, representing that the previous fall the Black Hawk band of Indians destroyed most of the crops and made several attempts upon the lives of the owners when they endeavored to prevent the depredations; that now they act in a more outrageous and menacing manner and their number, which amounts to 600 or 700, is to be further augmented if necessary, by the Potawatto- mies and Winnebagoes. A few days after another petition was sent, which after detailing similar outrages committed by the sav- ages, states that if relief does not arrive the inhabitants will be compelled to leave their crops and homes. Several depositions were also presented to the governor, corroborating the above evi- dence. B. F. Pike stated under oath that the number of warriors was about 300; that they had in various instances done much damage to the white inhabitants by throwing down their fences, destroying their fall grain, pulling off the roofs of their houses and positively asserting that if the Americans did not leave they would kill them.

Governor Reynolds, thus informed in regard to the state of affairs at the mouth of Rock River and believing that Black Hawk and his band were determined to retain possession of the country by force, resolved to effect their expulsion. A call was accordingly made for volunteers, and when it became known the whole north- western part of the State resounded with the clamor of war. Many of the old citizens, who 20 years before had fought these Indians in the war with Great Britain, still survived and urged their sons to appear on the tented field against the same enemy. The exigencies of the situation demanded that troops should reach the scene of action in the shortest time practicable, and therefore the 10th of June was appointed as the time, and Beards- town as the place for the assembling of the forces. No county south of St. Clair and east of Sangamon was included in the call, it being impossible for troops from the remote parts of the State to meet, organize and reach the place of rendezvous in the brief interval of 14 or 15 days, the allotted time. The governor circu- lated documents among the people and made speeches showing that the defence of the northwestern frontier required prompt and energetic action. Notwithstanding it was the most busy season of the year, hundreds abandoned their plows and cornfields, and more than twice the number called for volunteered. It was easier to obtain men than provide means of sustenance. Cols. Enoch C. March and Samuel C. Christy were appointed quartermasters, who, being extensive merchants, possessed superior facilities for obtain- ing supplies. These gentlemen were successful in the discharge of their duties and provisions were in readiness at the appointed time for the expedition to march.

The governor, aware that General Clark, the superintendent of Indian affairs stationed at St. Louis, had great influence with the Sac and Fox tribes, on the 27th of May, 1831, the day on which he made the call for volunteers, addressed a letter to him requesting his co-operation. In this letter he states: "I have called out about 700 militia to protect the citizens near Rock Island from Indian depredations. I consider it due the general government to state that in about 15 days a sufficient force will appear before the hostile Indians to remove them dead or alive west of the Missis- sippi, but perhaps a request from you would induce them to leave without the necessity of resorting to arms." On the 28th another letter was sent to General Gaines at Jefferson Barracks, in which he also stated: "I have received undoubted information that the section of the State near Rock Island is actually invaded by hostile bands of Indians headed by Black Hawk, and in order to repel the invasion and protect the citizens of the State, I have, under the provisions of the constitution of the United States and the laws of this State, called out the militia to the number of 700 men, who will be mounted and ready for service in a very short time. I consider it my duty to lay before you the above information that you may adopt such measures as you deem just and proper." Both generals Gaines and Clark considered the precaution of raising troops pursued by governor Reynolds unnecessary, believing that the forces of the regular army were sufficient to protect the frontier settlements. On the 2d of June, general Gaines replied to His Excellency that he had ordered 10 companies to Rock Island, 6 from Jefferson Barracks and 4 from Prairie du Chien, which he deemed sufficient for the protection of the frontiers, that if the entire Sac and Fox nation and other tribes united with the band of Black Hawk, he would call on him for additional forces to repel the invasion, but did not regard it necessary at that time.

Accompanied by six companies from the barracks, Gen. Gaines passed up the river in a steamboat to Fort Armstrong, situated on Rock Island, and on the 7th of June a council was held with the Indians. Black Hawk, Keokuk, Wapello, and a number of other chiefs and braves were present. Gen. Gaines stated in council that the President was displeased because the Sacs on Rock river refused to depart, that their great father only required that which was reasonable when he insisted that they should remove west of the river. Black Hawk replied by asserting that they had never sold their land and they were determined never to abandon them. Gen. Gaines thereupon inquired, "Who is Black Hawk? is he a chief, and why does he sit in council?" Black Hawk then arose from his seat, and gathering his blanket around him stalked out of the room without deigning a reply. When the council reconvened on the following morning Black Hawk was again present and said: "My father, you inquired yesterday who is Black Hawk, and why does he sit among the chiefs. I will tell you who I am. I am a Sac. My father was a Sac. I am a warrior and so was my father. Ask those young braves who have followed me to battle and they will tell you who Black Hawk is. Provoke our people to war and you will learn who Black Hawk is."

The result of the conference was that Black Hawk refused to leave, and Gen. Gaines informed him that if he and his band were not on the west side of the Mississippi in a short time he would be compelled to remove him by force. The American commander also wrote to governor Reynolds requesting the assistance of the volunteers and intimating that it might be necessary to call for more troops as Black Hawk was endeavoring to secure the co-operation of the neighboring tribes. It was hoped that by this augmentation of the forces the Indians might be intimidated, and thus prevent the effusion of blood, and in case of actual conflict the army would be enabled to act with greater efficiency.

Great enthusiasm was exhibited by the people in responding to the call for troops, and instead of 700, 1600 men offered their services. All were eager to enlist having made arrangements on leaving home to remain and take a part in the expedition. The

entire number could be provisioned and equipped, and it was deemed
folly to appear on the field without a force sufficiently large when
one more imposing and adequate could be secured. Among the
volunteers were many of the best and most energetic citizens of the
State, a number of whom afterward attained celebrity and still live
to enjoy the respect of their countrymen. The whole force consisted
of one brigade, subdivided into two regiments, and a spy and odd
battalion. The governor, who accompanied the expedition, appointed
Joseph Duncan, then a member of congress, brigadier general to
command the entire brigade, and Samuel Whitesides a major to
command the spy battalion. The other officers, not being regarded
so essential to the success of the campaign, were elected by the
volunteers.

Col. James D. Henry was chosen to command the first regiment,
Col. Daniel Lieb the second, and major Nathaniel Buckmaster the
odd battalion. Thus organized and furnished with the necessary
supplies, the brigade left their encampment near Rushville on the
15th of June for the seat of the Indian disturbances. Although
not highly disciplined, it was the largest military force that had
ever assembled in the State, and made a very imposing appearance
in its march over the then broad expanse of prairie wilderness.
Eager for a fray with the Indians the utmost vigilance was required on the part of the officers, to keep the men from indiscriminately killing every straggling savage they encountered in their
pleasant journey of four days to the Mississippi. A halt was made
on its banks eight miles below the old Sac village, where they were
met by a steamboat containing provisions, in charge of general
Gaines, who received them into the service of the United States.
A beautiful site was selected for an encampment, and as a battle
was considered imminent, the greatest watchfulness was exercised
during the night to guard against surprise, but no disturbance
occured. Here generals Duncan and Gaines concerted measures
of attack; the latter officer having been in the vicinity of the
Indian town for some time, thus became acquainted with the topography of the place. Previous to the arrival of the volunteers he
had possessed and fortified with cannon a commanding bluff in
range of the village, and in another direction had posted a strong
force of regulars to aid if necessary in the conflict. In accordance with the plan adopted, on the following morning General
Gaines with a force of regulars and cannon steamed up the river
in the boat, while the volunteers marched across the country, both
forming a junction at Woodruff's Islands in the channel of the
river opposite the Sac village. The boat having come within
range of the island, fired several rounds of grape and canister into
the dense growth of timber and thickets to test the presence of the
Indians, who it was feared might be concealed among them, to
intercept the passage of the volunteers across the stream. The
spy battalion, followed by the main body of the forces in three
columns, passed over a slough to the island, when it was discovered
that the rapid elevation of the land from the water had prevented
the shot taking effect more than 100 yards from the shore. Owing
to this circumstance the Indians might have been concealed in full
force without being discovered. Fortunately no enemy was found,
for the volunteers became so completely bewildered in the tangled
thickets as to disqualify them for effective resistance, and in case

of an attack the artillery looking down from the bluffs on what would have been the battle field, was too far away to distinguish friends from foes. On arriving at the river between the island and town, it proved to be a deep, bold stream at that point unfordable, and hence the progress of the troops was delayed till scows could be procured to ferry them over. When the town was finally entered it was found deserted, the inhabitants having the previous night crossed to the west side of the Mississippi. It was supposed that Generals Duncan and Gaines, before leaving camp, believed that the Indians would abandon their village, and now that such was the case, it served to explain the apparent neglect in ascertaining the presence of Indians and the seemingly unfavorable disposition of the forces. General Gaines appears to have been an efficient officer, anxious to settle the difficulties without the effusion of blood, and great credit was undoubtedly due Governor Reynolds and General Duncan for the promptness with which the troops were called out, organized and marched to the seat of war.

The number of warriors who fled across the Mississippi could never be definitely ascertained. Many of the straggling and disaffected Winnebagoes, and Potawattomies, doubtless united with the band of Black Hawk, and perhaps the number amounted to from 400 to 600. The Indians having escaped without injury, the volunteers took vengeance on the village by burning it to the ground, although the dwellings would have sheltered them from the incessant rains which prevailed during the day. "Thus perished this ancient village which had been the delightful home of 6000 or 7000 Indians, where generation after generation had been born, had died and been buried, where the old men had taught wisdom to the youth, whence the Indian youth had often gone out in parties to hunt or to war, and returned in triumph to dance around the spoils of the forest or the scalps of the enemy, and where the dark-eyed Indian maidens, by their presence and charms, had made it a scene of delightful enchantment to many an admiring warrior."[*]

Black Hawk and his warriors having departed the night preceding the destruction of their village, encamped on the west bank of the Mississippi, while the Americans took a position 12 miles above where Rock Island now stands. Gen. Gaines sent an order to Black Hawk, requiring him and his band to return and enter into a treaty of peace, or he would move on them with all the troops under his command. Several days afterward some of the chiefs made their appearance, but Black Hawk and the majority of them refusing to come, a more peremptory demand was made, which had the desired effect. He and about 30 chiefs of the British band of the Sacs, now came and in full council with Gen. Gaines, and Gov. Reynolds, on the 30th of June, 1831, signed an agreement of which the following is the first article.

"The British band of the Sac Indians, are required peaceably to submit to the authority of the friendly chiefs and braves of the united Sac and Fox nations, and at all times hereafter to reside and hunt with them upon their own lands, west of the Mississippi river, and to be obedient to their laws and treaties, and no one or more shall ever be permitted to recross said river, to the usual place of residence, nor any part of their old hunting grounds east

_____
[*]Ford's History.

of the Mississippi, without permission of the president of the United States or governor of the State of Illinois."

The truism that the brave are merciful, was well illustrated by the treatment extended by Gen. Gaines and Gov. Reynolds to the vanquished and unfortunate Indians, after the conclusion of the treaty. The larger part of the invading force had been deluded by listening to the bad counsel of Black Hawk and other leaders, and as a consequence, their helpless women and children, were then destitute of food and clothing. Gov. Reynolds in a conversation on the subject remarked, "I presume this is the last time the government will have any trouble with these Indians; the women and children are not so much to blame, and a support for them one summer, will be nothing to the United States. The government has possessed their fine country, and I cannot rest satisfied to leave them in a starving condition." Provisions were accordingly distributed among them at stated periods, exceeding in amount the quantity they would have raised. The volunteers seeing this exhibition of charity, ridiculed the adjustment of the Indian difficulties by calling it a corn treaty, and saying, "we give them bread, when we ought to give them lead."

The enemy being apparently humbled and quiet restored, the army was disbanded and returned home in the best of spirits, not a single person, by disease, accident or otherwise, having lost his life.

CHAPTER XXXIII

1832—SECOND CAMPAIGN OF THE WAR.

Black Hawk induced by White Cloud to recross the Mississippi—Refuses to obey the order of Gen. Atkinson to return—State Forces re-organized—March to Rock River and unite with the Regulars—Army proceeds up the river in pursuit of the enemy—Battle of Stillman's Run—Call for fresh troops—The old forces disbanded.

———

Prior to the expulsion of the Indians from their village, Naopope, a chief of the British band and second in command to Black Hawk, had started on a visit to Malden to consult his English father concerning the right of the Indians to retake possession of their lands on Rock river. According to his statement, he was advised by the authorities at Malden that the Americans, without a previous purchase, could not take possession of their lands. On his return he also visited Wa-bo-kies-shiek or White Cloud, the prophet of the Winnebagoes. His home was a village bearing the name of Prophetstown, situated on Rock river, 35 miles from its mouth. Like the prophet of the Wabash, he had great influence with his countrymen. He was a stout, shrewd looking Indian, about 40 years of age and claimed that one of his parents was a Sac and the other a Winnebago. A full and flowing suit of long hair graced his head, which was surmounted by a white head-dress several inches in height, resembling a turban and emblamatic of his profession. Sagacity and cunning were prominent traits of his character and essential to the prophetic pretensions by which he imposed on the credulity of his ignorant followers.

White Cloud informed his visitor that not only the British but the Ottawas, Chippewas, Potawattomies and Winnebagoes would assist his tribe in regaining their village and the lands around it. When Naopope in the summer succeeding the treaty, returned to his friends he communicated this information to Black Hawk who affected to believe it, and immediately commenced recruiting to increase the number of his braves. He also sent a messenger to Keokuk apprising him of the good news and requesting his co-operation. The latter, however, was a chief of too much sagacity to be misled by these promises of British and Indian assistance, and wisely admonished Black Hawk that he was deceived and should therefore abstain from hostile demonstrations. The latter, however, willing to credit any report that even faintly promised an opportunity to wreak vengeance on his old adversaries the Americans, rejected this good counsel and persistently

381

pursued his own plans. Having resolved to bid defiance to the
whites, in the winter of 1831-32, great efforts were made to obtain
recruits, and the number of his warriors embracing the chivalry
of the nation, was augmented to 500. His headquarters were at
the site of old Fort Madison on the west side of the Mississippi,
whence he moved up the river, his warriors proceeding on horses
and his women and children and baggage ascending in canoes. A
halt was made opposite the site now occupied by Oquawka, where
they were met by White Cloud the prophet. His mission was to
further strengthen Black Hawk's determination to recross the
Mississippi, by assuring him that he might depend on the assistance of other tribes. Naturally prone to mischief and entertaining a strong prejudice against the whites, he was at all times
ready to stir up strife without caring for the evils that might be
inflicted on those who listened to his advice. In a speech to the
warriors and braves, he told them that by following his advice they
had nothing to fear and much to gain; that the American war
chief would not interfere with them if they refrained from hostilities, and that strengthened by reinforcements the time would
come when they would be able to pursue a different course.
Pleased with this advice, on the 6th of April, 1832, they proceeded
to the mouth of Rock river and the whole party crossed the Mississippi and commenced ascending the former stream, for the
avowed object of entering the territory of the Winnebagoes and
raising a crop with them, when the real object was to secure them
as allies. After they had proceeded some distance they were
overtaken by an order from General Atkinson, then in command
of the regulars at Fort Armstrong, requiring them to recross
the Mississippi, which they refused to do, alleging that the general
had no right to make such a demand, as they were peaceably journeying to the village of their friends for the purpose of raising
corn. Before they had reached their destination another courier
was sent in pursuit, who this time informed them unless they returned force would be used to effect their expulsion. The Indians
replied that they would not be driven back, but did not intend to
make the first attack upon the whites. Black Hawk on arriving
among the Potawattomies and Winnebagoes, readily obtained permission to cultivate corn with them, but they refused to unite in
any acts of hostility against the United States, and denied having
given the prophet any assurances of co-operation.

The refusal of Black Hawk and his warriors to comply with the
demand of General Atkinson, and the imposing character of his
military operations, created a general panic along the whole northern frontier from the Mississippi to Lake Michigan. Most of the
settlers abandoned their homes and moved into the interior, while
messengers were at the same time sent to inform Gov. Reynolds
of the hostile attitude assumed by the Indians. The governor
understanding the belligerent character of the settlers and Indians, and knowing that the slightest indiscretion committed by
either party might involve the whole frontier in a bloody war, determined, on the 16th of April, to call out a large body of volunteers as the best means of averting such a calamity or meeting it
in case of its actual occurrence. Gen. Atkinson in command of the regular forces near the scene of the threatened hostilities, at the same time, made a requisition for troops, stating

the frontier was in great danger and that the force under his command was insufficient for its defence. Danger being imminent the 22d was made the time for meeting, which gave only 6 days for the troops to meet at Beardstown, again selected as the place of rendezvous. The governor, with great promptness, sent influential messengers to the northwestern counties of the State, in which levies were to be made and addressed the following letter to the citizens: "Fellow-citizens: Your country requires your service. The Indians have assumed a hostile attitude and invaded the State, in violation of the treaty of last summer. The British band of Sacs and other hostile Indians are in possession of the country on Rock river, to the great terror of the frontier inhabitants, and I consider the settlers in imminent danger. Under these circumstances I have not hesitated what course I should pursue. No citizen ought to remain inactive when his country is invaded and the helpless part of community is in danger. I have called out a strong detachment of militia to rendezvous at Beardstown on the 22d inst. Provisions for the men and food for the horses will be furnished in abundance. I hope my countrymen will realize my expectations and offer their services as heretofore with promptitude and cheerfulness in defence of their country."

Daily accounts respecting the operations of the Indians were received. Judge Young, Col. Strode and Benjamin Mills wrote to the governor urging the speedy protection of the frontiers as the Potawattomies and Winnebagoes had joined Black Hawk and the inhabitants were in great danger. On the receipt of this intelligence 200 men under the command of Major Stillman were ordered to guard the frontier near the Mississippi, and 200 un-under Major Bailey the frontier between the Mississippi, and the settlements on the Illinois. Such was the threatening aspect of affairs; the call of troops was now extended to every portion of the State, for the purpose of raising a reserve force of 5,000 men to be ready in case of emergency. Various causes operated to retard the progress of the campaign, and this precaution proved highly advantageous in the closing stages of the war. As in the preceding year, many of the most conspicuous men of the State volunteered, their prominence in public life giving them elegibility for potions in the organization of the forces.

Eighteen hundred men met at the place rendezvous and were divided into four regiments, an odd and a spy battalion. An election being held for field officers, Col. DeWitt was chosen commander of the first regiment; Col. Fry of the 2d; Col. Thomas of the 3d, Col. Thompson of the 4th, and Major James of the odd battalion. The governor, who participated in the campaign, placed Gen. Whitesides in command of the brigade, and Col. James D. Henry in command of the spy battalion. He also appointed Colonels Enoch C. March and Samuel C. Christy to procure supplies; as brigade quartermaster, William Thomas; as staff officers, James B. Stapp and Joseph M. Chadwick; as paymaster, James Turney; as adjutant general, Vital Jarrot, and as ordnance officer, Cyrus Edwards. On the 27th of April the army started from their encampment, a few miles north of Rushville, for Oquawka on the Mississippi river, with only a few days' rations, while Col. March was dispatched to St. Louis for additional supplies which were to be sent up the river to the

same place. After the arrangement had been made a letter came
by express from from Gen. Atkinson, informing the governor that
the hostile Indians had gone up Rock river, but the intelligence
came too late. Had it been received one day earlier the provisions might have been ordered to Peoria in greater proximity to
the enemy, and had the army marched to the same point it might
have ended the contest without giving the Indians an opportunity
to escape. Rains had recently prevailed and the progress
of the troops was retarded by the muddy prairies and swollen
streams. On arriving at Oquawka they hoped to find Colonel
March and the supplies from St. Louis, but they had not made
their appearance. The evening of the same day Captain Warren
and two companies from Shelby county also arrived and were
greeted with loud cheers for the energy which they exhibited in
swimming streams and overcoming other formidable obstacles encountered in their route. Great anxiety was now felt for the
safety of the supplies. A considerable advance had been made
into the wilderness and any accident which prevented or prolonged
the coming of the boat might necessitate the disbanding of the
army. On the 5th day the provisions were exhausted, and murmuring being heard among the men, the Governor engaged three
trusty persons to deliver a message to Gen. Atkinson informing
him of the destitute condition of the army, and requesting relief.
Although Rock Island was 50 miles distant, and it was necessary
to swim several streams in traversing the intervening country, the
journey was successfully accomplished and a boat load of provisions arrived the next day. The succeeding morning the steamboat William Wallace from St. Louis, also came in and the army,
which a short time before was in a suffering condition, had now a
two-fold supply.

Immediately on the receipt of provisions rations were issued to
the men and baggage wagons were loaded preparatory to moving
to Dixon, where, according to the latest intelligence, the enemy
was posted. Spies had previously been sent to obtain information of the Indians, but instead of returning with proper dispatch
they loitered with the officers of Fort Armstrong and finally returned on the boat which brought the supplies. When the army was
ready to march, a letter was brought from Gen. Atkinson informing
the governor that Black Hawk and his band had descended Rock
river, and requesting him to march immediately with the troops to
Fort Armstrong. Disappointment was felt at the reception of
this news, and perhaps the request would have been disregarded,
but according to the statement, the Indians had descended the
river, and it was folly to move up it to find them. Instead, however, of going to the fort, the force was marched to the mouth of
Rock river where they were received into the service of the United
States, and General Atkinson assumed command. It was now ascertained that the information in regard to the Indians was incor-
rect and the commanding general steamed up the river with an
armament of cannon and 400 regulars accompanied by the brigade, which rode through the swamps in the vicinity of the stream.

As the expedition advanced, dogs immolated to appease the
Great Spirit were frequently found at the various Indian encamp-
ments. This relic of barbarism and superstition common among
the oriental nations of antiquity, was employed by these Indians

when the nation was threatened with great calamity. The body of the animal, in these instances having the vitals removed, was fastened to a tree over a small fire with its head in the direction the Indians were traveling. Instead of rendering any assistance it only served to point out their trail to the pursuing foe.

On the 10th of May some spies sent in advance captured near Prophetstown, an Indian, from whom information was obtained that Black Hawk and his warriors were on Rock river above the town of Dixon. In accordance with this information the volunteers moved up to the town, where it was ascertained from scouts who had scoured the country, that the Indians had dispersed and it was determined to abandon the pursuit and await the arrival of Gen Atkinson with the steamboat and provisions. It was conjectured that Black Hawk and his band contemplated residing on the lands of the Potawattomies, and as a means of preventing the consumation of such a design, an embassy of five persons was sent to confer with the chiefs of that nation upon the subject. In consequence of cloudy weather the party became bewildered, and losing their way fell in with some of Black Hawk's band, who very adroitly endeavored to decoy them into the power of the principal Indian force. After much skillful maneuvering on horseback the savages retired and the Americans returned to Dixon greatly exhausted, having been without food or rest for two days.

Majors Stillman and Bailey, who had previously been ordered to protect the frontier were at Dixon when the army arrived at that place, and having done but little service, they besought the privilege of reconnoitering the country, and reporting the situation of the enemy. It was rumored that a small party of Black Hawk's force was encamped at the head of Old Man's creek 12 miles above Dixon, and in accordance with their request, the governor issued the following order: "Major Stillman: You will cause the troops under your immediate command, and the battalion under Major Bailey, to proceed without delay to the head of Old Man's creek, where it is supposed there are some hostile Indians, and coerce them into submission."

On the following morning, the Major with 275 men started on his mission, hoping to give a good account of himself when he returned. The expedition, after reaching Old Man's creek, although unauthorized to pass beyond it, continued their march 15 miles higher up the stream to Sycamore creek, where they dismounted for the purpose of spending the night.

Here they were within a few miles of the main lodgment of Black Hawk and a part of his braves, and while engaged in camp duties 3 unarmed Indians bearing a white flag made their appearance. The Indians giving themselves up, were taken into custody. Shortly 5 other Indians were descried on horseback upon rising ground about a mile distant. A party of Major Stillman's men immediately started in pursuit, and others followed as fast as they could mount; in a short time three-fourths of the whole detachment were scattered pell mell over the intervening prairie. In this irregular running fight, the troops at the camp knowing that blood had been shed, killed 1 of the 3 Indians who had been sent as envoys under the white flag, but the other 2 in the confusion escaped. The Americans having the fastest horses, overtook and killed 2 of the other party, and pursued the survivors to the edge

25

of the forest. At this juncture, Black Hawk and about 40 braves rose up from their ambush, and with a terrific yell, rushed on the assailants. Those who had just exhibited so much bravery in pursuit of the fleeing foe, now retreated with a corresponding swiftness. The frightful din attending the fugitives, who reached camp about dark, caused the remainder of the force to think that Black Hawk and his whole band were about to burst upon them like an avalanche. A panic ensued, and some with only a saddle or bridle, and others without either, mounted their horses and joined their comrads in the inglorious flight, leaving their wagons, ammunition and other property to the victors. Major Stillman ordered his men to retreat over the creek and rally on more elevated ground, but such was the consternation that no elevated ground was found till they reached the forces at Dixon.

The principal resistance offered to the pursuing Indians, was at Old Man's creek, a small stream rising in Ogle county and falling into Rock river at the town of Bloomingville. It has since been called Stillman's Run, in commemoration of the battle, a result incident to the delay caused in crossing its muddy banks. After passing the stream, Major Perkins, Captain Adams and about 15 other daring men made a stand, and by their heroic conduct partially checked the career of the Indians and saved the lives of others, who must otherwise have fallen victims of savage vengeance. Captain Adams, however, in saving the lives of his friends, sacrificed his own, his body being found the next day, near the two Indians whom in a personal encounter he had slain. None of the parties lived to tell the story of the terrific struggle, but from the evidence left behind it must have been of the most determined character. Their guns were broken into fragments, and the ghastly wounds inflicted by rifle balls, spears, butcher knives and tomahawks were frightful proofs of the efforts that had been made. The Americans greatly lamented the death of Captain Adams, and even the Indians, as a mark of respect for his bravery, neither scalped nor otherwise mutilated his body. Near was dismounted Major Hackleton, who had a severe encounter with with an Indian, in which he killed his tawny antagonist, and afterward made his escape to the camp at Dixon. Some others, in the confused and precipitate flight, occasionally fired on the pursuing savages, and as the result of the conflict, about 11 whites and 7 Indians lost their lives. The fugitives commenced arriving at Dixon about 12 o'clock at night, and from that time till morning they continued to come in small squads of 4 to 5 each, telling the most tragic stories of the disaster. Every one seemed to be impressed with the idea that his own party was all that escaped, and while telling the death of a comrade he would arrive and contradict the account.

During the night of the battle, which fully inaugurated the war, Gov. Reynolds made out a requisition for 2000 men to be in readiness for future operations, and orders were also prepared requiring Col. March to forward supplies for the men, and Major Adams to procure provisions for the horses. Letters were also written to Gens. Atkinson and Dodge, apprising the former, who had not yet arrived, that the army was without proivsions, and the latter, that Stillman was defeated, and the frontiers of Wisconsin were in danger. When the news of the defeat reached the camp, the officers were summoned to meet at the tent of Gen. Whitesides, and it was determined to march the next morning to the fatal field of the evening's disaster. Quartermaster Thomas anticipating the result of the council, obtained from John Dixon, then the only inhabitant in that part of the country, 8 or 10 oxen, as a temporary supply for the expedition. The animals were slaughtered and distributed among the men, who partaking of their flesh without bread or salt, started for the battle field. Arriving thither, the bodies of their fallen comrades were found frightfully mutilated, presenting a scene appalling to troops who had never before witnessed such a spectacle. Some were beheaded, some had their hands and feet cut off, while their hearts and other internal organs, were torn out and scattered over the prairie. The mangled fragments were gathered together, and buried in a common grave, over which a rude slab hewn from the trunk of a tree, was erected to mark the place. The troops encamped on the ground, and heavy guns being heard during the night, they were supposed to be signals for collecting the scattered warriors of Black Hawk. The men rested in their saddles, expecting every moment an attack, but the morning dawned without the enemy being seen. Major Henry and his battalion were then ordered to scour the surrounding country, but no traces of the foe being detected the whole detachment fell back to Dixon.

Perhaps no better material for an army could be found than Major Stillman and his men, and their defeat was not the lack of bravery, but the want of experience and discipline. No body of men under similar circumstances, would have acted more efficiently, yet for years afterward they were made the subjects of thoughtless merriment and ridicule, as undeserving as their expedition was disastrous.* Stillman's defeat spread consternation throughout the State and nation. The number of Indian warriors was greatly exaggerated, and the name of Black Hawk

NOTE.—"It is said that a big, tall Kentuckian, with a very loud voice, who was colonel of the militia, but private under Stillman, upon his arrival in camp gave to Gen. Whitesides and the wondering multitude the following glowing and bombastic account of the battle: 'Sirs' said he, 'our detachment was encamped among some scattering timber on the north side of Old Man's creek, with the prairie on the north gently sloping down to our encampment. It was just after twilight, in the gloaming of the evening, when we discovered Black Hawk's army coming down upon us in solid column; they deployed in the form of a crescent upon the brow of the prairie, and such accuracy and precision of movements were never witnessed by man; they were equal to the best troops of Wellington, in Spain. I have said that the Indians came down in solid column, and deployed in the form of a crescent; and what was most wonderful, there were large squares of cavalry resting upon the points of the curve, which squares were supported again by other columns 15 deep, extending back through the woods and over a swamp three-quarters of a mile, which again rested upon the main body of Black Hawk's army bivouacked upon the banks of the Kiswakee. It was a terrible and glorious sight to see the tawny warriors as they rode along our flanks attempting to outflank us, with the glittering moonbeams glistening from their polished blades and burnished spears. It was a sight well calculated to strike consternation into the stoutest heart, and accordingly our men soon began to break in small squads, for tall timber. In a very little time the route became general; the Indians were upon our flanks and threatened the destruction of the entire detachment. About this time Major Stillman, Colonel Stephenson, Major Perkins, Capt. Adams, Mr. Hackleton, and myself with some others, threw ourselves into the rear to rally the fugitives and protect the retreat. But in a short time all my companions fell, bravely fighting hand to hand with the savage enemy, and I alone was left upon the field of battle. About this time I discovered not far to the left a corps of horsemen which seemed to be in tolerable order. I immediately deployed to the left, when leaning down and placing my body in a recumbent posture upon the mane of my horse, so as to bring the heads of the horsemen between my eye and the horizon, I discovered by the light of the moon that they were gentlemen who did not wear hats, by which token I knew they were no friends of mine. I therefore made a retrograde movement and recovered my former position, where I remained some time meditating what further I could do in the service of my country, when a random ball came whistling by my ear and plainly whispered to me, 'Stranger, you have no further business here.' Upon hearing this, I followed the example of my companions in arms, and broke for tall timber, and the way I ran was not a little."*

*Ford's History.

carried with it associations of great military talent, savage cunning and cruelty. Gen. Scott, with 1000 United States troops, was sent to the northwest to superintend the future operations of the campaign.

The new levies under the proclamation of Gov. Reynolds, were to meet, some on the 3d of June, again at Beardstown, and others on the 10th of the same month at Hennepin, and efficient messengers were sent to convey intelligence of the requisition to different parts of the State. The greatest dispatch was required to enable forces in the most distant counties to assemble and march more than a hundred miles to the places of rendezvous in so short a period of time. The previous organization of the volunteers, however, greatly facilitated the labor of bringing the present call into the field.

The men in the service now asked to be discharged, urging that they had enlisted at a moment's warning, for the protection of the frontier, without providing clothes for themselves or food for their families at home, and both must suffer if the campaign was protracted. The term of enlistment being undefined, they had a right to return home, but the governor appealing to their patriotism, they agreed to remain 12 or 15 days longer. In the meantime, Gen. Atkinson arrived at Dixon with provisions, encamped on the northwest side of the river, and threw up embankments for the protection of his stores. The companies of Capts. Bailey and Stillman, were organized as a brigade under the command of Col. Johnson, and received into the service of the United States, and one part ordered to Ottawa for the defence of that place, while the other remained at Dixon to guard the stores.

On the 19th of May, the whole army consisting of volunteers and regulars, under the command of Gen. Atkinson, marched up the river in pursuit of the enemy. Toward evening news was received that several white families had been murdered by the savages, on Indian creek, not far from Ottawa. The story of the massacre is but a repetition of the bloody tragedies which always characterize savage warfare. About 70 warriors made a descent on the settlement, and in broad daylight stealthily entered a house in which 3 families had assembled, and murdered 15 of the inmates.*

On the receipt of the news, Gen. Atkinson ordered Gen. White-sides and Col. Taylor, afterwards president of the United States, to continue the pursuit of the Indians with the volunteers, while he with the regulars fell back to Dixon. After several days march, the trail of Black Hawk led the army to a village of the Potawattomies on Sycamore creek, where were discovered several relics of the tragedy on Indian creek, and the battle of Stillman's Run. The inhabitants had fled, and the trail separating led in different directions, a precaution doubtless taken to elude the pursuing force. It was the supposition that Black Hawk had visited the town to secure the co-opertion of the Potawattomies, who were perhaps deterred from rendering assistance by the overwhelming

*The fiends who perpetrated the butchery afterward related, with infernal glee, that the women squawked like geese, as they were pierced with spears, or felt the keen edge of the tomahawk entering their heads. The bodies of the victims were scalped and otherwise mutilated, the children were chopped to pieces with axes, and the women suspended by their feet to the walls of the houses, their clothes falling over their heads, leaving their persons exposed to the public gaze.

number of the whites. While the army lay at the village, a re-connoitering party was sent out to search for lost horses, and returning in the night, they discovered a large Indian force steal-ing away in the dark, evidently to avoid the whites, and to join their comrades, a large body of whom it was inferred was in the vicinity. The trail of the Indians led north, while the homeward route of the volunteers now about to return led south, and it there-fore became necessary to determine whether to continue the pur-suit or return home. Col. Taylor and Major Harney, of the regular army, and Gov. Reynolds urged them to remain in the service till the Indians could be overtaken and chastised. The volunteers, however, expressed great reluctance to a continuance of the pursuit. The private soldiers also were not only displeas-ed with the commanding general, but they had left their business in such condition as to require their presence at home. Gen. Whiteside, upon whom the principal command devolved in the absence of Gen Atkinson, although opposed to following the enemy, agreed to be governed by a majority of the officers, and the question being submitted to a vote, one-half were for pursuing the Indians and the other half for returning home. Gov. Rey-nolds seeing the demoralizing condition, caused them to be march-ed to Ottawa, and on the 27th and 28th of May they were discharged and the campaign thus ended without effecting any important results.

Chapter XXXIV.

1832—THIRD CAMPAIGN OF THE WAR.

Requisition for Additional Troops—Attack on Apple Creek Fort—Captain Stephens' Encounter with the Indians—Organization of the New Levies—Battle of Kellog's Grove—Battle of the Wisconsin.

———

Gen. Atkinson called upon the governor at the time these troops were mustered out, and at his suggestion a call was made for 1000 additional men to co-operate with the previous requisition and 1000 more to guard the frontiers. The danger of exposed settlements being very imminent, an appeal was made to the disbanded troops, and a regiment raised to serve till the new levies could be made available. After the election of Jacob Fry as colonel and James D. Henry as lieutenant colonel, the different companies of which it was composed were immediately dispatched to the most exposed localities. The regiment, after bravely guarding the imperiled frontier, was finally mustered out of service at Dixon, on the 19th of June by Col. Taylor. One of the companies under Captain Snyder, had some severe skirmishing with a body of some seventy Indians in the vicinity of Kellog's grove, in which 4 of the savages and 2 or 3 of his own men were killed. The new levies arrived, but before they could be organized or brought into the field, the Indians committed a number of murders in different parts of the country.

On the 6th of June Black Hawk and about 150 warriors made an attack on Apple River Fort, situated a quarter of a mile north of the present village of Elizabeth and within 12 miles of Galena. The fort was a stockade having strong block houses at the corners, and had been erected for the benefit of a small village of miners, who resided in their homes during the day and retired to the fort for protection at night. Three messengers chanced to be on their way from Galena to Dixon, and when within half a mile of the village, were fired upon by Indians lurking in ambush. One of them was wounded, but by the assistance of his two companions he reached the fort without further injury. The inhabitants, as usual during the day, were scattered abroad attending to business, when the report of guns apprised them of danger and they fled to the fort in advance of the enemy. The Indians came within firing distance, when the battle commenced and was continued with great fury for 15 hours, during which several attempts were made to burn and storm the fortifications. The assailants took possession of the dwellings in the village, and while some knocked holes in the

390

walls through which in safety they fired upon the fort, others destroyed provisions, broke crockery, and with devilish glee ripped open beds and bestrewed the houses and yards with feathers. There were only 25 men in the fort, but they fought with the impetuosity of desperation, deeming it better if they could not repulse their adversaries to die in defence of their families, than suffer capitulation and butchery afterward. The mothers and children partook of the same inspiration, and by moulding bullets and charging guns greatly assisted in warding off the assaults of the enemy. The Indians at length, finding they could not prevail against the garrison, raised the seige and departed, taking with them horses, cattle, flour and other provisions. The Americans sustained a loss of one man, that of the Indians could never be ascertained as their killed and wounded were carried away in the retreat. A messenger in the meantime had hurried to Galena for assistance, and Col. Strode of the militia marched to afford them assistance, but the enemy had left before he arrived.

On the 24th of June two men were killed near Fort Hamilton, situated among the lead mines 4 or 5 miles east of Galena. Gen. Dodge, of Wisconsin, who by chance visited the fort shortly after the tragedy was committed, immediately followed the trail of the savages to the Pekatonica, where they took refuge under a high bank of the river. The brave commander and his equally brave men immediately rushed on the sheltered foe and killed the entire number, having three of their own men mortally wounded in the assault. This action although small, exhibited the greatest daring on the part of those engaged in it.

About the same time Capt. Stephenson of Galena, and a portion of his company fell in with a party of Indians between Apple River Fort and Kellog's Grove, and pursued them till they took refuge in a small grove in the midst of the prairie. The Americans commenced a random fire into the timber but after the loss of a few men retired. Notwithstanding this loss neither officers nor men were yet willing to abandon the contest, and the party in a short time returned and charged into the grove, receiving the galling fire of the savages, who were so effectually protected by the trees it was impossible to dislodge them. The charge was renewed a second and a third time, and not until 3 additional men were killed and the captain supposed to be mortally wounded did the fighting cease. The Indians had greatly the advantage, and the rashness of making an attack under the circumstances is perhaps as much an object of censure as the heroic deeds performed are feats of admiration.

As previously arranged in the call for troops, the new levies met at Beardstown and Hennepin, but were afterward ordered to Fort Wilburn where a permanent organization was effected.* A promiscuous multitude of several thousand persons had assembled at this place, and the greatest patience and judgment was required to form them into an army. As many of the most prominent men in the State were present and wanted positions, there was great danger in the bestowal of offices that dissatisfaction might arise and thus seriously impair the efficiency of the army. It was

---

*This was a small fortification on the south bank of the Illinois, about a mile above Peru, and had been erected by Lieut. Wilburn, for the protection of the supplies entrusted to his care by Col. March.

however agreed in a consultation between the governor and captains of the various companies who had already been chosen, that the principal officers should be elected by the troops over whom they were to act. Three brigades were organized, and on the 16th of June Alexander Posey was elected general of the first, Milton K. Alexander general of the second, and on the 18th, James D. Henry general of the third. Gen. Atkinson received them into the service of the United States and acted as commander-in-chief of the force thus organized, which amounted to 3192 men. The governor appointed on his staff Benjamin F. Hickman and Alex. F. Grant as aids, James Turney as adjutant general, E. C. March as quartermaster general. Besides the main army 4 battalions were organized for special purposes, and commanded severally by Majors Bogart and Baily, and Colonels Buckmaster and Dement.

In view of the disasters which threatened the northern frontier of the State, the governor ordered a chain of forts to be erected and garrisoned from the Mississippi to Chicago. Indian war parties lurked in every defile, beset every solitary road, hovered about every settlement, and woe to the traveler or unprotected party of white men who attempted to pass through the country. Despite their vigilance their supremacy in the field was soon to end; beaten, humbled and bleeding they were to be driven before the conquerers, and their hunting grounds were to know them no more.

On the 17th of June, Col. Dement and his force were ordered to report themselves to Col. Taylor at Dixon, while the main army was to follow. Here Col. Dement was ordered to take a position in Kellog's Grove, where on the 25th of June he was visited by Mr. Funk of McLean county, who came during the night from the lead mines and informed him that the trail of about 300 Indians leading southward, had been seen the previous day, and that there was perhaps a large body of them in the neighborhood. A council of war was held the same night, which decided that Col. Dement and 50 picked men should reconnoitre the surrounding country the next day, while the remainder were to remain in the fort near the grove prepared for any emergency that might happen. This rude block house was an oblong building constructed of logs, contained 3 rooms, and was furnished with doors of strong material. At daylight on the following morning the party sallied forth, but the more advanced portion of it had not proceeded more than 300 yards, when several Indian spies were discovered on the adjacent prairies. Col. Dement and Lieut. Gov. Zadock Casey were mounting their horses preparatory to leaving the fort, when a messenger returned to make known the discovery. The news was soon communicated to the whole battalion; a phrenzy to fight the redskins took possession of the men, and contrary to orders they mounted their horses and started after them. At their approach the Indians fled, but Col. Dement suspecting that their intent was to decoy the whites into an ambuscade, galloped after them to induce them to return and thus prevent the occurrence of such a catastrophe. The excited volunteers, however, mistook his intentions, supposing he also was pursuing the Indians to kill them, and the chase was continued till they came near a bushy ravine in which Black Hawk and his men were concealed. The object contemplated by the hidden foe was now consummated, and no generalship of civilized warfare could have been better planned or more successfully executed than this strategy of the bookless men of the forest. Suddenly a war-whoop proceeding from the throats of 300 naked savages, who had previously prepared for battle by divesting themselves of their clothes, startled the Americans. Determined to profit by the surprise and the advantage of numerical strength, they rushed with the fury of demons upon their adversaries. Col. Dement and several other officers made several attempts to rally their panic-stricken men, but the danger of being out-flanked by superior numbers rendered their efforts futile. All subordination ceased, and each fugitive, prompted by the instinct of self preservation, shaped his course toward the fort with a speed equal to that with which a short time before he had left it. In the hurried and confused retreat which followed, 5 Americans who were without horses were killed, while the remainder reached the fort and dismounting entered it, closely pursued by the enemy. The fort was vigorously attacked for nearly an hour, but the force within returned the fire of the assailants with such rapidity and precision that they retired, leaving nine of their comrades dead on the field, and carrying others away with them. No one in the fort was killed but several were wounded by bullets which occasionally entered through crevices in the walls. Three balls passed through the apparel of Col. Dement, all of them touching his person, but none causing a wound. About 50 horses were killed, and suddenly swelling afterward it was supposed they had been pierced with poisoned arrows.

With the retreat of the Indians, sentinels were sent out to watch their movements, and work was commenced on the fort to get it in readiness for a night attack. The heavy timber of which it was built would withstand the effect of bullets better than that of fire, and lest an attempt should be made to burn it, barrels of water were provided, and a large number of wet blankets were hung on the walls.

At 8 o'clock in the morning when the battle had partially subsided, Col. Dement sent five messengers to Dixon, a distance of 50 miles, for assistance, and toward sundown Gen. Posey and his brigade made their appearance. Shortly after his arrival some Indian spies were seen to emerge from the adjacent thicket, where they had been watching to see if any additional troops came to the relief of the fort. Retiring to the main body of the enemy, a consulation was held, and doubtless further attempts upon the fort were abandoned, in consequence of the timely arrival of Gen. Posey.

Early the next morning an excavation was made with knives and tomahawks near the grove, and in this lonely grave were buried the mutilated remains of the five Americans killed the preceding day. When the melancholy task was ended Gen. Posey started after the Indians, but soon discovering by the trail that they had scattered, the pursuit was discontinued. Thus terminated this expedition. Nature had endowed in the highest degree with soldiery qualities those engaged in it, and the only reason their efforts were not more successful was the want of discipline, a disideratum which the immediate demand for their services had not permitted them to acquire.

After the battle of Kellog's Grove, the forces of Gen. Posey and Col. Dement returned to Dixon, where the regulars and most of the volunteers were concentrated under the command of Gen. Atkinson. To prevent the escape of the Indians if they attempted to recross the Mississippi, Gen. Alexander was ordered to the country south of Galena, and Gen. Posey to Fort Hamilton on the Pekatonica. While the army was at Dixon, 3 Potawattomie chiefs, Wapello, Billy Caldwell and Waubansee, came to Gen. Atkinson asking some protection against Black Hawk. The ire of the old Sac warrior was aroused because the tribe of these chiefs proposed an alliance with the Americans, who deemed it better to secure their co-operation than have them fight on the opposite side. Col. Fry and his regiment were accordingly sent in advance of the main army to Sycamore creek to afford protection, and to receive into the service 100 Potawattomie warriors, who had signified their willingness to unite with the whites. Much was expected from this accession to the army, but they soon returned home and little was realized, although commanded by Wabansee, a veteran chief of the tribe. Gen. Atkinson having heard that Black Hawk had fortified a position on the four lakes in southern Wisconsin, started thither for the purpose of bringing on a general engagement and thus terminating the war. Passing Sycamore creek he was joined by the Winnebago warriors, and on the 30th of June, encamped near Turtle village, a considerable town of the Winnebagoes, then deserted by its inhabitants. The night following was one of continual alarms, the whole command was frequently paraded in order of battle, but no enemy was seen except a few prowling Indians. The next morning the march was resumed, and on the 4th of July the army reached Lake Kush-ka-nong an expansion of Rock river, where they formed a junction with the forces of Col. Fry and Gen. Alexander. These having scoured the whole of the adjacent country and not finding the enemy, the march of the mounted men was continued up the east side of the Rock river to Burnt village, another town of the Winnebagoes situated on Whitewater, a tributary of the first mentioned stream. Here they were joined by Gen. Posey and a battalion of 100 men under Major Dodge of Wisconsin. The evening of their arrival at that place, a company of scouts came in and reported the main trail of the Indians 3 miles higher up the stream. Preparations were immediately made to follow it, and at an early hour next day a detachment proceeded up the river a distance of 15 miles, but no trace of the enemy being detected the detachment fell back to Burnt village.*

Eight weeks had now been spent in marching and countermarching to find the enemy, and the attainment of the object did not seem any nearer at hand than when the campaign was com-

[NOTE.—* "In this expedition the force came upon the trembling lands, which are immense flats of turf from 6 to 12 inches thick, extending for miles in every direction and resting on beds of water and quicksand. A troop or even a single horseman riding over them produced an undulating motion of the land from which it gets its name. Although the surface is quite dry yet there is no difficulty in procuring plenty of water by cutting an opening through the stratum of turf. The horses would sometimes force a foot through or fall to the shoulders, yet so great was the tenacity of the surface in no instance was there any trouble in getting them out. In some places the weight of the earth forced a stream of water upward, which carrying with it and depositing large quantities of sand formed mounds. The mounds as they enlarged increased the pressure on the water below presenting the novel sight of a fountain on the prairie, throwing its stream down the sides of the hillock then to be absorbed by the sand and returned to the waters beneath."]—Ford's Hist. Ill.

menced. The progress of the army was necessarily slow, the country was comparatively an unexplored wilderness of prairie and forest, none of the command had been through it, and it was therefore impossible to obtain reliable guides. A number of Winnebagoes followed who from necessity were frequently consulted, but their fidelity was of a doubtful character, and the information they communicated generally delusive. The result was short marches, frequent delays, fruitless explorations, giving the enemy every opportunity to ascertain the intentions and movements of the pursuing force and thus elude it. The efforts of the commanding general were further retarded by the distance from the base of supplies, and the great difficulty of transportation, in consequence of which the troops were frequently without provisions and rarely had sufficient for protracted operations. Owing to this difficulty, it now became necessary to disperse the army to obtain food. Accordingly Major Dodge and Generals Henry and Alexander were sent to Fort Winnebago, situate on the portage between the Fox and Wisconsin rivers, for this purpose, while Gen. Posey marched to Fort Hamilton for the protection of the adjacent frontier, the governor returned to his home at Belleville and Gen. Atkinson fell back to lake Kush-ka-noug. Here he erected a fort, which was called after the name of the lake, in which he expected to remain till the volunteer generals returned with supplies.

Fort Winnebago, a distance of 80 miles from the encampment on the Stillwater, was reached in three days, but the march thither over the intervening* swampy country so crippled some of the horses as to render them useless in the succeeding part of the campaign. Another calamity also befell the horses shortly afterward, which was worse than an ordinary battle. About 1,000 were peaceably grazing on the prairie when a stampede occurred, caused, as was supposed, by Indians attempting to steal some of them. The soldiers at the time were sound asleep in their tents, which were closely pitched together and the frightened animals in their mad flight rushed directly over the encampment, knocking the tents down on the faces of the men and trampling their weapons and camp equipage into the ground. Then coursing northward with great rapidity, the sound of their feet produced an appalling noise resembling the roll of distant thunder. The

[* "A view of the country from camp at Fort Winnebago presented the most striking contrariety of features. Looking toward the fort which was a neat structure among the green hills, two streams are seen, the Fox and Wisconsin, with sources several hundred miles apart, the former in the east and the latter in the north, gliding as if to mingle their waters, until within three miles of each other, when they sweep the one to the northeast, and the other to the southwest, as if they had met to bid each other a gallant adieu before parting, the Fox to mingle its sweet and limped waters in the Gulf of St Lawrence, and the Wisconsin to contribute its stained and bitter floods to the Gulf of Mexico. The course of the Fox is short, crooked, narrow and deep, and abounds in the finest variety of fish, whilst the Wisconsin is large, wide and comparatively straight, and is said to have no fish, owing perhaps to its passage through cypress swamps which renders it unwholesome for the finny tribes, and also causes the discoloration of its waters. Besides the rivers the face of the country is no less remarkable. The strip of land between the two rivers is low and marshy, with no other growth except a course variety of rush, and at high waters so completely inundated as to convert all that part of the United States east of the Mississippi into a vast island. A wisp of straw being thrown into the flood where the two currents meet will separate and one portion float into the northern and the other into the southern sea. East of the Fox river the land is generally undulating, presenting an equal distribution of prairie of the richest mould and timber of the finest growth. West of the Wisconsin commences those frowning steppes of rugged barren rocks covered with black and bristling pine and hemlock which toward the Mississippi terminates in a region mountainous, dreary, terrific and truly Alpine in all its features."—Ford's History.]

picket guards and sentinels fled to the camp, supposing an attack had been made by the Indians, the bugles sounded to arms, but many of the soldiers were temporarily injured and in the confusion which prevailed could not find their broken and scattered weapons. The Wisconsin river changed the direction of the stampede but did not stop its fury, for the frightened animals turned about and again ran into the midst of the camp, and the soldiers now aware of the situation, endeavored to arrest their headlong course but without success. It was supposed that most of them ran a distance of 30 miles before the alarm subsided. Some were followed a distance of 50 miles before they were found, and about 100 were permanently disabled in the surrounding swamps.

Two days were spent at the fort in regaining the horses, recruiting the men and procuring necessary supplies, during which some Winnebago chiefs said that Black Hawk and his force were encamped on Rock river, 35 miles above lake Kush-ka-nong, the headquarters of Gen. Atkinson. It was now evident that if the army attempted to return to Gen. Atkinson the Indians would perhaps escape to the west of the Mississippi, and the only opportunity of closing the war with profit to the country and honor to the service would be lost. A council of war was convened and it was the unanimous opinion of all the officers present that the exigency of the case demanded that they should disregard the orders of Gen. Atkinson, by marching directly upon the enemy with the intention of taking him by surprise or preventing his retreat further northward. The 15th of July was accordingly appointed as the time of starting, and Gen. Henry at once commenced reorganizing his brigade, and disencumbering it of the sick and dismounted men, who would retard the celerity of his march. Before, however, the day of departure came around, Gen. Alexander announced that his men becoming dissatisfied had determined not to accompany the expedition, and Major Dodge reported that so many of his horses were disabled that he could not mount a force sufficiently large to render any valuable assistance. At this juncture Capt. Craig arrived with a fine company of mounted men from Galena and vicinity, which uniting with the battalion of Major Dodge increased it to 120 effective men. Gen. Henry's brigade was reduced to 600 men, and even these associating with Alexander's malcontents, became so demoralized as to be at the point of open mutiny. A protest was handed to the former, signed by all his subordinate officers except the colonel who presented it, remonstrating against the enterprise as a violation of Gen. Atkinson's orders.

This was the turning point on which hinged the fate of the campaign, and but for the prudence and determination of Gen. Henry all would have been lost. He was perhaps the only man in the army who possessed the rare faculty of successfully commanding the militia by inspiring them with order and the honorable impulses of his own noble nature. He could command with sternness and not give offence, and while he excited the fear he always won the love of the most obdurate soldier. In this emergency he knew he was right and promptly ordered all the officers signing the protest to be arrested and marched to Gen. Atkinson, who he knew would approve his course when he became acquainted with the circumstances. This decided command from a general whom they knew had the courage to execute it, caused the officers to relent. The colonel who presented the shameful paper denied knowing its contents, and all promised with the greatest contrition that they would never again be guilty of insubordination. Gen. Henry, who understood human nature and knew how to profit by it, spoke to them with dignity and kindness, wisely forgiving the offence and thus securing their faithful co-operation during the remainder of the campaign.

At the appointed time Gen. Henry and Major Dodge, with two Winnebagoes for guides, started in pursuit of the Indians, and Gen. Alexander with provisions returned to Gen. Atkinson. The former while on their way to the infested region, were frequently thrown from a direct course by intervening swamps of several miles in extent, yet after three days hard marching they again encamped on Rock river. Here information was received that Black Hawk was entrenched on Cranberry lake, higher up the river, and relying on this information Henry determined to make a forced march to that place the following day. Adjutants E. H. Merryman and W. W. Woodbridge, accompanied by Little Thunder, a Winnebago chief, as guide, were sent to Gen. Atkinson to apprise him that they had discovered the situation of the enemy and were making preparations to move against him. The messengers started about dark and after proceeding about 8 miles southwest they struck the fresh trail of Black Hawk, who was making toward the Wisconsin river, evidently to elude his pursuers by crossing it. Little Thunder, panic stricken at the sight of the trail, without permission returned to the camp and revealed the discovery to the two Indian guides, who attempted to make their escape, but before their object was fully accomplished they were arrested and brought to the tent of Gen. Henry. Confessing that their motives for acting as guides was to give false information and thus favor the escape of Black Hawk, they now disclosed all they knew of his movements, with the hope of escaping the punishment which their perfidy deserved. General Henry humanely spared their lives, and to prevent his men who would have wreaked summary vengeance on them for their treachery, prudently kept it a secret. The messengers, when they found themselves deserted by Little Thunder, also returned to the camp, but just before reaching it one of them came near being killed by the fire of a sentinel. Early the next morning the same messengers and guide were again dispatched to Gen. Atkinson, and the army started in pursuit of the enemy, leaving all the heavy baggage behind in the wilderness. Those who had previously lost their horses, abandoned their blankets and all their clothing except what they wore, and carrying their guns, ammunition and provisions on their backs through thickets, swamps and prairie, kept pace with their comrades on horseback. The riders on reaching a slough through which their horses were unable to carry them, dismounted and waded across, driving their animals before them. The large fresh trail being strewn with various articles, belonging to the Indians, gave animation to the pursuing force; there were no more complaints among the men, and even the horses seemed to partake of the enthusiasm which prevailed. Towards evening there arose one of those terrific thunder storms common to the prairies, frightfully dark and accompanied by torrents of rain and peals of thunder. The men, however, dashed on regardless of the raging elements, through floods, marshes, and almost impenetrable clumps of timber, the horsemen frequently dismounting and marching afoot that the footmen might be relieved by riding their horses. The storm continued most of the night, and the exhausted men threw themselves on the muddy earth to obtain a little rest, having partaken of no supper except a little raw meat and some dough, the result of the drenching rain on the flour they carried in their sacks. A similar repast serving them for breakfast, by early daylight they were again in motion and after a march as hard as that of the previous day, they encamped on one of the four lakes, near where Black Hawk had rested the previous night. The men now eagerly embraced the opportunity which was offered to build fires and cook their suppers, having marched 100 miles without eating anything except raw food. As soon as their hunger was appeased, they again lay down to rest with nothing under them but the naked earth, and nothing over them but the starry canopy, and slept sweetly till aroused and called to arms. A sentinel who during the night discovered an Indian stealthily gliding toward the shore in a canoe, fired his gun which caused an alarm, but nothing further occurred to indicate the presence of an enemy. Early the following day the march was resumed with great vigor, all being elated with the hope of soon overtaking the Indians and terminating the war in a general battle. Crossing the river between two of the lakes, the army ascended an eminence, whence could be seen a panorama of wonderous beauty. Three of these lovely sheets of water environed by wooded hills and rolling prairies were in full view. The hand of civilization had not marred their primeval beauty and everything was wild and still, save the distant roar of the surging waters lashed by almost constant winds.

The Indians, however, were only a few miles distant endeavoring to escape, and the hurried march to overtake them gave but little time to contemplate the surrounding scenery. The path of the fugitives was strewn with all kinds of baggage highly valued by the owners, which they were compelled to throw away to accelerate their flight. Some of the horses were found dead, the result of exhaustion, and others were occasionally killed to afford their hungry riders the means of sustenance. About 12 o'clock on the 21st of July, 3 Indian spies were overtaken and killed, and shortly afterward the rear guard began to make faint stands as if desirous of bringing on a battle. It was, however, soon apparent that their object was to gain time, for after firing a few rounds they would dash ahead while the pursuing force was forming for battle. In this manner by 4 o'clock they gained the bluffs of the Wisconsin, and as the vanguard of the Americans, consisting of two battalions commanded by Majors Dodge and Ewing, came up they were fired upon by the Indians concealed in the timber which skirts the bluff of the stream. Gen. Henry soon arrived, and the entire force was formed in order of battle. Major Dodge's battalion constituted the extreme right of the line; Col. Jones' regiment the center, and Col. Collins' the left, while Major Ewing's battalion was placed in front, and Col. Fry's regiment in the rear as a reserve. A charge being ordered, Ewing's battalion and the regiments of Cols. Jones and Collins made a gallant onset upon the enemy, causing him to retire obliquely to the right and concentrate in front of the battalion of Major Dodge, who was then ordered to advance upon the foe, but considering his force inadequate and requesting assistance, Col. Fry's regiment was sent to his aid, when a vigorous charge was made from one end of the line to the other. Fry's regiment and Dodge's battalion entered the timber and tall grass, exposed to the fierce fire of the Indians, who maintained their ground till their adversaries could reach them with their bayonets, when they fled and took a new position in the head of a ravine farther westward, and leading to the low-lands of the river. Here they made a more stubborn resistance, but a handsome charge by Collins' and Jones' regiments and Ewing's battalion, forced some of them down the hollow, and others farther westward along the bluffs, whence they escaped to the bottom bordering on the stream. This was about a mile wide and next to the river, covered with heavy timber, while near the bluff it was swampy and overgrown with grass so tall as to be above the heads of the men on horseback. It was now near sun down, and Gen. Henry concluded it would be too hazardous to dislodge the enemy during the night, and accordingly remained on the battle ground.

The battle of the Winconsin was the first important victory obtained over the enemy during the war. The Indians had with them their women and children, and fully alive to the disastrous consequences which would attend defeat, fought with great determination. During the engagement Naopope, their commander, posted himself on an elevation near his warriors and gave his orders in a voice of thunder, which could be distinctly heard above the din of battle. It was said that of all men he had the loudest voice, but it ceased to be heard when his braves were driven from their position. Great praise was due the entire army, the officers having discharged their duties with great efficiency and the privates exhibited unusual bravery in the different charges made upon the enemy. Gen. Henry was young and inexperienced, yet in his coolness and the judgment displayed in the disposition of his forces acted the part of a veteran commander. He now concluded that if the Indians intended to continue the contest they would make an attack during the night, and as a precaution he increased the strength of the guard and caused fires to be built in front of the camp and kept burning till morning. Orders were given that the men should sleep on their arms, and they had not long been wrapt in slumber when they were aroused by the tramping of horses. It was supposed that the latter had been frightened by the approaching enemy, and the men were ordered to hold themselves during the remainder of the night in readiness for an attack. About 3 o'clock in the morning Naopope took a stand on the same elevation he had occupied during the battle, and spoke with a loud voice, in the Winnebago tongue, which in the calm of the night reverberated from hill to hill. It was ascertained when the war was over that he was suing for peace. He stated that his countrymen were in a starving condition and unable to fight the Americans, and that if they were permitted to peaceably return west of the Mississippi with their families they would do no further mischief. As the Indian guides had fled at the commencement of the battle there was no person in the camp who understood his language, and it was supposed he was giving commands to his warriors. The Americans expecting every moment to be attacked, Gen. Henry made a spirited speech in which he told them they were about to meet the savages who had butchered in cold blood so many of their helpless and unoffending citizens, reminded them of the obstacles which they had encountered and overcome during the campaign, and urged them not to tarnish the reputation they had gained in the battle of the preceding day. Every man then took his position and remained in it till early dawn, when Ewing's battalion proceeded to the top of the hill whence the voice proceeded, but only found the foot-prints of a few horsemen. The army then marched to the river and discovered that the Indians had crossed and made their escape among the mountains between it and the Mississippi. One hundred and sixty-eight of their fallen comrades were found dead on the field of battle, and the number of the wounded was perhaps proportionately large, as 25 of them were subsequenly found dead along the track of their departing trail. Gen. Henry had one man killed and 8 wounded. The great disparity in the loss of the Americans, and that of the enemy was accounted for on the supposition that the Indians had been taught to fire at men on horseback and consequently aimed too high to hit their adversaries, who dismounted before entering battle.

CHAPTER XXXV.

1832—CLOSE OF THE WAR.

Pursuit of the Indians—Battle of Bad-Axe—Arrival of Gen. Scott—Treaties with the Indians—Eastern Tour of the Prisoners— Death of Black Hawk.

It will be remembered that Adjutants Woodbridge and Merryman, piloted by Little Thunder, were sent the second time to Gen. Atkinson's headquarters. They arrived safely, and after conferring with him, they were ordered to return with instructions authorizing Gen. Henry to pursue the trail of Black Hawk, and if possible overtake and capture his force, and that when his provisions were exhausted he should go to the Blue Mounds for supplies, where he and his army would meet him. The messengers reached Gen. Henry during the recent battle, and the next day, as the army was without food and the means of rendering the wounded comfortable, it was determined to visit the Mounds for this purpose and replenish their stores. No one in the brigade, however, understood the topography of the country sufficiently well to act as guide. They had now penetrated 100 miles into an unexplored wilderness, and the Winnebagoes who had accompanied the expedition fled at the commencement of the battle and had not returned. A council was called to consider the means of overcoming the difficulty, and while in session a white flag was seen approaching, borne by a number of friendly Winnebagoes, who agreed to act as guides. Litters were constructed for the wounded, and on the 23d of July the army was again in motion, and after encountering a number of muddy creeks and a large extent of rough roads, they reached the Blue Mounds in safety. Here, as they had been advised, they found Gen. Atkinson, with the regular and volunteer forces under his immediate command, and a number of inhabitants, whose kind treatment made the wounded forget the hardships they had suffered in the journey thither.

It was now evident that Gen. Atkinson and other officers of the regular army were greatly mortified at the success of Gen. Henry, as they did not intend that the militia should acquire any renown in the war. Gen. Atkinson relying mostly on the regulars, had always kept them in front, but unexpectedly while they were snugly ensconced at Lake Kushkanong, Gen. Henry discovered and vanquished the enemy as effectually as if the veterans had participated in the engagement. This unmanly jealousy was further intensified by the fact, that the victory had been obtained in opposition to the council and orders of those who arrogated to themselves superior courage and knowledge in the practice and art of war.

All the generals were now together, but not all the men. Gen. Posey's brigade contained only 200 effective men; Gen. Alexander's 350, and Gen. Henry's being also greatly reduced, the three brigades combined were not much stronger than one at the commencement of the campaign. In addition to the volunteer force, there were now 400 regulars under the command of Gen. Brady and his subordinate officers, Col. Taylor and Majors Riley and Morgan. After spending 2 days at the Mounds, on the 25th of July the whole army, under direction of Gen. Atkinson, again started after the Indians. The regulars marched in front, Posey's and Alexander's brigades and Dodge's battalion came next, and lastly Henry's brigade in charge of the baggage brought up the rear. The position assigned Gen. Henry, the hero of the battle of Wisconsin, showed too plainly the ungenerous feeling that rankled in the breast of the commanding general. The whole army noticed the insult, and the brave men who were thus degraded knew they deserved better treatment, and justly claimed the post of honor and of danger. It was now evident that if other laurels were to be won they would decorate other brows. Gen. Henry and his men, were too true to their duties as soldiers to suffer this injustice to interfere with the success of the expedition, and therefore quietly trudged along in the rear, doing the drudgery of the army and taking charge of the baggage. On the 26th they arrived at Helena, with a view to crossing the Wisconsin at that place.

This village, formerly a promising town, was now abandoned by its inhabitants, and the houses were pulled down and converted into rafts on which to cross the river. During the construction of the rafts, scouts were sent up the river to the battle ground to ascertain if the Indians had returned thither as the course they had taken in their flight after the battle. A day was spent in making explorations, but no trace of the enemy being discovered the party returned. On the 28th the whole army had gained the opposite bank of the river, and after marching a distance of 5 miles fell in with the trail of the retreating fugitives. Before the discovery, the army was greatly disheartened, the distance to the Mississippi was supposed to be 80 miles, and it was seriously feared that ere the enemy could again be overtaken they would make their escape west of this stream. The men had become weary in hunting trails, but now it was found, the hope of again falling in with the Indians was revived and all murmurs ceased. The trail at first followed the course of the river, but soon turned northward among huge mountains, which never before had echoed with the tread of civilized men. Three weary days were consumed in scaling these precipitous elevations and crossing the intervening gorges, the one being covered with heavy timber and a dense undergrowth of briers and vines, and the other filled with swamps of deep black mud. The men were well supplied with provisions, and bore their labors with cheerfulness, but it was difficult for the horses to find grass, and many of them becoming debilitated by hunger were left to perish in these pastureless solitudes. The condition of the Indians was extremely deplorable. They were compelled to subsist on roots, bark and the flesh of horses, and their trail could be readily traced by blankets, kettles and other articles abandoned to hasten their flight. Death, too, had marked their course with the bodies of those who had been wounded, most of whom had died more for the want of proper medical treatment than from the fatal nature of their injuries.

At 10 o'clock on the morning of the 2d of August, the army reached the bluffs of the Mississippi, which at this point were some distance from the stream. The Indians having reached the margin of the river some time before the arrival of the Americans, were busily engaged in preparations to cross. Some had already reached the opposite shore, and some of the women had been put in canoes and started down to Prairie du Chien, but part of the latter were drowned, and those who reached the town were found in a starving condition. While thus employed they were attacked by the steamboat Warrior, which had been chartered for the purpose of conveying supplies to the army. On the 1st of August she was sent up the river to notify some friendly Indians that the Sacs were approaching, and to take them down to Prairie du Chien. On his way, Captain Throckmorton heard that Black Hawk was already encamped on the banks of the river, and he immediately made preparations for an attack. As the steamboat neared the camp of the Indians, they raised a white flag, which the captain affecting to believe was only used as a mask to cover their real designs, ordered them to send a canoe alongside his boat. The order being declined, they were allowed 15 minutes to remove their women and children, when a six-pounder, loaded with cannister, was discharged into their midst, followed by a severe fire of musketry. The battle continued about an hour, during which the enemy had 23 men killed and a proportionate number wounded. The fuel of the steamer now began to fail, and night coming on, she fell down the river to Prairie du Chien, intending to return the next day.

The captain of the Warrior, even if his surmises were correct respecting the perfidy of the Indians, was still liable to censure for the precipitancy with which he brought on the engagement. He and his men were beyond the reach of harm, and consequently both humanity and the rules of war required that he should have taken more than 15 minutes to discover the real motive of the Indians in hoisting the symbol of peace. Black Hawk himself asserted that he directed his braves not to fire on the Warrior, as he intended going on board in order to save his women and children, and that he raised a white flag and called to the captain of the boat for the purpose of effecting this object. His condition was now hopeless, his warriors, reduced in numbers, were exhausted by fatigue and hunger, while an overwhelming force ready to move against him, was just in his rear. It is therefore highly probable that he was sincere and anxious to end the contest, in which so many of his people had been slaughtered; and had the captain of the Warrior properly respected the flag of truce, which all civilized warfare holds sacred, the campaign would have terminated without the further effusion of blood.

Before the Warrior could return to the Indian encampment, which was on the Mississippi below the mouth of the Bad Axe, Gen. Atkinson arrived and commenced a general battle. Black Hawk, aware that the American force was in close proximity, to gain time for crossing, with 20 warriors, went back to meet them, his object being to make an attack and then retreat up the river to decoy the Americans from the principal force. Accordingly, when the army reached the bluffs of the Mississippi, it was fired upon from behind trees by the Indians, the tall grass growing among the timber greatly favoring their design. The order of battle being the same as at first: Major Dodge's battalion was in front, next the regulars, then the brigades of Alexander and Posey and lastly the command of Henry. At the first indications of opposition, Gen. Atkinson rode to the scene of action and in person directed the charge against the Indians, who of course fell back, and were pursued up the river by the whole army except the force under the immediate command of Gen. Henry and Major Ewing. In the hurried pursuit he was called on for one regiment to cover the rear of the pursuing forces, and the rest were left without orders. It now seemed that fortune was determined to distinguish her favorite son, despite the intention to disgrace him. He who during the whole march had been kept in the rear, now by the strategy of a few untutored savages who had triumphed over the science of the veteran general, was suddenly placed in front.

While Gen. Atkinson was ascending the river, the main trail leading directly to it was discovered by Major Ewing's men, who were in front. Henry being notified of the fact, followed to the foot of the bluffs bordering the valley, where he left his horses and arranged his men for an attack. Eight men were sent forward as a forlorn hope to draw the fire of the enemy, and thus disclose their situation in the drift wood and brush through which the trail led. The men moved boldly forward till they came in sight of the river, when they were fired upon by about 50 Indians, who were in advance of the main force. Five of the eight instantly fell, either killed or wounded, while the other three, protected by timber, remained in their position till the army came to their rescue. Henry immediately ordered a charge, before which the Indians retreated to the main body, amounting to 300 warriors and fully equal to the force contending against them. The whole force of the enemy becoming involved, fought with great bravery and determination, yet they had evidently been surprised and there was little concert of action. Closely pressed they fell back from position to position, until the bank of the river was reached, where retreat being impossible a frightful carnage ensued. The bloody bayonet in the hands of an excited soldiery, drove them into the water, when some of the survivors endeavored to swim the river and others sought refuge in a willow island 150 yards from the shore.

About this time Gen. Atkinson and that portion of the army which had been decoyed up the river, made their appearance at the scene of conflict. Henry had previously sent messengers to inform him that he had discovered the main force of the enemy, but the roar of battle apprised him of the situation before messengers had time to reach him. He came but found the battle substantially over, the dead and dying strewn upon the fatal field, disclosing the stern work which had been done in his absence. Seeing the position of the enemy, he immediately ordered a descent upon the island. A force consisting of the regulars, Ewing's and Dodge's battalions and Fry's regiment, charged through the water up to their arms, to dislodge them from their last refuge. When the island was gained most of the enemy who had fled thither were killed or captured, those attempting to swim to the opposite shore being either shot in the water or drowned. Large numbers of women and children lost their lives, owing to the fact that they were dressed so much like the men it was impossible to distinguish them in the high grass and weeds which obstructed the view. Some of them plunged into the Mississippi and were shot escaping in the promiscuous crowd which was buffeting the waves in the attempt to reach the opposite shore.*

It is supposed that the entire Indian loss amounted to 150 killed and as many lost by drowning in the attempt to swim the river. About 50, consisting mostly of women and children, were taken prisoners. The American loss amounted to 17 killed.

Soon after the battle was over, the captain of the Warrior steamed up the river and commenced raking the island, thinking that the Indians were still on it. The land forces hearing his guns, supposed he was firing a salute in honor of the victory, and fired a volley in acknowledgment, and it was not till she came to land that intelligence was for the first time interchanged in regard to the battles which had previously been fought by the respective forces.

Gen. Atkinson considering the war virtually ended, on the 4th of August, with the regulars, prisoners and wounded, on board the Warrior, fell down the river to Prairie du Chien, and the mounted men marched to the same place by land. The news of the battle had preceded the advent of the army, and when it arrived the Menomonee Indians were expressing their joy at the defeat of the Sacs and Foxes by music and dancing. Having obtained several scalps from the squaws of the enemy, they presented them to their own women, whose relatives had been murdered the preceding year at Fort Crawford by the same tribes. These trophies, held aloft on poles, constituted a prominent feature of the dance, which was conducted in the following manner: the men and women stood in two lines facing each other, while the squaws holding the scalps were situated between. The party was furnished with a rudely constructed drum, and each one who participated in the dance held in his hand a gourd partially filled with pebbles, which were rattled to keep time with the drum. Thus arranged, and equipped at the sound of the drum the exercise commenced, each dancer moving around the central group, supporting the scalps, and uttering a loud monotonous refrain, kept time by stamping with his feet and shaking his gourd. As the exercise was protracted the chant became louder and more animated, the jumping correspondingly higher and more boisterous, and the scalps were twirled in the air with increased vehemence. During

---

[NOTE.—Many painful scenes of adventure and horror were crowded into the 3 hours' continuance of the battle. A Sac woman, the sister of a warrior of some notoriety, found herself in the thickest of the fight, but at length succeeeded in reaching the river, when keeping her infant child safe in its blankets by means of her teeth, she plunged into the water, seized the tail of a horse with her hands whose rider was swimming the stream and was drawn safely across. A young squaw during the battle was standing in the grass a short distance from the American line, holding her child, a little girl of 4 years, in her arms. In this position a ball struck the right arm of the child and shattering the bone, passed into the breast of the young mother and instantly killed her. She fell upon the child and confined it to the ground till the Indians were driven from this part of the field. Gen. Anderson of the United States army, hearing its cries went to the spot and taking it from under the dead body, carried it to the surgeons to have its wound dressed. The arm was amputated and during the operation the half starved child did not cry, but sat quietly eating a hard piece of biscuit. It was sent to Prairie du Chien and entirely recovered.

the entire performance the bodies of the dancers were bent forward bringing their noses so close together as frequently to touch, and when finally they became exhausted the exercise ended.

The 2d day after their arrival, Gen. Atkinson having every reason to believe that the Winnebago chiefs had been treacherous, summoned them for the purpose of having a talk. He accused them of deception and rendering assistance to the Sacs, and Winnesheik, one of their number, having commanded the Indians in the recent battle, and his sons who were subsequently brought in wounded, were put in prison. Gen Street, the Indian agent, who was present at the conference, then told the chiefs that if they would bring in Black Hawk and the prophet, it would be well with them, and the government would hold them in future as friends. At this declaration, Decori, Cheater, and two other chiefs, at the head of a small party of Sioux and Winnebagoes, started after the two fugitives, who with 20 men, during the battle of the Bad Axe fled up the river. The Sioux and the Sacs had been at war for years, and the former eagerly embraced the opportunity now offered to avenge their wrongs by bringing them to punishment. The Winnebagoes, although first sympathizing with the hostile band, like civilized man in the hour of adversity, when friendship is mostly needed, proved unfaithful. As soon as war had demonstrated the comparative strength of the two belligerents, their cringing and crafty nature commenced pandering to the power of the conquerors.

On the 7th of August, Gen. Scott who with 9 companies of infantry had been sent from the eastern sea-board, arrived and assumed command. He started from Fortress Monroe, and in 18 days 4 of the companies reached Chicago, distant 1800 miles, which before the existence of the present railroad facilities was an unparelled feat of celerity. The whole force was destined for Chicago, but the virus of a disease more fatal than the sword preyed upon their vitals, and prevented the accomplishment of the object contemplated. The expedition, filled with patriotic ardor, arrived safe at Detroit, and while moored at its wharves two cases of a strange disease made their appearance and created unusual alarm. The army surgeons and local physicians were immediately summoned, but despite all their efforts two soldiers attacked were no more. The Asiatic Cholera, then a new disease on the continent of America was raging in the Atlantic cities, and had now broken out in the army, causing terror and gloom to rest on every countenance. The expedition passed on to Fort Gratiot, distant 40 miles, where 5 companies, numbering 280 men, who, either unwilling or unable to proceed further, were landed. Some of them died in the hospitals, and others fleeing to avoid the pestilence, wandered hopelessly over the country, shunned by the inhabitants, not through inhumanity, but the fear of contagion, till nature becoming exhausted they laid down in the fields and expired. The entire number with the exception of 9 perished, without a friendly hand to offer them assistance, or console them in the last moments of existence. Of the other 4 companies 30 died on the way to Chicago, and as a sustitute for burial, were heaved into the waters of the lake. Arriving at Chicago on the 8th of July, Fort Dearborn was converted into a hospital, and the families which had taken temporary refuge within its walls from the attacks of the Indians, were turned roofless on the prairie. In 30 days 90 inmates of the hospital became victims of the destroyer, and life was hardly extinct before they were cast, unwept and uncoffined, into pits, to prevent the spread of the epidemic.*

After the disease had abated, the march was resumed, and finally the remnant of the force which had started with such bright anticipations of glory, reached Fort Armstrong on the Mississippi, the latter part of August. Here not only many of the survivors perished, but the Indians were also attacked, and large numbers of them swept away. Gen. Scott arrived only in time to participate in the negotiations which followed the war, but in his humane exertions in behalf of the soldiers, he won laurels far transcending the glory of the most brilliant campaign against the enemy.

The further pursuit of the Indians being considered unnecessary, on the arrival of Gen. Scott the volunteers started for Dixon to be mustered out of service. Arriving thither on the 17th, they were discharged, and each soldier now released from military life returned to his home, kindred and friends, pleased with the congratulations which were ever extended, and feeling honored in having been instrumental in freeing the country from the ravages of the merciless foe.

Many of the noted men of the State had been engaged in the war, and many, at that time unknown to fame, afterward attained the highest honors in the gift of the country which they risked their lives to defend. Of the former class were Reynolds and Scott, men of State and national reputations. Of the latter, S. H. Anderson became lieutenant governor, James Turney, attorney general; W. L. D. Ewing, auditor of public accounts; Sidney Breese, chief justice of the State; John Thomas and John Dement, State treasurers; Thomas Ford and Joseph Duncan, governors of the State; Henry Dodge governor of Wisconsin, and General Taylor and Abraham Lincoln presidents of the United States. Jefferson Davis, the rival of the latter, also participated in the war, but his future career as the chief of the great rebellion, gave him a fame in striking contrast with that which was won by the martyr of liberty and the savior of his country.

Among the many who distinguished themselves in the war, there was no one more efficient as an officer, or more highly respected by the people of Illinois, than Gen. James D. Henry. His great sagacity and determination at Fort Winnebago, gave a new direction to the campaign and enabled the army to overtake the Indians. He was the chief commander in the battle of the Wisconsin, which followed the first decisive victory of the war, and the battle of the Bad axe which closed it, was the result of his generalship and not of the superior officers who endeavored to prevent his sharing in its dangers and honors.

*"The burial of the dead was entrusted to a sergeant, who executed his duty with military precision, as soon as life was extinct. On one occasion several were removed from the hospital to be buried at once. The grave had already been dug, and the bodies wrapped in blankets were laid by its side, the last military honors had been paid, and nothing more remained to complete the service but to tumble them one after another in, when a corpse appeared to move. A brother soldier resorting thither, his old messmate, opened his eyes and asked him for some water. The sergeant said they might take him back, as he was not yet ready for burial. The order was obeyed and the soldier lived many years thereafter." Brown's History of Illinois.

He was a native of Pennsylvania, and in the year 1822 emigrated to Illinois and located at Edwardsville. Born in poverty and obscurity, his earlier years were entirely devoted to manual toil, and when he attained the age of manhood he was hardly able to read or write. For some time after his arrival at Edwardsville, he worked as a mechanic during the day, and at night attended school for the purpose of improving his education. After leaving school, and engaging for a short time in the mercantile business, he removed in 1826 to Springfield, and was elected sheriff of Sangamon county. The integrity and sound judgment exhibited in discharging the duties of this office, attracted the attention of Gov. Reynolds, who at the breaking out of the war made him one of his aids. He was exceedingly modest and retiring till his passions were fully aroused, and then he showed an intensity of feeling and an iron will, which was irresistible so far as he had power to act. The fear of nothing except his maker ever entered his breast, and he knew and cared as little for danger and death as a marble statue. His extreme sensibility and diffidence never permitted him to appear in the society of ladies. At the close of the Black Hawk war, the citizens of Springfield gave him a splendid reception in honor of his services, but he never entered the apartments where the ladies presided. At the close of the war he was the most popular man in Illinois, and had he lived he could have been elected to any office in the gift of the people. His health and constitution were originally good, but the hardships of the war induced consumption, which caused his death, on the 4th of March, 1834, at New Orleans, whither he had gone for the benefit of the climate and medical treatment. Such was his singular modesty, that during his sickness in the city, he never mentioned his connection with the Black Hawk war, and no one knew he was Gen. Henry until after his death.

While Henry was duly appreciated at home, he never received abroad the honors to which he was entitled. The news of the war first made its appearance in *The Galenian*, a newspaper printed at Galena, and the only sheet issued north of Springfield. Dr. Philleo, the editor belonged to Dodge's battalion, and when from time to time he chronicled the events of the war and sent them home for publication, he gave his own command a prominence in the war to which it was not entitled. By a wilful perversion of facts, he never mentioned Henry except as a subordinate officer, while Major Dodge was spoken of as a general, thus creating the impression that the former commanded a brigade, and the latter a battalion, when the reverse was true. His letters were copied in the newspapers throughout the U. S., as authentic news, and in a number of cities it was asserted that Dodge was the principal commander of the war, and the names of Henry, Atkinson and Taylor, if mentioned at all, were only in connection with subordinate positions. This delusion was afterward of immense advantage to Major Dodge, but independent of the prestige thus acquired, he was a man of great popularity and influence.

On the 27th of August, Decori and Cheaters, after an absence of 20 days, returned with Black Hawk, the prophet, and a number of other prisoners. On handing them over to Gen. Street, Decori said: "Father, we deliver these men into your custody. We do not entrust them even to your brother, the chief of the warriors, but to you, because we know you, and we believe you are our friend. We want you to keep them safe; if they are to suffer we do not want to see it. Wait until we are gone before it is done. Father, many little birds have been flying about our ears of late, and we thought they whispered to us that there was evil intended for us, and we now hope they will let us alone." Gen. Street replied: "My children, you have done well. I told you to bring these men to me, and you have done so. I assured Gen. Atkinson that if these men were in your country, you would find them and bring them to me, and now I can say much for your good. I will go down to Rock Island with the prisoners, and I wish you as you have brought them, especially to go with me, with such other chiefs and warriors as you may select."

In pursuance of the treaty to be entered into, on the 10th of September Black Hawk, his two sons, Wishick, Naopope, the prophet, and a number of Winnebago chiefs, were sent down to Rock Island, where Keokuk and his warriors were to meet them. Likewise the remnant of Black Hawk's band also followed him to to the same place. Such was their utter destitution that they excited the compassion of all who saw them, and Gen. Scott, who was as sympathetic as brave, kindly bestowed on them everything that could supply their wants or relieve their suffering. On the 15th a treaty was made with the Winnebagoes, whereby they sold to the United States all their lands east of the Mississippi and west of Green bay. As a consideration, the government agreed to give them a large region of country west of the river, to pay them $70,000 in ten annual installments, to maintain schools for the education of their children for a period of 20 years, and to instruct them in agriculture and furnish them with cattle and implements for its practical introduction among them.

To escape from the cholera, which was still raging at Rock Island among the Indians and eastern troops, Gen. Scott and Gov. Reynolds, with the principal chiefs of the Sacs and Foxes, fell down the river to Jefferson Barracks, where they entered into a treaty with them also. They ceded to the government the tract of land embraced in the present limits of Iowa and a part of Wisconsin, and received in return, besides some minor considerations, an annuity of $20,000 for a period of 30 years. As a reward to Keokuk and his friendly band, a reservation of 40 miles square was made to them in Iowa, including their principal village. It was also proposed to Keokuk to establish schools for the benefit of his tribe, but he rejected the proposition, alleging that it might do well enough for the whites, but he had observed that it made Indians worse to educate them. By these treaties the United States obtained 30,000,000 acres of land, at a cost truly insignificant compared with their real value. Such, however, is the measures usually meted by the stronger to the weaker power, and such is the fate of savage races when brought in contact with the diplomacy of civilized men. Viewed in the light of a commercial transaction, such a disparity of values seems monstrous; but when we consider the Earth is the common heritage of the human family, and that an advanced state of the arts and sciences is essential to its development, we become reconciled to it as a necessity in the onward march of civilization.

The Indian prisoners who were to be retained during the pleasure of the President, were confined in the barracks till the following spring. Of the hundreds who visited them during the winter, one of them writes:

" We were immediately struck with admiration at the gigantic and symmetrical figures of most of the warriors, who seemed as they reclined in their native ease and gracefulness, with their half naked bodies exposed to view, rather like statues from some master hand than beings of a race whom we had heard characterized as degenerate and debased."

Keokuk visited them the following spring, and made great exertions for their release, offering to become responsible for their future conduct, but a message was received by Gen. Atkinson from the Secretary of War, ordering them to be sent to the national capital. Under the escort of an officer of the army on the 22d of April, 1833, they reached Washington, and had an interview with the President. Black Hawk closed his speech, delivered on this occasion, in the following words: " We did not expect to conquer the whites—they have too many houses, too many men. I took up the hatchet for my part, to revenge injuries which my people could no longer endure. Had I borne them longer without striking, my people would have said Black Hawk is a woman; he is too old to be a chief; he is no Sac. These reflections caused me to raise the war-whoop. I say no more, it is known to you. Keokuk once was here; you took him by the hand, and when he wished to return to his home, you were willing. Black Hawk expects, like Keokuk, we shall be permitted to return, too." The president informed them that they must go to Fortress Monroe and remain there till the conduct of their people satisfied him that they intended to comply with the stipulations of the treaty. He also assured them that their women and children, for whom they expressed solicitude, should be protected from their enemies. On the 26th of April, they set off for the Fortress, where they remained until the 4th of July following, when an order was received from the president directing their release and return home. The kind treatment of Colonel Eustice, in command of the prison, had so won the friendship of the captives, that when about to leave Black Hawk waited on the colonel and said: "The memory of your friendship will remain till the Great Spirit says it is time for Black Hawk to sing his death song." Presenting him hith a hunting shirt and some eagle's feathers, he added: "Accept these, my brother; I have given some like them to the White Beaver; accept them as a memorial of Black Hawk. When he is far away they will serve to remind you of him."

From Fortress Monroe they were taken to Baltimore, where they had another interview with the President, who informed them that Gen. Atkinson and Keokuk their principal chief were anxious for their return home, and that he had ordered Major Garland, who would accompany them thither, first to conduct them through some of the principal cities, that they might witness the power of the United States and learn their own inability to cope with them in war. "Go back," said he, "and listen to the counsel of Keokuk and other chiefs; bury the tomahawk and live in peace with the frontiers, and I pray the Great Spirit to give a smooth path and a fair sky for your return."

Leaving Baltimore they reached Philadelphia on the 10th of June, and remained long enough to see the principal objects of interest in the city and exhibited themselves to the curious thousands who flocked to see them. Black Hawk in referring to his conduct with the United States, said to the multitude about him: "My heart grew bitter against the whites and my hands strong. I dug up the tomahawk and led my warriors on to battle. I fought hard and much blood was shed, but the white men were mighty; they were many and my people failed." On the morning of the 14th they started for New York and arrived at the Battery, in the midst of a vast assemblage of people who had been drawn together to witness the ascent of a balloon. This novel spectacle greatly astonished the Indians, and one of them asked the prophet if the æronaut was going to the Great Spirit. On landing, the press of the multitude which crowded to see them was so great that they could not reach the hotel till they were placed in carriages and committed to the care of the police. While in the city they were treated with marked civility, being conducted with ceremony to theatres, public gardens, and other places of interest, and receiving many handsome presents.

Major Garland had been directed to conduct the prisoners as far north as Boston, but while in New York he was ordered to ascend the Hudson and proceed with them directly to their home in the West. In pursuance of the arrangements, on the 22d of June the party started westward, to the great disappointment of the Bostonians, who wanted an opportunity to see and lionize the savage disturbers of the Northwest. At Albany, Buffalo, Detroit, and other places along the route, the attentions paid them rendered their progress through the country a triumphal procession, instead of the custody of prisoners in the hands of an officer. In passing the site of the old Sac village at the mouth of Rock river, Black Hawk became melancholy and expressed many regrets at the causes which compelled him as an exile to leave it. The host of warriors whom he delighted to lead to battle were now no more; his village was reduced to ashes, his family was dispersed among strangers, and he a suppliant for a home in a foreign country. Finally, about the 1st of August, the party reached Rock Island, which had been selected by Major Garland as a suitable place for the liberation of the captives. The river at this place is a beautiful sheet of clear, swift running water, a mile wide and divided near the centre by Rock Island, which rises to a considerable height above the surface and stretches several miles up and down the river. It originally produced nuts and a variety of other wild fruits, and being in the rapids, it was a favorite resort for Indian fisherman who caught large quantities of excellent fish in the swift, pure waters that wash its rocky base. There was an Indian tradition that the island was inhabited by a good spirit which dwelt in a cave among the rocks. It had a plumage white as snow, wings much larger than those of the swan, and its voice in the Sac language was the sweetest music. The good spirit had sent it to teach the Sacs and Foxes wisdom and goodness and as a guardian divinity to preside over the destinies of the nation. In former times it had frequently been seen, but alarmed at the building of Fort Armstrong and the wickedness of the white men, it spread its snowy pinions and was seen no more.

The white-washed walls of the fort loomed up from the high bluffs at the lower extremity of the island, giving to the fortress the appearance of an enchanted castle when seen from a distance

in the beauty of the surrounding scenery. From its towers could
be seen the blue hills, which rising by a gentle acclivity from the
river follow its meandering course and bound the valley through
which it flows. The valley is several miles in width, and at that
time was interspersed with groves of timber, which gave it a vernal sweetness and beauty rarely equalled. Rock river could be
seen in the distance, forcing its pure waters over a rocky rapid
into the floods of the Mississippi. On the north bank of the former was the site of the Sac village, and directly opposite, on the
west bank of the latter, that of the Foxes, which time had consecrated as the Jerusalem of these tribes. No other locality could
have awakened in the mind of Black Hawk so many painful
memories. Here he had gamboled away his youth in its wooded
haunts; for half a century it had witnessed his power and influence, and now it was to become the scene of his submission to a
hated rival.

Immediately after his arrival, Major Garland sent out runners
to summon the neighboring Indians to meet him in council. Keokuk and his braves had been out on a buffalo hunt, and were about
20 miles below on their way to the fort in anticipation of meeting
the captives. He informed the messengers that he would be at
Rock Island at noon the following day, and accordingly, at the
appointed time his fleet was seen ascending the river, the wild
songs and shouts of his men echoing from shore to shore. A large
craft, covered with a spacious canopy and bearing the American
flag, moved in the van, carrying Keokuk and his three wives.
About 20 more canoes in the rear, each containing several warriors, completed the imposing pageant which gallantly moved
over the still waters. After ascending the stream some distance
above the fort and returning, a landing was effected on the eastern bank opposite the encampment of Black Hawk, where the
warriors spent several hours in painting their faces and equiping
themselves with implements of war. These preparations being
completed, the party passed directly across the river, and Keokuk
landing first turned to his warriors and said: "The Great Spirit
has sent our brother back to us, let us shake hands with him in
friendship. Then fully armed he slowly approached and saluted
Black Hawk, who was leaning on his staff in front of his lodge.
His followers, in like manner, having taken the old man by the
hand, the pipe was introduced, and after an hour of pleasant civ-
ilties, Keokuk and his braves arose and took leave of the captives,
promising to see them again at the council. The fort in the meantime had been fitted up for this purpose. A grand convocation of
Indians assembled the next day to witness the liberation of the
prisoners. At ten o'clock in the morning Keokuk and 100 warriors proceeded to the fort and were shown seats in the council rooms. Not long after the captives made their appearance, and
as they entered the room the chiefs who had preceded them gave
them a cordial greeting. Black Hawk and his son, who had previously objected to the council as unnecessary and painful to their
feelings, seemed much dejected. In the midst of the profound
silence, which for a time prevailed in the hall, Major Garland arose
and said to the assembled chiefs that he was much pleased at the
fraternal feeling which they had extended to the prisoners since
their arrival, and he trusted that this would continue, and there-

after they would dwell together in harmony and peace. He then caused a letter from the President to be read, admonishing the captives to cultivate the friendship of their neighbors, to hunt and support their families, and threatening the severest penalties if they again disturbed the frontiers. Keokuk replied: "We receive our brothers in friendship. Our hearts are good towards them. They have listened to bad counsel; now their ears are closed. I give my hand to them; when they shake it they shake the hands of all. I will shake hands with them and then I am done."

Major Garland, to be more explicit, again arose and stated that it must be distinctly understood that the two bands of the Sacs and Foxes must now be merged into one; that Black Hawk must listen to the council of Keokuk, and that the President would hereafter recognise the latter as the principal chief of the nation. When Black Hawk understood that he was required to conform to the advice of his rival, he became deeply agitated and his excited passions burst forth with uncontrollable violence. With intense indignation of countenance and the vehemence which characterizes the savage when roused to action, as soon as he could control his feelings sufficient to articulate, he exclaimed: "I am a man; I will not conform to the counsel of any one. I will act for myself; no one shall govern me. I am old; my hair is gray. I once gave counsel to my young men; am I now to conform to others? I will soon go the Great Spirit where I shall be at rest. What I said to our great father in Washington I say again. I will always listen to him. I am done." Keokuk apologized for his indiscretion, saying: "Our brother who has come to us has spoken, but he did it in wrath; his tongue was double and his words were not like a Sac. He knew they were bad. He trembled like the oak whose roots have been wasted by many rains. He is old; what he said let us forget. He says he did not mean it; he wishes it forgotten. I have spoken for him. What I have said are his own words."

Major Garland now informed the humbled chieftain that he was satisfied that his conduct in the future would be acceptable to the people of the United States, and that he and his fellow prisoners might now consider themselves at liberty. The council then adjourned, and early the next morning the Indians crossed the Mississippi and dispersed to their respective homes in the forest.

A violent war having subsequently broken out between the Sacs and Foxes and Sioux, in the autumn of 1837 Black Hawk again visited Washington with a deputation of chiefs who had been invited thither by the President, for the purpose of adjusting their difficulties. After their return he settled in what is now Lee county, Iowa, where he spent the winter. In the spring of 1838 he moved his family to the Des Moines, and built him a dwelling near the village of his tribe, 20 miles above the mouth of the river. He furnished his new wigwam after the manner of the whites, cultivated a few acres in corn, melons and other vegetables, and when visited by the Americans entertained them with true Indian hospitality. The following autumn he visited an Indian trader, near Burlington, and as the result of exposure, on his return he contracted a disease which terminated his life. His countrymen with the reverential respect which they had for the dead, assem-

bled to bury the mortal remains of their departed chief. The
body dressed in a uniform which had been presented to him in one
of his eastern tours by the Secretary of War, was borne to its last
resting place by four of his warriors. The grave was an excavation
6 feet deep, and into this the body was deposited in an upright posture, with the right hand resting on a cane which had been presented to him by Henry Clay. A mound several feet high was
thrown up over the grave, at the head of which was planted a
staff bearing the flag of the United States, and at the foot a post
on which was carved in Indian characters, the age of the deceased.
Those in attendance at the funeral expressed their sorrow after
the usual manner of the tribe, by shaking hands and uttering
prayers that the spirit of the chief might have a safe entrance
into the land prepared for the reception of souls.

Thus, after an adventurous and shifting life of 72 years, Black
Hawk was gathered to his fathers. The banner of war fell nerve-
less from his grasp; his voice at the council fire was heard no
more, and his restless ambition was stilled in the sleep of death.
While the rustling October leaves, moved by the sighing winds,
chanted a requiem over his ashes, the liberated shade sped to
the happy hunting grounds beyond the setting sun, which, according to Indian theology, only the good and the brave are permitted to enter.

Perhaps no one of his race excelled Black Hawk in humanity
and love of country. He always repelled with indignation the
charge that he murdered women and children, or mistreated his
prisoners. His patriotism is seen in the last speech he ever made
in the presence of the Americans, who had driven him from the
ancestral seat of his tribe: "Rock river was a beautiful country.
I like my towns, my cornfields, and the home of my people. I
fought for it; it is now yours; it will produce you good crops."
These sentiments were not only creditable to the heart of the
speaker, but essential in forming a just estimate of his motives
in contesting the removal of his people from their native land.
In his domestic relations, he was kind and effectionate, and unlike
other chiefs, never had but one wife.* After his campaign in the
British army, his first act was to visit his family. "I have
started," says he, "to visit my wife and children. I found them
well, and my boys growing finely. It is not customary for us to
say much about our women, as they generally perform their part
cheerfully, and never interfere with the business belonging to the
men. This is the only wife I ever had, or ever will have; she is a
good woman, and teaches my boys to be brave." In his private
relations his integrity was not questioned, and when in a public
capacity he disregarded treaties, he was actuated rather by

*It is said, however, upon good authority, that on a certain occasion, his vow of
exclusive devotion to one wife had well nigh been broken. While visiting a respectable frontier settler, many years since, he became pleased with the comely daughter
of his host, and having seriously contemplated the matter, decided in favor of the
expediency of adding the pale-faced beauty to the domestic circle of his wigwam. He
accordingly expressed his wishes to the father of the young lady, and proffered to
give him a horse in exchange for his daughter, but to his surprise, the offer was declined. Some days afterward, he returned and tendered two fine horses, but still the
father refused to make the arrangement. The old chief's love for the young lady,
growing stronger, in proportion to the difficulty of gaining her father's consent, subsequently he offered six horses for her, but even this munificent price was rejected by
the mercenary father. Black Hawk now gave up the negotiation, not a little
surprised at the high value which the white men placed upon their daughters

wrongs which he had suffered, than want of respect for his obliga-ions. A dispassionate view of the war and its causes, will show that he had grievances, and when it was impossible to redress them in a peaceable manner, appealed to arms as the only arbitrament.

CHAPTER XXXVI.

1834–1838—ADMINISTRATION OF GOVERNOR DUNCAN.

The Campaign—Life and Character of Duncan—More State Banks and what became of them—Slavery Agitation by Lovejoy—His Death.

———— .

At the general election of August 1834, Joseph Duncan was elected governor of the State. His principal opponent was ex-Lieut. Gov. Kinney, who was again an aspirant for gubernatorial honors. Duncan was elected by a handsome majority: 17,330 votes to Kinney's 10,224; Robert McLaughlin received 4,320 and James Adams 887 votes for the same office. The candidates for lieutenant-governor were Alexander M. Jenkins, who received 13,795 votes; James Evans, 8,609; William B. Archer, 8,573, and Samuel Webster, 69.

Gov. Duncan was born at Paris, Kentucky, February 23d, 1794. We have already noted his services in the war of 1812, under Col. Croghan at Fort Stephenson, when he was yet quite young. In Illinois he first appeared in a public capacity as major-general of the militia, a position which his military fame procured him. Subsequently he became a State senator from Jackson county, and is honorably mentioned for introducing the first bill providing for a free school system. In 1826, as we have seen, he gained great eclat by beating Daniel P. Cook for Congress, when in previous contests with the latter, such men as John Mc'Lean, Elias K. Kane, and Gov. Bond had met with disaster. From that time down to his election as governor, Duncan retained his seat in Congress. The first and bloodless year of the Black Hawk war he was appointed by Gov. Reynolds brigadier-general of the volunteers, and conducted his brigade to Rock Island. Duncan was a man of limited education, but with naturally fine abilities he profited greatly by his various public services, and gathered a store of knowledge regarding public affairs which served him a ready purpose. He possessed a clear judgement, decision, confidence in himself and moral courage to carry out his convictions of right. In his deportment he was well adapted to gain the admiration of the people. His intercourse with them was affable, courteous and dignified. He inspired confidence and attached to himself unswerving friends.*

During the gubernatorial campaign Duncan was absent in Washington attending congress, and did not personally participate in

---

*His portrait at the Governor's mansion presents him with swarthy complexion, high cheek bones, broad forehead, piercing black eyes and straight black hair.

it, but addressed circulars to his constituents. His election was
attributed to the circumstance of his absence, because his estrang-
ment from Jackson—erst his political idol—and the Democracy,
largely in ascendency in the State, was really complete; but while
his defection was well known to his Whig friends, and also to
the leading Jackson men of this State, the latter were unable to
carry conviction of the fact to the masses. The dissemination of
public events was not then facilitated by means of the telegraph
and press, as now. President Jackson had crushed the U. S. Bank
with an arbitrary if not tyranical hand; he had vetoed bills containing appropriations for improving the channel of the great
Wabash river and for the harbor at Chicago. These were Western measures which Duncan had greatly at heart, and hence he
refused to longer follow the dictatorial course of the "Military
Chieftain." His personal admiration of the old hero was changed
to hatred of his acts. This course, so far as his political fortune was concerned, was an error; but no one could say that
the step thus taken was not sincere. He had preferment to gain
by remaining attached to the dominant party, and nothing but
disappointment to look forward to in breaking with it. He committed the unpardonable sin in politics, and was charged with inconsistency and betrayal of his former supporters.*

These will ever be the the fossilized views of men regarding
party ties or affiliations. Under such circumstances no concession
is made by old party associates for the changed condition of the
times; for the death of former issues or the obtrusion of live ones,
unencountered in past strifes. No leniency for new public questions is extended between violent partizans; every man is guaged
by a party standard, irrespective of the principles he advocates.
Duncan stood bravely to his new colors and never regretted, it is
said, his change, made upon careful and candid examination of the
Jackson measures.

In his inaugural message, which was largely devoted to the discussion of national politics, Duncan threw off the mask and took
a bold stand against the course of the President. Notwithstanding his defection, and the fact of a large majority in the legislature being opposed to him, his recommendations relating to State
affairs were most fully seconded and carried out. The laying out
of public highways while the State was unsettled and they could
be made straight between most of the important points with little
expense or difficulty, as urged by him, was responded to by the
enactment of laws not only giving authority to county commissioners for these purposes, but by granting 42 State roads besides, and at the special session of the year following 40 more
were added. Equally liberal were they with reference to the canal
and charters for railroads.

To the subject of banking he called attention as follows:
"Banks may be made exceedingly useful in society, not only by
affording an opportunity to the widow, the orphan and aged, who
possess capital without the capacity of employing it in ordinary

* It is related that an old constituent rebuked him as follows: "Now Gov. Duncan,
we Jackson men took you up when you was poor and friendless; we put you in high
office and enabled you to make a fortune, and for all this you have deserted us and
gone to the Adams men. You was like a poor colt; we caught you up out of a thicket,
fed you on the best, combed the burrs out of your mane and tail, and made a fine horse
of you; and now you have strayed away from your owners."—Ford's History.
27

business, to invest it in such stocks; but by its use the young and enterprising mechanic, merchant and tradesman may be enabled more successfully to carry on his business and improve the country."

To this the willing Legislature, taking no lesson of the disastrous past, also responded by chartering a new State bank with a capital of $1,500,000, and the privilege to increase its stock $1,000,000 more. Six branches were authorized; and the old territorial Bank of Illinois, at Shawneetown, which had suspended business for upwards of 12 years, was revived with a capital of $300,000. In lieu of all taxes whatsoever, the State bank was to pay $\frac{1}{2}$ of 1 per cent. on capital actually paid in.

The legislature was not elected with reference to the creation of a new bank. It was not dreamed of by the people, who with much unanimity were averse to local banks, since the signal failure of the bank of 1821, the winding up of which, at a heavy loss to the State, had but four years before been provided for by the unpopular Wiggins' loan. The chartering of these banks was the opening of a Pandora's box out of which rushed that multitude of evil legislation which followed with a prompt step in the next few years, and which overwhelmed the State with debt and almost financial ruin. President Jackson had vetoed the bill to re-charter the U. S. Bank, which he regarded as "a permanent electioneering machine." Its old charter was about to expire and an inadequate supply of currency was dreaded; to meet which the Secretary of the Treasury "had encouraged the State and local banks liberally." This afforded to Democrats the pretext that President Jackson, while he opposed a concern of such magnitude and "electioneering influence" as the U. S. bank, was really in favor of multiplying local banks. But the bank party was not without other arts and plots to pass this measure. Every string of the human heart was played upon. A bitter feeling existed among the people in some portions of the State toward non-resident land owners, who held their lands at exhorbitant prices, while every improvement made in the vicinity added to their value.

The desire was to burden these lands with taxes and force them into the market at purchasable prices. The vote of an honorable senator, violently opposed to banks from principle, was obtained in consideration of the passage of a law to levy a tax for road purposes, in the military tract, where the great body of non-resident lands were located.* In the house, where the bank bill passed by a bare majority—27 yeas to 26 nays—a vote is said to have been obtained from a member opposed, in consideration of his election to the office of State's attorney.† Thus, says Gov. Ford, the making of a State's attorney made a State bank, and it

---

*[NOTE —The feeling of hostility toward non-residents found vent also, it is said, in trespasses upon their lands for timber, which was taken as if common property. The agents of the owners (the most unpopular men of the country) found no redress in the law, because with witnesses, jurors, and the sympathy of the court all on the same side, the blind-folded goddess of justice, in these cases blinded with prejudice, was of course with them. In this strait the distant land owners adopted the missionary plan, and sought to eradicate the sin of timber thieving, and to conciliate the favor of the people, through the gentle ministrations of the gospel, for which purpose preachers were sent out, the country divided into circuits and duly assigned. But the inhabitants were incorrigible, their feelings obdurate, and if they did not reject the gospel, they nevertheless continued to take the timber. To the land owners the gospel proved as ineffectual a protection as the law. —Ford's Hist.]

†The Journal shows that our late lieutenant governor, John Dougherty, was chosen to that office on the following day.

may be added, the bank was the incipient measure which led
to others, and brought unnumbered woes upon the people of the
State. The banks were not originally party measures.

One million four hundred thousand dollars of the capital stock
of the State bank were to be subscribed by individuals, and $100,-
000 were reserved for the State to take in such amounts as the
legislature should at any time deem proper. Shares were $100
each. The bank had the usual power to receive deposits, deal in
bills, gold, and silver, etc., but was prohibited from dealing in real
estate or personal property, other than to dispose of such as it
might be compelled to buy or bid in at sales upon judgments.
But it had power to borrow a million dollars to loan out on real
estate mortgages for five years. This provision was to conciliate
farmers, and extend to them long time accommodations. The
principal bank was located at Springfield, with a branch at Vandalia; other branches might be established and discontinued as
the officers should determine. Business was not to be commenced
until $600,000 was paid in in specie. Commissioners to open sub-
scription books for the capital stock, were appointed all over the
State. Nine directors, one of whom was to be chosen president,
were to manage the affairs of the corporation. The circulation
was not to exceed two and a half times the paid up capital stock.
No bills were to be issued of a less denomination than $5. If the
bank refused to redeem for ten days after demand, it was to be
closed and wound up. Such were some of the provisions of its
charter, which, rightly carried out, were not so bad.

The stock was eagerly taken, the subscriptions greatly exceeding the limits of the charter. Shortly after the passage of the
bank act, Thomas Mather, of Kaskaskia, John Tillson, of Hillsboro,
Samuel Wiggins, of Cincinnati, T. W. Smith, associate judge of the
supreme court, and Godfrey, Gilman & Co., of Alton, negotiated
for large sums of money in the east to invest in the stock. The
charter provided for the opening of the books in this State for 20
days before elsewhere, and to guard against undue influence from
large stockholders, as their number of shares increased, it proportionately lessened their votes for directors. To preserve the full
vote of the stocks, therefore, it became desirable to obtain small
subscriptions by citizens of this State, while they had the exclusive
opportunity. With the view to engross enough stock to direct the
bank, these parties procured, through numberless agents scattered
over the State, powers of attorney, from any person disposed to
make them, empowering them respectively to subscribe bank
stock for them and to absolutely manage it subsequently. Thus
there were many thousands of such subscriptions made by persons
whom it never cost a cent to own bank stock, and who remained,
perhaps, ignorant of the fact they ever were bankers. The stock
ran up to a premium of 13 per centum above par value.*

When the commissioners convened to award the stock, it was
moved that subscriptions made for residents should have precedence over those of non-residents, and that holders of proxies be
required to make oath as to the actual residence of the principals.
This proposition was supported by Judge T. W. Smith, between
whom upon the one hand, and the rest of the parties named upon
the other, the contest for the control of the institution obtained.

*Duncan's Message, 1836

It is said that he, of impeachment fame, was prepared to take such oath, and that he had in good faith paid for all his proxies out of his own money; but the others could not thus swear. The resolution therefore did not prevail; and Mather, Tillson, Godfrey, Gilman & Co., and Wiggins united against Smith, controlled the bank, and elected a directory in their interest, with Mather as the president. The bank was in Whig control—just enough democrats were chosen as directors to give a semblance of fairness to the proceedings.

At that time nearly the entire trade of the Upper Mississippi, including that of the lead mines of Illinois, was controlled by St. Louis. The ambition prevailed to build up Alton, within our own State, as the commercial rival of St. Louis. Alton, in 1834, had been elected as the seat of government after the 20 years limitation at Vandalia should expire; but this honor she now readily yielded in consideration of becoming the great emporium of the valley of the Mississippi. The Alton interest in the new bank was so large that, without a combination of all the residue of the stock, it possessed a controlling influence. The bank therefore loaned its aid to the building up of Alton, and to the diversion of the trade of the west to it. Godfrey, Gilman & Co., merchants, were accommodated to the amount of $800,000 to control and divert to Alton the immense lead trade of the mines on Fever river. The price of that commodity advanced directly 50 to 75 per cent., by reason of local competition alone. To exclude further competition several hundred thousand dollars were prodigally invested in mines and smelting establishments. The agent of the firm did not stop with this, but as if furnished with the purse of Fortunatus, recklessly extended his investments to Galena lots, which under the enchantment advanced in a short time, it is said, 2000 per cent. But this lavish enterprise to secure the lead trade for Alton failed to have a corresponding effect upon eastern markets. After holding the lead a long time in store in the east for an advance, sale had finally to be made under accumulated charges at a ruinous sacrifice. To Stone, Manning & Co., of Alton, several hundred thousand dollars were advanced to operate in produce; and Sloo & Co. received accommodations for like purposes, all proving equally disastrous. It was estimated that the bank lost by the Alton operations $1,000,000; but these reverses were not generally known.

The legislature was convened in extraordinary session, Dec. 7, 1835, and sat till Jan. 18th, following. In his message, among other measures, Gov. Duncan called attention to the subject of the banks, and recommended the subscription, by the State, of one million dollars provided for in the second section of the bank act, for which no steps had as yet been taken by the president and directors, and no vested right had yet accrued to any one. His Excellency, in his sanguine expectations, stated that by so doing the State treasury would realize $300,000 in premiums on the $1,000,000; that the stock of the bank was then at a premium of 13 per centum and that it would speedily rise to 30. The legislature did not fully fall in with his extraordinary expectations, but by act of Jan. 16, 1836, the $100,000 of the capital stock reserved for the State was authorized to be sold; additional branches of discount and deposit, not more than three, were also authorized;

and 50 days in addition to the 10 were allowed for the redemption of notes. These provisions were not to take effect until the bank first contracted with the governor to redeem the Wiggins' loan. By another act of the same date, the bank paper was authorized to be received in payment of the revenue of the State, college, school and seminary debts.

But the following year the legislature did not hesitate. At this session were authorized all those extravagant measures of internal improvement, which in a few years entailed upon the young State a debt so vast as nearly to bankrupt it. But of this farther along. By act of March 4, 1837, the capital stock of the State bank was increased $2,000,000, the whole to be subscribed for the State by the fund commissioners, an executive body of the internal improvement system. The capital stock of the Bank of Illinois, located at Shawneetown, was in like manner authorized to be increased $1,400,000, $1,000,000 being reserved for the State, and $400,000 for private subscription. The consent of the banks was first to be obtained, but either might accept the State subscription, to the amount authorized. In subscribing, the State was to advance the same per centum—$5 a share—as originally paid by private stockholders. The fund commissioners were authorized to sell the State's certificate of stock, and to use the surplus revenues of the United States from the sale of lands, as money might be needed from time to time for subscriptions. Five additional directors for the State bank were also provided, on behalf of the State, to be elected by the legislature, which still left a majority to private stockholders, although the State owned a majority of the stock by exceeding 20 per centum. The same was true of the Shawneetown bank, which was to have nine directors. This bank was also authorized to establish three branches, one at Jacksonville, at Alton and at Lawrenceville, with each such amount of capital as the mother bank could safely supply. The banks were designated as the places of deposit of all the public revenues, and the moneys borrowed by the fund commissioners to carry on the internal improvements of the State. They were to render quarterly statements of their financial condition to the commissioners, and the legislature might institute such examinations into their affairs, from time to time, as might be deemed requisite. No charges for disbursements were to be made by the State banks. The dividends accruing upon the State's stock, were first to be applied in payment of the interest upon loans; and the premium from State bonds, fondly expected to be at least 10 per centum, was to constitute a fund to be held inviolable for the payment of interest on loans effected to carry on the internal improvements. Many were the ingenious arguments, deduced from the fact that the first $1,500,000 had with great avidity been taken in the spring of 1835—the premium rising to 13 per centum—that the present stock would readily command ten per centum, and that the State's bank stock would yield a sufficient dividend to pay all interest on the bank bonds and leave a margin besides. When the State bonds were exposed in market by the commissioners, it was found that they would not only not bring a premium, but could not be negotiated even at par. In this strait the banks themselves came to the rescue, and, rather than the scheme should fail, took the bonds at par, amounting to $2,665,000.

The Shawneetown bank effected a sale of its share ($900,000), but the balance $1,765,000 taken by the State bank, was not disposed of; they however served the purpose of a capital for the bank, and its business was amplified correspondingly.

The banks, throughout their career, met with persistent opposition from influential party managers. This was greatly augmented by the fact that their officers, the president, cashiers, and a large majority of the directors, were whigs, which aroused the jealousy of democrats, causing them to charge that the banks were political concerns, operated for the advancement of party affairs. Jackson's expression respecting the United States bank —that it was a "gigantic electioneering machine"—was not forgotton. Judge T. W. Smith, who had drafted the charter of the State bank, and worked earnestly with democrats for its passage in the legislature, had ever since his defeat for its control, animated by that spirit which if it cannot rule is bent upon ruin, made war up-. on it, and now hesitated not to pronounce its charter unconstitutional. He was joined by many other sore party leaders.

By an act of congress, passed at the preceding session, it was provided that the surplus revenue of the United States, arising from the sale of public lands, &c., might be deposited with the different States. The bank accordingly solicited the treasury department at Washington to become the depository of the public moneys, but the credit of the State had been stabbed in the back, by its own disappointed citizens furnishing statements so derogatory, that the secretary declined the request. Among the more influential opponents of the banks was Judge McRoberts, then receiver of the public moneys at Danville. Party malice and private resentments outweighed the public good. The bills fell below par and from that time steadily depreciated. The notes of the bank were gathered up and presented for specie to enter land. Had the specie been re-deposited by the government, the relief from this annoyance would have been very great. But this, through the vengeful machinations of disappointed partisans, was not to be. The bank, to retard the constant ebb of specie from its vaults, had recourse to the plan of exchanging issues between the respective branches, and thus throwing the circulation as far from the place of redemption as possible.

Hardly were the banks in operation, with their enormously augmented capital stocks, when the disastrous financial revulsion of 1837 occurred. In May the banks of Illinois suspended specie payments. They were solvent, but the drain of specie at that time could not be borne. The charters provided that if redemption in specie was refused for 60 days together, they were to become forfeited and the banks should go into liquidation. They were the depositories of the moneys raised by the sale of State bonds; of the State revenue; in a word the fiscal agents of the State, and their suspension would involve the State and all its splendid scheme of internal improvements in common ruin. In this dilemma, the governor was urged by the canal commissioners to convene the legislature to legalize an indefinite suspension of specie payments by the banks. A special session was called July 10th, 1837, and the bank suspensions were legalized. But to his excellency's urgent appeal to repeal the pernicious system of internal improvements by the State, and remit the same to private enterprise duly encouraged, the legislature turned a deaf ear.

Parties in Illinois became almost divided upon the subject of the banks. Nearly all the leading democrats opposed them and the acts legalizing their suspensions, although they were authorized and their capital stocks were increased irrespective of party. The whigs were called bank-vassals and rag-ocracy, and charged to be bought and owned by British gold. The bank officers were sarcastically denominated rag-barons; and the money was called rags and printed lies. The whigs retorted that the democrats were disloyal, and destructive of their own government; that the banks were the institution of the State, and to make war upon the currency was to oppose its commerce and impede its growth and development. Although parties were in a measure divided upon the banks, with the democrats largely in the majority, this was not without benefit to those institutions. It gave them unswerving friends. Besides, the merchants and business men of that day were, with rare exceptions, whigs, who gave currency or not to the money as they pleased. Partisan zeal led them to profess that the banks were not only solvent, but that they were unduly pursued, and that the opposition to them was nothing but absurd party cry.

When the suspensions of the banks was legalized again in 1839, it was to extend until the end of the next general or special session of the general assembly. The legislature for 1840-41 was convened two weeks before the commencement of the regular session to provide means to pay the interest on the public debt, due on the first of January following. The influence and power of the banks over members were very considerable. The democrats now, however, thought that their time of triumph had arrived. It was by them contended, that that portion of the session preceding the time fixed for the regular session to begin, constituted a special session, and if the suspension was not further extended, the banks would be compelled to resume specie payment on the day the regular session should begin or forfeit their charters and stop business. Upon the other hand, it was contended that the whole constituted but one session. Much party animosity was, besides, manifested at this session. The fate of the banks seemed to hang upon the motion pending to adjourn the first part of the session *sine die.* It was perceived that the motion would prevail. To defeat it in the House, the whigs now essayed to break the quorum. But the doors were closed, a call of the House ordered, and the sergeant at arms sent in quest of the absentees. The whigs, being thus cut off from the usual avenues of retreat, bounded pell mell out of the windows, but without avail—enough were held in durance to make a quorum, and the *sine die* adjournment was carried. Among the members of the House we find the names of some of the most notable men in the annals of Illinois: John J. Hardin, Abraham Lincoln, Josiah Francis, &c., but whether these whigs participated in the window escapade is not definitely known. The session was the first in Springfield, and the house occupied what is now the old 2nd Presbyterian church, north of the new edifice occupied by the legislature in 1871.

The banks were now thought to be dead, and that nothing remained to be done but to wind up their affairs. But their enemies reckoned without their host. The splendid triumph of the democrats proved a barren victory. The regular session began on the 1st Monday in December, with the same members, and before the close of the month the banks obtained not only a further lease of life, and license to suspend specie payment, but were authorized to issue one, two, and three dollar bills besides, to effect change—silver having been driven out of circulation by the depreciated paper. The debtors of the bank were again allowed to give new notes by paying ten per cent. interest on their indebtedness. By what potency these additional privileges were procured must be left to conjecture. The State bank was the custodian of the public moneys and revenues of the State, as it were, a substitute for the treasury. Auditor's warrants, at a discount of 50 per cent, were drawn upon the bank and paid in its currency, worth a good deal more than the warrants, both in and outside of the State. All the State officers, including the members of the assembly, were for their pay in the power of the bank, and if these would do nothing to uphold the credit of that institution—their own creature—the honorable gentlemen might return to their constituents without other in their pockets than auditor's warrants! This, together with such judicious and timely accommodations to impecunious party leaders as the exigency dictated, enabled the bank to render the glorious democratic victory barren of results.

But the new lease of power did not last long. There were other influences arising from the inevitable laws of finance, more potent in their effects than acts of the legislature. When money is abundant credit is extended without stint. With the vast system of internal improvements and the large circulation of the banks, this was the condition of Illinois. The people were largely in debt on account of speculations which proved delusions, and also to the merchants; the latter in turn had received either accommodations at the banks or owed for goods abroad; contracts matured but nobody paid. The State revenues being inadequate to meet its expenditures—the people averse to higher taxation, and the legislators, with a tender regard to personal consequences, disinclined to impose them—the bank, to gain the favor of the legislature, taxed its resources to redeem the outstanding auditor's warrants, amounting to near $300,000. Its bills had gradually declined to 12 and 15 per cent. discount. Now came the bank directors themselves, as contractors to build the Northern Cross railroad, and added the last feather to the camel's back. For the building of the railroad they were to receive in payment canal bonds, which were at that juncture not negotiable. To obtain accommodations from the banks, these directors defeated a proposed order against expansion during the suspension.* Receiving loans for themselves to carry forward the public works on their contracts, they, to be consistent, voted like favors to others. The credit of the bank was put to its utmost tension. Its volume of money, further swollen, sank to a lower discount. And in Febuary 1842, the monster institution, with a circulation exceeding $3,000,000, snapped its thread of life and passed into dissolution, spreading devastation upon every hand, far and wide.

*See Gov. Ford's mistake as to this in his History of Illinois, 223-4.

The Bank of Illinois, at Shawneetown, was similarly involved. It loaned to the State, in the first place, $80,000 to complete the new State House at Springfield; early in the autumn of 1839, upon the earnest solicitation of Gov. Carlin and his engagement to deposit as a pledge $500,000 in internal improvement bonds, the bank advanced the Commissioners of Public Works $200,000. The collateral deposit was, however, never made nor the sum borrowed ever repaid. In June following, with a circulation of some $1,700,000, it also collapsed. The people were left destitute of an adequate circulating medium, and were not supplied until the ordinary processes of their limited commerce brought in gold and silver, and the bills of solvent banks from neighboring States, which was tardy enough, there being but little emigration to Illinois at that time. The banks and the State had been partners in speculation and they were now partners in embarrassment. The revenues were payable in the notes of these broken banks; the State paid no interest on her bonds, of which the banks held a large amount, and they were worth in market but 14 cents on the dollar.

But the old firm of Banks and State was to be speedily dissolved. By act of January 24, 1843,* to " diminish the State debt and put the State Bank into liquidation," the bank was given 4 years to wind up its business, but it was required to go into immediate liquidation and pay out all its specie *pro rata* to its bill holders and depositors, and issue to them certificates of indebtedness for the unpaid balances; $15,000 in specie, being however first reserved to the bank to pay the expenses of winding up its affairs. The new certificates were to be registered by the commissioner and made receivable in payment of any debt due the bank, or for the redemption of lands purchased by the bank under execution. The debtors of the bank upon paying instalments of 1-5 principal and interest, were authorized to execute new notes from time to time for their indebtedness. The bank was to deliver within five days to the Governor, State bonds, scrip and other evidences of debt equal to $2,050,000, he to surrender to the bank a like amount of State Bank stock, $50,000 being reserved for the final winding up of the affairs of the bank. All its banking privileges, other than those necessary to wind up its business, were to immediately cease; no property of the bank was to be sold on execution or otherwise, except for two-thirds of its appraised value. The bank might reserve from its sale such real estate as it deemed proper. Three days were allowed to file its acceptance with the Secretary of State. It was a very favorable act for the bank and an administration measure strongly seconded by a few leading Democrats, which caused it to prevail, as we shall see.

A somewhat similar bill, under the high sounding title of " An act to reduce the public debt one million dollars and put the Bank of Illinois into liquidation," passed at the same session, in relation to the Shawneetown bank. It was to surrender State stocks or other liabilities of the State equal on their faces to $1,000,000, half in five days and half in 12 months, when the governor was to assign to it an equivalent of State Bank stock. The charter of the Cairo bank was repealed. By these acts the immediate extinguishment of $2,206,000 was provided. But these acts were not passed with-

* See House Reports, 1842-3, 203-4-5.

out considerable opposition. The disposition on the part of many was to crush the banks, to which all the woe of the struggling country was ascribed, with one fell blow by a direct repeal of their charter, which they had frequently forfeited, however it might involve the best interests of the State in their disaster.

Prior to this, and in anticipation of this compromise legislation and the surrender by the State of her bank stock in exchange for her bonds, after the failure of the Bank of Illinois in 1842, the whole concern was purchased as a speculation by a company of sharpers, who elected themselves its officers. Some of the directors then secretly borrowed from the bank $100,000 in specie, which was transmitted to New York and purchased State scrip and $333,000 of the $804,000 of interest bonds hypothecated with Macallister and Stebbins in 1841 by Fund Commissioner Whitesides, for $261,500, contrary to law. Under the law these bonds were to be sold for what they would bring, but could not be hypothecated, as the recipients well knew. The favored directors, by connivance of the board, first paid the specie borrowed from the bank with $100,000 of these bonds, which cost them 30 cents on the dollar. Their unpaid stock notes were similarly discharged. A member of the legislature, fierce in his denunciation of bank corruption, availed himself of these bonds and paid a $10,000 note to the bank. After the bonds and scrip had passed into the control of the bank, they were, in 1844, tendered to Governor Ford in payment of the half million dollars of the State's bank stock, which was to be surrendered in 12 months after the passage of the Bank Liquidation law of 1843. The governor refused at first to receive these bonds; a law had been passed to settle with Macallister and Stebbins by paying interest on the sum actually advanced by them, and their surrender of the hypothecated bonds, making about 28 cents on the dollar; to have received a large share of these bonds at their face value would have defeated the law for this adjustment. Later it became patent, however, that Macallister and Stebbins had parted with many more of the bonds than the Bank of Illinois had received, and that they were unable to comply with the law if they had the will, and as the condition of the bank became constantly more hopeless and the president intended to return these bonds to New York, the governor, in the fall of 1844, received them conditionally, subject to the approval of the legislature. That body, unwilling to countenance the knavery of the bank officers, at first refused to ratify the contract of the governor, but at the succeeding session, 1846–'47, compromised by receiving the bonds at 48 cents on the dollar.*

Subsequently the State Bank of Missouri, jointly with several other creditors, brought a chancery suit in the United States' court for the district of Illinois against the Bank of Illinois, its officers and agents. By the decree in the cause, three receivers were appointed to take charge of the bank's assets, make sale and apply the proceeds in payment of the debts, the redemption of its issues, and to settle its affairs generally. By agreement but one of these trustees, Albert G. Calwell, qualified. Upon his death, soon after, Judge W. Thomas of Jacksonville, was appointed in his place, who acted in that capacity some 20 years. Early in the fall of 1871 he remitted to W. H. Bradly, clerk of the U. S. district court

---

* This chapter has in great part been gathered from Ford's History.

at Chicago, the special auditor, a batch of notes and certificates of $700 for cancellation. This it was supposed, would be about the last to be presented for redemption, and that the trust would be finally closed shortly after.

SLAVERY AGITATION—DEATH OF LOVEJOY.

The year 1837 is memorable for the death of Illinois' first martyr to liberty, Elijah P. Lovejoy. He was born at Albion, Kenebec county, Maine, Nov. 9, 1802. At the age of 21 he entered Waterville college, and after graduating with the first honors of his class, removed to St. Louis and commenced teaching. A year or two afterward he exchanged the occupation of a teacher for that of the journalist, became the editor of the *St. Louis Times*, and advocated the election of Henry Clay as president of the United States. Not long after he had entered this new field of labor, he united with the Presbyterian church, and determined to abandon it also for the clergical profession. Accordingly at the age of 30 he repaired to the theological school at Princetown, N. J., entered with great ardor upon his studies, and in 1833 was licensed to preach by the Presbytery of Philadelphia. The following summer was spent in preaching in Newport, Rhode Island, and at Spring Church, N. Y., after which he returned to St. Louis. Here he again assumed the editorial chair and issued the first number of the *St. Louis Observer*, a religious newspaper, Nov. 22d, 1833. Soon after he incurred the ill-will of the Catholic Church, by characterizing their proceedings in laying the corner stone of a cathedral on the Sabbath as a desecration of the day, and charging that the use of the United States artillery and cavalry, which were brought in requisition to give prestige to the occasion, was a prostitution of the purposes for which they were intended. From the clerical rancor excited by this out-spoken expression of opinion, he thought proceeded the persecutions which he subsequently encountered, though masked in the guise of abolition. The question of slavery even at that early day was one of absorbing interest, and it was impossible for a person with Lovejoy's vigorous intellect and fearless manner of speaking, not to become involved in its discussion and not incur the hatred of its advocates. The subject having arrested his attention he wrote an editorial on it, and left the city to attend a Presbyterian synod. During his absence it made its appearance in the columns of the *Observer*, and such was the commotion it excited, that the owners of the press were compelled to publish a card to allay the excitement and prevent a mob from destroying their property. On his return a paper was presented him by a number of leading citizens and the minister who received him into the church, in which they expressed the opinion that slavery is sanctioned by the bible, and asked him to desist from its further discussion. Though the authors of this request represented the intelligence and morality of St. Louis, if honest, how little they understood the personal rights of mankind, and how little they supposed this question was destined in less than half a century to shake the continent with civil commotion. This paper was inserted in the *Observer* and also a reply from Mr. Lovejoy, in which he claimed the right to publish his honest convictions. In answer to the biblical view given of slavery, he

reminds his censors of the golden rule—make not slaves of others
if you do not wish to be made slaves of yourselves. His statements, although couched in the most inoffensive language, again
excited the ire of the citizens, and the proprietors of the press
took possession of it to prevent a recurrence of the disturbance.
A friend, however, interposed and agreed to restore the press to
him, provided he would remove it to Alton, where he might use it
safely. The offer was accepted, but after he had gone thither to
make arrangements for publishing the paper, he was invited to
return to St. Louis. On going back he resumed his editorial labors
and continued them until the summer of 1835, when he again became involved in difficulties.

On the 23d of April, the police arrested a negro by the name of
McIntosh, who, while on the way to prison, drew his knife and
killed one and badly wounded another of the officers having him
in charge. In consequence of the murderous assault, a large
crowd surrounded the jail in which he was imprisoned, and taking
him thence they bound him to a stake and burnt him to death.
The community being largely in sympathy with the perpetrators
of this unlawful and fiendish act, it was a long time before they
were brought to trial. When at length the matter was presented
to a grand jury, the judge, by the most gross perversion of facts,
informed them that the *Observer* had caused the negro to murder
the policeman, and that there was no law for punishing them who
burnt him at the stake. A succeeding number of this sheet
repelled the flagrant charge made by the judge, alluded to the
fact that he was a Catholic, and intimated that his views respecting the enforcement of the law could only result from Jesuitical
teaching. The editor, aware that the statement would be followed
by another outburst of indignation and an attempt to destroy the
press, immediately caused it to be shipped to Alton, whither it
arrived July 21st, 1826. The day being the Sabbath, Mr. Lovejoy
proposed to let it remain on the wharf till Monday, but the
ensuing night it was secretly visited by a number of persons, who
broke it into pieces and threw it into the river. When this
dastardly act became known the next day, the people became
excited and the ensuing evening a large meeting assembled in the
Presbyterian church, to listen to addresses by Mr. Lovejoy and
other speakers. The former stated that he had come to Alton to
establish a religious newspaper, that he was pleased with the town,
and as most of his subscribers resided in Illinois, it would be best
for him to make it his future home; that he regretted his presence
had caused so much excitement, and the people must have a
wrong appreciation of his object; that he was not an abolitionist,
and had been frequently denounced by Garrison and others as
being pro-slavery because he was not in favor of their measures;
that he was opposed to slavery, ever had been and hoped he
always would be. This statement corresponds with his previous
declarations and position in regard to slavery. He always manifested a strong sympathy for the oppressed, and in common with
a large and intelligent class of persons at that time, in both the
north and south, regarded colonization as the best means of freeing the country from the curse of slavery. With the progress of
events, this scheme, though it had enlisted the regard of statesmen
and philanthropists, was abandoned for more practical views. Mr.

Lovejoy, who never permitted himself to fall behind the march of ideas, also took a more advanced position. In the same meeting he also said that "he was now removed from slavery and could publish a newspaper without discussing it, and that it looked like cowardice to flee from the place where the evil existed and come to a place where it did not exist to oppose it." With these declarations, extorted to a great extent by the tyranical censorship of the slave power, he no doubt after his arrival at Alton intended to comply. Indeed he might justly have concluded that it was useless to waste his time and energy in endeavoring to benefit a community which was endeavoring to exercise over him a bondage worse than that which fettered the body of a slave. Yet, as the contest between freedom and slavery grew warmer and earnest champions were needed to contend for the right, Mr. Lovejoy concluded that duty required him to again enter the arena of discussion.

As the result of the meeting, funds were raised, another press was sent for, and the first number of the *Alton Observer* was issued Sept. 8, 1836. Its editor, gifted with more than ordinary ability, soon extended its circulation, its discussions at first being mostly confined to subjects of a moral and literary character. By and by the question of slavery was also broached. Mr. Lovejoy, no doubt smarting under the unjust surveillance to which he was subjected at the starting of his paper, seemed now determined to exercise his constitutional rights to free speech, being willing that the laws of his country, not the dictation of ruffians, should decide as to whether he abused this privilege.

In the issue of June 29, 1837, at the instance of the American Anti-slavery Society, he favored the circulation of a petition for the abolition of slavery in the District of Columbia, and in the succeeding number he speaks of the importance of organizing an anti-slavery society for the State of Illinois. In the same paper he also indulged the following reflections, suggested by the 4th of July: "This day reproaches us for our sloth and inactivity. It is the day of our nation's birth. Even as we write crowds are hurrying past our window in eager anticipation to the appointed bower, to listen to the declaration that 'All men are created equal;' to hear the eloquent orator denounce, in strains of manly indignation, the attempt of England to lay a yoke on the shoulders of our fathers which neither they nor their children could bear. Alas what bitter mockery is this. We assemble to thank God for our own freedom, and to eat with joy and gladness of heart while our feet are on the necks of nearly 3,000,000 of our fellow-men. Not all our shouts of self-congratulation can drown their groans; even that very flag which waves over our head is formed from material cultivated by slaves, on a soil moistened by their blood, drawn from them by the whip of a republican task-master." As soon as this was read, the pro-slavery men assembled in the market house and passed a number of resolutions, in which, with strange incongruity, they claim the right of free speech for themselves, while they plot to deprive another of the same privilege. A committee was appointed to inform Mr. Lovejoy that he must cease agitating the question of slavery, and they accordingly dropped a letter in the post-office, containing a demand to that effect. The editor replied to the communication, by denying their right to dictate to him

what it was proper to discuss, and at the same time tendered them
the use of his paper to refute his opinions if they were wrong.
They, however, chose a more summary manner for ending the controversy. On the night of the 25th of August a mob made an assault on the office of the *Observer*, with stones and brickbats, and
after driving out the employes entered and completely demolished
the press. Mr. Lovejoy himself was afterward surrounded in the
street by a number of ruffians, it was believed, for the purpose of
offering him violence. These outrages were boldly committed,
without any attempt being made by the city officials to bring the
rioters to justice. The anti-slavery party of the town, of course,
were justly incensed at this wanton outrage and willful disregard
of individual rights, but being largely in the minority, all they
could do was to quietly submit and send for a new press. This,
however, the proscribed editor was never to see. Leaving Alton
shortly after to attend a presbytery, the press arrived September 21st, and in his absence it was demolished and, like its predecessor, thrown into the Mississippi. These unlawful proceedings
had now been perpetrated so often in St. Louis and Alton with
impunity, that not only these localities but other places were rapidly becoming demoralized. Not long after the destruction of the
third press Mr. Lovejoy visited his mother-in-law at St. Charles,
Mo. Here he was violently assailed by a crowd of ruffians, with
the avowed object of taking his life, and it was only at the interposition of his heroic and devoted wife that he escaped their murderous intent.

In the meantime the friends of Mr. Lovejoy sent for a fourth
press, and it was in connection with this that the tragedy occurred
which cost him his life. In anticipation of its arrival a series of
meetings were held in which both the friends of freedom and slavery were represented. The object of the latter was to effect a
compromise, but it was one in which liberty was to make concessions to oppression; in which the proprietors of the *Observer* were
to forego the legitimate use of their property to appease an ignorant mob, and in which right and modern progress were required to
submit to injustice and the exploded ideas of the past. Mr. Hogan,
the Methodist minister, endeavored to prove from the Bible the
inexpediency of the course pursued by Mr. Lovejoy and his friends,
in which he remarked: "The great apostle had said all things
are lawful for him, but all things are not expedient; if Paul yielded
to the law of expediency would it be wrong for Mr. Lovejoy to follow his example? The spirit of God did not pursue Paul to his
destruction for thus acting, but on the contrary commended his
course; Paul had never taken up arms to propagate the religion of his master, nor to defend himself from the attacks of his
enemies; the people of Damascus were opposed to Paul, but did
he argue with the populace the question of his legal right; did he
say I am a minister of Christ and must not leave the work of my
master to flee before the face of a mob."

This was strange advice to come from the abettor of a faction,
first to inaugurate violence, and at that very time conspiring
against the life of one who was legally void of offense. The rev-
erend gentleman seemed to think the aggrieved should exercise
forbearance, while the mob might insult and destroy with
impunity. Mr. Beecher, president of Illinois College, was

present and delivered addresses, in which he took a position almost as objectionable as that of Mr. Hogan. He believed that slavery was morally wrong, and should not be tolerated for a moment. He contended, that if the constitution sanctioned iniquity, it was also wrong, and could not be binding upon the people, that for his part he did not acknowledge obedience to the constitution, and as long as it tolerated slavery, he could not. But when he came to urge the rights of his friends to freedom of speech and the peaceable use of their property, he invoked all the guaranties of the constitution and government to protect them in the enjoyment of these privileges. He would now have others to submit to the law, while he was unwilling to do it himself. Mr. Lovejoy, who was more consistent than either of these gentlemen, contended only for his undoubted rights, and expressed, in a conciliatory manner his unalterable determination to maintain them. "Mr. Chairman," said he, "what have I to compromise? If freely to forgive those who have so greatly injured me; if to pray for their temporal and eternal happiness; if still to wish for the prosperity of your city and State, notwithstanding the indignities I have suffered in them; if this be the compromise intended, then do I willingly make it. I do not admit that it is the business of any body of men to say, whether I shall or shall not publish a paper in this city. That right was given to me by my Creator, and is solemnly guaranteed by the constitutions of the United States and this State. But if by compromise is meant that I shall cease from that which duty requires of me, I cannot make it, and the reason is, that I fear God more than man. It is also a very different question, whether I shall voluntarily, or at the request of my friends, yield up my position, or whether I shall forsake it at the demand of a mob. The former I am ready at all times to do when the circumstances require it, as I will never put my personal wishes or interests in competition with the cause of that master whose minister I am. But the latter, be assured I never will do. You have, as the lawyers say, made a false issue. There are no two parties between whom there can be a compromise. I plant myself down on my unquestionable rights, and the question to be decided is, whether I shall be protected in those rights? that is the question. You may hang me, as the mob hung the individuals at Vicksburg. You may burn me at the stake, as they did old McIntosh at St. Louis, or you may tar and feather me, or throw me into the Mississippi, as you have threatened to do, but you cannot disgrace me. I, and I alone, can disgrace myself, and the deepest of all disgrace would be at a time like this to deny my Maker by forsaking his cause. He died for me, and I were most unworthy to bear his name should I refuse, if need be, to die for him.

The boat having the obnoxious press on board arrived early in the morning, Nov. 7th, 1837, and the latter was immediately removed to the stone warehouse of Godfrey, Gilman & Co. The proprietors and their friends now assembled with arms to defend it. No violence was offered till the ensuing night, when a mob of about 30 persons came from the drinking saloons and demanded the press. This insolent and unjust demand was of course refused, when the assailants, with stones, brickbats and guns, commenced an attack on the building. Those within, among whom was Mr. Lovejoy, returned the fire, by which one of the mob was killed and several others wounded. This warm reception caused them to retire, some to bear away the dying man, others to summon reinforcements, but the most of them visited the adjacent grog-shops for the purpose of reviving their courage. Soon after, the bells of the city were rung, horns were blown, and an excited multitude came rushing to the warehouse, some urging on the drunken and imbruted mob, and others persuading them to desist. Ladders were placed against the side of the building, without windows, where there was no danger from within, and several persons ascended to fire the roof. Mr. Lovejoy and some others on learning their danger, rushed out and firing upon the incendiaries drove them away. After returning to the inside and reloading their pieces, Mr. Lovejoy, with two or three companions, not seeing any foe on the south side, again stepped out to look after the roof. Concealed assassins were watching, and simultaneously firing, five bullets entered his body, when he exclaimed, "My God! I am shot," and expired. With the fall of the master spirit, the defenders of the press surrendered it to the mob, who broke it into fragments and threw them into the river.

The following day a grave was dug on a high bluff, in the southern part of the city, and the body, without ceremony, was thrown into it and covered up. Some years afterward, the same elevation was chosen as the site of a cemetery, and in laying out the grounds, the main avenue chanced to pass over the grave of Lovejoy. To obviate the difficulty, his ashes were interred in a new locality, and within a few years past, a simple monument was erected over the spot, bearing the inscription: *Hic jacet Lovejoy; jam parce sepulto.*

Of those who participated in this infamous crime, it may be mentioned that the leader of the outlaws finally became a prisoner in the Ohio penitentiary; the person most instrumental in committing the murder was killed in a brawl in New Orleans, while many others, it is said, ended their lives in violence and disgrace.

The aggressive life and tragic death of Mr. Lovejoy, furnishes a subject for profitable reflection. In common with all true reformers, he possessed a grasp of intellect which enabled him to see and act in advance of his time, and hence was unappreciated by his less gifted cotemporaries. The world has often murdered the authors of its progress, and it is not strange that he lost his life. Every considerable advance in theology has had its persecutions and martyrs. The *magna charta* of English liberty was wrung from the grasp of tyranny by the death of patriots. France has battled and bled for republican government, yet her object is only half attained. The cause for which Lovejoy died finally triumphed, yet it cost one of the most bloody civil wars known to history. Such has been in general the past history of reform.

CHAPTER XXXVII.

STATE INTERNAL IMPROVEMENT SYSTEM.

In his message to the legislature at the special session begun December 7, 1835, Gov. Duncan said: "When we look abroad and see the extensive lines of inter-communication penetrating almost every section of our sister States—when we see the canal-boat and the locomotive bearing, with seeming triumph, the rich productions of the interior to the rivers, lakes and ocean, almost annihilating time, burthen and space, what patriot bosom does not beat high with a laudable ambition to give to Illinois her full share of those advantages which are adorning her sister States, and which a magnificent Providence seems to invite by the wonderful adaptation of our whole country to such improvements." Pennsylvania and other States were at the time engaged in extensive works of internal improvement. The legislature responded to the ardent words of the governor in a liberal manner, by chartering a great number of railroads, almost checkering the map of the State, and pledging its faith for $500,000 of the canal loan; but further than this they did not go; the supreme folly of the period being left for their successors to enact. After the adjournment, when the people contemplated the project of a vast system of internal improvements, as portrayed by His Excellency, they were fired with an inordinate desire to have it speedily in successful operation.

They were already inoculated with the fever of speculation, then rife throughout the west. Chicago, a mere trading post in 1830, had in a few years grown into a city of several thousand inhabitants. This remarkable city had now started upon her wonderful career of improvement, unsurpassed by individual effort in the annals of the world, steadily maintained to this day; and at present, after her terrible visitation by the fire fiend, also unsurpassed in the annals of the world for the magnitude of its destructiveness, since the days of Sodom and Gomorrah, she bids fair to eclipse all her former rapidity of growth. The story of speedy fortunes made in Chicago, which excited wonder and adventure 36 years ago, is still fraught with marvels. Early reports of the rapid advance of property in Chicago, spread to the east. Every vessel came crowded with immigrants, bringing their money, enterprise and industry to the enchanted spot of sudden opulence. They have not been disappointed. The rapid development of the town inspired emulation. Throughout the State, towns, and additions were plotted with the hope of profiting by the influx of emigrants. In some cases maps of splendidly situated towns would be taken to Chicago, to attract the attention of the emigrant, and auction sales of lots would be made far from the place of location. Others were sent east. It was said at the time that the staple articles of Illinois export were town plots, and that there was danger of crowding the State with towns to the exclusion of land for agriculture.* During the year 1836, lands to the amount of $5,000,000 were entered in Illinois. From this it was not unreasonably deduced that an extraordinary tide of emigration would speedily set into this State. Even the sober judgment of careful business men and staid farmers fluctuated, and they became fired with the idea of leaping into sudden fortune. The genius of speculation overspread the State with her golden wings, casting dazzling beams of bright promise across the paths of our people, beyond which it was difficult to see. They invested to the utmost of their credit, which at that time of bank expansion, was almost unlimited. To prevent their extensive purchases from becoming a drug upon their hands, and to further invite immigration and place the prosperity of the State upon a firm basis, by developing its resources—bringing its interior within the range of markets; settling it up; building up its towns and cities; having the muscle to wring from its vigorous soil the products of wealth, and enhance the price of property, was a great, a grand disideratum. All this could be accomplished, it was ingeniously argued, and doubtless demonstrated to many, by a general system of internal improvements, based on the faith and credit of the State. A new legislature was to be elected in August of that year, 1836. The dazzling scheme was now vigorously agitated. The press espoused the project. Public meetings were held all over the State, and resolutions, as the expressions of the people in favor of the scheme, were adopted. The subject was kept alive. The great natural surface advantages of the State for the building of railroads were dilated upon; the State which already possessed every element of greatness—extent of territory, richness of soil, variety of climate, almost bounded by navigable waters—lacked only these improvements to reach and develope its vast and inaccessible interior. Its broad and fertile prairies lay ready prepared, awaiting only population and the hand of industry to respond with abundant products, to freight these avenues of commerce connecting them with the markets of the world. That these views were in the main correct has by this time, with our 7000 miles of completed railroads, been demonstrated; but that the State should carry forward the herculean project was most vissionary, and proved most disastrous.

The legislature elected August 1836, was supplemented by an internal improvement convention, composed of many of the ablest men of the State, which was to meet at the seat of government simultaneously with the legislature. It is probable that the more zealous advocates of the project entertained doubts regarding the stamina of the honorable members of the legislature, when the vast project should be fully brought forward for action. The convention devised a general system of internal improvements, the leading characteristics of which was "that it should be commensurate with the wants of the people." It was an irresponsible body, determined to succeed in its one object, regardless of consequences. The wildest reasoning was indulged. Every theory

*Ford's History.

that the teeming brain of man could suggest was brought into requisition to further the success of the scheme. Possibilities were argued into probabilities, and the latter into infalibilities. Doubts regarding the advantages of the system were scouted; the resources of the State magnified a hundred fold, and the ultimate ability of the works to meet all their liabilities without detriment to the State, predicted with a positiveness as if inspired by the gift of prophecy. Governor Duncan in his message reiterated his recommendation to establish a general and uniform system of internal improvements, in which the State might take a third or half interest to hasten the works to completion, which would secure to her a lasting and abundant revenue, to be applied upon the principles of the plan proposed, "until the whole country shall be intersected by canals and railroads, and our beautiful prairies enlivened by thousands of steam engines, drawing after them lengthened trains, freighted with the abundant productions of our fertile soil." The production of the convention was confided to the hands of Edward Smith, of Wabash, chairman of the committee on internal improvements in the legislature, who, after the introduction of a set of resolutions covering the same ground, on the 9th of January, 1837, made a report on the memorial and the governor's message relating to the same subject, which it may safely be asserted is one of the most assuring, expectant, and hopeful papers to be found among the archives of Illinois. It occupies some 12 pages, and is replete with specious reasoning. The committee argued that public expectation, both at home and abroad, would be greatly disappointed if some system of internal improvement was not adopted at the present session; that the internal trade of a country was the greatest lever of its prosperity; that it was the legislator's duty, by his example, to calm the apprehension of the timorous and meet the attacks of calculating opposers of measures which would multiply the population and wealth of the State; that the surface of the State was peculiarly adapted to the construction of railroads, and that the practicability of removing obstructions to the navigation of our rivers could not be doubted; that a general system of internal improvements was then within the policy and means of the State, demanded by the people as expressed by their highly talented delegates, lately assembled in convention, and also looked forward to by the people abroad who had purchased lands here with a view to settlement, and whose expectations ought not to be disappointed by over cautious legislation, which would divert emigration to other States; that the cost of building railroads, from the uniformity of the country, and by analogy with similar works in other States, could be calculated with the utmost precision without previous surveys, ($8,000 per mile being the estimate); than an internal improvement fund should be constituted of all moneys arising from loans, sale of stocks, tolls, rents of land and hydraulic powers, interest on stocks, sale of State lands entered for the works, a portion of the deposits received from the national treasury, and portions of the annual land tax; that with the expiration of the government exemption in five years time, there would be 12,000,000 acres of land to tax; that by the disbursements of large sums of money, means would speedily be placed in the hands of the people to enable them to purchase their homes;

that the railroads as fast as completed both ways from the crossings of rivers and important towns, would yield the interests on
their costs; that in the advance of the routes of improvements the
State should enter lands to re-sell at an enhanced price; that a
board of fund commissioners should be elected, to consist of such
eminent financiers as to reflect great credit upon the State, and
thus add to its financial resources; and that with these active
resources at command no great financial skill was required of future legislatures to provide the ways and means to carry to completion the public works without burthening the people with taxation.   The works recommended, together with the estimated costs,
were as follows:

1st.	Improvement	of the	Great Wabash river	-	-	-	$100,000
2d.	"	"	Illinois river	-	-	-	100,000
3d.	"	"	Rock river	-	-	-	100,000
4th.	"	"	Kaskaskia river	-	-	,	50,000
5th.	"	"	Little Wabash river	-	-	-	50,000
6th.	"	"	Great Western Mail Route	-		-	100,000
7th.	"	"	Central Railroad from mouth of the Ohio to Galena	-	-		3,500,000
8th.	"	"	Southern Cross railroad		-		1,600,000
9th.	"	"	Northern Cross railroad		-		1,850,000
							$7,450.000

A bill covering these provisions was submitted by the committee, who concluded:

"The maxim is well understood by political economists, that the
wealth of a country does not consist so much in the abundance of its
coffers as in the number and general prosperity of its citizens.   In the
present situation of the country, the products of the interior by reason
of their remoteness from market, are left upon the hands of the producer, or sold barely at the price of the labor necessary to raise and prepare
them for sale.   But if the contemplated system should be carried into
effect, these fertile and healthy districts which now languish for the
want of ready markets for their productions, would find a demand at
home for them during the progress of the works, and after their completion would have the advantage of a cheap transit to a choice of markets
on the various navigable streams. . These would inevitably tend to build
towns and cities along the routes and at the terminal points of the respective railroads."

The legislature, in adopting "An act to establish and maintain
a general system of internal improvement," approved February
27, 1837, not only came fully up to the requirements of the convention, as reported by the committee, but went over two million
and a quarter beyond—$10,230,000, as follows: Toward the im-
provement of the Great Wabash, $100,000; the Illinois river,
$100,000; Rock river, $100,000; Kaskaskia, $50,000; Little Wa-
bash, $50,000; Great Western Mail Route from Vincennes to St.
Louis, $250,000, as follows: on the Purgatory swamp, opposite
Vincennes, $30,000, Little Wabash river bottoms, $15,000. on the
American bottom opposite St. Louis, $30,000, the balance on
bridges and repairs; for the Central railroad from Cairo to the
Illinois and Michigan canal and railroads from Alton to Mt. Car-
mel (Southern cross-road) and Alton to Shawneetown, $1,600,000;
Northern cross-railroad from Quincy to Indiana State line (present
T. W. & W.), $1,800,000; a branch of the Central from Hillsboro'
via Shelbyville and Charleston to Terre Haute, $650,000; from
Peoria via McComb and Carthage to Warsaw, $700,000; from

Alton to Hillsboro, and the Central railroad, $600,000; from Belleville via Lebanon to intersect the Southern cross-railroad, $150,000; from Bloomington to Mackinaw in Tazewill county, thence a branch to Pekin, $350,000; and finally, of the first moneys obtained, $200,000 were to be distributed among those counties through which no roads or improvements were projected.

A board of fund commissioners was provided to consist of three members, who should "be practical and experienced financiers," "who were to contract for and negotiate all loans authorized by the legislature on the faith and credit of the State for objects of internal improvements on the best and most favorable terms," sign and execute bonds or certificates of stocks, receive, manage, deposit and apply all moneys arising from said loans; make quarterly reports, &c., and keep a complete record of all their fiscal transactions. The commissioners chosen at this session by joint vote of both houses, were: Charles Oakley, M. M. Rawlings, and Thomas Mather. Their trust was enormous, and while they handled millions of the people's money, a bond was exacted of only $50,000. They were allowed a secretary and a per diem compensation of $5. For the purpose of promoting and uniting the various branches of improvement, a board of "Commissioners of Public Works" was created, consisting of seven members, one from each judicial district, to be elected biennially by joint vote of the General Assembly, and to continue in office for two years. An oath of office and a bond of twenty thousand dollars was required of each; no commissioner was permitted to retain in his hands more than $20,000 at any one time. Both commissioners and engineers were required to take an oath to keep secret, for the benefit of the State, all information they might receive relating to lands or choice town sites, that other persons might not enter or purchase them to the detriment of the State. A violation of this provision was to be deemed a misdemeanor, punishable by fine not exceeding $5,000 and incapacity of holding office. The commissioners were authorized to locate, superintend, and construct all the public works for the State, except the canal. They were to organize and meet semi-annually at the seat of government, at which times the general outlines of the operations were to be determined; examine and audit the expenditures of moneys on the works; make estimates of probable costs; serve authenticated copies on the fund commissioners, and make out a report of their proceedings for the governor to lay before the legislature. Certain duties or divisions of the work might be assigned among themselves; they were to cause examinations and surveys of rivers to be made, and generally to let the works to the lowest bidders, for which due notice was to be published and sealed proposals received; contracts were to provide for forfeiture in case of non-compliance, abandonment, &c., by contractors; no sub-letting was permitted.

Any vacant lands lying within 5 miles of any probable routes of the works were to be entered for the State. The railroads were to be built on the most direct and eligible routes between their specified termini. Individuals or private companies might connect any railroads or branches with the State works. Finally the board of public works were empowered to adopt and enforce all such rules and regulations as they might deem necessary and expedient, to carry into full effect the objects of the act.

The Northern Cross railroad, from Jacksonville to Springfield, was to be immediately constructed; but with regard to the other railroads, it was provided in section 25 of the act, that the work should be commenced simultaneously at each end, at important trading towns, and at their intersections with navigable streams, to be thence built in both directions. This provision, which has been called the crowning folly of the entire system, was the result of those jealous combinations, emanating from the fear that advantages might accrue to one section over another in the commencement and completion of the works, which evince, both the weakness and short-sightedness of human nature. We can appreciate the magnitude and enormity of the "grand system" better perhaps, by applying facts and figures to it. The census taken in 1835, returned the population of the State 271,727; in 1870 it is 2,539,891, or nearly ten times greater. The ratio of increase in the wealth of the State as fully as great.* The debt authorized for these improvements in the first instance was $10,230,000. But it was shortly found, that the estimates of the cost of the works were too low by half. We may with certainty assert, therefore, that the State was committed to a liability of $20,000,000, equivalent to $200,000,000 at the present time, with ten times the population, and more than ten times the wealth. Yet what would be the indignation of the people, if any legislature should now dare to impose the enormous liability of $200,000,000, or even half that sum, upon the State, notwithstanding its great wealth and resources?

The bill did not meet the approbation of the council of revision. It was assigned as a reason, "that such works can only be made safely and economically in a free government, by citizens or by independent corporations, aided or authorized by government." Allusions was also made to the undue influence over legislation that such vast public works would exercise. Notwithstanding these objections the bill was again passed by the constitutional majority and became a law. Messrs. E. B. Webb and John McCown, members of the House from White county, entered their solemn protest against its passage, setting forth their reasons at large, which were spread upon the journal.

Various combinations, or what is in modern parlence termed "rings," were formed in the legislature to effect the passage of the act. Previous to this all estimates of the cost of the canal, then in course of construction, were upon too low a scale. Its completion was very much desired by a large portion of the people, and it had been regarded as a work of great public utility with much unanimity among public men, but now farther aid was menaced to be withheld if other portions of the State were refused the improvements which their situations demanded. The canal was therefore connected with the general system, and a provision made pledging the faith of the State for a loan of $500,000 toward it. The canal is not yet done playing an important part in obtaining appropriations from the State treasury. To enlist the requisite number of members for its passage of the bill, provision was

*The taxable wealth of the State in 1839 was only $58,889,525, now it exceeds $500,000,-000.

made for improvements in almost every part of the State, and those out-of-the-way counties which could not be reached, were to share in a fund of $200,000, first to be raised. Alton, then munificently supplied with millions by the State bank to build her up as the mercantile center and metropolis of the west, would not be satisfied with less than the termini of three railroads. In 1834, she had received the highest number of votes as the seat of government, after the 20 years limitation at Vandalia should expire; but upon this she did not now insist—she preferred railroads. Several efforts were made to cut down the scheme to less dimensions, with failures each time, and not unfrequently more works added. Although the internal improvement convention had long since adjourned, there was still a powerful lobby busily engaged applying the pressure to pliant members of the legislature. The lobbies witnessed many oratorical efforts of ingenious and logical argument. The manifest destiny of government was protrayed in glowing colors; deductions from similar systems in progress in other States were made applicable to Illinois, and their certain success driven home and clinched with predictions; and who can argue against prophecy? The subsequent facts of signal and disastrous failure, were then hidden in the womb of time. What appears ridiculous and absurd now, was then by many confidently believed, because there were no facts to gainsay it, but much positive asserration that it would be a success.

The question of removing the seat of government from Vandalia, the 20 years limitation under the constitution having nearly expired, played no inconsiderable part in the passage of this measure. Sangamon county, then the most populous in the State, was represented by two senators and seven representatives, familiarly known as the "long nine," all whigs but one. Says Gov. Ford:

"Amongst them were some dexterous jugglers and managers in politics, whose whole object was to obtain the seat of government for Springfield. This delegation, from the beginning of the session, threw itself as a unit in support of, or opposition to, every local measure of interest, but never without a bargain for votes in return on the seat of government question. Most of the other counties were small, having but one representative, and many of them with but one for the whole district; and this gave Sangamon county a decided preponderance in the log-rolling system of those days. It is worthy of examination whether any just and equal legislation can ever be sustained where some of the counties are great and powerful and others feeble. But by such means 'the long nine' rolled along like a snow ball, gathering accessions of strength at every turn, until they swelled up a considerable party for Springfield, which party they managed to take almost as a unit in favor of the internal improvement system, in return for which the active supporters of that system were to vote for Springfield to be the seat of government. Thus it was made to cost the State about $6,000,000, to remove the seat of government from Vandalia to Springfield, half of which sum would have purchased all the real estate in that town at three prices; and thus by log-rolling on the canal measure, by multiplying railroads, by terminating three railroads at Alton, that Alton might become a great city in opposition to St. Louis, by distributing money to some of the counties, to be wasted by the county commissioners, and by giving the seat of government to Springfield, was the whole State bought up and bribed, to approve the most senseless and disastrous policy which ever crippled the energies of a growing country."

The first board of commissioners of public works, consisted of Murray McConnell, William Kinney, Elijah Willard, Milton K.

Alexander, Joel Wright, James W. Stephenson, and Ebenezer Peck. An effort was made to elect members of the legislature to this important place of trust. To evade the provision of the constitution, that "no senator or representative shall, during the time for which he shall have been elected, be appointed to any civil office under this State," and also the determination of Governor Duncan not to commission any member who might be chosen, a law was endeavored to be passed to over-ride the constitution and do away with a commission, notwithstanding the requirement that all civil officers shall be commissioned. In the light of a late decision of the supreme court, however, a commissioner is not an officer. Still, at the joint meeting of the two houses an effort was made to elect members as commissioners, but there were some scruples in the way; an adjournment for a day was had, when men were chosen, not members of either house.

It was now fondly hoped by those whose heads were not entirely turned that the fund commissioners would be unable to negotiate the bonds of the State. But this was soon swept away. Through the aid of the United States bank, then trading in State stocks, which served to bankrupt it, loans were effected in the summer of 1837; work was commenced at many different points before the end of the year. Throughout the State public expectation was wrought to the highest pitch over the scheme. Money became abundant by reason of local expenditures and in payments for estimates upon works. It had been confidently believed that the bonds of the State would bring ten per centum premium in market. Gov. Duncan had disposed of $100,000 in canal bonds the summer preceding at 5 per centum premium, which he considered too low and declined a larger sum at that rate. But now the commissioners could effect loans in this country only at par; London was tried with worse effect, "those in Europe were at 9 per cent discount. The bankers paid 90 cents on the dollar to the State, and, as is alleged, 1 per cent. to the fund commissioners, for brokerage."* Besides which a heavy contract was given for railroad iron at a most exorbitant price. Labor progressed meanwhile upon all the works.

---

*Ford's History.

CHAPTER XXXVIII.

1838–1842—ADMINISTRATION OF GOVERNOR CARLIN.

Continuation of the Subject of Internal Improvement—Collapse of the Grand System—Hard Times—Reorganization of the Judiciary in 1841.

———

While the unwieldy internal improvement system of the State was in full operation, with all its expensive machinery, amidst bank suspensions throughout the United States, a great stringency in the money market everywhere, and Illinois bonds forced to sale at a heavy discount, the general election of 1838 was approaching. Discreet men who had cherished the hope of a speedy subsidence of the public infatuation, met with disappointment. A governor and legislature were to be elected, and these were now looked forward to for a repeal of the ruinous State policy. But the grand scheme had not yet lost its dazzling influence upon the minds of the people. Time and experience had not demonstrated its utter absurdity. Hence the question of arresting its career of profligate expenditures did not become a leading one with the dominant party during the campaign, and most of the old members of the legislature were returned at this election.

Of the gubernatorial candidates, Cyrus Edwards (brother of the late governor,) whig, came out strongly for the system; while Thomas Carlin, the democratic nominee, well apprised of the public infatuation not yet sobered, failed to declare an emphatic opinion either for or against. This was the first time that the two political parties had the field to themselves in a gubernatorial campaign, unembarrassed by other tickets. In December preceding, the Democratic State convention had nominated James W. Stephenson for governor, and John S. Hacker for lieutenant governor. In April following, Hacker withdrew from the contest, and Stephenson, who was charged with being a defaulter, also withdrew, a sacrifice to the demands of party interests. The convention was recalled and met June 4th, when Thomas Carlin was nominated for governor, and S. H. Anderson for lieutenant governor. Carlin was elected, receiving 35,573 votes to Edwards 29,629. Anderson received 30,335 votes, to W. H. Davidson, the whig nominee for lieutenant governor, 28,716.

Gov. Carlin was born in Kentucky, near Frankfort, July 18th, 1789. His father was an Irishman. The education of young Carlin was meagre. In early manhood he applied himself to remedy this deficiency, being his own tutor. He was fond of reading through life. In 1803 his father removed to Missouri, then Spanish, where he died in 1810. In 1812 the subject of our

441

sketch came to Illinois and participated in all the "ranging" service incident to the war of that period, proving himself a soldier of undaunted bravery. He was married to Rebeca Huitt in 1814, and lived on the bank of the Mississippi opposite the mouth of the Missouri 4 years, when he removed to Greene county. He located the town site of Carrollton, and made a liberal donation of land for county building purposes in 1825. He was the first sheriff of Greene county, and afterward was twice elected a senator to the legislature. In the Black Hawk war he commanded a spy battalion, a post of considerable danger. In 1834 he was appointed by President Jackson receiver of public moneys and removed to Quincy. After the close of his gubernatorial term he removed back to his old home at Carrollton, where he spent the remainder of his life, as before his elevation to office, in agricultural pursuits. In 1849 he served out the unexpired term of J. D. Fry in the lower house of the legislature. He died Feb. 14, 1852, leaving surviving him his wife and seven children, out of thirteen born to them.*

Gov. Carlin was a man of remarkable physical energy and capacity. In stature he was above the medium height; light complexioned, a spare looking face, high forehead, long nose, and thin lips, giving to his mouth a compressed appearance. He was unyielding if not obstinate in disposition, possessed in private life an unblemished character, and was a democrat of the straightest sect. While he did not seek preferment, he did not reject office. Mentally he was not without vigor. His messages are smoothly and rather well written, but he did not attempt public speaking.

The lieutenant governor elect, Anderson, was a native of Tennessee. He proved an efficient officer, and attached to himself many warm friends through life. He resided in Jefferson county. After the expiration of his term of office, he received from President Polk the office of United States Marshal. In politics, it is needless to add, he was a democrat.

Upon the meeting of the legislature, 1839, the retiring governor, Duncan, in his message spoke in emphatic terms of the impolicy of the internal improvement system by the State; presaged the evils threatened by that measure, which experience had already sufficiently shown would have a most deleterious effect upon the property of the State; and urged that to correct the mistake, without too great a sacrifice of public or private interests, should occupy the most serious and patriotic deliberation of the legislature. But the incoming governor, contrary to the hope of many wise and discrete men, while he strongly assailed, in true Jacksonian style, the banks and their suspensions, which had been legalized, held the following language on the subject of internal improvements:

"The signal success which has attended our sister States in the construction of their extensive systems of improvements can leave no doubt of the wise policy and utility of such works. They open new channels of commerce and trade, furnish the farmer and mechanic the means of transporting the products of their labor to market, develope the natural and hidden resources of the country, and stimulate the enterprise and industry of the people. * * In the principles and policy of this plan, contrasted with that of joint stock companies and private corporations, I entirely concur. Had I occupied my present situation at the establish-

*From a memoir by his daughter, Mrs. E. C. Woodward.

ment of the system, I would have recommended its adoption on a less extensive scale, and the construction of the most important works first. Under the present plan of proceeding, however, near two million dollars have been expended, and whatever diversity of opinion may now exist as to the expediency of the system as originally projected, all must admit that the character and credit of the State forbid its abandonment.''

It was, therefore, to be expected that those who saw the folly of the State in the prosecution of this system, and had cherished the hope of a change, would be disappointed. The new legislature not only did not repeal or modify the expensive project, but made further specific appropriations and authorized additional works, involving an out-lay of near a million dollars: $50,000 for the improvement of Rock river; $150,000 to improve the navigation of the Little Wabash; $20,000 on the western mail route; $100,000 for a new railroad from Rushville to Erie, on the bank of the Illinois river; $20,000 to improve the navigation of the Embarras river; $20,000 for the Big Muddy; and $10,000 for a road from Cahokia Creek to Kaskaskia. Besides these specific amounts, the improvement of the navigation of the Illinois river was directed to be extended to Ottawa (which according to modern experience would have taken many millions more) and a lateral branch railroad from some eligible point on the Alton and Shelbyville railroad between Hillsboro and Alton to run to Carlinville. The governor was also authorized to negotiate a loan of $4,000,000 to prosecute the work on the canal. The lands and public works of the State were exempted from taxation. So thoroughly was the legislature still imbued with the idea of the State exclusively owning all the public works, that the chairman of the Committee on Internal Improvement, Mr. Smith, of Wabash, in reporting adversely upon a bill for ''an act to incorporate the Albion and Grayville Railroad Company,'' at this session, said: ''In the opinion of the committee, it is inexpedient for the legislature to authorize corporations or individuals to construct railroads or canals calculated to come in competition with similar works now in course of construction under the State system of internal improvements.''

Here let us stop and speculate over the probable future of our State, had this remarkable Mr. Edward Smith lived. As chairman of the committee on internal improvements, he drafted that glowing report of the committee which so fired the honorable members upon the subject of developing the resources of the State as to cause them to vie with each other in actually doing more than that not very modest document asked; and who, apparently, possessed the magnetic power to bring the members squarely up to the support of these improvement measures, like a skillful general marshaling his hosts for victory. He seemed to be born to command in this particular field of enterprise. Unfortunately, before the next session, Mr. Smith died, when the splendid system collapsed. Had he remained in life, with the peculiar force that characterized him in pushing through these measures, the final result of this herculean undertaking of the State becomes a subject of curious contemplation. It must have either bankrupted the State beyond all hope of redemption, or made her treasury the recipient of all the many millions of annual earnings of the vast net-work of nearly 7,000 miles of completed railroads at the present time, which now find their way into the coffers of private corporations, enriching them to an unlimited and uncontrollable extent. With such an enormous income by the State, the burthen of taxation would be entirely removed; we would be enabled doubtless to ship our produce to market for half of the present rates, which would double the value of crops and farms, and incidentally all other real and personal property; the cheapening of travel in a corresponding ratio would double the amount of it; we would visit our distant friends oftener, cultivate an extensive social intercourse by rail—indeed the whole country would be much as a city now is with its street railroads; promote harmony and good fellowship throughout the length and breadth of the State—in a word, have a very millenium in Illinois!

We have noted the fact that of the governor being authorized at the session of 1838-9 to negotiate a further loan of $4,000,000 for the canal. Money was stringent at the time both in Europe and America. The fiscal negotiations of the fund commissioners, made in Europe prior to this, were anything but satisfactory. Gov. Carlin, therefore, unwilling to put the new canal loan in the hands of these agents, and ambitious doubtless for the glory of his administration, commissioned ex-Governor Reynolds, the very last public man in the State, perhaps, for a duty so responsible and delicate, requiring an extensive and accurate knowledge of domestic and foreign fiscal affairs. The latter urged the association with himself of R. M. Young, then a senator in congress, to which the governor ultimately acceded. In their over-weening desire to raise money to carry forward the public works, both the fund commissioners and Gov. Carlin's financial agents made some very ill-advised and bungling loans, attended with heavy losses to the State.

Reynolds hurried immediately forward to New York, where he met and obtained the advice and assistance of Mr. Rawlings, one of the fund commissioners. They sold to Mr. Delafield, of N. Y., April 23, 1839, 300 bonds of $1,000 each, bearing 6 per cent. interest, payable half-yearly at Philadelphia and New York—the principal becoming due in 1860. In this the law was exceeded, because it provided only for annual interest. The whole of the 300 bonds were delivered, and payment was stipulated as follows: $50,000 within 15 days into the bank of the New York Banking Company, thence to be drawn out on not less than ten days sight drafts, in forty different installments; the next payment of $50,000 was not to be made till the 1st of August, 1839, in the notes of some bank or banking association of New York city, of a denomination not exceeding $10; and in like manner the remainder, commencing October 1st, in monthly installments of $50,000 each. Here was a sale of interest-bearing bonds made in April, the bonds all immediately delivered, and yet they were not finally to be paid for until the following January, 1840.

April 29, 1839, the same gentlemen contracted with Thomas Dunlap (whose performance was guaranteed by the United States bank of Pennsylvania,) to sell him 10 00 bonds due in 1870 of £225 each, annual interest 6 per cent.; and both principal and interest payable in London, "at the rate of 4s. 6d. sterling to the dollar." Payment for the bonds sold was to be made in ten equal monthly installments of $100,000 each, without interest, in $10 notes. This million dollars it was estimated by the house committee of the Illinois assembly, could be redeemed with 250,185 sovereigns, 11s. 2d., instead of £225,000, realizing a gain of 18,314 sovereigns, 8s. 10d. to the purchasers, equal to a loss of $91,250.34 to the State of Illinois. The contract was, besides, a glaring departure of the law, because the commissioners bound the State to pay in British coin £225,000, instead of $1,000,000; and while the State was paying interest on her bonds she not only did without the money for ten months but got no interest for that time. The money was to be paid in bills of the United States bank, but before the State actually received it, it became depreciated 10 per cent., making a loss of $100,000 on the amount. The total loss of this one transaction was near $200,000. The law required ready payment in cash for all bonds sold.

These transactions with Delafield and Dunlap, amounting to $1,300,000 in Illinois bonds, became in part the basis for starting into operation the New York free banking system, about that time authorized, which required a deposit of State stocks, in double value of the circulation, together with a small percentage of specie in the bank vaults. Our financiers thus enable several of the "wild-cat" institutions to start business, by furnishing them Illinois bonds on credit, and receiving in payment the money— after proper exchange with other banks doubtless—issued in pursuance of the charters, Illinois meanwhile paying interest for the privilege of advancing their bonded capital!

After the negotiations in New York and Philadelphia, the governor's agents, ex-Gov. Reynolds, and two of the fund commissioners, Gen. Rawlings and Col. Oakley, in May, 1839, repaired to Europe to effect further loans for the State. Judge R. M. Young, the other agent of Gov. Carlin, in custody of the bonds, subsequently joined them in London. The money market in Europe was tight, but the commissioners, whom the law required to be "experienced and skilled in finance," were not to be baffled. After considerable delay, Messrs. Young and Reynolds, on October 30th, 1839, deposited with John Wright & Co., of London, 1,000 bonds, representing $1,000,000, to be again reckoned in British coin of £225 each, authorizing them to sell or negotiate the bonds at a rate of not less than £91 for the £100. If more than 91 per cent. could be obtained for them, the surplus, not exceeding 4 per cent. was to be retained by Wright & Co. as commissioners; any excess beyond 95 per cent. for said bonds, was to be equally divided between the State and the said brokers. On this contract the brokers agreed to advance £30,000.

The law under which the financial agents acted, we will reiterate, expressly required ready payment in cash for all bonds negotiated, and that none should be sold for less than par. Although the bonds might be hypothecated, yet when the agents authorized Messrs. Wright & Co. to sell them at 91 per cent., they acted without warrant of law. The brokers sold about half a million dollars worth of the bonds, when they failed, with both the proceeds of these sales and the remainder of the bonds in their hands. The unsold bonds, being the property of the State, were afterward returned by the receivers, but the money received on those sold was adjudged as assets of the firm, in which the State was compelled to share pro rata with other creditors, amounting to a few shillings on the pound.

The Hon. E. B. Webb, from the house judiciary committee, to whom the accounts for the sales of bonds were referred, reported Jan. 29, 1840, saying: "The anxiety of the agents to procure money for the State, or their eagerness to succeed in effecting sales where others had failed, induced them to enter into contracts injurious to the best interests of the State, derogatory to her dignity, and in every way calculated to depreciate her securities." Resolutions were adopted by the house, disapproving of these transactions, whereby the State was required to receive in payment local bank bills, as under the contracts with Delafield and Dunlap, and the sales made on credit; condemning, as in contravention of law, the hypothecation of bonds with John Wright & Co., to be sold at 91 per cent.; declaring that the agents had transcended the powers vested in them, and that their London negotiation was void, copies were to be transmitted to J. Wright & Co., Covent Garden, London. By this time it had become patent that no more loans could be effected at par, as the law required. The dark cloud of infatuation which obscured the vision of the people began also to be dissipated, and as glimmers of light shone through they became clamorous against the large extent in which the works were feebly prosecuted simultaneously at all points. The ideas of Governor Carlin, in one short year's time, underwent a total revolution with regard to the grand system of internal improvement. He now found from correct data, that the State would speedily impose upon herself a debt of not less than $21,746,444, at an annual interest of $1,310,776, with a revenue of less than one sixth that amount—$200,000; that the then debt of the State exceeded already $14,000,000, which rested upon a community of less than half million souls, remote from markets, and with little commerce to bring in money. The giddy magnitude of the idea became appalling to his excellency, and he convoked the legislature in extraordinary session for December 9th, 1839.

In his message, after alluding to the spirit of speculation so rife in 1836, whereby not only individuals but deliberative bodies were lured from the paths of prudence and economy by this overweening delusion, he says:

"At this critical and most important crisis, a bill was introduced into the legislature, providing for a general system of internal improvements by the construction of nearly 1,300 miles of railroad, and the improvement of various rivers; and such was the zeal with which it was urged, and so numerous and powerful were its friends, that it passed through both houses by large majorities. No fear seemed to be entertained by its advocates, but the ability and resources of the State would prove equal to the accomplishment of such a herculean task, and they pointed with pride and exultation to that high rank in the scale of wealth to which the measure would finally elevate us."

His excellency, now discovering impending ruin and dishonor, invoked the legislature to the exercise of wisdom and unity of action in the adoption of such measures of reform as would best subserve the public welfare and save the State from bankruptcy and degradation.

The legislature, whose ruthless hand was destined to destroy the stupendous system, was composed in the main of the same members who had originally passed it; who had but one short year before supplemented and endorsed it by the addition of works involving a further expenditure of $1,000,000, now by their deliberate action to place the seal of condemnation upon their cherished offspring, was certainly most humiliating, and they hesitated in their course. If they could have wiped the system out, leaving no debt or memory of it behind, it would not have been so disagreeable, but when they reflected that their folly would cost the people $150,000 for every member, the politicians were smitten with fear regarding the future of their preferments. But thanks, the unpalatable task was performed. By the two acts of February 1840, it was provided that the board of fund commissioners and commissioners of public works be abolished; one fund commissioner was provided to perform the same duties as before required of the board, "except that he shall not be authorized to sell State bonds or borrow money on behalf of the State." He was to receive and take charge of the railroad iron purchased in Europe and pay the duty on it; receive back all bonds from persons failing to comply with their contracts, and register and burn the same; to audit and settle the accounts of the late board of fund commissioners and the late board of public works, and bring suit against each member in arrears in the Sangamon circuit court, for which purpose jurisdiction was given it to any county. Three instead of seven commissioners of public works were now provided who were to settle and adjust all liabilities under the internal improvement system, and give drafts for the amounts due contractors on the Fund Commissioners, whereupon such contracts were to be regarded as cancelled. If the drafts could not be wholly cashed, the amount paid was to be endorsed, and the residue to draw interest. All engineers and agents whose services were not indispensible to ascertain the amounts due contractors, were to be immediately discharged. The board was to secure and operate such roads or parts of roads as were completed, fix and establish tolls, and provide for their collection and payment over to the fund commissioners.

The progress of the work on the canal was not arrested; but of the remainder of the works of the grand system (with the exception of a part of the Northern Cross railroad) simultaneously begun in various parts of the State, nothing was ever done, except in detached parcels on every road, where excavations and embankments may even yet be seen—memorials of supreme legislative folly. That portion of the Northern Cross Railroad from Meredosia to Springfield, was afterwards finished at a cost to the State of $1,000,000; its income proved insufficient to keep it in repair and it was subsequently sold for $100,000 in State indebtedness. Of this road some 8 miles of track was laid in 1838, from Meredosia east, the first rail being laid May 9th. The first locomotive that ever turned a wheel in the great valley of the Mississippi was put on the track of this road at Meredosia, Nov. 8th, 1838. George W. Plant, afterward a prominent business man of St. Louis, was the engineer. The locomotive ran over the track 8 miles and back, carrying Gov. Duncan, Murray McConnel, one of the commissioners of the public works, James Dunlap and Thos. I. January, contractors, Charles Collins and Miron Leslie of St. Louis, and the chief engineer, Geo. P. Plant. Twelve years before only, 1826, the first railroad in the United States was built. connecting Albany and Schenectady, in New York. Her eager desire in the race of empire now gave to Illinois a check for 12 years before another railroad was built. This was the Chicago and Galena, finished as far as Elgin in 1850. Then dawned upon the State the great railroad era which has since covered her surface with a net-work of these iron arteries of commerce, affording rapid and easy communication with almost every county.

Thus, in 1840, after a short but eventful life of less than three years, fell by the hands of its creator the most stupendous, extravagant and almost ruinous folly of a grand system of internal improvements, that any civil community, perhaps, ever engaged in, leaving a debt of $14,237,348. While great disappointment pervaded the people at the failure of the splendid scheme, they were not surprised nor crushed with the news of its repeal. Indeed, their sobered senses had for some time taught them that to this extremity it must come at last, and they felt that sort of relief a man feels at the loss of half his fortune—he has learned his fate and is thankful it is no worse; possibly he learns a profitable lesson at the same time. While they felt chagrined, there was no one to blame in great part but themselves, for in many cases their representatives had but obeyed the voice of the people, as the voice of God. Many names since prominent, honored and great, are recorded in favor of the original passage of the measure, as may be seen by reference to the journal of the assembly of 1837.

Illinois was not the only State which embarked in these wild schemes of State undertakings. Indiana, in 1837, pursued the same course. Her bonds to upward $11,000,000 were disposed of, and after expending the proceeds improvidently, extravagantly, and doubtless fraudulently, there remained nothing to show for it but 40 miles of railroad, pieces of canal, and some unfinished turnpikes. Pennsylvania had taken the lead in like schemes of developing the State, for which she at one time owed a debt of $40,000,000, part of which was paid by the sale of the works. The same held good with Ohio; and Missouri, more recently, for the purpose of building railroads and other works of internal improvement, on the breaking out of the rebellion, found herself loaded with a debt exceeding a score of millions of dollars.

Hard Times.—With the collapse of the great internal improvement system, the suspension of banks and a depreciated currency, hard times obtained. The total debt of the State was as follows:

For bank stock,	$5,614,196 94
On account of internal improvements,	5,614,196 94
Canal debt,	4,338,907 71
State house,	116,000 00
School, college and seminary fund (borrowed)	808,085 00
Due State bank for auditor's warrants,	294,190 00
Annual interest upon this amount ($13,836,377,65)	830,188 77
Total,	$14,666,562 42

To meet this debt, outside of taxation, the State owned 42,000 acres of land, bought under requirements of the internal improvement law; 230,467 acres of canal donation remained undisposed of, besides 3,491 town lots in Ottawa, Chicago, and other places along the line of the canal; the State obtained shortly after by the distribution act of congress of 1841, 210,000 acres of land more from that source. These, together with the ill-advised European purchase of railroad iron, and the various pieces of unfinished railroads in different parts of the State, almost worthless, constituted the resources of the State to discharge a debt, which, considering our population (488,929 in 1840), as one-sixth of what it is now, our wealth, ($58,752,168 in 1840), as one-eighth of what it is now, and the value of money then and now at a difference of 100 per cent, which, owing to the large yields from the California, Australia, and other mines since, is an estimate perhaps not out of the way, was equal to a debt upon the State at the present of at least $150,000 000. This was indeed a heavy burden. The annual revenues—$117,821, in 1840—were no more than would meet the ordinary expense of the State government, leaving a deficit annually to the amount of the interest on the debt — $830,182, — to further yearly augment the debt. The State had sold and hypothecated its bonds until its credit was well nigh exhausted; the people were both unable and unwilling to pay higher taxes, and they were besides largely indebted to the merchants; the merchants to the banks, or for goods purchased abroad; while the banks, on account of suspending specie payment, owed every body who carried one of their rags in his pocket. None could pay in par funds, for they were not to be had.

In this condition of the State, it required great unanimity of action and harmony in counsel to carry it safely over the financial crisis. This did not wholly obtain. The character and genious of the people were very incongruous. Wide differences, social and political, of the two great geographical sections of the State, have prevailed even down to this day. The disparity in wealth between the north and south, the rapid settlement of the former after the close of the Black Hawk war, were not with without jealousy, of which public men partook and carried into the counsels of the State. This mutual misunderstanding of character and purposes was a stumbling block in the way of united and harmonious action in the adoption of the wisest measures for public relief. The canal, as it afterward proved, afforded the best and only avenue leading out of the financial embarrassments, and toward restoring the credit of the State. It stood independent, to a certain extent, of the other works of internal improvement, upon a landed capital of its own, the gift of the nation, and when the latter were abandoned, the work upon it was still more or less prosecuted. But the canal, from the want of unity in the sentiments of the people, now became the subject of bitter attack, for no other reason that it was in the northern part of the State.

Besides, there did not obtain with the people a clear conception of State policy. Men were elected to the legislature with reference to their national politics, greatly intensified by the exciting contest of 1840, and not with regard to the affairs of the State, then of deepest concern to the welfare of the people. Politicians were better acquainted with the devious ways of obtaining office than qualified to discharge its duties in accordance with enlarged principles of statesmanship. This is too much the case at the present time; people in the election of officers are actuated by a desire to confer favor upon the man, rather than choosing a servant who is to perform a service for them and the

29

public at large with wisdom and impartiality. It was therefore
difficult to make the questions of present embarrassment and
future State prosperity paramount, in a broad view, to all other
considerations.

By various expedients, means were provided to meet the accruing interest of 1841, on canal loans in New York and London, but
not so with regard to the interest on the State debt generally.
The fund commissioner, in his report, stated the difficulty of
meeting that which would fall due January 1st, 1841; the legislature, elected in August previous, was convoked some weeks earlier
than the time of the regular session, for the express purpose of
devising means to this end. This was the session by the *sine die*
adjournment of which it was attempted to crush the State banks,
or compel them to resume specie payments—a thing impossible
for them to do. Much conflict of opinion obtained among members and found expression in a flood of resolutions, as usual at the
outset of a session. The questions of difference were as to not
paying interest at all, or withholding it only on bonds for which,
by the mismanagment of the financial agents, the State had either
received less than par, or, as in some cases, nothing. To the
credit of the State it is to be recorded, that no idea of repudiation obtained among a large majority of the members. On the
contrary, the desperate remedy was proposed of issuing more
bonds and hypothecating them for what they would fetch in
market. The course pursued by the financial agents of the State
in disposing of bonds contrary to law, at less than par value on
credit, was severely animadverted, and that the State should pay
interest only on what money she had actually received on her
bonds was strenuously insisted upon. The opponents of this view
contended that bonds were articles of commerce, against which no
equities could arise while in the hands of innocent purchasers;
that the State must be held responsible for the conduct of its
agents; that the legislature in the selection of the fund commissioners, and the governor in the appointment of Messrs. Young
and Reynolds, had fully committed the credit of the State to their
hands, and if they blundered, the State was bound nevertheless
by their acts—she should have chosen agents more "skilled in
finance." In this conflict of views, legislation was well-nigh defeated altogether. Alfred W. Cavarly, of Green, now discovered
the happy expedient by which to extricate the legislature from its
dilemma. He prepared a bill of two sections, which became a law
Dec. 16th, 1840, empowering the fund commissioner to hypothecate not exceeding $300,000 of the State internal improvement
bonds, to raise a sufficient sum of money to pay the interest which
would *legally* fall due on the internal improvement debt in
January 1841; the bonds were to be redeemed any time before
1843, and not to draw interest unless forfeited. Thus was the
question of contention taken out of the halls of legislation, and
the decision of the *legality* of the loans imposed upon the commissioners—not an unfrequent expedient of deliberative bodies. The
legislature further authorized the issuance of State interest bonds,
to be sold in market for what they would bring, the proceeds to
be applied to the payment of interest and the redemption of hypothecated bonds—a most execrable measure. By another act, Feb.
27th, 1841, an additional tax of 10 cents on the $100 worth of

property was imposed, to be set apart exclusively as an "interest fund," pledged to pay the interest on these bonds; and the minimum assessment of all lands was to be $3 per acre. The fund commissioner, Mr. Barrett, by hypothecating internal improvement bonds, paid off the January interest, 1841; but by the time the July interest was to be raised, Illinois stocks had depreciated in market so that Mr. J. D. Whitesides, the new fund commissioner, hypothecated with Macallister and Stebbins, of New York, $804,000 in interest bonds for $321,600, as was promised him, but of which amount only $261,460 was ever by them paid. This was the origin of the notorious "Macallister and Stebbins bonds," of which more hereafter. Another law, showing the extremity to which this legislation went, was that of Feb. 27th, 1841, regulating the sale of property under execution. This serves to illustrate both the *hard times* and the inconsiderate and unjust legislation to afford relief to the debtor class at the expense of the creditor. It provided that property levied upon should be valued as in "ordinary times," to be made by three householders summoned by the officers, of whom the creditor, debtor, and officer should each choose one—placing it in the power of the officer to favor either party at his option; the property was not to sell unless it brought two-thirds of their valuation; no way was provided by which the creditor, if two-thirds of the valuation was not bid, could hold his lien—forcing him to stay collection or suffer a discount of 33⅓ per cent. The law was made applicable to all judgments rendered and contracts accruing prior to the 1st of May, without reference to the legal obligations of the time when contracts were entered into—being in violation of that clause of the constitution of the United States, declaring that "no law shall be passed imparing the obligations of contracts." In the case of McCracken vs. Howard, the supreme court of the United States subsequently held the law to be unconstitutional.[*] The law in the meantime had been instrumental, by various arrangements between parties, in extinguishing many debts. But this species of legislation seldom effects the benefits intended. It is apt to be harrassing and vexatious to both debtor and creditor, while experience teaches it to be distructive of all confidence between men in business, requiring prompt compliance with contracts; and it tends further to affect inimically the trade and commerce of the State. These views were enlarged upon in a solemn protest against its passage, signed by such names as John J. Hardin, D. M. Woodson, Lyman Trumbull, and many others.[†]

After July, 1841, no further effort was made to pay interest on the debt of the State. Her bonds declined rapidly in market to 14 cents on the dollar. In a few months, Feb. 1842, from proximate causes already stated, the State bank, with a circulation exceeding $3,000,000, finally went down; in June the Illinois bank at Shawneetown, with a circulation exceeding $1,500,000, also broke, thus rendering worthless about the only money there had been for some time in the country, and added materially to the pressure of the times. The banks had managed to keep up the value of their circulation far above the bonds of the State, but to conciliate an unfriendly legislature by advances on auditor's war-

[*]See 2d, Howard, 608.
[†]See House Journal, 1841.

rants, for the State house then building, and to carry forward the public works, an unwarranted expansion snapped their threads of life, spreading disaster round about them. The condition of this fair State, with her calamities thus augmented, was truly distressing. Abroad, her name was freely associated with dishonor; emigrants, dreading high taxation, gave it a wide berth, unless it were those who, having no character of their own, cared little for that of the State of their adoption; while the people here with rare exceptions were anxious to sell out and flee a country which presented no alternative but dishonor or exhorbitant taxation. The chances to sell were, however, in inverse ratio to the desire, and while impending financial ruin, disgrace, and the fear of taxation kept the State from gaining population as rapidly as had been her wont, the impracticability of effecting sales saved her against loss. In the meantime, an utter dearth and stagnation in all kinds of business prevailed. The notes of the banks were receivable in payment of taxes for which purpose they had been to a small extent hoarded by the people; but now the governor, auditor and treasurer, forbade their receipt by the collectors of the State revenue, except at specie rates—50 cents on the dollar. This step was unwarranted by the law, and condemned by the press and people in public meetings, irrespective of party until such a breeze was raised about the ears of the "officers of State" that they were fain to retract their pretentious proclamation, and taking the other extreme, suspended the collection of the taxes till the meeting of the legislature.

At this crisis in the fair fame of our State, there were not wanting men, in position to aid in moulding public opinion, who favored repudiation, both by the plan of omission and by directly declaring this purpose, and "setting the moral sense of mankind at defiance." Gov. Ford says:

"It is my solemn belief that when I came into office, I had the power to make Illinois a repudiating State. It is true I was not the leader of any party; but my position as governor would have given me leadership enough to have carried the democratic party, except in a few counties in the north, in favor of repudiation. If I had merely stood still and done nothing, the result would have been the same. In that case a majority of both parties would have led to either active or passive repudiation. The politicians on neither side, without a bold lead to the contrary, by some high in office, would never have dared to risk their popularity by being the first to advocate an increase of taxes to be paid by a tax-hating people."

Again he says:

"The people of Bond county, as soon as the internal improvement system passed, had declared in a public meeting that the system must lead to taxation and utter ruin; that the people were not bound to pay any of the debt to be contracted for it; and that Bond county would never assist in paying a cent of it. Accordingly, they refused to pay taxes for several years. When the system went down, and had left the State in the ruinous condition predicted by the Bond county meeting, many people remembered that there might be a question raised as to the obligation of payment. Public men everywhere, of all parties, stood in awe of this question; there was a kind of general silence as to what would be popular or unpopular. The two great political parties were watching each other with eagle eyes, to see that no one should get the advantage of the other. The whigs, driven to desperation by repeated ill-success in elections, were many of them in favor of repudiating, as a means of bettering their party. The Sangamon *Journal* and the Alton *Telegraph*, the two leading whig newspapers of the State, boldly took ground that the debt never could and never would be paid, and that there was no use to say anything about it.* Very many democrats were in favor of the same course, for fear of losing the power the democratic party already possessed.

It was thought to be a very dangerous subject to meddle with. At a democratic convention which nominated Mr. Snyder for governor, a resolution against repudiation offered by Mr. Arnold of Chicago, was laid on the table by an overwhelming vote of the convention, so as not to commit the party one way or the other. It was evident that this was to be a troublesome question, and a great many of the politicians on both sides were as ready to take one side of it as the other, and their choice depended upon which might finally appear to be most powerful The whigs were afraid, if they advocated the debt-paying policy, the democrats would take the other side, and leave the whigs no chance of ever coming into a majority; and the democrats feared that if they advocated a correct policy, the other side might be more popular, and might be taken by the whigs. I speak only of the leaders of parties, amongst whom on all sides there was a strong suspicion that repudiation might be more popular than taxation."

REORGANIZATION OF THE JUDICIARY.

Partisan Malice and Revolutionary Conduct.—By act of Feb. 10, 1841, the legislature repealed out of office the then 9 circuit judges, increased the number of supreme judges from 4 to 9, and, in addition to their duties as a supreme court and their functions as the council of revision, imposed upon them all the circuit court business in the State. Since 1835 the supreme judges, relieved of circuit duty, had acted solely as a court of appeals, errors and revision. The present change was a bitter partisan measure, in the language of Gov. Ford, "confessedly violent and somewhat revolutionary."

Three of the four supreme judges were of the whig party—the minority party of the State—while Judge Smith was a democrat. Gov. Ford says: "It is due to truth here to say, that Wilson and Lockwood were in every respect amiable and accomplished gentlemen in private life, and commanded the esteem and respect of all good men for the purity of their conduct and their probity in official station. Wilson was a Virginian of the old sort, a man of good education, sound judgment, and an elegant writer, as his published opinions will show. Lockwood was a New Yorker. He was an excellent lawyer, a man of sound judgment, and his face indicated uncommon purity, modesty, and intelligence, together with energy and strong determination. His face was the true index of his character. Brown was a fine, large, affable, and good looking man, had a tolerable share of tact and good sense, a complimentary, smiling and laughing address to all men, and had been elected and continued in office upon the ground that he was believed to be a clever fellow."

The State, in the exciting party struggle of 1840, had gone for Van Buren and both houses of the legislature were largely democratic. The supreme court had two years before offended the

---

*After the publication of Gov. Ford's history, in 1854. more than three years after his death, both the *Alton Telegraph* and *Illinois State Journal*, formerly the *Sangamon Journal*, denied having favored repudiation, either directly or indirectly; that they uniformly opposed it with zeal, and always advocated the liquidation of the entire public debt at as early a day as the means of the State would justify.—See Illinois State Journal, March 7, 1855.

sense of supremacy of the dominant party, in deciding a case of appointment to office by the governor. Pending before the same tribunal there was still another case fraught with political consequences far graver, which it was thence surmised would also be decided against the party in power. When men are themselves actuated by party feelings and prejudices in everything, they are apt to think others are similarly influenced, no matter what their position or how exalted in public life.

Alexander P. Field was and had been secretary of State, since his appointment by Gov. Edwards, having served through both the administrations of Govs. Reynolds and Duncan. In politics he was a whig, though originally, like Duncan, he had been a violent Jackson man. When Gov. Carlin came into office in 1838, he claimed the power of appointing a new secretary of State without a vacancy existing in that office. The claim was based upon the idea that a secretary of State under our first constitution, like a cabinet officer in the national government, was a confidential adviser of the governor, and for purposes of harmony in such relation, should be of the same political party with his excellency. The governor nominated John A. McClernand, then of Gallatin, to the senate for that office. But the senate, although democratic, by a vote of 22 to 18 passed a resolution, "That the executive does not possess the power to nominate to the senate a secretary of State, except in case of vacancy in that office, and that, inasmuch as the senate has not been advised of any vacancy in that office, the nomination of John A. McClernand be not advised and consented to by the senate." They were further of opinion that the tenure of office might be limited by the legislature; which had not been done, however. During the session, the governor sent to the senate several other names for that office, but all were rejected.

After the adjournment, he again appointed McClernand secretary of State, who thereupon demanded possession of the office from the whig incumbent, Mr. Field, but was refused. McClernand then laid an information in the nature of a *quo warranto* before Judge Breese, in the circuit court of Fayette county, and upon hearing, that court decided in favor of the complainant. Field took an appeal to the supreme court, where the cause was reversed. The question decided by the court, aside from the political or partisan bent given to it, derived importance from the fundamental principle of government involved. Quite an array of able counsel appeared on either side. For the appellant Field, there were Cyrus Walker, Justin Butterfield and Levi Davis; and for the appellee McClernand, S. A. Douglas, Jas. Shields and Wickliffe Kitchell, attorney general. Three separate opinions were written by the judges, Wilson and Lockwood concurring, Smith dissenting, and Brown, being connected by affinity, with the relator, declined sitting in the cause.[*] Chief Justice Wilson rendered the decision of the court in language clear, cogent and elegant, which is both exhaustive of the subject and convincing in its conclusions. The court decided that the governor had not the constitutional power at his will and pleasure, to remove from office the Secretary of State; that when that functionary was once appointed, the power of appointment was suspended until a

[*] See 2d Scam., Ill. reports, p 70.

vacancy occurred; that when the constitution created an office, and left the tenure undefined, the officer held during good behavior, or until the legislature by law limited the tenure or authorized some functionary of the government to remove the officer at will. The constitution was the charter of the governor's authority. All the powers delegated to him, or in accordance with that instrument, he was entitled to exercise and no other. While it was a limitation upon the powers of the legislative department, it was to be regarded as a grant of powers to the others. Neither the executive nor the judiciary, therefore, could exercise any authority or power, except such as was clearly granted by the constitution. In England the king was the source of power, and all rights and prerogatives not granted were adjudged to him, but here the theory is that the people are sovereign and the source of power, and that the executive could exercise only those powers specially delegated to him; and as it was not even pretended that any express grant of this character was to be found in the constitution, it must be denied. A grant by implication could not be maintained, because the enumeration of the powers of a department of government operated as a restriction and limitation of a general grant. "The executive power of the State shall be vested in a governor," was a mere declaration of a general rule. Besides, the power of appointment in case a vacancy existed, was given to the governor conjointly with the senate; and a nomination would not confer office without approval by the senate.

The decision caused a great partisan outcry against the " whig court," as it was called. The democrats, largely in the ascendancy in the State, were yet debarred from exercising uncontrolled power and the enjoyment of all the benefits and emoluments of office to which their ascendancy entitled them, by this decision, which proclaimed in their teeth, asit were, the existence of office for life incumbents.

But the other question, still pending and far more important, was fraught not only with preclusion from the secretary's office, but with the danger of losing political control of the State, and consequently all power and patronage. This was the celebrated Galena alien case. The alien vote was nine-tenths democratic, and sufficient in strength—about 10,000—that if precluded from the polls to determine the election in favor of the whigs at the approaching presidential election of 1840. As the McClernand-Field case was by the unscrupulous boldly charged to be partisan, it was now doubtless believed by many that the court in this case was prepared to violate a plain provision of the constitution. The constitution provided that " in all elections, all white male inhabitants above the age of 21 years, having resided in the State six months next preceding the election, shall enjoy the right of an elector."

The idea had gained currency that suffrage and citizenship were concomitant and indispensable qualifications to constitute a man an elector, and therefore the provision above quoted, if brought to the test before the proper tribunal, would be declared null and void. An agreed case had been made at Galena, where there was a large alien vote concentrated in and about the mining region, between two whigs, one of whom sued the other, who had acted as judge at the August election of 1838, and in that capacity received the vote of an alien, to recover $100 under the election law of 1829, for the use of the county, which it was supposed would present the constitutional question fairly. The suit was brought in the circuit court at Galena, Judge Dan. Stone, presiding; and as the case was admitted, he, without hearing argument, or probably giving the question much examination, decided that an alien, unlike a citizen, was not entitled to exercise the election franchise. The decision, when it became public, produced great apprehension in the ranks of the democracy, and steps were immediately taken to bring the case before the supreme court.

In view of the decision in the McClernand-Field case, it was further imagined that that tribunal would affirm the decision below, and that the remedy was the revolutionary one to reform the supreme court by adding a sufficient number of democratic members to change its political complexion, and thus either avoid the fearful contingency of such a decision, or, if too late for that, to have it overruled. This precedent is not without a tolerably close modern parallel in national affairs.

The case was ably argued in the supreme court at the December term, 1839, upon its merits and continued to the June term, 1840. This was during the heat of the presidential canvass of that year. If the case was now decided adversely to the aliens the State might be lost to the democracy. There was a general apprehension that such would be the decision. And now Judge Smith, the only democrat on the supreme bench, sharing in the apprehension, clandestinely pointed out to counsel a defect in the record, consisting in a clerical error. A motion to dismiss was thereupon founded, because it appeared by the record that the case argued was alleged to have occurred at a time when by the laws of the State, as the court must judicially take notice, no general election could be held, to-wit, on the 6th of August, 1839, the year meant being 1838. For the purpose of correcting the record a continuance was granted to the December term, which put it beyond the presidential election in November, 1840. The achievement of discovering the flaw in the record was accounted a remarkable stroke of legal acumen.

When the case came up finally for decision at the December term, 1840, it was found that the constitutional question upon which it was expected the case should turn, was not really before the court, but simply a question under the election law of 1829: If any judge of election shall knowingly admit any person to vote, not qualified according to law, he shall forfeit and pay to the county the sum of $100; and any person presenting himself to vote, and his qualification be suspected, he shall swear that he is a resident of the county; has resided in the State six months next preceding the election; is 21 years old and has not before voted at that election. The court held that, as it was admitted that one Kyle, upon the reception of whose vote the question was made, possessed all the qualifications required by the affidavit, under the law of 1829, it would have simply been superogatory either to challenge him or to have administered the oath to him; and therefore the court below, in fining the judges of election, erred, and the case was reversed. The broad and important question of alien suffrage under the constitution, did not arise in the case, and no opinion of the court was expressed upon it. Judge Smith, however, not to disappoint partisan expectation, took occasion, in a separate opinion elaborated at great length, to argue the constitutional question, quoting freely from a speech of James Buchanan made in Congress on the admission of Michigan as a State.*

Meanwhile the bill to reorganize the Supreme court was pending before the legislature, and with the rendition of this decision by the court, it was circulated about by the politicians, and boldly charged by Douglas, in a speech made in the lobby of the house, that the main question had been purposely evaded by the court to allay the apprehensions of democrats as to the alien vote, and to conciliate their favor, with the object of defeating the bill.

" Douglas," says Gov. Ford, " had been one of the counsel for the aliens, and it appeared from his speech, that he and Judge Smith had been in constant communication in relation to the progress of the case. Judge Smith, (I regret to say it of a man who is no more), was an active, bustling, ambitious and turbulent member of the Democratic party. He had for a long time aimed to be elected to the U. S. Senate: his devices and intrigues to this end had been innumerable. In fact he never lacked a plot to advance himself, or blow up some other person. He was a laborious and ingenious schemer in politics, but his plans were always too complex and ramified for his power to execute them. Being always unsuccessful himself, he was delighted with the mishaps alike of friends and enemies, and was ever chuckling over the defeat or blasted hopes of some one. In this case he sought to gain credit with the leading democrats, by the part he took, and affected to take, in the alien case as he had before in the case of the secretary of State. He it was who privately suggested to counsel the defect in the record which resulted in the continuance in June 1840, and during the whole time the case was pending, with the same view, he was giving out to Douglas and others, the probable opinion of the court. He affirmed that the judges at one time all had their opinions written ready to deliver, and all but himself decided against the aliens; and that the case would have been decided if he had not discovered the aforesaid defect in the record. Upon his authority Douglas denounced the court and brought all these charges against the whig judges, and endeavored to make it appear that they had now only evaded a decision for the time being, in the vain hope of stopping the career of the legislature. The judges on their part, denied all these charges; and Judge Smith uniting with the Whig judges, published their denial in the *Sangamon Journal* newspaper, published at Springfield." Gov. Ford further adds, "and there is now no doubt that the whole of it was false."

In this connection we subjoin the following correspondence:

"HOUSE OF REPRESENTATIVES, SPRINGFIELD, January 26, 1841.
"*To William Wilson, Theophilus W. Smith, Thomas C. Brown and Samuel D. Lockwood, Judges of the Supreme Court of the State of Illinois:*

"Mr. McClernand, a member of this house, (who is now speaking) has made the following statements, in substance, in his speech in favor of the bill to reorganize the judiciary of this State. 'I am authorized to say, and I do say on my own responsibility, if any such responsibility is needed, that the judges of the supreme court prepared an opinion against the right of foreigners to vote at the last June term of that court; but on account of objections made by counsel to a mistake in the record, they withheld their opinions, but did so most reluctantly.

"The opinion has gone abroad that these judges have made the decision recently delivered on the subject of the right of foreigners to vote, in order to defeat the bill under consideration and to prevent these judges from going on the circuit.

"This communication is made to call your attention to the statements, and I think it but due to yourselves that an answer should be made to

* See case of Thomas Spragins v. H. H. Houghton in the Ill. S. C. reports.

these [statements], as deductions may and will be made from silence which would seem to imply an acquiescence in the truth of these statements.

"Desiring to know whether these allegations are true, I trust an answer will be given.   Yours,
                                    "JOHN J. HARDIN."

                              "SPRINGFIELD, January 26, 1841.
"*John J. Hardin, Esq.*

"DEAR SIR: Your letter of to-day has just been received, and we proceed to answer it without hesitation.

"In doing so, we cannot, however, but express our great astonishment at the character of the statement to which you refer. You say that Mr. McClernand, a member of the house of representatives, has asserted in debate, in sustance [here follows a quotation of the language as given by Hardin.]

"To this statement we give the most unqualified denial in all its parts; neither of the members of the court having ever prepared or written any opinion against the right of aliens to vote at elections.

"In reference to the mistake in the record, the error alluded to was discovered by one of the judges, and suggested to the counsel in the cause, as interposing a supposed difficulty in coming to a decision, which, with a subsequent motion made by counsel for the plaintiff in error to dismiss the cause for that reason, and for the further reason, that the cause was a feigned and not a real one, produced the continuance of the cause, as will be seen by a copy of the motion herewith enclosed.

"As to the insinuation that the decision was made at this time to defeat the judiciary bill, we reply that it is in all its parts equally unjust, and without a pretence for its justification. Having been repeatedly urged to come to a decision of the cause, and having been moreover assured that individuals were industriously engaged in circulating reports that the judges had opinions written against the right of aliens to vote, and that as soon as the judiciary bill before the legislature was defeated, these opinions would be delivered. To refute these groundless assertions, on this subject, we concluded to decide the case without further delay, having no other means of refuting these aspersions.

"We have thus promptly complied with your request, and we cannot close this communication without remarking on the great injustice done to ourselves, not only by the statements referred to, but numerous other slanders which, in our situation, we have no means of repelling.

We have the honor to be, respectfully,
          Your obedient servants,
                              THOS. W. SMITH,
                              SAMUEL D. LOCKWOOD,
                              WM. WILSON,
                              THOMAS C. BROWN."

With this contradiction, McClernand, under date of January 29, called upon his informant, Mr. Douglas, to sustain him—inviting immediate attention to the subject. Besides Douglas, six other gentlemen, viz: A. R. Dodge, V. Hickox, J. H. Ralston, John Pearson, M. McConnell, and J. A. McDougal, all of whom derived their information from Judge Smith alone, furnished letters, some of which state positively that Smith had informed them distinctly that all the judges had their opinions written out and ready to deliver at the June term, and others that they understood from him that he (Smith) was thus prepared.* There is now no doubt that Smith made the former statement, nor is there any doubt that it was false.

"As to Judge Smith," says Gov. Ford, "he made nothing by all his intrigues. By opposing the reform bill, he fell out and quar-

---

*See Illinois State Register, Feb. 5, 1841.

relled with the leaders of his party. He lost the credit he had gained by being the democratic champion on the bench, and failed to be elected to the United States Senate; and was put back to the laborious duty of holding circuit courts."

The judiciary bill produced much excitement and party animosity at the capital, both among members and the goading, insatiate lobby vultures. It was no easy task for the dominant party to rally its force to the blind support of a measure so purely one of revenge. A great deal of opposition came from the friends and interests of the 9 circuit court judges, every one of whom would be repealed out of office and the majority of whom were democrats. However, the bill finally passed both houses. The council of revision returned it with their objections, urged at length.

The council regarded the requirement that the supreme court. with five additional judges, hold circuit courts in all the counties of the State; attend at the seat of government, and act as council of revision during the sessions of the legislature, and preside in the supreme court until all the business of that tribunal was disposed of, as physically impossible. Owing to the magnitude of the circuit court business, the nine circuit judges, for no fault of theirs, had been unable to attend to it and fully subserve the interests of the public. To thrust all this business upon the hands of the supreme judges, in addition to their other duties, would result in such delay in the administration of justice as to be equivalent to a denial of it. The law would prejudice the rights of citizens and the character of the State.

The bill, however, was re-passed, notwithstanding the objections of the council, in the senate, by a large majority, but in the house by barely one. A solemn protest by the undersigned members, many of whom have since attained imperishable renown, was spread upon the journal, February 26, 1841. After stating their objections at length, they sum up as follows :

1st. The bill violates the great principles of government by subjecting the judiciary to the legislature.

2d. It is a fatal blow at the independence of the judges, and the constitutional term of their office.

3d. It is a measure not asked for, or wished by the people.

4th. It will greatly increase the expenses of our courts or greatly diminish their utility.

5th. It will give the courts a political and partisan character, thereby impairing public confidence in their decisions.

6th. It will impair our standing in the opinion of other States and the world.

7th. It is a party measure for party purposes, from which no practical good to the people can possibly arise, but which may be the source of innumerable evils. * * The blow had already fallen, but they felt impelled to point out the danger of the measure, its impolicy and its usurpation, in order at least that the despotism of a momentary majority may not become a precedent for succeeding enormities, or future crimes. We have struggled ineffectually to guard the principles of our government from unhallowed innovation, and contended for the supremacy of the constitution.

(Signed): Joseph Gillespie, John J. Brown, Leander Munsell, William B. Archer, John F. Charles, Isaac Funk, Alden Hull, John Darnielle, Geo. W. Waters, Cyrus Edwards, James T. Cunningham John Bennett, Thos. Threlkeld, A. Lincoln, J. M. McLean, H. W. Thornton, Wm. A. Marshal, James M. Bradford John J. Hardin, Jeremiah Cox, Peter Menard, jr., W. H. Henderson, James Reynolds, W. W. Bailey,

D. M. Woodson, E. B. Webb, John Denny, Isaac Froman, Jas. A. Beal, Josiah Francis, Daniel Gray, James Parkinson, John Canady, Alexander Phillips, James N. Brown.

The five additional supreme judges elected by the legislature under this law were, Thomas Ford, (subsequently gov.) Sidney Breese, Walter B. Scates, Samuel .H. Treat, and Stephen A. Douglas,* all democrats. By this means all apprehension was allayed in the democratic breast regarding the continued support of the alien vote, so far as any interference from the supreme court was concerned. Nor did the majority of that court now question the right of the executive to appoint his own secretary of State; and had the question been now presented to the court, the McClernand-Field decision would have been overruled. Such is party influence upon the judiciary. One of the newly appointed judges, writing of this reorganization of the court says: The highest courts are but indifferent tribunals for the settlement of great political question; * * when any great political question on which parties are are arrayed comes up for decision, the utmost which can be expected of them is, an able and learned argument in favor of their own party, whose views they must naturally favor.† The court, however, as newly organized, proved not entirely acceptable to the dominant party; the judges generally enjoyed great personal popularity, but the bench became the subject of frequent malevolent assaults by the legislature. That body, fresh from an exultant constituency, imbued often with extreme partisan views, could illy brook any independence in the other departments of government.‡

At this session of 1844-5, the legislature, ostensibly as a measure of retrenchment, passed resolutions drafted by Mr. Trumbull, who was not a member though an aspirant for the ermine, calling

*The last named gentleman had been of counsel for the aliens, had derived his information of how the case was going to be decided in June preceding from Judge Smith, had obtained the continuance then on the defect in the record as pointed out by him, had made a violent attack upon the old judges by a characteristic speech in the lobby, and had furnished McClernand the data upon which the latter denounced the court; in view of all of which, it seems strange that he had sought and obtained a position side by side with the gentleman he had traduced and attempted so much to bring into disrepute. Partisan scheming and the cravings of office could not well go further.
The new judges were charged with partisan conduct, by the whig press of the period, in the secret appointment of a clerk of the supreme court. Ebenezer Peck, it seems, as a member of the legislature had originally opposed the judiciary bill; but his position became suddenly changed, and the bill passed the House by one majority over the objections of the council. After taking their seats, the new members of the court had no consultation with the old judges on the subject of the clerkship, and not a word was said in open court about removing the incumbent, Duncan. Indeed, one of them had given out that to avoid the imputation of being a partisan court, the clerkship was not to be disturbed. The public astonishment was not inconsiderable, therefore, when shortly after its adjournment, Peck announced himself as the clerk by appointment of the majority of the court.—*Sangamon Journal.*
†Ford's History.
‡At the session of 1842-43, there was an effort made to remove Judge Brown, on the ground of incompetency. This gentleman, whose home was at Shawneetown, upon the reorganization of that court, had been assigned to the remote Galena circuit, with the view to render his position uncomfortable and irksome, and worry him into a resignation. This failing, four lawyers from his circuit, viz: C. S. Hempstead, Thomas Drummond, Thompson Campbell, and A. L. Holmes, filed their specifications charging that he had not that natural strength of intellect, and lacked the legal and literary learning, requisite and indispensable to a proper discharge of the high and responsible duties devolving upon him as a judge of the supreme court; that his opinions delivered in that court were written and revised by others, and that his decisions upon the circuit had been the mere echo of some favorite attorney; and that by nature, education and habit, he was wholly unfit for his high position. Their stinging language indicated something more than a purpose to solely subserve the public good. The senate declined to participate in the examination of the charges. The house in committee of the whole went several times into the investigation of them, but finally asked to be discharged from their further consideration and so the matter ended and Judge Brown retained his seat.—House Journal, session 1842-43.

on the judges and governor to relinquish a portion of their salaries. This was refused, on the ground of the principle involved as to the right of the legislature to make such a request. It implied a control to a certain extent, of a co-ordinate department of government, however the request coupled with it the consent of the incumbents. Although their salaries were fixed, coercion was in this manner sought through the fear of losing public favor, interest, and popularity. It was an unworthy means, and destructive of the first great principle of free constitutional government —the independence of the co-ordinate branches to each other. The supreme court, as constituted under the act of Feb. 10th, 1841, was finally dissolved by operation of the constitution of 1848, the judges going out of office December 4th, that year.

CHAPTER XXXIX.

1842—1846—ADMINISTRATION OF GOVERNOR FORD.

*The Campaign—Life and Character of Gov. Ford—Lieut. Gov.
Moore—Means of Relief from the Financial Embarrassments—
The State at the Turning Point—Restoration of her Credit.*

As early as December, 1841, the State democratic convention
met at Springfield, and nominated Adam W. Snyder, of St. Clair,
and John Moore, of McLean, as their candidates for governor and
lieutenant governor at the election of August 1842. In the spring
following, ex-Gov. Joseph Duncan and W. H. Henderson became
the candidates of the whig party for the same offices. Charles
W. Hunter and Frederick Collins were also, respectively, candidates for the same positions. Mr. Snyder was an effective speaker
and possessed an ostentatious and plausable address. He had
been a member of congress and state senator, and in the latter
capacity, to gain the favor of the Mormons, who were looming up
in the State as a considerable political power by reason of their
unity, had been largely instrumental in the passage of the
obnoxious " Mormon charters," by which that modern sect were
placed above and beyond the laws of the State—constituted a
petty sovereignty within their corporate limits, whence they issued
forth, committed their depredations upon the neighborhoods outside, retired to their legal citadel of Nauvoo, and defied the process
of any court of the county to follow them.

The Mormons, driven from Missouri by a democratic governor,
denied protection by a democratic president, but in congress countenanced by Messrs. Clay and John T. Stuart, in 1840 had given
their support to the whigs. But now Joe Smith, their prophet,
issued his proclamation exhorting his followers in favor of Mr.
Snyder, and " declaring Judge Douglas to be a master spirit."
This mandate showed the whigs that the democracy had, by the
extension of these very liberal charters, woed the Mormons with
success. But the odium of this sect was already rapidly spreading over the entire State; and of this circumstance, Gov. Duncan
as the whig candidate, who was not concerned in the passage of
the obnoxious charters, sought to take advantage, and more than
retrieve from the people the whig loss by the Mormon defection.
Indeed things bore a very promising look in that direction. But
at this juncture Mr. Snyder sickened and died, and the new choice
as the standard bearer of the democracy for governor, fell upon
the Hon. Thomas Ford, who, although well known as a
jurist, was in no wise prominently connected with politics,

and certainly not with the passage of the obnoxious Mormon charters. The democracy apprehending the drift of public opinion, placed Judge Ford in the position made vacant by by the death of Mr. Snyder, because of his availability. It is doubtful whether any of the democratic leaders, in the then temper of the people toward the Mormons, could have been elected over so adroit and courageous a competitor as Duncan. The death of Snyder proved the triumph of the democracy.

Besides the odious Mormon charters and the alleged intrigues and corrupt bargains between certain politicians and the prophet, the other public questions of the day were, a revival of the work on the canal, repeal of the bank charters, and the claim of Wisconsin to 14 of our northern counties. The position of the new democratic candidate upon the questions was variously and oppositely reported in the public press of different sections of the State, to be everywhere in harmony with the varying, but prevailing, sentiments of the people. Much allowance ought to be made, however, for the statements of the press during a heated political campaign. Duncan charged Ford during the canvass with concealing his opinions on all these questions.

The following are the number of votes cast for governor in 1842: For Thomas Ford, 46,901; Joseph Duncan, 38,584; Charles W. Hunter, 909. For lieutenant governor: John Moore, 45,567; W. H. Henderson, 38,426; Frederick Collins, 905.

Thomas Ford was born at Uniontown, Pa., in the year 1800. He was a half-brother to George Forquer, his senior by six years. Their mother, after the death of her first husband, married Robt. Ford, who, in 1802 was killed in the mountains of Pennsylvania by Indians. She was left in indigent circumstances, with a large family, mostly girls. With a view to better her condition, she, in 1804, removed to Missouri, where it had been customary by the Spanish government to give land to actual settlers, but upon her arrival at St. Louis she found the country ceded to the United States, and this liberal policy, unlike as at present, changed by the new ownership. After some sickness to herself and family she finally removed to Illinois, and settled some three miles south of Waterloo, but the following year moved closer to the Mississippi bluffs. Here the boys received their first schooling under the instructions of Mr. Humphrey, for which they walked three miles.

Their mother, though lacking in a thorough education, was a woman of superior mental endowments, joined to energy and determination of character. She inculcated in her children those high-toned moral principles which distinguished her sons in public life. She exercised a rigid economy to provide her children an education, but George Forquer, her oldest son, at an early age had to quit school, to aid by his labor in the support of the family. He acquired the trade of a house-joiner, afterwards became a merchant, failed, and studied law, which his vigorous intellect enabled him to readily master in spite of a defective early education. He was determined and ambitious, had a good voice and became a fluent and elegant speaker. He filled many public offices; was a member of the legislature from Monroe, secretary of state under Gov. Coles, attorney general, senator from Sangamon, subsequently register of the land office at Springfield, and but for his early death would probably have been elected to the United States senate. Joined to his other intellectual qualities was rare merit as a writer. He was of an amiable and generous disposition, and was successful in accumulating a considerable estate.*

The younger brother, Thomas Ford, with somewhat better opportunities, received a better, though limited common school, education. His mind gave early promise of superior endowments, with an inclination for mathematics. His proficiency attracted the attention of the Hon. Daniel P. Cook, in whom young Ford found an efficient patron and friend. The grateful heart of the *protege* did not forget its benefactor. On page 73 of his History of Illinois, Ford pays that gentleman such unwonted compliments as no other of all his public cotemporaries receives at his hand. Through Cook, young Ford turned his attention to the law, but Forquer, then merchandising, regarding his education defective, sent him to the Transylvania University, where he remained, however, but one term, owing to Forquer's failure in business. On his return he alternated his law reading with teaching school for support. In 1829 Gov. Edwards appointed him prosecuting attorney; in 1831 he was reappointed by Gov. Reynolds; after that he was four times elected a judge, by the legislature, without opposition; twice as circuit judge, judge of Chicago, and as associate judge of the supreme court, when, in 1841, that tribunal through partisan malice was reorganized by the addition of five judges, all democrats. Ford was assigned to the 9th judicial circuit, and at the time of his nomination for governor was holding court in Ogle county. He immediately resigned his office, accepted the nomination and entered upon the canvass. In August he was elected governor. The offices which he held, although perhaps he was willing enough to have them, were unsolicited. He received them upon the true Jefferson principle, never to ask and never to refuse office.

As a lawyer, Gov. Ford stood deservedly high, but his cast of intellect fitted him rather for a writer upon law than a practicing advocate in the courts. In the latter capacity he was void of the moving power of eloquence, so necessary to success. As a judge his written opinions are sound, lucid and able expositions of the law. He was a stranger, in practice, to the tact, skill and insinuating address of the politician; but, as we may well infer from his history, no man of his time had a clearer perception of the wiles and sinuosities of that devious class than he. Yet despite this appreciation, his confidence in the honest purposes of others, joined to indecision or hesitation perhaps, enabled the unscrupulous to deceive him, and in the nondescript Mormon war cause him unwonted trouble and vexation.

As a man, Governor Ford was plain in his demeanor.† He lacked that sanguine and determined boldness and decision of character requisite to fit one for a great political leader. For

*Reynold's Pioneer History.
[† It is related that after the expiration of his term of office, upon the occasion of the assembling of the legislature, which always collected a horde of greedy seekers for subordinate positions at the capitol, a wag pointed him out to a certain "ring" as a formidable aspirant for door-keeper of the house. He was hunted up in his room at the hotel, in the small hours of the night, and approached for a bargain or combination. On discovery the "ring" felt mortified and the ex-governor perhaps not highly flattered.]

money getting he cared little more than would afford him a decent support, and scarcely that. He accumulated no wealth and upon his retirement from the gubernatorial chair he resumed the practice of the law. Gov. Ford was small of stature, slender, dark complexioned, with a profusion of black hair, sharp features, deep set eyes, a pointed, acquiline nose, with a decided twist to one side, and had a small mouth. His appearance was said to be somewhat cynical and he was, perhaps, not without vindictiveness. He was by nature a student, and the traits of his mind fitted him for close thought; though he lacked in imagery, the gift of genius. He had his weak trait; one besetting sin into which his convivial nature betrayed him, and which contributed to his early death.

As an author he deserves our special consideration. He has left to the State in which he was reared, trusted and honored with the highest office in the gift of the people, and which he dearly loved, a legacy in the form of a history, which, though but a fragment comprising his own time, and not topically arranged, will be more and more appreciated with the advance of years.

His writings show a natural flow of compact and forcible thought, never failing to convey the nicest sense. In tracing with his trenchant pen the devious operations of the professional politician, in which he is inimitable, his text is open perhaps to the objections that all his cotemporaries, many of whom have since had their names written high on the scroll of national fame, were mere politicians, and that he fails to discover little else in all their acts and deeds than the selfish promptings for place, power, or some local benefit. It has been inferred—indeed his book is somewhat calculated to to leave such an impression upon the mind of the reader—that it was dictated by spleen, and his enemies have charged it to be the jealous bile of disappointed ambition. But except, perhaps, as to his own administration this is a mistaken view. That he was an accurate observer of his own times, and that he relates events truly and describes men correctly, may aside from the internal conviction which his book produces, be inferred from the fact that he wrote concerning those who survived him, but who have never contradicted him.

The lieutenant-governor elect, John Moore, was born September 8, 1793, in Lincolnshire, England. Bereft of parents at the age of 20 he emigrated to America. Sojourning for a while in Virginia, he located in Hamilton county, Ohio, and about 1830 removed to Illinois, settling permanently at Randolph Grove, McLean county, where he pursued his vocation of wheelright; a trade which he had learned in England. His force of character was such that he speedily rose from obscurity. In 1831 he was elected a justice of the peace; twice afterward to the lower house of the legislature and in 1839 to the State senate. His sterling qualities of head and heart gained him distinction throughout the State, causing his party to designate him as its standard bearer for lieutenant-governor in 1842. On the breaking out of the Mexican war, animated by an ardent patriotism for the cause of his adopted country, he volunteered in the ranks, was chosen lieut. colonel of the 4th regiment, and participated in all its active services. After that, by the partiality of the people, he was twice elected State treasurer, and in that capacity earned the honored soubriquet of "Honest John Moore." He was long and favora-

30

bly known in the State as a consistent leader of the democracy, and died Sept. 23d, 1863.

With the advent of Governor Ford's administration, he sums up the condition of the State as follows:

"The domestic treasury of the State was indebted for the ordinary expenses of government to the amount of about $313,000. Auditor's warrants on the treasury were selling at 50 per cent. discount, and there was no money in the treasury whatever; not even to pay postage on letters. The annual revenues applicable to the payment of ordinary expenses amounted to about $130,000. The treasury was bankrupt; the revenues were insufficient; the people were unable and unwilling to pay high taxes; and the State had borrowed itself out of all credit; a debt of near $10,000,000 had been contracted for the canal, railroads and other purposes. The currency of the State had been annihilated; there was not over $200,000 or $300,000 in good money in the pockets of the whole people, which occasioned a general inability to pay taxes. The whole people were indebted to the merchants, nearly all of whom were indebted to the banks or foreign merchants; and the banks owed everybody, and none were able to pay."

In his message, the governor says:

"We have suffered all the evils of a depreciated paper circulation; the first of which is a great and sudden scarcity of money. The specie, which ought to be in circulation, is locked up in the banks; a large amount of the depreciated paper has been purchased up and held on speculation, and the residue has just been sufficient to keep money of a better character from coming among us. Consequently, we have been left without money, property has fallen unusually low in price, and the products of the farmer have been almost unsaleable. Two courses have operated to prevent an increase of population for a year or two past; one is the prevalent fear of exorbitant taxes; the other the reproach to which we are subject abroad. The remedy for this is obvious. Let it be known in the first place that no oppressive and exterminating taxation is to be resorted to; in the second, we must convince our creditors and the world that the disgrace of repudiation is not countenanced among us—that we are honest and mean to pay as soon as we are able."

In the legislature, which came into power simultaneously with Governor Ford, there was no party in favor of taxation to pay interest on the public debt. Some wanted to make no effort for five or ten years, but await the influx of immigrants, trusting that the future might develope something favorable; all would gladly yield up to the holders of the internal improvement bonds the public works as far as completed, and the lands, railroad iron and other property purchased to carry forward the system, in liquidation of the indebtedness, if they would finish the canal, but this was impracticable for obvious reasons. The great majority were neither willing to tax nor yet to repudiate. Governor Ford, in his message, said: "Although the elections in August last were conducted with warmth on the part of the candidates and people, not more than one or two individuals were found willing to offer their services upon principles of repudiation, and they were unsuccessful." The majority quieted their consciences by the adoption of resolutions recognizing both the moral and legal obligations to pay interest and principal, but that the present ability to do so was out of the question. Outside there were not wanting many who were outspoken in favor of repudiation, contending that neither the legislature nor the State financial agents possessed the power to legally obligate the people to the payment of debts incurred in a scheme of such gross and reckless infatuation as that of the internal improvement system of the State.

Another source of anxiety and trouble to thoughtful and conservative men, was the prostrate banks. They had been for a long time odious to the people on account of their oft infirmities. Any extremity pursued toward them would meet the hearty approbation of the people, however such course might be detrimental to the country. Hence politicians, who looked only to popularity with their constituents, were clamorous for the repeal of the bank charters. Illinois bonds in market were worth only 14 cents on the dollar at the time. The State owned bank stock to the amount of $3,100,000, which it was urged by the repudiating party should be returned to the banks in exchange for State bonds held as collateral; that the latter should be forced upon the market as assets, and with the proceeds pay the debts of the banks. This would have further depressed Illinois bonds. The bank stock was much more valuable than State bonds, the bills of the bank being worth about 50 cents on the dollar, yet the madness of the hour demanded a surrender and even exchange.

These were some of the obstacles in the way of harmonious deliberation for the best interests of the State. But fertile brains were immersed in thought to devise ways out of the embarrassing circumstances under which the State labored. The canal, upon which work had been longer continued than the other public works, was greatly advanced, requiring only some $3,000,000 more to finish it upon the first magnificent plan. It was now proposed to make of this work a fulcrum by which to raise the credit of the State out of its slough of despond. And as some sort of canal was better than none, it was further proposed to finish the remainder of it by abandoning the deep cut for the shallow, which could be accomplished at about half the price, or $1,600,000. The completion of the canal would inspire confidence abroad, invite emigration, and revive the drooping energies of the people at home. The plan was to induce the canal bondholders to advance this amount on the pledge of the canal, its lands and revenues, as a first mortgage, postponing all creditors who should refuse to contribute until the former were reimbursed. It seems that Justin Butterfield, an eminent lawyer of Chicago, was entitled to the credit of suggesting this plan, which, after a brief delay, proved successful. He first mentioned it to Arthur Bronson, a heavy operator in Illinois stocks, and a large landholder in the northern part of the State, who was on a visit to Chicago, in the summer of 1842, looking after his interests. Mr. Butterfield further imbued Mr. Michael Ryan with this idea, and the latter, when shortly after in New York, enlisted Mr. David Leavitt, Mr. Bronson, and other operators in Illinois stocks, both in London and New York, in the scheme. The plan received definite shape from these financiers, and upon the meeting of the legislature, December, 1842, awaited the sanction of that body.

But the more absorbing question of repealing the bank charters and winding up those institutions, boded evil to the success of the new canal loan, even if the bill to convey the canal in trust for the advance of $1,600,000, did become a law. The financial embarrassments of the State would probably become involved in an inextricable coil, to disentangle which would consume years of time. There was a question of law as to the vested rights of the banks under their charters, which they asserted their determina-

tion to contests with all the law's delay that the United States
courts afforded, if forcible liquidation was attempted. In the
meantime, their assest would be absorbed in litigation or squandered by villainous officials. It would, besides, produce mistrust
and a want of confidence in the minds of capitalists abroad, upon
whom we depended for the new loan to complete the canal. If
the bank charters could be repealed and banking corporations
arbitrarily crushed, what guarrantee was there that a succeeding
legislature would not treat the new canal company the same
way?

Gov. Ford, for the best interests of the State, determined upon
a just compromise with the banks, and labored earnestly to that
end. But with the convening of the legislature, the retiring
executive, Gov Carlin, (says Ford), "recommended repeal in his
valedictory message. When he first came to the seat of government he showed me his message, recommending wise, just, and
honorable measures to the banks. He also showed me what he
had prepared on the subject of repeal, assuring me that he had
decided not to put it in. But shortly afterwards, some of the
ultraists got a hold of him, and induced him to alter his message,
by recommending repeal. This recommendation embarrassed me
then, and has embarrassed me ever since. Here was a respectable recommendation of something more ultra than I thought was
warranted by the best interests of the State. It gave countenance
to the ultraists; they could rally around it, win a character for
stern and inflexable democrats. It at once put them ahead of the
new governor and his friends." As a further source of opposition
to the banks, Gov. Ford continues: "There was quite a party
out of the legislature, expectants of office and others, who
hoped that if the banks were repealed out of existence and
put into forcible liquidation, some of them might be appointed commissioners and put in charge of their specie and effects.
It was known that if the bank debts were paid pro rata, a large
amount of specie would remain on hand for a year or more, the
use of which could be made profitable in the meantime. Then
there were to be bank attorneys and agents in collecting and
securing debts; and the whole would furnish a handsome picking
for the buzzards and vultures who hang about lobbies and surround legislatures. As for myself, I decided at once in favor of a
compromise; and I gave notice to all these greedy expectants of
office, who were hanging around with eyes straining to devour
their substance, that if the banks were repealed, and the appointment of commissioners was vested in me, none of them could
expect an appointment. This I know cooled some of them."

The governor, who labored under a greater apprehension in regard to the power of the ultra anti-bank party than there was
perhaps any call for, drafted the bank bill himself, giving it
rather a higher sounding title than its provisions deserved or its
effects would warrant, namely "an act to diminish the State debt
and put the State bank into liquidation." The officers of the bank
were well apprised of its provisions and had agreed to them. "It
was then," says the governor, "shown to Mr. McClernand, chairman of the finance committee. Gen. Shields, Judge Douglas, and
myself, were invited to be present at the meeting. I was desirous
of having the bill introduced as a democratic measure, and

for this reason the whigs of the committee were not invited
to be present. The project was stated to the committee, and all
the members agreed to it but one, and he was soon argued out of
his objections by Judge Douglas. The next day it was introduced
into the lower house as a report from the finance committee.
This circumstance put Mr. McClernand in the position of being
its principal advocate; and it was soon known to be a favorite
measure of the new administration." It met with general favor
among the members.

The opposition to it came mainly from the outside expectants
of office in winding up the concern. Says Ford: "Lyman Trumbull, secretary of State, put himself at the head of this opposition.
In taking this ground, Mr. Trumbull was probably less influenced
by a hope of pecuniary advantages to himself, than by a desire to
serve his friends, to be considered a thorough-going party man,
and by a hatred of McClernand and Shields, who both favored
the measure.*

"As soon as McClernand took his position on the bank question,
Trumbull arrayed himself in opposition. He pretended that
McClernand's measure was not sufficiently democratic; in fact,
that nothing could be democratic in relation to the banks but to
tear them up and destroy them root and branch, and he hoped to
fasten upon McClernand the imputation of being a " milk and
water democrat,' and thus lower him in the estimation of the party.
At the instance of Ebenezer Peck, clerk of the supreme court, and
others, he put up a notice that he would address the lobby on the
subject, in the evening after the legislature had adjourned. Most
of the members attended to hear his discourse.

"The next day McClernand, who possessed a kind of bold and
denunciatory eloquence, came down upon Trumbull and his confederates in a speech in the house, which for argument, eloquence,
and statesmanship was far superior to Trumbull's. This speech
silenced all opposition thereafter to the bill in the house. The out-
door opposition, after this, forseeing signal defeat in the house,
turned their attention to the senate. * * * Trumbull took his
stand in the lobby and sent in amendments of every sort, to be
proposed by Crain, of Washington, Catlin, of St. Clair, and others.
The mode of attack was to load it down with obnoxious amendments, so as to make it odious to its authors; and Trumbull openly
boasted that the bill would be so altered and amended in the senate that the framers in the house would not know their own bantling when it came back to them. From this moment I determined

[* "His quarrel with McClernand sprung out of his appointment to the office of secretary of State two years before. McClernand was a member of the legislature in
1848, but not being an applicant then, Judge Douglas was appointed at the beginning
of the session without opposition. But when Douglas was elected a judge of the supreme court, toward the end of the session, McClernand incited his friends to get up
in his favor a strong recommendation from the members of the legislature for the vacant office. * * * Gov. Carlin had already allowed the members of the legislature and his political friends to dictate to him the appointment of McClernand on a
former occasion He had lately yielded to similar dictation in the appointment of
Douglas in opposition to his own wishes, for he had previously promised the office to
Isaac N Morris, of Quincy. [He] subsequently used his influence with the legislature
to get Morris elected to the office of president of the board of canal commissioners.
But this contest between McClernand and Trumbull took place at the close of the session, when the governor had nothing more to hope or fear from that legislature. * *
Trumbull was nominated to the senate; and McClernand and Shields as immediately
went to work in that body to procure the rejection of his appointment. They came
within a vote or two of defeating his nomination. Ever since then there has been no
good feeling between McClernand and Trumbull."—Ford's History.

to remove Trumbull from the office of secretary of State, [which was done]. The obnoxious amendments were rejected, and the bill passed by a large majority, and was approved by the council of revision. Judge Douglas, notwithstanding he had advised the measure before the finance committee, voted against it in council. [The bill passed the house by 107 for to 4 against.] A bill somewhat similar, passed in relation to the Shawneetown bank. By these two bills the domestic treasury of the State was at once relieved, and another debt of $2,300,000 was extinguished immediately.

"The legislature at this session also passed laws for the sale of State lands and property; for the reception of the distributive share of the State in the proceeds of the sales of the public lands; for the redemption of interest bonds hypothecated to Macalister and Stebbins, and for a loan of $1,600,000 to complete the Illinois and Michigan canal. By these various laws provision was made for the reduction of the State debt to the amount of eight or nine millions of dollars. * * From this moment the affairs of the State began to brighten and improve. Auditor's warrants rose to 85 and 90 per cent. State bonds rose from 14 to 20, 30 and 40 per cent. The banks began to pay out their specie, and within three months time the currency was restored, confidence was increased in the prospects of the State, and the tide of emigration was once more directed to Illinois."*

But the new canal loan of $1,600,000 met with delay in its negotiation. European capitalists were well disposed toward it, but there was no reliable evidence placed before them as to the value of the canal; nor were they willing to take the loan without some evidence of public faith and recognition of the obligation of the State, and some legislation for taxation to make at least a beginning to pay interest on the public debt.

In his message to the legislature of 1844-5, therefore, Gov. Ford recommended taxation. In September preceding, however, Mr. William S. Wait, of Bond county, through his published letter to the governor against taxation, had already afforded him an opportunity to make known his views in a public letter written in reply, which did great credit to his sentiments of honor and capacity as a sagacious statesman. It gained a wide circulation and produced so favorable an effect in Europe as to immediately cause the completion of the subscription to the loan. The State revenue was derived from a land tax, a portion of which had been in 1827 diverted to the counties then generally in debt, to aid them toward the erection of court-houses and jails, which had long since been built, and the governor in his message says:

"This land tax ought to be resumed to the State treasury. Frequent attempts have been made to effect this, but without success. The objection has always been that there was more land taxable in the old than in the new part of the State, and that the measure would be unequal. [Under the compact with congress in the enabling act of 1818, lands were not to be taxed till five years after their entry.] I would recommend that the additional revenue thus derived, and such additional tax as the legislature in its wisdom will provide for, be formed into a fund, the proceeds and increase of which shall be sacred and dedicated to the extinction of a portion, however small at first, of the interest on the public debt. Whatever we do in this way, ought to have the great-

*Ford's History.

est permanency. * * And thus by setting a limit to the fears and imaginations of men in relation to the huge phantom of expected taxes, we might reasonably calculate to restore ourselves in the estimation of mankind, turn the tide of emigration again into our country, accompanied by wealth and intelligence."

But from various causes quite an opposition had been raised to the administration. This grew out of the "Morman war," and the jealousies of political aspirants. Two bank commissioners, a secretary of state, three judges of the supreme court, and a U. S. senator had been appointed. For these offices there were many applicants, and the disappointed ones joined their influence to oppose the administration measures. Many charges were brought against the administration and an investigating committee was appointed, which, while it made a thorough inquisition of the executive offices and found nothing amiss, still did not possess the magnanimity to make any report at all—"the newest way of discrediting an administration," which ought to be patented, says his excellency.

The main administration measure at this session was a supplemental canal bill, and to provide for paying a portion of the interest on the State debt. It provided for a transfer of 1 mill from the county to the State tax, so as to make the State tax 3 mills, the latter to remain permanent, and together with all surplus moneys in the treasury constitute an "Interest Fund," to be sacredly set apart for the payment of interest on the public debt. The bill giving to the foreign bondholders two canal trustees and to the State but one, afterwards divided and passed in two laws, was prepared in accordance with the propositions of the foreign creditors, as made by the Boston committee, Governor Davis, of Massachusetts, and Mr. Leavitt, of New York, being present during the latter part of the session.

Besides disaffected democrats, a strenuous effort was made to array the whig party in opposition to this measure. To this end a secret meeting of the whig leaders was called to form a coalition with the southern democrats. But to these intrigues, fraught with mischief to the credit and prosperity of the State, Judge Stephen T. Logan, of Springfield, N. D. Strong, of Alton, and other whigs, set their faces as steel; and in the house these machinations met with signal defeat, the bill passing by some 20 majority. In the senate, after a substitue offered by Edwards and amendments by Worthington and Constable, (whigs,) all tending to its defeat, were voted down, that body refused to order the bill to a third reading—19 to 22. Now followed much parliamentary manuevering, and charges of bribery and corruption were freely made.

"The vote on the bill in the senate being reconsidered, it was referred to a select committee, together with another bill of an important character, which had already passed the house of representatives. It was known that one senator would not vote for the tax and the canal both in the same bill. By their connection the tax was made to appear as a local measure, intended only for the benefit of the north. The committee, therefore, divided the bill. They struck out of the canal bill all that related to a tax, and they struck out all of the bill referred with it, and inserted the taxing part in that. And these two bills being now reported back to the senate, the senate concurred in their passage as thus amended. They were sent back to the house the same hour for concurrence, which was given; and thus these important measures passed into laws; or rather they wabbled through the legislature. To Thomas M. Kilpatrick, senator from Scott, is due the honor of the good management in the senate, in dividing and amending the measure, and thus securing its passage. I give the facts, curious as they may appear, to illustrate the fertile genius of western men, and as a specimen of the modes of legislation in a new country."*

Thus was shown a recognition of our obligation to pay the public debt, and a willingness to contribute to do so as far as lay in our power. This, too, at a period of sore trial to the people of the State. For the two preceding seasons the crops had been a partial failure; the unprecedented freshets of the Mississippi, the Illinois and many other streams in the State, in 1844, had destroyed a large amount of property, and laid waste many a homestead; and an unusual amount of sickness had not only followed in the wake of the floods, but generally pervaded the country.

Another "Hard Times" measure, adopted at this session, was the reduction of interest to 6 per cent. During the flush times, prior to 1840, when money was abundant and unlimited, the people overtraded themselves, and, finally, on settlement, gave their promissory notes, bearing 12 per cent. interest, which they did rather than be sued and have their property sold under execution. The reader will have noticed that for twenty-five years the tendency of legislation in Illinois, and indeed all western states, a tendency not yet arrested, was to favor the debtor classes.

At the close of Gov. Ford's administration,† we find the domestic debt for the ordinary expenses of the State government to be only $31,212, instead of $313,000 as when he came into office; now, without the sum due from the general government to the school fund being paid, there was in the treasury $9,260, when at that time it did not contain enough to pay postage on a letter; now, auditor's warrants were worth over 90 cents on the dollar, then, not 50; now, people were in the main out of debt, then they were overwhelmed with private liabilities. The banks had been put into liquidation and gradually wound up, their depreciated circulation retired and replaced by a reasonable abundance of specie and the issues of solvent banks from other States. By exchanging the bank stock of the State for the bonds, and the sale of public property, about $3,000,000 of the public debt had been extinguished; and by the canal, then promising to be completed within the next year, some $5,000,000 more were effectually provided for in the enhanced value of the canal property, and the fact of its conveyance in trust to the foreign canal bond holders; being a reduction of some $8,000,000, extinguished and provided for, during Gov. Fords' administration, notwithstanding its begining under circumstances the most adverse and unpromising. The State, which for years before had been overwhelmed with debt; which had not for 4 years paid even interest on its bonds, and loth to even recognize its public debt; which was on the brink of repudiation—discredited throughout the civilized world, had dur-

*1 Ford's History.
†See his message, Dec. 1846.

ing his administration its credit greatly restored, and was enabled to borrow $1,600,000 to complete the canal. It now had a population of about 700,000, and the 1½ mill tax to be exclusively applied as interest on the public debt, would yield for the year 1846, $125,000. With the dissipation of the clouds of threatening dishonor, emigration, with an increasing tide, again sought our lands for homes, and population was augmenting faster than any previous time. The list of taxable property, and the aggregate wealth of the State, was rapidly on the increase. From the people here, erst so anxious to sell out and depart the State, the terrors of high taxation had been removed, and now when opportunity to sell and leave was almost daily presented, they were content to remain. The reputation of Illinois before the civilized world, now stood forth almost without spot or blemish, the peer in honor and credit of any in the sisterhood of States. The year 1845 was the turning point in her financial embarrassments, and marks the beginning of her since unabated prosperity and march to greatness.

"We may date the commencement of our returning prosperity to the passage of that law"—the law requiring the banks of this State to put their affairs in process of gradual liquidation—says Gov. French in his inaugural message. This law, we have seen, was conceived by the brain and drafted by the hand of Gov. Ford himself; through his admirable letter in reply to W. S. Wait, of Bond county, our foreign creditors took heart and subscribed the money for the completion of the canal; he had the courage to recommend taxation, and suggested the permanant tax or "interest fund" bill, which after a severe struggle became a law. We see thus the directing finger of Gov. Ford in every important measure which aided in restoring the credit of the State, and snatching it from the jaws of repudiation and dishonor. And this was done, not with the united support of his own party friends, but in the face of their many intrigues, jealousies and party machinations. Illinois was most fortunate in securing his services for its helm of State at this critical juncture of her financial career; and posterity will ever owe a debt of gratitude to him for his clear insight into the condition of her affairs, the measures which his genius brought forward for her extrication, and the fidelity with which he discharged the high trust reposed in him at this crisis in her history. In his valedictory message he says: "Without having indulged in wasteful or extravagant habits of living, I retire from office poorer than I came in; and go to private life with a full determination not to seek again any place in the government." Gov. Ford died, Nov. 2d, 1850, at Peoria, in very indigent circumstances.

CHAPTER XL.

THE ILLINOIS AND MICHIGAN CANAL.

Trials and Troubles Incident to its Construction.

The importance of a canal connecting the waters of Lake Michigan and those of the Illinois river, and thence by other navigable streams hundred miles in extent to the Gulf of Mexico, was at a very early time appreciated, and its consummation fondly cherished. The French traders and voyageurs in their explorations of the west, between one and two centuries since, passed with their boats from Lake Michigan into the Des Plaines at some seasons of the year, via the Calumet river and lake. The portage between the south branch of the Chicago river and the Des Plaines was only some five or six miles. Until the artificial connection between the waters of Lake Michigan and the Illinois river was practically essayed, it was regarded as of easy accomplishment; but the facts have shown the contrary. The canal, which in 1825 and prior was estimated at $640,000, has first and last, including the Chicago deepening for sanitary purposes, cost near twenty times that sum.

During the war of 1812, with the massacre at the mouth of the Chicago, and the retreat of the savages westward, national attention was first directed to the importance of this work, and the president in his message in 1814 brought the subject to the atten- of congress, and a select committee reported it as "the great work of the age," for both military and commercial purposes. "In 1816," says Gov. Edwards, who was one of the commissioners, "a tract of land bounded on Lake Michigan, including Chicago and extending to the Illinois river, was obtained from the Indians, for the purpose of opening a canal communication between the lake and the river. * * I personally know that the Indians were induced to believe that the opening of the canal would be very advantageous to them, and that, under authorized expectations that this would be done, they ceded the land for a trifle.'* In 1817, Major Long made a report to congress that "a canal, uniting the waters of the Illinois river with those of Lake Michigan, may be considered the first in importance of any in this quarter of the country, and the construction would be attended with very little expense compared with the magnitude of the object." Another report favorable to the canal was at that time made by Richard Graham and Chief Justice Phillips, of this State.† In 1819, Mr. Calhoun, secretary of war, directed the attention of congress to the

*Edwards' Life of Edwards.
†Ibid

474

canal on account of its importance for military purposes.* In 1822 congress authorized this State to construct the canal through the public lands, granting for the purpose a strip of ground 90 feet in width on both sides of it, and reserving the lands through which it might pass from sale until further direction. It was to be commenced within three and completed within twelve years. To the State was given the privilege of taking from the government land, material for its construction. Upon this slender beginning congress subsequently enlarged considerably.

In 1818, Gov. Bond, in his message, strongly recommended the construction of the canal; Governor Coles, four years later, did the same, and every governor of the State espoused its cause. No sectional question was made of it for many years. The legislature, at the session of 1822–3, appointed a board of canal commissoners "to make or cause to be made, estimates, etc., for completing said canal," and report to the next general assembly. Emanuel J. West, Erastus Brown, Theopilus W. Smith, Thomas Sloe, jr., and Samuel Alexander were appointed commissioners. The board employed Rene Paul, of St. Lous, and Justine Post, as engineers to survey the route and make out the estimates. They reported the route highly practicable and estimated the cost of the work at from $640,000 to not exceeding $716,110.71, which has proven to be very wide of the mark. The examination was superficial and no idea was formed of the amount of rock excavation which afterwards proved so formidable. These preliminary steps cost the State $10,589.87.†

By act of Jan. 19, 1825, the "Illinois and Michigan Canal Association," with a capital of $1,000,000 was incorporated. The company was to build and complete the canal within 10 year's time; to receive for its own use and benefit all the public lands which the United States, States, or individuals might donate in aid of the undertaking, and the tolls for 50 years after its completion; at the expiration of which time the canal and all its unsold lands were to be turned over to the State and the total sum expended in its construction, with 6 per cent interest, was to be paid.

The act, after its passage, incurred the strenuous opposition of the Hon. Daniel P. Cook, our only member in congress. A grant of land for the construction of the canal, upon the ground of its national character, was then with some degree of confidence looked forward to during the administration of Mr. Adams. The House committee, through Mr. Cook, had made a favorable report upon it. But the act of the legislature, by which any bonus to aid the work, was in advance turned over to a corporation of private individuals, would probably defeat the measure in congress. Mr. Cook published a long address to his constituents, under date of Oct. 28, 1825, forcibly attacking the canal policy of the State; urging the legislature to resume its possession and repeal the charter before any work was commenced, and the claim of vested rights should be set up. He demanded "that the rich harvest which it was destined to yield, should go into the treasure of the State;" and declared "that in less than 30 years it would relieve the people from the payment of taxes, and even leave a surplus to be applied to other works of public utility."

*Vol. 4 Pub. Doc. 15 Congress, 2d session.
†See Report of George Forquer, Senate Journal, session 1834-5.

These hopeful predictions have not been fulfilled. So sanguine was he, that to raise capital to build the canal, he was ready to sell or pledge a million acres of the school lands to carry forward the work. But no stock was ever subscribed by the "canal association;" the incorporators voluntarily surrendered their charter and the act was repealed.

This obstacle out of the way, the legislature, at the special session of January, 1826, called by acting Gov. Hubbard, transmitted to congress a very able memorial, drafted by Mr. Russell, of Bond, praying aid for the canal. We quote two sentences: "The construction of the canal, uniting the waters of Lake Michigan with the Illinois river, will form an important addition to the great connecting links in the chain of internal navigation, which will effectually secure the indissoluble union of the confederate members of this great and powerful republic. By the completion of this great and valuable work, the connection between the north and south, the east and west, would be strengthened by the ties of commercial intercourse and social neighborhood, and the union of States bid defiance to internal commotion, sectional jealousy, and foreign invasion."

The memorial, together with the efforts of our delegation in congress, Cook (in the house,) and Kane and Thomas (in the senate), but notably the first named, whose genial influence and untiring labors in this behalf have placed the State, and particulary Chicago, under lasting obligation to his memory, produced a favorable effect, and congress by act of March 2d, 1827, granted to the State of Illinois "for the purpose of aiding her in opening a canal to connect the waters of the Illinois river with those of Lake Michigan," the alternate   sections of the public lands on either side of the canal for five miles, along its entire route, which when set apart by the president were found to contain 224,322 acres. The lands were subject to the disposal of the legislature "for the purposes aforesaid, and no other." The canal was regarded as of national utility; it was to be commenced within 5 years thereafter and completed within 20; and if not so completed, the State was to pay the general government for all lands sold up to that time, and the remainder were to revert. This grant was the beginning of those enormous landed subsidies to western railroads which have become so frequent of late, but it will be noticed that this and the next, also in Illinois, for the construction of the Central railroad, were made to the State, whereas latterly the grants are to private corporations directly. It is a curious fact that the largely democratic State of Illinois obtained both these grants, by which she was more materially benefited than all else ever done for her, from whig administrations.

In 1829 the legislature organized a new board of canal commissioners, "to explore, examine, fix and determine the route of the canal," dispose by sale of the lands and lots and commence the work. Governor Edwards appointed Charles Dunn, afterwards U. S. judge of Wisconsin Territory, Dr. Gersham Jayne and Edmond Roberts, both of Springfield, as commissioners. For lack of funds little or nothing was done; times were rather hard, owing to the financial embarrassments caused by the old State bank of 1821. Feb. 15, 1831, an act amendatory of that of 1829, was passed. Under the provisions of these two acts, the board laid out the towns of Chicago and Ottawa, the map of the former, prepared by James Thompson, who made the surveys, bearing date August 4, 1830. When Thompson began his surveys of Chicago, in 1820, only 7 families lived outside of Fort Dearborn. Town lots and canal lands were sold to the amount of $18,924,83, and a re-examination and re-survey of the entire route of the canal were made, the engineer this time being Mr. Bucklin, whose estimate ran the work into millions instead of hundreds of thousands. The question of building a railroad over the route, instead of the canal was also considered. The commissioners reported their estimate to the legislature at the session of 1833, the cost of the canal at $4,043,386,50—still too low by about half—and the cost of a railroad at $1,052,488,19. The expenses of these examinations and surveys was $16,974,83. The board of canal commissioners, by act of March 1, 1833, was abolished. The incumbents were required to pay over all moneys, and deliver up all papers, vouchers, &c., of their transactions, to the State treasurer, and if upon examination any of the officers aforesaid had not faithfully and fairly accounted for all moneys &c., suit was directed to be commenced upon their official bonds," for which purpose, jurisdiction was given to the Fayette circuit court, its process running to any county in the State.

Meanwhile there were various projects of turning the construction of the canal and all its property gifts over to a company, and of building a railroad instead between Chicago and Peru. The distance was about 100 miles and the cost of a railroad was estimated at about $10,000 per mile. At the time, considering the expedition with which railroads are built, and the delay which has attended the completion of the canal, the former would doubtless have served the country more acceptably. A railroad would have been fully adequate to all the wants of the country and for passenger travel it is far preferable, while for the transportation of freight it offers the advantage of carrying in winter as well as summer. The consent of congress to divert so much of the avails of the canal lands as might be needed for this object was readily obtained. By act of March 2d, 1833, the State was authorized to use the lands granted for the canal, in building either a railroad or canal, as the legislature might elect; and the time for commencing either was extended five years.

In 1835 the governor was authorized to negotiate a loan not exceeding $500,000, "solely on the pledge of the canal lands and tolls," for the construction of the canal. The stock was to be called "Illinois and Michigan canal stock," and in no case to be sold for less than par. Governor Duncan told the legislature such was the universal estimate of the importance of the canal by all men of intelligence, that he had no hesitation in believing ample funds could be procured for its speedy completion. But the effort to obtain the loan proved a failure. Ex-Gov. Coles, residing at Philadelphia, was deputed to negotiate the loan for the full sum authorized. Under date of April 28, 1835, he wrote that capitalists were unwilling to take it because the bonds were not based upon the faith of the State. Nor were any funds for the payment of either principal or interest provided, except such as might arise from the lands and net revenues of the canal.

To meet these objections, the act of Jan. 9, 1836, was passed, which repealed the former act and authorized the same loan of $500,000 on the credit and faith of the State, irrevocably pledged for the payment of the canal stock and its accruing interest. James M. Strode, a senator then representing all the country north of and including Peoria, introduced this bill, which served as an entering wedge to the State treasury, and became the model for subsequent like legislation. The money borrowed, premiums on sales of stock, the proceeds of the canal lands and lots, and all other moneys arising from the canal, were to constitute a fund sacred to the canal till it was completed, except to pay interest on the stocks. The board of canal commissioners was constituted a body politic and corporate, subject to the control of the governor, one was to be the acting commissioner and general superintendent of the work, who was to report to the board. They were to hold till January following, when commissioners were made elective biennially. The salary of the acting commissioner was $1,200, and the compensation of the other two $3 per day when employed. Moneys from sale of stock or other sources were to be deposited in the State banks, to be thence drawn as needed by warrants on the treasurer. Immediate steps were to be taken for the construction of the canal, the contracts to be let to the lowest bidder. Materials for the canal were exempted from execution. Town sites were to be located and lots sold at auction. A sale of Ottawa lots, and the fractional section No. 15, adjoining Chicago, was made June 20, 1846; the latter under the extraordinary mania of speculation then rife regarding Chicago,* is said to have brought $1,503,495. The dimensions of the canal were to be not less than 45 feet at the surface, 35 at the base, and a navigable depth of at least 4 feet of water. Quarterly reports were to be made to the governor. The commissioners appointed by Gov. Duncan were William F. Thornton (acting commissioner), Gurdon S. Hubbard and William B. Archer, all whigs. The canal was to extend from Chicago to the mouth of the Little Vermilion, work to be begun at its northern terminus. Of the loan now authorized, Governor Duncan negotiated $100,000 in New York at a premium of 5 per cent., which he deemed too low and declined a larger amount at that rate. Subsequent experience showed that he should have taken more. The survey and estimate made at this time by chief engineer Goodwin, was $8,694,33.51—a hundred per cent higher than that of Bucklin—$86,000 per mile, being 4 times the cost of the Erie canal. The estimate was based upon a surface width of 60 feet, 40 at the bottom, and depth of water (to flow from the lake) of 6 feet. These dimensions were larger than the Erie, and would have made it one of the most splendid works of internal improvement anywhere to be found. But for such a work the estimate was yet too low. Contracts were let, and on the 4th of July, 1836, ground was first broken for the canal. The occasion was publicly celebrated at Chicago, by reading the Declaration of Independence, and the delivery of an able and appropriate address by Dr. Egan, picturing in glowing colors the future of Chicago and of the State of Illinois. Those glowing colors have been already dimmed by the reality.

* See Brown's History Illinois, p. 417. Note—Evidently a mistake.

Much of the route of the canal lay through marshy ground, inundated in the spring and fall, rendering it difficult of access. Forty thousand dollars was expended the first year upon roads leading to the work. The country bordering upon its route was but scatteringly settled, affording neither provisions nor shelter for laborers. Supplies had to be gathered from abroad. The work preceded the local demands of the country, other than those conceived in the brilliant imaginations of "corner" or "water lot" speculators in Chicago. Labor and provisions were high. The former from $20 to $30 per month and board. Pork at Chicago was from $20 to $30 per barrel; flour $9 to $12; salt $12 to $15; oats and potatoes 75 cents per bushel; and other articles of consumption in ratio.

To give a further idea of the difficulty of this great work, we reproduce from an exhaustive legislative report, made by the Hon. Newton Cloud in 1837, the following. The canal is treated in three divisions: The first, comprising a high level from Chicago to where it runs out (Lockport) distance 28 miles. On this, from Chicago river to Point of Oaks, a cut of 18 feet was required, to allow the waters of Lake Michigan to flow through. Half of the excavation for the entire 28 miles consisted of stratified and solid rock. The whole of this summit division was described as a sunken plain, largely underlaid with rock, the waters of the Des Plaines, Portage Lake, and the Saganaskee swamp extending over it and forming at times a continuous lake; 15 or 16 feet of the canal cut, on this division, lay below the surface of the Des Plaines and contiguous to it; and as drainage was impracticable, the difficulties and expense to be encountered from this object alone baffled the power of calculation. Besides, as the line was many feet below the river and the surface of the lake, subterraneous veins or fountains of water might be expected. In the rock cutting, much would depend upon the compactness of the rock and its capacity to exclude the suberincumbent water from the prism of the canal. If fissures, peculiar to lime stone regions, should be met with the work would be exceedingly slow, enormously expensive at any time of the year, and impracticable during rainy seasons. An abstract of the engineers estimate put the total cost of this division at $5,897,701.13; but the legislative committee, by referring to contracts already let, (which they cite) found that solid rock excavation per cubic yard would cost $2.50, instead of $1.54; earth excavation 40 cents, instead of 33; contingencies and superintendance 15 per cent. instead of 3, &c., &c.; whence they deduced that the summit level would cost $10,192,461, a difference against the engineer's estimate exceeding $4,250,000. These obstacles led to the consideration of the high level or shallow cut plan, as run by engineer Bucklin, ten feet above Lake Michigan, using the Calumet or Des Plaines rivers for feeders. They estimated that upon this plan the summit division, including the necessary feeders, might be constructed for one-fourth the cost, or $2,500,000. The Calumet was preferred for a feeder, because of its connecting 80 miles of navigation with the canal from the then contemplated internal improvements of the State of Indiana in that region. The middle division of 37 miles was estimated at $1,510,957; and the western division at $1,272,055—total $5,283,012. They further reported that by connecting the canal with the river at lake

Juliet, 60 miles would be saved; that the river could be locked and dammed thence to Peru at a cost of $576,665, reducing the cost of the entire work to only $3,551,665—the improvements of the river giving to the State, besides, a hydraulic power capable of running 700 pair of mill stones, yielding an annual rental of $210,000. None of these suggestions were adopted; though the State was, from financial embarrassments, afterwards forced into the adoption of the shallow cut plan.

By act of March 2d, 1837, supplemental to the law of Jan. 9, 1836, the canal commissioners were rendered independent of the governor. Besides an acting commissioner, one was to be president of the board and the other treasurer, the latter to give additional bond for the safe keeping and disbursement of the funds. In the absence of the acting commissioner, the others were to perform his duties. They were to, without delay, prosecute the canal to final completion upon the plan of 1836. A new survey and estimates, on the established route, were to be made under oath, with the view to ascertain if sufficient water could be obtained to feed the canal on the summit level. A route diverging from the main trunk was to be surveyed through the Aug-sag-nash-ge-ke swamp and Grassy lake to intersect the Calumet river, estimates to be made, and the canal built whenever the State of Indiana should undertake a corresponding work connecting therewith. A navigable feeder, from the best practicable point on Fox river to Ottawa, was to be constructed, and at the latter place, basins or a lateral canal connecting with the Illinois river were also to be built. Sales of Chicago lots to the amount of $1,000,000 were ordered; the governor was to borrow $500,000 upon the credit of the State, to be expended on the canal in 1838; to promote competition between contractors, no bond should be required, but a certain percentage on estimates reserved until the final completion of their jobs. Notwithstanding congress had many years before given license to the State to take materials from the public lands for the construction of the canal, the legislature now authorized the circuit courts to appoint men to appraise all damages arising to settlers upon them from the construction of the canal. Many claims were presented and allowed, costing the State many thousands of dollars. But at this time the canal had become connected with the great internal improvement system, and with the then inflated notions pervading the public mind nobody doubted either the credit or ability of the State to compass all these grand works, and such a power could not afford to be niggard to individuals with claims.

Up to January 1, 1839, the gross expenditures on the canal, derived from the various sources of loans, lot and land, amounted to $1,400,000. All of it, but about 23 miles between Dresden and Marseilles, was contracted, and the jobs let were roughly estimated at $7,500,000. The legislature, still infatuated with the huge State internal improvement system, at the session of 1838-9, encouraged the canal by directing the fund commissioners to loan to its fund $300,000, and authorizing the governor to make a further loan for it by the sale of $4,000,000 of State bonds. This was the canal loan, to negotiate which, Gov. Carlin, unwilling to put it into the hands of the fund commissioners, employed Messrs. Young and Reynolds, who made a very bungling job of it, entailing upon the State a loss of several hundred thousand dollars, by their various transactions with Dunlap, of Philadelphia, Delafield, of New York, and Wright & Co., of London. The latter, for a million dollars, except the advance of £30,000, proved almost a total failure; Delafield became unable to pay his installments, and was unwilling to surrender the bonds; and that of Dunlap was paid in such dribs of depreciated currency as to be of little avail in carrying forward the work.

In the meantime it became apparent that no more loans could be effected for the State without heavy sacrifice; the great system of internal improvements showed symptoms of a speedy collapse, and in February, 1840, the legislature put a period to its wild and reckless career. The work upon the canal was not interrupted by legislative action; provision was made to meet the liabilities or the State to contractors by issuing to them checks for the amounts found due on estimates, to bear interest at the rate of 6 per cent. The contractors had taken their jobs during the flush times (for Illinois) of 1836–7, when prices ruled much higher than in 1840. They could afford to lose 25 per cent. on them and still do well; and as the State hesitated to sell her bonds much below par, they engaged to receive them on their estimates at par. $1,000,000 were in that manner paid to them. Gen. Thornton, canal commissioner, was deputed to go to London with the bonds, where he effected a sale of $1,000,000 at 85 cents on the dollar, the contractors suffering the discount—being ten per cent. better than his instructions. By this expedient life was kept in the canal, though work on every other internal improvement had long since been abandoned. With the completion of their jobs some of the contractors proposed to receive, in like manner, the residue of their estimates, and $197,000 more was paid to them, when, with the final breaking of the State bank in February, 1842, an extraordinary depreciation of Illinois stocks in market took place, which put a period to this character of payments. After that no further payment was made to contractors for over two years, when the canal passed into the hands of the foreign bondholders, though work was not wholly intermitted upon many of the jobs during this time. The new board of canal commissioners, elected by the legislature at the session of 1841, were: Isaac N. Morris, president; Jacob Fry, acting commissioner, and Newton Cloud, treasurer.

After July, 1841, no further efforts were made to pay interest on the public debt. The financial embarrassments of the State became alarming. To add to the distress of the people, the State banks, early in 1842, broke down completely. The governor, auditor, and treasurer issued their circular, stating that the notes of these institutions would not be received in payment of taxes— nothing but gold and silver. The treasury was empty. There prevailed a dearth in trade and business amounting to stagnation; values declined; many despaired of the State's ability to ever pay off its enormous debt, exceeding $14,000,000, and equal to a present debt of at least $150,000,000, counting the lessened value of money and increased population, resources and capacity of the State. The people were unwilling to submit to higher taxation. Repudiation was openly agitated by not a few at home and abroad, and the fair name of Illinois became freely associated with dishonor.

31

In this crisis, besides the compromise legislation with the banks, the canal afforded the only practicable avenue out of the difficulty; its completion, it was thought, would give a new and powerful impulse to every department of business and industry throughout the State; and the advantages and facilities to be afforded by it would cause tides of emigrants and floods of wealth to pour into the State. The want of money and anxiety to have any sort of canal, now caused an advocacy of the high level or shallow cut, which could be completed at half the cost of the deep cut. The idea was to induce the holders of canal bonds to advance the money for its completion, upon a pledge of the canal, its lands and revenues in the nature of a first mortgage, and thus infuse life into a work now dormant, which would quicken everything else. Justin Butterfield, of Chicago, first suggested this idea; Michael Ryan, a canal engineer and State senator, in the summer of 1842, met Messrs. Bronson, Leavitt and other large canal bondholders in New York, and devised a plan for raising $1,600,000 to finish the canal on the shallow cut; and Gov. Ford recommended it in his first message,

In accordance with the above plan, the act of February 21, 1843, was passed authorizing the governor to negotiate a loan of $1,600,000, solely on the credit and pledge of the canal property, its revenues and tolls for a term of 6 years at 6 per cent. interest. payable out of the first moneys realized. The holders of the canal bonds and other evidences of canal indebtedness, were first entitled to subscribe the loan. A board of 3 trustees was established, 1 to be appointed by the governor and 2 by the subscribers of the loan—one vote for every $1,000 of stock. The former were to apportion their duties among themselves. The canal property was to be conveyed by the governor in trust, and to be managed by the trustees much in the manner of former proceedings. They might adopt such alterations of the original plan as they deemed advisable, without materially changing the location, having due regard to economy, permanancy of the work and an adequate supply of water. It was to be completed in a good, substantial, workmanlike manner, ready for use, if practicable, in two and a half years time. On payment of all debts the canal was to revert to the State. In the interest of economy, by another act, the number of canal officers were greatly reduced.

And now, when there appeared every favorable prospect for the speedy completion of the canal, it became involved in the meshes of national politics. Col. Charles Oakley and senator Michael Ryan were by the governor appointed agents to negotiate the new loan of $1,600,000. The treasury was empty; to give them an outfit $3,000 of the school fund was borrowed, which became the subject of attack upon Gov. Ford by Mr. Trumbull,* the lately removed secretary of State. The agents proceeded to New York; but with a view to the making of political capital, letter writers at home and partisan editors abroad attacked the canal policy of the State, in the hope that a measure so fraught with good should not redound to the credit of the dominant party. The action of the legislature was misrepresented, the party in power charged with disregarding the interests of the people, and the State creditors advised that if they advanced further funds, the succeeding legis-

*Ford's History.

lature would break faith with them and repeal their franchise. But these publications produced the opposite effect intended. The financial agents, with truth on their side, employed the public press in a series of articles in reply. The real condition of the State, the legislation adopted to reduce its debts, and its future prospects, were candidly and ably brought before the public, and the result was that the State stocks advanced in a week from 14 to 20 cents on the dollar, and in a short time doubled on that. Through the aid of David Leavitt, president of the American Exchange Bank of New York, which owned $250,000 canal bonds, the American creditors were called together, who resolved to subscribe their ratio of the new loan.

Thus assured, Messrs. Oakley and Ryan hastened to Europe with letters of these proceedings to Baring Brothers, of London, Hope & Co., of Amsterdam, and to Magniac, Jardine & Co., all wealthy bankers and creditors of the State. But these houses disappointed the ardent hopes of the State agents. They demanded something more substantial than newspaper articles, which had raised the spirits of the New York bond-holders. They wanted accurate data of the sufficiency of the canal property as security for both the present loan, and ultimately the payment of the entire canal debt, some $5,000,000 more; and further, some legislative effort at taxation and submission of the people thereto, in payment of interest on the public debt. It was finally arranged that Abbott Lawrence, Thomas W. Ward, and William Sturgis, of Boston, should designate two competent men to examine the canal and its property, estimate the value thereof, ascertain the total debt and report the whole; that $400,000 should be subscribed in America toward prosecuting the work; and that the governor recommend taxation in his next message to the legislature; whereupon the agents returned home in November, 1843. Ex-Gov. John Davis, of Mass., and W. H. Swift, a reputable engineer and a captain in the U. S. army, were selected by the Boston committee to examine the canal, its property and debts. This excited the political jealousy of the eastern press to a renewed interference with the domestic affairs of Illinois.

Gov. Davis' name was at the time mentioned in connection with the vice-presidency on the whig ticket in 1844. The *Globe* newspaper at Washington, the great organ of the democracy, boldly charged that Gov. Davis had been selected for this work with the view to influence the people of Illinois toward the support of the whig ticket, and in favor of the policy of the general government assuming the State debts. Senator Ryan came again to the rescue and published a merited and vigorous reply, in which Gov. Davis, the foreign bond-holders, and the people of Illinois, were ably defended, and the editor of the *Globe* deservedly rebuked for his impertinence.

The careful examination of the canal and elaborate report of Messrs. Davis and Swift, confirmed substantially the representations of Messrs. Ryan and Oakley, and they recommended the loan as a safe investment. Gov. Ford promised to recommend to the legislature increased taxation toward paying interest on the public debt. Thus armed, the sanguine financial agents again repaired to Europe, only to meet again with failure. The subscription of $400,000 was wanting. The foreign bond holders refused to perfect the new loan, alleging that the legislature and people should take some steps in good faith toward a recognition of their obligations to their creditors. Gov. Davis was sent for in the meantime, to proceed to London for fuller explanations of the details of the work and inspire greater confidence for the subscriptions. Thus the summer of 1844 passed; in December, the Illinois legislature would meet, and further effort was suspended to await the action of that body, of which Ryan was a senator. Ryan, chagrined at this failure, now yielded to the unworthy weakness of attempting to cast the blame upon Gov. Davis, from political motives. Through the public press of new New York, he reiterated the calumnies of the Washington *Globe*, against that gentleman, which he himself had formerly so ably refuted; and further charged him with causing the delay of the loan pending the presidential election. Messrs. Baring Bros. of London, took occasion, in an open letter addressed to Mr. Ryan, in a very plain manner to deny the charges.*

In the fall of 1844, after the election of the members of the legislature, but prior to their meeting, William S. Wait, of Bond, addressed a long letter to Gov. Ford through the public press, reviewing the illegal action of the State's financial agents in disposing of bonds, and bitterly inveighing against taxation to pay the public debt. The object was to elicit an expression from the governor as to repudiation or taxation. Now this was the very pretext the governor wanted, and he embraced it with alacrity. Although his excellency well knew the unpopularity of an advocacy of increased taxation, he replied in a very able letter, remarkable not only as a literary production of rare merit, but for its clear exposition of the embarrassed condition of the State, from which there was no hope of honorably escaping, except by taxation ; and while it was replete with broad, common sense and sagacious views, it characterized in fitting terms the disgrace of repudiation, breathing a noble spirit of self-abnegation and patriotism. The governor's reply was extensively re-published in newspapers, and elicited general commendation for its high tone. Mr. Leavitt, of the American Exchange Bank of New York, which held largely of the canal stock, was greatly encouraged, and after procuring subscriptions to the new loan in New York, joined Col. Oakley, who was still in that city, and early in the winter of 1844-45 they returned to Europe. The governor's letter had preceded them, and caused a marked change in the views of our London creditors, who now, without hesitation, subscribed liberally to the new loan, each more than originally intended. Thus, after many delays, (such are the vexations incident to a ruined credit) did the new loan of $1,600,000 become an accomplished fact, and the completion of the canal assured.

Mr. Leavitt and Col. Oakley, on their return home, joined by Gov. Davis, hastened to Illinois before the adjournment of the legislature. They arrived in Springfield the middle of February, 1845, where they became directly the curious objects of attraction as the envoys of Illinois' creditors. A prejudice was attempted to be excited against the administration policy of taxation, and these gentlemen were slyly denounced as moneyed kings, aristocrats,

---

*Letter of Baring Bros to Michael Ryan, in Ford's History.

etc.* But by their kindly and pleasant intercourse with the members, all prejudice against them was speedily dissipated. They reported the proposition of the foreign bond holders through the executive, and the finance committee brought in a bill, to which we have made allusion in the preceding chapter, which provided for raising by taxation an "interest fund" to be sacredly set apart for the payment of interest on the State debt; and as suplemental to the canal act of 1843, that the governor should execute and deliver, under the seal of the State, a deed of trust to the canal trustees, of all the canal property both real and personal, as the first mortgage, the subscribers of the new loan to have priority in the payment of their advances for both interest and principal, out of the proceeds of said trust property. The bill in its present form, met with decided opposition; it passed the house, but was defeated in the senate.

The expedient was now resorted to of dividing the measure, putting the provision for taxation and that relating to the canal into two separate bills. It was taking two bites at one cherry, for both bills became laws. The opponents, after the adjournment, took their departure in ill-humor, threatening that the southern part of the State should be thoroughly canvassed to arouse the people against the enormity of these measures. But when they found the friends of the measures as ready as themselves to enter the field, to expose their machinations and demagoguery, the purpose was abondoned. During the summer following, two conventions in that portion of the State, one at Marion and one at Fairfield, passed resolutions both in favor of the canal and of taxation to pay the public debt. In these measures of the legislature, the hydra of repudiation met its final quietus.

The canal, its lands and appurtenances were conveyed by the governor to the trustees, the bond holders under the act of 1843, having elected two, Messrs. William H. Swift and David Leavitt, the State trustee being Jacob Fry; the new loan was perfected in June, 1845; the new board was organized, the canal was accurately examined and careful estimates of its cost made; jobs were let and work was resumed in September, 1845. Thus, much of the working season was gone, the autumn proving unpropitious on account of sickness in the valley of the Illinois, and but little progress was made. The people were impatient at this tardiness. They were next promised that the canal should be in navigable order by July 4th, 1847, only to be again disappointed. Meanwhile a host of canal officials were drawing their large salaries with unerring fidelity. The foreign trustees received $2,500 each, the engineer the same, secretary $2,000, &c. There were a dozen or more subordinate officials. These were large salaries for the period, exceeding those of our State officials at the time by nearly 100 per cent. Estimates of work were made quarterly, but by the time they were approved by the foreign trustees, residing in Washington and New York, and the money sent on and paid out to the contractors and hands, 6 weeks were consumed. Much dissatisfaction and public clamor prevailed. Even the eastern press commented with severity upon the delay, while the money on deposit was drawing interest.

*Ford's History.

Finally, by the opening season of 1848, the Illinois and Michigan Canal, a stupendous public work, urged for 30 years, and in course of actual construction for 12, after many struggles with adverse circumstances, was completed. It was finished on the shallow cut plan, the datum line on the summit level being 12 feet above Lake Michigan. On this level, extending from the Chicago river to Lockport, the water was supplied by pumping.*

The success attending its first season's operations, yielding, as it did during that of 1848, $87,890 87 in tolls, seemed an earnest to the hopes of its warmest friends. For the first season its capacity for business was comparatively but slightly taxed, and its promises of revenues for the future from a largely increased business were undoubted. The law required that the lands and lots, constituting part of the canal fund, should within a very short time after its completion, be appraised and offered for sale. A sale was accordingly had in September, 1848, at Chicago and other towns, which yielded $780,758 87, less $11,060, on which payment was not made; which sum exceeded the original valuation of all the canal lands by 2 per cent., and was an excess over the appraisal of $40,724 87. The appraisal of all the canal lands and lots, before the sale, was $2,126,355 09; but if the remainder brought as great an advance over the appraisement as this sale, $3,500,000 would be obtained from this source; a most encouraging prospect, as this property would go far toward liquidating the canal debt, aside from its tolls.

The aggregate amount ultimately realized from the congressional grant of land to the canal, from 1830 to 1869, when the selling ceased, was $5,337,554. The total receipts for tolls, from the opening of the canal, in 1848, to the close of 1868, 21 seasons, were $3,997,281 22. The total expenditures on the canal, under the act of 1836, were $4,979,903; under the act of 1843, $1,429,-606—total cost $6,409,509. The entire canal debt at this time (1848) was some $6,000,000.†

*We have seen that Mr. Leavitt, early in the winter of 1844-5, returned to Europe, and the Governor's letter to Wait having preceded him, the foreign canal bond holders readily subscribed the new loan of $1,600,000. This agency of Mr. Leavitt, Gov. Ford said, " was entirely voluntary, and [he was] not advised that any compensation was expected." But in 1849 Mr. Leavitt brought forward a claim of $40,000 for negotiating the loan. As the foreign bondholders were disinclined to allow it, Mr. L renounced his demand and was re elected trustee Subsequently the claim was variously referred, but not decided. In 1854 he obtained the certificates of a number of bankers and prominent citizens of this State, stating that the 2½ per cent. was a reasonable charge. Gov. Matteson, after some hesitation, approved the claim, and certified it to the canal trustees. Josiah McRoberts. State trustee, drew a check for the amount, but withheld it till the claim was first approved by the board, which had to be done by mail, as the members resided apart. Capt Swift, the other member besides Leavitt, objected to the allowance, and McRoberts did not act further. Thus the matter rested until the administration of Gov. Bissell, when C. R. Ray, of the Chicago Tribune. relieved McRoberts. The Governor approved the claim and Ray paid it out of the canal fund, Swift entering a vigorous protest against it. Ray was furiously assailed for his action by the press of Illinois, and suit was brought against him and Leavitt to recover the amount. By agreement the matter was referred to Hon. B. F. Thomas, of Boston, and Edwin Bartlett, New York, as arbitrators. In 1859, the matter became the subject of investigation by our legislature, which reported against the allowance. An award was finally made by the arbitrators by which Leavitt was allowed $16,000, and after enjoying the money for 6 years, he disgorged $52,063 90, the costs of suit and $1,000 as compensation to the arbitrators.

†It is a curious fact that the early growth of Chicago was greatly in accord with the progress of the canal. The canal may be said to have made Chicago. When the survey of the site was commenced and platted, by order of the canal commissioners, in 1829, there resided upon its site only about a half dozen families outside the palisades of Fort Dearborn; but with the prospect of the inauguration of this great work, population began to pour in freely. The Black Hawk war perhaps checked it a little, but with the removal of the Indians, the tide of immigration was resumed. When, in 1835, the first canal loan of $500,000 was authorized, a new impulse was given to the settlement of the town, and with the additional legislation of January, 1836, her population, swollen to about 4,000, the extraordinary fever for speculating in town lots still rife,

In 1857 the arrearages of interest on the public debt, including that of the canal, were funded by the act of that year. The new loan of $1,600,000 and interest were finally paid off in 1858, and the same year the trustees commenced paying off the principal of the registered canal debt, the State aiding to the amount of $600,-000. But the incumbrances were not finally removed until Aug., 1871, when the trustees, after a faithful service of 25 years, turned over the canal to the State with a surplus of $92,099.61.

The legislature, by act of 1865, supplemented in 1867, authorized the city of Chicago to deepen that portion of the canal known as the summit level, a herculean feat which has been accomplished. The city was impelled by sanitary reasons to cut down the channel, turn the pure waters of the lake into the disease breeding Chicago river, reverse its current, allow it to course through the deepened canal into the Illinois in order to cleanse it. For this most necessary work to the city the State gave her a lien upon the canal revenues, after its old indebtedness was discharged, for a sum not exceeding $2,500,000, from which redemption might however at any time be made. The annual net revenues of the canal averaged only about $110,000, not near paying the interest on the outlay of the city. The canal, contrary to the ardent hopes of its early friends, who predicted for it a source of unfailing revenue sufficient to defray the expenses of the State government, utterly disappointed these fond expectations. The more there was expended upon it the more was demanded, and neither Chicago nor the State wanted it as a financial investment. But when on the 9th of October, 1871, the great metropolis was overwhelmed by the fire fiend and prostrated in ashes and want, the State, unable by the terms of the constitution to directly render the aid and succor that charity and the exigency demanded, through her legislature at the extraordinary session of October 13th, indirectly extended a noble bounty by redeeming the non-paying canal from her lien of some $3,000,-000.

There is a further history of the canal, as connected with the various efforts to obtain government aid to enlarge it to the dimensions of a ship-canal; the river improvements; the lock at Henry; and the repeated struggles in the legislature to procure appropriations; but the details would be voluminous, and uninteresting. We will only add that the year 1853 was the first to obtrude upon public recognition the disagreeable fact that the Illinois river required artificial aid to render it navigable through the boating season. That of 1853 lasted from March to December, 9 months; but from the first of July on, the river for its greater length was useless for craft of any considerable tonnage, curtailing the through carrying trade of the canal very greatly.

and the actual commencement of the work, we find the prosperity of that period to culminate. Shortly after came the great revulsion of 1837, which, with the collapse of the visionary internal improvement system of the State, two and a half years later, would have utterly prostrated Chicago but for the persistency with which the work on the canal was sustained. As it was her prosperity was checked materially for 7 years. In 1837 the taxable valuation of her real estate was $236,842. but in 1840 it lapsed to $94,437 ; and in the course of the next two years real estate was offered at less than 5 per cent of the price paid during the period of inflation in 1836 By 1843 the work on the canal, not having been entirely suspended, the population had slowly increased to 7,580 but with the resumption of work, in 1845, we find her inhabitants in that year speedily swollen to the number of of 12,088, and a corresponding increase in the value of taxable real estate ; and in 1848, with the completion of the canal, they had reached the number of 20,923 souls.—His. Chicago.

Had the navigation of the river during that long season not been interrupted, the tolls of the canal, it was estimated, would have reached $300,000 instead of $173,327. The fact is recognized all over the State, that as the country becomes settled many tributaries of the larger rivers become almost dry every season, and in all, by the removal of obstructions, the water runs speedily to a low stage. Surface water generally has fallen many feet in the past few years. Wells, which formerly afforded a bounteous supply at a depth of 16 to 20 feet, have gone dry and 25 to 40 feet are now required to reach water. Springs that have become historic and lakes that dotted our maps have disappeared, and while the health of the country has been materially improved, the scarcity of water is a very general complaint. To render the Illinois river permanently navigable during the forwarding season, there is no alternative but to thoroughly improve it by dredging and by locks and dams.

CHAPTER XLI.

1840-4—MORMONS OR LATTER DAY SAINTS.

Joe Smith—Prophetic Mission—Followers Remove to Missouri—Expulsion from the State—Settlement in Illinois—Obnoxious Nauvoo Charter and Ordinances—Arrest and Acquittal of Smith—His Assassination.

———

In the spring of 1840, a religious sect styled Mormons or Latter Day Saints, made its advent in Illinois, and located on the east bank of the Mississippi, in the county of Hancock. This strange people had previously resided in Missouri, but having been guilty of larceny and other crimes, they sought refuge in Illinois to escape the indignation of the inhabitants and the penalties of outraged law. They purchased a considerable tract of land and commenced building a city, which they called Nauvoo, a name signifying peaceable or pleasant. Joseph Smith, the founder and pretended prophet of the religion, was born at Sharon, Windsor county, Vermont, Dec. 23d, 1805. His parents being in humble circumstances, the prophet's opportunities for acquiring knowledge in early life were limited, and when to the want means is added the want of capacity, it is not strange that he lived and died a person of ordinary attainments.

In 1815 his father left Vermont, and settled on a farm near Palmyra, Wayne county, New York, where young Smith began to exhibit the traits which distinguished his subsequent life. Both he and his father became famous as water wizzards, professing to discover the presence of water in the earth from the movements of a green rod, and offering their services to point out suitable localities for the digging of wells. Many anecdotes formerly existed, respecting the vagrant habits of the son, who spent most of his time wandering in the woods, dreaming of hidden treasures, and endeavoring to find them by the use of charms. Such was the character of the young profligate when he made the acquaintance of Sidney Rigdon, a person of some intelligence and natural ability, who had conceived the design of starting a new religion. A religious romance, written by a Presbyterian clergyman of Ohio, who was then dead, falling into the hands of Rigdon, suggested this idea, and finding in Smith the requisite duplicity and cunning to reduce it to practice, it was agreed that he should act in the capacity of prophet. They then devised the story that Smith had discovered golden plates buried in the earth, near Palmyra, containing a record engraved in unknown characters, and that this romance was a translation of the inscription.

The fiction purports to be a history of the ten lost tribes of Israel, giving an account of their wanderings in Asia and subsequent emigration to America, where they flourished as a nation, and where Christ in due time appeared and established his religion as he had done among the Jews. It also contained the history of the American christians for several hundred years afterward, when in consequence of their wickedness, judgments were visited upon them and they were destroyed. According to the account several powerful nations inhabiting the continent were engaged in war, and at last a decisive battle was fought, between the Lamanites or heathen, and the Nephites or Christian, and the latter were defeated. This mighty contest, called the battle of Cumorah, was fought at Palmyra, New York; hundreds of thousands were killed on both sides, and all the Nephites, except a few who fled to the southern part of the continent, were exterminated. Among the survivors were Mormon and his son Moroni, who were righteous men, and who were directed by God to engrave the history of these important events on plates of gold and deposit them in the earth for the benefit of future generations.

Smith pretends that when he arrived at the age of fifteen he began to reflect on the necessity of preparing for a future state of existence, but the nature of the preparation was an unsettled question in his mind. He regarded this a consideration of infinite importance, for if he did not understand the way it was impossible to walk in it, and the thought of resting his soul's salvation on uncertainties was more than he could endure. If he sought information of the different sects of religion, they all claimed to be right, but as their doctrines were in many respects in direct conflict, it is impossible for most of them to be true. The vital issue to be determined was, if any of the conflicting systems of theology prevalent in the world are correct, which one is it; and until this question was decided he could not rest content. Under these circumstances he concluded to study the scriptures, and soon became convinced that if he sought wisdom of God he would be enabled to judge which of the opposing creeds conformed to the teachings of Christ. He therefore retired to a grove, in the vicinity of his father's house, and kneeling down, commenced calling on the Lord. At first the powers of darkness endeavored to overcome him, but continuing in prayer the darkness fled away, and he was enabled to ask for knowledge with great faith and fervency of spirit. While thus pouring out his soul in supplication, there appeared in the heavens above a bright and glorious light, which, as it drew near the tops of the trees increased in splendor and magnitude, the whole wilderness glowed with the most brilliant illumination. He expected to see the foliage of the trees consumed, but not perceiving any effect produced, he was encouraged to hope that he also would be able to abide its presence, and quickly he was enveloped in the midst of it without sustaining any injury. The natural objects about him soon vanished and he was caught away in a heavenly vision, in which two glorious personages appeared and informed him that his sins were forgiven, and that none of the existing eclesiastical organizations were accepted by God as his church and kingdom. After being especially informed not to go after them, and promised that in the fullness of time the true gospel should be made known to him, the vision disappeared.

Notwithstanding this glorious announcement, he afterward became entangled in the vanities of the world, but seeing the error of his way, and truly repenting, it pleased God to again hear his prayers. On the 21st of Sept., 1823, he retired to rest as usual, when his soul was filled with a desire to commune with some messenger who could make known the principles of the true church and his acceptance with God as promised in the former vision. While in this state of mind, suddenly a splendor, purer and more glorious than the light of day, burst into the room and the entire building was illuminated as if filled with a consuming fire. The unexpected appearance of a light so brilliant, caused in his whole system a shock which was soon followed by peace of mind and overwhelming raptures of joy. In the midst of this happiness a personage stood before him, whose stature was above the ordinary height of man, whose garments were perfectly white and without seam. Notwithstanding the glare which filled the room, the glory which accompanied him enhanced its brightness, and though his countenance was as lightning, the benignity of its expression banished all fear. This glorious being informed him that he was an angel sent from God to declare the joyful tidings that the covenant which had been made with ancient Israel concerning their posterity, was about to be fulfilled, and that the second coming of the Messiah was at hand, when the Gospel would be preached in its purity and a people prepared for the millennial reign of universal peace and joy. He was also informed that the American Indians were a remnant of the ancient Hebrews, who had come to the country; that for several hundred years after their arrival they enjoyed a knowledge of the true God, and that their sacred writings contain an account of the principal events that transpired among them during this interval. When, however, they neglected the religion of their fathers most of them perished in battle, but at the command of God, their sacred oracles were entrusted to a surviving prophet who buried them in the earth to prevent their falling into the hands of the wicked, who sought to destroy them. He was then told if he continued faithful he would be the highly favored instrument of bringing these important documents to light, but it must be done for the glory of God and none could be entrusted with them who would use them for selfish purposes. After giving him many instructions concerning the past and future, the heavenly messenger disappeared and the glory of God withdrew, leaving the mind of the prophet in perfect peace. Not many days thereafter, the vision was renewed and the angel appearing, pointed out the place where the records were deposited, and directed him to go immediately and view them.

According to the Mormon account they were deposited in a stone box, buried in the side of a hill, 3 miles from the village of Manchester, New York. When Smith first visited the depository, September 22d, 1823, the crowning stone was visible above the surface and a slight effort brought the contents to view. The words were beautifully engraved in Egyptian characters, on both sides of plates, eight inches long and seven inches wide, having the thickness of tin and the appearance of gold. Three rings passing through the edges of the plates united them in the form of a book about six inches in thickness. Besides the plates the box contained two transparent stones, clear as crystal, the Urim and Thummim of ancient seers, by which they obtained revelations of things past and future.

While contemplating the sacred treasure the heavens were opened, the glory of God shone about him, and he was filled with the Holy Ghost. The heavenly messenger who had visited him on previous occasions, again stood in his presence and said, look; and as he spake he beheld the power of darkness with an immense retinue of associates flee away. The angel instructing him declared that it was then impossible to possess the records, that they could only be obtained by prayer and faithfulness in serving God who had preserved them, not for the temporal but the spiritual welfare of the world. In them is contained the Gospel of Christ as it was delivered to his people of this land, and when brought forth by the power of God it shall be preached to the nations; the Gentiles receiving will be saved and Israel obeying it will be brought into the fold of the Redeemer. After it is known that the Lord has shown you these things the wicked will endeavor by falsehoods to destroy your reputation; nay, they will even attempt your life, but you observe the commandments, and in due time you shall bring them forth. When interpreted the Lord will appoint a holy priesthood, who will proclaim the Gospel, baptize with water, and have power to confer the Holy Ghost by the laying on of hands. In due time the ten tribes of Israel shall be revealed in the north country, where they for a long time have resided. The knowledge of the Lord shall be greatly extended, and your name shall be known among the nations by the works which shall be wrought by your hand.

On the 22d of September, 1827, after a probation of four years, during which he was frequently counseled by the angel, the records were delivered into his hands. When it was known among the inhabitants of the surrounding country that the prophet had seen visions and discovered the records, he was not only ridiculed and slandered but waylaid and assaulted, for the purpose of destroying the plates. These persecutions increased to such an extent that the house in which he lived was frequently beset by mobs, and finding his life thus exposed to constant danger he concluded to leave the place and go to Pennsylvania. During the journey thither he was twice overtaken by officers with search-warrants for the plates, but they failed in the accomplishment of their designs. After arriving in the northern part of Pennsylvania, where his father-in-law resided, by the aid of the Urim and Thummim, he made the translation of the plates known as the book of Mormon. This translation is from an abridgment composed by Mormon from the sacred writings of his forefathers, with additions subsequently made by his son Maroni, who survived him. The latter, in his continuation of the narrative, informs us that the Lamonites destroyed all the Nephites who escaped the battle of Curmorah, except such as forsook their religion, and that he, for the preservation of his own life, was compelled to hide himself.

This story, in its pretended miracles, visions and prophecies, is like other forgeries of the kind, which at different times have been imposed on the credulity of mankind. As dishonesty and ignorance will always exist, it may yet flourish and exert upon the future of the race an influence as controling as that of other systems which have preceded it in the past. While the holiest affections of the heart cluster about the religious element of man's nature, there is also a weakness connected with it which in all ages of the world has subjected him to the grossest impositions. In his social and political relations he exhibits a sagacity which, if it does not always protect him against abuse, is at least divested of the superstition which beclouds his religious aspirations and so frequently makes him the dupe of falsehood. He insists in his secular investigations upon the most rigid inductions, theories are subjected to the most searching analysis, and no doctrine can obtain credence unless sustained by indubitable facts; but in theology vague conjecture is substituted for positive knowledge, and errors which outrage the character of Deity and imbruit the intellect of man are accepted without even questioning their authenticity. To this infirmity of human nature, and the cupidity of designing men, Mormonism and other similar delusions owe their origin. If the parties who originate and manage them are intelligent they give them plausibility, but this is not important, for no system can be devised so absurd that fools will not believe it, and that knaves will not be found to profit by their ignorance.

According to the statements of the saints, after the book of Mormon was translated, the Lord raised up witnesses to testify to its truth. Oliver Cowdry, Daniel Whitmore and Martin Harris thus affirm: "We certify that we have seen the plates which contain the records ; that they were translated by the gift and power of God, for his voice hath declared it unto us, wherefore we know that the work is true, and declare with words of soberness that an angel of God came down from heaven and laid the plates before our eyes, and we saw the engravings on them." Eight other witnesses also declare: "Joseph Smith, the translator of this work, hath shown us the plates herein spoken of, which have the appearance of gold, and as many of the leaves as the said Smith hath translated we have handled with our hands, and we also saw the engravings thereon, all of which had the appearance of ancient and curious workmanship." The parties connected with these certificates were no doubt accomplices in the fraud, for if humanity could furnish a spawn base enough to originate the deception, plenty of men could be found sufficiently degraded to assist in its promulgation.

Another statement is given respecting the plates, by those in the confidence of the prophet, which does not coincide with the above certificates. It is said that the early followers of the prophet were desirous of seeing the plates, and importuning him for the privilege, he told them that they could not be seen by the carnal eye, that they must obtain a lively faith by fasting and prayer if they would have their holy curiosity gratified. Acting upon his suggestion, they engaged in continuous supplications that the hidden things of God might be made manifest, and when finally becoming impatient, Smith produced the box containing the treasure and opened it in their midst. Not seeing anything in it, they said, "Brother Joseph, we do not see the plates." The prophet answering said "Oh ye of little faith, how long will God bear with a wicked and perverse generation ? Down on your knees, brethren, every one of you, and pray God for the forgiveness of your sins and for the living faith which comes down from heaven." As commanded they fell upon their knees, and beseeching God with great earnestness for more than two hours for faith and spiritual discernment, they again looked and the plates were visible. In this case it has been suggested that the parties, operated upon by a fanatical enthusiasm, may perhaps have imagined they saw the plates, but it is far more probable that they had selfish ends to accomplish and wilfully misrepresented to impose on the ignorant.

On the 6th of April, 1830, the church of the Latter Day Saints was organized at Manchester, New York. Their numbers now rapidly increased, and with a view to securing a permanent location, in 1833, they moved to Missouri, purchased land in Jackson county, and commenced building the town of Independence. There the commission of petty crimes, and their arrogant presumptions that as saints of the Lord they had a right to the whole country, incensed the neighboring people against them. After some of their number had been ducked in the river, some tarred and feathered, and others killed, the whole community removed to Clay county, on the opposite side of the Missouri river. Remaining in this place only a short time, most of them went eastward, and located at Kirtland, Ohio, twenty miles from Cleveland, and commenced building a temple. In 1836 a large convocation of their elders met, and according to their reports, the work of the Lord had greatly increased in America, Europe and the islands of the sea.

About this time a financial institution, styled the Kirtland Savings Bank, was organized, and Smith appointed president. For the want of capital and integrity among the managers, it soon failed, under circumstances of more than ordinary depravity. Property to a large amount was purchased with the bills, and after the title became vested in the saints, the bank failed and its notes were never redeemed. Thus swindled, the people of the adjacent country, as at other places, became exasperated and a third hegira became necessary. Accordingly the prophet, apostles, elders and a great body of the saints, shaking the dust from their feet as a testimony against Ohio, started for Missouri; and this time settled in Davis and Calhoun counties. There they also purchased land of the United States, and built the town of Far West and other small villages. Still exhibiting the same conduct that at other places had involved them in difficulties, it was not long till they were accused of every possible crime. The breach thus opened between the saints and gentiles continued to widen, and in a few years both parties became so embittered that a resort to physical force was the only alternative by which the quarrel could be adjusted. The Mormon leaders declared that they would no longer submit to to the government of Missouri. Joe Smith, as he was generally called, ordered the circuit clerk, who was a disciple, not to issue any more writs againts the saints, and one of the elders, in a sermon, informed his people that henceforth they were not amenable to the laws of the State. Armed parties of Mormons commenced patroling the country and plundering the property of the inhabitants, who assembled in arms to protect themselves and drive the felons from the State. A company, under

Major Bogart, who had formerly commanded a battalion of rangers in the Black Hawk war, met one of these marauding parties, and a battle ensuing, the Mormons were routed after they had burnt two towns and ravaged a large extent of country. Gov. Boggs called out the militia for the purpose of either exterminating the plunderers or driving them from the country. A large force, commanded by Gen. Lucas and Brigadier Gen. Doniphan, surrounded them in the town of Far West, and although armed with the determination of resisting to the last extremity, they surrendered without an engagement. A large part of the stolen property was recovered, and, with the exception of the leaders, the Mormons were dismissed under promise to leave the State. Smith and other principal men were tried before a court martial and sentenced to be shot. The criminals would doubtless have been executed had not Gen. Doniphan, who considered the proceedings against them illegal, interfered and saved their lives. They were next arraigned before a civil tribunal, and indictments being found against them for murder, treason, robbery and other crimes, they were committed to jail, but before their trials came on they escaped from prison, and fled the State.

In the years 1839-40 the whole body of saints arrived in Illinois, and, according to their own account, the cruel treatment of their enemies, and their perils by field and flood, would make a story without a parallel in the annals of suffering. Representing that they had been persecuted in Missouri on account of their religion, and being the vanquished party, they soon excited the sympathy of our people. The inhabitants of Illinois have always been justly esteemed for their enlightened spirit of toleration, and the Mormons were kindly received as sufferers in the cause of religion. Several communities even vied with each other in offers of hospitality and efforts to induce the persecuted strangers to settle among them. As already stated, they finally located on the east bank of the Mississippi, in the county of Hancock, where they commenced building the city of Nauvoo, which they designed should be the center of their future operations in the conversion of the world to the new religion.

On their arrival in the State the effort of politicians to get their patronage soon brought them into notice. As they were already numerous and rapidly increasing in numbers, it was supposed that at no distant day they would exert a controling influence in the elections. Knowing their power in this respect, and intimating that they would support the men and measures most likely to promote their own welfare, both parties by acts of kindness and promises of help endeavored to win their support. In Missouri they had always sustained the democratic party, but having been expelled from the State by a democratic governor, and having afterwards been refused relief by Van Buren, a democratic president, in a spirit of retaliation, they voted for a time with the whigs. When, however, the legislature met in 1840, wishing to obtain the passage of several bills for the incorporation of Nauvoo and other purposes, they flattered both parties in order to secure their joint influence. With these objects in view Dr. John C. Bennett, a Mormon by profession and one of the most profligate men in the State, was sent as their agent to the seat of government to operate as a lobbyist. Arriving in Springfield, he applied to Mr. Little, the whig senator from Hancock, and to Mr. Douglas, the democratic secretary of state, who both promised him their influence, and when an act incorporating the city of Nauvoo was presented to the legislature, although in many respects in the highest degree objectionable, such was the dexterity with which these politicians managed their respective parties that it passed both houses without discussion or opposition. In the lower house it is said it was not even read, each party being afraid to oppose it for fear of losing the Mormon vote, and each in sustaining it verily believed it would secure their favor.

This act, which is a perfect anomaly in legislation, made the original boundaries of Nauvoo not only equal to the limits of some of the larger cities, but also provided for their indefinite extension. It reads: "Whenever any tract of land adjoining Nauvoo shall have been laid out into town lots, and duly recorded according to law, the same shall form a part of the city." The corporation was also empowered to deal in real and personal property for speculative purposes, a privilege not at that time conferred upon any other cities of the State by legislative enactment. One section of the law gave to the city council the extraordinary power to enact any ordinance not repugnant to the State and national constitutions, whereby they could nullify at pleasure the statutes of the State within the corporate limits of the city and over as much of the adjacent county as they could extend them. A mayor's court was established, with exclusive jurisdiction of all cases arising under the city ordinances, but subject to the right of appeal to the municipal court. The mayor and four aldermen as associates composed the municipal court, which was clothed with power to issue writs of habeas corpus, and had jurisdiction of appeals from the mayor's court, subject again to appeal to the circuit court of Hancock county. It made the Nauvoo legion, with the exception of being subject to the governor, independent of the military organization of the State, and its commissioned officers a perpetual court martial, having authority to enact such regulations as should be considered necessary for its welfare. The legion was made subservient to the mayor in executing the laws of the city, was entitled to its proportion of the State arms, and by subsequent enactments of the legislature any citizen of Hancock county might unite with it, whether he lived in the city or out of it. A bill was also passed incorporating the Nauvoo House, in which Joe Smith and his heirs were to have a suite of rooms in perpetual succession. By this unusual legislation the courts had little dependence on the constitutional judiciary, and the military establishment, empowered to regulate itself, was independent of the laws of the State. The different departments of the city government were blended into one, whereby the same public functionary could be entrusted with the discharge of legislative, executive, judicial and military duties at the same time, and such instances frequently occurred as the events which immediately followed prove.

In the year 1841, the Mormons organized a city government and Smith was elected mayor; presiding in the council as a legislator he assisted in making laws for the government of the city, and as mayor it was his duty to see that the laws were faithfully executed. By virtue of his office he was judge of the mayor's court and chief justice of the municipal court, in which situation he was the expounder and enforcer of the laws which he had assisted to make. In the organization of the Nauvoo legion it was made to consist of divisions, brigades, and cohorts, each of which had a general and over the whole as commander-in-chief Smith presided as lieutenant general. If to these multiform duties we add his calling as a real estate agent and his anticipated position as tavern keeper, the list of his vocations will be complete.

It has already been said that Smith and other leading Mormons escaped from jail in Missouri, and hence in the autumn of 1841, the governor of that State made a demand on Governor Carlin of Illinois for the arrest and delivery of the fugitives. A warrant was accordingly issued by which Smith was arrested and brought before Judge Douglas, who, at that time was holding court in Hancock and adjoining counties. In the trial which ensued, Smith was discharged on the plea that the writ by which he had been arrested was defective. The prophet, not being well enough versed in law to understand the legal nature of the question, regarded his acquittal as a great favor from the democratic party. In consequence of this decision the Mormons once more renewed their allegiance with that political organization and to strengthen the alliance, Bennett, who was then an alderman in Nauvoo and the major general of the legion, was made master in chancery and adjutant general of the State militia. At these signal marks of favor, Smith issued a proclamation exhorting his followers to unite with the democratic party, and the whigs on seeing themselves out-generaled in this manner, commenced a tirade of denunciations against the Mormons, their papers teeming with the enormities of Nauvoo and the wickedness of the party which would consent to receive the support of such miscreants.

As soon as the machinery of the government of Nauvoo was properly put in motion, ordinances were enacted in conflict with the laws of the State. The Mormons, believing that another attempt would be made by the governor of Missouri for the arrest of their leaders, declared that the public mind in that State was so prejudiced against them that a fair trial there was impossible, and should any of their fraternity be taken thither, if they could not be legally convicted and punished, they would be murdered by a mob before they could get out of the State. Determined to guard against any future demands of this kind, they commenced devising a scheme whereby they could protect themselves through the instrumentality of the city ordinances. A law was therefore passed by the common council virtually declaring that the municipal court should have jurisdiction whatever might be the nature of the offense, thus giving a latitudinarian construction to the charter, which was only intended to grant the right of administering justice in cases where imprisonment resulted from a breach of the city ordinances. Smith was afterward arrested by a writ from the governor, but it is unknown whether he was rescued by his followers or discharged in consequence of this ordinance.

A combination of circumstances now concurred in rendering the Mormons unpopular. Besides impolitic enactments, they were furnished by the State with three pieces of cannon and 250 stands of small arms, which jealousy and popular rumor increased to 30 cannons and 5,000 or 6,000 muskets. Many thought they enter-

32

tained the treasonable design of overturning the government, driving out the original inhabitants and substituting their own population in their stead, as the children of Israel had done in the land of Canaan.

In 1842, the Mormon population of Hancock county had increased to about 16,000, and several thousand more were scattered over various parts of the United States and Europe. Mr. Henry Caswel, an English gentleman of talent and respectability, ascending the Mississippi in a steamboat, gives the following graphic account of his observations respecting the Saints at that time:

"Having been told that three hundred English emigrants were on board to join the prophet at Nauvoo, I walked to that part of the vessel appropriated to the poorer classes of travelers, and beheld my countrymen crowded together in a comfortless manner. I addressed them and found they were from the neighborhood of Preston, in Lancaster; they were decent looking people and by no means of the lower class. I took the liberty of questioning them concerning their plans, and found they were the dupes of Mormon missionaries. Early on Sunday morning I was landed opposite Nauvoo, and crossing the river in a large canoe, filled with Mormons going to church, in a few minutes I found myself in this extraordinary city. It is built on a grand plan, accommodated to the site of the temple and the bend of the river. The view of the winding Mississippi from the elevation where the temple stands is truly magnificent. The temple being unfinished, about half past ten o'clock a congregation of perhaps 2,000 persons assembled in a grove, within a short distance from the sanctuary. Their appearance was quite respectable and fully equal to that exhibited at the meetings of other denominations in the western country. Many gray-headed old men were there and many well dressed females. Their sturdy forms, clear complexions, and heavy movements, strongly contrasted with the slight figure, the sallow visage, and the elastic step of the Americans. There, too, were the bright and unconscious looks of little children, who born among the privileges of England's churches baptized with her consecrated waters and taught to lisp her prayers and repeat her catechisms, had now been led into this clan of heresy, to listen to the ravings of a false prophet and to imbibe the principles of a semi-pagan delusion. Two elders shortly came forward and one of them having made a few common-place remarks on the nature of prayer, and dwelt for a considerable time on the character and perfections of the Almighty, proceeded in the following strain: 'We thank thee, O Lord, that thou hast in these latter days restored the gifts of prophecy of revelation, and of great signs and wonders as in the days of old. We thank thee that thou didst formerly raise up thy servant Joseph to deliver his brethren in Egypt, so hast thou raised up another Joseph to save his brethren from bondage of sectarian delusion, and to bring them into this great and good land, flowing with milk and honey, which is the glory of all lands, and which thou didst promise to be an inheritance for the seed of Jacob for evermore. We pray for this servant and prophet, Joseph, that thou wouldst prosper and bless him; that although the archers have sorely grieved him, and shot at him, and hated him, his bow may abide in strength, and the arms of his hands may be made strong by the hand of the Almighty God of Jacob. We pray, also, for thy temple that the nations of the earth may bring gold and incense, that the sons of strangers may build up its walls and fly to it as a cloud and as doves to their windows. We pray thee, also, to hasten the ingathering of thy people, every man to his heritage and every man to his land. We pray that as thou hast set up this place as an ensign for the nations, so thou wouldst continue to assemble here the outcasts, and gather together the dispersed from the four corners of the earth. May every valley be exalted and every mountain and hill be made low and crooked places be made straight and the rough places plain, and may the glory of the Lord be revealed and all the flesh in it together. Bring thy sons from afar and thy daughters from the ends of the earth, and let them bring their gold and silver with them.'

"After prayer the other elder commenced a discourse on the necessity of a revelation for America as well as Asia, and on the probability of continued revelations. At its close a hymn was sung, and a third elder came forward and observed that his office required him to speak of business, and especially of the Nauvoo House, and among other things said, 'the Lord had commanded this work and it must be done; yes it shall be done, it will be done; that a small amount of the stock had hitherto been taken, that the committee had gone on borrowing and borrowing till they could borrow no longer; that mechanics had been employed on the house, that they wanted their pay and the committee are not able to pay them; that he came there with seven thousand dollars and now had but two thousand, having expended five thousand on the work of the Lord;' that he therefore called upon the brethren to obey God's command and take stock. The address being concluded, others followed in the same strain, and appeared as familiar with wordly business and operations of finance as with prophecies and the book of Mormon. None, however, came forward to take stock, and one of the elders thereupon remarked, that as they had not made up their minds as to the amount of stock they would take, he wished them to come to his house on the next day for that purpose. The public exercises being closed, accompanied by a prominent member of the church, I next visited the temple. Its position is commanding, and designed to be one of the best edifices in the country. It is one hundred and twenty feet by one hundred, and when completed will be fifty feet up to the eaves. Its expense is estimated at three hundred thousand dollars. The baptismal fount is finished. It is a capacious laver, above twenty feet square, rests on the backs of twelve oxen, well sculptured, and as large as life. The laver and oxen are of wood painted, but are to be gilded. Here baptisms for the dead are celebrated as well as baptisms for the healing of disease. Baptisms for the remission of sins are performed in the Mississippi. I was next introduced to the prophet, and had the honor of an interview with him. He is a coarse, plebeian person in aspect, and his countenance exhibits a curious mixture of the knave and clown. His hands are large and fat, and on one of his fingers he wears a massive gold ring with some inscription upon it. His dress was of coarse country manufacture, and his white hat was enveloped in a piece of black crape, being in mourning for a brother. I had no opportunity of observing the eyes of Smith, he appearing deficient in that open, staid-fixed look which characterizes an honest man. The Mormon system, mad as it is, had method in its madness, and many shrewd hands are at work in its maintainance and propagation, and whatever may befall its originators, it has the elements of increase and endurance. Mormon missionaries have been sent forth and are now at work in almost every country in christendom. They have recently gone to Russia with letters of credence from the Mormon prophet. Their numbers in England, we have no doubt, are increasing rapidly, and it remains for christains of the present day to determine whether Mormonism shall work to the level of those fanatical sects, which like new stars have blazed for a little while and then sunk into obscurity, or whether like a second Mahomedanism it shall extend itself, sword in hand, till christianity is leveled in the dust."

In 1842, Dr. John C. Bennett was expelled from the Mormon church, and thereafter traveled through different parts of the country, avowing, in lectures and publications, that the Mormons entertained treasonable designs against the government. One of Bennett's principal objects was to induce the authorities of Missouri to bring another indictment against Smith for an alleged attempt to murder Gov. Boggs. Being successful in his endeavors, June 5, 1843, an indictment was found against the prophet and another prominent Mormon, and shortly afterwards a messenger presented himself to Gov. Ford with a new demand for their arrest. In pursuance of the laws of the United States, the writ was given to

a constable in Hancock county for execution. The Missouri agent
and a constable hastened to Nauvoo for the purpose of serving
it, but finding on their arrival that Smith was on a visit to Rock
river, they repaired thither, and made the arrest in Palestine
grove, in the county of Lee. The prisoner was then left in the
custody of the agent, who set off with him to Missouri, but had
not proceeded far, when he was met and captured by an armed
body of Mormons, who released the prophet and conducted him
in triumph to Nauvoo. A writ of habeas corpus was sued out in
the municipal court of that city, and Cyrus Walker, the whig candidate for congress, appeared as attorney for the accused. In a
labored effort of great length, he endeavored to show that this
court, which was composed of Smith and his friends, had jurisdiction to issue the writ, and proceed in the defense of the prisoner, under the ordinances of the city, and he accordingly was
acquitted. Mr. Hodge, the democratic candidate, was visiting
Nauvoo at the time of the trial, and both he and Walker were
called on in a political convention to give their opinion relative to
the city ordinance, empowering the municipal court to issue writs
of habeas corpus in all cases of imprisonment, and both solemnly
declared that they considered it valid. It is hardly necessary to
state that this advice was given for the purpose of obtaining
votes, as both candidates knew it was false. Instead of being
actuated by that integrity which combats and corrects public
opinion when wrong ,the only true passport to official position,
both willfully sanctioned an error for the accomplishment of selfish
ends.

The Mormons, on the other hand, in consequence of stupidity
and ignorance, were ever ready to be duped and brought in
antagonism to the laws of the State, by the chicanery of party.
If the action of the government bore hard upon them, however
justly it might be administered, they regarded it as wantonly
oppressive, or if judicious advice was given them, it was rejected
with scorn whenever opposed to their favorite schemes. Unscrupulous politicians becoming aware of this characteristic,
would first learn their predelictions and advise them accordingly,
whereby they became the sport of party and the victims of the
most corrupt men in the country.

On the release of Smith, the Missouri agent applied to Gov.
Ford for a military force to assist in arresting him, but the
application was refused. Smith having once been arrested, and
the writ returned as fully executed, the governor had no further
cognizance of the case except to issue a new warrant, provided
another requisition should be made for his re-arrest by the executive of Missouri. While it was readily admitted that Smith had
been forcibly rescued and suffered to go unpunished by a court
transcending its authority, yet it would have been an illegal and
perhaps dangerous expedient to attempt to call out the militia to
correct or reverse the decision.

The Mormons, emboldened by success in this trial, in the winter
of 1843-4, passed another ordinance to further protect their
leaders. They enacted a law providing that no writ issued from
any other place except Nauvoo for the arrest of any person in the
city, should be executed without an approval endorsed thereon
by the mayor; that if any public officer, by virtue of any foreign

writ, should attempt to make an arrest in the city without such an approval of his process, he should be subject to imprisonment for life, and the governor of the State should not have the power of pardoning the offender without the consent of the mayor.

The passage of this ordinance created great astonishment, and induced many to believe that there was a reality in the accusations which had been made against them, respecting the establishment of an independent government. After this law went into operation, if robberies were committed in the adjoining country, the thieves would flee into Nauvoo, and if the plundered parties followed them, they were fined by the Mormon courts for daring to seek after their property in the holy city. The Mormons themselves were frequently the guilty parties, and by this means sought both to retain the stolen goods and escape the just punishment of their crimes.

The most positive evidence that they contemplated the organization of a separate government, was based on the fact that about this time they sent a petition to congress, asking for the establishment of a territorial government, of which Nauvoo was to be the center. Another act characteristic of their vanity, was the announcement of Smith, in the spring of 1844, as a candidate for the presidency of the United States. His followers, sanguine of success, sent from two to three thousand missionaries into the field to convert the people, and labor for the election of the prophet. It was stated by dissenters in the Mormon church, that Smith also entertained the idea of making himself the temporal as well as the spiritual leader of his people, and that, for this purpose, he instituted a new order of church dignitaries, the members of which were to be both kings and priests.

He next caused himself to be annointed king and priest, but of a higher order than the others, who were to be his nobility, and to whom as the upholders of his throne he administered the oath of allegiance. To give character to his pretensions he declared his lineage in an unbroken line from Joseph the son of Jacob, and that of his wife from some other important personage of the ancient Hebrews. To strengthen his political power he also instituted a body of police styled the Danite band, who were sworn to protect his person and to obey his orders as the commands of God. A female order previously existing in the church, called spiritual wives, was modified so as to suit the licentiousness of the prophet. A doctrine was revealed that it was impossible for a woman to get to heaven except as the wife of a Mormon elder; that each elder might marry as many women as he could maintain, and that any female might be sealed to eternal life by becoming their concubine. This licentiousness, the origin of polygamy in the church, they endeavored to justify by an appeal to Abraham, Jacob and other favorites of God in a former age of the world.

After the establishment of these institutions, Smith began to play the tyrant over his people, as all persons of inferior intellect and unduly developed passions always do when others become subject to their will. One of his first attempts to abuse the power with which he was intrusted, was an effort to take the wife of William Law, one of his most talented and respectable followers, and make her a spiritual wife. Without the sanction of law he established offices in Nauvoo for recording property titles and issuing marriage licences, whereby he sought to monopolize the traffic in real estate* and control the marital relations of his people. The despotism thus practiced soon caused a spirit of insubordination and disaffection in the Mormon church and community. Law and the other leaders determined to resist the encroachments of Smith, and for the purpose of exposing the abuses growing out of the new institutions, they procured a press and commenced the publication of a newspaper. The appearance of the paper was the signal for opposition, and before the second number could be issued, by an order of the council, the heretical press was demolished, and the publishers ejected from the church. It is difficult to decide whether this trial, which is one of the most singular instances of adjudication to be found on record, was the result of insanity or depravity. The proceedings were instituted against the press instead of the owners, who were not notified to attend. No jury was called, the witnesses were not required to testify under oath, and the evidence was all furnished by the plaintiffs in the absence of the defendants. It was not difficult, under these circumstances, to prove that the publishers of the paper were the vilest of sinners, and that the press was the greatest nuisance, hence the order to have it abated.

The holy city becoming a dangerous place of residence for the seceding Mormons, they retired to Carthage, the county seat, and obtained warrants for the arrest of Smith and the members of the city council and others connected with the destruction of the press. Some of the parties having been arrested and discharged by the authorities in Nauvoo, a convention of citizens assembled at Carthage, and appointed a committee to wait on the governor for the purpose of procuring military assistance to enforce the execution of the law in the city. The governor, on learning the position of affairs, determined to visit the county and inquire into the nature of the complaints before he gave his official sanction to any particular course of action. When he arrived a message was sent to the mayor and common council informing them of the complaints made against them, and requiring that a committee might be sent to answer the charge. A number of persons were accordingly sent, and in the examination which ensued, it became evident that the whole proceedings of the mayor and common council were irregular and illegal. Though such proceedings could not be tolerated in a country claiming to be governed by law and order, yet they were excusable to some extent in consequence of undue statements frequently made to the Nauvoo officials by

*The Mormons made no efforts to conceal their design of monopolizing the lands in the vicinity of Nauvoo to the exclusion of those who had welcomed them with such genuine sympathy, when banished from Missouri. It is said, when they wished to possess the property of a gentile they offered what they considered a reasonable price for it, and in case of refusal they proceeded to enforce acceptance by various intolerable annoyances. Whittling was resorted to as one method of vexation. For this purpose three persons were appointed who, armed with sticks and jack-knives, took a position in front of the obdurate owner's residence and commenced whittling. If he went to church, the post office, market or other place of business, they followed him whittling. If he expostulated, became angry, threatened or swore, they answered by whittling. If idle boys laughed and jeered the victim, his tormentors demurely whittled. When he returned home the whittlers followed and again took their places in front of his house and continued their annoyance from early dawn till late at night. The irritated owner could not look from a window without encountering the insolent stare of his persecutors, who were still whittling. Generally a single day, it is said, was sufficient to make him submit, very rarely he held out two days, but never was able to endure more than three days of this ludicrous yet insufferable martyrdom.

some of the best lawyers in the State who, as candidates for office, sought their support by purposely exaggerating the extent of their authority.

The destruction of the press was a blow dealt against civil liberty, and hence among a republican people jealous of their rights, it was well calculated to raise a flame of excitement. The Mormon leaders, if honest, little understood the fact that a well conducted press is essential to a free government, and that a profligate one, by venality and falsehood, is sure to lose its influence and thus defeat the improper object it seeks to accomplish. Attempts to interfere with the freedom of the press causes the suppression of information which should be dessiminated among the people, and are always attended with a greater loss to civil liberty than can possibly result from the temporary indiscretions of a few imprudent publishers. Besides, when calumnies are circulated in this manner the authors are amenable to the law, which is the proper means of redress, and not the wanton destruction of property.

In the investigations made by the governor while at Carthage, it was proved that Smith sent a number of his followers to Missouri for the purpose of kidnapping two witnesses against a member of the church, soon to be tried for larceny; that he had assailed and brutally beaten an officer of the county for an alleged non-performance of duty, when in consequence of sickness he was not able to attend to it; that he stood indicted for perjury, having falsely sworn to an accusation of murder against a real estate agent, that he might be expelled from the city, and not interfere with his monopoly as a land speculator; and that the municipal court of which he was chief justice, had frequently discharged Mormons accused of crimes committed in various parts of the county, thus obstructing the administration of justice and making the common council of Nauvoo independent of the State government.

In addition to these actual infringements of law, other causes served to increase the tide of opposition now turned against the saints. The extravagance of their theological pretensions had incurred the ill will of other denominations of religion, while the effort to elect their prophet to the presidency brought them in conflict with the zealots and bigots of both political parties and covered them with ridicule. A fruitful cause of hostile feeling grew out of the fact that at several preceding elections they cast their vote as a unit, whereby it was evident that no one in the country could obtain official position without first securing their support. It was believed that Smith instructed the Danite band, which he had chosen as the ministers of his vengeance, and the instruments of the intolerable tyranny which he exercised over his people, that no blood, except that of the church, was to be regarded sacred if it contravened the accomplishment of his object. It was asserted that he inculcated the legality of perjury and other crimes, if committed to advance the cause of the true believers; that God had given the world and all that it contained to his saints, and since they were kept out of their rightful inheritance by force, it was no moral offense to get possession of it by stealing. It was reported that an establishment existed in Nauvoo for the manufacture of counterfeit money, and that a set of outlaws were maintained there for the purpose of putting it in circulation. Statements were circulated to the effect that a reward had been offered for the destruction of the Warsaw *Signal*, a newspaper published at Warsaw, in opposition to Mormon interests, and that Mormons dispersed over the country threatened all persons who offered to assist the constable in the execution of the law, with the destruction of their property and the murder of their families. There were rumors also afloat that an alliance had been formed with the Western Indians, and in case of war they would be used in murdering their enemies. In short, if only one-half of these reports were true the Mormons must have been the most infamous people that ever existed, and if one half of them were false they must have been the worst slandered.

Previous to the arrival of the governor the whole body of the militia in Schuyler and McDonough counties had been called out, and armed forces commenced assembling in Carthage and Warsaw to enforce the service of civil process. After the forces had appointed their officers, the governor, apprehensive that the Mormon leaders might be made the victims of popular fury, exacted a pledge from both officers and men that in the discharge of their duties they would, under all circumstances, keep within the pale of the law. All signified their willingness to co-operate with him in preserving order, promised to pursue a strictly legal course and protect the persons of the accused in case of violence. The constable and ten men were then sent to make the arrest, being instructed to inform the accused that if they peaceably submitted they would be protected, but if not, they must receive the consequences, as the whole force of the State, if necessary, would be called out to enforce submission.

In the meantime, Smith had declared martial law; his followers residing the country, were summoned to his assistance; the legion was assembled and under arms, and the entire city was one great military encampment, no ingress or egress being permitted except on the strictest examination. However, on the arrival of the constable and his escort, the mayor and members of the common council at once signified their willingness to surrender, and accompany them on the following morning to Carthage. Failing to make their appearance at the appointed time, the constable hastened away without attempting to make the arrest. It was subsequently ascertained that the cause of the hurried departure was the fear that the Mormons would submit and thus entitle themselves to the protection of the law. There were daring and active men traversing the country and making inflamatory speeches, with the hope that a popular movement might be inaugurated for the expulsion of the Mormons from the State. The constable and those who accompanied him were in the conspiracy, and endeavored, by the partial performance of their duty, to create a necessity for calling out an overwhelming force to effect this object. The artifice was, however, soon detected by the governor, and another opportunity given the accused to surrender. A requisition was also made on them for the return of the State arms, because the legion to which they had been entrusted had used them illegally in the destruction of the press, and the enforcement of martial law as a means of preventing civil process. On the 24th of June, 1845, in obedience to the last summons, Joe Smith, his brother

Hiram, the members of the city council and others, went to Carthage, and surrendered themselves prisoners to the constable, on the charge of riot. All entered into recognizance before a justice of the peace to appear at court, and were discharged. A new writ was, however, immediately issued and served on the two Smiths, and both were arrested and thrown into prison. The prophet, it is said, whether desirous of courting martyrdom or alarmed at the popular storm which threatened him, seemed to have a presentiment that he never would return to Nauvoo alive. According to the statement at Carthage, he remarked, "I am going like a lamb to the slaughter, but I have a conscience void of offence toward God and man."

The jail in which the prisoners were confined, was a stone building of considerable size, furnished with a suite of rooms for the jailer, cells for the close confinement of convicts, and a large apartment not so strong but more comfortable than the cells. The prisoners were first confined in the cells by the jailor, but at the remonstrance of the Mormons, and the advice of the governor, they were afterwards transferred to the large apartment, where they were more pleasantly situated, and where they remained till the occurrence of the tragedy in which they lost their lives. No serious apprehensions were entertained of an attack on the jail, nor was it supposed that the Smiths would make an effort to escape. At the time the prisoners were incarcerated, the forces at Carthage and Warsaw, amounted to 1700 men, most of whom were anxious to be led into Nauvoo to destroy the apparatus with which it was said the Mormons manufactured counterfeit money. It was also believed by the governor, that if an imposing demonstration of the State forces should be made, it might overaw the Mormons and exert a salutary influence in preventing the murders, robberies and burnings apprehended as the result of the proceedings against their prophet. In accordance with this view, arrangements were made for the marching of the troops on the 27, of June, and Golden's Point near the Mississippi, and midway between Warsaw and Nauvoo,was selected as the place of rendezvous. Before, however, the movement was fully inaugurated, the governor discovered his mistake, and immediately countermanded his previous orders for the assembling of the forces.

It was observed, as the preparations for marching advanced, the excitement prevading the public mind correspondingly increased, and threats were occassionally made to destroy the city and expel the inhabitants from the State. Subsequent developments rendered it evident that an agreement had been made by some of the most daring and reckless spirits, to fire on the forces of the State when they arrived in Nauvoo, and afterwards attribute it to the Mormons, as a means of bringing on a general engagement. The city at that time contained a population of 12,000 to 15,000 inhabitants, many of whom were helpless women and children, and humanity shudders at the wanton destruction of life and property that must have resulted from such blind and obdurate fury. Besides, if the disposition had existed to precipitate upon the city a calamity of this kind, the forces of the State were inadequate to afford such protection to the adjacent country as would have been necessary. After the surrender of the Smiths, at their request, Captain Singleton with a company from

Brown county, was sent to take command of the Nauvoo legion and guard the city. According to his report, when the legion was called out for inspection, they assembled 2000 strong and were fully equipped with arms. This was after the public arms had been taken away, and now they were prepared with weapons of their own for any emergency. The State forces had three pieces of cannon, 1200 muskets and rations for two days, after which they would have been compelled to discontinue operations for the want of subsistence. It was therefore deemed advisable to abandon the enterprise as impracticable, and the forces with the exception of three companies were accordingly disbanded. Two of these were selected to guard the jail, and the remaining one was retained as an escort for the governor, who proposed to visit Nauvoo for the purpose of inquiring into the charges preferred against the inhabitants, and to warn them that if any secret violence should be committed by them on the persons or property of those who had assisted in the execution of the law, it would inevitably be followed by the most summary retribution.

Leaving Gen. Demning in command of the guards, on the 27th, of June, the governor accompanied by Col. Buckmaster, and Captain Davis' dragoons, departed for Nauvoo, eighteen miles distant. Before proceeding far, Col. Buckmaster informed the governor that while at Carthage some circumstances of a suspicious character induced him to believe that an attack upon the jail was meditated. The latter, however was incredulous. It was notorious that he had gone to Nauvoo, and it was not probable that while there any outrage would be committed on the Smiths, which would endanger his own safety and that of his companions. Nevertheless, to guard against all possible contingencies, a messenger was sent back to inform the guard of danger, and to insist on their defending the jail at the peril of their lives, till the governor returned. It was also decided, to defer to some future time the examination of the misdemeanors alleged against the Mormons, that the company might immediately return and render assistance, in case the jail should be assaulted.

The parties arrived in Nauvoo about 4 o'clock on the 27th of June, and as soon as notice could be given, a large number of the inhabitants convened to hear a discourse from the governor. In the address delivered, the illegal action of their public functionaries was explained; they were advised of the infamous reports rife in all the country respecting their conduct, and the consequent prejudice and hostility engendered in the public mind, and admonished that in future they would have to act with great circumspection, or their lives and the safety of their city would fall a sacrifice to popular indignation. During the delivery of the speech, some impatience and excitement was exhibited by the auditors at the various allegations made against them, which they persistently denied as untrue. They claimed to be a law abiding people, and carefully observed its provisions, that they might in turn have the benefit of its protection. After the conclusion of the address, the question, as to whether they would conform to the laws of the State, in opposition to the advice of their leaders, was submitted to a vote, which resulted unanimously in favor of the proposition. Their subsequent conduct, however, proved that when guilty of the greatest extravagances, they would make the loudest professions of attachment to law and order.

The party left the city a short time before sundown, and had not gone far before they met two messengers, who informed them that the Smiths had been assassinated about five o'clock that afternoon. All were astounded at the reception of this intelligence, and fearful apprehensions were entertained respecting the consequences likely to ensue from the massacre. The Mormons were an infatuated, fanatical people, not likely to be influenced by the motives which ordinarily govern the conduct of men, and a desultory war might be the result. To prevent the news reaching Nauvoo the messengers were ordered into custody, and the governor hastened to Carthage to be in readiness for the outburst of excitement and lawlessness that might follow the dissemination of the intelligence. A courier was also despatched to Carthage to inform the citizens of the tragedy. They, however, appeared to understand the matter better than the messenger, and before his arrival had commenced removing their families across the river to guard against impending danger. The ensuing night they sent a committee to Quincy for help, and at an early hour on the following morning a large concourse of the citizens assembled to devise means of defense. At the meeting it was reported that the Mormons had attempted to rescue the Smiths; that a party of Missourians and others had killed them to prevent their escape; that the governor and his cortege, who were in Nauvoo at the time, had been attacked by the legion and forced to take refuge in a house, and that if assistance was not furnished within two days he would fall a victim to Mormon vengeance. A force of some 250 men was immediately raised, and by ten o'clock the same morning they embarked on a boat and steamed down to Nauvoo to assist in rescuing the governor. On arriving at the city the whole story proved a fabrication originated to intensify the excitement and cause a collision between the Mormons and State forces. Subsequent evidence also rendered it highly probable that the conspirators connected with the assassination contemplated involving the governor in the same misfortune. Circumstances warranted the conclusion that the assassins had arranged that the murder should occur while the governor was in Nauvoo; that the Mormons on hearing the catastrophe would suspect him as an accomplice, and at the first outburst of indignation put him to death as a means of retaliation. The motive for this treacherous attempt against the executive officer of the State was to arouse a spirit of opposition, and cause the extermination of the Mormons.

The governor arrived in Carthage about ten o'clock, and found the citizens in a state of consternation, some having left and others preparing to follow. One of the companies which had been left to guard the jail, departed before the attack was made, and many of the others left shortly afterward. General Deming, who was absent when the murder occurred, volunteered to remain and guard the town with the small force which remained, unless compelled to retire before superior numbers. The governor retired to Quincy and immediately issued orders for provisionally raising and equipping an imposing force, in case they should be needed.

CHAPTER XLII.

1844-6—MORMON WAR.

Manner of Smith's Death—Character of the Mormons—Apostles Assume the Government of the Church—Trial and Acquittal of the Assassins—Saints Driven from the Vicinity of Lima and Green Plains—Leading Mormons Retire Across the Mississippi— Battle at Nauvoo—Expulsion of the Inhabitants.

When the assassination of the Mormons became known, it appeared that the force at Nauvoo, agreeably to orders, had marched on the morning of the 27th in the direction of Golden's Point to form a connection with troops at that place, but after they had advanced about 8 miles they were met by a messenger from Carthage with an order to disband and return home ; the governor, who issued it, fearing he could not control the inflammable material he was collecting, determined to scatter it. About 150 of the men, instead of complying with the order, blackened their faces with powder, hurriedly started for Carthage and encamped some distance from the village. Here they learned that one of the companies left to guard the Smiths, had gone home and that the other, the Carthage Grays, was stationed in the square, 150 yards distant, and that Sergeant Franklin A. Worrel, with only 8 men, was detailed to watch the prisoners. As soon as messages could be interchanged it was agreed among the conspirators that the guns of the guard should be charged with blank cartridges and fired on the assailants, when they should attempt to enter the jail.

Gen. Deming, who had been left in command, discovering the plot to assassinate the Smiths, and having been deserted by the principal part of the troops, retired from the village, lest an attempt should be made on his own life. After perfecting their scheme of murder, the assailants scaled the slight fence enclosing the jail, and immediately disarming the guards, who according to agreement discharged their pieces, they ascended the flight of stairs leading to the room containing the prisoners. At the time the assault was made, two other Mormons, Richards and Tailor as visitors, were in the large apartment with the Smiths. Hearing the rush on the stairs, the imperilled men instinctively held the door by pressing their weight against it. The attacking party thus denied entrance, fired upon the door, and the bullets passing through it, killed Hiram Smith, who falling, exclaimed "I am a dead man." Tailor receiving 4 wounds, retreated under the bed, and Richards, after the door was burst open, secreted himself behind it, though afterward in relating the murder, he claimed that he stood in the midst of danger, warding off the balls with a consecrated wand. The prophet, armed with a six barrelled pistol which had been furnished by his friends, fought bravely in defence of his life, and wounded four of his antagonists before he was killed. At length when his pistol was exhausted, severely wounded, he ran to the window, and partly leaped and partly fell into the yard below; there with his last dying energies he gathered himself up in a sitting posture, but his disabled condition and vague, wandering glances excited no compassion in the infuriated mob, thirsting for his blood. The broils which had so long distracted the country, infused into the avengers the spirit of demons, and the shooting of Smith was not considered any more criminal than taking the life of a wolf or tiger. While in this position a party of Missourians discharged their guns at him, and he fell crying out "Oh Lord my God." Four balls had pierced his body and before the smoke cleared away the Mormon prophet was no more.*

When the tragedy was over horror succeeded the frenzied rage which had possessed the assassins, and in silence they hurried across the dusty prairies to Warsaw, 18 miles distant. The murder occurred at half-past five, and at a quarter before eight the fugitives dragged their weary limbs along the streets of Warsaw, at such an astounding rate had the lash of a guilty conscience driven them. An outburst of vengeance on the part of the Mormons was anticipated, but nothing of the kind occurred. The appalling disaster which had thus befallen the church was not followed by revenge, and it was a long time before they recovered from the stupor and despair attending it. A delegation repaired to Carthage for their dead, and on returning to Nauvoo they were buried with the honors belonging to the general of the legion.

"Thus fell Joe Smith, the most successful impostor of modern times. A man who, though ignorant and coarse, had some great natural parts which fitted him for temporary success, but which were so obscured and counteracted by the inherent corruption and vices of his nature that he could never succeed in establishing a system of policy which looked to permanent success in the future. His lusts, his love of money and power, always set him to studying present gratification and convenience, rather than the remote consequences of his plans. It seems that no power of intellect can save a corrupt man from this error. The strong cravings of the animal nature will never give fair play to a fine understanding; the judgment is never allowed to choose that good which is far away, in preference to enticing evil near at hand. And this may be considered a wise ordinance of Providence, by which the counsels of talented but corrupt men are defeated in the very act which promised success.

"It must not be supposed that the pretended prophet practiced the tricks of a common impostor; that he was a dark and gloomy person, with a long beard and grave and severe aspect, and a reserved and saintly carriage; on the contrary he was full of levity, even to boyish romping, dressed like a dandy and at times drank

* John Hay in the Atlantic Monthly of December, 1869

like a sailor and swore like a pirate. He could, as occasion required, be exceedingly meek in his deportment, and then again, rough and boisterous as a highway robber, being always able to satisfy his followers of the propriety of his conduct. He always quailed before power, and was arrogant to weakness. At times he could put on the air of a penitent, as if feeling the deepest humiliation for his sins, suffering unutterable anguish and the most gloomy forebodings of eternal woe. At such times he would call for the prayers of the brethren in his behalf with a wild and fearful energy and earnestness. He was full six feet high, strongly built and uncommonly well muscled. No doubt he was as much indebted for his influence over an ignorant people to the superiority of his physical vigor as to his cunning and intellect.*"

The Mormon church at this time, consisted of two classes, the rulers and the ruled, knavery in the one and credulity in the other being the heterogeneous characteristics which kept them together. The former consisted of unprincipled men of talent, who, abandoned in character and bankrupt in fortune, espoused the cause of Mormonism for speculative purposes, knowing it was an adventure in which they had nothing to lose, while it might be the means of retrieving their fortunes. Having neither respect for God nor man, and not reverencing any religion, they proposed, like Mahomet and others, to found a new system of theology, and if they could impose it on the credulity of mankind and live on the labor of their dupes, they had no higher object to accomplish. They formed a nucleus which attracted to Nauvoo adventurers and adepts in every species of crime, while the extraordinary powers which had been conferred on the city authorities enabled them to screen the guilty from the penalties of the laws they habitually violated. At their social entertainments, where music and dancing constituted the principal pastime, great attention was paid to dress, while little prudence was exercised in the selection of their company. There were in the same gay assemblage the brazen-faced desperado who despised the law, and the venal magistrate who protected him in his crimes, the wanton wife and the truant husband on an equal footing with those who respected the sanctity of marriage, the reckless adventurer in search of fortune, and the successful impostor in possession of ecclesiastical emoluments and honors. Discordant and incongruous in nature, they managed to keep time to the same music, and to forget minor differences, provided their principal objects, sensual pleasure and public plunder, were subserved.

The lay members of the church, on the other hand, were generally honest and industrious but ignorant, and the dupes of an artful delusion. In devotion to the principles which they professed, they were not surpassed by the believers of other creeds, for humanity exhibits little difference in this respect, whatever may be the system of religion. If the system is crude, the intelligent devotee rejects it, but if his want of knowledge allows him to believe it he will adhere to its dogmas with a tenacity equal to that exhibited by the enlightened advocate of a rational theology. With the great majority of the Mormons their religious belief amounted almost to infatuation, and they were, therefore, more

*Ford's History.

properly objects of compassion than persecution. Certainly no greater calamity can befall a member of the human family than to have the adoration which he offers the Deity perverted by the vagaries of such a monstrous superstition.

Mormonism, instead of perishing by the death of Smith, received a new impetus from his martyrdom. His followers now regarded him as a saint; his words on going to Carthage were adduced as fresh proof of his prophetic character, and a thousand stories were circulated respecting the meekness with which he met death. Prophecies were published that in imitation of Christ he would raise from the dead. Many confidently expected the fulfillment of these predictions, and in due time it was reported he was seen, attended by a celestial army, coursing his way through the heavens on a great white horse.

The principle that the death of the martyr is the seed of the church, proved true in regard to Mormonism. Smith, though well qualified to originate a movement of this kind, was unable to safely direct it through the complication of perils which always besets religious innovation. By dying he made room for Brigham Young, the present head of the church, who, by his superior administrative ability, perhaps, saved the Mormon theocracy from disorganization and its subjects from dispersion. Cunning and duplicity may be used by the founders of a sect, but great prudence and judgment best befits him who would afterwards harmonize its jarring elements and shape its future career.

The church, as originally organized, contained 3 presidents, Joseph Smith, Hiram Smith and Sidney Rigdon, and 12 apostles. The latter were abroad, and till they could return home the saints were in doubt as to the future government of the church. Rigdon, being the only surviving member of the presidency, claimed the government, and fortified his pretensions by declaring that the will of the prophet was in his favor, and that he had received several new revelations to the same effect. One of his revelations, requiring the wealthy to dispose of their possessions and follow him to Pennsylvania, rendered him unpopular, the rich being reluctant to part with their property, and the poor unwilling to be deserted by those whose patronage enabled them to live. When the apostles returned a fierce conflict arose between them and Rigdon for supremacy, which resulted in the expulsion of the latter from the church.

He afterwards retired with a small fragment of the saints, and established a little delusion of his own near Pittsburgh, while the larger part submitted to the apostles, with Brigham Young, a talented but dishonest and licentious man, as their leader.

Missionaries to the number of 3,000 were now sent abroad to preach in the name of the martyred Joseph, and Mormonism increased more rapidly than it had at any time in its past history. In their wild enthusiasm they were willing to compass sea and land to make a single convert, and everywhere they went they found the ignorant and credulous ready to become infatuated with their strange fanaticism. No other religion promised such great spiritual and temporal advantage with such little self-denial, and not only dupes but sharpers united with the church, and it is said that within 14 years after its organization it numbered 200,-000 members. The missionaries always informed their wondering and deluded converts that it was necessary to repair to the place of gathering where the sublime fullness of the gospel alone could be fully revealed and enjoyed. When removed thither, by seeing and hearing nothing but Mormonism, and associating with those who placed implicit confidence in its dogmas, they ultimately became so deluded as to believe the greatest extravagances and submit to the most intolerable despotism. Many by this system of training became devoted disciples, who would have spurned the empty pretensions and licentiousness of their religion, had it at first been presented to them in its real deformity.

About a year after the apostles had assumed the reins of government, they concluded to suspend for a time their efforts to convert the world, and accordingly their missionaries and all others connected with the church were called home. In a short time Mormons commenced pouring into Nauvoo from all parts of the world, and the infuriated elders, instead of expounding the gospel to the congregations which were regularly called together, indulged in a tirade of abuse against the gentiles, curses on the government and all who were not of the Mormon church or its tools. Nor were the anti-Mormons or those who opposed them idle. The death of the Smiths had not appeased their desire for vengeance, and more determined than ever to expel their adversaries from the country, they frequently called on the governor for aid. The Mormons also invoked the assistance of the executive in punishing the murderers of their prophet, and both parties were thoroughly disgusted with the constitutional provisons which imposed restraint on the summary attainment of their unlawful designs. The elections coming off in August, 1844, for members of the legislature and congress, and another pending for the presidency of the United State, further complicated the difficulties and enmities of the parties. The whig politicians, who were unable to secure their support, uniting with the anti-Mormons, sent invitations to the militia captains of Hancock and all the adjoining counties of Illinois, Missouri and Iowa to rendezvous with their companies in the vicinity of Nauvoo, preparatory to engaging in a wolf hunt, it being understood that the Mormons were the game to be hunted. Preparations were made for raising several thousand men; the anti-Mormons commenced anew the most exaggerated accounts of Mormon outrages, the whig press in every part of the United States came to their assistance, and the publications of the opposite party, which had hitherto been friendly, now quailed under the tempest which followed, leaving the denunciated and discredited sheet at Nauvoo alone to correct public opinion. Prominent politicians who had received the Mormon vote, were now unwilling to risk their reputation in defending them, so great was the cowardice of the one and the odious character of the other.

In the meantime, the anti-Mormon force, which had been summoned to meet in the guise of hunters, commenced assembling for the purpose of assaulting Nauvoo, and driving its inhabitants out of the country. To avert the blow, the governor, assisted by Gen. J. J. Hardin, and Cols. Baker and Merriman, raised a force of 500 men and marched to the scene of the threatened outbreak. When he arrived a large part of the malcontents fled across the river into Missouri. Flight, however, was unnecessary, for the State forces had not been long in the disaffected district before they espoused the cause of the rioters, and instead of driving them out as enemies, were disposed to receive them as friends. Despite his demoralized forces, the governor, whose sense of justice seems to have been in part sharpened by political motives, determined to follow the fugitives and arrest three of their leaders, against whom writs had been issued for the murder of the Smiths. Boats were procured and secretly landed a mile above Warsaw, and the troops marched to the same place, preparatory to crossing the river and seizing the accused.

In the meantime, however, Colonel Baker visited the encampment and effected arrangements for the surrender of the alleged assassins, and the further prosecution of the expedition was abandoned. Two of the suspected persons accordingly recrossed the river and surrendered themselves prisoners, it having been agreed that they should be taken to Quincy for examination; that the attorney for the people should be advised to admit them to bail, and that they should be tried at the next term of the Carthage court. The faith of the governor had been pledged for the protection of the Smiths, and he deemed it especially important that their assassins should be punished as a means of vindicating the honor of the State, restoring the supremacy of the law and preventing the recurrence of such infamous crimes in the future. Able lawyers were therefore secured to prosecute the prisoners, and the trial came off in the summer of 1845. The panel of jurors selected by the Mormon officials of the county was rejected, in consequence of being effected by prejudice, and two elisors were chosen, one a Mormon and the other an anti-Mormon, to select a new one. Ninety-six persons were presented, before any could be found sufficiently ignorant and indifferent to administer justice. They all swore they had never formed nor expressed an opinion as to the guilt or innocence of the prisoners, although at the same time they belonged to a military mob, which to the number of 1,000 men was in attendance with arms to overawe the Mormons and extort from the court the verdict in favor of the accused. The principal Mormon witnesses were Brackenbury, Daniels, and a Miss Graham. The first two had accompanied the expedition from Warsaw to Carthage, had witnessed the killing of the Smiths, and were able to identify the murderers. From Carthage they went to Nauvoo, where they united with the church and were boarded by the Mormons to secure their evidence at the trial. While here Brackenbury secured the services of a sign painter who executed the death and ascension of Smith, which he exhibited ostensibility for the spiritual edification of the saints, but more for the augmentation of his own private resources. Daniels, not to be outdone by his associate, wrote an account of the death of Smith, in which, among a great many other absurdities, he says he beheld descending from heaven and resting on the head of Smith, a bright light, which struck some of his murderers with blindness, and that he heard celestial voices confirming his mission as a prophet. Owing to these fictions, the evidence both of the showman and scribbler was rejected as invalid. Miss Graham was present and assisted in feeding the hungry mob at the Warsaw House, after it came straggling in from Carthage. Her nervous and sensitive organization, however, had been so wrought

33

upon by the Mormon delusion, that she was unable to distinguish her suspicions and fancies from actual facts, and so blended them in her evidence that it was contended she proved nothing except her own honest but insane zeal. Other witnessess were examined who knew all the facts, but under the dominating influence of a faction they refused to divulge them. The judge was held in duress by an armed mob, which filled the court house, and stamped applause or hissed defiance, according as they approved or disapproved the proceedings. The trial closed and though there was not a man in the jury, court house, or county, that did not know the prisoners had committed the murder, yet nothing could be proved and they were accordingly acquitted.

At a subsequent term of the court the Mormons were tried for the destruction of the heretical press. The tribunal in this case consisted of a Mormon court, a Mormon sheriff and a Mormon jury, selected on account of their partiality for the accused, as in the previous trial, yet all swore that they knew nothing of the guilt or innocence of the defendants, who of course were acquitted. No leading man of either faction could now be arrested without the aid of an army, and when thus secured, neither party would permit an impartial trial in their own county, and since a change of venue to a disinterested locality could not be effected without the consent of the accused, it was impossible to convict any one of a partisan crime. The administration of the criminal law was impossible, civil government was at an end, and the entire community was in a frightful state of anarchy.

During the summer and fall of 1845, several occurrences transpired, calculated to increase the irritation existing between the Mormons and their neighbors. A suit was instituted in the circuit court of the United States against one of the apostles to recover a note given in Ohio, and a marshal was sent to summon the defendants, but they refused to be served with the process. Indignation meetings were held by the saints, inflamatory speeches delivered by their principal men, and the marshal threatened for attempting to serve the writs, while it was agreed that no further attempts of that kind should be made in Nauvoo. About the same time an anti-Mormon made an assault upon Gen. Deming the sheriff of the court, and was killed by the latter in repelling the attack. The vanquished party had many friends, and his death occasioned a fresh outburst of passion. To allay the storm, the officer who was believed to be friendly to the Mormons was held to bail, although he had acted strictly in self-defence, and was therefore not guilty. It was also discovered in trying the right of property at Lima, in Adams county, that the Mormons had an institution connected with their church to secure their effects from execution. It was an association of five persons, any of whom was to own all the property, and in the avent of its being levied on for debt, they could refer the ownership to such a member of the firm as would defeat the execution. Incensed at this action, the anti-Mormons of Lima and Green Plains, held a meeting to devise means for the expulsion of the Mormons from that part of the country. It was accordingly arranged that a number of their own party should fire on the building in which they were assembled, in such a manner as not to injure any one, and then report that the Mormons had commenced the work of plunder and death. This plot was duly executed, and the startling intelligence soon called together a mob, which threatened the Mormons with fire and sword if they did not immediately leave the neighborhood. The Mormons of this locality had previously annoyed the inhabitants by petty larcenies, and now refusing to depart, the mob at once executed their threats by burning 125 houses and forcing the inmates to flee for their lives. The fugitives arrived in Nauvoo in the midst of the sickly season, carrying with them the infirm, whose pitiable condition excited the utmost indignation among the inhabitants.

As soon as the intelligence of these events reached Springfield, the governor ordered Gen. Hardin to raise a body of men sufficient to enforce the law, but before it was ready to march, the sheriff of the county took the matter in his own hands. Gen. Deming, the former sheriff, was dead, and J. B. Backinstos, his successor and a prominent Mormon, owing to unpopularity was unable to get assistance from the anti-Mormons, although many of them were strongly opposed to the riotous proceedings. He, therefore, hastened to Nauvoo and armed several hundred Mormons, established a permanent guard at Carthage, and swept over other parts of the county in search of the incendiaries. The guilty parties fleeing to the neighboring counties of Illinois, Iowa and Missouri, he was unable to bring them to battle or make any arrests. One man, however, was killed without provocation, another attempting to escape was shot, and afterwards hacked and mutilated as if he had been murdered by Indians, and Franklin A. Worrel, who had command of the jail, and betrayed his trust in consenting to the assassination of the Smiths, lost his life from the effect of a rifle ball discharged by some unknown person concealed for that purpose in a thicket. The anti-Mormons also committed one murder. A party of them set fire to a quantity of straw near the barn of an old Mormon ninety years of age, and when he appeared to extinguish the flames, he was shot and killed. The perpetrators of this cold blooded murder were afterwards examined before an anti-Mormon justice of the peace and discharged, though their guilt was sufficiently apparent.

The Anti-Mormons having left their property exposed in their precipitate retreat from the county, those who had been burnt out of their homes sallied forth from Nauvoo and plundered the whole country, taking whatever they could carry or drive away. Gen. Hardin finally succeeded in raising a force of 350 men, and marching to Carthage dispersed the guard which had been stationed at that place by the sheriff, checked the Mormon ravages, and recalled the fugitive anti-Mormons home.

While he was here a convention, consisting of delegates from eight of the adjoining counties, assembled to concert measures for the expulsion of the Mormons from the State. The people of these counties became fearful that Hancock would be deserted by the original inhabitants, and that their own homes and property would thereby become exposed to the depredations of the common enemy. The Mormons, on the other hand, believing the times forboded a series of fresh disasters, seriously contemplated emigration westward, having dispaired of establishing their religion in the midst of a people whose opinions and prejudices were hostile to its teachings. At this juncture they were advised by the governor and other prominent men that a withdrawal from the State was the only possible alternative for escaping the impending calamities and Gen. Hardin being sent with instructions for effecting this purpose, was successful in negotiating arrangements for their removal. It was agreed that the greater part of the Mormons should retire from the State during the following spring; that no arrests should be made by either hostile party for crimes previously committed, and that a military force should remain in the county to preserve the peace. A small force was accordingly left in command of Major Warren, who discharged his duties with such efficiency that the turbulent spirit of faction was kept in subjection.

During the winter of 1845-6, the most stupendous preparations were made by the Mormons for removal; all the principal dwellings and even the temple was converted into workshops, and before spring 12,000 wagons were in readiness. Previous to the departure indictments had been found against most of the apostles for counterfeiting the coin of the United States, and an application was made to the governor for a sufficient force to arrest them, but in pursuance of the amnesty agreed on for old offences, the application was dismissed. It was deemed impolitic to arrest the leaders and thus terminate the preparations for removal when it was notorious that they could command witnesses and evidence sufficient to render conviction impossible. With a view, however, to hasten their departure, the impression was made that a portion of the regular army would be ordered to Nauvoo as soon as navigation opened, to enforce the writs, and hence the leaders, on the 15th of February, with 2,000 of their followers, crossed the river on the ice and started westward in advance of the others. By the middle of May it was estimated 1,400 more, with their flocks, their wives and little ones, followed the former band, to seek a new home in the mountain fastnesses of the western wilderness.

Nauvoo, before the Mormon exodus, contained a population of 17,000 souls. Its buildings, commencing at the margin of the river and spreading over the upland, sparsely covered an area of 6 square miles. The temple, rising high above the adjacent objects, was built of compact polished limestone, obtained in the limits of the city. No order of architecture was observed in its erection, and the Mormons claimed that it was commenced without a plan and built in accordance with instructions received directly from heaven as the work advanced.` It was 128 feet long, 88 feet wide, 65 feet to the top of the cornice, and 165 to the top of the cupola. The basement was a large, imperfectly ventilated room, containing a baptistry, supported by 12 oxen, hewn out of limestone. In the main story was the audience room used for public worship. At the end of this large apartment were 4 seats, regularly elevated one above the other, on which were stationed, according to their respective rank, the elders who addressed the people. The second story also contained an audience room. and the third a large hall for educational purposes. Besides the large apartments there were in all the stories rooms connected with the. ecclesiastical and governmental interests of the people. From the top of the cupola a scene of enchanting beauty met the eye, from which few could turn away with indifference. Woodlands and prairies, diversified with gentle undulations and covered with farm houses, herds of cattle, fields of waving grain and other evidences of agricultural thrift, could be seen for a distance of 20 miles. Through this extensive landscape glided the Father of Waters, in whose floods repose a great number of islands, all in the range of vision, and captivating the eye of the beholder by their surpassing loveliness.

A small remnant of about 1,000, unable to dispose of their property, remained behind. These were sufficient, however, to control the vote of the county, and lest they should endeavor to make the attempt, their opponents discovered a pretext for new broils. For this purpose a party of Mormons who had been sent to harvest some wheatfields in the vicinity of Nauvoo, were severely whipped, the perpetrators declaring that they had disturbed the neighborhood by their boisterous conduct. Writs were sworn out in the city against those who had inflicted the castigation, and they were arrested and kept under strict guard until they could give bail. The anti-Mormons in turn procured writs for the arrest of the constable and posse who had served the first writs. The Mormons, believing that instead of being tried they would be murdered, refused to be taken, whereupon several hundred anti-Mormons assembled to enforce the process. The difficulty was, however, adjusted without making the arrest. A committee having been sent to Nauvoo reported the Mormons had agreed not to vote in the ensuing election, and that they were making every possible preparation for removal, and proceedings against them were suspended. Notwithstanding this agreement, when the election came off they all voted the democratic ticket, and so determined were they that their support should be efficient, all voted three or four times for each member of congress. Their excuse for violating their pledge was that the president of the United States had permitted their friends to temporarily occupy the Indian lands on the Missouri river, and for this favor they felt under obligations to support his administration. The want of good faith in this respect greatly incensed the whigs, and the certainty that many designing men were endeavoring to induce them to remain permanently in the country, revived the general opposition which previously prevailed against them. Writs were again issued for the arrest of prominent Mormons, and to create a pretext for assembling a large force to execute them, it was asserted by the constable that if the accused were taken and carried out of the city they would be murdered. Under these circumstances they refused to be arrested, and the posse summoned to enforce the law soon amounted to several hundred men. The Mormons in like manner obtained writs for the arrest of prominent anti-Mormons, and under the pretense of executing them called out a posse of their own people, and hence constable was arrayed against constable, law against law and posse against posse.

While the hostile parties were assembling their forces, the new citizens of Nauvoo, who had purchased property of the Mormons at the time of their exodus, applied to the governor for sufficient force to restore order and confidence. Major Parker, a whig, was accordingly sent, it being supposed, in consequence of his politics, he would have more influence with the malcontents, who were mostly of his party. When, however, he arrived the anti-Mor-

mon constable refused to be superseded by him, and declared that
he cared little for the arrests, thereby evidencing that his faction
was only using the process of the law as a pretext for accomplishing their real object, the expulsion of the Mormons.   The anti-
Mormon faction continued to increase till it numbered 800 men, and
while they were preparing to march on Nauvoo the inhabitants
were preparing for a vigorous defense, a portion of the new citizens uniting with them, and some assisting their enemies.   At
this stage of the proceedings Mason Brayman, a citizen of Springfield, was sent by the governor to inquire into and report the
nature of the difficulties.   When he arrived an attempt was made
to effect a reconciliation.   It was agreed by the leaders of both
factions that the Mormons should remove from the State in two
months, and that their arms in the meantime should be placed in
the custody of a person appointed to receive and redeliver them
to the owners at the time of their departure.   When this
agreement was submitted for ratification to the anti-Mormon
forces it was rejected.   Gen. Singleton and Col. Chittenden, their
commanders, then withdrew and the governor was informed by
Mr. Brayman that the better portion of the anti-Mormons would
abandon the enterprise and return home.   Subsequent events, however, proved that Mr. Brayman was mistaken in his conjectures.
When Gen. Singleton retired, Thomas S. Brockman, a dishonest
and vulgar man, bigoted and bitter in his prejudices against the Mormons, was put in command.   Brockman immediately marched
his forces to Nauvoo and commenced skirmishing with the inhabitants, while Mr. Brayman, owing to the threatening aspect of
affairs, hastened to Springfield to obtain further assistance for
the defense of the city.   In this emergency, troops could not be
called from a distance in time to be made available, and hence an
effort was made to procure them in the neighborhood of the conflict.   Orders were issued to Major William T. Flood, commander
of the militia of the adjoining populous county of Adams, authorizing him to raise a volunteer force sufficient to restore the observance of law.   The excitement by this time had spread through
Adams and all the adjoining counties, and it was evident that if
the State attempted to raise a force a much larger one would
march to the assistance of the insurgents, and hence this officer
declined making any effort.

To meet this contingency he had previously been instructed, in
case he failed to raise the required force, to hand over his command to some one who would properly execute it.   Major Flood,
however, without immediately authorizing any one to act in his
stead, hastened to Nauvoo to use his influence with the antagonistic factions for the restoration of peace.   Failing in his mediation, he entrusted his authority to the Mormons, who selected
Major Clifford to command them.

The forces under Brockman numbered 800, and were armed
with muskets and five pieces of small cannon, belonging to
the State, given them by independent militia companies in the adjacent counties.   The Mormon forces, including a portion of the
new citizens, at first amounted to 250 men, but before
any decisive fighting commenced, were diminished by desertion to 150.   Their weapons consisted of sixteen-shoot-
ing rifles, common muskets, and five pieces of cannon,

hastily and rudely constructed by themselves from the shaft of a steamboat. Acting on the defensive they took a position in the suburbs of the city, a mile east of the temple, and threw up breast works for the protection of their artillery. The attacking force was sufficiently numerous to have simultaneously marched on both flanks of the besieged, beyond the range of their battery, and thus have taken the city without firing a single gun. Brockman, however, approaching directly in front, stationed his men about half a mile from the battery, and each party commenced a fire from their cannon, while some of the combatants with small arms occasionally approached closer, but never sufficiently near to do any damage.

The contest was thus continued at a great distance, with little skill till the ammunition of the besiegers was exhausted, when they retired to their camp to await a fresh supply. In a few days ammunition was brought from Quincy, and the conflict again resumed, and kept up several days, during which the Mormons admitted a loss of one man killed and 9 wounded, and the anti-Mormons of 3 killed and 4 wounded. It was estimated that some 800 cannon balls were fired on each side, and the small number killed can only be accounted for on the supposition that the belligerents either kept at a safe distance, or were very unskillful in the use of arms. The contest was finally ended by the interposition of an anti-Mormon committee from Quincy. According to the terms of capitulation dictated by the superior force of the besiegers, the Mormons were to surrender their arms to the committee. All, with the exception of trustees for the sale of their property, were to remove out of the city, and the anti-Mormon posse was to march in and have a sufficient force there to guarantee the performance of the stipulations. The posse with Brockman at its head, accordingly started on its mission, followed by several hundred spectators, who had come from all the surrounding country to see the once proud city of Nauvoo humbled and delivered into the hands of its enemies.

As soon as they got possession of the city Brockman, whose vulgar soul became intoxicated with success, commenced acting the part of a tyrant. Arrogating to himself the right to decide who should remain and who should be driven away, he summoned the inhabitants to his presence, and at his dictum most of them were compelled to leave their homes in a few hours in a destitute condition. It was stipulated that only Mormons were to be expatriated, yet at his behests armed ruffians commenced expelling the new citizens, ducking some of them in the river, and forcing others to cross it at the point of the bayonet. In a few days the entire Mormon population and the new citizens who had co-operated with them in resisting the mob, were expelled. The latter class had strong claims to be treated with more generosity by the conquerors. Having been attracted to Nauvoo from various parts of the United States by the low price of property, and knowing but little of the previous difficulties, it was but natural that they should offer their services to defend the town from mob violence and their property from destruction. They saw that the Mormons were industriously preparing to leave, and therefore considered the effort to expel them not only unnecessary but unjust and cruel.

The mob, however, under the influence of passion, could see no merit in this portion of their adversaries, and in the flush of victory dealt out indiscriminate brutality to all.

Brockman having sufficiently glutted his vengeance, returned home, leaving 100 of the lowest and most violent of his followers to prevent the return of those who had been driven into exile. This remnant of the mob continued its acts of violence and oppression till they heard that a force was moving against them from the seat of government, when they also departed.

In the meantime, the Mormons were thrown houseless on the Iowa shore, without provisions and means to procure them, and were in a starving condition. It was also the height of the sickly season, and many had been hurried away while suffering with disease to die from exposure and privation. Without food, medicine or clothing, the mother watched her sick babe till it died, and then became herself a victim to the epidemic, finding the grave a refuge from persecution and a balm for her sufferings. After this distress became known all parties hastened to their assistance, the anti-Mormons vieing with the Mormons in furnishing relief. The people of the State at first looked with indifference upon these outrages, but the hardships attending them at length began to cause reflection. They had seen a large tract of country compelled to submit to the domination of a self-constituted power, the legitimate government trampled under foot and a reign of terror substituted in its place.

With this change of sentiment, a force was raised in and near Springfield, of 120 men, and the governor proceeded with it to the scene of the disturbance. The principal object the expedition was to restore the exiled citizens to their new homes and property, a large part of the latter having been stolen in their absence. When the force arrived the riotous population was greatly incensed at the governor and could hardly find language sufficiently strong to express their astonishment that he and the people of other counties should interfere in the domestic affairs of Hancock. Public meetings were held in Nauvoo and Carthage, at which it was resolved to again drive out the citizens as soon as the State forces should be withdrawn.

Writs were also again sworn out against some officers of the State forces, with a view to calling out a posse and expelling them from the county, but the mob failed to enlist more than 200 or 300 men, and these hesitated and finally abandoned their design of making the arrests or resorting to violence. To prevent further outbreaks a small forces was left in the county till the assembling of the legislature on the 15th of December, 1846, when the cold weather put an end to the agitation and they were withdrawn. The western march of the Mormons who left the State the preceding spring, was attended with greater suffering than had been endured in their banishment from Missouri. On the 15th of Feb., 1846, the leaders crossed the Mississippi and sojourned at Montrose, Iowa, till the latter part of March, in consequence of the deep snow which obstructed the way.

When finally the journey was resumed, the fugitives taking the road through Missouri, were forcibly ejected from the State and compelled to move indirectly through Iowa. After innumerable hardships, the advance guard of emigration reached the Missouri river, at Council Bluffs, when a United States officer presented a requisition for 500 men to serve in the war against Mexico. Compliance with this order so diminished the number of effective men, that the expedition was again delayed and the remainder, consisting mostly of old men, women and children, hastily prepared habitations for winter. Their rudely constructed tents were hardly completed before winter set in with great severity, the bleak prairies being incessantly swept by piercing winds. While here cholera, fever and other diseases, aggravated by the previous hardships which they had endured, the want of comfortable quarters and medical treatment, hurried many of them to premature graves Yet, under the influence of religious fervor and fanaticism, they looked death in the face with resignation and cheerfulness, and even exhibited a gayety which manifested itself in music and dancing during the saddest hours of this sad winter. At length welcome spring made its appearance; by April, the people were again organized for the journey, and a pioneer party, consisting of Brigham Young and 140 others, was sent in advance to locate a home for the colonists. On the 21st of July, 1847, a day memorable in Mormon annals, the vanguard reached the valley of Great Salt Lake, having been directed thither, according to their accounts, by the hand of the Almighty. Here, in a destitute wilderness, midway between the settlements of the east and the Pacific, and at that time a thousand miles from the utmost verge of civilization, they commenced preparations for founding a colony. Those who were left behind arrived at different times afterward, in companies sufficiently large to preserve discipline and guard against the attacks of the Indians who continuously hovered about them for purposes of plunder. At first they endured great sufferings for the want of food; immense numbers of grasshoppers having come down from the mountains and consumed a great portion of their crops. According to the Mormon historian, the whole would have been destroyed had not the Almighty sent great flocks of gulls which devoured the grasshoppers and thus saved the people from famine and death. The lands, as soon as they were properly irrigated, produced abundantly all the necessaries of life; and at length plenty alleviated the privations of hunger, and peace followed the fierce persecutions which had attended them in their former place of residence. New settlements were made as fresh companies of emigrants arrived, and in a short time the space occupied by the colonists extended nearly a hundred miles north and south, and Salt Lake City, the present capital of the territory, became a populous city. Nestled in a sea of verdure, at the base of the surrounding mountains, washed on the west by the Jordan, and commanding a view 25 miles southward, over a luxuriant plain silvered with fertilizing streams, it is now one of the most romantically situated cities on the continent. So picturesque is the valley, and its metropolis especially, when decked in the beauty of spring, that the traveler when he crosses the desert, imitating the enthusiasm of the saints, is wont to liken it to the New Jerusalem, surrounded by green pastures, and fountains of living water.

Chapter XLIII.

1846.—ILLINOIS IN THE MEXICAN WAR.

We cannot enter into details regarding all the causes of this war. Proximately, it grew out of the annexation of Texas. In 1836 the American settlers in that country defeated the Mexican forces at San Jacinto, captured Santa Anna, the dictator of all Mexico, and under duress wrung from him a treaty acknowledging the independence of Texas. But this treaty the republic of Mexico ever repudiated. From 1836 on, overtures were frequently made to the United States by the "Lone Star," for admission into the Union. Mexico took occasion several times to inform the government of the United States that the annexation of Texas would be regarded as a *casus belli*. The question entered into the presidential contest of 1844, and the election of Polk was construed into a popular approval of the step. Congress no longer hesitated, and on the 1st of March, 1845, gave its assent to the admission of Texas into the Union. Mexico immediately broke off diplomatic intercourse with the U. S. In July the army of occupation, under Gen. Zachariah Taylor, was ordered to Corpus Christi. During the following winter, while Mexico was in the throes of revolution, during which Parades came to the surface as president, and while the administration sought an adjustment of the questions of boundary, through an envoy (Mr. Slidell), it ordered the army of occupation to a point opposite Matamoras, to take possession of the territory long in dispute, lying between the Nuces and the Rio Grande. This was a repetition of the diplomacy of Frederick the Great in Silesia. The Mexicans occupied the territory at the time with a military force stationed at Brazos Santiago, which, on the approach of Taylor to Point Isabel, withdrew west of the Rio Grande. Many outrages and robberies upon our citizens residing in Mexico had also been perpetrated through official sanction, with losses amounting to several million dollars, which our government had labored to have adjusted, but with very tardy progress.

On the 28th of March, 1846, Taylor's army of some 4000 troops took position on the left bank of the Rio Grande within cannon shot of Matamoras, opposite. On the 24th of April Gen. Arista assumed command of the Mexican forces. On the same day Gen. Taylor, having learned that a large body of Mexicans had crossed the Rio Grande 20 miles above, detached a force of 60 men, under Captains Thompson and Hardee, to reconnoitre the enemy. They fell in with what they supposed was a scouting party, but which proved to be the advance guard of a strong body of the enemy posted in the chapparal. The American commanders, contrary to the advice of their Mexican guide, charged and pursued the guard across a clearing, and in an instant their forces were surrounded by the main body of the Mexicans, who fired upon them, killing 16 and taking prisoners the remainder. A wounded soldier was sent into Taylor's camp by the Mexican commander, with a message that he had no traveling hospital to render him the needed medical aid.

Thus were hostilities actually commenced. Notwithstanding it was reasonably well known that war was almost inevitable from the advance of the army of occupation, which was about all the army the country had, all military preparation to meet such a calamity was calmly avoided. This gave it the appearance of a surprise. Reports of this disastrous engagement reached Washington May 9th, together with many painful rumors that Taylor was surrounded and cut off from his base of supplies at Point Isabel. Consternation was rife; the president sent into congress an extraordinary message, declaring that Mexico had "at last invaded our territory, and shed the blood of our fellow citizens on our own soil." Congress, with an alacrity unusual, two days after, passed an act declaring that "by the act of the republic of Mexico a state of war exists between that government and the United States;" authorized the president to accept the services of 50,000 volunteers, and appropriated $10,000,000 to carry on the war. The intent was to conquer a peace in short order with an overpowering force.

All this was in the midst of the public excitement incident to the Oregon boundary question—"54 40 or fight," being our motto. Mr. Polk had been elected with the understanding that he would insist upon the line. The notice terminating the joint occupation of Oregon had passed congress, April 23d. But now happily with one war on our hands a collision with Great Britain was avoided by adopting the 49th parallel of north latitude, and sacrificing all that vast region of the northwest, equal to several States; but we gained largely in the southwest.

The call for volunteers was apportioned mostly to the western and southern States. The requisition upon Illinois was for "three regiments of infantry or riflemen." The pay was $8 per month, but with commutations it amounted to $15.50. The enlistments were for 12 months from the time of mustering into service at the place of rendezvous. The men were to uniform themselves, for which they would be allowed. The selection of officers was left to the volunteers, in accordance with the militia laws of the State whence they were taken. The number of privates were limited to 80 men in each company. Under date of May 25th, Gov. Ford, commander-in-chief of the militia of the State, issued his general order calling upon the major and brigadier generals and other militia officers to aid in raising and organizing the three regiments. As the militia had for a long time been in a disorganized state, it was further ordered that the sheriffs convene the regiments or old battalions *en masse*, and enroll such volunteers as might offer in their respective counties. The governor proposed to receive the first full companies that offered. The company officers were to act under their certificates of election until commissioned. And now many portions of the State seemed alive with the zeal of patriotism. The animating strains of martial music were wafted upon the air, everywhere inspiring the soldierly impulse. Our public men rallied the people with spirited, patriotic and effective appeals. The militia generals issued their orders convening their brigades, and exhorted them to volunteer and "maintain their honorable position on the present occasion." We note the first of these orders as by the gallant J. J. Hardin, who "enrolled himself as the first volunteer from Illinois."[*] The responses to the demands of patriotism were prompt, eager, and overwhelming. It was esteemed an honor to be permitted to contribute to the nation's call. In 10 days time 35 companies duly organized were officially reported to the governor, while the busy notes of preparation still resounded from all parts of the State. By the middle of June the requisition was exceeded by more than 40 companies. The ladies, too, animated by the patriotism of their brothers, with a free will formed sewing societies and made uniforms and garments for the volunteers.

The place of rendezvous was appointed at Alton. Brigadier General James Shields[+] was by the governor designated to inspect and muster into service the Illinois volunteers; this was not his excellency's province, however, and the war department sent out Col. S. Churchill, Inspector General of the United States Army, to supervise the mustering in. This gentleman entertained throughout the war an affectionate regard for the Illinois troops. From the governor's office the 30 full companies were ordered, by letters addressed to their respective captains, to repair to the place of rendezvous as fast as uniformed. Of course, out of the more than 75 companies, some fragmentary and others replete to overflowing, more than half were disappointed. Much fault was now found with Governor Ford, here and there over the State, by the disappointed ones, who, in their chagrin, charged him with partiality, favoritism and dishonorable conduct, in the acceptance of companies, using language anything but temperate.[‡]

The first regiment of Illinois volunteers was organized July 2d, as follows: The first battalion consisted of companies commanded by Captains J. D. Morgan, of Adams; Elisha Wells, of Cook; Noah Fry, of Greene; J. S. Roberts, of Morgan; and W. A. Richardson, of Schuyler. The 2d battalion consisted of companies under the command of Captains Lyman Mowers, of Cook; T. Lyle Dickey, of LaSalle; A. W. Crow, of Jo Daviess; William Weatherford, of Morgan; and Samuel Montgomery, of Scott. Gen. John J. Hardin was elected colonel with great unanimity; Captain William Weatherford was elected lieutenant colonel, and W. B. Warren, major—all three of Morgan county. B. M. Prentiss was appointed adjutant, John Scanlan commissary, S. M. Parsons

---

[*]See Illinois State Register, May 29, 1846.

[+]NOTE.—Judge Shields, who resided at Washington, as Commissioner of the General Land Office, on the outbreaking of the war, ever full of the martial spirit, promptly repaired to Illinois and labored efficiently to rouse the patriotic sentiments of the people, bringing with him the President's promise of a brigadier-generalship, the Illinois regiments to constitute his brigade. Rumors in advance of the fact of his appointment reached Illinois and considerable dissatisfaction grew out of it at home, but the President nominated him and he was confirmed. Criticisms and sneers at his military qualifications were freely indulged, but when his gallant behavior at Cerro Gordo, and his great services at Churubusco and Chepultepec were heralded over the country, together with the well deserved praises of his superior commanders, it appeared that a better choice from civil life could not well have been made, and his own State rewarded him with the highest office a foreigner can hold.

[‡]See Capt. G. W. Aiken's letter dated Benton, June 20th, in Illinois State Register of July 10, 1846. See also proceedings of the Clark County Company at a public meeting in Marshall, July 6th, published in Illinois State Register, July 17, 1846.

quartermaster, E. A. Giller sergeant-major, A. W. Fry drum-major, Dr. White surgeon, and Dr. Zabriskie* assistant surgeon. W. J. Wyatt was also a captain in this regiment.

The 2d regiment was organized on the same day. It consisted of companies under the command of Captains Peter Goff, of Madison county; J. L. D. Morrison, of St. Clair; Erastus Wheeler, of Madison; A. Dodge, of Kendall, Jersey and Madison counties; W. H. Bissell, of St. Clair; E. C. Coffee, of Washington; H. T. Trail, of Monroe; John S. Hacker, of Union; L. G. Jones, of Perry; and H. L. Webb, of Pulaski. Captain Wm. H. Bissell was elected colonel by 807 votes against 6, one of the latter being in his own company and 5 in Captain Morrison's. Capt. J. L. D. Morrison was elected lieutenant colonel, and Capt. H. F. Trail major. Lieut. A. Whitesides was appointed adjutant, and Lewis J. Clawson sutler. Julius Raith, Joseph Lemon and Madison Miller were also captains in this regiment.

The 3d regiment was composed of the following companies: Captains Ferris Forman, of Fayette county; J. C. McAdams, of Bond; M. K. Lawler, of Gallatin; Theo. McGinnis, of Pope; W. W. Wiley, of Bond; J. A. Campbell, of Wayne; W. W. Bishop, of Coles; S. G. Hicks, of Jefferson; James Freeman, of Shelby; and J. P. Hardy, of Hamilton. Capt. Forman, of Fayette, was elected colonel; W. W. Wiley, of Bond, lieutenant colonel, and Samuel D. Marshall of Gallatin, major. Lieut. J. T. B. Stapp was appointed adjutant. Philip Stout and B. S. Sellers were also captains in this regiment. Col. Churchill, of the U. S. army, inspected and mustered it into service. The 1st numbered 877 men, rank and file; the 2d 892, and the 3d 906. The inspecting officer pronounced them as fine a body of men as ever he saw mustered. It was a subject of remark how little intoxication there was among the volunteers.

In the meantime the Hon. E. D. Baker, then a member of congress from the Sangamon district, had received authority from the secretary of war to raise an additional regiment of Illinois volunteers. Gov. Ford issued his order of approval under date of June 5th, and authorized companies raised, or to be raised, to join this regiment by permission of Mr. Baker. He also authorized him to appoint the time and place of rendezvous for the regiment, and to provide for its sustenance, equipment and transportation. The following companies constituted this regiment: Captains Pugh, of Macon county; Elkin, of McLean; Roberts, of Sangamon; Harris, of Menard; Morris, of Sangamon; Newcomb, of DeWitt; Hurt, of Logan; Jones, of Tazewell; McKonkey, of Edgar—9 companies. The 10th company did not join until after its arrival at the place of rendezvous, Alton. It was at first expected that this would be either Captain Garrett's, of Chicago, or that of Captain Eagan, of LaSalle; but these failing to arrive in time, Captain Murphy's, of Perry, formed the 10th company. The regimental officers elected were: E. D. Baker, colonel; ex-Lieut. Gov. John Moore, of McLean, lieutenant colonel; and Capt. T. L. Harris, of Menard, major. The regiment lacked a few privates of being full; but Illinois had raised a larger number of volunteers

---

*Capt. Roberts resigned at Alton, and the brave Zabriskie, who fell by the side of the noble Hardin at Buena Vista, was chosen in his place.

than any other State in the Union.   Lewis W. Ross and A. W. Wright were also captains in this regiment.

Immediately after the arrival of the 4th regiment at Alton, a question of rank arose between its colonel, Baker, and Col. John J. Hardin, of the 1st regiment. Col. Baker had been elected at Springfield, and his commission ante-dated that of the other colonels, whence he claimed seniority. This was resisted by Colonel Hardin, who charged such irregularity in Baker's choice as to be no election at all by the regiment, first, because the governor had never ordered the election; second, because there were but seven companies present to participate in the election; therefore the improper issuance of the commission could not give priority to Col. Baker. The matter was referred to a court of inquiry, consisting of Captains Bishop, Dickey, Crow, Jones, Elkin, Hicks, McAdams, Wiley, Coffee, Roberts and Morgan, with G. T. M. Davis as clerk. After due investigation Col. Hardin was declared the senior officer* At a meeting of the officers of the 3 first regiments, subsequently, a formal protest was signed and forwarded to the president against the appointment of officers on the recommendation of members of congress.† The 4th regiment passed on to Jefferson Barracks.

After the disaster to Captain Thompson's reconnoitering party on the 24th of April, and before the news reached Washington, the important battles of Palo Alto and Resaca de la Palma, May 8th and 9th, were fought and won by Taylor's forces, on the route between his camp and Point Isabel, his depot of supplies, which the Mexicans sought to cut off. They had also bombarded Taylor's camp opposite Matamoras, called Fort Brown, but the siege was raised by the arrival of the victorious army on the 10th of May, and Matamoras was surrendered without a further struggle. Thenceforward the Rio Grande was assumed as the base of military operations, and the Mexican villages at the mouth of the San Juan having also surrendered, Comargo, 180 miles above the mouth of the Rio Grande, was selected as the depot of supplies for Gen. Taylor's army. Thither the various volunteer regiments which were to reinforce Taylor's army were to be sent.

But while Gen. Taylor was passing the Rio Grande and directing his columns toward the interior of Mexico, the cabinet at Washington formed the plan of moving a corps on Santa Fe, and another to march on the capital of Chihuahua, believed to be the centre of much wealth and strength—a gross mistake. It was also supposed that the northern States of Mexico were ready for revolt. The former, called the army of the west, was assembled at Fort Leavenworth and placed under the command of Gen. Kearney; and the latter, under Brig. Gen. John E. Wool, was called the army of the centre, the troops for which were ordered by the war department to assemble at Antonio de Baxar, on the San Antonio river, whence they were to proceed westward to Chihuahua. The troops for these expeditions were the volunteers, scattered at the time in different parts of the U. S., strangers to the vicissitudes of war, and remote from the points of rendezvous. But the celerity of their assembling, their prodigious marches and *esprit du corps* are among the wonderful incidents of that war.

---

* Illinois State Reg. July 10, 1846.
† See Mo. Republican July, 1846.

The Illinois regiments were not all formed into one brigade, as many had fondly hoped. The 1st and 2d were assigned to the army of the centre, and the destination of the 3d and 4th was Comargo. They proceeded by water. The 1st and 2d left Alton, July 17th, 18th and 19th, on board the steamers Convoy, Missouri and Hannibal; were transhipped at New Orleans, and finally debarked at Levacca, on Matagorda Bay, July 29th. Gen. Wool accompanied them from Alton. They arrived at Pallida creek, 12 miles from Levacca, August 7th, and commenced their march 4 days later. The route to San Antonio de Bexar was over an arid prairie under a tropical sun, whose rays were cooled but little by the frequent showers. At the crossings of the head streams of the Antonio and the Guadaloupe, the parched and weary volunteers of the north found the only good water to quench their thirst, or shade for rest. An Illinois soldier wrote: "Heat—heat—heat; rain—rain—rain; mud—mud—mud, intermingled with spots of sand gravel, form the principal features of the route from Levacca to San Antonio. Loaded wagons, of course, moved slowly over the roads, and our troops moreover were scourged on the route by the mumps and measles."* On the 23d, the 1st and 2d Illinois regiments were encamped on the San Antonio, 2 miles below the Alamo, at Camp Crocket.

The 3d regiment (Col. Forman's) took its departure from Alton, July 22d, on board the steamers Glencoe and John Aull. On the next day the steamers Sultana and Eclipse took on board the 4th regiment (Col. Baker's) at Jefferson Barracks. It came first to St. Louis and made a parade through some of the streets, and in front of the Planters' Hotel executed with nice precision its evolutions and drill. It was handsomely uniformed and was much admired. The boats got off the same evening, and the troops, after considerable detention at the mouth of the Rio Grande and Matamoras, arrived at Comargo toward the close of September.

Our northern troops reached the enervating southern climate in the very heat of summer; they were used to a more bracing air, a variety of wholesome food, well cooked, good water, cleanliness of clothing and body, comfortable bedding and regularity of work and rest. All this was changed in their new life of the soldier, with its irregularities, its excitements, its unrest and its restraints. The food was new and untried, its quality often inferior, and its preparation unskillful. The result was a percentage of sickness unprecedented, and a death rate extraordinary. The suffering of our once hale, yet brave young men, in this respect, was fearful. The burden of messages home was sickness—measles, diarrhœa, ague—the first named very fatal.

Gen. Taylor's army, reinforced by volunteers, had gradually concentrated at Comargo, and about the first of September began to march up the valley of the San Juan, towards the important city of Monterey, whither the Mexicans, after evacuating Matamoras, had retreated. Taylor's force, after leaving a strong garrison behind, consisted of about 7,000 effective men. On the 19th of September, Monterey was reached. Gen. Ampudia was in command of the city with an army of 6,000, and some raw recruits, though up to the time of attack Gen. Taylor supposed it to consist of only about 3,000. The defences of the city, both

* "Rondenac" to Nat. Intel. Niles Regis. 71—90

natural and artificial, were very strong; and Gen. Ampudia for 3 days made a vigorous resistance. On the 24th he sent a flag to the American commander requesting a cessation of firing. After negotiation, terms of capitulation were entered into by which the Mexicans evacuated and surrendered the city, and retired beyond a line formed by the pass of the Rinçonada, the city of Linares and San Fernando de Presas, beyond which the forces of the United States were not to advance during a period of 8 weeks, or until the orders of their respective governments could be received. The war department disapproved the armistice, and under date of October 13th, directed Gen. Taylor to give notice that it should cease. By the middle of November, Saltillo was occupied by Gen. Worth's corps.

The army of the centre under Gen. Wool, some 3,000 strong, began its march westward September 25th. Its declared object was to aid in establishing the independence of the northern States of Mexico. Its route lay over a great barren region of country, rendering its subsistence extraordinarily expensive. With it were the 1st and 2d Illinois regiments. The 3d and 4th regiments on the Rio Grande, did not reach Comargo in time to participate in the movements of Taylor's army up the pleasant valley of the San Juan and the reduction of Monterey. On the Rio Grande a great dearth in army movements prevailed, rendering the volunteer officers, eagerly seeking the "bubble reputation at the cannon's mouth," extremely impatient. Gen. Shields was now, however, detached from his brigade, consisting of the 3d and 4th Illinois regiments, and ordered to join the moving column under Gen. Wool. In addition to his staff, Gen. Shields called upon. Gen. Patterson, in command of all the forces at Comargo, for an escort, for which he received from the 1st battalion of the 4th Illinois, 18 privates, a lieutenant, sergeant and corporal. They were mounted and had 6 pack mules. Their destination was the Presidio, where they arrived before the middle of October, the 1st and 2d Illinois being now assigned to Shields' brigade. At the time (Oct. 14th) Bissells' regiment, which had not started with the advance, was a week behind. After the detachment of Gen. Shields from his brigade on the Rio Grande, the question of rank or seniority, which, as we have before noted, had its origin in Illinois, came up between Colonels Forman and Baker, of the 3d and 4th regiments. The order to Gen. Patterson was to assign the senior colonel to the command of the brigade. The question, however, was left open for the present, Baker, taking the temporary command. Gen. Shields remained in his new position but a short time, when he was again detached and returned to Matamoras. An entire change in the conduct of the war had been planned at Washington. This consisted in an attack on Tampico, (which invited deliverance from Mexican misrule), the invasion of Tamaulipas, and most important, the descent on Vera Cruz. In November Gen. Scott was assigned with full power to the conduct of the expedition against Vera Cruz. Gen. Taylor had been instructed to organize a force in accordance with these plans, for which purpose Generals Twiggs, Quitman and Pillow were ordered from Monterey, and Gen. Patterson from Matamoras, to march by way of Victoria and concentrate at Tampico. This was a hard and apparently needless march for Gen. Patterson's division, to which the 3d and 4th Illinois regiments belonged. It should have gone by water, as was first intended. The troops did not get finally started till in December. Gen. Shields in the meantime had preceded his brigade by water and on December 19th he took formal command of Tampico. On the 22d he issued his police regulations, which were of a rigid character. Tampico had been captured by Commodore Perry, but was garrisoned by land forces.*

We propose first now to follow and sketch the career of the 1st and 2d Illinois regiments. They were in Gen. Wool's expedition, planned by the cabinet at Washington, to march to Chihuahua and to promote the revolt of the northern States of Mexico. The army, some 3,000 strong, broke camp near San Antonio, Texas, September 26, 1846. Two months later it crossed the Rio Grande at San Juan, better known as the Presidio, an old Mexican town, containing many Jesuit ruins, distant 182 miles. Thence their route lay over a level but now desolate plain, through the dilapidated town of Nava, in the midst of it, by the Grove of the Angels, to San Fernando de Rosas. This place was embosomed apparently in an artificial grove, surrounded on 3 sides by a fine stream of clear water, and stretching off in every direction were fertile plains. It contained some 4,000 inhabitants, was neatly built up in the Mexican style of architecture, the material being stone and adobe. It was a perfect oasis in the long and weary marches of the army. The army thence traversed over spurs of mountains, through rugged defiles, to the valley of the Santarita, and emerged by a tortuous gorge upon the broad plain of San Jose, stretching 30 miles away before them. Through it flowed two rivers, 4 or 5 feet deep, with currents so swift that it was difficult to hold a footing in fording. But with considerably delay, by the aid of ropes, all the forces, cannon, provision trains, &c., were passed over. On the 24th of October, the army entered the city of Santa Rosa. The inhabitants, numbering some 3,000, offered no resistance, but furnished the supplies required. This place was situated at the base of the Sierra Gorda, a range of mountains rising 4,000 feet above the level of the plain. Through these they now ascertained there were no defiles westward affording passage to other than mule trains. It was impossible to lead an army over them. It became apparent that the martial ambition of the War Department exceeded its geographical knowledge, which had thus been obtained at a cost of many millions to the treasury of the nation. The only alternative was to push hundreds of miles out of the way south, to Monclova and Parras, and strike the great road from Saltillo to Chihuahua. This course was decided upon, and the army again took up its weary line of march over the most rugged, mountainous and sterile country it had yet passed, about the only vegetation met with being the *Maguey*, celebrated as the plant from which an intoxicating liquor, called *mescal*, is distilled.

After a short halt at the hacienda of Senor Miguel Blanco, they finally emerged into the valley of Monclova; crossing which, Gen. Wool encamped his column before the city of that name. This was in consequence of the formal protest of the prefect, the first show of opposition with which the army had met thus far on the route. Gen. Wool immediately took possession of the town, November 3d, and displayed the American flag from the top of the

* See letter from Secretary of War to Gen. Taylor, Oct. 22, 1846.

34

governor's palace on the principal plaza. In the meantime, Gen. Taylor had ordered Gen. Wool, with whom he had communicated several times, not to advance beyond Monclova until the termination of his armistice with Ampudia. Being now some 700 miles from Lavacca, Gen. Wool determined to establish a depot of supplies at Monclova, for which purpose he employed the time to collect large quantities of stores and provisions and in reconnoitering the country, while he also perfected the discipline of the troops. After the delay of a month, the "Centre Division," except 250 men left to guard the depot at Monclova, once more took up its line of march for Parras, distant 180 miles. The route was south, and led through a number of towns before reaching Parras, containing about 6,000 inhabitants, located near the centre of the best grain region of Mexico, at the base of the Bolson de Malpami, 100 miles southwest from Saltillo and 300 miles from San Luis de Potosi.

This key to Chihuahua (distant 450 miles) was reached on the 5th of December. By this time the conquest of Chihuahua had been abandoned, and, as we have seen, other plans of prosecuting the war were in process of execution. Scott was in supreme command; the army of occupation had dispersed from Monterey, Taylor being at Victoria, and Patterson ordered from Comargo to Tampico. Santa Anna was collecting a large force at San Luis Potosi, threatening Monterey, the Rio Grande, and all the conquests of Taylor's army. Gen. Wool therefore left Parras, after 12 days' stay, to throw himself across the probable route of Santa Anna's advance, and on the 21st of December occupied Agua Nueva, his movement culminating just two months later in the severest and most important battle of the war, that of Buena Vista. Thus was completed a fatiguing march of near a 1,000 miles, made in about 6 weeks time (deducting stoppages at Monclova and Parras), over a barren and desolate country, through which supplies were transported at an infinite expense, which proved utterly fruitless of results; and viewed at this day seems to have been planned without consideration, if not conceived in folly. Throughout the arduous and excessive marches the Illinois troops conducted themselves as veterans.

Battle of Buena Vista.—It becoming more and more apparent that Santa Anna meditated a descent upon Saltillo, and probably the entire country over which the army of occupation had fought, Gen. Taylor, in January, 1847, left Victoria and established his headquarters at Monterey. Directly, further information of Santa Anna's purposes were discovered in the capture of C. M. Clay, and Majors Borland and Gains at Encarnacion. Leaving 1,500 men behind, Taylor now advanced with all his available force to Saltillo, distant 40 miles. After a short halt he proceeded forward to the camp of Gen. Wool at Agua Nueva, the whole effective forces concentrated there now being swollen to about 5,000 men, all volunteers except 500.

Agua Nueva was situated at the southeast corner of the elevated and well watered valley of Encantada, where the great road from San Luis Potosi entered it. From thence north to Saltillo, a distance of 20 miles, the road followed the pass of Buena Vista, which varied in width from $1\frac{1}{2}$ to 4 miles, but at a point 6 miles south of Saltillo contracted to the "Narrows"—La Angosturea.

Meandering through the Pass was a small stream of water, which had washed out at the Narrows a net work of gullies 20 feet deep, with precipitous banks. On the east side of the stream the ground was elevated to the height of 60 or 70 feet. Into this, at right angles from the Narrows, extended 3 gorges of unequal length, varying from perhaps a $\frac{1}{4}$ to $\frac{1}{2}$ mile, the southernmost being the longest and deepest. Between these were high ridges running back into a plateau, which extended to the mountain further east about $\frac{1}{2}$ a mile. Between the gullies and the table land thus cut into ridges there was a narrow strip of ground for the road, down on the lower level, leaving hardly room for two wagons to pass. Back of the plateau a deep ravine ran up to the mountain, and to the south of it there was also a ravine, broad, but not so difficult to cross. Precisely two months before the battle, Gen. Wool, on a trip to Saltillo, pointed out this defile as the spot of all others for a small army to fight a large one. And it was in fact a perfect Thermopylæ.

When, therefore, Santa Anna with his splendid army of 20,000, poured into the valley at Agua Nueva, early on the morning of the 22d of February, hoping to surprise Taylor, he found nothing but destroyed dwellings, burning stacks of grain, and a small mounted force, which gave him room without parley. Everything indicated a hurried departure, which his ready imagination construed into a precipitate retreat. Thus deluded, after a bare halt, he made pursuit, hoping to overtake the Americans and convert their retreat into a rout. He urged forward his famished and jaded forces 14 miles farther, without adequate rest or nourishment, and when he did overtake the Americans it was at these very "Narrows," where he could not recede without defeat or avoid battle without dishonor.

Gen. Minon, who had hovered around Gen. Wool's forces for a week, had been dispatched with 2,000 cavalry by a circuitous route to the east, to threaten Saltillo and cut off their retreat; and Gen. Urrea, with 1,000 rancheros, had been sent by a circuitous route to the west of the road.

The approach of the Mexicans through the Pass was made visible at a considerable distance by the clouds of dust raised. Our troops had halted north of the Narrows, about 1$\frac{1}{2}$ miles, at the hamlet of Buena Vista. After refreshment on the morning of the 22d, they were marched back and placed in position on the field by Gen. Wool. Gen. Taylor was away 6 miles, at Saltillo, directing the defences of the depot of supplies. Capt. Washington's battery of 8 pieces was placed to occupy the road at the Narrows, supported by the 1st Illinois regiment, Col. Hardin, posted on the high road to the east of it. Still farther to the east, on the main plateau, was the 2d Illinois regiment and one company of Texans (Capt. Conner's,) under Col. Bissell. Captains Morgan's and Prentiss' companies of the 1st Illinois, and Captains Hacker's and Wheeler's of the 2d Illinois, were despatched under command of Major Warren to Saltillo, to guard the train and depot against attack from Gen. Minon. To the left of the 2d Illinois, near the base of the mountain, were the mounted Kentucky and Arkansas regiments, Colonels Marshall and Yell; and on the ridge to the rear of the Illinois troops, as a reserve, were placed the 2d and 3d Indiana regiments (Gen. Lane's brigade), the Mississippi rifles,

the 1st and 2d dragoons, and the light batteries of Captains Bragg
and Sherman. The 2d Kentucky regiment (of foot), Col. McKee,
occupied a ridge, around which the road divided to the rear of
Washington's battery.

As the Mexican cavalry came clattering down the road, the first
intimation they received of an enemy in the way was to behold
him thus stationed in battle array. Before they came within
range their bugles sounded a halt, and they directly wheeled to
the right behind a protecting elevation of ground. As those in
the rear came up, the whole were formed into three columns, one
to carry Washington's battery and the others to turn our left;
with still a large reserve. The enemy had 20 guns, among which
there were three 24-pounders, three 16, five 12, besides a 7-inch
howitzer. Before attacking, Santa Anna sent Gen. Taylor a flag
of truce, assuring him he would be cut in pieces, and summoning
him to surrender, which was promptly declined. It was now 3
p. m. In the meantime Gen. Wool had passed along the lines,
addressing a few spirited words to our troops. He reminded his
own column, mostly Illinoisans, of their protracted and impatient
marches, but that every one would now have an opportunity to
win all the distinction desired. In honor of the day the watch-
word was: "The memory of Washington."

The enemy opened with a brisk cannonade upon our right and
centre, but he fought mainly to get possession of the two
slopes of the mountain rising from the plateau on the east, to
turn our flank. This was met by the Kentucky and Arkansas regiments (dismounted), and a portion of the Indiana brigade, armed
with rifles. A movement was also made on the west, to meet
which Bragg's battery was sent across the stream on an eminence
opposite the Narrows, supported by McKee's 2d Kentucky. A desultory fight was kept up till nightfall, but the two armies did not
become fully engaged. Gen. Taylor, who had returned, departed
for Saltillo to look after the safety of the stores and the protection of his rear.

During the day Col. Hardin's 1st Illinois threw up a parapet
along his whole front, cut a trench across the road to the brink
of the gullies, in front of Washington's battery, and covered his
position with an epaulment, leaving an opening for the advance
of the battery choked with two wagons loaded with stones, their
wheels locked that the enemy should not profit by it. The troops
bivouacked on the field without fires, resting upon their arms. The
night was cold and dreary, with rain and gusts of wind, causing
them to suffer with cold. Santa Anna made a spirited address to his
troops, reciting in burning words the wrongs heaped upon their
country by the barbarians of the north, their *vivas* being distinctly
heard by the Americans. The delicious strains of his own band
till late in the night, playing the exquisite airs of the sunny
south, mellowed by distance, were fully audible to our troops.
But at last silence fell over the hosts that were to contend unto
death in that narrow pass on the morrow.

The battle was resumed early on the morning of the 23d, and continued without intermission until the shades of night precluded
further effort. Never did armies contend more bravely, determin-
edly, stubbornly and arduously than these on this long and toilsome day. It was again opened on the mountain slope to the east

of the plateau by Gen. Ampudia's division of light infantry, heavily reinforced. At 2 a. m. they clambered up the mountain to flank our riflemen, who had kindled fires, and at dawn the engagement became general. Gen. Wool sent reinforcements to our riflemen, under the command of Major Trail, of the 2d Illinois, consisting of Captains Lemon's and Woodward's companies, and Captain Conner's Texans, and a 12-pound howitzer and two guns under Lieut. O'Brien, which did great execution upon the Mexicans, as they poured upon our men in the number of eight to one.

About 8 a. m. the enemy made a strong demonstration against our centre, doubtless for a feint. His force was soon dispersed by the well directed shots from Washington's battery; but in the meantime he was collecting a large force in the broad ravine south of the main plateau, under Gen. Pacheco, while Gen. Lombardini's division marched up the ridge (which hid the former) in plain view, supported by dragoons and lancers, the whole in their splendid uniforms presenting a beautiful sight. The object was to form a junction on the south side of the main plateau, and, that gained, overwhelm our forces. The plateau at the time was occupied by the 2d Illinois, Col. Bissell's, and the 2d Indiana, Col. Bowles', the latter of Gen. Lane's brigade. The object of the enemy was perceived; and to prevent the junction of his two divisions, Gen. Lane ordered forward Lieut. O'Brien with three pieces of artillery and the 2d Indiana in support. They proceeded between 200 and 300 yards in advance of all other troops, turning down the ridge up which Lombardini's division was advancing. No sooner had they formed than the Mexicans opened upon them, the odds against them being as ten to one. There, isolated, they stood and fought the cohorts of Santa Anna with terrible effect. But a Mexican battery, south-east of them and somewhat to their rear, began to play a murderous cross fire of grape and cannister upon them. The unequal contest was maintained not less than 25 minutes; to get out of the range of this battery Gen. Lane now ordered his force still forward and to the right, 50 yards farther, which was promptly done; but at this juncture, perhaps from a misapprehension of Gen. Lane's order, Col. Bowles cried out to his regiment, "cease firing, and retreat", which was obeyed not only with alacrity but precipitancy. It was sought to rally the men back to their position, but without effect. The battery, with the loss of one piece, got away.

Pacheco's division, having by this time made the ravine, joined Lombardini's, and the two poured upon the main plateau, so formidable in numbers as to appear irresistible. At this time the 2d Illinois, Col. Bissell, six companies, a squadron of cavalry, and Lieutenants French and Thomas with their pieces of artillery, the whole having already advanced to a closer point, came handsomely into action and gallantly received the concentrated fire of the enemy, which they returned with deliberate aim and terrible effect; every discharge of the artillery seeming to tear a bloody path through the heavy columns of the enemy. Says a writer: "The rapid musketry of the gallant troops of Illinois poured a storm of lead into their serried ranks, which literally strewed the ground with the dead and dying." But, notwithstanding his losses, the enemy steadily advanced, throwing a large body between the left of the Illinoisans and Sherman's battery, which had come up, so that our gallant regiment received a fire from three sides, front, left flank and left rear; but they maintained their position for a time with unflinching firmness against that immense host—to have charged which would have been speedy and complete destruction. At length, perceiving the danger of being entirely surrounded, it was determined to fall back to a ravine. Col. Bissell, with the coolness as if on ordinary drill, ordered the signal "cease firing" to be made; he then, with the same deliberation, gave the command, "Face to the rear! Battalion, about face; forward march!"—which was executed by the Illinoisans with the regularity of veterans to a point beyond the peril of being outflanked. Again, in obedience to command, these intrepid and subordinate men halted, faced about, and, under a murderous tempest of bullets from the foe, resumed with promptness and precision their well-directed fire on his left, as he essayed to cross the plateau and gain their rear. The conduct of no troops anywhere could have been more admirable. Will it add any encomium to state that they had never till that day been under fire?—that in the space of less than half an hour they had seen drop by their side their fellows to the number of 80—officers and men? How different from the four companies of the Arkansas regiment, which (dismounted) were ordered to the plateau, but gave way and dispersed after delivering their first fire!

There now came to the aid of our struggling and shattered regiment four companies from the 1st Illinois under the gallant Hardin himself, the 2d Kentucky, Col. McKee, and Capt. Bragg, with two pieces of artillery. Here on the plateau now the battle long in even balance hung. In the meantime the enemy's left, 4,000 strong, was repulsed by the iron tempest from Washington's battery. But behind his serried ranks on the plateau, next to the base of the mountain, his cavalry swept past, driving the Kentucky and Arkansas mounted volunteers back. Seeing this, our riflemen abandoned their position with great loss under the pursuit of Ampudia's light infantry, who poured down in great masses on a section of the plain half a mile north of the plateau, completely turning our left. With the exception of Col. Hardin's parapet, and Washington's battery at the narrows, both held and supported by a portion of his regiment, our forces had now been driven from every first position on the field, and our loss was immense. Gen. Wool had conducted the brilliant achievements of our army up to this time; but the demand for reinforcements was now imperative. It was at this critical period that Gen. Taylor arrived from Saltillo, accompanied by the Mississippi Rifles, Col. Jefferson Davis, a squadron of dragoons, Lieut. Col. May, two companies of infantry, Captains Pike and Preston, and a piece of artillery. This force, tried in the storming of Monterey, threw themselves with intrepid gallantry against Ampudia's hordes as they came pouring down the plain flushed with victory. From their unerring rifles men dropped as grass before the scythe. The tide of victory was checked; and the 3d Indiana coming to their support, the Mexicans were driven beyond range.

In the meantime Santa Anna had, with infinite labor, brought his battalion de San Patricio (deserted Irish soldiers from our army) forward with a battery of 18 and 24-pounders, enfilading with grape and cannister the whole plateau. But by a vigorous sortie his heavy column was broken near its centre, a portion flying north towards Ampudia; the other, with Santa Anna in their midst, (his horse shot,) pressing southward, and Hardin,. Bissell and McKee, with their forces dashing in pursuit to a point within close musket range, where they poured a rapid and most destructive fire into his ranks till he gained the cover of the ravine. His battery, however, held its position. Directly after, Gen. Taylor ordered Bragg's and Sherman's batteries to another part of the field, leaving but 4 pieces on the plateau. The 1st and 2d Illinois and the 2d Kentucky regiments, together with 4 pieces of artillery, were now stationed near the heads of the first and second gorges, holding in check the enemy's 1st and 2d attacking columns filling the ravine next south of the plateau. For a long time the contest was maintained without decided advantage to either side on the plateau, the main theatre of the battle.

We have not space to follow in detail all the gallant fighting around on our left. Suffice it to say that the pieces of Bragg, Sherman, Reynolds, and Kilburn, the Mississippi Rifles, the 3d Indiana and a fragment of the 2d, and Major Trail with two companies of the 2d Illinois, and Capt. Conner's Texans, the 1st and 2d dragoons, and Colonels Marshall's and Yell's mounted Kentucky and Arkansas volunteers, and others, with signal success, beat back the enemy, cavalry and infantry, from the hacienda de Buena Vista, around on our left under the base of the mountain.

But now we have to relate the saddest, and for Illinois, the most mournful event of that battle-fatigued day. As the enemy on our left was moving in retreat along the head of the plateau, our artillery was advanced well within range, and opened a heavy fire upon him, while

"Colonels Hardin, Bissell and McKee, with their Illinois and Kentucky troops, dashed gallantly forward in hot pursuit. A powerful reserve of the Mexican army was just then emerging from the ravine, where it had been organized, and advanced on the plateau opposite the head of the southernmost gorge. Those who were giving way rallied quickly upon it; when the whole force, thus increased to over 12,000 men, came forward in a perfect blaze of fire. It was a single column, composed of the best soldiers of the Republic, having for its advanced battalions the veteran regiments. The Kentucky and Illinois troops were soon obliged to give ground before it and seek shelter of the 2d gorge. [The enemy pressed on, and] arriving opposite the head of the 2d gorge, one half of the column suddenly enveloped it, while the other half pressed on across the plateau, having for the moment nothing to resist them but the 3 guns in their front. The portion that was immediately opposed to the Kentucky and Illinois troops, ran down along each side of the gorge in which they had sought shelter, and also circled around its head, leaving no possible way of escape for them except by its mouth, which opened upon the road. Its sides [which] were steep—at least an angle of 45 degrees—were covered with loose pebbles and stones, and went to a point at the bottom. Down there were our poor fellows, nearly 3 regiments of them [1st and 2d Illinois and 2d Kentucky,] with but little opportunity to load or fire a gun, being hardly able to keep their feet. Above the whole edge of the gorge, all the way around, was darkened by the seried masses of the enemy, and was bristling with muskets directed upon the crowd beneath. It was no time to pause; those who were not immediately shot down, rushed on toward the road, their numbers growing less and less as they went; Kentuckians and Illinoisans, officers and men, all mixed up in confusion, and all pressing on over the the loose pebbles and rolling stones of those shelving, precipitous banks, and having lines and lines of the enemy firing down from each side and rear, as they went. Just then, the enemy's cavalry, which had gone to the left of the reserve, had come over the spur that divides the mouth of the 2d gorge from that of the 3d, and were now closing up the only door through which there was the least shadow of a chance for their lives. Many of those ahead endeavored to force their way out; but few succeeded; the lancers were fully 6 to 1, and their long weapons were already reeking with blood. It was at this time that those who were still back in that dreadful gorge heard, above the din of the musketry and the shouts of the enemy around them, the roar of Washington's Battery. No music could have been more grateful to their ears. A moment only, and the whole opening, where the lancers were busy, rang with the repeated explosions of spherical-case shot. They gave way. The gate, as it were, was clear, and out upon the road a stream of our poor fellows issued. They ran, panting down towards the battery and directly under the flight of iron then passing over their heads into the retreating cavalry. Hardin, McKee, Clay, Willis, Zabriskie, Houghton—but why go on? It would be a sad task indeed to name over all who fell during this 20 minutes' slaughter. The whole gorge, from the plateau to its mouth, was strewed with our dead; all dead; no wounded there, not a man; for the infantry had rushed down the sides and completed the work with the bayonet."*†

On the plateau our artillery did its utmost to hold at bay the hordes of Mexicans while reinforcements pressed forward to this the center of conflict. The enemy fought with a perfect abandon of life. The heavy battery steadily held its ground. The remnants of the 2d and 1st Illinois regiments, after issuing from the fatal gorge, were reformed and again brought into action, the former under the modest but intrepid Bissell, and the latter, after the fall of the noble Hardin, under the command of Lieutenant Colonel Weatherford. The 2d regiment took a position to the right of our batteries, and the 1st somewhat toward the left of them. The enemy also brought reinforcements to the field. A brisk artillery duel was now steadily maintained; but gradually, with the setting of the orb of day, the cannonade and rattle of small arms slackened, and when night spread her pall over the field of carnage, it ceased altogether, and the gloom of silence succeeded. Both armies, after the long day's struggle, occupied much the same position as in the morning; the enemy, with his overwhelming numbers, having gained but little ground. Early on the following morning the glad tidings spread rapidly among our gallant troops that he had, under the cover of darkness, retreated; and victory once more perched upon the banners of the Americans.

Our total loss was 746—killed, 264; that of the enemy, 2,500. The loss of the 1st Illinois regiment was 45—killed, 29; of the 2d, 131—killed, 62. This battle, as it was the heaviest and most stubborn, proved also to be the turning point of the war—like that of Saratoga in the war of the revolution. It ended the campaign in that part of Mexico.

In the movement against Vera Cruz, the 3d and 4th Illinois regiments, Colonels Forman and Baker, together with a New York regiment, Col. Burnett, constituted the brigade of General Shields. After reconnoitering the city by Gen. Scott, the spot selected for the landing place of the army was the main shore to

*Colton's History of the Battle of Buena Vista; to which, with Gen. Taylor's official report, we are largely indebted for our account of this battle.
†Col. Bissell in a speech subsequently made at Jacksonville (?), said that neither Hardin nor any of the three Colonels had orders for their last furious charge made upon the retreating army across the plateau, (Taylor being away); that it arose by a species of common consent between them, for as Hardin started, he (Bissell) followed, and McKee, with his Kentuckians, fell in in support of the movement. He stated further that it was that terrible charge which saved the fortunes of the day.

the west of the Island of Sacrificios, and south of the city. The men were landed March 9, 1847, by surf-boats, companies A, F and G of the 4th Illinois, under the immediate command of Lieut. Col. John Moore, being among the very first to participate in that admirably executed achievement in which not a man was lost. On landing, the troops of Shields' and Pillow's brigades were assigned to the advance, and they cleared hill after hill of the Mexicans, who, with a feeble effort at resistance, took refuge in the chaparral. The army, after experiencing very warm weather, alternated with a "norther"—a cold and blinding sand storm—and sleeping on sand banks at night, gradually gained in its approaches upon the city, completing the investment in about 3 days' time.

Nearly two weeks later, after due summons and refusal to surrender, our artillery opened its terrible fire of shot and shell upon the city and the far-famed castle of San Juan de' Ulloa, reputed to be the strongest fortress on the continent. After a stubborn resistance to the dreadful effects of our mortars, howitzers and Paixhan guns in the battery on shore, at a distance of 800 yards, and the broadsides of our ships of war for 5 days, the city and castle both, unable to cope with the advance in science which American artillery had made, surrendered. Our loss in men was very trifling. During the bombardment there were thrown into the walled city 3,000 ten inch shells of 90 pounds each, 200 howitzer shells, 1,000 Paixhan shot and 2,500 round shot—a half million weight of metal. The wreck of the city and its mourning attested both the power and the sadness of war.

On the 8th of April the army began its forward movement on the Jalapa road. Four days later it reached the Plan del Rio at the Pass of Cerro Gordo. Here a deep river breaks through the mountain, whose sides tower aloft 1,000 feet. Winding along through this gorge, on the north side of the river, ran the national road, the only highway by which our army could gain the interior. On these ramparts of nature, Santa Anna, by a series of rapid marches, after his defeat at Buena Vista, had concentrated an army of 15,000 men, and had further fortified the position by entrenchments and the erection of batteries, which, one above another, commanded a sweep of the road and frowned grimly upon our army below. It was concluded, after a thorough reconnoisance by Gen. Scott himself, that the position was impregnable. The plan was next formed of cutting a new road through the chaparral to the north of and winding around the base of the mountain, thence to ascend and unite with the national road in the rear of the enemy's position. The plan was feasible only with great toil and labor, but our brave men were equal to the task. So well was the enemy's attention employed by movements in his front, that for 3 days he was not apprised of this work, when he assailed the laborers with grape and musketry. Twiggs' division was thereupon advanced along the new route, which was nearly completed, and carried the eminence occupied by the enemy and protected the working parties. During the darkness of the night following, by almost superhuman exertion, a 24-pounder battery was silently lifted hundreds of feet to the top of this height. This was done by Gen. Shields' brigade, the 3d and 4th Illinois and the New York regiment. It was a herculean labor gallantly performed.

Everything being ready, in accordance with the order of battle, Twiggs' division, by a somewhat farther route, was to turn and assail the position of the enemy directly on his rear; still beyond, but in supporting distance of him, were ordered the volunteer regiments under Gen. Shields, the 3d and 4th Illinois and the New York, which were to carry a battery of the enemy's on his extreme left (Santa Anna's), gain the national road and cut off his retreat by that route; Pillow's brigade was to attack his river batteries in front. At a given signal the general attack on the enemy's line was to begin. Pillow's assault was repulsed; Twiggs' men advanced from the rear with a plunging fire in their front and a rolling one on either flank, climbed the rocky ascent, and under the lead of Col. Harney, stormed the enemy's center, carried the fortifications, routed his main body, and turned his guns upon the fugitives as they fled, while Shields' brigade assaulted and carried the enemy's battery on the extreme left, dispersed its supporting infantry, gained the Jalapa road, cut off his retreat in that direction and prevented his rallying beyond. In the storming of this battery, the heroic Shields received a grape shot through his lungs. He fell apparently mortally wounded; his obituary was published in many newspapers throughout the country; he recovered, however, and is still in life. The command of his brigade devolved upon Colonel E. D. Baker, of the 4th Illinois, from whose official report we extract the following:

"At daylight on the morning of the 18th the brigade was under arms, and moved at an early hour to turn the Cerro Gordo and attack the extreme left of the enemy's position, on the Jalapa road. This was effected over very difficult ground, through thick chaparal, and under a galling fire of the enemy's guns on the heights. Upon approaching the main road the enemy was found upon and near it, with a field battery of six guns, supported by a large force of infantry and cavalry. Whilst forming for the attack, and under a heavy fire from the enemy's guns, Brig. Gen. Shields, who had gallantly led his command, fell, severely, if not mortally, wounded. I then directed a company to deploy as skirmishers on the right flank, and ordered a charge upon the enemy's line, which was accomplished with spirit and success by those companies, which were enabled by the nature of the ground to make the advance. They were promptly and gallantly supported by the remainder of the 4th regiment Illinois volunteers, under Major Harris. The 3d regiment under Col. Forman, and the New York regiment, under Col Burnett, being ordered by me to move to the right and left upon the enemy, the rout became complete at that point, and the enemy fled in great confusion, leaving his guns and baggage, a large amount of specie, provisions and camp equippage in our hands. Portions of the 3d and 4th Illinois volunteers and several companies of the New York regiment, all under the immediate command of Gen. Twiggs, pursued the enemy on the Jalapa road as far as Encerro, when they were passed by the dragoons and halted for the night."*

Col. Baker further expressed his obligations to Cols. Forman and Burnett, and to Major Harris for the coolness, promptitude and gallantry with which they carried into execution the several dispositions of their commands; also to his regimental staff (the 4th), Capt. Post, A. C. S., and Adjutant Fondey; and to the staff of the brigade, Lieuts. R. P. Hammond, 3d artillery A. A. A., and

*Col. Forman says that "Baker's report in the main is correct, except that the regiments fought under their own commanders—we knew what we had to do and did it."

G. T. M. Davis, A. D. C., for their assistance and their promptness in the discharge of their duties.

His loss was: 4th regiment, 6 officers, (2 being killed—Lieuts. Murphy and Cowordin), and 42 non-commissioned officers and privates; 3d, 1 officer and 15 non-commissioned officers and privates; the New York regiment, 1 officer and 5 privates—total of 70 in the brigade. The loss of our army was 417—killed, 64, and wounded, 353. The enemy's loss in killed and wounded is not known; but we took 3,000 prisoners, 5,000 stands of arms and 43 pieces of artillery.

Gen. Twiggs in his report speaks in glowing and enthusiastic terms of the conduct of the Illinois regiments, both in the storming of Santa Anna's battery and in the pursuit of the flying enemy, under his immediate command. The battle of Cerro Gordo, as it was one of unsurpassed difficulty, proved also one of the most brilliant and important in the war. Its results were to lay open the road to the capital, and place the empire of Mexico under the feet of the conqueror. The gallant troops of Illinois shared to no inconsiderable extent in the dangers, toils and hardships, as their large ratio of losses attests; and their heroic deeds have reflected imperishable honor and glory upon our State.

The battle of Cerro Gordo was the last in the war with Mexico in which any Illinois troops participated. At Jalapa, the year's time for which they had been enlisted having nearly expired, and it being ascertained that the 3d and 4th regiments would not re-enlist, Gen. Scott disbanded them; the campaign on the Rio Grande having been virtually ended by the battle of Buena Vista, the 1st and 2d regiments were disbanded at Comargo, and all our troops of the first four Illinois regiments returned home about the same time, Lieut. Col. Moore with companies B, G and K, of the 4th, reaching Springfield June 4th, and 300 men of the 1st arriving at St. Louis May 31st, 1847. The latter brought home the remains of their beloved colonel, Hardin; and the people of Morgan county invited the entire regiment to accompany them to their final resting place at Jacksonville. The funeral (July 12th,) was one of the largest and most imposing ever held in the State.*

The soldiers generally on their return home were received with mark of affection, and tendered, as they well deserved, the enthusiastic welcomes of the people. Public dinners, complimentary toasts, flattering addresses and fulsome speeches were profusely showered upon them; the newspaper press vied with the orators of the period in praises of the heroic deeds of our volunteer soldiery, while, as aspirants for office, all mere civilians had to stand aside and leave the track for the proud patrons of Mars, or be crushed in the result. Mere civil accomplishments or services will ever as nothing be in the average popular mind compared with the deeds heralded by the pomp and circumstance of glorious war. The Mexican war was such a wonderful lever to office and political preferment that some envious Whigs, whose party had opposed it, took early occasion, it was said, to declare themselves in favor of the next war, whatever it might be for!

---

*Col. Forman brought home and presented to the State a 6 pound gun, now in the arsenal at Springfield, as a trophy from the Mexican battery in the battle of Cerro Gordo, stationed near Santa Anna's headquarters, which was taken by the Illinois troops shortly after the fall of Gen. Shields.

More Volunteers.—In the meantime, the government having determined to raise 6,000 more troops, a call upon Illinois had been made for ten additional companies of infantry, or one regiment more, and one company of cavalry, by the secretary of war, W. L. Marcy, under date of April 19th, 1847. The enlistments were to be during the war; the other terms were the same as under previous calls; Alton was again designated as the place of rendezvous. Under date of April 27th, the commander-in-chief (Gov. French), by M. K. Anderson, adjutant general of the Illinois militia, issued his general orders calling for volunteers. In less than two weeks had not only the 11 companies reported and been accepted, but 8 more were tendered, which had to be rejected. Emulation never ran higher; expresses hurried to Springfield with the utmost dispatch to secure places on the list before it should be filled. The disappointment to those who were too late was most bitter.

The following were the accepted companies, which, under date of May 10th, were ordered to march to the place of rendezvous:

Company A, Clinton county, Thomas Bond, captain.
Company B, Williamson county, J. M. Cunningham, captain.
Company C, Marion county, Vautrump Turner, captain.
Company D, Brown county, John C. Moses, captain.
Company E, St. Clair county, G. W. Hook, captain.
Company F, Cook county, Thos. B. Kinney, captain.
Company G, LaSalle county, Henry J. Reed, captain.
Company H, Williamson county, James Hampton, captain.
Company I, Shelby county, R. Madison, captain.
Company K, Pike county, W. Kinman, captain.

The cavalry company was from Schuyler county, Adams Dunlap being the captain.

The 5th Regiment of Illinois volunteers was organized of the foregoing companies, at Alton, June 8th, 1847. E. W. B. Newby of Brown county, was elected colonel; Henderson Boyakin, of Marion, lieutenant-colonel; and J. B. Donaldson, of Pike, major, excellent selections. The regiment took its departure by steamboat 6 days later for Fort Leavenworth. Its destination was Santa Fe, whither it marched across the plains from Fort Leavenworth in the hottest part of the summer, the consequence being an unusual amount of sickness, traceable in great part to this exhaustive march. While the days were extremely warm, the nights were frequently very cold; the troops greatly fatigued, would lie down of nights with their blood heated beyond a healthy standard; ere morning they would be chilled by the transition of the atmosphere; besides several times on the journey they were overtaken by severe storms, against which there was no shelter; thus the seeds of disease were sown and its virulence intensified. The measles had already appeared among them at Fort Leavenworth. By the first of December the loss of the battalion stationed at Santa Fe was reported at 68, of which 42 were by death.

In October, at Santa Fe, the regiment was divided into two battalions, the first, together with a battalion from a Missouri regiment, under Col. Newby, the senior officer, being ordered to move in an expedition south to El Paso. The 2d battalion, under Lieut. Col. Boyakin, remained as a garrison at Santa Fe. The regiment saw no service in conflict with the enemy, the war by that time being virtually over. We will note, however, that these Illinoisans were the first to organize a lodge of the Masonic order at the remote post of Santa Fe.

6th Regiment of Illinois volunteers. We have noted the fact that when in April a new call upon Illinois for ten companies of infantry and one of cavalry was made, that in less than two weeks time 19 offered, and still more continued to offer, not knowing that the 5th regiment was full. Much disappointment was felt at their rejection; but their hope was speedily revived. Under date of May 20th, the secretary of war wrote to Gov. French: "Yielding to the earnest solicitations of the patriotic citizens of your State, the President has instructed me to request that your excellency will cause to be raised and rendezvoused at Alton another regiment of volunteer infantry." The enlistments were to be for the same period and have the same organization as those of the 5th regiment, but its destination was Vera Cruz.

The organization of the surplus companies had been held intact until the President's pleasure in the premises could be ascertained Accordingly, when the requisition came to hand, Gov. French, on the very same day (May 29), notified the expectant companies of their acceptance; ordered them to the place of rendezvous to be mustered in, and the war department, two days later, that the companies were all organized and ready to march.

The following are the companies of the 6th regiment:

Company A, of Madison county, Franklin Niles, captain
Company B, Madison county, Edward W. Dill, captain.
Company C, Fayette county, Harvey Lee, jr., captain.
Company D, Greene county, John Bristow, captain.
Company E, Macoupin county, Burrell Tetrick, captain.
Company F, Cook county, James R. Hugunin, captain.
Company G, Boone county, William Shepherd, captain.
Company H, Will and Iroquois counties, G. Jenkins, captain.
Company I, Jefferson county, James Bowman, captain.
Company K, Jo Daviess county, C. L. Wright, captain.

Company A, Captain Niles, was ordered into the 5th regiment, and Capt. Collins' company from Jo Daviess, took its place in the 6th.*

For colonel of the 6th regiment, Capt. Collins, of Jo Daviess, was elected, receiving 472 votes, to Capt. Wright of the same county 334; lieutenant-colonel, Capt. Hicks of Jefferson, received 448, to Lieut. Omlveny of Monroe, 379; for major, Lieut. Livington, of Jefferson, received 340; Capt. Shepherd, of Boone, 220; Capt. Lee, of Fayette, 142, and H. Hunter, 102. Lieut. Fitch, of Greene, was appointed adjutant, W. G. Taylor quartermaster, and J. B. Hines sergeant-major. At New Orleans the 6th regiment was divided, the first battalion, companies A, D, E, F, H, being sent to Vera Cruz under the Col. Collins, and the 2d in command of Lieut. Col. Hicks, to Tampico. The division caused no little dissatisfaction among the men. The 2d battalion saw no service other than garrison duty. The 1st arrived at Vera Cruz, August 31st, and after remaining in camp Bergara awhile, was ordered out on the national road and stationed at the San Juan Bridge. Here a skirmish with guerrillas was had, in which one private was killed and

* NOTE.—Captains David C. Berry, James Burns, Ed. E. Harney and John Ewing also served in this regiment. The Roster in the Adjutant-General's Office, in giving the regiments which served in the Mexican War is very imperfect and inaccurate. It gives the 5th regiment as the 1st. We have collated our facts from the press of the period.

two wounded. Col. Collins was very sick nearly all the time; indeed, more than the usual amount of sickness attended the whole regiment. Reports were current in the press that one-fifth of its force, in five months after leaving camp at Alton, found a grave in Mexico, not from the foe, but by sickness. The 1st battalion lost 7 out of its 20 officers; and the battalion at Tampico, while it suffered as greatly in men, lost but one officer.

Under date of June 30, 1847, the Hon. R. W. Young, commissioner of the General Land Office at Washington, wrote that the Secretary of War consented to accept two more companies of cavalry from Illinois, which had been raised. Capt. William Prentice's to rendezvous as Gov. French direct, and Capt. W. B. Stapp's of Warren county, to rendezvous at Quincy, on horseback, and proceed thence to St. Louis by steamboat.*

The destination of these cavalry companies was Vera Cruz, to operate against the enemy's guerrilla parties, and keep open the roads from the gulf to the City of Mexico. Captain Lawler of Shawneetown, also raised a cavalry company; and to show the troublesomeness of this arm of the service, we will state that, owing to delays on the river—near 2 weeks being occupied in going to Baton Rouge—he was compelled at that point to land, rest and recruit his exhausted horses.

After his return, Col. E. D. Baker, in pursuance of his request, was authorized to raise a battalion of five companies from the veteran volunteers, recently returned. The battalion was not raised; the fall of the City of Mexico speedily followed, virtually ending the war, although the treaty of Guadalupe Hidalgo was not made till February 2, 1848.

* See Illinois State Register, July 8, 1847. Josiah Little also raised a cavalry company. He was commissioned Sept. 24, 1847.

CHAPTER XLIV.

CONSTITUTIONAL CONVENTION OF 1847, AND SOMETHING OF THE ORGANIC LAW FRAMED BY IT.

After the violent political struggle of 1824 concerning the admission of slavery into the State, the question of calling a convention to revise or amend the first constitution was not again revived for a period of 18 years. At this time such was the hight of partisan feeling aroused against the supreme court in deciding the McClernand-Field case against the wishes of the dominant party, and the unnecessary apprehension that the Galena alien case would also be decided against the wishes and interests of the democracy, involving a possible loss of its political supremacy in the State, that the legislature, at its session of 1840–1, passed a resolution recommending to the electors at the general election of 1842 to vote for or against the calling of a constitutional convention. But in the meantime the judiciary was reorganized by the addition of five judges to the supreme court, all democrats, to overbalance the whig judges. The democracy having by this act secured their political supremacy in every branch of the government, had no further use for a convention to remodel the constitution, and at the August election the resolution failed to carry, though the whig party, against whom it was originally aimed, ardently supported the call.

Still the insufficient limitations of the old constitution became more apparent from year to year, and in 1845 the legislature again passed a resolution recommending to the electors to vote for or against a constitutional convention at the ensuing general election of August, 1846. The democratic press this time urged the people to vote for the call of the convention, publishing the resolution to be voted for as a standing advertisement and part of the regular democratic ticket; but the whig press, if not opposed to the call, deeming, perhaps, that its espousal of the question might tend to defeat it, was totally silent upon the subject, and did not once direct the attention of the people to the importance of the measure. Being thus a democratic measure, the call prevailed.

In the passage of the act to provide for the meeting of the convention, the main question over which there was any considerable contest, was whether it should consist of as many members of the then general assembly, apportioned upon the population of 1840 (476,183), or whether the number should correspond to the new apportionment act of that session, based upon the census of 1845 (662,125). The contest was between the north and south parts of the State; the former, which had been benefited most by the immi-

543

gration of the preceding years, was in favor of a representation based upon the census of 1845. The constitution reads: " The general assembly shall, at the next session, call a convention to consist of as many members as there may be in the general assembly." Mr. Dougherty, since lieutenant governor, introduced a bill fixing the number of delegates to correspond with the number of members of the then two houses, and Mr. N. B. Judd, of Cook, offered a substitute based upon the census of 1845, which finally prevailed and became a law.

. A special election of delegates was fixed for the 3d Monday of April, 1847, who were to meet in convention at Springfield on the first Monday of June following. During the canvass the whig press in the strong democratic districts argued plausibly and truly that for a duty so important as the framing of a new organic law for the State, which was to affect not only the present but perhaps future generations, when present political questions might be classed with the things that were, the ablest talent of the State should be called upon, irrespective of party predelictions ; but at the same time good care was taken by them to bring out and support none but their own partisans. The democratic press, having the utmost faith in the permanency and well-being of democratic principles, came squarely out and urged its party to rally as one man and secure such a majority in the convention as would insure the infusion of pure democratic principles into the instrument which was to be the guide for future legislation ; to attain which care should be taken to select candidates whose democracy was unimpeachable. The election resulted in a return of a greater proportion of whig delegates than was to be expected from the relative strength of the two parties, although the democracy had a considerable majority.

The democracy required the convention, as paramount to all other considerations, 1st, to abolish all life offices or long tenures, and to provide for an elective judiciary, from the supreme court down; 2d, to prohibit the legislature from ever again creating a bank—all the financial evils which had ever afflicted the people of Illinois, it was charged, had proceeded from the oppressions of banks ; 3d, to limit the power of the legislature to borrow money, which had been another great source of calamity to the people. This power should be so limited as to prevent the legislature from pledging the credit and faith of the State in all cases except, perhaps, in great emergencies, as of threatened danger from invasion, and then only to defray the expenses of the State government. If such a provision had been embodied in the constitution of 1818 the financial embarrassments growing out of the reckless internal improvement system of the State would not have oppressed the people. It required, 4th, a veto power to the governor equal to that of the president of the United States. The veto power, notwithstanding the terrible ordeal of its denunciation, had been a favorite democratic measure ever since Jackson had saved the country, as it was supposed, by refusing his assent to the re-charter of the U. S. Bank. Of course the democracy were opposed to any change in the qualifications of an alien elector.

The whigs wanted, 1st, a longer residence than 6 months before any man should be entitled to exercise the elective franchise, and that no alien should be entitled to that sacred privilege of an

American citizen until he was first naturalized; 2d, to take from the legislature the power of electing or appointing officers for the people, particularly as it regarded the members of that body, and thereby prevent that bargaining and corruption which grew up in the general assembly, and to prevent that body from exercising nearly all the powers of government, executive as well as legislative; 3d, to limit the number of representatives in the general assembly, and to fix the age at which men should be eligible to seats in that body, and thus prevent the many mischiefs growing out of legislation by young men whose minds were immature; 4th, to fix the ages at which men might hold the office of judge, and at which judges should retire from the bench; 5th, to prevent a majority of the two-thirds which constituted a quorum in the legislature from finally passing a bill.

There were also many provisions mooted by the press and people, upon which there was no political or party division. The most important and generally demanded were retrenchment and economy; to disconnect the supreme judges from legislative duty as a council of revision; to abolish eligibility to several offices at the same time; to limit the power of the legislature in contracting debts and imposing taxes; to organize a more efficient tribunal for the management and control of county affairs than the county commissioner's court; to limit the powers of government so as to secure the people against oppression by those in authority, (in view of what was done during the hard times of 1842, when the officials of the executive department required that nothing but gold and silver should be paid for taxes, while there was nothing but depreciated bank rags in the country, the State having made the issues of the State bank receivable for taxes); to provide against successive special sessions of the legislature at the will and pleasure of the governor without specifying the character of the business to be transacted; to fix the pay of members, and to devise some way to prevent an accidental majority from continuing or adjourning sessions for the sake of compensation.

Among the democratic delegates there was not entire unanimity upon the bank question. The following is one of the bolts launched at the recussants by the press of that party:

"These bank-democrats occupy rather paradoxical ground. They assert that banks are pernicious, dangerous and anti-republican, but inasmuch as the bank paper of other States naturally circulates among us, it is our true policy to establish these engines of evil as a measure of self-defense. They admit that we are injured by the paper of other States, and they propose to mitigate the injury by producing it themselves—if any mischief is to be done, the citizens of the State ought to have the privilege and enjoy the profits of doing it. If other States choose to injure us, we ought to seek redress by injuring ourselves."*

The convention met on the 7th of June, 1847, and concluded its labors on the 31st of August following. When its work first came before the people (for unlike the constitution of 1818, this was to be passed upon by them), nobody seemed entirely satisfied with it, yet all concurred that the new was preferable to the old constitution. Judging it from the partisan stand-point of that day, it must be confessed that the the greater success in grafting it with their peculiar views was with the whigs. The old allowed

*Ill. State Reg.
35

aliens and citizens alike to vote after a residence of 6 months, to
maintain which feature when supposed to be in danger in 1840,
the democracy waged a fierce warfare against the supreme court,
resulting in a partisan reorganization. Yet the very thing feared
from that court was now embodied in the constitution; every
elector must first be a citizen, and second have a residence of one
year in the State. The elective principle by the people was extended to the filling of every office, a thoroughly democratic provision, and the only one which ought ever to obtain under any
republican government. Yet the democracy, for obvious party
reasons, desired to confine this to the life offices—the supreme
judges—leaving the great bulk of the offices to be doled out, if
not bargained, as before by the legislature, and thus fasten their incumbents upon every county in the State, regardless of local political majorities. For like party reasons the whigs desired to deprive the dominant party of the power to elect this great crowd
of officers—judges and clerks, both circuit and county—to the
legislature, but favored life officers for the supreme bench. In
this particular, fortunately for the State, the partisan cravings
of both, to a certain extent, were defeated, yet the deprivation of
the power to elect all the host of the former by the legislature was
a greater loss to the democracy than the latter was to the
whigs. This took from the legislature a fertile source of patronage by depriving it of the choice of some 200 county officers from
time to time, who by their intimate relations to the people are in the
situation to exercise a most potent political influence. During
the pendency of the constitution before the people, the provision
relating to 3 county judges, called the "puppy court," was made
to do peculiar service against it. Upon the subject of banks, too,
the democracy may be said to have been in a manner defeated.
The democratic convention of February, 1846, the largest ever
assembled in the State, had declared that the creation of any new
banks, either State or other banking institution whatever, should
be frowned upon by the party; and throughout the sitting of the
convention the press of that party was strenuous in its opposition
to banks of any kind. Yet banks, other than State banks, were
not prohibited by the constitution, though a general banking
law was required to be submitted to a vote of the people.

We note but a few features wherein the constitution of 1848 differed from that of 1818. Profiting by the lesson of experience
taught by the State internal improvement system, whose enormous debt was then pressing heavily upon the people, no debt was
allowed to be contracted by the legislature exceeding $50,000, and
that only to meet casual deficits or failures in revenue; nor was
the credit of the State to be extended to any individual, association or corporation. Article 14, separately submitted, provided
for the yearly collection of a tax of 2 mills upon the dollar, in addition to all other taxes, the proceeds of which were to be paid
out in extinguishment of the public debt, other than the canal
and school indebtedness, pro rata to such holders as might present their evidences. This was a noble self-subjection of the people to a tax for an indefinite time at that dark period of public
and private embarrassment, for which we ought to profoundly
honor them.

Regarding tax titles, the law of 1839 was one of peculiar hardship, rendering their defeasance most difficult by throwing the *onus probandi* as to any irregularity in the manner of acquiring them upon the real owners of the land. A deed was *prima facie* evidence that the land was subject to taxation; that the taxes were unpaid; that the lands were unredeemed; that it had been legally advertized; that it was sold for taxes; that the grantee was the purchaser; and that the sale was conducted in the manner required by law.* It was possible for a man to lose the title to his land, although residing on it and having paid his taxes. All this was radically changed by section 4, article 9 of the new constitution, introduced by Judge Lockwood, the requirements of which the courts have construed strictly, and it may well be inferred that since then not many tax titles have stood this ordeal of the organic law.

The legislature was required to encourage internal improvements by passing liberal general laws of incorporation and for other corporate purposes; special acts for which were not to be granted unless the objects could not be attained under the former. It seems that in the legislatures since scarcely any corporate objects could be attained under general laws, for throughout the sway of the constitution of 1848, were not only no general incorporation laws of any degree of perfection passed, but from session to session were granted, with most lavish hand, private and special acts of incorporation for every conceivable purpose, passed in packages of hundreds at a time, making huge tomes, whose contents and provisions were equally unknown to the general public and the honorable members whose names stand recorded in favor of their enactment. This species of legislation, in many cases, has been attended with the most pernicious results, as the people to their cost can testify.

The judges of the supreme and circuit courts were made ineligible to any other office of profit or public trust in this State or the United States during the terms for which they were elected, and for one year thereafter. This clause, as it reads, has been repeatedly violated by the election of judges to congress; and while it is true that body has held that it is the sole judge of the qualification of its members, and that State laws or constitutions in such cases are of no binding force, it is equally true that the gentlemen thus elected had sworn upon their installation as judges to observe the constitution of Illinois in all its provisions, without any reservation as to the clause in question, or they could not have taken their seats upon the bench.

In the legislature bills were to be read on three different days before becoming laws, and on final passage the ayes and noes were to be recorded. This well intended provision was most shamefully violated in actual practice in after years by a reading of the title of a bill only, and by the so-called "omnibus" system, by which hundreds of bills—many providing for private jobs and corrupt schemes—were passed at once, few of the members knowing their contents.† The reading of bills the first and second time by their title only gave rise to the reprehensible practice of introducing

*Blackwell Tax. Tit. 84.
†It seems that the Hon. J. Y. Scammon, of Cook, first suggested the passage of bills by the package.

and passing along in their order what was known as "skeleton bills"—bills with simply a head, but no body, the latter being afterward supplied.*

But the chief feature of the constitution of 1848 was its rigid economy. The salary of the governor was fixed at $1,500; supreme judges—three, made elective—$1,200 each; circuit judges, $1,000 each; auditor of public accounts, $1,000; treasurer and secretary of State, each, $800; the compensation of members of the general assembly was fixed at $2 per day for the first 42 days' attendance, and $1 a day thereafter. It was a hard times' instrument. Retrenchment in everything, as inaugurated by Gov. Ford and then with severity being carried out by Gov. French, was the order of the day. But in this particular the constitution rather overdid the thing. The true medium between paying our elective servants a just compensation and allowing our represent atives the exercise of a sound discretion in all the transactions of public business, and at the same time to bind them down so that they may work no mischief or injury to those who choose and delegate them, is, perhaps, difficult of attainment. It is one of the problems connected with a representative form of government.

In evidencing the severe economy of the new organic act, we will mention that the amount of warrants drawn upon the treasurer on account of the general assembly for the session of 1845 was over $55,000; and that the total amount of mileage and *per diem* compensation paid to the members and officers of the two houses for the first session under the new regime in 1849, was not quite $15,000, a material reduction—exceeding 300 per centum. But in this connection, to show that we are a progressive people, and at the same time indicate the proficiency which our Solons have attained in the "ways that are dark", we will give the total amount of legislative expenditures for the same purposes on account of the last session, that of 1869, under the same economical constitution, which were $206,181, exclusive of printing, paper and binding, making nearly $75,000 more. The four items of newspapers, stationery, postage and pocket-knives alone amounted to $54,322.†

The salary of the governor, it was provided, was "not to be increased or diminished;" and by way of emphasis in fixing the compensation of the other officers which we have enumerated, the words "and no more" were added. Yet by indirection, under pretense of paying a gardener to take charge of the grounds surrounding the executive mansion, we find in 1861 $2,500 was appropriated to be expended or not by the governor, as he pleased, being intended as an increase of his salary. Afterwards this unlawful gift was annually increased to $4,500. Indeed, the auditor's office shows that the incumbents of the executive office have received, from December, 1860, to December, 1872, twelve years, $66,000, to which they were not entitled. All the State offices became immensely profitable in fees—running the emoluments of their incumbents into thousands of dollars, instead of the hundreds fixed by the constitution. The compensation of the supreme judges was evasively increased to $4,000, by allowing them each a chief

*See debate in senate. Feb., 1857.
†Convention Journal 1870. p. 218

clerk at $1,600 and $1,200 for an assistant (neither of which they employed), instead of $1,200, their constitutional salary; and to the circuit judges, in defiance of the words $1,000 " and no more," were yearly given an additional $1,000 each, for revisions and suggestions of changes in the laws, a labor which they were not expected to, and did not, perform; besides which a docket fee of $1 for each suit brought was wrung out of litigants, also for their benefit. But the abuses which crept into the legislative department were still grosser and more alarming. The *per diem* compensation of members, which for the session of 1861, for instance, amounted to $8,800, was supplemented by postage $8,892, newspapers $1,1812, pencils $2,664, few of which items were actually received, but the money taken in place of them, on "commutation" as it was called with State officers, and thus by indirection they got $8 per day each, instead of $2 "and no more." The practice was subsequently increased by various subterfuges of rent for committee rooms never used nor paid for, &c., to sometimes amount to more than $20 a day for each member. Ten cents a mile was allowed to each as necessary traveling expenses to and from the seat of government. While it would be difficult to travel more than 200 miles from any point in the State to the capital, the journals show honorable members to have charged and received pay for 1,200 miles going and coming. Thus did our public servants debauch themselves, one department the other. But notwithstanding its abuses, the constitution of 1848 was, in many particulars, a great improvement upon that of 1818.

That the whigs had succeeded more than the democrats in stamping that instrument with their principles, soon had its influence. The whig press advocated its adoption constantly and urgently, while the democratic press, where it did not oppose, was lukewarm in its advocacy, yet candor compelled an acknowledgment that the elective principle as applied to every important office was a thoroughly democratic idea, which covered a multitude of bad provisions; that on the whole, the new was preferable to the old, and it justly regretted the "abrogation of the provision permitting foreigners to a participation in the right of suffrage after a residence of 6 months, the same as the most unlettered native," predicting that that would prove pernicious by diverting emigration from the State. No evil had resulted, and, it may be added, never will, from admitting foreigners to this privilege. It is a most foolish proscription. The provision limiting the power of the State to borrow money, and prohibiting the credit and faith of the State in aid of any individual or corporation, was a most excellent one.

The people had ample time to consider its provisions, and they did not fail to see its great superiority over the old organic law. For the points of party significance in it, which at best might prove but transitory, they could not afford to throw away the many safe and excellent limitations for their protection against the chances of a wild, reckless and extravagant legislature to involve them in ruin.

The black clause—prohibiting negro immigration—met with considerable opposition in the northern part of the State, particularly in Cook county, which voted two to one against it; but the greatest general opposition was to the 2 mill tax. The following is the vote upon the constitution and the separate articles:

For the constitution proper, 59,887; against it, 15,859.

For article XIV—negro clause, 49,066; against it, 20,884.

For article XV—2 mill tax, 41,017; against it, 30,586.

The vote for ratification or rejection was taken on the first Monday in March, 1848; and the new constitution went into operation on the first of April following. The election of governor was anticipated two years, and accordingly the first general election under it took place in November, 1848. The commencement of the regular legislative sessions was deferred from December to January, the first convening at that time in 1849.

CHAPTER XLV.

1846-1852—ADMINISTRATION OF GOVERNOR FRENCH.

Lives and Character of the Gubernatorial Candidates—Funding of the State Debt—Refusal of the People to give the Legislature Control of the 2 Mill Tax—Township Organization—Homestead Exemption—The Bloody Island Dike and a Speck of War—State Policy regarding Railroads.

The Democratic State Convention of 1846, to nominate candidates for governor and lieutenant governor, met at Springfield on the 10th of February. There was no lack of aspirants for either of these positions. In connection with the first we will name six in the order of their supposed strength, before the meeting of the convention: Lyman Trumbull, John Calhoun, (he of subsequent Lecompton Constitution notoriety), Augustus C. French, Walter B. Scates, Richard M. Young, and A. W. Cavarly, an array of very able and prominent names. The contest was supposed to lie between the first two mentioned, but the balloting gave a different exhibit. After sundry efforts by their friends, it was found that neither could be nominated, and as usual in such cases, both parties went over to the support of another. Trumbull received the highest number on the first ballot, it is true, but French, as the coming man, was already next, and on the 2d ballot advanced to the front. On the 4th ballot all the names except those of French, Calhoun and Trumbull being withdrawn, the friends of Calhoun, fearing the ultimate success of Trumbull, also withdrew his name. The friends of Trumbull saw in this move their inevitable defeat, and for the sake of harmony, they also withdrew the name of the latter. French was thereupon proclaimed the nominee of the convention for governor, amidst a great tumult of shouting and exultation. Owing to the many able and determined democratic aspirants, and the strong attachment of their respective friends, the whigs had indulged a hope that the convention would break up in disorder, but in this they were disappointed. Trumbull's effort in 1845 to defeat the canal had been revived against him and industriously circulated by Gov. Ford and others, as being still his position, which doubtless proved his discomfiture.

For lieutenant-governor, the names of J. B. Wells, Lewis Ross, William McMurtry, Newton Cloud, J. B. Hamilton and W. W. Thompson, were presented for nomination. On the 4th ballot all the names except the first two mentioned, were withdrawn, when the voting resulted in the choice of Wells, who received 132 to

551

Ross 95 ballots. The resolutions adopted strongly condemned the resuscitation of the old State banks, and declared against any more of any kind in this State.*

The whigs, who were in a hopeless minority, seemed averse for a time to holding a State convention. Their press discussed the idea of some suitable candidate running by general consent without nomination. Names to this end were proposed, of which we may mention that of James Davis of Bond. It was also proposed that the Whig State Central Committee should make the ticket. Finally, on the 8th of June, a convention was held at Peoria, over which Major Richard Cullom, of Tazewell, presided, which nominated Thomas M. Kilpatrick, of Scott, for governor, and Gen. Nathaniel G. Wilcox, of Schuyler, for lieutenant-governor.†

Kilpatrick was born in Crawford county, Penn., in 1807. His early education consisted solely in instruction from his mother. He lost his father at the age of 15, became a mechanic, married in 1828, and removed to Illinois in 1834. In 1840 he beat Murray McConnel for the State senate. In 1844 he was elected to the lower house of the legislature, where he was greatly instrumental in the passage of the school law of that period. He was a man of easy manners, pleasant address, strong, practical sense, and withal quite a forcible speaker on the stump. In this campaign, however, he deemed it doubtless a waste of time to canvass the State, and contented himself with issuing an address to the people, in which he opposed repudiation of the State debt and argued the ample resources of the State to pay, if properly developed. He looked forward to the completion of the canal as a means to arouse the despondent energies of the people. As Illinois was then the only State destitute of banking facilities, he favored banks based exclusively on specie; and a revision of the constitution (a convention call for that purpose was then pending before the people), saying: "At the commencement of the session, the capitol is crowded with aspirants from different parts of the State seeking different offices; each has his friends among the members; a system of electioneering intrigue and log-rolling commences, which enters into the discussion and passage of almost every bill, until these offices are disposed of; and it is not unfrequently the case that the success of the most important measures of State policy depend upon the election of some little fourth-rate lawyer to the office of district attorney. I attributed the bad legislation mainly to this influence."‡

In the campaign, the whigs exposed Gov. French's record and connection with the passage of the internal improvement system, and urged it against his election; but in the meantime the war with Mexico broke out, regarding which the whig record was unfavorable. The war was the absorbing and dominating question of the period, sweeping every other political issue in its course. The election of August, 1846, resulted in the choice of the democratic candidate, A. C. French, over Kilpatrick, his principal competitor, by 58,700 votes for the former, to 36,775 votes for the latter. We say principal competitor, because Richard Eells (abolition) was running for the same office and received 5,152 votes.

---

*See Illinois State Register, Feb. 27, 1846.
†Illinois State Journal.
‡See Illinois State Journal.

For lieutenant-governor, Joseph B. Wells, the democratic candidate, received 55,221 votes; Nathaniel G. Wilcox, whig, 29,641, and Abraham Smith, abolition, 5,179 votes.

By the constitution of 1848, a new election for State officers was ordered in November of that year, before Governor French's term was half out. He was re-elected for the term of 4 years. Gov. French thus is the only man who has ever held the office of governor in this State for 6 consecutive years. At the election of 1848 there was no organized opposition to him, though a number of other gentlemen were honored as the recipients of the votes of the people. Augustus C. French received 67,453 votes; Pierre Menard (son of the first lieutenant-governor), 5,639; Charles V. Dyer, 4,748; W. L. D. Morrison, 3,834; and James L. D. Morrison, 1,361. William McMurtry, of Knox, was elected lieutenant-governor (in place of Joseph B. Wells, the incumbent, who did not run again), receiving 65,304 votes. O. H. Browning, Henry H. Snow, Pierre Menard and J. L. D. Morrison, were also honored by votes for this office, ranging from 2,000 to 5,000.

Gov. French was born in the town of Hill, New Hampshire, August 2, 1808. He was the descendant in the 4th generation of Nathaniel French, who emigrated from England in 1687, and settled in Saybury, Massachusetts. In early life young French lost his father, but continued to receive instruction from an exemplary and christian mother until he was 19 years old, when she also died, confiding to his care and trust four younger brothers and one sister. He discharged his trust with parental devotion. His education in early life was such mainly as a common school afforded; for a brief period he attended Dartmouth College, but from pecuniary causes and care of his brothers and sister, he did not graduate. He subsequently read law, was admitted to the bar in 1831, and shortly after removed to Illinois, settling first and practising his profession at Albion, Edwards county. The following year he removed to Paris, Edgar county. Here he attained eminence in his profession, and entered public life by representing that county in the legislature. A strong attachment sprang up between him and Stephen A. Douglas. In 1839, French became receiver of the United States land office at Palestine, Crawford county, at which place he resided when elevated to the gubernatorial chair. In 1844 he was a presidential elector, and as such voted for James K. Polk. After the expiration of his term of office as governor, he occupied for some years the professor's chair of the law department of McKendree College, at Lebanon, and did not reappear in public life except as a member of the constitutional convention of 1862.

In stature, Gov. French was of medium height; squarely built, well proportioned, light complexed, with ruddy face and pleasant countenance. In manners he was plain, agreeable, and of easy approach by the most humble; neither office nor position changed him in his bearing toward those he had met while in the more humble walks of life. Though by nature diffident, and at times apparently timid, yet when occasion demanded he was outspoken and firm in his views of public questions and convictions of duty. As a speaker, while he did not approach to the higher arts of oratory, he was chaste, earnest and persuasive. In business he was accurate and methodical, and as the executive of this State administered its affairs with great economy, prudence and discretion. He was an honest and conscientious man in all his transactions, and the State was fortunate in securing his services just at the time she did. While strong common sense, vigilance in looking to the public welfare, and conscientious convictions of duty are often more desirable in an executive officer than brilliancy or genius, it was peculiarly so at this juncture in the affairs of the State. In the pecuniary embarrassments of those times the credit of the State had been in a measure restored, and the overwhelming debt properly directed in the course of ultimate extinction during the administration preceding, yet it still required a clear, careful executive brain to bring order out of chaos, and a steady hand to guide the ship of state into the haven of safety. When Gov. French quitted the helm, in 1852, it was with the proud consciousness that her credit was fully restored, and her indebtedness, which had for many weary years pressed her incubus-like to the earth, would be faithfully and honestly discharged; that prosperous days had at length dawned for her people; that her unexampled resources were upon the eve of development, and that she would now make giant strides toward wealth, greatness and empire, in all of which his excellency had borne a just and faithful part. He was zealously devoted to the best interests of the State, ever acting for the public good, without regard to personal advantage or aggrandizement. He lived in his exalted station with much frugality. As the first governor under the hard times constitution of 1848, he received simply the salary provided, $1,500, and no more. The legislative art of evading this stringent provision by allowing the executive $4,500 for a gardener, had not as yet been evoked, nor would it, we may safely say, have been sanctioned by an acceptance of the douceur.

In 1845 a tax of $1\frac{1}{2}$ mills on the dollar was authorized, to be exclusively applied in payment of accrued interest upon the public debt. The proceeds of this tax were applied to all the interest-bearing debts of the State alike, including the canal bonds, leaving only about half of the tax to be applied to the interest accruing upon the debt proper, and causing a yearly deficit of unpaid interest exceeding $300,000, which was unprovided for. The canal, subject to all its arrearages, under the loan of $1,600,000, had been transferred in trust to the new subscribers. To carry forward the work so well begun of grappling with the monster debt, Gov. French recommended the registration and funding of the debts. The uncertainty, he urged, which hung over the exact amount of our liabilities, had produced a vague and painful apprehension in the public mind that the efforts then making to meet a portion of it were of little avail, to correct which, and elicit its true amount, this course should be adopted. Excluding the canal debt, the residue of all bonds or scrip should be converted into uniform transferable stock. For the arrears of interest due upon the bonds, a deferred stock of similar character, differing only in that it bore no interest for a number of years, was recommended. The expense of funding, it was thought, would be less than the loss already suffered from counterfeiting the coupons. In accordance with these views the legislature passed two funding acts, one authorizing the funding of the State bonds, and the other funding the State scrip and accrued interest on the debts. The funding of accrued interest met with considerable opposition, on the ground that the effect would be to cause the State to pay compound interest after 1857. But the measures passed, and by 1850 the entire State debt, excluding that of the canal, was nearly refunded in uniform securities, which greatly simplified the debt, and precluded further losses from the free counterfeiting of the bonds, both to the State and holders of the bonds.

The State of Illinois, as a condition to her admission into the Union, like many other States, had entered into a compact not to impose a tax upon the land sold by government within her limits for five years after sale, which was a serious clog upon her revenues. During the period of our financial embarrassment, the legislature earnestly petitioned congress to remove this restriction; to these appeals, urged with much force by Senator Breese, that body had finally acceded. And now, by act of February 19, 1847, the legislature provided that all lands hereafter sold by government within this State should be immediately subject to taxation. This measure materially increased the revenue of the State, as after the close of the Mexican war, the distribution by the government of land warrants among the soldiers as bounty, caused a large quantity to be thrown upon the market, and great numbers were located in Illinois. Indeed, so cheap did land warrants become, that they operated greatly to check the sale of State lands, which were held higher; and to avoid sacrifice, the legislature peremptorily suspended from further sale the public property, as provided by act of March 4, 1843, to wind up the internal improvement system.

The legislature, in 1847, in accordance with the recommendation of the governor, authorized the sale of the Northern Cross Railroad, from Springfield to Meredosia, now the T., W. & W. Upon the purchaser was imposed the duty of putting it in good repair, safe for the transportation of persons and property. The road and its equipments sold for $100,000 in State bonds, though it had cost the State not less than $1,000,000. The salt wells and canal lands in the Saline reserve in Gallatin county, granted by the general government to the State, were also authorized to be sold by the governor to pay State indebtedness.

The 2 mill tax provided by the new constitution to be annually distributed in payment of the principal of the public debt, other than the canal, and which, in 1849, amounted to $165,788 71, was found to work badly and unprofitably to the best interests of the State. The legislature passed a resolution submitting to a vote of the people an amendment to the constitution, to accord to that body the discretion of using the fund arising from this tax in the purchase of State bonds, in open market, at their current rates, at any time, instead of keeping the fund idle in the treasury until the 1st of January in each year, then to be apportioned and credited pro rata at a par valuation on the bonds presented, no matter at what discount they might be rated in market. In this there would undoubtedly have been a saving to the State, by her agents going upon the market and buying in her own paper at a discount, the same as any individual might operate; but the people, who felt it to be more honorable that the State should pay the full amount, refused to sanction this scheme or to entrust the general assembly in meddling with this sacred fund, and the amendment failed for want of that majority of votes which the constitution required to secure its adoption. The question, though urged again upon the people by the governor, was never again presented for their action, one reason being that the time required to again bring it to a vote would essentially lessen its importance, as the bonds were rapidly approximating a par valuation in market. Such were some of the efforts made during Gov. French's administration to gain the mastery of the monster public debt.

In 1850, for the first time since 1839, the accruing State revenue, exclusive of specific appropriations, was sufficient to meet the current demands upon the treasury. Prior to this it had been the practice to issue a surplus of auditor's warrants to meet deficiencies. Of course when the treasury was not in a condition to redeem these warrants, they depreciated, resulting in great losses both to the holders and the State by their lessened value, and the prolonged time of their redemption. But these embarrassments and sacrifices were now happily overcome. The aggregate taxable property of the State at this time was over $100,000,000, the annual constitutional 2 mill tax yielded a revenue, after allowing a proper margin for defaults and casual losses, of about $190,000, and the population was 851,470 souls.

Township Organization.—In 1849, in accordance with the permission of the new constitution, and in obedience to the demand of the people from the northern part of the State, who had observed its practical working in the eastern States, the first township organization act was passed by the legislature. But the law, in attempting to put it into practical operation, disclosed radical defects. It was revised and amended at the session of 1851, substantially as it has existed up to the present revision of 1871. The adoption of the township organization system marks an era in the management of fiscal affairs in many of the counties of this State.

The system of township government had its origin in New England. But the root of this form of local government may be traced to the districting of England into tithings by King Alfred, in the 9th century, to curb the wide-spread local disorders which disturbed his realm.* Upon this ancient idea of tithing districts, the Puritans grafted their greatly improved township system. The county system originated in this country with Virginia, and was also derived from England. The tobacco planters of the Old Dominion, owning their laborers more completely than did the barons of England their vassals, lived isolated and independent on their large landed estates in imitation of the aristocracy of the mother country. They also modeled their county and municipal institutions with certain modifications suitable to the condition of the new country after the same prototype; whence has spread the county system into all the southern and many of the northern States. All of the northwest territory, now constituting five States, after the conquest of Clark, was by Virginia, in 1778, formed into a county under her jurisdiction, called Illinois. The

---

*See further Blackstone's Commentaries, B i. p. 114–116.

county feature was afterwards retained in all the States carved out of the northwestern territory. The county business in Illinois was transacted by 3 commissioners, in the respective counties, who constituted a county court, which, besides the management of county affairs, had usually other jurisdiction conferred upon it, such as that of a justice of the peace and probate business. By the constitution of 1848, owing to the influence of eastern or New England settlers in the northern portion of the State, township organization was authorized, leaving it optional for any county to adopt or not the law to be enacted. Our township system, however, is not closely modeled after that of the New England States. There, a representative is sent directly from each town to the lower branch of the legislature. In New York, owing to her large extent of territory, this was found to be impracticable, and a county assembly, denominated a board of supervisors, composed of a member from each town, was there established. This modified system we have copied, almost exactly, in Illinois.

Townships are often compared by writers to petty republics, possessing unlimited sovereignty in matters of local concern; and boards of supervisors are popularly supposed to be vested with certain limited legislative powers. But neither is the case. Both the county and township boards are mere fiscal agents. They hold the purse strings of the counties; they may contract, incur debts or create liabilities—very great powers, it is true—but they cannot prescribe or vary the duties, nor control in any manner the county or township officers authorized by law. While the county court, consisting of three members, is a smaller, and, therefore, as a rule, more manageable or controllable body by outside influences, there is little doubt that a board of supervisors is not only directly more expensive, but also that a thousand and one petty claims of every conceivable character, having often no foundation in law or justice, are constantly presented, and, being loosely investigated and tacitly allowed, aggregate no insignificant sum. A board of supervisors also acts or is controlled more by partisan feelings. There ought to be uniformity throughout the State in the management of county affairs. No little confusion seems to pervade the laws at the present time relating to our two classes of counties.

Homestead Exemption.—The general assembly, at its session of 1851, first passed the act to exempt homesteads from sale on executions. This subject had been brought before the legislature repeatedly by Gov. French in his messages. The principle of this beneficent law was not a new or untried one. Its practical effects upon the social relations of communities had been fully and successfully tested in different States. The claims of society in maintaining the integrity of the family relation, which is the foundation of all society, it was argued, were superior to those of the individual; that some men, then as now, were to be found mean enough to specially evade honest debts, did not argue that such a law, in the interests of a higher duty from man to man, would not subserve, as a rule, a beneficent purpose, by shielding the widow and orphans, the aged and decrepid, from the cruel demands of the Shylocks of the world. Prior to this, the exemption of certain articles of personal property, which had been the law for a number

of years, had not proven inimical to the true interests of the creditor. For the $60 worth of property exempted, suited to the debt-
or's condition or occupation in life, he might select a yoke of oxen
for the cultivation of land, but no land was by the law allowed him
from which to raise something wherewith to support his family or
discharge his debt.

The provisions of the law (which was in force up to July 1st,
1872,) are too well known to recapitulate here. It exempted from
levy or forced sale, under any process or order of court, the lot of
ground and the building thereon occupied as a residence and
owned by the debtor, being a householder, and having a family,
to the value of $1,000. The law of 1872 raises this to $1,500. The
benefit of the act was extended to the widow and family, some or
one of them continuing to occupy the homestead until the youngest
child should become of age, or until the death of the widow.

The Bloody Island Dike—A Speck of War.—Owing to the formation of sand-bars in the Mississippi river opposite the lower part
of St. Louis, which it was apprehended would divert the channel
of the river to its left bank, and greatly injure, if not destroy, the
harbor of that city, the municipal authorities thereof, to prevent
that threatened calamity, passed an ordinance, February, 1848,
making appropriations to construct a dike or dam across the eastern channel of the river, from the foot of Bloody Island to the
Illinois shore, to force the main current of the water over to the
St. Louis side. This effort, made at a great expense to the treasury of that city, was met with determined opposition in Illinois,
as defiant to the sovereignty of this State and an infringement
upon the rights of our citizens. It was urged that the work
would change the channel in the upper Mississippi; that the effect
would be to inundate the American Bottom; that the river would
cut around the dike, drive the full force of its current towards
Cahokia creek, and destroy Illinoistown; and that the ferry would
be changed up the river to the island, to get to which the company
would charge enormous tolls over the dike.

The work was commenced by St. Louis within the rightful jurisdiction of this State, without permission from our legislsture or
notice to the governor, but solely with the consent and approbation
of the proprietors of the island, and the main shore opposite. Come
years prior, it seems, congress had made appropriations at different times for the improvement of St. Louis harbor, part of which
had been expended in the removal of a sand-bar at the south end
of the harbor. These appropriations, together with the consent
of the owners of the ground where the dike was to be built, St.
Louis claimed as a sufficient license for her invasion of the sovereignty of Illinois with this work. The rising cities of Alton and
Quincy, watchful of their rights and jealous of their big commercial neighbor, through their municipal boards passed resolutions
expressive of their apprehensions that these improvements would
be attended with danger to the navigation of the great commercial
highway of the west, and prove detrimental to their interests. The
executive of the State was called upon to inquire into the matter,
and to take such steps as would protect the sovereignty of this
State and the rights of its citizens. A large number of letters

from different citizens poured in upon his excellency to the same end.

Governor French thereupon addressed a letter to the municipal authorities of St. Louis, recapitulating the representations made to him as to the threatened dangers of this work, urging them to pause in their manifest encroachments upon the sovereignty of this State, and the rights of its citizens, which, if persisted in, would require him to employ suitable means to arrest.

To this somewhat bellicose document Mayor Krum, of St. Louis, replied, claiming the general government had some years previously projected and partly constructed certain works opposite the city, with the view to improve the navigation of the river, and at the same time improve the harbor of St. Louis; that the works now being prosecuted were substantially the same, originally designed and in part constructed by the U. S.; that to the unexpended balance of the appropriations by congress for this purpose, St. Louis had likewise added moneys to further the said object; joined to this high authority he plead also the consent of the owners of the ground where the work was being erected, and assured his excellency that the contemplated improvements would in no wise infringe either the sovereignty of the State of Illinois, or the rights of any citizen. After alluding to the influences at work to create a false impression upon the public mind, he closed, trusting that no inconsiderate steps would be taken on the part of the authorities of Illinois without due deliberation.

This answer, intended to disarm opposition and allay feeling, was not satisfactory in Illinois. It was not believed that the dike, in any manner, entered into the plan of improvement by the general government, but that it was the offspring of and solely prosecuted by St. Louis. Neither was it conceded that the general government had the right to carry forward this work within the rightful jurisdiction of this State. It was further inferred that the work was to be vigorously pushed forward by St. Louis, and that the equivocal agency of the general government was held out as a cloak to ward off molestation in its prosecution.

In view of the fact that it was sought to associate the general government with the project, the governor proposed to submit the question as an agreed case, to the U. S. circuit court, then sitting at Springfield, as the speediest and most satisfactory mode of settling the controversy. But this proposition was declined. Subsequently, in a letter to Gov. Reynolds, he writes that there is left him but one alternative, either to check the work or have some agreement that it shall await the meeting of the legislature.* A committee of the common council of St. Louis, with power to treat, visited Governor French at Springfield. His excellency offered to lay the matter before the next general assembly, but as that involved a considerable loss of time, the commission was unwilling to accede to it. The governor could not grant permission to proceed with the work. In the meantime an injunction, issuing from the St. Clair circuit court, had been served upon the contractors. But the work was proceeded with in contempt of the order of court. The governor now inaugurated "strong measures to cause the injunction to be respected." To this end, H. S. Cooley secretary of

* See Illinois State Register, July 14, 1848.

State, was sent to Illinoistown, to investigate the matter. He learned that a large number of men were employed, that steamers towed stone-laden barges from the St. Louis quarry, and that between 200 and 300 tons of rock were deposited upon the dike every night, notwithstanding the injunction; that 12 feet of wall was up, and that in 4 weeks time the whole line, from the Island to the main shore, would be built above the water's edge. At Belleville he found the war feeling so strong that a general disposition was manifest to enforce obedience to the writ of injunction. The sheriff of St. Clair county went beyond his bailiwick and served the writ upon the Mayor in St. Louis, who treated the matter rather lightly. Writs of attachment for contempt were now issued for the arrest of every person found violating the process of the court. If these civil measures failed and the sheriff's posse proved insufficient, the governor was determined to resort to military force, and all the able-bodied men of St. Clair county appeared ready to back him in the enforcement of the civil process. It might be inferred that war was imminent. The sheriff arrested two of the principal workmen on the dike and conveyed them before Judge Koerner to be tried for contempt. The press, both of St. Louis and Illinois, became violently inflamatory, portraying all manner of dire results to grow out of these acts, much as if an actual state of war existed.

In the meantime the governor's envoy found in mingling with the citizens of St. Louis that the people took very little interest in the trouble, and that the city authorities had no disposition to defy the process of a court of Illinois; that outside of the efforts of the Wiggins ferry company, which owned in great part the island, and the contractors, who wanted to earn their money, very little concern was felt in the dike controversy. It was represented that beyond a desire to hold the city harmless in its contract, (wherefore no effort was made to impede or restrain the work of the contractors) the authorities had no immediate interest in it; that willful contempt or double-dealing toward the authorities of Illinois, while their committee was on a peace mission to the governor, was not designed. It was the ferry company, owning the island, which would monopolize the causeway or dike leading to it from the main shore; the distance of its transit across the river would be shortened by half; the "St. Clair ferry," (partly owned by the State), together with Illinoistown, to which it ran, would by the new ferry landing be thrown so far out of the direct line of travel as to destroy both, and a new town, (the present East St. Louis,) would spring up on the island, more convenient and with shorter ferryage, which would enable that company to hold the traveling public to their own terms without successful competition, and bid defiance to the State. For these reasons the Wiggins Company took a deep interest in the successful accomplishment of the work.*

The injunction suit came up for hearing in September, before Koerner, then one of the supreme judges, at Belleville. After elaborate argument by Mayor Krum and Mr. Blannerhasset of St Louis, and Col. Bissell, in favor of the work, and Messrs. Keeting and Trumbull against it, the jurisdiction of the State

* See letters of Gen. Cooley to Gov. French, Illinois State Register, August 4th and 11th, 1848.

court was held to be concurrent with that of the federal; the power of the State to prohibit obstructions being placed in her highways or the construction of this dike in her navigable waters, was equally clear. The bill and writ were sustained as to Hall, Cannon and Bennet, three contractors served with process in St. Clair county, but as to the city of St. Louis, a foreign municipal corporation, and John Schreiber, served in St. Louis, out of the jurisdiction of the court, it was dismissed. An appeal to the supreme court was taken from the decision dismissing the case as to the city of St. Louis and Shreiber.[*]

The dike had been built up to the water's level, and the main contention now was over the attempt to build it 12 feet higher and level with the shore for a highway, belonging to and in the control of a private company, traversing the navigable waters of the State. Another point was the consequential impairment of the St. Clair ferry below, in which the State had an interest. In defense, it was claimed that the obstructed channel never was navigable, which was the fact, except perhaps on occasion of extraordinary freshets, and that it had been cut within 20 years through lands belonging to the old Wiggins ferry company, which, with St. Louis, was making this dike, and thus reclaiming their own land.

The legislature, at its session of 1849, settled the trouble by the passage of resolutions which provided that the city of St. Louis should file a good and valid bond with the secretary of state, binding the city to construct a safe and commodious highway over the dyke; and that the owners of the property on the island and main shore secure the undisturbed right of way to the public over it forever without tax or toll. The right of way was not to extend to chartered companies (except the St. Clair ferry) and turnpike companies. The city of St. Louis was also to secure to the St. Clair ferry a landing in the city, all of which was done, and thus was the cloud of war dispelled.

A committee was also appointed, consisting of J. L. D. Morrison, (from the aggrieved county), A. J. Kuykendall and Herbert Patterson, to examine the works, who reported, February 1, 1851, that the dike was then completed, being a solid stone wall across the chute, sunk in 40 feet of water, 36 feet wide and elevated to a level of 3 feet above the lower store doors on the levee in St. Louis, leaving the distance from the island across the river but 800 yards. A thriving city was predicted, to which at no distant day the workshops, boatyards and manufactories of St. Louis would in a great measure be transplanted, and where the tired artisan or mechanic, after his day's labor in the city, would repose in a cheaper and more comfortable home than he could enjoy in the crowded city. The result of the building of the dike has shown, after a lapse of 20 years, that stability has been imparted to the Illinois shore of the turbulent river, that Bloody Island has been permanently joined to the main land, and, while much remains to be done to build up a considerable city there, a half score of railroads centre already in East St. Louis.

[*] See 5 Gilman, 368.

36

" STATE POLICY."

Tribute Levied upon Illinois Produce in the St. Louis Market— Railroads Disappoint Ambitious Towns, &c.—From 1849 until the special session of February, 1854, there prevailed in the legislation of Illinois what was known as the "State Policy." The object was to so locate and fix the termini of cross railroads as to build up great commercial marts and mighty cities within the limits of this State; and if this did not follow, railroads should not go where they would contribute to the commerce and wealth of cities without the State. The "policy" was directed against St. Louis, a foreign city, ostensibly to favor our aspiring domestic cities falling within her competition, situate on the hither bank of the Father of Waters; those on the Wabash, Vincennes and Terre Haute were also included.

The reasons urged in favor of this policy were many and novel, and forcible enough to in a measure hold the best interests of the State in thrall for a period of six years. A general railroad incorporation law was opposed and defeated, on the grounds that any railroad company, foreign or domestic, could choose its route across the State in any direction without consulting the interests of the section of country through which it passed, which was not only highly unjust, but amounted to an infringement of the right of private property; it might be detrimental, and would certainly be in bad faith to other roads already built or chartered. If a road was built on the line of and in direct competition with the great public work of the State, the canal, the result would be to diminish its revenue, injurious to the State, the reversioner, and unjust to the bondholders of that work. It was gravely argued that no shrewd capitalist would make an investment at all, and that all improvements of that character must be arrested, because under a liberal general railroad incorporation law a ruinous competition would inevitably grow up. It was scouted as unworthy and insulting to our State pride to contend that the great cities of the Mississippi valley could not be built up in Illinois. All the railroads from east to west, north of the Ohio river, seeking termini with or beyond the Mississippi, must pass over Illinois territory. Let but these roads be compelled, by the statesmanship of Illinois, to converge to a point on that river within our border, and capital would center there, storerooms and warehouses spring up, dealers and commission merchants would be there, produce and shipping would gather there whence to seek an outlet to the Atlantic seaboard; in a word, a great commercial mart and the busy hum of a mighty city would be there. While the resources of the State were being developed, and property generally upon the lines of railroads increased in value, at the termini would be built up a city to rival in a few years St. Louis, which paid one-third of the revenue of Missouri, with debt and tax-ridden Illinois contributing half to her capital and substance, trade and prosperity.

Again and again were strenuous efforts made to pass an efficient general railroad incorporation law in accordance with the express provision of the constitution: "The general assembly shall encourage internal improvements by passing liberal general laws of incorporation for that purpose;" and again and again did the people from that portion of the State whose nearest, most direct and best market was St. Louis, petition the legislature to grant charters for railroads across the State from Vincennes, Terre Haute and other points on the Wabash, to terminate at a point opposite St. Louis, but were as often refused, and bill after bill containing such charters were invariably rejected.

At the close of the winter session of 1849 the members of the general assembly, to the number of 18 or 20, representing that belt of counties across the State opposite St. Louis, mainly affected by this exclusive policy, issued a stirring address to their constituents and all the section immediately concerned, setting forth that justice had been denied them by the legislature, and strongly appealing to them to send delegates to the number of not less than ten from each county to a railroad convention to be held in Salem in June, 1849, to take into consideration their grievances, and devise such measures as might be deemed necessary in the emergency to secure for their section those rights under the constitution from which they had been so unjustly debarred. To the north, it was charged, nothing had been refused, while to the south nearly everything had been denied—but not by northern votes alone !

The convention met at the appointed time and was attended by a large concourse of people; at least 4,000 earnest men were assembled, and over 1,000 delegates from the counties aggrieved. Ex-Gov. Zadock Casey presided. Mr. Wait, of Bond county, presented an able address, setting forth in apt language the grievances of that belt of country across the State through which the Ohio and Mississippi railroad would run, pointing out the advantages of St. Louis as a market, and boldly declaring the interests of that section of the State to be identical with those of that foreign city. The exclusive policy of the legislature was rebuked in severe terms for denying them the railroad charters which they sought for their section ; the governor was requested to convene the legislature in extraordinary session, and a general railroad incorporation act, with liberal provisions, was demanded from it ; and finally the people throughout the country were recommended to assemble in their home districts and take steps to urge these measures without ceasing.

It was generally supposed at this time that the governor would convene the legislature for the purpose of electing a United States senator in place of Gen. Shields, rejected by the senate in March previous for want of eligibility. As anticipated, the governor, on the 4th of September, issued his proclamation for a special session in October, 1849, inviting action upon several subjects, among them the establishment of a general railroad incorporation law.

To counteract the influence of the Salem convention, a "State policy" meeting was called at Hillsboro, in Montgomery county, for the 20th of July, 1849, to consider and take action in reference to railroads crossing the State east and west, and terminating at suitable points for building up commercial cities and towns within the borders of our own State. The convention did not meet, however, until October. For the occasion an immense barbecue was prepared, and it was said some 12,000 people attended. Many public men and politicians participated in the proceedings, and much bombast, portraying the great question of "State policy" in glowing colors, was indulged. Among the participants may be noted the names of Joseph Gillespie, Robert Smith, Cyrus Edwards, A. N. Starbird, W. Pickering, Gen. Thornton, W. D. Latshaw, and others. These names show that the Alton interest was largely represented. Resolutions were adopted in favor of the "policy;" approving the action of the legislature at its last session in refusing charters to railroads leading to St. Louis; condemning the call of the extra session of the general assembly by the governor for that month, and asking its immediate adjournment after the election of a United States senator, without acting upon any other question.

Here it may be mentioned that the action of the Missouri legislature contributed not a little to incense the people of Illinois against St. Louis. That body had, in the winter of 1849, preceding, passed an act levying tribute upon all property sold within the limits of Missouri, being the growth, produce or manufacture of any State other than her sovereign self. The amount of saletax required to be paid was $4 50 on every $1,000 worth of merchandize sold, for 6 months from and after the 21st of August, 1849. Commission merchants in charging this amount back to their consignors, were required to make out sworn returns, much, it is presumed, after the manner of our late government income tax. It was estimated upon accurate data, that the commerce of Illinois alone, in the market of St. Louis, would yield, by this sale tax, $150,000 annually to the treasury of Missouri. It was a scheme by which to lift the burden of government and taxation from the people of Missouri, where it belonged, and impose it upon the people of Illinois, Iowa and Minnesota. A law so obnoxious to every principle of justice, gave immediate rise to much dissatisfaction and clamor among the people, with severe denunciation of the offending State by the press; it is but just to say, however, that the press of St. Louis also contemned the law and its enactors, charging that the legislature of Missouri, was controlled by influences outside of and antagonistic to that city, rather than promotive of her interests. The law was clearly inimical to the constitution of the United States. Such a tax if at all admissable, congress alone has the power to levy, on condition that it be made uniform throughout the United States. Subsequently the supreme court of Missouri set the law aside. But it may be well imagined that it contributed not a little in arousing feeling and prejudice among our people and law-makers against St. Louis. The dike, too, afforded an opportunity to array prejudice against that city, and neither was slowly taken advantage of.

The legislature, at the called session of October, 1849, again refused special charters to the Vincennes and St. Louis railroad, a general railroad incorporation law was however established, but so defective in its provisions that no company could well organize or operate under it without further legislation. The subjoined declaration of principles of State policy, drawn up by Wesley Sloan, of Pope, the sage of Golconda, which passed the house, Nov. 3, 1849, by 43 to 27, and the senate with only 2 dissenting votes, illustrates the animus of the legislature upon the subject of railroads, better than anything else:

Resolved 1st. That the geographical position of the State of Illinois, considered in connection with the construction of railroads within her limits, is one of the greatest natural advantages which she possesses, and which under a judicious system of legislative policy must be very instrumental in promoting her general welfare as a State.

"2d. That the prosperity of a State or nation, consists not only in the virtue and intelligence of a brave and energetic people; in the richness of her soil and mineral resources, but also in the number and extent of her flourishing towns, cities and villages.

"3d. That any internal improvement, whether constructed under a general or special law, tending in its operation to impede the growth and prospects of cities, towns and villages, within our own borders, ought not to be encouraged.

"4th. That the construction which should be given to the 6th section of the 10th article of the constitution is, that the general assembly shall encourage improvements that are of an internal character and advantage, and not such as are mainly intended to promote external interests.

"5th. That a railroad commencing at our eastern boundary, running across the State and terminating at a point on the Mississippi river opposite St. Louis, and also uniting with continous lines of railroads extending eastwardly through our sister States, either to Cincinnati or the Atlantic cities, would be immensely advantageous to St. Louis, at the same time 'that it would impede the growth and prosperity of the cities, towns and other localities on the Illinois side of the Mississippi river.'

"6th. That the connection of the Mississippi river by continuous lines of railroads with the Atlantic seaboard, is of vital importance to the whole Union, and we willingly invite the construction of railroads passing through other States, to our eastern boundary, promising to grant to them the right of way, and reserving to ourselves only the privilege of fixing the termini; a privilege we constitutionally claim, and which we are entitled to exercise by reason of our geographical position.

"7th. That the construction of the great Central Railroad is a subject of vast importance to Illinois, and all laws, having for their object the completion of the same on proper principles, ought to be encouraged; provided such laws do not infringe too much upon our natural advantages growing out of the geographical position of the State."*

The passage of these resolutions by the very decided majorities we have noted, was rather alarming. And now the internal policy of the State, so emphatically announced, was attacked without gloves by the foreign press, and our own, partly, too. The newspapers of St. Louis and Cincinnati, directly affected by the refusal of the legislature to grant a charter to the Ohio & Mississippi Railroad Company, were unsparing in their abuse. The State policy was denounced as selfish, narrow and contemptible— we were re-enacting the fable of the dog in the manger. The press of New York chiming in, characterized our "State policy" as unreasonable, vain and churlish; we would neither help the parties affected by it, nor permit them to help themselves; to the great railroads pushing their lines from the Atlantic cities westward, conferring permanent benefit and untold wealth along their routes, when they arrived upon our eastern border we exclaimed in the blindness of our own interests, thus far shalt thou go and no farther, because they wanted to go to St. Louis, the great commercial centre on the Mississippi. It was urged that Illinois stood in the light of her own interests; that our shortsighted policy was proving ruinous to the south and middle parts of the State; that it was the Alton influence, as opposed to St. Louis, which had produced the conflict between the three sections

* See laws of Special Session, 1849.

of the State, but that after all the north was taking advantage
of it, using Alton to pull the chestnuts out of the fire for Chicago.

Alton had been ambitious of commercial distinction for many
years, always waiting Micawber-like for some fortuitous circumstances, or involved in some ingenious schemes to accomplish this
grand object. But these, without energy, labor and capital will
not alone succeed in building up a great city. It will be remembered by the reader that the State bank in 1835 was bankrupted
within two years after it started by its efforts to supply the capital to monopolize the lead mines of Galena, divert all the up-river
trade from St. Louis, and build up Alton, nearly opposite the
mouth of the Missouri, as the emporium of the Mississippi valley.
The completion of the canal, also, it was fondly hoped, would
check the prosperity of St. Louis. Canal boats, it was maintained, might with safety and expedition be towed down as low
as Alton, but the increased difficulties and dangers in the current
of the Mississippi, below the mouth of the Missouri, would prevent their being taken to St. Louis, while freight could at all
times be brought as cheaply from New Orleans to Alton as to St.
Louis.

Thus by the deceptive cry of this grand internal State policy,
and various combinations formed in consequence thereof, hostile
legislation was evoked toward that part of the State which by
nature is not so well adapted to the construction of railroads as
the great prairie regions of the center and north, and which should
rather have received the fostering care of friendly legislation than
the blight of this policy, whose effects are not entirely removed to
this day. The great northern portion of the State, seeking an
outlet by railroads to markets on the lake, and mainly within our
own borders, was not inimical to the exclusive policy; but while
that region was liberally rewarded with railroad charters for its
development, it was not without aid, infatuated let us hope, from
the south to impose the "policy" upon the latter.

Notwithstanding this withering policy, and the just strictures
upon it by our own and the foreign press, which disseminated a
knowledge of it far and wide; and also that the State generally
had been greatly retarded in her onward career by an enormous
public debt, without equivalent, weighing her down like an incubus, there was not, as we approach the close of the decade terminating with 1850, another State in the Union increasing so rapidly in population, wealth and resources. Not Illinois alone, but
the entire northwest was settling up rapidly. The whole of this
vast wilderness in 1820, contained only about 850,000 souls, (being
less than Illinois had in 1850), while now it numbered 5,000,000.
The action of steam had cheapened and immeasurably increased
the speed of transportation and immigration. The completion of the canal had given an impetus to the agricultural
resources of Illinois, long needed. It had also been indirectly a
means of wonderfully improving her financial affairs. With the
advent of Gov. Ford's administration, it was officially announced
that there was not money enough in the State treasury to pay
postage on a letter. Since then the new loan of $1,600,000 had
been made, with which the canal had been completed, yielding now
an annual revenue in tolls of over $125,000; canal lands worth half
million dollars had been sold, far above the appraisement; 3-5ths

of the $1\frac{1}{2}$ mill tax authorized in 1845 now paid $12 out of every $60 of annually accruing interest; and if the two mill tax authorized by the new constitution could have been diverted in that way the whole annual interest on the internal improvement debt proper could have been paid. Auditor's warrants were worth 95 cents on the dollar. Such was our improved condition at this time, brought about by a rigid economy in expenditures, a thorough system of retrenchment under the new constitution, and a wise administration of public affairs under Govs. Ford and French.

And now came in addition such glad tidings which, but for the thorough schooling in these rigid economies and dearly bought experiences, might have sent us again headlong into a wild course of profligacy and schemes of infatuation. This was the magnificent donation by congress of some 3,000,000 acres of land to the State, which secured the building the Illinois Central Railroad; also at the same session, the grant to the State of all the unsold swamp lands within her limits, estimated at 1,500,000 acres; and what was also of incalculable benefit to many a family, the act of congress granting bounty land to the brave men who periled their lives in the but recently closed Mexican war. With these encouraging and hopeful aids, joined to an ever thronging emigration pouring in upon our rich prairies, stifling legislation could no longer retard our march to empire.

In the fall of 1850, a new legislature, fresh from a new people— new in great accessions, and also in that they had cast off their garments of despondency, and were full of hope—was elected. This body met in January, 1851, and while it did not inconsiderately crowd important bills through, performed a great deal of labor, giving life to those measures which have become the instruments of an enduring greatness to this empire State, and from which, with proper additions since, we behold to-day unfolding the full glory of a grand future. These instruments were mainly important railroad charters, which in number were even then said to mark up the surface of the State into a network of these improvements.

The incubus of "State policy" was not altogether shaken off, but a good beginning was made by granting a charter to the Ohio and Mississippi railroad company. Mr. Douglas, taking a broader view than the confines of Illinois, was prompted to address a letter from Washington to Uri Manly, of Coles, saying if he were a legislator he would certainly grant a charter for the proposed road from Illinoistown to Terre Haute, and also to Vincennes, and to other lines across the State when any considerable portion of the people desired it. He would give a preference to the towns and cities of Illinois where it could be done without injury or injustice to others, but he would never sacrifice the great agricultural interests for the benefit of a much smaller interest in the towns. The country was not made for the towns, but the towns for the convenience of the country.* The Hon. Y. R. Young, M. C., also wrote to Mr. W. S. Waite, of Bond county, that good faith on the part of the legislature required them to charter all cross railroads contemplated, as most probably the Illinois Central railroad grant of land would not have been obtained if the delegation in congress had withheld the positive assurance that the State would change

* Vide Ill. Reg., Jan., 1851.

her policy in relation to cross roads. That such assurances were given was also corroborated by Mr. Douglas and Col. W. H. Bissell, the latter writing that he felt quite sure votes were obtained in that way, and that the result showed that they had but very few to spare in the final trial.* Thus was the legislature induced to yield and grant just one cross road leading to St. Louis. But that was all.

And now, to illustrate the bad faith of soulless corporations—the many disappointments and heart-burnings which they have caused, and the bitter curses they have invited from rising towns and ambitious cities throughout the length and breadth of the State, it may here be mentioned in connection with this road, which gave one of the earliest cases of the kind, and which, too, will serve as a type of many others whose local history cannot well be obtained, that, after being a suppliant for years before the legislature for just the right of way, and in its obsequiousness full of the most honorable and humble promises, no sooner had it obtained its charter than it turned and violated them, becoming perfectly oblivious to everything else except what was expressed in that instrument. Belleville, at that day, was an ambitious and flourishing young city. In the passage of the charter for the Ohio and Mississippi railroad company, it is alleged that it was distinctly understood that the interests of Belleville should not be sacrificed, and therefore the naming of that place as a point in the charter was magnanimously omitted. This magnanimity that corporation failed to appreciate, and grievous disappointment followed. Belleville thereupon tendered a subscription of $50,000 on condition that she be made a point; she entreated and remonstrated, but a deaf ear was turned to all her requests. Belleville was left some six miles to the south. She held an indignation meeting and declared it inconsistent with the honor, interests or duty of any citizen to participate in the ceremonies of breaking ground at Illinoistown for that road, February 8, 1852. On that occasion was presented the singular spectacle of Cincinnati, Vincennes and St. Louis, three foreign cities, taking possession of the soil of Illinois upon which to inaugurate a great improvement, without our countenance or approbation, but we were powerless to prevent it. Other places in this State, similarly aggrieved by other roads, are Uniontown, Salem, Charleston, Shelbyville, Urbana, &c., &c. Verily, in our legislation upon the subject of railroads, and the granting to them of valuable franchises, we have gone from one extreme to the other. While our action toward them in respect of the State policy was entirely too narrow and illiberal, savoring too much of proscription, when chartered privileges were extended to them it seems that the bars were let clear down, and we failed to retain any sufficient control over them. These, to-day, giant foreign corporations, some of whom erst begged in a most suppliant manner of this sovereign State merely for the right of way, now set up their vested rights and defy not only legislative but constitutional control.

The "State policy" maintained its supremacy longer with regard to the Atlantic and Mississippi railroad, known as the "Brough" road, from Terre Haute via Vandalia to St. Louis direct, than any other. This road was regarded as in direct conflict with the Alton

* Ibid

interest, and a ruinous competition to the Terre Haute and Alton road, then building. Col. John Brough, a leading public citizen of Indiana, was at its head, and showed much determination to accomplish it. When he was denied a special charter by the legislature of 1851, a company was organized under the general laws of 1849; subscription books to the capital stock were opened in New York city, capital $2,000,000, shares $50 each; $470,000 were speedily subscribed, and Col. Brough, the president, issued his bulletin, announcing his intention to build a road from Terre Haute to St. Louis, not only without, but against, legislation. The idea that St. Louis should have two railroad highways across the State of Illinois was simply monstrous to Alton. An Alton newspaper of November, 1852, says:

"At the close of the last session of our legislature we expressed the opinion that Col. John Brough, of Indiana, would be satisfied with the explicit refusal of our State to grant a charter of incorporation to his pet project * * and that he would abide by the several times repeated decision. The citizens of Illinois had reason to suppose that they were rid, for all time to come, of this pretended friend, but real enemy, to their best interests. It seems, however, that this valiant Indiana colonel is determined, notwithstanding his former repulses, to continue his unsolicited and officious intermeddling with the domestic policy of this State."

But it was found impracticable to build the road under the law of 1849, and application was again made to the general assembly of 1853 for a special charter. Col. Brough was personally present and labored earnestly to succeed, but the State policy party, after strenuous opposition, led by Messrs. Wynn, Kuykendal and others, were again enabled to defeat the bill. Another bill looking to the accomplishment of the same result, perhaps, was for a charter of the Terre Haute and Vandalia railroad, but the jealous and watchful State policy party, regarding this as a piecemeal resurrection of the "Brough road," promptly defeated it. The extension of the Belleville and Illinoistown charter eastward across the State, the Terre Haute and Marshall branch, and several others, which looked to approach the Mississippi at St. Louis, all met with signal defeat. The triumph of the State policy party was complete, and the press in its interest boldly proclaimed that it had waxed stronger than ever.

About this time, too, Chicago was greatly exercised over the Joliet Cut-off grievance, a road which would save to the public from the east, west or south—not desiring to make the detour to Chicago— 60 miles in transportation or travel, going and coming. Yet Chicago, for some fancied benefit, was anxious that that circuit should be maintained and enforced, *nolens volens*, upon all freight and passenger transportation. It is but just to say, however, that in this there was not entire unanimity. Notably the Chicago *Democrat* became all at once the most ardent advocate of State policy, and strongly urged this enforced deviation upon the public, denouncing Joliet and her citizens prominently connected with the steps taken to build a short railroad directly east, in unmeasured terms of abuse.

It was at the session of 1853, that Joseph Gillespie, champion of the Alton interest, introduced into the senate a bill by which all these existing chartered railroad corporations were to be protected for ten years against the building of any competing roads within 25 miles distance, unless existing corporations first

consented thereto. This amazing proposition was a fit climax to
all the monstrous, absurd and pernicious schemes of the State
policy party. While many of the other States of the Union, animated by a noble spirit of enterprise, were removing legal obstructions and instead adopting broad and liberal railroad incorporation laws, throwing wide open their borders, and inviting
capital from abroad to build railroads and create competition
wherever it inclined, it was cooly proposed in the great State
of Illinois, which needed development very badly, to draw a cordon of exclusiveness around her borders, and within to combine
with soulless corporations in the monopoly of all improvements,
and hand over to them, bound by the strong chords of the law,
the people of the State to be fleeced without stint. The bill
failed to become a law.

The Salem railroad convention of 1849 having ultimately proved
successful in obtaining a charter for the Ohio and Mississippi railroad, another convention now met at the same place, Nov. 25, 1853,
to urge upon the governor the calling together of the general assembly in extraordinary session. The counties of Clark, Cumberland, Effingham, Crawford, Fayette, Jasper, Edwards, Bond,
St. Clair, Jackson, Monroe, Williamson, Randolph, Clinton, Jefferson, Perry, Marion, Clay, some 19, all south of the
Terre Haute and Alton railroad, whose best and most accessible
market would be St. Louis, were ably represented by their most
public spirited and enterprising men. The Hon. Zadock Casey
was unanimously chosen chairman. A committee was appointed
of which the Hon. Sidney Breese was chairman, to draft an address, setting forth their grievances and urging the governor to
convene the legislature. Action upon seven measures was demanded, but the railroad grievance was the main one. The committee say:

"The special acts and the general law, so-called, for railroad incorporation demand action that would alone justify an extra session. Restrictions upon the accomplishment of useful enterprises might be removed by an act of ten lines, opening the way to immediate construction of works that would bring in capital from abroad and enhance the
value of real estate to the amount of several millions of dollars. That
Southern Illinois has a peculiar interest in this important measure, she
has no disposition to deny. Look at the single fact that in the vast and
increasing railroad enterprises, which is giving new life to the State, and
which already exceed 2,000 miles in extent, less than 300 are permitted
to Southern Illinois."

A committee of some 20 was appointed to present the address
in person to the governor. It had the desired effect. The governor
issued his proclamation, convening the legislature in Feb., 1854.

This special session was a very busy, and in many respects, a
most important one for the State. But we now can only notice
the subject in hand. The State policy was narrowed down to the
one object of again defeating the "Brough road," for which purpose a great effort was made, aided by foreign lobbyists interested
in the Terre Haute and Alton road. But their efforts failed; the
liberal policy triumphed, the charter "recognizing and authorizing
the construction of the Mississippi and Atlantic railroad" passed
in both houses by decisive majorities. Exit "State policy"—a
policy which has done much to hinder and retard the growth and
development of the southern portion of the State, and whose
blight has lingered more or less to this day.

CHAPTER XLVI.

THE ILLINOIS CENTRAL RAILROAD.

Congressional Grant of Land—Holbrook Charters—Bondholders' Schemes—The 7 per cent. of its Gross Earnings—Passage of its Charter—Benefits to the Company, the State and Individuals— Note: Jealousy of Politicians on Account of its Glory—Correspondence of Messrs. Breese and Douglas.

The subject of this chapter marks an era in the progress of the State. The grand scheme of connecting, by means of iron bands of commerce, Lake Michigan with the great watery highway of the Mississippi Valley at the confluence of the Ohio, had long been a desideratum with our people. It had constituted part of the State internal improvement system of 1837, and some work on the line was actually done, but was abandoned with the general collapse of that system. The Central Railroad, from the southern terminus of the canal to Cairo, was subsequently revived by legislation, procured by scheming brains with an eye to the future, but the whole subject lacked vitality until the passage of the act of congress of September, 1850, granting to the State a munificent donation of near 3,000,000 acres of land through the heart of Illinois in aid of its completion. This noble tribute by the nation had its birth simultaneously with and amidst the throes of the great adjustment measures of 1850, which, during that long and extraordinary session of Congress, shook the Union from center to circumference. Twice before had a similar bill passed the senate, and twice had it failed in the house, but now it was a law, and the State possessed the means to complete the great work. The final passage of the measure was hailed with demonstrations of great joy by the people and press of our State.* Illinois internal improvement bonds made a bound forward of 10 per cent. in the New York market. At this time the amount of railroad completed in the State consisted of a section of the Northern Cross Railroad, from Meredosia and Naples, on the Illinois river, to Springfield; the Chicago & Galena, from the former city as far as Elgin; and a 6 mile coal track across the American bottom from opposite St. Louis to the mines in the bluffs.

---

*After the adjournment of congress, Senators Douglas and Shields, on their return home, were tendered a public dinner at Chicago in honor of the occasion, but for reasons of delicacy they declined becoming the exclusive recipients of such attentions, awarding to their colleagues of the house—where the final battle was fought and won—Messrs. McClernand, Harris, Wentworth, Young, Richardson, Bissell and Baker, the principal merit of its passage. The honors for the success of the measure were a fruitful source of jealousy among our public men.

The act granted the right of way for the railroad through the public lands of the width of 200 feet, from the southern terminus of the Illinois and Michigan Canal to a point at or near the junction of the Ohio and Mississippi rivers, and for branches to Chicago and Galena; also the privilege to take from them materials of earth, stone and timber for its construction. But the main grant to the State was the alternate sections of land designated by even numbers for 6 sections deep on each side of its trunk and branches; for the lands sold or pre-empted within this 12 mile belt or area, enough might be selected from even numbered sections to the distance of 15 miles on either side of the tracks equal in quantity to them. The construction of the road was to be simultaneously commenced at its northern and southern termini, and when completed the branches were to be constructed. It was to be completed within ten years, in default of which the unsold lands were to revert to the United States, and for those sold the State was to pay the government price. The minimum price of the alternate or odd numbered sections of the government land was raised from $1 25 to $2 50 per acre. While the public lands were thus by the prospect of the building of this road rendered more saleable at double price, it followed that the general government not only lost nothing in dollars and cents, but in point of time was actually the gainer by this splendid gift. The land was taken out of market for two years, and when restored, in the fall of 1852, it in fact brought an average of $5 per acre. The grant was subject to the disposal of the legislature for the purpose specified, and the road and branches were to be and remain a public highway for the use of the government of the United States, free from all tolls or other charges for the transportation of any troops, munitions or other property of the general government. This provision, had it applied to the rolling stock as well as the use of the rails, would doubtless have saved the general government during the rebellion many hundreds of thousands of dollars; but it has been construed adversely to the rights of the government in this particular. For the purpose of continuing the road south to Mobile, all the rights, privileges and liabilities, with regard to the grant of the public lands and in every respect as conferred on this State, were extended to Alabama and Mississippi. Such is a synopsis of the important provisions contained in this, the first land subsidy made by congress in aid of railroads, latterly so lamentably frequent as to well nigh despoil the country of its public domain.

Upon the passage of the bill, Mr. Douglas immediately prepared a petition, signed by the congressional delegations of all the States along the route of the road from Mobile north, describing the probable location of the road and its branches through Illinois, and requesting the president to order the suspension of land sales along the lines designated, which was immediately done.*

The act of congress threw upon the legislature of Illinois the entire duty of making a prudent, wise and satisfactory disposi-

---

*At the same session congress passed an act granting to the State of Akansas the swamp and overflowed lands unfit for cultivation, and remaining unsold within her borders, the benefits whereof were extended by section 4 to each of the other States in which there might be such lands situated. By this act the State of Illinois received 1,500,000 acres more. These lands were subsequently turned over to the respective counties where located, with the condition that they be drained, and for school purposes.

tion of the magnificent grant. The point of departure of the Chicago branch from the main trunk was not fixed by the act, and this delicate duty the legislature, it was generally expected, would take in hand. Before the meeting of that body, in January, 1851, much contention pervaded the press of the State regarding the location of the main trunk, and particularly the routes of the branches. Many worthy and ambitious towns were arrayed against each other. The LaSalle interest wanted the Chicago branch taken off at that point. Bloomington, looking to a continuation of the Alton & Sangamon road (now the Chicago, Alton & St. Louis) to that place, wanted the Chicago branch to connect her with the lake. Shelbyville, which was a point on the old line of the Illinois Central, not dreaming but that she would have the main trunk, was grasping for the departure thence of the Chicago branch also, and lost both. Another route, which ought to have commanded great strength, was proposed on the most direct line from Cairo, making the point of connection with the main trunk in Pulaski county, and taking off the Galena branch at Mt. Vernon, thence through Carlyle, Greenville, Hillsboro, Springfield, Peoria, Galena and on to Dubuque. But of course it was to the interest of any company to make the location where there was the largest amount of vacant land that could be brought within the belt of 15 miles on either side of the road. And this proved the controlling influence ultimately, both in the location of the main stem and the branches.

The disastrous failure of only a dozen short years before, as connected with the Utopia of the internal improvement system by the State, was not forgotten; and now when the means of achieving great good for developing the State were in hand, the stump and press teemed with advice as to the best mode of disposing of the grant of land, which, it may be added, was seldom free from bias or a look to local advantages. Swarms of land speculators and town site owners, it was anticipated, would infest the lobby at the next session of the legislature. The people were very properly advised that to guard against the influences and intrigues of these sharks they must select their best and ablest men to represent them.

The Holbrook Charters.—One of the phantoms which loomed into public recognition, casting its shadow across the path of bright promise for the State, was what was known as the "Holbrook Charters," whose incorporators, it was feared, would step in and swallow up the congressional grant of land under the broad terms of their franchises.

The Cairo City and Canal Company was originally incorporated for the purpose of constructing dikes, levees or embankments to secure and preserve Cairo city and adjacent lands against the freshets of the rivers. The cutting of a canal to unite the Mississippi with the Ohio through Cash river, was also authorized. In the fall of 1835 the Hon. Sydney Breese, through a well-considered published letter, had first called attention to the plan of a central railroad, connecting the southern terminus of the Illinois and Michigan canal at Peru with the confluence of the Ohio and Mississippi rivers at Cairo. An effort was made at the special session of 1835–6 to unite this project with the canal, for which an appropri-

ation of $500,000 was then granted. This failing, a charter for the
railroad was granted, supplementing this project with the Cairo
City Company, the corporators being Darius B. Holbrook, (who
was also the president of the company,) Miles A. Gilbert, John S.
Hacker, Alexander M. Jenkins, Anthony Olney and William M.
Walker. Application was then first made to congress for aid by
pre-emption. One year later the State entered upon the great internal improvement system, and, unwilling to brook a rival, applied to the Cairo company to surrender the charter for the building of this railroad through the centre of the State, which was
complied with on condition that the State build the road on a
route leading from Cairo through Vandalia, Shelbyville, Decatur,
Bloomington, Peru, and via Dixon to Galena. The State expended
more than a million dollars, it is said, on this route before the
"grand system" collapsed in 1840. Subsequently, by act of March
6, 1843, the road, in the condition that it was abandoned, was restored to the Cairo company under the title of the Great Western
Railway Company, with the power to construct the road from
Cairo via the places named, to a point at or near the southern terminus of the Illinois and Michigan canal, in such manner
as they might deem most expedient. The Cairo Company was
vested with the title and effects of the old Central railroad. All
the usual franchises were granted to the Great Western Company
as part of the Cairo Company, and in section 18 it was added that
" all lands that may come into the possession of said company,
whether by donation or purchase," were pledged and mortgaged
in advance as security for the payment of the bonds and obligations of the company authorized to be issued and contracted under
the provisions of the charter. By act of March 3, 1845, the charter
of this Great Western Railroad Company was repealed; but by
act of February 10, 1849, it was revived for the benefit of the Cairo
City and Canal Company, with the addition of some 30 names as
incorporators, taken from all parts of the State, many of whom
were well-known politicians. The company thus revived was authorized in the construction of the Central Railroad to extend it
on from the southern terminus of the canal—LaSalle—to Chicago
"in strict conformity to all obligations, restrictions, powers and
privileges of the act of 1843." The governor was empowered to
hold in trust for the use and benefit of said company whatever
lands might be donated to the State by the general government,
to aid in the completion of the Central or Great Western Railway,
subject to the conditions and provisions of the bill (then pending before congress and expected to become a law,) granting the subsidy
of 3,000,000 acres of land. The company was further authorized
to receive, hold and dispose of any and all lands secured to it by
donation, pre-emption or otherwise. There were other details of
minor importance, but these sufficiently indicate the nice scheme
entertained by the long-headed speculators.

But Douglas, though absent at Washington, was not to be
hoodwinked by these schemes against the best interests of
the State. At the special session of the legislature in the autumn of 1849, in his able speech delivered to that body, October
23d, he demonstrated that a fraud had been practiced upon it the
winter preceding in procuring from it this charter; and that had
the bill in congress donating this land met with no delay on this

account, this vast property would have gone into the hands of Holbrook & Co., to enrich these scheming corporators, with little assurance, as they represented no wealth, that the road would ever be built. Congress had an insuperable objection to making the grant for the benfit of a private corporation. The connection of these Holbrook companies with the Central railroad, in the estimation of congress, presented an impassible barrier to the grant. But this legislature, which had granted the charter, refused to repeal it.

To obviate the difficulty, Mr. Holbrook, president of the companies, who ardently sought the success of the road, executed a promise of release to the governor, December 15th, 1849, a duplicate of which was transmitted to Mr. Douglas at Washington. But the senator did not regard this release as valid or binding upon the company, because it was without the sanction or authority of the stockholders, or even the board of directors. While he did not impute any such motive, the company, he believed, was still in the condition which would enable it to take all the lands granted, divide them among its stockholders, and retain its chartered privileges without building the road. He was unwilling to give his approval to any arrangement by which the State could possibly be deprived of any of the benefits resulting from the expected grant. For the protection of the State, and as an assurance to congress, the execution of a full and complete release of all rights and privileges, and a surrender of the charters, and all acts or parcels of acts supplemental or amendatory thereof, or relating in any wise to the Central railroad, so as to leave the State, through its legislature, free to make such disposition of the lands, and such arrangement for the construction of the road as might be deemed best, was demanded. These requirements were deemed not unreasonable by the agents of the company at Washington, the Hon. John A. Rockwell, of Connecticut, and Mr. G. W. Billings, and a few days after a release, in duplicate, was executed in New York, one copy of which was forwarded to the governor of Illinois, and one retained by Mr. Douglas, to be used, if necessary, in congress, containing these conditions:

"1st. That the legislature of said State shall, within the period of TEN YEARS from the 1st of January, 1850, construct and finally complete, or cause to be constructed and completed, a railroad from Cairo to Chicago, and that the southern terminus of said road shall be the city of Cairo. 2d. That the legislature of said State shall, during its next session, elect whether to accept or decline this release upon the conditions herein stated. 3d. That until said State, through their legislature, shall have made their election, this company may *with the approbation of the governor of the State*, proceed in the construction of said road, and if said charter shall be released as aforesaid to said State of Illinois, the said State shall, within one year from the time of said election, refund to this company the amount which between that period and the present time, shall have been expended in the construction of said road, with 6 per cent. interest thereon, and shall assume all *bona fide* contracts *hereafter* made by this company in the construction of the same, which shall have been previously approved by the governor of said State."

Nothwithstanding this release, after the passage of the bill granting the land by congress, there was a doubt in the minds of the people of Illinois, which was freely canvassed pending the election of the legislature, which was to dispose of the splendid donation to the best interests of the State, regardless of local considerations or sectional desires, that the Cairo company, through its president, could and would repudiate the relinquishment of its charters, or use some expedient to induce the general assembly to fail in accepting it according to its 2d stipulation, which would enable that concern to resume its former position and grasp the large grant of land under the provisions of its charter of 1849. The following curious letter, over the name of the president of the company, which appeared in the *Illinois Advocate* at Lebanon, and floated about considerably in the public press of the day, seems to evince a desire to hold on, and it doubtless gave color to the public apprehensions:

"NEW YORK, Sept. 25, 1850.

"*Hon. E. O. Smith:*

"DEAR SIR: I can truly say that I am under obligations to those who with Gov. Casey prevented the repeal of the charter of the Great Western Railway Company. It was granted in good faith and under no other that the State can now grant. I am happy to say that when I explained the bill to Judge Douglas, and that my object was to have the road made for the best interest of the whole State, I would return the charter rather than have any opposition from the State, he was satisfied; and the consequence has been that we have worked together at Washington this winter, and have obtained the grant of land from congress toward making the road. We are now sure that the road from Cairo to Peru, Galena and Chicago will be built. I am now organizing the company to commence the work this fall, and put a large part of the road under contract as early as possible. We shall make the road on the old line of the Central route, through Vandalia, Shelbyville, Decatur and Bloomington. I rejoice with the people of Illinois that this important road to the whole State, will now be made.

"Very respectfully,   D. B. HOLBROOK."

This was construed as a pretension on the part of the president, that the State could not grant any other charter than that which his company owned, to complete the Central railroad, implying a repudiation of the release. Here was also a claim to a share of the glory in procuring the grant from congress, and the assertion that his company was ready to resume the work (mentioning the route of the road) indicated that the Cairo company was master of the situation. Further, the Chicago *Commercial Advertiser*, a newspaper in Holbrook's interest, in no very elegant language, and not devoid of bitterness, boldly set up for him a repudiation of his release of the charters, by the following avowal:

" Judge Douglas has declared the first release of the Cairo company illegal and defective; but that he obtained a second one that was legal, before he would vote for the grant of land. That will likely be found equally so. For, although he is an ex-judge, it is doubted if he knows enough of law to either dictate or draw a legal release in such a case; and his whole concern in the matter may be looked upon as much a piece of political trickery as his bragging about it is bombastic, and that he had no more influence in procuring the grant than the barking of a poodle dog.   *   *   The Cairo Company have never asked anything of the State but the privilege to expend their own money in it, which would never injure, but do much good to the State.   *   *   *   If Breese, and Casey and Holbrook can be killed off by the politicians of Illinois, look out for more plunder."

These pretensions brought down upon the Cairo companies, and particularly their president, the severest animadversions of the press and many politicians. But the companies were not without friends in the legislature and out of it. It is probable that the release signed in New York was not authorized by the Illinois resident corporators under the revival act of 1849.

In November, before the meeting of the legislature, Walter B. Scates, one of the new corporators of the Great Western Railroad Company of 1849, addressed a letter of invitation to all his co-corporators, duly named, to meet at Springfield, January 6, 1851, for the purpose of taking such action as might be deemed expedient for the public good by surrendering up their charter to the State, or such other course as might be desired by the general assembly, to remove all doubts and questions relative to the company's rights and powers, and to disembarrass that body with regard to the disposal of the grant of land from congress for the building of the much needed Central railroad.

With the opening of the general assembly there were not wanting wealthy capitalists ready to avail themselves of this munificence of the nation, who proffered to build the Central railroad and its branches. The following memorial explains itself:

" To the Honorable the Senators and Representatives of the State of Illinois, in General Assembly convened:

The memorial of Robert Schuyler, George Griswold, Gouverner Morris, Jonathan Sturgis, George W. Ludlow and John F. A. Sanford, of the city of New York, and David A. Neal, Franklin Haven and Robert Rantoul, jr., of Boston and vicinity, respectfully represents:

Having examined and considered an act of congress of the United States, whereby land is donated for the purpose of ensuring the construction of a railroad from Cairo, at the mouth of the Ohio, to Galena and the northwest angle of the State of Illinois, with a branch extending to Chicago on Lake Michigan, on certain conditions therein expressed ; and having also examined the resources of the tract of country through which it is proposed that said railroad shall pass, and the amount of cost and space of time necessary to construct the same, the subscribers propose to form a company with such stockholders as they may associate with them, including among their number persons of large experience in the construction of several of the principal railroads in the United States, and of means and credit sufficient to place beyond doubt their ability to perfom what they hereinafter propose, make the following offer to the State of Illinois for their consideration :

The company so formed by the subscribers will, under the authority and direction of the State of Illinois, fully and faithfully perform the several conditions, and execute the trust in said act of congress contained. And will build a railroad, with branches between the termini set forth in said act, with a single track, and complete the same ready for the transportation of merchandise and passengers, on or before the 4th day of July, which will be in the year of our Lord 1854.

And the said railroads shall be in all respects as well and thoroughly built as the railroad running from Boston to Albany, with such improvements thereon as experience has shown to be desirable and expedient, and shall be equipped in a manner suitable to the business to be accommodated thereby.

And the said company, from and after the completion of said road, will pay to the State of Illinois, annually, — per cent. of the gross earnings of said road, without deduction or charge for expenses, or for any other matter or cause : *Provided,* that the State of Illinois will grant to the subscribers a charter of incorporation, with terms mutually advantageous, with powers and limitations as they in their wisdom may think fit, as shall be accepted by the said company, and as will sufficiently remunerate the subscribers for their care, labor and expenditure, in that behalf incurred, and will enable them to avail themselves of the lands donated by the said act, to raise the funds, or some portion of the funds, necessary for the construction and equipment of said road."

Mr. Rantoul, one of the memorialists, was the accredited agent of the others, with full power to act. He attended personally at Springfield during the sitting of the legislature, and the above proposition, coming from gentlemen of such high financial standing, was very favorably received from his hands, particularly as it offered the completion of the road and branches in a much shorter space of time than was by any one anticipated. He was willing to adjust the conditions of the contract so as to render the completion of the road certain, and without a possibility of the misapplication of the lands, or the bestowal of a monopoly upon the company, which was ready to give any guarantee that might reasonably be asked to guard the State against loss from defalcation, both as respected the prosecution of the work and the application of the proceeds of the sales of lands. The terms generally were regarded as highly advantageous, both to the State and the company, and they were ultimately made the basis of the Central railroad charter.

But opposition to the gift of land from the nation being turned over by the State to a private corporation was not wanting. The magnitude of the grant was so overpowering to the minds of some persons that they fancied and argued that the State, by proper management of the means, might build not only the 700 miles of railroad, but pay off the public debt of many millions besides. If the State could have managed its finances and property with the economy, sagacity and flexibility of a private corporation, much of this doubtless could have been done. Mr. John S. Wright, of Chicago, published a pamphlet, insisting that the State would be everlastingly dishonored if the legislature did not devise laws to build the road and disenthral the State of its enormous debt besides out of the avails of this grant.

Three-fourths of the lands donated, it is true, in quality of soil and fertility were unsurpassed, and there was a most excellent bargain in them so soon as iron arteries of commerce could be extended to them; but there they lay, and had lain for 25 years, free to any purchaser at $1.25 an acre, and recently, with the abundance of land warrants thrown upon the market by the soldiers of the Mexican war, they might be had at about 70 cents per acre, but they remained unentered. The bargain in them was to be imparted to them by the construction of a railroad, and the bringing of them within the range of markets. It was a question of development, for which large and ready capital was necessary. Even if the credit of the State would have commanded the requisite capital to build the road, judging by her experience then some 12 years past, it is questionable whether she ought to have undertaken it. Certainly there was no such disposition on the part of the legislature. The shortness of time in which the road was proffered to be built was a cardinal consideration. The great interior of the State, then of no taxable value to the treasury, being almost a howling wilderness, would in some three years' time be penetrated by a commercial highway, and brought within ready access of the great markets af the world throughout the year. From the great lakes and upper Mississippi on the north, to the extreme peninsula of the State on the south, a back-bone of well-settled country, populous towns and flourishing cities, with ribs extending out on either side, would spring into being, and the life currents of commerce and prosperity would speedily flow strong and healthy from the sentre to the extremities.

The bill lingered in the legislature much longer than its ardent friends had anticipated, to their no little anxiety. Many amendments were offered and rejected, such as requiring payment for the right of way to pre-emptionists, or settlers upon the government land, the same as to actual owners, though their benefits, and the enhanced value of their lands by the building of the road would be 500 per cent. The point of divergence for the Chicago branch was strenuously attempted to be fixed, but was finally left with the company anywhere "north of the parallel of 39d. 30 m. of north latitude." Much discussion was had upon the location of the main stem, what towns it should touch between its termini designated in the congressional grant, but all intermediate points failed of being fixed in the act except a single one, the N. E. corner of T. 21 N., R. 2 E. 3d P. M., from which the road in it course should not vary more than five miles, which was effected by Gen. Gridley, of the senate, and by which the towns of Decatur, Clinton and Bloomington were assured of the road.

A scheme was also developed, but never yet explained, by which it was proposed to place this grand enterprise into the hands of the state bondholders, adding a bank. It was known as the bondholders' plan. Early in January the legislature received a voluminous printed bill for a charter, the provisions whereof, closely scrutinized, contained about as hard a bargain as creditor ever offered bondsman. It was coolly proposed, among other provisions, that the State appoint commissioners to locate the road, survey the routes for the main stem and branches, and select the lands granted by congress, all at the expense of the State; agents were further to be appointed by the governor to apply to land-holders along the routes, who might be benefited by the road, for subscriptions, also at the expense of the State.

" All persons subscribing and advancing money for said purpose, shall be entitled to draw interest upon the sums advanced, at the rate of — per cent. per annum from the day of said advance, and shall be entitled to designate and register an amount of 'New Internal Improvement stock of this State' equal to four times the amount so advanced, or of stock of this State known as 'Interest Bonds,' equal to three times the money so advanced; and said stock, so described, may be registered at th eagency of the State of Illinois, in the city of New York, by the party subscribing, or by any other persons to whom they may assign the right at any time after paying the subscription, in the proportion of the amount paid; and said stock shall be endorsed, registered and signed by the agent appointed by the governor for the purpose, and a copy of said register shall be filed in the office of the auditor of public accounts, as evidence to show the particular stock secured or provided for as hereinafter mentioned."

The lands were to be conveyed by the State to the managers of the road; to be by them offered for sale upon the completion of sections of 60 miles, expenses to be paid by the State; the money was to go to the managers, but the State was to receive certificates of stock for the same; two of the acting managers were to receive salaries of $2,500 and the others $1,500—large sums at that time; the company, with the sanction of the governor, to purchase iron, &c., pledging the road for payment; and the road, property and stock, to be exempt from taxation. The bill also embraced a bank in accordance with the provisions of the gen-

enral free banking law adopted at that session, making the railroad stock the basis. It also provided that if the constitution was
amended (which failed to carry,) changing the 2 mill tax to a
sinking fund to be generally applied in redemption of the State
debt, that then the stock registered under this act should also participate in the proceeds thereof.

Here was a scheme to fasten upon the State treasury a horde
of high-salaried officials to eat out the substance of the people,
empowering the company to create additional officers and fix their
compensation at pleasure; no limit was fixed for the completion
of the road; extended advantages were offered to holders of interest bonds, then low in market, to control the road to an amount
of four times their actual outlay, mortgage it for iron, attach a
wild-cat bank to the enterprise, and strangle it to death. But
the measure was so preposterous that it received little countenance.*

The next apprehensions of the friends of the measure were the
efforts interposed early in February, through the Holbrook influence, to delay action at the then session of the general assembly,
which would revive the Cairo city company's charters by the
terms of their release. To this end a resolution was offered in the
senate instructing the committee on internal improvements to
prepare and bring in a bill providing for the appointment of agents
to locate the road, with a view to future construction, and to
select the lands under the grant of congress. It is one of the
unfortunate features incident to representative forms of government that for selfish and partisan ends men will entail large losses
indirectly upon a tax-ridden community. So now men were not
wanting who exerted themselves to create a hobby for their future
political advancement by efforts to delay a work which would in
a short time render the central portion of the State populous by
pouring into it a flood of immigration to build towns and cities
and improve the country, create wealth and increase by millions,
annually, the aggregate taxable property of the State—so badly
needed to relieve her of an oppressive debt. For "the State might
own, in fee simple, many millions of acres of land and yet be all
the poorer for it, unless the lands by settlement and improvement
were rendered capable of yielding a revenue." Such were some
of the arguments held up to these men.

It will be remembered that the memorialists, in their proposition to the legislature to obtain the charter, offered, among other
things, to pay the State of Illinois annually a certain per centum
of the gross earnings of the road, without deduction for expense
or other cause. The amount was left blank, to fix which, however, became subsequently a matter of no little scheming and
trouble. In the first gush of desire to obtain the splendid grant
of land from the State, it is said, the corporators would have
readily consented to fill this blank at 10 per centum of the gross
earnings. But unfortunately for the tax payers and the treasury
of the State, as is charged in the press of the day, the shrewd

*The origin of the bondholders' plan was involved in mystery. Dr. Holford, the
largest of the Illinois bondholders, denounced it, and declared he had no hand in it.
Mr. King, of New Jersey, the next largest, also refused to endorse it. It was a question from whom did it emanate; who was it that wanted to rob Illinois and grind her
farther in the dust? It was manifestly an underhanded scheme for purposes of speculation. Had the bill become a law, the beneficiaries would doubtless have avowed
themselves readily enough.

capitalists employed a gentleman as their attorney—a citizen of Illinois and member of congress at the time, than whom none was more popular and wielded a greater influence at home—an orator, statesman and soldier of renown—who had within the year emerged from an affair of honor with no little eclat, and which gained national notoriety—who left his seat in congress and attended at Springfield in the capacity of a lobbyist for the company, and the result was the State conceded a deduction of 3 per cent. from that figure, the amount being fixed at 7 per centum, and that in lieu of all taxes, State or local.*   The gross earnings of that corporation now amount to about half a million dollars annually.   No little effort has been made to get rid of the payment of this percentage into the State treasury, but since the lands turned over to the company have yielded so well in price, repaying the cost of the road perhaps twice over, the people set their faces against it, and have been exercised by no little anxiety that this now wealthy corporation would succeed in buying up enough members of the legislature at some future session to relieve it of this percentage.   To satisfy the popular clamor a limitation has been irrevocably fixed in the organic law of 1870, which places the subject beyond the control of further legislative meddling, and the public anxiety is allayed.†

In the legislature, after procrastinating action until the heel of the session, Mr. J. L. D. Morrison, of the senate, brought in a substitute for the pending bill, which, after being amended in several important particulars—that by Gen. Gridley has already been noticed—was passed finally with but two dissenting votes; and shortly after, the house took up the senate bill and passed it without amendment, also by two dissenting votes, and it became a law February 10, 1851.   The law is so accessible that it is unnecessary to give a synopsis of it.   The final passage of the bill was celebrated in Chicago by the firing of cannon and other civic demonstrations in honor of the glorious event.

But in the spring following, when the surveys of the Chicago branch were under way, there arose quite a fever of excitement in that city, fearing that the branch road would be carried to the Indiana line to form a junction with the Michigan Central, and thus practically become an extension of the latter road to Cairo, leaving Chicago northward of this thoroughfare about 20 or 30 miles.   Prominent gentlemen addressed a letter to Mr. Douglas, requesting his opinion respecting the power of the company to make such a divergence from a direct line.   Mr. Douglas replied at length, denying the power of the company to do so; citing the language of the charter that the Chicago branch should diverge "from the main trunk at a point north of the parallel of 39 deg. 30 min., and running on the most eligible route *into* the city of Chicago;" that one object in the grant of land by Congress was to render saleable the public land in Illinois which had been 20 or 30 years in market; that the union with another road negatived the provision of free transportation of United States troops

and property forever from Chicago to Mobile—from the lakes of
the north to the Gulf of Mexico, &c.

There was some delay in commencing the work, occasioned by
the Commissioner of the General Land Office at Washington,
Justin Butterfield. The company had negotiated a loan of $400,-
000, but before it could be consummated it was necessary that
there should be a conveyance of the lands from government.
The commissioner, who was from Chicago, construed the grant as
entitling the company to lands for the branch on a straight line
to Chicago, which would avoid the junction with the Michigan
Central. But this construction was reversed by the President and
Secretary of the Interior. In March, 1852, the necessary documents of conveyance were finally secured, contracts were let, and
the work carried forward. The road was completed with little interruption.

As an instructive example of how money may quicken other
property into manifold life, scattering its gains in many unexpected directions, the Illinois Central railroad is a subject in point.
This work was one of the most stupendous and ingenious speculations of modern times. By means of it a few sagacious capitalists became the owners of a first-class railroad, more than 700
miles long, in full running order, complete in rolling stock and
every equipage, and millions of acres of land, worth in the aggregate perhaps, $40,000,000, without the actual outlay of a cent of
their own money. This project was among the first to illustrate
the immense field there was opening up in this country for bold
and gigantic railroad operations by capitalists; and as contrasted
with the State internal improvement scheme of 1836–7, it was
furthermore an example of the superiority of private enterprise
over State or govermental undertakings. The State at that time,
with a population of about 350,000, mostly small farmers, authorized a loan exceeding $10,000,000, to construct public works. One
of these was the Central Railroad, upon which a considerable
sum was expended. Hard times and a general collapse followed
in rapid order. Now, with this grant of land from the general
government, not far short of 3,000,000 acres within a belt of 15
miles along the route of the road, to aid its construction, these
gentlemen, backed by credit and capital, step forward, propose to
take the lands and build the road, which is to belong to them
when built. The State accepts the offer, incorporates the gentlemen's scheme by perpetual charter, and endows them with this
munificent domain and all the property and remains of the old
Central road. After the road is put in operation, the company
pays the State annually 7 per centum of its gross earnings in lieu
of all taxes forever. Having acquired a vested right, the State
has no other than police control over the company, and as it is a
foreign corporation, disputes between them must be settled in
foreign, i. e. U. S., courts. The minimum valuation of the lands
acquired, so soon as the road should be completed, was $20,000,000,
exceeding by $6,000,000, the cost of the road, estimated at $20,000
per mile, which in Illinois, was liberal, because she presented the
most uniform and favorable surface for the construction of railroads of any other State in the Union. Two-thirds of the land
was stipulated as security for the principal of the construction
bonds; 250,000 acres to secure the interest fund, and the remain-

der as a contingent fund. The construction bonds found ready sale at par, and built the road. The land sales yielded interest to set off in part the accruing interest on the bonds. The redemption of the bonds completed, the road and all its appurtenances remains the property of the fortunate gentlemen who had the sagacity to see how it could be built without costing them a cent.

But they did not reap all the developed benefits of this grand enterprise. The alternate sections of land reserved by the federal government within 15 miles of the route of the road, numbered as many acres as the grant to the State; it had been for 20 odd years in market at $1 25 per acre without sale, but now when again put in market in the fall of 1852, it was eagerly taken up and readily brought from $3 to $7 per acre, and more, had not settlers and speculators combined not to bid against each other. As it was, the sales averaged $5 per acre. The government thus realized a profit of some $9,000,000 by its munificent policy of giving away half its lands in this locality. This was indeed casting bread upon the water, which after many days returned several fold. The lands in the railroad belt, so long neglected by buyers, were situated as follows: In the Kaskaskia land office district, 23,681 acres, over 30 years on the market; Shawneetown, 401,873 acres, over 30 years; Vandalia, 344,672 acres, over 25 years; Danville, 345,702 acres, over 20 years; and in the Dixon 465,949 acres, over 10 years.

But besides the general government, the State too, was at the same time benefited by having its unsettled interior opened up to tides of thronging immigrants; its rich soil brought into cultivation; population increased, and its resources and taxable wealth augmented by many millions of dollars. The products of the newly developed region found a ready avenue to the markets or the world. Chicago, too, was thus furnished with another iron tentaculum to reach far into the interior of the State for commercial food to give increase to her marvelous life. But the greatest immediate benefit resulting from the building of the road and branches, accrued to the lands within due and proper marketing distance of the lines, estimated at the enormous amount of $10,000,000 acres in private hands, selected early because of their choice quality, which were directly enhanced at least $4 per acre and rendered more saleable. Here was an increase of wealth, amounting to $40,000,000.

[NOTE.]—Reference has already been made to the jealousy which the success of obtaining this subsidy from Congress, excited among some of our public men as to who was entitled to the meed of praise for carrying the measure through, and the honor of originally suggesting the plan or line of such a railroad. It was a conception and labor worthy the pride and ambition of any man. Visions of office, emolument and fame were doubtless discovered in it. While some apparently shunned it but to make it sure, others boldly claimed the credit. In this connection we are tempted to extract from the piquant correspondence between the Hons. Sidney Breese and S. A. Douglas. The former had been a senator in congress up to March 4th, 1849, when he was succeeded by Gen. Shields. In 1850 he was elected to the Legislature. Under date of December 23, 1850, among other things in reply to the Illinois State Register, regarding his favoring the "Holbrook Charters," he says:

"The Central Railroad has been a controlling object with me for more than 15 years, and I would sacrifice all my personal advantages to see it made. These fellows who are making such an ado about it now have been whipped into its support. They are not for it now, and do not desire to have it made because I get the credit of it. This is inevitable. I must have the credit of it, for I originated it in 1835, and, when in the senate, passed three different bills through that body to aid in its construction. My successor had an easy task, as I had opened the way for him. It was the argument contained in my reports on it that silenced all opposition, and made its passage easy. I claim the credit, and no one can take it from me."

This fell under the eye of Senator Douglas, at Washington, who took occasion to reply on January 5th, 1851, at length, giving a detailed history of all the efforts made in congress to procure either pre-emption or grant of land in aid of building this road, saying : "You were the champion of the policy of granting pre-emption rights for the benefit of a private company [the Holbrook,] and I was the advocate of alternate sections to the State." The letter is quite long, but very interesting, and may be found in the *Illinois State Register*, and papers of the State of that period generally.

Judge Breese rejoined under date of January 25, 1851, through the columns of the same paper, at great length, claiming that beside seeking to obtain pre-emption aid he also was the first to introduce "a bill for an absolute grant of the alternate sections for the Central and Northern Cross Railroads," but finding no favorable time to call it up, it failed. "It was known from my first entrance into congress that I would accomplish the measure, in some shape, if possible ;" but the Illinois members of the house, he asserts, took no interest in the passage of any law for the benefit of the Central road, either by grant or pre-emption. He claims no share in the passage of the law of 1850 : "Your (Douglas',) claim shall not, with my consent, be disparaged, nor those of your associates. I will myself weave your chaplet, and place it, with no envious hand, upon your brow. At the same time history shall do me justice. I claim to have first projected this great road, in my letter of 1835, and in the judgment of impartial and disinterested men my claim will be allowed. I have said and written more in favor of it than any other. It has been the highest object of my ambition to accomplish it, and when my last resting place shall be marked by the cold marble which gratitude or affection may erect, I desire for it no other inscription than this, that he who sleeps beneath it projected the Central Railroad."

He also cited at length his letter of October 16, 1835, to John Y. Sawyer, in which the plan of the Central Railroad was first foreshadowed, which opens as follows · "Having some leisure from the labor of my circuit, I am induced to devote a portion of it in giving to the public a plan, the outline of which was suggested to me by an intelligent friend in Bond county, a few days since." • •

To this Douglas, under date of Washington, Feb. 22, 1851, surrejoins at considerable length, and in reference to this opening sentence in the Sawyer letter, exclaims, "How is this ! The father of the Central railroad, with a Christian meekness worthy of all praise, kindly consents to be the reputed parent of a hopeful son begotten for him by an intelligent friend in a neighboring county ! I forbear pushing this inquiry further. It involves a question of morals too nice, of domestic relations too delicate, for me to expose to the public gaze. Inasmuch, however, as you have furnished me with becoming gravity, the epitaph which you desire engrossed upon your tomb, when called upon to pay the last debt of nature, you will allow me to suggest that as such an inscription is a solemn and a sacred thing, and truth its essential ingredient, would it not be well to make a slight modification, so as to correspond with the facts as stated in your letter to Mr. Sawyer, which would make it read thus, in your letter to me : "*It has been the highest object of my ambition to accomplish the Central Railroad, and when my last resting place shall be marked by the cold marble which gratitude or affection may erect, I desire for it no other inscription than this :* HE WHO SLEEPS BENEATH THIS STONE VOLUNTARILY CONSENTED TO BECOME THE PUTATIVE FATHER OF A LOVELY CHILD, CALLED THE CENTRAL RAILROAD, AND BEGOTTEN FOR HIM BY AN INTELLIGENT FRIEND IN THE COUNTY OF BOND." We find no further correspondence. See Illinois State Journal, March, 1851.

CHAPTER XLVII.

OUR FREE OR STOCK BANKS—1851-1865.

*How a Bank might be started—Ultimate Security of the Bill holder—
The Small Note Act—Panic of 1854—Revulsion of 1857—Winding up.*

Notwithstanding the State, in 1851, was in the hands of the
democratic party by an increased majority, and that this dominant party had for years in its State platforms fulminated resolutions against the enormity of banking as the source of all our
financial woes, the legislature, also largely democratic, nevertheless passed another general banking law, authorizing free or stock
banks. The democratic governor vetoed the bill, but it was
promptly passed over his objections, and the people of the State,
notwithstanding their experiences of the disastrous results from
the banks authorized in 1821 and in 1836-7, and in spite of their
teachings and democratic majority, approved it by their votes at
the election of November of that year. As a rule, the masses
favor any scheme which promises an abundant currency—they are
naturally for expansion—while capitalists favor contraction.

Directly after the adoption of the constitution of 1848, the establishment of another banking system was agitated. The project
advanced was to divide up the State into 3 banking districts,
with boards of bank trustees for each. As security, banking
associations were to deposit United States stock and a certain portion of gold, when circulating notes as money were to be issued to
them. The democratic press made a great outcry against the
whig scheme, as it was called, to fasten again upon the then once
more thriving and prosperous State the withering curse of banks.
This plan, which proposed but one class of securities—United
States 6's—was certainly preferable to that adopted two years
later, which allowed as security the stocks of any or all the States.
The former presented the advantage of having a uniform security for all the banks of the country, giving a like uniformity of
value to their issues all over our broad domain ; while to the latter, with bonds of any State, many far from home perhaps, the
fluctuations of a varying market would severely attach. But in
principle the State stock banks were the forerunners of the present national banking system.

The banking law of 1851 required as a basis or security for all
banks operating under it, the deposit with the auditor of, 1st,
United States stocks; 2d, stocks of any other State; 3d, stocks
of Illinois valued at 20 per cent. below the market price. Stocks

on which the interest was not annually paid could not be deposited except in double amounts. If they depreciated in the market, further deposits were to be made. The depositors were entitled to the interest accruing on the bonds. When the deposit of stocks was perfected, the auditor was authorized to have engraved and issue bank notes to the owners in nearly equal amounts, not less than $50,000, to circulate as money. The notes on presentation at the bank were required to be redeemed in specie, the amount to be kept on hand not being specified, and for refusal and after protest it became liable to 12½ per cent damages in lieu of interest. On failure of the bank, it was to be wound up by sale of its stocks at auction in New York, and the proceeds were first to be paid out on the circulating notes. If the stocks and other effects of the banks proved insufficient, then the stockholders became liable respectively to the amount of their stocks in their private property, to pay the bill holders. Interest was fixed at 7 per cent., and loans might be made on real or personal property. Dealing in real estate was not allowed, other than to sell that which fell into their hands as security. The usual banking privileges of buying and selling exchange, coin, &c., were extended to them. A board of 3 bank commissioners, with power of examination into their affairs, was also provided; and the officers of the banks were required to render quarterly statements to the auditor, under oath, as to their condition.

With these provisions, it was thought that the notes would certainly be safe. Indeed the law was first regarded as so stringent that few would attempt banking under it—certainly mere speculators would not. The bill holders appeared to be ultimately secure. New York, we have seen, as early as 1838, authorized banking on State stocks, and by the time Illinois, which subsequently copied the New York law, embarked in the project, half the States of the Union ran wild after the discovery of the new and safe scheme, by means of which the capitalist, contrary to Franklin's aphorism, might "eat his cake and have his cake"—invest his money in bonds, deposit them, and from the hands of the auditor have his money again and own his bonds too.

While the banking bill was pending before the people, the friends of the measure, to secure its adoption, pointed to the fact that the State was inundated with millions of the notes of banks of foreign States, of the value, solvency, or genuineness of which little or nothing was known here; that by allowing aliens to furnish us a circulating medium we not only paid tribute to them but yielded our State pride; that it was but just to ourselves and to our interests to replace this exotic trash by a sound and safe currency of our own; that the basis for banks required by this law made them not only perfectly secure to the bill holders, but that a home currency, within easy reach of the places of redemption and its ready convertibility into specie, would directly drive out the foreign bills; that with the greater abundance of money, times would become easy, produce would rise in price, lands enhance in value, the influx of emigrants be augmented, and general prosperity would shower its glad smiles upon all our people with a profuse hand. Experience shows that the masses are but too ready to grasp at a project which promises plenty of money to-day, although assured that it will be worthless to-morrow.

· Its opponents argued that under the new law, the currency proposed to be introduced was susceptible of multiplication to an indefinite amount, and if the bill carried, an avalanche of paper money might be thrown into circulation, dazzling and bewildering the senses of the people, leading them into a wild, headlong mania of speculation, the sequel to which, as had ever been the case, must be disaster and ruin. With an inflated currency property would attain to unhealthy prices, purchases would be made at perhaps half cash, balance on time, secured by mortgages on the premises. While the obligations were maturing a contraction would take place, stagnation ensue and prices be depressed below the normal standard; claims would be pressed upon debtors, mortgages foreclosed, and many an unwary purchaser would be stripped of his all under the hammer of the sheriff, his vendor buying back the property at less than the mortgage claim, leaving an unsatisfied judgment still hanging over him. The bank measure was held to be a project to swell the coffers of the rich from the labor and necessities of the poor.

They further showed that the bank securities might be of unstable value, which would rise and fall in the market with the operations and machinations of financiers; that money based upon them would be subject to similar fluctuations; that these pledges of stock were as nothing to the man with this money in his hand which he desired to convert. Let but an actual case of suspension be contemplated. To sell the stocks and redeem the notes required time and was attended by circumlocution. The poor or needy cannot wait. Want and exigence press from myriad directions. Now the broker steps in, himself perhaps a shareholder in the suspended bank, and offers 50 or 75 cents on the broken promises. The holder of this money received in exchange for his labor or other equivalent, cannot wait the ultimate redemption by the auditor, but is compelled to suffer a shave to this depth. The broker, however, is in no such stress; he quietly awaits the sale of the stocks, the redemption of the notes with the proceeds, and realizes the 25 or 50 per cent. which his thousands of victims have lost, and with the gains starts another bank.

The 6th section of the bank bill provided for the association of persons "to establish offices of discount, deposit and *circulation*," with an aggregate capital stock of not less than $50,000. This section served the opponents of the bill a good turn before the people. It was deduced thence and asserted that the bill was a trick, concealing deceptive phraseology; that it provided for two classes of banks, one secured by the pledge of public stocks, the other totally irresponsible, allowing its issues to "circulate" on no other basis than pen, ink and paper to write out its articles of association, money enough to pay for recording and posting copies thereof to Springfield to be filed with the secretary of state; that the former were to catch the votes of the people, but the latter concerns were to furnish the currency. The phraseology of this section in connection with the word "circulate," it must be confessed, was somewhat ambiguous.*

---

*The Chicago *Press*. December, 1852, says it has warned the people that paper would be issued not secured by stocks, and there were then various issues of certificates of deposit in the similitude of bank notes, signed and subscribed by the officers, designated by the utterers to circulate the same as bank notes.

Notwithstanding these arguments against it, the people in November, 1851, elected the bank bill, and it became the law of the State. The vote stood 37,626 for to 31,405 against it. This poll was less by 7,000 than half the votes cast at the gubernatorial election one year later, being 153,882.

The constitution provided that no banking law should be enacted except by the sanction of a majority of the people voting for it at a general election. A special election, it was doubtless thought by the framers, would not call forth a full expression of the sentiment of the people upon such a measure. In their haste to have the people pass upon the bank bill, the legislature created a general election for this purpose, by repealing all the county treasurers out of office, and ordering a new election for those officials at the same time the bank bill was to be voted upon. With this action of the legislature, after the election, the defeated opponents of the measure found much fault, and it was severely denounced. It was claimed that a presidential, biennial election for members of congress, or the state legislature alone, were *general* elections, where the bill would have been fully discussed before the people. The spirit of the constitution was doubtless violated by the legislature.

The apprehensions that the law was so stringent that few, if any, banks would be organized under it, was speedily dispelled. Within the first year the democratic press cried aloud that the country was flooded with paper money to an alarming extent. Property rose in price, and a speculative spirit became rife. All who could command the means were enlarging the area of their territorial possessions and debts were freely incurred. The mania of 1836-7, it was urged, would be repeated, and irretrievable ruin overtake thousands. Indeed the new plan of stock banking became very general throughout the Union, and there was no little expansion. But in Illinois much of all this was owing to the inauguration of the railroad era just at that time, and enhancements had a solid basis, very unlike the period of 1836-8.

When the organization of banks under the new loan was commenced, nothing further was heard of the great part the associations under section 6 were to play; no issues were uttered without the deposit of stocks by any associations. But as the law stood and the courts afterwards held, the deposit of $50,000 in bonds was a sufficient compliance with its provisions as to capital. The amount of specie capital to be kept on hands was a question of risk for the banks, the law not fixing any amount. This caused much of the business of free banking to go into the hands of irresponsible and non-resident persons, who, having no object or interest further than to get their notes into circulaton and leaving the bill-holders to take care of them, located their concerns in remote and inaccessible places, where no legitimate banking business could or was expected to be done, and flooded the country with "wild cats." And as such banks did not often keep any place of business in the apparent location thereof, the power of demand and protest was destroyed.*

How a Stock Bank Might be Started—While doubtless many of these free banks were started with an actual paid up capital,

---

* See Report House Committee, 1861.

and did a regular and legitimate banking business, for the remuneration was ample, it is also true that the following perfectly feasable manner of organization under the law, was freely recognized and often approachably put into practice. A few sharp operators, hailing from, it mattered little where, with ready money enough to meet the expenses of getting up the bills, notify the auditor in the proper way, that they have organized a company to start the, say "Absolute Safety Bank of the town of Wildcat, in Brush county; capital $200,000." They now contribute perhaps $5,000 for the cost of engraving the plates, printing the bills and other incidental expenses. Having credit they obtain letters and next apply to a broker and borrow on short time, say Missouri 6's or stocks of other States, to the amount they want. Perhaps as security they hypothecate or mortgage other property, either to the broker or some well known financier. By the time the notes are printed, countersigned and registered the bonds are taken to Springfield and deposited. The auditor, in accordance with the law, turns over to them their nicely executed bright new bills, representing $200,000, declared by law to be money. Appropriate and exquisite devices, representing perhaps stacks of money bags, out of which a stalwart Indian is pouring the yellow eagles in great heaps of precious gold, embellish the crisp "promises on demand.' The bills are next taken or sent, say to Georgia, or some other distant State where a similar banking system is in operation, and there swapped for the issues of various banks, the more scattered the better, so as to have them from home as far as possible. The money received in exchange is now either directly paid over for the bonds bought or deposited, or perhaps brought home and vested in grain, pork or beef, which is shipped east, the bills of lading transmitted to the broker, who pays out of the proceeds for the bonds advanced, and forwards the residue, perhaps a handsome margin besides, to the bankers in Illinois. And thus the money is turned. In the meantime the bank at Wildcat is opened for a few hours each day, but no piles of bank notes appear on its desks, no exchange is bought or sold, no accommodations are granted or discounts made. No drearier looking bank ever opened its doors. But then in the out of the way place of its location there is little demand for these ordinary transactions of a bank. Notwithstanding the rather sorry looking appearance of this concern with its capital of $200,000, the owners are making the interest on the bonds deposited, amounting to double the original capital invested in the bank. If the bills are a long time in finding the retreat for their redemption, it is a good thing for the ingenious bankers. To guard against their ready presentation for this purpose the institution has been located in Brush county, where it may be both difficult to find and tedious of access, and where a small amount of coin in the vault serves to sustain it against failure. Perhaps, by fortunate investments, the bank prospers; the owners add some paid up capital, and with these means a general banking business is engaged in. Of the banks located in cities, or at conveniently accessible points, it was noted that the same companies would start several banks with a large nominal capital for each, though the actual banking, or the uttering of their bills, was restricted to the minimum amount allowed by the law. This would enable them, by shifting coin from one to another in times of a run to get along with perhaps half or less of the ordinary amount of specie kept on hands for redemption. Redemption of each bill separately was allowable at this time, and separate protests were likewise required. In 1857 the legislature amended the law so that in presenting notes for payment it was not required to receive redemption for each note separately, but the whole amount might be presented as a general obligation and one payment demanded.

In the summer of 1859 the Grayville bank sought to restrain the auditor from putting it in liquidation, because its bills were protested in amounts of $6,000 and $8,400 upon the ground that this amendment was null and void, not having been submitted to a vote of the people for ratification like the original law. A readiness to redeem separately was alleged. In 1860 Willard & Adsit of Chicago presented a number of bills for redemption to the Reapers' Bank at Fairfield. Payment was commenced in dimes and half dimes, occupying a whole day in redeeming $150. After this trifling, the remainder was protested for non-payment and forwarded to the auditor, who being about to force the bank into liquidation, was enjoined. But Judge Wilson, of Chicago, decided that "a bank had no right to throw such obstacles in the way of a prompt and speedy redemption." But, however the bonds were obtained for banking purposes, the issues based upon them added to the currency of the country and benefited very many people; and with a faithful auditor to look after these securities, who, in case they depreciated in market would promptly call on the banks affected to make good the margin declined with additional deposits, no ultimate loss could well occur to the bill holder.* Nothing would permanently have depreciated these state securities except the unprecedented occasion offered by the rebellion of 12 States of the Union.

---

*As a good commentary on the argument of ultimate security to the bill holder, however, upon which much stress was laid at the time by the advocates of the stock bank system, and also as illustrating the manner of hindering and throwing obstacles in the way of a ready redemption in specie that might be made use of by bankers, the following pleasantly related experience, current at the time, though applied to Indiana, fitted Illinois as well, and will, we trust, prove not uninteresting to the reader. It is the invention of some fertile newspaper genius of the time, and first appeared in the Cincinnati *Commercial*:

Suppose a gentleman should be so unfortunate as to fall heir to a five dollar note upon one of these institution, and desires to realize upon it specie or exchange. ‡ * what is he to do? First, find the bank! that of course ; and that is not always an easy matter. Banks in Indiana lurk in out-of-the-way places. Like the insect hunted by the entomological Hibernian, when you find them they ar'nt there. They don't affect corner lots, but shun the din of crowded cities. nestling close under the lee of primeval forests, marked by an ancient Indian trail or solitary cow path. They are things to be found by the bee hunters, are seen far off by the midnight Nimrod in search of coons, with the moonlight sleeping upon their shingle roofs and primitive cornices. Capital has become modest, and wealth retires from the world into the cloisters of the deep old woods, or the holy solitudes of the prairies, conversing with nature—laying up its treasures "where neither moth nor rust doth corrupt," and where none [but the auditor of state] can find them.

But suppose that the institution is revealed, and the monetary anchorite stands confessed,; suppose that the business hours have arrived, and the shingle whose opposing sides give each other the lie, faces the sun with the announcement—"bank open"— we see the aforesaid heir, with rapid steps, approach the edifice. He enters; he draws his pictorial evidence of a promise from his pocket book; he approaches the counter, presents his note to the paying teller, and a coloquy ensues:

"Can you give me specie for this?"
"No."
"Sight or short time eastern exchange !"
"Nothing."
"Why ?"
"You are making a run on our institution; this species of presentation we are bound to resist. You are trying to break us, sir—to make us stop payment, sir; you can't do it, sir."
"But haven't you stopped payment when you refuse to redeem ?"
"No, sir; ours is a stock institution. There's your ultimate security, sir, deposited

"The Foreign Small Note Act."—With the meeting of the legislature, in 1853, a contrariety of opinion obtained among the members as to the power to amend, modify or repeal the general free banking law. One view was that the original act having been submitted to a vote of the people for their sanction, it was now their law and beyond the control of the legislature, fixed as the laws of the Medes and Persians; that the voice of the people had imparted to it its vitality, and it must live to procreate its nursling banks until the same mighty voice deprived it of its existence; that by the terms of the constitution the people had to sanction such law by their vote, first authorized by the legislature; and that the same routine had to be undergone with all its amendments. A "supplemental" banking law without all this routine was, however, ventured upon and adopted by the legislature. But its reception by the people indicated that the legislature might have spared themselves this trouble; for the want of obedience to this law was not based upon any technical ground of want of power by the legislature. It was probably more a question of convenience.

This was the well known "foreign small note act," by which to foster home banks and prevent the retirement of specie from circulation, a penalty of $50 was imposed for every foreign bank bill of a less denomination than $5, uttered after the 1st of August, 1853. It was sought to absolutely squelch the foreign small trash. Bankers and general dealers, or their employees, guilty of this offense were to be additionally punished by imprisonment in the county jail; and no suit could be maintained upon any obligations the consideration of which was these small notes of banks of alien States. Great latitude in pleadings under the act was specially enjoined.

---

with the auditor. We can't break, sir; we can't stop payment. Look at the law! Look at the (auditor's) circular!"

"But have you no specie on hand?"

"Yes, sir; and we are bound to keep it. The law obliges us to keep 12½ per cent. of specie on hand. If we pay out every time one of you fellows call, how can we keep it on hand?"

"Then I shall proceed and have the note protested."

"Very well, sir. You will find a notary public at Indianapolis, provided he is at home, which is only about 140 miles from here. But, sir, you had better go home, and rely upon your ultimate security. We can't pay specie—find it won't do; but you are ultimately secure; you can't lose your money, though you never get it. Remember that."

We will suppose our gentleman so unreasonable as not to be satisfied with the presentation of the paying teller of the great principle of ultimate security. He finds his way to Indianapolis, makes protest in due form, and, note in hand, proceeds to the auditor of state, where another dialogue ensues:

"Sir, I have a note of the Squash Bank, at Lost Prairie, with certificate of protest, which I want to deposit in your hands, with a request that you make collection as speedily as possible."

"Certainly, sir."

"How long before I can expect to realize upon the ultimate securities of the institution? Thirty days, is it not?"

"Not quite as soon as that sir. I shall give notice to the officers of the Squash Bank. If they pay no attention to it, I shall offer its securities in my hands for sale; but in discharging my duty to all the creditors of the institution, I shall not proceed to offer any of its assets in this market until after at least 60 days' notice in New York, London and Paris, so as to insure the largest and best price for the securities; and not then, if, in my opinion, the ultimate interests of all concerned will be promoted by a further extension! Hem!"

"But, my dear sir, how long will it be before I can realize upon my demand?"

"Can't say, sir; stocks are down just now—may rise in a year or two—depends somewhat upon the fate of the war in Europe. But never fear, your ultimate security is undoubted. If you should never get it, you will never lose it; remember that. Rely upon your ultimate security and you are safe."

"D—n ultimate security! I want my money."

"Well, sir, if that's your game, when you get it, please give us the information."

The exceeding stringency of the provisions overleaped themselves. While no law was ever more generally understood, both
as regards its provisions and the time when it was to go into
effect, for the press constantly invited attention to it, urging its
observance in every particular, so no law was ever more totally
ignored by everybody, or became a more complete dead letter
from the start. It was violated throughout the length and breadth
of the State many thousands of times daily in the multiform business relations of society, without the least attention being paid to
it. The floods of foreign small notes continued to infest our communities and retained their ground.

The Panic of 1854.—In the fall of 1854 there was, for a short
time, quite a monetary crisis in the country. Among the
free banks of especially Ohio and Indiana there were a number of failures, and much alarm prevailed. Missouri and Virginia
bonds had been thrown in large amounts upon the New York
market, and declined to 95 and 93 cents; though their interests
had been regularly kept up. Dame rumor, with her many tongues,
doubtless considerably enlarged upon the facts, and much distrust
obtained in Illinois. Chicago was flooded with Georgia shin-
plasters. Brokers sought to take advantage of the public solicitude to precipitate a panic; its effects, however, did not extend
much beyond the city. There, a heavy run was made on the banks
by bill holders and depositors, and a pretty general suspension
took place.

In the meantime, W. B. Fondey, of the bank commission, counselled the people that the panic was a mere brokers' trick, that no
default had been made in interest payments on the depreciated
bonds, and therefore it could only be temporary, and warned them
not to part with their money at discount or sacrifice. The merchants of Chicago had steadily taken the money in exchange for
goods, and the wholesale dealers, feeling assured of the ultimate
security of the stock banks, and perceiving no adequate cause for
the panic, also lent their support in sustaining the banks, and the
result was that in a few days they resumed business, and the panic
only gave them greater confidence with the people. The storm
was successfully weathered, and those banks whose deposits were
depreciated complied with the call of the commissioners, and put
up an additional margin of security.

After the flurry the press took up the subject of revising our
banking law. The discrimination of 20 per cent. against Illinois
bonds as a banking basis was demanded to be removed. Under
the law of 1849 private persons might make valid agreements for
interest at 10 per cent.; not so, however, the banks—they were restricted to 7. In this connection the bank commissioners, ex-Gov.
A. C. French, P. Maxwell and W. B. Fondey, in their report of
Dec. 30, 1854, say it had been the custom with banks to loan their
money to other corporations and associations composed for the
most part of the same stockholders, to be re-loaned by them as
individuals at an advanced rate of interest, 10 per cent., and the
result was that the community had not been enabled to get money
any cheaper than formerly, while the difference of 3 per cent. in
the rate of interest obtained in this manner, had induced the
banks to evade the intention of the law, and pursue a course cal-

culated to weaken the confidence which they should endeavor to inspire in the community where located. It was also urged that those banks which wanted to, should be permitted to withdraw their bills from circulation and take up their bonds with the auditor in sums of $5,000 or $10,000, instead of all but 10 per cent., as the law then stood. But the legislature of 1855 disregarded all the objections with the single exception of the last, and simply allowed banks to surrender to the auditor their bills in sums of $1,000 for their securities.

Two years later, however, another legislature put Illinois bonds on an equal footing with those of other States as a basis for banking, all to be valued 10 per cent. less than the market price; allowed banks to discount paper or make loans at the rate of 10 per cent; forbade the location of banks at places of less than 200 inhabitants; made the issues redeemable at the places where dated, in packages, to be treated as a single obligation, and which might thus likewise be protested for non-payment.

The Revulsion of 1857.—On the first of January, 1857, the whole number of banks which had been organized since the law took effect in 1851, was 61, eleven had been closed voluntarily or by protest and forfeiture of charter, leaving 50 in operation, with a circulation of $6,480,873, on a basis of stock security whose cash valuation was $6,663,389; and up to the time when the financial crash swept the country in September of this year banking capital and operations were largely on the increase.

The period of the existence of the banks up to this time had been one of unparalleled prosperity in this State. Its rapid strides to opulence and empire had never been equalled before, nor have they since. Our taxable wealth had nearly trebled itself, being, for the year 1851, $137,818,079, and for the year 1857, $407,447,367. This period being within the railroad era, the increase of wealth was either solid or based upon a just and reasonable expectation of values, though something was attributable to bank expansions. The whole country was prosperous, stimulated greatly by the number of free banks then very generally in vogue. It is in periods of this sort, when times are good, paper money abundant, and confidence strong, that communities incline to the abandonment of the old, slow but safe pursuits, for the tempting prospects of realizing large gains on small capital in short times. There was an inflation of values throughout the west, which affected landed property in cities, towns and country. Chicago corner lots shared in this to a wonderful degree. A spirit of speculation was rife, but it was more intensified in the east than the west. There large amounts of western unproductive property had been bought purely on speculation, with money borrowed from the abundant coffers of the banks at home, depending upon its steady advances in quoted values to meet payments as they matured; here purchases were made, many of them on better time, and the property developed and made productive. When the financial storm burst upon the country its disastrous effects were therefore more severely and more lastingly experienced in the east than the west. As western lands and lots had been in great part the means, but not the cause, of the monetary crisis, so now western industry and western products became the medium of unlocking the wheels of

38

commerce and righting the business of the country. The eastern currency sent west to move the crops, had been, on the first mutterings of the approaching storm, very generally recalled. Western merchants had bought very largely on time in the east. It now became the duty of the western producers to throw their staples of grain, pork, beef and other commodities into the market on time to release these merchants and debtors, which was nobly done.

In January, 1857, an effort had been made, mostly on the part of western brokers, to discredit some of the stock securities of Illinois banks, which created some alarm. St. Louis merchants issued a circular stating that they would continue to receive the notes of the discredited banks as heretofore. The determined stand thus taken inspired the public with confidence, and the brokers' scheme proved a failure. Later, the securities of some of the banks having sustained a diminution in value, the bank commissioners, on the 8th of May, made a requisition on them to file, within 40 days, additional security. All responded but two. By the 27th of July, such was the fluctuation of stocks in market, and the signs of the impending revulsion, that it became necessary to make a similar requisition, this time on 29 banks, being more than half of those in the State. They were given 90 days to make good the margin. These 29 banks had a deposit of stock securities of $4,560,000, of which $2,738,000 were Missouri 6's. The total number of Missouri bonds upon which banking was done in Illinois was at this time not less than $4,500,000 ; notwithstanding which the brokers and merchants of St. Louis now refused Illinois currency, causing much embarrassment to our people in the central and southern parts of the State. One of the bank commissioners visited St. Louis, and, before a meeting of her merchants, brokers and business men, made a masterly exposition of our banking system, and failed not to show to those gentlemen that the credit of Missouri, whose bonds formed nearly three-fourths of the bases of our banks, was also involved in their attempts to bring Illinois currency into disrepute. His action was also seconded by candid and intelligent discussions by the newspapers of the city. The whole was crowned with the success of restoring Illinois currency to its former standing in St. Louis at gold par. This was a noble stand for a foreign city to take, but a severe shock to her commerce. Chicago banks and business men arranged a different standard for this currency, nominally known as a par standard—par for that city —which was never less than 10, and generally 15 per cent. below a real par representing a specie equivalent.

Owing to the general prosperity of the country and the public feeling of security, many of our banks which desired to do only a legitimate business, had been tempted into excessive issues. Now the large number of suspensions and failure of banks, insurance and trust companies in other States, carrying down with them many of the staunchest mercantile houses in the country, created a panic which bore heavily upon our banks, brokers, capitalists and business men generally. The discredited banks protested their inability of complying with the requisition of the commissioners, but these functionaries were firm in their demand. And the banks, notwithstanding their condition and the disastrous monetary crisis prevailing, with but very few exceptions, struggled nobly through the prostrating storm, and subsequently enjoyed a larger share of public confidence than at any former period* The financial standing of the State among all the private and corporate calamities of that period stood unshaken.

The effects of the revulsion of 1857 was stated as follows: Whole number of firms in the U. S. (except California) which failed was 204,061; liability $299,801,000; assets $150,021,000; total loss $149,780,000, of annihilated commercial wealth. The number of firms failing in Illinois, was 316, with an aggregate liability of $9,338,000. Of these 117 belonged to Chicago, with a liability of $6,562,000. The remaining 199 Illinois firms had a liability of $2,766,000.† If the losses in Illinois averaged with that of the country at large they were about $4,500,000. These incredible sums must have been largely speculative. In Chicago, legitimate business received only a staggering blow, but speculation was totally prostrated. The depreciating effects on the prices of real estate, with the harrassing influence of maturing payments, were not checked for 2 years; and the business of erecting buildings, or in some cases finishing those begun, was stopped. Workmen in large numbers forsook the city, improvements languished, store-rooms and houses stood vacant, rents declined, and vendors and mortgagees received back the property sold, with the added improvements, finished or otherwise, and the forfeiture of one or more payments by purchasers besides.

The revulsion of 1857, unlike that of 1837, involved mostly only individuals and certain speculative and commercial centres. Had the State been involved by its connection with the banks, as 20 years before, the extent of this mad panic torrent upon the entire people, with the expanded credits and inflated prices of the period, is fearful to contemplate. But thanks to the provision of the constitution, forbidding State connection with banking operations. And the collapse coming when our abundant crops were matured, with exchange in our favor, the mines of California pouring their volumes of precious metals into the current of specie exchange, the panic could not and did not produce a lasting effect upon the prosperity of the State. Still the taxable wealth of the State the second year after the revulsion was reported $40,000,000 less than in 1857.

Before 1860 the free banking system had amply demonstrated that, however a law might compel a banker to fully secure his issues by pledge of State stocks, it was practically impossible to engraft upon it peremptory and immediate redemption of issues in specie.‡ The notes of Illinois banks were current only in our own State, and to any considerable extent beyond they were at a discount of one per cent. or more.‖ Before the close of this year the banks had increased to 110, with a circulation of $12,320,964, which constituted almost exclusively, the currency of this State. The bank securities on deposit were valued at $13,980,971. Of the 14 banks withdrawn from existence up to this time in the 9 preceding years, some voluntary and others by forfeiture under the law, the securities of all save one had been ample to redeem

* See Bk. Com.'s. Report, Jan. 1869.
† B. Doglas & Co.'s Com. Agency, N. Y. Herald.
‡ See Report H. Com. 1861.
‖ Bissell's Message 1859.

every note, dollar for dollar in specie; and in the exceptional case there was only a loss of 3 per cent.* This demonstrated their ultimate security to the bill holder in ordinary civil times.

And now with this large volume of home currency, based for the most part upon the stocks of southern States, in the midst of rapid and solid prosperity to this State, was wantonly precipitated the great and disastrous war of the rebellion. State after State shot madly from the orbit of the Union. Confidence in their securities was disturbed. Before the close of November, 1860, 18 banks were already in discredit on account of depreciated securities, and were subjected to the call of the commissioners. Eastern exchange advanced to 8 per cent. Business men held meetings to counsel together and devise ways out of the financial trouble that was thickening daily. In the impenetrable political darkness of the times, the bank commissioners left the banking interests of the State to the correction of the legislature. That body, which met in January, 1861, revised the free banking law by restricting banks thereafter to be organized, to the deposit of U. S. and Illinois stocks as security, which would also enhance the salable value of our State stocks; granted to existing banks 6 months' time after call in which to make good any margin suffered by the decline of their securities in market, before being forced into liquidation or their assets could be reached for failure to redeem; designated Chicago and Springfield as general points of redemption, through agents of the banks, at a discount of $\frac{3}{4}$ of 1 per cent., the money having for some time been 1 per cent. below par, which was in accordance with the recommendation of Chicago business men; raised the interest damages on notes protested for non-payment from $12\frac{1}{2}$ to 25 per cent., and allowed the auditor to surrender bonds deposited pro rata to holders of notes protested, or on banks in process of liquidation from other causes. If the legislature had not thus temporized, but with a due appreciation of that juncture in national affairs, rigidly forced every bank in default into liquidation on 10 day's call, and required the auditor to sell the securities immediately, if the market was a little depressed by the abundance of bonds cast upon it, it would have would have wound up almost every one, and the final result would have been better for both the bill-holders and the banks.

The legislature at this session passed also another general banking bill predicated solely upon a specie basis. We will not synopsize this measure; suffice it, the people, tired of a rotten bank currency which the history of the State showed had been furnished by every banking system which had ever yet been in operation, they, by their votes cast at the November election of 1861, rejected it. Besides, a revision of the constitution had been ordered, and it was not deemed advisable to hamper in any way the convention soon to meet.

But besides this legislation, the days of free banking in Illinois, as in every other State, were numbered. Secession was on the rampage. In the latter part of March, but before open hostilities, Chicago brokers threw out the issues of 32 Illinois stock banks. Forty odd were now uncurrent. This act was purely arbitrary, for the auditor's report showed many of these to stand as well as many of those bank-quotable. Perhaps it was shrewdly calculated

* Gov. Wood's Message, 1861.

that the masses, with small amount of uncurrent money, would sacrifice it blindly at the first broker's office. St. Louis continued to receive this currency. Prior to this, owing to the general distrust, in which country shared perhaps more fully than city, large amounts of the Illinois issues had accumulated in Chicago, where they were current, making trade brisk. Before long the Merchants' Loan and Trust Company, anticipating an early heavy depreciation, and having perhaps first worked off its supply, refused to further take this currency. The other banks, with their coffers full of it, attempted to sustain it, doubtless with no other view than to gain time to get rid of it. Hence it remained current in trade, and large amounts were sent to the country to buy produce, which advanced rapidly in price; but as the country was fully infected with the distrust, the money showed evidence of exceeding nimbleness, and would return to the city faster than it could be shoved off. Local trade was unusually active. In this straight, to keep the stuff up, leading business men and bankers in Chicago actually pledged themselves, and signed and issued a circular, to take the money at par during the war. But the pledge was broken a very few days after. Other distinctions now obtained in this currency, such as "Illinois preferred," which the seller of produce could only obtain at a deep shave. Exchange on New York speedily advanced above the "preferred" to 13 per cent. While the farmer thus got a few cents more for his grain, it cost him a heavy per centage to exchange for good money, or he paid it out in double profit to the merchant. The list of discredited banks rapidly increased. All the stock banks, regardless of the State stocks which formed their security, shared more or less in the depreciation, but after the breaking out of actual hostilities those based upon southern stocks declined directly to 50 cents on the dollar.

With the meeting of the legislature in extraordinary session, April, 1861, there were various schemes mooted to have the State guarranty the ultimate redemption of this free bank money of the Illinois banks. Some plans embraced all of the $12,000,000 of circulation, and others half, selecting those secured by the best stocks. In behalf of the latter proposition petitions were freely circulated among the people praying the legislature to this end. This plan was by a certain portion of the press denounced as an invidious distinction. To obviate the constitutional provision, the power of the legislature was claimed upon the ground of necessity, this money in that desperate crisis constituting the sole circulating medium of the people of the State. There was a senate bill guarantying the issues of certain banks, and there was an effort made to have the State take this bank currency for its war bonds, authorized at that session, but all failed.

After this the money got into a still more mercurial and unsettled condition. No one knew what his money would be worth on the morrow. Of course the wiles and arts of the brokers added no little to this instability, and the perplexity of the people. Before June every important city and many different railroads issued from day to day their special, and sometimes their exclusive, lists of banks, whose notes they designated as current. These lists were, for the most part, arbitrary. Every tradesman, and even farmers, carried in their pockets bank lists of this kind, often only to hear of new break-downs and revised lists just after having taken in some of the money. It was a period of annoyance, trial and vexation.

The banks, from their location—often at remote and inaccessible points—had earned the not inexpressive soubrequet of "wild cats;" and now, since their general depreciation, their issues received the rather inelegant appelation of "stump-tail." To aid in hurrying forward the approaching end of their reign, the press in many ways lent its powers of ridicule.*

By the time the rather abundant wheat crop of 1861, notwithstanding the devastation of the army worm that season, went into the market, the stock banks were driven to the wall, and gold and silver sent from the east was paid into the farmer's hand, though the prices ranged low—60 to 70 cents per bushel. By 1863 all except 17 of the 110 banks were in process of liquidation, with the circulation reduced from about $12,000,000 to about $566,163. The retirement of this vast circulation was effected mainly by the bill-holders voluntarily surrendering the money for the bonds deposited, for which purpose every facility was extended to them by the auditor in accordance with the law. Five banks had organized under the amended act of 1861, with an aggregate circulation of $51,945. By the first of January, 1865, the circulation of Illinois banks had dwindled down to $132,436, all secured by Illinois 6's —$175,034. Some of the free banks were under the act of congress of 1863 converted into national banks; and it was the national banking law, taxing the issues of all other banks 2 per cent., which has finally wholly extinguished them.

---

*(One of the banks became the property of the Hon. J. Young Scammon, a well known wealthy resident of Chicago, who, to give them currency, endorsed all its notes. Mr. Wentworth, of the Democrat, who had fought the "wild cats" with an unflagging will, heading his editorials on that subject with a family group of wild cats in various suggestive attitudes, when this Scammon money came to his hands, which was not slow, printed across the back of each note, his favorite family group of wild cats, and set it afloat again. These caricatures, it was said, had the effect to greatly stimulate the proprietor of the notes to retire them.)

CHAPTER XLVIII.

1853–1857—ADMINISTRATION OF GOV. MATTESON.

Democratic and Whig Conventions—Sketches of the Gubernatorial Candidates—Financial Condition and Physical Development of the State—Legislation, 1853–5—Maine Law and Riot at Chicago— Our Common Schools and trials in the establishment of the Free School System.

The Democratic State Convention of 1852, to make a ticket for State officers, met in Springfield April 20th. The political outlook for that party appeared clear all around the horizon auguring an easy victory at the coming November election. Hence there was no lack of aspirants for place on a ticket of such promise. For the position of governor seven names were presented. For some time previous it had been confidently expected that the Hon. David L. Gregg, then secretary of State, an accomplished gentleman of learning, varied political experience, and great influence with his party, would receive the nomination. Quite a number of counties had instructed for him, the public press in its comments and surmises, had settled on him with a degree of certainty, causing the opposition to discharge their batteries at him, as if his nomination had been consummated. The attack upon him was mainly on account of his religion, he being a Catholic. The evening before the meeting of the convention, a sermon of a political bearing, violently attacking Romanism, was preached at the Capital, which was largely attended by the assembled members of the convention. Some controversy was indulged afterward as to whether the minister was a whig or democrat. One thing, however, was certain, it was preached to influence the action of the convention in the defeat of Mr. Gregg. How much influence it had we do not say. No sooner had members begun to collect than it was whispered about that it would never do to nominate Gregg because of his catholicism; and this objection was industriously but quietly urged against him in the convention. After his sacrifice there was an effort to smother the matter, but it could not be done. Mr. Gregg knew and felt it all the time, but he was to true to party to bolt the ticket, and he gave it the support of all his power. In a letter to I. N. Morris, scouting the idea that the convention was governed by such intolerant motives, he nevertheless adds, "it is doubtless true that a few men in the convention sought to stir up religious prejudices with the view of accomplishing my defeat." Aside from this quiet persecuting intrigue, the convention was entirely harmonius.

The convention was organized with the Hon. J. A. McClernand as its permanent chairman. The names presented for the position of governor on the ticket, together with the number of votes on the first ballot, were as follows: D. L. Gregg, of Cook, 84 votes; Joel A. Matteson, of Will, 56; John Dement, of Lee, 53; F. C. Sherman, of Cook, 23; Thomas L. Harris, of Menard, 16; Lewis W. Ross, of Fulton, 7; and D. P. Bush, of Pike, 6. Joel A. Matteson afterwards received a majority of the votes cast and was declared the nominee of the convention for governor. Gustavus Koerner received the nomination for lieutenant-governor; Alexander Starne, secretary of State; Thomas H. Campbell, auditor, and John Moore, State treasurer.

The platform stood by the compromise measures of 1850, and non-intervention; against meddling with the domestic affairs of other States to stir up strife and hatred; for free homesteads to heads of families on the public domain; and declared in favor of Douglas for the presidency—that he "embodied all the elements of popularity and success to such a degree as to stamp him as the man for the coming crisis." State affairs received no notice at its hands, and as the free banking law was in full operation, democratic hostility to banks, so strenuously asserted in 1846-'48, was not repeated.

The Whig State Convention of 1852, met also at Springfield on the 7th of July. It was but sparingly attended. The regularly appointed delegates failed to appear and their places were in part filled by proxies taken from the grand and petit juries, litigants and witnesses in attendance upon the U. S. district and circuit courts then in term. It was organized by the choice of the Hon. O. H. Browning, of Adams, as chairman, who in his opening speech candidly remarked in effect, that it was not expected that the ticket to be by them nominated would carry the State, but it would prove important in tending to hold up the hands of their party friends in those States where there was hope of success for Gen. Scott, candidate for the presidency.

The ticket was mostly made by acclamation. Aspirants for the barren honors were not numerous as in the case of the democracy. The Hon. E. B. Webb, of White, was nominated for governor; J. L. D. Morrison, of St. Clair, for lieutenant-governor; Buckner S. Morris for secretary of State; Charles Betts for auditor; and Francis Arnz, a German, then on a visit to Europe, for treasurer. Owing to the wide-spread disgust in the whig ranks regarding the compromise measures of 1850, and the national whig platform, which approved them, it was planned on the part of the managers that with the endorsement of the nomination of Gen. Scott, to show party loyalty, it might be best to quietly stop, leaving candidates free to assume such grounds upon the slavery question and fugitive slave law, either pro or con, as might be deemed to accord best with the varying sentiments of different localities in the State. But this plan was sadly deranged by Mr. Herndon, of Sangamon, who unexpectedly, introduced a resolution, approving the Baltimore platform. Here was a dilemma. To refuse to adopt what was clearly their duty as national whigs, would be to break their party adhesions and become despised disorganizers; to do so, division and estrangement in their ranks, at home was inevitable. The whig party, in the north of this State especially, was largely anti-slavery. Herndon was firm, and the resolution passed, it is said, with feelings of melancholy and mutterings of discontent. It was first omitted from the published report of the proceedings, but the alert democracy promptly called attention to the dereliction, whereupon the official proceedings were republished "to correct the many inaccuracies of the first report."*

The abolitionists, who probably expected to gain by the large defection in the whig party, also brought out a State ticket with Dexter A. Knowlton, of Stephenson, for governor, and Philo Carpenter, of Cook, for lieutenant-governor.

Mr. Webb, the head of the whig ticket, was a lawyer, deeply read in his profession, and of excellent standing in the State. He had been for many years State's attorney, and repeatedly represented his county in the legislature. He did not possess the gifts of oratory. In 1836, as a member of the legislature, he opposed the adoption of the State improvement system, and spread his protest upon the journal, containing language of prophesy, whose verification in a few years, was but too emphatic. In 1855 he was a candidate for the supreme bench against Judge Breese, who was elected. While yet a boy his father removed to Carmi, Illinois, where Mr. Webb continued to live, and died in 1859. When the writer personally knew him in the latter years of his life, he was exceedingly fond of a small social circle of friends with whom to discuss the political and other questions of the day, and to talk over old times in his peculiar didactic and instructive manner.†

The whig candidate for lieutenant-governor, Col. Don Morrison, was also by profession a lawyer. He had served with acceptability in both the State and national legislatures, and as lieutenant-colonel of the 2d Illinois regiment in the Mexican war. He was a native Illinoisan; an orator of distinguished manners, daring address, and an ardent whig. He had been very successful in accumulating a large and valuable landed estate, which he still lives to enjoy. Neither of these candidates was tinctured with the growing anti-slavery sentiments of the party at that day.

Beside the disappointment of public expectation in the defeat of Gregg before the democratic convention, the nomination of Matteson for governor did not at first give general satisfaction to the party in all parts of the State. From the south, hostile to all banks, the press indicated the impression to be that the head of the ticket had warmly advocated the adoption of the general banking law; that he favored a U. S. bank, or any kind of "wild cat system;" that he had not besides been sound on the Wilmot proviso; was against the compromise measures of 1850, and favored free soilism. The democratic organ at the capital called on the Joliet paper (where Matteson resided,) to give to the democracy a "full and explicit statement of [his] views" upon the important subjects named. To Koerner was ascribed a position upon these questions in perfect accord with the sentiments of the party.

* See Illinois State Journal.
[NOTE—†For his own amusement, unaided by any teacher and perhaps before he was aware of his proficiency, he became a most excellent French scholar, without being able, however, to his knowledge, to pronounce a word of the language correctly. This was done by regularly reading the *Courier des Etat Unis*, a French newspaper printed in New York, for which he was a subscriber. The writer has heard him read in English fresh from its columns, time and again, translating with such readiness that one would suppose him to be reading from an ordinary American newspaper.

It was said that if the ticket had been reversed as regards these candidates it would have been preferable—"but as it is we adhere to it," commanded the party drill-sergeants. Two short years or less demonstrated the fallacy of these apprehensions by the going over of Koerner to the anti-Nebraska party, and Matteson's support of the repeal of the Missouri compromise.

The campaign of 1852, as might have been expected by the whigs giving up the contest in advance, was attended by little excitement; nothing of interest occurred, and upon its close in November, resulted in an overwhelming victory for the democracy. Joel A. Matteson received 80,645 votes, Edwin B. Webb 64,408, and Dexter A. Knowlton 8,829.

Joel A. Matteson was born August 8, 1808, in Jefferson county New York, whither his father had removed from Vermont three years before. His father was a farmer in fair circumstances, but a common English education was all that his only son received. Joel first tempted fortune as a small tradesman in Prescott, Canada, before his majority. He returned thence home, entered an academy, taught school, visited the large eastern cities, improved a farm his father had given him, made later a tour south, worked there in building railroads, experienced a storm on the Gulf of Mexico, visited the gold diggings of northern Georgia, whence he returned via Nashville to St. Louis and through Illinois to his father's home, and married. In 1833, having sold his farm, he removed with his wife and one child to Illinois, and took a claim on government land near the head of Au Sable river, in the present Kendall county. At the time there were not exceeding two neighbors within a range of ten miles, and only three or four houses between his location and Chicago. He opened a large farm; his family was boarded twelve miles away while he erected a house on his claim, sleeping, during this time, under a rude pole shed. Here his life was placed in imminent peril by a huge prairie rattlesnake sharing his bed. In 1835 he bought largely at the government land sales. During the speculative real estate mania which broke out in Chicago in 1836, and spread all over the State, he sold his lands under the inflation of that period, and removed to Joliet. In 1838 he became a heavy contractor on the Illinois and Michigan canal. Upon the completion of his job in 1841, when hard times prevailed, business at a stand, contracts paid in State scrip; when all the public works except the canal were abandoned, the State offered for sale 700 tons of railroad iron, which was purchased by Matteson at a great bargain. This he shipped and sold at Detroit, realizing a very handsome profit, enough to pay off all his canal debts, and leave him a surplus of several thousand dollars. His enterprise next prompted him to start a woolen mill at Joliet, in which he prospered, and which, after successive enlargements, became an enormous establishment. In 1842 he was first elected a State senator, but, by a bungling apportionment, John Pearson, a senator holding over, was found to be in the same district, and decided to be entitled to represent it. Matteson's seat was declared vacant. Pearson, however, with a nobleness difficult to appreciate in this day of greed for office, unwilling to represent his district under the circumstances, immediately resigned his unexpired term of two years. A bill was passed in a few hours ordering a new election, and in ten days' time Matteson was returned re-elected and took his seat as senator. From his well-known capacity as a business man, he was made chairman of the committee on finance, a position which he held during this half and two full succeeding senatorial terms, discharging its important duties with ability and faithfulness. Besides his extensive woolen mill interest, when work was resumed on the canal under the new loan of $1,600,000 he again became a heavy contractor, and also subsequently operated largely in building railroads.* He had shown himself a most energetic and thorough business man.

Matteson's forte was not on the stump; he had not cultivated the art of oily flattery, or the faculty of being all things to all men. His qualities of head took rather the direction of efficient executive ability; his turn consisted not so much in the adroit management of party, or the powerful advocacy of great governmental principles, as in those more solid and enduring operations which cause the physical development and advancement of a State —of commerce and business enterprise, into which he labored with success to lead the people. As a politician he was just and liberal in his views, and both in official and private life he then stood untainted and free from blemish. As a man, in active benevolence, social virtues, and all the amiable qualities of neighbor or citizen, he had few superiors. His messages present a perspicuous array of facts as to the condition of the State, and are often couched in forcible and elegant diction. The helm of State was confided to no unskillful hands.

Gustavus Koerner, the lieutenant-governor elect, was born in 1809, in the old free city of Frankfort-on-the-Main, Germany, and received in his youth the usual thorough common school education of that country. At the age of 19 he entered the University of Jena; in 1832, at Heidelberg he took the degree of doctor of laws, and was soon after admitted to the bar of his native city. While at Jena the French revolution of 1830 inspired him, like many other ardent youths, with the principles of liberty. Thus imbued, he could illy brook the decrees of the Germanic diet suppressing the freedom of the press, and prohibiting public discussions of political questions, and connected with a political association having for its aim an enlarged liberty and more perfect union of the Germanic States, he became implicated in a revolutionary movement against the government, which proved a failure, when he sought exile. Finding no security in France, then under Louis Philippe, in May, 1833, at the age of 22, he embarked at Havre for America, and on arrival proceeded to Illinois, and settled in Belleville. Here he determined to pursue the practice of the law, notwithstanding the obstacles of a foreign tongue, of which he had but a student's knowledge, and immediately commenced a diligent course of reading, attended the Lexington law school, and afterward became the law partner of Adam W. Snyder and James Shields. He attached himself to the fortunes of the democratic party, and took an active part in politics. In 1840 he edited a German campaign paper named *Messenger of Liberty*, and carried the electoral vote of Illinois to Washington. In 1842 he was elected to the lower house of the legislature, and in 1845 appointed a judge of the supreme court, by Gov. Ford, vice Gen. Shields, resigned. In 1848 he was appointed consul to Hamburg. This

* See speech of D. L. Gregg. 1852

place was procured for him by his political friends, knowing well his ardent wishes to revisit the scenes of his youth during the then struggle of that country for liberty. But when the effort was crushed, and crowds of political refugees fled the oppressed fatherland, Koerner, not having started, resigned his commission.* In 1854 he went off with the anti-Nebraska movement, since when he has acted with the republican party. He presided over the State republican convention in 1858, when Mr. Lincoln was designated as a candidate for U. S. senator. In 1860 he was a delegate at large to the Chicago convention. On the breaking out of the rebellion he raised the 43d Illinois regiment, but before it was fully organized he was appointed a colonel on the staff of Gen. Fremont. In 1862 he was appointed minister to Spain, which place he resigned in 1865. Since then he has acted in various public capacities for the State. He was in 1872 the liberal republican and democratic candidate for governor, but was defeated.

The new administration was entrusted with the helm of State at a time when she was rising with great rapidity from the long and gloomy spell of pecuniary embarrassment following the failure of the internal improvement system of 1837. The building of the great net-work of railroads was just fairly inaugurated, and about 400 miles of track completed. The first year of this administration the increase of taxable wealth in the State amounted to $75,-865,328, equal to about 51 per cent. Only a small portion of this unprecedented increase was reasonably attributable to the new assessment law. The commerce of Chicago, with a population of 50,000, had gone beyond $20,000,000, and the trade and commerce of the Illinois river and canal amounted to $42,345,000. The State debt, principal and interest, on the 1st of January, 1853, was $17,-398,985.35, which, as the State increased at the rate of 10 per cent. and the debt at 6 per cent., was estimated to be extinguishable in 11 years' time—by 1864.

In his elaborate inaugural message, indicating that a master of finance had cast his eye over the field of State, Gov. Matteson alluded to her flattering prospects; how she was in the track of empire; the great number of railroads in course of construction, and bespoke the liberality of the legislature in granting further charters, and affording every proper encouragement to bring new fields of labor into market. True to the place of his abode, he recommended the building of a State prison in the northern part of the State. The Alton penitentiary was then crowded with 227 convicts. He also recommended the adoption of a free school system, and if that should be deemed premature, at any rate to authorize a general superintendent of the common schools. The new free banking law he did not want to see disturbed by the legislature, but those unauthorized institutions still operating under the semblance of banks and issuing their notes, should be stopped. He also desired a re-submission to a vote of the people the question of changing the distribution of the 2 mill tax; and such amendment of the constitution as would give to the foreigner a speedier right of suffrage, out of which, he argued at length, no evil could grow. In his view the hard times constitution was too parsimonious in the salaries and fees fixed for officers; the judi-

---

*See D. L. Gregg's speech, 1852.

ciary should be placed above pecuniary want, upon that high ground which would command the confidence and respect of intelligent men. He regarded the compensation of members of the general assembly so low as to be attended with embarrassments. This he desired also amended. The constitution was not amended, however, in any of these or other particulars for 17 years; and these objections, urged from so high a source, doubtless contributed to the first feeling and impulse that license taken with its rigid provisions would not perhaps incur any great public obloquy, which was subsequently improved upon until their violations were practiced by every department of government in the grossest manner.

During the legislative session of 1853 was enacted the small bank bill law, which was, from the start, as dead a letter as law ever became; also acts to use the surplus fund of the treasury in the purchase of State indebtedness; to condemn the right of way for purposes of internal improvement; to build the present government mansion; incorporate the State Agricultural Society; sell the State lands, of which 128,954 acres, valued at $747,190, were still on hand, and granting the right of pre-emption on them; re-enact the law prohibiting the retailing of intoxicating drinks, fixing the license at from $50 to $300; and, under the partisan lash, that inhuman and disgraceful act, preventing free negroes and mulattoes from settling in the State, under severe penalties, was passed.

In 1855 was passed that law, more than any other upon our statutes fraught with untold benefactions to the youth of our State, to maintain a system of free schools; also an act authorizing the erection of 150 additional prison cells to the Alton penitentiary. The most important measure bearing upon the treasury of the State, at this session, was the act for a settlement of old canal claim damages, dating back beyond 1840, in favor of certain contractors, &c. The commission appointed for the final adjustment of these claims consisted of S. H. Treat, John D. Caton, and Walter B. Scates. By resolution it was ordered that with the State census to be taken in 1855 should be separately returned the name, residence and postoffice address of all the deaf and dumb, blind and insane persons in the State. A resolution relative to the calling of a convention to alter the constitution was also again submitted to the people, to again meet defeat.

During the 4 years of Matteson's administration the taxable wealth of the State was about trebled, being for the year 1851, $137,818,079, and for the year 1856, $349,951,272; there were raised and paid out on the public debt, $7,079,198, reducing it from $17,398,985 to $12,843,144; in the meantime taxation had been reduced, and the State had resumed paying interest in New York as it fell due. While the public debt was thus being reduced, the means of its ultimate extinction were rapidly on the increase. When Matteson came into office, less than 400 miles of railroad were constructed in the State; when he went out, the number would vary little from 3,000, "penetrating almost every section and filling the country with activity and business." During his term, the population of Chicago was nearly doubled and its commerce more than quadrupled.

The Maine Liquor Law in Illinois.—In 1855 the legislature passed a very stringent prohibitory liquor bill, commonly known as the "Maine law"—being a total prohibition of both the sale and manufacture of spirituous, vinous or malt liquors, under heavy penalties of fines, imprisonments, or both, and destruction of liquors. It contained certain exceptions in favor of the making of cider, wines and beer and ale for export. Importers were allowed to sell in the original packages only. The law was not to go into effect unless approved by a majority vote of the people at a special election to be held in June of that year.

In 1851 had been adopted a somewhat stringent act known as the "quart law." It was designed to strike at tippling establishments, in prohibiting the sale of spirituous and mixed (not malt) liquors in less quantity than a quart, by forbidding them to be drank on the premises where sold or given away; and by repealing all laws granting license for these purposes. The penalty was a fine of $25. The law produced a great outcry of popular indignation, and was in 1853 repealed. While the legislature was thus bowing to low clamor, the friends of temperance were not idle. A State temperance convention met at the capital in January. Delegates to the number of 200, from all parts of the State, were in attendance. The leading participants were S. D. Lockwood, formerly supreme judge, the distinguished pioneer and divine, J. M. Peck, D. D., Hons. B. S. Edwards, S. W. Robins, Thomas M. Taylor, G. P. West, W. C. Vanmeter, Judge Grover, &c. Believing intoxicating drink to be the great incentive to crime, they sought to reform society by abolishing this terrible temptation. The Maine law was undergoing trial in several States at the time. The use of the hall of representatives was denied them after a protracted debate in the house, by a vote of 33 to 36. The convention drafted a bill similar in its provisions to the Maine law, which was presented to the general assembly for adoption, but met with speedy defeat; some of the strongest temperance members believing that moral suasion, and not arbitrary legislation, was the only mode of approaching a free, thinking people like the Americans, voted against it. At the special session of February, 1854, the friends of temperance again assembled at Springfield. The attendance was chiefly from the northern part of the State. The prohibitory bill was again introduced in the legislature, and this time favorably reported upon by the select committee on temperance. Mr. Palmer (since governor,) moved the submission clause as an amendment, but for want of time no final action was had upon it.

There were at the time grave doubts as to the constitutionality of such a law; but at the June term of the Supreme court, in the case of Jacksonville *vs.* Godard, these were in a measure removed. Jacksonville by ordinance had declared the sale of liquors a nuisance, making the offense punishable by fine. It was contended by the defendant that liquor was property, and that the right to acquire property, and holding, using and disposing of it was both natural and constitutional, and could not be invaded by any municipality under authority of the State; the right might be regulated but not destroyed. The court held that this doctrine as a universal principle was not tenable. It depended upon the kind of property; its use and disposal. We surrendered both natural and social rights in the political state, which was necessary and paramount for the well being of society. These police powers destroyed neither Magna Charta nor any constitution. The act and the thing, with its use, must be judged by its effects, and when they brought it within the reason and mischiefs of the law the power of government must regulate them. We had a right to our gold and silver, and the disposal of it, yet could not coin it, We might labor and rest, yet were disallowed to become idlers, vagrants or vagabonds. We might dispose of our property, yet had no right to gamble it off. And to punish the effect we might remove the cause. Judge Scates delivered the opinion of the court.

The prohibitory bill came again before the legislature in 1855. That body was unexpectedly republican, or rather "fusion" by a combination of whigs and anti-Nebraska democrats. For the first time in the history of the State, since the organization of the whig and democratic parties, it was not in the control of the latter. The bill, after being amended by the senate, passed both houses, and under the submission clause went before the people for approval.

It may not be uninteresting to give an idea of the arguments advanced for and against the measure. The opponents held that drinking men must be restrained, if restrained at all, by convincing their judgment that dissipation led to ruin and death; by a conviction that temperance was the way to prosperity, happiness, health and longevity; that their sympathies must be enlisted in the cause by moral suasion, which was the only effectual lever to bear on such a work; that penal and prohibitory laws had in every instance, proved a total failure, and were calculated to provoke resistance. It was hard to establish the belief that liquor was not property which men might not defend from destruction, and the principle was the same whether ten dollars worth of liquor was destroyed or ten millions worth.*

The friends of the bill argued that as the people of this State were law abiding they would not resist so beneficent a law. Every man in society or government had to yield something of his savage liberty—the liberty of each was circumscribed by the equal liberty of all. The effect of intemperance in producing crime and pauperism called for taxation to defray and support a double wrong. It might destroy a husband or son, in whom the wife or mother had a right of support—a form of property. If liquor was property, so was iron, yet convert that iron into counterfeiting tools it became contraband and lost the character of property. All things were sacred until desecrated. Man was entitled to personal liberty, yet inebriation would subject him to arrest under police regulations; liberty was regulated by law; governments were instituted among men to promote their general welfare, and prevent wrong and injury to the rights of persons and property. The general good of the people was the object of all law, and whatever stood in the way of its attainment should be removed by appropriate legislation. Finally, it simply resolved itself into a question whether intemperance was an evil, and whether intoxicating liquors produced intemperance.†

---

* Illinois State Register, April 1853.
† Journal (Ill. State,) March, 1855.

The Hon. B. S. Edwards, a lawyer of ability and eminent standing, framed the bill, and labored earnestly before the people to secure its adoption; many others, influenced by philanthropic motives, did the same. The State received a pretty thorough canvassing by speakers and the press. But politicians, a craven set, with an eye ever to the future of their personal advancement, stood aloof from it. The opponents circulated garbled copies of it among farmers, with forged interpolations, forbidding the manufacture and sale of cider. The bill read, if a man was found drunk and committed a breach of the peace, he should be arrested. From this the words "committing a breach of the peace" were omitted. It was further characterized as the great abomination of modern times—it circumscribed the privilege of the citizen, it outraged his free conscience, and by its adoption liberty would be crushed. The bill was defeated before the people by a small aggregate majority. The southern counties voted mostly against it, and the northern, with the exception of Cook and Rock Island, for it.

Maine Law Riot in Chicago.—Section 36 of the prohibitory bill provided that "all laws authorizing the granting of licenses to sell spirituous, intoxicating or mixed liquors shall be repealed from and after the date of the passage of this act"—February 12th. Section 39 read: "The provisions of this act shall take effect on the first Monday of July next," provided that if a majority of the ballots to be deposited were against prohibition then the act was to be of no force or effect whatever. Section 39 being a later expression of the will of the legislature than the conflicting provision of section 36, according to numerical order, ought plainly to have prevailed. In March the city council of Chicago, said to have been Knownothing, required all persons selling liquor to take out license at the rate of $300 a year. Many of the saloon-keepers were Germans. These, acting under legal advice as to the construction of the State prohibitory law, that the city had no legal authority to issue licenses from February to July, and that every person choosing to had the right to sell liquor within that period according to section 36, refused to comply with the requirements of the council, and continued to sell liquors. Warrants were issued, and some 30 German saloon-keepers were arrested. The question being an important one, it was concluded to try them before Judge Rucker. On the day set Germans thronged the court room until it was impossible to proceed with the trials. The police cleared the room, and the crowd retired to the next, from which, on account of their noise, they were also excluded. With the beating of drums the crowd now took possession of the sidewalk on Randolph street, excluded the passing pedestrians, and, armed with bludgeons, knives and pistols, speedily developed into a mob, insulting every one coming within range, and bidding defiance to the police. The latter attempted to open the sidewalk by force, and a general melee ensued, resulting in the death of two policemen, as many Germans, and the serious wounding of a great number. The streets were cleared, and order re-established by the aid of the military; 53 Germans were arrested and lodged in jail. It was a day of outraged law, disgrace and blood for Chicago. On the next day (Sunday,) the city was put under martial law.

OUR COMMON SCHOOLS.

Trials Incident to the Establishment of the Free School System.— The free school system, entered upon in 1855, marks the turning point in the history of common school education of the State. The right of the State to maintain such a system is founded upon the idea that where ignorance predominates vice and crime are its inseparable concomitants, and that by education the masses will be elevated, society benefited, offenses lessened, and good government promoted. But the main incentive to its establishment in Illinois was the great necessity that efficiency be infused into the cause of education; and the awakening of the people from the deep lethargy into which they had sunk to an appreciation of its importance. Keeping in view the wonderful power of money upon all the affairs of men, it was invoked in this case to stir them up, and a law was devised which offered essentially a premium to stimulate them to take hold of those benefits which had been tendered them for 10 years past under then existing laws, but which they had steadily refused to fully accept. The main feature of the law is bringing the strong hand of government, operating through the taxing power, to bear upon the property of the State, and causing it to contribute to the education of its youth. To effect this was no easy task. Many old and deep-rooted prejudices as to taxation for this purpose had to be eradicated; the judgment of men as to its power and rightfulness was to be convinced; false ideas of economy for ten years sedulously pursued by the State, were to be unlearned; ignorant parents enlightened; and teachers of the requisite qualifications and earnestness obtained. It was a problem both difficult and delicate; but indefatigable men labored unceasingly for its solution, and it was finally accomplished; and the law and its results point an instructive lesson in the science of government.

The ordinance of 1787, declared knowledge in connection with religion and morality; " to be necessary to the good government and happiness of mankind," and enjoined that "schools and the means of education shall forever be encouraged." Accordingly, congress, in the Enabling Act for this State, April 18, 1818, appropriated 3 per cent. of the net proceeds of the sales of the public lands, lying within her limits, for the encouragement of learning, 1-16th parth thereof to be exclusively bestowed on a college or university. Two townships, one then and one sometime prior, were besides donated for founding and maintaining a seminary of learning. The proceeds of the 3 per cent. fund and the sales of the seminary lands, were blended in 1835, and borrowed by the State at 6 per cent., the interest to be annually distributed for school purposes. In 1845 the receipts of the proceeds of the 3 per cent. school fund were suspended for a time. Owing to the embarrassed condition of the finances, this State, like many others, had stopped paying interest on her public debt, and congress, by resolution, ordered the 3 per cent. fund to be withheld from them and applied toward the payment of interest on bonds held in trust by the general government. This action was denounced at home as a grievous and unwarranted wrong, but our delegation in congress raised no voice against it. After the Mexican war the free entry of lands by land warrants caused the 3 per cent. fund to be materially lessened, and the legislature, in 1849, authorized its proceeds to be invested in Illinois bonds, then low in market, which would have been a wise expedient for the 8 preceding years but now nothing much came of it. The seminary fund received additions from time to time, as sales were made, and in 1861, the residue of the land was turned over to the agricultural college, the principal of the fund being $59,838. The State in 1857 had set apart the interest of the college and seminary funds for the maintenance of the normal university, except one-fourth for the deaf and dumb asylum. In 1837 the legislature added to the common school fund the proceeds of the surplus revenue of the U. S., distributed to the several States by act of congress, amounting at that time, to $132,856, the State paying interest thereon at the rate of 6 per cent. This fund thus escaped being swallowed up in the vortex of the internal improvement system of that period. The several sums thus derived may be called the permanent State common school fund, the whole amounting, when the free school system was entered upon in 1855, to $951,504, yielding an annual interest of $57,700, one-fourth of which was distributed to the deaf and dumb asylum.

But a more important and really munificent donation from congress was the 16th section of every congressional township, or if sold, lands equivalent thereto, as contiguous as might be, for the use of the inhabitants of such township for school purposes. This amounted to 998,448 89-100 acres, which, had it been properly husbanded and managed, would have given the people such an ample school fund as would have saved them from local taxation. One trouble of most new countries is that immigrants come empty-handed and are both averse and unable to pay taxes. Such was emphatically the case in Illinois at an early day. To the sentiments of a people, law makers, seeking office at their hands, will bend, and the result in Illinois, was that as early as 1828, with an empty treasury and the fear of providing adequate revenue by taxation, the legislature unfortunately authorized the sale of the school lands, and borrowed the proceeds to defray the current public expense. At first the lands were leased and squatted on to a large extent. The occupants shortly desiring better titles, possessing the elective franchise, and being united by a common interest, their influence with our law-makers was sufficient to procure the passage of laws to sell them at very low prices, and thus this magnificent gift of the nation for the highest of purposes, was in great part squandered. The seminary township largely shared the same fate. By 1855 the township fund amounted to $1,441,427, yielding then an annual interest of $111,191. In 1868 the principal was $4,873,232, varying in different townships from $100 to more than $100,000, owing to losses and mal-administration in the one case, and provident management, a later settlement of the districts, and fortuitous circumstances as to location in the other.

In 1855, as we have noted, the interest on the several school funds thus borrowed by the State, was first distributed to the counties according to the number of children under 21 years, to be paid to teachers at a rate of not more than one-half due them for services rendered in the preceding 12 months, the overplus, if any, to constitute forever a county school fund, a wise provision, but lost in the subsequent changes of the law. Of course there was no county fund made if the distributive share was less than one-half the sums due to teachers; hence there are some counties without this fund. The aggregate county fund in 1855 was about $50,000. In 1852 the balance of the swamp and overflowed lands, after paying for drainage and levees built to reclaim them, was granted to the counties where situate, their proceeds to be equally divided among the townships for educational purposes, roads and bridges, as might be deemed expedient. In 1853 the fines collected and criminal forfeitures on bail were further added to the school fund and school property was exempted from taxation.

The first free school system of this State was adopted 30 years before the present one. Schools flourished in almost every neighborhood, and the law "worked admirably well."* Gov. Coles, in his message to the legislature of 1824-5, directed attention to the liberal donation of congress in lands for educational purposes, asking that they be husbanded as a rich treasure for future generations, and in the meantime to make provision for the support of local schools. Later during the session, Joseph Duncan, afterwards governor, then a senator, introduced the bill for this act. The preamble declares that:

"To enjoy our rights and liberties, we must understand them; their security and protection ought to be the first object of a free people; and it is a well established fact that no nation has ever continued long in the enjoyment of civil and political freedom which was not both virtuous and enlightened. And believing that the advancement of literature always has been and ever will be the means of more fully developing the rights of man—that the mind of every citizen in a republic is the common property of society, and constitutes the basis of its strength and happiness—it is therefore considered the peculiar duty of a free government, like ours, to encourage and extend the improvement and cultivation of the intellectual energies of the whole."

It was provided that common schools should be established, free and open to every class of white citizens between the ages of 5 and 21; and persons over 21 might be admitted on such terms as the trustees should prescribe. Districts of not less than 15 families were to be formed by the county courts upon petition of a majority of the voters thereof; officers were to be elected, sworn in, and their duties were prescribed in detail. The system was full and complete in all particulars. The legal voters were empowered at the annual meeting to levy a tax, in money or merchantable produce at its cash value, not exceeding ½ of 1 per cent., subject to a maximum limitation of $10 to any one person. But aside from this tax, the best and most effective feature of the law, in principle the great stimulant of our present system, was an annual appropriation by the State of $2 out of every $100 received into the treasury, and the distribution of 5-6 of the interest arising from the school funds, apportioned among the several counties according to the number of white children under the age of 21 years, which sums were then re-distributed by the counties among their respective districts, none participating therein where not at least 3 months school had been taught during the 12 months preceding. In this law were foreshadowed some of the most valuable

* Gov. Ford.

features of our present efficient free school system. But it is asserted that the law of 1825 was in advance of the times ; that the people preferred to pay their tuition fees, or do without education for their children, rather than submit to the bare idea of taxation, however it might fall in the main upon the wealthier property-holders for the benefit of all ; and the law was so amended in 1827 as to virtually nullify it, by providing that no person should be taxed for the maintenance of any school unless his consent was first obtained in writing, and the continuance of the State appropriation of $2 out of every $100 received into the treasury, being its very life, was denied. The legislature of 1827, unlike its predecessor, not only in this but many other respects, was one of the worst that has ever afflicted the State.

After that there were repeated amendments and revisions of the school law by the legislature, but for the want of the vital principle of the taxing power, little efficiency was imparted to the cause of education in Illinois. For 18 years, it may be said, the darkness of ignorance hung over the land, unrelieved by a ray of promise in the right direction. Still, zealous men labored indefatigably in the cause. In 1844 an earnest common school convention met in Peoria, and, after deliberation, Messrs. John S. Wright, of Chicago, H. M. Weed, of Lewiston, and Thomas M. Kilpatrick, of Winchester, drafted a memorial to the legislature in favor of an efficient common school system, which is an able and exhaustive document on the subject.* To arouse public interest and stir up the masses to the necessity of educating their children they deemed of prime importance, and to this end pleaded earnestly for a State superintendent of public instruction, as a separate and distinct officer, with a fair salary, whose duty it should be, among other things, to travel into every county and neighborhood in the State, deliver lectures to the people, impress upon them the importance of education, carefully examine such schools as there were, note the operation of the existing law, learn the wishes and plans of the people, and from sources outside of the State collect such valuable information as could be obtained respecting improvements, &c., and report from time to time to the legislature. That such an officer would see to it that the public moneys raised were rightfully applied and made useful in the highest degree. Gov. Ford added his recommendation, saying such an officer "must be a rare man, endowed with talents, zeal and discretion of the highest order." They further declared education a public benefit, indispensable to the welfare of the State, and as much entitled to support from general taxation .as the judiciary, or the maintenance of public highways; and asked why single out education from all other public benefits and exempt a man's property from paying its expense. Well knowing, however, the then crippled condition of the State treasury, resulting from the late internal improvement scheme, they asked no contribution from it, but boldly recommended local taxation, and frankly acknowledged that their every effort was intended as a lure to draw the people into the grasp of the awful monster, a school tax. Let them but give permission to use this monster to those so inclined, and others, seeing the result, would fall into his embrace. In

* See Ill. Reports, 1845.

other words, allow such townships or districts as wanted, by a majority of their legal voters, to adopt this method of sustaining their schools. The local tax would incite inquiry, and insure the faithful use of the public money, both from the State treasury and the township fund.

The legislature at the session of 1844–5, unable to resist the force of this reasoning, yielded its partial assent. Actuated by a feeling of economy, under the pressure of the times, the secretary of State, already burdened with the business of his office, was made ex-officio State superintendent of public instruction; and in reference to local taxation it was required that a two-thirds legal vote of any district concur in ordering the tax. Considering the influence of large property holders, who were mostly opposed to the assessment of taxes for school purposes, it may well be imagined that little school revenue was thence derived. Indeed the whole of the local school taxes for the years 1846-47 did not amount to 1 mill on the $100 of taxable wealth of the State. The auditor was to distribute the interest of the State school fund according to the number of children in each county under 20 years, based upon the preceding census, and these distributive shares were again to be distributed by the counties to the townships according to the number of children in each, under 21. But if no school had been taught for 10 months preceding, the money was to be added to the principal of the township fund. Many of the features of the law of 1845 are incorporated in that of 1855.

As a qualification for teaching, the law required a knowledge of reading, writing, arithmetic, geography, grammar and history, which, strange as it may now appear, was far too high a standard, and many districts were deprived of their distributive shares of the State school fund on this account.

Thus, while the statute books were swollen with school laws, this, like many others which preceded it being most voluminous and anything but clear, repelling nearly all from reading it, the cause of education was not carried into as vigorous and efficient operation as might have been done under the law, and a most lamentable apathy still pervaded the people. In many counties in the northern part of the State, and notably in Cook, the schools were in a flourishing condition. But out of the 99 counties in the State, the secretary of State, ex-officio superintendent, in 1846, was able to obtain reports from 57 only, as to the condition of their schools. The county school commissioners received very inadequate compensation, and were mostly negligent of their duties or incompetent.

In 1847 the standard of the qualification for teachers was lowered, or sought to be brought within the reach of the material that existed, by amending the school law so as to allow the granting of certificates for any one or more of the before named branches, as the applicant might desire; and the requirement of a $\frac{2}{3}$ vote to levy a local tax was was modified to a majority of all the legal votes of any district—whence it followed that a simple absence could defeat the tax, and as might be expected, great difficulty was experienced to induce a sufficient number of voters to assemble, and efficiency was still in abeyance. In 1849 the qualification of teachers was raised to the former grade, subject, however, to the will of directors, as to any of the branches, and a certificate of that kind was valid. The local tax which might be levied was limited to 25 cents on the $100, its purpose to be designated. Incorporated towns and cities were allowed to go to 50 cents on the $100. In 1851 a majority of the legal voters, attending at any legally convened meeting for the purpose, were allowed to levy a local tax not exceeding $1 on every $100 of the taxable property of the district. The taxable wealth of the State at this time exceeded $100,000,000, and $1,000,000 might have been raised, which added to the State school fund annually distributed, and that of the township, would have furnished the people an ample fund for a complete free school system. But it depended upon their election to avail of it, and instead of $1,000,000 and more, we find that for the year 1852 the total local ad valorem school tax in the whole State amounted to only $51,000, being less than one-twentieth part of the limits of the law. Mr. Gregg, secretary of State and superintendent of public instruction at the time, says: "I am not aware that in a single instance has this been done [that is, the full benefit of the law availed of], nor can any motive be assigned for the action of the people in this respect, unless it grows out of a preference for the system which now prevails." The school law, in educational effects, was a dead letter.

As stated in the outset, the problem remained how to lift public sentiment from the slough of apathy into which it had sunk, to the great importance of education. Happily, from many parts of the State the question of a general free school system was beginning to be agitated. The press, which had long stood aloof, took hold and began to discuss the subject in earnest. The *Illinois Teacher*, a publication devoted to the cause of education and numbering among its contributors many of the ablest teachers, exerted a wide influence and did efficient service. The financial condition of the State, too, was undergoing a most desirable change. Our rapid increase in population and wealth was dissipating the clouds of embarrassment which for 10 years had cast their shadow over the land, and the people beheld the future bright with promise. The railroad era had dawned upon the State, a new impulse was given to its development, and its strides to empire were unequaled. Gov. Matteson, in his inaugural message, in a forcible manner directed attention to the great importance of a broad and comprehensive common school system, free to all alike, and supported by a tax upon all the property in the State, to fit the rising generation in its intellectual capacity for the proper direction of the grand future of the State. Still there were in the then views of the people many weighty objections to a scheme of such extraordinary State dictation, as it was called. It was regarded as wholly at war with the property rights of the individual, exacting and oppressive to those unable or unwilling from various motives, to favorably view or participate in the common advantages to be derived from it; and the legislature adjourned without having accomplished anything toward a solution of the problem.

In December, 1853, anticipating an extra session of the legislature, two large common school conventions met, one at Jerseyville composed of many adjoining counties, and one at Bloomington, for the whole State. These conventions, whose earnest spirit was widely felt, indicated not only a growing dissatisfaction with the existing common school system, but evinced a ripened determination in the public mind to make a radical change. These movements, and the very general approbation of their expressions, were so emphatic as to produce a decided impression upon the general assembly, which met in February following, and took the first step in the right direction, by the enactment of a law separating the office of superintendent of public instruction from that of secretary of State, the former being neglected on account of the arduous duties of the latter, and creating it a distinct department of State government, the incumbent to receive a salary of $1500. Besides other duties, he was required to draft a bill embodying a system of free education for all the children of the State, and report it to the next general assembly. On the 15th of March, 1854, Gov. Matteson appointed the Hon. N. W. Edwards State superintendent of common schools. This most important office, at that juncture, was bestowed upon Mr. Edwards on account of his long experience in public life, and from the conviction that he would carry into effect the hopes of the people and the designs of the legislature in creating it. In January following he submitted to the general assembly a full report upon the condition of the public schools throughout the State, ably urged the education of the children in the State at the public expense, and presented a well-drawn bill for a complete system of free schools, which, with some alterations, became a law. And thus the great desideratum, long sought, was found ; and the earnest and indefatigable men, who had labored unceasingly to advance the cause of education, and who had never faltered even in the darkest hours of the State's finances, were rewarded by beholding the completed machinery prepared for its accomplishment.

The act bore date Feb. 15, 1855, and embraced all the essential principles now in force. In them, as we said in the outset, is evinced something of the science of government. We have noted the educational needs of the people, and how they might have provided the means under the laws for free schools in every district of the State, but they would not. It remained, therefore, to compel them, not by force or the strong arm of the government, but in a way whose results would be fully as efficient. And this was accomplished by recognizing and enforcing the principle that the State has the sovereign right to levy and collect a sufficient tax from the real and personal property within its limits, and expend it in giving its youth a common education. For State purposes the school tax was fixed at 2 mills on the $100. To this was added the interest from the permanent school fund, when the whole would be given back to the people, $\frac{2}{3}$ of it in proportion to the number of children under 21 in each county, and the residue to the townships, whole or fractional. In allowing territory to control $\frac{1}{4}$ of the fund, which is unvarying in the distribution, new or sparsely settled counties were stimulated to the establishment of schools, which otherwise could not have coped with the denser settlements. But before the State fund could be shared in, certain prerequisites must be complied with. A free school had to be maintained for at least 6 months in the year, and it was made imperative upon the directors of every organized school district to levy such a tax annually as if added to the public funds would be sufficient for that purpose: and, as if fearing that this might not prove successful, it was made collectable the same as the State and county tax. Other taxes might still be voluntarily added by a vote of the people, to extend the term of schools, build or repair school houses, purchase sites, &c. The local tax made thus obligatory, is, however, the main resource of our free school system, which, in 1868, aggregated $4,250,679. The public school funds having reached the hands of the township trustees, a new rule obtains as to their distribution among the districts. To encourage school attendance, half of the funds are apportioned on the exhibits of the teachers' schedules, and half in proportion to the number of children under 21 years old in each district. Such are the leading and sagacious combinations of the scheme to bring education nearer to the people, and induce them to partake of it. This is the force resorted to by government to render the system efficient. It is essentially the offering of large yearly premiums to every district to establish and maintain a free school for its youth.

The new school system showed directly a marked improvement in educational efforts and results. Of the number of children in the State, under 21, only about one-third attended any kind of school before its establishment, now the average reached nearly half; before, the total number of schools was 4,215, now the number rose directly to 7,694; before, the average monthly wages of teachers were $25 for males and $12 for females, now they were reported at $45 and $27, respectively; and while for 1854 the school fund (interest) distributed was only $37,155, for 1855 it was $665,025—$606,809 being the yield of the 2 mill tax. The cause of education thus at once received an impetus which has since not only been well maintained but gained velocity, until to-day the free school system of Illinois, among the very best in the Union, is one of the proudest and noblest monuments which she has erected along the highway of her career toward greatness, and who will dare to raise his ruthless hand to tear it down?

But now a new feature of opposition to the new school system was suddenly developed, which clouded the vision of some of its staunchest friends, and threatened its destruction. This grew out of the collection and distribution of the 2 mill tax, which acted very unequally in the different counties. Thus, from Cook was collected $30,000 more than she received back as her distributive share; Sangamon paid into the State treasury $23,132, and received back $11,027; and from all the wealthier and more populous counties, with varying amounts, the same results obtained; while others—for instance White—contributed $2,579 as her share of the 2 mill tax, and received back a distributive share of $5,409, a gain of over 100 per cent.; Pope paid in $1,055, and received $4,239, and Hardin paid $894, and received back $2,417, being more than 4 times the sums raised. While the people had been gradually brought to view as but right that one man's property might be taxed to defray the expense of teaching another's child, the idea that one county should similarly contribute to another, perhaps hundreds of miles distant, was regarded as the essence of injustice. In many parts of the State their complaints were loud and deep, and meetings were held in 1856 severely denouncing the law, and requiring of candidates for the legislature pledges to favor its modification or repeal. It was manifest that a flagrant wrong existed somewhere, and it rested, doubtless, in great part with the unequal valuations of real and personal property in the different counties, as in Sangamon lands were valued at $12.54; in Christian, $3.06; in White, $2.52, &c.; but equalization of assessments could not wholly remedy it—the spirit and cardinal principles of the free school system were that the property and wealth of the State should bear the burden of educating its youth, no matter in whose hands it was, or where situate. The framers of the law had builded better than they knew, and with this broad idea, comprehended in its fullest sense, the efforts at amendment by the legislature in 1857 proved abortive. It is the vital principle of the law to-day.

There being still a great dearth in teachers, and with the view also to attain uniformity in the modes of teaching and conducting schools, at the session of 1857 the State Normal University was established at Bloomington.

CHAPTER XLIX.

DUELS IN ILLINOIS, AND ATTEMPTS AT DUELS.

Affairs of Honor and Personal Difficulties.

The soil of Illinois has been blood-stained but comparatively a few times by the barbarous code duello. Those fierce and implacable passions which in controversy know no final argument but mortal combat have not found congenial culture on the level plains of the Prairie State. The records and details of the actual duels fought are particularly meagre, obscure and unsatisfactory. But we are tempted to give what there are. Of the first duel fought within the present limits of this State by residents, the names of the principals even are not transmitted. All that we have been able to find recorded regarding it may be found in Reynold's Pioneer History, in the words following:

"At the time the English troops came to take possession of Fort Chartres, [1765], two young officers, one French and the other English, had a misunderstanding at the Fort. This quarrel arose as did the war of the Greeks against the Trojans, on account of a lady. These officers fought with small swords early on a Sunday morning, near the fort, and in the combat one was killed. The other left the fort and descended the river. I was informed of the above duel nearly 50 years ago, by a very aged Frenchman. He informed me of the details, and said he was present and saw the combat." Reynolds wrote this about 1850, and he must have received the information when he was barely 12 years old.

The next duel of which we have any record, occurred in 1809, and may be found in the same book. It proved a bloodless affair at the time, but an angry quarrel grew out of it, resulting afterwards in the dastardly assassination of one of the principals. The duel was arranged between Rice Jones, son of John Rice Jones, a Welchman, the first and also one of the ablest lawyers Illinois has ever known, and Shadrach Bond, afterwards the first governor of the State. Jones, the elder, settled at Kaskaskia in 1790, but upon the formation of the Indiana territory, which included Illinois, removed to the capital, Vincennes, where he attained prominence. The son possessed a high order of intellect, was well educated, and located at Kaskaskia in 1806 to practice the profession of the law. He drifted into politics, and by his rare ability speedily attained to the leadership of his party. He was elected a member of the territorial legislature, which met at Vincennes. His talents, prominence and influence was distasteful to the opposite party, if it did not arouse jealousy in his own.

618

The question of public interest, and no little virulent excitement at the time, was the division of the territory by the detachment of Illinois. Young Jones and Bond became involved in a personal controversy; a challenge and acceptance followed, and the parties met for mortal combat on an island in the Mississippi, between St. Genevieve and Kaskaskia. The weapons were hair trigger pistols. After taking their positions Jones' weapon was prematurely discharged. Bond's second, named Dunlap, was disinclined to allow it as an inadvertence, claiming that according to the code it was Bond's fire next; but the latter, unwilling to take so murderous an advantage of his adversary, exclaimed that "it was an accident," and refused to fire. To conduct so noble the nature of Jones at once responded in an amicable spirit. The two principals reconciled their difficulty and quitted the field without further conflict. But the ignoble conduct of Dunlap rankled and led to a relentless quarrel between him and Jones. Hatred grew apace until finally the malignant heart of Dunlap prompted him to assassinate Jones in the public streets of Kaskaskia. The latter was standing on the sidewalk at the time, conversing with a lady, his arms resting on the railing of a gallery, when Dunlap crept up behind, unobserved, and with a pistol shot Jones dead in his tracks. Thus fell by the hand of a cowardly assassin, through a feud engendered by the most foolish miscalled code of honor, in the 28th year of his age, perhaps the most promising young man of the period. His untimely death, coupled with the manner of it, shocked the whole community, which sincerely mourned his loss. His murderer escaped to Texas and successfully evaded the just punishment due him from an earthly tribunal. In 1810 a law was adopted by the governor and judges, to suppress the practice of dueling, which constituted a fatal result in dueling murder, making the aiders, abettors or counselors principals in the crime.

Still later, in the same work, giving a sketch of the well known and dauntless pioneer Rector family, consisting of 9 sons and 4 daughters, and recounting the deeds of valor performed by some of them in the west during the war of 1812, the author records that "Thomas Rector, one of the younger brothers, had a duel with Joshua Barton, on Bloody Island, opposite St. Louis, and was as cool in that combat, as if he were shooting at a deer on the prairie. These young men espoused the quarrel of their elder brothers, and Barton fell in the conflict." No date or other particulars further than above quoted, are appended, but it occurred probably sometime during the war of 1812. Bloody Island, within the jurisdiction of Illinois, was more frequently the convenient and safe battle ground resorted to by St. Louis or Missouri belligerents for the settlement of their personal difficulties by the barbarous rules of the bloody code, than Illinoisans, and this is said to have given origin to the horrid name by which the island was known.

The next and last duel which resulted fatally between Illinois citizens and upon its soil, was fought within the limits of Belleville, in February, 1819, between Alonzo C. Stuart and William Bennett. It grew out of a drunken carousal in which besides the combatants, many citizens of St. Clair county participated. Stuart and Bennett fell out, and with the view to having some

rare sport and making a butt of Bennett, it was proposed among
the outsiders that these two, to settle their quarrel, should fight
a sham duel. Stuart was let into the secret but Bennett was kept
in the dark. Both parties readily agreed to the duel. Nathan
Fike and Jacob Short acted as seconds. The weapons selected
were rifles, which were loaded with powder only. The combatants fearlessly took their position on the field at 40 paces, and at
the proper signal, Bennett fired with good aim, and to the horror
of every one present, Stuart fell mortally wounded in the breast
and expired almost instantly. Stuart, to lighten the merriment
against his antagonist, had not fired his weapon at all, but Bennett, probably suspecting a cheat or trick, and animated by malice
was proven on the trial to have secretly slipped a ball into his
rifle. Stuart was a most estimable citizen and his untimely death
was deeply and generally regretted.

Bennett and the two seconds, Fike and Short, were arrested and
imprisoned. In the spring they were indicted for murder. Daniel
P. Cook was prosecuting attorney, and Thomas H. Benton, of St.
Louis, appeared for the defendants. A separate trial was granted
and the two seconds were acquitted. The transaction was condemned, yet as it clearly appeared that the seconds intended no
harm, the verdict was generally approved.* Next Bennett was to
be tried, but having learned that the testimony elicited in the other
cases was damaging to him, he broke jail and made his escape
into Arkansas. His whereabouts was some two years later discovered, and by means of artifice, ("which was not approved,"
says Reynolds, the judge, who sat in his trial), he was taken back
to Belleville, tried in 1821, at a special term of the court, convicted of murder, sentenced and executed.

Gov. Bond was strenuously and clamorously besieged for a
considerable time with petitions praying a pardon for the doomed
man, but without avail. He, who on the field, as we have seen,
was unwilling to take an advantage of his deadly foe, would not
yield to entreaty in this case, and William Bennett dangled at
the rope's end till he was dead, in presence of a great multitude
of spectators, who doubtless took in a great moral lesson. To
the advocates of the code, his fate must have appeared peculiarly
hard. They may have well conceived that Bennett, in ignorance
of the sham intended, by putting a ball into his rifle was but
doubly assuring his defense against an adversary who was entitled to an equal chance with him. But fatal dueling was murder
in the eye of the law, as it ever should be.

Stone Duel.—Among the motly and heterogenious collection of
men at the Galena lead mines in 1829, representing almost every
nationality of the civilized world, together with a sprinkling of
Indians, on the holy Sabbath might be witnessed, within the limited area of the town, the preaching of the gospel, dancing, all
manner of gambling and horse-racing under the hill—it was, perhaps, not astonishing to them that a duel, exceptionable and
outlandish in form, should there also be fought. This was nothing
less than a deadly set-to by the throwing of stones. The chastisement inflicted by such a combat is something fearful to con-

---

* Reynolds' Life and Times.

template—better be shot into fragments than bruised and mangled to death with stones. The name of but one of the principals in this fight is recorded—the same Thomas Higgins of whom we have already related a marvelous Indian rencontre during the war of 1812. A quarrel between him and another was arranged to be settled by this cruel wager of battle. A pile of stones carefully assorted, both as to number and size, was placed within easy reach of the stand or post of the respective combatants, who took their positions ten paces apart. The dreadful conflict was to open by the hurling of these stones at each other on a given signal from the seconds. The stones flew fast and thick for a moment, but the battle was of short duration, Higgins proving too brave, dexterous and powerful for his adversary, who fled in great precipitation to save his life.*

We now approach a period of something less than two years in the annals of of Illinois, exceedingly rife with belligerent bluster. The legislative session of 1840–1, attended by much political strife and vengeful partisan legislation, was also fruitful of threatened combats and "affairs of honor" between members and other official dignitaries. Indeed, one honorable senator, Mr. Hacker, fond of making a good point, improved the occasion to move the suspension of the dueling law for two weeks, to accommodate all the doughty and chivalrous gentlemen with full opportunity to settle their personal difficulties. The occasion of this was a personal question between two senators, Messrs. E. D. Baker and Judge Pearson. The former, smarting under the epithet of "falsehood," threatened chastisement to the latter by a "fist-fight" in the public street. Pearson declined making a "blackguard" of himself, but intimated a readiness to fight as gentlemen, according to the code of honor.†

The exciting presidential contest of 1840 resulted in the defeat of the democracy. The chagrin of the dominant party in Illinois, which had gone democratic, seems to have impelled them to proceed to any length to secure absolute control of every department of government in the State. The two questions before the legislature in 1840–1 to secure these revengeful partisan ends, were a repeal of the State bank charters, and the reorganization of the judiciary. It had been assumed by the democrats that the supreme court, which was composed of 3 whigs and 1 democrat, would decide the Galena alien case, pending for some time, against the aliens, and against the wishes and interests of that party. To prevent this, or to overrule a decision fraught with such dire results to that party, 5 democratic judges were added to the court. The measure, looked upon as a revolutionary one, was resisted step by step by the whigs; the debates incident to it took a wide range, were often bitter in personal invective and defiant contradictions, and threats of combats and affairs of honor were not unfrequent. Among others in these debates, the Hon. J. J. Hardin shone with unwonted power and brilliancy. In one of his speeches the Hon. A. R. Dodge, of Peoria, discovering, as he thought, an indignity personal to himself, took exception, and an "affair" seemed imminent. The controversy was referred to "friends," the

*Reynolds' Life and Times.
†See Ill. State Register, Feb. 12, 1841

speaker Hon. W. D. Lee Ewing, and Wm. A. Richardson acting
for Dodge, and J. J. Brown and E. B. Webb for Hardin. These
respective, and we will add, sensible and judicious "friends," reported as follows:

"In the matter of controversy and misunderstanding existing between
the Hon. J. J. Hardin and the Hon. A R. Dodge, the undersigned (the
respective friends of the parties,) believe that no cause of quarrel now
exists; the Hon. J. J. Hardin disavows the imputation of falsehood as
applied to the Hon. A. R. Dodge personally—but was and should be understood as denying the charge that the whig party was opposed to extending the right of suffrage to unnaturalized foreigners; and to the
charge in general terms he applied the epithets "falsehood and calumny,"
and not to Mr. Dodge; the undersigned, on this statement of the case
and the facts, pronounce the difficulty honorably and amicably arranged
and settled, and should be so received by those gentlemen.
Hereunto we set our hands."

Another "affair" growing out of the same partisan measure,
which gained considerable notoriety at the time, and which went
a step farther, was that of the Hon. Theophilus W. Smith, one of
the supreme judges, and the Hon. John A. McClernand, then a
young member of the house. McClernand, as we have seen, had
some two years prior received the appointment of secretary of
State from Gov. Carlin, but the old incumbent, A. P. Field, a whig,
refused to yield up the office to him, in which the supreme court
had sustained him. Much partisan feeling had been stirred up
against the court in connection with this case. McClernand now
took a leading and very active part in the passage of the act
which returned the old supreme judges to the drudgery of circuit
duty. He made an acrimonious speech against the whig members
of the court, charging that a majority of that tribunal had opinions
prepared at one time to decide the alien case adversely to that
class, and that but recently the whig judges, with the view to influence legislation upon the judiciary bill, had evaded the constitutional question in the case, and decided it upon an unimportant
point. He had this information, it seems, from S. A. Douglas,
but held himself personally responsible also for the assertion.
Judge Smith (democrat,) had given currency to these reports
against his associates, but now, at the request of J. J. Hardin, he
joined them in a published card denying that such ever was the
fact. A number of gentlemen in their cards sustained McClernand
that Smith had given out such reports. The issue of fact being
thus narrowed down against this functionary of the supreme
bench, and placed thus in no very enviable position before the
public and his associates, he was stung to the sending of a note to
McClernand by the hands of his "friend," Dr. Merriman (said to
have been an old rover of the high seas, and who, we shall see,
was mixed up in nearly all the "affairs" of that period,) penned
in such discreet language that it might be construed into a challenge or not; but the impetuous McClernand promptly accepted it
as a challenge, holding his second responsible if his principal should
attempt a different interpretation, and, without further parley, as
the challenged party, named the place of meeting, which was to be
in Missouri; the time, early; the weapons, rifles; and distance, 40
paces.* This meant business, as the phrase now goes. We have

_____

* The Ill. State Journal of Friday, March 5th, 1851, in evident allusion to this case,
gives the distance at 60 yards

been unable to obtain a view of the correspondence between the belligerents, which was not published, but learn from reliable authority, that with this serious aspect of the case, Josiah Lamborn, the attorney general of the State, lodged a complaint before a justice of the peace at Springfield, whereupon a warrant issued and the pugnacious gentleman of the judicial ermine was arrested and placed under bonds to keep the peace. The "affair" being thus interrupted, Judge Smith took his departure for Chicago to enter upon the duties of his circuit. This unexpected termination of the "affair" afforded no little merriment to the old-time wags and jokers about the capital.

Shields and Lincoln.—In the summer of 1842, at the worst period of the hard times, when both the State bank with its branches and the Shawneetown bank had finally collapsed with a circulation of $4,500,000, about the only circulating medium the people had; the notes hardly worth 50 cents on the dollar, gold and silver very scarce, business prostrated and the people dejected, Governor Carlin, Auditor Shields and Treasurer Carpenter, as "officers of State," issued their proclamation, notifying the various tax collectors that the revenue would have to be paid into the treasury in specie or at specie rates, that the State bank notes would not be taken at their face value, and that they would be held responsible for any deficit between their current value and specie. Whereupon the collectors demanded gold and silver or its equivalent from the people in payment of their taxes. This was a great hardship at the time. An act of 1836 had authorized the collection of taxes in State bank paper, giving discretion, however, to the governor, auditor and treasurer, to suspend this provision of the law and demand payment in specie. The notes of the Shawneetown bank were not covered by the law. But by another act of 1839, it was declared generally and without reservation, that the paper of both the State banks and Shawneetown bank should be received in payment of taxes—the act of 1836 not being in terms repealed. These State officers, however, took the view that the law of 1836 was still in force, and they deemed it their duty to protect the interests of the State by demanding the revenue in specie or its equivalent. They held that the law of 1839, allowing payment of taxes in bank paper meant and intended that that paper should be received only at its actual value on a specie standard. This action of the State officials provoked much feeling and opposition throughout the State. Indignation meetings were held by the people, irrespective of party, for it concerned all alike, the action denounced and resistance to its enforcement threatened. It was charged that these officials aimed only at securing their fees and salaries in specie from a distressed people. The democratic press, to a certain extent, like the whig, characterized it as an unwarrantable assumption of authority. The pressure became so great that in a short time a supplemental proclamation was issued suspending the collection of the taxes of 1842 until the meeting of the legislature. Whatever may have been their power to enforce the collection of taxes in specie, the suspending of the collection altogether was certainly beyond their province.

Mr. Lincoln, in an article published in the *Sangamo Journal*, of September 2d, 1842, dated "Lost Township, Aug. 27," and signed "Rebecca," attacked this action of the "officers of State" pretty roughly, though done in a jesting style. The form of a dialogue is adopted, representing a democratic neighbor of "Aunt Becca's," who has "tugged" hard getting out his wheat to raise bank paper enough to pay his taxes and a small school debt which he owes, and just after he gets his money, in looking over the *State Register*, he is confronted with the proclamation forbidding tax collectors and school commissioners to receive bank paper, whereupon he indulges in some intemperate language against these officials in general, denouncing them as a hypocritical set who disgrace their places, which ought to be filled with men who will do more work for less pay and take fewer airs while doing it. Auditor Shields is especially assailed. He alone had signed the supplemental proclamation suspending the collection of the revenue for the current year. He is called a liar and a fool—dull as a "cake of tallow"—for presuming to make an order so illegal. But that was not all. Shields was a bachelor, and his appearance at a fair in the city is caricatured, his demeanor criticised, and he is named a "conceited dunce." The article is somewhat long, cutting and humorous, but abounds in such indelicate allusions generally as to render it unfit for insertion in this work. The fanciful idea, as represented by some of the since great man's biographers, that it was a poetical effusion of a lady, and that when the author was demanded Mr. Lincoln in a spirit of gallantry gave his name, may be dismissed as a delusion.

The mercurial blood of the Milesian gentleman thus assailed, was sent to the top of the tube. He demanded of the editor, Simeon Francis, the name of the author, and that of Mr. Lincoln was given to him. Having a pre-arranged trip to make to Quincy on public business, on his return, in company with Gen. Whiteside as his "friend," he pursued Mr. Lincoln to Tremont in Tazewell county, where the latter was attending court, and immediately sent him a note, stating that his name had been given him by the editor as the author of the Rebecca paper "and requiring a full, positive, and absolute retraction of all offensive allusions" made to him in relation to his "private character and standing as a man, or an apology for the insults conveyed." In the meantime Dr. Merriman and William Butler of Springfield, having learned the errand of Shields to Tremont, had started a few hours later, and by riding all night had preceded Shields and Whiteside in their arrival there. They informed Mr. Lincoln what he might expect. In the evening of the same day, September 17, Mr. Lincoln answered Shield's note, refusing to offer any explanation on the grounds that Shields' note assumed the fact of his (Lincoln's) authorship of the article in the *Journal*, not pointing out what the offensive part was, and accompanying the same with menaces as to consequences. Mr. Shields on the same day, addressed him another note, disavowing all intention to menace; inquired if he was the author of the article in question and if so, asked a retraction of the offensive matter relating to his private character. Still technical, Mr. Lincoln returned this note with the verbal statement "that there could be no further negotiation until the first note was withdrawn." Mr. Shields now sent a note designating Gen. Whitside as his friend, to which Mr. Lincoln instantly replied by naming Dr. Merriman as his friend. This was on Monday morning the 19th of September.

These two "friends" now secretly pledged their honor to each other to agree upon some amicable terms and compel their principals to accept them; and to procrastinate the matter adjourned further proceedings to Springfield, whither all parties repaired except Shields, whose horse was lame—the two seconds, Whiteside and Merriam, riding in the same buggy, though part of the time Whiteside rode with Lincoln. Merriman says that the "valorous general" beguiled the tedium of the journey by recounting his exploits in many a well fought battle, dangers by flood and field, doubtless with a view to produce a salutory effect on his nerves and impress him with a proper notion of his fire-eating propensities. They arrived at Springfield late Monday night, and Mr. Lincoln to prevent arrest, left early on Tuesday morning for Jacksonville, in company with Mr. Butler, leaving the following instructions as a guide to Dr. Merriman:

" In case Whitesides shall signify a wish to adjust this affair without further difficulty, let him know that if the present papers be withdrawn and a note from Mr. Shields, asking to know if I am the author of the articles of which he complains, and asking that I shall make him gentlemanly satisfaction, if I am the author, and this without menace or dictation as to what that satisfaction shall be, a pledge is made that the following answer shall be given:

" I did write the " Lost Township" letter which appeared in the *Journal* of the 2d inst., but had no participation, in any form, in any other article alluding to you. I wrote that wholly for political effect. I had no intention of injuring your personal or private character or standing as a man or gentleman; and I did not then think, and do not now think, that that article could produce or has produced that effect against you; and had I anticipated such an effect would have forborne to write it. And I will add that your conduct towards me, so far as I know, had always been gentlemanly; and that I had no personal pique against you, and no cause for any."

" If this should be done, I leave it with you to manage what shall and what shall not be published. If nothing like this is done, the preliminaries of the fight are to be:

1st. *Weapons*—Cavalry broad swords of the largest size, precisely equal in all respects and such as are now used by the cavalry company at Jacksonville.

2d. *Position*—A plank ten feet long, and from 9 to 12 inches broad, to be firmly fixed on edge, on the ground, as the line between us which neither is to pass his foot over on forfeit of his life. Next a line drawn on the ground on either side of said plank, and parallel with it, each at the distance of the whole length of the sword and 3 feet additional from the plank; and the passing of his own such line by either party during the fight, shall be deemed a surrender of the contest.

3d. *Time*—On Thursday evening at 5 o'clock, if you can get it so; but in no case to be at a greater distance of time than Friday evening at 5 o'clock.

4th. *Place*—Within 3 miles of Alton, on the opposite side of the river, the particular spot to be agreed on by you.

"Any preliminary details coming within the above rules, you are at liberty to make at your discretion, but you are in no case to swerve from these rules or pass beyond their limits."

The position secondly prescribed for the combatants on the field looks a good deal like the cropping out of one of Lincoln's irrepressible jokes; as if both were placed out of harm's way, and that they might beat the air with their trenchant blades forever

40

and not come within damaging reach of each other. But it must be remembered that Shields' adversary was wonderfully provided with reaching powers.

These instructions to Dr. Merriman, together with the terms of the hostile meeting, were read by him to Gen. Whiteside, who, in the absence of his principal, declined agreeing upon terms of settlement until they should meet in Missouri. Besides, Shields and Whiteside both held State offices, the latter being fund commissioner, and to have accepted the challenge would have interfered with their oaths of office and the laws of the State. All parties now left for the field of combat, Mr. Lincoln (who had gone before,) and his party via Jacksonville, where they were joined by Doctor Bledsoe, and where they procured the weapons; and Shields, whom Whiteside went to meet, via Hillsboro, where they were joined by Gen. Ewing, and at Alton, which they reached in advance of the other party, they were further joined by Dr. Hope.

Both parties shortly after, being Thursday, crossed the river to Missouri. In the meantime Gen. Hardin and Dr. English had also arrived, who now, as the mutual friends of both parties, presented the following proposition:

"ALTON, SEPT. 22, 1842.

"_Messrs. Whiteside and Merriman:_ As the mutual personal friends of Messrs. Shields and Lincoln, but without authority from either, we earnestly desire a reconciliation of the misunderstanding which exists between them. Such difficulties should always be arranged amicably, if it is possible to do so, with honor to both parties. Believing ourselves that such arrangement can possibly be effected, we respectfully but earnestly submit the following proposition for your consideration: Let the whole difficulty be submitted to four or more gentlemen, to be selected by yourselves, who shall consider the affair, and report thereupon for your consideration.   JOHN J. HARDIN,
                                                                                  R. W. ENGLISH."

This proposition was submitted to the respective principals, who both signified a disposition to accommodate the affair, and it was accepted with slight modification—Mr. Shields declining to settle the matter through any other than the friends he had already selected. The following correspondence then took place, which ended this most ridiculous controversy:

"MISSOURI, SEPT. 22, 1842.

"_Gentlemen:_—All papers in relation to the matter in controversy between Mr. Shields and Mr. Lincoln, having been withdrawn by the friends of the parties concerned, the friends of Mr. Shields ask the friends of Mr. Lincoln to explain all offensive matter in the articles which appeared in the _Sangamo Journal_ of the 2d, 9th and 16th of September, over the signature of Rebecca, and headed 'Lost Township.'

It is due to Gen. Hardin and Mr. English to state that their interference was of the most courteous and gentlemanly character.   JOHN D. WHITESIDE,
                                                                                  WM. LEE D. EWING,
                                                                                  T. M. HOPE."

'MISSOURI, SEPT. 22, 1842

"_Gentlemen:_ All papers in relation to the matter in controversy between Mr. Lincoln and Mr. Shields having been withdrawn by the friends of the parties concerned, we, the undersigned, friends of Mr. Lincoln, in accordance with your request, that an explanation of Mr. Lincoln's publication in relation to Mr. Shields in the _Sangamo Journal_ of the 2d, 9th and 16th of September, be made, take pleasure in saying that although Mr. Lincoln was the writer of the article signed Rebecca in the _Journal_ of the 2d, and that only, yet he had no intention of injuring the personal or private character or standing of Mr. Shields as a gentleman or a man, and that Mr. Lincoln did not think, nor does he now think, that said article could produce such an effect, and had Mr. Lincoln anticipated such an effect he would have forborne to write it; we will further state that said article was written solely for political effect, and not to gratify any personal pique against Mr. Shields, for he had none, and knew of no cause for any.

It is due to Gen. Hardin and Mr. English to say that their interference was of the most courteous and gentlemanly character.

E. H. MERRIMAN,
A. T. BLEDSOE,
WM. BUTLER.*

Shields and Butler.—Out of the Shields and Butler *fiasco* grew directly another affair of honor, this time between Gen. Shields and Mr. Wm. Butler. The latter gentleman had been one of Mr. Lincoln's seconds, and says that he was for the fray. Disappointed in this, immediately after the bloodless termination of that affair, he wrote a not very complimentary account of the conduct of the belligerents, from Alton, to the *Sangamo Journal* (which the writer has been unable to find after careful search,) in which he thinks he bore fully as severely upon his principal as his adversary. The latter, however, who again evinced that the blood of Donnybrook coursed in his veins, on Butler's arrival home from St. Louis at once addressed him a curt, menacing note, by the hands of his former friend, Gen. Whiteside, which was promptly accepted as a challenge, and the inevitable Dr. Merriman designated as his friend, through whom the preliminaries were, without further circumlocution, submitted to Gen. Whiteside about 9 p. m. on the same day, October 3d, 1842. These were:

Time—Sunrise on the following morning.

Place—Col. Robert Allen's farm—(about 1 mile north of the State House).

Weapons—Rifles.

Distance—100 yards.

The parties to stand with their right sides toward each other—the rifles to be held in both hands horizontally and cocked, arms extended downwards. Neither party to move his person or his rifle, after being placed, before the word fire. The signal to be: "Are you ready?—fire!—one—two—three!" about a second of time intervening between each word. Neither party to fire before the word fire, nor after the word three. The word to be given by the friend of the challenged party. The principals to be attended by one friend each, who were to be placed midway between the principals, 30 yards back from a straight line between them, to the rear of each.†

These terms were indignantly refused by Mr. Shields' friend, claiming that he had waited all day for the answer which now came at 9 p. m. while his principal was attending a social party. He, as a State officer, had also uniformly refused to violate the laws of the State by dueling within its limits to which he would not subject his principal, also a State officer. The terms were satisfactory with the exception of the place, which he further claimed the challenged party had no exclusive right to dictate, and that the time should be a matter of agreement. The language used was curt and abrupt. It seems that the terms were further unfair in the position assigned to the combatants on the field, with their right sides towards each other, in that it would give Mr. Butler the advantage, he being left-handed, as was alleged. Gen. Whiteside, late on the night of the 3d sought Dr. Merriman at his lodg-

* Both Gen. Whiteside and Dr. Merriman published cards in the *Sangamo Journal*, the former in that of Oct. 7, 1842, and the latter on the 14th of the same month, detailing, with some variance, all the circumstances of this affair, from both of which we have gathered this account.

† See Sangamo Journal, Oct. 7, 1842.

ings, to hand in his objection, but did not find him. No meeting took place on the morning of the 4th. During the day, however, owing to a rupture between the seconds, Mr. Shields addressed another note to Mr. Butler, explaining the status of his second, cheerfully accepting the preliminaries himself, and offering to go out to a lonely place on the prairie to fight where there would be no danger of interruption; or, if that did not suit, he would meet him on his own conditions when and where he pleased. This note was declined by Mr. Butler, claiming that the affair was closed, and this was the end of it.

Whiteside and Merriman—And now the doughty seconds wound up this series of affairs by one of their own; which grew out of the next preceding one. We have already said that Whiteside's refusal of Butler's terms was couched in curt and abrupt language, and that the place of combat could not be dictated to him, for it was as much his right as Merriman's, who, if he was a gentleman would recognize and concede it. To this the latter re-replied, October 4, 8 a. m : "That the arrogant, dictatorial, rude, and ungentlemanly character" of this note precluded the possibility of his communicating farther on the subject to which it alluded, which was sent by the hands of Capt. Lincoln, who now served his former second in the same capacity of "friend." Whiteside then wrote to Merriman: "I have to request that you will meet me at the Planters' House, in the city of St. Louis, on next Friday, where you will hear from me further." Merriman now wrote: "I wish to know if you intend that note as a challenge; if so, my FRIEND will wait upon you with the conditions of our meeting." At 4 p. m. Whiteside replied: "You shall have a note of the character you allude to when we meet at the Planters' House, on Friday next, at St. Louis." Merriman rejoined, denying Whiteside's right to name the time and place for the adjustment of their difficulty, but proffered to meet him on that day at Louisiana, Mo. When this last note was presented to Gen. Whiteside, he replied verbally: "Lincoln, I cannot accept anything from him now. I have business at St. Louis, and it is as near as Louisiana." *On the 5th of October, Gen. Whiteside addressed another note to Dr. Merriman, which was delivered by Gen. Shields, offering to accept the proposition to meet at Louisiana, Mo., but the doctor, deeming the affair closed, now declined to re-open it, and the matter was dropped.†

It seems that out of all these bellicose manifestations one engagement or one hostile pass at least might have been had. But it was better that they all terminated pacifically, as they did.

Drs. Hope and Price had a duel in Texas during the Mexican war. Dr. Hope was a well known gentleman from Alton. We have seen his name connected with the Shields-Lincoln affair as one of the seconds. The 1st and 2d Illinois volunteers, Colonels Hardin and Bissell, were encamped at San Antonio, two miles from the Alamo. Dr. Hope was surgeon to the 1st regiment. The difficulty grew out of Dr. Price's repeating a conversation having

*Sangamon Jour. Oct. 7, 1842.
†Ill. State Reg. Oct. 14, 1842.

occurred in Dr. Hope's tent. The latter, feeling himself aggrieved, flogged the former in the streets of San Antonio, whereupon Price sent him a challenge. Major Cross, of the United States army, acted as the second of Dr. Price, and Capt. Williams, of the Kentucky Life Guards, acted for Dr. Hope. The engagement was fought September 14, 1846, and Price was badly wounded in the abdomen.*

Pratt and Campbell.—The next affair of this sort was the occasion of fixing in the constitution of 1848 the stringent clause relating to dueling. During the sitting of the convention, in 1847, which framed that instrument, when the question of alien suffrage was under consideration, Mr. O. C. Pratt, from JoDaviess, a democrat, opposed foreigners enjoying the elective franchise until they were naturalized. His colleague, Thompson Campbell, also a democrat, who favored great leniency in this respect to aliens, attacked and taunted him with having obtained the votes of foreigners for his position (to which he was elected by only 9 majority) on pledges to them that he would require no more than a year's residence and a declaration of intention, citing an occasion where some 60 or 70 foreigners were at work on some public works. Pratt denied this, attributing his colleague's mistake to the presence there of a barrel of beer and a keg of whisky. Campbell denounced the insinuation as unqualifiedly false, and that if he (Pratt) was a man he would notice it, and settle it personally. On the same day, Wednesday, Pratt sent him a note requesting his presence at the Planters' House, St. Louis. Campbell answered that he would be there on Monday following, but repaired thither immediately, putting up at the Planters' Hotel. His "friend" in St. Louis was Col. Ferd. Kennett. Late on Saturday night Pratt also arrived, with his "friend," taking lodgings at the Monroe House. But the business of the belligerents, "on bloody deeds intent," who thus sought a foreign jurisdiction to arrange their preliminaries and settle their difficulty by the duello, had leaked out; indeed it was well known, and one Blennerhassett, an alderman, made affidavit to the fact, and late on Saturday night both parties were arrested and placed under heavy bonds to keep the peace. This plan of giving an "affair" notoriety ought to be effective in these days of telegraph and newspaper enterprise to gain a name for bravery, and at the same time by judicious arrests run no danger of sustaining personal injury. It is a wonder that it is not more improved. These gentlemen new returned and resumed their seats in the convention.

By the old law of this State the penalty for dueling, when the issue was fatal, was death, the same as in case of murder, but for these "affairs" it was disability from holding office of honor, trust or emolument, and small fines after conviction. The law was without restraint; there never had been a conviction for this lesser offense, because parties always evaded the law by going beyond the jurisdiction of the State to carry out their purposes. The facts and circumstances of the Pratt-Campbell affair, as well as the repeated evasions of the law, well known to the members of the convention, stimulated them now to effectually circumvent and

*See Ill. State Reg. Oct. 16, 1846.

break up the practice, more common among officials and political
aspirants, as will have been noticed, than others. Hence they
devised and framed an oath of office, and incorporated it in the
constitution, so broad in its terms of disfranchisement and the
structure of its language as to cover not only Illinois, but all the
world besides. Not perhaps that Illinois could punish the per-
jurer, who, having committed an offense of the kind outside its
jurisdiction, should he take this oath of office, but rather to ap-
pall the conscience of those public men who would be most likely
to yield to such murderous practices. The mischief aimed at was
the suppression of the outrageous practice of dueling, without
respect to place, circumstance or time, save only that the offense
should date since the adoption of the constitution.

The oath may be found in the constitution of 1848, article 13,
section 26. Mr. R. B. Servant, of Randolph, introduced and
moved its adoption. It passed the convention by 74 yeas to 44
nays—neither of the above combatants voting. Among the nays
appears the name of Gen. Whiteside, who, it might thence be inferred, notwithstanding the *fiasco* with which we have seen his
name connected, still believed in the code of honor.

Harris and Henry.—The Mexican war, which proved such a God-
send to democratic politicians that a noted and witty whig, whose
party was out in the cold, shortly after its close announced himself in favor of the next war, was also fruitful of personal difficulties. During the election campaign of 1848, Dr. A. G. Henry, in
a speech at Beardstown, charged Major Thomas L. Harris, one of
the truest and noblest men of Illinois, then running for congress,
with "skulking at the battle of Cerro Gordo; that he could prove
this, and would repeat it to his face the following week." Here
was a good opportunity for an "affair." When Harris arrived at
Springfield he asked an interview with the doctor. But that gentleman answered: "I have no business with Major Harris, and
do not desire a personal interview." Harris then demanded that
he make good his Beardstown statement. The doctor now denied
having uttered exactly this language; disclaimed wanting to do
Harris knowingly an injustice, but that he could not be deterred
from saying what he believed to be true; offered to refer the matter to John Calhoun and James Barrett, of Harris' party, and at
their instance would make a public apology, adding that he would
leave town the following morning to meet his speaking appointments. Major Harris then proved by four good citizens, who published their card, that the doctor had made the statements referred to at Beardstown, and in the words given, whereupon he denounced him to the world as a liar, a scoundrel and a coward—
and that was the last of this affair.*

Davis and Bissell.—After the constitution went into operation,
no other duels or attempts at duels have been engaged in or had
an origin within the jurisdiction of Illinois, to the knowledge of
the writer;† and there were only three outside of its limits to

_____

*See Ill. State Reg. Oct. 6, 1848·
†Of course this does not mean to include the duels of parties outside the State, who
found in Illinois a safe and convenient rendezvous for the settlement of their personal difficulties. Various islands in the Upper Mississippi within the jurisdiction of
Illinois—notable, Bloody Island—have been the scenes of these barbarous frays between citizens or residents from neighboring territories and States, the latest being
between B. Gratz Brown and Gov. Reynolds, of Missouri.

which our citizens were parties.   Two of these resulted fatally,*
and the other attained national celebrity and was no little source
of pride to Illinoisans at the time; and as it was subsequently
the occasion of much political and personal censure and abuse, in
connection with the constitutional oath of office, we here insert it.

During the long and angry contest in congress over the adjustment of 1850, southern members, more than ever, indulged their
gasconade in vaunting southern chivalry, defending slavery and
portraying the beauties and advantages of disunion.   To dispar-
age northern courage and exaggerate southern valor, the then
late Mexican war was dragged in as proof and illustration.   Mr.
Seddon, of Virginia, encouraged by other southern gentlemen,
went further and attempted, in commenting on the battle of Buena
Vista, to award the entire credit of saving the fortune of the day
at a very critical period of that battle to a Mississippi regiment,
of which Jefferson Davis had been the Colonel, for the purpose
of maintaining the southern boast that there was more personal
bravery and prowess in that section than in the north.

Mr. Bissell was a new member, with a good record in that war
as the colonel of the 2d regiment of Illinois volunteers.   Shocked
at these utterances, and fired with the disgrace attempted to be
cast upon his section, he on the 31st of February, 1850, essayed a
reply to these ceaseless tirades of braggadocio, which. proved to
be one of the keenest, most incisive and brilliant speeches ever
spoken in the halls of congress, not only in vindication of his own
section, but in pricking the vain assumption of the other.   This
speech stamped Bissell at once with national distinction and fame.
The chivalry were touched to the quick ; and failing to answer
him in debate, it was sought to crush him in another way.   The
following passage was ostensibly claimed to be the offensive portion, and the since well-known chief of the southern confederacy
was put forward to test Bissell's mettle:

"This proneness, however, [to underrate the bravery of others and
vaunt their own,] is not always harmless," exclaimed Bissell, "and I
must now refer to a subject which I would have gladly avoided. I allude to the claim put forth for a southern regiment by the gentleman
from Virginia, [Mr. Seddon,] of having met and repulsed the enemy on
the field of Buena Vista, at the critical moment when the Indiana
regiment, through an unfortunate order of their colonel, gave way.
Justice to those living, as well as those who fell on that occasion, demands of me a prompt correction of this most erroneous statement. And
I affirm distinctly, sir, and such is the fact, that at the time the 2d Indiana regiment gave way the Mississippi regiment, for whom the claim
is gratuitously set up, was not within a mile and a half of the scene of
action, nor yet had it fired a gun or pulled a trigger. I affirm further,
sir, that the troops which at that time met and resisted the enemy, and
thus, to use the gentleman's own language, 'snatched victory from the
jaws of defeat,' were the 2d Kentucky, the 2d Illinois and a portion of
the 1st Illinois regiments. It gives me no pleasure, sir, to be compelled
to allude to this subject, nor can I see the necessity or propriety of its introduction into this debate. It having been introduced, however, I
could not sit in silence and witness the infliction of such cruel injustice
upon men, living and dead, whose well-earned fame I were a monster
not to protect. The true and brave hearts of too many of them, alas,
have already mingled with the soil of a foreign country ; but their
claims upon the justice of their countrymen can never cease, nor can my
obligations to them be ever forgotten or disregarded. No, sir, the voice

---

*Both in California—Ferguson and Lippincott being the Illinoisans—the former was
killed and the latter now holds office here.

of Hardin, that voice which has so often been heard in this hall, as
mine now is, though far more eloquently, the voice of Hardin! aye, and
of McKee and the accomplished Clay—each wrapped in his bloody
shroud—their voices would reproach me from the grave had I failed in
this act of justice to them, and the others who fought and fell by my
side.

"You will suspect me, Mr. Chairman, of having warm feelings on this
subject. Sir, I have; and have given them utterance as a matter of
duty. In all this, however, I by no means detract from the gallant
conduct of the Mississippi regiment. At other times and places on that
bloody field they did all that their warmest admirers could desire. But,
let me ask again, why was this subject introduced into this debate?
Why does the gentleman say 'troops of the north' gave way, when he
means only a single regiment?* Why is all this but for the purpose of
disparaging the north for the benefit of the south? Why, but for the
purpose of furnishing material for that ceaseless, never-ending theme
of 'southern chivalry?'"

As soon as it transpired that Davis, upon this slender pretext,
and as if he could vary a historical fact by a duel, had challenged
Bissell, all Washington was on the *qui vive*. The query ran from
mouth to mouth, "will he accept—will he stand fire?" Those who
knew the man were emphatic in their answers that he would. It is
said that Daniel Webster came over to the hall of the house for
an introduction to this northern man who proposed to meet the
southron in his favorite method of settling a dispute, saying, "I
wish to look him in the eye." Bissell was called and the two
grasped hands heartily. As Webster withdrew with an elastic
step and a kindling eye, he observed to a high dignitarry of the
government who understood the object of his visit, "He will do,
the south has mistaken its man," which was the fact. Bissell
promptly accepted the challenge. He left the preliminaries to his
friends, except weapons and distance, these he determined upon
himself, selecting the common army musket, to be loaded with a
ball and three buck-shot; the combatants to be stationed at 40
paces, with liberty to advance to 10. This evinced a cool and determined purpose to fight to the death, and the fire-eaters stood
amazed. Davis had designated S. W. Inge as his friend, and Bissell named Major Cross, of the U. S. army. The meeting was to
take place on the following day, Feb. 28th, the rendezvous being
understood.

But at a late hour in the evening another effort at reconciliation
was made by the mutual friends who had been of counsel in the
affair, Judge Dawson, of Georgia, and Col. W. A. Richardson, of
Illinois. After further conference it was agreed that the challenge,
and all correspondence therewith connected, should be treated as
withdrawn, and that Col. Bissell add to his first letter, to be inserted after the word regiment in the last paragraph, "but I am willing to award to them the credit due to their gallant and distinguished services in that battle." The reconciliation thus effected
was satisfactory to the parties immediately concerned, and a source
of gratification to their friends.

In the meantime it was said that President Taylor, the father-in-
law of Col. Davis, having been apprised of the arrangements for
the hostile meeting, accompanied by Col. Bliss, his private secretary, had instituted legal proceeding to check the intended hostile

*The 2d Indiana. Col. Bowles.

event, but prior to this interference, which was after midnight, the foregoing amicable understanding had already been arrived at.

We subjoin the memorandum and correspondence:

"[MEMORANDA No. 3.]

"Met Gen. Shields and Major Cross at 8 o'clock p. m., to arrange terms of combat. Before entering upon business Judge Dawson, of Georgia, and Major Richardson, of Illinois, entered, and proposed submitting to us a proposition which they hoped would obviate a meeting. We consented on both sides to hear it, and the following proposition was then submitted: That all correspondence be withdrawn subsequent to Col. Davis' first letter, and that Col. Bissell add to his first letter a statement (to come in after the word regiment, at the foot of the first page,) as follows, to-wit: ' But I am willing to award them the credit due to their gallant and distinguished services in that battle.' This being in substance the same proposition offered by me (embraced in memorandum No. 1), of course I expressed my willingness to accept it. After consulting, Gen. Shields and Major Cross expressed their willingness to make the addendum, which was accordingly done. By mutual consnet, all correspondence subsequent to Col. Bissell's amended letter was withdrawn, and thus the difficulty was adjusted.

S. W. INGE."

"Washington, D. C., Feb. 27, 1850."

The matter being adjusted on this basis, the following appeared in the *Union*, of Feb. 28, 1850:

"WASHINGTON, Feb. 24, 1850.

"*Gentlemen:* In order to remove any erroneous impression which may have been made o the public mind, by the surmises of letter writers, in relation to a correspondence which has passed between Col. Davis and Col. Bissell, we take the liberty of requesting you to publish the following correspondence, which will show that the matter has been most honorably adjusted to the gratification and entire satisfaction of the mutual friends.

JAMES SHIELDS,
S. W. INGE."

After which follow the first two letters subjoined, Bissell's being amended by the words inclosed in brackets in the 2d paragraph:

"WASHINGTON, D. C., Feb. 22.

"SIR: I am informed that in yesterday's debate you asserted that at the time it was claimed for the Mississippi regiment, on the field of Buena Vista, to have passed through the scattered files of the 2d Indiana regiment, and to have met the Mexican forces, who had routed and were pursuing that regiment, the Mississippi regiment was not within one mile and a half of that particular spot. Not having been able to find a "report" of your remarks, and being the proper person to answer any charge which a responsible man may make against the Mississippi regiment referred to, I take this mode of asking whether the information I have received is correct.
" Yours respectfully, JEFF. DAVIS."

"HON. Mr. BISSELL."

"WASHINGTON, Feb. 22.

"SIR: In your note of this date, you inquire whether I asserted in yesterday's debate that 'at the time it was claimed for the Mississippi regiment, on the field of Buena Vista, to have passed through the scattered files of the 2d Indiana regiment, and to have met the Mexican forces, who had routed and were pursuing that regiment, the Mississippi regiment was not within one mile and a half of the spot."

"The best answer I can give to your inquiry is to state what I did say, which was this, that "at the time the 2d Indiana regiment gave way, the Mississippi regiment was not within a mile and a half of the scene of action.' This substantially, was all I said in reference to the Mississippi regiment. I also said that the 2d Kentucky regiment, the 2d Illinois and a portion of the 1st Illinois regiments, were the troops that at that time, met and repulsed the advancing column of the enemy. In my remarks, I referred to what occurred 'at that particular spot' at that particular time.

Having answered your inquiry, I deem it due in justice alike to myself and the Mississippi regiment to say that I made no charge against that regiment, [but I am willing to award them the credit due their gallant and distinguished services in that battle]. My only object was to do justice to the character of others, living and dead, whose conduct fell under my own observation on that occasion—a duty imposed upon me, by remarks previously made in the course of the same debate.
Very respectfully, yours, &c., W. H. BISSELL."

"HON. JEFF DAVIS."*

---

* Illinois State Journal, March 2, 1850.

Lane and Douglas.—In the spring of 1856, shortly before the
National Democratic convention, there was an evident attempt
made to chafe and provoke Mr. Douglas into an affair of honor.
There were doubtless many anxious to thus embroil Illinois' great
senator at that particular juncture of his public career. The
occasion of this was the presentation to congress of the Topeka
constitution, accompanied by a forged memorial, praying admission into the Union. The genuine memorial took the high, not
to say revolutionary, ground, that congress had no power to establish governments for the territories, and that the Kansas Nebraska act was unconstitutional and void; that the people owed
no allegiance to them, and that they asserted their inherent right
to overthrow the territorial government without the consent and
in defiance of the authority of congress. Gen. J. H. Lane had
been chosen one of the senators, and naturally desiring to take his
seat as such, perceived that this document would probably not
tend to further his chances to that end. A forged copy, couched
in more obedient phraseology, was therefore presented to congress.
The trick was disclosed, however, and Mr. Douglas, as chairman
of the committee on territories, denounced it in unmeasured terms,
as was his right and duty, as a fraud and forgery, and it was rejected. The quidnuncs and Washington letter writers hostile to
Mr. Douglas, immediately snuffed a battle from afar. Rumors became rife of an expected hostile meeting according to the code of
honor, between the fierce border general and the great champion
of popular sovereignty. A determination seemed to be evinced
to intensify the affair in every way possible. The time and minutest details of the expected hostile event were carefully announced. Mr. Douglas, however, was not deceived. He divined
the purpose to be to give the matter notoriety, provoke the sending of a hostile message, get arrested, and come out of the affair
with a name for bravery. When the message of Gen. Lane, therefore, under date of April, 1856, finally came, asking "for such
an explanation of your language as will remove all imputation
upon the integrity of my action or motives in connection with
that memorial," Douglas answered, reiterating in scathing
phrase, all the facts of the case and concluded—"My reply is
that there are no facts within my knowledge which can remove
all imputation upon the integrity of your action or motives in
connection with that memorial."[*] After that there were no further rumors of a duel, but Gen. Lane, sixty days later, published
an abusive card in the Washington papers, which injured the
author more than Senator Douglas.

---

* See Ill, State Register, May 8, 1856.

1852-1856—ORGANIZATION OF THE REPUBLICAN PARTY

The Illinois Wilmot Proviso—Dissolution of the Whig Party—Repeal of the Missouri Compromise—Intense Political Feeling—Douglas denied Free Speech in Chicago—Know Nothingism—Democratic and Republican Conventions of 1856—Result of the Campaign—Lincoln's Plea for Harmony at the Chicago Banquet.

After the Missouri compromise of 1820, the question of slavery, ever an angry one, did not again attain national prominence for something like 30 years. The cause of its revival grew out of the annexation of Texas and the acquisition of territory from Mexico. The object for which the former was sought and secured—involving a war with Mexico; the avowed purpose of the most active friends of the movement, the annexation of Texas being a paramount issue of the national campaign of 1844; the influences which prevailed in securing the administration to the south ; and the overt aim and official declarations of its supporters, although foreign to the purpose of this work to either trace or analyze, all point to the extension of slavery.

Slavery was distasteful generally to the north, but particularly so to a large portion of the whig party at this time. It was more generally obnoxious in an early day of the government than at a later period, but it did not become a question of party fealty until efforts were made to extend its area ; and had slavery not become aggressive for territorial expansion, it would have taken a long time probably for the anti-slavery party to have risen above the contempt with which it was generally regarded in its early days.

In August, 1846, pending the deliberations of congress to appropriate $2,000,000 for the executive to prosecute negotiations with Mexico, looking to the acquisition of territory, Mr. Wilmot, of Penn., moved the celebrated proviso (almost in the words of the 6th article of the ordinance of 1787): "Slavery, or involuntary servitude, except as a punishment for crime, shall be forever prohibited in any territory which may be acquired from Mexico." When this amendment came up for action in the house it prevailed by a majority of 6, the only names from non-slave-holding States recorded against it being from Illinois, viz : Messrs. Douglas, Ficklin, Hoge and McClernand—a fair counterpart to the action of the Illinois senators on the admission of Missouri a quarter of a century before. Mr. Douglas, subsequently, in the senate, moved a substitute for the "proviso," prohibiting slavery in the acquired territory north of 36d. 30m., which was lost.

To show that the sentiment of the north was averse to the extension of slavery, and that the northern democracy was not yet wholly in the grasp of the slave propagandists, the legislature (largely democratic), at its regular winter session of 1849, passed joint resolutions instructing our senators and representatives in congress to use all honorable means in their power to procure the enactment of such laws for the government of the territories of the U. S., acquired by the treaty of peace with Mexico as should contain the express declaration that "there shall be neither slavery nor involuntary servitude in said territories otherwise than in punishment for crime whereof the party shall have been duly convicted." The "Wilmot proviso" had had much odium cast upon it by this time, and this modification of it by omitting the word "forever" would apply to territorial conditions only, leaving States to be formed out of it free to establish or exclude slavery—a vastly different thing! The discovery of this nice distinction, practically without a difference, it was thought by no means recognized the odious "proviso," fast becoming a party test. A portion of the Illinois democracy at the time held that congress had no constitutional right to either establish, prohibit, or in anywise interfere with slavery in the territories.

The proceedings in both houses incident to the passage of these resolutions of instruction were exciting and protracted, and the debates, in which all the leading members shared, exceedingly able and not without acrimony. They were adopted in the house by 38 to 34, all the whigs (24) and 14 democrats voting for them, while the 34 noes were all democrats; in the senate the vote stood 14 to 11, all the whigs (7) and 7 democrats voting aye, the 11 noes being all democrats.

There was some question at the time as to whether our delegates in congress would obey these instructions. Pending the compromise measures of 1850, a mass meeting in Chicago called upon Senator Douglas to obey the resolutions in their spirit as well as technical letter, or resign. Douglas had ever opposed the Wilmot proviso. Now, having written the compromise bills and reported them from the committee on territories without the proviso, an amendment was offered in the precise language of the Illinois instructions. He believed in the right of instruction, but rather than resign his seat and knowing that it would not prevail even with the vote of Illinois, he denounced it in severe terms, and then in obedience to instructions, voted for it.

At the session of the legislature in 1851, the so-called Illinois Wilmot proviso resolutions were rescinded. It was further resolved to sustain the executive of the U. S. in his determination to enforce the fugitive slave law; and as the adjustment measures passed by congress, comprising the admission of California, the establishment of territorial governments for Utah and New Mexico upon the principle of non-intervention, the settlement of the Texan boundary, amendment of the fugitive slave law of 1793, and abolition of the slave trade in the District of Columbia, were eminently calculated to remove all controversy and restore peace, quietude and confidence between the two sections of the country, they met their hearty concurrence. Our delegation in congress was further instructed to resist all attempts to disturb or unsettle them. The resolutions were adopted in the house by a vote of

49 to 11, and in the senate by 22 to 2. The democratic press congratulated the people upon the removal of this stigma from the State, which indicates the advance the question of slavery was making as a party issue. In rescinding the resolutions, both democrats and whigs largely participated, while but two years prior every whig in both houses had voted to adopt them. In the meantime the agitations incident to the great adjustment measures of 1850, which shook the Union to its centre, had taken place and been fraternally settled, and this action of the legislature was an earnest of its acceptance in good faith, and a hearty acquiescence in the national compromise of that period by both whigs and democrats.

Under this fraternal feeling the national election of 1852 resulted in favor of the democratic party by an overwhelming majority. This was hardly expected. They had cast their representative men overboard and selected Mr. Pierce, at the instance of the South (Virginia bringing him forward in convention) on account of availability, while the whigs had for their candidate a soldier chieftain of renown, who had carried our flag to victory from Canada to the City of Mexico, in the person of Gen. Scott. While many whigs had labored with patriotic zeal in the adoption of the adjustment measures of 1850, there was still a very large anti-slavery element in that party throughout the North, which gave but a sullen acquiescence to the compromise; many of the leaders spit upon the Baltimore platform. Besides, in the election of Taylor in 1848, the whigs had swerved from principle for personal considerations, and while crowned with success, forfeited the confidence of the country. With the overwhelming defeat in 1852, and the northern disaffection in its ranks, symptoms of dissolution in that grand old party were now everywhere manifest. It was pronounced in *articulo mortis* by its leaders, and its abandonment daily advocated.

In Illinois the democracy were in such ascendency in 1852 that when the whig State convention assembled to put forth a ticket, it was candidly stated by the chairman in his opening speech, that they had no hope of success, but it was highly important to make a decent show, and thus encourage and uphold their friends abroad.

After the accession of President Pierce democracy was not without its mutterings of discontent. In the election the Van Buren breach of 1848 was bridged over, it seems largely by the "cohesive power of public plunder" in prospect, but disappointment in the division of the loaves and fishes now caused a wide and deeper hostility than ever, in many portions of the country. The troubles of a country emanate from uneasy and ambitious politicians, its safety reposes in the tranquil masses.*

During a period of dead calm in general politics, the opposition for the October contest in Ohio in 1853, sought to fuse all the various party factions and unite them against the party in power, and the Republican party was in a manner forshadowed by their platform of principles: opposition to the fugitive slave law and the further extension of slavery; freedom of the public lands; equal taxation and the suppression of intemperance. This was known as the Giddings ukase. The movement met with defeat.

* Benton.

The various party elements released by the dissolution of the whig party, together with other disaffected elements, were at this period drifting hither and thither, ready and eager to catch or cling to this rock or that vine, to crystalize about any strong object which offered them a hopeful opposition to the party in power; but they were as yet unwilling to embrace unadulterated abolitionism. A large portion of the whigs were still conservative and disinclined to give in their adhesion to a new party. Blind to the plain purposes of the South, they reasoned justly that to base a party on geographical boundaries in one section of the country, rather than upon the broad constitution for the whole, was to justify the same in the opposite section, in utter disregard not only of the solemn injunction of Washington's farewell address, but revolutionary in spirit and result, if not intent, and utterly subversive of all fraternity of action in the nation at large. Reposing confidence in a continuance of the tranquility afforded by the compromise of 1850, they saw no exigency which justified the sacrifice of the peace and harmony 25,000,000 of people for the imaginary benefits to result to 3,500,000 Africans in our country.*

Some great question to convulse the tranquility of the country and awaken the slumbering sentiments of the masses to a new conflict of political opinion was therefore required; and to crystalize their first horror and astonishment into a new party was the duty of the hour. Expectants did not have to wait long. At the session of congress of 1853-4, the repeal of the Missouri Compromise, by the organization of Kansas and Nebraska into territorial governments, presented an ample field for the arts and skill of party disciplinarians, and the opportunity was well improved. The Missouri compromise, since 1820, had inhibited slavery from that vast and temperate region which faced the turbulent river of that name for 500 miles on the west, and extending southward to the line of 36 d. 30 m. All this extensive and supposed fertile territory was thus opened to the introduction of the blight and curse of slavery, otherwise so well adapted for millions of free and happy homes. The fact was regarded as an unparalleled outrage, and the excitement throughout the north was extraordinary; nor was the public mind at all appeased by the fact that it was tendered the south by northern men.

Mr. Douglas, as chairman of the committee on territories, was the author of the Kansas-Nebraska bill, yet the superogatory amendment (according to his view), which, in express terms, repealed the restriction as to slavery, was offered by Mr. Dixon, of Kentucky, a whig. Mr. Douglas promptly accepted it, feeling that he could not consistently do otherwise, for his original bill, drawn in accordance with the principles of non-intervention, recognized in the compromise measures of 1850, of which he was the real author, rendered the inhibition in effect nugatory. While such was the case with regard to the organization of Utah and New Mexico, it is also true that the Missouri restriction was not expressly repealed; nor was it ever intimated during the protracted discussions in congress, in 1850, that such would be the effect.

* Resolutions of Whig Convention.

The measure was of such absorbing interest that long before it became a law the people in public meetings gave expression to their indignation in many parts of the country. Early in February, 1854, when it was apparent that the bill would become a law, a large meeting was held in Chicago, to place the ban, as was said, upon the movements of Senator Douglas. It was comprised of citizens of all parties, but more largely participated in by former prominent supporters of the senator than others. Speeches commendatory of his course were made by R. S. Blackwell, S. S. Hays, E. C. Larned, T. L. Dickey, Mr. Mannierre, Mark Skinner, and others. Of the resolutions adopted we subjoin the following: "That the passage of the [Nebraska] bill for the repeal or molestation of the Missouri compromise, will destroy the harmony which now exists between the north and the south, create sectional disturbances and perpetual agitation of questions which have heretofore been regarded as settled by the unanimous consent of the nation." The immediate action of the legislature, then in extraordinary session, was invited to the subject, and instructions demanded for our congressional delegation to vote against the bill.*

The question speedily got into the legislature, which was largely democratic, and hardly required the Chicago invitation. Two sets of resolutions were introduced, one known as the Gillespie, strongly condemning the purposed action of congress, and the other by Mr. Omelveny, approving the Nebraska bill as but another application of the principles of adjustment of 1850. After a protracted debate, in which Messrs. Logan, Snyder and Singleton (whig) took a leading part in advocacy, the Omelveny resolution passed in the House by 30 to 22—3 whigs and 27 democrats for, and 11 democrats and 11 whigs voting against.

Mr. Douglas was the champion of the measure in congress. This drew upon him much of the public resentment. The excitement invaded the portals of the church. Twenty-six ministers of the gospel at Chicago addressed him a letter on the iniquity of repealing the Missouri compromise, to which he replied in admirable temper, objecting to the use of the Sabbath as a day for electioneering, or converting the pulpit into a place for stump speeches; "the purity of the christian church and our holy religion, and the preservation of our free institutions require that church and state be separate, that the preacher on the Sabbath day shall find his text in the Bible; shall preach Jesus Christ and him crucified; shall preach from the holy scriptures, and not attempt to control the political organizations and political parties of the day."

After the passage of the measure, the indignation vented by an enraged people did not abate, and the brunt of it continued to fall upon its gifted champion. Illinois' great senator was denounced as a traitor to his section and the cause of human liberty, from New England to California; the press of the north teemed with abuse and censure; he was burnt in effigy along his route home, and in the chief city of his own State denied the right of free speech in vindication of himself by a tumultuous mob.

Douglas Denied Free Speech in Chicago.—Four years before, when the city council passed resolutions denouncing the compro-

*See House Jour. Feb. 22, 1854.

mise measures as a violation of the laws of God and the constitution, enjoining the city police to disregard the fugitive slave law, and all good citizens to disobey it, Mr. Douglas, in a speech of great force and convincing eloquence, attacked this action with such effect as to revolutionize the sentiment of the people, and the next day the council reconsidered the resolutions by 12 to 1. His power in vindication of himself was now justly dreaded. It was sought to squelch him. Before his arrival the opposition press cried out: "We have pretty good reason for believing that Senator Douglas will arrive in the city to-day or to-morrow. If so, it will be seen that the renegade is endeavoring to sneak home quietly, and avoid the odious public demonstration which, he must know, awaits him. The people are ready for him."* And after his arrival we find the following language:

"Had Douglas dared to come to Chicago soon after the passage of the Nebraska infamy, when the sting of the wound was yet rankling fresh in the hearts of his insulted constituency, and when their blood was yet boiling at the treachery of their servant, to whom they had entrusted so much, he would have been met with a storm of indignation, and scorn, and retribution, which might have swept him from the earth, and relieved the world of the disgrace and suffering which he may yet entail upon it.   *   *   Stephen A. Douglas has no claims upon the courtesy or kindness of the people of Chicago, but he has the deepest reasons to fear their detestation, their abhorence, their rebukes, and their vengeance. He has betrayed us; he has disregraded us; he has insulted us; he has disgraced us; he has injured us· in our reputation, our fair fame, our honor, and our pecuniary interest.   *   He is now in our midst. If he is content to remain in the obscurity into which he has sunk, we shall not pull him forth.   *   *   But if, in his madness and his folly, he attempts to get up what he calls a 'vindication' of his crimes   *   it will not be our fault if he arouses a lion which he cannot tame. Let him add no more insults to those which he has already heaped upon us. There is a point beyond which the people will not endure."

We give these extracts to show the hight   to which political feeling was aroused.

Douglas, however, nothing daunted, caused an announcement to be made that he would address the people in vindication of the Kansas-Nebraska bill on Saturday evening, September the 1st. In the meantime rumors were rife on the streets regarding the efforts making to prevent his speaking, and others, that he should have a hearing at any cost; that thousands of 6-shooters would be on the ground to enforce the freedom of speech. His friends openly indulged in the taunting remarks that his opponents would be silenced and "made to crouch at his feet like whipped curs," and the like. On the afternoon preceding the speaking, one of the opposition newspapers issued an inflammatory hand-bill, asserting that an "Irish body guard" had been organized to prevent Americans participating in the meeting. Knownothingism was beginning to make a show in the land. A threatening letter was sent to Douglas from the secretary of an organization formed since his arrival, which required him to leave the city or remain silent; "if he disregarded the notice the organization was pledged, at the sacrifice of life, to prevent his being heard." Shortly after noon the flags of all the shipping were displayed at half-mast; and at a quarter past 6 p. m. the city bells began to toll, and continued to fill the

*Tribune, Aug. 1854.

air with their mournful tones for over an hour. The subject was sought to be impressed with an air of mourning.

At the appointed hour of meeting in the evening the vast space in front of the North Market Hall was thronged with men. Crowds of visitors from a distance, some as far as Detroit and St. Louis, had arrived by every train, desirous to hear him.

On the appearance of the senator on the open balcony, when, after a suitable allusion to the excitement of the occasion, he attempted to launch out into the subject of his address, he was at once greeted with hisses and groans followed by a wild tumult of shouting and outrageous noise. He folded his arms across his breast, and with a silent determination calmly surveyed the angry, seething multitude around and beneath him. Anon, upon the cessation of the din, he stretched forth his hand to resume his speech, only to have his voice drowned by a redoubled uproar, and there, fearlessly above that surging and maddened mass of men, stood the "Little Giant" for four hours, essaying time and again to speak only to be overpowered by the hooting and demoniac yells of the infuriate multitude of ten thousand. The most opprobrious epithets were hurled at him, and the most insulting words were shouted and bandied back and forth by the crowd. In vain did well known gentlemen circulate among the throng and counsel order—but there was no order. It was an intolerable outrage offered to a distinguished citizen and a man of towering intellect. No violence or collision occurred, however, as had been feared. It was said that Douglas' manner tended to add to the flame of passion already high. Inspired by a conscious feeling of excelling power, he appeared rather as a master than a servant of the people. This peculiarity has frequently been observed of him—doubtless it was hightened at this time. An opposition paper, describing the scene, says of him: "Dictator flashed from out his eye, curled upon his lip, and mingled its cold irony in every tone of his voice and every gesture of his body. At this, as in water face answereth to face, so the heart of man to man." Many of the opposition felt deeply mortified that Mr. Douglas had not been permitted to speak.

Prominent among the early mass meetings in Illinois, irrespective of party, but in which leading democrats acted a controlling part for the purpose of sinking all previous party predelictions, and pledging themselves to unite in the organization of a new party to make common cause against the extension of slavery, either by the abrogation of the Missouri compromise or the annexation of more territory for the use of slavery (the acquisition of Cuba then being in the public eye), was held at Freeport in the spring of 1854. Many other meetings of a similar character, all showing how earnestly the people took this matter to heart, were held during the summer of 1854, mostly in the northern portion of the State. We subjoin a summary of one held in Kane county August 19, 1854:

"We, the people of Kane county. in mass convention assembled, irrespective of party, in view of the long-continued encroachments of the slave power, culminating at last in the repeal of the law of freedom in all the hitherto unorganized territories of the Union, will co-operate with the friends of freedom throughout the State in an effort to bring the government back to just principles; to restore Kansas and Nebraska to the po-

41

sition of free territories ; to repeal the fugitive slave law ; to restrict slavery to the States in which it exists; to prohibit the admission of any
more slave States into the Union ; to exclude slavery from all the territories over which the general government has exclusive jurisdiction ; resist the acquirement of any new slave territory, and the repeal of the inhuman and barbarous black laws of this State."

These were the sentiments of the people to a large extent.

The Tazewell *Mirror* (whig) proposed a "State convention of
all parties and divisions of parties opposed to the repeal of the
Missouri compromise, to be held at some convenient place in the
State early enough in point of time to make arrangements for the
fall elections of 1854." But this proposition did not meet with
general favor. While the old whigs in Illinois stood almost as a
unit in opposition to the repeal of the Missouri compromise, they
were yet unwilling at that time to lose their identity to accomplish
one single object which it was supposed would prove transitory,
and it was apprehended that when the Nebraska matter was disposed of the disaffected democrats would do as they had done in
the election of Pierce in 1852, after supporting Van Buren in 1848.
The whigs argued that as their antagonism to the Nebraska swindle was well known, all that the disaffected democrats and free-
soilers had to do was to join them, and unitedly place the seal of
condemnation upon it.

In the north part of the State, however, in every congressional
district, and also that of Madison in the south, anti-Nebraska or
fusion candidates were brought out, anti-Nebraska platforms
adopted (a notable one at Bloomington), and the whigs may be
said to have been fully merged with all the opposition elements.
But in the central or capital district it was otherwise ; there, while
the whigs had a large majority, and Mr. Yates, their idol, had
taken extreme ground upon the question in congress, they yet
dared not adopt an anti-Nebraska platform for fear an abolition
plank would drive off the national whigs ; and if the whigs should
adopt a national platform the free-soilers and abolitionists would
be driven off. The whigs there inclined more to know-nothingism.

On Tuesday, October 3d, 1854, however, a small anti-Nebraska or fusion State convention, which assumed the name of
Republican, met at Springfield. It was attended by some 26 delegates, and chiefly managed by leading and ever ardent abolitionists—Mr. Lovejoy, of Bureau, Ichabod Codding (the Tom Corwin
of Illinois), of Cook, Erastus Wright, of Sangamon, &c. The convention was held at arms length by the great body of anti-Nebraska democrats and whigs, both on account of insignificance in
point of numbers and the political status of its fuglemen. It
has never been generally acknowled as the first State republican
convention. There was, besides, but one State officer to elect, the
treasurer. It concluded its labors on the 5th by nominating J.
E. M'Clun of M'Lean, for that office. The Hon. John Moore, the
old incumbent, was the democratic candidate. McClun's name
was in a few days after withdrawn, and that of James Miller, a
whig of the same county, substituted. A platform of principles
was adopted, as follows:

Whereas, The present congress by a majority of the members elected to the house,
has deliberately and wantonly re-opened the controversy respecting the extension of
slavery under our national jurisdiction, which a majority of the people had understood to be closed forever by the successive compromises of 1820 and 1850 ; and

Whereas, This congress, aided and impelled by the federal executive, has by the act currently known as the Nebraska bill, designedly subverted so much of the compact commonly termed the Missouri Compromise. as excluded slavery from that vast region of our continent stretching from the Mississippi to the Rocky Mountains, and from the parallel of 36 d. 30 m. to the northern boundary of our Union, the State of Missouri alone excepted; therefore.

Resolved, That the State of Illinois affirms and maintains the right and the duty of the general government to prohibit and preclude the extension, establishment or perpetuation of human slavery in any and every territory of the U. S. and in any territory, possession and country over which this country now has or may hereafter acquire exclusive jurisdiction.

Resolved, That the doctrine affirmed by the Nebraska bill, and gilded over by its advocates with the specious phrases of non-intervention and popular sovereignty, is really and clearly a complete surrender of all the ground hitherto asserted and maintained by the federal government, with respect to the limitation of slavery, is a plain confession of the right of the slave-holder to transfer his human chattels to any part of the public domain, and there hold them as slaves as long as inclination or interest may dictate ; that this is an attempt totally to reverse the doctrine hitherto uniformly held by statesmen and jurists, that slavery is the creature of local and State law, and to make it a national institution.

Resolved, That as freedom is national and slavery sectional and local, the absence of all law upon the subject of slavery presumes the existence of a state of freedom alone, while slavery existed only by virtue of positive law.

Resolved, That slavery can exist in a territory only by usurpation and in violation of law, and we believe that congress has the right and should prohibit its extension into such territory, so long as it remains under the guardianship of the general government.

Resolved, That we willingly concede to neighboring States all the legal rights on our soil included in the sacred compact of the constitution, but we regard the trial by jury and the writ of habeas corpus as safeguards of personal liberty so necessary that no interests of any citizen of our own State ever are or can be permitted to suspend them; and therefore no citizen of other States can fairly ask us to consent to their abrogation.

Resolved, That we recognize no antagonism of national interests between us and the citizens of southern States, nor do we entertain any feelings of hostility toward them, but we recognize them as kindred and brethren of the same national family, having a common origin, and we hope a common and glorious destiny.

Resolved, That in that fraternal spirit we call upon them to aid us in restoring the action of government to its primitive usage. under which we have so long enjoyed prosperity and peace. as the only guarantee of future harmony, and a certain, if not the only, means of perpetuation of the Union.

Resolved, That the river and harbor improvements, when necessary to the safety and convenience of commerce with foreign nations, or among the several States, are objects of national concern, and it is the duty of congress, in the exercise of its constitutional power, to provide for the same.

Resolved, That we heartily approve the course of the freemen of Connecticut. Vermont, Iowa, Ohio, Indiana, New York, Wisconsin, Michigan and Maine, postponing or disregarding their minor differences of opinion or preferences, and acting together cordially and trustingly in the same cause of freedom, of free labor and free soil, and we commend their spirit to the freemen of this and other States, exhorting each to renounce his party whenever and wherever that party proves unfaithful to human freedom

The following State central committee was designated : Judge David J. Baker of Madison, Maj. U. D. Coy of Knox, N. C. Geer of Lake, A. G. Throop, of Cook, Edwin S. Leland of La-Salle, M. L. Dunlap of Cook, Hon. A. Lincoln of Sangamon, H. M. Sheets of Stevenson, Z. Eastman, of Cook, J. F. Farnsworth of Cook, J. B. Fairbanks of Morgan, Ichabod Codding of Chicago.*

We cannot forbear to relate an episode which occurred during the sitting of the convention, which, by its brilliancy, doubtless aided to cast that body in the shade. On the 4th day of October a mass meeting, by previous appointment, was held at Springfield, at which Mr. Douglas, Gen. Singleton and Major Harris (running for congress against Yates,) were to speak. A large assemblage of people had gathered from far and near, in consequence. It was also the occasion of the first State fair at Springfield, which had drawn a large attendance from all over the State, and was a great success. It had been rumored that Judges Breese and Trumbull, anti-Nebraska democrats, both looking to Shields' place in the United States senate, would be present to answer Douglas. Mr. Lincoln, too, looking forward to that exalted position, had carefully prepared for the occasion, and the two former

* See Chicago Tribune, Oct. 7, 1854.

failing to appear at the appointed time, he divided the time and discussed the all-absorbing question of the day with Mr. Douglas. This was the first occasion that these great rival champions, who have occupied so large a share of public attention, and whose just fame has sunk deep into the patriotic heart of the nation, measured their strength in debate; and the intellectual efforts of both, carrying the assembled multitude alternately by storm, are spoken of in the highest of terms by their respective friends. The meeting, on account of the weather was held in the hall of representatives.

Mr. Lincoln spoke first, occupying two hours. He (whig) claimed to be national in his views; was opposed to disturbing slavery where it existed in the States; would sustain an efficient slave law, because of the clear grant of power in the constitution for the recovery of fugitives from labor; believed that congress had the power, and should exercise it, to prohibit slavery in the territories, citing the ordinance of 1787. He also took the broad ground derived from the declaration of independence, that the white man had no right to impose laws upon the blacks for their government without their consent; and concluded with a vigorous attack upon Douglas personally, taking as his text the celebrated apostrophe of that gentleman in 1849, that the Missouri compromise was canonized in the hearts of the American people, which no ruthless hand would dare to be reckless enough to disturb. He spoke with singular power, and being deeply moved himself, carried his audience with him step by step in wrapt attention to his eloquence, until his argument broke like a sun over their understanding. *Mr. Lincoln's speech was heartily endorsed by the convention.

Mr. Douglas, in answer, showed that the principle of legislation in the adjustment measures of 1850, supported by patriot whigs and democrats alike as a finality, was precisely the same as that embodied in the Kansas-Nebraska bill, and that the insertion of the words declaring the Missouri line inoperative and void by a southern whig, was mere surplussage, and did not change the legal effect at all; that aside from those words the act was the same in its grant of legislative powers as that of Utah and New Mexico, which had met the approbation of all parties except ultra abolitionists. The argument of his adversary, his friends claimed, was met, point by point, repelling his assaults and exposing his sophistry in a scathing and triumphant manner, as only the Little Giant, with his ready powers of debate, of all men in America could have done, carrying conviction home to the minds of his hearers until their pent up enthusiasm, knowing no bounds, burst forth in ringing applause from a thousand throats.

The closing hours of the convention were also graced by the presence of Messrs. Breese and Trumbull, who had been heralded to answer Douglas, but failed to arrive until the day after the great debate. The hour of their speaking was deferred till 4 p. m. for the convention to close its labor, when Mr. Breese made the opening speech of about an hour's duration, in which he denounced the repeal of the Missouri compromise, declaring he would have suffered his right arm to be cut off rather than have

*See Ill. Jour. Oct. 1 1854.

voted for that measure, had he been in the senate.* In the absence of Douglas, John Calhoun (of subsequent Lecompton constitution notoriety,) took the privilege to reply, saying that with regard to the personal dislike to Mr. Douglas which appeared to animate Judge Breese, he had nothing to do; and then proceeded to show that the compromise of 1850 superseded the Missouri compromise, by establishing the principle of non-intervention, to which both national whigs and democrats were committed; he taunted the speakers with not meeting Douglas at his apointment, but waiting until the enemy had departed, and then, Parthian-like, discharging their poisoned arrows after him. Calhoun had few equals in point of ability, but he lacked energy and was the slave of the cup. In the evening a very large audience assembled in respresentatives' hall to hear the very able argument of Judge Trumbull, and doubtless also to hear the self-appointed and inimitable Calhoun in reply. Trumbull made the "one question of the repeal of the Missouri compromise the text," scouting the idea that he was ever either a whig or abolitionist."† McClernand's position was the same. Indeed, those who had affiliated with the democratic party rebelled ostensibly only against Nebraskaism being made a party test or tenet, because it revived slavery agitation; and they studiously masked all appearances of, and disclaimed all sympathy with, anti-slavery sentiments in the sense of abolitionism.

The weeks' discussion at Springfield, as it was called, did not result in establishing a unity of position, or cause a full espousal of a new party organization by all the opposition; the convention was not openly subscribed to, and the whig press feared to approve or notice it; but in all the trimming of the period there was entire unanimity in thorough opposition to the repeal of the Missouri compromise.

The incipient republican party of Illinois made a vigorous and spirited campaign. Messrs. Chase and Giddings, of Ohio, lent it their aid, and spoke words of cheer and encouragement to the new and untried party in many counties of our State; the result was the development of a strength in the election astounding to the democracy, gratifying to themselves, and unexpected to all. They emerged from their first political conflict, in 1854, in a manner triumphant. The only State officer to elect was the treasurer, and the tried and incorruptible veteran incumbent, honest John Moore, it is true, was re-elected, but what was far more important in a political point of view, five out of the nine congressmen were republican, viz: Washburne, Woodward, Knox, Norton and Trumbull. Yates, personally popular, but forsaken by the pro-slavery whigs, was lost. The straight Nebraska democracy were in a minority in the general assembly, lost the organization of both houses and the election of a United States senator. Thus closed the first contest in Illinois between the incipient party of freedom, though sectional, and the old democratic party, which, to hold in its grasp a united south, was leaning too much to slavery. In Illinois the scepter of power had departed from the hands of the democracy.

---

*See Ill. Reg. Oct. 12, 1854.
†See his Letter Oct. 14, 1854, in Ill. Register.

THE KNOW-NOTHING, OR AMERICAN, PARTY.

The curious student who will take the trouble, may easily trace something of a connection from the old federal party down to the know-nothingism of half a century later. The former culminated under the elder Adams in disaster and disgrace, by the enactment of the alien and sedition laws and its final overthrow in the election of Mr. Jefferson. From that time, however, nativist organizations existed more or less in the larger cities of the Union, where their contests were mostly personal and local, meeting with varying success and failure. Later, in State and national elections they mostly co-operated with the whig party, and occasionally sought to commit it to their narrow doctrines. Upon the dissolution of the whig party this element devised a new secret organization more subtle in its operations, and by its mysterious ways enticing the young and unwary (for the human mind loves a mystery) with principles proscriptive of foreigners and intolerant of catholics.

The dark ceremonies of the order, conducted with mysterious secresy, were peculiarly impressive. In admissions to membership much solemn parade was made, sacred oaths administered, and horrid penalties required to be underwritten by candidates for violating any behest of the order; and to all inquiry the member was to "know nothing." They were bound by their oaths to deny that they belonged to the order. In this feature of the institution is found the meaning of the name "Know-nothing." It was significant of their obligations. The local organizations were denominated lodges, the meetings of which were usually held under cover of night, as if their deeds were evil, by aid of dark lanterns, in lonely and unfrequented places, in the recesses of forests, prairie hollows, deserted or untenanted buildings, unfinished attics, &c., repairing thither stealthily, though none pursued—conduct most unbecoming patriotic citizens of a free country. Lodges sent delegates to the council which nominated candidates, designated other delegates to other councils or conventions, issued orders, &c., all of which the members had solemnly sworn to implicitly support and obey, under penalty of expulsion, proscription, personal indignity if not outrage.

At first their nominations were made from the other political parties, and by their secret and united weight they would generally turn the scale as to them seemed meet. Thus emboldened, the operations of the order were extended and finally its own distinctive nominations openly announced for either local or other offices. Advancing with clandestine and rapid strides, it attained political supremacy in several States, and cast a large vote in many others. Still aspiring, in 1856, a presidential ticket was put forth. But it may be said that the Know-nothing order lost power so soon as it openly made separate and distinct nominations from its own party and quit secretly espousing the nominations of other parties. While many of the pretensions of all parties are hollow—advanced to make political capital among the masses—the cry of "Americans to rule America" by the ostracism of foreign-born citizens and proscription in religion, the two cardinal tenets of the party, was both unrepublican and unconstitutional —unrepublican, because in conflict with the Declaration of Independence, which charges the King of England with "endeavoring to prevent the population of these States; for that purpose obstructing the laws for the naturalization of foreigners, refusing to pass others encouraging their emigration hither;" unconstitutional, because that instrument says: "No religious test shall ever be required as a qualification to any office of public trust under the United States." Further, the constitution not only permits but fosters the freest discussion. With frequent appeals to the people, a tribunal than which none is higher, with the duty of the citizen to arraign and investigate the conduct of government, and scrutinize the operation of the laws, what can justify political organizations which avoid the open day meet in darkness and seclusion, which offer no ground to open combat, whose principles are a sealed book, and whose adherents, under sworn obligations, "know nothing?" It tended to segregate foreign-born and Catholic residents into communities distinct in feeling and in political and religious interests, and to excite in their breasts the animosities and hatreds of race by fastening upon them politically the brand of Helots. Every consideration of expediency no less than justice demand that this large and valuable element be in every way encouraged to amalgamate freely with the masses in order that its character and impulses may be rendered homogeneous with the vast aggregate of American society.

At first the order had no clearly defined position upon the slavery question. It sought to ignore it for a time; but that all-absorbing subject which enlisted both the sympathy and cupidity of men, and excited them as no other public question has ever done, would not down at the bidding of the secret cabal. It had to be met and it ultimately proved its ruin.

In Illinois the order was not early developed, neither did it take deep root. In combination with the whigs of central and southern, and the free soilers of northern, Illinois, it fused and entered with its strength into the contest of 1854. Perhaps its most determined effort was then made on W. B. Archer for congress in the 7th district, which, singularly, resulted in a tie vote, though Allen was said to have had *one* majority. In 1855 it presented the most disjointed issue, and made the largest effort ever essayed by it in Illinois. In the spring of that year the State council, which met in Chicago, endorsed for supreme judge of the central division the Hon. Stephen T. Logan, and for clerk S. A. Corneau, both of Sangamon; and the conclave issued its secret edict to the members of the lodges requiring obedience to its behests. In the council, it is said, the contest for the control of its organization was warmly waged between the open anti-slavery members and those who sought to dodge that obtrusive issue.

Judge Logan (probably not personally identified with the order, it being its practice to support candidates irrespective of their personal connection with them,) was known far and wide as a deep read lawyer and able jurist, and had been a whig leader for a long time.* The democratic ticket for the same offices was composed of O. C. Skinner, of Adams, for judge, and W. A. Turney, of Morgan, for clerk. Mr. Skinner was comparatively a young man for

---

* In the constitutional convention of 1847 Judge Logan had advocated a proposition requiring 15 years citizenship (20 years residence,) from a foreigner as a qualification for the office of governor.

a place on the supreme bench ; not generally known, but of good ability. Under the circumstances Logan's election was confidently expected ; but he met with overwhelming defeat, being beaten some 10,000 votes. In November before Sangamon had sent him to the legislature by 800 majority ; now he was repudiated in his own county by 1,100 majority. This was but further proof that the embittered slavery question dominated every other political tie, however oath-bound. It was a manifestation of the old whig pro-slavery sentiment which felt that Logan had been too closely allied in the legislature the winter before with the anti-slavery fusion which elected Mr. Trumbull to the U. S. senate, and which now broke its old adhesions and went en masse to the democracy, where it may be found to-day in central Illinois.

The national K. N. council, after a protracted and stormy session at Philadelphia, February, 1856, nominated Filmore and Donaldson and adopted a platform recognizing the principles of the Kansas-Nebraska act, whereupon the northern members bolted the convention and repudiated the platform. Thus the overshadowing question of slavery ruptured and overthrew know-nothingism, though the organization was kept up, both State and national, for some time after.

On the 6th of May, 1856, the know-nothing State council of Illinois convened at Springfield. The attendance exhibited a portentious falling off in numbers. The deliberations were conducted with closed doors. On the part of many of the managers who played with the order only for republican purposes, a strong effort was made to defer proceedings until after the meeting of the State republican convention on the 29th inst. But this scheme was defeated, and the following ticket was brought out: For governor, W. B. Archer, of Clark ; for lieutenant-governor, M. L. Dunlap, of Cook ; for secretary of State, A. Thornton, of Shelby ; for treasurer, James Miller, of McLean ; for auditor, Dr. Barber, of Washington ; and for superintendent of public instruction, E. Jenkins, of Fayette. Mr. Danenhower, of Cook, and Joseph Gillespie, of Madison, were appointed senatorial electors. The Philadelphia K. N. platform, totally at variance with republicanism, was adopted, and the nomination of Filmore and Donaldson ratified.

Mr. Archer, who was at Washington contesting the seat of J. C. Allen in congress, refused to accept, and subsequently participated in the national republican convention which nominated Fremont. Buckner S. Morris, of Cook, was substituted. Others refused to accept, and T. B. Hickman, of Fayette, was substituted for Mr. Dunlap; W. H. Young, of Logan, for Mr. Thornton. James Miller, of McLean, without accepting his nomination, received the same place on the ticket of the Bloomington convention a few days later. Indeed, it is said that many members of the council went direct to Bloomington, and that some received places on the republican ticket. At the November election of 1856 the K. N. ticket polled about 20,000 votes, and this was about the last effort of the order in Illinois.

Besides know-nothing, the American party was also designated "Sam," from "Uncle Sam" or U. S., the initials of United States. The personally figurative representative of slavery was often spoken of as "Sambo," denoting, in concrete, the anti-slavery party. Hence the slavery question in the K. N. council was spoken of as a set-to between "Sam" and "Sambo." At Philadelphia "Sam" carried the day, but the victory was dear as defeat. The terms of reproach applied to the party were Hindoos or Thugs, the latter an association of robbers and murderers of India. This, from the fact that its course was marked by riots and the destruction of life and property. These, it will be remembered, were fearful in the years 1854–5 in many of our large cities—Baltimore, Louisville, St. Louis, Cincinnati and other places.

It is well that such organizations, from the condition of enlightened society, must ever prove short-lived, as did this. Their tendency is to diffuse distrust, suspicion, hatred, insincerity; they disturb the order and quiet of society, poison confidence, and eventuate in mobs and crimes. This order taught men to think lightly of the principles of liberty as set forth in the Declaration of Independence, and of treason by administering oaths in violation of the constitution; it profaned religion by appeals to the weak prejudices of bigotry and fanaticism; and planted the seeds of riot, arson and blood-shed, by arraying the people of one race or nationality in deadly hostility against the other. Its name should be anathema.

During the year 1855 the republican organization gave renewed evidences of vitality and increasing strength. In Ohio, Mr. Chase was elected by a large majority. The democracy of Illinois felt impelled to look to their position, and immediately after began to prepare for the great contest, nearly a year ahead. A stirring address, dated December 1, 1855, was issued by the State general committee, of which the Hon. J. A. McClernand was chairman, directing the appointment of delegates to the State democratic convention, to be held at Springfield, May 1st, 1856. A portion of the address, which, by its terse, argumentative diction, reveals the author in the chairman of the committee, is here quoted, as portraying in a manner the intense and acrimonious party feeling of that day:

"The malcontents, the intolerants, and the religious bigots of the country, have determined upon making a desperate effort to seize the reins of government. Their only wish and hope is to excite popular passion and upon it ride into office and power. They have raised their black flag, with "Abolition" upon the one side, and "Disunion" upon the other, surmounted with the know nothing death's head and cross bones, and with hideous outcries are rallying their motley forces for the coming struggle. They pretend to be the peculiar friend of the negro, while they would make slaves of white men; they pretend to be the friends of freedom, yet murder men for exercising a plain constitutional right; they pretend to love liberty, while they denounce the constitution as a 'league with hell;' they make loud professions of policy while they persecute others for difference of religious opinions, and slander and belie all who entertain sentiments different from their own. One day they profess to be charmed by 'that rich Irish brogue and that sweet German accent,'* and the next they shoot down, burn and murder men, women and children for not being born in the same country as themselves; they illustrate their principle of 'Americans ruling America' by mobbing the elections, breaking up the ballot boxes, and destroying the votes; they urge their own will as higher than the constitution, while they deny to the people of the territories the right to have any will at all; they seek to revolutionize government by violence when its acts conflict with their own; they resist the constitutional acts of congress by armed mobs, which is treason by the law. Devoid of po-

*Gen. Scott's speech while a candidate for president.

litical principle themselves, they are for fusion with men of every shade
of political principle, and men of no political principle, so they can
'vote a vote,' and add strength to their political organization. In bold
contrast and aloof from all this confusion stands the democratic party."*

The convention met according to the time and place designated,
and nominated the Hon. W. A. Richardson, of Adams, as their
candidate for governor, on the 3d ballot; the old treasurer, John
Moore, being his strongest opponent, and leading him on the first
ballot 23 votes. The nomination of Richardson was not unexpected. It was foreshadowed by a little circumstance that took
place the preceding summer. A company of Chicago militia
made Senator Douglas a complimentary visit at his residence on
the lake shore, below the city, and during the afternoon's entertainment, in their hilarity, nominated Col. Richardson for governor. He, more than perhaps any other member from the free
States had proven himself the firm and reliable friend and supporter of the senator in the passage of the Kansas-Nebraska bill
through the lower house of congress. The fusion press, which
constantly taunted the democracy with the dictatorship of Douglas, took this circumstance of a social occasion and settled upon
Richardson as the candidate with whom the State convention had
nothing else to do but to confirm; in which they proved to be
correct. Col. R. J. Hamilton, of Cook, was nominated for lieutenant governor; W. H. Snyder, of St. Clair, for secretary of state;
honest John Moore, of McLean, the old incumbent, again for
treasurer; Samuel K. Casey, of Jefferson, for auditor, and J. H.
St. Matthew, of Tazewell, for superintendent of public schools.

In the platform the convention affirmed that congress had no
rightful authority to establish, abolish or prohibit slavery in the
States or territories; approved non-intervention and popular sovereignty, the compromise of 1850, and declared that the restoration of the Missouri restriction would be a flagrant violation of
the constitution and the principles of self-government; asserted
the national right of all men to religious freedom, declaring their
opposition to proscription of foreign born citizens; and instructed the delegates to the Cincinnati national democratic convention
to vote for Stephen A. Douglas for president.

During all this time, it may well be imagined, the leaders of
the new party, which had met with unexpected success in 1854-5,
were not idle. While they were sanguine, they were also cautious
in taking extreme or advanced anti-slavery ground. They sought
to form a coalition of all the various factions, odds and ends
outside of the democratic party opposed to the Nebraska measure, with a view rather rather to success than the espousal of radical principles. The democracy characterized this coalition as the
"speckled progeny of many conjunctions." But success, it was
well reasoned, would do more to confirm lukewarm friends than
unanswerable arguments. In this connection we quote the apt
language of the Chicago *Tribune* at the time:

"THE BLOOMINGTON CONVENTION.—Only two weeks will intervene between the present time and the day fixed for holding the anti-Nebraska
State convention at Bloomington. But, though the time is short, we
wish to correct one misapprehension that has gone abroad in relation to
the proposed gathering. It is this: that the convention is to be exclusive-

*See Ill. Reg., Dec. 4, 1855.

ly republican. Such is not the case. The republicans, so far as we are informed, consent to be represented there purely as anti-Nebraska men, and if there is anything in their political creed. which points to more radical measures than old line whigs and anti-Nebraska democrats can consent to, they have expressed their willingness. without dissent, to put such things in abeyance, and unite upon the platform upon which all northern men, who are not avowedly pro-slavery, ought to stand. As one of the organs of republican opinion, we have no hesitation in saying that we advise our friends throughout the State to such a course of action. We say further, that we know of no man who is identified with the republican party who desires or would accept a nomination from the convention, for any place whatever. The republicans of the north wish to testify their sincerity by taking the places of privates in the ranks, reserving the right to do battle wherever the fight is fiercest. They expect that the nominee for governor will possibly be a man who differs with them upon some matters connected with national politics, but they do not demand uniformity of belief—do not expect it. We know not who may be on the ticket with Col. Bissell, and we do not care what they are called, or what may be their political antecedents, so that they are men of personal and political integrity, who may be depended upon to carry out the views that they will announce. The republicans ask nothing."

On the 22d of February, 1856, an anti-Nebraska editorial convention had met at Decatur, with Paul Selby as chairman, and W. J. Usrey as secretary, which gave a free airing to its political views, both State and national, as editors are wont to do. They demanded, in a set of resolutions, the restoration of the Missouri compromise; opposed the demands of slavery for territorial expansion as inconsistent with freedom; declared there was an urgent demand for reform in the State administration; stood to the free school system; and asked all who concurred in their views of national questions to drop all party differences upon other issues and unite in a common effort to give these practical effect. For this purpose they recommended a delegate State convention to be held Thursday, May 29, at Bloomington. They designated a State central committee, one from each congressional district, to make the call, fix the ratio of representation, and take such other steps as would secure a full representation from all parts of the State. We name the committee in the order of the number of their respective districts: W. B. Ogden, Chicago; S. M. Church, Rockfort; G. A. D. Parks, Joliet; T. J. Prickett, Peoria; E. A. Dudley, Quincy; Wm. H. Herndon, Springfield; R. J. Oglesby, Decatur; Joseph Gillespie, Edwardsville; D. L. Phillips, Jonesboro. Gov. Koerner and Ira O. Wilkinson were designated for the State at large.

Accordingly the republican State convention of 1856, met at Bloomington, in Major's Hall, May 29th. Out of the 101 counties nearly one-third were unrepresented, namely: Alexander, Pulaski, Massac, Johnson, Pope, Hardin, Saline, Gallatin, Hamilton, White, Wayne, Wabash, Clay, Crawford, Jasper, Effingham, Cumberland, Clark, Douglas, Fayette, Shelby, Brown, Jefferson, Franklin, Williamson, Jackson, Perry and Monroe, nearly all in the southern part of the State. The Hon. John M. Palmer of Macoupin, was chosen permanent chairman. The following were chosen as vice presidents: J. A. Davis of Stephenson, Wm. Ross of Pike, James McKee of Cook, J. H. Bryant of Bureau, A. C. Harding of Warren, Richard Yates of Morgan, H. O. Jones of Piatt, D. L. Phillips of Union, Geo. Smith of Madison, J. H. Marshall of Coles,

J. M. Ruggles of Mason, G. A. D. Parks of Will, John Clark of Schuyler. Secretaries: H. S. Baker of Madison, C. L. Wilson of Cook, John Tilson of Adams, W. Bushnell of LaSalle, B. J. F. Hanna of Randolph.

The proceedings of the convention were harmonious. The nomination of the Hon. W. H. Bissell of St. Clair, who was simply an anti-Nebraska democrat, had been generally agreed upon before the convention met, by the press and people. The Belleville *Advocate* had first brought forward his name in connection with this office, in March preceding, which was shortly seconded by the opposition press generally and in meetings of the people. He was very popular, but his health had been impaired by paralysis of his lower extremities and there was apprehension as to his ability to make a vigorous canvass. But in a letter to Geo. T. Brown of Alton, dated May 24, he wrote that he was recovering from his infirmity, and hoped for entire restoration; that his general health and capacity for business were as good as ever; and while he might not be able to engage in an active canvass he would not decline the nomination if tendered him. After the reading of this letter to the convention, public expectation was confirmed by his unanimous nomination. Francis Hoffman of DuPage, a German, was also unanimously nominated for lieutenant governor.* O. M. Hatch of Pike, was nominated for secretary of State, the Hon. Jesse K. Dubois of Lawrence, for auditor, and James Miller of McLean, for treasurer. These last named gentlemen were charged with being members of the know-nothing order, which was doubtless the fact; that the two former had attended every State council of that order since its organization, and been delegates and prominent leaders in its late State convention held at Springfield on the 6th inst.† At the same know-nothing convention, we have seen that Mr. Miller had been honored with the nomination for the same place on the ticket at Bloomington. But to the nominating committee at the latter place he stated that he had not nor did not intend to accept the place on the know-nothing ticket. W. H. Powell of Peoria, was nominated for superintendent of public instruction. These latter names were selected by a committee of 9, one from each congressional district, appointed by the chair. They were: S. W. Lawrence, Cyrus Alden, W. W. Orme, J. D. Arnold, A. Williams, A. Lincoln, T. A. Marshall, Thos. McCluken and Ben. T. Wiley, named in the order of their respective districts. The candidates selected by them were confirmed by the convention.

The following is the platform adopted:

Resolved, That foregoing all former differences of opinion upon other questions, we pledge ourselves to unite in opposition to the present administration and to the party which upholds and supports it, and to use all honorable. and constitutional means to wrest the government from the unworthy hands which now control it and to bring it back in its administration to the principles and practices of Washington, Jefferson, and their great and good compatriots of the revolution

Resolved, That we hold, in accordance with the opinions and practices of all the great statesmen of all parties, for the first 60 years of the administration of the government,

---

* This gentleman found during the canvass that he was ineligible for that office—not having been naturalized 14 years, a qualification prescribed by the constitution, and he resigned his place on the ticket. The convention subsequently met again and substituted the name of John Wood of Adams. an old whig. B S. Edwards. at the same time, received 20 votes, Dr. Egan 17, J. M. Ruggles 10, Joseph Seiffiger 8, S. M. Church 11, and Leonard Swett, 8.

† We have it from undoubted authority that the candidate for auditor not only refused to come into the convention but cursed it for its abolitionism while he accepted the place upon its ticket.

that under the constitution congress possesses the power to prohibit slavery in the territories ; and that whilst we will maintain all constitutional rights of the south, we also hold that justice, humanity, the principles of freedom as expressed in our declaration of independence. and our national constitution and the purity and perpetuity of our government require that that power should be exerted to prevent the extension of slavery into territories heretofore free.

Resolved, That the repeal of the Missouri compromise was unwise, unjust, and injurious; an open and aggravated violation of the plighted faith of the States, and that the attempt of the present administration to force slavery into Kansas against the known wishes of the legal voters of that territory, is an arbitrary and tyrannous violation of the rights of the people to govern themselves. and that we will strive by all constitutional means to secure to Kansas and Nebraska the legal guaranty against slavery of which they were deprived at the cost of the violation of the plighted faith of the nation.

Resolved, That we are devoted to the union and will, to the last extremity, defend it against the efforts now being made by the disunionists of this administration to compass its dissolution, and that we will support the constitution of the United States in all its provisions, regarding it as the sacred bond of our union, and the only safeguard for the preservation of the rights of ourselves and our posterity.

Resolved, That we are in favor of the immediate admission of Kansas as a member of this confederacy, under the constitution adopted by the people of said territory.

Resolved, That the spirit of our institutions as well as the constitution of our country, guaranties the liberty of conscience as well as political freedom, and that we will proscribe no one, by legislation or otherwise, on account of religious opinions, or in consequence of place of birth."

Resolutions approving of the course of Senator Trumbull, and condemning that of Senator Douglas were also adopted; one by Mr. Wentwork, in favor of an economical administration of the affairs of the State; and one by O. H. Browning, that the proceedings of the convention be signed by all the officers, and published. The State central committee appointed consisted of J. C. Conkling of Sangamon, Asabel Gridley of McLean, B. C. Cook of LaSalle, and C. H. Ray and N. B. Judd of Cook.

It will be observed that the platform omits to demand the repeal of the fugitive slave law, omits to assert the right of trial by jury for the captured slave, and omits to claim the writ of *habeas corpus* in his behalf; nor is the institution of slavery denounced as the sum of all villainies. The Hon. Owen Lovejoy, an original abolitionist, who had vainly endeavored in the legislature, in 1855, to commit the new party to a declaration against the admission of more slave States into the Union and in favor of the repeal of the fugitive slave law, which, by the way, received a large vote in that body at the time, now in the convention strove to have a plank inserted in the platform which would reflect a more advanced position for the party, but was defeated. But with a keen insight into the future, he observed that while he would like to have inoculated them with the virus more thoroughly at the time, he didn't care much ; for having been exposed to the infection they would all take the disease in the natural way, and break out all over with it before the campaign was ended anyhow—which was the case.

The *personnel* of the republican ticket thus made showed that the Chicago *Tribune*, bespeaking for advanced republicanism a subordinate part—the post of honor as privates in the battle— was taken at its words, for not a pure and simple republican received a place on the ticket. It was a coalition which the republicans were content to support with the hope of future reward. They did not reckon without their host. Success, the touchstone of all human undertakings, attended them, and cemented all these various elements into one great and homogeneous party, leading to the most radical results. With success, all the halting, the timid and the doubting ones, now perhaps beholding the reward of office in the future, became immediately the most pronounced and unyielding, if not radical, partisans.

It has been supposed that the whig and know-nothing parties were wholly absorbed by the republican party. Such is only partly true. It is true in the northern part of the State, perhaps, but not in the central and southern parts. In the latter, while the democratic party contributed largely toward its ranks, it received back a greater number of whigs. The Germans, wholly democratic in Madison and St. Clair counties, went over almost in a body, but the whigs of Sangamon, Tazewell, Morgan and Adams largely joined the democracy, where they are to this day.

The repeal of the Missouri compromise was both a party blunder and mistaken statesmanship. The south, with a sectional institution in its midst, ought to have broadly appreciated the great north with its giant steps toward empire, its teeming millions, its innumerable work-shops, skilled laborers and vast industries. In the face of this, while it had practical control of the government, its policy was to excite into being the party whose principles, however they may be said in the abstract to have been national by approximating to the landmarks of the fathers, were sectional, because it opposed the spread of an institution which was itself sectional; and it became national only through the operation of a war madly precipitated by the south. The party which ostensibly sought only to restrain the sectionalism of the south, has accomplished greater and mightier deeds than the most ardent abolitionist of 25 years ago could have dreamed. And what it has done it has done so thoroughly that it can never be undone. It has abolished slavery; raised more than 5,000,000 of negroes to citizenship, and enfranchised them—all this by constitutional provisions.

W. H. Bissell was elected governor by a plurality of 4,729 votes over Col. Richardson; Morris, K. N., receiving 19,241 votes for the same office, while Buchanan's plurality over Fremont was 9,164; Filmore, K. N., receiving 37,451. The legislature was democratic. The democracy had thrown no obstacles in the way of the opposition dividing upon Filmore, but rather encouraged it; but the main reason why Buchanan carried the State and Richardson failed was owing to the former's want of identification with the repeal of the Missouri compromise, though he had accepted the Cincinnati platform and dilated upon the beauties of popular sovereignty. It was, in spite of this, believed that in his convictions and policy he would be apart from its principles, and break faith with its devoted friends—an opinion which proved prophetic within the year of his installation. The Missouri *Democrat*, while it espoused republicanism and supported Bissell, by a strange inconsistency, labored even with republicans to separate Buchanan in the public mind from the outrage of the repeal of the Missouri compromise.

We close this chapter by the concluding portion of Mr. Lincoln's speech made after the election at the republican banquet in Chicago, Dec. 17, 1856:

"All of us who did not vote for Mr. Buchanan, taken together, are a majority of 400,000. But in the late contest we were divided between Fremont and Filmore. Can we not come together for the future? Let every one who really believes, and is resolved, that free society is not, and shall not be, a failure, and who can conscientiously declare that in the past contest he has done only what he thought best—let every such an one have charity to believe that every other one can say as much. Thus let by-gones be by-gones. Let past differences as nothing be, and with steady eye on the real issue, let us re-inaugurate the good old 'central ideas' of the republic. We can do it. The human heart is with us—God is with us. We shall again be able not to declare that 'all States, as States, are equal,' nor yet that 'all citizens, as citizens, are equal,' but to renew the broader, better declaration, including both these and much more, that 'all men are created equal.'"

CHAPTER L.

1857-1861—ADMINISTRATION OF GOVERNOR BISSELL.

Life and Character of the Governor—Gross Attack upon him in the Legislature on Account of his Dueling Affair—Turbulence of Party Strife and want of Official Courtesy—Disgraceful Action in Organizing the House—Apportionment Bills of 1857-9 —The Canal Scrip Fraud—The McAllister and Stebbins Bonds.

———

Aside from the general excitement incident to our quadrennial political campaigns, that of 1856, owing to its sectional character, was more than ordinarily bitter. The contest for State and local offices in Illinois, where the new republican party had developed unexpected strength two years before, was unusually acrimonious and personal. Of the candidates for governor, Richardson canvassed the State thoroughly, but Bissell, owing to his physical ailment, was unable to do so, and made but one speech, which was to his old neighbors at Belleville. But his character throughout the campaign was the target of vindictive assaults, some of which he felt himself impelled to deny as utterly untrue. In letters addressed to the Quincy *Herald* and Springfield *Register* he took occasion to repel the charges that in 1851, as the paid attorney for the capitalists who sought the incorporation of the Illinois Central Railroad, he had been authorized to offer 10 per cent. of the gross earnings of the road for the charter, or that he had from his knowledge of public men in the legislature, labored as a lobbyist with Mr. Rantoul to obtain the reduction to 7 per cent. to the lasting detriment of the treasury of the State.

Upon Richardson was concentrated and poured out all the pent up rage of the opposition. He, it was urged, as a northern man, next to Douglas, had advocated in congress with determined zeal, persistence and effectiveness the disturbance of the Missouri compromise, and was joint author in opening the Pandora's box to precipitate the evils of slavery agitation upon the entire country, and a border war upon the ill-fated territory of Kansas, to crush out her freedom for the purpose of enlarging the area of human bondage. These impassioned appeals told with effect upon the people—Bissell was elected by a plurality of 4,729 votes over Richardson. The legislature, nearly balanced, was politically opposed to the governor elect. The senate stood, 13 democrats, 11 republicans and 1 American (K. N.); house, 37 democrats, 31 republicans and 6 Americans, besides a contested election case from Peoria, which was the occasion of a fierce partisan struggle, as we shall see.

656

William H. Bissell was born April 25, 1811, in the State of
New York, near Painted Post, Yates county. His parents were
obscure, honest, God-fearing people, who reared their children under the daily example of industry and frugality, as is the wont of
that class of eastern society. Young Bissell received a respectable but not thorough academical education. By application he
acquired a knowledge of medicine, and in his early manhood came
west and located in Monroe county, Illinois, where he engaged in
the practice of that profession. But he was not enamored of his
calling; he was swayed by a broader ambition, and the mysteries
of the healing art and its arduous duties possessed no charms for
him. In a few years he discovered his choice of a profession to
be a mistake; and when he approached the age of 30 sought to
begin anew. Dr. Bissell, no doubt unexpectedly to himself, discovered a singular facility and charm of speech, the exercise of
which acquired him ready local notoriety. It soon came to be understood that he desired to abandon his profession and take up
that of the law. During terms of court he would spend his time
at the county seat among the members of the bar, who extended
to him a ready welcome.

It was not strange that he should drift into public life. In 1840
he was elected as a democrat to the legislature from Monroe
county and made an efficient member. On his return home he
qualified himself for admission to the bar and speedily rose to
front rank as an advocate. His powers of oratory were captivating: with a pure diction, charming and inimitable gestures,
clearness of statement, and a remarkable vein of sly humor, his
efforts before a jury told with almost irresistible effect. He was
chosen by the legislature prosecuting attorney for the circuit in
which he lived, in which position he fully discharged his duty to
the State, gained the esteem of the bar, and seldom failed to convict the offender of law. In stature he was somewhat tall and
slender, and with a straight, military bearing presented a distinguished appearance. His complexion was dark, his head well
poised, though not large, his address pleasant and manner winning. He was exemplary in habits, a devoted husband, and kind
and indulgent parent. He was twice married, the first time to
Miss James, of Monroe county, by whom he had 2 children, both
daughters, now living in Belleville. She died soon after 1840.
His second wife was a daughter of Elias K. Kane, formerly
United States senator from this State. She survived him but a
short time, and died without issue.*

When war was declared with Mexico, in 1846, he enlisted and
was elected colonel of his regiment, over Hon. Don. Morrison, by
an almost unanimous vote—807 to 6. For his opportunities he
evinced a high order of military talent. On the bloody field of
Buena Vista he acquitted himself with intrepid and distinguished
ability, contributing with his regiment, the 2d Illinois, in no small
degree toward saving the wavering fortunes of our arms during
that long and fiercely contested battle.

After his return home, at the close of the war, he was elected
to congress, his opponents being the Hons. P. B. Fouke and Joseph
Gillespie. He served two terms in congress. He was an ardent
politician. During the great contest of 1850 he voted in favor of

*Letter from the Hon. Joseph Gillespie.

42

the adjustment measures, holding the following language on the doctrine of non-intervention : "It is a principle, sir, upon which I have always stood, and from which I have no idea of departing, a principle maintained and cherished by my constituents, and one which they will be slow to surrender." But in 1854, when the same principle was sought to be applied to the organization of the territories of Kansas and Nebraska, involving a repeal of the Missouri compromise, he opposed that unnecessary assault upon the domain which for 30 years had been consecrated to freedom, and upon its consummation became identified with the organization of the republican party.

On account of exposure in the army, the remote cause of a nervous form of disease gained entrance to his system, and eventually developed paraphlegia, affecting his lower extremities, which, while it left his body in comparative health, deprived him of locomotion, other than by the aid of crutches. While he was generally hopeful of ultimate recovery, this mysterious disease pursued him without once relaxing its stealthy hold to the close of his life, on the 18th of March, 1860, over 9 months before the expiration of his gubernatorial term, at the early age of 48 years. He died in the faith of the Roman Catholic church, of which he had been a member since 1854. When it is remembered that William H. Bissell, in the short period of 16 years, without early educational advantages, abandoned at the mature age of 30 years one profession by casting aside his pharmacopia, his vade mecum and armamentum chirugicum—quitting the dull and laborious routine of a country doctor, and resolutely turning his attention to the profession of the law, as affording him a wider field for his active imagination and aspiring ambition ; attained speedily at the latter eminence as an irresistible advocate ; distinguished himself as a soldier ; as an accomplished orator took front rank in the halls of the national legislature ; and as the standard bearer of a new party marching toward national freedom, was elevated to the first position of his State by the partiality of a grateful and confiding people, his life may be considered a brilliant success.* Yet, in the annals of this State, as will be seen, no public man was ever subjected to contumely so gross, abuse more harrowing, or pursued with malice more vindictive ; and that these cruelties caused him many a heart-pang, casting a shadow over his exalted position, or embittered his closing days, is not a foreign inference.

It was during his first congressional term, before he was stricken with paralysis, that his high sense of gallantry was deeply wounded by an effort on the part of the southern chivalry, through Mr. Seddon, of Virginia, to depreciate the valor of northern troops at Buena Vista, while the victory upon that field—"snatched from the jaws of defeat"—was attributed solely to southern troops, and particularly claimed for the Mississippi rifles, a regiment commanded by Jefferson Davis, the late rebel chief. The discussions in congress, growing out of the acquisition of territory, of a character to bode dissolution to the Union for a time, were attended by unusual explosions of turbulent passions. Personal insults and menaces to northern members, with a view to their intimidation, were frequent. These insults and the braggadocio of swaggering disunionists to overawe the north, which were submitted to in many

*Gov. Palmer's funeral oration, May, 1861.

instances with a meekness to cause one even now to blush with indignation, Bissell's ardent nature could not brook, and the vile slander of Seddon was repelled in a speech replete with facts, stinging rebuke and moving eloquence, which acquired for him national fame, and was a source of pride to his section and State. Such bold utterances in such accomplished oratory was more than the vaunting chivalry could bear. He was challenged by Jefferson Davis to mortal combat. Bissell had indulged in honorable debate, warm, it is true, but in terms decorous withal, and in manner courteous, yet his life was sought. It was explicable only on the ground that the challenge was addressed to the entire north. It could not change or vary the fact of history connected with the battle of Buena Vista. But when Bissell coolly accepted the challenge, without unseemly parade, evincing not only his individual intrepidity but an earnest of a deliberate intention to fight, which won him the admiration and gratitude of the country, the matter was accommodated.

But the constitution of Illinois, besides the regular oath of office prescribed the following in addition :

"I do solemnly swear that I have not fought a duel, nor sent or *accepted* a challenge to fight a duel, the probable issue of which might have been the death of either party, nor been a second to either party, nor in any manner aided or assisted in such duel, nor been knowingly the bearer of such challenge or aceptance, since the adoption of the constitution ; and that I will not be so engaged or concerned, directly or indirectly, in or about such duel during my continuance in office : so help me God."

The democracy, which had indulged confident expectations of success in the election of 1856 to the very last, when they found the scepter of power, so long wielded by them in Illinois, pass from their grasp, their chagrin and mortification knew no bounds. During the canvass their press and stump orators had not been silent on Bissell's disability on account of this affair with Jeff. Davis, and after the election, the pressure and onslaught in this direction was furious and unintermittent. The disease-smitten man was pursued with a bitterness and ghoul-like spirit painful to read, using the circumstance of accepting the challenge, erst a source of such pride to every citizen, as a means now to prostrate him. Their press teemed with comments upon the deliberate intention of so distinguished, exalted and honorable a personage as the governor of this great State committing the dark and fearful crime of perjury.

But these assaults, that they should have no deterring effect upon their object, were met by the republican press, politicians and orators, at meetings and banquets celebrating the great victory, in various parts of the State, by every known art of encouragement, legal sophistry, and assurances that the governor elect could and would without hesitation, take the oath of office prescribed by the constitution. It would not do to lose the fruits of a great victory on account of a paltry oath of office. The constitution, it was exclaimed, by the simplest rules of law could not and did not have any extra-territorial jurisdiction, wherefore he could not perpetrate an infraction of it where it did not extend— he was a *rectus in curia* in this respect. Bissell himself published a letter in the Alton *Courier*, in which he went over the whole legal grounds applicable to the question, resting upon the fact that he was beyond the legal jurisdiction of the constitution of Illinois. He furthermore regarded the objections so vehemently urged as a political persecution of himself, the result of mortification consequent upon democratic defeat, and announced his determination to take the required oath. In this he was applauded by his party, declaring that he was right, that the people looked to and relied upon him, that his incorruptible integrity was above reproach, and that he would take no step or do aught which his conscience could not fully justify.

He further, it seems, took counsel from and fortified himself with the opinions of the best legal talent of the State among his political friends. At the time of Bissell's election as governor he had been an invalid exceeding three years, his paralysis rendering him for much of the time physically helpless, and it is not in accordance with physiological law that the mind connected with such a body should maintain its wonted vigor, strength of purpose or independence of will the same as if the system was unimpaired; and though he himself wrote at the time of the meeting of the Bloomington convention that his intellect knew no abatement of its vigor and strength, " it was manifest to his friends that his active career was ended."* A man smitten with incurable disease leans upon the support of his friends, and is then more than ordinarily influenced by them. Did they not, therefore, assume a culpable responsibility in putting him forward for this place, and after election further impel a step which exposed him to the envenomed shafts of an implacable political enemy, if not fraught with serious consequences to the peace of his conscience? Democrats derisively avowed that his moral constitution was not spared by the blow which prostrated his nervous system.

In January, 1857, Governor-elect Bissell and family arrived by the Chicago and Alton railroad at the seat of government. Governor Matteson met them with his carriage at the depot, and conducted them to the elegant mansion to which they had been invited by the flattering partiality of the people of this great State. On the 13th inst., at 2 p. m., the two houses of the general assembly, which had been in session since the 5th inst., preceded by their respective officers and escorted by Capt. Hopkins' artillery and a large concourse of citizens, proceeded to the executive mansion in pursuance of a joint resolution to witness the installation of the governor-elect. The oath of office having been taken, and the ceremonies and congratulations over, the two houses returned to the hall of the house of representatives, the lobby and gallery of which were crowded. Lieutenant-Governor-elect Wood was then sworn in by Chief Justice Scates, and the inaugural message of Governor Bissell received and read to the two houses, after which the senate retired to their chamber, where Lieutenant-Governor Wood delivered a neat and appropriate address.

Governor Bissell's inaugural message was short and a very ordinary document, noticeable only in that it stepped out of the usual course in "distinguishing" the incorporators of the Illinois Central railroad company, "that our people in future may never forget to whom they are mostly indebted for the great work of that road." For the handsome grant of land that those gentlemen got from the State, more than enough to build and fully

---

* Palmer's funeral oration, May, 1871.

equip that road, one would suppose that the people did not owe them much either in debt or gratitude. But the portion of this message particularly offending to the democratic majority was a cursory view and discussion of the all absorbing slavery question as connected with Kansas. Now in this there was perhaps nothing unusual, but the out-going governor, Matteson, in his complete and admirable valedictory message, then a week old, had studiously avoided the subject of politics in any phase whatever, and had invoked harmony in council with his distinguished successor. This, then, was the fire-brand for an explosion, doubtless but too gladly received, and a most extraordinary debate, both as to character and duration, sprung up.

In the house, Mr. I. N. Arnold, upon the conclusion of the reading of the message, made a motion to have the usual number of 20,000 copies printed. This was the signal for attack. Mr. Logan (now senator in congress), moved to amend by inserting 10,000, and followed up his motion by a speech of two days duration, which in severity of language excels perhaps anything that that gentleman has ever uttered. It shocked the better sense of all considerate men not wholly devoured by partisan malignity, and must have deeply wounded the sensitive feelings of Bissell's high strung nature rendered more acute by a long entailed, enfeebling nervous disorder. To many democrats the speech was no suprise. Due preparation, participated in by some of the party leaders, had early been made. Material for evidence to cover the entire ground had been carefully collected, and an orator to execute the unfeeling task selected with skillful penetration. In August preceding, Col. Richardson had written to Jefferson Davis for a copy of the correspondence between the latter and Col. Bissel, connected with their dueling affair. In the published correspondence the challenge and its acceptance, or the memorandum of final settlement had never appeared. Davis had to write to California to Mr. Inge for it, and it had now arrived to be used to convict Bissel of perjury. Major Harris had written from Washington, stating he knew Bissell had accepted a challenge from Davis, for he had copied it. The Hon. P. B. Fouke, who was present in Springfield, furnished a written statement that Bissell in the canvass against him 1852, for congress, had urged his acceptance of this challenge in his own favor, because he was ineligible to any State office on account of the constitutional oath of office. Col. John Crain said he had heard Bissell state the same in a speech at Nashville in 1851. The Hon. W. R. Morrison wrote that Bissell during the late canvass for governor, had said in his hearing, that he did accept the challenge from Jeff Davis, &c.; all these letters are paraded in the speech of Logan, Jan. 13–14, 1857.

Thus fortified, Logan exclaimed: "If corruption enters into high places, it is my duty as a faithful public servant, to drag it from its polluted den and expose its hideous deformity to public criticism and contempt." He would "demonstrate to the world a degree of moral turpitude without parallel in the history of the State. No governor of Illinois has ever sought retirement to take the oath of office"—the oath was taken at the executive mansion, as we have seen. "We might infer from this, that a guilty and bleeding conscience had sought seclusion rather than stand erect upon this floor and pass the fiery ordeal. The secluded and unusal place at which it was taken may afford grounds for an inference as to the working of a mind goaded to desperation by a weighty conviction of moral turpitude." That the executive had said "he must commit perjury to hold the office of governor; and then hear of his taking the very oath which he said would amount to perjury; I am lost in amazement—standing before the people with falsehood upon his lips, and averring his own guilt of a reckless disregard of all that can inspire confidence in man; * * the moral sense of a million and a half of the people has been shocked by that fearful oath. Truth, sir, has been crushed to earth. The high standard of moral rectitude has been broken. The votaries of virtue and honesty have been vanquished, and one universal wail, from Chicago to Cairo, has been heard in consequence of the prostration of the executive chair by the hands of a man whose lips are quivering with falsehood. * The constitution of my beloved State lies prostrate in the dust— bleeding and mangled. * * I warn young men and old against the example set. I pray God that we may never again witness such an occasion; Virtue and Truth bereft of all their charms, while the hideous and hateful gods of vice hold dominion over the people." Such are only a few salient extracts from this long speech.†

The array of able names, both democrat and republican, as members of the house at this session, is excellent. Much party feeling had been already elicited, as we shall see, in the first efforts to organize the house, and the debates incident to this question, nominally upon the printing of the governor's message, were not only generally participated in but were protracted, exciting and exceedingly acrimonious. We cannot do more than to state that the position of the friends of the governor, in defense of him, was generally the same as has already been indicated—that the *locus delicti* was the District of Columbia; that he had offended no law of Illinois, either statutory or organic, for neither could have legal jurisdiction beyond the State; wherefore his excellency might safely and truly swear that he had not accepted a challenge to fight a duel since the adoption of the constitution. And Mr. Denio, in the debate, asserted that Davis "to this day declares to Gov Bissell, through Senator Trumbull, that he did not consider the notes exchanged between them equivalent to a challenge." But the documentary evidence shows this to be untenable.

The *locus delicti*, which the governor and his friends set up and used as a defense, was not in question. That the offense committed in the District of Columbia was defined as an offense by our statutes is true, but that it was not punishable here is equally true. It was circumstances and evasions of that character, however, that the constitutional oath sought to compass and prevent. The intent of the law may be gathered from the circumstances of its passage. To mark the popular abhorence of the duello, and to impose upon its votaries the disability of holding office in spite of their constant evasions of its punishments by going beyond the confines of the State, was the aim of its framers, and it has failed of efficacy in only two instances. The offense now and here was not in accepting a challenge in Washington, but in swearing at this time, in Illinois, that he had not. The reasoning in the one

* See Ill. State Register, Feb. 1857.

case does not appear to fit the other. Was Bissell then only a *de-facto* governor?

The courtesy of printing the usual number of copies of the message was denied. Attacks on the private character of his excellency continued throughout the session. No annoyance or embarrassment that could be inflicted was spared him. In the passage of the bill establishing the northern or Joliet penitentiary, recommended in his message, his customary privileges as a co-ordinate branch of the law-making power were encroached upon, and the appointment of the commissioners taken from him. The dignity of official position, and the courtesies and amenities incident thereto, were, to a great extent, sunk out of view.

In the senate, which contained a democratic majority of one, no discourtesy was shown to the governor by a refusal to order the printing of the usual number of copies of his message. In that chamber, besides, general harmony and good feeling prevailed throughout the session, and business moved along with acceptable dispatch. Lieutenant-Governor Wood, a gentleman of fine, commanding personal appearance, presided in an impartial manner, and his conciliatory deportment, meeting out to all the senators the same courtesy, was received and met in return by a like mark of respect and cordiality.

The house, notwithstanding its many able and talented members, was the theatre of much turbulence and partisan strife throughout the session. It was said to have opened as a mob and closed in a rout. In political complexion it stood, democrats 38, republicans 31, and Americans 6. There were, however, two contestants to this democratic majority, and in the Peoria case of Eastman, republican, against Shellabarger, democrat, it would seem that Eastman was justly entitled to the seat. A few votes cast for O. L. instead of C. M. Eastman had been thrown out, and the certificate awarded to Shellabarger, whereas had they been counted the former would have had the majority.

In the first effort to effect a temporary organization of the house was enacted one of those unseemly squabbles, which, while they are not unfrequent in this free country, are nevertheless a disgrace to any deliberative body. The republicans were primarily in fault. By uniting the 6 Americans with their 31 members they had planned to secure the organization of the house in accordance with the usages of the lower house of congress and the British parliament. For this purpose Mr. Bridges, clerk of the house for the preceding general assembly, a republican, was on hand to call the house to order and temporarily organize it; to act as temporary speaker, and in that capacity exclude all contestants from voting, which would leave the republicans in a majority, and throw its permanent organization into their hands. But the democrats were on the alert, and the trick was suspected. The moment the old clerk essayed to call the house to order, F. D. Preston nominated John Dougherty for speaker *pro tem.* A scene of unparalleled confusion and uproar, mixed with personal menace, now ensued, Preston, in stentorian tones and with much firmness, putting Dougherty's nomination to vote and declaring it carried, and Bridges, persistent in his right to organize the house, calling the roll for this purpose, and many members answering in recognition of his right. Mr. Latshaw was declared secretary *pro tem.* in the same manner that Dougherty had been chosen speaker, and he also was calling the roll of members. Above the din a motion was now made for the sergeant-at-arms to eject the old clerk, Bridges. Amid the great uproar it was declared carried, and at once executed with a rush, by his forcible removal, in which quite a number of the honorable gentlemen volunteered their assistance. The greatest confusion prevailed, muscle was triumphant and order was restored. The victory was with the democrats; Shellabarger, one of the Peoria contestants, was retained in his seat, which gave them a clear working majority and the organization of the house. As there were many able members in the house, this Peoria contested election case, as well as the question of printing the governor's message, elicited their full power of debate, and many fine and eloquent speeches from both sides were made during the session.

Early in the session an apportionment bill, based upon the State census of 1855, was introduced into the house by the republicans. The population of Illinois, in 1850, was 851,470, and in 1855, 1,300,251—an increase of 447,781—about 50 per cent., or one-third her entire population in 5 years. This gain was two-thirds in the northern parts of the State, the main republican strongholds. The bill was therefore at once spurned by the democrats, who offered a substitute which was provocative of the most stubborn parliamentary resistance at every step by the republicans. Such measures are nearly always passed in the interests of the dominant party. Both bills sought to secure ascendency in the next legislature, when a United States senator was to be elected to Douglas' place.

The constitution required districts to be composed of contiguous territory, bounded by county lines. The substitue was claimed to be unconstitutional, in fact a perfect libel on the theory of equal representation, in that it "gerrymandered" the State into all sorts of deformity, the mere cornering of counties in many instances being deemed a sufficient contiguity of territory for the formation of districts; in one district 3 votes were made equal to 4 in another; in another 5 were made to equal more than 9 in still another; and that in a certain contingency one county would be without representation at all. With much show of reason, doubtless, the opposition regarded the substitute as a most villainous piece of party legislation, and they exhausted every parliamentary effort and device to defeat it, but failed. The bill was passed toward the heel of the session. It now went to the governor for his signature. That functionary, it was confidently expected, would veto it; the surprise, therefore, was simply astounding when his secretary, on the last day of the session, with other bills reported his approval of it to the house.

And now everything was bustle, there was hurrying to and fro. His excellency was confronted by disappointed but determined political friends, and within an hour he sought to recall his message of approval, alleging it to have been made by mistake. Some republicans openly boasted that they had compelled the recall and the veto. An informal note explanatory of the circumstances was sent to the house, followed afterwards by his veto and return of the bill. The chagrin and mortification was now changed from the republican to the democratic side. The house, where it originated, refused to receive back the bill, or allow the veto message to be read or entered upon the journal, as the constitution required, and both were taken to the office of the Secretary of State, and there filed. It was held that after the governor had announced his approval of the bill it became a law, and passed forever beyond his control, and the only way to reach it would be by repeal.

The republican members signed a protest, which was spread upon the minutes, as was the undoubted right of any two or more. But now that party feeling was thoroughly aroused, the protest was not allowed to stand. On motion, it was expunged from the journal. This conduct, both with reference to the rejection of the veto message and the expunging of the protest, was contrary to the constitution, revolutionary and most reprehensible. With these partisan acts, and amidst the greatest uproar, without indulging the ordinary courtesy of passing a resolution of thanks to the speaker, the hour of the *sine die* adjournment having been postponed by stopping the clock, this deliberative body finally, late in the night, adjourned in a rout.

Some democrats having confidence in the legality of the point upon which the house acted, that the governor could not recall his approval, the act was by mandamus carried up to the supreme court to test its validity. But the opinion of that tribunal was adverse. The constitutionality of the objectionable provisions of the bill were not passed upon, but whether the forms of legislation which it followed rendered it valid or not. Judge Caton, delivering the opinion of the court, held that while a bill is in the possession and control of the executive, within the period limited by the constitution, it has not the force of law, and he may exercise a veto power, and so return to the house where it originated, with his name erased, notwithstanding he had once announced his approval of it.

Apportionment Bill of 1859.—Two years later, at the close of the session, another bedlam, more outrageous and undignified than the foregoing, was enacted by the legislature. The occasion was again an apportionment measure. The democracy, through the herculean labors of Douglas in his senatorial canvass against Mr. Lincoln, were in a small majority in both houses, although the popular vote of the State was against them. Seeing the close of their rule approaching, probably in the next election as it proved, they sought to perpetuate their power, and possibly with the view to elect a democratic successor to the then hated Trumbull in the United States senate, in 1861, by so shaping the senatorial and representative districts as to give them the general assembly and accomplish the ends in view.

The bill, it seems, was indeed a most unfair gerrymander, looking solely to partisan ends. Counties separately entitled to representatives were grouped with others, and large districts formed whose aggregate democratic vote would overbalance their small republican majorities, and thus force upon them representatives they did not want. Instead of forming districts out of contiguous and compact territory, they were stretched over two degrees of latitude. To the republican counties of the State, whose population was stated at 646,748, were accorded 33 representatives, while to the democratic counties, with a population of 477,678, were given 41 representatives.

The bill was introduced the third week of the session and the democratic majority forced it along in its order. The republicans who were ably represented, particularly in the house, fought it at every step. Thus all the legislation behind this bill was held in abeyance on its account. The 42 days contemplated by the constitution as the limit of the session, were frittered away in resolutions, parliamentary contention, and buncomb speeches. When it finally passed, first the lieutenant-governor, whose signature was required to it, was said to be absent during the night session, and refused to sign it except at the capital. Next Gov. Bissell retained it a week before he sent in his veto. In the meantime everything of importance was delayed. The enrolling clerks, in obedience to orders it was said, retarded their labors. Chairmen of the engrossing committees had their pockets crammed with bills, which they would neither report themselves nor disgorge for others to do it. Private bills of friend and foe were kept back, so great was the feeling of determination. Confident of veto, it was determined to repass the bill over it before any other business should be transacted. It was the main appropriation bill, through non-action upon which the ends of the majority were sought to be accomplished by failing to provide the means for carrying on the government and administering the laws during the coming two years' interregnum. The republicans sought to pass it out of the regular order but failed. It was well understood that with the passage of this bill they would leave all else in the lurch, stampede, and break a quorum to defeat the hated apportionment.

Finally the governor sent in his veto. The house had met at 9 A. M. Immediately after prayer, the Hon. L. S. Church announced the governor's private secretary, and as he commenced to read a violent tumult ensued. The democrats almost in a body sprang to their feet, vociferating fiercely, while above the din rapped the speaker with his gavel, crying " silence—order—there is no quorum present. No communication can be made to the house in the absence of a quorum! Doorkeeper put that man out"—meaning the secretary. Others shouted "Knock him down," "Kick him out," &c., with other threats and imprecations. The door-keeper started to execute the speaker's order, but by this time the secretary had read the veto message, and delivering it and the bill to a page, turned to depart. As the page started to the clerk's desk, the speaker ordered the papers to be returned to the secretary, and Mr. Green of Massac volunteered to execute the order. He snatched them from the boy's hand, pursued the secretary into the lobby and thrust them at him. Upon refusal they were violently cast on the floor. Mr. Church gathered them up, folded them together, walked leisurely up the aisle and laid them carefully on the speaker's desk. That gentleman, with a contemptuous expression, brushed them off. They were examined by several members and thrown back, when Mr. Green picked them off the floor and thrust them in his pocket, with the remark that he had as much right to them as anybody and he would assume the responsibility; meanwhile the wildest disorder prevailed.

When quietude was restored, a call of the house showed only 42 members present, less than a quorum, and the house adjourned.

The objections of the governor to the apportioment bill were that its effect would be to continue the control of the general assembly in the hands of a minority of the people; that the new county of Ford was placed wholly within both the 9th and 18th senatorial districts; that in the matter of giving excess the 10th section of the the 10th article of the constitution was disregarded; that there was an unnecessary departure from single districts—a glaring instance being the 32d, composed of the counties of Champaign, Piatt, DeWitt, Macon, Moultrie, Shelby and Effingham, to which 3 representatives were given, when the census showed that the 7 counties would divide neatly into 3 separate districts, &c.

Messrs. S. A. Hurlbut, A. W. Mack, L. S. Church, Leonard Swett and J. A. Davis, republicans, offered a protest against the action of the house in its rejection of the veto message, setting forth in scathing language the conduct of the house and the speaker, as detailed; quoting also the governor's message to make it appear of record. The speaker, Hon. W. R. Morrison, doubting the the necessity of receiving the protest without the house first passing upon the propriety of its language, held it for advisement, but subsequently, with the modification of some of its allusions to individual members, not himself, he admitted it, and it was spread upon the journal. The democrats spread a counter protest against receiving the first protest upon the journal.

In the meantime the not unexpected republican hegira took place—a few being left behind to attend to the protest and look after things generally. The quorum was broken, the re-passage of the apportionment bill over the governor's veto prevented, and all the unfinished business brought to a dead-lock; involving hundreds of bills, both public and private, including the general appropriation bill necessary to keep the wheels of government in motion. The result was not so bad, however, as was at first anticipated. The appropriations for the northern penitentiary and the asylums at Jacksonville had been gotten through early in the session, as also for the payment of the semi-annual interest on the State debt; and the judges, by a law of 1849, could draw their salaries on vouchers certified from the governor to the auditor. The conduct of the republicans in leaving was revolutionary, and the whole proceedings not only undignified but discreditable to the State. If the minority, not appreciating that in their capacity as legislators they acted for the whole State and the entire people, sought only to discharge partisan duty to their constituents, then they should have defeated the re-election of Douglas, and, indeed, they might in the same way have altogether prevented legislation. After waiting two days for the return of the delinquents, the democrats adjourned the general assembly *sine die.*

Upon the death of Gov. Bissell, March 18, 1860, the Lieut. Gov., John Wood, by virtue of his office, became governor for the unexpired term of near 10 months time Bissell was the only executive of the State who died in that office.

THE CANAL SCRIP FRAUD.

In the winter of 1859 was brought to light the most stupendous individual fraud ever perpetrated upon the State of Illinois. It was greatly intensified in that all the attendant circumstances pointed to a gentleman as the perpetrator, who but a short time before had been honored with the most exalted station in the gift of the people of the State, and who carried into his retirement their confidence and esteem. The fraud consisted in the re-issue of $224,182 66 of 90 days redeemed canal scrip, dating back some 30 years. Owing to the pecuniary necessities of that period, the canal trustees had issued $265,237 ninety-day checks, dated May 1st, and $123,317, dated August 1st, 1839. Much looseness had been observed in the original issue of these checks as well as in their redemption, they having been put aside without being cancelled. A superabundance of them had been prepared (not knowing how many might be needed) all signed and executed except filling in the name of the treasurer. They remained unregistered and untrimmed until detached and signed, when the amount of the different denominations were entered in a book, which served as a memorandum of the actual amount in circulation. These checks had been put in circulation in 1839 for a temporary purpose from the canal office at Lockport, and were redeemed partly by the State bank branch at Chicago, in payment for dues to the canal, and otherwise. It appears from the reports of the canal officers to the legislature, in 1840, that all of both these May and August issues had been redeemed, except $822, and in 1842-3 only $323 remained outstanding.

During the session of the legislature, in 1859, Gen. Jacob Fry, for many years canal trustee, called at the auditor's office and showed Mr. Dubois, auditor, one of these old canal checks, which had been offered for sale in Springfield, and cautioned the State officers against receiving such scrip, explaining how it was long since redeemed, and that what was then in circulation must be fraudulent. He was referred to the fund commissioner's office—the governor having been ex-officio fund commissioner since 1843—where he learned to his amazement that scrip of that description to a very large sum had been funded, and that new bonds of the State under the funding acts had been issued therefor. The checks were duly signed W. F. Thornton, president, and countersigned by Jacob Fry, commissioner, and by those gentlemen, and also Mr. Joel Manning, recognized as the same $50 and $100 checks issued by them in 1839, and redeemed and carefully packed away in a box, but now doing service again, after exchange as free-bank deposits. With this revelation consternation became rife in every State department, in which the legislature participated, the people generally shared, and the newspaper press fairly reveled. Nor was this lessened when it also transpired that the whole of this scrip thus fraudulently converted was presented by no less a personage than ex-Gov. Matteson.

In the State senate, Mr. Marshall of Coles, introduced a resolution, which was adopted, instructing the finance committee to inquire into certain State stocks said to be issued and based on counterfeit or spurious scrip, empowering them to send for persons and papers, and to report to the senate the result of their investigation. This committee consisted of S. W. Fuller, chairman, B. C. Cook, A. J. Kuykendall, Z. Applington, S. A. Buckmaster and Silas L. Bryan. They report:

"It appears that in December, 1856, just before the close of his term of office, about $13,000, in amount, of the checks above described, were, by Gov. Matteson, presented to Enoch Moore, secretary of the fund commissioner, and new State bonds issued therefor. That during the year 1857, about $93,500 additional of the same checks were, by Governor Matteson, presented to the same officer, who issued new bonds for that amount—and that at divers times there has been paid to Governor Matteson, from the State treasury, an amount of money, for principal and interest, to make, with the bonds so issued to him, the sum of $223,-182 66, on account of the canal checks so presented by him. The greater part of the checks are recognized by Gen. Thornton, Gen. Fry and Mr. Manning as the genuine $50 and $100 checks of May 1st and August 1st, 1839, by them issued and redeemed, and as part of the redeemed checks packed by Mr. Manning and Gen. Fry in the box deposited in the bank at Chicago, in the year 1840. There are also found among the checks funded by Gov. Matteson, two packages of the checks, dated August 1st, 1839, amounting to $10,500, which are fresh in appearance, have the edges untrimmed, but fully signed by the commissioner and secretary of the canal commissioners, and used by the treasurer of the board, but wanting the name of the treasurer filled in upon their face, and lying upon each other in consecutive numbers."

It appeared also in testimony before the committee that Gen. Fry, treasurer of the canal board, and Joel Manning, secretary, in the fall of 1840, counted and packed in a large sealed box the checks redeemed and other evidences of canal indebtedness, and they believe some of the partially executed checks; that Mr. Manning took the box to Chicago and deposited it in the Branch State Bank, where it remained undisturbed until 1848, when it, with other boxes and packages left there by the canal officers, was removed to the canal office in Chicago. This box and other divers packages of redeemed canal indebtedness, were receipted for by successors to predecessors from time to time as changes in that office occurred. And none of these 90 day checks were seen in circulation from 1840-1 down to 1859. Gen. Hart L. Stuart testified that for years after 1847 he bought altogether near half a million dollars worth of all kinds of Illinois canal indebtedness, advertising therefor in Chicago and New York, but among all his purchases he saw only about $100 of the 1839 canal checks.

In 1853 Gov. Matteson appointed Josiah McRoberts State canal trustee, who went to Chicago to receive from ex-Lieut.-Gov. J. B. Wells the assets of the canal office, among which was this sealed box, corresponding to the above description. He received also another box with a loose lid or cover, containing broken packages of canal indebtedness, defaced with a canceling hammer, but on counting the contents they were found to be short in many instances of the amounts noted on the wrappers. He also found divers packages of canal indebtedness in the office, partially broken, and part of the contents missing. And "he was advised by Gov. Wells, his predecessor, in substance, that the vouchers and affairs of the canal office would not hold out, or prove correct, but such as were there then of the papers, vouchers and furniture of the office, he received from Gov. Wells."

McRoberts then advised Gov. Matteson that the books, vouchers, &c., of the canal office had been turned over to him, among which there was much useless matter which should be disposed of; and by the governor's direction he packed all the evidences of canal or other indebtedness received from Wells in a trunk and a box (an ordinary shoe box,) for transmission to Springfield. In so doing he tried to put the same sealed box "into the trunk and shoe box, but it was too large, and he broke it open and packed the contents either in the trunk or shoe box, or a part in each, which, he cannot certainly state. After packing the trunk and shoe box, he locked and sealed the trunk and box," directed them to Gov. Joel A. Matteson, at Springfield, Illinois, put them on board the railroad at Chicago, and came with them to La-Salle, with Gov. Matteson, and there left them in charge of Gov. Matteson, who directed them to be sent to the Central Rail road depot at LaSalle, *en route* for Springfield, Illinois, in charge of Gov. Matteson, who was then going to Springfield.

"There is no distinct evidence before the committee that the shoe box has ever been seen since, but the trunk was found during the course of this investigation in a basement room of the capitol at Springfield. It was opened (there were upon it some appearances of having been sealed twice, as if opened and sealed again), and the contents found to consist of a great variety of evidences of canal indebtedness, some complete, that had been in circulation and redeemed and cancelled, and some unfinished scrip, also cancelled with a hammer, the whole contents counted to near $2,300,-000, of all sorts, although Mr. McRoberts stated in his report to Gov. Matteson, in 1853, that the contents of the trunk and box delivered by him to Gov. Matteson, in the spring of that year, were only estimated to amount to $680,000." The uncancelled checks were not found in the trunk, and no trace of the box was ever discovered.

Thus the box and trunk, which the evidence and attendant circumstances all show contained the redeemed and unused canal checks of 1839, were directly traced into the custody of the governor; he subsequently appeared with the identical bonds in his possesion, and had them exchanged or funded for new State bonds by the secretary of the fund commissioner, to the amount of $223,-182.66; and he appeared further as the sole beneficiary of their proceeds. A *prima facie* case was thus strongly made out against the ex-governor, and the *onus probandi* was shifted to him to relieve himself of the charge.

Under this grave state of the case, it was only shown in defense that the governor, after his retirement in the winter of 1857, took rooms at the St. Nicholas Hotel in Springfield, where he bought largely of the public indebtedness of the State—$380,000 of all sorts, other than canal checks of 1839. Mr. Niles testified that $200,000 of this sum was funded for and on account of Clark, Dodge & Co. "Messrs. R. E. Goodell (a son-in-law of the governor), Wm. Smith and Mr. Nesbitt, swore that Gov. Matteson received from the Merchants' and Drovers' Bank, at Joliet, from December 12, 1856, to about the first of May, 1857, a little over $200,000, which Mr. Smith understood was to be used in buying State or canal indebtedness. Mr. Goodell states he knew that Gov. Matteson was about that time buying public indebtedness; and Mr. Nesbitt, that he brought to him packages of money, which he delivered to him at his room in the St. Nicholas Hotel." Gen. I. B.

Curran and A. H. Moore testified "that they, each, at different times, were in his rooms at that hotel, and saw him buying of persons unknown to them, and apparently strangers in the town, canal scrip and checks, to an amount, on some occasions, of about $5,-000, which he paid for in cash at the time, except in one or two instances he was noticed to give a check." Curran thought purchases were made ocasionally at 75 cents on the dollar for principal, to which was added the accrued interest; and he also thought that he observed purchases to the amount of $30,000 to $50,000, and that some of these were 90 day checks. Moore swore that he thought he had observed the governor pay from $1.20 to $1.30 for principal and interest of public indebtedness due. A letter from Governor Bissell stated that shortly after his accession he was frequently applied to by letters and persons strangers to him, desiring to dispose of evidences of State indebtedness, and he uniformly referred them to Gov. Matteson as dealing in such evidences.

Thus while the trunk full of cancelled and worthless evidences of State indebtedness was readily found, no successful effort appears to have been made to show what became of the box containing the uncancelled and unused canal scrip; and while Matteson obtained the new State bonds and money, he failed to show where he got the 90 day canal checks exchanged for them, shown to have been in the lost shoe box.

From the time the exchange was effected in 1857, up to the time of its detection in 1859, neither Gov. Bissell, although ex officio fund commissioner, nor any other State officer, the fund commissioner's clerk, Mr. Moore, who had also been Matteson's clerk, alone excepted, knew anything of the transaction. Governor Matteson was not personally examined before the committee of investigation. Messrs. Grimshaw, Browning and Koerner were present on behalf of the State, and Messrs. Stuart and Edwards of Springfield, as counsel for Gov. Matteson. The examination was reported in detail, and may be found in full in the weekly *Illinois State Journal* of April 27, and May 4th, 11th and 18th, 1859.

The committee forebore to express any opinion of the guilt or innocence of any party concerned, and were apparently glad that Gov. Matteson had saved them "the necessity of determining many embarrassing questions arising out of the foregoing statement of facts, by offering to indemnify the State against all loss or liability by reason of moneys paid him, or bonds issued to him on account of said canal checks." The governor's letter to this effect, dated Springfield, February 9th, 1859, appears with their report. This letter, notwithstanding its fair language that he had "unconsciously and innocently been made the instrument through whom a gross fraud upon the State has been attempted," and his "earnest desire for the preservation of [his] own reputation pure and spotless, rendered [him] unwilling to retain these bonds, although purchased by and issued to [him] *bona fide* and for a valuable consideration," was commonly regarded as a confession of the transaction.

These funded bonds were on deposit with the auditor of State as security for the State bank (so-called) located at Shawneetown, a free or stock bank owned by Gov. Matteson. To indem-

*See Ill. Reports 1859, vol. 1, 644.

nify the State against loss by these securities thus fraudulently obtained for the canal scrip, the governor and his wife, under date of April 21, 1859, mortgaged his Quincy property to the State.*

The committee asked leave to sit during vacation for further investigation, which was granted, and in 1861 they made a voluminous report, embracing a general examination into the different classes of indebtedness of the State. They found in the course of their investigation additional frauds upon the State perpetrated during the period in question, with various kinds of scrip, amounting in the aggregate, estimating principal and interest up to January 1, 1861, to $165,346.

To pay off a claim of $38,214 44 to Mr. Kenedy, authorized by the legislature in 1846-7, Gov. French had commenced to reserve, undefaced, internal improvement scrip paid in for State lands sold, but as this was slow in coming in, he, in September, issued bonds to Kenedy, which paid him off. In the meantime $4,501 64 of the land scrip had accumulated, and the governor caused a descriptive list of it to be made and filed away, which was found by the committee; but the scrip was fraudulently funded May 14, 1857, amounting then, principal and interest, to $6,656 79. In December, 1841, Gov. Carlin placed in the hands of the canal commissioners 298 bonds of $1,000 each, 195 were paid out, 101 returned, and 2, Nos. 105 and 106, reserved in blank for Messrs. J. G. and D. L. Roberts, who never called for them, and they were never paid out to any one. The bonds were dated July 1, 1841, and fully executed except inserting the name of the payee. The committee now found the two bonds in the auditor's office cancelled. "The evidence before the committee tends to show that the name of J. Cratty, the payee of bonds Nos. 105 and 106, aforesaid, is in the handwriting of Joel A. Matteson; that while 19 bonds, numbered consecutively from 126 to 144 inclusive, were paid out to Cratty by the commissioners, these two never were, but were reserved as above stated. The loss to the State, as we have seen, was estimated at $165,346, besides the $223,182 66, based upon the uncancelled canal checks of 1839, total $368,528 66. The committee conclude: "Whether this scrip thus fraudulently taken from the State was the scrip which was in the box and trunk above mentioned cannot be determined, because no descriptive lists of the scrip was kept. The only facts in evidence before us tending to throw light upon that subject are above stated."

In the spring of 1859 the offense was brought to the attention of the grand jury of Sangamon county by three of the State officials, Messrs. Dubois, Hatch and Miller, who by their letter of April 27th, furnished that body a list of witnesses in various parts of the State, all of whom had been before the senate committee. The witnesses were subpœnaed, and the evidence elicited was such that the grand jury, by a vote of 16 to 7, determined to indict; but on the next day their action was on motion reconsidered. The inquiry was extended, but nothing new being elicited they again determined to find a true bill, only to be again reconsidered. And now sundry members of the jury began to falter in their determination, and when they again bal-

* See Book N. of Mortgages, pp. 550-22. Adams Co.

lotted the bill was refused by a vote of 10 for to 12 against—5 having reversed their opinions. Many rumors and surmises, both of a political and financial character, gained currency in connection with these "backings and fillings" of that body.

A grand jury's investigations are *ex parte*. It is not their province to inquire into the defense. The attorneys of the accused governor planned a letter, which reached the jury through the prosecuting attorney, suggesting (besides some witnesses who had testified favorably to Matteson before the committee) the names of Capt. O. H. Pratt of LaSalle and Dr. A. R. Knapp of Jerseyville, as parties who would make important disclosures. According to the rumors of the period, which were exceedingly numerous, the captain and the doctor mentioned were expected to shift the brand from the governor, and fix it upon ex-Lieut. Gov. J. B. Wells, then deceased, who, we have seen, when he yielded up the canal office to his successor, McRoberts, had remarked "that the vouchers and affairs of the canal office would not hold out." But the scheme failed; though these rumors promptly brought to the capital of Illinois Judge Wells, of Massachusetts, his brother, who unwilling that the imputation rest longer on idle and mischievous rumors, demanded that the charge be avowed and the grounds distinctly set out—when they immediately ceased.*

The sum subsequently recovered by the State, under decree rendered in the Sangamon circuit court against Matteson, was $255,500. On the 27th of April, 1864, the master's sale of the ex-governor's property took place at the door of the court house in Springfield, to satisfy the decree. The property sold realized $238,000, leaving a deficit to the State of $27,500. The State became the purchaser of the larger share of it. His splendid mansion and grounds at Springfield, which cost $93,000, brought only $40,000. This property was afterwards redeemed and never passed out of the possession of the family; a son-in-law being the reputed owner, and the ex-governor making his very retired home there. Never did a governor retire from office in Illinois with more respect by the people of both parties; with more general confidence in his integrity or administrative ability; with prospects for future political preferment of exceeding high promise; but the disclosure of these frauds upon the State, prostrated as by a single blow all these cherished hopes, and to-day there are doubtless many people in Illinois who even do not know that such a man is in life among us.†

THE MACALISTER AND STEBBINS BONDS.

Attempted Swindle by Funding them in 1859.—And now at the very hight of the great hue and cry of corruption, theft, robbery, &c., raised in connection with the canal scrip fraud, over which the republican press fairly gloated with demoniac delight, and while in the full tide of its onward career, a shadow was suddenly thrown across its track by a dark cloud replete with ominous portent, implicating the existing State government in an attempted

* The full proceedings of the grand jury are published in the weekly Ill. State Journal of July 13, 1859.
† The ex-governor died in the winter of 1872-3 at Chicago.

swindle upon the treasury of the State, amounting to $244,268, by the refunding of the Macalister and Stebbins bonds, so-called, which struck consternation into the ranks of the leaders. The democratic press, which had stood almost dumb under the revelation of the canal check fraud and meekly received the vehement blows of its adversary, was not slow to avail itself of the opportunity thus afforded to off-set the former, and it rallied to the onset with a will. While the two wrongs did not make one right, it was nevertheless a great relief (such is human nature) for the latter to find grounds to charge the former equally with culpability.

In 1841, June 17th, John D. Whiteside, fund commissioner, received an advance of $261,460 from Macalister & Stebbins, bankers in New York, for a short period, and as security, hypothecated with them 804 State bonds of $1,000 each, bearing 6 per cent. interest from May 1, 1841. Eight days later he delivered to them 30 $1,000 6 per cent. internal improvement bonds; on the 1st of July following he gave them an order on Nevins, Townsend & Co., of New York, for a further batch of 41 bonds of $1,000 each, which they received; and on the 27th of October following, they received from Michael Kenedy $38,215 44 in canal scrip—the whole aggregating $912,215 44 of Illinois interest bearing indebtedness, which that firm received to secure their advance of $261,460 to the State. The receipt of these sums they acknowledged in their account current rendered in 1842, during the session of the general assembly, being 28 64-100 cents on the dollar of security in their hands. Upon the bonds and obligations received by them, after the first 804, they had agreed to make further advances to pay the State's July interest for 1841, if it was found necessary, but the State stopping her interest payments, the advance was never made; and under her then financial embarrassments, the $261,460 advanced was not repaid; the hypothecated bonds, according to the contract with the fund commissioner, became forfeit, and Macalister & Stebbins claimed their full redemption in money. But it was answered that this contract was made in violation of law; that it was the duty of the lender to have inquired into the fund commissioner's legal authority to hypothecate these obligations, and as he had manifestly been overreached by the arts and cunning of money-jobbers, the State, at the bar of conscience, would only repay the amount actually received with the interest agreed to be paid. But these just terms of settlement were refused, after which the pledged securities were known as the "Macalister & Stebbins' bonds."

In 1847 (Feb. 28th,) the legislature passed "an act to authorize the funding of the State debt." By its provisions the Macalister & Stebbins bonds were specially excluded from its operation. The new "certificates of indebtedness" authorized by it were designated "New Internal Improvement Stock of the State of Illinois," of $1,000 each. "Certificates" for matured interest of over 6 years were to be issued, not to draw interest till after 1857, being without coupons, as the interest was stipulated in the body of the certificates. A "transfer agent" was to be appointed in New York to attend to the funding of the complicated Illinois indebtedness.

Three days after a supplemental act was passed to authorize a settlement with Macalister & Stebbins, by the provisions of which

36 cents on the dollar were offered, in new bonds on the amount hypothecated; the bonds to bear upon their face the words, "liquidation bonds," which, it will be observed, would have made two classes of Illinois funded bonds. By its terms the law expired on the 4th of July, 1847, and as the holders of the bonds refused to surrender them, or settle according to its provisions, nothing more was done.

Subsequently better counsel prevailed, and at the session of the legislature in the winter of 1849, Wm. H. Bissell, then a member of congress from Illinois, was sent by Macallister & Stebbins to Springfield to make as good a bargain with the State as he could for the redemption and settlement of these securities. "An act" was passed "to prevent loss to the State on the Macalister & Stebbins bonds." It was enacted that upon surrender of the bonds and scrip hypothecated with Macalister & Stebbins, amounting in the aggregate to $913,215.44, together with the interest coupons, the governor was to settle and pay the amount of money originally advanced with 7 per cent. interest thereon from the date of deposit to the time of settlement, in $1,000 bonds due after 1865, bearing 6 per cent. interest, payable semi-annually in New York, *pro rata* out of the interest fund. The old bonds to be surrendered in such amounts at a time as $20,000 of the new bonds would settle; and all heretofore surrendered to be credited in full at 26 cents on the dollar of the 804 bonds first hypothecated. The new bonds, like those provided for in the act of 1847, were to bear upon their face the words "liquidation bonds." Hence no "new internal improvement stock" could legally be issued for these bonds; these liquidation bonds were a distinct class. The greater portion of the Macalister & Stebbins bonds were funded under this act at the rate offered, but not all—114 having passed out of their hands.

During the session of the general assembly in 1857, Dr. W. W. Roman, member from St. Clair, introduced a bill which became a law, entitled "An act to fund the arrears of interest accrued and unpaid on the public debt of the State of Illinois." It authorized the governor to take up all arrears of interest due and unpaid, and to issue to the holders thereof bonds of $1,000 each, the same as those authorized by the funding act of 1847; for old bonds without coupons, interest certificates were to be issued to the holder, for which new bonds were to be issued upon presentation; and "any holder of canal or internal improvement scrip holding less than $1,000 may present the same with interest certificates enough to make $1,000 or more, and the governor shall issue a bond as before stated for such amount."

After its passage it was apprehended that the law was broad enough in its terms to include the outstanding Macalister & Stebbins bonds. To prevent such a construction, a joint resolution was promptly passed: "That no bonds or certificates for arrears of interest upon the Macalister & Stebbins bonds, *held by lien*, shall be issued by the governor to the holders of the aforementioned indebtedness, to their agents, or to any person or persons claiming under them."

The outstanding 114 Macalister & Stebbins bonds of $1,000 each had passed into the possession of other parties in New York, who alleged that they had purchased them some 16 years ago at public auction without the knowledge that the State refused to pay them at par. They now, under the law of 1857, made application to the governor to have them funded at par, which was refused. They next applied to the supreme court for a *mandamus* to compel the governor to fund them, but the writ was also refused, the court holding that the executive is a co-ordinate and independent branch of the government, and that they had no power to command him to do an official act. No opinion was expressed relative to the power of the governor, under the law, to issue the bonds; but Judge Breese, in delivering the opinion of the court, added: "If the governor asks our opinion on the point of duty, we will cheerfully give it; but we refer him to the high tribunal of his own conscience and the public judgment."

But notwithstanding the refusal of Gov. Bissell at this time to fund them, and apparently in the face of the joint resolution above quoted, he subsequently changed his mind, signed the requisite number of new bonds in blank, as did also the treasurer, Miller, and sent them on to New York to be filled up, as was the reprehensible custom of the time. In 1859 he further ordered the State transfer agent, Edward Bement, resident in New York, to fund the old Macalister & Stebbins bonds at their full value, principal and interest, in the "New Internal Improvement stock" of 1847, authorized by the funding act of that period, which in express terms forbade the funding of these bonds. The principal, $114,000, was accordingly funded, February 5th, 1859, leaving $78,660, the arrears of interest, still unfunded. The bonds were held at the time by the New York Bowery Insurance Company, $85,000; the Mechanics' Banking Association, $26,000; and Morris Ketchum, $3,000. Under the existing laws of the State, the governor had no power to settle with these parties upon any other terms than those proposed by the law of 1849, at 28.64 cents on the dollar; and the just liability of the State on these outstanding Macalister & Stebbins bonds, including interest, was less than $45,000, whereas by this action it would have been directly $192,683, and ultimately $244,268—a loss of near $200,000.

The transaction seems to have been kept a profound secret. But at this time the canal scrip fraud having transpired, a bill was introduced into the legislature abolishing the funding agency in New York, and ordering the books of the office, containing the evidences of this transaction, to be forwarded to Springfield—and now on "a more careful examination of the law [the governor] became doubtful of his authority in the matter, and immediately telegraphed Mr. Bement to stop funding, which was done at once."[*] Immediately after this the governor informed the auditor of the fact. "I was for blowing it at once," said that functionary, "but he [the governor] insisted that that would lessen his chances of having the bonds returned, and I reluctantly consented to keep still for a time."[†] A correspondence was immediately opened by the governor with Mr. Bement and the holders, to negotiate with them for their surrender, which did not at once succeed. In May the books of the New York funding agency were brought to Springfield. The auditor, professing now to derive his information from them, broke the subject to the treasurer, who was already apprised of it. These gentlemen, before the

---

[*] See Dr. Mack's letter to the Chicago Journal, July 12, 1859.
[†] See Dubois' letter, Ill. State Jour., July 20, 1859.

treasurer started to New York to pay the July interest on the State bonds generally, agreed and determined positively between themselves "that nothing should ever be paid upon the bonds of either principal or interest, while [they] were in the offices." With this resolution on their part, the closure of the transfer office in New York, and the fact that the new bonds issued under the law of 1849 were *inscribed* bonds—not transferable except upon the books—they could not be used or placed upon the market at any price; nothing could be done with them, and as neither principal nor interest had been paid to any considerable extent, the State could not be, and was not, financially, harmed. The scheme was nipped in the bud; though before the transfer agency was closed in New York Mr. Ketchum succeeded in having his three new or funded certificates of $1,000 each transferred on the books to a Mr. Graham.

"The plan embraced the funding of the 114 bonds under the general law of 1847, which expressly prohibited its being done; to issue for them 'New Internal Improvement Stock,' to the credit of which new stock was to be placed, the aggregate of pro rata interest which the State had paid in *cash* on its bonds since 1847, amounting on these $114,000 of 'stock' to $37,298, which sum would be payable on the 1st of July, 1859, the first interest pay day after the funding of the bonds, (the bonds being funded on the 5th of February, 1859); in addition to which two sums there was issued certificates for interest due from date of the original bonds surrendered, up to the passage of the law of 1847 under which they were funded, amounting to $41,388 83; and the holders were entitled to the further sum of $41,382, being the balance of the 12 year's interest *remaining* uncredited to the 'new stock,' for which, under Dr. Roman's law of 1857, they would be entitled to certificates"*—making a total of $244,268 83, or just about $200,000 more than the State justly owed.

During the summer of 1859, Dr. Mack was sent to New York to negotiate for the surrender of the refunded bonds. As the holders found they could not make them available—being inscribed bonds they could not be sold without transfer on the books—the State department unwilling to recognize them or pay interest on them either accruing or in arrear, they were finally, in October, 1859, surrendered. The holders were unwilling, however, to settle by the law of 1849. Six years later, at the session of 1865, the legislature passed a law compelling the surrender of the Macalister and Stebbins bonds, under penalty of a forfeiture of interest after July, and principal after January following, 1866. The amount allowed to be paid by this law on each $1000 was $248 13.

The action of Gov. Bissell in ordering the funding of the Macalister and Stebbins bonds is difficult to explain. He apparently disregarded the Dr. Roman resolution, misremembered the mandamus proceedings in 1857 to compel him to do what he now did, and violated the law of 1847, under which the funding was done, which expressly forbade it; while even if he had been legally authorized to pay their full value of principal and interest, as only about 28 cents on the dollar had ever been received for them by

Letter of "Investigator" to Chicago Times, Aug. 1859.

the State, it was plainly contrary to the justice and equity of the case, and popular opinion would have sustained him in a refusal, for the protection of the treasury of the State.*

NOTE—*When the transaction gained the light, during the height of the canal scrip fraud investigation, Bissell's enemies, stimulated doubtless to additional partisan feeling, or influenced by personal animosity, put the very worst construction possible upon it, and the most corrupt motives of combining with New York sharpers to rob the treasury were attributed to his excellency. A long letter from New York to the Chicago *Times.* dated August 20, 1859, signed "Investigator," evinces a "working up of the case" with apparently damaging effect to his excellency. From it, it seems, that an old Belleville acqaintance of Bissell's, through letters of introduction from him, in 1858, gained credit enough in New York to buy 111 of the bonds, with their accrued interest of $120,000 besides, for $85,000. He brought an installment to Illinois to get funded, but owing to a quarrel as to how the profits were to be divided between him and his confederates, the sale was rescinded, and after some threats with the law, the bonds were given back. Next, the New York owners, one of whom was Morris Ketchum, a close friend of the governor's and one of the original Illinois Central Railroad incorporators, having also resigned the State transfer agency, his partner, Bement, being appointed in the place, all with a view to the consummation of this fraud, it is hinted, tried their skill and ultimately succeed, as we have seen, in having the bonds partially funded; and with all these efforts. Bissell, who had the power to fund the bonds, is sought by letters, conjectures and deductions, to be connected as a corrupt sharer in the profits of the transaction. The letter is the careful, elaborate and able argument of a legal prosecutor, who manifestly has much personal feeling in the matter. It contains a complete history of the Macalister and Stebbins bonds, and many of the points against the governor appear to be well sustained by his own correspondence. At the meeting of the democratic State convention at Springfield, in January, 1860, Hon. J. L. Don Morrison avowed himself its author, and in a speech supplemented his charges against his excellency by the production of a number of letters from him to the New York parties and his Belleville acquaintance †

Prior to Morrison's convention speech, Bissell had been under many inflictions; but this was too much and in the *Illinois State Journal* of January 11, 1860, he published a stinging reply, evincing the rekindling of his old flame of scathing invective. He attributes the causeless attack upon him to the envy and jealousy of his assailant, as the key to all his malice; they were neighbors, both living in Belleville—one, obscure, had been honored with office repeatedly; the other, wealthy and conspicuous. had met with constant disappointment in this respect. He denied receiving one cent during his long official career that did not properly and legally belong to him; pronounced the "Investigator" letter "a tissue of vile assumptions, inferences, deductions and downright lies;" accused Morrison of dishonorably suppressing a letter of his to Penseneau [the Belleville friend) rejecting a dishonorable proposition in reference to the funding of the Macalister and Stebbins bonds, which would have "blown his pitiful cobwebs sky-high," and by way of counter charges, proceeds negatively to intimate his assailant's connection with many dishonorable acts. overreaching widows and orphans, &c., to obtain titles to lands, prompting the Old Ranger to exclaim: "If that man keeps out of the penitentiafy 20 years he will be the richest man in Illinois.

---

†See Ill. State Register, Jan. 10, 1860.

CHAPTER LII.

OUR SENATORS IN CONGRESS.

Their Lives and Characters—Senatorial Contest between Lincoln and Douglas in 1858.

———

Edwards and Thomas.—Upon the meeting of the first State legislature in October, 1818, Ninian Edwards, who had been the able and popular territorial governor up to that time, and Jesse B. Thomas, one of the federal judges during the entire separate territorial existence of Illinois, were elected as senators to congress; the former on the first ballot by a large majority, 32 out of the 40 votes, and the latter on the 3d ballot by 21 out of the 40 votes cast; Leonard White receiving 18, and Michael Jones 1.

The full term of a senator is 6 years, or 3 congresses. The constitution of the U. S. divides the senators into 3 classes, one going out with the expiration of each congress. Upon the admission of a State the new senators draw lots for classes. Edwards drew the 3d class, being the existing 15th congress which expired with the 3d of March, 1819, and Thomas the class which expired with the 17th congress on the 3d of March 1823. Both were re-elected for full terms. Edwards in 1819, till March 4th 1825, and Thomas at the session of 1822–3 till March 4th, 1829.

Of Edwards we have already spoken fully, as governor. Thomas, as a federal judge, had borne himself with much dignity upon the bench, but it is recorded that he did not apply his talents to the mastery of the law. By nature he was rather a politician, an avocation which absorbed his better abilities through life. Without talent as a speaker, he exhibited shrewdness and tact in the management of men and questions. We have already noted the manner of his election as a delegate to congress by the Indiana territorial legislature in 1808, his pledge being that he procure the separation of Illinois from Indiana, a valuable public service to us, which he fully discharged. Both senators actively supported, in 1820, the admission of Missouri as a slave state. Mr. Thomas gained considerable notoriety for originally suggesting the line of 36d. 30m., known as the Missouri compromise. With this proviso the Missouri bill passed the senate, 24 to 20; the senators of all the slaveholding States, with one from Indiana and two from Illinois, the last admitted State into the Union, voting for it. Mr. Randolph, the leader of the ultra southern faction in the house, indignantly characterized the compromise as a "dirty bargain," and the northern men by whose co-operation it was carried as "doughfaces," which was the origin of that appelation. Thomas was the intimate friend of Mr. Crawford, advocating his election to the presidency in 1824, but after the success of Adams, came over to the support of his administration. During the convention struggle he advocated the engrafting of slavery upon our constitution. After the expiration of his last senatorial term he removed to Ohio, where he died in 1853.

John McLean.—In 1824 Edwards resigned the senatorship to accept the mission to Mexico tendered him by President Monroe. On the meeting of the legislature in November of that year, John McLean was elected to fill the unexpired term of Edwards, the latter having thrown up the Mexican mission, being his competitor. McLean is said to have been in many respects, the most gifted man of his period in Illinois. He was born 1791, in North Carolina. At the age of 4 years his father's family removed to Logan county, Kentucky, where he received such limited education as the new country afforded. He studied law, and in 1815, at the age of 23, came to Illinois and settled at Shawneetown, with little means and less credit, but endowed with great natural talents and swayed by a lofty ambition. He speedily became conspicuous at the bar and in political life. Three years after, he became a candidate for congress, Daniel P. Cook being his opponent. The contest was one of the most animated and vigorous ever made in the State, characterized throughout by a high-toned courtesy, which eminently distinguished both competitors. They were young men of rare promise and alike won the esteem of the people. McLean was elected by a small majority, but at the next election Cook succeeded over him and continued to hold the place until 1826, when Duncan beat him. McLean was frequently a member of the legislature and speaker of the house.

He looked the born orator; with a large symmetrical figure, fine light complexion, a frank, magnanimous soul, he exercised that magnetism over his auditory which stamped him as the leader of men. Possessed of strong common sense, a lively imagination, a pleasant humor, ready command of language, his oratory flowed with a moving torrent, almost irresistible to the masses of his day. With these native attributes and a compass of intellect exceedingly great, consciousness of power caused him to rely perhaps too much upon them to the exclusion of that discipline, constant and painstaking study which make the profound scholar. He was twice elected to the U. S. senate, the last time, December 6th, 1828, unanimously, as the successor of Jesse B. Thomas, for a full term; but he only served the first session, and after coming home died at Shawneetown in 1830, in the very prime of his manhood, at the age of 39 years. His death was a great public loss, and the legislature, as a fitting testimonial to his memory, named the large, fertile and now populous county of McLean in honor of him.

Elias Kent Kane—was elected a senator in congress November 30, 1824, for the term commencing March 4, 1825, and terminating March 3, 1831—to the place of McLean. The latter, at the time of his election, 7 days before for the 3 months unexpired term of Edwards, was also a candidate for the long term, and, not doubting his choice, immediately departed for Washington; but a new candidate appeared in the field, and after a protracted struggle, he failed becoming his own successor, and Elias K. Kane was elected. This was on the 10th ballot, when Kane received 28 votes, and Samuel D. Lockwood, the next highest, 23. Mr. Kane was a native of New York; had received a thorough education, being a graduate of Yale College, studied law, and in 1814, when quite young, sought the south and west, and located finally at Kaskaskia. He was possessed of a strong, clear mind; was a close reasoner, a profound lawyer, an agreeable speaker, a lucid writer and attained eminence in his profession as well as in public life. When the wheels of the new State government were put in motion, in October, 1818, Gov. Bond appointed him secretary of State. Afterwards he was a State senator. December 11, 1830, he was re-elected, on the first ballot, to the U. S. senate for the full term from the 4th of March following, J. M. Robinson, his principal opponent, receiving 6 votes; but before the expiration of his 2nd term, his health, which had long been feeble, gave way, and he died at Washington, December 12th, 1835. He was a man of purity of character, honesty of intention, amiable and benevolent in disposition, and very generally esteemed. The legislature named the county of Kane in honor to his memory.

David Jewett Baker—was, November 12th, 1830, appointed by Gov. Edwards to fill the unexpired term of John McLean, deceased; but the legislature, between which and his excellency there was little accord, meeting shortly afterwards, refused to sanction the executive choice, and on the 11th of December, 1830, elected John M. Robinson instead. Baker was born in Connecticut, in 1792, and after receiving a collegiate education, and studying law, in 1819 with his young bride removed to Illinois, and located at Kaskaskia. He was a studious, painstaking lawer, and attained a standing with the ablest of the Illinois bar. He was long probate judge of Randolph county. He eschewed politics, except in 1824, when he actively, both with pen and tongue, opposed the introduction of slavery into Illinois. For his warm utterances, the then chief justice of the State, Thomas Reynolds, afterwards governor of Missouri, attacked him with a bludgeon in the streets of Kaskaskia. During his short stay in congress he originated the measure for disposing of the government lands in tracts of 40 acres, which facilitated the settlement of the State—the law up to that time not permitting the entry of less than 160 acres. In 1833 he was appointed by Jackson U. S. attorney for Illinois, and re-appointed in 1837 by Van Buren. In 1840 he united with the whig party. In 1848 he was defeated for supreme judge by Mr. Trumbull, in the 3d grand division. In 1854 he helped to organize the republican party. He died at Alton, August 10, 1869. *

John M. Robinson—had the following opponents: Theophilus W. Smith, Thomas Mather, R. M. Young, J. Kitchell and ex-Gov. Bond, but his strength increased at every ballot, and on the 5th obtained a majority. Gen. Robinson was a Kentuckian by birth, with a liberal education and a lawyer by profession. While still a young man he came to Illinois and settled at Carmi, where he married, and continued to make his home; a member of his

*See Weekly Illinois State Journal, Aug. 11, 1869.

family—a daughter, the only survivor—still resides there. He was tall and erect in stature, well proportioned, of light complexion, with large head, pleasing countenance and winning address—a fine specimen of manly beauty. A distinguished trait of his character was sociability; indeed, his convivial disposition carried him into frequent excesses. His title of general was derived from a connection with the militia organization of the State. He was re-elected to the U. S. senate December 20th, 1834, on the first ballot by a vote of 47 to 30—R. M. Young being his opponent—for a full term, which expired March 3d, 1841. In 1843 he was elected one of our supreme judges, but within two months after, April 27th, died at Ottawa, away from home, whither his remains were taken.

William Lee D. Ewing—was elected December 29th, 1835, to serve out the unexpired term of Elias K. Kane, deceased. This election was a protracted struggle. His competitors were James Semple and R. M. Young, both of whom led him on the first ballot, the vote standing, Semple 25, Young 19 and Ewing 18. On the 8th ballot Young was dropped, the 9th and 10th stood a tie, but on the 12th Ewing received 40 to Semple 37, and was elected. Gen. Ewing was a gentleman of culture, a lawyer by profession, and had been much in public life. He had been receiver of the public moneys at Vandalia and lost a $1,000 deposit by the robbery of the State bank in 1823. He was speaker of the State senate in 1834, and by virtue of that position had been acting governor for 15 days. His title of general was of militia origin, and he attained some distinction in the Black Hawk war. He was a Kentuckian, above medium hight, and of heavy build, with auburn hair, blue eyes, large-sized head and short face. He was genial, social, friendly and affable, with fair talent, though little originality. Under Gov. Ford he was elected State auditor.

Richard M. Young—succeeded to the seat of Gen. Ewing, and served out a full term from March 4, 1837, to March 4, 1843. He was elected December 14, 1836, on the 3d ballot, Samuel McRoberts being his principal opponent; Archie Williams and Gen. Ewing also received some votes, the former 21 and the latter 13. Judge Young was gifted with fine colloquial powers, and his intercourse with men was managed with an urbanity, smoothness and address well calculated to impress them with his excellence and worth, in which lay the secret of his success, rather than force or energy of character, or vigor and compass of mental endowments. His talents, which were respectable and above mediocrity, derived additional lustre from these amiable attributes. He was a Kentuckian, of spare build, rather tall, educated, and a lawyer by profession. In 1824 he was elected by the legislature one of the 5 circuit judges, and assigned to the 2d circuit. During his senatorial term in 1839, he was appointed by Gov. Carlin one of the State agents in connection with ex-Gov. Reynolds, to negotiate the $4,000,000 canal loan, for which purpose they repaired to Europe, and their advances of $1,000,000 in Illinois bonds to the house of Wright & Co., of London, proved a heavy loss to the State. Still, under party operations, before his senatorial term expired, he was made, February 3d, 1842, a supreme judge, a position which he held until 1847. He died at Washington, in an insane asylum.

From this time on the caucus system was resorted to by parties to determine their choice of candidates for offices, including that of United States senator, and aspirants to that exalted position were no longer distracted with the whims of individual legislators. The scheming or party pipe-laying was now all with the view to secure the favor of leaders and the manipulators of the caucus. Whom king-caucus designated as the party nominee no one was to gainsay. The system was adopted by the minority as well as the majority party, but it is to be noted that Illinois never had a whig senator throughout the existence of that party. The first democratic senatorial caucus resulted in the selection of perhaps the most uncompromising party man in the State.

Samuel McRoberts—the first native Illinoisan ever elevated to the high office of a United States senator from this State, was born April 12, 1799, in what is now Monroe county, his father residing on a farm. He received a good English education from a competent private tutor, Edward Humphrey, and attained also some proficiency in latin, but his naturally strong mind inclined him to mathematics. At the early age of 20 he was appointed circuit clerk of Monroe county, a position which afforded him opportunity to become familiarized with forms of law, which he eagerly embraced, pursuing at the same time a most assiduous course of reading. Two years later he entered the law department of Transylvania University at Lexington, Ky., where, after 3 full courses of lectures, he graduated with the degree of bachelor of laws. He commenced the practice of law in competition with such men as Kane, Reynolds, Mills, Mears, Blackwell, Star, Clark, Baker, Eddy, McLean. &c. In 1824, at the age of 25, he was elected by the legislature one of the 5 circuit judges. As judge he first publicly exhibited strong partisan bias. In 1824 he had been a violent convention advocate, and now, in defiance of a release by the legislature, he assessed a fine against Gov. Coles for settling his emancipated slaves in Madison county, without giving bond that they should not become a public charge; he also removed a circuit clerk in the same county, and appointed another in his place, from partisan motives, which caused a great outcry at the time and contributed largely to the repeal of the circuit court system in 1827. In 1828 he was elected a State senator; in 1830 appointed United States district attorney for this State; in 1832 receiver of the public moneys at the Danville land office, and in 1839 solicitor of the general land office at Washington. When the State banks of 1837 passed into whig control by their organization, Judge McRoberts, with others, opposed them, and they were refused the land office moneys as deposits, to aid in crippling them. On the 16th of December, 1840, Samuel McRoberts was elected United States senator for a full term, commencing March 4th, 1841. He received on the first ballot 77 votes, Cyrus Edwards, the whig nominee, 50, and E. D. Baker, 1. He died March 22, 1843, at Cincinnati, at the house of his old friend, Judge James Hall, formerly of Shawneetown, on his route home from Washington, in the vigor of intellectual manhood, at the age of 44 years.

Judge McRoberts was a little above medium hight, sparely built, of a nervous-bilious temperament, and had a good head.*

*He had a defect in one eye.

He was swayed by a stubborn will, a high ambition, and
unbounded energy. His mind was clear strong and precise, and
he was a deep read lawyer. He was ever a voracious student,
given to over-exertion. While he exerted a cogent influence over
his party, he was yet without the smooth and oily arts of the
ordinary politician. He governed by the power of will rather
than address and blandishment.

Sidney Breese—succeeded R. M. Young to the United States
senate for a full term, from March 4, 1843. He was the democratic
caucus nominee and was elected December 17, 1842, on the first
ballot, by 108 votes to his opponent, Archibald Williams', 49.

He was born about the close of the last century, in Oneida
county, N. Y., received a collegiate education and graduated with
distinction from Union College. He had been the school-fellow
of Elias Kent Kane, who was his senior. After the latter was
appointed secretary of State, in 1818, he wrote for young Breese
to join him, which he did by the close of the year, and read law
with him. Aside from the ability of his preceptor, this gave him
the advantage of forming a wide acquaintance in the new State.
In 1820 he essayed the practice of the law in Jackson county, but
met with failure in court before a jury, and, overwhelmed with
mortification, resolved to abandon his profession. The next year
he became postmaster of the ancient town of Kaskaskia. In 1822
Gov. Bond appointed him circuit attorney, in which position Gov.
Coles retained him, but Edwards did not. In 1831 he prepared
and published "Breese's Reports" of our supreme court decisions,
being the first book ever published in the State. The next year
he took part in the Black Hawk war—being a major. On the
establishment of the circuit court system, in 1835, he was chosen
judge, in which capacity the McClernand-Field case came before
him—an exciting political question—concerning the power of
the governor to remove the incumbent of the office of the secretary of State, which he decided with an elaborate opinion in
favor of the relator, but which the supreme court reversed. Upon
the reorganization of that court, in 1841, resulting in great part
from this question, he was elected one of the five democratic
supreme judges.

As senator, he occupied the seat of his old school-mate and
friend, E. K. Kane. Upon the expiration of his term he was
elected, in 1850, to the legislature, and was made speaker of the
house. In 1855 he was again elected circuit judge, and two years
later, on the resignation of Judge Scates, again elevated to the
supreme bench, where he has held a position ever since; and
here it is, by his numerous and able opinions, that he has made a
lasting record in the annals of this State, being a finished scholar
and profound jurist.

In congress he favored the annexation of Texas, our title to
Oregon up to the line of 54d. 40m., and carrying the war
with Mexico into the heart of that country. To his connection
with the land grant for the benefit of the Illinois Central
railroad. we have alluded—his original plan being a pre-emption
instead of a grant. He procured the passage of acts for the sale
of the mineral lands at Galena and other places, and the repeal
of the 5 years exemption from taxation of the public lands in this

State, which were valuable aids to the State at that juncture of her financial distress. He made also an able report in favor of a grant of land to a railroad from Lake Michigan to the Pacific.

James Semple—was appointed United States senator by Gov. Ford, in 1843, as the successor of Samuel McRoberts, deceased, and after serving for one session as such appointee, the legislature, December 11, 1844, confirmed his appointment by electing him for the unexpired term of his predecessor, by a vote of 102 to John J. Hardin 47. In politics Semple was a democrat, and the caucus nominee of his party, as was Hardin of the whigs. He had been much in public life. He was speaker of the house in 1836-7, when the State Internal Improvement measure was passed; afterward Charge de Affairs to New Grenada and judge of the supreme court. Gen. Semple was a fine looking man, and detested the plots and intrigues of politicians. Many of the older residents of Alton and Springfield will remember him as the projector of the "steam wagon" which lay for years a wreck on the prairie south of Springfield. He wrote an elaborate history of Mexico, which has never been published.

Stephen Arnold Douglas—became the successor of Semple. He received the Democratic caucus nomination and was elected December 14, 1846, on the first ballot, by 100 votes to Cyrus Edwards, the whig nominee, 45. Douglas was not unknown in the national legislature, having already served parts of 3 terms in the lower house. With the advent of this remarkable man, whom we do not hesitate to call great, into the U. S. senate, Illinois, took at once high rank in that august body, redounding not only to her glory, but solid advantage such as no State before nor since has received from the hands of congress. We allude to the procuring of the Illinois Central railroad land grant, a herculean task, in which he received the earnest support of his colleague and the entire delegation in the lower house. Douglas, though young in years, was directly acknowledged the peer of the great statesmen, Clay, Webster and Calhoun, with whom he served his first term. Since his death, Trumbull has maintained a high position for Illinois down to the present time. Douglas became his own successor in 1853, and again in 1859; but we defer a more extended sketch of his life and character to an account of the celebrated senatorial contest between him and Mr. Lincoln in 1858, contained in this chapter.

James Shields—was chosen to succeed Sidney Breese for a full term from March 4th, 1849. He was the caucus nominee of the democracy, largely in the ascendant in Illinois. The contest—an exciting one—was over the caucus nomination. Breese strove earnestly to become his own successor, and John A. McClernand, ambitious for the exalted seat, was also in the field. Both were greatly the superiors of Shields in ability and probably in art and address, but the latter had the advantage of military glory before which mere civil services, however valuable, have ever paled. Neither was he a novice in civil official experience. Born in county Tyrone, Ireland, in 1810, he emigrated to the U. S. in 1827, and settled in in Illinois, 3 years later. In 7 years time, without being naturalized, he was sent to the legislature from Randolph county. Gov. Carlin appointed him auditor, and in 1843, he was elected a supreme judge. Under President Polk he was commissioner of the general land office at Washington. In the Mexican war he entered by favor of the president as a brigadier-general and was afterward breveted major-general for gallant services. He was a fortunate soldier. Borne from the field of Cerro Gordo shot through and through, and reported at home as killed, he recovered in time to take a conspicuous part in the triumph of our arms under Scott in the valley of Mexico. In this latter campaign such was his soldierly conduct that the State of South Carolina voted him a handsome and costly sword, inscribed with the battles of Cherrebusco and Chepultepec, and the following sentiment:

"FROM THE STATE OF SOUTH CAROLINA,

"TO GENERAL SHIELDS.

"In testimony of her admiration of gallantry in the Mexican war, and as a tribute of gratitude for his parental attention to the Palmetto regiment."

From Mexico, after the fall of the capital of that country, had first come the announcement by letter that the gallant soldier would be a competitor for senatorial honors before the ensuing legislature of 1849. On his way home, at Washington, a public dinner was tendered him and Gen. Quitman, at which, in a speech Shields spoke incautiously in glowing terms of Gen. Scott, then under ban with the administration. Breese forseeing in this soldier of renown a formidable competitor for his place, did not attend the banquet. Before long Shields was ordered to Tampico, but on his route thither, at New Orleans, a dispatch from the War department ordered him back to Washington, to testify in the trial of Gen. Pillow. The order to return to Tampico was not renewed, and Shields came to Illinois and moved about among his friends. Now he was appointed governor of remote Oregon, which created the impression upon the public mind that the object of the administration, which did not relish his fearless praise of Gen. Scott, was to banish him beyond being a competitor against Breese for the senate, but he did not accept the governorship of that remote post.

In the senatorial canvass it was urged against Breese that he differed with his colleague on a subject of vital importance to the State, the procuring of the Illinois Central railroad grant of land; against McClernand it was objected that his principles of democracy were so thoroughly Jacksonian that consistency would lead him to oppose the vital interest of the west, the improvement of rivers and harbors; and against Shields, that he was ineligible, because, as a foreigner, he had not been naturalized long enough to entitle him to a seat in the U. S. Senate, the constitution of the U. S. requiring a citizenship of 9 years, Shields having been naturalized in October, 1840. These valid objections failed, and he was elected.

Shields repaired to Washington to take his seat on the 4th of March following. And now this most impulsive son of Erin committed a most foolish blunder, to call it no worse, as public men are wont to do when they write letters. To overcome the question of his ineligibility, which would probably be raised against his taking a seat in the senate, he addressed Mr. Breese a letter under date of February 23, 1849, charging him, among other "meannesses," toward him, with propagating this in Illinois, saying: "Had I been defeated by you on that ground, I had sworn in my heart that you never should have profited by your success; and depend upon it, I would have kept that vow, regardless of consequences." But that being past, he demanded of him then a letter, acknowledging, in effect, that in 1840, when he (Shields,) talked of going to Canada in case of war, that he (Breese) as circuit judge, offered to give him something in the shape of a final naturalization certificate to take along—to simply proof in case of difficulty; adding, "and refuse this request, I here give you fair warning—let the consequences fall on your own head—I shall hold myself acquitted both before God an man for the course I shall feel bound to pursue toward you."

But Breese did not scare as well as it was evidently hoped. He refused compliance with the demand, which he construed as a threat of assassination, publishing his refusal, together with Shields' letter, in the newspapers. Shields, in a subsequent letter, attempted to explain this away. When his credentials were presented in the senate on the 5th of March, objections to his eligibility were promptly interposed; Douglas, however, succeeded in having him sworn in, which enabled him to participate in the debate. After due investigation, a resolution was reported that Mr. Shields was not eligible at the commencement of the term for which he was elected, and that his election was void. Before its adoption he tendered his resignation, and thus addressed the senate: "To my own State, sir, I shall appeal, and hear what she has to say; and if she deserts me now, if my State shall not answer to the appeal I am about to make to her, I will say further that it is my intention (though I have endeavored to prove my fidelity to my country by every act of my life,) never to offer myself again for office in the United States." As his resignation should have been tendered to the governor rather than the senate, the resolution was adopted.

The question at home now was as to the power of the governor to fill the vacancy thus occasioned. The constitution of the U. S. says if vacancies happen by resignation or otherwise, during the recess of the legislature of any State, the executive thereof may make temporary appointments until the next meeting. Was this such a vacancy as the constitution contemplated that the governor had power to fill by appointment, and thus save the expense of a called session? The question was thoroughly discussed in the public press, and by letters from public men, both for and against. Mr. Douglas, perhaps fearing a new election before Mr. Shields would become eligible, held that the governor had the power;* but that functionary, in a long letter published, disclaimed the power,† and finally, in September of that year, issued his proclamation, convening the legislature in extraordinary session, October 22, 1849, to elect a U. S. senator, including in his call a number of other subjects for legislative action. Under the decision of the

---

*See his letter in Ill. State Register, Aug. 30, 1849.
† Ibid, June 21, 1849.

U. S. senate Gov. French had it in his power to cut off Shields
from this position, but he convened the legislature for a time just
after Shields would be rendered eligible by being 9 years naturalized.

After the call the canvass waxed exceedingly warm. The whig
press openly espoused the cause of Shields, crying out persecution,
and charging that those democrats who usually controlled the
party in the State had determined to sacrifice the gallant soldier,
and that to attain their ends wicked means were being employed.
Breese, McClernand and Shields were again the candidates, and
the friends of the respective aspirants were exceedingly active.
The contest was again for the caucus nomination. The friends of
McClernand, fewest in number, supposing that such a state of
hostility existed between the respective adherents of Breese and
Shields, that neither would yield in caucus, but would finally as a
compromise concentrate upon their candidate, proved very tena-
cious. 21 ballotings were had; on the first Shields received 28,
Breese 21, and McClernand 18; on the last, Breese 20, McClernand
12 and Shields 37—a majority. The highest for Breese was on
the 7th ballot, 29; the highest for McClernand on the 2d, 19.
Shields was again elected senator, and thus ended the very bitter
struggle.

Lyman Trumbull—succeeded to the seat of Senator Shields for
a full term from the 4th of March, 1855; and became his own
successor in 1861. Since the first organization of the democratic
party, and dating beyond that to 1824, when it was in its formative stage, those who afterwards constituted it never failed of
electing men of their political views and principles to the U. S.
senate from this State. Their defeat now was attended by a
bitterness and depth of feeling unprecedented. The occasion we
have already traced to the repeal of the Missouri compromise,
resulting, unexpectedly to all parties, in this State going anti-Nebraska at the election of November, 1854.

At the meeting of the legislature the choice of a U. S. senator
was to be the political event of the session. The exact political
status of that body after the election was not at once fully realized,
and while the democracy were apprehensive they yet hoped to
prevail. But upon its assembling in January, 1855, it became
speedily apparent that by a fusion of all the anti-Nebraska members the democracy were in a minority. The house, on the 2d
day, was organized by the election of anti-Nebraska officers: Thos.
J. Turner, of Stephenson, being chosen speaker by 40 votes over
J. P. Richmond, of Schuyler, democrat, 24. The senate acted
more tardily on account of the conduct of Messrs. Jarnigan and
Morton, Nebraska democrats, representing anti-Nebraska districts,
in absenting themselves. The fusionists, however, prevailed, and
organized both houses.

Alarm now seized the democracy. Their press cried out to the
fold: the wolf is on his walk—let the old party awaken to the
danger which threatens it from the allied isms; traitors are conspiring to stab deep into its vitals; nefarious schemes are concocted and combinations of an unholy ambition formed, moved
unto by a deep-seated antipathy against the truest and best men

of the State.* Anon intimidation and cajolery were both tried upon the disaffected wanderers from the democratic fold. They were denounced as malcontents who illy requited the past favors bestowed upon them at the hands of the democracy by their base attempts to disrupt the old party—ingrates, prompted by malice and jealousy to rule or ruin. They were apprised that the people were vigilant and would narrowly scrutinize their every act, artifice and departure from principle, and would not fail to visit signal retribution upon those who braved, defied and trampled upon the popular will. The name of Douglas—a tower of strength, and dear to the democratic heart—was invoked; it was necessary that his colleague should be a man who would uphold his hands to battle for the success of those great principles of non-intervention which were founded in justice, and which by the magic of his genius would eventually triumph and overwhelm all its opponents with confusion.†

All this was preliminary to the senatorial election. The contest was tardily approached and was not finally reached until the 8th of February, owing partly to a snow blockade which kept many members from the capital beyond the time of the temporary adjournment. James Shields, the regular democratic caucus nominee, was placed in nomination by Mr. Graham; Abraham Lincoln, the idol of the old whigs and strongly anti-Nebraska, by Stephen T. Logan; and Lyman Trumbull the nominee of the less than half a dozen anti-Nebraska democrats, by John M. Palmer. Archibald Williams, W. B. Ogden, Joel A. Matteson, Cyrus Edwards and W. B. Kellogg were also put in nomination. 51 votes were necessary to a choice on joint ballot. On the first, Shields received 41, Lincoln 44, Trumbull 5, and the others named each 1. On the 7th ballot Shields was out of the field and Matteson being substituted, received on the 8th 46 votes, the utmost strength of the democracy. On the 10th Mr. Lincoln's name was withdrawn and the whig vote being concentrated on Mr. Trumbull, he received 50 votes direct, and before the result was announced, Mr. Sullivan changed from Williams to Trumbull, electing him by just the requisite number.

Neither persuasion nor menace could move or intimidate the Trumbull phalanx of five. Mr. Lincoln, though ambitious of senatorial honors, for he had been elected a member of the same legislature, but supposing he could be elected senator, had resigned shortly after; now when it became apparent that he could not succeed, he pressed his friends to support Mr. Trumbull, which was ultimately done, (with tears by his old friend, Judge Logan, it is said), not that they loved him less, but the cause of freedom demanded it. Governor Matteson, though he was not the caucus choice of his party, not being in full accord with Douglas on the question of harbor and river improvements in the west, the levy of tonnage duty for this purpose, &c., the democracy boasted (as was done by Mr. Moulton upon the floor of the house, notwithstanding their knowledge of an anti-Nebraska majority,) that in the last resort enough members, influenced by a high regard of personal consid-

---

* See Ill. State Register, Jan. 1855.
† See the press of the period.

44

eration for his excellency, would rally to his support and triumphantly elect him. But they reckoned without their host.*

Mr. Trumbull, at the time of his election to the senate of the
U. S., was about 43 years old. He was born in Connecticut, where
he received a good education. Subsequently he turned his attention to the law and later settled in Illinois to practice his profession, which he did with marked success, speedily attaining distinction as an able lawyer. In 1840 he was elected to the legislature. When Douglas was elected a supreme judge in 1841, Gov.
Carlin, resisting legislative dictation, appointed Trumbull to the
vacant office of secretary of State, over McClernand, but he came
near being defeated in the senate by the efforts of the latter and
his friends, out of which grew some ill-feeling. At the opening of
Gov. Ford's administration, he incurred the displeasure of that functionary by opposing his policy toward the State banks, causing his
dismissal from office. The same year and the following one, he
sought the congressional nomination in the Belleville district,
but failing, upon the meeting of the legislature he aspired to
the senatorial nomination against James Semple, the governor's
appointee, and failed again. In 1846 his name appears among the
candidates for governor, but failed through the influence of Gov.
Ford, and on account of his opposition to the canal. He immediately sought and obtained the candidacy for congress in the
Belleville district, but was defeated by over 2,000 majority, though
the district was largely democratic. As a politician Trumbull
lacked that hearty and cordial geniality of manner which wins
popularity among the masses. His intercourse with the people, if
not formal, left the impression of reserve, and his nature was re-
pellant rather than magnetic. But no such disadvantage obtained
with him in regard to politicians—over such as might be reached
by the force of intellect he ever exercised a large influence. However, after these repeated trials for place, in 1848 he was elected
one of the supreme judges under the new constitution, which
office he resigned July 4, 1853, on account of insufficient salary.
By nature, study and habit he was admirably fitted for the bench;
with a mind strong, clear and penetrating, which, while it inclined
to detail, never lost its broad grasp of principle—here he was
capacitated for great eminence. He was an able, searching and
comprehensive constitutional pleader. He was ever a strenuous
and ultra democrat, but in 1854, unable to brook the repeal of the
Missouri compromise, he opposed his party upon that question,
and was in November elected to congress as an anti-Nebraska
democrat, which place he resigned to accept the senatorship.

His record in congress, which is national, and not our province
to give, stands very high. He was for many years the able chairman of the judiciary committee, and few congressional acts of
importance but what bear the impress of his far reaching mind.
As an orator he is devoid of imagery and ornateness of diction,

* The whigs for a long time felt sore over the defeat of Mr. Lincoln and the forcing
of an obnoxious candidate upon them by the arbitrary conduct of only 5 men. In
1856 the Hon. J. H. Matheny, a whig, in a Filmore speech at Petersburg, using most
scathing language toward Mr. Trumbull, boldly charged a pre-arranged bargain between all the anti-Nebraska elements to the effect that Trumbull was to be elected to
congress, which was done: that the abolitionists were to have the offices on the convening of the legislature, which they got; and that the whigs were to have the U. S.
senator, which they did not get. The charge was denied at the time by a brother-in-
law of Mr. Trumbull, and in 1858, Mr. Lincoln, during his senatorial canvass with Mr.
Douglas, in his speech at Charleston characterized it as a "cock and bull story."]

but as a close, clear, compact and systematic thinker, with an excellent memory, a wide acquaintance of public affairs, and an extensive knowledge of the law, he was the most formidable debater of the august senate. As a practical expounder of the principles of his party, he eclipsed Mr. Seward. He ever has been a hard student, but notwithstanding his mental labor he bears his near three-score years well and looks youthful.*

DOUGLAS AND LINCOLN.

Senatorial Campaign of 1858.—The contest between these gentlemen for a seat in the U. S. senate is not only the most memorable in the annals of Illinois, but involving great national issues at the time, assumed a scope beyond the mere personal success of the contestants, and an importance which arrested public attention from all parts of the Union. Douglas was the leading representative man of the democracy, and Lincoln being pitted against him, became the same for the republican party. It was called the battle of the giants, and results grew out of it, both as relates to the men concerned and the principles involved, the most momentous to the nation since its foundation was laid in the blood of the Revolution.

To appreciate this contest fully we are compelled to present a short view of the status of parties at the time.

The all-absorbing political question was that of slavery. Since the day that Whitney invented the cotton-gin, slave labor had gradually become so profitable that the whole south favored the enlargement of its territorial area, and so far as the south, acting as a unit, could control the democratic party, it was pro-slavery. To this was arrayed in sectional antagonism the new republican party, which, while it professed to be anti-slavery only so far as extending the territorial area of slavery, had through sympathy swept into its ranks as co-workers all the old abolition element of the country. Between these two, thus presenting a dangerous sectional issue, it was attempted to interpose the broad national doctrine of non-intervention, or as it was called, popular sovereignty, of which Mr. Douglas was the acknowledged champion. This principle, honestly applied to the organization of the territories, and fairly carried out, offered the only peaceable solution for the fierce sectionalism of the period. But this plausible theory was practically subjected to the grossest abuses. Kansas and Nebraska had been organized upon it, but no sooner done than emigrant aid societies were formed throughout the north sending thither men armed with Sharp's rifles to locally organize the territory in the interests of freedom, while the slaveholders of the south with their emissaries pressed over the borders to effect the first organization in the interests of slavery. Two parties with totally opposite views thus strove for supremacy in a new country where there was no legal restraint imposed upon them, and it is not strange that collision and an actual border war followed.

[* Gov. Matteson refused Mr. Trumbull his certificate of election as senator in 1855, because the constitution provided that "the judges of the supreme and circuit courts shall not be eligible to any office or public trust in this State or the United States, during the term for which they are elected, nor for one year thereafter." But the senate of the U. S., when the question was raised, held that it was the judge of the qualification of its members, a right which no State law, either organic or statutory, could take away or circumscribe.]

While the south viewed popular sovereignty as the short cut to
all the ends of abolitionism, the democratic party, of which, by its
unity it was the controlling party at Cincinnati in national convention assembled, solemnly affirmed it as its creed. Mr. Buchanan,
its nominee, in his letter of acceptance said "that the people of a
territory, like those of a State, shall decide for themselves whether
slavery shall or shall not exist within their limits." The nation
gave its confidence to these fair promises only to be deceived.
After Buchanan's accession to power, with a cabinet mainly of
southern men about him, he threw off the mask, and in his manifesto to the New England memorialists, said: "slavery existed at
that period—when the Kansas-Nebraska bill was passed—and
still exists in Kansas under the constitution of the U. S. This point
has at last been decided by the highest tribunal known to our
laws [alluding to the Dred Scott decision]. How it could have
been seriously doubted is a mystery."

During the summer of 1857 was concocted in Kansas the infamous Lecompton constitution. After the election of the pro-slavery
delegates—the free State men not voting—and when the character
of their work was well anticipated, rumors were current that the
president would sustain it; and after the adoption of its pro-
slavery clause by a largely fraudulent vote, in which all the great
historic names of the country, from George Washington down,
were recorded in its favor—the free State men not voting at all,
because the constitution proper, which also recognized slavery,
not being submitted—upon the meeting of congress he boldly and
in shameless defiance of his previous pledges to the country, urged
the admission of Kansas under this fraud.* He made it the test
of party fealty, and brought to bear in its favor the full power of
his official patronage. Douglas, in a speech at Milwaukee, in 1860,
says:

"If you look into the Lecompton constitution you will find that the
original document made Kansas a slave State, and then the schedule
submitted another slavery clause to the people to vote for or against; if
they voted for it, Kansas was a slave State, and if they voted against it
still it was a slave State. When I reached Washington, three days before
the meeting of congress, I went directly to the president, and had a talk
with him upon this subject, in which I informed him, as a friend, not to
send the constitution into congress for acceptance I told him that it
was a violation of every pledge we had made to the people; a violation
of the fundamental principles of the democratic party, and a violation
of the principles of all parties in all republican governments; because it
was an attempt to force a constitution upon an unwilling people. He
begged me not to say anything upon the subject until we should hear the
news as to how the vote stood on the slavery clause. The vote, you remember, was to be taken on the slavery clause on the 21st of December,
three or four weeks subsequent to this convention. I told the president
that if he would withhold his recommendation until the vote was taken
on that clause I would withhold my speech against the measure. He
said he must recommend it in his message, and I replied that if he did,
I would denounce it the moment his message was read. At last the
president became somewhat excited upon the subject, and he arose and
said to me: 'Mr. Douglas, I desire you to remember that no democrat

* "My political life has no greater error to atone for than my neglect to crush this
reptile of Pennsylvania when I had him in my power. He was the cause of a bitter
war between two men of this republic (Clay and Jackson,) who should not have been so
estranged. His representations caused the charge of 'bargain and sale,' and when
brought home to him he meanly left me to face it. Friends interfered to save him from
being exposed, and I listened to them."—Jackson's opinion of Buchanan, expressed
to Moses Dawson in 1837. See Washington *Republic*.

ever yet differed from an administration of his own choice without being crushed.' Then he added: 'Beware of the fate of Tallmadge and Rivers.' I arose and said : 'Mr. President, I wish you to remember that General Jackson is dead, sir.' From that day to this he and I have been trying the question whether General Jackson is dead. And one thing is certain —the people of Illinois decided in 1858 that James Buchanan was not General Jackson."

At the opening of congress in the fall of 1857, the slave propagandists, assured of the powerful aid of the executive, proclaimed loudly that Kansas must be admitted under the Lecompton constitution unconditionally, supplemented with their oft repeated threats of disunion. But the great champion of popular sovereignty, unwilling to do this violence, both to the law of his country and the pledges of his party, now promptly stepped forward and fought the battle of freedom for Kansas, almost single-handed of his party in the senate, but well seconded in the house by the democrats of the Illinois delegation, ably led by the lamented Thomas L. Harris. In disregard of old and dear party ties, the popular sovereignty democrats stood side by side with the republicans in congress, and the recreant president with his disunion allies were defeated in their outrageous scheme to force slavery on the unwilling people of Kansas.

From a volume entitled "Our Living Representative Men," by John Savage, we copy a few graphic sentences describing a memorable scene in the United States senate, on the occasion of Mr. Douglas' delivering his celebrated anti-Lecompton speech, March 22, 1858. Besides citizens from all parts of the Union and members of the house, the dignitaries and representatives of foreign courts at Washington were in atendance :

"If the immense mass of people who crowded the galleries, the lobbies, the stairways and the ante-rooms of the senate is any evidence of interest in the question of debate, then Kansas is the most interesting topic of the day. * * Senator Douglas entered the chamber just after a fainting lady had been carried out of the gallery. * * He was congratulated by men of all parties, and soon was engaged in an earnest confab with Green, upon whose spirits, however, the Little Giant did not seem to make any especial change. * * * *
Gwin and Seward rose simultaneously and moved to admit the ladies to the floor of the senate, and a perfect flood of beauty poured into the chamber. The appearance of Senator Douglas was the token for around of applause. The sight must have been as deeply gratifying to him as it was entrancing to that mother and daughter, Mrs. Douglas and her mother, who, from the reporters' gallery, looked upon the scene with that anxious pleasure which tell the physiognomist that they, of all the gay and brilliant crowd, had the deepest interest in it. For three hours Senator Douglas spoke—he warmed up by degrees, lifting the head and heart of the multitude with him, until one almost felt as if he were in Europe during the revolutions, listening to some powerful tribune of the people expounding their rights and inspiring them to such action as made America a republic. He went through his public course. The period embraced some of the most prominent and vital acts in the history of American poltics. He showed—not as a defence, but in a proud, manly, and almost defiant spirit—what his acts had been ; he echoed his own words ; he was proud of his deeds—deeds and words which were recognized portions of the policy of the democratic party.
As he proceeded, with emphatic and measured dignity, to define his position in the present crisis—what the duty of a senator from a sovereign State was, and the responsibility he owed to the people whose voice culminate in him—he held the multitude chained with that peculiar eloquence which, based on common sense and the rights of man, reaches its destination without the aid of winged rhetoric. Such eloquence

does not dazzle, it convinces, it does not stretch the fancy, but solidifies the head; it does not hold the breath, but makes one breathe freer, for it cheers the heart.

The great burst of applause which broke from the galleries and rolled over the chamber was a nobler testimony to the principles enunciated by the eloquent senator than might be written. He was there the defender of the people, the representative of the State, and not the vassal of the executive, nor the valet of the administration, to do its bidding without consulting their own judgment or the interests of the people. He stood forth as the champion of State sovereignty." He grew in enthusiasm with the progress of his subject, and the effect was electric.

Thus was conveyed a lesson which should have taught the chief magistrate of this nation that there may be popular leaders more powerful than the executive, with all his enormous patronage at his back; but his perception was blinded by mortification, and he looked only to revenge, and for this purpose pursued Douglas, who looked forward to a renewed senatorial term at the ensuing session of the legislature, with all his official power and patronage, into Illinois.

The adherents of the president in this State, the federal officers and appointees, and other recipients of his bounty and favors, joined by the broken down politicians and place hunters, whose future depended not upon the preservation but rather the destruction of the democratic party, and also those moved by envy or hatred of the "Little Giant," were rallied and thoroughly organized. A few democratic newspapers yielded to subsidy, but more were directly established; and itinerant orators were employed to perambulate the State through its length and breadth. The adherents of the president were designated as Danites. A secret politico-military order in Kansas, of whose fearful oaths and frightful doings, horrid accounts had been published, was denounced in congress by Mr. Douglas, and characterized as an imitation of a cut-throat Mormon band, called Danites. One of the reputed leaders of the Kansas order was employed in Illinois as a general post office agent, in which capacity he traversed the State constantly, notoriously doing more to organize the administration oposition against Douglas, by threats of dismissal or intimidation, than ferreting out government delinquencies.

The democracy of Illinois met in convention at Springfield, April 21, 1858, to nominate candidates for State treasurer and superintendent of public instruction, and particularly to declare its status with regard to the great question of variance between the president and Senator Douglas. In 97 of the 101 counties resolutions had already been passed by the democracy, approving the course of the Illinois delegation in congress upon this Lecompton question. Two conventions met at the appointed time and place, both claiming to represent the true democracy of the State, one sustaining popular sovereignty and approving the course of our delegation in congress during the Lecompton struggle, the other endorsing the administration and repudiating Douglas as affiliating with republicans. The latter was but sparingly attended, the representation being from 24 counties, and its proceedings were somewhat spiritless. John Dougherty (since lieutenant governor) presided. Ike Cook, a Chicago postmaster, was chief manager, and Dr. Leroy, John L. McConnel, R. B. Carpenter and B. F. Blackburn were the speakers. As it was partly composed of seceders, no ticket was made, and an adjournment till the 9th of June was had, when it met again with a somewhat larger attendance. John Dougherty was nominated for treasurer, and ex-Gov. John Reynolds for State school superintendent, both by acclamation. The "nationals" met with much encouragement from the republicans, but now, in their long platform of principles, they paid their respects to them as follows: We deem the principles and policy of the black republicans as utterly opposed to the spirit in which the Union was formed, and the success of that party would be disastrous to its prosperity—which was not so palatable to the latter. The president was very much dissatisfied with these meagre and spiritless affairs; county meetings and district conventions were therefore held, and administration legislative tickets were generally put in the field with the hope of diverting votes enough to carry the State for the republicans.

The regular democratic convention was largely attended, 84 counties being fully represented, embracing more of the eminent and distinguished men of the State, than was common on such occasions. Ex-Lieut. Gov. John Moore presided. The ticket made was W. B. Fondey for treasurer, and ex-Gov. French for superintendent of public instruction. While the resolutions of the convention were firm in their tone, they did not openly and decisively mention Douglas by name and applaud his course, nor did they condemn the president in direct terms. It was sought rather to avoid an open rupture with the administration. A resolution offered by Judge Drummond, "That this convention view with regret the course pursued by the present administration in removing good men from office for the expression of opinions upon any given proposition," was, upon motion of Judge O. C. Skinner, promptly laid on the table. This looks like a piece of arrant truckling to an arbitrary and recreant president. It was hoped that the Kansas troubles would prove evanescent and that party unity would be preserved. The convention did not nominate or recommend Mr. Douglas as the senatorial candidate, as did the republicans Mr. Lincoln, some time after. But his candidacy was generally conceded. There were other aspirants in the democratic ranks, but when it was perceived what herculean blows were requisite in the fight, the field was left by common consent to the Little Giant.

But with the efforts and exceptions mentioned, the democracy generally, both press and people, sustained Senator Douglas. During the darkest hour of the Lecompton struggle, the republican press, laying aside party, heartily praised the course of Douglas and his colleagues of the house for their noble stand in vindication of law and popular right, against the slave oligarchy, with a treacherous president at its head. During the canvass Mr. Greeley, a warm admirer of the character of Douglas, however he warred against his political principles, held the following language in the New York *Tribune* regarding his or Mr. Lincoln's success:

"There is a contingency in which even he [Mr. Lincoln] might be elected, that would cause such election to be viewed with regret by republicans in other States. * * We allude to secret coalition between republican leaders and the little faction of postmasters, tide-waiters and federal office seekers, who, for the sake of their dirty pudding, present and hoped for, pretend to approve the Lecompton fraud, and are now hounding on the track of Senator Douglas. Any conspiring or conniv-

ing with this pack on the part of republicans of Illinois, no matter by
what name glossed, under what pretext veiled, would be regarded by
republicans in other States with profound disfavor."

Of Douglas, he held the following language :

"They have seen him separate himself from a triumphant and almost
invincible administration, which had honors to dispense and millions
to disburse, braving the denunciations of party organization and party
progress, which have for 20 years borne him onward from triumph
to triumph, and from indigence and obscurity to opulence and distinction—they have seen him incur the deadly and unquenchable
hatred of the slave power, blasting in a moment all the reasonable hopes
of obtaining the presidency through the machinery and spell of the
democratic party. * * When a statesman so high in position, in power,
in hopes, separates himself from a triumphant majority to fight a
momentous battle on the side of a minority, to whom he had always
stood in deadly opposition, it is scarcely reasonable to attribute that
change to any motive which does not honor his conscienciousness and
his courage. And it seems to us particularly ungracious in those to
whom he has lent the weight of his powerful arm to unite with his
and their implacable enemies, in disparaging his motives, belittleing his
influence, and paralyzing his exertions. * * However pointed may be
our future differences, we shall never forget that in the Lecompton
struggle he proved faithful, in defiance of great temptation, not to our
principles but to his own, * * If this course was taken, the consequences braved by Mr. Douglas, solely upon the strength of his convictions of right. and of the moral weight of the pledges given in the
Nebraska bill and the Cincinnati platform, no public man in our day
has evinced a nobler fidelity and courage "

But this out-spoken approval of Douglas' course by the republican press outside of the State was bitterly and defiantly resisted
in Illinois. The administration organs had read him and his followers out of the democratic party, and the reflection had been
indulged that he might find a lodging place in the republican, but
the press of the latter party, knowing well the man, scouted this
as an egregious falacy. Their political hatred of their old foe was
revived with all its former animosity, and they proclaimed that
there was no conflict into which the republicans of Illinois entered
so heartily, so thoroughly, so unitedly as this. They desired to
be avenged on him with an intensity not to be appreciated by
outsiders, and for the purpose in hand asked to be let alone in
the fight by the sentimental philosophers and enthusiasts abroad.*
The feeblest efforts, sayings and purposes of the Buchanan men, to
divide the democracy of the State, were greedily taken up, paraded
before the public and heralded abroad in a magnificent form.
The strange anomaly was exhibited of a most persistent praise
and flattery bestowed by the republicans upon the slave party,
while those who had in congress stood side by side with them in
the defeat of the Lecompton iniquity, received only their abuse
and slander. All this to promote the schism in the democratic
party, and redound to the benefit of their own.

The State republican convention met at Springfield, June 15, 1858
and was organized by selecting ex-Lieut.-Gov. Koerner as president.
It was largely attended, 87 counties being represented, and much
enthusiasm was exhibited. James Miller, the then incumbent, was
re-nominated for treasurer without opposition. For the candidacy
of the office of superintendent of public instruction ten names
were presented. The second ballot showed the contest to lie be-

*See Chicago papers of June, 1858.

tween W. H. Powell, the then incumbent, and Newton Bateman, of Morgan, who on the third ballot received the nomination.

In their declaration of principles they "disclaimed all intention of attempting, either directly or indirectly, to assail or abridge the rights of any of the members of the confederacy guarantied by the constitution, or in any manner to interfere with the institution of slavery in the States where it existed." They denounced the administration; differed with the decision of the U. S. supreme court in the Dred Scott case; maintained the right of congress to prohibit slavery in the territories, and its duty to exercise it; approved the then recent decision of the supreme court of Illinois declaring that property in persons was repugnant to the constitution, and that slavery was the creature of local or municipal law. Charles L. Wilson offered a resolution, which was unanimously adopted amidst shouts of applause: "That Abraham Lincoln is the first and only choice of the republicans of Illinois for the U. S. senate, as the successor of Stephen A. Douglas."

DOUGLAS AND LINCOLN.—These two most eminent and illustrious men of Illinois and of the nation deserve at our hands somewhat more extended biographical sketches than are generally given in this work, which we deem it proper to make before proceeding to detail their great contest for senatorial honors.

Stephen Arnold Douglas—was born April 23, 1813, at Brandon, Vermont, "a good State to emigrate from," as he has said. His father, who died when Stephen was an infant of 3 months, was a physician of considerable eminence, and a native of New York. His grandfather was a Pennsylvanian, and a soldier in the Revolution, being with Washington at Valley Forge and at Yorktown. His great grandfather was also native born, but the remote ancestry was from Scotland, and, it has been said, traceable to the blood of the Douglas. In youth Stephen received the ordinary school education of his native State, and was an apt and diligent pupil. At 15, unable to gratify an ardent desire to prepare for college, owing to his mother's straightened circumstances, he apprenticed himself to the cabinet trade. In 18 months afterwards, finding it too hard for his constitution, he abandoned it and entered the academy at Brandon. The following year, his mother having married a Mr. Granger, whose son had previously married his eldest sister, the family removed to Canadagua, N. Y. Here Stephen resumed his academical course, and also commenced to read law. At the age of 20 he started west to seek an eligible location. At Cleveland he was long detained by sickness. Recovering, he went to Cincinnati, and thence by river to St. Louis, finding his way, late in the fall of 1833, to the village of Winchester, Scott county, Illinois, whither he walked from Jacksonville, in quest of a school to teach, his exchequer being reduced to 37½ cents. His first work was clerking at a vendue, which yielded him $6, but he obtained, shortly after, a school of 40 pupils at $3 a quarter. He kept up his law studies meanwhile, and the following March was admitted to the bar by the supreme court sitting at Vandalia. He now betook himself to the practice of the law, and speedily won distinction in his profession. Within a year of his admission to the bar, before he was 22 years old, he was chosen by the legislature attorney general of the State. In 1836 he was elected to the legislature from Morgan county, being the youngest member in that body. At this session the internal improvement folly of the State was entered upon. In 1837 he was appointed by Van Buren register of the land office at Springfield. The same year he was nominated for congress, and at the election of August, 1838, came within 5 votes of an election out of 36,000 cast, his opponent being the Hon. John T. Stuart, whig. He now devoted himself assiduously to his new profession, and proved himself an able lawyer and successful advocate. His tact and skill in the examination of witnesses was unrivalled. In 1840 he entered with great ardor into the exciting presidential campaign, canvassing the State thoroughly, by addressing 207 meetings in favor of Van Buren. Upon the meeting of the legislature in December of that year, he was appointed secretary of State by Gov. Carlin, who was unable to withstand the pressure in his favor. During the session, from partisan motives, the supreme court was reorganized, in which Douglas took an active part through lobby addresses, &c., and was also elected to a seat upon the bench, rendering the court democratic. The supreme judges had to perform circuit duty, Douglas being assigned to the Quincy district.

In the 4th volume of the "Law Reporter," Boston, 1842, may be found a letter from a lawyer, who had emigrated to Illinois, giving the following description of him on the bench:

"The judge of our circuit is S. A. Douglas, a youth of 28, who was the democratic candidate for congress in 1838, in opposition to [J. T.] Stuart, the late member. He is a Vermonter, a man of considerable talent, and, in the way of despatching business, is a perfect 'steam engine in breeches.' This dispatch is the only benefit our circuit will derive from the change. He is the most democratic judge I ever knew. While a case is going on he leaves the bench and goes among the people, and among the members of the bar, takes a cigar and has a social smoke with them, or often sitting in their laps, being in person say five feet nothing, or thereabouts, and probably weighing about 100 pounds. I have often thought we should cut a queer figure if one of our Suffolk bar should accidentally drop in."

But Douglas' manners upon the bench were unexceptional. He was studious, clear, comprehensive and expeditious, and it may be said that a more popular judge never wore the ermine in this State, notwithstanding his youth and slight figure.

In 1843 he was first elected to congress by a majority of about 400. He was twice re-elected, his majority being increased each time—the last time to 3,000. In the lower house he is said to have been cautious and sparing of debate, studious and closely observant, and when he did arise for a speech it was apt, forcible, and to the purpose. His early education was not so thorough and scholastic as it might have been, as he well knew, but this fact could never have been gathered from his speeches. Ashamed to be either uninformed or misinformed, he was a studious toiler throughout his busy and boisterous political life, amidst all its engrossing cares and unceasing occupation, and a wide and varied reader of history and its kindred of politics and law. Contact with public affairs gave scope to his understanding and depth to his judgement, and his knowledge became vast, complete and accurate. One of his first masterly efforts in congress to attract national attention, was his speech on the bill to refund to Gen.

Jackson the fine imposed upon him for placing New Orleans under martial law at the time of the battle in its defence on the 8th of January, 1812. The venerable hero of that glorious event subsequently thanked Douglas for this able vindication, saying: I knew when I proclaimed and enforced martial law that I was doing right; but never, until I read your speech, could I express the reasons which actuated my conduct.

In 1847 Douglas entered the senate, which was the arena of his herculean labors. His name, young as he was, became speedily associated with the great national issues which affected the destiny of this people. He moulded and gave them direction in public affairs. Between the aggressions of the south and the resistance of the north over the angry subject of slavery in our territories, it has been said that there is no escape from the conclusion that the genius of Douglas offered the only peaceable solution of a common national ground upon which all could meet in the theory of territorial sovereignty. To it, through his labors, the democratic party was committed in 1856, gained a triumph at the polls and then was basely betrayed by Buchanan and the south. But Douglas was true and faithful to it to the last and defended it whenever and wherever assailed. And while he was personally pursued by bitter, implacable, open political opponents, his darling idea, which was empire or ruin with him, was more grossly betrayed by perfidious friends who rode into power upon it.

The most striking peculiarity in the *physique* of Mr. Douglas was his stature which was greatly below the medium hight—not above 5 feet. His trunk was ample, compact and erect, with full chest and square, well defined, though not broad shoulders; but his extremities were disproportionately short. In the latter years of his life he grew stout, though not obese. His figure would have been fatal to the divinity of the Appollo Belvedere. While his diminutive stature would arrest attention, his facile and natural dignity of manner, not to say grace, with an air, as if born to command, would cause idle curiosity in the contemplation of his person to pass into speedy forgetfulness by the respect and attention which he inspired. His splendid head, covered with a heavy suit of dark hair, nicely poised upon his shoulders and connected by a short neck, was massive in its brain developement, conveying, under animation, the impression of almost infinite power. The ample forehead was squarely built up over the wide arches of his heavy brows, under which rolled a pair of large, restless, deep-set, dark blue eyes, capable of shooting out glances of electric fire, when under the impulse of the powerful brain battery back of them. His nose was broad and short, with flaring nostrils, denoting coolness and courage. At its junction with the projecting forehead it left a peculiar transverse crease. His mouth was ample, cleanly cut, with lips finely arched, the whole evincing decision, and by the depression at the angles, conveying a mingled idea of sadness and disdain. His chin, backed by a firm jaw, squared well to the general outline of his face, indicating ardor, strength and vigor. He wore no beard, but presented smoothly shaven cheeks and handsome throat with slight double-chin. The general contour of his face was regular, and its muscles wonderfully mobile, giving a pleasing and winning countenance; his complexion, though somewhat dark, with his usually good health,

was clear; the exuberance of his animal spirits was extraordinary.
He was of the vital temperament. Such is a brief physical
description of the "Little Giant."*

As an orator Douglas possessed the peculiar magnetism of
imparting to his auditory the hue of his sentiments and views—
swaying their will or directing their sensibility at pleasure. He
affected no senatorial airs, betrayed no aristocratic spirit, but
naturally and easily identified himself with the democracy. He
had been the genial companion of many an early pioneer, and his
intimate knowledge of the people and sympathy with them,
enabled him on the stump to convey to their common understanding, in their own accustomed vehicles of thought, his reasoning
upon the political questions of the day, often enforcing and clinch-
ing an argument to those who remembered the frontier times by a
peculiar border figure, carrying conviction to their minds as
evinced by a spontaneous outburst of applause at frequent intervals. But his most inseparable attributes were rapidity and boldness of thought, and his dexterity in debate—of which he became
a consummate master—cropped out in early life, giving promise
of unequaled power in his first efforts on the stump. He had the
faculty of summoning all his mental resources with a promptitude
which served admirably the occasion, even if required instantly
in reply to a powerful antagonist in the senate. Therefore, while
his forte lay to a certain extent in his matchless power upon the
hustings, he swayed a no less power in the caucus or the august
senate. His manner of treating a subject was bold and inde-
dependent, always striking the hard and strong points. To halting friends he appeared at times to be overbearing; and there
was a vein of cold irony in his nature which, with a defiant tone
in his remarks, a haughty manner and a curling of the lip, sunk
deep into the heart of an enemy. Energy and activity, courage
and fortitude, were of the essence of his nature. The assaults
that would excruciate some men only excited a smile of derision
on his intrepid face. Elastic in both body and mind, he was capable of performing an incredible amount of political labor in the
open field. Thus with sagacity as if inspired by genius, a mind

* This soubriquet originated very early in his public life. In 1833 President Jackson added to his refusal to recharter the U. S. Bank, the removal of the deposits.
Great was the consternation of the people, and a general panic prevailed. Party feeling ran extremely high, the president's supporters were unsettled in their views and
thousands differed with him on these measures Douglas had just located at Jacksonville and opened a law office in a room in the court-house. The whigs of Morgan
county, from their number and standing, were arrogant and audacious in their denunciation of the administration. Douglas mingled freely with the people, who usually
crowded the county seat on Saturdays, and among them, was outspoken in his approbation of the acts of the administration. He and the editor of the democratic paper
at Jacksonville, deeming it advisable to rally the undecided, effect an organization of
the administration party, and define its position, in opposition to the views of many
friends, called a mass meeting, and prepared a set of resolutions endorsing the bank
policy of the administration. On the day of the meeting the court house was thronged
with people of both parties. Douglas being comparatively a stranger, declined to offer
resolutions, but as it soon became apparent unless he did it would not be done, he
boldly advanced and read them, following with a few brief explanatory remarks.
Immediately upon his conclusion, Josiah Lamborn, a whig of great influence and
oratorical powers, attacked the resolutions and their reader in a severe and caustic
manner. The blood of Douglas was up; this was his first political effort, but he met
his antagonist with such arguments, so vehement and effective, that the excitement
of his friends reached the highest point of endurance; they cheered, seized, and bore
him aloft through the crowd and around the public square, in gratitude and admiration, applying to him such complimentary titles as "high-combed cock," "little giant"
&c., which last, by its peculiar appropriateness, adhered to him to the last. His effort
that day, in a measure, changed the political destiny of Morgan county. It was long
remembered, and the old veterans of Morgan always held that Douglas never equalled
this speech of March, 1834.—*Sheahan's Life of Douglas.*

matured by careful study, a judgment clear and decisive; a courage which shrank from no danger, amounting at times to apparent audacity, yet always tempered with discretion; a will to yield to no difficulty, and unappalled by any obstacle; appreciation of the people and the rare faculty to lead them, Douglas was a statesman of the very first order.*

Douglas' speeches contain few rhetorical flourishes. But they are models of exact language, orderly and systematic in thought, full and comprehensive in grasp. There is never a strained effort at mere beauty of word painting. The architecture of his sentences, as well as the ideas, are solid, massive masonry, with broad foundation laid on firm rock, and the details and working plans so accurate as to be perfect in their adaptation, with nothing amiss or foreign and no surplus or waste material. So well and thoroughly are his sentences woven together that it is difficult to extract from his speeches any separate sentence conveying, text-like, a summary of the whole. While they are complete they yet seem parts necessarily connected with the whole. His

*Rev. W. H. Milburn.

Note—To further illustrate Douglas' power among the people, we subjoin a chatty but graphic sketch by the editor of the Newburyport (Mass.) Herald (republican), who was a fellow passenger in the cars with Mr. Douglas through Illinois on occasion of opening the Ohio & Mississippi railroad, and afterwards:

'That man with a big, round head, a brow almost as broad as Webster's, and a quick, active eye that rolls under the heavy projecting brow, watching every other man, and not allowing a motion to escape him—with arms too short for his body, which is full and round as though it never lacked the juices that supply life; and with small duck legs, which, had they grown as thick as his back-bone (and they would, probably, if Providence had not foreseen that he would want back-bone more than legs in his battle of life,) would have made him of respectable stature,—that little man is no less than the great politician of the west, who has attracted more attention in the last four years than any other man of the nation, and done more to give direction to public affairs than even the president, with a million and a half of voters at his back, and the army, navy and treasury of North America at his command. It is the 'Little Giant,' Stephen A. Douglas, with whom we parted company at Vincennes, and who has slowly come along, feeling the public pulse to learn the political health of the 'Suckers' up to Springfield, the capital of the State.

"The means of success in Senator Douglas are very apparent. First, he is really and intellectually a great man. Eastern people who view him only as a low politician, should disabuse their minds in relation to one who is to exercise a wide influence in the affairs of the country, and very probably, for he is yet young, to be the head of the republic. He is massive in his conceptions, broad and comprehensive in his views, and in a good measure is endowed with all those powers of mind that make a statesman.

But he is greater still in energy of character. There are those that think that a defeat of him next year would be his death in politics; but the man who sprung from a cabinet-maker shop in Vermont, and without father or friend worked his way to an honorable place upon the bench of judges, who entered Illinois with less than 50 cents in money, and not one cent in credit, and has acquired great wealth, and the highest station and influence, is not ready to be whipped out. But if he is great in mind, and greater in energy, he is greatest in those winning manners for which the world calls him a demagogue. Scarcely a man, woman or child in the cars escaped his attention, or passed by unspoken to. At one moment he talks with the old, stern visaged politician, who has been soured by a thousand defeats and disappointments; in the next, to that well formed and genial Kentuckian, who has just sought a free State; now he sits down with the little girl approaching her teens, and asks of her school studies; and he pats the little boy on the head, and in presence of his mother and proud father (what father is not proud to see his boy noticed?) says a word of his mild eyes and glossy locks. Again the lady is approached with a fair word and a bland smile, and goes home pleased to tell her father how he looks, and then half a dozen are about him, all standing together. He can talk religion with the priest as well as politics with the statesman; he can congratulate the newly appointed Buchanan office-holder, who has supplanted his friend, tell the displaced friend of the good time coming, when his wing shall be up; and at every station, more regularly than the conductor, Mr. Douglas is upon the platform with a good-bye to the leaving, and a welcome to the departing traveler—a shake of the hand with one man that stands at the depot, and a touch of the hat to another. He knows everybody; can tell the question that affects each locality; call the name of every farm owner on the way; tell all travelers something of the homes they left, that they never knew themselves, and suggest what place they deserve in heaven. Now, such a man as that, in contact with everybody, knowing everybody, and at the bottom wrapped up with the one idea of preferment, power and dominion among men is not easily to be put down; and his opponents might as well believe at once, that when they fight him they fight a strong man—a little giant indeed. He would be popular in Boston or anywhere else, and half the 'three thousand clergymen' he denounced would have their hearts stolen if he could speak to them a half hour.'

arguments succeed each other like the weighty blows of an enormous trip-hammer, shaping the subject in hand with irresistible power, flattening the points opposed to him, and possibly the adversary under its mighty tilts.

In the circle of Washington life, Douglas, with the honors of a senator, appeared with a natural grace and dignity rarely excelled. At the social board or in dinner table conversation, Col. Forney in his sketches of public men, says: "Douglas was almost unrivaled. His repartee was a flash, and his courtesy as knightly as if he had beeen born in the best society."*

Abraham Lincoln.—The life of one who has become so exalted in American history as Abraham Lincoln, must ever possess a charm to the reader in its minutest detail. But the great acts with which his name is associated are national, and it is foreign to the scope of this work to give more than a cursory glance at the man as he appeared in Illinois. We desire rather to speak of his meagre early life, his attributes of person, character and mind—his qualities of head and heart—as they appeared here, than the great events with which he was subsequently connected, however the latter may have flown from the former. His broad executive capacity, so suddenly developed under great trials, constituting the sublimest events in our history; his fidelity to the right, and his courage and firmness which grew out of that, it may here be said, were not without astonishment to those who knew him best in Illinois, and who imagined that they comprehended all that was to be learned of his character.† Possibly it was so to himself. The great lesson of man—know thyself—is ever least understood.

The most striking contrast between Mr. Lincoln and his antagonist for senatorial honors, was in their physical appearance. It would be difficult to find two men with the requisite capacity for so exalted a position, more opposite in physical development than these. Mr. Douglas, as we have seen, was low of stature, scarce 5 feet, erect, with trunk large and rotund, and extremities unduly short. Mr. Lincoln, on the other hand, was tall, exceeding 6 feet, spare, angular body, with a slight forward inclination, extremities long and lank, the upper terminating in huge hands and the latter in large feet. His shoulders, of medium breadth, drooped slightly forward, giving him the appearance of being hollow-breasted. As it is a fact, it is not derogatory to say of him that his appearance was somewhat ungainly. He was of the nervous bilious temperament. His head, covered with thick masses of dark hair, was large, with a receeding but ample forehead, well and prominently developed at its base, and under the arched and projecting brows rolled his clear, dark-blue eyes of more than medium size, with a mild and benignant expression, speaking the sympathetic soul within. His nose was his most prominent facial organ—high, thin, straight, neither long nor short,—a fine nose, expressive of even force of character. His ample mouth, while it indicated enough of decision and strength of will, was totally devoid of anything like disdainful expression. It would have been difficult for Mr. Lincoln, capable as he was to express in his face inimitable grotesqueness, to have curled his lip in contempt, defiance or disdain. His chin, mostly covered with whiskers, was of fair prominence; though it lacked that squareness which gives a full and agreeable development to the lower face, while at the same time it is indicative of ardency and combativeness—it was not the military chin. His cheeks were gaunt, and the general outline of his face, as has been aptly said, was that of craggy grandeur. It wore a habitual expression of sadness; yet his countenance could beam with a kindliness of heart which gave license for the approach of the humblest, and revealed a largeness of soul replete with a charitable and forgiving disposition. His health, though never apparently robust, was uniformly good, and he was capable of great physical endurance.

Abraham Lincoln was born in La Rue (now Hardin) county Kentucky, about 2 miles south of the village of Hoginsville, February 12th, 1809. (He was thus the senior of his competitor by 3 years.) Here his father had taken up a land claim of 300 acres, rough, broken and poor, containing a fine spring, known to this day as the "Linkum Spring." Unable to pay for the unproductive land, the claim was abandoned, and the family moved from place to place in the neighborhood, being very destitute. These removals occurring while Abraham was scarcely more than an infant, has given rise to different statements as to the exact place of his birth. It is said that in that part of Kentucky four places now claim the honor. In 1816 the family started westward, following the Ohio river, and settling in Spencer county, Indiana. Two years later the mother died, and also an only sister; the thriftless father married again, and Abraham worked in the neighborhood on farms, and in clearing away the dense forest underwent the sturdy discipline of toil. He received the meagre education which the new country afforded, but his boyhood had few advantages of culture, and he was emphatically self-made.* "I have not a fine education; I am not capable of entering into a disquisition upon dialectics, I believe you call it"—he himself complained in his Chicago speech in answer to Douglas at the opening of the senatorial canvass in 1858. He was of, and grew up among, the common people, the hard-handed yeomanry of toil. His warm and benevolent heart was thus early taught to sympathise with labor, and later his brain appreciated the importance of its freedom.

He grew to manhood rapidly, and such were his qualities of head that before he attained to majority he was employed as supercargo to take a flat-boat load of produce to New Orleans, which he did giving full satisfaction. In 1830 the family removed to Illinois, settling on the south side of the north fork of the Sangamon river, 10 miles southwest of Decatur, in Macon county. Here young Lincoln spent his first winter in Illinois, during which he aided in building for the family a cabin, stables and other buildings; mauled and split rails, cleared and fenced in 10 acres of ground. From this place the rails which played so important a part in the campaign of 1860 were procured.† The following

---

* It is asserted that he learned to cipher on a smooth clap board by the light of a cabin fire after getting through with the day's labor, while working on the Crew farm in Indiana. When the board was written over with figures, recourse was had to a drawing knife to shave it down, and with the clean surface thus presented it was ready for further use. The books that he could get to read were very few, but the Bible was evidently one of them.

†One Charles Hanks, a cousin on the mother's side, who had all the time lived within two and a half miles of this place, published in 1860 a letter saying, that 5 years afterward the entire fence was burned up, and that he helped to build a new one: but his brother John maintained the genuineness of the rails. See Decatur papers 1860.

spring, being now of age, he aided in conducting a flat-boat down
the Sangamon, became acquainted with the country, and later
found employment as clerk in a country store, at a village on its
west bank named New Salem, a mile from the present Petersburg,
whither its tenements were finally removed.   Lincoln, with a
partner, succeeded his employer, the stock of goods probably not
large and the purchase being made on time.   The merchants, as
merchants are wont to do, speedily failed.   Lincoln now turned
his attention to surveying, but when the Black Hawk war broke
out, in 1832, he volunteered and was elected captain of his company.   He served three months but was in no engagement with
the enemy.   The same year he became a candidate for the legislature but was defeated.   He was an Adams man, the whig party
not yet having assumed its name.   He now pursued surveying
and occupied his spare time in reading law.   In 1834 he again
offered for the legislature and was elected as a member for Sangamon, the village of his residence, since Menard county, was then
still in Sangamon.   He was for four successive terms re-elected
from the same county, but after his first session, by the advice
of a friend, to whom he ever felt grateful, he gave up the business of
surveying, settled in Springfield and thenceforward gave his attention wholly to the law.   During his 8 years in the legislature he was a
serviceable member, belonging to the minority party all the time,
and attained some distinction.   He was twice the whig candidate
for speaker, which was a compliment but an empty honor.   In
1837 he sustained the visionary scheme of the State Internal
Improvement system, which nearly bankrupted the State, doubtless like all others, with the best, but mistaken intentions.   Still
it is to be remembered that as one of the "long nine" from Sangamon, who acting constantly as a unit, artfully contrived many
combinations during that eventful session, always with an eye
single to removing the capital from Vandalia to Springfield.   Out
of all the reckless schemes of that session, the constituents of Mr.
Lincoln in Springfield were the only ones who ever derived any
permanent benefit from any of them.   He was a vigorous opponent
of the partisan reorganization of the supreme court in 1841.

He now (1842) devoted himself exclusively to the practice of his
profession, in which he attained a high standing as a lawyer, and
particularly as an advocate.   Before a jury he had few equals
either in originality, humor or pathos.   His most effective oratory
was of the persuasive order.   While he sought to lead a jury by
the force of logical reasoning and striking similes, whatever his pos-
tulate, he seldom attempted to drive them either by intimidation
or the power of detailed argumentation, to awaken perhaps their
obstinacy or tire them into listlessness.   He would contrive to put
them in good humor by apt and original turns on his antagonist,
his inimitable manner and complete acting being his most effective
aids for this purpose ; gain their favor ; enlist their interest ; then
touch their sympathies by the power of his pathos, and wring from
them a verdict.   His most effective weapons with which to assail
or demolish the arguments of opposing counsel, either of attack or
defense, were his powers of ridicule, originality and quaint logical
reasoning.   To the beginner at the bar he was kind, indulgent
and ever ready to render assistance without ostentation.   He was
full of humor, overflowing with anecdote, and loved a neat, harm-

less practical joke. With rare capacity for treasuring up anecdotes, he had a fund to aptly illustrate almost every circumstance in life. Many were original with him, as he had an eye constantly on the look-out for the humorous or grotesque in everything, and a good point never escaped his attention, nor suffered in the rendering. Among the older members of the Illinois bar his humorous sayings, oddities, and pointed anecdotes are yet current.

During the presidential contest of 1844, Mr. Lincoln canvassed the State for Henry Clay, the beloved chief of all the old whigs. In 1846 he was elected to congress, taking his seat in the lower house at the same time that Douglas entered the senate. He was the only whig in the Illinois delegation, and in common with his party, opposed the Mexican war. He introduced a set of resolutions shortly after, proposing an inquiry as to the exact spot upon Texan soil where American blood was first spilled by the Mexicans. These resolutions gained some notoriety for their quisical and witty character, and have been generally known as his "spot resolutions." He supported the "Wilmot proviso" attached to the bill appropriating $3,000,000 for the war—being the same which Mr. Douglas moved to amend by prohibiting slavery from all acquired territory north of of 36d. 30m., but which was lost. Mr. Lincoln declined the candidacy for re-election in 1848. In 1849 he first received the complimentary vote of his party for U. S. senator. He was again their candidate in 1855, but through the obstinacy of a handful of anti-Nebraska democrats, Mr. Trumbull was elected, as we have seen.

Mr. Lincoln was truly great in many traits of his character. Chief among these may be mentioned his fidelity to the right, firmness to principle, fortitude to duty, honesty and tenacity of purpose, and moral courage, united to such amiable attributes as kindness of heart, forbearance for others, enduring patience, modesty and gentleness of disposition. All these virtues he possessed in an eminent derce. Some of his old, intimate and loving friends* say that he was ambitious, but his ambition was so tempered with patience, that it never would have, as it did not, overleap itself.

His opposition to slavery was grounded upon its inherent moral wrongfulness—that it was a great evil, socially, politically, and materially. His conscience revolted at its injustice, its degradation and cruelty. His heart naturally sympathized with the oppressed. Douglas, born and reared in free States, while he doubtless regarded slavery as a clog and hindrance to the material advancement of a people or State, never disclosed by any expression, either written or spoken, his conception of its moral enormity. The refrain of his speeches was ever to let the people decide it in their own way—"I do not care whether slavery is voted up or down."

Mr. Lincoln's speeches and writings bear the stamp of strong individuality—peculiarly Lincolnian—which crops out in nearly every paragraph. They abound in short pithy sentences, separate and distinct in themselves, approaching to aphorisms. Many of them are stamped with immortality. They are sublime conceptions of great truths, clothed in few but ample words, which will live in the remote cycles of time, when his more painstaking sentences and carefully-studied arguments may be lost under the moldering

* Hon. J. K. Dubois.
45

dust of ages. "Slavery is founded in the selfishness of man's nature—opposition to it in the love of justice," he exclaimed at Peoria in 1854. "Repeal the Missouri compromise—repeal all compromises—repeal the Declaration of Independence—repeal all past history—you still cannot repeal human nature. It still will be in the abundance of man's heart that slavery extension is wrong, and, out of the abundance of his heart his mouth will continue to speak." Evidently he was deeply read in the book of books, the Bible, as the last sentence above shows, and he possessed the happy faculty of weaving its sublime sentiments with his own thoughts and expressions. His speeches bore abundant testimony to this. Politicians should ever bear in mind this broad text from him, that ours is a "government of the people, for the people and by the people." But time and circumstances considered, it will be difficult to find sentiments outside of the inspired book more touchingly beautiful than the closing paragraph of his last inaugural address : "With malice toward none, with charity for all, with firmness in the right as God gives us to see the right, let us strive on to finish the work we are in, to bind up the nation's wounds, and care for him who shall have borne the battle, and for his widow and his orphans—to do all which may achieve and cherish a just and lasting peace among ourselves and with all nations."

To fully appreciate Mr. Lincoln as an orator he must be both heard and seen—he conveyed so much meaning by gesture and manner. And even then many of his sentiments were so terse that it was impossible to do him justice ; nor can this be done by a casual reading after him. He seemed to be aware of this himself, for in preparing his early writings or speeches for the press, understrokes for italics and capitals were freely resorted to, to give them power and emphasis.

Both these senatorial candidates used simple, plain but exact language, and eschewed mere word-painting. They sought to reach the understanding of the common people, and indulged little in the sweeping roundness of grand oratory. The best speeches of Mr. Lincoln's life are said to have been made four years prior to this contest, when the Missouri compromise was first repealed, in answer to Douglas, who sought to justify himself before the people. Mr. Lincoln was looking forward at the time to become the successor to Shields in the senate. One made at Peoria October 16, 1854, is recorded, and is a chaste and powerful argument. It received a wide circulation. The one made 12 days before at Springfield, in debate with Mr. Douglas, being the first time that these champions measured their strength, is not recorded. It is said to have greatly exceeded the former in boldness of sentiment, force of argument, beauty and moving eloquence. It was made in the representatives' hall in presence of the first State republican convention, when that party was in its chrysalis state, and a great throng of people from all parts of the State attending the first State fair. A contemporary writer describing it says : Every mind present did homage to the man who took heart and broke like a sun over the understanding; he shivered the Nebraska iniquity as a tree of the forest is torn and rent asunder, by hot bolts of truth.*

* See Ill. State Journal, Oct. 18, 1854.

Such is our brief summing up of the lives and character of these great representative men, upon whose contest in Illinois for the senatorship rested the eager eyes of the entire nation, so important were the political issues for which they contended. The combatants were not unacquainted with each other's strength, for as we have seen they had previously crossed their trenchant blades of argument, logic and debate in the political arena.*

THE CANVASS.

We have seen that the State republican convention in June declared Mr. Lincoln the first and only choice of its party for the senatorial seat of Mr. Douglas. Mr. Lincoln was not unprepared for this action of the convention. The choice of Trumbull over him in 1855 had gained him the sympathy of his party, and he was thence tacitly looked forward to as the successor of Mr. Douglas four years later. This he appreciated himself. When Douglas, (who well understood this also,) therefore, in June, 1857, during a lull in political excitement, found, or created, an occasion, through the invitation of the U. S. grand jury sitting at Springfield, to air his political views and possibly forestall public opinion, Mr. Lincoln was on the alert, and after some time for preparation, two weeks later answered Douglas' speech from the same stand, and had it also published. The convention now (June 16, 1858,) took a recess until 8 o'clock in the evening, when Mr. Lincoln addressed them in a carefully prepared speech, whose opening sentences—truly Lincolnian—aftewards attained so much celebrity, we subjoin:

"If we could first know *where* we are, and *whither* we are tending, we could then better judge what to do, and how to do it.

"We are now far into the fifth year since a policy was initiated with the *avowed* object, and *confident* promise, of putting an end to slavery agitation.

"Under the operation of that policy, that agitation has not only *not ceased*, but has *constantly augmented*

"In my opinion it *will* not cease until a *crisis* shall have been reached and passed—'A house divided against itself cannot stand.'

"I believe this government cannot endure permanently half *slave* and half *free*. I do not expect the Union to be *dissolved*—I do not expect the house to fall—but I do expect it will cease to be divided. It will become *all* one thing, or *all* the other. Either the *opponents* of slavery will arrest the further spread of it, and place it where the public mind shall rest in the belief that it is in the course of ultimate extinction; or, its *advocates* will put it forward, till it shall become alike lawful in *all* the States, *old* as well as *new*—*north* as well as *south*. Have we no *tendency* to the latter condition?"

—proceeding to argue that we had under the Nebraska doctrine and the Dred Scott decision.†

These at the time bold and advanced political sentiments were uttered 4 months prior to the enunciation of Mr. Seward's cele-

*The following figure, to illustrate the relative merits of the contestants, current at the time, views this civil battle from a military standpoint. We leave the reader to estimate its fairness: Douglas marshalled all his facts with the view to concentrate them with terrible and irresistible onslaught upon a given point of his adversary's line of battle, and with great power and energy attempts to rout the enemy from his strongest position. Lincoln in his argument breaks out all along his entire battle line in sudden charges, unsurpassed in brilliancy of execution, affording subjects for the poet's pen to live in heroic verse for perhaps countless ages

†See Ill. State Journal, June 19, 1858. The above is from a draft made by Mr. Lincoln himself, italics and all.

brated "irrepressible conflict" doctrine, which rendered that statesman the common target for all the opposition political shafts
throughout the land. Mr. Lincoln's had not only precedence, but
they were more comprehensive and direct; and is it any wonder
that political sentiments so axiomatic dwelt in the hearts of the
people, and subsequently turned the nation's eye upon the man
whose mind conceived them? But they also furnished Mr. Douglas a handle with which to ring upon his opponent, with incessant
repetition, all the changes of detested abolitionism, disunion and
civil war with its horrid concomitants, until they told with deep
effect upon the masses.

The republican press demanded for Mr. Lincoln, with frequent
iteration, a free political fight, which was no less freely tendered
by Mr. Douglas, who, before he left Washington, matured his
preparations for a vigorous and thorough stumping canvass, to
embrace the ample field of the entire State. Nowithstanding his
open rupture with the administration, which was pursuing him
into Illinois, the grudging support of the State democratic convention at its meeting in April forced him into a plan of campaign somewhat conciliatory toward the administration, but war
to the knife against the anti-slavery heresies, as he called them,
enunciated in the platform of principles adopted by the State
republican convention, and particularly against the advanced anti-
slavery position of their senatorial nominee. The republicans, to
promote the chism in the democratic ranks, encouraged the Buchanan followers in various ways by favorable notices of their
meetings, publishing their proceedings, flattering their efforts, &c.

Douglas, on his arrival from Washington, was received at Chicago by an immense concourse of people with shouts and huzzahs,
amidst the roar of cannon, music from bands and the escort of a
blaze of fire-works. He entered directly upon the campaign by
addressing his first speech from the balcony of the Tremont Hotel
to a perfect sea of human faces upturned in the thronged street
below. He re-affirmed his doctrine of popular sovereignty with
great force, stood by the platform, and acquiesced in the Dred
Scott decision while it remained the law. He then paid his
respects to Mr. Lincoln, who was present on the balcony, taking
for a text his convention speech, that a house divided against
itself cannot stand—that the government could not endure half
slave and half free, which he assailed with a logical power and
vehemence unsurpassed in his generation, leaving a deep and
abiding impression upon his auditory. He further denounced the
unholy alliance of the republicans with the unscrupulous pro-
slavery Buchanan office-holders to compass his defeat, as unnatural, declaring his purpose to fire his broadsides, as the Russians
did at Sebastopol, regardless of which were hit, Turk or Christian.

At the conclusion of his speech, loud calls were made by the
crowd for Mr. Lincoln. He declined speaking, but made an
appointment for the following evening, when he replied to Mr.
Douglas from the same stand. A larger, denser and more enthusiastic crowd, if that were possible, greeted the republican chieftain, the windows and balconies of the houses on both sides of
the street and the street itself being literally packed with men
and women. Procession after procession with bands of music
arrived on the ground amidst a brilliant pyrotechnic display. Mr.

Lincoln on his appearance was hailed with a storm of applause. He denied the charge of an alliance between the republicans and the federal office-holders, but the former would certainly do nothing to prevent the democratic schism, and reminded Douglas that if he was the "rugged Russian bear," it was a very suggestive circumstance that the "allies" did take Sebastopol—which was very happy. He declared Douglas' great doctrine of squatter sovereignty as old as the Declaration of Independence itself; that governments derived their just powers from the consent of the governed; but ridiculed the idea of its compatibility with the Dred Scott decision, which held slavery to exist in all the territories by virtue of the constitution, with which neither congress nor the territorial legislature could interfere. Hence no man could consistently stand both by that decision and the Cincinnati platform, which declared the sovereignty of the territories absolute as that of the States. He maintained the power of congress to exclude slavery from the territories, notwithstanding the decision of the supreme court.

But Douglas' great assault upon his convention speech, that a divided house could not stand, that the government could not endure half slave and half free—had the effect to throw him upon the defensive, from which he did not recover during the canvass. He plead—"I did not say that I was in favor of anything in it. I only said what I expecttd would take place. I made a prediction only; it may have been a foolish one perhaps."

Mr. Lincoln had taken bold and advanced ground. We who have lived to see his words fulfilled can hardly appreciate their full import as applied to those times. The striking deductions that Douglas made from them, apparently irresistible in their conclusions then, and which have become history since, tended to drive their author into the then detested ranks of the abolition-disunionists, hated of nearly all men, and need we wonder at Mr. Lincoln's shrinking from the position thus logically assigned to him, or at the defense of himself, as we have quoted? Douglas did not intermit his blows upon this point during the canvass, but hammered and battered away at it continuously. It was his stronghold, and under it he crowded his antagonist unceasingly. Indeed some republican papers got to denying that Lincoln ever uttered the sentiment. It lost him the senatorship then, but its unceasing iteration placed him prominently before the country, and two years later it gained for him the presidency. A prophet is not without honor save in his own country.

And now blazed forth in full splendor that remarkable canvass all over the State. The prairies seeemed animated with political fervor and discussions. The people did or talked little else. The business of railroads increased enormously. The trains were alive with the people and excursions were the order of the day. In attendance upon the great leaders were swarms of politicians, replaced from time to time as rapidly as they dropped off, besides journalists, reporters and others drawn by the excitement of the occasion. The ladies not unfrequently met the trains containing the leaders and attendants and spread for them bounteous repasts. Indeed creature comforts were occasionally furnished on the cars. Up and down the State and through its length and breadth, by rail, by carriage, raged the great political battle of the giants.

The people seemingly were aglow with the fire of their respective party leaders. The contest was the most exciting in our history.

. As an illustration of what was kept up all over the State, both on occasion of the joint debates and the separate discussions, we will describe Douglas' first trip, made on the Chicago & Alton railroad to Springfield, Mr. Lincoln being also aboard. Douglas and a party of friends left Chicago Friday morning, June 16th. The train, although it was the regular passenger, was tastily decorated with flags and banners, inscribed with the name of the senator, appropriate mottoes, such as "champion of the people," "popular sovereignty," &c. At Bridgeport a numerous body of laborers quit their work to cheer the senator as the train swept by. At Lockport a moment's halt was made, and hearty greetings were exchanged with the assembled friends, amidst the handkerchief wavings of welcome from numerous ladies. At Joliet its arrival was announced by the booming of cannon, and upon the senator's appearance the thousands assembled rent the air with their cheers. He had only time to thank them for their cordial welcome. A numerous party of friends here joined them for Springfield. A platform car was attached to the rear of the train, carrying a cannon to herald their approach at every station along the route. At Wilmington the salute of a 6-pounder was answered by this piece on board. A large concourse of people had assembled, and as the train drew up a fine band played "Hail to the Chief!" followed, on the appearance of the senator, by air-splitting cheers from the crowd, men swinging their hats, and ladies waving their handkerchiefs, making a scene of indescribable enthusiasm and joy. Tender greetings and kindly expressions were exchanged with the representative of the great principle of self-government. At every station these glowing scenes were repeated.

At Bloomington, where it was appointed for Douglas to speak, suitable arrangements for his welcome had been made. The day was inauspicious, but the people had gathered in large numbers through rain and mud. The Bloomington Guards in full uniform, citizens, mounted, on foot and in carriages, formed into line as an escort to the civic hero. A salute of 32 guns was fired on the approach of the train, and the appearance of the senator was followed by the usual expressions of enthusiasm greatly augmented. Douglas entered a carriage and a procession was formed which moved through the principal streets, lined on either side with dense masses of people, the windows and balconies of the houses filled with ladies waving their handkerchiefs. The Laudon House, the stopping place, was appropriately decorated with flags and mottoes of welcome for the occasion. At night there was a grand pyrotechnic display, the court house was brilliantly illuminated, and Douglas addressed the people in the public square. Mr. Lincoln was called out, but excused himself on the ground of its being Douglas' ovation.

On the following morning a special train took the party, which was further joined by the Bloomington Guards with their cannon and a large number of citizens, to Springfield. The train was appropriately decorated with beautiful flags and inscriptions.

At Atlanta both Douglas and Lincoln were called out by a large assemblage of people, and both excused themselves from speaking. At Lincoln a halt was made for dinner. The town was crowded with people, and the reception was splendid. The principal street was spanned by a triumphal arch—a graceful combination of leaves, flowers and evergreens, and small banners with mottoes, surmounted by a large one inscribed "Douglas Forever." The Lincoln House was also beautifully decorated, and, after partaking of a sumptuous repast, Douglas made a brief but happy address, received the congratulations of his friends, when the excursionists sped on their way towards the capital, the previous scenes being repeated at every station. At Williamsville, committees from counties south, east and west of Sangamon, met the train, and the party being greatly increased, two engines were brought into requisition; and thus with cannons firing, bands playing martial airs, the train, amidst the greetings, shoutings, and joys of a large multitude, sped into the capital city. A halt was made at Edwards' Grove, where, notwithstanding the occasional rain, the people from far and near had waited by thousands, and were now addressed by Douglas for three hours in one of his most masterly efforts.*

At night Mr. Lincoln spoke in the city. He had not heard Douglas. We subjoin the opening remarks:

"Fellow-Citizens: Another election which is deemed an important one is approaching, and, as I suppose, the republican party will, without much difficulty, elect their State ticket. But in regard to the legislature we, the republicans, labor under some disadvantages." This he attributed to a want of change in the apportionment of representatives in the legislature, still based upon the census of 1850, which bore with unequal effect upon the north part of the State, the republican stronghold, which had nearly doubled its population since then, while in the south part no corresponding increase had taken place.

He further alluded to some disadvantages of a personal character, in the following humorous vein:

"There is still another disadvantage under which we labor, and to which I ask your attention. It arises out of the relative positions of the two persons who stand before you as candidates for the senate. Senator Douglas is of world-wide renown. All the anxious politicians of his party have been looking to him as certainly, at no very distant day to be the president of the United States. They have seen in his round, jolly fruitful face post-offices, land-offices, marshalships, and cabinet appointments, chargeships and foreign missions, bursting and spouting out in wonderful exuberance, ready to be laid hold of by their greedy hands. (Great laughter.) And as they have been gazing upon this attractive picture so long they cannot, in the little distraction that has taken place in the party, bring themselves to quite give up the charming hope; but with greedier anxiety they rush about him, sustain him, give him marches, triumphal entries, and receptions beyond what even in the days of his highest prosperity they could have brought about in his favor. On the contrary, nobody has ever expected me to be president. In my poor, lean, lank face nobody has ever seen that any cabbages were sprouting out." [See Illinois State Register, July 22, 1858.]

How differently two year's time showed the result. But notwithstanding all these disadvantages, one week later he addressed Douglas a note dated Chicago July 24th, by the hand of the Hon. N. B. Judd, for an arrangement to "address the same audiences the present canvass." Mr. Douglas answered on the same day that under the advice of the democratic State central committee a list of appointments running into October had been made for him, at which legislative and congressional candidates would also

---

*Condensed from Ill. State Register of July 19, 1858.

be present occupying the whole time. His wily nature led him
further to suggest that in company with Mr. Lincoln would be a
third candidate for the senate, canvassing the State for the sole
purpose of dividing the democratic vote, who would also claim a
portion of the time from the same stand; and further in the same
politic vein expressed his surprise that Mr. Lincoln should have
waited till after his appointments were out when they had been
together a number of times before; but while not at liberty to
change his appointments he took the responsibility to stipulate
for joint discussions in 7 congressional districts, one in each, they
having already both spoken in the 2d and 6th—Chicago and Springfield. He named Ottawa, Freeport, Quincy, Jonesboro, Charleston, Galesburg and Alton, the speaking to alternate by opening
for 1 hour, answering 1½, and replying ½—he taking the openings
at the first and last places. Mr. Lincoln replied protesting against
the insinuations of unfairness, which, he thought groundless and
unjust; denied any knowlege of his plan of appointments;
thought Douglas had the advantage in the openings and closings
of the speaking, and accepted the proposition. But their separate appointments were such also that they usually followed each
other in rapid order, in one place, Sullivan, on the same day.

The champions first met for joint discussion at Ottawa. They were
attended by short-hand reporters, many leading newspapers abroad
had their special correspondents on the ground, and the speeches
were carefully taken down and widely circulated. It is not our
purpose to give a synopsis of the debates, which have been fully
published, but to draw attention to a few leading occurrences.

Douglas here propounded 7 questions to Mr. Lincoln, all based
upon a resolution that he mistakenly supposed the first State
republican convention had adopted at Springfield, October 4,
1854, and which had recognized Mr. Lincoln by placing him on
the State central committee. The leading question was whether
he favored the unconditional repeal of the fugitive slave law?
The resolution proposed " to repeal and entirely abrogate the fugitive slave law;" but Mr. Lincoln had already declared his reluctant support of a just and equitable fugitive slave law, because the
constitution was mandatory upon that point, and the republican
conventions of 1856-8 had omitted to declare against the rendition of fugitives from labor. Douglas, to prove Lincoln's position extreme or inconsistent, as also the republicans generally,
made use of this resolution—into which he was led by the Springfield *Register*, which had published it with the proceedings of the
convention. It was really a resolution adopted by a Kane county
meeting; but Mr. Lincoln was not aware of the mortifying mistake Douglas had fallen into. The republican press, however,
soon unearthed it, and the opportunity to assail Douglas thus
afforded was fully availed. Its columns teemed with charges of
"bold and deliberate forgery," "unparalleled mendacity," "dastardly infamy," &c.*

At Freeport, 6 days after, Mr. Lincoln answered Douglas's inter-
rogatories, this one in the negative, and then propounded 4 to

* To show the depth of party and personal feeling against Douglas at the time, the
Chicago *Press & Tribune* spoke of him at Ottawa, as follows: "He howled, he ranted,
he bellowed, he pawed dirt, he shook his head, he turned livid in the face, he struck
his right hand into his left, he foamed at the mouth, he anathematized, he cursed, he
exulted, he domineered—he played Douglas."

Douglas, which the latter proceeded to answer immediately, making them the subject of his speech. While this proved his ready and wonderful powers of debate, it would have perhaps been well to have deliberated some time as Mr. Lincoln had done. The 2d interrogatory was: "Can the people of a United States territory, in any lawful way, against the wishes of any citizen of the United States, exclude slavery from its limits prior to the formation of a State constitution?"

The Dred Scott decision was, that congress had no right to prohibit a citizen of the United States from taking any property which he lawfully held into a territory of the United States; and that if congress could not do this, it could not authorize a territorial government, in the absence of any distinction in property, to exclude slaves, which were property under the constitution. In his Chicago speech, Douglas had said that to this decision of the august tribunal of the supreme court he bowed with deference. Now he said: "I answer emphatically that in my opinion the people of a territory can by lawful means exclude slavery before it comes in as a State. Mr. Lincoln knew that I had given that answer over and over again." But in the very next breath he intimated that this could only be done by the adoption of unfriendly police regulations, by the territorial legislature withholding the needed local or municipal laws, without which slavery could not exist a day anywhere.

The Freeport speech caused Douglas to be severely denounced, not only at home but abroad, by republicans, for his gross inconsistency and change of front, and throughout the south as having at last shown his cloven foot; they could have no further confidence in a northern man who unnecessarily espoused their interests against his own section.

After this the general scope of their discussions was not materially enlarged. It was slavery in the territories and the rights of the people in relation thereto, Mr. Lincoln insisting that congress, notwithstanding the *obiter dictum* of the supreme court in the Dred Scott decision, had the right, the same as when the ordinance of 1787 was adopted, to exclude slavery, and ought to exercise it; and Mr. Douglas holding that the vexed question ought to be referred to the people of the territory immediately concerned, to settle as their other domestic institutions in their own sovereign way, subject only to the constitution of the United States. Mr. Lincoln did not assume an attitude of hostility to slavery in the States, other than that he desired it "to be put in course of ultimate extinction," the language of his first convention speech. He did not repeat or enlarge upon the extreme ground of this speech, but constantly guarded against it, though Douglas throughout the debates essayed to push him on to it.

Whilst there were but 7 joint discussions, the two champions had their separate programmes for speaking so arranged for them that they addressed very nearly the same crowds in many counties of the State, sometimes on the same day, but oftener with only a very short time intervening. In Sullivan, Moultrie county, where they spoke on the same day, a serious collision between their respective crowds was imminent for a time. Mr. Lincoln had purposed deferring his speech to the last, but as a separate stand had been erected by the republicans in the north part of the town, they formed a procession of their forces, and in marching thither attempted to go right through the other crowd in the street where Douglas was speaking, and out of their way. This was not to be brooked; a parley ensued, during which the band wagon was attempted to be driven through the crowd and a conflict was the immediate result. But through the commanding voice of Douglas, beyond a few blows, a general melee was averted.

At Winchester, his first home, Douglas' enthusiastic greeting was deeply touching. The old county of Scott was never so aroused before. His arrival was announced by the roar of cannon and the glad shouts of a large assemblage. Here among these people the now great senator had first cast his lot a penniless stranger. Here he had taught school, and among his auditory were gray-haired sires and fond old matrons who had entrusted to him the education of their children, and pupils whom he had taught. All the old settlers well remembered him in his poverty and obscurity, and doubtless the entire community were now animated by that pleasant pride and affection which said "we are the makers of this great man"—glorying in his fame and prosperity—and with that feeling welcomed the whilom schoolmaster in his present character of the great American statesman. Let the reader trust both the heart and mind of Douglas to suitably deal with the occasion of such a kindly re-union, and display to the utmost those wonderful powers of eloquence which were placed under additional tribute by the time, circumstance and place. He alluded, in the most touching manner, to his advent and residence at Winchester, his early struggles and honest efforts for a beginning in a strange land; the ready imagination of his hearers readily suggesting the rest, while many a tear of joy crept down furrowed cheeks as the spontaneous outburst of cheers from friend and political foe rent the air, and attested the opinion of all in entire approbation of his subsequent career, more exalted, but among true Americans, not more honorable. The audience and occasion were suggestive of a rich vein of sentimental topics to the orator, and none escaped him or were omitted. It is a source of regret that this speech, so well calculated to give us a fuller insight into the depth of Douglas' better nature, was not recorded.

The result of the election returned to the legislature, in the house, 40 democrats and 35 republicans; the senate stood 14 democrats and 11 republicans, giving the former 8 majority on joint ballot. The republicans carried the State by a plurality, the vote standing: republicans, 124,698; democrats, 121,190; Buchanan democrats, and scattering, 4,863.

And now the administration clique, defeated in their efforts to beat Douglas, fell out among themselves, and blamed each other for the result. It seems that some of the Buchanan office-holders, like Ike Cook and others, favored the direct support of the republicans at the polls, while others, like R. B. Carpenter,[†] etc., made the fight against Douglas and the republicans, both, on principle. Many charges of subserviency, gross deception of the president as to their strength, blunders, follies and villainies, were bandied back and forth. Col. John Dougherty, the administration candi-

*See Ill. State Register, Sept. 25, 1858
†See his letter to Chicago Democrat, Nov., 1858.

date for treasurer, who had received less than 5,000 votes out of the one-fourth of a million cast, issued a manifesto to the people of Illinois, through the Cairo *Gazette*, "reading the entire democratic party out of the party, and insisting that their delegates should not be admitted to the Charleston convention [in 1860]."* The Buchanan party now affected to believe that Douglas would be defeated before the legislature; but when the time came there were no opponents to him before the democratic caucus,† though he was absent, and he was re-elected by 54 votes to Mr. Lincoln 46. He telegraphed back from Baltimore—"Let the voice of the people rule."

Thus terminated this unprecedented senatorial contest, which was waged throughout with a vigor and spirit which had no parallel in the history of parties in this or any other State. Both the great political organizations fought with a fierceness which never lagged for a moment, but increased with every coming day. With Douglas, apparently, his political fortune was at stake. The republicans, after the election, complimented Mr. Lincoln for the strong and noble fight he had made, what no other man in the State could have done for the cause; and they consoled him in the language of Pope:

> "More true joy Marcellus exiled feels
> Than Cæsar with a *senate* at his *heels*."

Mr. Lincoln was thus brought conspicuously before the nation as one of the ablest leaders of the opposition; and, in the humble opinion of the writer, this great contest, which primarily resulted simply in the making of a U. S. senator of one of the contestants, directed the public eye to the merits of the other, and caused him to become the standard bearer, two years later, of that party whose cardinal principle demanded freedom for the public domain, and which, aided by the divisions in the ranks of the democracy, carried him by their voices triumphantly into the presidential chair; which the south deemed a sufficient affront for disunion.

Having consumed so much space to complete the sketch of our senators in congress, we can only say that to the seat of Douglas, after his death in 1861, succeeded, 1st, the Hon. O. H. Browning by appointment from Gov. Yates; 2d, the legislature in 1863, being democratic, and fierce in partisan spirit, Browning failed of confirmation, and the Hon. W. A. Richardson was elected for the remainder of Douglas' unexpired term. In the three executive appointments to senatorial vacancies in the history of the State—Baker in 1830, Semple in 1843, and Browning in 1861—only one, that of Semple, has been confirmed by the legislature. In 1865 Richard Yates was elected to the same seat for a full term, and he in 1871 was succeeded by Gen. John A. Logan, who is the second native Illinoisan that has ever filled that exalted office for this State.

---

* "Not having the fear of numbers before his eyes, he boldly ruled the 121,000 democrats who voted for Douglas. out, to graze upon the common, as unworthy to associate with him, and sat the autocrat of the party in Illinois"—said the St. Louis *Republican* at the time.

† Though in September Judge Breese in a letter to Mr. Boyakin, of the Belleville *Democrat*, wrote: "I demand as a right to know who requested you to say as you have said in an editorial in your paper of the 4th. that "Judge Breese is not, nor will he be, a candidate for the U. S. senate in opposition to Mr. Douglas."

CHAPTER LIII.

1861–1865—ADMINISTRATION OF GOVERNOR YATES.

*Party Conventions of 1860—The two Great Labor Systems of the
Country in Direct Antagonism—Life and Character of Gover-
nor Yates—Lieutenant Governor Hoffman—Condition of the
State and Comparative Growth since 1850.*

———

The republican State convention of 1860 met at Decatur, May
9th. Every county except Pulaski was represented. The Hon.
Joseph Gillespie, of Madison, was chosen to preside over its
deliberations. For the candidacy of governor there were three
aspirants: Norman B. Judd, of Cook, Leonard Swett, of McLean,
and Richard Yates, of Morgan. On the first ballot Judd received
245 votes, Swett 191, Yates 183 and James Knox 12; on the third
ballot Judd received his highest number, 263; on the fourth all
the Swett men but 36 went to the support of Yates, giving him
363 votes, which nominated him. Judd had incurred the formidable opposition of the Chicago *Democrat*, then a power with the
republican party of the State. Francis A. Hoffman, of DuPage,
was next nominated as a candidate for lieutenant governor by
acclamation. The remainder of the ticket was: For auditor, Jesse
K. Dubois; for treasurer, William Butler; for secretary of State,
O. M. Hatch, and for superintendent of public instruction, Newton Bateman—all incumbents. The Bloomington platform of 4
years before was re-adopted with a stronger plank regarding the
right of foreigners, doubtless to sweeten the slightly remaining
taint of know nothingism that democrats might scent about republican garments. They also declared for a homestead act by congress, and the immediate admission of Kansas as a free State. A
resolution was adopted that Abraham Lincoln was the choice of
the republican party of Illinois for president, and the delegates
from this State were instructed to use all honorable means to
secure his nomination at the Chicago convention, and to vote for
him as a unit. A motion to strike out the last clause was
defeated.

Mr. Hoffman, candidate for lieutenant governor, it will be
remembered by the reader, was nominated for the same place on
the republican ticket in 1856, but shortly after was found not to
be eligible to the office if elected, he being a German and not a
citizen for 14 years as the constitution required. He now refused
to run for the position, alleging ill health. The State central committee put the name of Hon. Vital Jarrot, of St. Clair, on the
ticket in his stead. But the congressional convention of the 3d

district at Bloomington refused to ratify his nomination, whereupon he also declined to run. The objection was that it gave both gubernatorial candidates to the southern portion of the State. The State convention was thereupon recalled and met again, this time at Springfield, August 8th, on occasion of the great republican mass meeting at the home of Lincoln, one of the grandest outpourings of the people and largest civic demonstration with which any public man was ever honored. In convention, on motion of Mr. Jarrot, Mr. Hoffman had leave to withdraw his letter of declination, and his nomination was again unanimously confirmed.

The State democratic convention of 1860 met at Springfield in the hall of the house of representatives, June 13th. Hon. Wm. McMurtry, of Knox, presided. On the first ballot to nominate a candidate for governor, J. C. Allen, of Crawford, received 157 votes; S. A. Buckmaster, of Madison, 81; J. L. D. Morrison, of St. Clair, 88; Newton Cloud, of Morgan, 65; W. B. Scates, of Cook, 14; J. A. McClernand and B. S. Edwards, both of Sangamon, 2 each. On the second ballot it was soon disclosed that Allen was the favorite, and all the other competitors being withdrawn before the announcement of the vote, Allen's nomination was made unanimous. The balance of the ticket was: For lieutenant governor, L. W. Ross, of Fulton; secretary of State, G. H. Campbell, of Logan; auditor, Bernard Arntzen, of Adams; treasurer, Hugh Maher, of Cook; superintendent of public instruction, Dr. E. R. Roe, of McLean. Their resolutions reaffirmed the principles of the Cincinnati platform of 1856, approved the course of the delegates to the Charleston convention, and expressed their confidence in Stephen A. Douglas for president.

On July the 11th, the Buchanan or Breckinridge democracy met in convention also at Springfield, and put the following State ticket in the field: For governor, Dr. Thomas M. Hope, of Madison; lieutenant governor, Thomas Snell, of DeWitt; secretary of State, B. T. Burke, of Macoupin; auditor, Henry S. Smith, of Knox; treasurer, W. H. Cather, of Adams; superintendent of public instruction, J. H. Dennis, of St. Clair; the electors at large being John Dougherty and Thompson Campbell. Eleven counties out of 102 were represented by 53 delegates, 41 of whom were currently reported at the time as federal office-holders.

The Bell-Everett State convention met at Decatur, Aug. 16, 1860. Thirty counties were represented by an aggregate of 92 delegates. They nominated the following ticket: For governor, the Hon. John T. Stuart, of Sangamon; lieutenant governor, Henry S. Blackburn, of Rock Island; secretary of State, James Monroe, of Coles; auditor, James D. Smith, of Sangamon; treasurer, Jonathan Stamper, of Macon; superintendent of public instruction, D. J. Snow, of Sangamon; electors at large, M. Y. Johnson, of JoDaviess and D. M. Woodson, of Green.

Thus 4 tickets were in the field. The political contest of 1860 over the question of slavery was the most momentous in the history of this nation. The two great labor systems of the country, free and slave, representing their respective sections, were brought into direct antagonism for the first time in a presidential election. The southern wing of the democratic party, spurning Douglas and his theory of popular sovereignty at Charleston, split from its northern associate, and eagerly brought forward the labor system of its section and opposed it to that of the north. The issue thus presented was so clearly defined that it was impossible to long occupy any middle ground. The power of Douglas alone held his followers to one for a time, but it was apparent that all between would soon be but a chaotic mass, whose particles, drifting hither and thither, must find lodgment on the side within whose sectional or local focus of attraction they chanced to come. The inexorable logic of events disclosed the completion of an inevitable destiny. The house was indeed divided against itself, and the irrepressible conflict was at hand. The canvass proved both an exciting and determined one, and the fearful consequences have passed into history, abundantly and ably written up by other hands.

The victory at the polls for the republicans of Illinois in 1860 was complete. They carried the presidential and State tickets, and gained both houses of the legislature, each by a small majority. For governor, Yates received 172,196, Allen 159,253, Stuart 1,626, Hope 2,049 and Chickering 1,140. The vote on the presidential ticket was: for Lincoln, 171,106; Douglas, 158,254; Bell-Everett, 4,851; and Breckenridge, 2,292. With few exceptions the adherents of the latter two tickets—particularly the leaders of the Breckinridge faction—were shortly afterwards absorbed by the republican party, where some of the Buchanan men have since attained distinction, both for their radicalism and success in obtaining office.

Richard Yates was born January 18, 1818, on the banks of the Ohio river, at Warsaw, Gallatin county, Kentucky. His father, in 1831, moved to Illinois, and settled (after stopping for a time in Springfield,) at Island Grove, Sangamon county. Here, after attending school, Richard joined the family. Subsequently, he entered Illinois College, at Jacksonville, where, in 1837, he graduated with first honors. He chose for his profession the law, the Hon. J. J. Hardin being his instructor. After admission to the bar he soon rose to distinction as an advocate. Gifted with a fluent and ready oratory, he soon appeared in the political hustings, and being a passionate admirer of the great whig leader of the west, Henry Clay, he joined his political fortunes to the party of his idol. In 1840 he engaged with great ardor in the exciting "hard cider campaign" for Harrison. Two years later he was elected to the legislature from Morgan county, a democratic stronghold. He served three or four terms in the legislature, and such was the fascination of his oratory, that by 1850 his large congressional district, extending from Morgan and Sangamon north to include La Salle, unanimously tendered him the whig nomination. His opponent of the democratic party, was Major Thomas L. Harris, a very popular man, who had won distinction at the battle of Cerro Gordo, in the late war with Mexico, and who, though the district was whig, had beaten for the same position, two years before, the Hon. Stephen T. Logan by a large majority. The contest between Yates and Harris, animating and persevering, resulted in the election of the former. Two years later, the democracy ungenerously thrust aside Major Harris and pitted John Calhoun against Yates, and, though Calhoun was a man of great intellect, and when aroused, of unsurpassed ability as a political debater—whom. Mr. Lincoln had said he would dread more in debate than any man in Illinois—the result was as before. It was during Yates' second term that the great question of the repeal of the Missouri compromise came before congress, against which he early arrayed himself, and took decided and advanced anti-slavery ground in a speech of rare oratory and remarkable power, which gained him national reputation. But we have seen that at this formative period of the republican party, the whigs of central Illinois, unwilling to join their fortunes with a sectional party, went with the democracy, and in 1854, Major Harris being again his opponent for congress, Yates was defeated on the Nebraska issue by only about 200 votes in the district which had given Pierce two years before 2,000 majority over Scott. Six years later he was elected governor by the party, for the aid in the formation of which he had suffered this defeat.

Richard Yates occupied the chair of State during the most critical period of our country's history. In the fate of the nation was involved the destiny of the States. The life-struggle of the former derived its sustenance from the loyalty of the latter. The position of governor of a great State was, therefore, important and responsible, as it was capable of being exerted for vast good or immense evil. Need it be said that in this trying period he discharged his duty with patriotic fidelity to the cause of the nation? Gov. Yates had many valuable attributes for his high station in this ordeal of the country. His loyalty was as undoubted as it proved itself true. He was the close personal friend of President Lincoln. His ardent devotion to the Union was founded upon a deep love for it. While he had been early identified with the formation of the republican party, he had not been connected with the old abolitionists, among whom were persons who preferred the success of their hobby to the safety of the Union. But above all, he had a deep hold upon the affections of the people, won by his moving eloquence and genial manners. He inspired strong attachments among his partisan friends. Nature had fashioned him to be admired by the masses. Handsome, erect and symmetrical in person, with a winning address and a magnetic power, few men possessed more of the elements of popularity. His oratory, into the spirit of which he entered with apparent forgetfulness of self, was scholarly and captivating, the hearer hardly knowing why he was transported. Though less logical than eloquent, he reasoned well, and always inspired deep and enduring partisan attachments. He was social and convivial to an eminent degree, traits of character, which, however, were subjected to little of puritanic denial; but in the very excesses of his appetites he has carried with him the sympathies of the people, almost irrespective of party, on account of his many noble attributes of head and heart.

The very creditable military efforts of this State during the war of the rebellion, in putting her quotas, aggregating the enormous number of about 200,000* soldiers in the field, were ever promptly

*In 1850 Illinois had a population of 851,470, and according to the army register for 1851, her militia numbered 170,359, 4,168 of whom were commissioned officers: in 1860, she had a population of 1,711,951, which would have given her at the breaking out of the rebellion, in 1861. a militia force of 350,000, and out of this number nearly 200,000 volunteers were furnished.

and ably seconded by his excellency: he was ambitious to deserve the title of the soldiers' friend. His proclamations calling for volunteers are impassionate appeals, urging the duties and requirements of patriotism upon the people; and his special messages to the last democratic legislature of this State, pleading for material aid for the sick and wounded soldiers of Illinois regiments, breathe a deep fervor of noble sentiment and feeling rarely equalled in beauty or felicity of expression. Generally his messages on political or civil affairs were able and comprehensive; though on these subjects, particularly the former, his style is perhaps too florid and diffuse. There were no State civil events of an engrossing character during Gov. Yates' administration; two years of it, however, were replete with partisan quarrels of great bitterness, during the sitting of the constitutional convention of 1862, and the sessions of the last democratic legislature in 1863, which latter body he finally squelched by his act of prorogation. These the reader will find summed up further along. The operations of Illinois regiments in the field are also elsewhere recorded in detail.

Lieut. Gov. Hoffman was born at Herford, Prussia, 1822. He was the son of a bookseller, and educated at the Frederich William Gymnasium of his native town. At the age of 18 he emigrated to America, landing penniless in New York. Borrowing $8 he started west, and after a toilsome journey reached Chicago in 1840. Moneyless and unable to speak the English language, he taught a small German school at Dunkley's Grove, DuPage county, at $50 a year, with the privilege of "boarding around" among its patrons. Next, having studied theology, he was ordained a minister of the Lutheran church. In 1852 he removed to Chicago, studied law, was successful in the real estate business, became a free-banker in 1854, and as such, with the secession of 1861 and the downfall of our "stumptail" currency, failed. He had annually published, in German, a review of the commerce and finances of Chicago, and scattering thousands of copies in his native land, materially benefited her growth; and as commissioner of the foreign land department of the Central Railroad Company, he was instrumental in inducing many thousands of German families to purchase lands and settle in Illinois.

He early took an active interest in public affairs. In 1847 he was a member of the famous River and Harbor convention at Chicago. In 1853 he was elected alderman for the 8th ward of that city. He was among the first of the prominent Germans of the northwest to advocate the anti-slavery cause by writing for the first German newspaper of Chicago, and translating from the German for the *Democrat*. In 1848 he supported Van Buren for the presidency; with the repeal of the Missouri compromise he aided in the organization of the republican party, and in 1856 canvassed the State for Fremont. Well educated, a clear mind, decision and energy, he acquitted himself with dignity and impartiality as the presiding officer of the Senate during a period replete with partisan strife, and the most perilous in our history.†

Comparative Growth of the State since 1850.—The national census of 1860 revealed for Illinois a population of 1,711,951, against

†See "Biographical Sketches of leading men of Chicago," by A. Shuman.

851,470 in 1850—an increase of over 100 per cent. in the preceding decade. This ranked her as the fourth State in the Union in point of population, and entitled her to 14 members in the lower house of congress.

The following table from the census reports show her increase in wealth during this period:

Classes of Property.	1850.	1860
Real and personal	$156,000,000	$871,000,000
Value of farms	96,000,000	432,000,0 0
Value of farming implements	6,000,000	18,000,000
Value of orchard products	446,049	1,145,936
Value of live stock	24,000,000	73.434,000
Value of animals slaughtered	4,972,000	15.0.0,000
Wheat raised, No. bushels	9,414,000	24,159,003
Corn raised, No. bushels	57,546.600	115,296,000
Barley, No. bushels	110,000	1,175,000
Buckwheat, No. bushels	184,000	345.000
Potatoes, No. bushels	2,514,060	5,799,964
Hay, tons	601,952	1,834,265
Butter, lbs	1,200,000	28,337,000
Tobacco, lbs	841,394	7,014,234
Total No of acres improved	500,000	13,251,000

This shows the aggregate wealth of 1850 to have multiplied five times in one decade; the value of farms 4½ times. But while the census of 1860 gave us a total property value of $871,000,000 the assessed value for the same year was not quite $390,000,000. Illinois was the first corn and wheat producing State in the Union; in value of her live stock she was second; in cattle, Texas and Ohio were ahead; in the number of horses, Ohio was also ahead, having 622,829 to Illinois 575,161; in the number of improved acres, New York alone led her by about 1,000,000 acres.

The permanent debt of the State in 1860 was $10,277.161.

CHAPTER LIV.

ILLINOIS IN THE WAR OF THE REBELLION.

*Slavery—Sectional Antagonism—Secession—Inauguration of Lincoln
—Call for Volunteers—Proclamation of Gov. Yates—Uprising of
the People.*

In 1861 the Great Rebellion assumed a definite shape, and a civil war of the most astounding magnitude followed. The primary cause of the antagonism which existed between the Northern and Southern sections of the Union was the institution of slavery. Other agencies doubtless served proximately to intensify the hostility unfortunately engendered, but in every instance, if not directly connected with this great national evil, their remote origin could be traced to it.

The federal constitution recognized slavery, but its framers supposed that in the different States where it existed the benign influences of free institutions and the palpable advantages of free labor, would extirpate it without the intervention of the general government. These happy anticipations at first seemed likely to be realized. Commencing with the more northern of the slave States the work of emancipation gradually extended southward till it reached Virginia, Maryland and Kentucky, where its further progress was stayed. The growth of cotton in the Gulf States had in the meantime become a source of vast wealth, and the belief that slavery was essential to its cultivation greatly modified the repugnance with which it had hitherto been regarded. The remaining slave States, now actuated by pecuniary considerations, abandoned the idea of emancipation and accepted slavery as a permanent institution. The invention of the cotton-gin and other machinery gave a new impetus to the cultivation of cotton, and the fabrics manufactured from it, and those engaged in this great branch of industry soon resolved not only to protect slavery where it existed, but demanded new territory for its future expansion. In carving new States out of the vast unoccupied portion of the national domain, a bitter sectional contest arose as to whether the new members of the confederacy should belong to the empire of freedom or slavery. The opponents of slavery were desirous of restricting it to its original limits, but the cotton States threatened to withdraw from the Union if their demands were not granted, thus causing grave apprehensions for the safety of the republic unless the question could be amicably adjusted. Pending the admission of Missouri into the Union a compromise was at length effected, making the southern boundary of that State the

722

line of demarkation between free and slave territory. This was supposed at the time to be a final settlement of the dangerous question, for no one proposed to interfere with slavery within its original limits.

The recognition and protection thus offered inspired new confidence in the advocates of slavery, and so enhanced the value of its capital that they ultimately became the principal elements of southern wealth. With her capital thus invested the south necessarily became agricultural, and hence the agitation that arose in regard to the tariff, culminating in the attempt of South Carolina to nullify the laws of the U. S. for collecting duties. Notwithstanding repeated threats on the part of this refractory member of the Union to withdraw, the sturdy determination of Jackson secured the enforcement of law, but the cause which had produced the disturbance still existed, and soon disclosed itself in another form. By the treaty with Mexico vast accessions of territory were made to the national domain, and southern politicians insisted on the repeal of the Missouri compromise, declaring they had a right under the constitution to take their chattels to any part of the western territory and compete with the north in the formation of new States. The question was brought before the national legislature, and this compact, originally established for the benefit of slavery, for the same purpose was now annulled, thereby renewing sectional agitation and animosity. The fertile plains of Kansas, situated within the region which had been consecrated to freedom, were rapidly attracting population, and a fierce struggle immediately arose to decide whether the territory should be admitted into the Union as a free or slave State. As its character in this respect must now be determined by the vote of actual residents, emigrants in great numbers were hurried into it from the rival sections. After a protracted contest the champions of slavery, finding themselves in the minority, and knowing the result of the ballot would be against them, endeavored to gain ascendency by intrigue and violence.

The startling fact now became apparent, even to the southern mind, that while slavery enabled the few who owned and controlled it to amass princely fortunes, and live idle and profligate lives, it correspondingly impoverished the States in which it existed. At the adoption of the federal constitution both sections started with perhaps equal natural advantages, but one having free and the other compulsory labor, an immense disparity now existed between them in all the elements of power and civilization. The North, with its vastly preponderating population, could now people and control the greater part of the unoccupied territory, and with the repeal of the Missouri compromise the South had given the legal right to it.

During the years of increasing excitement the general government remained uncommitted to either section, but the States in which the contest originally commenced daily became more hostile, and in some instances laws were enacted calculated to further inflame the public mind. A remarkable fact, however anomalous it may appear, was that the extreme northern and southern States, the most remote from the evils complained of and the least likely to be affected by the issue which entered into the controversy, manifested the greatest hostility. In many northern localities the

impression prevailed that the rendition of slaves to their masters
was wrong, and the enforcement of the fugitive slave law met
with strong opposition, while in the South those who expressed
themselves condemnatory of slavery were subjected to indignities
which even barbarism would hesitate to impose. Truth ever
demands investigation, and error ever shuns it, consequently
those who in the interest of slavery imposed restraint upon free
speech virtually acknowledged they were endeavoring to uphold
an institution intrinsically wrong. This moral despotism set up
in the midst of the republic further exasperated the northern mind,
the indignation becoming so unmanageable in some instances as
to transcend the requirements of law and order.

As a result of the sectional feeling, conventions assembled in
the different parts of the South ostensibly for commercial purposes, but in reality to plot treason against the general government. The church, for a long time involved in the controversy, in
some of its branches, endeavored to maintain conservative ground,
while others were torn asunder by the violence and antagonism
of the contest. Southern clergymen, while preaching redemption
from spiritual bondage, strangely insisted that the political bondage of the African, which imbruited both the soul and body of
its victims, was a divine institution. Southern disunionists also
endeavored to poison the public mind with the impression that
the future triumph of the republican party would be a justifiable
pretext for dissolving the Union. Said Jefferson Davis in a speech
at Jackson, Miss.: "If an abolitionist be chosen president of the
United States you will have presented to you the question
whether you will permit the government to pass into the hands of
your avowed and implacable enemies. Without pausing for an
answer, I will state my own position to be that such a result would
be a species of revolution by which the purposes of the government would be destroyed, and the observances of its mere forms
entitled to no respect. In that event, in such manner as should be
most expedient, I should deem it your duty to provide for your
safety outside of the Union." Said the unscrupulous politician,
W. L. Yancy: "The remedy of the south is in a diligent organization of her true men for prompt resistance to the next aggression. It must come in the nature of things. No additional party
can save us; no sectional party can ever do it. But if we could do
as our fathers did, organize committees of safety all over the cotton
States, and it is only by these that we can hope for any effective
movement. We shall fire the southern heart, instruct the southern mind, give courage to each and at the proper moment, by one
organized concerted action, we can precipitate the cotton States
into a revolution."

While the political horizon was assuming this alarming aspect
the presidential contest of 1860 gave additional intensity to sectional excitement. The supporters of Mr. Breckenridge evinced
the greatest hostility toward the republicans, and openly declared
their determination never to submit to the government if it should
pass into their hands. Formerly similar denunciations and threats
caused the most serious alarm, but now they had become so common that in the fierce storms of political excitement that swept
over the country they were little regarded. The protracted contest at length terminated in the election of Mr. Lincoln. It was

evident to all who were conversant with the progress of events that the supremacy which the south had so long maintained in the government was at an end. The southern malcontents must now either submit to republican rule or put in practice their oft-repeated threat to dissolve the Union. The latter alternative was chosen.

As the result of this election was flashed over the telegraph wires, it was hailed as a pretext for secession. The cities of the Gulf States were nightly illuminated, and preparations were immediately commenced for the coming conflict. Ignoring the moral sense of mankind, which had long since condemned slavery, they proposed to found a nation recognizing the absolute supremacy of the white man and the perpetual bondage of the negro. Long accustomed to the exercise of arbitrary power over the body and soul of the bondman, they had lost all sympathy for free institutions, and while ostensibly proposing to establish a republic, their ultimate object was doubtless the upbuilding of a monarchy. States and nations when subjected to great evils which the governing power refuses to rectify have the right of revolution, but the abettors of the present movement had no such justification. The dominant party had come into power strictly within the pale of the constitution and law, and with a platform fully recognizing the right of each State to manage its domestic institutions in its own way. It is true the incoming president had given it as his opinion that the government could not remain permanently half slave and half free, but this was in view of the fact that natural law rendered the two conditions wholly incompatible, and not because he wished to make the civil law a disturbing element. On the contrary, he had said in a speech at Cincinnati the previous year, "I now assure you that I neither had nor now have any purpose in any way of interfering with the institution of slavery where it exists. I believe we have no power under the constitution of the United States, or rather under the form of government under which we live, to interfere with the institution of slavery or any other institution of our sister States."

But independent of grievances, the south maintained that the several States on entering the Union, reserved to themselves the right to secede from it whenever they deemed their interest rendered it expedient. In the north it was contended that the power, if not expressed, is implied in the fundamental law of all governments to protect and indefinitely prolong their existence that the framers of our constitution never intended to incorporate in it any provision for its destruction; that its checks and balances for preserving harmony in the different departments of government were designed to make it a mighty fabric capable of resisting the most adverse vicissitudes of coming time; that the doctrine of voluntary secession if admitted would disintegrate all existing governments, and reduce society to a chaos, that mankind, whether in an individual or corporate capacity, must therefore submit to just restraint in order to secure the beneficent ends contemplated by good government. It was contended moreover the States of Louisiana, Florida and Texas cost the general government between $200,000,000 and $300,000,000, and it was unreasonable to suppose that they could withdraw at pleasure after the obligation incurred by the expenditures of this vast sum of money, that a primary object of their acquisition was to obtain control of the Mississippi, and the people of the northwest could never consent that it should flow hundreds of miles through foreign jurisdiction and thus be compelled to submit to the arbitrary imposition of duties upon their commerce.

When, however, the hour finally came for committing the overt act which should dismember the great republic, even the reckless conspirators, who had for years derided the warnings of statesmen, and stigmatized them as Union-savers, trembled in view of the consequences which must follow. The people especially, among whom there were many loyalists, hesitated to enter the yawning abyss, whose dark and angry depths the ken of human wisdom was unable to fathom. Some of their wisest and most patriotic leaders, till borne down by the tide of revolution, continually endeavored to avert the impending calamity.

Said A. H. Stephens in the Georgia convention pending the discussion of secession: "This step once taken can never be recalled, and all the baleful and withering consequences that will follow must rest on this convention for all coming time. When we and our posterity shall see our lovely land desolated by the demon of war which this act of yours will inevitably invite and call forth ; when our green fields and waving harvests shall be trodden down by a murderous soldiery, and the fiery car of war sweeping over our land, our temples of justice laid in ashes, all the horrors and desolations of war upon us—who but this convention will be held responsible for it? and who but him who shall have given his vote for this unwise and ill-timed measure shall be held to a strict account by this suicidal act by the present generation, and probably cursed and execrated by posterity for all time, for the wide and desolating ruin that will inevitably follow this act you now propose to perpetrate?"

At this critical period, pregnant with the unnumbered woes that afterwards befell the country, the representatives of Illinois in congress all united in condemning secession, and maintaing the right of coercion. Douglas, in his last speech before the distinguished body of which he was a member, remarked : "Sir, the word government means coercion. There can be no government without coercion. Coercion is the vital principle upon which all governments rest. Withdraw the right of coercion and you dissolve your government. If every man would do his duty and respect the rights of his neighbor there would be no necessity for government. The necessity of government is found to consist in the fact that some men will not do right unless forced. The object of all government is to coerce and compel every man to do his duty who would not otherwise perform it, and hence I do not subscribe to this doctrine that coercion is not to be used in a free government. It must be used in all governments, no matter what their form or what their principles." Mr. Trumbull, his colleague, in speaking of compromise said, if they wanted anything, let them go back to the Missouri compromise and stand by it. All agreed that congress had no right to interfere with slavery in the States ; but he would never, by his vote, make one slave, and the people of the great Northwest would never consent by their act to establish slavery anywhere. He did not believe the constitution needed amending, but was willing to vote a recommending to the States to make a proposal to call a convention to consider amendments.

During the interval of time from the election to the inauguration of Mr. Lincoln, the conspirators hurried forward their unhallowed scheme. The seven extreme Southern States adopted ordinances of secession, each declaring it had again resumed its place among the independent nations of the world, with full powers to declare war, establish commerce, contract alliances, and perform all other acts pertaining to independent States. In order to meet the fearful responsibilities thus incurred, they immediately seized a large number of the forts and arsenals within their limits, and invested the others with troops to enforce their submission. In many instances those in command basely betrayed the government that had educated and given them positions. Delegates from the several rebellious states assembled at Montgomery, Alabama, and organized a provisional government, adopting the constitution of the U. S., modified so as to suit treason and slavery, and electing Jefferson Davis president, and Alexander H. Stephens vice-president. Rumors in the meantime prevailed that armed rebels were about to march against the national capital, and Gen. Scott organized the militia of the District of Columbia, placed regulars in the navy yard, and adopted other precautionary measures to prevent an attack. Yet the president, while admitting that secession was treason and revolution, said that the federal government had no power to coerce into submission rebellious States. Even when the nation was crumbling into fragments, and an energetic effort might, to a great extent, have prevented the terrible ordeal of blood through which it subsequently passed, he pleaded for further concessions to its implacable enemies. Patriots all over the land had keenly felt the indignities and insults so defiantly perpetrated by rebels, whose arrogance, instead of being severely punished, only met with encouragement under the imbecile rule of Buchanan. It was, therefore, with no little anxiety and impatience that all looked forward to the incoming administration, hoping that those about to assume the reins of government would have the wisdom to comprehend the situation of the country, and the courage to punish the traitors who were endeavoring to ruin it. On the 11th of February, 1861, the president-elect left his home in Springfield preparatory to assume the grave responsibility which devolved on him as chief magistrate of the nation now rent with civil feuds and upon the eve of a bloody war. A large number of his old friends assembled at the depot to bid him farewell, and express their sympathy in view of the perilous and momentous duties that awaited him. Said he:

"My friends, no one, not in my position, can appreciate the sadness I feel at this parting. To this people I owe all that am. Here I have lived more than a quarter of a century, here my children were born, and here one of them lies buried. I know not how soon I will see you again. A duty devolves upon me which is perhaps greater than that which has rested upon any other man since the day of Washington. He would never have succeeded except for the aid of Divine Providence, on which he at all times relied. I feel that I cannot succeed without the same divine aid which sustained him. On the same Almighty Being I place my reliance for support, and I hope you, my friends, will pray that I may receive that divine assistance, without which I cannot succeed, but with which success is certain. Again I bid you all an affectionate farewell."

Hitherto he had maintained a quiet reserve respecting the momentous crisis in national affairs, but now as he journeyed toward the capital of the republic he found it impossible to longer remain silent. In all the principal cities through which he passed vast crowds assembled to greet him and listen to the brief speeches made in connection' with the interchange of civilities. In these guarded utterances he did not commit himself to any definite line of policy save to express his intention to leave unmolested the institutions of the disaffected states, his devotion to the Union and his desire to maintain it without a resort to arms. The vast extent of the conspiracy was not yet fully understood, and he in common with a great many others still hoped for a peaceful solution of the difficulties. At Cincinnati he said

" *Mr. Mayor and Fellow-citizens:* I have spoken but once before this in Cincinnati. That was a year previous to the late presidential election. On that occasion, in a playful manner but with sincere words, I addressed much of what I said to the Kentuckians. I gave my opinion that we as republicans would ultimately beat them as democrats, but that they could postpone the result longer by nominating Senator Douglas for the presidency than in any other way. They did not in any true sense nominate Mr. Douglas, and the result has come certainly as soon as ever I expected. I told them how I expected they would be treated after they should be beaten, and I now wish to call their attention to what I then said. When beaten you perhaps will want to know what we will do with you. I will tell you so far as I am authorized to speak for the opposition. We mean to treat you as near as we possibly can as Washington, Jefferson and Madison treated you. We mean to leave you alone and in no way interfere with your institutions. We mean to recognize and bear in mind that you have as good hearts in your bosoms as other people, or as we claim to have, and treat you accordingly. Fellow-citizens of Kentucky, brethren may I call you, in my new position I see no occasion and feel no inclination to retract a word from this. If it shall not be made good be assured the fault shall not be mine."

Arriving in New York he said :

"In my devotion to the Union I am behind no man in the nation, but I fear too great confidence may have been placed in my wisdom to preserve it. I am sure I bring a heart devoted to the work, and there is nothing that could ever induce me to consent willingly to the destruction of this Union, in which not only the great city of New York, but the whole country has acquired its greatness, unless it should be the object for which the Union itself was made. I understand that the ship was made for the carrying and preservation of the cargo, and so long as the ship is safe with the cargo it shall not be abandoned."

While thus speaking to large assemblies in different cities, rumors reached him that an attempt would be made to assassinate him on the way to the capital, or if he reached it an armed mob would assemble and prevent his inauguration. These reports were at first regarded with incredulity but when he reached Philadelphia he was warned by Gen. Scott that if he attempted to pass through Baltimore in the day time his life would be exposed to imminent danger. Acting on the advice of those who knew the extent of the danger and the vast importance of his reaching the seat of government in safety, he left his family at Harrisburg and proceeded in disguise on the night train to Washington. Had it been known that such malignity existed that such a crime was meditated against the life of him whose only cause of offense consisted in assuming the important responsibilities to which he had been constitutionally called by a majority of his countrymen,

a half a million of men would have volunteered to escort him
through the rebellious city. Unexpected by the conspirators who
had marked him for their prey, and his friends who were making
preparations for his reception, he arrived in Washington on the
morning of the 23d of February. On the 4th of March he was
inaugurated president of the United States in the presence of a
vast multitude who had assembled to witness the imposing spectacle. His inaugural address is a state paper of more than ordinary ability, and whatever may have been the suspcions previously entertained in the South in regard to his policy after this
expression of his views, the rebellion was wholly without a justifiable pretext. While the most ample assurances are given of protection in the Union, he also refers to his obligations to maintain
it, and his determination to do it. Its great length renders it
impracticable to repeat it in full, but the following passages are
characteristic of its spirit :

"Apprehensions seem to exist among the people of the Southern
States that by the accession of a republican administration that their
property and their peace and personal security are to be endangered.
There has never been any reasonable cause for such apprehension.
Indeed, the most ample evidence to the contrary has all the while existed and been open to their inspection. It is found in nearly all the
public speeches of him who now addresses you. I consider that in view
of the constitution and laws the Union is unbroken, and to the extent
of my ability I will take care as the constitution expressly enjoins upon
me that the laws of the Union be faithfully executed in all the States.
Doing this I deem it only a simple duty on my part, and I shall perform
it so far as practicable unless my rightful masters, the American people,
shall withhold the requisite means, or shall in some other authoritative
manner direct the contrary. Physically speaking, we cannot separate.
We cannot move the respective sections from each other, nor build an
impassable wall between them. A husband and wife may be divorced
and go out of the presence and beyond the reach of each other, but the
different parts of our country cannot do this. They cannot but remain
face to face, and intercourse either amicable or hostile must contiue
between them. Is it possible then to make that intercourse more advantageous or more satisfactory after separation than before? Can aliens
make treatise more easily than friends can make laws among friends?
Suppose you go to war, you cannot fight always, and when after much
loss on both sides, and no gain on either, you cease fighting the identical
old questions are upon you. In your hands, my dissatisfied fellow countrymen, and not in mine, is the momentous issue of civil war. The government will not assail you. You can have no conflict without being
yourselves the aggressors. You have no solemn oath registered in heaven
to destroy the government, while I shall have the most solemn one to
preserve, protect and defend it. I am loth to close. We are not enemies,
but friends. We must not be enemies. Though passion may have
strained it must not break our bonds of affection. The mystic chords
of memory stretching from every battle field and patriot's grave to
every living heart and hearth-stone all over this broad land will yet
swell the chorus of the Union, when again touched, as surely they will
be, by the better angels of our nature."

At the time of Mr. Lincoln's accession to power several members of the Union claimed that they had withdrawn from it, and
styling themselves the "Confederate States of America," had
organized a separate government. The remaining slave States
were convulsed with excitement, and traitors taking advantage
of the magnanimity which the new administration would fain
have exercised, with fiendish eagerness were endeavoring to precipitate them also into revolution. The confederate authorities,

emboldened by this forbearance, and acting on the assumption of their independence, sent commissioners to Washington to amicably arrange all differences growing out of their separation from the United States. They, however, failed to receive any recognition, and were informed by Mr. Seward, Secretary of State, that the action of their States was an unjustifiable and unconstitutional aggression upon the authority of the federal government. The convention of Virginia being in session at the time, also sent commissioners to ascertain from Mr. Lincoln the policy he intended to pursue in regard to the Confederate States. In reply, the president reaffirmed the opinion previously expressed in his inaugural that he would repossess the property and places belonging to the United States, and collect the duties on imports. He likewise informed them that he would not needlessly invade any State, yet when such conduct as the firing upon Fort Sumter rendered it necessary he would repel force by force.

This celebrated fortress was situated in Charleston harbor, and just prior to the assault had been occupied by Major Anderson as a place of greater strength and security than Fort Moultrie, from which he removed. Notwithstanding the fact that South Carolina was in open revolt, Mr. Buchanan had allowed the most formidable works to be erected around the fort. Had permission been granted to Major Anderson with his heavy artillery he could have swept the adjacent shores and thus have prevented the preparations which he daily witnessed for his overthrow. As the batteries commanded the entrance to the harbor cut off supplies from the sea, and the hostile shore refused to furnish provisions, an attack for the reduction of the fort was wholly unnecessary. When, however, the preparations were completed, Beauregard, who had deserted the flag of his country, hurriedly opened fire upon it, as if fearful that starvation might, by giving him peaceable possession, frustrate his desire for an opportunity to inaugurate civil war by a bloody assault. After a furious cannonade of 34 hours the fort was wrapped in flames, and Major Anderson and his small band of heroes were forced to capitulate.

Thus had been struck the first blow of the conflict which summoned vast armies into the field, brought State into collision with State, and drenched the land in fraternal blood. When the news of the bombardment and surrender reached the North, the whole country rocked with excitement. Longer forbearance was now impossible, and President Lincoln immediately issued a proclamation calling for 75,000 volunteers. The proclamation stated that combinations existed in several of the States too powerful to be suppressed by ordinary judicial proceedings, and that the force to be raised would be employed to repossess the property of the United States in the hands of the insurgents and enforce the observance of law. It also summoned congress to meet on the 4th of July to institute in view of the extraordinary condition of public affairs such measures as the safety of the nation might demand.

The details connected with raising the troops having been arranged by the war department, Gov. Yates was informed that the quota of Illinois was six regiments. On the 15th of April, the day on which the intelligence was communicated by Mr. Cameron, the secretary of war, the governor issued the following proclamation :

"I, Richard Yates, governor of the State of Illinois, by virtue of the authority vested in me by the constitution, hereby convene the legislature of the State, and the members of the 22d general assembly are hereby required to be and appear in their respective places in the capital on Tuesday, the 23d day of April A. D. 1861, for the purpose of enacting such laws and adopting such measures as may be deemed necessary upon the following subjects: The more perfect organization and equipment of the militia of the State and placing the same on the best footing to render assistance to the general government in preserving the Union, enforcing the laws, and protecting the property and rights of the people; also, the raising of such money and other means as may be required to carry out the foregoing object, and also to provide for the expense of such session."

General orders one and two were issued from headquarters at Springfield, the first commanded divisions, brigades and regiments to hold themselves in readiness for actual service, and the second providing for the immediate organization of six regiments.

The president's proclamation at the South was regarded as a declaration of war, and Davis issued a similar one calling for volunteers and granting letters of marque for privateers to prey on northern commerce. The shouts of approval with which it was received everywhere in the north showed the people were greatly in advance of the government as to the propriety of using military force. They had long writhed under the murderous stabs thrust by traitors at the vitals of the nation, and now when this restraint was removed, and the time had come for action, the rebound of popular feeling and indignation was overwhelming. The prairies, hamlets and cities of Illinois became ablaze with excitement. Pulpits thundered with anathemas against the crime of treason, secular orators spoke eloquently of the flag which, as the symbol of the nation's majesty, had been so ruthlessly insulted, and newspapers teemed with proclamations and preparations for war. All ages, sexes and conditions as if moved by a common impulse partook of the enthusiasm. The aged and feeble again assumed the burdens of civil life that the young and vigorous might grapple with the sterner duties of war ; the wealthy provided for the families of the indigent whose natural protectors were guarding the life of the nation. Fair woman laid the incense of her sympathy and devotion on the altar of her country; and even children, imbibing the inspiration, converted their play grounds into camp and parade grounds, and miniature drums and cannon became the common toys of their nursery.

A similar uprising occurred in all the loyal States of the Union, and men and money, the sinews of war, were furnished with lavish profusion. Within two weeks after the president issued his proclamation, beside a large surplus of rejected applicants, there were a hundred thousand men preparing for active operations, while more than thirty millions of dollars had been offered by private individuals, corporations, and legislatures to procure arms and munitions.

CHAPTER LV.

1861–1864—ILLINOIS IN THE REBELLION.

Unprecedented Success in Furnishing Men—Patriotic Efforts of Women—Military Operations Within the State.

———

Enlistments.—Almost simultaneously with the call for troops enlistments commenced, and within ten days 10,000 volunteers offered service, and the sum of near $1,000,000 was tendered by patriotic citizens to procure supplies, for which the State, in the sudden emergency, had made no provision. At the time the requisition was made the military law of the State was imperfect, and in many respects in conflict with the regulations of the war department, while perhaps not more than 30 military companies were to be found in the entire State. In some of the larger towns and cities, however, there were a number of well-drilled companies which volunteered, and proved a valuable acquisition in the organization of the immense forces subsequently sent to the field. It was early thought that Cairo was in danger of seizure by the rebels, and these companies formed the nucleus of the force hurriedly gathered and sent thither for its defense. On the 19th of April, 1861, Simon Cameron, secretary of war, telegraphed Gov. Yates to take possession of this important strategic point as soon as a force could be raised for that purpose. . The governor forthwith sent a dispatch to Gen. Swift, of Chicago, to raise and equip as large a body of men as possible for immediate service, and sent a messenger by rail with full instructions for the occupation of Cairo. With commendable promptness this officer, on the 21st of the month, got on board the southern bound train of the Central railroad with four pieces of cannon and the following companies: Company A, Chicago Zouaves, Captain Hayden, 89 men; Company B, Chicago Zouaves, Captain Clybourne, 83 men; Chicago Light Artillery, Captain Smith, 150 men; Captain Harding's company, 80 men; Turner's Union Cadets, 97 men; and Lincoln Rifles, Captain Mihalotzy, 66 men. These were followed, on the 22d, by Captain Houghtelling's Light Artillery, of Ottawa, 86 men; Captain Hawling's Light Artillery, of Lockport, and Captain McAlister's Light Artillery, of Plainfield.

Of the volunteers who offered their services under the call of the governor only 6 regiments could be accepted under the quota of the State. These, in accordance with an act of the legislature, which met on the 23d, were designated by the numbers commencing with 7 and ending with 12, as a mark of respect for the 6 regiments which had served in the Mexican war. The entire force was styled the 1st Brigade of Illinois volunteers. The regulations of the war department required each regiment to consist of 1 colonel, 1 lieutenant-colonel, 1 major, 1 adjutant, 1 regimental quartermaster, 1 surgeon, 1 surgeon's mate, 1 sergeant-major, 1 drum-major, 1 fife-major, 10 captains, 10 lieutenants, 10 ensigns, 10 drummers, 10 fifers, 40 corporals, 40 sergeants and 640 privates. Thus organized a regiment numbered 780 men, rank and file, and the entire brigade 4,680. Gen. Prentiss was placed in command, and proceeding to Cairo with the larger part of the force, he relieved Gen. Swift. The commanding officer of each regiment, the call under which it was organized, the time and place it was mustered into service, and the aggregate strength are given in the subjoind schedule, taken from the report of the adjutant general. There was a large surplus of men in camp, and such was the patriotic desire to enter the service that many of them wept when refused admission.

The legislature, anticipating another call for troops, authorized the formation of 10 additional regiments of infantry, 1 of cavalry, and a battalion of artillery. The law provided that one regiment should be furnished by each congressional district, and one by the State at large. Over 200 companies immediately volunteered, and from this large number the required force was selected and ordered into camp. The act creating the regiments had hardly passed the legislature before the president issued a call for 42,000 volunteers to serve for three years unless sooner discharged. The quota of Illinois under this call was only 6 regiments, and a messenger was sent to Washington to urge upon the war department the importance of accepting the entire force organized by the State. It was believed that more men would be needed, and as they were already in camp, and had made considerable proficiency in drill, to disband them would cause distrust in the wisdom of the government. As the result of persistent importunity the four

SCHEDULE—*Showing statement of volunteer troops organized within the State, and sent to the field, commencing April, 1861, and ending December 31, 1865, with number of regiment, name of original commanding officer, call under which recruited and organized, date of organization and muster into United States' service, place of muster, and the aggregate strength of each organization.*

INFANTRY.

No.	Commanding officer at organization.	Call under which recruited and organized.	Date of organization and muster into U. S. service	Place where mustered into the United States service.	Aggr. str'gth since organizat'n.
7	Col. John Cook	Aug. 15, 1861	July 25, 1861	Cairo, Illinois	1747
8	" Rich'd J. Oglesby.	"	"	"	1853
9	" Eleazer A. Paine.	"	"	"	1265
10	" Jas. D. Morgan...	"	"	"	1759
11	" W. H. L. Wallace.	"	"	"	1384
12	" John McArthur...	"	"	"	1675
13	" John B. Wyman..	May 15, 1861	May 24, 1861.	Dixon	1112
14	" John M. Palmer..	"	May 25, 1861.	Jacksonville.	2015
15	" Thos. J. Turner..	"	May 24, 1861.	Freeport	2028
16	" Rob't F. Smith...	"	"	Quincy	1833
17	" Leonard F. Ross..				1259
18	" Mich'l K. Lawler.	May 15, 1861	May 28, 1861.	Anna	2043
19	" John B. Turchin..				1095
20	" Chas. C. Marsh....	May 15, 1861	June 13, 1861	Joliet.	1817
21	" Ulysses S. Grant..	"	June 15, 1861	Mattoon	1266
22	" Henry Dougherty,	"	June 25, 1861	Belleville	1164
23	" Jas. A. Mulligan	Authorized by the Sec.	June 18, 1861	Chicago	1982
24	" Fred'k Hecker..	- of War, July, 1861...	July 8, 1861.	Chicago	989
25	" Wm. N. Coler.....				1082

remaining regiments were accepted, and the entire force was mustered into service, as shown in the schedule.

Owing to the great expense connected with the equipment of cavalry and the opposition of Gen. Scott to the employment of any considerable force of this arm of the service, the governor accepted only 5 companies but designated the remaining 5, which should be received in case the governor should need them. The battalion of artillery authorized by the legislature was never organized as contemplated in the law, yet several companies, some of which were in Gen. Swift's expedition, were received into the service, as per schedule.

The more than knightly ardor with which the young men of the State at first exhibited was still unabated, and several thousand being denied the privilege of serving in regiments of their own State, went abroad and enlisted in the forces of other States.

In view of the alarming aspect of the rebellion, the secretary of war, in May, June and July, 1861, authorized some 17 regiments of infantry and 5 of cavalry. These regiments were speedily filled up, and in answer to an application for furnishing additional forces, the secretary of war replied that no more troops would be received till authorized by congress. Congress convened July 4th, and consequent upon the battles of Bull Run and Wilson's Creek with the national capital imperilled and Fremont's force threatened by superior numbers, empowered the president to call into the service 500,000 volunteers; 13 regiments of infantry, 3 of cavalry, as a part of the quota of the State under the call were forthwith tendered; the people impatient at the slow progress of the war, would have increased this force by thousands had they been permitted. From the 14th of August till the 3d of December, it was agreed to accept all the infantry which should be willing to enter the service. As the result, 11 regiments of infantry, 4 of cavalry, and 8 companies for the 2d regiment of artillery volun-

26	Col.	John M. Loomis..	July 25, 1861............	Oct. 31, 1861.	Camp Butler.......	1602
27	"	Nap. B. Buford...				1193
28	"	A. K. Johnson....	July 25, 1861............	Aug. 3, 1861.	Camp Butler.......	1939
29	"	Jas. S. Rearden..	"	July 27, 1861.	Camp Butler.......	1547
30	"	Philip B. Fouke..	"	Sept. 30, 1861.	Camp Butler.......	1878
31	"	John A. Logan....	"	Sept. 8, 1861.	Camp Butler.......	1973
32	"	John Logan......	"	Dec. 31, 1861.	Camp Butler.......	1711
33	"	Chas. E. Hovey.	Authorized by the Secretary of War, in May, June and July, 1861.	Aug. 15, 1861.	Camp Butler.......	1660
34	"	Edward N. Kirk.		Sept. 7, 1861.	Camp Butler.......	1558
35	"	Gus. A. Smith..				1012
36	"	Nich. Greusel..		Sept. 23, 1861	Aurora	1593
37	"	Julius White...		Sept. 18, 1861	Chicago............	1157
38	"	Wm. P. Carlin....	July 25, 1861.	Aug. 15, 1861	Camp Butler.......	1388
39	"	Austin Light....	Authorized by the Secretary of War, in May, June and July, 1861.	Decemb. 1861	Chicago............	1807
40	"	Steph. G. Hicks.		Aug. 10, 1861	Salem..............	1277
41	"	Isaac C. Pugh..		Aug. 9, 1861	Decatur	1211
42	"	Wm. A. Webb..		Sept. 17, 1861	Chicago............	1824
43	"	Julius Raith	July 25, 1861.	Dec. 16, 1861	Camp Butler.......	1902
44	"	Chas.Noblesdorff	Authorized, Sec. War, May, June, July, 1861	Sept. 13, 1861	Chicago............	1512
45	"	John E. Smith..		Dec. 26, 1861	Galena.............	1716
46	"	John A. Davis...	July 25, 1861.	Dec. 28, 1861	Camp Butler.......	2015
47	"	John Bryner......	Sec. War, July, 1861...	Oct. 1, 1861	Peoria.............	2051
48	"	Isham N. Haynie	July 25, 1861.	Nov. 18, 1861	Camp Butler.......	1874
49	"	Wm. R. Morrison.	"	Dec. 31, 1861	Camp Butler.......	1482
50	"	Moses M. Bane...	"	Sept. 12, 1861	Quincy.............	1761
51	"	G. W. Cumming..	Authorized Sept. 20, '61	Dec'61 Feb'62	Camp Douglas.....	1550
52	"	Isaac G. Wilson..	Authorized July 1, '61	Nov. 19, 1861	Geneva	1519
53	"	W.H.W. Cushman	Authorized Sept.16, '61	March 1862	Ottawa	1434
54	"	Thos. W. Harris..	Authorized Oct. 3, '61	Feb. 18, 1862	Anna	1720
55	"	David Stuart	Authorized July, 1861	Oct. 31, 1861	Camp Douglas.....	1287
56	"	Robert Kirkham..	Authorized Aug, 14, '61	Feb. 27, 1862	Shawneetown......	1180
57	"	Silas D. Baldwin	"	Dec. 26, 1861	Camp Douglas.....	1754
58	"	Wm. F. Lynch ...	Authorized Sept. 25, '61	Dec. 24, 1861	Camp Douglas.....	2202
59	"	P. Sidney Post ...	July 25, 1861	August, 1861	St. Louis, Mo......	1762
60	"	Silas C. Toler.....	Authorized Oct. 3, '61	Feb. 17, 1862	Anna..	1647

teered and were accepted. On the 3d of December an order was promulgated which stopped all further recruiting, except for the completion of companies already in process of formation. With the enlistment of over 4,000 for this purpose during the remainder of the month, the record of the year was completed. Despite the rebuffs and opposition frequently manifested by the war department, the State at the close of the year had in camps of instruction over 17,000 men, had sent to the field nearly 50,000, and consequently had exceeded her quotas about 15,000.

On the 2d of April, 1862, all the corps authorized previous to December, were full and the officers who had been detached for recruiting purposes were ordered to rejoin their regiments. Many of the old regiments, however, as the result of disease and recent battles, had been reduced below the proper standard, and recruiting was still continued for the purpose of replenishing them with their complement of men. Early in May Washington was threatened by a large force of the enemy, and Mr. Stanton, secretary of war, telegraphed Governor Yates on the 25th instant, for more troops and several regiments of infantry and cavalry were filled up and sent to the field.

On the 6th of July, 1862, the president issued a call for 300,000 volunteers to serve for 3 years, and on the 7th of August another call for 300,000 militia, to serve for a period of nine months. The secretary, believing that a draft would be necessary, ordered the enrollment of the militia that it might take effect on the 18th of August if the quota under the first call was not completed by that time. This vigorous determination on the part of the government was hailed with demonstrations of approval by the people of the State, and everywhere preparations were commenced to make a response commensurate with the magnitude of the requisition. The adjutant-generals' office was at once thronged by messengers from every part of the State, demanding for their several

No.	Name	Authorized	Mustered	Location	Strength
61	Col. Jacob Fry	Authorized Aug. 14, '61	March 7, 1862	Carrollton	1385
62	" James M. True	Authorized Oct. 3, '61	April 10, 1862	Anna	1730
63	" Francis Mora	" "	" "	Anna	1228
64	Lt. Col. D. D. Williams	Authorized Aug. 14, '61	Dec. 31, 1862	Camp Butler	1624
65	Col. Daniel Cameron	" "	May 15, 1862	Camp Douglas	1084
66	" Patrick E. Burke	Transf'd from Mo. 14th	April, 1862	St. Louis, Mo	1694
67	" Rosell M. Hough	May 25, 1862	June 13, 1862	Camp Douglas	979
68	" Elias Stuart	"	June 20, 1862	Camp Butler	889
69	" Jos. H. Tucker	"	June 14, 1862	Camp Douglas	912
70	" O. T. Reeves	"	July 4, 1862	Camp Butler	1006
71	" Othniel Gilbert	"	July 26, 1862	Camp Douglas	940
72	" Fred'k A. Starring	July, 1862	Aug. 21, 1862	Camp Douglas	1471
73	" Jas. F. Jaquess	"	" "	Camp Butler	968
74	" Jason Marsh	"	Sept. 4, 1862	Rockford	989
75	" George Ryan	"	Sept. 2, 1862	Dixon	987
76	" Alonzo W. Mack	"	Aug. 22, 1862	Kankakee	1110
77	" David P. Grier	"	*Sept. 2 9 cos.	Peoria	1051
78	" W. H. Bennison	"	Sept. 1, 1862	Quincy	1028
79	" Lyman Guinnip	"	Aug. 28, 1862	Danville	974
80	" Thos. G. Allen	"	Aug. 25, 1862	Centralia	928
81	" Jas. J. Dollins	"	Aug. 26, 1862	Anna	1187
82	" Frederick Hecker	"	" "	Camp Butler	961
83	" Abner C. Harding	"	Aug. 21, 1862	Monmouth	1286
84	" Louis H. Waters	"	Sept. 1, 1862	Quincy	956
85	" Robert S. Moore	"	Aug. 27, 1862	Peoria	959
86	" David D. Irons	"	" "	Peoria	993
87	" John E. Whiting	"	Sept. 22, 1862	Shawneetown	994
88	" F. T. Sherman	"	Aug. 27, 1862	Camp Douglas	907
89	" John Christopher	"	*Aug. 25, 9 cos	Camp Douglas	1285
90	" Timothy O'Mera	"	Nov. 22, 1862	Camp Douglas	95?
91	" Henry M. Day	"	Sept. 8, 1862	Camp Butler	1041
92	" Smith D. Atkins	"	Sept. 4, 1862	Rockford	1265
93	" Holden Putnam	"	Oct. 13, 1862	Princ'tn & Chicago	1036
94	" Wm. W. Orme	"	Aug. 20, 1862	Bloomington	1091

counties the privilege of volunteering, and thereby securing exemption from the draft. This preference for volunteering, and an urgent request that the quota of the State under both calls might be immediately ascertained, was made known to the secretary of war. Information was duly received that the entire number was 52,296, and volunteers would be accepted till the 15th of August for forming new regiments, and after that for filling old ones already in the field. The State had now furnished 16,978 in excess of previous quotas, and it was at first intended that this surplus should be deducted from the present requisition. This, however, was afterwards countermanded and it was therefore necessary to raise the entire number in 13 days or submit to the alternative of a draft. The result is thus eloquently given in the language of Adjutant-Gen. Fuller:

"These new volunteers must come, if come at all, from the farmers and mechanics of the State. The farmers were in the midst of harvest, and it is no exaggeration to say that, inspired by a holy zeal, animated by a common purpose, and firmly resolved on rescuing the government from the very brink of ruin, and restoring it to the condition our fathers left it, that over 50,000 of them left their harvests ungathered, their tools and their benches, the plows in their furrows, and turning their backs on their homes, and before 11 days expired the demands of the government were met and both quotas were filled. Proud indeed was the day to all Illinoisans when the announcement was made that the enlistments were full. And when the historian shall record the eventful days of August, 1862, no prouder record can be erected to the honor and memory of a free people than a plain and full narrative of actual realities. It is not my province in this report to bestow fulsome praise or write glowing eulogies, but when I remember what we all witnessed in those days; when I remember the patriotism and unselfish impulse which animated every soul, and the universal liberality of those who were either too young or too old to enlist to aid those who were eager to join their brethren in the field; when I remember the holy ardor which aged mothers and fair daughters infused into husbands, sons and

95	Col.	Lawr'n S. Church.	July, 1862.		Sept. 4,	1862	Rockford	1427
96	"	Thos. E. Champion	"		Sept. 6,	1862	Rockford	1206
97	"	F S. Rutherford..	"		Sept. 8,	1862	Camp Butler	1082
98	"	J. J. Funkhouser.	"		Sept. 3,	1862	Centralia	1078
99	"	G. W. K. Bailey..	"		Aug. 26,	1862	Florence, Pike co..	936
100	"	Fred. A. Bartleson	"		Aug 30,	1862	Joliet	921
101	"	Chas. H. Fox.....	"		Sept. 2,	1862	Jacksonville	911
102	"	Wm. McMurtry.,	"		"		Knoxville	998
103	"	Amos C. Babcock.	"		Oct. 2,	1862	Peoria	917
104	"	Absalom B. Moore	"		Aug. 27,	1862	Ottawa	977
105	"	Daniel Dustin....	"		Sept. 2,	1862	Chicago	1001
106	"	Rob't B. Latham..	"		Sept. 17,	1862	Lincoln	1097
107	"	Thomas Snell.....	"		Sept. 4,	1862	Camp Butler	944
108	"	John Warner.....	"		Aug. 28,	1862	Peoria	927
109	"	Alex. J. Nimmo..	"		Sept. 11,	1861	Anna	967
110	"	Thos. S. Casey....	"		"		Anna	873
111	"	James S. Martin..	"		Sept. 18,	1862	Salem	994
112	"	T. J. Henderson...	"		Sept. 12,	1862	Peoria	1095
113	"	Geo. B. Hoge.....	"		Oct. 1,	1862	Camp Douglas	1258
114	"	Jas. W. Judy.....	"		Sept. 18,	1862	Camp Butler	990
115	"	Jesse H. Moore...	"		Sept. 13,	1862	Camp Butler	960
116	"	Nathan H. Tupper	"		Sept. 30,	1862	Decatur	952
117	"	Risden M. Moore.	"		Sept. 19,	1862	Camp Butler	995
118	"	John G. Fonda....	"		Nov. 29,	1862	Camp Butler	1101
119	"	Thos. J. Kenney..	"		Oct. 7,	1862	Quincy	952
120	"	Geo. W, McKeaig.	"		Oct. 29,	1862	Camp Butler	844
121	Never Organized							
122	Col.	John I. Rinaker..	July, 1862.		Sept. 4,	1862	Carlinville	934
123	"	James Moore.....	"		Sept. 6,	1862	Mattoon	1050
124	"	Thomas J. Sloan..	"		Sept. 10,	1862	Camp Butler	1130
125	"	Oscar F. Harmon.	"		Sept. 4,	1862	Danville	933
126	"	Jonth'n Richmond	"		"		Chicago	998
127	"	John VanArman..	"		*Sept. 5,	9 cos	Camp Douglas	957
128	"	Robert M. Hudley	"		Dec. 18,	1862	Camp Butler	866
129	"	Geo. P. Smith.....	"		Sept. 8,	1862	Pontiac	1011

brothers—I say when I remember all these things, I cannot but feel justified in departing from the dull routine of statistics and bestow upon the subject this parting notice."

A vast army was thus suddenly ushered into existence, and the government being unable to supply tents, how to provide comfortable quarters became an important consideration. In many counties, therefore, large numbers were temporarily lodged under the sheds of fair grounds till barracks could be erected at the principal camps of instruction at Springfield and Chicago. It was also difficult to procure clothing. The vast multitude of recruits in the different States, and the sudden emergency which had called them forth, taxed the government to its utmost capacity to furnish equipments. Before the close of the year, however, there were clothed, armed and sent from the State 59 regiments of infantry, and four batteries of artillery, aggregating a force of 53,819 men. There was also enlisted during the same time for the 14th cavalry, and for old regiments an additional number, which, added to the former, makes a grand total of 58,416 men, an excess of 23,097 over the quotas of the State.

The last call for troops was on the 19th of December, 1864. The number required was 300,000, and if not raised by voluntary enlistments, by the 15th of February following the State was to be drafted. Past experience had shown that troops could be more readily secured by the formation of new organizations, and application was made to the war department for the privilege of raising ten additional regiments. Permission was granted, and a number of persons who had distinguished themselves in the service, but whose terms of enlistment had expired, commenced recruiting, each authorized to raise a single company. Formerly one person had been permitted to raise a whole regiment, but it required a much longer time for its accomplishment than where the work was sub-divided among a number. This modification in the practice which had hitherto prevailed operated with astonishing success. The adjutant general's office was again thronged with applications

130	Col. Nathaniel Niles...	July, 1862	Oct. 25, 1865.	Camp Butler	932
131	" George W. Neeley.		Nov. 13, 1862.	Camp Massac	880
132	"' Thos. C. Pickett. }	"'	June 1, 1864.	Camp Fry	853
133	" Thad. Phillips...		May 31, 1864.	Camp Butler	851
134	" W.W.McChesney		"	Camp Fry	878
135	" John S. Wolfe...	100 day organizations	June 6, 1864.	Mattoon	852
136	" Fred A. Johns..	tendered by the Gov-	June 1, 1864.	Centralia	842
137	" John Wood......	ernor of Illinois, April	June 5, 1864.	Quincy	849
138	" J. W. Goodwin..	21, '64, and accepted	June 21, 1864.	Quincy	835
139	" Peter Davidson..	by the President,	June 1, 1864.	Peoria	878
140	" L. H. Whitney..	April 23, 1864.	June 18, 1864.	Camp Butler	871
141	" Stephen Bronson.		June 16, 1854.	Elgin	842
142	" Rollin V. Ankney		June 18, 1864.	Camp Butler	851
143	" Dudley C. Smith		June 11, 1864.	Mattoon	865
144	" Cyrus Hall........	July, 1864	Oct. 21, 1864.	Alton, Ills	1159
145	" George W. Lackey	100 day's organization	June 9, 1864.	Camp Butler	880
146	" Henry H. Dean....	July, 1864	Sept. 20, 1864.	Camp Butler	1056
147	" Hiram F. Sickles.	December 19, 1864.	Feb. 18, 1865.	Chicago	1047
148	" Horace H. Wilsie..	"	Feb. 18, 1865.	Quincy	917
149	" Wm. C. Kueffner..	"	Feb. 11, 1865.	Camp Butler	983
150	" Geo. W. Keener...	"	Feb. 14, 1865.	Camp Butler	933
151	" French B. Woodall	"	Feb. 25, 1865.	Quincy	970
152	" F. D. Stephenson..	"	Feb. 18, 1865.	Camp Butler	945
153	" Stephen Bronson..	"	Feb. 27, 1865.	Chicago	1076
154	" McLean F. Wood..	"	Feb. 22, 1865.	Camp Butler	994
155	" Gustavus A. Smith	"	Feb. 28, 1865.	Camp Butler	920
156	" Alfred F. Smith...	"	March 9, 1865.	Chicago	975
...	" J. W. Wilson......	Spec auth'ty Sec. War.	Dec. 1, 1861.	Chicago	985
...	" John A. Bross.....	*Sept. 24, 1863		Quincy	903
...	Capt. John Curtis......	100 day's organization.	June 21, 1864.	Camp Butler	91
...	" Simon J. Stookey	100 day's organization.	June 21, 1864.	Camp Butler	90
...	" James Steele....	April 15, 1861	June 15, 1864.	Chicago	86

47

for authority to raise companies, and as fast as a sufficient number was secured for a regiment it was organized and marched to the front. Early in February it was feared that recruiting was going on so rapidly that more volunteers would offer than could possibly enter the 10 regiments, and the draft was temporarily postponed. These regiments were soon completed, and it was directed that the remaining companies arriving under voluntary enlistments should be disposed of in filling up old regiments. This course was continued till the 13th of April, 1865, when, by an order of the war department, recruiting ceased throughout the U. S. The State now only lacked 4,896 of completing her quota. These would have been speedily obtained had not the termination of the war rendered it unnecessary.

Toward the close of the war, in consequence of an imperfect enrollment of those subject to military duty, it became evident that the State was furnishing thousands in excess of what a correct estimate would have required. So glaring had this disproportion become, that under the last call the quota in a number of sub-districts exceeded the number of able-bodied men. Yet the people, when it was found inexpedient to correct the enrollment, determined to raise the number required, believing that in the extraordinary exigencies of the times the safety of the country demanded the sacrifice. Let the thousands of brave men which the State thus voluntarily laid on the altar of the country forever remain a proud monument of the patriotism which so triumphantly sustained it in the hour of danger.

The office of the Adjutant General, which played such an important part in the organization of the troops, was occupied at the commencement of the war by Thomas S. Mather. The duties of the office were then executed by virtue of the militia law of 1845, and acts amendatory thereof. Mr. Mather held the office till November, 1861, when Gen. Allen C. Fuller assumed control. The latter incumbent, possessing superior qualifications, soon reduced the military records of the State, hitherto sparse and confused, to order, and systematized the business of the office. A fruitful source of disorder grew out of the acceptance by the war department of what were termed independent regiments. The correspondence of the first 22 regiments of infantry and 4 of cavalry were addressed directly to the war department, and for a time their officers were disinclined to furnish the adjutant general with muster rolls, and other official information. To remedy this evil and promote

CAVALRY.

1	Col. Thos. A. Marshall	Auth'd by Sec'y War..	June, 1861....	Bloomington........	1206
2	" Silas Noble........	July 2, 1861...........	Aug. 24, 1861.	Camp Butler.......	1861
3	" Eugene A. Carr....	July 25, 1861...........	Sept. 21, 1861.	Camp Butler.......	2183
4	" T. Lyle Dickey....	Authorized July, '61.	Sept. 30, 1861.	Ottawa	1656
5	" John J. Updegraff	Auth'd Aug. 27, 1861...	Dec. 1861.....	Camp Butler.., ...	1669
6	" Thos. H.Cavanaugh	July 25, 1861...........	Nov.61 Jan '62	Camp Butler.......	2248
7	" Wm. Pitt Kellogg	July 25, 1861...........	Aug. 1861....	Camp Butler.......	2282
8	" John F. Farnsworth	Authorized July, 1861.	Sept. 18, 1861.	St. Charles.........	2412
9	" Albert G. Brackett	Authorized July, 1861,	Oct. 26, 1861.	Camp Douglas.....	2619
10	" James A. Barrett..	Auth'd Sept. 5, 1861....	Nov. 25, 1861.	Camp Butler.......	1934
11	" Robert G. Ingersoll	*July. 1861.............	Dec. 20. 1861	Peoria	2362
12	" Arno Voss.........	Auth'd Sept. 28, 1861.	Dec'61 Feb '62	Camp Butler.......	2174
13	" Joseph W. Bell....	Auth'd Nov. 27, 1861...	"	Camp Douglas.....	1759
14	" Horace Capron.....	July, 1862..........	Jan. 7, 1863	Peoria.............	1565
15	" Warren Stewart...	July, 1861.............	org'd Dec25'63	Camp Butler, ...	1473
16	" Christian Thielman	April, 1861, July, 1862.	Jan.Apl. 1863.	Camp Butler.......	1462
17	" John L. Beveridge.	1863................	Jan. 28, 1864.	St. Charles.........	1247

harmony between the federal and State authorities, the secretary of war promulgated order 18, which contains the following provision: "The governors of the States are legally the authorities for raising volunteer regiments and commissioning their officers. Accordingly no independent organizations, as such, will hereafter be recognized in the U. S. service. Copies of the rolls of muster into service will be sent as soon as practicable to the governors of the States to which they belong by the commanders of brigades, regiment or corps, heretofore recognized as independent of State organizations, and all vacancies of commissions in such regiments and corps will be hereafter filled by the respective governors according to law." Mr. Fuller retained possession of the office till January 1, 1863. Thence to the installation of Gen. I. N. Haynie, January 14, 1865, the duties of the office were discharged by Lieut.-Col. Edward P. Niles, who, from the commencement of the war, had been intimately connected with its routine. By the provisions of an act to provide for the appointment, and to prescribe the duties of, the adjutant general, approved February 2d, 1865, the office became an organized department of the State government. In accordance with the law

FIRST REGIMENT—ILLINOIS LIGHT ARTILLERY.

	Field and Staff.					7
A	Capt. C. M. Willard....	April, 1861			Chicago.	168
B	" Ezra Taylor	"			Chicago.	204
C	" C. Haughtaling..	"		Oct. 31, 1861.	Ottawa.	175
D	" Ed. McAllister..	July, 1861		Jan. 14, 1862.	Plainfield	141
E	" A. C. Waterhouse			Dec. 19, 1861.	Chicago.	148
F	" John T. Cheney.	"		Feb. 25, 1862.	Camp Butler.	159
G	" Arthur O'Leary.	"		Feb. 23, 1862.	Cairo	113
H	" Axel Silversparr.	"		Feb. 20, 1862.	Chicago.	147
I	" Edward Bouton	"		Feb. 15, 1862.	Chicago.	169
K	" A. Franklin	"		Jan. 9, 1862.	Shawneetown.	96
L	" John Rourke...	"		Feb. 22, 1862	Chicago.	153
M	" John B. Miller ..	July, 1862		Aug. 12, 1862.	Chicago.	154
	Recruits.					883

SECOND REGIMENT—ILLINOIS LIGHT ARTILLERY.

A	Capt. Peter Davidson..	July, 1861		Aug. 17, 1861.	Peoria.	116
B	" Riley Macison....	April, 1861		June 20, 1861.	Springfield	127
C	" Caleb Hopkins....	July, 1861		Aug. 5, 1861.	Cairo	154
D	" Jasper M. Dresser	Auth'd, Sept. 1861.		Dec. 17, 1861.	Cairo.	117
E	" Adolph Schwartz	"		Feb. 1, 1862.	Cairo.	136
F	" John W. Powell.	"		Dec. 11, 1861	Cape Girardeau, Mo.	190
G	" Chas. J. Stolbrand	"		Dec. 31, 1861.	Camp Butler.	108
H	" Andrew Steinbeck	Auth'd Sept. 15, 1861.		Dec. 31, 1861.	Camp Butler.	115
I	" Charles W. Keith.	"		Dec. 31, 1861.	Camp Butler.	107
K	" Benj. F. Rogers...	"		Dec. 31, 1861.	Camp Butler.	108
L	" Wm. H. Bolton...	Authorized 1861.		Feb. 28, 1862.	Chicago.	145
M	" John C. Phillips.	Authorized 1862.		June 6, 1862.	Chicago.	100
	Field and staff.					10
	Recruits.					1171

INDEPENDENT BATTERIES.

Bd of Trade	Capt. James S. Stokes.	July, 1862		July 31, 1862.	Chicago.	258
Springfield	" Thos. F. Vaughn	"		Aug. 21, 1862.	Camp Butler.	199
Mercantile	" Chas. G. Cooley	"		Aug. 29, 1862.	Chicago.	270
Elgin	" Geo. W. Renwick	"		Nov. 15, 1862.	Elgin.	242
Coggswell'.	" Wm. Coggswell.	Auth'd Sept. 15, 1861.		Sep. 23, 1861.	C'mp Douglas	221
Henshaw's	" Ed. C. Henshaw.	July, 1862		Oct. 15, 1862.	Ottawa	196
Bridges....	" Lyman Bridges..	Auth'd Jan. 1, 1862.		Jan. 1, 1862	Chicago.	252
Colvin's ...	" John H. Colvin.	Auth'd July, 1863.		Oct. 10, 1863.	Chicago.	91
Busteed's..					Chicago.	127

RECAPITULATION.

Infantry... 185 941
Cavalry... 37,082
Artillery... 7,277

Gen. Haynie provided a seal of office. Previously, to give validity to commissions and other official instruments, it was necessary to procure the seal and signature of the secretary of State. After a suitable imprint was provided, this indirect method of transacting the business of the office was discontinued. The extensive reports, issued under the supervision of Gen. Haynie, contain all the military information that can be interesting to the reader or useful in the organization of future armies, and may justly be regarded as a monument of industry, of which the State should be proud.

From data thus furnished, the whole number of enlistments during the war was 256,000, average strength 299,963, number killed in action, 5,888; died of wounds, 3,032; of disease, 19,496, in prison, 967; lost at sea, 205; aggregate, 29,588.*

Medical Department.—At the instance of the Secretary of War, the governor appointed a board of medical examiners consisting of A. H. Johnson, president, and O. M. Ryan, secretary. The medical profession sharing the enthusiasm that animated the masses, tendered their services to the government with a zeal which, in many instances, surpassed their qualifications for the work they were required to perform. They went forth in large numbers from the prairie, the village and country where their undiversified practice little qualified them for the more arduous and extensive duties of the army.

The board met on the 18th of June, 1861, in Springfield, and in accordance with the army regulations they proceeded to "investigate carefully the physical ability, moral character and professional attainments of each candidate. To accommodate the large number who applied for positions, sessions were held in Chicago, Alton, Cairo and the field. The importance of the work which they performed may be inferred from the fact that much the larger part of the mortality connected with armies results from diseases instead of the sword, and that many of those who proposed to assume the responsibilities of physicians had never received the first rudiments of a medical education. It is but justice to state that the selections made by the board were judicious, and that the medical treatment enjoyed by our volunteers was efficient. Many not only evinced a high order of skill in the practice of surgery and therapeutics, but what was of more importance, with a paternal solicitude instituted the most rigid sanitary regulations for the prevention of disease.

Camps.—The two principal camps in the State were Camp Butler, at Springfield, and Camp Douglas, at Chicago. The immediate location of the former was near where the Toledo, Wabash & Western railroad crosses the Sangamon river, and that of the latter just by the last resting place of the great statesman after whom it was named. Each was provided with commissary and ordnance warehouses, general prison and small pox hospitals, company and prison barracks, officers' quarters and other structures necessary for the outfit of an extensive encampment. Both places—especially Camp Butler—became the principal points for the rendez-

*Computation by Adjutant General E. L. Higgins.

vous and instruction of volunteers and mustering them out of service after the war.

As the result of the battle of Fort Donelson some 10,000 prisoners were sent to these camps, and thereafter they became places of custody for other prisoners captured in the war. Their treatment by the officers in charge was always humane, though if the statements of rebel writers could be credited, they suffered more hellish barbarities than were perpetrated in the prison pens of the South. Of the 30,000 prisoners received at different times at Camp Douglas 3,500 died, about 10 per cent., while of the number of prisoners received at Belle Isle more than 50 per cent. died from exposure, starvation and brutality. The site of Camp Butler is still preserved as a national cemetery, in which many of the gallant sons of Illinois sleep in honored graves. Other camps were formed in different parts of the State, but they in general subserved only temporary purposes.

Women of Illinois.—We have spoken of the patriotic sons of Illinois, her daughters must not be omitted. Perhaps the brightest page in the history of the State is that which records their efforts in behalf of the soldier. Their devotion to the national cause was rather the promptings of inspiration than the ordinary impulse of patriotism, and its defenders were objects of their deepest sympathy. Women in all ages have prompted men to deeds of noble daring, while with the progress of civilization in modern times her influence has become more potent than presidents, cabinets or crowns. It is a true adage that she who rocks the cradle rules the world. In the hallowed associations of home are born and nurtured the great intellects, large hearts and the staunch integrity which has accomplished all that is noble in the history of the race.

The women of Illinois, in common with others all over the land, were the first to commiserate the sufferings of the soldier, and the first to make efforts to afford relief. In this they were actuated not only by a heroic love of country, but their kindred were enduring the privations of war, and who like them could feel for their distress? Though physically incapacitated to share with them the toil and perils of battle, yet before its smoke and the echoes of its artillery passed away they could bind up their wounds, and by their self-denial inspire them with a holier ardor for the cause they were defending. How many weary sufferers on the field of carnage, in the lonely hospital relieved by their bounty and cheered by their presence, none but the recording angel can tell.

Their labors soon assumed an organized form; hundreds of relief societies sprang up all over the State, and proportionately as the terrible effects of the war increased, the warm current of their sympathies and charities augmented. These consisted of food, clothing, medicine, hospital delicacies, reading matter and thousands of other articles in such quantities as to necessitate the chartering of cars, and in some instances steamboats to carry them to their destination.

The counties of the State next became enlisted in the work of benevolence. In the 69 where records were made and reported, the sums donated as bounties to volunteers for the support of sol-

diers' families and other objects amounted to more than $1,500,-
000. In this estimate the donations of 33 counties, and the unrecorded benevolence of thousands of individuals all over the State,
is not included.

Another form which the work assumed was the establishment
of soldiers' homes in the principal cities. In these places of refuge the traveling soldier, when he had no one else to care for him,
was provided with board and lodging free of cost. During the
war the several homes in Illinois and other parts af the West furnished lodging for 600,000 men and meals valued at $2,500,000.
The relief thus afforded was not intended as a substitute but as
supplemental to that of the government. The troops of Illinois
participated in some of the most gigantic struggles of the war,
in which no government system, however provident or elastic, can
do more than mitigate the suffering. In these bloody conflicts
the private benevolence of the people nobly seconded the efforts
of the government, and could the relief afforded by both have been
tenfold more effective, the wounded would still have suffered
unspeakable privations and agony.

The sanitary commission greatly assisted in arousing and giving direction to the benevolent enterprise of the State. The first
members of the society were appointed on the 9th of June, 1861,
by the Secretary of War. They met and organized in Washington the same month, and in the autumn of the same year Dr.
Newberry, one of the most efficient members, organized the
Northwestern branch at Chicago.

"This was one of the most efficient of all its auxilaries in collecting
supplies, and its various tributaries scattered throughout the States of
Illinois, Iowa and Wisconsin, did more for the relief of the soldier
probably in proportion to their means, than those of any other section
of the country. Nowhere had the commission warmer or more enthusiastic friends than at Chicago. It was most fortunate in enlisting at an early
period the active sympathy of some of the most influential and trusted
men of that important place. The names of the gentlemen who conducted its operations, Judge Skinner, E. B. McCagg and E. W. Blatchford were alone a tower of strength to its cause throughout the Northwest and the commission reaped the benefit in the vast contributions of
that region of their wide spread reputation and active exertions."*

The most successful effort in turning the great tide of popular
sympathy into the channel of the commission, occurred at Chicago
in May, 1865. The means employed was a fair in which not
only Illinois, but her sister States of the West, were largely represented. Though all gave it a hearty support the conception of
its plan and the success with which it was carried out was mostly
due to the efforts of Madams Hoge and Livermore. These ladies
who are the personification of benevolence and energy wrote
appeals, distributed circulars, and addressed public meetings till
the great heart of the Northwest was moved to its utmost depths.
Union Hall, the principal building, occupied the whole of Dearborn Park and was brilliantly illuminated with gas from floor to
apex. In the centre were tastefully arranged in booths and on
tables the consecrated offerings of churches, and rare and beautiful contributions from the nations of Europe. In the two
wings business and industry were represented by goods and
machinery, less ornamental but more useful. Eastward a whole

* History of the Sanitary Commission.

block was covered by Floral Hall, whose contents appeared like a crystalized vision of beauty, in which both nature and art had been laid under contribution for their most exquisite productions. Bryan's Hall, then the largest room in the city, was used as a depository for battle-torn banners and other trophies of the war, indicative of Illinois and western valor.

Generals Grant and Hooker, Senator Yates, and a large number of other distinguished personages, gave the prestige of their presence to the occasion. A vast multitude thronged the different avenues of approach to the city, and though the rebellion had suddenly collapsed and the necessity for raising funds had greatly ceased, the gross proceeds amounted to more than $300,000 and the net profits to $250,000.

Military Movements in the State.—The operations of the immense hosts furnished by the State within her borders, was limited in extent. We have already spoken of the occupation of Cairo, located at the junction of the Ohio and Mississippi rivers and Illinois Central railroad, which was early regarded as a strategic point of more than ordinary significance. Its near proximity to Kentucky, Missouri and Tennessee, whose governments were controlled by disloyal men, rendered it liable to seizure. One of the first acts of the garrison was to suppress the traffic in lead and other contraband merchandise carried on by Galena, St. Louis and Cincinnati, with the rebellious cities on the Lower Mississippi. Among other contraband shipments Gov. Yates received intelligence that two steamers, the C. E. Hillman and John D. Perry, carrying arms and ammunition, were about to descend the river from St. Louis and telegraphed Col. Prentiss to stop them and take possession of their cargoes. In due time the vessels made their appearance and were immediately boarded and brought to the wharf. A large number of arms and other military stores were seized and confiscated, a proceeding at the time somewhat informal, but subsequently approved by the Secretary of war. To prevent the recurrence of similar attempts on the part of the rebels to obtain supplies all further shipments to posts under insurrectionary control were interdicted.

The State was almost destitute of arms, and the Cairo expedition had been equipped to a great extent with shot guns and rifles, taken from the stores in Chicago. According to the report of the ordinance qartermaster, the arsenal contained only 362 muskets, 105 rifles, 133 musketoons, and 297 pistols. In addition to these there were a number of other arms in possession of different militia companies of the State, of antique patterns, and far inferior to weapons of a more modern construction. Under these circumstances an effort was made to obtain arms from the arsenal of New York, and a messenger was sent to Washington for a similar purpose. It, however, soon became evident that this destitution was not confined to Illinois, but as the result of Floyd's treachery, common to all the Northern States. According to rebel newspapers, there had been deposited at different points in the South 107,000 stand of muskets, and 200,000 pistols for the avowed purpose of overturning the government to which they rightfully belonged. Furthermore, of the home squadron, consisting of 12 vessels, carrying 187 guns and 2,000 men, only 4 small vessels, carrying 25 guns and 280 men, were available, the others having been dispersed to distant seas.

While the subject of procuring arms was under advisement, the messenger who had been dispatched to Washington returned with an order on the arsenal at St. Louis for 10,000 muskets. This repository of military stores was now closely watched by traitors, and a mob of them were ready to seize the arms which it contained the moment an attempt should be made to remove them. While those in charge of the requisition were looking about for competent men, and considering an available plan for getting possession of them, Captain Stokes, of Chicago, volunteered to undertake the hazardous enterprise. Gov. Yates at once put into his hands the order issued by the secretary of war, and hastening to St. Louis, he found the arsenal surrounded by a disorderly, treasonable rabble. After a number of unavailing attempts to pass through the crowd, he at length reached the building, and communicated to the officer in charge the object of his visit. The commander informed him that the arsenal was surrounded by hundreds of spies in communication with the secessionists of the city, and that the most trivial movement might excite suspicion, and bring an overpowering force upon the garrison at any moment. Although he doubted the possibility of complying with the requisition, it was evident that delay would render it more difficult, and permission was given to Captain Stokes to make the attempt. These apprehensions were well founded, for the next day information was received that Gov. Jackson had ordered 2,000 armed men down from Jefferson City, and was evidently contemplating by this movement the capture of the arsenal. Two batteries had already been planted by his friends, one near the arsenal, and one on the St. Louis levee, and were either designed for this purpose, or some other treasonable object. Captain Stokes immediately telegraphed to Alton to have a steamer descend the river and about midnight land opposite the arsenal, and proceeding to the same place with 700 men of the 7th Illinois, soon commenced lowering the heavy boxes containing the guns from the upper to the lower portion of the building. At the same time, to divert attention from his real design, he caused 500 unserviceable muskets to be openly placed on a different boat. As intended, this movement was soon detected, and the shouts and excitement upon their seizure, drew most of the crowd from the arsenal. Captain Stokes ordered the remainder, who were acting as a posse, to be shut up in the guard house, and as soon as the boat came along side commenced freighting her with guns. When the 10,000 muskets were aboard he asked permission to empty the entire arsenal, and was told to go ahead and take what he wanted. He, therefore, instead of confining himself to the requisition, besides cannon and a large number of other valuable accoutrements, took 500 carbines, 500 pistols, and 20,000 muskets, leaving only 7,000 to arm the St. Louis volunteers. When all was on board and the order was given to start, it was found that the immense weight of the cargo had bound the bow of the boat to a rock, which at every turn of the wheel was crushing through the bottom. The arms had been piled in large quantities about the engines to protect them from the battery on the levee, and assistance was immediately summoned from the arsenal to remove them to the stern. Fortunately, when this was partially effected the boat fell away from the shore and floated into deep water.

"Which way?" said Captain Mitchell, of the steamer. "Straight in the regular channel to Alton," replied Captain Stokes. "What if we are attacked?" said Captain Mitchell. "Then we will fight," was the reply of Captain Stokes. "What if we are overpowered?" said Mitchell. "Run the boat to the deepest part of the river and sink her," replied Stokes. "I'll do it," was the heroic answer of Mitchell, and away they went past the secession battery, past the St. Louis levee, and in the regular channel on to Alton, where they arrived at 5 o'clock in the morning. When they touched the landing, Captain Stokes, fearing pursuit by some of the secession military companies by which the city of St. Louis was disgraced, ran to the market house and rang the fire bell. The citizens came flocking pell-mell to the river in all sorts of habiliments. Captain Stokes informed them as to the state of affairs, and pointed to the freight cars. Instantly men, women and children boarded the steamer, seized the freight, and clambered up the levee to the cars. Rich and poor tugged together with might and main for two hours, when the cargo was all deposited on the cars, and the train moved off to Springfield amid the most enthusiastic cheers."*These arms thus rescued from the very grasp of traitors, served to equip the first regiments of the State, and on many a bloody field became the terrible avengers of those who sought to use them against their country.

---

* Patriotism of Illinois.

CHAPTER LVI.

1861—1862. ILLINOIS IN MISSOURI.

Battles of Lexington, Monroe, Charleston, Fredericktown, Belmont and Pea Ridge.

———

Having given a brief sketch of the operation of Illinois at home let us look abroad at the exploits of her soldiers in the field.

In the valley of the Mississippi, east of the Alleghanies, and on the Southern seaboard, every commercial highway was blockaded by the terrible enginery of war, and every mountain pass and salient out-post echoed with the tramp of hostile squadrons. In the disposition of the Union armies, Illinois troops were mostly confined to operations on the Mississippi, the Tennessee, the Cumberland, the White, the Red, the Savannah, and in the battles of Belmont, Pea Ridge, Donelson, Shiloh, Corinth, Perryville, Vicksburg, Jackson, Stone river, Chickamauga and Lookout Mountain, Missionary Ridge, Peach Tree Creek, Jonesboro, Atlanta, Savannah, Franklin and Nashville, and they won fame for themselves and a proud record for the State.

Military operations in the West commenced with the occupation of Cairo. Missouri lying westward, with a treasonable executive and a population partly disloyal, soon became involved in civil strife. Gov. Jackson appointed Sterling Price brigadier general of the State troops, which were to be organized and equipped for action. He managed to get the police of St. Louis under his control, and endeavored to persuade the people of the city and State to cast their destiny with their brethren of the Southern Confederacy. Acting upon his advice a body of armed men, notoriously hostile to the government, and in communication with traitors in the seceded States, met near the city, styling their place of rendezvous Camp Jackson, in honor of the governor. Captain Lyon, then in command of the arsenal, had in the meantime been empowered by the president to enroll 10,000 loyal men to maintain the authority of the government within the limits of the State. With the promptitude which the emergency demanded, he appeared on the morning of May 10th with a force of 6,000 men before the hostile camp, and demanded its surrender. Taken wholly by surprise, and threatened by a superior force, there was no alternative but to submit, and accordingly 20 cannons, 1200 rifles, and a large amount of ammunition fell into the hands of the Unionists. The force, after dispersing the rebels retired to the city, and being assaulted with showers of stones and pistol shots from disunionists, they fired into their ranks and killed some of their leaders. Great excitement ensued, and but for the vigorous interposition

746

of Lyon the commercial metropolis of Missouri would have become the scene of strife between warring factions. His course being highly approved at Washington, he was raised to the rank of brigadier general, and placed in command of the government forces then operating in the State.

Perceiving that the militia force under Price, although organized with the professed intention of preserving peace, was also treasonable in its sympathies and ulterior designs, he ordered them to surrender their arms. When this demand was made Jackson issued a proclamation calling 50,000 State militia to repel federal invasion, thus further disclosing the real *animus* of the organization under his control. With a view of arresting further proceedings of this kind, Lyon started in steamers for Jefferson City with a force of 2,000 men, and arriving thither he found that Jackson had evacuated the city and retreated to Booneville, higher up the river. Following him to the latter place, he, on the 17th of June, met and completely routed the rebel force, and most of their military stores fell into his hands. With the Union force in rapid pursuit Jackson and his followers fled to the southwestern part of the State, where he expected assistance from Price. He was, however, met in Jasper county by 15,000 men under Col. Franz Sigel, a spirited officer, who was pushing forward to prevent his junction with reinforcements. On the 4th of July Sigel had an engagement with his force near Carthage, and although outnumbered two to one, inflicted upon him a severe blow, the rebel loss being 50 killed and 150 wounded, while his own was only 13 killed and 31 wounded. Sigel's ammunition being exhausted, he was compelled to fall back, first to Mt. Vernon, and then to Springfield, where he met Gen. Lyon. The retreat was fortunate, for the next day Price, reinforced by several thousand men from Texas and Arkansas, under command of McCulloch, advanced to the support of Jackson. This force continued its march in the direction taken by Sigel, and took a position on Wilson's creek, with the intention of moving against Springfield, only ten miles distant. Lyon's force at the latter place was only 5,000 men, and many of these were inexperienced recruits, who had just taken the place of 3-months troops, while he was confronted with 20,000 enemies. A council of war was held, and in view of the demoralizing effect a retreat would have upon the Union cause, it was decided to risk a battle with even this superior force.

Accordingly on the 8th of August Lyon led his forces against the enemy. A bloody fight ensued, in which Lyon, at the head of one of his regiments, in a heavy charge against the foe, was pierced through the heart by two bullets, and fell lifeless from his steed.

The command now devolved on Major Sturgis, and after three hours' hard fighting the enemy was driven from the field. The Union troops, being now without ammunition, retired to Springfield, where Sigel took command, and conducted them to Rolla. The loss of the enemy was reported at 1,347, ours at 1,235, besides the death of Lyon, who was himself a host. His glorious past, the purity of his life, and almost reckless daring, had made him the idol of the people, and when stricken down the nation was filled with mourning. Rebel authorities endeavored to magnify this battle into a victory, notwithstanding the fact that 20,000 of

their men had been met by 5,000 federals and so badly disabled
that they could not pursue the latter when they retreated. As
Price was unable to resume operations for more than a month, it
was evidently a Union triumph, although dearly purchased at the
cost of Lyon's life.

Early in July, 1861, Fremont was entrusted with the chief command of the western department, embracing the State of Illinois,
and the States and territories between the Mississippi and the
Rocky Mountains. He found the situation of affairs in his new
field of labor very unpromising. Pope was in northern Missouri
with a small force, Prentiss at Cairo with a few regiments. Confront-
ing these and ready to pounce upon them with irresistible might
whenever the varying fortunes of war furnished an opportunity, were
20,000 men under Pillow at New Madrid, and 30,000 under Price in
the southwest part of the State. One of Fremont's first acts was to
reinforce Cairo and Bird's Point, on the opposite side of the Mississippi, both imperiled by the overwhelming forces on the river
below. On the 30th of August he issued a proclamation placing
the whole State of Missouri under martial law, and declaring the
property of rebels confiscated, and their slaves free men. Public
opinion, however, was not yet prepared for emancipation, and
President Lincoln annulled that portion relating to slavery.

Battle of Lexington.—After recovering from the battle of Wilson's creek, Price started northward to the Missouri river, it was
supposed to get possession of Jefferson City, and reinstate the authority of Gov. Jackson. Despite small detachments sent out to
intercept his movements, he turned his course to the northwest,
and on the 11th of September set down before Lexington, on the
Missouri, 300 miles above St. Louis. Col. Mulligan, in command
of the 23d Illinois infantry, 1st Illinois cavalry, and about 1,200
Missouri troops, had previously taken position between Old and
New Lexington, distant about half a mile, and commenced fortifying it. His entire force was less than 3,000, while the assailants
were estimated at nearly 20,000, and consisted, according to rebel
statements, of the elite of the Confederate army. As early as the
12th an assault was made on his works, but the fierce and derter-
mined manner in which it was met soon convinced Price that even
with his overwhelming numbers, it would not be prudent to attempt to carry the place by storm. Accordingly, as a means of
gradual approach, bales of hemp, saturated with water, to prevent
ignition from the hot shots of Mulligan's guns, were rolled in
front of his batteries. Mulligan, in the meantime, had burnt a
portion of the old town to prevent the enemy taking shelter in it,
and sent messengers by different routes for more troops.

Price, who had been waiting for ammunition, received a supply
and on the 18th 13 guns, posted in commanding positions, opened
their fiery throats upon the federal intenchments. The Union
commander had five small brass pieces which were brought into
position and worked with great gallantry, being charged with
rough shot manufactured for the occasion in a neighboring foundry.
Price having previously seized the boats in the river, and fortified
the adjacent bluffs, the besieged troops were cut off from water,
and suffered the most intense agonies of thirst. This hardship
was further aggravated by the stench arising from the putrid car-

casses of horses which in large numbers had been slaughtered by the fire of the rebel guns. It, however, rained at intervals, and the thirsty men, by spreading their blankets till they became saturated with water, and then wringing them in camp dishes, were enabled to prolong the seige till the 20th, when they surrendered.

Col. Mulligan facetiously remarks of the home guards, a portion of the Missouri troops under his command who refused to fight, that they were "invincible in peace and invisible in war." Col. Estvan, of the rebel service, in writing of the capitulation, said : "This surrender does not cast the slightest discredit on Col. Mulligan, his officers and men. After having exhausted all their means against an enemy three times their strength, they had no choice but capitulation. The booty was considerable. In addition to arms, clothing and ammunition, we took more than a million dollars in hard cash. These dollars nearly rendered our fellows frantic, for this was the object which had induced the majority of them to take up arms against their former government."*

A writer in the Chicago *Post* thus speaks of Mulligan's command known as the Irish Brigade, of which he was a private :

"On the 17th the enemy commenced erecting breastworks of hemp bales from behind which they continued to fire as they rolled them towards us. About 3 o'clock of the same day they charged over our entrenchments, upon Col. Peabody's home guards, and planted their flags on the top of our breastworks, The Irish Brigade was ordered to leave its position on the opposite side to retake the ground which Peabody had lost. We fired on the run, and continued on the double quick. The rebels scattered and fled like a flock of sheep, but left the top of the breastworks covered with dead and wounded. In this single charge we killed and wounded some 55 and lost about 30. They had no bayonets, and most of their weapons being shot guns we did not give them time to use them. They fired at random. Col. Mulligan received a buck-shot through one of his legs, which lamed but did not disable him ; six or seven passed through his blouse. Six different times during the ensuing night the rebels were allowed to approach the ditch on the side next the city. When they got sufficiently near, our boys on the inside would explode a mine, hurling them promiscuously in every direction, and slaughtering them by hundreds. Six mines were thus sprung under their feet, and they evidently began to regard that side of the entrenchment as a dangerous locality."

Col. Mulligan, who by the gallant though unsuccessful defense of Lexington, won the esteem of Illinois, was born in 1829, in the city of Utica, New York. While a child his father died and his mother moved with him to Chicago. At the age of 24 he commenced studying law in the office of Isaac N. Arnold, M. C. from the Chicago district, and in 1856 was admitted to the bar. At the commencement of the war he was captain of a militia company, the Shields Guard, in the drilling of which he acquired a knowledge of military tactics. At the fall of Sumter he threw his soul into the cause of the Union, assisted in forming the Irish-American companies of Chicago into a regiment, known as the Irish brigade, of which he was elected colonel. The conduct of the regiment at Lexington and elsewhere was brave and efficient.

Fremont had sent reinforcements to Mulligan, and unfortunately his men had hardly laid down their arms when the succoring force made its appearance on the opposite side of the river.

---

* This admission but illy comports with the oft-repeated statement of rebels that they had taken up arms to resist the aggressions of the north.

He left St. Louis on the 27th, for the purpose of meeting Price and giving him battle at some point on the Missouri. His force was composed of five divisions, commanded respectively by Gens. Pope, Sigel, Hunter, Ashboth and McKinstry, amounting in the aggregate to 39,000 men. The wary rebel general, however, soon apprised of his intentions, commenced retreating southward and by offensive cavalry feints succeeded in placing the Osage between him and his pursuers. Fremont still following, on the 28th of October the advance divisions of his army entered Springfield and drove a portion of the rebel force from the town. As soon as he came up preparations commenced to give the enemy battle, but unfortunately at this juncture when the army was eager for the contest and everything seemed to promise success, he was relieved of his command.

This was not entirely unexpected as his relations with the war department had for some time been unsatisfactory. Its occurrence at this critical time, however, was a matter of regret, for whatever errors may have been committed, the retreat of the army and the abandonment of this portion of the State to rebels, which followed, was far more disastrous. The failure to promptly send troops to the relief of Mulligan caused a storm to break out against him, and his enemies never afterwards became reconciled. He was charged with defrauding the government in purchasing supplies for the army; with surrounding himself with favorites to the exclusion of meritorious officers, and finally incompetency in the management of his department; it should, however, be mentioned in extenuation of these charges, that the failure to relieve Lexington was rather the result of adverse circumstances than the fault of Fremont; that his attempt to free the slaves of rebel masters, although rejected at the time, subsequently became the policy of the government, and that had he been enabled to carry out his plans for the descent of the Mississippi, which his successors mouths afterward adopted, it would have saved the country thousands of lives and millions of treasure.

Battle of Monroe.—Besides the battle of Lexington, a number of minor engagements occurred in Missouri during Fremont's administration, in which the troops of Illinois bore a distinguished part. A spirited fight occurred between Col. R. T. Smith of the 16th Illinois and the rebel Gov. Harris, in command of 2,500 confederates stationed at Florida. The federal officer with a force of 600 men detached from his own regiment and the 3d Iowa, left his camp at Monroe, 30 miles west of Hannibal, to engage the enemy. On nearing the ford on Salt river, he was suddenly attacked and Capt. McAlister of the 16th Illinois, mortally wounded. Finding himself confronted by greatly superior numbers Col. Smith fell back to Monroe and stationed his force in an academy. Here he maintained his position till the arrival of reinforcements from Quincy, under ex-Gov. Wood, when the enemy was charged and routed with a loss of 70 men and a large number of horses.

Battle of Charleston.—On the 19th of August an engagement occurred at Charleston, of which Gen. Fremont gives the following account: "Report from commanding officer at Cairo says that

Col. Dougherty of the 22d Illinois, with 300 men sent out yesterday at 7 o'clock from Bird's Point, attacked the enemy at Charleston, 1,200 strong, drove him back, killed 40, took 17 prisoners and 15 horses and returned at 2 A. M. to Bird's Point, with a loss of 1 killed and 6 wounded." A correspondent of the New York *Tribune* relates the following of Lt. Col. Ransom of the 11th Illinois: "He was urging his men to the charge when a man rode up and called out "Do you know you are killing our own men?" Ransom replied "I know what I am doing; who are you?" The reply was "I am for Jeff Davis." Ransom replied, "You are the man I am after," and instantly two pistols were drawn. The rebel fired first, taking effect in Col. Ransom's arm near the shoulder. The colonel fired, killing his antagonist instantly.

Battle of Fredericktown.—Another spirited engagement came off on the 21st of October near Fredericktown. Gen. Grant then commanding the southwest district of Missouri, with headquarters at Cairo, hearing that the town was occupied by a rebel force under Gen. Jeff. Thompson, sent Col. Plummer, of the 11th Missouri, to operate against them. This regiment was composed of Illinois men who enlisted in Missouri. The completion of the quota rendered it impossible to obtain admission to the service at home, and hence they went abroad. The force of the latter consisted of his own regiment, the 17th Illinois, Col. Ross, the 20th, Col. Marsh, White's section of Taylor's Chicago battery and Captains Stewart and Saunders' companies of Illinois cavalry. On his arrival at Fredericktown he found it in possession of Col. Carlin, 38th Illinois, whose command, in addition to the 38th, included the 21st and 23d Illinois, Colonels Alexander and Harvey and several companies of infantry and cavalry from Wisconsin and Iowa. The entire force under the leadership of Col. Plumber rapidly pursued and overtook the enemy, when a severe engagement followed. The 17th Illinois and Taylor's battery commenced the attack in the rear, while the other regiments deployed to the right and left as they came up and delivered their fire. The left of the rebel force soon gave way, and their retreat was converted into a rout. The right under Thompson supported by a battery maintained its position longer, but the battery was at length captured and the rout became general. The retreating foe was pursued a distance of 20 miles, and lost in the engagement 200 men by death and 80 by capture. The federal loss was 6 killed and 60 wounded.

Gen. Hunter, who was sent to succeed Gen. Fremont, arrived on the 3d of November, and declining an engagement with Price commenced retreating in the direction of St. Louis. Price followed him and endeavored to destroy the Northern railroad for the purpose of cutting off communication with St. Louis. On the 18th of November Gen. Halleck reached that city, and relieving Gen. Hunter, took command of the Western Department. He immediately issued a proclamation fixing the penalty of death against all persons engaged in destroying railroads and telegraphs, and by superior strategy succeeded in circumventing the designs of Price. On the 7th of December Pope was placed in command of the troops in Northern Missouri, and pushing forward he occupied a position between Warrensburg and Clinton. Operating from this

position he enabled Col. J. C. Davis to meet and completely rout
the enemy near the mouth of Clear creek. This victory was
immediately followed by an epedition to Lexington for the purpose
of destroying a foundry and a small fleet in possession of rebel
troops. This was speedily accomplished, and with it almost the
entire region between the Missouri and Osage rivers fell into the
hands of the federals.

Battle of Belmont.—In the meantime Gen. Grant made an
attempt to capture the rebel force at Belmont, on the Missouri
side of the Mississippi. Henceforth the history of this officer
is too well known to require recital. With his past history we
are not so familiar. Ulysses S. Grant was born in Clermont county,
Ohio, April 27, 1822. At the age of 17 he was admitted ·to
the military academy at West Point, and graduated June 30,
1843. Immediately after his graduation he received the brevet
of 2d lieutenant, and was placed in the 4th regiment of United
States infantry, then stationed in Missouri. During the war
with Mexico his regiment was ordered to join the army of
occupation under Gen. Taylor, and subsequently he participated
in the battles of Palo Alto, Reseca de la Palma and Monterey.
On the arrival of Gen. Scott he was transferred to his command,
and in the battles of Vera Cruz and Molino del Rey his bravery
was so conspicuous, he was made 1st lieutenant on the battle field.
In the battle of Chepultepec, which followed, he further distinguished himself and was again promoted, receiving the brevet of
captain in the regular army. With the cessation of the war he
returned home, resigned his commission and lived a private life till
the commencement of the rebellion.

In April 1861, he waited on Gov. Yates and tendered him his
services, modestly stating that he had been educated at the expense of the government; that he now thought it his duty
to assist in defending it, and would regard it a privilege to
be assigned to any position where he could render himself useful. The first important duty with which he was entrusted was
the organization of the first regiments furnished by the State
under the call of April 15, 1861. Evincing in the performance of
this work his superior military qualifications, the governor placed
him in command of the 21st Illinois, his commission as colonel dating from the 15th of June, 1861. At the time he took command the
regiment was demoralized and incomplete, but in 10 days afterward he filled it to the maximum standard and brought it to a
state of discipline seldom attained in so short a time. Being
ordered to Northern Missouri, his regiment proceeded on foot from
Springfield to the Illinois river, thence on the cars to Quincy,
where its first duty was the protection of the Quincy & Palmyra
and the Hannibal and St. Joseph railroads.

On the 31st of July Grant was placed in command of the troops
at Mexico, in the North Missouri District, commanded by Brig.
Gen. Pope. Early distinguishing himself in the field, his claims
for increased rank were recognized by his friends in Illinois before
his worth was fully appreciated in Washington. His vigorous
prosecution of the campaign in North Missouri, however, soon
won universal recognition, and he was promoted August 23d to
the rank of brigadier general, his commission dating from May

17th. After his promotion he was placed in command of the District of Cairo, embracing in its jurisdiction Southern Illinois and Missouri and that part of Kentucky west of the Cumberland. The force now under his command consisted of two brigades numbering 2,850 men. The first under Gen. John A. McClernand consisted of the 27th, Col. Buford; 30th, Col. Fouke; 31st, Col. J. A. Logan; Capt. Dollins' company of 4th cavalry and Taylor's battery of light artillery. The second, under Col H. Dougherty, comprised his own regiment, the 21st Illinois, and the 7th Iowa, Col. Lauman. The entire force except the last regiment was from Illinois.

Grant's first movement was to seize Smithland and Paducah respectively at the mouths of the Cumberland and Tennessee, and use them as the base of future operations in the rebel States. Having garrisoned these places, his next movement was to dislodge a rebel force stationed at Belmont, on the Missouri side of the Mississippi. The entire force under his command was embarked on board the gunboats Tyler and Lexington and landed November 7th, 1861, at Lucas' bend, about two miles from the camp of the enemy. As soon as debarkation was effected a line of battle was formed, Buford commanding the right, Fouke the center and Logan the left. The advance toward the camp was a continuous running fight, in which a storm of the enemy's missiles battered and tore down the timber in the faces of our men. Passing over all obstacles and surmounting all opposition the three divisions vied with each other for the honor of first reaching the rebel position. The scene became terrific, men grappled with men, column charged upon column, musketry rattled, cannon thundered and tore frightful gaps in the contending forces. Presently the 57th planted its colors in the midst of the hostile encampment, and a loud and prolonged shout was heard above the din of battle. Next, the 21st captured a 12-pound gun battery, one of the enemy's principal defences, when a final impetuous, irresistible charge drove him in every direction and left the field in possession of the federals. The victory was complete. The captured camp was immediately fired, and all the rebel baggage and ammunition destroyed.

In the meantime a heavy rebel force was thrown across the river from Columbus and moved up to repair the disaster, while batteries opened upon our men from the opposite shore. Unable to cope with such formidable numbers, a retreat became necessary to avoid being cut off from the boats. The command was therefore given to retire, but before it could be executed the passage became blocked up with rebel forces. The boys of Illinois and Iowa, however, had fought their way forward, and they now in opposition to a foe of greatly superior numbers fought their way back. Every regiment suffered severely, but it was believed the enemy suffered worse. Grant in his official report gives the loss of the former at 84 killed and 150 wounded; that of the latter was not known.

The object of the battle was to prevent the enemy from sending reinforcements to Price and Thompson in Missouri. But how this was to be done does not appear, when the impossibility of holding the position under the heavy guns of Columbus was apparent. Though the propriety of the expedition

48

may be questioned the valor of Illinois was undoubted. Gen. Mc-
Clernand was in the midst of danger displaying great coolness and
skill in handling his forces. Gen. Logan exhibited the intrepidity and judgment which distinguished him in subsequent
battles, and Col. Dougherty at the head of his brigade was three
times wounded and at length taken prisoner. Says McClernand:

"I cannot bestow too high commendation upon all I had the honor to
command on that day. Supplied with inferior and defective arms, many
of which could not be discharged, many bursting in use, they fought an
an enemy in woods with which he was familiar, behind defensive works
which he had been preparing for months, in the face of a battery at Belmont and under the huge guns at Columbus, and although numbering
three or four to our one, we beat him and captured several stand of colors,
destroying his camp and carrying off a large amount of property already
mentioned. To mention all who did well would include every man of
my command who came under my personal notice. Both officers and
privates did their whole duty, nobly sustaining the character of Americans and Illinoisans. They shed new luster upon the flag of their country
by holding it in triumph through the shock of battle and the din of arms.
The blood they so freely poured out proved their devotion to their country and serves to hallow a just cause with glorious recollections. Their
success was that of citizen soldiers."

Battle of Pea Ridge.—The forces operating in Missouri at the
close of January, 1862, were combined under the command of Gen.
S. B. Curtis, a distinguished officer of the U. S. army. Early the
following month they pushed rapidly toward Springfield, where
on the 12th they encountered Price with about 4,000 men. Sharp
skirmishing ensued and the rebel general fleeing during the night
to avoid an engagement, was pursued for more than 100 miles.
Stopping in the vicinity of the Boston mountains he was re-inforced
by McCulloch and Van Dorn, whereby his army was augmented
to near 40,000 men, and he was again enabled to resume offensive
operations. Curtis thus threatened, had distributed portions of
his command for garrison duty along his extensive line of communication, and now had left only 12,000 men and about 50 pieces
of artillery. His several divisions had been sent in various directions for the purpose of obtaining forage and dispersing rebel
bands gathering at different points in the southeastern part of the
State. The 1st and 2d were under Sigel near Bentonville, the 3d
under Davis near Sugar Creek, and the 4th under Carr at Cross
Hollow. Early in March intelligence was received that Van Dorn
who assumed chief command, was advancing to make an attack

A correspondent of the Chicago *Post*, writing of Belmont, says: "An incident worthy of being recorded occurred during the recent battle. Col. Phil. B. Fouke, of the
31st Illinois, and Col. John V. Wright, of the 13th Tennessee, both members of the last
congress, were warm friends and occupied seats together. When the war broke out
before they had left Washington, Mr. Wright received the appointment of colonel
from the governor of Tennessee. When about to separate Mr. Wright said: 'Phil., I
am going into the war, and I suppose you will be in it also, and I promise if we meet
on the battle field that I will take care of your men if you will take care of mine.'
The pledge was mutual, and the next time they met was on the bloody field of Belmont.
At one time during the fight Col. Fouke's men were lying down waiting for the enemy
and he was standing on a log in full view waiting for them, when about twenty of
Wright's men leveled their muskets at him, which movement being seen by Col. Wright,
he looked in the direction and recognized Col. Fouke, ordered his men to desist, saying
that man was his friend and he did not want him harmed. This interposition doubtless saved Col. Fouke's life as these Tennesseeans are crack shots. Col. Wright was
was afterwards severely wounded, but the next day sent his adjutant to inform Col.
Fouke that he had not forgotten his pledge. Before the battle was ended Col. Fouke's
regiment took a number of Col. Wright's men, and he religously obseved his share of
the pledge, looking after the wants of the prisoners as though they were his own
men."

and the several divisions of the Union forces were ordered to concentrate on Sugar Creek, a point regarded favorable for effective resistence. Sigel in bringing up his division was assailed by large numbers of the enemy, and for five hours compelled to cut his way through their midst to effect a junction with the others.

On the 6th of March, 1862, the entire force was brought together on the western edge of Pea Ridge, and in anticipation of an engagement, slept on their arms. The battle commenced at early dawn and raged furiously the whole day, during which Van Dorn succeeded in marching round the Federal army, and took a position in the rear. Curtis was thus compelled to change his front, and although exposed to the continued fire of the enemy, the movement was executed with the most intrepid gallantry. In the centre and on the left the battle raged with increased fury, and when evening put an end to the carnage, McCulloch and Mc'Intosh, two of the most efficient rebel officers, were among the slain. The weather was cold and the army lay down to pass a comfortless night, being unable to kindle fires without drawing the attention of the enemy. During the night the rebels effected a junction of their forces, and as the rising sun lighted up the battle ground, they recommenced the conflict, confident of overwhelming the federals by superior numbers. The latter, however, were handled with great skill and Sigel served the artillery with such accuracy that the rebel line in a short time was seriously shaken and finally forced from the field. The routed army fled in the direction of Keitsville and was followed a distance of 12 miles, when further pursuit, in consequence of the wooded and broken country, became impracticable. That portion of the battle field pounded by our artillery presented a ghastly scene of dismounted cannons, shivered carriages and mangled bodies. Price's loss was estimated at 3,000 in killed, wounded and missing. A novel feature introduced at this battle was the employment of some 2,500 Indians seduced from their allegiance by the rebels. They were of little service to their allies in fighting the living but vented their brutal ferocity in mutilating the bodies of the dead.

The Illinois troops participating in the engagement were the 35th, Col. G. A. Smith; 36th, Col. Greusel; 37th, Col. J. White; 57th, Major Post; 3d cavalry, Col. E. A. Carr; a battalion of the 15th cavalry, Capt. Jenks, and Davidson's Peoria battery. All acquitted themselves in such a manner as to reflect honor upon the State. Day Elmore, a drummer of the 36th, exchanged his drum for a musket and fought with the bravery of a veteran during the intire battle.

After this engagement large numbers of the Missourians who had fought with the rebels, were permitted to return home, and on taking the oath of allegiance, the State for a short time enjoyed comparative quiet. In June, at the suggestion of Gen. Curtis Missouri was erected into a separate military district, and Gen. J. M. Schofield, who had served with distinction as chief of the lamented Lyon's staff, was placed in command. Marauding bands again began to be troublesome, and Schofield, on the 22d inst., issued a proclamation holding rebel sympathizers and their propery responsible for the depredations committed in their respective districts. Encouraged by Price at Helena, numerous rebel emissaries next spread themselves over the State, and while openly professing Union sentiments, they secretly organized a force estimated at 40,000 men, and agreed upon signals whereby they could suddenly seize all the important points in the country. To prepare for the conspiracy Schofield obtained from the general government authority to organize the militia, and as the loyal people readily submitted to the enrollment, and the disloyal refused, thus disclosing the real character of each man. Some 20,000 men were reported for military duty, and to raise funds for their support, the wealthy in St. Louis county who refused to serve, were required to furnish $500,000. A bloody struggle was now going on in the north-east portion of the State between bands of guerillas and the militia. By the 1st of September as many as a hundred small engagements had occurred in which Illinois troops largely participated, and some 10,000 rebels were killed, wounded or driven from the State. At this date the rebels under Hindman, in northern Arkansas, numbering 50,000, were also contemplating an invasion of south-western Missouri. As the result, battles of considerable magnitude were fought at Fort Wayne, Cane Hill, and Fayetteville, in which the rebels sustained such serious losses that Hindman abandoned his designs.

CHAPTER LVII.

1861–1862—ILLINOIS ON THE CUMBERLAND, TENNES-SEE AND MISSISSIPPI.

Battle of Forts Henry and Donelson—Capture of Columbus. New Madrid and Island No. 10.

We must now go back to the commencement of the operations for opening the Mississippi. The course of this magnificent river from north to south and the intercourse necessarily existing among the inhabitants of its fertile valley will always render it impossible to form them into separate nationalities by arbitrary boundaries. Running entirely across the rebel confederacy and making it vulnerable to the assaults of a fleet, the government at an early day commenced making preparation for offensive naval operations. Columbus, Kentucky, situated on the east bank, 20 miles below Cairo, had been seized as early as Sept. 1861, and so fortified as to be termed the rebel Gibralter. Its massive works and heavy guns rendering capture by a direct assault almost impossible, it was determined to cut off its supplies and thus compel its abandonment by an expedition up the Tennessee and Cumberland rivers. Near where these streams flow across the northern boundary of Tennessee, the rebels had erected two strong fortifications known as Forts Henry and Donelson. After mature deliberation, Gen. Halleck decided first to attack the former of these strongholds, and then moving across the intervening land, attack the latter. For this purpose Commodore A. H. Foote, as gallant an officer as ever sailed the deep, with a fleet of 7 gunboats, the St. Louis, Cincinnati, Carondelet, Essex, Tyler, Lexington and Mound City, and Gen. Grant, with a co-operating land force from Cairo and Paducah, were sent up the Tennessee. On the 5th of February, 1862, the land forces disembarked from their transports and prepared to spend the night, during which a thunder storm burst on the encampment, portraying in its terrific grandeur, the fury of the coming battle. Grant ordered Gen. Mc'Clernand commanding the first division, to take a position in the rear of the fort for the two-fold purpose of guarding against reinforcements, or preventing the escape of the garrison as the exigencies of the engagement might require. His division consisted of 2 brigades commanded respectively by Cols. Oglesby and W. H. L. Wallace; the first comprising the 8th, 18th, 27th, the 29th, 30th and 31st Illinois infantry, Dresser's and Schwartz's batteries; the 2d, the 11th, 12th, 45th and 48th Illinois infantry, Taylor's and McAlisters' batteries and 4th cavalry.

The 2d division under Gen. C. F. Smith, was thrown across the river and ordered to proceed up the Kentucky shore and occupy the heights adjacent the fort, which the enemy had begun to fortify. The 9th, 12th, 28th and 41st Illinois constituted a part of the force.

Owing to the badness of the roads, none of the land forces arrived soon enough to share in its capture. About 10 o'clock Foote steamed up toward the fort, which standing in a bend of the river, had complete command of the channel for a long distance below. Being a bastioned earth work and mounting 17 guns of the largest calibre, it was deemed capable of resisting any assailing force however formidable. An island lay in the stream about a mile below, under cover of which the fleet advanced without becoming exposed to the fire of its long ranged rifled guns. The wooden vessels remained at the island while the ironclads emerging from behind it, and proceeding in the direction of the fort were met by the ponderous shot of the fort. The boats immediately returned this greeting, and their screaming missiles fell with such rapidity in and around the fort as to cause some 4,000 infantry to flee with precipitation. Coming within closer range the breastworks were plowed up and dashed in the face of the garrison, gun after gun was dismounted, and within an hour from the commencement of the engagement, the stronghold was surrendered. Sixty prisoners and a large amount of military stores fell into our hands. Unfortunately the infantry which fled at the commencement of the engagement, were beyond the reach of pursuit, before Mc'Clernand and his Illinois men could arrive and intercept them. The principal damage inflicted on the fleet was sustained by the Essex. A 24-pound shot passing in at a porthole, and plunging into one of her boilers, caused the steam to escape and completely envelope the crew. Some in their terrible agony throwing themselves out of port holes into the river while others struggling in vain to escape, sank gasping for breath, scalded in the fiery vapor.

This important victory was the first won on the western waters; the telegram announcing the event was read in both houses of congress, and a vote of thanks tendered Commodore Foote. The fleet under Lieut. Phelps was sent up the river to capture two rebel boats which were pursued so closely that their crews blew them up to prevent their falling into the hands of the pursuers. The expedition sailed up the river as far as Florence, destroying the bridge of the M. & O. railroad connecting Bowling Green, Memphis and Columbus, and compelling the rebels to burn five of their valuable steamers. All along the route Phelps met with many cheering evidences of loyalty among the people of Tennessee and Kentucky, old men and women flocking to the shore, and shedding tears at again beholding the old flag.

Donelson.—The fall of Henry opened the way for an advance upon Donelson. This formidable rebel stronghold was situated on the west bank of the Cumberland, and served as an outpost for the defense of Nashville, 80 miles higher up the river. The ground upon which it was situated is about 100 feet above the level of the river, which at that point bends toward the west, and after running a few hundred yards turns again and pursues its general course northward. To command the river northward and guard against a naval attack, two batteries of heavy ordnance had been planted at the foot of the bluff near the edge of the water. The fort itself was an irregular work enclosing about 100 acres, and except on the river side surrounded at the distance of a mile with rifle pits. On the west side a formidable abatis ran between the fort and rifle-pits, while from every commanding point along the whole line, howitzers and field-pieces, pointed their grim muzzles directly at the face of the besieging army. These almost impregnable works were occupied by 20,000 impetuous fire eaters from the southwest under command of Floyd, Pillow, Buckner, and Johnson. Additional troops being necessary to effect its reduction, Gen. Grant ordered forward all the available forces in his district, while troops from Cincinnati and the right wing of Gen. Buel's division from Kentucky, under Gen. Crittenden, were hurried forward and placed at his disposal. The army thus augmented, consisted of 3 divisions under McClernand, Smith and Wallace and numbered some 25,000 men, the elite of western troops.

On the morning of the 12th, Gen. Grant, with Smith's and McClernand's divisions started for Fort Donelson and by noon arrived within two miles of the enemy's outposts. After driving in the rebel pickets, and investing the works, Col. Haynie of W. H. L. Walace's brigade, McClernand's division, with the 17th, 48th and 49th Illinois, was sent to make an assault on the enemy's middle redoubt. "Forming a line of battle they moved in fine order across the intervening ravines and mounted with the coolness of veterans the steep height on which the redoubt stood. The enemy screened behind their embankments, poured into the exposed ranks a terrible fire of musketry. Still the brave Illinoisans, undaunted, steadly advanced. But at this critical juncture it was found that the line was not long enough to envelope the works and the 45th Illinois was ordered to their support. While these movements were being carried out the enemy sent forward heavy reinforcements of men and field artillery, which soon swept the advancing line with murderous effect. But onward pressed the undaunted regiments leaving their dead and wounded strewing the slope till they came to the foot of the works, where an abatis presented a tangled wall of jagged points, through which no soldiers under heaven could force their way in the face of such a fire. Braver officers never led men to death, but they found they had been sent to accomplish impossible work, and gave the reluctant command to fall back.*"

This determined assault rendered it evident that the task before the army was one of no ordinary magnitude, and it was deemed best to await the arrival of Wallace's division and the fleet under Foote, before attempting any further demonstrations. Meanwhile the pleasant weather which had previously cheered the army suddenly changed· A continous storm of sleet and snow prevailed during the night of the 13th and the army, destitute of blankets and tents, was compelled to suffer the unmitigated rigors of winter. On the 14th an irregular fire of sharp-shooters occasionally interluded with bursts of artillery, was kept up but un-

* Headley's Rebellion

attended by important results. The same day the expected reinforcements came up and the commander of the fleet put his
boats in motion for an assault on the batteries at the foot of the
bluff, the wooden vessels in the rear and the iron-clads in front.
Coming within range, the contest commenced and continued to
increase as the distance between the combatants diminished. The
loud explosions of the guns shook the adjacent shores and reverberating far inland, spread dismay among the rebellious inhabitants. Still farther and farther they advanced, discharging their
heavy ordnance directly into the batteries, and in turn exposed to
the storm of shot and shell rained down upon the river. The fire
of the batteries at length began to slack, but unfortunately before
they were entirely silenced, a shot destroyed the steering apparatus of the Louisville and another disabled the St. Louis, and both
crafts unmanageable, rapidly drifted with the swift current from
under the enemy's guns.

Grant now determined to strengthen his line of investment so
as to render egress impossible, and await the repair and farther
co-operation of the boats. The rebels, however, becoming alarmed
at finding themselves almost literally walled in by the besieging
forces, resolved to open an exit and escape to the country. Accordingly early in the morning of the 15th, the enemy, some 7,500
strong, emerged from his works and in separate columns, hurled
himself against McClernand's division on the right of the federal
line. Oglesby's brigade, the 8th, 18th, 29th, 30th and 31st Illinois
received the first concussion. Next Wallace's, the 11th, 20th, 43d
and 48th; Morrison's, the 17th and 49th, and McArthurs', the 9th,
12th, 29th and 41st were struck by the angry foe, and the entire
division for four hours alone contended with his overwhelming
numbers. It was an irregular battle-field of hill, ravine and forest;
and concert of action among the several regiments engaged at
different points of attack was difficult. Stubbornly, gallantly,
enthusiastically, however, the sons of Illinois met the onslaught,
the advancing and receding roar of musketry and cannon through
the forest marking the shifting tide of battle. At length from the
incessant pounding of shot, shell, and cannister, the extreme
right of the line began to crumble away and the exultant enemy
concentrating at a single point, and hurling himself in overwhelming masses against the division, it was compelled to fall back, not
however, till the regiments had exhausted their ammunition, and
some of them had lost near a third of their men.

Never fought braver men than ours on that bloody day, some
of the companies remaining rooted to their position till the
enemy's forces rolled about and swallowed them up. Some of the
regiments were literally cut to pieces, while the loss of officers was
great beyond proportion. Col. Quinn of the 20th, Major Post of
the 8th, Captain Rigby of the 31st, Lieut.-Col. Smith of the 48th,
Capt. Craig, and Lieuts. Skeats and Mansker of the 18th, Capt.
Shaw and Lieuts. Royce and Vore of the 11th, Adjutant Kirk-
patrick of the 13th, Capt. Mendell of the 7th and Capt. Brokaw
of the 49th, were among the many who laid down their lives on
the fatal field that liberty, right, and progress might live. In the
retrograde movement, McAllister's battery having exhausted the
150 rounds of ammunition with which it went into action, was
captured while waiting a fresh supply.

In the early part of the assault McClernand, fearful he might be overborne by superior numbers, sent to Wallace, whose division occupied the center of the line, for reinforcements. The latter sent Cruft's brigade to his assistance, but being imperfectly guided, it was carried too far to the right to render successful aid. The enemy still advancing, he next interposed Thayer's brigade between them and the retiring regiments, which had expended their ammunition. The force was immediately placed in line by pushing forward Wood's Chicago battery to the road along which the foe was moving, posting the 58th Illinois and 1st Nebraska on the right of the battery, and 58th Ohio and a portion of the 32d Illinois on the left. Behind the line thus formed at right angles with the road, the 76th Ohio and 46th and 57th Illinois were stationed as reserves. Hardly were these arragements complete before the rebels emerged from the woods and dashed up in front of the brigade. A blinding sheet of flame burst forth from cannon and musketry, causing the exultant foe to recoil and fall back to the elevated ground previously taken from McClernand. Battered and buffeted by the blows which had been previously dealt him, his further advance was stayed, and this was the last offensive movement he was able to make.

At 3 o'clock Gen. Grant made his appearance on the field, having been in consultation with Commodore Foote in reference to another attack by the fleet. He immediately ordered the division of Gen. Smith, containing the 7th, 43d, 50th, 57th and 38th Illinois to move against the enemy in their front, and a renewed attack on the right. At the request of Gen. McClernand, whose division had borne the brunt of the battle, Gen. Wallace took the advance. Placing the 8th Missouri and 4th Indiana in the lead, and pushing the 17th and 49th Illinois far along the enemy's flank, he gave the command, "forward." Knowing well the fearful object his men had to accomplish, he gave them the simple instruction to ascend the height in columns of regiments and then act as circumstances might suggest. The men pleased with the confidence reposed in their judgment, and nerving themselves for the bloody work, moved forward and commenced ascending the hill, when plunging volley after volley tore through and decimated their ranks. Nothing short of annihilation, however, could stay their advance, and in the face of the murderous fire they bounded to the summit and drove the rebels behind their inner works.

While this important success was achieved on the right, Gen. S. F. Smith, with the 2d and 7th Iowa and 52d Indiana, performed an equally brilliant exploit on the left. After feigning an attack in a different direction, he commenced ascending the steep hill on which was posted the rebel force he proposed to attack. The enemy perceiving his design at once opened a destructive fire upon the advancing regiments, yet without discharging a single gun in reply, they swept up the slippery heights. Mounting higher and higher they at length gained the summit from which volcano-like had been hurled the storm of fiery projectiles encountered in the ascent. A determined bayonet charge quickly ended the contest, and high above and within the rebel ramparts their colors were flung to the breeze, while a prolonged shout announced the welcome victory to their comrades on other parts of the field. The position was immediately fortified, and when the sun went down the enemy was again confined within his works.

Convinced that they could not hold the works, Floyd and Pillow passed the command over to Buckner, and during the night with about 5,000 men embarked on board steamboats and escaped up the river. The following morning, although our troops had marched from Fort Henry with only such food as they could carry in their haversacks, and for three nights had been exposed to the rigors of winter, yet at early dawn they eagerly awaited orders to renew the conflict. The besieged anticipating an immediate attack, and satisfied that all further attempts to extricate themselves from the iron grasp with which they were bound would be futile, ran up a flag as evidence of submission. Correspondence was immediately interchanged respecting terms of surrender. Grant to the overtures of the rebel general said: "*No terms other than unconditional and immediate surrender can be accepted. I propose to move immediately upon your works.*" Buckner thought the terms ungenerous, but was compelled to submit, and Sunday morning February 16th, 1862, Donelson, of almost fabulous strength, fell into the hands of the federal conquerers. The spoils obtained consisted of 46 cannon, 20,000 stand of arms, 3,000 horses and a large amount of commissary stores; while as the result of the victory Bowling Green, Nashville and Columbus became untenable. The federal loss in men was 446 killed, 1,735 wounded; that of the enemy 231 killed, 1,007 wounded and 15,000 captured.

The people of the North expressed their appreciation of this great victory by public meetings, illuminations and other similar demonstrations; Grant congratulated his soldiers upon the triumph gained by their valor; while Davis and other rebel authorities were deeply mortified at their disgrace, and Floyd and Pillow were suspended from command.

Besides the Illinois infantry already enumerated, Schwartz's, Dresser's, Taylor's, Wood's, McAlister's and Willard's batteries, McClernand's division and Stewart's, O'Harnett's, Carmichael's, Kellogg's and Dickey's cavalry of the same command also participated in the battle. The want of space renders it impossible to mention the many instances of Illinois valor noticed in the reports of the battle. Says Mr. Stevenson, author of Indiana's Roll of Honor: "Upon McClernand's division was first hurled the rebel thunder. Under fire from several batteries an immense mass of infantry charged upon his line. Sudden as was the attack, the gallant sons of Illinois were ready to meet it. Into the enemy's teeth they poured a steady, deadly fire. Taylor's battery and McAlister's guns met them with a storm of grape and shell, and a brigade charging drove four times their number back into their embankments. The struggle was hand to hand. The bayonet, the bowie-knife and the but end of the musket were freely used. Scarce a regiment, company or battery from the State failed to distinguish itself, and if there was failure it was for the want of opportunity. A New England poet reading the telegrams of the battle as they came in, and admiring the audacity of Illinois' daring, wrote the following stanzas:

"Oh, gales that dash the Atlantic's swell
  Along our rocky shores,
Whose thunder diapason swell
  New England's glad hurrahs.

"Bear to the prairies of the West
  The echoes of our joy,
The prayer that springs in every breast,
  God bless thee, Illinois.

"Oh, awful hours when grape and shell
  Tore through the unflinching line,
Stand firm, remove the men who fell,
  Close up and wait the sign.

"It came at last, now lads the steel,
  The rushing hosts deploy,
Charge boys, the broken traitors reel,
  Huzza for Illinois.

"In vain thy ramparts, Donelson,
  The living torrent bars,
It leaps the wall, the fort is won,
  Up go the stripes and stars.

"Thy proudest mother's eyelids fill,
  As dares her gallant boy,
And Plymouth Rock and Bunker Hill
  Yearn to thee, Illinois."*

The news of the surrender reached Nashville as the people were assembling at church. A dispatch had been received the previous evening from Pillow claiming the victory, and now they were meeting in the sanctuary to offer thanks to the God of battles for the success of their cause. The truth fell like a thunderbolt. Joy and exultation gave place to alarm, and the whole population in a short time was in commotion. Gov. Harris, it is said, rushed wildly through streets crying, the enemy will soon be in the city, and the terrified inhabitants seizing every available means of conveyance fled as if from certain destruction. Says Pollard, "An earthquake could not have shocked the city more." The congregations of the churches were broken up in confusion and dismay. Women and children rushed into the streets wailing with terror, trunks were thrown from three-story windows in the rush of the fugitives, and thousands hastened to leave their beautiful city in the midst of the most distressing scenes of terror and confusion and plunder by the mob.

On the 24th of February, the Union forces under Buell entered and took possession of the city. A general order was issued promising protection to all peaceably disposed citizens, and on the refusal of the municipal authorities to take the oath of allegiance they were ejected from office. Andrew Johnson was appointed military governor of the State, and while he was entering on the vigorous prosecution of his duties the federal army was slowly moving southward in the rear of the fugitive enemy.

Occupation of Columbus.--Columbus, from the formidable character of its fortifications called the Gibralter of the West, was

---

*Atlantic Monthly.

selected as the next place of attack. The force designated to operate against it was the fleet under Commodore Foote, and a co-operating force of infantry under Gen. W. T. Sherman. The latter consisted of the 27th and 55th Illinois and 74th Ohio, the former of 6 gun and 4 mortar boats in charge of Capt. Phelps, of the United States navy. The ponderous mortars, of which there was only one on each boat, weighed 17,000 pounds, and threw shells of more than 200 pounds a distance of three miles. Such was the deafening effect of the concussion when fired, the gunners were compelled to take refuge behind the timber work which enclosed them to escape the shock.

With everything in readiness the entire force, the infantry on transports, slowly and cautiously descended the Mississippi, till on the 4th of March the bluffs of Columbus became visible. Preparations were commenced to open fire when a strange flag was discovered floating above the works, different from the rebel colors, and it became questionable who were in possession of the place, our own forces or those of the enemy. To solve the mystery Capt. Phelps and 50 Illinois volunteers made a dashing reconnoisance in a tug directly under the water batteries, but failed to elicit a single hostile shot. It was now evident that the town had been evacuated. A rush was made for the shore, and in less than five minutes the flag of the 21st Illinois proudly waved over the fort which the chivalrous southrons regarded as impregnable. Cheer after cheer from soldier and tar rent the air at this happy consummation of the expedition. The strange bunting which had been discried, proved to be a flag improvised from pieces of calico by soldiers of the 2d Illinois cavalry, who the previous day, to the number of 400, had galloped from Paducah and taken possession of the town. Gen. Polk with 20,000 men had been intrusted with the custody of this almost impregnable fortress, but finding himself completely turned on both sides of the Mississippi, the result of Union triumphs in Missouri, and the conquests of Henry and Donelson, he was compelled to evacuate it without striking a single blow in its defense. Says an officer in the expedition: "I could not resist landing to examine the works, which are of immense strength, consisting of tiers upon tiers of batteries on the river front, and a strong parapet and ditch strengthened by a thick abatis on the land side. The fortifications appear to have been evacuated hastily considering the quantities of ordinance stores, a number of anchors, the remnant of the chain which was once stretched across the river, and a large supply of torpedoes remaining. Desolation was visible everywhere, huts, tents and barricades presenting their blackened remains, though the town was spared."

Capture of New Madrid.—The tide of victory following the current of the Mississippi, New Madrid and Island No. 10, were soon added to the list of Union triumphs. On the 22d of February, the anniversary of Washington's birth day, Gen. Pope was ordered by Gen. Halleck to dislodge a large rebel force stationed at New Madrid. On the 24th of March his force arrived at Commerce, and on learning that Jeff Thompson with a rebel force, was in the neighborhood, it was determined to give him battle. Accordingly two companies of the 7th Illinois cavalry, and the 26th Illinois infantry was sent in pursuit and soon encountered the foe, having a mounted force of 2,000 men and 3 pieces of artillery. A dashing charge was immediately ordered. The rebels after delivering a scattering volley, hurriedly fled, with our men in pursuit. As the chase was continued at short intervals, squads of the enemy broke into the woods and fired at our men as they passed, till not more than one-fourth of the original number remained in the road. These to expedite their frantic flight, left their track strewed with coats, hats, blankets, guns and other baggage; 3 pieces of artillery were run down and captured, and thus for 20 miles the precipitate flight and pursuit was kept up till the flying foe sought shelter under the friendly guns of New Madrid.

The main column of our forces arrived on the 3d of March, when Pope, not knowing the exact position of the enemy, sent forward 3 regiments and a battery of artillery to make a reconnoisance. On coming within ranging distance they were met by shells from gunboats stationed in the river, when they fell back and encamped beyond their reach. The rebel entrenchments might have been easily carried, but it would have been impossible to hold them in consequence of the destructive fire of the gun-boats. It was therefore deemed best to order 4 seige guns from Cairo before making the attempt. In the meantime a force under Col. Plummer, consisting of the 11th Missouri and the 26th and 47th Illinois, was sent with all speed to occupy Point Pleasant, 12 miles below, for the purpose of blockading the river and cutting off reinforcements. This was successfully accomplished though not till the rebel force was increased to 9 gunboats and 9,000 infantry and several batteries of artillery. The rebel fleet was commanded by Commodore Hollins, and the land forces by McCown, Stuart and Gant. The siege guns arrived at sunset on the 12th, and the 10th and 16th Illinois, Cols. Morgan and Smith, were detached to cover the position chosen for the battery, and assist in its erection. Although exposed to constant volleys of musketry, rifle pits were excavated, and the guns mounted ready for action. within 35 hours after they had been shipped from Cairo. At early dawn, on the 13th, the battery opened with telling effect, and in a few hours disabled several of the gun-boats and dismounted the heavy pieces of artillery in the enemy's main works. While this furious cannonade was maintained throughout the day on the right, Paine's division, containing the 51st and 64th Illinois, supported by Palmer's, forced their way up to the rebel works on the right, compelling the rebel pickets to seek shelter within their works. At nightfall, during a blinding thunder storm, the hostile force hurriedly fled, leaving their dead unburied, their suppers untasted on the tables, their candles burning in their tents and other evidences of a disgraceful panic.

The details of the battle show that the Illinois troops who participated in it fought with no ordinary bravery and success, and added additional lustre to their previous record. Gen. Pope in his official report says:

"The 10th and 16th Illinois, commanded respectively by Cols. Morgan and J. R. Smith, were detailed as guards to the proposed trenches, and to aid in constructing them. They marched from camp at sunset on the 12th, and drove in the pickets and guard of the enemy, as they were ordered, at shoulder arms, and without returning a shot, covered the front of the entrenching parties, and.occupied the trenches and rifle pits during the whole day and night of the 13th, under a furious and incessant cannonading from 160 pieces of heavy artillery. At the earnest request of their colonels, their regimental flags were kept flying over our trenches though they offered a conspicuous mark to the enemy. The coolness, courage and cheerfulness of these troops, exposed for two nights and a day to the incessant fire of the enemy at short range. and the severe storm which raged the whole night, are above all praise."

Capture of Island No. 10.—Pope now planted his batteries on the banks of the river and shut up the rebel fleet between himself and Island No. 10, the next place of attack. The island, situated just above New Madrid and 45 miles below Columbus, was fortified with eleven earth works and 70 heavy cannon. The day after the capture of New Madrid, Foote, with the fleet, made his appearance above it, effected a reconnoissance of the adjacent shores and placed his mortar boats in position for attack. On the morning of the 16th of March, 1862, the bombardment commenced, but the rebel batteries were targets too small to be hurt by shells thrown at an angle of 45 degrees a distance of three miles. The slightest breath of air operating on a projectile thrown so great a distance was sufficient to frustrate the nicest mathematical calculations, and hence the cannonading continued day after day without beneficial results. The gunboats could easily have prevailed against the hostile works but for the danger of becoming disabled and drifting helplessly in the swift current directly under the enemy's guns. Pope was expected to co-operate with the fleet, his plan being to gain the Kentucky shore, where he could operate directly agains the foe and cut off his retreat in case of an attempted escape. The want of transports being the only difficulty attending the execution of this plan, the following expedient was adopted:

Near where the fleet lay there was a slough running inland which connected with a stream emptying into the river below the island, not far from New Madrid. Pope determined to open this for the passage of transports round the island, having previously sent Col. Bissell to ascertain the practicability of the undertaking. The levee was cut, and the surface inland being lower than the bank of the river, when the opening was effected water passed through in a stream of sufficient depth to float ordinary transports. The route to be opened was 12 miles in length, one-half of it extending through a growth of trees, many of which were two feet in diameter. To admit the passage of boats it was necessary to saw them off four feet below the surface of the water for the space of 50 feet in width. The machinery employed for this purpose was placed on boats and operated by twenty men who, in some instances consumed several hours in the removal of one tree. The transports slowly advancing as the channel was opened, at length again entered the turbid Mississippi, the crew chanting "On the other side of Jordan" in lieu of "Jordan is a hard road to travel," with which they had previously beguiled their labors.

During the accomplishment of this splendid achievement of engineering skill, two other feats were performed equally brilliant, but of a different character. The rebels in possession of Union City, becoming very troublesome, Col. Buford, of the 12th Illinois infantry, with his own regiment, two companies of the 2d Illinois cavalry and 400 other troops was ordered to dislodge them. Entering the town by forced marches he surprised and dispersed a large force of the enemy under the command of the notorious Henry Clay King. Panic-stricken they fled in every direction, leaving their horses, arms and a considerable amount of other property as spoils for the victors. On the following day Col. Roberts, of the 42d Illinois, with twenty of his most daring men, having provided boats with muffled oars, made for the island for the purpose of destroying the upper battery. As the night advanced the surface of the river became ruffled with fitful gusts of wind; presently the corrugated edge of a cloud rose up from the western horizon, and the muttering of distant thunder presaged an approaching storm. Favored by the darkness and the roar of the coming storm they reached the shore and started for the battery about 200 yards distant. When arriving at the ditch in front of the works a vivid flash of lightning made their presence known to the sentinel, who fired his gun and fled, evidently thinking the whole Lincoln army was after him. The flash also revealed the situation of the guns, and hardly had the reverberating thunder died away in the distance before that which a fortnight's bombardment had failed to accomplish was consummated. Six heavy guns were spiked, among which was a superb 9-inch pivot gun, called Lady Davis, in honor of the rebel president's wife. The romance of war does not furnish a deed of more dashing gallantry than the performance of these men, who all returned unharmed.

Before the transports could be made available in moving troops to the opposite shore of the river, it was necessary to get some of the gunboats below the island to protect them in case of an attack. Accordingly on the night of the 3d of April, the Carondelet with her vulnerable parts protected, was cut loose and started down the river for the purpose of running the rebel batteries. A storm of great fury had again burst on the river, and completely shrouding the boat in darkness, it rapidly moved forward on its perilous mission. As it approached the island the soot in the chimney caught fire and suddenly, with spectral glare, lighted up the river. The flue caps were immediately opened and fortunately the flames subsided before the enemy discovered their real character in the blinding darkness of the storm. A second time while the crew were congratulating themselves on their miraculous escape, the flames burst forth, casting a brilliant light in the face of the foe, rendering further concealment impossible. Suddenly signal rockets from the island and Kentucky shore streamed up in the darkness; drums beat to quarters and cannon and musketry opened upon the boat in deafening roar. The storm was still unabated, and warring elements played in wild response to hostile batteries. Flashing guns alternating with gleams of lightning, peals of thunder answering to booming cannon, and drenching torrents of rain, intermingled with falling missiles, enveloped the crew in a pageant of terrific grandeur. Calm, however, as if about to enter a peaceful harbor, they put on steam and steered directly under the enemy's guns. Owing to the difficulty of depressing their guns so as to cover the vessel, she ran the fiery gauntlet without sustaining the slightest injury. The firing of a signal gun announced to friends above and below the island, the successful result, and as the boat neared the wharf at

New Madrid it was greeted with the wildest enthusiasm. Soldiers almost frantic with joy, seized the sailors and carried them up the banks of the river to the nearest hotel, where they became objects of absorbing interest. On the night of the 6th the Pittsburgh also successfully performed the same feat, completing the preparations for the reduction of the island.

Paine's division, in which were the 22d and 51st Illinois was now embarked and crossed over the wild floods of the Mississippi, presenting in its passage, one of the most magnificent spectacles ever witnessed. Stanly and Hamilton's divisions followed, and by 12 o'clock the ensuing night, April 7th, all the force required, was safe on the Kentucky shore. As soon as the rebels discovered that a lodgment had been effected they evacuated the island as untenable and concentrated at Tiptonville, situated at the lower extremity of the 12 miles of batteries which stretched along the Kentucky side of the river. The three divisions, Paine's command in advance, immediately started in pursuit. The enemy 7,000 strong, under McCown, was encountered and driven back into the swamps, where he was forced to unconditionally surrender. Says Pope: "Gen. Paine fortunate in having the advance, exhibited unusual vigor and courage, and had the satisfaction to receive the surrender of the enemy. Three generals, 5,000 prisoners, 17 steamboats, 74 heavy pieces of artillery, 10,000 lbs. of powder fell into the hands of the victors."

Besides the Illinois regiments mentioned, the 7th (cavalry) and the 60th also participated in the battle and demeaned themselves with the alacrity, courage and prudence which should ever characterize the citizen soldiery of the republic. Their acknowledged efficiency furnishes ample proof that the soldier is not a machine moved and controlled independently of his volition, but that intelligence and moral worth are as essential to his success as they are in other pursuits of life, however exalted.

Maj. Gen. John Pope, to whom we are indebted for the two preceding brilliant victories, was born at Kaskaskia, Illinois, March 12th, 1823. His father, Nathaniel Pope, was a prominent actor in the early history of Illinois. His son John graduated at West Point in 1842, fought his way through the Mexican war, and for his meritorious conduct was made captain by brevet, his commission dating from Feb. 23d, 1846. In 1849 he commanded an expedition sent out from Minnesota to test the practicability of obtaining water by artesian borings in the great plain which stretches with such terrible aridity between Texas and New Mexico. The enterprise proved a failure. The interval from 1854 to 1859 he spent in exploring the Rocky Mountains and was promoted to a captaincy in the corps of topographical engineers. When the rebellion commenced he was made brigadier-general of volunteers and assigned to command the district of North Missouri, where after dispersing the predatory rebel bands, he made his way to New Madrid and Island No. 10.

CHAPTER LVIII

1862—ILLINOIS IN NORTHERN MISSISSIPPI AND ALABAMA.

Battle of Pittsburg Landing—Mitchell's Campaign—Siege of Corinth

---

While these events were transpiring on the Mississippi a battle of much grander proportions was raging on the banks of the Tennessee. The rebel line of defense, extending from Columbus eastward through Forts Henry and Donelson to the Alleghanies, having been broken by federal forces the enemy fell back and established a new one farther southward on the Memphis and Charleston railroad. This great thoroughfare runs eastward from Memphis through Corinth, Florence, Huntsville, Chattanooga and other important places, hence the rebels regarded its defense essential to the preservation of Northern Mississippi, Alabama and Georgia. The Union forces, after having secured possession of the Tennessee, kept it open by means of gunboats as far as Eastport, Mississippi, and made it the base of operations. The rebel authorities aware of the tremendous issues at stake, commenced concentrating all their available forces at Corinth, situated at the intersection of the Memphis and Charleston and the Ohio and Mobile railroads. Johnson after his escape from Donelson, led his forces through Nashville to this strategic point, and hither also came Price from Western Arkansas, Bragg from Pensacola, and Polk from Columbus.

For the purpose of tapping this great central line of transportation reaching from the Mississippi to the sea, on which the rebels were rallying, Halleck ordered forward the different divisions of the Union army. About the middle of March Grant, with the conquerors of Donelson, moved forward to Savannah, when the division of Lew. Wallace was thrown across the river at Crumps landing, about 2 miles above, and those of Prentiss, Smith and McClernand at Pittsburg landing, 5 miles higher up the stream. Buel, who with a separate army from the department of the Ohio, had taken possession of Nashville, and on learning in the meantime the destination of Johnson also started to co-operate with the forces on the Tennessee.

Pittsburgh Landing, where most of Grant's army was now posted, was the point of debarkation for Corinth, Purdy and some other towns on the west side of the river. The bank here rises to a height of 80 feet and is cloven by ravines, through one of which the Corinth road ascends to the general level of the country where it sends off branches to neighboring towns. From the river an irregular plateau sweeps inland, bounded on the north and west by Snake Creek, on the south by Lick creek, both small streams, emptying into the Tennessee 5 miles apart, one below and the other above the landing. Variegated with ravines and ridges, partly wooded and partly cultivated, it lay like a picture in a frame, green with the opening verdure of April. Three miles from the landing, on the Corinth road, near the centre of the field, was a small church styled Shiloh, from which the subsequent battle received its name. On the 4th of March Grant had been superseded by C. F. Smith, one of his commanders, who shortly afterwards was attacked by a fatal disease, when his division was transferred to W. H. L. Wallace and Grant was re-instated.

Sunday morning, April 6th, the several divisions of his army were situated as follows: Commencing on the right near the river below, and sweeping round in the form of an irregular semi-circle to the river above were the divisions of W. H. L. Wallace, McClernand, Sherman, Prentiss and Hurlbut, while that of Lew. Wallace was still at Crump's Landing. The confederate army consisted of 3 corps and the following principal officers: A. Sidney Johnson, first in command, P. T. G. Beauregard second, and Polk, Bragg and Hardee, corps commanders. It was well known in the rebel camp that Buell was rapidly advancing from Nashville to reinforce Grant, and it was determined to attack and defeat the latter before he was strengthened. By the aid of spies Johnson was apprised of the daily progress made by Buell, and when on the 3d of April his junction with Grant became imminent, he started with all his available forces for Pittsburg Landing. Owing to bad roads the whole day was consumed in reaching the Union outposts, and after some slight skirmishing the army encamped with the expectation of making an attack on the morrow. Fortunately a severe storm fell the next day and the contemplated attack was postponed till the Sabbath morning following. Buell in the meantime pushed forward with all possible dispatch over the muddy roads and gained a day, which, as the sequel shows, was of vital importance. The rebels, although unable to make an attack moved up to to within a mile of the Union pickets, and though some skirmishing had occurred, their presence in force was unsuspected.

As previously arranged, with the early gray of the Sabbath's dawn, the confederate army started across the narrow belts of woods which separated them from the unsuspecting federals. On emerging from the timber such was the impetuosity of their onset they swooped down in compact masses on our advanced outposts before the small force which had been sent out to reconnoitre could return and apprise them of their danger. So sudden and complete was the surprise of the federals that some of them were overtaken preparing for breakfast, some sitting listlessly in their tents, while others still wrapt in unconscious slumbers, were bayoneted before they had time to rise from their beds. Prentiss and Sherman who were considerably in advance, thus rudely awakened by the thunders of battle, immediately dispatched messengers to the other divisions to apprise them of the enemy's approach and request their co-operation. The latter by his stirring appeals and the reckless exposure of his person in the midst of the greatest dangers, succeeded in restoring confidence, and his divisions, in which were the 40th and 55th Illinois, half dressed, fell into line. The sudden charge of the foe and the want of preparation to receive him, caused one of his brigades to fall back in confusion and McClernand came up with the 11th, 30th and 43d Illinois to fill the gap. Convinced from the roar of cannon that the engagement was becoming general, he apprised Hurlburt of Prentiss' danger and requested his assistance. The contest along Sherman's line became desperate and bloody, the rebels dashing up to the very muzzles of Waterhouse's guns, and in a hand to hand fight, contending for their possession. Although further re-inforced by the 14th, 15th and 46th Illinois from Hurlburt's division and Schwartz's, Dresser's, Taylor's and McAlister's batteries from McClernand's, his battered and bleeding forces were driven from their position and their camp despoiled by the the shouting enemy. By his protracted stand and frightful sacrifice of men the enemy was, however, partially checked and the army escaped the calamity of being driven into the Tennessee.

In the meantime the division of Prentiss, containing the 61st Illinois, had become involved and almost annihilated. At the first intimation of danger, he hastily formed his line, but unfortunately it was in an open field. The enemy soon came streaming through the woods, and taking advantage of the shelter they afforded, poured volley after volley into the ranks of the exposed troops and covered the field with their slain. While Prentiss stubbornly refused to retire before this wasting slaughter. Hardee massing his impetuous brigades, forced them through the gap between him and Sherman, and flanked him on the right, while Jackson with his Mississippi fire-eaters, sweeping round in an opposite direction, turned his left. Hurlburt hastened to his assistance but came too late. Batteries were immediately opened on both sides of the division, and ploughing a passage through it Prentiss and 3,000 men were surrounded and taken prisoners. As the captured troops were borne to the rear of the victorious foe, the remnant of the division, in a confused mass, was driven in the opposite direction.

We have seen that when the conflict commenced the convexity of the Union line was turned from the river, now, by the beating back of the center, it formed an arc in the direction of the stream. Prentiss and McClernand, constituting the two wings, still retained their positions, and Hurlbut moving to the center had been forced back. The conflict had been fierce, terrific, determined and bloody; great forest trees were riven into fragments by the incessant crash of artillery, and the fatal field lay ghastly with huge piles of victims. Grant, as at Donelson, was absent, and each command was compelled to act upon its own responsibility.

The division of McClernand, containing the 8th, 11th, 17th, 18th, 20th, 29th, 31st, 42d, 43d, 45th, 48th and 49th Illinois, which had supported Sherman in the first onset of the battle, when the latter fell back, became exposed to a dangerous flank movement on the right. Dresser was ordered forward with his rifled guns to the vulnerable point, and for a time checked the inflowing tide of assailants. Schwartz and McAllister, in other parts of the line, rendered efficient aid, and rebel charge after charge was repulsed, but only to make room for fresh regiments to pour in and repeat them with redoubled fury. When at length it became necessary to retire before the overwhelming pressure, there were not artillery horses remaining alive sufficient to remove the batteries, and portions fell into the hands of the enemy. By 11 o'clock the division was driven back to a line with Hurlbut.

The division of the latter, comprising the 14th, 15th, 28th, 32d, 41st and 46th Illinois, as the others were falling back, took a position in the edge of a wood fronting an open field over which the enemy must pass to attack him. Thither also Sherman, with a faint hope of saving the army from annihilation, led the battered fragments of his command. The rebel officers, determined not to be checked in their advance toward the river, into which they proposed to hurl the defenders of the Union, threw forward their victorious legions with almost resistless momentum. Three times they emerged from the timber on the opposite side of the open space, and three times were they swept back by the hurricane of fire which met them, leaving their gory track covered with the dead and dying. Gallantly leading his columns in these tremendous charges, Johnson was pierced with a ball, and stretching out his arms fell on one of his aids and expired. Undeterred by loss of men or leader, fresh regiments dashed into the deadly vortex with renewed vigor, and finally exhausted and overwhelmed by numbers, the federals were compelled to retire and join their discomfited companions in the rear.

After Prentiss had been driven from his position. the onset of the enemy fell with tremendous force on the 7th, 9th, 12th, 50th, 52d, 57th and 58th Illinois, a part of the division of W. H. L. Wallace, which had been moved to an advanced position in the Union line. Serving his batteries planted on commanding ridges with great skill, and his infantry fighting with the determination of battle-scarred veterans, four times he repulsed the enemy with terrific slaughter. The other divisions had, however, given way, and his also, under the concentrated fire of Polk's and Hardee's united columns, was compelled to yield, its brave commander falling mortally wounded in his attempts to resist the overwhelming flood.

It was now 5 o'clock. All day the battle had raged, but the field cleft by ravines and obstructed by timber, had rendered the contest irregular and indecisive. When it commenced Grant was at Savannah, and until his arrival on the field each division commander managed his own force to suit the exigencies of the engagement. There was little unity of action. Hearing the heavy and continuous booming of artillery, he hurried to the scene of conflict and arrived about 9 o'clock, but skillful generalship could not then avert the evil caused by surprise, nor screen him from the angry criticism which he encountered. In the desultory conflict the principal resistance was afforded by McClernand, W. H. L. Wallace and Hurlbut, the divisions of Sherman and Prentiss having become too much demoralized by the morning's surprise to render the aid which otherwise would have been furnished. Lew. Wallace, at Crump's Landing, had been ordered to form on the Union right, but unfortunately was misled by a change in the position of the army. What in the morning had been the federal right was now the enemy's rear. Though apparently he might have hurled his fresh troops against the jaded enemy, doubled up his left and thus have given a more favorable issue to the contest, he retraced his steps, and moving along the river did not arrive till nightfall, when the battle was over.* Had the enemy known the vulnerable condition of our right and made his principal attack in that direction instead of the left, his success would doubtless have been more complete.

The tide of battle which had hitherto drifted adversely, was now to change. The exultant threat of treason, that it would overwhelm the defenders of the Republic in the dark waters of the Tennessee, was never to be executed; but, beaten and humbled, its minions were to be driven from the field. The army in the morning was extended out in a semi-circle of 5 miles; now it was in a compact body around the landing, and though bleeding and reduced in numbers, it still presented a bold front. There was a lull in the conflict, caused, perhaps, by preparations of the enemy for the final charge which was to execute his threat. This pause was also improved by our jaded and imperilled men. Fortunately there had been deposited on the bluff a number of siege guns and other heavy ordnance designed for future operations against Corinth. These with the fragments of field artillery which had escaped capture Col. Webster chief of Grant's staff hurriedly placed in position. This defense was rendered more effective by a deep ravine which, on the left separated the Union from the Confederate army, the latter now concentrated in that direction. Hardly had our guns been mounted when a shower of projectiles, some of which exploded on the opposite bank of the river, announced his coming, and presently every avenue of approach was crowded by his dark masses of infantry. Streaming across the ravine they scaled the opposite gun-crowned slopes. But as soon as they had gained the summit they were met by a blinding fire and swept back bleeding into the gorge. Flushed, however, with previous success, they were easily rallied, and while they were advancing and recoiling in a series of final charges, the gun-boats Lexington and Tyler opened upon them with their heavy guns. All day they had been anxious spectators of the combat, moving restlessly up and down the river in vain seeking an opportunity to co-operate. Now, however, the foe was in range and they sent their ponderous shells screaming dismally and deathly into his ranks, opening huge gaps and exerting a moral effect upon the hostile army more fatal than the physical results of their death-dealing explosions. The rebel officers tried in

* Wallace's arrival was awaited with all the anxiety which an imperiled condition of the army could inspire. The suspense increasing, about 3 o'clock a staff officer rode up to the 2d battalion of the 4th Illinois cavalry and asked for volunteers to go on the perilous mission of meeting and urging upon him the importance of hurrying forward his division. Lieut. Frank Fisk and Sergeant Henry Sturges immediately rode to the front and called for others to join them. A party of seven was soon formed, and dashing by the enemy's left in easy range of his musketry, and bounding over Owl Creek they found Wallace near its intersection of the Corinth road, made known their errand, and advised a direct attack upon the enemy. He replied that his artillery had not yet come up and the movement would leave it exposed and liable to capture. They also pointed out the elevated ground occupied by the rebels, and the impossibility of his using his artillery, and insisted that it was better to abandon his own guns than lose the advantage of an assault on the exposed rebel flank. These arguments were, however, rejected, and the heroic little band safely returned and reported the result. They were then instructed to ride among the soldiers and proclaim that Wallace was at hand with 10,000 fresh troops. The effect was electric, the loud answering shout of our almost overpowered men rising above the din of battle.

vain to get their men to face the new engines of destruction, but were compelled to fall back beyond their range. Shortly after the gun-boats came into action the glittering arms of Buel's advanced division were seen across the river. It had arrived at Savannah 30 hours before, and Nelson, the commander, detecting in the deep and continuous roar of artillery the existence of battle, pushed forward to render assistance. A brigade immediately crossing the stream and rushing directly to the front, greatly revived the spirits of the exhausted army.

The sun now as if to end the slaughter, withdrew his light from the gory field—a field literally covered over with piles of victims, some torn into fragments, others exhibiting but little evidence of the means by which they had lost their lives; some still writhing in the agonies of death, and others less injured crying for help. Interspersed among them were the fragments of guns and their carriages, splintered trunks and branches of forest trees, all indicating the fury of the battle storm which had wrought their destruction. Night came on but the period of repose which it brought afforded little rest to either belligerent. As soon as the position of the enemy was ascertained, the two gun-boats again commenced throwing among them immense shells which, exploding far inland, gave back reports resembling those of replying guns. This heavy cannonade, with slight intermission, was continued the whole night, and the exhausted enemy aroused from his imperfect slumbers, was forced back farther and farther from the river.

The landing also became the scene of important operations. Crittenden's division of Buel's army having reached Savannah, was brought up on steamers and placed in position. The next news received was that McCook's division had also arrived at Savannah, but owing to the lateness of the hour, it was not brought up till the next morning. The heavy explosions of artillery reverberating far up and down the Tennessee had apprised the commanders of these gallant divisions of what was going on, and regardless of almost impassable roads they pushed forward to participate in the battle. With this augmentation of its forces the Union army was able to act on the offensive and accordingly the several divisions were assigned places for an attack the next morning. Commencing on the right and extending to the left were the commands of Nelson, Crittenden, Hurlbut, McClernand, Sherman, and Lew Wallace, the latter including the divisions of Prentiss and W. H. L. Wallace. Each took the place assigned it, and as is usually the case after a heavy cannonade a storm arose and the remainder of the night was spent in a drenching rain. When morning dawned the Confederates beheld with surprise Buell's handsomely deployed columns and doubtless with increased anxiety thought of the work still before them. Their consternation was farther increased when the strains of martial music announced the arrival of McCook's division which at once advanced and took a position between Crittenden and Hurlbut.

Nelson's and Crittenden's divisions, eager to measure their strength with the foe, first commenced the attack. For a time the contest was an artillery duel of grand porportions and proportionately bloody. Notwithstanding the severe fire, one of Nelson's brigades charged across the open space between the two lines and captured one of the hostile batteries. Before the prize, however, could be removed, its captors were driven back with a loss of one-third their number. This reverse only partially checked the forward movement of the division over the ground which their less fortunate comrades had lost the day before. Crittenden next became involved; one of his brigades made a desperate attack on a battery of the enemy, and this time after capturing retained it. Exasperated by the loss of his guns he charged with redoubled fury to recover them, stubbornly refusing to yield till the ground was strewn with the victims of the bloody struggle. The tide of battle sweeping farther on the right at length fell upon McCook, whose men fought with the heroism of veterans, driving the enemy before them as they moved forward.

About 10 o'clock the rebels rallied in some heavy timber, and, under cover of a furious cannonade, threw themselves with great impetuosity mostly against Nelson and Crittenden and turned them back. At this juncture the artillery was taken to the front and opened a murderous fire directly in the face of the shouting foe, dashing up in pursuit of the retreating Federals. The movement of both lines was arrested, but the incessant play of artillery and musketry went on with increased effect, the commanders on both sides holding their men to the grim work as if to determine which could stand pounding the longest. In the meantime Buel came up, and, seeing that the enemy's line was badly shaken by the continuous volleys ploughing through it, ordered a charge as the most successful method of ending the contest. Cheer after cheer rent the air as the war-begrimmed legions of the two divisions swept down like a dark cloud on the recoiling foe till all the ground which had been lost in this part of the field the day before was regained. Still unwilling to lose all the prestige of previous success, the rebels again halted in front of McCook's division in a clump of timber near Shiloh Church where for an hour they stubbornly maintained their position. Reinforcements from Sherman and McClernand were, however, sent up, when an irresistible charge swept them from their place of refuge and the battle on this part of the field was over.

On the right the contest had been equally severe and bloody. As Wallace in the morning moved forward he halted on an elevation overlooking the field in front, and suddenly a strong rebel column emerged from the woods and formed in line of battle parallel with his own division. Both immediately became engaged, and Wallace threw forward sharp-shooters to pick off the rebel artillerymen till he could get his batteries with infantry supports on the open field in front. For an hour the flash and roar of guns was incessant when Sherman with the remnant of his heroic division, came up, and, regardless of danger, dashed forward across the field; midway between the two lines he met such a destructive fire he was compelled to return, having received a wound and lost his horse by the fearless exposure of his person. Leaping into the saddle of another, and arousing the enthusiasm of his men, he gave the order, "forward," and again they started on the perilous mission with the brave Col. Marsh, of the 20th Ill., as their leader. Sweeping across the field and gaining in the woods, beyond, a position that flanked the enemy, the latter retreated in hot haste to another part of the timber farther from danger. Here he made a determined stand and a second time compelled Sherman to recoil before his murderous fire; but a second time he rallied his men and rushed into battle though bleeding from 2 wounds, and having had 2 horses shot under him. Other forces in the meantime came up, the position was taken and the discomfitted rebel hosts driven from the field. Thus the action commenced on the left and, as if the foe was feeling for a vulnerable point, swept along each division to the right when he struck his last blow and retired. In the final charge on this part of the field, McClernand's and Hurlbut's divisions participated and added new laurels to those which they had previously won.

On the following morning Gen. Sherman with his cavalry and two brigades, were sent in pursuit of the enemy. Proceeding along the Corinth road they encountered the cavalry of the enemy which temporarily checked their advance. A line of battle was, however, soon formed, and Col. Dicky's 4th Ill. cavalry, leading in a dashing charge on the rebel force, put them to flight. After caring for the wounded and burying the dead, the weary troops returned, finding the road strewn with blankets, haversacks and muskets, which the rebels had abandoned in their flight.

No official statements of the numbers engaged in this battle was made by either party. In the first day's fight, however, the Confederate army was considerably in excess, while on the 2d the Federal having been reinforced by Buell, was largest. The loss of the former was 1,728 killed; 8,012 wounded, and 959 missing; that of the latter 1,735 killed; wounded 7,882; and 3,956 taken prisoners. The rebels having fled, the mournful task of burying the dead of both armies fell to the lot of the conquerors. Nearly 4,000 victims, recently brothers of the same great national family, lay pulseless and still in the sleep of death. They were consigned to their graves, and would that the demon of hate and the carnage of war had been buried with them.

Gov. Yates, who had already earned the appellation of "soldiers' friend" by his devotion to the interest of those engaged in the performance of military duty, immediately proceeded to the battle field to look after the wounded. His appeals for the means of affording relief met with a response from the people commensurate with the extraordinary necessities that existed. Every city and village of the State poured forth contributions; physicians and nurses volunteered their services, and steamboats laden with every appliance for ministering to the distressed, were sent on their errands of mercy. Such an extensive slaughter had been unknown in the history of the war, and notwithstanding the profusion of means which had been furnished, many of the soldiers still suffered from unavoidable neglect. The Governor therefore returned home, and, procuring another corps of surgeons and additional stores, a second time repaired to the scene of suffering. As fast as transportation could be obtained, the wounded were conveyed to northern homes and hospitals where facilities for more skillful treatment could be furnished.

Illinois was more largely represented in the battle than any single State. On its death-smitten field her citizen-soldiers traced in characters of blood a record of deeds which will be read not only in the patriotic homes of the broad prairies, but wherever free institutions have a votary or the honor of the republic awakes an echo in the human heart.

It was upon the troops of Illinois and those immediately associated with them in the first day's battle, that the enemy dealt his heaviest blows and received in turn a stroke which rendered his subsequent defeat comparatively easy, both sustaining a loss hitherto without a parallel in the history of the war. Though our divisions were driven back as the result of surprise and superior numbers, the advance of the enemy was finally checked, and when the gallant cohorts of Buell came to their rescue, were preparing for offensive operations, and largely shared in the magnificent charges which subsequently bore our blood-stained banners triumphant over the field.

The contest was one in which cannon and musketry played the most conspicuous part. Yet, in the constant shifting of brigades and divisions the cavalry guarded their movements, protected their exposed wings or dashed over the field with important dispatches. The 2d, 4th, Charmichael's, O'Harnett's and Dollins', were among the organizations from Illinois, and distinguished themselves by their soldierly conduct.

Among the bravest of the heroes who died on the bloody field of Shiloh, that their country might live, was Gen. William Henry L. Wallace. He was born on the 8th of July, 1821, at Urbana, Ohio. His father, in 1833, removed to Illinois, and settled in the vicinity of LaSalle. After 4 years residence he removed to Mt. Morris, Ogle county, for the purpose of giving his family the benefit of tuition in Rock River seminary. Young Wallace completed a course of study in the institution and, after some preliminary study of the law, repaired to Springfield to enter the office of Logan and Lincoln, lawyers of great celebrity and legal ability. While in the capital he formed the acquaintance of T. Lyle Dicky, also a lawyer of ability, to whom he became attached and shortly afterward went to Ottawa and entered the office of his new friend. He was admitted to the bar in 1845, but the Mexican war breaking out the following year, Wallace abandoned his profession and enlisted in the regiment raised by the brave and eloquent Hardin. He was mustered in as orderly sergeant, Co. I, commanded by Judge Dicky, whom they elected as captain. After their arrival in Mexico, the Judge, in consequence of his ill health, was compelled to resign, and was succeeded by his 1st Lieut., B. M. Prentiss, and Wallace became adjutant. In this capacity he bravely encountered the thunders of Buena Vista and was by the side of his gallant colonel when he was stricken down in this memorable conflict. When the rebellion commenced he was among the first to respond to the call of the government for troops, and exerted himself to arouse the people to the magnitude of the struggle. In May he was chosen colonel of the 11th regiment, and June 20th, 1861, was placed in command of Bird's Point. In February following he was promoted to the command of a brigade in McClernand's division, participated in the capture of Forts Henry and Donelson and acquitted himself with great bravery in the heavy charges in the last day's battle. From Donelson his brigade was ordered to Pittsburg Landing, and upon the death of the brave C. F. Smith, Wallace was placed in command of his division. In the appalling fury of the first day's conflict, his division, in conjunction with Hurlbut's, for a time stood between the army and destruction, but without supports their isolated advance had to be abandoned. Recklessly exposing his person in the accomplishment of this movement he was shot through the head and fell insensible from his horse. His comrades essayed to carry him from the field, but, pressed by the pursuing enemy, they sadly laid him down on the field and abandoned him to his fate. On the following day the lost ground was regained and Wallace was found still alive. The enemy, perhaps out of respect for his bravery, had placed a pillow under his head and covered his body with a blanket. His wound was, however, mortal and he died, greatly regretted by the army whose confidence and affection he had won by his many noble qualities.

Benjamin F. Prentiss, the brother-in-arms of Wallace, was the first Illinoisan to secure the commission of a brigadier general, the first to command a division, and the first to be captured. He was born in 1819, at Belleville, Va., whence his father removed to Missouri, and thence in 1841 to Quincy, Ill. His first military experience was in the Mormon war, being 1st Lieut. of the Quincy rifles, commanded by Gen. Morgan, which visited Hancock county during the prevalence of its civil feuds. In the call for volunteers to serve in the Mexican war, he entered the same company with Wallace, and as we have already seen by the resignation of Capt. Dicky, he was elected to fill his place. In the battle of Buena Vista his company won merited distinction for its superior drill and soldierly efficiency. Returning to Quincy he engaged in mercantile pursuits until the commencement of the rebellion. When intelligence was received of the outrage on the national flag at Sumter, he reorganized the Quincy rifles, and within a week afterward was on his way to Cairo. Here as soon as there was a sufficiency of men to organize a brigade, he was elected its general. At the close of the 3 months term, for which his men had enlisted, he was made brigadier general by appointment of the President and sent to Southern Missouri. Next he was ordered to report to Gen. Grant at Pittsburg Landing, whither he arrived 3 days before the battle, and was selected to take command of a division. We have already spoken of his capture in the battle. In his passage through the Southern towns as a prisoner, it is said the Southrons crowded to see the Yankee general, and that he made them a number of rousing Union speeches such as had not for many months been heard in their sunny latitude. He and his men were conveyed to Montgomery, Alabama, where they were parolled, after which they returned home by way of Nashville.

Major Gen. Stephen A. Hurlbut, the commander of the 4th division in the battle of Shiloh, was born at Charleston, S. C., Nov. 29th, 1815. Having studied law in his native city, he moved to Belvidere Illinois, and commenced the practice of his profession. Two years afterward he was elected a member of the constitutional convention, and subsequently served several terms in the legislature. Lincoln, aware of his ability and patriotism, appointed him one of the first civilian commanders of the war. He was first ordered to North Missouri, where he rendered efficient service in protecting railroads against rebel marauders by holding the districts through which they ran responsible for their destruction. After having taught the "borderers" that treason was expensive as well as dangerous and unlawful, he was transferred to Grant's command, participated in the battle of Donelson, and thence moved to Pittsburg Landing.

Battles may be divided into 3 classes: decisive engagments, such as bring them on and those that flow from them. Prominent among the great battles of the first class was the contest of Shiloh; not only because it changed the complexion of the war in the West, but on account of the permanent advantages derived from it. Both parties claimed it as a victory, but it was some time after the immediate reverberations of the battle before its true significance was fully appreciated. Beauregard, the hero of Sumter and Manassas, had been called west by a deputation of citizens to extricate them from impending danger, determined upon a change of policy. Hitherto the Confederates had ridged their broad valleys with parallels of earthworks and scattered their troops for defensive operations, but Beauregard, reversing the order, commenced their concentration for aggressive movements. He proposed first to move against Buell, but the prompt demonstrations of Grant on the Tennessee made a counteracting force in that direction a more pressing necessity. Accordingly he assembled his troops at Corinth where they were hurled upon Grant at Shiloh with the intention next of overwhelming Buell, and finally sweeping northward through Tennessee and Kentucky to the Ohio. Shiloh was then in a great measure a contest for supremacy in the valley of the Mississippi, and the terrible fierceness with which it was fought, only corresponded with the momentous interests involved. From its terrible shock, the rebel army recoiled, too much broken to afterward act on the offensive, while its commander bitterly regretted the necessity which compelled him to abandon his long cherished schemes of Northern conquest. But for this success it would have been impossible to check the rebel army till it had recovered all that portion of the great valley from which they had recently been driven, and the war would have thus been indefinitely prolonged.

Victory not only forced the foe to abandon all further attempts to overrun the North, but caused the loss of a large additional scope of territory. As the fall of Donelson compelled the relinquishment of the first Confederate line of defense, so the repulse of Shiloh resulted in the abandonment of the second. Thus the whole of Middle and Eastern Tennessee became exposed to the Union army, whose columns could now penetrate to the very centre of the Confederacy; but even here the effect did not cease. The Confederate authorities becoming alarmed at the dangers threatening their defenses on the upper Mississippi, commenced the concentration of their naval forces at Memphis. This transfer proportionally weakened the means of protection at the mouth of the river, and thus greatly facilitated the capture of New Orleans which occurred shortly afterward.

Mitchell's Campaign.—At the same time the 3 divisions of Buell's army left for Nashville to co-operate with Grant, 10,000 men started southward under the command of Gen. Mitchell. The objective point of the expedition was Huntsville, Ala., where, by severing the Memphis & Charleston Railroad, it was proposed to cut off reinforcements and supplies destined for Corinth. After arriving in Nashville he remained there till the 4th of April, engaged in organizing his army, building bridges, and otherwise preparing for his campaign. When everything was in readiness the march was resumed on the 7th, and Fayetteville was reached and occupied without opposition. Here much anxiety was felt in regard to the issues of the expedition, for should our army either in Tennessee or Virginia, meet with a reverse, the destruction of Mitchell's force would be almost unavoidable. While harrassed by these forebodings, Col. Turchin of the 19th Illinois came forward and asked permission to move at once upon Huntsville before delay should add new perils to those which already threatened. Gen. Mitchell assented and with the 18th and 37th Ind., 4th O. cavalry and the 19th and 24th Illinois, he left Fayetteville on the morning of April 10th, 1862. With the Illinois regiments in advance the brigade toiled over roads rendered extremely difficult by the precipitous hills, swampy glades, and tangled forests of the country. Frequently it became necessary, in consequence of its impassable condition, to harness two or three teams to a single wagon and in some places to drag the guns by hand. The indomitable energy of Turchin, however, pervaded his men, and they struggled on over almost insurmountable obstacles without complaint. When night came on they partook of a hearty repast and threw themselves round their camp fires till the moon went down and the march could be resumed with greater security. The roads now became better, and the progress being more rapid, in the grey light of morning, the city became visible behind a grove of cedars. A battery was immediately placed in position and presently two trains came dashing up on the railroad toward Stevenson. The one in advance was chased a distance of ten miles by a squad of cavalry, but the engineer crowded on steam and the iron horse proved too fleet for those bestrode by the cavalrymen. The one in the rear, less fortunate, was brought to by a shot from the battery and all its passengers were made prisoners.

In the meantime Col. Mahilotzy, of the 24th Illinois, dispatched a force to tear up the track in the direction of Decatur, to prevent the escape of other trains in the future. The order was then given to advance on the town, and an exciting cavalry race ensued for the honor of first entering it. Three troopers became the winners, who, dashing far in advance of the others, entered and captured 170 rebels before they had time to rise from their couches. The inhabitants of the city were still wrapt in sleep, dreaming, perhaps, of "Southern Independence or troubled with Yankee nightmares," when the clatter of cavalry in the streets first apprised them of danger. On being awakened they rushed half naked into the streets to ascertain the character and object of the unexpected visitors, and learned, with deep mortification, that their beautiful city was in the hands of the enemy. A reign of terror succeeded, all classes being seized with consternation, except the negroes, who, though naturally the most timid, on this occasion maintained a wonderful equanimity. The mayor, after regaining to some extent his composure, determined to expel the intruders, but the other forces soon came up and he abandoned his design. As the result of capturing the city, 17 locomotives, 150 cars and a large amount of war material fell into the hands of the victors. The rolling stock was soon put in motion for the transportation of troops, and within three days, not only Huntsville, but Stevenson, Decatur, Tuscumbia and 107 miles of railroad were in the possession of the Unionists. The signal guns of Turchin's force which had occupied Tuscumbia, could now be heard at Corinth, the centre of the enemy's operations.

The great dispersion of Mitchell's division for the purpose of holding the captured towns and such a great extent of railroad, soon rendered his situation precarious. The enemey began to gather in force and threaten him; no reinforcements had reached him, and a large part of the subsistence which had been sent by Halleck was burnt to prevent its falling into the hands of the enemy. Gen. Turchin, finding his position at Tuscumbia becoming untenable, fell back to Decatur, where, after crossing the Tennessee river, he burnt the bridge just in time to prevent the enemy from following him. This was the only crossing between Bridgeport and Florence, hence its destruction was a severe blow on rebel operations in that part of the country. On the 27th of April Turchin evacuated Decatur and continued his retrograde movement to Huntsville.

Shortly after an episode occurred at Athens, on account of which the 19th Illinois was severely, but unjustly, censured. The town had previously been occupied by an Ohio regiment, to which the inhabitants made loud professions of loyalty. While in peaceable custody of the place the regiment was unexpectedly fired upon by a squad-of rebel cavalry, and returned to Huntsville under the impression that the attack was made by a large force of the enemy. As they left Athens, notwithstanding the previous professions of the inhabitants, guns were discharged at them from dwellings; women derided them with the vilest epithets, while a crowd of rebels followed in the streets and threw upon them the most disgusting garbage. Turchin's brigade was next ordered to take possession of the town, but no enemy was found. The inhabitants were again loyal, but the 19th Illinois, remembering the indignities which had been offered their comrades, retaliated by the destruction of property. This outrage, as it was termed, was the legitimate fruit of the previous provocation, and would never have occurred had not the people who so loudly complained, been the aggressors.

In the meantime the rebels were concentrating a force at Bridgeport, a small town near Chattanooga, which gets its name from the bridge over the Tennessee at that point. Mitchell having ascertained the position of the force, on the 29th of April approached their encampment under cover of a hill, and made his presence known by firing a volley of grape and cannister into their midst. Some immediately fled, while others, seizing their guns, endeavored to make a stand, but the Federals, with fixed bayonets, charged upon and quickly put them to flight. In their retreat they attempted to blow up the bridge, but were too closely pursued to succeed. Another portion of the enemy stationed on the railroad after the firing commenced debouched into an open field and formed a line of battle. By mistake, he moved up toward one of Mitchell's batteries which had been planted for their reception. When within easy range a terrific fire of cannister was poured into their ranks, and both cavalry and infantry, taken by surprise, threw down their arms and fled in confusion. Thus ended the battle of Bridgeport, and with it virtually terminated Mitchell's campaign. In his report to the Secretary of War he said: "The campaign is ended and I now occupy Huntsville in perfect security, while in all Alabama, north of the Tennessee, there floats not a flag but that of the Union." As the sequence of his operations and successes in northern Alabama, a number of minor expeditions were sent in various directions after roving bands of rebel cavalry, but the numbers engaged and the results accomplished were not important.

Gen. Basil Turchin, whose genius and energy contributed so largely to the success of the campaign, was born in the valley of the Don, Russia, Jan. 18, 1822. At the age of 14 he entered the military school of St. Petersburg, and after his graduation his remarkable military talent rapidly gained him promotion. At the outbreak of the Crimean war he received an appointment on the staff of the Crown Prince, the present Emperor of Russia, planned and superintended the coast defenses of Finland, among the most elaborate and scientific feats of military ingineering in Europe. Having in early life formed a partiality for free institutions, in 1856 he emigrated to the United States, and was employed as an engineer on the Illinois Central railroad. When he saw that the liberty for which he had abandoned his fatherland was in danger of being blotted out by the overshadowing power of slavery, he at once rushed to its rescue. He was appointed Colonel of the 19th Illinois, one of the most maligned though efficient regiments in the service. Immediately after its organization it became noted for the excellence of its drill; nor was it long in the field, as we have seen, before the fighting qualities of both men and commander made it the synonym of success.

Siege of Corinth.—While Mitchell was thus engaged in severing the rebel communications between the east and the west, two hostile armies were gathering at Corinth for another deadly struggle. So long as this strategic point remained in the hands of the rebels, it endangered Nashville on the one hand, and retarded operations against Memphis on the other. Hither Beauregard had led his army from the fatal field of Shiloh, and hither Halleck had come to superintend in person the operations of the Union forces. Having ordered Pope and his army from New Madrid, and reorganized his other forces, he assumed the leadership of the whole, placed Grant second in command and transferred his army to Thomas. Pope's command was placed on the right, Buell's in the centre, and that of Thomas on the left, the entire army occupying a semi-circle of six miles and numbering 108,000 men. Thus arranged the army began to advance but moved cautiously, it being a part of Halleck's plan to approach the rebel works in front after the manner of a siege while he cut the railroads in their rear and on each flank.

On the 30th of April, 1862, a reconnoisance was made toward Purdy, on the Ohio & Mobile railroad, about 20 miles north of Corinth. The force detailed for this purpose was commanded by Lew Wallace, consisting of 2 batteries of artillery, 2 regiments of infantry and 3 of cavalry, 2 of the latter being the 4th and 11th Illinois. At night the infantry and artillery encamped midway between Pittsburg Landing and Purdy, while the cavalry commanded by Col. T. Lyle Dickey, pushed on till they arrived at the town. The prevalence of a storm and the intense darkness of the night, however, rendered inexpedient any attempt at the reduction of the place, and they returned to the encampment. The next morning Col. Dickey again advanced on the town, and, having severed its connection with Corinth by destroying a portion of the railroad, the principal object of the expedition was accomplished.

Farmington.—A second reconnoisance was made on the 3d of May in the direction of Farmington, a commanding position four miles east of Corinth, in possession of a rebel force of 5,000 men. The men engaged in this expedition were almost entirely from Illinois, consisting of the 10th, 16th, 22d, 26th, 27th, 42d, 47th and 50th regiments of infantry, Yates sharp-shooters and Houghtaling's battery of light artillery, the whole under the command of Paine and Palmer. The force moved forward five miles on the Farmington road where they met the enemy, and in a skirmishing fight drove him back some distance to an eminence from the summit of which his artillery for a time checked their advance. Houghtaling's battery moved immediately to the front and opened such destructive fire on his position that he fell back to Farmington. Here he again made a stand when the same battery was brought up and opened on his left, and an Ohio battery on his right, from the combined fire of which he retreated with the federal cavalry in hot pursuit. Farmington fell into the hands of the Unionists. The enemy returned on the 9th and made a determined effort to flank and cut off from the main army the forces which occupied it. A fierce battle of five hours duration commenced, in which Paine and Palmer, who were peremptorily ordered not to bring on a general engagement, slowly retreated. This was preminently an Illinois battle, and an exhibition of Illinois prowess, although the 2d Iowa cavalry greatly distinguished itself in charging on the enemy's batteries.

Finally, on the 28th of May, after some other fighting by detached portions of both armies, Halleck sent forward three heavy reconoitering columns against Corinth to feel the strength of the enemy's entire line, and unmask his batteries. The rebels hotly contesting the ground at the several points of approach on the right centre and left, but were driven back. On the 29th Pope and Sherman opened upon the rebel entrenchments with their powerful guns and drove the enemy from his advanced battery. But while the movement of the federal army, entrenched in successive parallels, was slowly converging on the hostile works with their heavy siege guns, Beauregard, aware that he was unable to cope with such a formidable force, was secretly withdrawing from the town to prevent capture. During the entire succeeding night from Halleck's advanced position could be heard the rumbling of cars and the shrieking locomotive whistles, terminating at daylight with several loud explosions. Skirmish parties were immediately thrown out and a general advance being ordered, the troops entered Corinth and found it deserted. All the heavy ordnance had been carried away while commisary stores, powder and other valuable property, which, for the want of transportation could not be removed, was destroyed. The news of the evacuation soon spread from regiment to regiment and from division to division till the air echoed with jubilant

shouts in every part of the widely extended field. The mayor came
forward and surrendered the town, and the national ensign was
hoisted over the public buildings where the rebel flag had so long
defiantly floated its treasonable folds. The rebels fled with great
precipitation notwithstanding their oft-repeated boasts to immo-
late the Yankees if they ever ventured beyond the Tennessee. The
pursuit of the fugitive enemy was immediate and the same day a
cavalry force overtook his rear guard on Tuscumbia creek 8 miles
south of Corinth. The retreat and pursuit was continued for several days with skirmishing at various points, and finally ended
in the occupation of Guntown and Baldwin by the federals, and
Tupello by the confederates.

The lengthening list of regiments which Illinois added to the catalogue of battles in the siege of Corinth attained its greatest dimensions. The following array of numbers constitute a roll of honor
which patriots and heroes will ever revere: The 7th, 10th, 11th, 12th,
14th, 15th, 16th, 17th, 18th, 22d, 26th, 27th, 28th, 29th, 30th, 31st,
34th, 35th, 38th, 41st, 42d, 43d, 45th, 46th, 47th, 48th, 51st, 52d,
53d, 55th, 57th, 60th, 64th, and 66th. Most of these were brigaded
and officered as at Shiloh and Island No. 10, and advanced upon
Corinth in Thomas' corps. Prominent among the many organizations which were distinguished in the fighting about the besieged
city were a portion of the 2d, 4th, 7th and 11th cavalry, and the
batteries of Waterhouse, Houghtaling, Bouton and Silverspare.
Lieut. Baker, of Yates' sharp-shooters was the first to enter the
rebel works, and Col. Stuart, of the 55th, was the first to hoist the
federal flag over the captured city. Gen. Sherman thus alludes
to Logan: "I feel under special obligations to this officer, who,
during the two days he served under me, held the entire ground
on my right extending down to the railroad. All the time he had
in his front a large force of the enemy, but so dense was the forest he could not reckon their strength save what he could see on
the railroad."

Chapter LIX.

1862—ILLINOIS IN KENTUCKY, NORTHERN MISSISSIPPI AND MIDDLE TENNESSEE.

Battles of Perryville, Bolivar, Britton's Lane, Iuka, Corinth and Stone River.

Shortly after the reduction of Corinth important changes occurred in the Army of the West.

On the 27th of June, 1862, Pope left to take command of the Army of the Potomac. On the 23d of July Halleck, by order of the President, assumed command of the armies of the United States, and Grant occupied Northern Alabama and West Tennessee.

Buell, on the 10th of June, started eastward to counteract the designs of Bragg, who was collecting a large force for an offensive movement northward. One corps of his army was stationed at Knoxville, under the command of E. Kirby Smith, and two at Chattanooga under Polk and Hardee. The troops under the immediate command of Buell numbered 25,000, with an auxillary force of 13,000, at different places in Northern Alabama and Middle Tennesse, under the command of the gallant Mitchell. Buell's first object was to repair the railroads which had previously been destroyed by raiding parties of rebel cavalry, and thus maintain ready access to his depot of supplies at Nashville. The performance of this important work was entrusted to Mitchell, who soon restored the road between Nashville and Murfreesboro; but unfortunately, Forrest, with 3,000 cavalry, immediately afterwards made a descent on the latter place, captured the small garrison, again destroyed the railroad and escaped with his prisoners and a large amount of booty to Chattanooga. Next the startling intelligence was received that the force under Smith, had burst through a gap of the Cumberland Mountains, for the purpose of invading Kentucky. Passing without opposition through the State, he approached within seven miles of Cincinnati, but finding the city prepared to receive him, he retired without attempting its capture.

When war exists one of the belligerents must be subdued before peace can be restored; and however prudently it may be conducted, the destruction of life and property is unavoidable. The forces employed if divested of the restraint common to regular military organizations, frequently forget the object of legitimate warfare, and plunder indiscriminately both friend and foe. Such was the character of the marauding parties which the rebels now employed as a means of obtaining supplies and avenging their imaginary wrongs. Frequently they dashed into a village or district and having seized the property of the inhabitants, if any dared to resist they were either shot or dragged into captivity. Lying in wait for railroad trains, they were not content with destroying the road and robbing the mails, but murdered the passengers. If dispersed at one point they suddenly appeared at another, and renewed their depredations, seriously interfering with the business of the country without leading to any decisive military advantages.

Almost simultaneously with the passage of the Cumberland Mountains by Smith, Bragg with an army of 60,000 men, crossed the Tennessee for a similar offensive movement. Buell had extended his line of operations along the Memphis and Charleston railroad to Huntsville, where he had established his headquarters. Owing to the manifold dangers which now beset him, instead of penetrating farther eastward as contemplated, he found it necessary to return for the purpose of guarding the movements of Bragg. The latter proceeding by way of Pikeville, Sparta and Carthage, entered Kentucky on the 5th of September. During the march, Buell harrassed his rear; on the 17th drove his forces out of Mumfordsville, and deducing from his movements that he was aiming at Louisville, he hastened thither in advance.

The inhabitants were laboring under the most serious apprehensions for the safety of the city, and when his advancing columns awoke them from their nightly slumbers, the cry "Buell has come," was repeated as when his advent was greeted by the imperiled army at Shiloh. Anticipating an attack by the rebel army, a large number of fresh troops had been hurriedly pushed forward from Illinois, Indiana and Ohio for the protection of the city, when some misunderstanding arising between Gens. Davis and Nelson, as to whose command they belonged, the latter was shot and killed by the former. After the adjustment of this difficulty, Buell's army was reorganized, he being first and Thomas second in command, and its three corps being commanded by Generals A. M. McCook, Crittenden and C. C. Gilbert.

Battle of Perryville.—Thus officered and numbering near 100,000 men, the army on the 1st of October left Louisville in pursuit of Bragg, who being unable to proceed farther northward, commenced returning. Buell following in his wake by way of Bardstown, heard there was a large force of the enemy at Perryville. He determined to move against him and accordingly ordered his three corps to advance without delay by different roads. On the 7th of October, 1862, Gilbert's corps moved along the Springfield pike to within 5 miles of Perryville when heavy skirmishing commenced. Mitchell's, the leading division, was formed in line of battle across the road and Sheridan's division, containing the 36th, 44th, 73d, 85th, 86th, 88th and 125th Illinois, was shortly after brought up and stationed beyond Doctor's Creek on Mitchell's right. This movement brought McCook's brigade of Sherman's division, within 2½ miles of the enemy's position and early in the morning of the 8th he deployed the 85th Illinois on his right, the 52d Ohio on his left, while the 125th Illinois was placed as a reserve, and the 86th Illinois pushed forward as pickets. The rebel pickets now commenced the contest by a severe fire on the 85th, which, without having previously been under fire, charged up the hill on which the enemy was posted, and drove him from his position. Exasperated at their discomfiture the rebels now massed their forces on the right and left of the brigade, and for an hour poured upon the devoted men a furious fire of shrapnel. Stubbornly, heroically they breasted the storm till Barrets' 2d Illinois battery was brought into position when the rebels were three times driven from their guns, which at length were permanently silenced. The 125th Illinois had in the meanwhile been ordered up to support the battery and so efficiently was the task performed that the rebels retired leaving the federals in possession of the field which they had so heroically won.

In the meantime Jackson's and Rousseau's divisions, A. M. McCook's corps, the former containing the 34th, 80th, 89th and 123d Illinois and the latter the 19th, 24th and 39th Ill., were brought up and formed on Gilbert's left. Bragg fearing the arrival of Crittenden, determined to take advantage of his absence by an immediate assault with his entire force. Accordingly about 11 o'clock his batteries opened from 6 different positions, and were answered by the federal artillery, but no effect being produced on either side, the firing ceased. The lull, however, only presaged the coming storm. Again the rebel guns opened with redoubled fury and presently the dark masses of the enemy were seen emerging from the woods. Bragg had concentrated the flower of his army against the left center of the Union line, while Buckner massing another force, moved against Jackson's division further to the left. The latter gave way and Rousseau next becoming involved, for half an hour the fighting was terrific and the carnage fearful. In the heat of the conflict the 24th Illinois was ordered up for the defense of a vulnerable point in the line, and although frequently assailed by overwhelming numbers, they tenaciously maintained their position. While the battle was thus raging on the left Gens. Mitchell and Sheridan attacked the enemy on the right and driving him from the field, ended the contest.

During the afternoon Mitchell's division, in which were the 21st, 25th, 35th, 38th, 42d, 58th, 59th, 74th and 75th Illinois, had been moved up to the support of Gen. Sheridan, who was hard pressed by the enemy. Col. Carlin of the 38th Illinois, with a brigade, pushed forward on the right and upon ascending a hill, discovered a strong force of the enemy ready to hurl themselves against Sheridan's overtasked men. Ordering a charge his men met the advancing rebels with such irresistable momentum as to completely pierce their centre and put them to flight. He then pursued the fugitives a distance of two miles, when finding in the ardor of pursuit he had isolated himself from the other forces, he returned before the confused enemy could take advantage of his situation. While in this advanced position his own regiment, the 38th Illinois, captured an ammunition train of the enemy, and its guard, numbering 140 men.[*] As an evidence of the heroism with which the 59th and 75th exposed themselves and the deadly ordeal through which they passed, the former lost 153 out of 325, and the latter 221 out of 700. In another part of the field the 80th and 123d behaved with great gallantry, the first having 11 killed, 32 wounded, and 13 missing and the 2d 35 killed, 119 wounded and 35 missing.

[*] Mitchell's Report.

Other regiments, though not specially mentioned in the reports of the battle, fought as bravely, loved the cause as devotedly and are as much entitled to our respect and gratitude as those who have a more pretentious record. That none could have shunned danger is evident from the fatal effects of the battle, which McCook says, for the number engaged, was the bloodiest conflict of modern times. According to Buell's report, the entire federal loss in killed, wounded and missing was 4,000; that of the enemy being about the same. Had Crittenden's corps, which did not arrive till after the fighting was over, been present, the result might have been different.

As Bragg retreated it was supposed he would make a stand on Dick river, and Buell accordingly sent Crittenden forward to engage him in front while McCook and Gilbert were to turn his flank and compel him to fight or surrender. The sagacious Confederate, however, suspecting the design of his adversary, evacuated his position and resumed his march. Possessing an accurate knowledge of the country and skilfully using the advantages which it afforded, he managed to elude the Union troops. The pursuit was continued as far as London, when its farther prosecution was deemed inexpedient. Bragg thus escaped laden with the rich spoils gathered in Kentucky; and Buell falling back to Nashville, was superseded by Rosecrans.

The Richmond authorities evidently supposed that the people of Kentucky were ready to espouse the cause of the confederacy if they could have some assurance of protection when the decisive step was taken. One object of the invasion was, therefore, to inspire the necessary confidence, and much disappointment was felt at the apathy with which these overtures were received, and, therefore, except a large amount of supplies Bragg carried with him to Tennessee, he derived no advantage from the expedition.

Battle of Bolivar.—After the reduction of Corinth Grant's army occupied Northern Alabama. His forces having been seriously weakened by detailing a portion of them for the defense of Louisville, a strong rebel force of cavalry, under the command of Armstrong, undertook the capture of Bolivar, for the purpose of severing the railroad at that point and thus interrupting the federal lines of communication. Col. Crocker with a small Union force was in command of the town, and as soon as he learned the intentions of Armstrong, he dispatched, on the 30th of August, 1862, two companies of the 11th and four of the 2d Ill. cavalry, Cols. Puterbaugh and Hogg, and the 20th and 78th Ohio infantry, to give him battle. About noon Col. Leggett, who had charge of the force, met a large body of rebels, who immediately endeavored by a flank movement on the Middleburg road, to get in his rear. Here with the two companies of the 11th Ill. cavalry and some mounted infantry he engaged the enemy, and after an hour's fighting, drove him back. After the first struggle was over a portion of the Ohio infantry arrived, and Leggett, leaving a sufficient force for the protection of his left, massed the remainder of his troops on the road where it was evident the enemy was making preparations for a second attack, for the purpose of gaining his rear. Hardly had this disposition of the forces been made, when the enemy charged with great impetuosity down the road, but was twice repulsed by the deadly fire of the infantry. Finding this part of the field impregnable, the foe next turned on the left, where had previously been posted the four companies of the 2d Ill. cavalry, under Col. Hogg. Col. Leggett soon discovered that a full regiment of rebel cavalry was preparing to swoop down upon and gobble up his small force, and sent him word to fall back if he had any doubt as to his ability to resist the intended charge, "For God's sake don't order me back," were the memorable words of the daring cavalryman. "Then meet them," replied Leggett, "and may God bless your effort." Immediately giving the command "Forward" to his men, and putting spurs to his steed, with a daring that heeded not the dangers to which he exposed himself, dashed forward in advance of his force. Thus isolated, he became a conspicuous mark for rebel sharpshooters, and fell pierced by nine bullets. The next moment the two lines came together with a crash, from the effects of which both recoiled. In the meantime reinforcements of infantry came, and a battery opening upon the hostile force, drove them from the field. The victory was complete, but dearly bought at the sacrifice of the heroic Colonel. Chivalrous, generous and daring, in his death Illinois lost one of her noblest sons, liberty an admiring votary and the profession of arms a hero of more than ordinary courage. Says Col. Leggett in his official report: "The 2d Ill. cavalry was on the field so short a time, I can only particularize their commander, the lamented Col. Hogg. A braver, truer man never lifted his sword in defense of his country. He was brave to a fault, and fell while leading one of the most gallant cavalry charges of the war.'

Battle of Britton's Lane.—Armstrong next attacked a force of 800 men under command of Col. Dennis, while on his way from Estinaula, Aug. 30, 1862, to Jackson, Tenn. Having been ordered to the latter place with his force, consisting of the 20th and 30th Illinois, two pieces of artillery and two companies of cavalry, on the 1st of September his vanguard encountered at Britton's Lane a rebel cavalry force of 5,000 men. A battle immediately commenced, in which he lost his trains, yet after fighting heroically for four hours he remained master of the field, and inflicted a loss on the enemy of 400, while that of his own was only 5. The great disparity in numbers engaged in this contest and the results which followed fully refutes the rebel idea that one Southron was equal to five Northern men.*

Battle of Iuka.—After the reduction of Corinth, Grant's line of communication with Buell was threatened by the rebels under Price, who, after their destruction, proposed to cross the Tennessee and co-operate with Bragg in his invasion of Kentucky. With these designs in view he had already taken possession of Iuka, a small town on the Memphis and Charleston railroad, about 20 miles southeast of Corinth. To dislodge him from this position Grant directed Gen. Ord, with 18,000 men, to move forward by way of Brownville, and to make a direct attack, while Gen. Rosecrans with another force was to proceed by way

---

* Ross' Report.

of Jacinto, to operate on the flank of the enemy and cut off his retreat in case he should make his escape southward. At 10 o'clock on the morning of the 19th of September, 1862, Hamilton's division of Rosecrans' force encountered the rebel pickets, and drove them back a distance of six miles. The pursuit was then discontinued, and Rosecrans waited, according to previous under-standing, to hear the sound of Ord's artillery as a signal to move forward. About noon a dispatch was received from Grant revers-ing the previous order of battle, and Rosecrans now becoming the attacking party, pushed forward till he discovered the enemy posted on a commanding ridge about two miles from the village. Skirmishers were immediately thrown out, under cover of which Hamilton's division moved up and commenced an attack. The engagement soon became general; the rebels in overwhelming numbers fighting with great determination till night put an end to the contest. The 11th Missouri, composed of Illinois soldiers, distinguished itself in the battle by the terrible blows which it in-flicted on the enemy. At the time the brave men of this regiment offered their services to the government, the quota of Illinois was complete, and they went to Missouri where they sought and ob-tained admission into the service.

During the night the troops lay on their arms expecting to re-new the fight the next morning, but when the time arrived they found the enemy had fled. Rosecrans immediately sent his cavalry and the 47th Illinois after them, but not being sufficiently strong to effect any important result, after a pursuit of 25 miles, the force returned. Owing to some unfortunate mistake, the force under Ord did not arrive at Iuka till the next day, and the enemy thus doubtless escaped an overwhelming defeat.

Battle of Corinth.—Gen. Grant with a portion of the forces re-tired to Jackson, Gen. Ord to Bolivar, and on the 20th Rosecrans fell back to Corinth, where he soon learned that the enemy was col-lecting his forces to again offer him battle. Price, Van Dorn and Lovell were concentrating their forces, amounting in the aggregate to over 40,000 men, for the purpose of crushing the comparatively small Union force before it could be reinforced. Rosecrans, in in his preparations for an attack, so arranged his defenses that if he could draw the rebel forces under them, they might be defeated, notwithstanding their superior numbers. For this purpose as they approached, Davis' division, containing the 7th, 9th, 12th, 50th, 52d and 57th Illinois, was thrown out to meet them, and after some heavy skirmishing and considerable loss, retired in the desired direction, followed by the enemy. The next day Price moved his forces up, as contemplated by the strategy, directly toward the point covered by the heavy artillery. When within range they were met by a destructive fire, but despite the frightful rents which were opened in their ranks, they steadily moved on till they reached the crest of the hill where Davis' division was now posted. Under the heavy pressure the division gave way and the assailing force, seeing the advantage gained, rushed forward with redoubled speed, Rosecran's headquarters being entirely engulfed by the inflowing tide. Hamilton's division, containing the 56th Illinois, was next compelled to retire, and instantly the rebels made for Fort Stevenson, the key of the position. Here their first onset was repulsed, but quickly rallying, they again came forward with increased determination and commenced leaping over the bulwarks into the fort. At this juncture the 56th Illinois, which had been concealed in a ravine, rushed forth as if rising from the earth, and, charging into the fort, drove the astonished rebels out as rapidly as they had entered. This onslaught was immediately seconded by Hamilton's whole division which swept forward with such resistless might that the rebel host broke wildly for the woods throwing away their arms as a useless encumbrance in their flight.

While Price was thus foiled on the right, VanDorn's men came up on the left in front of Stanley's division, and, facing the heavy guns of batteries Willaims and Robinette, Col. Rogers leading the charge with a body of Mississippi and Texas troops with a heroism worthy of a better cause, colors in hand, leaped to the top of the breastworks, when he was pierced with bullets and fell back lifeless into the ditch. A concealed Ohio regiment next rose up and pouring into the ranks of his followers a continuous musketry fire at short range, put them to flight.

A supporting brigade, maddened by the terrible fate of Rogers, with wild shouts dashed upon the 11th Missouri, composed of Illinois men, and some Ohio regiments, and instantly, friend and foe were locked in a hand to hand death struggle. When bayonets, pistols and sabres failed, the fist was used as a substitute, while the yells and imprecations which were uttered, sounded as if wrung from the throats of demons. Northern brawn proved too much for the impetuosity of the Southrons and the latter gave way. As they fled the batteries double-shotted, played upon and decimated their ranks; arms were thrown away to expedite their flight, which soon become a rout, and terminated the battle. The federal loss was estimated at 315 killed, 1,812 wounded; and that of the enemy 1,423 killed, and from 5,000 to 6,000 wounded. Among the wounded Union officers were Gens. Oglesby and McArthur, both of whom exhibited undaunted bravery and great skill in the management of their commands. Yates' sharp-shooters went into the fight on the morning of the 4th, and came out with a loss of 73 men killed, showing that ragardless of consequences they had braved the battle's fiercest storm, adding new laurels to the military renown which the troops of the State had previously acquired. The magnificent charge of the 56th has already been mentioned. The 7th, 50th and 57th, for a long time sustained the pressure of a greatly superior force of the enemy, drove them back and recaptured several guns previously taken by the enemy.

The rebels left closely pursued by a fresh brigade under the command of McPherson, who captured a large number of prisoners and valuable materials of war. To ensure the safety of the fugitive army it was necessary for it to detail a force to occupy the Hatchie river bridge over which it must pass to prevent its falling into the hands of the federals. This movement was, however, too late. Gens. Hurlbut and Ord, aware of this necessity, had sent a force in advance, and when the rebels came up and made a stand on the north bank of the river, they were immediately charged by the Union troops and driven across the river, losing 2 batteries and several hundred prisoners. In this onset the 28th, 32d, 41st, and 53d Illinois, bore a conspicuous part and Gen. Lau-

man, who commanded the brigade, in his official report highly
compliments his subordinate Illinois officers for their great skill
and bravery in leading the men in the charge.

Stone River or Murfreesboro.—As previously stated Rosecrans
superceded Buell, and on the 27th of October commenced reorganizing the army. His command was the remnant of the brave men
who, under Anderson, Mitchell, and Buell had repelled the invasion of Kentucky and carried the national banners almost to the
centre of the confederacy through Middle Tennessee. A new military district styled the Department of the Cumberland was created in which it was to operate, comprising Middle and East
Tennessee and such portions of Northern Alabama and Georgia,
as might be wrested from the power of the rebels. With his army
augmented and strengthened by new recruits he left Louisville,
his base of supplies, and proceeding by way of Bowling Green,
reached Nashville on the 10th of November and took a position
near the city. From this time till Christmas he improved in dis-
ciplining the army and furnishing it with clothing and other indispensible supplies.

The rebels on the other hand, were not idle, and before the close
of November had massed at Murfreesboro' an army of about
50,000 men under Bragg. The rebel commander, under the impression that Rosecrans was going into winter quarters, sent a
large cavalry force into Kentucky under Morgan and another
under Forrest, into West Tennessee, for the purpose of destroying
the railroads and cutting off the communications of the advanced
Union forces from their respective bases of supplies. Bragg's
army being weakened by these detachments, Rosecrans judged it
an opportune time to give him battle, and accordingly on Christmas eve, 1862, a consultation was held to concert measures for an
aggressive movement. Arrangements being perfected the next
morning, in torrents of rain the army started for Murfreesboro',
Thomas' corps moving in the centre, McCook's on the right and
Crittenden's on the left. As the day wore away the tedium of the
march was relieved by the occasional rattle of musketry or the
explosions of cannon, heralding encounters with advanced
squads of rebel pickets. Heavy rains prevailed and the army
was compelled to feel its way over the muddy roads through a
foggy atmosphere in opposition to skirmishing parties of the
enemy. Sunday December 28th the army rested, Rosecrans being
averse to active operations on the Sabbath unless the exigency of
his situation urgently demanded it. In the afternoon of Monday,
Gen. Palmer leading the advance of Crittenden's corps moved up
in sight of Murfreesboro' and sent a dispatch back that the
enemy was retreating, Crittenden, thereupon was ordered to occupy
the town but advancing and finding the rebels still in possession,
he fell back having exposed himself to great danger in consequence of the misapprehension.

A stormy night supervened which so saturated the ground
that the following day the artillery carriages in passing over the
fields sank up to their axels in mud. Rosecrans rose at an early
hour and carefully pushed his columns forward over the miry
ground through cedar brakes in front of the enemy. By
noon the army was in position, stretching from Stone River across

the country in a southerly direction as far as the Franklin pike, a distance of 3 miles, Crittenden on the left with 3 divisions, Vaucleve, Wood, and Palmer, Thomas in the centre with two divisions, Negley and Rousseau, and McCook on the right with 3 divisions, Sheridan, Davis' and Johnson's. Outstretched between the Union army and Murfreesboro' and parallel with the former was the rebel line. Breckenridge's division lay across the river on the extreme right, under Polk in the centre were 2 divisions, Wither's and Cheatham's, and under Hardee on the extreme left were 2 divisions, Cleburne and McCown. The rebel centre was masked in dense cedar forests, while the river was in the rear, which being fordable, could in case of necessity readily be crossed and made available as a means of defense. During the night the rebels massed their forces on the right of Rosecrans, who inferring their intention, met with his corps commanders and planned the battle of Murfreesboro. It was decided to hold the right stationery, while the left under Wood and Vancleve crossing Stone river, were to drive Breckenridge from his position, occupy Murfreesboro and finally get in the rear of the enemy. Bragg had also decided to act on the offensive, his plan being similar to that of his adversary. Both intended to strike with the left of their respective lines, and had accordingly massed their forces to suit their plan of operations.

At early dawn on the last day of the year, while Rosecrans' left was crossing the river, McCown's division emerging from the fog which had settled on the battle-field and striking our right under Johnson, hurled it back at a single blow and captured two of the batteries before a gun could be fired. The next division under Davis in which were the 35th, 59th, 73d and 75th Illinois, after a determined resistance, met with a similar fate. It was only when the exultant foe came in contact with Sheridan's, containing the 36th, 44th, 51st and 88th Illinois that its terrific onset was stayed. Directly in front of a battery vomiting forth death, and exposed to a cross fire from two others, the hostile columns moved till within close range when a musketry fire poured into the faces of the men sent them staggering back. Rallying again and strengthened by the victorious divisions which had crumbled Johnson's and Davis' command to fragments, they again bore down on Sheridan with the determination to overwhelm him. Hastily attaching his right to the rear of Negly's division, and placing his artillery in the angle formed by the two lines, lanes were plowed through the advancing masses. Repulsed they three times renewed the assault but with such appaling slaughter that Vaughn's brigade of Polk's division lost one third of its men and all the horses of its brigade and staff officers except one were killed. Sheridan was seriously damaged, having all his brigade commanders killed and losing 1,630 men. With his ammunition exhausted he also was compelled to retire, losing 9 guns, owing to the difficulty of getting them through the dense cedar thickets which covered his rear. Negly, exposed by the movement, was soon outflanked and compelled to cut his way out of overwhelming numbers. A magnificent charge by the 19th Illinois, 11th Michigan and 21st Ohio, forced the enemy back in confusion and the environed divisions passed out, removing their guns in safety. The force of the rebel onset next falling on the division of Palmer, his two right brigades were soon pushed back with the others, leaving Hazen alone to cope with the hostile surging masses.

By the sudden and terrific assault of the enemy, Rosecrans' offensive movement on the left was paralyzed, and he commenced massing his artillery on a knoll in the plain whither his shattered divisions had retreated. He also commenced forming a new line, on the completion of which entirely depended the ability of Palmer to maintain his position till the broken forces could be restored to order and placed in position. He saw at a glance the danger which threatened the entire army, and with a determination commensurate with the stupendous interests involved, determined to maintain his position or perish in its defense. The rebels on the other hand, aware that he was the only obstacle between them and victory, rushed on him with tenfold fury, only to be swept back by the terrific fire which met them.

Time was thus gained and the new line sufficiently perfected to receive the enemy, and presently the gray costumed confederates emerged from the cedars, their long lines of burnished weapons like a forest of glittering steel flashing in the sunlight, as they swept forward over the plain. With fearful grandeur the pageant moved up within range, when the federal batteries, which had been previously posted on the eminence, opened upon them with merciless volleys, gashing and distorting their compact ranks. Rosecrans observing the effect of the fire on the enemy, dashed up to the line where hostile shot were falling like a hail-storm, and ordered a charge. The men catching the inspiration of their leader, sprang to their feet and with a shout swept them back to their cedar coverts. Four times they rallied and returned to the conflict, but the tempest which assailed them, more fatal than the blasts of the simoon, piled up the plain with heaps of their mangled carcasses. Finding at length that neither numbers nor desperate daring could prevail against Rosecrans' front, they determined to make a final attempt on his left. Breckenridge's division of 7,000 fresh troops was brought into the contest. Advancing in an imposing manner till they encountered the fire of the Union artillery, when they turned and disappeared from the field. The day's fighting was over; many a dying soldier looked for the last time on the azure sunset, and soon the ghastly field was enshrouded in the pall of night.

A council of war was held during the night to consider the propriety of continuing the contest. There was a scarcity of ammunition, seven generals and 20 colonels had been killed, and 7,000 men or about one-seventh of the entire army were either killed, wounded or missing. It was found, however, that there was ammunition sufficient for another day's battle, and after making slight changes in the disposition of his forces, Rosecrans waited till morning for a renewal of the conflict. Morning came, but the enemy had been too severely punished to make another aggressive movement, and New Year's day was mostly spent by both armies in recruiting their exhausted energies for another death struggle on the morrow. At 3 o clock Jan. 2d, a double line of skirmishers was seen advancing from Breckenridge's position across the river, with heavy columns of infantry a short distance in the rear. Soon the moving mass burst like a swollen torrent on VanCleve's division, and partially forced it back into the stream. Prior to the assault, Rosecrans was making preparations to execute the original plan of swinging his left round against Breckinridge, and securing the hight on which his division was posted. For this purpose he had mounted 58 guns on an eminence enfilading the attacking force, and so destructive was the cannonade, that in less than half an hour Bragg lost 2,000 men.

Bleeding and torn, the enemy turned and fled as if from the crater of an exploding volcano, closely pressed by the Union troops. A violent storm prevented the renewal of hostilities on the 3d, and the succeeding night Bragg retired to Tullahoma, leaving his antagonists in the possession of the field. The Union army was again victorious, but another such a victory would have ruined it. It had lost one-third of its artillery and one-fourth of its men, nearly 2,000 of them being killed. The loss of the Confederates was equally severe, being in killed, wounded and missing 14,700. Just prior to the battle they had celebrated the festivities of Christmas by dancing in halls carpeted with American flags; now defeated and humiliated, they were compelled to depart, leaving the national emblem which they had insulted proudly floating over the city of their giddy revels.

The battle of Stone River, with its fearful perils, persistent fighting and deeds of desperate daring, furnished a rare opportunities for the troops of Illinois to further distinguish themselves. Nor was it misimproved, as the proud record of their skill and bravery in the midst of the most appalling dangers abundantly prove. Many of the Illinois regiments were, however, placed in situations where overpowering rebel assaults in greatly superior numbers rendered success frequently impossible. Yet there is associated with the stern resistance which was offered a moral sublimity that almost surpasses the glory of victory itself, especially when we remember the patriotism which prompted and the adverse circumstances attending it.

No regiment in the battle evinced more intrepid courage or rendered greater service than the old regiment of Gen. Kirk, the 34th Illinois. Early on the morning of the first day's conflict, when the rebels, in overwhelming numbers assaulted the right of the Union line, Kirk's brigade became exposed and the 34th Illinois, stationed in front, soon became engaged. Although exposed to a terrific fire, they stood as if rooted to the earth, and by their well directed volleys kept the rebel host at bay till reinforcements could come to their support. A flank movement of the enemy at length rendered Kirk's position untenable, and brought the 34th into a hand to hand contest. In the bloody strife which ensued five color bearers heroically laid down their lives to prevent the standards of their regiments from falling into the hands of the enemy. But neither courage nor skilful generalship could cope with superior numbers, and the old flag was at last seized by traitors, and Kirk compelled to fall back. In directing his troops he had two horses shot under him, when, after receiving a severe wound and faint from loss of blood he was carried to the rear. Col. Dodge took command, and with a portion of the men fell back to the Nashville Pike. The remainder joined the 29th, 30th and 34th Indiana, supported by the 79th Illinois, and hurriedly prepared to again meet the advancing rebels. The latter coming up and hurling themselves with great violence on the Union flank, the 79th receiving the principal shock, was compelled to fall back, followed by the rest of the force. Another stand was immediately made, and again the 79th was exposed to a destructive artillery fire, and withdrew to the Nashville Pike, where Rosecrans was forming a new line. Among the fallen heroes, with which the track was strewn was the mortal remains of its Colonel, the brave Sheridan P. Read. While gallantly leading his men regardless of menacing dangers, he was shot and instantly expired.

When on the morning of the first day's battle Gen. Kirk's brigade was broken to pieces by the fierce onset of the enemy, the fragments fell back through the 89th Illinois, which brought that regiment into action. The men lay down on their faces till all the fugitives had passed from their front, when they arose and delivered a well directed fire into the ranks of the foe only 50 yards distant. Before this volley the colors of the rebel advance were lowered, but the other regiments were falling back and the 89th was ordered to follow.

From this time till night-fall, at every available point they inflicted heavy blows on the enemy, and suffered terribly from the incessant fire of rebel musketry and artillery. As an evidence of the fiery ordeal to which they were exposed, they came out of the conflict with a loss of 149. Though warring against fate itself and success impossible, the regiment seriously damaged the enemy and won a proud name by its heroic and determined resistance.

But to no regiment from the prairie State nor to any engaged in the battle does the country owe a greater debt of gratitude for what it accomplished, than the 19th Illinois. Reference has already been made to its magnificent charge on the morning of the first day's battle. A more daring feat was, however, executed in the afternoon of the second day. Vancleve's division having been thrown across the river to operate against Breckenridge, the latter at the head of his own and two other divisions hurled them with irresistible force against his antagonist. Two of the Union brigades were instantly shivered by the concussion, and the other pushed back into the river, when Negley, riding to the front and comprehending the situation shouted, "Who will save the left?" "The 19th Illinois," was the immediate response of Scott, the commander of the regiment. Then giving the command, "forward," his men sprang to their feet and pouring a destructive fire into the face of the foe, leaped forward with fixed bayonets. Plunging into the river they scaled the opposite banks despite the volleys and bristling bayonets of a whole rebel division posted on the stream to dispute their advance. On gaining the summit of the shore, the rebels, astounded at the audacity of the charge, turned and fled for the protection of their batteries. The 19th Illinois, 11th Michigan and 78th Pennsylvania in close pursuit. In vain the Confederates endeavored to rally at every available point, or sought to secure themselves by intervening timber, but determined men were after them, and not even an army of devils could have interposed an obstacle to their progress. With accelerated velocity charging up to the muzzles of the enemy's guns, and leaping the parapets, the battery was captured. The victory was complete, but more than a third of the men had fallen or disappeared along the highway of death which they so gallantly trod.

Another charge splendid in execution and important in results, was made by the 88th and 36th Illinois. A heavy rebel column was advancing across an open field, on the border of which these regiments were drawn up to receive them. The 88th lay down till the enemy approached within 40 yards, when they arose and after firing two rounds, both regiments bounded forward and swept their adversary from the field.

Gen. Woodruff, who was on the right of the Union line, highly complimented the officers and men of the 25th and 35th Illinois. Three of their companies under Major McIlvain as skirmishers in front of the brigade, behaved with great gallantry, and both regiments during the entire battle inflicted heavy blows on the enemy. He says: "I desire to call the attention of the commanding officer to the gallant conduct of Lt. Col. Chandler, commanding the 35th Illinois, whose cool, steady courage, admirable deportment and skillful management, evinced the soldier true and tried; and who, at all times, proved himself worthy of the trust he holds. Major McIlvain, of the same regiment, who had the supervision of skirmishers, I cannot praise too much. His good judgment and skillful handling elicited encomiums of well merited compliments at all times. He was cool, determined and persevering. Capt. W. Taggart, who succeeded to the command of the 25th Illinois, behaved as a soldier should, efficient and ever ready to execute orders."

"While we remember the noble dead let us pay a tribute of respect to the gallant Col. L. D. Williams, of the 25th Illinois, who died in the performance of his duty. He fell with his regimental colors in his hands, exclaiming: "We will plant it here, boys, and rally the old 25th around it, and here will we die!" The 25th lost in killed, wounded and missing 142 men, the 35th, 81 men.

The 74th Illinois, Col. Marsh, while on its way to Murfreesboro, inflicted serious damage on a greatly superior force of the enemy, and in the subsequent battle it established a reputation for bravery and other soldierly qualities. The 100th and 110th in conjunction with the 41st Ohio, kept back the heavy masses of the enemy in his efforts to overwhelm the brigade of Gen. Hazen. The amunition of the 110th becoming exhausted, the men clubbed their muskets and fought with the coolness of veterans, although they had never before been under fire. The 21st, 22d and 84th, in common with other Illinois regiments, passed through the battle's carnage and came out reduced in numbers but with increased reputation. Where the shafts of the enemy fell thickest, or valor most needed, they were found with strong arms to battle for the nation's life.

The moral prestige attending the battle of Murfreesboro was greater than the resulting material benefit. The rebel authorities during the early part of the summer had pushed forward their aggressive movement with comparative immunity beyond the bounds of the Confederacy. Expectation raised by the brilliant spring campaign in the West had become disappointed at the results of the army in the East. The public mind was brooding over the repulse and frightful slaughter of Fredericksburg. When therefore the tidings of Murfreesboro were read in the cities and hamlets of the North, the people became more hopeful, and with increased determination, resolved that the nation's honor and integrity should be maintained. If the Union army had received a blow it was evident it had dealt a counter-stroke which sent its reeling and disabled enemy from the field and its sacrifice was not in vain. Moreover the skillful generalship and determined fighting which had triumphed when the first onset of the battle had placed success almost in the grasp of the foe gave additional lustre to the victory. But while its moral effect gave confidence to the federals it correspondingly depressed the confederates. In the shock of Stone River the spirit of Bragg's army was broken and subsequent efforts were feeble, compared with the dash and vigor of its first campaign. As a remote sequence Rosecrans next planted his standards within the rocky bulwarks of Chattanoooga from which the enemy was unable afterward to dislodge him. The Union army thus entrenched in the heart of the confederacy won new triumphs under Grant, and subsequently Sherman sent its veteran columns to Atlanta and thence to the sea.

CHAPTER LX.

ILLINOIS IN THE VICKSBURG CAMPAIGNS.

1862–1863—Movements on the Mississippi—Battle of Coffeeville, Holly Springs, Parker's Cross Roads, Chickasaw Bayou and Arkansas Post.

———

Topographically considered North America must ever be the home of one people. The destiny of the Mississippi Valley, the repository of the vast resources which past ages have accumulated for the benefit of man, will be the destiny of the continent. The immense river system by which it is drained, having its source in the regions of the remote north, and its outlet in the distant south will, through the agency of commercial intercourse, neutralize the diversity of race, caused by climatic differences and thus prevent the rise of separate nationalities. Further more the wide area thus bound by commercial ties, is not only inseparable but will so dominate in population and power over the continental borders which surround it as to extend over them the same institutions and a common government. Should an attempt be made to close the gateways to the Pacific through the Rocky Mountains, there are not elements of power in the region beyond to cope with the force that would be arrayed against it. The St. Lawrence, the principal outlet to the Atlantic, although now subject to foreign jurisdiction, must ultimately become wholly subservient to the great valley. Nor is access to the sea through the Mississippi any more likely to be permanently disturbed by a rival power on the south than are its resistless floods to be held by artificial barriers. The great heart of the continent with its exhaustless resources must through the vast river systems with which its surface is furrowed, send life sustaining supplies to its most distant extremities.

At least so thought the hardy race of freemen who dwell on the Mississippi and its hundred tributaries, when the rebels attempted to obstruct its navigation, and in their might resolved that its commerce, in common with its waters, should flow undisturbed to the sea. Measures for the accomplishment of this object were first projected by Fremont, and commenced by the formation of the fleet and army under Foote and Grant at Cairo. Subsequently it gave character to the military operations of the West and ended with some of the most brilliant victories of the war.

In erecting defences for the Mississippi the confederate authorities had to make them sufficiently formidable to withstand the attacks of the Union fleet on the one hand, and the operations of the land forces on the other. In the first particular they were far more successful than in the second, as the fate of nearly all their fortified forts was determined by contests between armies on the field. Columbus, the first position taken by the rebels, although

invincible in a naval assault, when uncovered by the capture of
Donelson, its guns and garrison were transferred to Island No.
10. Foote with the navy, followed to the same place, but after a
bombardment of three weeks, he was unable to prevail against it.
Pope's victory on the Kentucky shore, in the meantime, however,
rendered it untenable and its munitions were sent to Fort Pillow,
situated on Chicasaw bluff, 75 miles above Memphis. This stronghold withstood a bombardment of six weeks without sustaining
serious injury, but at length becoming entangled in the evil fortunes attending the Confederate army at Corinth, it was like the
other places unavoidably abandoned.

Commodore Foote, suffering severely in the meantime from
a wound received at Donelson, was relieved of his command and Capt. Davis appointed in his place. The latter
immediately started in pursuit of the rebels who next fled to
Memphis, and on the 5th of June anchored his squadron
above the city and prepared for an engagement the next day.
Five boats and two rams constituted his naval force, while the
rebels had 7 boats, which in addition to their armament of guns
were so constructed as to act as rams. The following morning, as
the lofty spires of the city were glittering in the rising sun, the
federal fleet slowly drifted down the river till that of the enemy
was discovered near the western shore. Davis then ordered his
boats to steam up the stream to give the men an opportunity to
breakfast before going into the fight. The rebels regarding this
as a retreat and elated with the hope of an easy victory, immediately started in pursuit, firing round after round as they advanced. The contest now commenced with terrible earnestness,
and in an hour and twenty minutes the entire rebel fleet, except
one boat, was either captured or destroyed. Van Dorn, the rebel
leader, who sat upon his horse a spectator of the fight, exclaimed:
"It is all over with us," and galloped away. The federal tars,
none of whom had been killed, were now ready for breakfast. On
the 4th of June, 1862, the fleet proceeded southward to the mouth
of White river, which it ascended for the purpose of removing
rebel obstructions and opening communications with northwestern Arkansas.

The first movement for opening the mouth of the Mississippi
was the occupation of Ship Island in December, 1861. The following winter Gen. Butler took charge of the land forces, numbering 8,000 men, and prepared to co-operate with the fleet under
Commodore Farragut. The latter arrived at the Island on the
20th of February, 1862, and by great labor got his heavy ships
over the bars into the river and commenced ascending its turbid
currents. At 3 o'clock on the 24th of April he came within range
of Forts Jackson and St. Philip and the rebel navy, when 500
cannon opened with deafening roar their ponderous missiles,
weaving a fiery net work on the face of the sky, and falling with
a thunderous crash into the midst of the opposing forts and fleets.
Breasting the furious battle storm the federal squadron continued on
its way toward the city of New Orleans, whither it arrived on the
25th to the great astonishment of its rebellious inhabitants. Gen.
Butler took immediate possession and a portion of the fleet was
sent up the river under Commodore Lee. It was not known
what obstructions the enemy had interposed in the long

stretch of miles through the confederacy, and the expedition moved slowly and cautiously. Taking possession of Baton Rouge, Natchez and other places, on the 15th of May arrived at Vicksburg and the city at once became famous in the annals of the rebellion.

Only three days before the arrival of Lee, Beauregard had commenced the erection of batteries on the high bluffs overlooking the river. Had he come three days sooner the vast expenditure of treasure and blood which the subsequent reduction of the place cost the country, might have been saved. The work of fortifying was prosecuted with such energy that when Lee demanded the surrender the rebels were ready to defend it and refused to comply. Concluding that his force was insufficient for the reduction of the works he wated till the 28th, when having received additional boats from New Orleans, he commenced the bombardment. Still the force proved inadequate for the enemy meanwhile had proportionally increased the strength of the fortifications. The seige, nevertheless, was continued till Farragut with the entire fleet of gun and mortar boats, about the middle of June, anchored in the river below the city. Four regiments of infantry under Gen. Williams, also came up up and commenced cutting a canal across the narrow peninsula west of the city that the boats in passing might avoid the batteries located on the channel of the river. The fleet of Commodore Davis next came down the river, and it was determined with the combined force to again attempt the reduction. Accordingly the bombardment was renewed at close range and broadside after broadside was fired into the batteries without apparent effect. Although the gunboats were unable to silence them, several succeeded in running by them and joining the fleet above.

July the 15th the monotony of naval warfare was broken by the appearance of the powerful iron plated ram Arkansas, which steamed down the Yazoo, and after disabling two of the federal gunboats, sought safety under the fortifications. It was now feared the ram might destroy the morter fleet below, and the boats which had passed up the river were ordered to return, and finally on the 27th, the entire squadron withdrew from the city. Farragut fell down the river to New Orleans, while Davis in connection with Curtis, made a successful expedition up the Yazoo. The canal also proved a failure, and Williams retired with his force to Baton Rouge and the 70 days of the Vicksburg seige were at an end. During its continuance some 25,000 shot and shell were thrown into the town by the fleet when it became evident that like the other strongholds on the river above, it would require the co-operation of the land forces to effect its reduction. Let us now see how this was to be effected.

We have seen that after the second battle of Corinth, Kentucky and Middle Tennessee became the principal theatres of western military movements, and a large portion of Grant's force was sent to augment the army of Buell and that of his successor, Rosecrans, and hence he found it impossible to co-operate with the naval operations for the opening of the Mississippi. When, however, in the latter part of the year 1862, he could command the requisite number of men, a movement against Vicksburg, the great stronghold of the river, again became the principal military

51

enterprise of the west. The line held at this time by the Union army was the Memphis and Charleston railroad, the right wing resting on Memphis and the left on Corinth. In front and occupying the line of the Yazoo and Tallahatchie its principal tributary, were the forces of Van Dorn and Price, which, during the month of November, were concentrated under Gen. Pemberton. To eliminate this force the real defense of Vicksburg from the numberless bayous and swamps peculiar to the country occupied, was now the problem which Grant had to solve.

He accordingly ordered Sherman, commanding the right wing of the army at Memphis, to fall down the river and operate against the rebel line near Vicksburg, a cavalry force from the trans-Mississippi army to cross the river and menace the railroad connections in Pemberton's rear, while he proposed to press him in front. The cavalry force under Gens. Hovey and Washburne, as arranged, crossed the river at Helena and destroying the railroad, Pemberton was forced to fall back to Grenada 100 miles further south. Grant immediately followed and on the 3d of December, established his headquarters at Oxford, making Holly Springs through which he passed, his principal depot of supplies. As the result of these movements 3 engagements occurred with the enemy, in rapid succession.

Battle of Coffeeville.—After the occupation of Oxford Colonels Dickey and Lee, with the 4th and 7th Illinois, and three other regiments of cavalry, on the 6th day of December, 1862, advanced from Watervalley for the purpose of capturing Coffeeville, situated 11 miles north of Grenada. A short distance from the town they encountered the enemy, and after vainly endeavoring to dislodge him from his position, Col. Lee pushed forward a 10-pounder and opened upon them. A full rebel battery immediately replied and soon after a large force of infantry rose up from the ground where they had been concealed and poured volley after volley into the ranks of the federal skirmishers, compelling them to retire with severe loss. The Union officers, seeing their inability to cope with such a large force prepared to fall back, leaving part of the 4th Illinois to cover their retreat. This small protecting force, however, was immediately driven by five regiments of rebel infantry who soon overtook the principal force and a retreating fight commenced. For a distance of three miles the contest was stubbornly maintained, the retiring force halting at different points, sufficiently long to pour a volley into the ranks of their pursuers and then resume their march. Night at length terminated the work of death and the federals retired without further molestation to their camping ground. The loss of the 4th Illinois in killed, wounded and missing was 17; that of the 7th, 34, and that of the entire force 99. Among the killed was the veteran McCulloch, Lieut. Col. commanding the 4th, who fell at the head of his regiment.

Battle of Holly Springs.—Among a number of other important cavalry expeditions thrown out in different directions, that of Col. Dickey was sent to destroy a portion of the Mobile and Ohio railroad. He left camp with the 7th and a portion of the 4th Illinois cavalry and subsequently joined by some troopers from Iowa, on the 16th and 17th they destroyed the railroad from Okalona to Saltillo, a distance of 34 miles. The force was now ready to return but hearing that there was a large body of rebel cavalry at Pontotoc, Dickey determined to move in that direction and take observations. In the reconnoisance some 22 regiments were discovered which subsequently proved to be the cavalry of Van Dorn who was on his way to capture Holly Springs. The next day the force hastened to return, and without further detention arrived at Oxford and reported the movement of the rebel cavalry to Gen. Grant. The latter immediately divined VanDorn's object and telegraphed Col. Murphy, the commandant of Holly Springs that he would be attacked the next day, and that reinforcements would be sent to him.

As intimated, on the 20th of December the rebel cavalry dashed into town and the infantry guarding the government stores, only 100 in number, were soon overwhelmed and forced to submit. The remaining infantry dispersed in different parts of the town on picket duty, unable to act in concert, were captured in small detachments. The cavalry, 6 companies of the 2d Illinois, were compelled to cut their way through thousands to avoid a similar fate. The rebels had come prepared with canteens filled with turpentine and immediately used it in firing the railroad trains. one of which was laden with cotton. Soon all the railroad buildings, some 30 dwellings, 1,800 bales of cotton, and the great arsenal which the rebels themselves had built, and in which Grant had deposited immense quantities of army supplies, were wrapped in flames. By degrees the conflagration spread to the square where large quantities of powder had been stored, and suddenly an explosion occurred which shook the earth and tore all the adjoining buildings to fragments. Whiskey was found among the spoils and the rebel soldiery previously intoxicated by victory and now maddened by the effects of spirits, shouted and yelled in unison with the raging elements. It was known to Van Dorn that a number of cotton buyers were in town and squads of cavalry were detailed to go round and conduct them to his headquarters. Each was closely questioned as to his business, then searched, and his money handed over to a receiver. In this manner more than $100,000 were taken from private individuals.*

As Murphy's force of 1,800 men was sufficiently large to defend the place till the arrival of aid, he was severely and justly censured for his culpability. In pleasant contrast with his cowardice was the conduct of the Illinois cavalry, which was thus complimented by the correspondent of the *Missouri Democrat:* " Six companies of the 2d Illinois cavalry were completely surrounded in the town by at least as many thousands, and were called on to surrender, to which demand they made reply by dashing on the enemy's forces and nobly cutting their way out. Not a more gallant deed has been done during the war. Six hundred against 8,000, and still they hewed their way through them and escaped."

---

* Some of the speculators managed to save their funds by placing them in the custody of the ladies with whom they were boarding One gentleman who had arrived in town only the day before, entrusted some $40,000 to his landlady who, although a strong secessionist, faithfully returned it. It is said a number of ladies wore belts during the rebel occupation of the town, containing northern funds amounting in some instances to $50,000, and in no instance was the trust reposed in them betrayed.

Battle of Parker's Cross Roads.—Grant's communications were also threatened by the operations of Forrest. On the 18th of December, Gen. Sullivan in command of Jackson, learning that Forrest in charge of a band of rebel cavalry, had crossed the Tennessee to capture the town, commenced preparations to prevent the consummation of his design. Having been reinforced by two brigades under Gens. Fuller and Brayman, the next day he sent out the 43d Illinois to oppose the advance of the enemy. The regiment having concealed itself, awaited the appearance of Forest, when it fired a destructive volley into the midst of his men. Not being sufficiently strong to check the rebels it slowly retired till Gen. Brayman's brigade was thrown out and drove them back. Having heard on the 21st that detachments of Forrest's men had destroyed a portion of the Mobile and Ohio Railroad, and captured Humboldt, Trenton and a number of other stations, Gen. Haynie was ordered to repair the damages. With the 106th, the 119th Illinois, 1 company of the 18th and 90 men of the 11th Illinois cavalry, and a brigade of Iowa troops, he proceeded on the railroad to the first break and commenced repairing it. Having put the road in running order he moved to Humboldt, where he was reinforced by the 126th and the 122d Illinois and the 7th Tennessee. Thence moving to Trenton he learned the situation of Forest and communicated the information by telegraph to Gen. Sullivan, who immediately joined him with all his available force. Forrest was advancing toward the Tennesse which he desired to cross and Gen. Sullivan at once seized the bridges on the most available routes, and the enemy, as the only alternative, moved southwest and got on the Lexington road. The federal commander soon became apprised of this movement and sent Col. Dunham of the 5th Indiana, with a brigade, to intercept him. On the morning of the 31st of December, 1862, the force reached Parker's Cross Roads, a short distance south of Clarksburg, and Col. Dunham was surprised to find himself confronted by several thousand rebels, commanded by the redoubtable Forrest, and the road through which he must pass nearly encircled by rebel cavalry. Escape being impossible, Col. Dunham formed his men in solid column and soon they were enveloped in a storm of shot and shell.

Although outnumbered two to one they returned the fire with such well directed aim and invincible determination, that the enemy was kept back till their amunition became exhausted when, by a sudden flank movement, they were completely surrounded, Bayonets were now substituted for powder and bullets, and still they persisted in fighting. Forrest, believing their position hopeless and not knowing whether it was possible for a Yankee generall ever to consider himself whipped, ordered a cessation of hostilities and sent a flag of truce to demand a surrender. Dunham replied, "Give my compliments to the general and tell him I never surrender. If he thinks he can take me let him try." Some of this pluck and independence was doubtless based on an expectation of reinforcements. Nor was this anticipation unfounded. While the rebel general was considering what course to pursue, Gens. Sullivan and Haynie came up with their forces and prepared for action. Stricken with amazement at their sudden appearance the rebels fled, despite the almost frantic exertions of their officers to hold them in position. The loss of the enemy in killed, wounded and prisoners, as reported by Forest himself, to a captured federal officer, was fully a thousand. The national loss was one hundred, mostly sustained by the 122d Illinois. This gallant regiment and a portion of the 18th Illinois, constituted part of Col. Dunham's brigade and were thus complimented in his report: "The 122d Ill. deserves especial notice. It is comparatively a new regiment and part of it was at one time more exposed to the enemy's fire than any other; at any rate it suffered more in killed and wounded. Its gallant colonel fell severely wounded, yet its courage never flagged and it met every duty and danger with unwavering resolution. The detachment of the 18th Illinois acted for the most part with it and deserves the same commendation."

The frequent raids on Grant's communications and the destruction of his stores at length compelled him to fall back to Holly Springs and abandon his original plan of forming a junction with Sherman on the Yazoo.

Battle of Chicasaw Bayou.—The latter in the meantime had embarked his division in transports at Memphis, steamed down the Mississippi, formed a junction with the fleet of gun-boats under Admiral Porter, ascended the Yazoo and at Chicasaw bayou made an assault on the enemy. This bayou is the northern portion of an old channel of the Yazoo extending from the present river to the Mississippi near Vicksburg and with the exception of one or two places was still filled with water. Immediately east are the Walnut Hills, a high range of land trending northeasterly from Vicksburg to Haines' bluff where they impinge against the Yazoo. From the Mississippi, a distance of 15 miles, the sides and summits of the highlands frowned with rebel rifle pits and batteries, while, at their base, ran the Vicksburg and Yazoo City road along which the enemy could push his artilley and infantry if any attempt should be made to cross the bayou.

It was this exterior line of the Vicksburg defenses that Sherman intended to pierce when, on the 26th of December 1862, he debarked his army of some 40,000 men. The bayou could only be crossed at 3 points, where the torrents from the hills had washed sufficient quantity of material to form a natural causeway for the passage of troops. On the morning of the 27th Steele's division on the right, passing around the north end of the bayou, endeavored to move along the west side to silence a battery commanding one of the passages, Morgan's division, containing the 118th Illinois, proceeded around the south end, while Morgan L. Smith's, and A. J. Smith's, the former containing the 55th and 113th Illinois, and the latter the 77th and 108th, further southward advanced toward the lagoons connecting the bayou and the Mississippi. Before, however, the engagement properly commenced, Steele found it impossible to reach the hostile battery, and was ordered to return and reinforce Morgan L. Smith, the united force moved rapidly forward and soon commenced skirmishing with the enemy who, during the entire day, stubbornly resisted but were slowly driven back. Blair's brigade of Steele's, and Decourcey's, of Morgan's division, while feeling the enemy, unmasked a battery which immediately opened on them. The battery was soon silenced and the 13th and 16th Illinois made a gallant charge on the rebels, and when nightfall ended the contest they were driven a quarter of a mile from their original line.

During the night the enemy received reinforcements, and at dawn on the 28th, heavy cannonading was commenced on Blair's brigade and Morgan's division. The latter also brought forward artillery, and after a sharp exchange of shot and shrapnel, preparations were made for a charge. Blair's brigade and Gen. Wyman with the 13th and 16th Illinois, were drawn up for the assault. The order was given to advance and Gen. Wyman placing himself at the head of the 13th, arrived within 80 yards of the rebel batteries and succeeded in unmanning 2 of the guns. Here raising his sword in the air, as he was about giving the command to charge, he was pierced through the body by a minnie rifle ball. Col. Gorgas immediately ran to his assistance, when he raised himself up and seeing his regiment in confusion, exclaimed, "For God's sake Colonel, leave me and attend to these men." As directed Col. Gorgas at once rallied the men, took the battery and in conjunction with Gen. Blair drove the enemy from the field. Wyman's wound proved to be mortal and he died in the arms of an attendant on the battle ground immortalized by his valor. He had entered the service as Colonel of the 13th Illinois, and for his bravery on the field, was commissioned brigadier-general by the president and was highly esteemed for his many virtues by all who knew him.

On the 29th it was proposed to make a concerted attack with a view of crossing the bayou and carrying the heights beyond. Morgan's division reinforced by the brigades of Blair and Thayer moved forward as a storming column under a furious cannonade. Blair's men succeeded in crossing the bayou and capturing two lines of rifle pits, and while he returned to get reinforcements, fought with   desperate energy to reach the summit of the hills. The rebel riflemen whom they had driven back, retired into a growth of willows higher up the hill. Into this covert the the 13th Illinois fearlessly charged, and in a hand to hand contest quickly dislodged them. Thayer's brigade also gained the rifle pits, but being unable to get supports, both brigades were compelled to retire. An assault by M. L. Smith's division was likewise unsuccessful. One regiment, the 6th Missouri, crossed the bayou but the opposite bank was too abrupt to be ascended and the succeeding night it was ordered back. A. J. Smith's division bridged the bayou within two miles of Vicksburg, but the enemy was so strong in his front an assault was not deemed advisable. The day thus ended with defeat, although the national troops fought and exposed themselves with almost reckless daring. The 13th Illinois especially exhibited a bravery which neither overwhelming numbers nor the terrific fire to which they were exposed during most of the battle could effect. The loss of the federal troops was, killed, 191; wounded, 982; missing, 756.

The position of the enemy naturally strong, was rendered almost impregnable by every appliance of military art. Signals were established on the highest peaks and batteries planted on every available bluff and their guns wherever an assault was attempted, could be turned with destructive effect. Sherman, therefore concluding it impossible to force the confederate line of defences determined to throw a large force in transports up the Yazoo to pass round them. It was proposed to effect a landing at Haines' Bluff during the night, and Steele's division was embarked for this purpose, but a heavy fog settled on the river and the enterprise was abandoned.

The entire army now got aboard transports and sailed down the Yazoo to the Mississippi where Gen. Mc'Clernand awaited in the steamer Tigress to assume command. The conception and organization of the expedition was in a great measure the result of his sagacity and labors and he was now regarded as a suitable person to conduct its future operations. As early as the 28th of September, while on a visit to Washington he submitted an elaborate plan for the opening of the Mississippi. It not only contemplated the reduction of Vicksburg by moving a column of some 60,000 men by way of the Mississippi and Yazoo, but proposed to follow up the advantages of victory by siezing important cities, railroad centers and other points of military value, east of the river. Its author, as the subsequent events of the war in the Southwest abundantly prove, had grasped the full significance of the enterprise and the best method of conducting it to a successful completion. He sums up its importance in a military view as follows:

1st. Because it would afford the means of cheap and easy communication between our troops dispersed at different points on the Mississippi river and its navigable tributaries, and because it would facilitate their concentration at any one or more of those points.

2d. Because it would cheapen the cost of supplying our men and animals at or near New Orleans, with provision and forage. It would do that by substituting the overflowing granaries of the Northwest for the remoter sources of such supplies in the East.

3d. Because in securing to us the command of the Mississippi, it would enable us to stop the communication between the revolted States and their armies east and west of Red river, thus isolating each section as to the other, destroying the unity of their plans and combinations and cutting off the rebel forces east of that river from their wonted source of supplies in Texas.

The president and secretary of war having approved his plans as early as October, he received the following dispatch from the latter, urging him to hasten forward the expedition. Mr. Lincoln in the order which conferred upon him the authority for this purpose, thus speaks of this enterprise: "I feel a deep interest in the success of the expedition and desire it to be pushed forward with all possible despatch, consistent with other parts of the military service."

In accordance with these instructions, Gen. McClernand forwarded from Illinois, Indiana and Ohio, some 40,000 men for this purpose, and on the 18th of December the following despatch was sent from the War Department to Gen. Grant at Oxford, Miss. "The troops of your department including those from Gen. Curtis' command, which join the down river expedition will be divided into 4 corps. It is the wish of the president that Gen. McClernand's corps shall constitute a part of the river expedition and that he shall have the immediate command under your direction." Gen. McClernand left Springfield on the 25th of December for Memphis where he received communications from Grant in relation to his new command. Thence descending the Mississippi to the mouth of the Yazoo, he assumed command as previously stated.

He now styled his forces the Army of the Mississippi, and desiring to devote his undivided attention to the general interests of the expedition, retained Gen. Sherman in command of the 15th army corps, and assigned the 13th to Gen. Morgan. The former consisted of two divisions commanded by Steele and Stuart, the first containing the 13th Illinois infantry, the 3d and a company of the 15th Illinois cavalry; and the 2d the 113th and 116th Illinois infantry, Willard's and Taylor's batteries and two companies of Thielman's battalion of Illinois cavalry. The latter corps also consisted of two divisions, the 1st commanded by A. J. Smith, containing the 77th, 97th, 108th, 131st Illinois infantry, and the Chicago Mercantile battery ; the 2d commanded by P. J. Osterhaus, of the 118th Illinois.

Capture of Arkansas Post.—The same day he assumed command he started with the army for Arkansas Post, or Fort Hindman, situated on a bend of the Arkansas river about fifty miles from its mouth. It was a strong bastioned fortification surrounded by a deep moat and furnished with ten guns. Two of them were Columbiads surrounded by immense casements, one on the river side and the other in the northeastern bastion. On the bank of the river below was a line of rifle pits and a number of embrasures made in the levee for the use of cannon. This rebel stronghold formed the key to Little Rock, 117 miles above and was the source whence a number of rebel detachments had proceeded for the purpose destroying the supplies destined for the forces operating on the Mississippi. Only a few days before the Blue Wing a government transport laden with valuable stores had been destroyed by a predatory party of this kind and Gen. McClernand now proposed to end these annoyances by the capture of the fort.

The expedition ascended the Mississippi to the mouth of White River and after a short pause entered its narrow channel which wound serpent like through dense forests centuries old and grey bearded with Spanish moss, whose dim aisles strangely reverberated with the whistles of the struggling engines and sent back in weird echoes the voices of men on board the fleet. After threading this mere ribbon of waters the boats turned into the Arkansas where the channels of the two rivers unite and continued to ascend the latter stream. On arriving within three miles of the fort they drew near a great plantation on the eastern side of the stream for debarkation. Night came on before this could be effected and a strong picket force was thrown out between the fleet and the rebels who could be heard busily engaged in felling trees in the woods beyond to strengthen their defense.

At early dawn the work of landing commenced, each boat approaching the shore and pouring forth its crowds of soldiers. Regiments, brigades and divisions soon collected and commenced stretching out in line to the right for the purpose of investing the works. After toiling for several hours in this direction, impassable bayous and swamps were encountered and the right and centre of the line were compelled to return. When night came on they entered a more practicable route near the enemy's works and by 5 o'clock the next morning reached the opposite side of the bend and were able to command the river above and below the fort. When the investing line was thus made complete, Steele's divison occupied the right, and those of Stuart, Smith, and Osterhaus extended toward the left in in the order mentioned.

Admiral Porter with three iron clads and a fleet of light draft gunboats had accompanied the expedition to co-operate with the land forces. While the latter was making the necessary detour to surround the fort, Porter pushed forward the fleet to ascertain the range and strength of the enemy's guns. Opening within 400 yards of the works he soon demonstrated the superiority of his fire by partially silencing the hostile batteries. During the engagement the Ratler, one of the light draft boats, ran by the fort and commenced an enfilading fire, but becoming entangled among snags was compelled to return. The attack was made late in the afternoon of Saturday, and night soon coming on ended the contest. Sunday morning, the 11th of January 1863, the enemy, finding himself greatly outnumbered, had retired to his inner defenses, where, owing to their great strength he hoped to make a successful resistance. All the federal batteries having been placed in position at 1 o'clock, a simultaneous assault commenced by both navy and army. The fire was terrific, the rebel batteries sweeping the plain in front of the works with cannister while they hurled at the gunboats their own shot recently taken from the Blue Wing. Twice charges were made by different commands, but so destructive was the fire they were compelled to return without reaching the coveted goal. Meanwhile a tremendous concentrated fire from the surrounding federal batteries on land and water was rapidly silencing those of the fort. Their huge shells, after continual pounding at the great casemates at length affected an entrance, and, exploding within, tore the rebel artillerists into fragments. As the afternoon wore away the fire was increased till the bomb-proofs were battered to pieces and all the heavy guns were either broken or dismounted. The infantry had, in the meantime, fought its way foward and just as it was about to charge into the fort a white flag was run up and the battle ceased. At 4½ o'clock the national troops took possession of the works. Seven stand of colors, 17 cannon, 5,000 prisoners, besides large numbers of other munitions fell into the hands of the conquerors. The loss of the latter was 129 killed, 831 wounded, and 17 missing.

This signal triumph coming after the reverses of Grant and Sherman, greatly encouraged the army and thus prepared for the arduous labors yet to be performed in the reduction of Vicksburg, the primary object of the campaign. The government became more hopeful, and its chief magistrate returned thanks to Gen. McClernand and his brave army for the important services which they had rendered the country. One fourth of the troops who fought in the battle and shared in the glory of victory were from Illinois. The commanding general, John Alexander McClernand, was born in Kentucky of Scotch parents, who while he was young, removed to Shawneetown, Illinois. Here he studied law and soon rose to distinction in the practice of his profession. His first military experience was acquired in the Black Hawk war, during which in the performance of a number of gallant actions, he evinced superior address and daring. In 1836 he was elected a member of the legislature, in which he was made commissioner and treasurer of the Illinois and Michigan Canal. In 1838 he was tendered the office of lieutenant-governor, which he declined, not having attained the constitutional age of 30 years. He served two additional terms in the legislature, and while still a member in 1843, was elected a representative to the 28th congress. During the session, as one of the committee on public lands, he brought forward a bill donating land to aid in the completion of the Illinois and Michigan Canal. He was four times re-elected to congress. During the summer of 1850 he prepared and introduced the first draft of the famous compromise measures and the same year drafted a bill, granting land to aid in the construction of the Illinois Central Railroad. While still a member of congress, in 1861, at the instance of Gov. Yates, he took command of a volunteer force at Cairo and assisted in suppressing the contraband trade then carried on by means of the Mississippi and Ohio rivers. We have already spoken of his operations at Donaldson and Shiloh. As a soldier he was vigilant, sagacious and brave.

As a memorial of Illinois valor, one of the broken guns of the fort was sent to Gov. Yates, and is still preserved as a State relic.*

[* The following correspondence occurred in connection with its presentation:
"His Excellency Richard Yates, Governor of Illinois:

"I have the honor to send you a broken Parrott piece, captured by the force under my command at Arkansas Post. The piece was broken by a shot from one of the guns of my batteries. Please accept it on behalf of the noble State you so worthily represent, as an humble testimonial of the esteem and admiration of the brave men whose valor wrested it as a trophy from the enemy.   J. A. McCLERNAND,
                                        "Major-General Commanding."

"*Maj. Gen. J. A. McClernand, Vicksburg, Miss.*
"DEAR SIR: I have the honor to acknowledge the receipt of the broken Parrot gun captured by the army under your command at Arkansas Post, and to express my acknowledgement in the name of the people theretor. It also gives me great pride and satisfaction to do so, from the fact that I regard the victory at Arkansas Post, gained under able and energetic generalship of a distinguished officer and citizen of Illinois, as second in importance and consequence only to Fort Donelson, in which that officer also prominently participated. Fort Donelson and Arkansas Post, dear general, I regard as the two great and positive victories of the war in the West. May your participation in the third be equally prominent and attended by as substantial advantages and glorious results.
"With sentiments of respect and esteem, I am your most obedient servant.
                                        RICHARD YATES, Governor."

CHAPTER LXI.

1863—ILLINOIS IN THE VICKSBURG CAMPAIGNS.

Battles of Port Gibson, Raymond, Jackson, Champion Hills and Black River, Grierson's Raid—Siege and Capture of Vicksburg

McClernand next proposed to strike a blow at Little Rock, but Gen. Grant arriving at the fort a few days after the battle, ordered the army to Young's Point opposite the mouth of the Yazoo whither he arrived on the 29th of January, 1863. His forces, greatly strengthened by the addition of McPherson's corps from the river above, and the fleet under Commodore Porter, he was ready to resume more immediate operations for the reduction of Vicksburg. For this purpose it was necessary to get his army on the east side of the Mississippi and in the rear of the city, a feat which he found extremely difficult to perform. Five different expedients were tried, three of which were to get around the batteries on the Mississippi at Vicksburg, and two round those of the Yazoo at Haines' Bluff. The first was an attempt to complete the canal commenced by Gen. Williams, but unfortunately when nearly finished a flood in the Mississippi rendered it impracticable. The second was a canal from Millikin's Bend through a number of bayous communicating with the Tensas river, and thence to the Mississippi at New Carthage. The third was an inland passage by way of Lake Providence, the Tensas, Washita, Black and Red rivers. The 4th and most promising plan was to get from the Mississippi into the Yazoo above the batteries at Haines' Bluff through Moon Lake and the Coldwater and Tallahatchie rivers. The 5th was to effect a circuit of the Haines' Bluff batteries by way of Steel's bayou, connecting with the Yazoo 7 miles above its mouth thence by Black bayou, Dear Creek and Sunflower river to the Yazoo, some 60 miles above its mouth.

Such is the remarkable hydrographical character of the region in which the army was operating, that by cutting the levees of the Mississippi, and removing obstructions from the channels of bayous, passages could be opened for the advance of the gunboats and transports along the several routes mentioned. Vast labors were expended and the whole of February and March consumed in attempts to avoid the hostile batteries by these routes, and when in two or three instances success was almost attained, some unexpected or unavoidable obstacle intervened and they were all finally abandoned. A man of less determined fibre than Grant would have been overwhelmed by the repeated failures. Defeat, however, only nerved him for renewed exertions. When one expedient failed another was quickly substituted, and at length the city which had so long defied the approach of his army was laid under seige and compelled to surrender.   811

The number of probable operations for its reduction was now reduced to one, that of moving the army on the west side of the river, crossing below the rebel fortifications and ascending on the Vicksburg side. The conception of this plan was easy, but its execution appalling. As a requisit gunboats and transports must descend the Mississippi in opposition to the hostile batteries to furnish facilities for crossing, and the army, when on the eastern side of the river, must cut itself off from its base of supplies and depend upon the contingency of beating the enemy in the field before another could be established. The commanding general unmoved by these perils, determined to hazard a trial. Accordingly the 13th army corps, commanded by McClernand, consisting of 4 divisions in charge of Gens. Osterhaus, A. J. Smith, Carr and Hovey, and containing the 33d, 77th, 97th, 99th, 108th and 120th Illinois infantry, portions of the 2d and 3d Illinois cavalry and the Peoria and Chicago Mercantile batteries, on the 29th of March left Milliken's Bend above Vicksburg for New Carthage below. McPherson with the 17th corps, followed as fast as the imperfect roads would permit. Vast bogs intersected with bayous were encountered, and it became necessary to construct causeways over the one and bridges over the other. Arriving at New Carthage it was found to be an island, the rebels having flooded the entire region round by cutting the adjacent levees of the Mississippi. Under these circumstances the march was continued to Grand Gulf farther down the river, where the lowest of the Vicksburg works was located.

In the meantime Porter was making preparations to execute the fearless enterprise of descending the river with a portion of the fleet. It being deemed best not to compel the crews of the boats designated for this purpose to accompany them, volunteers to man them were called for. Soon more men offered their services than could be accepted. Logan's division of the 17th corps, alone furnishing the number required. Of the 65 men furnished by the Illinois troops for this daring feat the 81st furnished 16, the 8th 14, the 45th 13, the 31st 9, the 20th 8, the 30th 4, and the 11th 1. It was arranged that 8 gunboats should proceed in single file down the river and engage the batteries, while 3 accompanying transports should pass unnoticed near the western shore. A little before midnight the boats with their lights concealed, moved like huge phantoms down the stream. Despite the attempt at concealment they were discovered and suddenly a sheet of flame, keeping pace with the advancing boats, flashed along the 8 mile of rebel batteries which lined the bank of the river. Simultaneously the fleet replied, and for miles distant the tortuous windings of the Mississippi echoed with the thunders of artillery. It was hoped in the general commotion the frail transports might escape unobserved, but suddenly a huge bonfire threw a glare over the waters with such brilliancy that the most minute objects could be seen, and they soon became targets for the enemy's guns. From the effects of shot one of them was set on fire and soon became a mass of flame, while another was rendered unmanagable, but fortunately a gunboat towed it beyond the range of the batteries without further injury. The rest of the fleet, although exposed for an hour to an incessant fire, passed through in safety, and with the exception of one killed and two wounded, the crews were favored with like immunity. This unexpected success induced Grant to order 6 more transports and 12 barges to run the blockade, and from the list of eager applicants who at once volunteered to man them in the dangerous experiment, the requisite number was chosen by lot.* With the completion of the preparations the boats started down the river, and with strange good fortune most of them got below without injury. Having now a sufficient number of transports and gunboats to afford the necessary protection it was determined to effect a passage of the river at Grand Gulf. The rebels in the meantime, had erected batteries on the adjacent heights and a combined land and naval attack was planned for their reduction. Porter commenced the assault but a bombardment of 5 hours failing to make any serious impression, and Grant being unwilling to expose his men in an attack by land, ordered a continuance of the march to Bruinsburg, farther down the river. When night came on the gunboats again opened on the batteries, and under cover of the fire the transports, safely passed below while the land forces passed unobserved through the forest to the place selected for crossing. The next day, without farther disturbance, the army was ferried to the opposite shore, and Grant as the reward of unparalled perseverance, at length had the satisfaction of seeing it in a situation where he could effectually operate against the enemy. This result was partly due to the vigor with which it had been executed, and partly to the success with which the attention of the enemy had been drawn in a different direction. Sherman, with Blair's division, had steamed up the Yazoo, and feigning an attack, successfully diverted the attention of the rebel commander from the real object which Grant sought to accomplish at Bruinsburg.

After the passage of the river, McClernand with the 13th corps pushed forward in the direction of Port Gibson, and on the 18th of May encountered the enemy four miles from the town. The force proved to be 11,000 men under Gen. Bowen who had marched from Grand Gulf, when it became known that Grant had succeeded in crossing the river. Carr's division in advance was met by a light fire of artillery and musketry which it soon silenced. The troops rested on their arms the short remainder of the night, where at dawn the enemy was found strongly posted on a narrow ridge with impassable ravines on either side. McClernand having made a reconnoisance of the situation at an early hour, a portion of the 35th Illinois was moved to the rear of the position signalized by the night attack with orders to hold it till relieved by Gen. Osterhaus. In a few minutes their skirmishers were at the outposts of the enemy and a sharp fire of artillery and musketry ensued. Osterhaus soon marched to their relief and in a fierce struggle of an hour's duration succeeded in driving the enemy from this position. While he was thus engaged on the right Gen. Carr made an assault on the left which, after several hours' furious fighting, terminated in a magnificent charge by the division of Gen Hovey. As the result, the enemy was driven back several miles and lost one stand of colors, two guns and 400 prisoners.

* One incident will illustrate the spirit which animated the troops. A small boy whom the fates had favored with a successful number, was offered $100 for his privilege which he refused to accept and afterwards lived to tell of the part he performed in the dangerous feat.

A second position was taken by the retreating army in the bottom of a creek where it was sheltered by timber and had the advantage of an open field in front. The commands of Carr and Hovey followed till they arrived at the slope overlooking the creek when the battle again commenced. The rebels massed a large force for the purpose of turning the federal right but their exposed flank was promptly supported by Smith's division till Hovey got his artillery in position and drove them back. A second time they concentrated their forces for a similar purpose but Carr's division with detachments from Hovey's and Smith's, and after an obstinate struggle again beat them back, when night ended the contest. The confederates hastily retreating under cover of darkness across Bayou Pierre, burnt the bridges in their rear, while the Union army the next day occupied Fort Gibson.

The loss of the latter in killed and wounded was some 600, but the victory was worth the cost. Five guns and 4,000 prisoners fell into the hands of the victors. Furthermore, Grant had now secured a firm lodgement on the high plateau east of the river upon which, as exigency might demand, he could move against any point of the rebel line. Also with the retreat of the vanquished army the garrison withdrew from Grand Gulf and it became the base of supplies for the Union army.

Illinois was largely represented in the battle, and its auspicious termination was largely owing to the sturdy blows dealt by her hardy sons. As Logan's division of McPherson's corps came up in time to participate in the action, the Illinois troops engaged were detachments of the 2d and 3d cavalry, the Peoria light artillery and Chicago Mercantile battery, and the 8th, 11th, 20th, 30th, 31st, 33d, 45th, 77th, 81st, 97th 99th, 108th, and 118th regiments of infantry. Of the latter the 33d, 99th and 118th, are mentioned in the official reports of the battle as having fought with great success and daring.

Bowen, after his defeat at Port Gibson, crossed Big Black river and was ordered thence by Pemberton to the vicinity of Vicksburg. As the result of the victory Grand Gulf was evacuated and Grant changed his base of supplies from Bruinsburg to that place, and followed the retreating rebels as far as Hankinson's ferry, where they crossed the river. Here, while awaiting the arrival of Sherman's corps, he made a feint in the direction of Vicksburg to conceal his contemplated operations eastward. General Johnson, who at this time had supreme command of the confederate forces of the West, was with Bragg in Tennessee, but in constant communication with Pemberton. Grant was therefore afraid to move directly on Vicksburg lest Johnson with a force from the East should assail him in the rear. To avoid a contingency of this kind he directed McClernand and Sherman to move along the eastern side of Black river so as to strike the Vicksburg railroad at Edward's station, while McPherson was to make a detour farther eastward and destroy the rebel stores and lines of communication.

Battle of Raymond.—On the morning of May 12th McPherson's advanced cavalry met near Raymond a strong body of rebel infantry. A severe engagement ensued in which the 2d Illinois cavalry behaved with great gallantry and lost several men. Owing to the situation of the foe in the woods, it was found impossible for mounted men to dislodge him, and Logan's division was ordered forward to make an attack. The column advanced toward the wood and fought with great determination although exposed to the murderous fire of an almost concealed enemy. Shortly after the fighting commenced a battery was pushed forward to assist in dislodging him and made such havoc that after an attempt to charge and take it, he was compelled to fall back to a new position. Here he was again assailed by the same troops strengthened by additional forces. In resisting an attempt to turn our left flank the 20th Illinois fought with Spartan courage. Having lost their colonel, Stevenson's brigade containing the 8th Illinois, with fixed bayonets bounded forward to the rescue and the rebels were driven in wild disorder from the field.

Battle of Jackson.—Retreating to Jackson they were followed by the 3d corps of the Union army. Sherman and McClernand had been ordered to Edward's station but Grant in the meantime learning that fresh accessions of rebel troops were daily arriving at Jackson, and fearing that McPherson's force might not be adequate to cope with them, countermanded the order. On the morning of the 14th, McPherson's advanced divisons, closely followed by Sherman's, came up with the main force of the enemy about three miles from the city. Artillery was opened on both sides and after firing for sometime without any decisive results, the infantry were led into action. With measured tread and colors flying the Union columns slowly ascended the hill on which the rebel force was posted, suffering terribly from the tremendous volleys hurled at them from the summit. When within 300 paces they delivered their first fire and with a shout that rose above the report of artillery rushed upon the astonished confederates who broke and fled in the wildest terror, throwing away their knapsacks, blankets and muskets, to accelerate their flight.

This was one of the most spirited charges of the campaign and no regiment engaged in it fought with more bravery and success than the 56th Illinois. The 30th, 33d, 48th, 114th and 118th also participated in and largely contributed to the successful issue of the battle. Among the generals of this and the two preceding engagements, Gen. Logan was conspicuous for the indomitable energy and skill with which he handled his men.

The rebels retreated northward on the Canton road and the rebellious capital of Mississippi became the prize of the conquerors. The governor and others holding official relations with the local and confederate governments left the day before with the funds and archives of the State.

Battle of Champion Hills.—Grant leaving Sherman to destroy the railroads, bridges, arsenals and other public property, turned the remainder of the army westward to pay his respects to Pemberton. The latter illy conceiving the military necessities of his situation, now rapidly became entangled in toils from which at length extrication was impossible. Johnson in the meantime had arrived and beheld with regret the confederate army separated in detachments with that of Grant between them. He saw that with his interior communications now cut off by the destruction of the railroad to Jackson, that Vicksburg might become the grave of an army but could be of no possible use to the confederacy. He therefore ordered Pemberton to make a detour northward round the federal army and form a junction with the forces which had been expelled from Jackson. Pemberton, however, had a plan of his own which was to move in the opposite direction and cut off Grant's supplies. With this intent he set his columns in motion in the afternoon of the 15th, moving from Edward's station in the direction of Raymond. But Grant, now had no base of supplies, having cut himself loose from Grand Gulf as early as the 11th, and was now pushing forward with the intention of overpowering all opposition and opening a new base on the Mississippi by way of the Yazoo. Little recked he of communicating with Grand Gulf, and the luckless Pemberton was sallying forth on a bootless errand. Nor had he gone far before the advancing Union pickets convinced him that his movements instead of harming his adversary, was only compromising his own safety. He therefore resolved to return to the station and then move northward in the direction of Brownsville in conformity with the previous advice of his superior officer. This was a good resolution but it came too late, for while he was dallying, the Union army had moved up to the same place and was ready with its heavy guns to dispute his advance. As the only alternative the confederate force was hastily drawn up for action, the left division under Stevenson occupying a thickly wooded height of Champion Hills, while the centre and right divisions under Bowen and Loring extended across Baker's creek to a number of abrupt elevations and yawning ravines. Logan's and Crocker's divisions of McPherson's corps, were thrown round the above mentioned height so as to flank the confederate left. Hovey's division of McClernand's corps advanced against Stevenson leaving the other division of the corps to engage Bowen and Loring.

A courier was sent to Jackson with orders for Sherman to hasten forward with his command, and in less than an hour he was on the road to the scene of conflict. Hovey's division which first engaged the enemy was in deadly grapple with him before the others, owing to the unfavorable nature of the ground, could come in striking distance. The situation in which he operated compelled him to contract his lines and expose his men to the fierce fire of the rebels who, under cover of heavy timber, suffered little. After facing, with heroic tenacity for an hour, the relentless fire of an enemy greatly exceeding him in numbers, and having every advantage of position, he was compelled to give way. He, however, retired only a short distance when two brigades of Crocker's division were sent to his aid and he reformed and again went into action. Logan in the meantime had turned the enemy's left and commenced operating in his rear which partially relieved the pressure in front. Seeing the advantages of the position he had gained he rode up to Grant and informed him if Hovey could make another dash at the enemy, it would enable him to come up and capture the greater part of the confederate forces. Preparations for this purpose were made, but before it was executed Pemberton, seeing his position was compromised, commenced drawing off. Simultaneously the national troops pressed forward and the rebel host breaking, fled in a panic and rout from the field. Although the brunt of the battle fell on Logan and Hovey, there was severe fighting on the enemy's right by Carr and Osterhaus. The impassable character of the ground on which they fought prevented them from getting into action as soon as the others, but when at length this difficulty was overcome they greatly assisted in turning the tide of battle in our favor.

A great many instances of heroism are mentioned in the reports of the battle. Logan's division, composed largely of Illinois troops, engaged the enemy on his left and succeeded in capturing more than 1,000 prisoners and 12 pieces of artillery. An officer was sent to inquire how the contest was going on in his front. "Tell Gen. Grant," he replied, "my division can't be whipped by all the rebels this side of hell. We are going ahead and won't stop till we get orders."* Gen. Leggett commanding his second brigade, containing the 30th Illinois, was ordered up to protect the right of Hovey's division, seriously threatened by the enemy. The rebels suddenly emerged from the woods and prepared for an attack, when the 30th Illinois charged upon them and drove them back in confusion. In the afternoon, on the extreme right, the 8th Illinois and 32d Ohio charged upon and repulsed one of the enemy's most effective batteries. A section of Co. D, Illinois artillery is also favorably mentioned in the reports.

Besides the regiments mentioned, the 17th, 31st, 55th, 58th, 72d, 75th, 77th, 79th, 81st, 93d, 97th, 108th, 113th, 118th and 124th were a part of the troops engaged in the battle, and with the aid of their comrades from other States added another victory to the list of Union triumphs.

Pemberton's force was estimated at 30,000, somewhat exceeding the Union troops engaged, as all of Grant's divisions did not arrive in time to participate in the battle. The victory cost us in killed, wounded and missing, 2,500 men, but gave in exchange 200 pieces of artillery and 1,500 prisoners, besides inflicting a serious loss of killed, wounded and missing on the enemy.

Battle of Black River Bridge.—So quickly was the retreating army followed that Loring's division became completely detached and was compelled to make a circuit in a southwesterly direction round the federal army and report to Johnson. The main force retreated to Black River, and with the exception of two brigades, crossed the stream. The latter to dispute the advance of the pursuing army took a position within a bayou which leaves the river above and sweeping round in the form of a semi-circle, unites with it below. In addition to the natural defences offered by the miry channel of the bayou, breastworks were thrown up, and cannon placed within the enclosure swept the plain beyond and commanded the bridge across the river. On the morning of the 17th of May, McClernand's and McPherson's corps moved directly against the position of the enemy, while that of Sherman advanced in the direction of Bridgeport, higher up the river for the purpose of crossing at that point. The rebel pickets were soon encountered and McClernand, who was in advance, hastily deploying his division, on each side of the road brought on a hot engagement in the forest which skirts the banks of the river. Artillery was placed in position and served with such effectiveness, that

* Cincinnati Commercial

the enemy soon fled behind his works to escape its fury. McClernand now resolved to carry the works by storm and Gen. Lawler's
brigade of Carr's division immediately signified their readiness for
the charge. By moving round on the right under cover of the
river bank, he had gained a position from which the rebel defences
might be easily assaulted. The order forward was given, and the
eager men plunging across the bayou and scaling the breastworks,
regardless of the fatal fire that covered their track with fallen
comrades, with fixed bayonets, drove the rebels from their guns.
The victory was complete. To Carr, one of Illinois bravest officers,
and his gallant division more than any other, its honors are due.
Constituting the advance of McClernand's corps, they not only
commenced the engagement, but ended it in the splendid charge
which placed them in possession of the skillfully constructed
works. Prominent among the regiments which distinguished themselves were the 33d, 48th and 77th Illinois. The fruits of the victory were 1,500 prisoners and 18 pieces of artillery.

The army on the opposite side of the river, witnessing the defeat, set fire to the bridge and hastily retreated in the direction
of Vicksburg. The afternoon of the same day the inhabitants of
the city were startled by the influx of the fugitives, who, exhausted by privations and hardships, tumbled almost helplessly
into the surrounding entrenchments. The night after the battle
bridges were thrown across Black river, and Sherman, still
holding the right, took possession of Haines' Bluff, as the demoralized confederates departed, while McClernand and McPherson,
moving farther southward, closed in on the doomed city.

In the daring and successful passage of the Vicksburg and
Grand Gulf batteries, in the audacity which abandoned one base
of supplies, with the necessity of crushing an enemy of unknown
strength before another could be established, and in the determined courage and endurance which wrung success from the
most untoward circumstances in five consecutive victories, the
campaign may be regarded as one of the most brilliant furnished
by the annals of the war. The celerity of movement and
strategy by which the enemy was separated and beaten in detail,
rank it with Napoleon's celebrated Italian campaign. Port Gibson, Raymond, Jackson, Champion Hills, and Black river, will
always occupy a proud place in the history of the nation, endure
as a monument of Illinois valor, and perpetuate the names and
generalship of Grant, McClernand, Carr, McArthur, and other
brave men of Illinois who so gallantly maintained the reputation
of the State.

It was now evident, if the siege was successfully maintained that
famine would ultimately bring the garrison to terms. Johnson,
however, was making great efforts to collect a relieving force, and
Grant, therefore, to avoid all possible contingencies, determined
to make an attempt to carry the place by storm. The demoralized
condition of the force within favored immediate action, and
accordingly an assault was made in the afternoon of the 17th.
No permanent advantage was gained, although the 127th Illinois
and 83d Indiana, succeeded in planting their colors on the exterior slope of the enemy's entrenchments. Notwithstanding the
want of success, it was beleved under more favorable circumstances, a second attempt might be attended with better results,

and the two succeeding days were spent in making the necessary preparations. At 10 o'clock on the morning of the 22d the 3d corps, Sherman's on the right, McPherson's in the centre, and McClernand's on the left, moved forward, but such was the nature of the ground that only narrow fronts could be brought into action. The garrison reserved its fire till the storming force were in close range, when they opened with the most deadly effect. Many turned back as if from instant destruction, but others, disdaining to retire, pushed on, and portions of each corps succeeded in reaching the breastworks. Conspicuous in McPherson's corps, was the brigade of Gen. Ransom, containing the 11th, 72d, 95th and 116th Illinois. The brigade sprang forward with a shout when the order was given to advance. At the distance of a few paces a storm of grape and cannister tore through the different regiments disabling Col. Humphrey of the 95th, killing Col. Nevins of the 11th, and for a short time checking the advance. At this juncture Gen. Ransom rushed forward to the head of the brigade and, seizing the colors of the 95th, and waving them overhead, shouted, "Forward men, we must and will get into the fort. Who will follow?" The column again moved forward directly in the face of the wasting volleys, and, on reaching the works, fought for half an hour to effect an entrance. Finding at length this was impossible, the regiments were reformed and marched back without the slightest confusion or the appearance of a single struggle. Within 15 minutes after the charge was ordered, Gens. Lawler's and Landrum's brigades, the latter containing the 97th, 108th and 131st Illinois, were at the works. Twelve men entered a bastion, 11 of whom were killed, while the survivor, aided by sharp-shooters on the parapet, captured and brought out 12 rebels. It being instant death to the force within to expose themselves above the works, they lit the fuse of shells and threw them among the federals who coolly picked them up and threw them back in time to explode. The Mercantile battery of Chicago, approached within a few feet, and fired into an embrasure, and as a reward for their bravery Gen. McClernand presented them with two Napoleon guns captured at Black river. No permanent entrance could be effected and at night the forces were recalled.

Grant, now concluding that the position of the enemy was too strong, both by nature and art, to be carried by storm, sat down before it in regular siege.

Grierson's Raid.—Leaving the beleaguered stronghold to the care of the investing army, we will now relate one of the most brilliant episodes of the war, the raid of Gen. B. H. Grierson. While Grant was closing round Vicksburg with his gallant troopers, he was dashing through Mississippi to destroy the railroads and prevent the enemy from sending forward supplies and reinforcements.

On the 17th of April with 3 regiments of cavalry, the 6th and 7th Illinois, and the 2d Iowa, he left Lagrange Tennessee. Arriving at Houston on the 20th, Col. Hatch with the 2nd Iowa was sent to Columbus to destroy a portion of the Mobile & Ohio Railroad, and if able to capture the town. On the way he was attacked by 800 rebel cavalry, which he repulsed, and at night reached the railroad at Okalona. Having burnt the depot, barracks and hospital, he started on his homeward march. Before going far, a force of cavalry made a dash at his rear, and again he overthrew them, inflicting on them a loss of 26 men while his own sustained little injury. The remainder of the march was without opposition and the regiments arrived in Lagrange with 20 prisoners, 50 negroes and 500 horses and mules.

Col. Grierson was now left with only the Illinois regiments to cope with the numerous forces of rebel cavalry which were scouring the country in every direction to intercept him. Their opposition and the attending dangers, however, instead of discouraging him and his brave followers, only gave zest to the enterprise which they now proposed to finish by a headlong dash to Baton Rouge, through the heart of Mississippi. To divert attention from their principal movements and damage the enemy, Capt. Forbes, with 35 men, were sent on a detour eastward to destroy the telegraph and another portion of the M. and O. R. R. at Macon. They left their comrades with stout hearts but little hope of seeing them again, as they would have to pass through a country swarming with enemies and march at least 50 miles farther than the main force. Capt. Graham, with a battalion was also sent to burn a shoe factory in the neighborhood, and succeeded in destroying a large amount of leather and several thousand boots, shoes, hats and caps, besides capturing a quartermaster, who had come to get supplies for the rebel army at Port Hudson.

With these preliminary arrangements, Col. Grierson pushed forward for Pearl river bridge, the reaching of which was now an object of vital importance. Hostile bands of cavalry were on the alert, and should their scouts who preceeded him destroy it, the result would be fatal. With an earnestness, therefore, commensurate with the risk involved, they urged their way forward. Grierson with his kindling eye and thoughtful face, leading the van. Nearing the bridge and hearing the sound of persons engaged in its destruction, they drove spurs into their foaming chargers to increase their speed, and swooping down on the destroyers as an eagle in pursuit of his prey, quickly dispersed them. The entire party reaching the opposite shore in safety, again dashed forward, and on the 24th reached Newton Station on M. & O. R. R. Here they captured 75 rebels, tore up the railroad track, burnt 4 car loads of ammunition and 2 warehouses filled with commissary stores, and destroyed the bridges on the west side of the station. Tarrying only long enough to complete the work of destruction, they were again on the wing, and after an exhausting ride by way of Garlandville, Raleigh and Westville, were ready to recross the river at Georgetown ferry. Gaining the ferry, as in case of the bridge, was a matter of life or death; for although they moved with great rapidity, the news of their exploits usualy preceded them, and it was believed that the citizens were now arming to stop their progress. Arriving at the river the proprietor of the ferry made his appearance, and in a careless way, asked if they wanted to cross, supposing them to be a force of Alabama cavalry which was expected in the neighborhood. Col. Prince of the 7th, imitating his provincial vernacular, replied in the affirmative, and added that "it took more time to wake up his negro ferryman than to catch the d—d conscripts."

Thoroughly deceived by his Yankee interlocutor, and apologizing for their detention, he awoke his negroes, who ferried them over, and then with true southern hospitality, invited them to breakfast, believing he was entertaining the 1st regiment of Alabama cavalry. As soon as the repast was over the party resumed their march and shortly afterward captured a courier, flying with the startling intelligence that the Yankees were coming and that the ferry must be destroyed. At Hazlehurst on the New Orleans and Jackson railroad, the next place visited, a large number of cars were destroyed, containing powder, shell and other supplies for the confederate army.

At this point Capt. Forbes sent to destroy the railroad at Macon rejoined them. In his return he unwittingly became the hero of a daring adventure. Entering Newton station where he expected to meet with the men under Grierson he was astonished to find himself in the midst of 3000 rebels in the act of debarking from the cars. With remarkable presence of mind he hoisted a flag of truce, and, boldly riding up, demanded the surrender of the force, in the name of Col. Grierson. The rebel officer in command, supposing Grierson's whole force which rumor had magnified to a mighthy host, was close at hand, asked an hour to consider the demand. Forbes granted the request with feigned reluctance, and started for the pretended troops in reserve to whom the confederate was to send his reply at the expiration of the time. The raiders, amused at the sell, dashed away, giving the enemy a long time to consult in regard to terms of the capitulation, and a long distance to travel before they could make them known. The entire command left Hazlehurst on the 27th and, pushing along the N. O. & J. R. R., through the stations of Bahala, Brookhaven and Summit, tore up the railroad destroyed its rolling stock, and immense quantities of commissary's stores and munitions on the way to Vicksburg, Port Hudson and Grand Gulf. On leaving the railroad they reached Baton Rouge on the 2d of May, the objective point of the expedition. Within the last 30 hours without eating or sleeping, they had ridden 80 miles, destroyed a number of bridges and large quantities of military stores, swam one river, had three skirmishes with the enemy, and took 42 prisoners. So exhausted were the men that they slept on their horses till the report of carbines roused them to action, and when the fray was over again relapse into slumber.

A resume of their operations shows that in the brief interval of 16 days they had ridden from the northern to the southern part of Mississippi, and, although operating between two great rebel lines of communication, the Mobile & Ohio and New Orleans and Jackson railroads, by skillful manœuvers, usually succeeded in eluding the enemy. In their march of 800 miles they took 500 prisoners, destroyed from 50 to 60 miles of railroad, 2 locomotives, 200 cars and military stores, and other property valued at $40,000; while they crossed into the Union lines with 1,200 horses and mules and 500 negroes.

The most determined efforts were made to capture them. A thousand cavalrymen from south of Port Hudson, 1,300 from Mobile, and 2,000 from the vicinity of Columbia, were sent for this purpose, but Grierson's strategy rendered their efforts abortive. Their safe arrival in Baton Rouge, whither the story of

their adventure had preceded them, created the greatest enthusiasm and rejoicing. Many refused to believe what they had heard
till they saw the men and listened to a recital of their feats. So iminent were the dangers and so complete the success, it seems more
like a feat of romance than an occurrence of actual life. The rebels were taught, notwithstanding the efficiency of their cavalry,
they could be "outrode, outwitted and out fought," and hence the
moral results achieved were no less important than the physical.

Siege and Surrender of Vicksburg.—From the investment of the
city till the surrender, little occurred to diversify the routine of
duty performed by the investing army. On the 22d of June, the
rebels in a sortie drove the 14th Illinois from their trenches which,
as a working party, they were engaged in excavating round the
city. The succeeding night the 41st Illinois and some other forces,
were ordered to the same trenches and the rebels again sallied
forth and demanded their surrender. The colonel of the 41st instantly ordered the artillery to open and in a severe fight the rebels were driven back to their works.

On the 25th the miners of McPherson's corps blew up
the rebel Fort Hill. Having deposited a ton of powder in an excavation under the fort, and selected the 45th Illinois to occupy
the breach, the mine was sprung. Almost noiselessly the ground
was lifted up as if some subterranean monster had suddenly risen
from his lair and tossed aside his covering of earth. A yawning crater some 20 feet in width was opened, and hardly had the cloud
of white smoke which issued from it cleared away, before the battle-scarred veterans of the 45th were at their post. The rebels
crowded up to the breach with great rapidity, and the fight on both
sides was one of desperation. For want of room the federal regiments subsequently engaged, went in one at a time, and as each
exhausted its amunition another took its place. In this manner
the 23d, 25th, 39th, 31st, 46th, 56th and 124th, Illinois, successively entered the vortex of fire and struggled like demi-gods to
quench its flames.

The object of these mining operations was to possess important
points in the enemy's line of defenses and thereby press him back
toward the river. When, however, it became evident that the
garrison was short of provisions, the excavations of parrallels
and mines was discontinued. The supply of food, though it
had been carefully husbanded, and the flesh of mules extensively
used, was now nearly exhausted. A failure of amunition also ensued, the ardor of the garrison was dampened by protracted privations, and the citizens living in caves to avoid danger, found
their suffering too great to longer continue the siege.

Induced by these stringent necessities, Pemberton, on the 2d of
July, displayed a white flag on the ramparts in view of the investing army, and an officer being sent to ascertain its meaning
learned that he wished to confer in regard to terms of capitulation. Correspondence was interchanged, resulting in a personal
interview between the two chiefs of the contending forces, and
finally in the unconditional surrender of the city and confederate
army. So great was the number of prisoners to avoid the expense of
their maintainance and transportation to northern prisons, they were
paroled. It was also believed that the demoralization consequent

upon their return home after defeat, would more than counterbalance the efforts of those who might be again induced to take up arms. The stars and stripes were hoisted over the conquered stronghold, thus symbolizing the nation's majesty in the presence of her erring and rebellious children.

Only three days after the fall of Vicksburg, as the immediate result of the victory, Port Hudson surrendered to the besieging force under Banks. The campaigns for the opening of the Mississippi were now at an end. To Illinois far more than to any other State, the nation is indebted for this successful termination. Her representatives in the long list of bloody battles and brilliant victories were the 8th, 11th, 13th, 14th, 17th, 20th, 23d, 25th, 28th, 29th, 30th, 31st, 32d, 33d, 35th, 38th, 41st, 45th, 46th, 47th, 48th, 51st, 53d, 55th, 57th, 63d, 72d, 75th, 76th, 77th, 81st, 93d, 95th, 97th, 99th, 108th, 113th, 114th, 116th, 118th, 120th, 124th, 126th, 127th and 131st regiments of infantry, Willard's Peoria and the Chicago and Mercantile battery, the 6th, 7th and portions of the 23d, 15th and Thielman's cavalry.

Step by step they had hewed their way toward the gulf, stronghold after stronghold had fallen beneath their stalwart blows, and now the last fetter which treason had forged to bind the Father of Waters, was riven asunder. No victory of the war was so decisive in its results as the capture of Vicksburg. It has been truthfully said that the possession of the Mississippi valley is the possession of America. Had the Richmond government been able to maintain the power it set up in the lower part of the great valley, the upper portion would have gravitated into the confederacy as naturally as its waters fall into the gulf. Furthermore the river not only served as a means of defense but was the dividing line between two great sections of the revolted territory. That lying on the west, although less important than the Atlantic region, was nevertheless the vast storehouse whence supplies had been drawn for the support of the armies in Virginia and Tennessee. Now isolated Texas could no longer contribute her vast herds of cattle, Arkansas her serials and Louisiana her sugar. With a fleet of federal gunboats patrolling the river, concert in the military operations of the severed States was impossible, and in those of the west the war was virtually at an end.

To the material effects of the blow the moral must be added to fully appreciate the extent of the damage sustained by the confederacy. The surprise and consternation consequent upon the Mississippi disaster fell like a thunderbolt from a clear sky on the people of the south. The spirit of their high vaulting chivalry was broken, and gloomy doubts brooded in the minds of many as to the possibility of ever realizing the success of their cause. The confederate authorities were early convinced of the importance of the Mississippi. At the time Grant commenced his descent against Vicksburg, Jefferson Davis harangued the people of Jackson on the necessity of preserving the Mississippi, as the great artery of the country and the only means of securing the perpetuity of the new government. Pollard in referring to its loss, says: "It compelled as its necessary consequence, the surrender of other posts on the Mississippi and cut the confederacy in twain. Its defense had worked exposure and weakness in other quarters. It had about stripped Charleston of troops; it had taken many thousand

of men from Bragg's army, and it had made such requisition on
his force for the newly organized lines in Mississippi that he was
compelled or induced, wisely or unwisely, to fall back from Talla-
hassee, Tullahoma to give up the country on the Memphis and
Charleston railroad and probably to abandon the defences of Middle Tennessee."

Brigadier-General John A. Logan, whose deeds and fame
are so inseparable blended with the opening of the Mississippi,
was born at Murfreesboro, Jackson county, February 9th,
1826. In common with others, at that early day in Illinois,
his educational privileges were limited. Natural ability, however,
triumphed over all obstacles, and he early become noted for the
proficiency of his attainments. At the outbreak of the Mexican
war he entered as a lieutenant in the 1st regiment of Illinois volunteers, and valiantly fought with his comrades till they returned
home. Resuming the duties of civil life, he commenced the study
of law in the office of his uncle A. M. Jenkins, formerly lieuten
ant-governor of the State. On the completion of his studies he
rapidly rose in his profession and obtained a wide-spread popularity.
In 1852 he was elected prosecuting attorney of the 3d judicial district. In the fall of the same year he was chosen to represent the
counties of Franklin and Jackson in the legislature, and was re-
elected in 1856. After the expiration of his last term in the legislature he was twice elected to congress, and while still a member
in 1861, he returned home, and upon the organization of the 31st
Illinois, was chosen its colonel. Of his subsequent operations in
the war we have already spoken. From the iron fibre of his composition and his deeds of fiery valor, he has been styled the Murat
of Illinois bravery

CHAPTER LXII.

1863—ILLINOIS IN THE CHATTANOOGA CAMPAIGN.

Battles of Chicamauga—Wauhachie—Lookout Mountain and Mission Ridge—Relief of Knoxville.

After the battle of Murfreesboro several months were spent by Rosecrans in recruiting his army, procuring supplies and opening up lines of communication to again advance on Bragg. Rigid discipline was enjoined and no effort spared to create in the minds of his men a proper appreciation of the work before them.

While these preparations were going on a number of minor engagements occurred in Middle Tennessee, in which Illinois troops were prominent actors. On the 3d of February, 1863, Forrest made a determined attack to recapture Fort Donelson, garrisoned by the 83d Illinois, but was repulsed. March 20th the 8th, 80th and 123d Illinois and some other troops under Col. Hall had a severe encounter with Morgan's cavalry near Milton, and the latter were forced to retreat. Again on the 20th of April the 24th, 80th, 98th and 123d Illinois, assisted by a force of cavalry, overtook a body of rebels at Woodbury and drove them from the town.

At length, the Washington authorities, believing that Bragg's army had been weakened to strengthen that of Lee's, insisted on a forward movement. The rebel commander, after his defeat, retired to Tullahoma and Shelbyville, making Duck River his line of defense. His position in the towns was strongly fortified, while the occupation of the roads leading south, as well as the natural features of the country gave him additional security in case of an attack. Rosecrans determined to neutralize these advantages by a flank movement on the left and compel him either to retreat or fight outside of his fortifications. Accordingly on the 24th of June the Union army set out from Murfreesboro, Thomas' corps in the centre, McCook's on the right and Crittenden's on the left. By a feint on Shelbyville with a portion of his army, he deceived the enemy, causing him to uncover Liberty, Hoover's and other principal gaps in the Cumberland Mountains through which the main advance was to be made. After hard fighting these were possessed by the national troops, the enemy's position at Shelbyville flanked and Bragg compelled to evacuate his works and escape to Tullahoma. Dispositions were immediately made to get in his rear and destroy his communications at the latter place, but he immediately abandoned it and retired in the direction of Chattanooga, pressed as far as practicable by the Union troops. Thus in a campaign of nine days, during which the roads were rendered nearly impassable by one of the most extraordinary rain storms ever known in the country, the enemy was driven from his entrenched position and Middle Tennessee relieved from rebel domination. Also in the various rencountres which occurred, there were captured 1,634 prisoners, six pieces of artillery and a large amount of stores.

The next step in following up the enemy was Chattanooga, the approaches to which were strong by nature and rendered more so by art. Rosecrans having put the railroad in operation to Stevenson for the transportation of supplies, commenced crossing the Cumberland Mountains, whose towering masses of rock lay between him and the stronghold he wished to subdue. Availing himself of the mountain passes previously captured, he reached the Tennessee and, descending it, prepared to cross in the vicinity of Chattanooga. The city being impregnable to a direct attack, Rosecrans decided to flank it on the west and south, and either force Bragg to evacuate it or suffer isolation from his base of supplies. With the exception of Hazen's division the enemy crossed the river below the city and commenced moving into Lookout valley. This, with the parallel valleys of Chattanooga and Chicamauga, extends southward from the Tennessee, which, at this point, runs in a westerly direction. Creeks bearing the names and coursing through each valley fall into the river, the two most western below the city and the one farthest east above it. Separating the waters of the creeks are Lookout Mountain and Mission Ridge, the former abutting on the river opposite Chattanooga and the latter a short distance above.

Hazen was instructed to watch the fords and make Bragg believe that the main body of the national troops was still on the north bank of the river. His force, although numbering only 7,000 men, was accordingly so dispersed; the heads of columns and camp-fires could be seen simultaneously at the fords along the river a distance of 70 miles. So adroitly was the ruse managed that McCook's corps had advanced up the valley 45 miles, and Thomas' 13, while Crittenden was on the river only 8 miles from Chattanooga before it was discovered by Bragg. He was now in a quandary. He could easily maintain himself against any assault of his adversary within his fortifications, but how long could he defy starvation when the investing army had cut off his supplies. If he attempted to defend both Chattanooga and his communications his army would be divided and easily beaten in detail, and, if he abandoned the city, it would provoke a clamor, among the people of the South eagerly watching his movements. The last expedient was, however, chosen as the least of three evils, and abandoning the city and its well constructed fortifications, he moved his army up Chicamauga valley in the direction of Lafayette.

Crittenden having taken possession of the town without opposition, was ordered to leave a brigade as a garrison, and with the remainder of his corps pursue the retiring army up the valley. Rosecrans, believing that Bragg was in full retreat, and that his chief object should be to intercept him, McCook and Thomas were ordered through the passes of Lookout and Mission mountains to get in advance of him on the south. In making this disposition of his forces, like many other good generals before him, he was deceived. Bragg was not retreating, but concentrating, in the vicinity of Lafayette, the most numerous army that had ever fought under rebel standards west of the Alleghanies. Buckner had been summoned from Knoxville, Johnson had been drawn upon for one of his strongest divisions, and Lee, satisfied that Richmond was not in danger, dispatched Longstreet's heavy corps of veterans from the Rapidan. Ere this was known Crittenden, deflecting easterly, had collided with a portion of his force in the vicinity of Ringgold. Thomas had developed it near Lafayette, and McCook had completely turned his position on the south.

In this detached condition of the Union corps a rare opportunity was offered Bragg to crush them in detail. All it required was to fall on Thomas with such a force as to overwhelm him, then turn down Chicamauga valley, and throwing himself between the city and Crittenden crush him, and finally, turning up Lookout valley, intercept and capture McCook. Failing to immediately avail himself of his advantages our generals discovered their mistake and rapidly commenced concentrating to avoid its consequences. Thomas at once pushed down the valley to within supporting distance of Crittenden, while McCook, whose isolation was greater, marched back into Lookout Valley and descending it, recrossed the mountains at Stephen's Gap. By this zig-zag course he effected a junction with the other corps and eluded Bragg, who had posted a heavy force to intercept him in the direct route down the Chicamauga. In the meantime affairs on the Chicamauga had assumed an alarming aspect. Bragg had received reinforcements, and, endeavoring to get between his antagonists, and Chatanooga, a race commenced between their respective armies on opposite sides of the creek in the direction of the city. This movement evinced a determination on the part of Bragg to turn our left, and Thomas was ordered to that end of the line, leaving Crittenden's and McCook's on the right. Its 7 divisions, Wood's Van Cleves', Palmer's, Reynold's, Johnson's, Baird's and Brannan's, now concentrated, extended down the west bank of the Chicamauga in the order mentioned, some 12 miles southward of Chattanooga. Negley's, Davis' and Sheridan's were yet several miles south of the main force, and Granger's at Rossville, but after the commencement of the battle, they came up and participated, swelling the entire force to some 55,000.

Early on the morning of the 19th of September, 1863, clouds of dust were seen hanging over the road beyond the creek, caused by the heavy columns of the enemy moving in the direction of Chattanooga. At 10 o'clock the loud explosion of artillery on the extreme left signalled the commencement of battle, and Thomas, riding forward to ascertain the nature of the attack, found Brannan's division hard pressed. To his surprise, also, the enemy had crossed the creek, and all the advantages which it afforded as a means of defense was lost. The impetuosity of the assault came near sweeping his entire corps from the field before it could be rallied and reinforced. When at length this was effected, its sturdy regulars, stung by the disaster they had sustained, and catching the resolution of their commander, threw themselves with irresistable force against their assailants. Even Longstreet's veterans strove in vain to check the advance, and were swept back the distance of a mile, and all the lost ground recovered—the

charge which struck the left, extended toward the right, causing
that end of the line to sway backward and forward according to
the varying success of the combatants. At the centre such was
the violence of the assault that Davis, who had come into the
fight, was thrown to the right and Van Cleve to the left,
and the rebels pouring into the gap the battle seemed to be
lost. At this juncture Hazen massed some 20 pieces of
artillery at the threatened point and discharging a cross-
fire of grape and canister into the charging columns,
forced them back. On the extreme right no very serious demonstrations were made till the afternoon, when several rebel brigades charged on one of our batteries and captured 3 of its guns.
These were afterward retaken and the assault at this end of the
line in the end proved a failure. At different times during the
day victory was almost within the grasp of the enemy, but when
night ended the conflict, the two armies stood face to face on
ground that offered little advantage to either.

During the night, Longstreet with additional veterans from the
army of Virginia, reinforced Bragg, swelling his army to 70,000,
and giving him an excess over Rosecrans, of 15,000. The latter
made some slight changes in the disposition of his divisions to
strenghten the left, against which it was expected the rebels would
next hurl their greatly preponderating forces. With these preparations the troops rested in the bleak September air of the mountain region on the ground where they had so persistently fought.

At daybreak the armies were drawn up for battle, but a dense
fog filling the valley and rendering objects invisible, it did not
commence till near 8 o'clock. The time was improved by further
strengtening Thomas, whose force now constituted about half of
the entire army. Rude breastworks were also thrown up on his
front, which afforded great protection in the subsequent battle.
As soon as the fog disappeared the rebel squadrons moved up in
an overwhelming charge. Thomas received the brunt of the onslaught. Bragg was again endeavoring to interpose his army
between that of Rosecrans and Chattanooga, which the preceding
day he had failed to effect. For a time the battle raged with
frightful carnage and varying success. The rebels, however, when
repulsed, continued to swarm up with fresh troops and augmented
numbers, and at length threw themselves with such momentum on
Thomas as to force him back. A new position was, however,
taken and all further attempts to turn his flank and get into Chattanooga proved abortive.

The right, in the meantime, had suffered irreparable disaster.
Negley's and Van Cleves' divisions, having been ordered to the
support of Thomas, opened a gap which the division commanders
on the right were ordered to close, but owing to a misunderstanding in regard to the movement and the consequent delay, Longstreet threw Hood's command into the breach. The result was
fatal. Davis' division moving up for the same purpose, was struck
and severed by the blow which smote it. Palmer and Van Cleve
on the opposite side, shared a similar fate, and soon the whole
right wing crumbled into fragments, was sent in impotent disorder in the direction of Chattanooga. Rosecrans, with other prominent officers was swept along by the tide, and on arriving in the city
he commenced preparations to defend the place and save the frag-

ments of the army, for it seemed to be utterly routed and at the mercy of the enemy. The result, though sufficiently bad, did not prove in the end so disastrous as was supposed.

Thomas, subsequently styled the rock of Chicamauga, gathering his bleeding forces and massing his guns in a semi-circle on the side of Mission Ridge, stood like a wall of adamant between the routed divisions and the enemy. Squadron after squadron attempted to breast the terrific fire of his artillery but were melted away like frost work in the blaze of the morning sun. Four of the 9 divisions of the army had been swept entirely away, and with the remnants of the remainder he kept the entire rebel army at bay. About 4 o'clock a new peril threatened him. The enemy pressing him in front and on both flanks, discovered a gorge on the right crossing the ridge on which he was posted, and commenced streaming through it to get in his rear. The danger was seen, but he could not spare a single man to avert it. In a few minutes he would be surrounded by a shouting foe and compelled either to surrender or be cut to pieces. Fortunately, at the very moment on which hung the fate of his army, Granger came up and offered the necessary assistance.

Posted at Rossville, and hearing the continuous thunder of battle in the direction of Thomas, he waited impatiently—anxiously for orders to join the conflict. As the tumult swelled and deepened, though contrary to orders, he was unable to resist its loud appeal for help, and started where his intuitions told him assistance was needed. On arriving he reported himself to Thomas, and was at once ordered to the point of danger. His troops, in which was the 115th Illinois, although new recruits, comprehending the momentous issues at stake, were soon breast to breast with the veterans of Hindman, now pouring through the gap and triumphantly shouting. In 20 minutes the gorge was carried and Thomas was saved, but 1,000 of our brave men had been killed and wounded in the charge. Longstreet, the rebel Achilles of the battle, determined to retake it, and repeatedly charged up to the very muzzles of our guns, double-shotted with grape and canister. Finding at length this point impregnable, Bragg determined to improve the remainder of the day in a final assault on the front and left. The national troops, having exhausted their ammunition, waited in the gathering gloom of twilight with fixed bayonets, to receive them. When within striking distance, they precipitated themselves on the enemy with such vigor as not only to rout him but capture some 200 prisoners.

Rosecrans, having informed Thomas to use his own judgement as to the propriety of longer holding his position, he concluded to fall back to Rossville—the want of ammunition, food, and water being the principal inducements for the change. After reaching this place a new line was formed and the advance of the enemy awaited. Although hovering near, he had been too severely punished to renew the attack, and on the night of the 21st Thomas fell back to Chattanooga. Rosecrans estimated his losses in the bloody conflict at 36 pieces of artillery and 16,000 men and claimed the capture of 2,000 prisoners. Bragg admitted a loss of 18,000 men and claimed the capture of 51 guns and 8,000 prisoners. He also vauntingly announced a great victory, yet he evidently either lacked the ability or the courage to improve it.

Thomas offered him battle the next day, and although outnumbering the federals two to one, he declined it. Furthermore, if Bragg had gained a victory its fruits were confined to the battlefield, while Rosecrans had secured Chattanooga, the strategic object of the campaign.' The key to the mountain system extending to the heart of the confederacy, it also served as an impregnable bastion to command the rebel lines of communication which traversed its rugged passes.

Says Pollard: "Rosecrans still held the prize of Chattanooga and with it the possession of East Tennessee. Two-thirds of our nitre beds were in that region and a large proportion of the coal which supplied our founderies. It abounded in the necessaries of life. It was one of the strongest countries in the world, so full of lofty mountains that it has been called, not inaptly, the Switzerland of America. As the possession of Switzerland opened the door for the invasion of Italy, Germany and France, so the possession of East Tennessee gave easy access to Virginia, North Carolina, Georgia and Alabama."

The representatives of Illinois in the bloody conflict were the 10th, 16th, 19th, 21st, 22d, 24th, 25th, 27th, 34th, 35th, 36th, 38th, 42d, 44th, 51st, 73d, 74th, 75th, 78th, 79th, 80th, 84th, 85th, 86th, 88th, 89th, 92d, 98th, 100th, 104th, 110th, 115th, 123d, 125th and 127th. Cols. Chandler and Mihalotzy and a long list of others, were among the slain. The 21st lost 238, 22d 235, 35th 152, 38th 18, 51st 90, and 79th 121.

The battle of Chicamauga was made the subject of remark both among rebels and Unionists. Bragg, by failing to take advantage of the victory which he so pompously claimed, completed the overthrow of his reputation, which had been tottering since the battle of Stone River. Rosecrans, suffering greatly in fame, was finally relieved of his command, and Thomas, whose superior fighting qualities had saved the army from destruction, was placed in his stead.

To secure greater unity of design and co-operation, and thereby greater efficiency, the separate armies operating in the region of Chattanooga were placed under the command of Grant. He immediately telegraphed Thomas to hold Chattanooga at all hazards, and received in reply assurances that starvation was the only contingency that could lead to its abandonment. Had he been forced to relinquish it, all its possession had cost would have been thrown away, and the struggle for ascendancy in the valley of the Mississippi again to re-enact. To prevent such a disaster Grant immediately commenced preparations to forward supplies and reinforcements. On the 22d day of September, Sherman, then on Big Black river, was notified by a dispatch to send over one of his divisions, and the next day Osterhaus was steaming up the Mississippi on the way to Chattanooga. Four days after, in accordance with further instructions, Sherman and his entire corps embarked in steamboats and started for the same place. At Memphis he commenced the repair of the Memphis and Charleston R. R., with the design of using it for the conveyance of his supplies as he advanced. While vigorously engaged in pushing forward this enterprise directly in the face of the enemy, he was ordered to abandon it and proceed directly forward to effect a junction with the other forces at Chattanooga.

The partial reverse at Chicamauga also induced Halleck to detach two divisions from the army of the Potomac and send them under Hooker to operate in the same field. Grant himself arrived on the 23d of October, and seeing the precarious condition of supplies, instituted measures to place them beyond the reach of future contingencies. Both troops and animals were already suffering for the want of provisions which had been brought in wagons over the numerous mountain ridges separating Chattanooga from Middle Tennessee. Bragg, aware that he could neither flank nor carry by storm the stronghold which he had so recently lost, was endeavoring to get possession of the river and the railroads leading to it with the intention of starving our army out of it.

For the two-fold purpose of obtaining relief and facilitating the operations of Hooker, who was approaching the city by way of Lookout valley, Grant determined to seize the heights on the west side where it connects with the Tennessee. After a reconnoisance, 1,500 picked troops under Hazen were sent in pontoons down the river to Brown's ferry adjacent the heights, while a co-operating force of 2,500 secretly followed on the north bank of the river. The pontoons carrying the advance party noiselessly floated down the stream to the point chosen for debarkation. Here a picket alarm aroused the neighboring camps of the enemy and Hazen's men jumped quickly ashore and formed to repel an attack. The former, wholly taken by surprise, after a feeble resistance retreated up the valley, and the spurs on the east side of it were seized and fortified. The pontoons were next employed to pass over the force on the opposite side, and at daylight the heights, which gave Grant the key to Bragg's position, were made impregnable. During the day Hooker came down the valley, and having dispersed the rebel forces on the river below, it was opened to navigation and all fears of starvation removed. A bridge was thrown across the river opposite, and should Bragg mass his forces either against Hooker or Chattanooga, we now had the shorter line of concentration.

Battle of Wauhatchie.—The rebels, alarmed at the demonstrations in Lookout valley, determined, on the night of the 28th of October, to interpose a counteracting movement. Bragg, unable to cope with Hooker's entire corps, made an assault on Geary's division encamped at Wauhatchie, the point where he had effected an entrance into Lookout valley. About midnight they rushed forward with loud yells and great impetuosity, but found their antagonists wide awake and ready to receive them with a fire fierce and deadlier than their own. Hooker, hearing the report of guns, and anxious for the safety of Geary, immediately sent forward Schurz's division of Howard's corps to his aid. As the force rapidly marched forward in the moonlight they were suddenly and unexpectedly fired upon by 2,000 rebels posted on an adjoining hill. One of brigades moved on to the assistance of Geary while the other halted to charge the heights. The latter, immediately scaling the steep acclivity with fixed bayonets, cleared the rifle pits on its summit. In the meantime the wild hills which girt Geary about were ablaze with flashes of musketry and exploding shells. Although several times nearly overwhelmed,

he clung to his position and at length forced his assailants back
and compelled them to seek refuge in their works on Lookout
Mountain.

The 101st Illinois was among the heroes of the battle, and materially aided in the enemy's overthrow.

Battle of Lookout Mountain.—Bragg, weakened by detaching
Longstreet's corps to operate against Burnside at Knoxville, now
concluded to remain in his trenches and act on the defensive. His
position stretched across the valley of Chattanooga, and high on
the western and northern slopes of Lookout and Mission Ridge
was one of great natural strength. The valley here is narrow and
was so enfiladed by batteries planted on the sides of the adjacent mountains as to render it wholly impregnable to a direct
assault. Hooker, holding the valley of Lookout, confronted the
enemy on the adjacent mountain. Thomas occupied a central position in the valley of Chattanooga in the front of the city, and
Sherman was ordered to seize the northern extremity of Mission
Ridge. With the 15th army corps he moved from Bridgeport and
on entering Lookout valley, dispatched Ewing's division up it to
threaten Bragg's extreme left and thus divert attention from
his right, where he was ordered to operate. With the remainder of
his force he crossed the bridge at Brawn's ferry, and, proceeding
unobserved along the north bank of the river, he recrossed it
near the mouth of the Chicamauga and seized the position assigned him before the rebels had time to interpose any serious opposition. Ewing's division was now ordered back to rejoin Sherman, but the bridge having given away, he returned and fought
under Hooker.

The latter in the meantime climbing the precipitous steeps of
Lookout, had planted his veteran standards high on its cloud-
capped summit. To favor Sherman's movement he had been directed to threaten the enemy. With this object in view, on the
morning of the 24th his forces were in motion, but the rain of the
previous days had swollen Lookout creek and swept away the
pontoons prepared for crossing it. While rebuilding the bridge
Geary was ordered to move up the valley and cross at a more
available point. Favored by a heavy mist the force unobserved
crossed the creek and secured a lodgment on its western bank.
By 11 o'clock the bridge was completed, and the force augmented
to some 9,000 men, swept down between the creek and the mountain, carried the rifle-pits at its base and captured a large number
of prisoners. Next commenced the fearful ascent of the mountain, our men enthusiastically climbing over splintered crests and
yawning chasms, directly under the muzzles of the enemy's batteries. Soon the flashes and thunderpeals resembling the crash
of heaven's artillery, announced the storm of war raging in the
clouds above. When the dense masses of fog that had become
banked against the side of the mountain rolled away, and the splendid pageantry of battle burst on the vision of the thousands who had
been shrouded in the mist-clouded valleys below, charging
squadrons, shouting multitudes and clashing arms appeared high
above them, as if the gods, having espoused the cause of the contending armies were warring to decide their fate. Our columns,
flushed by success, in the face of a plunging fire of heavy ordnance,

rushed on the foe capturing many prisoners and hurling the remainder of his forces down the pricipitous eastern declivity of the mountain. The entire army with almost painful excitement having witnessed the sublime scene, responded with loud acclaim to the shout which rose from the conquering columns, till the wild mountain gorges became vocal with the echoes and seemed to partake of the rejoicing.

The Illinois regiments in and otherwise connected with the battle were the 12th, 34th, 35th, 59th, 60th, 73d, 75th, 101st and 115th.

Battle of Mission Ridge.—Sherman, after having gained a foothold on Mission Ridge, improved the succeeding night in fortifying his position, and was ready on the morning of the 25th to move against the enemy. The ridge he occupied was not continuous but a succession of eminences. A deep gap lay between him and the elevation on which the enemy was posted, and should he get possession of this, there was still a second higher and farther back whose guns commanded it. At early dawn Gen. M. L. Smith was directed to move along the east base of the ridge, Col. Loomis the west base and Gen. Corse with the 40th Illinois, supported by the 20th and 40th Ohio, along the crest. The latter advanced to within 80 yards of the enemy's works where he gained a secondary crest and commenced an assault, but was unable to carry the works of the rebels, and they unable to drive him from his position. Smith and Loomis were however gaining on each flank, and Bragg massing his forces to protect the most vulnerable points of his position, the battle raged with constantly increasing fury. From every salient point and projecting spur, batteries flamed and thundered, wrapping the combatants in a cloud of smoke. As the day wore away this fearful pounding was continued without intermission and without either belligerant gaining any decided advantage. Grant meanwhile had been listening to the stern work in which his favorite lieutenant was engaged, and anxiously waiting for the time to come when he could relieve him by a move on the centre. At length, when Bragg had weakened this part of his line to support his right, and Hooker had come down from the heights of Lookout without a co-operating force, Thomas was ordered to advance.

That portion of Bragg's position which he was now to assail lay on a bald rugged height of Mission Ridge, 800 feet above Chattanooga. A line of rifle pits protected its base, while on its summit were batteries which had achieved fame in previous battles supported by veteran regiments. As soon as the command was given Wood's, Baird's and Johnson's divisions under Granger, immediately started rapidly forward. So openly and deliberately was the movement that the enemy regarded it as a review, and those in the rifle pits, surprised, fled precipitately up the mountain as the assaulting columns approached. The rebels greatly astonished at the attack made at the base of the mountain were more so when they beheld the national troops climbing its precipitous sides to assail them on its summit. Nearly 30 pieces of artillery commenced hurling at them grape and canister to dispute the ascent yet the works were carried simultaneously at six different points. A shout made known the result, and soldiers clinging to steeps and spurs and deep in the valley below, answered with a loud response. Bragg, seeing

53

all was lost, commenced withdrawing, closely followed till night-fall, which put an end to further movements. The next day the pursuit was continued and the enemy overtaken in a gap of the mountains near Ringgold. Here he made a stubborn resistance but was finally forced from his strong position, the 13th Illinois bearing an honorable part in the fight.

The Illinois regiments in the magnificent charges of Mission Ridge and the co-operative struggles, were the 12th, the 19th, 22d, 26th, 27th, 35th, 42d, 44th, 48th, 51st, 59th, 63d, 73d, 79th, 80th, 84th, 86th, 88th, 89th, 93d, 104th and 115th. The 26th lost 101 men, the 42d, 45 and the 51st, 30. They were first in Sherman's and first in Thomas' advance, and first to surmount the battery crowned crests of the ridge.

Considering Bragg's almost impregnable position on the summits of the mountains and the daring and skillful generalship used in wresting it from his grasp, the battles in the vicinity of Chattanooga must be regarded among the most remarkable on record. Though outnumbered toward the close of the campaign, the lofty eyry in which he had perched his forces gave him decidedly the advantage. Failing to hold it the passes which it overlooked and commanded now became salient points for the farther advance of the national armies, and Chattanooga became henceforth as serviceable in the cause of the Union as it had hitherto been defiant to loyalty. The Union loss in the series of engagements, terminating in this auspicious result, was reported 5,600; that of the enemy in killed and wounded at 2,500; prisoners 6,000; artillery 40 guns.

Siege and Relief of Knoxville.—The sequence of the campaign was the relief of Burnside at Knoxville. While in command of the department of the Ohio before it had been merged into that of the Mississippi and Grant assumed command, Burnside undertook an expedition into East Tennessee to relieve the loyal inhabitants. The people of this region had been devotedly attached to the Union and as a consequence had suffered terribly from conscription persecution and spoilation. The dungeon, bullet and halter, used to crush out their loyalty, had only served to intensify it, and Burnside was welcomed among them with every expression of delight. He immediately took possession of Knoxville, and shortly after the battle of Chicamauga Longstreet was sent with an army of 20,000 to crush him before he could be reinforced.

After severe fighting the city was closely environed and preparations made to carry it by storm. The garrison, consisting in part of the 65th and 112th Illinois, entertained no doubt of their ability to defend themselves, but their supplies were nearly exhausted and the danger of starvation compelling a surrender was iminent. Messengers had informed Grant of their destitution and as soon as the fate of Chattanooga was decided Granger was ordered to Knoxville with a relieving force. Grant, however, on finding his command inadequate, substituted Sherman's, containing the 27th, 44th, 48th, 60th and 80th Illinois, although it was imposing a severe task on his brave but exhausted men. Leaving their surplus clothing behind to augment their speed, they had marched by land from Memphis, fought their way through the battles of Chattanooga, and now, without a moment's respite, and without suitable apparal for the altered temperature of the advanced season—without a word of complaint they cheerfully set out the night after the order was issued, and by morning they had made 15 miles, and at night of the succeeding day 26 more, though the rebels had delayed their advance by burning bridges and otherwise interposing obstacles.

Longstreet had entertained hopes that starvation would induce Burnside to surrender, but after hearing of Bragg's defeat and that a relieving force was coming, determined, on the 29th of November, to carry the place by storm. A storming column accordingly made its appearance, and for hours a deadly struggle ensued. More than 1,000 in killed and wounded was the cost of the assault, but the fort was not taken. Sherman, fearing the garrison might despair of success, when his army was within 40 miles of the beleagured place, sent forward a brigade of his fleetest cavalry to announce his coming. The clatter of their hoofs were heard on the night of the 3d of December, and the beseiged army with inexpressible delight received the welcome intelligence. The march was continued till the night of the 5th, when news was received that Longstreet had raised the seige and retreated into Virginia. Sherman immediately halted the army, and after personally visiting Knoxville and having an interview with Burnside, returned with it to Chattanooga.

Chapter LXIII.

1864—ILLINOIS IN THE ATLANTA AND NASHVILLE CAMPAIGNS.

Battles of Rocky Face Mountain, Resaca, New Hope Church, Peach Tree Creek, Atlanta, Jonesboro', Alatoona, Spring Hill, Franklin and Nashville.

Grant, the former colonel of the 21st Illinois, had now fully won the confidence of the people, and congress reviving the grade of lieutenant-general on the 2d of March, 1864, he was commissioned as the generalissimo of the nation's armies. For a long time there had existed a feeling of dissatisfaction in regard to the want of concert in the movements of the armies in the east and west. It was too frequently the case when a success occurred in one part of the field the enemy was permitted to send a relieving force from another, and thus neutralize the effect of victory. Whether this was the fault of Halleck or not, public opinion required a new head for the army, and Grant whose fitness was wisely estimated by his past successes, was raised to the high position which only Washington before him had filled.

If the task before him was not more difficult than that of his predecessor, the field of his operations was far more extensive. "Never before had one commander surveyed such a vast field of operations and looked over such a mighty array subject to his single control. From the Potomac to the Rio Grande, for 5,000 miles arose the smoke of camp fires, and the shouts of embattled hosts, evoking his leadership. To aid him in the gigantic task before him 600 vessels lined the rivers and darkened coasts for 2,500 miles, while 4,000 guns lay ready to send their stern summons into rebel defenses.[*]

As a consequence of Grant's promotion, Sherman was placed in command of the department of the Mississippi, comprising the armies of the Cumberland, Tennessee and Ohio. The army of the Cumberland, consisting of the 4th, 14th and 20th corps, was commanded by Thomas; the 4th corps by Howard; and its divisions by Stanley, Newton and Wood, the 14th by Palmer, and its divisions by Davis, Johnson and Baired; the 20th corps by Hooker, and its divisions by Williams and Butterfield. The army of the Tennessee, consisting of the 15th corps and portions of the 16th and 17th, was under McPherson; the 15th corps was under Logan and its divisions under M. L. Smith, J. E. Smith,

---

[*] Headle .

836

Osterhaus and Harrow; the 16th corps under Dodge and its divisions under Ransom, Corse and Sweeney; the 17th corps under Blair, and its divisions under C. R. Woods and Legget. The army of the Ohio was under the leadership of Schofield.

The cavalry consisted of Kilpatrick's and Garrards' divisions of the army of the Cumberland, E. McCook's brigade of the army of the Tennessee and McCook's division of the army of the Ohio.

Sherman, the central figure of the drama now about to be enacted in Georgia, had by great energy and skillful generalship acquired a prestige of great value and assistance in playing the difficult role that fell to his lot. He had won high scholastic honors in the military curriculum of West Point. As the commander of a brigade at Bull Run he exhibited noticeable soldierly skill; at Shiloh, as the head of a raw division, both Grant and Halleck declared that they were indebted to him for the success of the battle; and finally, in the well earned plaudits as the commander of a corps in the recent battle of Chattanooga, other laurels were won and his present promotion secured. His principal subordinate officers were men of repute, generals whom the stern ordeal of war had tried and proved to possess a high order of military talent.

Grant, before repairing to his new field of labor, had a long interview with Sherman, in which the plans of the campaigns it was proposed to institute against Richmond and Atlanta were fully discussed. It was decided to simultaneously move from the Rapidan and Tennessee, with two great armies southward, and so vigorously press the confederate forces both east and west that relieving parties could not be sent from one department to another. It was also settled that the campaigns should commence about the first of May, and Sherman accordingly set out from his winter quarters around Chattanooga, with an army of near 100,000 men and 254 guns.

Johnson, who assumed command after Bragg's ill-starred campaign, confronted him with an army of some 60,000 men, consisting of 3 corps under Polk, Hardee, and Hood. To compensate for his want of numbers he had selected and fortified his position, and the national army, as it followed him into Georgia, was forced to keep open a long line of communications, which greatly reduced the number of men available for the field. His army lay at Dalton, so strongly fortified that an attack in front was impossible. Barring his approaches in this direction was Rocky Face Mountain, here cloven by Mill Creek, on the banks of which the railroad found a passage to the town. This narrow defile, the only gateway to the rebel position, was artificially flooded and swept by artillery placed on its rocky abutments, while inaccessible spurs, frowning with batteries protected his flanks.

Battle of Rocky Face Mountain.—Sherman now commenced that series of movements which won for him the appellation of the "Great flanker," and by which he proposed to turn Johnson's craggy citadel and compel him to fight outside of its impregnable fastnesses. Resaca is situated 18 miles farther southward on the railroad, and for this purpose McPherson was sent on a westward detour through Ship and Snake Gaps to cut off the confederate communications at that point. To cover this movement Thomas entered the Mill Creek Gap, and on the 8th and 9th of May, 1864, made a bold push for the summit of the mountain, the 42d, 44th, 51st, 59th, 79th, 88th, 89th and 107th Illinois, fighting with great determination, but without dislodging the enemy. His attention was, however, diverted from McPherson, who unmolested arrived within a few miles of Resaca.

Battle of Resaca.—A reconnoisance, however, showed that the town was too strong to be carried, Johnson having provided for such contingency by sending thither troops at the first intimation of danger. It was designed not only to make the enemy retreat southward by getting on his base of supplies, but to have McPherson strike him on the flank and the rest of the army in the rear after he had been dislodged from his position. McPherson being unable to accomplish his part of the programme, all the remaining forces, with the exception of Howard's corps, which was left to watch Dalton, were sent to his aid, and Johnson, seeing his position was no longer tenable, suddenly evacuated it and fell back to Resaca. Sherman finding him strongly fortified, determined to institute another flank movement, and turn him out of it. For this purpose on the 14th he pontooned the Ostenaula, which crosses the railroad south of Resaca, and on the 15th Sweeney's division and a force of cavalry were sent to break the railroad behind Calhoun and Kingston. Simultaneously, McPherson's, Thomas' and Schofield's forces assaulted the right and centre of the rebel line. The former driving Polk from his position, planted his artillery on commanding heights, and swept the confederate bridge over the river, while Sweeney, unmolested, crossed farther down the stream. The crossing of the stream, as is usually the case in exposed situations, was attended with a number of brilliant incidents. As Dodge's corps moved up to Lay's ferry a heavy fire was opened upon them from the opposite bank to prevent its crossing. Six companies of the 66th Illinois and 81st Ohio were sent across in pontoons to dislodge them, during which a storm of bullets was encountered, toppling many of them over into the water, and ruefully singing their requiems as they disappeared beneath the waves. Undaunted by the loss of their comrades, they gained the shore, and charging up the bank, soon drove the enemy from his position. The next day and succeeding night the fight was renewed. Hooker, driving the enemy from several points, captured 4 of his guns and a large number of prisoners. A short time after midnight the enemy gave way and retreated across the Ostenaula, leaving Resaca the prize of the invading army. In the several engagements our loss amounted to some 5,600, that of the confederates being much less, as they fought behind breastworks.

The Illinois regiments present were the 27th, 42d, 44th, 48th, 51st, 52d, 59th, 60th, 64th, 75th, 80th, 84th, 86th, 88th, 89th, 92d, 98th, 101st, 102d, 104th, 105th, 107th, 111th, 112th, 115th and 127th. Outnumbering the troops of any other single State, the victory was largely an Illinois triumph. On one occasion our men had been ordered back, which evoked exultant shouts from the enemy, who supposed we were repulsed. The color-bearer of the 127th Illinois, becoming exasperated, and, regardless of danger, returned to an embrasure and defiantly flaunted his standard in the face of the astonished enemy. His life was the foreit of his temerity, for he and others after him who attempted to take up the colors were shot.

Battle of New Hope Church.—The main body of the army now moved after the retreating enemy, while Davis' division, following the Ostenaula to Rome, captured 8 heavy pieces of artillery and destroyed rolling mills and foundries of great value to the enemy. At Adairsville and Kingston, Johnson held strong positions, but, after a sharp brush with the pursuing army, in which the 42d, 44th, 59th, 80th, 84th and 88th Illinois became engaged, he abandoned them and occupied Altoona, a place strong by nature and more so by art. By Johnson's last movement, the valley of the Etowah was abandoned to Sherman, who now began to think it was the intention of his adversary to draw the Union army far into the interior before risking a general engagement. He nevertheless accepted the issue, and determined to make another attempt to draw him out of his entrenchments for the purpose of fighting him on open ground. Accordingly, with supplies for 20 days, on the 20th of May, he set out with the army on a westward detour to Dallas, intending, after arriving thither, to seize and destroy the railroad west of the town. Johnson quickly divined the object of the movement, and Hooker, in our van, encountered a stubborn resistance at New Hope church, in the vicinity of Dallas. Altoona had been evacuated and the rebel army was stretched from Dallas to Marietta on the railroad, the rugged character of the ground occupied giving it every facility for opposition and defensive operations. Sherman, pushing up his forces toward the enemy's entrenchments, brought on heavy skirmishing, which, on the 29th, culminated in a fierce assault on Johnson's position, the assailants suffering heavy loss and gaining no permanent advantage.

The next day the rebels made an assault on McPherson, occupying the Union right. Our men were sheltered by earthworks, up to which the rebels advanced in one of those overwhelming charges for which they were distinguished, and, with a shout which rose above their crashing volleys. The federals reserved their fire till the surging masses came within deadly range, when they opened with such destructive effect that the storming party was compelled to retire. Again and again they rallied and marched up almost to the muzzles of our guns, refusing to desist till the ground on which they fought was covered with heaps of dead and dying. In the terrible onslaught the former colonel of the 52d Illinois, now styled Bull Dog Sweeney, on account of his stubborn fighting qualities, with his division twice received the rebels and sent them in disorderly masses from the field. The Illinois regiments engaged at New Hope church and its vicinity, were the 42d, 44th, 48th, 51st, 52d, 59th, 60th, 64th, 79th, 80th, 84th, 86th, 88th, 101st, 104th, 105th and 111th.

Battle of Kennesaw Mountain.—After this death grapple, several days were spent in skirmishing, when Sherman again determined to turn the position of the enemy. He therefore gradually moved his forces in the direction of the railroad and Johnson, closely watching him, led his troops to Marietta, whence he fell back to Kennesaw mountain. This towering height, and its almost equally formidable neighbors, Pine and Lost mountains, now loomed up before the pursuing army, dark with panoplied hosts and their inaccessible spurs frowning with batteries. Sherman, after reconnoitering the new situation of the enemy, commenced forcing a passage between Pine and Kennesaw, which caused him to concentrate on the latter so as to cover Marietta and the railroad. In effecting these changes, the fighting was desultory, but severe, the rebels from their high position being able to minutely scrutinize the movements of our men and pour down upon their heads a pelting rain of iron.*

Johnson, seeing the Union army gradually approaching his position, on the 22d of June, ordered Hood to make an assault on Hooker's corps, which had moved to an advanced position. The onset was fierce and determined but repulsed with heavy loss to the enemy in killed, wounded and prisoners. Sherman now determined to deal a counter blow, and, on the 27th, after a heavy cannonade, Thomas and McPherson, at different points, moved simultaneously up to the rebel works. Soon the mountain, volcano-like, became wrapped in fire and shook from base to summit under the incessant peals of heavy guns. Our men fought with unparalleled devotion, and portions of Newton's and Wood's divisions succeeded in capturing the first line of rebel works, but the side of the mountain above them was abrupt and inaccessible, and they were compelled to return.

The entire loss of the army in the fatal charge was 3,000. A large part of this fell on the Illinois troops, as might be expected from the long list of regiments. The 12th, 27th, 31st, 32d, 35th, 38th, 42d, 44th, 48th, 51st, 52d, 55th, 59th, 60th, 64th, 65th, 79th, 80th, 84th, 86th, 88th, 89th, 101st, 104th, 107th and 111th, were in the hottest part of the engagement and correspondingly suffered.

This was Sherman's first defeat and perhaps the greatest mistake of the campaign. He had so frequently outflanked the enemy that an idea prevailed, both among his own and the rebel officers, that he would not make an assault, and he says he ordered the attack partly for the moral effect. The best method of procedure in every case is to secure victory with the least expenditure of life, and, therefore, his pretext hardly seems satisfactory. Besides, in this instance, the chances of success were in favor of the enemy, and the assault proving unsuccessful, the moral effect was in his favor also.

After the bloody repulse he buried his dead and again resorted to flanking, which, as the result shows, should have been tried in the first place. McPherson was sent on the right toward the Chattahoochie, and Johnson, as soon as he became aware of the movement, departed from his fortified heights, and also hurried to the river. Sherman pushed after him with the hope of striking a

---

*While thus making observations, Gen. Polk, the Episcopal bishop of Louisiana, was struck by a 3-inch ball from our guns, and instantly killed. In company with Johnson and Hardee, the group was discovered on its lofty lookout, and, at the instance of Sherman, a gun was turned upon it and fired. The missile passed directly over the party, which caused them to dismount and retire to a place of safety. Polk, however, refusing to remain under cover, returned, and a second shot directed with unerring aim, struck and tore his body into fragments. Our men having discovered the meaning of the signals employed by the enemy by reading the dispatches sent along his lines, learned soon afterwards that he had been killed.

fatal blow when he attempted to cross, but the wary confederate had provided for this contingency by seizing and fortifying a position on its banks. This was held till the passage of the men was effected when he retired into his works around Atlanta, where he was destined to meet his final overthrow.

Battle of Peach Tree Creek.—The Chatahoochie here is a large stream running in a southwesterly direction and near where the railroad crosses it, receives the waters of Peach Tree creek, a deep tributary falling into it from the west. Within the angle formed by the streams and 8 miles distant from each, Atlanta, the principal objective point, is situated. The rebels, taking advantage of the peculiar conformation of the streams, had arranged their lines of defense with a view of disputing the passage of these natural barriers which lay between them and the national army. To surmount this difficulty was the problem which Sherman had to solve. With his army on the west side of the river below the mouth of Peach Tree creek. he could easily approach the city on the south and west where it was comparatively defenseless, but to cross it in the face of a powerful foe, and risk a battle with it in his immediate rear, was a dangerous undertaking. Another plan was to cross the river above the mouth of Peach Tree creek, where little opposition would be encountered, and then turning southward, risk the contingencies of crossing the smaller stream. The latter alternative was adopted as the least difficult, but, during its execution, Johnson was relieved of his command.

This was only one of the many acts of stupendous folly which characterized the Richmond authorities during the latter days of the confederacy and materially hastened its downfall. He had skillfully used the advantages of defense offered by the rugged mountain passes through which he had been driven; yet, because he had failed to annihilate his adversary, who exceeded him in numbers, the rebel president was displeased and superseded him. Says Pollard : " He lost 10,000 men in killed and wounded, and 4,700 more from other causes, a fact which proves his men never failed to meet the invading army whenever an opportunity offered to strike a damaging blow." The fiery and impetuous Hood was placed in his stead, and, commencing a furious offensive warfare, and remorselessly slaughtered his men when there was little prospect of success. Hood, in taking command of the rebel army, found it, in consequence of reinforcements, some 5,000 stronger than at the commencement of the campaign, while that of his adversary had also been kept up to the original standard, and, flushed with triumph, was better prepared than at first to grapple with the foe.

As the army was developing a line along Peach Tree creek, Thomas on the right, Schofield in the centre, and McPherson on the left, Hood, on the 20th, massed his forces and endeavored to penetrate a gap between Thomas and Schofield which Sherman was trying to fill. The assault, although as sudden as a thunder clap, was received by Palmer's, Hooker's and Howard's corps, with such determined resistance that defeat was impossible. Musketry and artillery mowed them down by hundreds, yet, with a devotion worthy of a better cause, they continued to crowd up in the wasting fire which no amount of blood was able to quench. The great sacrifice did not avail, for, after a five-hours' battle and the loss of 5,000 men, they were driven back to their entrenchments.

Battles of Atlanta.—The main army now closed in on the fated city, in the form of a semi-circle of two miles radius, and Hood determined to strike another offensive blow to extricate himself from its toils. Moving up on the extreme left, the most vulnerable part of our line, he massed his forces for an assault. McPherson, in command of this wing, had made a wide circuit by way of Decatur, and it was Hood's intention to fall on and crush him before he could properly get in position. Accordingly, on the 22d the latter was impetuously assaulted, the charging squadrons sweeping along the whole line, for a time it seemed almost irresistable. The first blow fell on Blair's corps, but soon that of Dodge, which, moving around him in the rear to form on his left, became involved. Dodge, finding his right about to be turned, ordered a charge on the enemy's flank by the 12th Illinois and 81st Ohio, which, sweeping up to the foe, captured two stand of colors and left the ground covered with his dead. Hardee had entered a gap between the two corps, when Sweeney's division met him, and by stubborn fighting, in which the 9th Illinois bore a distinguished part, kept him at bay till other forces could arrive and assist him. While Dodge roughly handled the rebels and took many of them prisoners, their assaults on Blair were more successful. With their customary daring they rushed up and both armies fought on opposite sides of the same breastworks on which were planted their respective standards. The orders of officers were unheard, and each combatant rallying round his colors struck such blows as seemed likely to do the greatest execution.

In the meantime a heavy force of the enemy got in our rear and captured 12 guns. Sherman sent word to Logan, whose corps was on Blair's right, that he must charge and retake them. Two batteries placed on commanding hills, were now ordered to open upon the enemy, and under cover of their converging fire, he massed and pushed irresistibly forward his charging columns. All the guns were retaken except two, which had been carried from the field, and when night put an end to the contest, Hood found himself again foiled, and his forces exhausted.

The Illinois regiments in the two preceding battles were the 16th, 26th, 27th, 30th, 31st, 35th, 38th, 42d, 44th, 48th, 51st, 52d, 53d, 55th, 59th, 60th, 64th, 73d, 74th, 75th, 80th, 84th, 86th, 88th, 89th, 92d, 101st, 102d, 104th, 105th, 107th, 111th, 112th, 115th and 129th. In the heavy charging and counter charging of the opposing forces in the battle they frequently became intermingled in hand to hand contests. On one occasion, Col. Flynn, of the 129th Illinois, met a rebel colonel, and while their regiments were engaged in a death grapple they had a combat from behind trees, with guns, each dodging round his covert so as to give and avoid shots. One of our batteries planted on the Atlanta road did such terrible execution upon the enemy, a heavy column was sent up to capture it. The 74th Illinois, stationed on the right of the road, and the 88th on the left, poured into the assaulting force such a destructive fire, it was compelled to forego the prize, and pay dearly for the attempt to get it. One stand of colors was captured by the 129th, two by the 105th. The 104th distinguished itself by the determined stand it made in an advanced position, where the enemy first came thundering down on our lines. In this stubbornly contested battle, the rebel loss was 18 stand of colors and 8,000 men, of whom 3,000 were killed and 1,000 taken prisoners. Our own loss amounted to 3,000, of whom 1,000 were made prisoners.

Among the dead was Gen. McPherson, who, at the time he lost his life, was riding unprotected in the rear. While proceeding in fancied security he came unexpectedly upon a detachment of rebels who shot him, and his steed escaping wounded and rider-less out of the forest, gave the first intimation of his fate. He was a young man of fine personal appearance, of rare ability as an officer, and possessed a heart abounding in kindness and win-ning for him the esteem and affection of all who came near him. It is said Sherman burst into tears when he heard of his death, and the whole army expressed the most intense sorrow. By order of the president, Gen. Howard assumed command of the Army of the Tennessee. Gens. Hooker and Palmer resigned, and their respective places were filled by Gens. Stanley and Davis.

With this assault the direct operations on the north and east terminated. Sherman determined to try a flank movement on the south and west. To assist in this movement Stone-man, with 5,000 cavalry, was ordered to move round the city on the left, and McCook, with 4,000 on the right, to destroy Hood's communications. The latter moved along the west bank of the Chattahoochie, and crossing the West Point railroad, tore up a portion of the track, and proceeding thence to Fayetteville, cap-tured 250 prisoners, 500 wagons and 800 mules. Next Lovejoy, on the Macon railroad, was visited, to form a junction with Stoneman, who had arranged to meet him at that place. The latter failing to come, he destroyed part of the road, after which, being confronted by a force of Mississippi infantry on their way to join Hood, he was forced to return with a loss of 500 men. Stoneman had started with the magnificent project of sweeping down the Macon road, capturing the city, and then turning on Andersonville and releasing our suffering soldiers confined in its prison. Sherman gave his assent to it, with the understanding that he should meet McCook at Lovejoy, and with the united forces proceed to Ander-sonville. Stoneman, however, failed to comply with his part of the engagement, and as the result he made his appearance before Macon with an inadequate force, and in attempting to retire he and 1,000 of his men were captured by the cavalry of the enemy.

The army of the Tennessee now moved round the city on the right, and Hood, detecting the movement, prepared to risk another offensive battle. On the 28th his infantry poured in dense masses from the west side of the city, and moved in magnificent style up to Logan's corps on the Bell Ferry road. Our troops having learned from experience Hood's method of warfare, hurriedly made breastworks, and with comparative immunity, as the rebels came within range, slaughtered them by hundreds, forcing them to retire. Six different times, however, they were reformed and pushed up to our works by their infuriated officers, and it was only when their loss reached some 5,000 men, and the survivors could no longer be driven to the slaughter, that the battle ceased.

Sherman now continued the movement of his force on the right, with the view of disabling the railroad on which the city depended for supplies. Hood also determines to make a similar attempt against the communications of the Union army. Wheeler, in command of his cavalry, was therefore sent northward and succeeded in breaking the Chattanooga railroad and capturing 900 beeves, a part of our supplies. Sherman, however, foreseeing emergencies, of this kind had built and garrisoned blockhouses for the protection of his bridges. In these he had stored vast quantities of provisions, whereby he could subsist his army till any ordinary breakage in his line of communication could be restored. The withdrawal of Wheeler, therefore, while it would not be of any serious consequence to Sherman's supplies, was on the whole an advantage. Without any effective opposition, he now sent his own cavalry to operate on the roads in Hood's rear, while he followed with the rest of the army to complete the work of destruction, compel his adversary to abandon the city.

Battle of Jonesboro.—Sending the sick, wounded and surplus stores to his entrenched position on the Chatahoochie, and leaving Slocum with the 20th corps to guard them, the advance of the remainder of the army was continued in a southwesterly direction. Before Hood was apprised of the movement, the West Point road was destroyed and the army approached Jonesboro to tear up the Macon road. For the want of cavalry Hood had sent one-half of his army under Hardee to the same place to guard his communications, and on the morning of August 31st, each army learning the position of the other, prepared for battle. Howard was on the right, Schofield in the centre and Thomas on the left, or nearest Atlanta. Hood attacked the former with great vigor hoping to overwhelm him before the others could come to his assistance. Our men, expecting an assault, had hurriedly thrown up breastworks, and, with compartively slight losses, frightfully slaughtered the charging columns. After two hours of carnage the assailants retired, having lost in the attack 2,500 men, of whom 400 were killed. Sherman, hearing the din of battle on his right, pushed forward Thomas and Schofield in the direction of the conflict. At 4 o'clock Davis' corps came up and at once charging on the enemy's position, captured 8 guns and inflicted on him a loss of 5,000 men. Almost one entire brigade was captured.

The Illinois regiments in the battle were the 38th, 42d, 44th, 48th, 51st, 52d, 55th, 60th, 65th, 79th, 80th, 84th, 86th, 88th, 89th, 92d, 104th and 111th. Side by side with their equally brave comrades of other States they fought for the Union which, instead of being disrupted by treason, is destined to expand by the accession of new States till one language, the same institutions and a common government extend over the whole continent.

The succeeding night ominous sounds were heard in the direction of Atlanta, 20 miles distant, which proved to be the rebel magazines which Hood was blowing up preparatory to leaving the city. After destroying a large amount of other property by the light of 1,000 bales of cotton to which he had applied the torch, he led the bleeding remnant of his army from the scenes of his bloody and bootless assaults. He was pursued the next day a distance of 35 miles, when our army, greatly fatigued, returned and occupied the stronghold which they had so valorously won.

The effect produced on the despondent public mind by the campaign now closed, was almost magical. When the two great Union armies started southward in the early spring, it was believed by many the succeeding summer would witness the end of the rebellion.

But how often are the fondest anticipations dispelled by the stern logic of events. Midsummer came and Virginia, the great charnel house of the nation's defenders, was again dug over to make graves for the army which had crossed her borders. Before summer was ended more Union troops had perished than in all the previous campaigns of the war on the same ill-fated field.

As the months wore away hope was succeeded by sober reflection and finally by despair, when it beame known that Lee had destroyed a force equal to his own army, and was still defiant. In the midst of this gloom and national humiliation, Sherman's series of victories was crowned by the fall of Atlanta, and the shout which rose from the sturdy sons of the West was taken up and prolonged by pealing bells, booming cannon and the loud responses of millions throughout the North. A joy as hopeful as the preceding despair had been gloomy, succeeded, and never, after the autumn of 1864, was a reasonable doubt entertained that the republic would not only live, but maintain intact the integrity of her wide domain.

But the material advantages must not be overlooked. Atlanta was one of the principal manufacturing cities of the South, from whose rolling mills, foundries and other labratories, had proceeded large supplies of munitions for the rebel armies. It was the centre of the great railway system, commencing in the eastern and western portions of the confederacy, and the heart of the rich grain-growing region of Georgia which had contributed large quantities of serials for the sustenance of Lee's army. All these sources of supply, after the capture of the city, became tributary to Sherman's army. A rebel newspaper, in expatiating upon the consequences, declared that the fall of Richmond in a material point of view could not have been half so disastrous.

NASHVILLE CAMPAIGN.—As the result of Sherman's inroad into Georgia and the downfall of Atlanta, the southwest suddenly became the principle focus of confederate alarm. As soon as its significance become fully known, the Richmond president hurriedly made his appearance at the scene of danger and found the defiles of the Alleghanies, which he had claimed would furnish citadels for a century's warfare, pierced in a single campaign, and the stalwart invader ready, by another advance, to bisect the remainder of his domain. By frantic appeals to the desponding Georgians he succeeded in reinforcing Hood, but still being unable to cope with the federal army in open field, he proposed to draw it out of Georgia by operating on its long line of communications. With this intent he left his camp at Palmetto, and re-crossing the Chatahoochie on the 5th of October, 1864, made an assault on Allatoona for the purpose of breaking the railroad and capturing Sherman's supplies. The latter, sending Thomas to guard against demonstrations north of the Tennessee, and leaving Slocum in possession of Atlanta, started after Hood, and came up in time to save his supplies.

A fierce battle had been raging, in which the little garrison lost 700 men or near a third of its entire number. From the Spartan valor with which the 39th Iowa and the 7th and 93d Illinois met the enemy, Gen. Corse, their commander, was styled the Leonidas and Allatoona pass the Thermopylæ of the campaign.

Hood next appeared before Resaca, but remembering his bloody reception at Allatoona, he was content after disabling the railroad to leave without molesting the town. Sherman, endeavoring to bring on a general engagement, followed him as far as Gaylesville on the Coosa, when it became evident that the object of the retreat was to transfer the war from Georgia to Tennessee, and the pursuit was abandoned.

The national commander, accepting the issue, ordered the 4th and 23d corps, under Stanley and Schofield, and all the cavalry, except one division, under Kilpatrick, to report to Thomas at Nashville, who was now entrusted with the department of the Tennessee, with discretionary powers as to the use of all its available military resources. Not, however, intending by this disposition of his forces to be deprived of the fruits of his victories in the previous campaigns, he lead the remainder of his command back to Atlanta preparatory to making his grand march to the sea.

Hood approached the Tennessee at Decatur and made an attack on it as a *feint* to cover his crossing at Florence, farther westward. Schofield and Stanley were ordered to keep the field and check his advance as much as possible till Thomas could concentrate his forces, scattered at widely separated points of his department. November 24th they encountered Hood at Columbia, and while Schofield remained to prevent his crossing Duck river, Stanley followed our heavy trains to Spring Hill, whither he arrived just in time to save'them from capture by the rebel cavalry. The enemy, in the meantime, effected a passage of the river 6 miles above the town, and when night fell, Schofield started after Stanley and found the rebels encamped in force at Spring Hill, only half mile from his line of retreat. More anxious to place Harpeth river between them and our long trains than to interfere with their nocturnal repose, he pushed on with all possible dispatch.

Battle of Franklin.—Marching and fighting the next day and night, November 30, he halted on the south side of Franklin for his trains to cross the Harpeth, and get fairly on their way to Nashville. The river on the north and east sides of the village forms a right angle, and slight breastworks thrown up on the south and west sides, formed a rude square, which inclosed and protected the most of the Union army. Works were also thrown up on Carter's Hill, a few hundred yards in advance of the position where it is crossed by the Franklin and Columbia pike. Hood in close pursuit, came up the same day at 4 o'clock, and with his accustomed impetuosity, commenced an attack. Expecting to crush our little army by sheer weight of numbers, he shouted to his men: "Break these, and there is nothing to withstand you on this side of the Ohio river." So overwhelming was the onset that Wagoner's division, occupying Carter's Hill, was swept back through our general line, and 8 of his guns captured without materially checking its progress. The exultant victors rapidly formed on the inside of the Union works to follow up the advantages of their triumph, when Opdyke's brigade, of Wood's division, suddenly moved against them, their bayonets flashing back the rays of the setting sun as they were brought down for a charge. A struggle, fierce and bloody, followed, terminating in the expulsion of the enemy from their entrenchments, the recovery of all our guns, the capture of 10 battle-flags and 300 prisoners. Hood, more exasperated than disconcerted by his reverse, moved round to the right of our line, and made a number of bloody assaults to again break it, but without success. At 10 o'clock the battle ceased. Hood having sustained a loss of 702 prisoners, 3,800 wounded, among whom were 7 generals, and 1,750 privates, and 6 generals killed. The Union loss was officially reported at 189 killed and 1,014 wounded, the latter including Gen. Stanley, who was temporarily superseded by T. J. Wood.

The severe blow inflicted on the enemy at Franklin, assured his defeat at Nashville. To none, more than the troops of Illinois, are we indebted for this desirable result. The 44th, 73d, 74th and 88th constituted a part of Opdyke's brigade, which was accorded the honor of saving the battle. Gen. Wood, to whose division it belonged, accompanied by Gen. Thomas, sought out the colonel of the 88th and thus addressed him : "Col. Smith I desire to report to you, in the presence of Gen. Thomas, that which Gen. Stanley said to me respecting you and the troops you command: that with the exception of Col. Opdyke, commanding the brigade with whom you share the honor, to your special gallantry and exertions, more than any other man, is owing the repulse of the rebel columns and the safety of the army." The 51st lost 149 men, and the 72d 9 officers and 152 men. The 72d, having lost its colors, subsequently retook them and captured 2 flags belonging to the rebels. The other Illinois regiments in the engagement were the 38th, 42d, 49th, 59th, 65th, 84th, 89th and 112th.

Battle of Nashville.—Schofield, having saved his valuable trains and dealt the enemy a fatal blow, drew out of his defenses about midnight, and by noon the next day was safe in the sheltering fortifications of Nashville. Hitherto Hood, with a force of some 40,000 infantry and 12,000 cavalry, had only to contend with 20,000 Unionists, but when he arrived at Nashville the respective strength of the two armies was reversed. The original garrison of the city had been reinforced by a portion of the 16th corps under A. J. Smith, Steedman's division from Chattanooga, and now by the accession of Schofield's army, so that when he effected to lay the place under siege, it was evident that Thomas considerably outnumbered him in the way of infantry. The latter was, however, greatly inferior in cavalry, and, on this account, deferred an engagement till additional forces could be procured and he should be able to follow up his advantages when he put his adversary to flight. The Secretary of War was immediately apprised of the fact, and Gen. Wilson, chief of cavalry, was ordered to impress all the serviceable horses he could find in Tennessee and Kentucky, to supply the defficiency. Grant, becoming nervous over the delay and the displays of rebel audacity in the heart of Tennessee, left his camp near Richmond and started westward to superintend in person the movements of the national troops. On reaching Washington and hearing the Nashville reports, he was satisfied that his Tennessee lieutenant was fully equal to the emergency of his situation, and, like Sherman of Georgia, did not require any supervision.

The employes of the commissary, quartermaster and railroad departments were immediately set to work on the fortifications, and soon two lines of defense, furnished with forts, redoubts and rifle pits, encircled the southern side of the city. On the north side the Cumberland was patrolled by a fleet of gun-boats, which served as a defense to the city, and to prevent Hood from throwing cavalry across the river to operate on the national line of communication. Hood occupied a range of hills some four or five miles from the city, and evidently wished to completely invest it, but the fleet prevented the consummation of his design. By the 14th of December, the day preceding the battle, Thomas' forces were collected and placed in position, Steedman holding the extreme left, Wood, in command of Stanley's corps, the left centre, Smith, with the 16th corps, the right centre, and Wilson's cavalry the right, while Schofield, with the 23d corps, was held as a reserve.

The plan of battle ordered for the next day, December 15th, was to make a feint on the enemy's right, and then, falling with an overwhelming force on the left, force it back on the centre. The morning broke auspiciously, and Steedman pushed forward a heavy force of skirmishers, who drove back the enemy's pickets till the movement was checked by a deep railroad excavation defended by batteries. Hood at an early hour was aroused by firing on his right but before he could ascertain the cause, Wood and Smith struck his left, which now became the focus of solicitude. Crumbling to pieces under the heavy concussion it was soon hurled back in confusion on the centre. Wilson's cavalry, meanwhile hanging like a thunder cloud on their flank and rear, captured two batteries and, dismounting, turned them on their late owners. The centre and principal salient of the rebel army rested on Montgomery Hill, to which his hurrying squadrons of infantry and artillery were now sweeping to reverse the unpropitious tide of battle. At 10 o'clock Wood moved against this strong position and carried it, Col. Post, of the 59th Illinois, leading the charge. Efforts in other parts of the field were attended with similar success, and Hood was compelled to abandon his entire line of defense and seek a new position at the foot of Harpeth Hills, two miles in the rear of the first.

The national troops fought with great alacrity and success, and their day's labor was rewarded with the capture of several battle flags, a large number of small arms, 16 pieces of artillery, and 1,200 prisoners. The disposition of the Union troops for the next day's battle remained the same as on the first, with the exception of Schofield's army, which, during the day, had moved into position between Wood's corps and Wilson's cavalry. Hood, contracting his line from six to three lines in length, took a strong position on Overton's Hill, where he awaited the coming battle.

At an early hour the next day Wilson was ordered on a reconnoisance round the enemy's position, and if practicable, to cut off his line of retreat in the direction of Franklin. Hood was superior to Thomas in the strength of his cavalry, but he had made the mistake of sending a portion of his force down the Cumberland after our transports, and suffered a portion to dash itself to pieces against the impregnable defenses of Murfreesboro, which left Wilson almost without opposition. While the cavalry was executing this movement, the entire front of the Union army advanced to within 600 yards of the enemy's line, and Wood and Steedman made an assault on Overton's Hill, Post, as on the day before leading the charge. The enemy, anticipating an attack, had covered the slopes of the hill with abattis, and, opening with grape, canister and musketry, repulsed the assailants with heavy loss.

Meanwhile Smith and Schofield, farther to the right, with leveled bayonets had marched straight over the works in their front, and in one fell swoop completely turned the enemy's flank. Hearing the victorious shouts, Wood and Steedman immediately reformed their broken line and a second time moved against the key of the rebel position. Scaling the hill and charging over the abattis directly in the face of a terrible fire, they captured the fort and its 9 pieces of artillery, which had so fearfully slaughtered their comrades in the first assault. The charge was final; the discomfitted rebels hurriedly fled through Brentwood Pass leading to Harpeth river, and the day being spent the Union army rested on the field it had so nobly won.

Wilson's cavalry started in pursuit early the next day, and four miles north of Franklin captured 413 of the rear guard. Again attacking them at the village, they were forced to decamp, leaving 1,800 of their wounded in the hands of the pursuers. The fugitive army was followed till it crossed the Tennessee, but, as it burned the bridges after it, and heavy rains rendered the roads almost impassable, it was not again overtaken.

Among the batteries which achieved distinction at the battle of Nashville, none thundered louder or sent its bolts with more deadly effect, than that of Lyman Bridges. During the engagement it was commanded by Lieut. White, Capt. Bridges having become chief of artillery. The 72d Illinois had a number of severe encounters with the enemy, and in a high degree exhibited the soldierly qualities for which it had been previously distinguished. The 47th, 48th, 114th and 122d were in A. J. Smith's command, which on the morning of the 15th, made the magnificent charge on the enemy's left, crumbling it to pieces and hurling it back on the centre. The 59th Illinois lead the storming columns against the rebel works on Montgomery Hill, and was the first to plant its colors within the entrenchments. The next day it was in the famous assault on Overton's Hill, in which it lost one-third of its number. The 80th captured 3 guns and 100 prisoners; the 122d 4 pieces of artillery and one battle flag. The other Illinois regiments in the battle were the 38th, 42d, 44th, 49th, 51st, 65th, 73d, 79th, 84th, 88th, 89th, 107th, 112th, 114th, 115th, 117th and 119th.

To the confederacy the results of the Nashville campaign were overwhelming. Thomas, in auditing his accounts after its brilliant actions, found he had captured 1,000 officers, over 12,000 men, while more than 2,000 threw down their arms and took the oath of allegiance. Among the spoils were 3,000 small arms, 72 heavy pieces of artillery and immense quantities of military stores.

54

But the crowning stroke was the destruction of the confederate army of the West. With the elimination of the invaders from Tennessee, it only remained for the Union army to resolve itself into separate columns and proceed to other fields. Sherman, with his veterans of a hundred battle fields, was now enabled to reach the Atlantic almost without opposition. Schofield, with a heavy body of infantry, proceeded to the coast of North Carolina to co-operate with him and converge on Richmond; and Canby, with another large force, advanced by way of the Mississippi to Mobile for the reduction of the adjacent forts, while Wilson, without a foe to confront in the West, dashed in a raid through Alabama and Georgia. The days of the rebellion were numbered and the silver tracery of the dawn of peace began to light up the cloud of war.

CHAPTER LXIV.

1864—1865—ILLINOIS IN THE MERIDIAN CAMPAIGN—RED RIVER EXPEDITION—REDUCTION OF MOBILE—SHERMAN'S MARCH TO THE SEA—REDUCTION OF WILMINGTON—MARCH THROUGH THE CAROLINAS—CLOSE OF THE WAR.

———

Consequent upon the reduction of Vicksburg and the opening of the Mississippi some military movements occurred in the Southwest, in which our troops were honorably engaged.

Meridian Campaign.—After Sherman marched to the relief of Knoxville, he returned to Vicksburg and organized a force to operate against Bishop Gen. Polk, in command of an army at Meridian, also to destroy the Southern Mississippi and the Ohio and Mobile railroads. For this purpose Gen. W. S. Smith, with a large cavalry force was ordered to proceed from Memphis on the 1st of February, 1864, while Sherman, with 2 divisions of the 16th army corps under Hurlbut, and 2 of the 17th under McPherson, left Vicksburg on the 4th. Meeting with little opposition they entered Morton on the 9th, where McPherson was halted to tear up the surrounding railroads. Hurlbut moved on to Meridian, but Polk, apprised of his approach, decamped, covering his retreat with a cavalry force under Lee.

Smith failing to arrive with his cavalry, pursuit was deemed useless. Having no enemy to fight, a warfare was commenced on the railroads entering the town—Hurlbut on the north and east destroying 60 miles of track, one locomotive and eight bridges, and McPherson on the south and west, 55 miles, 53 bridges, 19 locomotives and 28 cars. The Tombigbee being now between the army and Polk, and no other foe in striking distance, Sherman headed his columns toward the Mississippi, whither he arrived without further noticeable incidents.

His losses in the campaign were 21 killed, 68 wounded and 81 missing. The Illinois organizations in the expedition were the 8th, 15th, 30th, 31st, 49th, 58th, 76th, 112th, 117th, 119th, 124th the 5th cavalry and Powell's battery. Its leader, as we have seen, next repaired to Chattanooga preparatory to entering upon his Georgia campaign.

Red River Expedition.—During the spring of 1864 an expedition was projected to drive Price from Arkansas, Taylor from Louisiana, and Magruder from Texas. This was to be effected by the joint efforts of three columns, one moving under Steele, from Little Rock, another under Banks from Brownsville, and a third under A. J. Smith, from Vicksburg, concentrating at Shreveport. On the 12th of March, 1864, Admiral Porter, with the fleet, and A. J. Smith with the 1st and 3d divisions of the 16th army corps, and the 1st and 4th of the 17th, in transports, started up Red River, on which the objective point is situated. At Semmesport Smith debarked his forces and started to operate against Fort De Russy, a strong quadrangular work furnished with bastions and covered with railroad iron. The assailants moving up on the 14th, Dick Taylor, in command of the fort, marched out to meet them, when Smith, by a skillful movement, threw himself between the rebels and the fort, which, after a sharp fight, he forced to surrender, the 47th, 49th, 58th, 81st, 95th, 117th and 119th Illinois demeaning themselves with great gallantry in the engagement, the 58th being the first to plant its colors on the works.

As the expedition again moved toward Shreveport, the force under Banks, en route for the same point, encountered a rebel force at Pleasant Hill, and Smith, advised of the situation, marched to his assistance. Gen. Robinson, commanding the advance Union cavalry, had engaged that of the enemy under General Green, after which the latter fell back to Saline Cross Roads where the main force under Taylor lay masked in the forest. Thither he was followed on the 8th of April by the Union cavalry, now reinforced by two divisions of the 13th army corps under Gen. Ransom. The latter suspecting danger, proposed to await the arrival of the force under Smith, before renewing the attack. Banks, however, overruling his advice, ordered an assault. Taylor's men concealed in the woods were posted in the form of the letter V, into the open base of which our men unwittingly advanced. The 2 wings of the enemy were immediately thrust forward and like huge tentacula closed in on them and before they could escape lost 2,000 men and 16 guns, 6 of which belonged to Taylor's Illinois battery.

Battle of Pleasant Hill.—The remainder of the forces returned to Pleasant Hill, whither had arrived Gen. Franklin with the 19th corps and the force under Smith. The troops of the latter were placed in position behind a low ridge on the right the 19th corps on the left. Ransom's men in the rear as a reserve, and 4 guns of Taylor's battery on an eminence commanding the approaches of the enemy. On the 9th he advanced and made an assault on Emery's division thrown in advance of Smith, which, according to previous arrangement, fell back. This brought the assailants directly up to the crest of the ridge behind which were concealed the Vicksburg veterans of Smith, who, to the number of 7,000, immediately rose up, and, pouring an incessant blaze of musketry fire into their faces, caused them to stagger back, when a bayonet charge was ordered which swept them from the field.

The 49th, 58th, 77th, 117th and 119th Illinois bore themselves honorably in the contest and largely contributed to the result.

The Union losses in the two battles aggregated the enormous number of 3,000 men, 21 pieces of artillery, 130 wagons, and 1,200 horses and mules. Steele, in playing his part of the programme, was equally unfortunate, and with heavy losses and great difficulty, fought his way back to Little Rock, whence he had started. Thus endes in irretrievable disaster, the ill-starred expedition, which, in its return, came near being entirely cut off in consequence of a low stage of water in the river.

Brigadier-General T. E. G. Ransom, who at Sabins' Cross Roads warned his superior officer of danger, and made such heroic efforts to repair the disasters caused by his mistake, was born at Norwich, Vermont, November 29, 1834. Having completed his education in the university of his native town, in 1851 he removed to Peru, Illinois, and engaged in the practice of engineering. At the organization of the 11th Illinois, in April, 1861, he was elected a major. For his bravery and skill in the battle of Donelson, he was promoted to the colonelcy of his regiment; again, as the reward of distinguished service at Shiloh and Corinth, he was raised to the rank of major-general. After the battle of Pleasant Hill, in which he commanded a division and received a wound from which he never recovered, he temporarily took charge of the 17th army corps in Georgia. While gathering new laurels in the Atlanta campaign, he died of a disease contracted by previous exposure. He was retiring, modest, and unusually brave. Devotedly attached to his men, while an invalid he was frequently advised by his physician to quit the field, but replied, "*I will stay with my command till I am carried away in my coffin.*"

Reduction of Mobile.—After the disastrous Red River expedition, the department of the Arkansas and Gulf, including Texas, and Louisiana, were united in one, styled the West Mississippi, and Major-Gen. Canby placed in command. In the spring of 1864, all the rebel posts had either been successfully blockaded, or captured, except Wilmington and Mobile. To Canby was now assigned the task of reducing the latter, while the former, as we shall see further on, fell beneath the sturdy blows of the conquerors of Nashville.

The entrance to Mobile bay is by two inlets, one on each side of Dauphin Island. They were guarded by Forts Gaines on the island, and Morgan and Powell on the mainland opposite. Hither Farragut led his fleet of some 18 vessels, and as a co-operating land force, Canby in July, ordered 5,000 men under Granger, from New Orleans. The latter were debarked on Dauphin Island, on the 4th of August, to operate against the adjacent fort, and the following morning the fleet moved up the principal channel, its gallant commander lashed in the maintop of the Hartford to overlook the field of action. Seeing his vessels arrested by torpedoes, he dashed ahead under the tremendous volleys of the enemy's guns, and in an hour and a quarter was above the forts. The others, animated by his fearless heroism, followed, emptying broadsides after broadsides into the hostile works, and partially checking their fire. Next commenced the capture of the great iron-clad ram Tennessee, which Farragut declares was one of the "fiercest naval engagements on record." During the month the 3 forts surrendered, and the door was opened for a farther advance toward Mobile.

This was not effected till the following spring. In the meantime the 13th corps, under Granger, was reinforced by A. J. Smith with the 16th, arriving mostly by way of New Orleans, and a force in command of Steel from Pensacola. The army marched up on the east side of the bay in the direction of Forts Spanish and Blakely, which it was necessary to reduce before the fleet could reach the city. The first being more accessible, an investing force containing the 8th, 11th, 28th, 29th, 33d, 47th, 72d, 77th, 81st, 91st, 95th, 99th, 108th, 117th, 119th and 124th Illinois, was pushed up, the artillery, a part of which was Coggswell's battery, placed in position, and on the 4th of April a tremendous bombardment opened on the fort. On the 8th the assault was renewed, and after a furious cannonade, at 3 o'clock, 2 brigades of Carr's division, containing the 72d, 81st and 124th Illinois, moved forward in an impetuous charge, and mounting the ramparts, carried 300 yards of the works. The advance position was held till the next day, when the garrison finding that further opposition was useless, capitulated.

The same day Gen. Steel made a successful assault on Fort Blakely. Amidst a furious battle storm, shells exploding overhead, and torpedoes underfoot, Garrard's division made its way up in front, and Rinnaker's and Gilbert's brigades on the right, and simultaneously leaping the parapets, the stronghold was won. The 8th Illinois was the first to enter and hoist its colors over the works; the 58th and 117th are also honorably mentioned in connection with the charge. The other Illinois organizations in the engagement were the 11th, 29th, 33d, 72d, 76th, 77th, 81st, 91st, 99th, 119th, 122d infantry, and Coggswell's battery. Our loss in the assault was 1,000 men, while the fruits of the victory were more than 3,000 prisoners, 4,000 stand of arms, and 32 pieces of artillery.

Mobile was now uncovered and the national columns put in motion to effect its capture. On the 12th, however, news was received of its evacuation, and the army entered without opposition. Its approaches had been carried with unparalleled gallantry, caused by the exciting intelligence of the fall of Richmond and other great events, marking the close of the war. The beginning of the end was at hand.

Brigadier-General Eugene A. Carr, who so brilliantly closed his rebellion record in the assault on Fort Blakely, was born in Erie county, New York, March 30th, 1830. In 1848 he removed with his father to Galesburg, Illinois, which, up to the time of the rebellion, was his recognized home. At the age of 16 he entered the Military Academy of West Point. After his graduation he was commissioned 2d lieutenant of mounted riflemen, and for several years was engaged in suppressing Indian hostilities on the western plains. Subsequently he was assigned as aid to Gov. Walker in the border ruffian war of Kansas. As a captain in the regular army, he took an active part in the battles of Springfield and Wilson's Creek, Missouri. Next we find him at the head of the 3d Illinois cavalry and a division commander under Curtis. In the latter position he served with such distinguished success that on March 7th, 1862, he received the commission of brigadier general of volunteers.

March to the Sea.—Sherman, after sending a portion of his forces to co-operate with Thomas in Tennessee, still retained under his immediate command some 60,000 infantry and artillery, and 5,000 cavalry. These forces were organized in two great wings, the right under Howard, comprising the 15th corps, Gen. Osterhaus, and the 17th, Gen. Blair; and the left under Slocum, comprising the 14th corps, Gen. Davis, and the 20th, Gen. Williams. The cavalry was led by Gen. Kilpatrick, a daring trooper, who had already won distinction by his fearless encounters with the enemy. For the results of the campaign, so valuable to the cause of the Union and so fatal to that of the rebellion, the nation is largely indebted to Illinois organizations: the 7th, 9th, 10th, 12th, 14th, 15th, 16th, 20th, 26th, 30th, 31st, 32d; 34th, 40th, 41st, 45th, 48th, 50th, 52d, 53d, 55th, 56th, 57th, 60th, 63d, 64th, 66th, 78th, 82d, 85th, 86th, 90th, 92d, 93d, 101st, 102d, 103d, 104th, 105th, 110th, 111th, 116th, 125th, 127th, 129th regiments of infantry, companies C and H 1st, and company I, 2d artillery and 11th cavalry. As his troops would have to subsist on the country through which they marched, Sherman issued stringent regulations to prevent, as far as possible, the excesses incident to this method of obtaining supplies. Brigade commanders were ordered to organize foraging parties, under one or more discreet officers, to collect provisions, aiming always to keep on hand 10 days supply for the men and 3 days for the horses. Soldiers were not to enter the houses of the inhabitants, and were to leave with each family a reasonable amount of food for its maintenance. The cavalry and artillery were authorized to press horses and wagons when needed, discriminating between the rich and the poor. Corps commanders were empowered to accept the services of able-bodied negroes, and to burn mills, bridges, cotton gins, &c., whenever local hostilities were manifested; but no such devastations were to be suffered if the inhabitants remained quiet.

Could these humane regulations have been properly enforced, many unpleasant occurrences connected with the expedition would have been avoided. Says an officer who commanded in it: "In all cases where the foraging parties were under the direction of discreet officers, no improprieties were committed, and only necessary supplies were taken." Following, and preceding them, however, were swarms of strangers and vagabonds, such as always hover about large armies, to indulge their propensities for violence and plunder. These, with impunity, frequently entered the houses of the planters and relieved them of their silks, jewelry and other articles of value, and to climax their depredations, burnt the houses of their victims and committed acts of violence upon their persons.

Before Sherman put his columns in motion, Rome was set on fire and its foundries, machine shops, hotels and stores were burnt, and everything that could be of value to the army was taken. A few days afterwards the torch was also applied to Atlanta and all its public buildings, theatres and costly mansions were consumed in a common conflagration. The few remaining inhabitants alarmed at the devouring flames, rushed through the streets and fled from the perishing city. The railroads in the rear were destroyed, and about the middle of November the famous march was commenced.

Howard with the right wing moved along the Georgia Central Railroad, and Slocum with the left along the parallel road leading to Augusta. The latter tore up the track as he advanced, reached Madison without opposition, and while the soldiers were engaged in destroying its depot, a band of stragglers becoming drunk on the contents of wine cellers, sacked the stores and shops of the citizens. The ravages were continued till the main body of the army came up, when it was quickly brought to a close and guards stationed to protect what remained of the town. From Madison Slocum moved directly on Milledgeville, and the legislature then in session, hurriedly fled, carrying with them the funds, archives and other valuables belonging to the State. The rebels at first supposed that Sherman was only on a raiding expedition, but now they were compelled to admit that a powerful invading army was moving directly through the heart of Georgia, and unless it could be met the most disastrous circumstances must follow.

Howard, in the meanwhile, had advanced and destroyed the railroad after him till within a few miles of Macon, where there was a large force protected by breastworks well mounted with cannon. The rebels supposed of course the city would be laid under siege, but Sherman not attaching as much importance to it as its defendants, concluded to pass it by with but slight recognition. Wishing, however, to cross without opposition the Ocmulgee, which runs by the place, Kilpatrick was sent to make demonstrations against it and thus conceal the real movement intended. The latter charged up to the breastworks of the town, and while the alarmed garrison was preparing for defense, Howard quietly slipped across the stream at Griswoldville below the city. Leaving here a portion of the 15th corps to cover his rear, he pushed on in the direction of Milledgeville, whither he arrived the day after its occupation by Slocum.

The Macon rebels, exasperated at finding themselves outwitted, made a furious assault on the force left at Griswoldville, but were repulsed with the loss of 1,000 men.

The army having now consumed a week, and marched a distance of 95 miles, was again united in the capital of Georgia. At Millen, located on the Central railroad, some 80 miles south, was a great prison pen where thousands of our captured soldiers had suffered unspeakable privations, and Sherman's next object was to liberate them. With this design in view Kilpatrick was directed to move in the direction of Augusta, to create the impression that that place, rather than Savannah, was the objective point of the expedition. Wheeler, with the rebel cavalry, was encountered on the way, and, after some severe skirmishing with him, Kilpatrick learned that the enemy had removed the prisoners from Millen, and, deeming it useless to persist in the hazardous march after the motive which prompted it had ceased, commenced falling back. Closely pursued he retreated and fortified a strong position, and when Wheeler came up, although he fought with the greatest determination, he was repulsed at all points without difficulty.

After the attack Kilpatrick joined the left wing and moved on its flank. Though the prisoners had not been liberated, the cavalry demonstrations served to keep the enemy in doubt as to the real destination of the expedition, and consequently unable to concentrate his forces at any salient point. Sherman meanwhile with the other wing, leaving Macon far in his rear was advancing on Millen, whither he arrived on the 2d of December.

The railroad and other public property behind him was completely destroyed, while the country traversed abounding in the

necessaries of life, was despoiled of large quantities of provisions.
His men had fared sumptuously on chickens and turkeys and a
profusion of other luxuries, besides collecting large quantities for
future consumption. This was a necessary precaution, for the army
was now about to enter a long strip of country covered with pine
forests comparatively destitute of food. Millen being the seat of
the above mentioned bastiles where large numbers of Union prisoners had sickened, starved and died, it required great efforts to
keep our indignant men from laying it in ashes. The prison was
a stockade inclosing 15 acres, and hard by was the burying ground
containing 650 graves as the result of one month's mortality.

From Millen Sherman next swept down on each side of the
Ogeechee in the direction of Savannah, Kilpatrick careering in
front and making the green arches of the pine forests echo with
the tramp of his squadrons and the shrill notes of his bugles. On
the 9th of November, Howard struck the canal connecting the
Ogeechee and Savannah, 10 miles in the rear and west of the city.
The thunder of signal guns could now be heard booming over the
swamps from the fleet, awaiting Sherman's advent upon the coast.
Col. Duncan was sent down the Ogeechee, and three days afterward, stepping on board of one of Dahlgren's vessels, once more
put the army in communication with the outer world. The next
day Sherman advanced to within 5 miles of Savannah, and laid the
city under siege, the 26th, 30th, 32d, 48th, 53d, 64th, 93d, and
102d Illinois constituting a part of the investing force. Having,
however, only brought field pieces in the long marches through
Georgia, it was necessary to get siege guns from the fleet before
he could make a successful assault. These could only be brought
up the Ogeechee, hence Fort McAlister, commanding the mouth,
must first be reduced.

The enemy, in guarding against the fleet, which had previously assailed it, failed to strengthen its landward defenses, and Sherman
ordered a bold attack on this point, hoping its vulnerable character might facilitate its capture. Hazen with his well tried division
and a detachment of the 17th corps, consisting in part of the 26th,
48th, 90th, 111th and 116th Illinois, was selected for this purpose,
but having to throw a long bridge over the Ogeechee in the place
of one previously burnt by the rebels, it was not till the afternoon
of the 13th of December that the fort was reached, and preparations completed for the assault. The fortress stood on the right
bank of the river and could only be reached over a level plain
three-fourths of a mile wide swept by heavy cannon. These opened
upon the charging columns as soon as they commenced moving
up, but produced little damage as the advance was made in a
single line. The plain, however, was sown with torpedoes, which,
exploding, threw up piles of dust on the men and sent many of
them mangled and lifeless into the air. Pushing on regardless of
danger they tore open an abatis, forced a passage over a ditch
thickly studded with pikes, and, with a bound, made for the parapets. Rushing in, on every side for an instant was heard the clash
of steel and the whistling of bullets, mingled with the shouts of
the combatants, and victory was complete.

Sherman, who had witnessed the charge from the top of a rice
mill across the Ogeechee, when he saw the national colors run up,
called for a boat, and being rowed over, warmly congratulated

Hazen and his brave troops for having captured the key to Savannah. Communication was opened with the fleet, and Sherman visited Admiral Dahlgren and made arrangements with him to send some heavy siege pieces from Hilton Head for the reduction of Savannah. The guns arrived on the 17th and Slocum was ordered to place them in position. At the same time Sherman started to secure the co-operation of General Foster, commanding the department of the South, in intercepting the rebels, should they attempt to make an exit in the direction of Charleston. Encountering high adverse winds he did not proceed far before he was overtaken by a steam vessel and informed that Hardee, in command of the garrison, had already accomplished that which he was endeavoring to prevent. The movement at the time was unsuspected, and when discovered the fugitives were beyond the reach of pursuit. Before leaving they destroyed the navy yard, two iron clads and a large number of smaller vessels, besides great quantities of military stores and provisions. Gen. Geary pushed up to the city next day and received its surrender from the mayor, and Sherman, returning, sent the following dispatch to the president: "I beg to present you as a Christmas gift the city of Savannah with 150 heavy guns and plenty of ammunition, and also about 25,000 bales of cotton."

Thus auspiciously ended the campaign which the European press had predicted would meet with total failure, and which many of our own journals spoke of as one of doubtful issue. Much of its success was due to the skill with which Sherman had deceived the rebels respecting his objective point whereby the large forces stationed at Macon, Augusta and Savannah, which might have been concentrated to oppose his advance, were rendered ineffective.

Its results may be summed up as follows: The army in the brief space of 24 days had destroyed 320 miles of railroad substantially made, a conquest of Georgia and again divided the confederacy. With an inconsiderable loss of men, 1328 of the enemy had been made prisoners, there had been captured 167 guns, 25,000 bales of cotton, and foraged from the country 1,300 beeves, 16,000 bushels of corn and 5,000 tons of fodder. This abundance had been gathered in the region where the Union prisoners of Andersonville had been starved to death, or idiocy, under the pretext that their captors were unable to furnish them with the necessaries of life. Some 4,000 mules and 5,000 horses had been impressed into the service, while 10,000 negroes, abjuring the servitude of their masters, followed the national flag, and thousands more would have been added to the number had not some of the officers driven them back. Sherman partially atoned for this cruelty by assigning lands on the sea islands, deserted by the rebel owners, to those who were so fortunate as to reach the coast.

Sherman remained in Savannah over a month, resting his army and preparing for more arduous labors. Correspondence had been interchanged between him and Grant, respecting his future movements, and the South looked with alarm at his anticipated departure from the city. Some thought he would strike at Charleston, others Augusta, but a greater object was to be accomplished than either. As arranged by Grant, he was to lead his gallant army through the heart of the Carolinas, and after destroying the railroads and seizing their capitals, he was to co-operate with the forces operating against Richmond. One rebel army watched him at Augusta, and another at Charleston, thus affording him an opportunity to pursue his favorite strategy of threatening both places and preventing the concentrating of a force against his real line of march. Howard, on the right, was ordered to Pocataligo, a station on the railroad leading to Charleston, to menace the city, and Slocum on the left and Kilpatrick with the cavalry to threaten Augusta. The former started on the 15th of January, 1865, the 17th corps going by water, and the 15th by land. At Pocataligo, a depot of supplies was established and demonstrations made in the direction of Charleston, causing the rebels to keep all their available forces ready for the defense of the city.

Incessant rains prevailed, and Southern South Carolina being a region of swamps, became saturated with water and the roads almost impassable. The streams, which lay in front of Sherman, unable to carry off the surplus water, the country for miles on each side of them was submerged. These difficulties proved far more formidable than those offered by the rebel army, although Gov. McGrath had impressed every white male citizen of the State, between the ages of 16 and 60, to augment its numbers.

The next point aimed at by Howard, was midway on the South Carolina Railroad. Before this could be reached it was necessary to cross the Salkahatchie, behind which, at River Bridge, was posted a rebel force and artillery, to dispute its passage. Mower's and G. A. Smith's divisions, however, affected a lodgment on the opposite side below the bridge, by wading for 3 miles through chilly waters, from 2 to 5 feet in depth. The rebels fled precipitantly beyond the Edisto, while the Union corps pushed rapidly for the railway at Midway, which it reached on the 7th and commenced tearing up the track.

The extraordinary freshet in the Savannah had detained Slocum in the city till the 2d of February, when the flood partially subsiding, he succeeded in crossing the stream. The demonstrations of Kilpatrick kept the force at Augusta shut up in its fortifications, apprehending an attack, while Slocum, encountering little opposition, moved rapidly forward, and also struck the South Carolina railroad farther westward, and assisted in its destruction. Sherman's army now lay between Augusta and Charleston, and the forces stationed at the two places hopelessly divided and unable to act in concert. Leaving the left wing still engaged in breaking up the railroad, the right started northward for the Edisto, where they found the bridge partially destroyed, and a force on the opposite side to prevent their crossing. Forces' division dropping down the river, landed a number of pontoons, and passing over, pounced upon the astonished rebels and put them to flight. The bridge was soon repaired, and the national troops on the south side of the river rapidly moved on Orangeburg, again waking up the enemy. After a slight brush with him, in which the 30th, 31st and 32d Illinois became engaged, they tore up the railroad.

Sweeping on through the heart of the rebellious State, Howard on the 16th drew up on the banks of the Saluda, in front of its capital. Almost simultaneously Slocum appeared on the same stream, having met with no opposition, except from Wilson's cavalry, which Kilpatrick alone was sufficient to keep at a prudent distance. The 15th, 30th, 31st, 32d, 48th and 63d Illinois, with other advanced forces, drove back the rebel cavalry and the river was crossed without opposition. The mayor, finding the city at the mercy of the Union guns, surrendered it. Sherman, before entering, issued an order for burning the public property, its schools, colleges, asylums and other buildings, which could not be made available in war, being exempted. The main body of the army passed west of the city, and the 15th corps marching through it, encamped on the Camden road beyond.

Col. Wade Hampton, commanding the rear guard of rebel cavalry, ordered all cotton belonging to the inhabitants to be collected and burned. Piles of the inflammable material were ignited in the heart of the city, and, swept by the wind, soon communicated fire to the adjacent buildings. At dark the flames got beyond the control of the brigade on duty in the city, and Wood's entire division was brought in to assist in subduing them. Still the devouring element raged uncontrolable, lighting up the midnight sky with the brightness of noonday, and filling it with myriads of brands, which drifting in eddying circles on the buildings, extended wider and wider the conflagration. At 4 o'clock in the morning the wind ceased and the fire was checked, but the princely abodes of many who had been prime movers in the rebellion, together with the old state-house, which 4 years before had rung with acclamations at the passage of the first secession ordinance, were now shapeless masses of glowing embers. Says Sherman: "I disclaim, on the part of my army, any agency in the fire, but on the contrary, claim that we saved what of Columbia remains unconsumed. And without hesitation, I charge Gen. Wade Hampton with having burned his own city of Columbia, not with malicious intent, or as the manifestation of a silly Roman stoicism, but from folly and the want of sense, in filling it with cotton and tinder. Our officers and men on duty worked well to extinguish the flames, but others, not on duty, including the officers long imprisoned there, rescued by us, may have assisted in spreading the fire after it had once begun, and may have indulged in unconcealed joy to see the ruin of the capital of South Carolina."

The fall of Columbia involved that of Charleston. Hardee, declining isolation and capture, evacuated the city. This he effected on the 18th of February, by the westerly line of the coast railroad, the only avenue of escape which the federal blockaders and invasion had left intact. Before his departure he fired the arsenal, commissary stores and cotton warehouse, the latter containing 4,000 bales, which perished in the flames From the burning cotton, fire was communicated to a large quantity of powder stored in the northwestern depot, causing an explosion which sent the building a whirling mass of ruins through the air, destroyed 200 lives, and shook the city to its foundations. Spreading thence, the flames were soon leaping and crackling among the adjoining buildings, and 4 squares were consumed before they could be extinguished. The city was formally surrendered to Gen. Gilmore and the national flag again hoisted over the ruins of its public buildings, where, for the first time in the history of the republic, it had been ruthlessly assailed by those who owed it allegiance.

Forts Sumter and Ripley and Castle Pinkney submitted gracefully to a similar embellishment, and the formidable armaments unharmed passed into our possession. Gen. Gilmore reported 450 pieces found in all the defences, many of them 8 and 10-inch columbiads, and 7-inch rifled cannon of foreign construction.

History furnishes few such reverses as that which in the brief space of 4 years had befallen the city. Here rebellion had been spawned for the purpose of rendering perpetual the servile condition of the black man, and now a regiment of the emancipated race, wearing the national uniform, was the first to march as conquerors through its scarred and blackened streets. Everywhere ruin had been wrought by the long and continuous bombardment of the fleet. Many of the once palatial buildings were now the blackened wrecks of conflagration, some yawning and tottering with seams caused by exploding shells, or pounded to a mass of rubbish and strewn in the adjacent streets. As if to make the desolation more complete, a large part of the city which had escaped the guns of the besiegers had been set on fire by its defenders and thus met a common doom.

There was a feeling prevalent in the army that South Carolina, the cradle of secession and rebellion, should be made to feel some of the evils which she had been so active in bringing on her sister States. Hence not only her cities, but her rural dwellings, rice mills, and pine forests and other property, were fired and served as a bon-fire to signalize the advance of the invading army. In Georgia little private property was destroyed; here little escaped. The devastation was forbidden, but could not be prevented where so many of the army, if not directly connected with it, evidently regarded it as justifiable retaliation.

Let no one imagine that he can see in the deplorable fate of South Carolina the special displeasure of an angered God. Let him rather regard her calamities as the inevitable penalty which always attends the infraction of moral and physical law; whether the wrong doer be an individual, State, or nation. Our forefathers wantonly disregarded the rights of the negro when they kidnapped him on the coast of Africa and introduced him a slave into the American colonies. Again they were guilty of a moral breach when they sought to make his degradation perpetual by tolerating slavery in the national constitution. From this abnormal element in our political and social fabric sprang sectional discord, treason, and civil war with its rapine, burnings and slaughters. The blood shed by the sword in the war was the penalty for that which had been drawn by the lash from the backs of the bondsmen; the desolation caused by the destruction of cities, was the price paid for the wealth which had been piled up by long years of unrequited toil; and the wail which went up from homes all over the land had its precurser in the cry wrung from the families of the oppressed when ruthlessly torn asunder by the dealers in human souls. Crime and punishment are cause and effect and cannot be separated. No one can trample on the just and inevitable laws of God without suffering, and if the transgression is continued he must of necessity perish, not by a special bolt from heaven, but as the unavoidable consequence of his own crime.

Sherman, leaving at Columbia provisions to sustain for some time its destitute and houseless population, resumed his march, moving in the direction of Charlotte. Hither had preceded him under Beauregard the garrison of the devastated capital, and hither Cheatham had lead the dilapidated divisions of Hood's old army which had survived the blows inflicted on it in Tennessee. Notwithstanding the heavy storms and almost impassable roads, he continued in his course till the 23d, when suddenly, heading his columns for Fayetteville, N. C., Charlotte, like other points which had been threatened, was left far in the rear. His line of march now lay across the Catwba and Great Pedee, which, 100 years before, had enabled Green to elude the pursuit of Lord Cornwallis. Kilpatrick, while manœuvering with the enemy, to enable our army to cross the river without opposition, was surprised by a force of rebel cavalry and driven back into a swamp, losing all his guns and most of his staff. He, however, rallied his men, and, charging upon the rebels while they were plundering his camp, put them to flight and retook his captured guns.

The army having rapidly crossed Pedee, bringing the 30th and 31st Illinois into action and capturing 25 guns, the opposing force, the ill-starred garrisons of Mobile and Charleston, under the luckless Hardee, hurriedly retreated to Fayetteville. Hither they were closely followed, and, after a sharp fray, on the 11th of March, with the 15th, 30th and 31st Illinois, retreated up Cape Fear river.

While the army lay in Fayetteville, the steam tug Davidson, and gun-boat Eolus steamed up from Wilmington, bringing news of the capture of that city and other important events, which had transpired during the six weeks that our army had been forcing its way through the interminable swamps and over the swollen streams of the Carolinas.

Reduction of Wilmington.—The capture of Wilmington, in which the 65th, 107th and 112th Illinois participated, was intimately connected with, and had an important bearing on the operations of Sherman. As tending to facilitate his movements Grant, on the 14th of January, ordered Schofield from Tennessee to the seaboard of North Carolina. His instructions were to debark at Wilmington if the place should be captured, but if not, to land at Newbern. In accordance with this arrangement he transported his corps to the latter place, but detached Cox's division to co-operate with Porter in the reduction of Wilmington, still in possession of the enemy. The only obstacle which now remained to prevent the advance of our fleet to the city, was Fort Anderson, a place of immense strength inclosing about 4 square miles. To effect its overthrow, a movement was commenced up the river on the 11th of February, and, on reaching the fort, Cox's division, by wading through a difficult swamp, took a position in the rear. On the 18th the gun-boats opened on the works, while Schofield made arrangements to intercept the garrison in case of retreat. Hoke, in command, finding himself likely to be surrounded by a formidable force, and Sherman's army in a position to isolate him as it had done Hardee at Charleston, the succeeding night evacuated the place and pushed northward to form a junction with Johnson. The works were occupied, and 700 prisoners and 50 pieces of artillery passed into the hands of the victors.

Sherman now directed Schofield to meet him in Goldsboro, and, after destroying the arsenals of Fayetteville, and costly machinery which had been brought from the armory of Harper's Ferry, resumed his march. Hardee having fled on the approach of our army, moved further up the river and fortified a position on the left bank near Areysboro. Here he encountered the 60th, 86th, 101st, 102d and 105th Illinois, under Slocum, who was moving in the same direction to make a feint on Raleigh and thus conceal Sherman's movement on Goldsboro. The enemy's position was almost inaccessible on account of swamps, yet it was necessary to dislodge him, and Wood's division of the 20th corps was thrown forward to develop his lines. Immediately charging upon the outer works the division captured three guns and a considerable number of prisoners. Kilpatrick, farther to the right, was, however, vigorously attacked and driven back, gallantly fighting. Slocum in the meantime had ordered up three additional divisions, which, falling upon the enemy, forced him to retire within his entrenchments, where he was held during the remainder of the day. The succeeding night being stormy, under cover of the darkness Hardee abandoned his position and retreated over the road to Smithfield.

Hitherto Sherman had succeeded in interposing his army between the scattered detachments of the rebel forces, but now they were rapidly concentrating, and it became necessary to move with more caution. There were gathering about him Cheatham, with Hood's forces from Tennessee; Hoke, with the recent garrison of Fort Anderson; Hardee, with that of Charleston, and Wheeler's cavalry reinforced by Wade Hampton. These forces, numbering 40,000 veterans, were under the command of Johnson, Sherman's old antagonist, rendering it necessary for the latter to keep his columns within supporting distance. Slocum, after making the feint on Raleigh, wheeled to the right and took the road to Goldsboro, whither Howard, on his right, with his forces was also marching.

Hopes were entertained by Sherman that the army might reach its destination without further opposition. Suddenly, however, as Slocum on the 18th neared Bentonville, he found himself confronted by the whole of Johnson's army. Before dispositions could be made to receive the unexpected enemy, two brigades were driven back on the main force with a loss of three guns. Slocum, as soon as possible, deployed four divisions behind barricades and stood on the defensive. Kilpatrick hearing the roar of artillery, also dashed up and moved his forces on the left. Hardly had these preparations been made when Hoke, Hardee and Cheatham swept up their massive columns, hoping by sheer weight of numbers to overwhelm and break the Union line. The whole fury of the assault spent itself within an hour, yet, in this time the rebels made six successive charges, all of which were successfully repulsed. The rapid volleys of our batteries did immense execution upon the foe, who, divesting himself of artillery, had hurried up expecting to crush Slocum before he could be supported. Howard, however, in obedience to orders from Sherman, came up the next day, and the rebel general finding himself opposed by an army of 60,000 strong, decamped the succeeding night, and retreated in the direction of Raleigh. The following day, the 23d of March, the army, without further opposition, entered Golds-boro, whither Schofield two days before had preceded it.

The battle of Bentonville, honored by the presence of the 30th, 53d, 56th, 60th, 63d, 64th, 86th, 92d, 101st, 104th and 105th Illinois, was the last engagement of the campaign. It is needless to say they, in common with the rest of their comrades, fought well. The results speak for themselves. A track of country from Savannah to Goldsboro, 40 miles wide and nearly 500 long, had been successfully overridden. The immediate fruits of the march were Mobile, Charleston and Wilmington, which, hitherto, had defied some of the most destructive naval enginery the world has ever seen, while it largely contributed to the downfall of the confederate capital. Walled in on one side by the army of Grant, with Sherman rapidly approaching on the other, its evacuation was a military necessity.

Close of the War.—Sherman temporarily turned over his army to Schofield and hastened to City Point, where he had an interview with Gen. Grant and President Lincoln. The object of the meeting was to concert measures for striking the death blow of the rebellion. An important part in the closing drama was assigned to the army of the West, but the end was at hand. Before any important movement could be effected, Lee surrendered, and the civil war, whose throes had convulsed the continent and disturbed the commerce of the world, existed only in history.

The slave power, corrupt, defiant and rebellious, had now measured its strength with the republic, and the latter had triumphed. Not a stripe was erased from her banners; every star still revolves in the frame work of the constitution; her domain is unbroken. May she still continue to prosper till her expanding dominion is only limited by the billows which at every point of the compass, break upon the ocean's shore; till her proud destiny becomes a realization of the prophecies written in her coal-fields, beds of iron and seams of gold; till all nations, taught by her example, are released from political oppression, and man attains the full measure of happiness forshadowed in the divinity of his nature.

How much the nation is indebted to Illinois for the auspicious termination of the war, may be inferred from the fact that in the two great movements which severed the insurgent States, and so greatly paralyzed their efforts, her soldiers were more largely represented than those of any other member of the Union. Furthermore, we must place on the credit side of her balance sheet a large amount of legal talent, superior generalship and executive ability; for Trumbull was our lawyer, Grant our soldier, and Lincoln our president.

From the scene of its dangers and triumphs, Sherman's army proceeded to the national capital to share in the great review, which came off on the 23d and 24th of May, as a fitting close of the struggle in which it had been so long engaged. At the appointed time, in presence of the president, the members of his cabinet, foreign ministers, and other eminent personages, the united armies of the East and West moved along Pennsylvania avenue. Never had more gallant legions been entrusted with the destinies of empire than those which received the congratulations of the dense masses which packed the spacious streets. The pageant was grand, yet grander far was the scene when the mighty host which could have overrun a hemisphere, peacefully, joyfully melted away into regiments and returned to their distant homes.

Again the cities and villages of Illinois were aglow with enthusiasm when the lengthened trains and crowded steamboats poured forth the thousands who had gone forth to battle. Everywhere they were met with expressions of welcome. Ovations were prepared for their reception, and long absent friends who had followed them with their sympathies through weary marches and perilous battles, gave them a happy greeting. The greatest reward, however, was the proud consciousness of having served and saved their country. Laying aside their military costume, they again assumed the habiliments and duties of civil life, and to-day the State is bounding forward in the career of greatness and power as the result of their thrift and enterprise.

Many who had been instrumental in saving the nation, never lived to see the consummation of their labors. On the Father of Waters; where the Tennessee wanders; by the southern sea; along the track of the great contending armies, may still be seen their last resting places. As long as vernal suns shall cause the earth to bloom, may the sons and daughters of freedom strew with flowers their graves and from the remembrance of their deeds, gather new inspiration to direct them in discharging their duties to the country they died to save.

CHAPTER LXV.

POLITICAL AND PARTY AFFAIRS DURING THE REBELLION.

Sentiments of the Illinois Democracy in the Winter of 1860–1861—Patriotic Feeling on the breaking out of Hostilities, irrespective of party, as inspired by Douglas—Revival of Partisan Feeling—Constitutional Convention of 1862—Its high pretensions—Conflict With the Governor—Some Features of the Instrument framed; it becomes a party measure—The vote upon it—Party Convention of 1862—The last Democratic Legislature—Frauds in passing bills—Reaction among the People against the Peace Movement—Military Arrests—Suppressing the Chicago Times—Secret Politico-Military Societies—Democratic Mass Convention of June 17th, 1863—Republican Mass Convention, September, 1863—Peace Meetings of 1864—Note, Chicago Conspiracy.

———

During the winter preceeding Mr. Lincoln's first inauguration as president, when State after State was shooting madly from the orbit of the Union by passing secession ordinances, conservative men generally, to avoid the horrors of impending civil war, were anxious to conciliate the existing misunderstanding and restore harmony between the different sections of our country. Several propositions were offered in congress as plans for compromise; one by Mr. Douglas; one by Mr. Crittenden, and one known as the "Border State Proposition." With the feeling of compromise the democracy of Illinois were fully imbued, and for the sake of peace, they would have conceded much.

On the 16th of January, 1861, a Democratic State convention met in Springfield to give expression to their sentiments upon the state of the Union. Ninety-three counties were represented by over 500 delegates. The venerable Zadock Casey presided. More than 28 years before he had presided over the Illinois senate, when the legislature declared the position of the State upon the nullification of South Carolina, sustaining President Jackson in his proclamation, and instructing our senators and representatives in Congress "to unite in the most speedy and vigorous measures on the part of the government for the preservation of the peace, integrity and honor of the Union; and we do most solemnly pledge the faith of our State in support of the administration of the laws and constitution of our beloved country;" resolving further "That disunion by armed force is treason, and should be treated as such by the constituted authorities of the nation." But this convention of 1861 adopted a preamble and set of resolutions, counselling concession and compromise, and the acceptance of any of the propositions pending in congress to restore harmony between the sections; declared that an effort to coerce the seceding States, would plunge the country in civil war, and denied the military power of the government to enforce its laws in any State, except in strict subordination to the civil authorities; believed "that the perilous condition of the country had been produced by the agitation of the slavery question, creating discord and enmity between the different sections, which had been aggravated by the election of a sectional president;" condemned the party leaders, madly bent on fraternal strife; did not recognize any conflict in the diversity of the domestic institutions and industries of the country, but rather discovered grounds for a more lasting and perfect union in its variety of soil and climate, and modes of thought of the people; denied the right of secession; commended the proposed Louisville convention, and proposed a national convention to amend the constitution so as to produce harmony and fraternity throughout the whole Union.*

In the proceedings of this convention may be found the names of men, who, in antagonism to the high national ground occupied by Mr. Douglas, ever sought to place the democracy of Illinois in a false light before the country during the rebellion. These resolutions foreshadowed the views which two years later, in a modified form, re-appeared in the Armistice resolutions of the 23d general assembly, and again in the enunciations of the so-called Democratic mass convention of the 17th of June, 1863. But the full force of the rebellion was not yet, in January, 1861, realized. The bluster of extremists was so great in those days that much of it was disregarded. When the war was actually upon us, many other names seen there as participants, by their patriotic and gallant conduct, gave the lie to these enunciations. And prior to this, in December, 1860, the Hon. John A. McClernand, a leading representative democrat in congress from this State, in the discussions incident to the state of the Union, had exclaimed that

"The sacred obligations of patriotism would prompt every loyal citizen, whether in the North or in the South, to defend and maintain the integrity of the Union and the authority of its common government against the inroads of violence. * * Is it coercion of a State for us to do what we are sworn to do—to support the constitution and the laws and treaties as the supreme law of the land? Is it coercion for us to maintain peaceably if we can, forcibly if we must, possession of the treasure and other property of the United States? Is it coercion for us to stay the violent and lawless hand that would tear down the noble structure of our government? Sir, it is a perversion of all language; a mockery of all ideas, to say so."

Mr. Douglas, devotedly attached to the Union, and anxiously laboring for conciliation and compromise, exclaimed to the South: "What are you afraid of? You have now, and will have when Mr. Lincoln becomes president, two-thirds of the government, the supreme court, and both branches of congress." Unable to assign a sufficient reason, it was answered that they could not endure

---

* Illinois State Register, Jan. 17, 1861.

the disgrace of a man in the White House, elected president by
the Republicans. "Well," replied Douglas, "If the South se-
cedes and takes up arms against the government, there will then
be an end of compromise. You and your institutions will perish
together."

The legislature of Virginia had adopted resolutions, extending
invitations to the other States of the Union, to appoint commissioners to meet at Washington, February 4th, 1861, with similar
commissioners from that State, to consider and suggest plans for
the adjustment of the unhappy differences between the North and
South. The basis of adjustment suggested by Virginia was the
" Crittenden Compromise;" or to so amend the federal constitution that "property in African slaves should be effectually protected in all the territory of the United States, now held, or hereafter to be acquired south of the parallel of 36 deg. 30 min., during the continuance of territorial governments therein." The
legislature of Illinois (Republican) authorized the governor to appoint 5 commissioners, as above, to be at all times, however, subject to the control of the general assembly, but disclaimed any
admission, by their response to the invitation of Virginia, that any
amendment of the federal constitution was requisite to secure the
people of the slaveholding States adequate guarantees for their
rights, or that it was an approval of the basis of settlement proposed by Virginia; and declared it simply an expression of their
willingness to unite in an earnest effort to adjust the present unhappy controversies. The resolutions in that form did not meet
the approval of the democrats. In the senate every democrat, but
one, voted against them. The governor appointed the following
gentlemen as commissioners: Ex-Governor John Wood, Ex-Governor Koerner, (who declined, and the Hon. John M. Palmer was
named instead), Judge Stephen T. Logan, Hon. B. C. Cook
and Hon. Thomas J. Turner, all republicans. The conference of
these commissioners, known as the "Peace Congress," was duly
held at Washington, but their labors were unsatisfactory from the
start, incurring the severest criticism from every direction and
their recommendations resulted in nothing.

The first determined expression from leading republican sources,
and supposed to reflect the views of the new administration as to
the course to be pursued with the rebels, came, also, from
an Illinoisan. On the 28th of March, 1861, Mr. Trumbull,
in the senate of the United States, offered a resolution that "in
the opinion of the senate the true way to preserve the Union [was]
to enforce the laws of the Union; that resistance to their enforcement, whether under the name of anti-coercion or any other name,
was disunion; and that it was the duty of the president to use all
the means in his power to hold and protect the public property of
the United States, and to enforce the laws thereof, as well in the
States of South Carolina, Georgia, Alabama, Mississippi, Florida,
Louisiana and Texas, as within the other States of the Union."
It was not acted on; no fixed policy was settled upon or seemed
to exist at the time.

When the news of the rebels opening their batteries upon Fort
Sumter was received at Washington, Douglas, the great champion
of popular rights, who truly represented more than nine-tenths of the
mass of the Illinois democracy, freed immediately of all partizan feel-

ing, rose at once to the duty of the hour. He called upon President Lincoln and tendered him his sympathy and support in his efforts to preserve the Union and maintain the government. It was a touching scene to see these old political antagonists thus meet to bury the political hatchet and address themselves only to the patriotic work before them. The president was deeply gratified by the interview. To the west Douglas telegraphed, "I am for my country and against all its assailants." The fire of his patriotism spread to the masses of the north, and democrat and republican rallied to the support of the flag. In Illinois the democratic and republican presses vied with each other in the utterance of patriotic sentiments. From the former we quote a few sentences:

"The fratricidal blow has been struck! Civil war is upon us. The rebels have opened batteries on Sumter, and the prospect of a long and bloody strife is before us. * * The government has been resisted in the performance of its legal functions. Rebels to the national authorities have fired upon the flag of the country and assaulted one of its garrisons when effort was being made to reinforce and provision the noble Anderson and his gallant little band. * * Whatever may be men's opinions as to the causes which have brought war upon us, there is but one feeling, and that is in behalf of the national government and the flag of the Union. This is as it should be with the true patriot. Whatever may be his opinions of the causes of the war with his country's enemies, he is for his country and his country's flag, and his hearty support, morally and physically, if necessary, should be rendered to the country's cause. * * Civil war is our present condition, and the patriot can only sympathize with his government and with the flag, beneath the folds of which we have achieved our national eminence, with which are associated so many glorious memories, and with which are blended all our hopes of future greatness, happiness and prosperity of civil and religious liberty, and the cause of democratic republican government." "Whatever may be our party leanings, our party principles, our likes or dislikes, when the contest opens between the country—between the Union and its foes, and blows are struck, the patriot's duty is plain—take sides with the stars and stripes. As Illinoisans, let us rally to one standard. There is but one standard for good men and true. Let us be there; through good and through evil report, let us be there; first, last and all the time."*

Large and numerously attended mass meetings met, as it were with one accord, irrespective of parties, and the people of all shades of political opinions buried their party hatchets. Glowing and eloquent orators exhorted the people to ignore political differences in the present crisis, join in the common cause, and rally to the flag of the Union and the constitution. It was a noble truce. From the many resolutions of that great outpouring of patriotic sentiment which ignored all previous party ties, we subjoin the following:

"*Resolved*, That it is the duty of all patriotic citizens of Illinois, without distinction of party or sect, to sustain the government through the peril which now threatens the existence of the Union; and of our legislature to grant such aid of men and money as the exigency of the hour and the patriotism of our people shall demand."

Governor Yates promptly issued his proclamation, dated the 15th of April, convening the legislature for the 23d inst. in extraordinary session.

That body remained in session ten days. Their labors were chiefly addressed toward placing the State in proper position for defense, and to enable it to respond to the requisitions of the general government. In addition to the 6 regiments under the call of the president, they authorized the organization, by the State, of ten regiments of infantry, one of cavalry, and one batallion of light artillery, to repel invasion, suppress insurrection, &c. The entire militia of the State, including all able-bodied men between the ages of 18 and 45, was to be organized; $3,500,000 were appropriated for war purposes: $1,000,000 for the equipment of the ten regiments of infantry; $500,000 for the purchase of arms and the establishment of an arsenal, and $2,000,000 for general war purposes.

* Illinois State Register.

The opinion of the Supreme Court, then sitting at Ottawa, was first taken as to the power of the legislature to transcend the constitutional limitation of $50,000. The extraordinary emergency was decided to be sufficient.

The Executive department was also provided with a fund of $50,000 for extraordinary expenses. An act was also passed requiring war claims to be audited by three commissioners. Messrs. J. H. Woodworth, of Chicago, Wm. Thomas, of Jacksonville and C. H. Lanphier, Springfield, (the latter a democrat,) were by the governor appointed.

Political or party questions were not obtruded to mar the harmony of the special session, other than a resolution by Aaron Shaw—"That, while we are ever ready to stand by, and defend with our fortunes, and our lives, the constitution, the honor and flag of our country, we will frown upon and condemn any effort, on the part of the federal government, which looks to the subjugation of the Southern States." Mr. Burr, democrat of Scott, from the committee on federal relations, reported a substitute, which was adopted by 67 to 0, disclaiming a purpose to subjugate the people of any State to any other duties than those imposed by the constitution and laws made in pursuance thereof.

On the evening of the 25th of April, Mr. Douglas, who had arrived at the capital the day before, addressed the general assembly and a densely packed audience, in the hall of representatives, in that masterly effort, which must live and be enshrined in the hearts of his countrymen so long as our government shall endure. Douglas had ever delighted in the mental conflicts of party strife; but now, when his country was assailed by the red hand of treason, he was instantly divested of his party armor and stood forth panoplied only in the pure garb of a true patriot. He taught his auditory—he taught his country, for his speeches were telegraphed all over it—the duty of patriotism at that perilous hour of the nation's life. He implored both democrats and republicans to lay aside their party creeds and platforms; to dispense with party organizations and party appeals; to forget that they were ever divided until they had first rescued the government from its assailants. His arguments were clear, convincing and unanswerable; his appeals for the salvation of his country, irresistible. It was the last speech, but one, he ever made.

Thus everything moved in accord, as it should at such a time. The demon of party seemed swallowed up in the awakened patriotism. Everything was harmony, concord and unity, actuated by but one purpose, to uphold the flag and maintain the integrity of the Union.

The first ripple across this smooth sea, in which apparently was engulphed all party animosity, arose from the appointment of a successor to the lamented Douglas, who died on the 3d of June, 1861. Some of the leading republican newspapers of the State, actuated by sentiments that rose above party, demanded of Gov. Yates the appointment of a Democrat to fill the vacancy. But the lesser though more numerous republican lights, who, so long as there was nothing to lose or gain, had been loud in praise of burying the party hatchet during the war for the Union, now, however, opposed this magnanimous concession, so well calculated to promote harmony, and severely denounced this step and the indecent haste of their party associates to guide the political sentiments of the State. They did not want to thus buy the loyalty of the democracy, they said. The democracy was not to be trusted in the emergency which threatened the perpetuity of the Union—citing the anti-coercion resolutions of the January State democratic convention, that the government had no constitutional power to put down insurrection by military force. From this domestic warfare the democracy stood aloof; they did not expect the senatorship, a political office, as a gift, at the hands of the republicans. But it may well be imagined that the taunts and flings of the latter were not promotive of the amity and unity of feeling so auspiciously begun. While the advocates of such appointment gave thus an earnest to sink the partizan out of view during the war, they ought to have foreseen the inability of his excellency to throw off party shackles and rise to the grandeur and independence of such an act. Their good intentions resulted only in harm. The governor appointed a republican, the Hon. O. H. Browning, of Quincy, a gentleman who, by his legal attainments, occupied a front rank at the bar of Illinois, and who, by education, large acquaintance with public affairs, natural ability and gifts of oratory, was in every way qualified to adorn the senatorial office.

In the meantime the national administration proceeded with the work of official decapitation fully as much as in times of profound peace, with no common danger threatening and no other public feeling than party animosity, and a scramble for the loaves and fishes. While the dominant party press cried "Union" and "no party" during the war, they approbated at the same time the course of the administration, and said: "The democrats belong to that political tribe which, for years, have been giving aid and comfort to Southern traitors, and are now only for the Union by the force of circumstances and not inclination; that the republican party, after driving the disunionists out of office at Washington, should not allow their sympathizers to hold office anywhere else in the country; that the people expected the political axe to be applied."*

Democrats and republicans had alike rallied with alacrity to the defense of the nation. The former voted unlimited supplies of money, men and credit, to an administration which, in its civil appointments, drew the line of strict party separation—a poor requital, indeed, for the generous surrender of party feeling in the moment of great peril to a common government; and while the republicans were thus revelling in the full enjoyment of the spoils of party victory, it could hardly be expected that partizan feeling should be entirely sunk out of view by the democracy thus irritated.

The Constitutional Convention of 1862.—In November, 1861, quite an important election was to take place for delegates to revise the constitution. This convention had finally been authorized by a vote of the people, after several previous attempts and failures. The legislature at its winter session of 1861, with some reluctance, owing to the changed condition of the nation, had

*See Republican press of the period.

passed the act for the election and meeting of this important body. When the convention was called times were good and the State in a prosperous condition; now they were hard, banks daily breaking, money worthless, and produce extremely low.

It was to consist of 75 members, corresponding to the number of representatives in the lower house of the general assembly, to be elected from the same districts. The legislature elected in 1860 was republican—the house by five majority and the senate by one. Yet the election of delegates to the constitutional convention, but one year later, resulted in 45 democrats, 21 republicans, 7 fusionists, and 2 doubtful; the latter 9 acting in the convention mostly with the democrats. From this result, which was entirely unexpected by the republicans, it may well be inferred that the democrats, like their opponents, had also not, when the scramble for office was at stake, sunk all party issues out of view while the war should last. Indeed, for party organization and alertness, democratic leaders have ever out-maneuvered their opponents, probably because the rank and file of their party have ever been tractable. It seems that the democracy in some republican districts readily agreed to a fusion upon an equitable or satisfactory division of candidates, but in districts where they had clear majorities, this cognate rule was ignored, a straight party ticket brought out, and elected.

Among the delegates were many well-known politicians of the State. In the list of names may be recognized ex-governors, ex-congressmen, ex-State officials, ex legislators, learned jurists who held on to their seats upon the bench while they were remodeling the organic law, distinguished lawyers, experienced editors, and able civilians.

The convention assembled January 7th, 1862, and at once took the high position that, after due organization, the law calling it was no longer binding, and that it had supreme power; that it represented a virtual assemblage of the whole people of the State, and was sovereign in the exercise of all power necessary to effect a peaceable revolution of the State government, and to the reestablishment of one for the "happiness, prosperity and freedom of the citizen," limited only by the federal constitution. Notwithstanding the law calling the convention required that, before entering upon their duties, the members should each take an oath to support the constitution of the United States, and of this State, they utterly refused to include the latter, denying the right of the legislature to prescribe their oath of office, and holding it inconsistent for them to swear to maintain what it was their duty to tear to pieces.*

They claimed their authority from the vote of the people at the election of 1860, and not from the subsequent act of the legislature, which had exhausted its power by authorizing their election and could attach no condition to their duties; that if the legislature could bind them in their oath, it could in the articles to be amended, and thus in advance render null the voice of the people and the labors of the convention.

*See remarks of Mr. Anthony, of Cook, a republican, who first called attention to this view.

They went farther, and asserted their supremacy, not only with reference to the framing of a constitution, but assumed the right to control the executive departments of the State government—the governor and subordinate State officials—the courts and all cognate matters; that they were sovereign with regard to both existing laws and the constitution, as it was their pleasure to will. This was high and extraordinary ground to take, though not entirely new. Nor did the convention stop with the mere claim of these extraordinary powers—it essayed to exercise them. This led directly to an onslought from the republican press of the State, which grew in sharpness as its sitting progressed. The convention was denounced as an illegally organized body—a mere mob, exercising usurped powers, &c.

The legislature, at its special session of April, 1861, had, it will be remembered, with a liberal hand, appropriated $3,500,000 for war purposes. When the convention met it speedily ascertained that the governor had not stopped with the expenditure of the appropriation, but, without authority of law, had greatly exceeded its limits—the aggregate claims audited by the military auditing board amounting to $4,885,886. This was in express violation of the law. But these liabilities had been contracted in a crisis of extraordinary peril to our country, to feed, clothe, equip and organize the troops of Illinois at a time when the government itself was inexperienced in every step it took, and should certainly not have caused the arraignment of the governor as being false to his official trust and obligations. He had a right to and doubtless did rely upon the people for his acquittance, so long as it was shown that these expenditures were necessary, and the money was rightfully applied, to promote the comfort and efficiency of our troops. Besides, the general government was under obligations—which it has fully discharged—to reimburse the States for necessary expenditures in the equipment of their volunteers.

But in the fall of 1861, the U. S. quartermaster's department sent its agent to Springfield to take charge of all expenditures incident to the supplies and equipment of Illinois troops.*

This did not accord with the wishes of his excellency. To the agent's request to relieve the State, the governor replied that he availed himself of the right conferred by act of Congress upon each State to furnish supplies for its troops. Contracts for supplies were still given out, one for clothing alone amounting to over $800,000.*

The State was for a time threatened with a loss of $130,000, on account of inferior clothing purchased by the governor's agent, in Philadelphia. Finally, but not till in January, 1862, upon a sharp demand from the Secretary of War, the expenditures and rich drippings of the quartermaster's department were turned over to the general government. In this instance, however, the conduct of the governor, by thus fixing a liability upon the State beyond the war fund provided, in the face of the demand of the war department to relieve the State, cannot certainly be extenuated upon the grounds of necessity.

*See Q. M. Gen. Meigs' letter to the Governor Sept, 28, 1861.
*See correspondence of Q. M. Gen. Meigs.

The convention made many of these matters the subject of inquiry. They demanded of the governor, by resolution, to know whether the general government had notified him of its readiness to relieve the State of the further expenditures in the organization, equipment and maintenance of troops enlisted in this State for the service of the U. S.; whether the general government had not sent its agent here for that purpose, and if so why the arrangement had not been made; also all correspondence with the general government in relation thereto. They called upon him (by resolution of Mr. Wentworth, republican) to furnish the convention the names and pay of all persons appointed to office by him since the beginning of the war, and out of what appropriations they were paid; what civil officers or agents he was empowered to appoint under the constitution; and whether the militia of the State called into service had been permitted to elect their own officers, and if not, by what authority he had exercised those functions, &c. The Illinois Central R. R. Company, which, in its grant of land from Congress, was bound, in express terms, to render to the general government transportation for troops and munitions of war, free of charge, had brought against this State a claim for military transportation of $116,719, which had been audited and approved by a majority (Messrs. Thomas and Woodward) of the State military auditing board. The company wanted to set off this claim against the semi-annual dividend of 7 per centum of its gross earnings. The convention instructed the new board of army auditors (the auditor, treasurer and governor,) to suspend all action in relation to this claim until further notice from them. His excellency, in several lengthy communications, complied with the demands of the convention, setting forth in detail all his transactions inquired about; but finally, in a short letter, dated February 5th, 1862, after stating that he had, from the beginning, maintained that the claims of the Central railroad could not be brought against the State of Illinois, but were property chargeable against the general government, he sharply defined his independence by saying, "he did not acknowledge the right of the convention to instruct him in the performance of his duty."

The convention went still further. Instead of revising the constitution simply, it also assumed legislative powers and put its finger into almost every conceivable State affair. It attempted to crush the free banks by instructing the auditor not to issue to any more bank notes to circulate as money, unless the bank first showed, by the affidavits of two credible witnesses that it had on hands, always previous thereto, a cash capital of not less than $50,000; that it had never refused to redeem its circulation in specie; and that at the time of application for further issues, it had actually, and in good faith, a paid in capital of $50,000. The requirements of these impossibilities from the banks was, perhaps, well enough, to save the people from further losses by "stump-tail" currency.

It also passed, by a vote of 39 to 23, an ordinance ratifying the amendment to the constitution of the U. S., proposed by joint resolution of Congress, March 2, 1861: Article XIII—"No amendment shall be made to the constitution which will give to Congress the power to abolish or interfere within any State with the domestic relations thereof, including that of persons held to labor or service by the laws of said State." The convention had not been called for the purpose of ratifying this amendment, and Congress, which has the selection of the mode of ratification, had designated the legislatures. Some leading democratic members protested against this step, not that they did not approve the amendment, but because the convention had not legislative power to act in the premises.

A resolution was introduced to inquire into the feasibility of electing a U. S. senator in place of the appointee of the governor. And this step was encouraged by the democratic press, as it encouraged all the proceedings. In these ways the bitter hostility of the entire republican press of the State was provoked, and it did not halt or hesitate, but came to the charge with a will. The cry of usurpation was raised. It was charged that the convention went out of its legitimate sphere to provoke a collision with the State authorities; it was denounced as a mob of political demagogues who sought by every means to discredit the war for the Union, destroy the government and build up secession democracy on its ruins. The strictures of the press were unparalleled in grossness and severity.*

And now, February 18, 1862, the convention, by a vote of 50 to 16, passed an ordinance appropriating $500,000 for the exclusive purpose of relieving the wants and sufferings of Illinois sick and wounded soldiers battling for the Union and the constitution. To raise the necessary funds, 10 per cent. bonds were to be immediately issued, redeemable at the pleasure of the State. The governor, treasurer, and finance committee of the convention were constituted a commission to properly expend this fund. But this most generous action was characterized by Republicans as a Democratic effort to make political capital out of the war. The convention was ridiculed as having gone off on a buncomb ordinance, and its members sneeringly denounced as eleventh-hour patriots. The bonds bearing the enormous rate of 10 per cent. interest, it was argued, would astonish the financial centres of the country; that the whole scheme was meant to aim a blow at the credit of the State, to give aid and comfort to the rebellion. So difficult is it for one party to please another, with the most liberal acts even, in favor of a cause espoused by both. Notwithstanding a resolution directing the preparation of the bonds and their sale, the State officials, all Republicans, wholly ignored the behests of the convention, and the ordinance became a dead letter. The sick and wounded Illinois soldiers received no State aid, said the Democrats, because it was not the act of the dominant party. As the convention possessed probably no legislative power, the ordinance was doubtless a nullity, and the bonds would have been worthless in market.

Some Features of the Instrument framed:

SEC. 30, Article 11, provided that "The people of this State have the exclusive right of governing themselves as a free, sovereign and independent State, and do and forever shall enjoy and exercise every power

---

*A correspondent of the Chicago Tribune boldly charged that 31 members of the convention belonged to the Knights of the Golden Circle—commonly reputed to be a treasonable political organization in sympathy with the rebellion. This foolish and unsupported charge was dignified by the convention with the consideration of a resolution to inquire and ferret out whether any member did belong to any such order, or was in treasonable correspondence with the Confederacy; the resolution went to its grave by reference.]

pertaining thereto, which is not and may not thereafter be by them expressly delegated to the people of the United States of America, or prohibited to the State by the constitution of the United States."

In this Republicans discovered lurking the abominable heresy
of State sovereignty and the right of secession, which set a State
above the nation, and had proven the bane of the Union; which
fostered sectionalism and made of one's own countrymen aliens.
Long before the labors of the convention were concluded, blind
partisanism, lashed into fury, was arrayed against whatever might
be produced by it, good or bad. When the work was finally completed and published, it was at once ruthlessly attacked by the
Republicans, notwithstanding its many excellencies and great improvement upon the old constitution. Its provisions were such
that where responsibility could be attached it was done; everything was fixed, determined and rigidly enforced upon the respective departments of government, with nothing left to chance or
mischievous interpretation. It guarded the interests of the people,
lessened taxation, and sought to compel an honest administration
of public affairs generally. It relieved from the useless 2 mill tax
of the old constitution, saving to the people $1,000,000 annually.
It abolished the grand jury system in all cases except felony.
This inquisitorial institution, though venerable with age, is a cum-
brous and expensive machinery in the administration of justice
illy adapted to the flexibility of our day. The statistics of 1861
showed that out of 4,682 indictments found in this State, but 330
convictions were had, leaving upon the residue an indelible stain
for the finger of scorn to point at, perhaps to the second generation. The constitution placed a curb upon railroad corporations,
both existing and prospective, and effectually limited all monopolies. The 7 per cent. fund, arising from the gross earnings of the
Central Railroad, was definitely fixed so that no future legislature
might be tampered with for its removal. Special legislation was
prohibited, cutting up, by the roots, the occupation of the lobby
cormorants. All of which provoked the ardent hostility of the
many large and influential interests affected, which thus reinforced
the partisan opposition to it with a powerful auxillary.

But upon the other hand, it should also be said that in contradis-
tinction of the ancient theory, that the State is the fountain of justice which can do no wrong, it contained a provision for bringing
suits against the State prostrating its sovereignty at the feet of every
one, and opening a Pandora's box to let loose all manner of frauds
upon the common treasury. Apportionments, whether fair or
otherwise, always give partisan offense, and it was so with the
work of the convention. A revision of the census of 1860, entitled
Illinois to 14 instead 13 congressmen, the State having been
apportioned for 13 by the legislature in 1861. The convention
plan gave to each political party 7 members; but as the Republicans felt that they had a popular majority in the State, they preferred a congressman at large. The opponents further charged
that while by the census of 1860, the Republican counties contained a population of 942,005, and the Democratic 769,748, yet
by the apportionment for members of the legislature, the latter
would have 19 of the 33 senators, and 57 of the 102 representatives, and that it was so contrived that if the former should carry
the State by a popular majority the general assembly would still

be democratic. In making State officers elective biennially instead of quadrennially, the convention committed its gravest blunder by dismissing from office the incumbents, whose terms would be but half expired, and ordering a new election in November, 1862; while the circuit and county clerks, mostly democratic, were retained till the expiration of their full terms. This was an unjust partisan discrimination, which the people would not brook, and they defeated the instrument in June following. Six different propositions were separately submitted to a vote of the people. The constitution proper, the article prohibiting banks, and the congressional apportionment, were all defeated, the former by a majority of 16,051. But the article prohibiting negroes and mulattoes from settling in the State, was carried by 100,590 majority; that prohibiting their voting, by 176,271, with only 35,649 votes against it; and the requiring these provisions to be carried into effect by appropriate legislation, by 154,524 majority. Such was then still the overwhelmingly dominant sentiment of the people of this State with regard to the political status of the black man. Three months after this overwhelming expression of the people of Illinois, Mr. Lincoln issued his preliminary proclamation of freedom, to the African bondsmen of America; and in November following, the State, which in June cast over 16,000 votes majority against the constitution as a party measure, went largely against the Republicans, the Democrats electing 9 out of the 14 congressmen, including the congressman from the State at large by 16,355; the State Treasurer and Superintendent of Public Instruction, and carried both houses of the general assembly. The summer of 1862 had witnessed the great uprising of the people in the ready volunteering of 600,000 men, and more, until the government refused them. After the proclamation, contrary to the predictions of Greeley, Andrew and Yates, such patriotic scenes were not again witnessed. The conscript law, threatened drafts and local bounties afterward supplied the demand. Had the constitution been adopted in June, the State, by the election of a governor and State officers in November, would have wholly passed into the hands of the democrats—whether for good or evil, is left to the conjecture of the reader.

Democratic and Republican Conventions of 1863.—On the 16th of September, 1862, the State Democratic Convention was held at Springfield in Cook's Hall. The attendance was not full, the call being for 529 and the attendance 381. The contest for congressman at large lay between Col. T. Lyle Dickey, of LaSalle, a war democrat, himself and sons having enlisted in the service for the Union, and James C. Allen, of Crawford. The latter was nominated on the first ballot, by 17 majority, which was regarded as an anti-war triumph. Alexander Starne, of Pike, was chosen as the candidate for treasurer, and John P. Brooks, of Rock Island, for superintendent of public instruction. At this stage of the proceedings no little commotion was produced by W. B. Scates, of Gen. McClernand's staff, offering a series of resolutions, favoring a vigorous prosecution of the war, " whether slavery survived or perished," adopting the language of Mr. Lincoln; and using the language of Mr. Douglas—" There are only two sides to the question—every man must be for the United States or against it.

There can be no neutrals in this war; only patriots and traitors. The more stupendous our preparations, the less blood shed and the shorter the struggle;" that it was the duty of American citizens to rally around the flag of their country; approving, also, of the president's call for 600,000 volunteers. The resolutions were immediately tabled by a large majority.

Of the resolutions reported by the committee on platform, through the Hon. W. A. Richardson, and unanimously adopted, we give the first and second in full, with a synopsis of the remainder:

"*Resolved*, That the constitution, and laws made in pursuance thereof, are, and must remain the supreme law of the land; and as such, must be preserved and maintained in their proper and rightful supremacy; that the rebellion now in arms against them must be suppressed; and it is the duty of all good citizens to aid the general government in all legal and constitutional measures necessary and proper to the accomplishment of this end.

"*Resolved*, That the doctrines of Southern and Northern extremists are alike inconsistent with the federal constitution, and irreconcilable with the union and harmony of the country. The first have already involved us in civil war, and the latter, if permitted to retain ascendency, will leave the nation but little hope of the restoration of the Union in peace."

They further protested against congress pledging the nation to pay for all slaves that should be emancipated; condemned as tyrannical, the recent arbitrary arrests of our citizens by the general government, and their transportation beyond the State, demanding their immediate restoration for trial at home; denounced the military interference with the freedom of speech and the press; viewed with alarm the reckless extravagance pervading every department of government; considered the new excise law as unjust and oppressive to the agricultural States; commended strict economy in State affairs, and the payment of taxes in United States treasury notes; sustained the president in his recent declaration to "save the Union the shortest way under the constitution;" asked from the authorities of Illinois the enforcement of the negro-exclusion clause, recently added to the constitution; and tendered their thanks to the volunteers of Illinois, for their gallant services at Belmont, Donelson, Shiloh, Lexington and Fredericktown. The convention was held about a week prior to the issuance of the proclamation of freedom.[*]

The Republican, or Union State Convention, as it called itself, met September 24, 1862, two days after that proclamation. Out of 340 delegates entitled to, 328 attended. For congressman at large there were a dozen candidates, but the Hon. Eben C. Ingersoll, of Peoria, a strong war democrat, who, immediately after the adjournment of the Democratic Convention, had taken occasion, in a published letter, to denounce its secession proclivities, and made a strong call for a State convention, composed of true, loyal democrats, who would draw a line between union and disunion, without an "if" or a "but," was now taken up by the Republicans, and nominated on the 4th ballot, his strongest opponents being such original republicans as H. P. H. Bromwell and Jackson Grimshaw. William Butler, of Sangamon, was nominated for treasurer, and Newton Bateman for superintendent of public instruction.

The committee on platform, through Lawrence Weldon, made their report, which was adopted, and which we condense. It denounced the rebellion as the most causeless known to history;

_____
[*] See Illinois State Register, Sept. 17, 1862.

acknowledged but two divisions of the people—the loyal, ready to make any sacrifice for the integrity of the Union and the preservation of liberty, and those who openly or covertly endeavored to sever the former and yield the latter; called upon all patriotic citizens to rally for an undivided country and one flag, and the prosecution of the war to any extent or sacrifice; cordially approved the proclamation of freedom as a great and imperative war measure essential to the salvation of the Union, pledging all truly loyal citizens to the support of the president in its enforcement; commended the patriotic and efficient aid of loyal democrats, but deprecated the course of those political leaders, who, while studiously avoiding all harshness toward the conspirators of the south, found fault with the administration for its manner of prosecuting the war; favored a system of direct taxation to suppress the rebellion, but demanded an equitable modification of the existing excise law; commended, as a work of great national importance, the construction of a ship canal, connecting Lake Michigan with the Mississippi river; expressed gratitude to the governor for his labors to bring into the field the Illinois troops, and his efforts to care for them in sickness; and that the Illinois volunteers were entitled to our lasting gratitude for nobly periling their lives in battle, from Kansas to the Potomac.* We have already stated that the election in November, 1862, resulted in a complete victory for the democrats. The State ticket was carried by an average of over 16,000 majority, showing a change of 32,000 votes since June, when the Republicans defeated the new constitution by 16,000 majority. Democrats attributed this remarkable change in the sentiments of the people to the proclamation of freedom of September 22, 1862.

The Last Democratic Legislature of Illinois.—The political status of the 23d General Assembly, elected November, 1862, was as follows: Senate, democrats 13, republicans 12; House, democrats 54, republicans 32. With the meeting of this body on the 5th of January, 1863, flushed with the democratic triumph at the polls, not only in Illinois, but other Northern States, a large outside force of well-known politicians, like vultures to their feast, also collected at the capital. These, joined by some of the members, arranged a public meeting at the Hall of Representatives for the evening of the first day of the session, in which every part of the State was represented. V. Hickox, of the State Democratic Committee, presided, and Capt. Thos. W. McFall, of Quincy, was made secretary. A committee of 16 on resolutions, one from each congressional district, and three from the State at large, was appointed, embracing the following prominent names: I. N. Morris, L. W. Ross, John T. Lindsay, E. D. Taylor, S. A. Buckmaster, John T. Stuart, John Schofield, O. B. Ficklin, W. A. Hacker, H. M. Vandeveer, A. C. Harrington, M. Y. Johnson, C. H. Lanphier and B. L. Caulfield. Messrs. W. A. Richardson, S. S. Marshall, Richard L. Merrick and W. C. Goudy addressed the vast audience, denouncing the president as a usurper, criticising the conduct of the war in unmeasured terms and characterizing it as barbarous and disgraceful.

---

* See Illinois State Journal, Sept. 25, 1862

The committee reported the following resolution, which was vociferously applauded and unanimously adopted :

Resolved, That the emancipation proclamation of the President of the U.S. is as unwarrantable in military as in civil law; a gigantic usurpation, at once converting the war, professedly commenced by the administration for the vindication of the authority of the constitution, into the crusade for the sudden, unconditional and violent lliberation of 3,000,000 of negro slaves; a result which would not only be a total subversion of the federal Union, but a revolution in the social organization of the Southern States, the immediate and remote, the present and the far-reaching consequences of which to both races cannot be contemplated without the most dismal forebodings of horror and dismay. The proclamation invites servile insurrection as an element in this emancipation crusade – a means of warfare, the inhumanity and diabolism of which are without example in civilized warfare, and which we denounce. and which the civilized world will denounce, as an ineffaceable disgrace to the American name."

The committee were instructed to report further on the evening of January 8th, to which time the meeting adjourned---a day sacred from its patriotic associations—when this scene was again rehearsed.

At that time the Hon. I. N. Morris, of the committee, reported a set of 11 resolutions, condemning the administration for suspending the writ of *habeas corpus* in the arrest of private citizens, and their incarceration in political bastiles ; the dismemberment of Virginia; and "That while we condemn and denounce the flagrant and monstrous usurpations of the administration, and the encroachments of abolitionism, we remain equally hostile to the Southern rebellion." They further commended a cessation of hostilities with the rebellious foe, to allow, as they said, the people of the North and the South to express their wishes for peace, and a maintenance of " the Union as it was and the constitution as it is," through a national convention to meet at Louisville, Kentucky, to which the legislature was invited to send a suitable number of discreet commissioners in behalf of Illinois. In these resolutions we find foreshadowed and prescribed the subsequently notorious armistice or peace resolutions of the legislature, which were attended with so much partizan strife and loss of time.

The speeches made in support of the resolutions were of the most inflammable anti-war character. The speakers on this occasion were Judge O'Melveny, Hon. O. B. Ficklin, R. L. Merrick, B. Caulfield and T. Lyle Dickey, the latter the only one who counselled moderation, saying that to stir up a counter-revolution to oppose revolution could only result in the destruction of our whole political fabric. Detraction of the president for issuing the proclamation of freedom, denunciation of the policy of his administration, criticism of the conduct of the war, and opposition to it, were indulged as on the preceding occasion, with added force and bitterness of expression. They charged that the war had been perverted, for political reasons, from a war for the restoration of the Union, to a costly struggle of blood and treasure, purposely protracted for the accomplishment of partizan ends. It was demanded that not another dollar or a single man should be contributed to carry on such a monstrous contest. The people of the New England States were charged with causing all the trouble leading to the deplorable war; and a reconstruction of the Union by joining with the South, leaving them out, was advocated. Not a word was uttered in denunciation of the rebels. The inconsistency of the republican party was shown by quoting the Chicago platform of 1860: "That the maintenance inviolate of the rights of the States, and especially the rights of each State to order and control its own domestic institutions, according to its own judgment exclusively, was essential to that balance of power on which the perfection and endurance of our political faith depends." The violation of the president's promise to the country was shown by quoting from the inaugural address: "I have no purpose, directly or indirectly, to interfere with the institution of slavery in the States where it exists; I believe I have no lawful right to do so, and have no inclination to do so." And the republican congress, after the Bull Run disaster, had pledged the nation "that this war was not waged, on their part, in any spirit of oppression, or for any purpose of conquest or subjugation, or purpose of overthrowing or interfering with the rights or established institutions of the States, but to defend and maintain the supremacy of the constitution, and to preserve the Union, with all the dignity, equality and the rights of the several States unimpaired."*

But the numerous military arrests for treasonable utterances which the general government had, for some time, caused to be made—some of the sufferers being present—afforded the orators the rarest field for the display of their declamatory powers, and R. T. Merrick, gifted with a singular power of eloquent denunciation, shone with unwonted brilliancy. Forcible resistence to these unlawful aggressions upon the rights of the citizen was freely counseled. This was doubtless a political blunder on the part of the general government by which little good was accomplished. In many instances insignificant, if not contemptible treason-spouters were arrested and imprisoned, men never heard of before beyond their immediate neighborhoods, who, upon their return found themselves notorious, sympathized with, and, often by many sanctified into martyrs and heroes.

Thus duly impressed, and their course mapped out for them by the democratic leaders, the dominant partizans of the 23d General Assembly were not slow to follow it. They refused, for a long time, to print the usual number of copies of the governor's long and able message. In the House, M. W. Fuller, of Cook, on the 8th of January, introduced a resolution adroitly quoting the language of Gen. Jackon's farewell address: "The constitution cannot be maintained, nor the Union preserved in opposition to public feeling, by the mere exertion of the coercive powers of the government." Mr. Wenger, of Tazewell, one to the effect that after an unsuccessful war of two years' duration to crush the rebellion, hostilities ought to be immediately suspended and a national convention appointed to settle the difficulty. In the Senate, Mr. Vandeveer, of Christian, on the 21st of January, offered a preamble and set of resolutions, to the effect that the people of the loyal States had acquiesced in, rather than approved of the coercive policy of the federal administration; that the government was impoverished, the people weighed down with an onerous debt and the land filled with cripples, widows and orphans, without restoring the Union; and that as the Union was brought about by concession and compromise, they should memorialize congress to obtain an armistice and cessation of hostilities for a national

*Crittenden resolution, 1861.

convention to assemble at Louisville to adjust the difficulties. Mr. Underwood, of St. Clair, also, with a like view, offered a preamble and resolution soliciting congress to obtain the consent of the States to call a national convention to amend the constitution of the U. S.

And now the legislature took a pleasure trip to Joliet and Chicago. At the latter place a large democratic mass meeting for the occasion gave expression to the popular opposition to the Lincoln misrule, as it was called. Members participated in the proceedings, and, by resolution, the Springfield meetings of the 5th and 8th of January were approved.

On the 4th of February, Mr. Wike, of Pike, from the committee on federal relations, reported to the House the notorious armistice resolutions:

The preamble asserted the supremacy of the constitution in time of war as well as peace, and its suspension, whether by the North or South, to be alike disunion: that it could not be maintained by coercion, but by appeal to the people peacefully assembled through their representatives ; that to it the allegiance of the citizen was alone due—not to any man, officer or administration; that the act of the federal administration in suspending the writ of *habeas corpus*, the arrest of citizens not subject to military law, without warrant or authority, transporting them to distant States, incarcerating them in political prisons, without charge or accusation, denying them the right of trial by jury, witnesses in their favor, or counsel for their defense; withholding from them all knowledge of their accusers, and the cause of their arrest; answering their petitions for redress by repeated injury and insult; prescribing, in many cases, as a condition of their release, test oaths, arbitrary and illegal; in the abridgement of freedom of speech, and of the press, by imprisoning the citizen for expressing his sentiments, by suppressing newspapers by military force, and establishing a censorship over others, wholly incompatible with freedom of thought and expression of opinion, and the establishment of a system of espionage, by a secret police, to invade the sacred privacy of unsuspecting citizens; in declaring martial law over States not in rebellion, and when the courts are open and unobstructed for the punishment of crime: in declaring the slaves of loyal, as well as well as disloyal citizens, in certain States and parts of States, free; the attempted enforcement of compensated emancipation; the proposed taxation of the laboring white man to purchase the freedom and secure the elevation of the negro: the transportation of negroes into the State of Illinois, in defiance of the repeatedly expressed will of the people; the arrest and imprisonment of the representatives of a free and a sovereign State; the dismemberment of the State of Virginia, erecting within her boundaries a new State, without the consent of her legislature are, each and all, arbitrary and unconstitutional—a usurpation of the legislative functions, and a suspension of the judicial departments of the State and federal government—subverting the constitution—State and federal—invading the reserved rights of the people, and the sovereignty of the States, and, if sanctioned, destructive of the Union—establishing, upon the common ruins of the liberties of the people, and the sovereignty of the States, a consolidated military despotism. And we hereby solemnly declare that no American citizen can, without the crime of infidelity to his country's constitutions, and the allegiance which he bears to each, sanction such usurpation. Believing that our silence will be criminal, and may be construed into consent, in deep reverence for our constitution which has been ruthlessly violated, we do hereby enter our most solemn protest against these usurpations of power, a d place the same before the world, intending therby to warn our public servants against further usurpations. Therefore,

Resolved by the House of Representatives, the Senate concurring herein, That the army was organized, confiding in the declaration of the president, in his inaugural address, to wit: that he had no purpose, directly or indirectly, to interfere with the institution of slavery in the States where it existed, and that he believed he had no lawful right to do so ; and upon the declaration of the federal congress, to wit: that this war is not waged in any spirit of oppression or subjugation, or any purpose of overthrowing any of the institutions of any of the States; and that inasmuch as the whole policy of the administration, since the organization of the army, has been at war with the declaration aforesaid, culminating in the emancipation proclamation, leaving the facts patent that the war has been diverted from its first avowed object, to that of subjugation and the abolition of slavery, a fraud, both legal and moral, has been perpetrated upon the brave sons of Illinois, who have so nobly gone forth to battle for the constitution and the laws. And while we protest against the continuance of this gross fraud upon our citizen soldiery, we thank them for their heroic conduct on the battle field that sheds imperishable glory on the State of Illinois.

Resolved, That we believe the further prosecution of the present war cannot result in the restoration of the Union and the preservation of the constitution as our fathers made it, unless the president's emancipation proclamation is withdrawn

Resolved, That while we condemn and denounce the flagrant and monstrous usurpations of the administration, and encroachments of abolitionism, we equally condemn and denounce the ruinous heresy of secession, as unwarrantable by the constitution, and destructive alike of the security and perpetuity of our government, and the peace and liberty of the people; and fearing, as we do, that it is the intention of the present congress and administration, at no distant day, to acknowledge the independence of the Southern Confederacy, and thereby sever the Union, we hereby solemnly declare that we are unalterably opposed to any such severance of the Union, and that we never can consent that the great Northwest shall be separated from the Southern States comprising the Mississippi valley. That river shall never water the soil of two nations, but, from its source to its confluence with the Gulf, shall belong to one great and united people.

The fourth resolution recommended the assembling of a national convention at Louisville, Ky., to adjust our difficulties, restore peace, fraternity and political fellowship among the States.

Resolved further, therefore. That to attain the object of the foregoing resolution, we hereby memorialize the congress of the U. S., the administration at Washington, and the executives and legislatures of the several States to take such immediate action as shall secure an armistice, in which the rights and safety of the government shall be fully protected for such length of time as may be necessary for the people to meet in convention as aforesaid. And we therefore earnestly recommend to our fellow-citizens everywhere, to observe and keep all their lawful and constitutional obligations, to abstain from violence, and to meet together and reason each with the other, upon the best mode to attain the great blessings of peace, unity and liberty.

And be it further resolved, That to secure the co operation of the States and the general government, Stephen T. Logan, Samuel S. Marshall, H. K. S. O'Melveny, William C. Goudy, Anthony Thornton and John D. Caton, are hereby appointed commissioners to confer immediately with the congress and the president of the U. S., and urge the necessity of prompt action, to secure said armistice, and the election of delegates to, and early assembling of said convention. and to arrange and agree with the general government and the several States upon the time and place of holding said convention, and that they report their action in the premises to the General Assembly of this State."

The resolutions elicited a long and acrimonious debate in both houses, to the delay of nearly all other business. Every parliamentary expedient to retard legislation, centering chiefly upon the appropriation bills as usual, was resorted to. The public press took sides, the republicans against, of course, and the democrats for. But among the latter there were many notable exceptions who deprecated the extremity to which the resolutions looked; who appealed to the magnanimity of the democratic majority to cease the bitter strife, unlock the wheels of legislation and allow the important labors of the session to go on. This went unheeded; and finally, two days before the recess, the resolutions were adopted in the House by a vote of 52 yeas to 28 nays.

Thus did the House of Representatives of the State of Illinois, a body fresh from a loyal people whose patriotism never flinched, after being first systematically debauched in their sentiments by the political meetings at the opening of the session, commit themselves upon the record, and attempt to thrust the State also into the erroneous position before the world, that the war for the Union was a failure, that secession was a right under the constitution which could not be met or defeated by the sword, and that a cessation of hostilities with an armed and defiant rebellion was necessary. Nay, if we construe the last clause of the 3d resolution with the repeated utterances of their speakers and leaders, as well as the entire resolution, wherein a man of straw is set up regarding their fears of recognition of the Southern Confederacy, we see a quasi declaration for a union of the Northwest with the South as more desirable than the connection with the hateful abolitionists of the East.

These legislators were not elected for the purpose which mainly engrossed their attention; they assumed unauthorized power and proved themselves recreant to their trust. No peace could have been made with the defiant rebels at that time, nor for a long time afterwards. It was folly to talk of peace at that stage of the war. The Indiana legislature at the time passed similar resolutions.*

---

* It was a curious conjuncture that on the 26th of January, 1863, a preamble and set of 8 resolutions were introdu ed into the Confederate Congress at Richmond by Henry S. Foote, of Tennessee, the fifth of which reads as follows:

"The government of the Confederate States, in consideration of the change in the public sentiment, which has occurred in several Northern States, wherein political elections have been recently held—sympathizing most kindly with those by whose manly exertions that change has been brought about—would be willing to conclude a

Part of the programme in connection with the passage of the peace resolutions was the joint resolution of Senator Underwood, providing for a legislative recess from the 14th of February till the 2d of June, by which time the peace commissioners might report progress of their negotiation for an armistice. This resolution was violently fought in the senate, and when a vote could be staved off no longer, the republican members bolted the chamber, leaving the senate without a quorum; but enough were finally brought in and the resolution passed. When it was brought up in the house a similar attempt was there made, which failed likewise, and the resolution was adopted.

But the armistice resolutions shared a different fate in the senate. They had been the subject of acrimonious debate in that body, the same as in the house, for a longtime, having been deferred from time to time, and now, early in the week (the recess having been fixed for the following Saturday,) to avoid a vote, the republican members absented themselves, breaking the quorum for business. The further consideration of the distasteful resolutions was deferred till Friday night. The republicans came in and business progressed. In the meantime the democrats lost a member by sudden death, in the person of Senator Rogers, of Clinton. This left the senate a tie, with the presiding officer, Lieut.-Gov. Hoffman, who had the casting vote in such contingency, against the democrats. And thus the armistice resolutions failed of adoption in the senate and went over to the June session; whereat a portion of the democratic press sent up its wailings and lamentations about the great disappointment which the people would feel at this result; and the democratic members of the senate, who had consented to the staving off of a vote upon the resolutions to the evening before the close of the session, were handled without gloves.

As a fitting commentary upon this wasted session, and also to indicate the violence of party feeling, we will reproduce the notable speech of Jacob Funk, a senator from McLean, made a day or two before the close of the session, the occasion being the introduction of some trifling resolutions to stave off a vote upon the general appropriation bill. It also deserves to be preserved for its uniqueness, and as offering a fair but now curious oratorical type of the early settler of the West, and his manner of settling disputes; true, brave, and patriotic, though devoid of the breadth of diction imparted by education. It created a great sensation at the time, and was republished all over the Northern States. It was delivered in a stentorian tone, gathering in the people from around the capital square, till the hall was densely packed. The speaker's great fervor and pathos, born of conviction, wrought the audience to the highest pitch of excitement, and upon its conclusion, both members and spectators thronged about him with congratulations:

just and honorable peace with any one or more of said States, who (renouncing all political connection with New England) may be found willing to stipulate for desisting at once from the further prosecution of the war against the South, and in such case, the government of the Confederate States would be willing to enter into a league, offensive and defensive, with the States thus desisting, of a permanent and enduring character." But in the 4th resolution, the confederates declared their unalterable opposition, in the event of peace, to form any commercial treaty with the New England States, "with whose people, and in whose ignoble love of gold and brutifying fanaticism, this disgraceful war has mainly originated."

"Mr. Speaker—I can set in my seat no longer and see so much by-playing going on. These men are trifling with the best interests of the country. They should have asses' ears to set off their heads, or they are traitors and secessionists at heart. I say there are traitors and secessionists at heart in this senate. Their actions prove it. Their speeches prove it. Their gibes and laughter and cheers here nightly, when their speakers get up to denounce the war and the administration, prove it. I can set here no longer and not tell these traitors what I think of them; and while so telling them, I am responsible, myself, for what I say. I stand upon my own bottom. I am ready to meet any man on this floor in any manner, from a pin's point to the mouth of a cannon, upon this charge against these traitors. [Great applause from the galleries.] I am an old man of sixty-five. I came to Illinois a poor boy; I have made a little something for myself and family. I pay $3,000 a year in taxes. I am willing to pay $6,000; aye $12,000! [striking his desk with a tremendous blow, sending the ink whirling in the air.] Aye, I am willing to pay my whole fortune, and then give my life to save my country from these traitors that are seeking to destroy it. [Tremendous cheering.]

Mr. Speaker, you must excuse me; I could not sit longer in my seat and calmly listen to these traitors. My heart, that feels for my poor country, would not let me. My heart, that cries out for the lives of our brave volunteers in the field; that these traitors at home are destroying by thousands—would not let me. My heart that bleeds for the widows and orphans at home, would not let me. Yes, these traitors and villains in the senate [striking the desk with his clenched fist, that made the chamber resound] are killing my neighbors' boys, now fighting in the field. I dare to say this to these traitors right here, and I am responsible for what I say to any one or all of them. [Cheers.] Let them come on now right here. I am sixty-five years old, and I have made up my mind to risk my life right here, on this floor, for my country. [This announcement was received with great cheering. Here the crowd gathered around him—his seat being near the railing—to protect him from violence, while many sympathetic eyes flashed defiance.] These men sneered at Col. Mack, a few days since. He is a small man, but I am a large man. I am ready to meet any of them in place of Col. Mack. I am large enough for any of them, and I hold myself ready for them now and at any time, [Cheering from the galleries.]

Mr. Speaker, these traitors on this floor should be provided with hempen collars. They deserve them. They deserve hanging, I say [raising his voice and striking the desk with great violence.] The country would be the better of swinging them up. I go for hanging them, and I dare to tell them so, right here to their traitorous faces. Traitors should be hung. It would be the salvation of the country to hang them. For that reason I must rejoice at it. [Cheers.]

Mr. Speaker, I must beg the pardon of the gentlemen in this senate who are not traitors, but true, loyal men, for what I have said. I only intend it and mean it for secessionists at heart. They are here in this senate. I see them gibe and smirk and grin at a true Union man. Must I defy them? I stand here ready for them and dare them to come on. [Cheering.] What man, with the heart of a patriot, could stand this treason any longer? I have stood it long enough. I will stand it no longer. [Cheers.] I denounce these men and their aiders and abettors, as rank traitors and secessionists. Hell itself could not spew out a more traitorous crew than some of the men that disgrace this legislature, this State and this country. For myself I protest against and denounce their treasonable acts. I have voted against their measures; I will do so to the end. I will denounce them as long as God gives me breath; and I am ready to meet the traitors themselves here or anywhere, and fight them to the death. [Prolonged cheers.] I said I paid $3,000 a year taxes. I do not say it to brag of it. It is my duty, yes, Mr. Speaker, my privilege to do it. But some of these traitors here, who are working night and day to put some of their miserable little bills and claims through the legislature, to take money out of the pockets of the people, are talking about high taxes. They are hypocrites, as well as traitors. I heard some of them talking about high taxes in this way, who did not pay $5 to the support of the government. I denounce them as hypocrites as well as traitors. [Cheers.]

The reason they pretend to be afraid of high taxes is that they do not want to vote money for the relief of the soldiers   They want to embarrass the government and stop the war. They want to aid the seccessionists to conquer our boys in the field. They care about high taxes! They are picayune men anyhow, and pay no taxes at all, and never did, and never hope or expect to. This is the excuse of traitors. [Cheers,]

Mr Speaker, excuse me. I feel for my country, in this her hour of danger, from the tips of my toes to the ends of my hair. That is the reason I speak as I do. I cannot help it. I am bound to tell these men to their teeth what they are, and what the people, the true, loyal people, think of them. [Cheering, which the speaker attempted to stop by rapping on his desk but really aided, not unwillingly.]

Mr. Speaker, I have said my say. I am no speaker. This is the only speech I ever made, and I don't know that it deserves to be called a speech. But I could not sit still any longer and see these scoundrels and traitors work out their hellish schemes to destroy the Union. They have my sentiments; let them one and all make the most of them. I am ready to back up all I say, and I repeat it, to meet these traitors in any manner they may choose, from a pin's point to the mouth of a cannon."

With a parting whack on his desk, the loyal old gentleman resumed his seat, amidst the din of cheering and the clapping of hands.

LEGISLATIVE FRAUDS.—The very last hour of this session was disgraced by the perpetration of one of those parliamentary swindles which in modern times are not infrequent in deliberative bodies. The partisan strife which obtained between the constitutional convention and the governor, was, if anything, intensified between this legislature and that functionary. At the special session of 1861 the executive department had been provided in the most liberal spirit with a fund of $50,000 for extraordinary and contingent expenses, which was largely looked to as aid for the sick and wounded Illinois soldiers in the field. But owing to the great number of agents employed to visit different camps and accompany the regiments, to look after the sanitary wants of the volunteers; extra surgeons sent down the rivers in anticipation of battles; steamboats chartered, also in expectation of battles, to go and bring home the wounded and disabled soldiers, all of which, and much more, was in constant operation during the winter of 1861-2, prompted doubtless, by the most charitable of motives, but exhibiting in some instances a prodigal disregard of economy and a lavish display of means, amounting almost to recklessness, and resulting in the wounded and disabled soldiers, for whom ostensibly much of this parade was made, receiving only $1,119 out of the $50,000 appropriated.*

Much fault had been found by the Democracy at home with his excellency in the distribution of this fund. Both he and his many agents were charged with having been more zealous during their perigrinations among the Illinois volunteers in distributing documents to defeat the new constitution than in alleviating their suf-

* The State Treasurer, June 16, 1863, gave the following items of expenditures, as paid out of that appropriation: Steamboat trips by the governor and party: $8,887; for the quartermaster's department, $9,874; receipts of John Wood, $3,264; for Adjutant General's office, $7,748; Commissary General's Office, $3,043; trips to Washington by Messrs. Yates, Trumbull, Kellogg and others, $4,449; messenger and clerk hire in governor's office, $8,463; J. K. Forest to Cairo and back, $120; sick and wounded Illinois soldiers, who fought at Belmont, Forts Henry and Donelson, and at Shiloh, $1,119. The war demonstrated sanitary efforts to be most efficient in the hands of private enterprise. Untold blessings were meted out by the sanitary bureaus in charge of noble and devoted men and women, who, unlike politicians in the employ of the State, did not seek personal glorification among the volunteers, but truly to mitigate the sufferings of the sick and wounded.

ferings. Indeed, Gov. Yates in all the exuberance of his patriotism, was ever charged by the Democracy as being actuated by partisan motives, and guided by considerations of personal ambition; that in all his transactions with the raising of the vast number of Illinois volunteers and in his appointments, he looked forward to political aggrandizement; and that in his ardent desire to earn the honorable soubriquet of the "soldiers' friend," he discovered untold preferment to himself. And both the convention, and now the legislature, doubtless mainly from partisan motives, refused further to solely entrust him with the distribution of more sanitary funds. Early in the session (January 7th) an appropriation of $10,000 in gold had been made for the Illinois sick and wounded soldiers in view of the battle of Murfreesboro, and the probable advance upon Vicksburg. Three commissioners, (Lewis D. Erwin, W. W. Anderson, and Ezekial Boyden), were appointed to distribute this fund, who sold the gold for paper, realizing a large premium, and the whole, it seems, was carefully expended with great relief and benefit to the needy soldiers, who received over 80 per cent. of it. But the Governor was anxious for another $50,000. He sent in a special message upon the subject, couched in terms of rare beauty and felicity of expression, evincing a noble sympathy for our struggling soldiery in upholding the flag of our country. It was a plea such as few men are capable of making, and should have gone to the most caloused heart.

The senate had passed two appropriation bills of precisely similar titles. These bills were numbered respectively 202 and 203; they were in the same handwriting, and when folded looked alike, except as to their numbers. No. 203 provided for the payment of the salaries of executive officers, the ordinary expenses of the executive department, the adjutant general's office, and the various other usual items of appropriation. This was acceptable to the Democrats. No. 202 provided besides all these items, a contingent fund of $10,000, and $2,500 for the hire of a gardener, both to be expended at the option of the governor; and an appropriation of $50,000 to the "aid of the sick and wounded Illinois soldiers; to defray the contingent expenses of the executive department; for the pay of clerks in the governor's office; of messengers on public service; of assistants in the adjutant general's office, quartermaster general's office and the commissary general's office, lithography, postage and other incidental expenses," all to be expended by order of the governor.

From this array of participants in the $50,000 fund, the sick and wounded soldier, although first mentioned, it may be well imagined, would very likely be the last to receive a slender share. The Democrats opposed No. 202, as providing his excellency with a "corruption fund," but were willing to pass No. 203. When the latter came up for action in the house, a short time before the adjournment, it was upon demand twice read at large to be certain that the $50,000 item was not in it. The third time the bill was read by its title only and passed, 59 to 2. The chief clerk who had been out, came in as the roll was being called upon the passage of the bill, and being informed that it was necessary to use haste in reporting the bill back to the senate, as the hour of adjournment was at hand, he sat down to write the message to that effect, but at this juncture, by some adroit prestidigitation, the obnoxious bill, No. 202, was substituted and received the endorsement of having passed, due to No. 203. It was immediately reported back to the senate, as hastily sent to the governor, approved, and returned to the senate where it orginated.

The house had not proceeded far with other business, when the noise and apparent exultation among Republican members at the north end of the hall, and the adjacent lobby, revealed the fact that Democrats, notwithstanding their vigilance, had been tricked in the passage of this obnoxious measure. A scene of the wildest confusion ensued. Information was menacingly demanded of the speaker; a resolution was introduced, recalling the bill from the hands of the governor, but, as many members had in the meantime left for home, it failed for want of the requisite three-fourths vote. A protest, detailing the circumstances of the fraud, was signed by 41 Democratic members and spread upon the journal. The treasurer was requested not to honor any drafts upon the fund thus fraudulently appropriated. Accordingly, when the governor shortly after drew upon the fund, he found that guardian of the people's strong box, (a Democrat), recalcitrant. A writ of mandamus was sued out of the Supreme Court, then sitting at Ottawa, a day before its adjournment, against the treasurer, requiring him to show cause why he did not pay the warrants drawn upon that fund; but before answer could be made the court adjourned. It is probable that it was designed in advance by the suitors that the case should not go to trial, rendering public all the facts connected with the passage of the bill, in which rumor at the time involved a certain noted Democrat, a member and high official of the house. And thus the perpetrators of this legislative swindle have escaped deserved exposure and merited public disgrace.*

The winter session of the 23d general assembly proved a most unprofitable one to the people. The dominant party, engrossed with the peace resolutions, passed but one measure of public advantage, that of abolishing the State quartermaster and commis-

---

* Another most audacious legislative swindle, well illustrating the careless manner of enacting laws under the old constitution, and the tricks by which corrupt men, both as lobbyists and members, gained advantages, was the "Chicago Gridiron bill," as it was nicknamed, passed by this general assembly at the June session. The title of the bill, "An act to incorporate the Wabash Railway Company," was calculated to convey the deceptive idea of a railroad in the Wabash region of the State, instead of which it gave to a few sharpers in Chicago most extraordinary franchises over the streets of that city. It provided for the exclusive construction of horse-railways through 18 of the principal streets of Chicago, across 4 of its most important bridges, and on any common highways in either or all of the towns of South Chicago, Hyde Park, Lake, Worth, West Chicago, Lyons, Jefferson, Cicero, and Proviso, adjacent to the city, and from to time to change, enlarge and extend the location thereof. It allowed the corporators to impose and collect such tolls as it should fix, without restraint from the city council. This was an immense monopoly, affecting the material interests of the whole city. It was a subject properly for the city council of Chicago, but neither that body nor the people, which they represented, knew aught of this monstrous movement which sought to filch from them the control of their own streets and highways, though the recess had intervened between its passage in the senate and in the house.

It was introduced into the senate by a member from the southeastern part of the State, which added to the deception, and in a loose way permitted to pass that body in January, without being read other than by its title, the Senate relying upon the statement of the member introducing it, that it was simply a bill for an ordinary railroad charter, containing the usual privileges. Its provisions were not generally known to senators who passed it, or to the public until a few days before it was manouvered through the house on the 8th of June, under the pressure of interested members and a powerful lobby influence. And now, the swindle having transpired, the angry protests against it from the people of Chicago came loud and deep, the newspaper press of the State joining its voice to the indignant refrain. The governor vetoed it, and in his message of June 19th, 1863, exposed its horrid enormity very fully. This message was addressed to the general assembly which he had dissolved nine days before—the "rump" being still in session.

sary departments, which, since their supercedure by the general government, not without reluctance from Gov. Yates, as we have seen, had become useless and expensive encumbrances. Every other of its party measures met with disaster. The *habeas corpus* and illegal arrest bills; the prohibition of negro immigration; the congressional apportionment, and the armistice resolutions—succeeding alone with the recess resolution; while the Republicans, by their vigilance, fidelity and courage, succeeded in the defeat of all these, they were also balked, as we have described, in the full fruition of their only affirmative measure, the $50,000 appropriation for the sick and wounded Illinois soldiers.

Reaction among the People against the Peace Movement of the Legislature.—Both during the session after the armistice resolutions had been brought forward and throughout the recess, the people, being awakened by these schemes of the politicians who thus sought to place Illinois on record as an anti-war State, held public meetings all over the State, giving expression to their loyal sentiments, and evincing the strongest devotion to the war for the Union. From Egypt the Douglas democrats sent out their resolves "that, as citizens of Illinois and as democrats, we are in favor of the continued and vigorous prosecution of the war until the supremacy of the constitution is acknowledged in every State of the Union; that the errors of the administration, while they should not be adopted by the people, form no excuse for any loyal citizen to withhold his support from the government;" that they were inflexibly opposed to the secession heresy of a Northwestern Confederacy, &c., recommending to the "true democracy to organize and be prepared to resist all schemes of disloyal men looking to a further disruption of the Union."

It was a gloomy period of the war. The turning point in the great civil conflict had not been reached. Vicksburg—strong and defiant—had not only not surrendered, but repulsed the national troops under Sherman in January preceding. Nor had Gettysburg been fought. The great captains of the war had not been revealed on our side. In the West, the battles of Shiloh, Perryville and Murfreesboro had proven little better than defeats; while in the East, Fredericksburg, speedily followed by Chancellorville, had spread a general gloom. Said the New York Tribune: "If 3 months more of earnest fighting shall not serve to make a serious impression on the rebels—if some malignant fate has decreed that the blood and treasure of the nation shall ever be squandered in fruitless efforts, let us bow to our destiny, and make the best attainable peace." It was at the time no doubt honestly believed by many that the States could not be re-united by military coercion—that the war was a failure.

Gold, the most sensitive index of the fortunes of the war, was steadily on the rise. Rebel bonds bore a premium in the London market. The picture was a dark and dreary one and, in the West, relieved only by the brilliant military exploit of Gen. McClernand in the capture of Arkansas Post.

But amidst all these dreary scenes—the demand of the democracy for peace, the low ebb of the tide in the fortunes of the war, and the discouragement of the many staunch friends of the Union—the heart of the soldier remained undismayed. Hardly an Illinois regiment, learning the situation at home, and the false and dishonorable attitude in which the legislature sought to place the State before the country, but what held meetings and expressed their abhorrence of the " fire in the rear, " as it was termed —repledged their loyalty to the Union and devotion to the flag— breathing the noblest of patriotic sentiments commingled with purposes of the most determined valor. These resolutions poured in in great profusion, the columns of the republican press being fairly laden with them. The democracy charged the voluminous loyal expressions to be merely the dictates of those " whose shoulders were adorned with the stars, eagles and bars. " If such was the case it but showed discipline in the right direction. Few of the masses, even under our form of government, exercise either original or independent political opinions.

It was the unworthy action of this legislature that precipitated the defection of such men as John A. Logan, Isham N. Hainie, John A. McClernand, and a host of others from the democratic ranks.

In his address to the soldiers of the 17th army corps, dated Memphis, Feb. 12th, 1863, Gen. Logan, in allusion to the "falsifying of public sentiment at home," said: "Intriguing political tricksters, demagogues and time-servers, whose corrupt deeds are but a faint reflex of their corrupt hearts, seem determined to drive our people on to anarchy and destruction. The day is not far distant when traitors and cowards, North and South, will cower before the indignation of an outraged people. March bravely onward!" Gen. Hainie, in a private letter, gave his unqualified endorsement to every paragraph, line and word of Gen. Logan's address. Gen. McClernand, in his letter to John Van Buren, dated Feb. 22d, 1863, denounced these democratic factionists as "Northern peace mongers, who 'will be carried away,' if not by the torrent of public opinion, eventually by force of arms." For the expression of such sentiments, these gentlemen were now read out of the party by the peace organs of the democracy.

There were also a number of anti-war meetings held in different parts of the State under the management of the democratic leaders, declaring hostility to the policy of the war as then prosecuted by the national administration, which culminated in the large mass meeting of the 17th of June, at Springfield, of which more further along.

The party nomenclature of the period as applied to democrats also evinced deep partisan feeling and was of the most insulting character: " Copperheads, " " Snakes, " " Butternuts," "Secesh, " &c. The origin of these opprobrious epithets, we will not stop to give.

Military Arrests.—Of the many arrests of our citizens by military authority we can only relate one or two of the most notable. A Capt. Linsley, by order of Col. Carrington of Indianapolis, was stationed at Terre Haute to arrest deserters in Vigo and surrounding counties of Indiana, nothing being said about Illinois. In March, 1863, he sent two sergeants into Clark county of this State who arrested four deserters. The mother of one of them, at the instance of the Hon. John Schofield, acting as her attorney, to procure her son's release swore out a warrant charging the officers with kidnapping. The sergeants were arrested and taken before the Hon. Chas. H. Constable, circuit judge, the court being then in session at Marshall. In their examination the judge doubted the sufficiency of the papers exhibited as authority for the sergeants to make the arrests in Illinois. Their attorney, R. L. Dulaney, then attempted to prove that the men alleged to be kidnapped were in fact deserters from the federal army, whom any one might arrest as in the case of any criminal. This was not allowed to be shown by the judge. He bound them over in a bond of $500 and discharged the deserters. At the request of the sergeants, Judge C. gave them a written statement:

"That Messrs. McFarland and Thomas Long, have been arrested and brought before me for examination on a charge of kidnapping, and that I have deemed it my duty to hold them over in a bond of $50u to appear next Thursday morning, to answer farther to said charge, and I have ordered the discharge from custody of James Gammen, Hugh Scott, M. Belcher and Jno. Tanner, four men whom they had arrested upon the ground that they were deserters from Co. K, 30th Ill. Vol."

The sergeants procured bail without difficulty, though they were strangers. Subsequently, on the day of their trial, and while it was in progress, Col. Carrington, with a force of 250 infantry, surrounded the court house at Marshall, and with 50 dismounted cavalrymen in citizens' dress entered the court room without exciting surprise, and at the very moment the adjournment of court for dinner was announced, stepped forward and arrested Judge Constable before he had quitted the bench. The infantry were stationed outside to quell any attempt at rescue by the citizens. There was no molestation, however. Judge Constable, who was taken by surprise, was considerably unmanned at this summary exhibition of military power.*

The prisoners were released, and the judge trying them was torn from his judicial seat in the midst of his labors, his court adjourned by military power, and he conveyed a prisoner to a foreign State. Could audacity, apparently, in a free government, outside of the theatre of actual war, go further? Yet of all the military arrests made in this State, this was the most justifiable. The offense consisted in no mere disloyal gasconade, but in substantial acts which, by the discharge of four deserters and the imprisonment of two officers, was an actual interference with and injury to the military effort of the government to suppress the rebellion.

About the 1st of April Judge Constable was brought from Indianapolis to Springfield and delivered over to the civil authorities. An affidavit was filed before the U. S. Commissioner, charging him with encouraging desertion by ordering the release of the four deserters from the custody of the officers. By agreement the examination was had before Judge Treat, of the U. S. district court, the district attorney, Lawrence Weldon, appearing for the government, and Stuart & Edwards for the prisoner. After hearing all the evidence, the defendant was discharged.

Later in the spring of 1863, W. H. Green, a State Senator from Massac, and G. W. Wall, of Perry, were arrested by order of the provost marshal. The charges do not appear. In the Senate Mr. Green had signalized himself as an ardent supporter of the armistice resolutions, laboring earnestly to bring that body to a vote upon them. The republican press brought forward many of his

---

*See Terre Haute Express.

anti-war utterances, such as " we (he and his constituents) stand
upon the border as peace makers, and we intend that unless it be
over our dead bodies, there shall be no fraternal blood shed," &c.
Mr. G. took occasion to deny some of these charges, in a published
letter. He was also found fault with for wearing a " butternut"
suit, &c. General Buford required each of these gentlemen to
take the oath of allegiance to the U. S.; to write letters to the commander of the post confessing the acts for which they had been
arrested, with expressions of regret and promises of future con
duct comporting with that of loyal citizens; and to declare they
had not aided deserters to escape nor discouraged enlistments,
whereupon they were released from arrest.*

Many others of our citizens too numerous to mention were arrested, some taken to Washington bastiles and others incarcerated in Fort Lafayette, in New York harbor. It was about this
time that the noted arrest of Mr. Vallandigham of Ohio was
made.

Suppression of the Chicago Times.—But the general government
did not stop with military arrests and imprisonment of the citizen for his exercise of the right of free speech; it also laid its
hand of power upon the freedom of the public press. The
suppression of the Chicago *Times*—a newspaper which exercised an unusual license in its criticism of the policy of
the administration and the conduct of the war—formed the
most notable event of that sort in Illinois. This was done by order of Major Gen. Burnside, in command of the department of
the Ohio, dated Cincinnati, June 1st, 1863. Brig. Gen. Jacob
Ammen, in command of the district of Illinois, stationed at Camp
Butler, was charged with its execution. The cause assigned in
the order was "the repeated expression of disloyal and incendiary
sentiments" by that newspaper. The same order (No. 84), in paragraph 1, included the N. Y. *World*. Gen. Ammen was directed
to allow no more issues of the paper to appear, and if necessary
to "take military possession of the *Times* office." The editor was
also notified of the order by telegraph from Gen. Burnside, June
2d. Late in the night of that day Messrs. Storey and Worden,
the proprietors, made application to Judge Drummond, of the U.
S. court for the Northern district of Illinois, for an injunction to
restrain Gens. A. E. Burnside, Jacob Ammen, and Capt. Jas.
S. Putnam, of Camp Douglas, detailed to act, from carrying
into effect the order of suppression. About midnight the court
granted a temporary restraining order upon the defendants, until
the application could be heard and determined in open court. Learning which, Capt. Putnam hastily departed to his post at Camp Douglas, gathered a sufficient military force, returned, and about 4 o'clock
in the morning of the 3d, executed Gen. Burnside's order by
taking possession of the *Times* office, in defiance and contempt of
the order of the civil tribunal. In the meantime the *Times* issues
of the 3d of June, in great part, had been struck off and found
circulation.

Here was presented the grave question of a collision between
the civil and military authority of the U. S. A stay of proceedings in court was granted on the same day to give time for service

<hr>

*See Illinois State Register, May 6 1863

on Gen. Ammen. Judge David Davis, presiding in the U. S. Circuit Court at Springfield, was telegraphed to come to Chicago and join in hearing the application for the injunction, with which he complied.

Meantime the excitement created in Chicago was intense. On the evening of the same day a large concourse of citizens met and expressed their deep indignation against this military despotism. On the following day the intensity of the popular feeling having steadily increased, fears were entertained that an outbreak of mob violence would attack the *Tribune* establishment (republican). A secret meeting of prominent republicans, and a few democrats, was now held in the circuit court room, to devise ways to preserve the peace of the city. It was participated in by Senator Trumbull, Hon. I. N. Arnold, Wm. B. Ogden, Judge Van Higgins, (a heavy stockholder in the *Tribune*,) S. W. Fuller, Jas. F. Joy, C. Beckwith, A. C. Coventry, Judge Dickey, S. S. Hayes, A. W. Harrington and others. A petition to the president was prepared representing that the peace of the city, if not the welfare of the country, would be promoted by rescinding the order suppressing the *Times;* that this was asked upon the ground of expediency alone, without regard to party; and his favorable consideration was respectfully asked. The petition was telegraphed to the president. Messrs. Trumbull and Arnold sent an additional dispatch especially inviting his prompt and serious consideration of the very grave state of affairs. By half-past six p. m. of the same day, he replied by telegraph unconditionally revoking the order of suppression. But one number of the *Times'* issues, that of Thursday, June 4th, failed to appear. Pecuniarily it may well be guessed the paper was not long injured, as by this it gained largely in its sales.

After thus saving it from the fury of the gathering mob, the *Tribune* said: "The order of revocation was, and is universally felt, to be a most unfortunate blunder. * As the matter stands it is is a triumph of treason. The minions of Jeff. Davis have won a victory by which they will not fail to profit. * Oh! for a Gen. Jackson while this war lasts, and it would not last long." The republican press was generally chagrined at the wavering conduct of the president, and in a tone of irony exclaimed: "It is not true that any republican has telegraphed to Washington to seek the presidential revocation of Gen. Grant's order to suppress Pemberton's issues of shot and shell at Vicksburg." The Belleville Zeitung (German republican), somewhat profanely said: "May the devil take the 'honesty' of Lincoln and his cabinet. We are for the energy and power of action of Fremont. Let Fremont be our next president."

In the meantime Judges Davis and Drummond had been hearing the able arguments of counsel on the application for an injunction, but the president's revocation stayed all further proceedings in court, and, what is to be regretted, no opinion was rendered upon this very interesting question. From Judge Drummond's remarks upon the motion to defer the application till after service, we gather the following:

"As the officer of the government, I will seek to maintain that government, but I believe that the constitution and the laws furnish ample means to suppress the rebellion. * When there are military operations going on—when there are armies in the field in hostile array, in battle, in movement, then the civil law ceases and then comes in the martial law. But the armies of the U. S., the major generals of the U. S., act under the authority of law, and the military law is just as much under the constitution and under the law as is the civil law, precisely. * It is desirable that we should know whether we live under a government of law or under a government of force. * I believe that we live under a government of law, and I trust that every citizen of the community also rests under the same belief, and that all, each for himself, will remember that we live under a government of law."

Secret Politico-Military Societies.—The year 1863 was also prolific in the organization of secret political orders with semi-military attributes. They were variously known as "Knights of the Golden Circle," "Union Leagues," the "S. B's," (whatever that stood for) &c. The former of these was of democratic and the two latter of republican origin. Various circumstances contributed to the wide extension of these orders. The open clamor for peace on the part of many leading democrats; the opinion that the war was a failure—indirectly conceded by some of the staunchest republican newspapers; the unpopularity of the conscript law with the $300 exemption clause and its frequent denunciation, these, joined with the political excitement by the peace resolutions of the legislature, and the many expressions from public meetings in opposition thereto, produced a serious impression among the people not unmingled with feelings of personal insecurity. During this year, too, many deserters were at large, prowling about the neighborhoods of their homes, often leading their friends or relatives into difficulties with the secret agents of the government in pursuit of them, who, when they became known, of course swaggered and boasted not a little of their prowess and the terrible retribution to be visited upon certain localities supposed to harbor them. There were also at home rather an unusual number of soldiers on furlough—roistering blades, pompous in their neat, blue uniforms —into whose ears were poured by partizan friends tales of horror, how the venomous "Copperhead democrats" purposed resisting the draft, subvert the State government, and form an alliance with the rebel confederacy. The soldiers, thus incited by narrow and prejudiced republicans, often swaggered about insulting good citizens and making threats of dire vengeance, which they felt it their duty and privilege to wreak, and sometimes they went so far as to actually perpetrate indignities and outrages upon really unoffending democratic civilians. The general government, too, as we have seen, was making numerous military arrests for the mere utterance—often but an idle or thoughtless boast—of disloyal sentiments.

There was consequently little open discussion of the war indulged on either side in many portions of the State. A deep feeling of mistrust regarding the thoughts and purposes of one's own neighbor was all-pervading. The air was rife with whispers of direst portent as to the treatment to be visited upon this or that citizen, who should have uttered this or done that disloyal thing. The State was under martial law; and it was generally felt that outrages growing out of the political condition of the times, or perpetrated at such a period, would either meet with ready excuse and escape of punishment, upon the one side, or a summary visitation of revenge from the other. Each was thus steeled against the first overt act. Under these circumstances men of prior partizan affiniteis, even if not then in full accord upon the great question of the war, instinctively sought to bind themselves together by ties of the strongest oaths for mutual protection, which doubtless did not always stop with provisions against personal indignities and local outrages alone, but may have included purposed resistence to the lawful demands of the government in the enforcement of the conscript law to carry on a war odious to their political sentiments.

For greater efficiency, here and there these combinations, on both sides, partook of the character of military organizations; but it is questionable if any were furnished with arms other than home affairs, shot guns, &c. The drilling was often done with corn stalks. The associations of one side caused the other to do the same; while the utmost quiet prevailed as to the usual wrangles and discussions incident to all public questions of great interest in this country. Both sides feared and guarded against precipitating a general collision. No one knew what a personal affray might instantly develop as to the number of sworn assistants on either side, nor what weapons were concealed, ready to leap forth upon the first emergency. To such considerations an active imagination was of course ready to add its legions of numbers and dire results. In some respects this mutual forbearance, born of caution, may have been well. But these secret associations by skillful and industrious agencies were extending their power and influence all over the country.

All secret political societies are dangerous to the State and to the liberty of the people. The very fact of their secrecy stamps them as wrongful and hazardous. Secrecy eviscerates true democracy or republicanism of its essential principles. To deny an open comparison of views and a free discussion of questions affecting the public weal, or the rights of the citizen, is to remove the underlying safeguards of an intelligent liberty. It is but just to say that the democratic press counselled the people against them.

The republican press, with untiring industry, circulated reports that the democrats were preparing and intended to resist the draft under the conscript law. A regiment was organized and armed by the State, by order of Adjutant General Fuller, "for the purpose of guard and protection of the State of Illinois"— meaning that it was to aid in enforcing the draft. Col. R. H. Hough was assigned to its command. This ill-advised step, one would suppose, was rather calculated to provoke the armed collision so much dreaded. Many indeed feared, that, by these various means, a struggle might be brought about in the State. Judge O'Melveny, a fierce anti-war democrat, wrote: "I still think we are nearing convulsion in the North. It must be with us the last alternative, but free speech ought to be made the issue —no point more available; to surrender it, is to perish; and if fate and destiny so will it, let the democracy go down with the constitution and with liberty in one common struggle for life and power." So much was said of secret traitorous political organizations, and their threatened violent resistance to the draft under the conscript law, that Judge Davis, of the U. S. circuit court, during the June term at Springfield, charged the grand jury that there were secret organizations with "grips, signs and pass-words, having for their object, resistance to law, and the overthrow of the government. * If anywhere in this State bad men have combined

together for such wicked purpose, bring them to light and let
them receive the punishment due their crimes"—charging them
further with reference to any kind of resistance or obstruction to
the enforcement of the draft, and the aiding or abetting of deserters by advice, assistance or harboring them.

While the many rumors of lawless conduct on the part of these
organizations, with which the press teemed, were exaggerated, all
was not smoke. A number of atrocious murders were committed,
and armed resistance offered to the arrest of deserters
in many portions of the State, which we have neither the
space nor disposition to give in detail. Of the counties
in which these disreputable proceedings occurred, we may
mention (commencing south and proceeding north) Union, Williamson, Richland, Clark, Coles, Fayette, Montgomery, Greene,
Scott, Tazewell and Fulton. The most pertinacious resistance
was offered in Scott and Greene, whither a detachment of over 100
mounted soldiers was sent to ferret out the camps of lawless men
hid among the glades and swamps bordering the Illinois river.
The most fatal collision occurred in Coles, at Charleston, on the
22d of March, 1864, between citizens in attendance upon circuit
court, under the lead of Sheriff O'Hara, and the re-enlisted veterans of the 54th Illinois regiment. Four soldiers were killed and
8 wounded, one mortally; of the citizens, 3 were killed at the time;
one accidentally. Some time after, two of the O'Haras were waylaid and assassinated in the woods.* Assaults upon various men
were made in Edgar and some other counties. A raid, projected
from Cass, was made upon Jacksonville to intimidate the federal
authorities in the discharge of their duties. In Hancock, Adams,
Pike, Calhoun and other counties bordering the Mississippi, incursions were made by rebel "bushwhackers" from Missouri, who
were said to be but too freely countenanced and harbored. It is
also doubtless true that these scenes of lawlessness uniformly
occurred in regions where unconditional unionism was in minority
and the loyal sentiment of the people overborne. But aside from
these comparatively petty outbreaks of a few misguided, perhaps
lawless men in scattered localities, no serious purpose to any considerable extent really ever existed to resist the draft in Illinois,
or to obstruct the operations of the laws of the general government. The great mass of the people, Democrat as well as Republican, were ever willing and ready to obey the law, both State
and national, dutifully, quietly and cheerfully.

Prorogation of the Last Democratic Legislature.—The 23d general assembly, upon the expiration of its recess, met again, June
2d, 1863. Besides a number of bills of a private or local character,
patriotic resolutions, resolutions of thanks to the Illinois volunteers for their valor in the field, and resolutions of a political char-

---

* Much disaffection obtained between citizens (who often gave vent to treasonable
utterances by shouting for Jeff. Davis, &c.,) and soldiers, and many personal indignities were inflicted by the latter upon the former. In Coles, it is said that soldiers, perhaps when intoxicated, out of mere wantonness, would seize farmers, (many of them
doubtless, belonging to the order of the Golden Circle), from their wagons and compel
them to take an oath of allegiance manufactured for the occasion: "You solemnly
swear to support the administration, Abraham Lincoln, all proclamations now issued,
and all that may hereafter be issued, so help you God." At Vandalia a Mr. Smith was
made to take the oath, and afterwards, in an altercation, killed. One of the soldiers
escaped, and his associates, on examination were discharged. Citizens, doubtless American Knights, to the number of 50 or 60, sought to revenge the murder, but failing in
this, burnt a railroad bridge and committed other depredations.

acter, covering the military order suppressing the Chicago *Times*, the military arrests of Illinois citizens, particularly the case of Judge Constable, were numerously introduced. The consideration of the latter character of resolutions elicited warm debate and consumed much valuable time. At this time the army in the West, containing nearly all the Illinois troops, had been active in its approaches upon Vicksburg, and all the severe fighting in the investment of that rebel fortress was over. The casualties to Illinois volunteers were great, and the demands for sanitary aid pressing. On the first day of the session, therefore, in the senate, Mr. Green, who had but recently been the subject of military arrest, as we have seen, introduced a bill, appropriating $50,000 for the sick and wounded Illinois soldiers. In the house a similar bill was introduced by Mr. Fuller, appropriating $100,000 to be disbursed by a commission, consisting of Messrs. John T. Stuart, C. H. Lanphier, and W. A. Turney, all opposed to the administration policy of the war. A bill for taking the Illinois soldiers' vote was also introduced.

On the 3d day of the session, in the senate, a proposition to adjourn *sine die* was extensively discussed and made the special order for the following day. On Monday, June 8th, three Democrats being absent, the senate, on motion of Mr. Vandeveer, a Democrat, passed a resolution by a vote of 14 to 7, to adjourn *sine die* on that instant, at 6 P. M. This the house amended by inserting the 22d of June at 10 A. M. instead. The senate refused to concur by yeas 11 to nays 12. By the constitution, in case of disagreement between the two houses with respect to the time of adjournment, the governor was empowered to adjourn the assembly to such a day as he deemed proper. Such conjuncture now obtained. On the 9th the senate transacted but little business. There was also disagreement upon the house soldiers' relief bill, the senate having added the names of the governor and the treasurer to the commission, to which the house refused to accede. On the morning of June 10th, in the house, shortly after a motion by Mr. Lawrence to take up the general appropriation bill had, at the instance of Mr. Fuller, been laid on the table, and while not a Democrat was dreaming of such a move, the governor's private secretary entered the hall, and being announced by the door-keeper, but without recognition from the chair, (Mr. Burr), read hurriedly, but in a loud tone, his message adjourning the general assembly to the Saturday next preceding the 1st Monday in January, 1865.

This unexpected stroke fell upon the dominant party like a clap of thunder from a clear sky. Their chagrin and anger knew no bounds. They were beaten by the hated governor in parliamentary tactics. Amidst the unexampled din and confusion, all sorts of motions were made. The Republican members at once withdrew, breaking the quorum. The speaker vacated the chair, and the house took an informal recess. In the senate, upon the reading of the prorogation message, a similar scene of excitement took place. Lieutenant-Governor Hoffman said: "In obediance to this order, I do now adjourn this senate until the Saturday preceding the 1st Monday in January, A. D. 1865." He then vacated the chair and retired from the chamber. Senator Underwood was called to the chair. In the afternoon 13 senators were present—

the 12 Republican members having left. In the house 44 members were present; a majority in either house, but not enough to do business, the constitution requiring the presence of two-thirds of the members in each house to constitute a quorum. Regarding the prorogation as illegal both houses continued the session.

It is probable the absconding members knew of the governor's purpose, judging from the promptness with which they and the lieutenant-governor took their departure. Yet upon the other hand, in the senate, Mr. Vandeveer, a Democrat, made the motion to adjourn, on which the disagreement occurred.

Prior to the prorogation in the house a motion had been adopted for a conference committee to reconcile the differences upon the soldiers' $100,000 relief bill. This was, in the present strait, proffered to be accommodated by the house agreeing to the senate amendment to insert the names of the governor and treasurer with the other commissioners. A joint resolution was thereupon adopted, inviting the co-operation of enough Republican members to help pass this much needed measure. If a quorum had been obtained and the bill regularly passed, it would have been void because of the legality of the prorogation, as subsequently decided by the supreme court. But the Republicans showed no disposition to accede to this request, although the legality of the adjournment was then generaly doubted by both parties. The fiat had gone forth, political capital was a stake, to retract was to prove vacillating and contemptible, and they braved it through.

The sincerity of the Democrats—who believed the bill might be legally passed if a quorum could be obtained—in making this proposition, has been doubted, as inferred from the fact that there had been ample time to pass the bill. True, they had showed no haste, but after the disagreement, there was at stake the pride of consistency with either house, for which some allowance should be made. It cannot be possible that such trifling was intended; that the olive branch was held out only as a lure and deceitful snare. It may also be safely asserted, that the bill would have passed had more time been allowed and the prorogation not been interposed. But for the sake of gratifying the vanity of partisan triumph, the law-makers were dispersed, and this beneficent measure failed. Besides this measure, which appealed directly to one's sympathy and humanity, there were others pending of great public utility, which were thus also defeated; the bill for the sale of coin and the payment of interest in treasury notes; an appropriation to the State Normal University; the general appropriation bill; an appropriation for the erection of a monument to Douglas, and some needed local measures, all in an advanced state of maturity.

Immediately after the prorogation the Democrats prepared a protest, setting forth in detail the injurious consequences to the public of the governor's "monstrous usurpation" of power, signed by 56 representatives and 13 senators. A counterblast to this, addressed to the people of Illinois, was published by 3 Republicans of the senate, and 6 of the house, acting as a committee for this purpose, in defense of the Republican members and the act of the governor. Both were extreme partisan documents, full of accusations of corruption, and devoid of neither errors of fact nor intemperate language.

After the prorogation, the "rump," or moot legislature, as it was variously called, still kept up the session technically. The roll call was studiously avoided so as not to have it appear from the journals that a quorum was not present, and thus the legality of their acts would turn upon the validity of the prorogation alone, which was to be tested in the Supreme Court. On the 23d and 24th of June business was transacted. The governor was informed that they were about to close, asking if he had any further communication to lay before them. He replied that he had not, and did not recognize their legal existence. A joint resolution was thereupon passed, taking a recess until Tuesday after the first Monday in January, 1864.

Before the close of the year a decision was obtained from the Supreme Court, sustaining the validity of the prorogation. This was the first political question that had been before the Supreme Court since the alien case in 1840. A portion of the Democratic press assailed the court (which was Democratic in political sentiment) with great virulence, charging that the

"Decision was not only wholly wrong, but had been made from unworthy motives. It was time that judges who made wrong decisions, to avoid the lash and propitiate the impending anger of their political opponents, should be made to feel the indignation of their former friends whom they had thus betrayed. The Democratic party had asked, and would ask for nothing but impartial fairness at the hands of the judges, and no consideration of delicacy would impel it to silence, if it felt that unworthy personal motives had moved them to deal unfairly with it. We had fondly hoped that in Illinois there was a State court in whom the people could confidently repose as a barrier to frightful invasions of executive power. This hope is dispelled, and we are overwhelmed with sorrow and mortification in view of it."[*]

The deep chagrin of the Democrats at the dispersion of the legislature by the governor is eloquently portrayed by a member, before the Supreme Court, in his capacity as attorney in one of the cases involving the validity of the prorogation. He exclaims: "Malignant partizanship could go no farther. The annals of political warfare display no grosser infraction of the dignities and amenities of private or official life. * * Since the members of the long parliament were driven from their seats with opprobrious epithets by Cromwell, there has been no such exhibition of virtuperative lawlessness."[*]

We will carry this parallel further by adding the concluding part of Cromwell's address to the commons, and see where it leads: "But now I say, your time hath come. The Lord hath disowned you. The God of Abraham, and of Isaac, and of Jacob, hath done with you. He hath no need of you any more. So, he hath judged you and cast you forth and chosen fitter instruments to Him to execute that work in which you have dishonored Him." History repeats itself. The chronicler of the scene adds: "Sullen, humiliated and unpitied, for they had lost the respect of honest men of all denominations, the members of that parliament now sneaked away to find a miserable refuge in the dispised obscurity of private life, deserted by the people in their turn, whom they first deserted at the dictates of a depraved and poor ambition."

The Great Democratic Mass Convention of June 17th, 1863.—The Democratic State committee had issued a call on the 28th of May for a mass convention to assemble at Springfield, June 17th, 1863, being the anniversary of the battle of Bunker Hill, for the purpose of consultation and deliberation upon the state of the coun-

---

* From the Chicago Times.
*See M. W. Fuller's brief.

try, and to give expression in an authoritative form to the views
of public policy entertained by the Illinois Democracy. Prominent democratic orators from foreign States were advertised to
be present to speak, confer and counsel with the Illinois Democracy.

The result was the most extraordinary gathering, in respect of
numbers, fine personal appearance, high character of the men in
attendance and the spirit which pervaded them, that ever
assembled in Illinois. Not less than 40,000 men were present,
representing all parts of the State. It was not a gala day assemblage of men, women and children, but of solid looking, well
attired men, whose countenances betokened thought, earnestness
and determination. They were evidently political leaders of more
or less influence in whatever sections they belonged. Their outward appearance indicated not only this, but also that the great
body of them were men of means. While all classes were more or
less represented, the solid element greatly predominated, giving
tone and character to the whole. No drunkenness, brawling or
semblance of unseemly conduct marred the occasion. No taunting acts of disloyalty by the display of secession flags, shouting
for Jeff Davis, or like conduct calculated to provoke a breach of
the peace, was manifested. A disturbance of the peace while this
immense crowd was in the capital city, leading to a serious out
break, perhaps a collision with the soldiers, was greatly feared by
some prominent officials. Gen. Ammen, commandant of Camp
Butler, took the precaution to order that no soldier be allowed to
leave camp during the whole of that day. But this crowd, though
large, was not a mob. It was composed rather of respectable,
well-to-do and reflective citizens who—whatever their opinion
regarding the war, and that was for peace—would not precipitate a collision voluntarily. Yet it may be well considered,
had it been forced upon them they were not the men to quail;
doubtless many were well prepared for such a contingency. They
had come, not for an excursion to seek relief from and vary the
monotony of home life, but, moved by a feeling of deep earnestness, to compare views and take counsel of one another, and
repledge their devotion to that democratic faith that was in them,
which stood steadfast for the "Union as it was and the constitution as it is ;" to condemn the aggressions of arbitrary power both
State and National, and denounce the "abolitionizing" of the conduct of the war. Prominent republicans had themselves asserted
that "the problem would be [when the war was past] to combine the forms of republican government with the powers of a
monarchical government."* They met to place their ban upon the war
at a time when many earnest hearts were trembling for the cause of
the Union, and when discouragement might be doubly effective.
In the west, Vicksburg was invested, it is true, but it had not
fallen. In the east the victorious legions of Lee, fresh from the
blundering contests on the Rappahannock, and inspired by a
contempt for the Union forces under Hooker, with the utmost
audacity moved clear around him, boldly crossed into Maryland
and deliberately pushed forward to Pennsylvania, while the country stood amazed, and the deepest anxiety pervaded every breast.
Gettysburg, though not far in the future, was not foreseen.

*See Forney's Press.

The meeting was held at the old Fair Ground or Camp Yates, about one mile due west of the old State House. The day was oppressively warm. To give an idea of some of the leading participants we will append a few names:

Senator W. A. Richardson, president; vice presidents; Hons. Chas. A. Constable, Wm. McMurtry, Peter Sweat, J. M. Young, Aaron Shaw, O. B. Ficklin, Wm. F. Thornton, J. W. Merritt, H. M. Vandeveer, B. F. Prettyman, Chas. D. Hodges, John S. McDonald, James Robb, W. H. Gilman, Virgil Hickox, James E. Ewing, E. D. Taylor, A. D. Wright, I. P Rogers, John V. Ayer, A. Withers, David A. Gage, Sargent Gobble, John Cunningham, Noah Johnson, M. Y Johnson, B. S. Edwards, S. Staats Taylor, John Pierson, C. L. Higbee, R. L. Merrick, S. S. Hays, Cyrus Epler, R. M. B. Wilson, John D. Wood, S. A. Buckmaster, Jacob Bowman, S. J. Cross, J. M. Epler, Robert Halloway, Henry Dresser, J. L. D. Morrison, J. K. Stitt, James C. Robinson, W. A. J. Sparks, F. C. Sherman, J. S. Bogan, John C. Champlin, C. A. Walker, and Dr. N. S. Davis. Among the speakers in attendance from abroad we notice the names of Daniel Voorhees, of Indiana, S. S. Cox of Ohio, and Chris. Kribben and Gen. McKinistry, of St. Louis, and from our own State, Richardson, S. S. Marshall, J. R. Eden, Jas. C. Allen, Ex Gov. John Reynolds, J. C. Robinson, Greathous. Bryan, Connolly, Wescott, Chas T. E. Merritt, M. Y. Johnson, J. L. D. Morrison, W. M. Springer, and a host of others. Speaking was constantly had from six different stands, enthusiastic crowds thronging about each.*

The position of the Democracy of Illinois was declared at length in 24 separate paragraphs, which we summarize, except the two last. They declared the supremacy of the constitution of the United States, as well in time of war as peace, which they were ready and willing to obey, as also all laws made in pursuance thereof, so long as they remained upon the statute books, claiming the right to constitutionally change them; they quoted the bill of rights, and upon it arraigned the federal administration for violating nearly every one of its guarantees to the citizen; they condemned the arrest and banishment of Vallandigham, demanding his restoration; denounced the arrest of Judge Constable and the imprisonment of Hon. W. H. Carlin and other citizens of the State, demanding their release; condemned the suppression of the Chicago *Times;* declared their determination to exercise the right of electing public officers in defiance of the demands of power; adhered to the doctrine of State sovereignty; denounced martial law in this State; denounced the recent act of prorogation of the legislature by Gov. Yates as a high-handed usurpation by one department of government of the rights of another; charged the governor with not only not protecting the citizen in his constitutional rights, but violating them himself; denounced secession as a ruinous heresy, and offered their cordial co-operation in securing to the seceded States equal rights if they would return to their allegiance.

"23. That the further offensive prosecution of this war tends to subvert the constitution and the government, and entail upon this nation all the disastrous consequences of misrule and anarchy. That we are in favor of peace upon the basis of a restoration of the Union, and for the accomplishment of which we propose a national convention to settle upon terms of peace, which shall have in view the restoration of the Union as it was and the securing, by constitutional amendments, such rights to the several States and the people thereof, as honor and justice demand.

"24. That we denounce as libellers of the Democratic party, and willful instigators of mischief, those fanatics who are engaged in representing the democracy as wanting in sympathy for our soldiers in the field. Those soldiers are our kindred, our friends and our neighbors, whose interests are identified with our own; whose prosperity is our pleasure; whose suffering is our pain; and whose brilliant achievements are our pride and admiration. Promptly rushing to arms as they did, in answer to the call of their country, they merit our warmest thanks, our sympathy and our support; and we earnestly request the President of the United States to withdraw the "Proclamation of Emancipation," and permit the brave sons of Illinois to fight only for the "Union, the constitution and the enforcement of the laws."

The assembled multitude testified their faith in the last of these declarations by their works on the spot, in contributing the munificent fund of $47,400 for the sick and wounded Illinois soldiers. This very liberal response was one of the noblest and most touch-

*See Illinois Register, June 18th, 1863.

ing scenes ever witnessed. When the call of the committee for this purpose was announced, wallets flew out of pockets thick and fast, and thousands of upraised hands held waiving aloft innumerable greenbacks, inscribed with the interesting $ figures of 5's, 10's, 20's, 50's, &c., impatiently waiting for the passing hats to come round to gather them in. The hats were filled and crammed, passed to the committee, emptied, passed back again and as quickly refilled. Some individual subscriptions were as high as $500. And thus the errand of mercy prospered; the glorious contagion of a philanthropic enthusiasm spreading the while, encouraged with inspiring cheers, while many a thoughtful eye, set perhaps in a stern countenance, dropped a silent tear in sympathy with this beautiful manifestation of a grateful patriotism. Thus were wrought up those tender emotions of love of country, which transported the fond recollections of affectionate hearts after the absent ones, gallantly defending the union and our homes against the cohorts of treason. The warm hearts of these contributors pulsated in unison with a genuine patriotism, albeit their unyielding heads, influenced by partisan feelings, enunciated what we now know to have been a wrongful stand against the further prosecution of the war for the Union. Doubtless they were thoroughly honest in their belief at the time, but its results upon this nation, if carried out, must have been attended with unnumbered woes.

In this munificent offering "the soldier's friend" and his goading backers, who, rather than forego the opportunity of wreaking a partisan triumph by the prorogation of the legislature in defeating the appropriation of $100,000 for the sick sick and wounded Illinois soldiers, doubtless discovered a merited rebuke. It has been asserted that this feeling prompted the large contribution rather than the dictates of a generous philanthropy. But a good deed should not be attributed to bad motives; to do good to those that despitefully use you, is of the highest christian spirit. Crowds of men are not likely to seek revenge in such noble and generous actions; neither was this assemblage the legislature which had been affronted. Col. W. R. Morrison was selected to disburse the fund raised at this meeting, for the relief of the sick and wounded Illinois soldiers.

While this meeting was "called" to give authoritative expression to the views of public policy entertained by the Illinois democracy, the position here assigned to them in the 23d declaration, was but the position of those who framed it, or of that assemblage, not that of the great mass of the party. It was not a delegate but a mass convention, each attendant representing himself and no one else. By this declaration it was proposed precisely to do all the rebels had ever asked—to be let alone. It did not express the sentiments of the Democracy of Illinois. The Democracy had ever been the war party of the country, in all the wars it ever had. The great body of the rank and file were loyal to the core and unconditionally for the war, contending, with rare exceptions, that there was no other honorable alternative but to prosecute it until the authority of the government was acknowledged and respected over all the broad domain of our country. The leading spirits of this meeting forsook the exalted loyal stand of the party as correctly defined by Mr. Douglas, and placed themselves in perfect antagonism with his patriotic utterances, that while the war lasted there could be but two parties in the country—" patriots and traitors." They assumed to speak for the Democracy of Illinois, without delegated authority so to do, and assign to them a position before the country which they abhorred. Their unworthy efforts met with a withering rebuke from the people and they dealt the party a last blow, from which it has not recovered. If not in *articulo mortis*, it has been paralized ever since in the State.

The first fruit of these legislative and convention proceedings was exhibited in the elections of November, 1863, for county officers, which resulted in favor of the Republicans by an aggregate majority of 30,000 votes. A full vote was not polled, it is true, yet there was an actual Union gain of 5,000, and a comparative gain of 46,000 votes over the preceding year.*

On September 3d, 1863—the country having been in the mean time encouraged by the victory of Gettysburg and the fall of Vicksburg— the meeting of the 17th of June was offset by an immense Union gathering at Springfield. Hons. Henry S. Lane, J. R. Doolittle, Zachary Chandler, Gov. Yates, Gens. R. J. Oglesby, John A. McClernand, I. N. Haynie, B. M. Prentiss and many others, addressed the vast assemblage. Mr. Lincoln sent a long and patriotic letter, addressed to the chairman, J. C. Conkling, which was read. Many other patriotic letters from prominent gentlemen in various parts of the country were likewise read. A vigorous prosecution of the war for the Union was urged by all the speakers, and in all the letters—that that was the only true way to an honorable peace.*

The peace efforts of a faction of the Illinois Democracy may be said to have culminated in 1863. With the approach of the election contest of 1864 we discover a manifest weakening in the wonted unanimity of their demands for peace. The desire for party success was stronger than any other political sentiment. The leaders, not unmindful of the expression of the people of Illinois at the polls in November, 1863, were inclined to greater caution in taking advanced unconditional peace ground. Indeed many were the other way. McClellen had loomed up as the most available Democratic candidate for the presidency. It could not be expected that the hero of Antietam, who it was supposed would carry the soldiers' vote to a man, could consistantly be run as an unconditional peace man. Accordingly when the first State Democratic Convention of 1864 met at Springfield, June 15th, they contented themselves with appointing delegates to the national convention, and State presidential electors, without putting a ticket in the field, or adopting a platform, deferring that matter by an overwhelming majority to the action of the national convention shortly to meet at Chicago. A buncomb resolution was adopted to stand by Vallandigham (who had just returned from exile), and the democracy of Ohio (then, also, assembled in convention) in the preser-

---

*Out of the resolutions of the 17th of June sprung a curious quarrel between the peace policy and no policy factions of that meeting, led respectively by Col. Richardson and Gen. Singleton. The "declarations," it seems, were prepared and passed upon the day before by a self constituted committee of congressmen, judges, office holders and office seekers, whose retreat, the latter as he asserted for a long time. could not discover. He claimed the paternity of the 23d "declaration" with only the word "offensive" in the first line added by the committee. Doubtless honors are easy upon that point by this time.

*See Illinois State Journal, Sept. 9th, 1863.

vation of their liberty, but the reiteration of the former bold stand
for peace, for which the masses in Illinois in their expression at
the polls had shown no relish, was shrewdly avoided. This was
regarded as a McClellen triumph, and a rebuke to the peace-on-
any-term's party. But the peace faction against which the tide
was thus strongly setting, was not to be squelched without making
an effort. With the view to influence the approaching State convention, a mass meeting to the number of perhaps 20,000 assembled at Peoria, August the 3d, under the management of the leading peace men of the State. The meeting was also said to have
been called by "a secret organization whose members acted with
the Democratic party. "*General Singleton, author of the 23d declaration of the 17th of June, 1863, presided; and Amos Green,
Grand Commander of the Order of American Knights in Illinois,
who, subsequently, in the trial of the Camp Douglas conspirators
at Cincinnati, turned state's evidence, H. M. Vandeveer, W. W.
O'Brien and others, reported a series of resolutions, in the 2d
of which they "declare that the coercion and subjugation of sovereign States was never contemplated as possible or authorized
by the constitution, but was pronounced by its makers an act of
suicidal folly. But whatever may be the theory of constitutional
power, war, as a means of restoring the Union, has proved a failure and a delusion," etc.; and in the 3d, "that the repeal and
revocation of all unconstitutional edicts and pretended laws, an
armistice, and a national convention for the peaceful adjustment of
our troubles, are the only means of saving our nation from unlimited calamity and ruin."*

In the meantime another Democratic mass convention had
been called to assemble at the capital. The Peoria meeting,
doubtless fearing that the policy to harmonize all the discordant
elements manifest in the party would there prevail, now resolved
to then re-assemble at Springfield, being the 18th of August following, and stamp that meeting, also, with their character. Accordingly, upon that occasion, General Singleton claimed that the
Springfield meeting, which was very largely attended, was but a
continuation of the Peoria meeting; that the officers were already
chosen, and nothing remained to be done but for him as president
to call the multitude to order, listen to the speaking, and pass the
Peoria peace resolutions. But his assumptions met with earnest
protest; however, for the sake of harmony, it was agreed in caucus that Singleton should preside, that the Peoria resolutions
should be reported stripped of two objectionable clauses, and in
addition to pledge the party to the Chicago nominees. This was
strenuously opposed by the ultra peace faction, who declared they
would appeal to the people. The meeting was forthwith called to
order, General Singleton became chairman and addressed the
masses in a forcible and able speech. He was followed by Henry
Clay Dean, of Iowa, in an eloquent effort. The Peoria resolutions
unchanged were then offered for adoption, as also those of June
17th, 1863, and by the chair declared passed. The caucus resolution pledging the efficient support of the Illinois Democracy to the
Chicago nominee for president, whoever he might be, was then

*See correspondence Chicago Times.
*See Illinois Register, Aug. 5th, 1864

offered. It was sharply attacked and laid on the table. Next the Peoria and 17th of June resolutions were offered for adoption at stand No. 2, and there, also, declared passed. The resolution pledging unconditional support to the Chicago nominees was now again offered. A bitter debate, not unmixed with gross personalities, was instantly aroused, resulting this time in the adoption of the resolution. And now the cloven foot having been revealed to the multitude, when the latter resolution was again moved at stand No. 1, amidst much confusion and opposition it was there, also, vociferously adopted. The presiding officer, who had been assailed as a disorganizer, thereupon retired from the meeting in disgust.*

Thus this meeting, after adopting the Peoria and 17th of June resolutions, demanding an armistice, pronouncing the war for the Union a failure and unconstitutional, and proposing an almost unconditional peace with defiant rebels, in the next breath pledged themselves in advance to support a war Democrat for the presidency. But this glaring inconsistency only indicated after all that many of the democratic leaders, in their ardent and ultra opposition to the war for the Union, had been really less disloyal in their true feelings and sentiments than partisan and factious. They were anti-war men because it was not, as they thought, the war of their party. They did not love the Union less, but office more. The partisan strife for place, power and position is a terrible thing in our country, and not at all on the wane.

Nor was this meeting more inconsistent than the Chicago Democratic national convention of 1864, which met a few days later, in the adoption of their platform and the choice of a candidate to be placed upon it.

The 2d resolution declared it as the sense of the American people "that after four years of failure to restore the Union by the experiment of war, during which, under the pretense of military necessity or power higher than the constitution, the constitution itself has been disregarded in every part, and the public liberty and private rights alike trodden down, and the material prosperity of the country essentially impaired; justice, humanity, liberty and the public welfare demand that immediate efforts be made for the cessation of hostilities, with a view to an ultimate convention of the States or other peaceable means to the end that at the earliest practicable moment peace may be restored on the basis of the Federal Union of the States.

To which the distinguished military chieftain, Gen. McClellen, a strong war Democrat, who had dispersed the Maryland Democratic legislature at the point of the bayonet, replied in his letter of acceptance:

"But the Union must be preserved at all hazards. I could not look in the face of my gallant comrades of the army and navy, who survived so many bloody battles, and tell them that their labors and the sacrifice of so many of our slain and wounded brethren have been in vain."

CHICAGO CONSPIRACY.

During the autumn of '64 a conspiracy was detected at Chicago, which had for its object the liberation of the prisoners at Camp Douglas, the burning of the city, and the inauguration of rebellion in the north. Gen. Sweet, who had charge of the camp at the time, first had his suspicions of danger aroused by a number of enigmatically worded letters which passed through the Camp postoffice.

From subsequent developments he became convinced it was the intention of the conspirators to carry out their nefarious designs during the session of the National Democratic Convention in August, but before the time arrived defensive measures were instituted, and the leaders deemed it best to postpone the consummation of their object till the presidential election. They were, however, again destined to be foiled. On the 2d of November, a citizen of St. Louis, an avowed secessionist, but in reality a government detective, followed a criminal from that city to Springfield, and thence to Chicago. Here, while on the alert for the fugitive, he met a former acquaintance, a member of the order of American Knights, from whom he learned that the rebel

*See Illinois Register, Aug. 19th, 1864.

Marmaduke was in the city. After a short interview he met Dr. Edwards, a citizen of Chicago and a rebel sympathizer, who asked him if he knew Southern soldiers were in town. The detective answering in the negative, his interlocutor further informed him that Marmaduke was stopping at his house under the assumed name of Burling, and mentioned as a "good joke" that he had a British passport made out under the same cognomen by the American Consul. The detective, in his report to the Provost Marshal General of Mo., says: "The same evening I again met with Dr. Edwards on the street going to my hotel. He said Marmaduke desired to see me and I accompanied him to his house. There in the course of a long conversation Marmaduke told me that he and several officers were in Chicago to operate with other parties in releasing the prisoners of Camp Douglas, and in inaugurating a rebellion in the north. He said the movement was under the auspices of the American Knights, and was to begin operations on the day of the election. The detective immediately called on Col. Sweet and communicated to him the startling intelligence, and the latter telegraphed for troops. There were in the camp 8,000 prisoners, among whom were Morgan's freebooters. Texas Rangers and others precocious, daring and ready for reckless adventure. To guard the large force there were only 700 effective men, and the commandant felt as though there was a mine beneath him, and only 70 hours remained in which to prevent its being sprung with disastrous consequences to the garrison and adjacent city. Disclosures soon reached him from other sources whereby he learned the full particulars of the gigantic scheme. The blow was to be struck on the 8th of November, and Camp Douglas was the first objective point. The 8,000 prisoners when liberated were to be joined by the 5,000 knights of Chicago, making a nucleus of 13,000 about which would gather Canadian refugees, bushwhackers from Mo., prisoners from other Camps, and members of the same' order in other localities. The city of Chicago was first to be sacked and burned, after which a similar fate was to be meted out to the other cities of the north. A general uprising of the treasonable element in the loyal States was to follow, and simultaneously Hood was to move on Nashville, Buckner on Louisville, and Price on St. Louis.

It must not be supposed these seemingly extravagant arrangements were without some prospect of success. Investigations before military commissions in different parts of the west indicated the existence of treasonable societies of almost fabulous extent. A report of the Judge Advocate General of the U. S. disclosed "the existence of a military organization having its commander-in-chief, general and subordinate officers, and 500,000 enrolled members, all bound by a blind obedience to their superiors, and pledged to take up arms against any power found waging war against a people endeavoring to establish a government of their own choice."

Col. Sweet duly apprised the police of Chicago of the presence of the conspirators, and at 2 o'clock in the morning preceding the election, made a descent on their respective places of lodging. Among the arrests were the rebel officers Grenfell, Morgan, Adjutant General Marmaduke, brother of the general, Cantrell, of Morgan's command, Buckner Morris, treasurer of the Sons of Liberty, Charles Walsh, a member of the order were also arrested. In the house of the latter were found two cart-loads of loaded pistols, and in another part of the city two boxes of guns. The startling intelligence of the arrests spread with lightning rapidity, and as the sun rose up from the bosom of the lake and looked down on the miles of palatial residences, stores and well-filled houses marked out for rapine and burning, their inhabitants were in arms, patrols were marching and countermarching through the entire city which presented the appearance of an extended military encampment. Thus in one short hour the scheme which was to transfer the theatre of the war to the free states, and apply the torch to northern cities, collapsed and its reckless projectors were in the custody of the officers in the narrow cells of a prison.

Early in January, 1865, Gen. Hooker, commandant of the Northwestern Department, convened a court martial in Cincinnati to try the leaders of the conspiracy. They were charged with violating the laws of war by attempting to release the prisoners confined at Camp Douglas, and conspiring to lay waste the city of Chicago. The trial lasted till April, when Walsh was sentenced to three years' imprisonment in the penitentiary, Grenfell to be hung. Rafael Semmes, captured after the first arrests, to two years imprisonment. Of the other prisoners one committed suicide by shooting himself, one escaped from custody and the remainder were acquitted. After remaining in prison 9 months all the convicts except Grenfell, whose sentence was commuted to imprisonment for life, were pardoned.

CHAPTER LVI.

1865—1869—ADMINISTRATION OF GOV. OGLESBY.

Republican and Democratic State Conventions of 1864—Lives and Character of Oglesby and Bross—Prosperity and Condition of the State during the Rebellion—Legislation, Political and Special, in 1865-7—Board of Equalization established—Location of Agricultural College—Illinois Capitals and their removals—History of the Penitentiary.

The Republican, or Union State Convention of 1864, was held at Springfield, May 25th. A. J. Kuykendall, of Johnson, was chosen to preside. For Governor four names were proposed. On the first or informal ballot, Allen C. Fuller, of Boone, received 220 votes; Richard J. Oglesby, of Macon, 283; Jesse K. Dubois, of Sangamon, 103; and John M. Palmer, of Macoupin, 75. On the next ballot Oglesby was nominated, receiving 358 out of 681 votes cast. William Bross, of Cook, was nominated for lieutenant governor; Sharon Tyndale, of St. Clair, for Secretary of State; O. H. Miner, of Sangamon, for Auditor; James H. Beveridge, of DeKalb, for Treasurer; Newton Bateman, of Morgan, for Superintendent of Public Instruction; S. W. Moulton, of Shelby, for Congressman for the State-at-large. Thus far all was harmony, but now came trouble. The committee on platform gave the national administration but a quasi endorsement, saying that the president's "war measures were planned with an honest purpose; that it was not necessary to approve of every act of the administration to enable them to say Mr. Lincoln was an honest man and prudent statesman; and that in the main the acts of the administration had been highly conducive in suppressing the existing rebellion, and should Mr. Lincoln receive the nomination of the Baltimore convention they would give him their earnest support."*

This resolution excited intense opposition and was laid on the table. A new committee was appointed and in the evening a new set of resolutions were reported and adopted after a protracted sitting. The administration was strongly indorsed, and the delegates to the Baltimore convention instructed to use all honorable

----
*See Illinois State Register, May 28th, 1864.

means to secure the re-nomination of Mr. Lincoln for the presidency; a determination was expressed to prosecute the war until the cause of the Union triumphed; slavery was charged as the cause of the rebellion; they breathed the sentiments of a genuine patriotism and noble sympathy for the soldiers; extended thanks to the governor and all the State officials; indorsed the 13th amendment abolishing slavery; and asserted the Monroe doctrine—that it was the duty of the U. S. to reinstate republican institutions on the continent of America, which looked to the French operations in Mexico.

The Democratic State Convention of 1864 also met at Springfield, but not till September 6th. The Hon. S. S. Hayes, of Cook, presided. The Chicago national democratic platform was adopted. James C. Robinson, of Clark, was nominated for Governor; S. Corning Judd, of Fulton, for Lieutenant Governor; John Hise, of LaSalle, for Auditor; Alexander Starne, of Pike, for Treasurer; William A. Turney, of Morgan, for Secretary of State; John P. Brooks, for Superintendent of Public Instruction, and James C. Allen, of Crawford, for Congressman for the State-at-large.

The election in November, 1864, resulted in favor of the republicans on the State ticket by an average majority exceeding 31,-000 votes. The estimated gain of the republican vote on 1862 was over 69,000. The Legislature was republican, as follows: Senate 14 republicans to 11 democrats; House 51 republicans to 34 democrats; Union majority on joint ballot 20. Eleven out of the 14 congressmen elected were also republicans.

Richard J. Oglesby was born July 25th, 1824, in Oldham county, Kentucky. Bereft of parents at the tender age of eight, his early education was neglected. When 12 years old he removed with an uncle to Decatur. He was subsequently apprenticed to the carpenter's trade, worked occasionally at farming, studied law, essayed to practice it at Sullivan, this State, returned to Decatur, volunteered in the Mexican war, was elected 1st Lieut. Co. "C," 4th Illinois regiment, and participated in the battle of Cerro Gordo. On his return he sought to perfect his law studies by attending the lectures at Louisville, took the gold fever then raging and crossed the plains to California, returned, and, in 1852, first appeared in politics as a Scott elector. Later he visited Europe and the Holy Land, returned, and, in 1858, offered for congress, but was beaten by the same competitor he had for governor in 1864. In 1860 he was elected a State Senator, but the following spring when the rebellion broke out, his ardent nature quickly responded to the demands of patriotism, and, as colonel of the 8th regiment, he tendered it as the second raised by the State for that conflict. He was shortly entrusted with important commands, and for a time stationed at Bird's Point and Cairo. At Fort Donelson his brigade was in the van, and, on the morning of the last day, the first to be attacked by the enemy, resulting in the loss of 500 men before reinforcements came to his support. At Corinth his and Hackleman's brigades held the rebels at bay during a large part of the afternoon; but in a daring charge the latter was killed, and Oglesby dangerously wounded in the left lung was borne from the field in expectation of immediate dissolution. On his recovery he was promoted for gallantry to a major generalship, and in the spring of 1863 assigned to the command of the 16th army corps, but owing to the trouble of his wound, (he carried the rebel lead in his person) he relinquished active service within three months after.

Governor Oglesby is a fine appearing affable man, with regular, well defined features and rotund face. In stature he is a little above medium height, large frame and somewhat fleshy. His physical appearance is striking and prepossessing, while his straight-out, not to say bluff, manner and speech are well calculated to favorably impress the average masses. Ardent in feeling and strong in party bias, he inspires deep partisan prejudices in others. He is quite an effective stump orator. With a vehement, passionate and scornful tone and gestures, tremendous physical power, which, in speaking, he exercises to the utmost; with frequent descents to the grotesque, and with abundant homely comparisons or frontier figures, expressed in the broadest vernacular and enforced with stentorian emphasis, he delights a promiscuous audience beyond measure; while his bitter invective, bestowed without stint upon the opposition must gratify the extremest feeling of partisan hatred and animosity.

Lieut. Gov. Bross was born in Sussex county, New Jersey. His youth was mostly spent in the wilds of Pennsylvania, aiding his father in the hard toil of a lumberman and rafting on the Deleware. He acquired, however, a classical education, and afterwards, for many years, taught school. In 1848 he removed to Chicago and became a partner in the publishing house of Griggs, Bross & Co. But in Illinois he is chiefly known by his career as an editor. In 1852 he united with John L. Scripps and started the *Democratic Press*, a political and commercial newspaper. He was originally a democrat, but with the repeal of the Missouri compromise this paper forsook the democracy and aided in forming the republican party. In 1858 it was "consolidated" with the *Tribune*, and in 1860 the name of "Press" was dropped. No paper has perhaps exercised a larger influence upon the politics of Illinois, while at an early day it was the leading commercial medium of the northwest. Mr. Bross is a man of sound practical sense, varied and extensive information, exact, thorough, and untiring in effort. He had shown himself an able statistical, commercial and political writer. Energy and resoluteness are of the essence of his nature, and with wonderful rapidity of utterance, as presiding officer of the senate, he was capable of dispatching a large amount of business in those days of omnibus legislation. He is of medium height and robust frame, with angular features, high forehead, and ruddy complexion. Honest himself, he despises the tricks and arts of the politician; and his own achievements being the result of industry, he entertains little reverance for genius.[*]

Governor Oglesby was duly inaugurated January the 17th, 1865,[*] but before proceeding with his administration it is proper that we take a short retrospect at our material prosperity during the rebellion.

---

[*]See Ward's speech in senate Jan. 11, '69, and Western Monthly, June, '69.

[*]The day before the time first set for Gov. Oglesby to assume the duties of his office, death visited his home at Decatur, and took therefrom his only son, an intelligent and sprightly lad of 6 years, a great favorite with the bereaved parents. This caused the inauguration to be postponed for one week.

Notwithstanding the demands of the war had drawn upon Illinois to the extent of near 200,000 men—hale, vigorous and without physical blemish, taken from the most active producing classes—the great industries of the State had not only speedily recovered from this enormous draft, but her material prosperity, retarded the first one or two years, was unparalleled by any other State. The census of 1865 revealed a population of 2,141,510, being an increase of 429,559, or near 25 per cent. since 1860 ; and nearly every department of production and industry exhibited a like ratio in advancement, as evidenced by the area of land under cultivation, and its yield of agricultural wealth, the triumph of invention and substitution of machinery for manual labor, the augmentation of skilled laborers and mechanical production, the rapid growth of our cities, villages and increase of fixed capital, the excellent remuneration for all employment, the high prices for all products, and above all the abundance of money which stimulated all manner of business to unusual activity.

While this material prosperity prevailed with the close of the war, and for some time before, the times were hard with us during the first two years of the civil conflict. The writer saw corn, our great staple, sell in 1862, in Central Illinois, as low as 9 cents a bushel. The failure of our local banks, which in a manner left us without a currency, contributed not a little to the condition of the times. Prosperity during the war was first experienced in the Eastern States, where the lavish expenditures of the government for clothing and munitions of war caused money to be profusely scattered from the outset. With us, beef and pork, and the products of the soil, were the first to experience an advance in prices.

Corn, our most unfailing crop, made its first great bound upward immediately after the severe frost of August 29th, 1863. Lands remained for a long time a drug. This class of property the experience of centuries has shown to ever be the last to rise in price, but once starting it excels all other, as it affords the safest and surest investment, and not unfrequently the largest speculative return. Finally the tide of abundant money set into Illinois and began to influence realty. Now, to many of our people, was heard abroad in the land the pleasant voice of the stranger inquiring the price of lands, and seeking to invest his abundant and daily cheapening money in lots, lands and farms. Population, with a renewed current, was pouring over our borders ; houses in cities and towns became scarce ; rents rose beyond precedent, and the prices of lands passed the most sanguine expectation. An enhancement of 100 per cent was not unusual; many of our people never dreamed of such prices, and that all in cash too. Many transfers were made, the proceeds re-invested to better advantage, and comparative independence acquired by owners. The abundance and cheapness of money, and high prices of property enabled others of our people to extinguish mortgages, which had hung like a pall over their homes ; and thus thousands of families were placed in comfortable circumstances and rendered happy. While an intestine war piled a debt on the nation by the billion, upon the individual were conferred benefits and unexpected independence. But, while some, for years dissatisfied, now that they could get perhaps double their prices, were content to hold their property and neither loose nor profit by the times, others,

it is sad to relate, who had never hoped to realize old values, eagerly sold with the first advance of prices, failed or neglected to rein-
vest, easily spent or squandered the proceeds, and are to-day
renters. It was generally better to buy than sell—to be in debt
for lands purchased than hold credits for property sold. Debts
did not increase except by accruing interest, while the money
wherewith to pay them, cheapened sometimes in a few days 25 to
50 per cent, taking gold for a standard.

The permanent debt of the State, funded and unfunded in
1865, was $11,178,561, being an increase since 1860 of only about
$1,000,000, notwithstanding our heavy war appropriations and
expenditures. But the general government, it may be remarked
parenthetically, largely refunded to the States their advances on
account of the war. From December, 1864, to December, 1868,
our bonded debt was reduced $7,651,796, leaving a balance of
$5,989,158. The total taxable property of the State in 1864 was
$356,878,837; in 1868, $475,379,194. The total number of acres in
cultivation for 1868, was 8,603,599, of which 5,193,747 were in corn.

Legislative.—After 1864 our field is barren of interesting or important political or party events. Peace came to the Union in the
following spring; and the results of elections in the State have
since been uniformly the same, and generally so overwhelmingly
republican as to not only afford little show for equal party contests over any question, but to well nigh crush all hope in the
democratic bosom. That party has made in consequence several
ineffectual flank movements and taken new departures, until, in a
manner, its time-honored tenets are abandoned, and it seems to be
in the throes of dissolution. Gov. Oglesby, in his inaugural message, commenting upon the majority of the preceding election, said:
" So marked, indeed, has been the expression of the popular will,
I do not fail to recognize in it the absence of mere party triumph."

The political events of the legislative session of 1865 were the
election of Ex-Gov. Yates to the U. S. Senate, and the ratification
of the 13th amendment to the constitution of the United States
abolishing slavery. Early in the session a joint resolution was
passed, instructing our delegation in congress to vote for this
amendment. On the 1st of February, a telegram was received by
the legislature from Senator Trumbull, announcing its passage in
congress. The utmost precipitation now obtained in both houses
to ratify the measure so immediately as to place Illinois in the
van of prompt loyal States, and it was passed the same day.

This legislature also signalized itself by repealing the notorious
" black laws," part of which, although a dead letter, had held
their place upon the statute books since 1819, to the disgrace of
this free State, in the opinion of many of our citizens. In opposition it was earnestly argued by the democrats that these laws
were a positive requirement under the amendment to the State
constitution adopted by an overwhelming majority of the people
in 1862. The governor had urged the repeal in his message,
petitions numerously signed by colored men of the State and sent
in, prayed for the same. Another partisan measure was the cutting down of the 4th judicial circuit, Judge Constable's, from 6 to
2 counties, to punish that functionary for his decision in the
Clark county deserter-kidnapping case, some 2 years previously.
This was done in the face of the remonstrance of the people of the

circuit. And in the very opening the house, it seems, passed a resolution, inviting only "the loyal clergy of Springfield to open each day's session with prayer." The law requiring the registration of electors was also enacted at this session. The imposition of this restriction upon the elective franchise has ever been most distasteful to democrats; and they opposed its passage by all the arts known to parliamentary rules. By recent modification it now applies only to cities of 5,000 inhabitants and over.

But it was this legislature which, owing to the increasing demands of activity throughout the State, first gave itself up almost wholly to the enactment of special, local and private laws. The pressure of an insatiate lobby was extraordinary all winter long. Now was entered upon in full plenitude, that pernicious legislation, continued afterwards with a most prodigal hand, of granting special privileges and protection, by charter, for every conceivable object of association or business, without reserving a check or right of subsequent control in case of oppression. And to-day, in answer to the loud demands of the people to curb and repress one class of these corporations in their exorbitant and ruinous charges for freight and passage, they defiantly set up their vested rights and chartered franchises, and it is the great question whether or not the legislature is powerless in the premises.

Among the measures of general interest, not political or partisan, were the increased fees allowed to county officers. To compass this, a systematic pressure was brought to bear upon the legislature. Conventions of sheriffs, circuit clerks, county clerks, and prosecuting attorneys were held at the capital. These respectfully deliberated upon their schedules of fees and prepared their bills to be enacted into laws, and as to the demands of these county officials, who are a power in elections, what could the august legislature of the State of Illinois do but to yield to them. The raising of the fees, which were already ample, has cost the people many millions. To wind up for instance a small estate by passing through all the various stages of the courts and the hands of these officers, it would be found at the end to be wound up indeed! And the most difficult feat of legislation is the reduction of fees or the abolishment of an office, however oppressive the one or useless the other.

Gov. Oglesby interposed his veto to but one bill during the session, which was an amendment to a charter for a Chicago horse railway, granted in 1859 for 25 years and now sought to be extended 99 years. This long period of time was an insuperable objection with his excellency, which he elaborated at length, but as the measure was promptly passed over his veto by both houses, he doubtless deemed it useless to further attempt to check their headlong career.

The various appropriations made at this session amounted to $1,120,000. The constitution limited the expenditures of the legislature to 1½ mills on the dollar of assessed value of the real and personal property of the State, then aggregating about $333,000,000 and yielding, at this rate, $759,000, which made an excess in the appropriations of $361,000, and which was regarded as invalid and denounced by the Democrats as prodigal.

The members, finding there was gold in the State treasury, that commodity being then at a high premium in market, coveted it in payment of their mileage and per diem. But in this enterprise they were baulked. The auditor possessed no authority to issue to them warrants different in character from those for any other purpose and without a specification to that effect the treasurer could not pay out the gold; thus this precious little scheme was nipped in the bud, which gave very general satisfaction to the people. No law of a general useful character or public interest was perfected at the session of 1865, if we except the turning over of the canal to Chicago to be deepened.

1867.—The session of 1867 was still more productive of private and special acts than the preceding. Indeed this class of legislation now reached perhaps its culminating point in successful audacity. The omnibus* was very active throughout the session, and that vehicle, by which laws were passed by the wholesale, was time and again freighted with bills, exceeding 200 in number. The occasion was most propitious for every axe presented to receive ready grinding. The contests over the location of the Industrial College, the Capital, the Southern Penitentiary, and the canal enlargement and Illinois river improvement, dominated everything else. For these engrossing measures members yielded a ready assent to all others. It was a long and arduous session of 53 days, during which an unprecedented amount of work was accomplished. The monopolists and corporation kings, in faultless attire and with amiable manner, were out in full force. The lobbyists, which fairly swarmed the halls and toyed with the "rings," gloated in the magnitude and number of their successes. The senate, as a partial protection against the wiles of this ubiquitous and cheeky race, adopted a resolution, forbidding any one but senators and clerks of committees demanding the perusal of bills in the custody of the secretary.

There were also a number of very important public laws passed. Among these may be mentioned the act establishing the State Board of Equalization. This measure was advocated by the governor in his message. The great need of it may be inferred from the varying assessments of the same kinds of property in different portions of the State. Horses, in Kane county, were valued at $15 52 per head—in Franklin, at $60 08; cattle, in Piatt, $24 04 —in Jo Daviess and Putnam, $4 36; mules, in Madison, $129 86 —in Hamilton, $10 69; swine, in Douglas, $3 50—in Jefferson, 50 cents. The burdens of taxation ought ever to be distributed with the utmost uniformity.

There was also passed the important law enabling parties to suits or civil actions to testify as witnesses, which worked a radical change in the time-honored rule of the common law. And there was the law, adopted at the instance of the philanthropic Mr. Bovee, which, in a manner, abolished capital punishment— or rather which allows the jury in case of murder to fix the punishment either by hanging, or imprisonment in the penitentiary not less than 14 years.

But the question of most absorbing sectional interest, not excepting that of the capital removal, the canal enlargement, or the Southern penitentiary, was the location of the Agricultural or Industrial College. This had been a disturbing element two years before. Under the terms of the land grant the question had now

* This was the term applied to the passage of bills by the bundle, practiced under the constitution of 1848.

58

to be met. Congress, by act of July 2, 1862, donated to the several States and territories, which should, within five years from the date thereof, provide colleges for the benefit of agriculture and the mechanic arts, land, or its equivalent in scrip, at the rate of 30,000 acres for each senator and representative in Congress. The amount apportioned to Illinois was 480,000 acres. The legislature in 1863 had signified to the Secretary of the Interior the acceptance of the grant, and the government land scrip was now in the hands of the governor. If one such college at least was not provided by July 2d, the State should return the scrip or pay for it.

To this munificent grant from Congress many places in the State were eager to add further donations, in some instances exceeding that of Congress, to secure the location of the college. In the bidding for that object, invited by the legislature, there was a generous competition. Jacksonville, Lincoln, Pekin, Bloomington and Champaign, participated in it. The best offer was that of the last named place, and consisted of 970 acres of farm land, a large college building (completed with special reference to this object) and its site of 10 acres of ground in the city, and $100,000 ten per cent. interest-bearing Champaign county bonds, the whole estimated at $555,400. The Bloomington bid, estimated at $470,000, was the next best. A legislative committee was charged with the duty of visiting the various points contending, and of inspecting the property proffered to be donated. It was also a season of numerous legislative visits, and the enterprise of the friends of Champaign caused one to be made to that place.

Champaign being the highest bidder, it was next sought to stave off the location and refer it to a commission. But this finesse did not succeed. Having invited competition the legislature could not consistently do otherwise than accept the best bid and make the location accordingly; and it was but proper and eminently just that Champaign was selected as the Industrial University seat.

Little time of this long and laborious session was wasted in partisan debates, a circumstance as unusual as it was praiseworthy. The political events were the re-election of Lyman Trumbull to the U. S. Senate, and the adoption of the 14th amendment to the constitution of the U. S. conferring citizenship upon the blacks, which was resisted, on the part of the democrats, by all the known rules of parliamentary warfare. A set of resolutions was adopted by the House, 43 to 15, against rebels settling in Illinois, and exercising the elective franchise which none but the truly loyal should exercise, and that a bill should be framed forever excluding from office all traitors voluntarily taking the oath of allegiance to the rebel confederacy, and those who left home to escape the draft, encouraged or concealed deserters, or by force of arms opposed the draft. The feelings here manifested are by this time greatly mitigated.

Illinois' Capitals—Our Several Seats of Government.—The location of the Capital of any country has ever been a subject of prime importance; and it is no less so with the States of this Union than it has been with the empires of the old world. It is a subject which, for obvious reasons, has ever been attended with bitter disputations, jealousies and rivalries between contending points for the honors or fancied benefits to be derived from it.

County seat questions are notoriously acrimonious, and often for a considerable time work a blight upon the prosperity of the sections contending. In some States the seat of government question has only found a quietus by the establishment of two capitals, while in others, particularly in the growing West, the flow of population, or possibly the desire of legislators to serve the interests or caprices of their constituents, has prevailed to keep the subject in a ferment, causing frequent changes. Illinois, in her short career as a State, has had three locations for her capital, and more agitations for its removal. The first seat of government in Illinois was at Kaskaskia, where it remained during the 9 years of our territorial existence and for two years afterward. It was then removed to Vandalia, where it remained for 20 years, since when it has been at Springfield.

When Congress, in 1809, erected Illinois into a separate territory, it was provided that Kaskaskia should be and remain the seat of government until the legislature should otherwise direct.

"The sessions of this august body were held in a large, rough building, in the centre of a square, in the village of Kaskaskia, the body of it being of uncut limestone, the gables an l roofs, which was of the gambrel style, of unpainted boards and shingles, with dormer windows. The lower floor, a large and cheerless room, was fitted up for the House, whilst the council sat in a small chamber above, around a circular table, and, it is said, when the labors of the day were over, the interesting game of "Loo" at once succeeded. This venerable structure was, during the time of the French occupancy of the country, prior to 1763, the headquarters of the military commandant, and doubtless within it. many an arbitrary edict was framed, to be executed with all the severity attendant upon the administration of military law by military men."*

The Convention which framed the first State Constitution also met in this "old stone house."

"It was provided by this instrument that the seat of government should remain at Kaskaskia until the general assembly should otherwise direct; and that body was required, at its first session, to petition Congress to grant to the State a quantity of land of not more than four and not less than one section, or to give to the State the right of pre-emption in the purchase of that quantity, the land to be situated on the Kaskaskia river, and as near as might be, east of the third principal meridian, on that river. Should the petition be granted, the general assembly, at their next session, were required to appoint five commissioners to make the selection of the land, and provide for laying out a town upon it; which town, it was declared, should be the seat of government for the term of 20 years. * When the question was before the convention two points were in contemplation by the members and outsiders; one was Carlyle, just then located on the Kaskaskia river by two Virginia gentlemen, and an elevated site, higher up the river, known as 'Pope's Bluff,' the property of Nathaniel Pope. He and his friends were of course very desirous the seat of government should be located there, while the proprietors of Carlyle had no less desire that the latter place should be the favored spot. While the subject was under discussion in doors and out. there come to look in upon that body a noted hunter and trapper, one Reeves by name, who had his cabin still higher up the river, and near where the third principal meridian crossed the stream. He spoke in glowing terms of the beauties of Reeves' Bluff; 'that Pope's Bluff nor Carlyle, wasn't a primin' to his bluff,' &c. Such was the force of his representation, that the language 'on the Kaskaskia river, as near as might be east of the third principal meridian,' was adopted by the convention; and when the legislature, at the session of 1819, appointed the commissioners to select the land granted by congress, they fixed upon the old hunter's home. 'Reeves' Bluff.' It proved to be a most beautiful spot, a heavily wooded tract, covered by gigantic trees under whose shades the former lords of the soil might have held grave council. A town was laid out with a handsome public square and broad streets, and christened 'Vandalia,' but these vandals did not suffer one of these forest kings to remain on the square, but cut them down to the ground, leaving not one to sigh in the summer wind or bend to the blast."

Gov. Ford, page 35 says:

"After the place had been selected, it became a matter of great interest to give it a good sounding name, one which would please the ear, and at the same time have the classic merit of perpetuating the memory of the ancient race of Indians by whom the country had first been inhabited. Tradition says that a wag who was present, suggested to the commissioners that the 'Vandals' were a powerful nation of Indians who once inhabited the banks of the Kaskaskia river, and that 'Vandalia,' formed from their name, would perpetuate the memory of that extinct but renowned people. The suggestion pleased the commissioners, the name was adopted, and they thus proved that the name of their new city (if they were fit representatives of their constituents) would better illustrate the character of the modern than the ancient inhabitants of the country."

* Judge Caton's address at the laying of the corner stone of the new State House, Oct. 5, 1868, using Judge Breese's language. The headquarters of the French military commandants were at Fort Chartres. "the centre of life and fashion in the West." Monette's Val. of the Miss. Vol. 1, 164—2 Ibid.

The location was in the midst of the wilderness, northeast of the settlements.

"Lots were sold at public auction on credit, at fabulous prices, few of which were paid for in full. The enterprising and scheming came to it, some from the old world, and soon the nucleus of a town was formed. Measures were inaugurated for the erection of a State House which culminated in a plain two-story frame building, of rude architecture, set upon a rough stone foundation and placed in the centre of the square, the lower floor of which was devoted to a passage and stair-way to the upper story, and a large, plain room, devoid of ornament, (for the accommodation of the House;) the upper floor was divided into two rooms, the largest for the accommodation of the Senate and the smaller one for the office of Secretary of State, the Auditor and Treasurer occupying detached buildings, hired for that purpose. No ceremonies were observed in laying the corner-stone of this unsightly structure; no music disturbed the solitude of the forest, then in its primeval beauty; no crowd in pageantry lent excitement to the scene; no sound was heard save the rap of the mason's hammer and the sharp click of the trowel."*

The archives of State were removed from Kaskaskia to Vandalia early in December, 1820, at one load in a small wagon. They were in the care of Sidney Breese, then clerk to the Secretary of State, Mr. Kane, and the route being quite difficult, the driver and he had to cut a road through the woods at several points. The Auditor, Elijah C. Berry, with his family, occupied the new State House at the time, but soon moved out into a cabin. The day on which the session of the legislature opened in Vandalia, was most beautiful. "The sun shone in cloudless splendor and the temperature of the air was autumnal; all was excitement and all seemed pleased." This structure was destroyed by fire about 2 o'clock in the night December 9, 1823. So rapidly did the flames spread that not a single article of furniture was saved. The U. S. Land Receiver's office was kept in one of its rooms, and the books, papers and every article pertaining to the office was consumed. The cause of the fire was not ascertained. The house had been occupied the day preceding for the sale of non-resident lands for State taxes. A subscription paper was immediately started by the citizens of Vandalia to rebuild it. In three days $3,000 was raised. "It was succeeded by a commodious brick building, of sufficient dimensions, built in part at the expense of the citizens of Vandalia. The corner-stone was laid without any public display; it still stands, renovated and embellished by the people of Fayette county, and is now devoted to the administration of justice and the various public offices of the county."*

Eight years before the expiration of the 20 years' term for which the capital was to remain at Vandalia, the question of removal was already agitated in the legislature. The initiative came from Greene county, strongly seconded by the delegation from Sangamon. The house passed a bill providing for the appointment of commissioners to permanently locate the seat of government; but the senate amended it by striking out all after the enacting clause and submitting the following places to be voted for by the people at the next election for the legislature: The geographical centre of the State, Jacksonville, Springfield, Alton, Vandalia, and Peoria, the point or place receiving the highest number of votes to be the permanent seat of government. The house, at the instance of Cyrus Edwards, sought to further amend this by having the two places receiving the highest number of votes voted for again at the succeeding general election. The

*Caton's address—Breese's words.
*Caton s address—Breese's words.

senate amendment, after some reluctance by the house, was finally
agreed to. As the time for taking the vote approached, the places
ambitious for this high and honorable distinction in the State be
stirred themselves to obtain concert of action. Spirited addresses
were issued to the people, ably setting forth the many excellencies and great advantages of the respective places contending.
The election took place in August, 1834. Alton received 7,511
votes; Vandalia, 7,148; Springfield, 7,044; the geographical centre (Illiopolis), 744; Peoria, 486; and Jacksonville, 272.

Alton was thus designated as the seat of government after the
20 years at Vandalia should expire. But it requires something
besides votes to erect capitol buildings. No appropriation was
made or further steps taken by the legislature to second this choice
and nothing came of it. Still the removal question would not
down; it continued to be canvassed by the press at the various
points whose expectations had been raised by the election and influenced the local elections in many parts to no inconsiderable degree. Springfield, particularly, felt greatly encouraged by the
vote of 1834. By the apportionment of 1835 Sangamon county
was accorded 2 senators and 7 representatives in the legislature.
That county, in the incredibly short space of 15 years, had become
the most populous in the State. The tide of emigration had begun
to set into the north part of the State with a steadily augmenting
current, and it became apparent that the seat of government could
not be long retained at Vandalia, so far from the centre of population. It was a period before we had railroads, and travel to and
from the capital, conducted in the same primitive manner it had
been all over the world since its earliest dawn, made distance no
inconsiderable object.

In the summer of 1836, the great fever of land and town lot
speculation of that period spread from Chicago, like an epidemic,
all over the State, and the legislature at the session of 1836-7
fully embarked in the disastrous policy of the State internal improvement system. And now the opportunity for the actual removal of the capital had come. In the general rage for developing the infant resources of the State, the delegations from almost
every county had improvement axes to grind, and to attain their
objects hesitated not to lend their aid in grinding those of all the
rest. What we call in modern parlance "rings," were thus
readily formed, and every bill of importance was passed without
inquiry, until everybody was satisfied, including that for the removal of the seat of government. The Sangamon delegation of 9,
known as "the long nine," because they averaged 6 feet in hight,
some more and some less—there being precisely 54 feet in the
stature of them—were able, persistent and dextrous manipulators,
acting upon all questions as a unit, and exercising thus a most
potent influence. They gave it doubtless, a long pull, a strong
pull, and a pull altogether. They were: Senators—A. G. Herndon and Job Fletcher; Representatives—Abraham Lincoln,
Ninian W. Edwards, Dan Stone, John Dawson, W. F. Elkin, Andrew McCormick and Robert L. Wilson.

The act required that the two houses meet in Representatives
Hall on the 28th of February, 1837, at 10 o'clock, A. M., and proceed to select a suitable point or place for the permanent location
of the seat of government, after the expiration of the constitu-

tional term at Vandalia. The election was to be conducted much
after the manner of choosing a U. S. Senator. During the ballotings, 29 places were voted for, of which we will only give the 6
highest. Springfield started with 35, and on the 4th received 73,
a majority; Vandalia started with, and continued to receive
throughout the 4 ballotings, 16 votes; Alton started with 15 and
ran down to 6; the highest Jacksonville received was 15, and the
lowest 10; Peoria came in on the 2d ballot with 8, increased to 11,
but on the 4th was down to 8; Illiopolis started with 3, increased
to 10 and fell back to 3. No other place received a higher number than 4 votes. $50,000 was appropriated for the purpose of
erecting a state house, but the act was to be null and void unless
$50,000 more was donated by individuals secured by their bond, pay-
able to the treasurer by the 1st of May following, to be approved
by the governor, and to become due as he should direct; and also,
unless not less than 2 acres of ground, upon which to erect the
State House, be donated and conveyed without expense to the
State. The donation of $50,000 was to be exclusively applied
toward the erection of the building. The act of February 5, 1833,
was repealed. By a supplemental act of March 3d, 1837, the
county commissioners of Sangamon county were authorize'd to
convey to the State, for the use of the people, the public square at
Springfield. Archibald Job of Morgan, and A. G. Henry and
Thomas Houghton, of Sangamon, were appointed commissioners
to superintend the erection of the State House at Springfield.
They gave bonds in $10,000, and received a per diem compensa-
tion of $3 each. The legislature first met at Springfield (in ex-
traordinary session), December 9, 1839; but as the new capitol
was not then completed, the house was accommodated in the 2d
Presbyterian church, the senate in the 1st Methodist (an old frame
structure) and the supreme court in the Episcopal.*

As early as during the war of 1812, the troops and rangers, in
their various expeditions against the hostile Indians on the Peoria
Lake, noted the country of the Sangamon as one of surpassing
attraction. The Indians well appreciated this fertile region, for
in the Potawatamie tongue the word Sangamo meant "the country where there is plenty to eat," in our phrase "the land flowing
with milk and honey." It was not, however, until some years
after the close of that war that the hardy pioneer pressed into it.
Then, with little delay, along the borders of the timber, the log
cabin of the adventurous settler began to rear its humble walls,
and the smoke from its ample chimney went curling heavenward.
The "St. Gamo Kedentry," as it was pronounced in the vernacular, soon became famous, and emigration set freely in that direction. In the autumn of 1819, a weary emigrant family, originally
from North Carolina, with its teams, encamped on the right bank
of Spring Creek, in the west part of the present city of Springfield. This was the end of their journey. Soon the camp fires
were lighted, and parents and children gathered about the homely

* Springfield afterwards paid off one-third of her $50,000 bonus with the evidences of
State indebtedness, which after the failure of the internal improvement system, at one
time, as we have seen, touched 14 cents on the dollar in market But this transaction,
which has been occasionally animadverted, was perfectly legitimate. The last installment of $16,666 67 was obtained from the State Bank on one year's time, at 6 per cent,
101 of the best citizens executing their promissory note to the bank; and it was this
note that was afterwards paid off with internal improvement scrip, which the State
has ultimately redeemed dollar for dollar.

supper-board for the first time on the spot of their home in the wilderness. In the morning the echoing ring of the ax resounded in the adjacent forest, and in a few days a rough cabin home sheltered John Kelly and family, the first white settlers of the site since become the capital of this great State. The county of Sangamon was organized in 1821. On the 10th of April, the same year, the temporary county seat was fixed at Kelly's, the stake for a court house being set at the northwest corner of the present 2d and Jefferson streets, and in honor Spring Creek and Kelly's field, was christened Springfield. On May 1st, a term of court was held at Kelly's cabin. In 1823 the public lands having been previously surveyed, were offered for sale by government. A town had been laid off and plotted under the name of Calhoun, but as settlers came in, the name of Calhoun was gradually dropped and that of Springfield revived. In the name of Springfield for the capital of this State, there is nothing suggestive of meaning or of origin—nothing to perpetuate any aboriginal race, deed, or historical name. Besides it is so common that in using it the name of the State has ever to be added to give it definiteness. When you speak of Kaskaskia, Vandalia, Peoria, LaSalle, Chicago, or Illiopolis—the last best of all—your reference is clear, without adding Illinois. Not so when you mention Springfield, for there are places of that name in many States.*

Springfield, at the time of the location of the seat of government, contained some 1,100 inhabitants. The corner stone of the Capitol was laid July 4th, 1837. The brilliant orator, E. D. Baker, then a resident of the place, pronounced a beautiful and thrilling address on the occasion. The estimated cost of the structure was $130,000, but this, as usual, in such cases, proved too low by nearly 100 per cent.

When the Capitol was first reared it was the wonder of the country round. It was admired by the people as a model of architectural beauty, and supposed to be ample enough to answer the purposes of the State for all time. But such has been the march of Illinois to empire that in less than a quarter of a century the public demand became rife for a new structure commensurate with our growth, our pride and pretensions. Our population in that time has been more than quadrupled, being, in 1840, 476,183, and in 1865, 2,141,510. If, under the restrictions of the constitutions of 1848 in the number of our legislators, we did not actually lack for room to accommodate the two houses, our pride as a State was touched whenever we cast a glance at the squat

* The present capital gave early promise of rare capacity for legislative finesse. The county seat of Sangamon was permanently located at Springfield in 1825. Prior to that an election for the legislature turned upon the question of location. One of the candidates, W. S. Hamilton, favored Sangamo Town, a beautiful elevated bluff on the river, 7 miles northwest from the city, a most charming town site. Jonathan H. Pugh was the Springfield candidate. Hamilton, son of the great Alexander Hamilton of Revolutionary fame, was elected, and the aspirations of Springfield seemed crushed. But unwilling to yield, she raised a fund and sent her defeated candidate, a man of considerable ability, to Vandalia as a lobby member. His tact and skill in the management of honorable members made him more than a match for his competitor on the floor. Hamilton failed of having an act passed, fixing the county seat at Sangamo Town; Pugh did succeed in having special commissioners appointed to make the location. These came to Springfield to examine the sites. Conveyance was prepared to take them over to Sangamo Town. On the way they passed over so much low and wet ground, and through so many sloughs and mud holes, particularly as they approached the proposed site, that their minds were made up. They decided in disgust that it would never do to fix a county seat at a point so surrounded by swamps. Whether the route was chosen by accident or design does not appear, but it has been shrewdly suspected that so much good luck for Springfield was not wholly accidental.—Taken from a volume of the Springfield City Ordinances.

and unshapely pile representing the Capitol of the fourth State
of the Union. Public edifices in all ages and countries have been
types, or marked the greatness and dignity of the rulers or people who have reared them. This seems to be a law of man's civilization.

In 1865 Senator Lindsey introduced a bill into the legislature to
remove the seat of government to Peoria. This was the first renewal
of the agitation. Chicago, Jacksonville and Decatur, (the latter
probably dreaming of benefits because one of her burghers
occupied the gubernatorial chair), were also clamorous for the
capitol. The Chicago Tribune, in an elaborate leader, favored
removal, and so did many other papers. Springfield was much
faulted for its inferior hotel accommodations and their exorbitant charges. The senate special committee, to which the question had been referred, reported in favor of removal to Peoria,
and no little alarm was experienced in Springfield. Later the
Chicago bill was laid upon the table in the house by 61 to 16, and
the star of capital removal, erst so refulgent, waxed dim, and
gradually dipped its bright disk below the horizon. But it was
apparent that the question must be again confronted with the
dawn of another legislature. The building of a new State House
could not be much longer delayed.

Intimations from various parts of the State began to be early
thrown out that powerful influences would be brought to bear in
favor of removal at the next session of the legislature. To the
various objections brought against Springfield as the capital,
that city, keenly appreciating the consequences which might ensue to her prosperity, did away with the chief one, the want of
hotel accommodations, by building the Leland, than which, except
perhaps in size, there is not a more elegant and commodious hotel
in all its appointments, in all the State. She further resolved to
take the threatening question by the forelock, and in November,
1866 one of her most capable public-spirited citizens, the Hon.
J. C. Conkling, was elected to the lower house of the legislature.
All the tact and address of her prominent citizens were besides
brought into requisition. The county board agreed to take the
old State House and square for a court house at $200,000; the
city council offered to furnish the Mather lot, some six or eight
acres, which cost $62,000, and cause it to be conveyed free to the
State as a site for the new capitol—which was to be so elegant
and ornate in architecture, so grand and ample in its proportions,
as to control by its cost and magnificence the seat of government
question for a long time. Upon the assembling of the legislature,
the honorable members became the objects of much polite attention. The ladies, with all the agreeable arts of the sex, lent the
charm of their presence in attendance upon the sittings of the
two houses. Invitations to pleasant social gatherings, to parties
and receptions at elegant private mansions, were frequent. The
Leland, just finished with the commencement of the session, was
opened with a grand ball and supper, to which the members and
high dignitaries from various parts of the State present in the
city, with their ladies, received free tickets of invitation. And
now, with the assembly in a proper frame of mind, the bill providing for the erection of a new State House at Springfield, was

introduced. It appropriated $450,000, as a commencement, $200,-000 of which were to be the proceeds of the sale of the old State House to the county of Sangamon, its use being reserved until the new one should be completed.*

The bill was not free from opposition in the legislature; but from many other local measures pending, such was the high expectation of benefits in various parts of the State, that, while each section looked to its own interest, little was done toward forming combinations for the defeat of this. One of the very earliest to be introduced was the location of the Industrial University. It was the general understanding of the people that the legislature at that session would take steps to secure the congressional grant for that school. A number of places were bidding high for its location. Jacksonville, Pekin, Lincoln, Bloomington; and Chicago wanted to divide the fund; but in the eastern portion of the State the Champaign interest was all-absorbing and dominated everything else. The south was moving for the Southern penitentiary, while Chicago was engrossed with her park bills and the canal extension and enlargement, in which Peoria and the Rock River country were also deeply interested. The immediate opposition to the State House bill was therefore in the main narrowed down to the efforts of Decatur, which presented the very munificent offer for its location of a fine 10-acre lot of ground, and $1,000,000 in money from Macon county, whose entire taxable wealth on realty amounted to only $2,422,000. The proposition was said to be backed by the Illinois Central R. R. Much indignation was vented upon this effort to huckster or hawk the location of the seat of government. The names of seven commissioners to superintend the erection of the building and disburse the funds appropriated, were also so judiciously chosen and distributed as to impart to the measure much strength.† Besides, it was urged that the present capital had become historic ground; that it was illustrated by the life and residence of the best, the purest, and the noblest of American statesmen, Abraham Lincoln, and sactified by his grave.‡

The bill became a law February 25, 1867. This was the senate bill of Mr. Cohr's; it limited the total cost of the new capitol to $3,000,000.

The commissioners, in March, advertised for plans and specifications to be submitted by July 15, offering $3,000 for the successful design. But, while the act for the new State House met generally with approval, some leading Chicago newspapers,* chagrined probably over the canal legislation, continued their assaults upon the measure, bitterly charging it to be a fraud and swindle upon the people. The aspiring city of Decatur, too, illy brooked her disappointment in not becoming the Capital. And now, May 13, 1867, at her instigation and cost, a writ of *quo warranto*—an inquiry into the right or power to act—was granted against Philip Wadsworth and the other commissioners, impleaded by Judge Wilson of the Superior Court of Chicago, and judgment of ouster entered. The legal objection urged, was that the commissioners

---

*For a copy of Voris' humorous bill to dislocate the Capitol, see the Ill. State Register, Feb. 22, 1867. It provided for a perigrinating legislature by railroad, to stop at every place where a notice appeared that legislation was wanted.

†See Bailey's speech.

‡Hurlbut's speech.

║Times and Tribune.

were *officers*, whose appointment under the constitution should have been made by the governor and confirmed by the senate, and who could not be designated in the bill as had been done. On appeal to the Supreme Court, that body, at the September term following, reversed the decision of Judge Wilson, holding that the Commissioners were not *officers*, and therefore rightfully entitled to carry out the law.

From the great number of designs submitted by architects from various parts of the Union, that of J. C. Cochrane, of Chicago, was chosen and adopted. Its style does not exclusively follow any one of the ancient or classic orders of architecture, but harmoniously blends these with modern art, imparting massiveness, strength and durability, while preserving external grace and airyness. The ground plan is in the form of a great cross or 4 wings, whose grand outlines are 359 feet north and south by 266 east and west, exclusive of the porticos. The basement story, excavated to the depth of 10 feet, will contain the boilers for the heating apparatus and the elevators, storage room for fuel, and other weighty articles. Next above is the first story, 19 feet high, on which are located the adjutant-general's office and museum, the geological museum of specimens, and artists' rooms, &c. The floor is to be laid in mosaic marble, imbedded in cement, the whole supported by brick arches. That part of the ceiling constituting the floor of the rotunda, is to be of glass. Next above is the principal story, 22 feet in hight. The grand corridors, running the whole length and breadth of the building, crossing each other at right angles on the glass floor of the rotunda, will be beautifully finished with variegated marble pilasters projecting from the walls, forming panels, and opening from them on this floor are located all the rooms of the different State departments, including the Supreme Court-room and Clerk's office, and the state geologist's office. With the Treasurer's office are connected 4 massive stone fire proof vaults. The floors are supported by wrought iron beams imported from Belgium. The next, or 2d principal story, is 45 feet in altitude. Here is the great hall of the house of representatives, in the southern arm of the cross, 66 by 100 feet, and the senate chamber, 62 by 75, in the northern wing. Here too, on the main floor, are rooms for the speaker, clerks, sergeants-at-arms, post-office, State library, &c., &c. On three sides of each of the grand legislative halls, half way up, are to be magnificent galleries, from which will extend back floors, divided up into committee rooms. The means of communication between the different stories are by grand marble stairways and two steam elevators. The roofs over each wing are to be of the mansard style, slated on the sides and covered with copper. Through the centre of these will rise the stately dome 320 feet from the ground, surmounted by a lantern 16 by 25 feet, crowned with ball and pinnacle. An iron stairway will ascend inside the dome to the floor of the lantern. The rotunda is to be 76 feet in diameter, and from its glass floor to the fresco painting on its ceiling, will present a clear, dizzy view of 217 feet. The north, south, and east wings are to have porticos of ten stone columns, each 45 feet in elevation. The east wing is to be the principal front, and here, from each corner of the portico, 90 feet wide, will rise a turret 132 feet in altitude. The north portico will be surmounted by a statute of

Lincoln, and that on the south by one of Douglas. The outside walls of the structure are of cut stone, taking 750,000 cubic feet, and their linings, together with the partitions, will take 20 millions of brick; 1,200 tons of wrought iron and 1,800 tons of cast iron will be consumed in its building. Such is but an imperfect outline of the new capitol, which, in its massiveness, durability, symmetry, beauty and grandeur, will symbolize the extent, the resources, the power and pride of our young giant State.

Owing to the litigation, the year 1867 was little fruitful of results in building. The next year the foundation, 8 feet thick, was well brought under way, and the corner stone laid, October 5th. In 1869 the legislature appropriated $650,000, to be expended only after ascertaining that the work could be brought within the original maximum limitation of $3,000,000, and reduced the number of commissioners from 7 to 3. The stone work was to be procured from the penitentiary at Joliet. The constitutional convention, influenced by the constant cry of a portion of our State press, forbade the legislature expending more than $3,500,000 on the grounds, construction and furnishing of the new State house, without first submitting the question to the voters of the State.

In 1871 a further appropriation of $600,000 was asked. Bills for this purpose were early introduced, and that in the senate readily passed. But in the house opposition was developed. The canal and Illinois river improvement project was again on foot. The Chicago press, perhaps with a view to making it a lever for the river improvement measure, attacked the State house appropriation bill with exceeding virulence. Startling developments in regard to the building contracts, the character of the work, &c., were threatened. The removal of the capital was advocated. Peoria came forward with a proposition to reimburse the State to the full amount ($805,303 08) already expended on the new structure, donate a beautiful ten acre lot as a site, and furnish free of rent, for 5 years, accommodations for the meetings of the general assembly, in consideration of the location of the capital there. An offer so munificent was well calculated to arrest attention. This, with her other indebtedness, would have placed Peoria under obligations to about half of all her taxable wealth. To avoid the constitutional objection which forbids the creation of a debt exceeding 5 per cent. on assessed values, her private citizens of undoubted character and ample means tendered their bond for the amount. The capital removal question now ran up to fever heat all over the State. A large committee from Peoria, duly empowered, visited Springfield, and for a time creature comforts lacked in neither style nor abundance. The two houses accepted an invitation of a free excursion to Peoria. The occasion proved one of unusual enjoyment to the members, who were treated with distinguished consideration. Upon arrival there carriages were provided and the visitors taken to view the site for the capitol on the bluff, than which there is not a more charming and commanding spot in all the State. A steamboat trip past the city and a few miles up the lovely lake was next in order, followed by a banquet at the hotel, and a grand ball at night. On their return the members were accompanied by a large lobby force.

These movements were of a character and magnitude to fairly alarm the capital city. Its council hastened to pass an ordinance, tendering a guaranty of additional ground for the capitol. The gallery of the house and the lobby were daily thronged by her anxious citizens, deeply intent on its proceedings. To remove the capital it was necessary first to defeat the appropriation bill. This was the test. The house was a large, unwieldy body of 177 members, and its rules were such that by dilatory motions—parliamentary "fillibustering"—time could easily be consumed so as on no day to reach the order of business in which the bill stood on the calendar. All manner of parliamentary tactics were practiced to kill time and tire out the house. Quantities of weary memorials on the capital question found their way in and were diligently insisted upon to be read at length, and when this was refused speeches were made on the right of petition. Thus the time of adjournment for the recess, April 17th, was reached without action on the bill, notwithstanding a majority of the house were for it.

The feeling of depression at Springfield was very great. Gov. Palmer next convened the legislature on the 24th of May, and required, among many other important measures omitted, action on the State house appropriation. Bills for this purpose were again introduced and pressed duly forward under the rules. The previous scenes were re-enacted by the opposition; but the calendar was not so full. And now the move was to tack on a submission clause. The Peoria lobby, reinforced from other parts of the State, was again on hand. Day by day the beauty and fashion of Springfield thronged the galleries of the house like a bright galaxy, as they were, and patiently set out the weary hours with the punctuality of members, eagerly and anxiously watching the dilitory movements below. Gradually but slowly the measure was pressed along in its order Finally, when every parliamentary resistance was under the rules exhausted, a vote was reached at 10 o'clock at night, June 7th, and the bill passed by 100 yeas to 74 nays. Peoria's apple of.hope was turned to ashes. The senate the next day substituted the house bill and passed it. It provided for a bond of the citizens in the penal sum of $500,000, conditioned that the obligors procure such additional ground as the State might require, not exceeding 4 acres, to be demanded within two years after the building is ready for use. Thus ended the last effort to remove the capital. The agitation of the question had a most depressing effect upon the building business and the price of real estate at Springfield for a full year or more.

The Penitentiary—A Resume of its History.—In June 1867, Governor Oglesby convened the Legislature in extraordinary session, inviting action upon ten subjects, chief of which was to provide for the taxation of the shares of banks, State and National. The assembly, however, acted upon but five. But before the session was two days gone another occasion arose to again convene that body, which was done for the 14th inst. This was the abandonment of the penitentiary by the lessees, which threw upon the hands of the State 1,058 convicts to be immediately provided for, fed, clothed and put to work.

To go back 40 years, the first step taken toward the establishment of a penitentiary in this State was at the legislative session in 1826–27. The need of a State's prison had been greatly felt for some time. The jails of the country were very inferior, and the breaking of them by the more energetic and desperate offenders was of frequent occurrence. The State was poor and oppressed by the broken currency of the First State Bank. There was, however, at the time a project on hand for the legislature to memorialize congress to allow the State to sell 30,000 acres of the Ohio and 10,000 acres of the Vermillion Saline lands. The Saline reserves, which had been granted to the State in 1818 on condition that they be never sold, had become useless for the manufacture of salt, but they retarded the settlement of the country. Congress readily made the concession, the lands were sold, and the proceeds, according to previous arrangements, were divided between the eastern and western sections of the State—the former applying its share toward the improvement of the Great Wabash, the draining of Purgatory Swamp opposite Vincennes, and of the Cache river flats; the latter devoting its share toward the building of a penitentiary. Governor Edwards opposed the measure, and great efforts were made to further divide the fund for the benefit of local river improvements, but all failed.

Ex-Gov. Bond, Dr. Gersham Jane and W. P. M'Kee were appointed the first penitentiary commissioners. They selected the site at Alton, for which ten acres of ground were donated. Besides the proceeds of the Saline land sales, the legislature, in 1831, appropriated $10,000 toward the completion of the penitentiary. The first building, which was a neat stone structure, contained 24 cells, and was ready for occupation in 1833. The system of State prison confinement in Illinois has ever been (except in the case of some special sentences) what is known as the congregated in contradistinction of the dreadful solitary plan, in vogue in Pennsylvania and elsewhere.

The criminal code had been adapted the preceding legislative session to the penitentiary system by abolishing the barbarous punishment of whipping, the stocks and pillory, and substituting confinement and hard labor. A close observer of the effects of this change (Gov. Ford) states that the increase of crime for 15 years following greatly exceeded the relative increase of the population in Illinois.

For the first 5 years the State conducted the prison herself. A warden was biennially elected by the legislature, who received a salary of $600, and 3 inspectors were also elected, whose powers and duties were much the same as those of our present penitentiary commissioners. They received $2 a day each for the time actually employed, not to exceed $100 each annually, however. Whether candidates for this position were numerous or not we are unable to say.

Under the law of 1837 the inspectors were authorized, in their discretion, to farm out the convicts and give a bonus of $800 annually besides. Accordingly, on the 10th of June, 1838, the penitentiary, then containing 38 convicts, passed from the control of the State into the hands of a lessee, Mr. S. A. Buckmaster. Thence forward the lease system was continued for 29 years—from 1838 to 1867. In 1842 it was leased to Isaac Greathouse and N. Buckmaster, but without a bonus from or expense to the State. In 1845 it was re-leased to S. A. Buckmaster for a term of 8 years, the bonus—$5,000 annually—now coming to the State; besides which he agreed to feed, bed and guard the prisoners, pay physi-

cians' bills, fees of the inspectors, and save the State harmless from
all expense. The lease was subsequently extended 5 years on the
same terms. Under the lease system the lessee was vested with
the powers of a warden.

As the number of convicts increased additional cells were built
from time to time, and other buildings, such as the warden's residence, etc., for all of which the State paid. In 1847 there were 96
cells authorized to be constructed. By 1857 the cells numbered
256, and the convicts, averaging two to a cell, far exceeded the
capacity of the institution. At this time the penitentiary was
leased to S. K. Casey for 5 years, on the same terms as the Buckmaster lease of 1845. The legislature at the same session provided for the building of a new prison with 1,000 cells, which, it
was thought, would be ample for generations to come; but the
limits of its capacity were reached in less than 7 years. The old
prison was to be sold. The inspectors were discontinued, a
superintendent provided, and 3 commissioners charged with the
supervision of the new structure. They were instructed to contract with the lessee and employ the convict labor in the building of it. The new prison was located at Joliet on a tract of
72 19-100 acres of land. Its construction was commenced the same
year, temperary structures for the workmen being provided. In
May, 1859, prisoners were forwarded in batches of 40 or 50, and
in June, 1860, the Alton penitentiary was finally abandoned. An
area of 16 acres is at present inclosed within the main walls of the
Joliet prison, which are 6 feet thick and 25 high. The prison
proper contains 900 congregate cells, 100 separate, and 100 for
females.

In 1863 a 6 year lease was given by the State to J. M. Pitman,
who was to keep, provide and work the convicts, and save the
State harmless and free of all expense. No bonus was to be paid
either way. Three others, Boyer, Buck and Buckmaster, each a
one-fourth interest, bought in under Pitman. Owing to disagreement between them, Buckmaster, in April, 1864, bought out all
his partners and received an assignment of the lease to himself,
Pitman surrendering his charge as warden to Gov. Yates. Buckmaster took in a number of partners, the two Mitchells, Acres, Job
and Judd, he retaining a one-third interest.

At this time, 400 cells were completed, but 500 in the west wing
still remained unfinished. The commissioners, under the pressure
for room (the number of prisoners being very great and steadily on
the increase), authorized the new firm to finish these cells, which,
together with repairs and other changes, made a claim against
the State by January, 1867, considerably exceeding $100,000.

It now became apparent that State appropriations beyond a limited amount of a few thousand dollars could no longer be looked
forward to, and the firm having found purchasers, on the 28th of
January, 1867, in consideration of $200,000, transferred the stock,
fixtures and lease to Messrs. Burns and Hatch. The latter admitted to the partnership three others----Bane, Osburn and Dus-
tin----and sanguine in their new vocation, the firm obtained from
the legislature an extension, or rather a new lease for 8 years from
and after the expiration of their assigned lease in 1869, upon the
same terms. They were thus the lessees till 1877.

Up to this time, owing to the State's expenditures for work done, which was well paid for, as public corporations always pay, the leasing of the convict labor had proved more or less profitable to the lessees, notwithstanding the high prices of provisions and clothing, and the constantly augmenting number of convicts during the war and immediately after, many of whom were physically disabled. But now, with the speedy completion of the building, State appropriations must cease, and the lessees were thrown upon their own business enterprise for manufacturing contracts and outside jobs. These things had been for a long time of secondary consideration. The penitentiary work had consequently suffered in character and it could illy compete in price with other like manufactured articles.

The new lessees in a short time apprehended the situation, but instead of attempting to improve the management of the concern, the discipline of its inmates and character of the work like business men of energy and pluck, they were appalled by the prospect. They saw nothing but utter ruin before them, as they alleged, and threw upon the State their threatening losses. They notified the governor they should abandon the institution on the 30th day of June, 1867. It is ever thus in contracts between States and individuals; the former are bound, but the latter will find methods to either secure profits to themselves, or if loss threatens, to cast it upon the State.

In this emergency the governor, as we stated in the outset, convened the legislature to take action in the premises, either by again leasing the penitentiary, or to provide for the State taking control of it. The policy of State control had been mooted before upon humanitarian grounds. It was urged as the duty of the State to retain custody and control of its convicts, provide them employment, look after their welfare, and seek to reform them; and that the hiring of them out for private gain was unchristian and in conflict with public morals. The governor advocated an abandonment of the lease system, believing that the penitentiary could be made self-sustaining. A committee was appointed to make a thorough investigation of the conduct and workings of the prison during the recess, which the leigislature took until the 25th of June, ensuing. At this time it was determined that the State retain control of the penitentiary. Three commissioners were provided for (to be then appointed but made elective at the next regular election), a warden, chaplain, physician, matron, &c., and thus, on the 1st day July, 1867, the penitentiary passed again into the control of the State, the first time for 29 years. At this time 900 cells and the warden's residence were completed; $175,000 had been expended thereon, the original estimate of the entire cost being but $550,000. It is however, a superb structure, complete in all its appointments and fully equal to any in the United States. The convicts numbered 1,000. It proved a grievous burden to the State at first. Large sums of money were demanded and obtained. Everything was to buy almost—machinery, stock and tools. The sum of $300,000 was appropriated. In 1869, $350,000 more were appropriated to defray its expenses, $50,000 going to pay the late lessees for stock, machinery &c. In 1871 $175,000 more were required to pay deficits.

The choice of commissioners by the people, rendering them independent of executive supervision, did not tend to promote that
harmony and unity of action among them requisite to the attainment of success. In the spring of 1869, they were found to differ widely upon important points in the management of the establishment, and in 1871 the legislature thoroughly revised the
law for the government of the penitentiary. The appointment
of commissioners was vested in the governor after the expiration
of the terms of the then incumbents, and they were to be subject to
removal by him at his discretion. It was also made the executive's
duty to semi-annually visit the penitentiary and examine its affairs thoroughly. The commissioners were empowered to hire out
the labor of the convicts on sealed bids, a special or semi-lease
system which seems to be the secret of its present success. Since
then its management has steadily improved, the discipline is of
the highest order, and under the last year of Gov. Palmer's administration the penitentiary has become self-sustaining and in
future will probably yield a surplus.

CHAPTER LXVII.

1869–1873—ADMINISTRATION OF GOVERNOR PALMER.

Republican and Democratic State Conventions—Life and Character of Governor Palmer—Legislation, the Tax Grabbing Law, Lake Front Bill, Land Companies, &c.—The Constitution of 1870— The Great Chicago Fire.

When, in 1867, Gen. Palmer failed to obtain the Republican caucus nomination for U. S. senator, the feeling in his party became very general to reward him for his eminent services with the governorship, and he was thence tacitly looked forward to as the Republican candidate for that office in 1868. But the object of this high distinction was far from seeking it. In March, 1865, he wrote that the invalid condition of one of his children would compel his absence from the State during the ensuing campaign, and as he would consequently be unable to do his full share of labor in the canvass it was not proper that he should become the head of the ticket. Aspirants enough now sprang up for the exalted position, but they had no desire to embarrass Gen. Palmer. The Hon. R. G. Ingersoll, under date of Chicago, April 3d, asked him to state explicitly whether he was a candidate or would accept the nomination. He answered by telegraph, "I am not, and do not intend to be a candidate for governor." But his objections, it was thought by some of the Republican press, might be overcome, and the Carlinville *Free Democrat*, his former home organ, thought that "for some time past it had observed strenuous efforts made in certain quarters to compel Gen. Palmer to announce *a priori* that he would not serve the Republican party if nominated for governor;" that the *party* had not asked him to take the position; that while he was not thrusting himself forward, it spoke with assurance, he would not decline the nomination if tendered him by the Peoria convention. To this the *Illinois State Journal* replied: "We are requested to state that this is not the position which Gen. Palmer occupies." Still it was thought he was in the hands of his friends; that if the nomination was pressed upon him he would regard the voice of the convention as a summons to duty which must be obeyed.*

The Republican State convention of 1868 met at Peoria, May 6th. Franklin Corwin presided. An informal ballot to select a candidate for governor resulted: For John M. Palmer, 263 votes; Robert G. Ingersoll, 117; S. W. Moulton, 82; J. K. Dubois, 42.

-----

* Chicago Post.

59

The friends of Anson S. Miller refused to submit his name against Gen. Palmer. After a spirited debate with reference to Palmer's candidature, Gen. Rowett from Macoupin telegraphed to him: "It is asserted that you will be nominated for governor. Will you accept?" He replied promptly, "Do not permit me to be nominated. I cannot accept." Whereupon he was immediately nominated; the first formal ballot being, for Palmer, 317; Ingersoll, 118; Moulton, 52; Dubois, 17. Previous to this, however, a letter from him to Horace White had been read, stating that if nominated he would be governed by the duty of the hour. But for Gen. Palmer's repeated objections, he would undoubtedly have been selected by acclamation. He more than came within the Jeffersonian rule, neither to seek nor refuse office.

The remainder of the ticket was made up, either on the first ballot, or by acclamation, of John Dougherty of Union, for lieutenant-governor; Edward Rummel of Peoria, secretary of state; Charles E. Lippincott of Cass, auditor; E. N. Bates of Marion, treasurer; Washington Bushnell of LaSalle, attorney-general; and for penitentiary commissioners, after some delay and discussion, the old board, Andrew Shuman of Cook, Robert E. Logan, of Whiteside, and John Reid of Will, were re-nominated. Gen. John A. Logan was nominated for congress from the State at large.

The platform reannounced the Republican doctrine; condemned the policy of President Johnson; denounced all forms of repudiation, and affirmed that the indebtedness of the United States should be paid according to the letter and spirit of the law under which it was contracted; that the principal of the debt should be a heritage of the future; instructed in favor of U. S. Grant as the Republican nominee for president and the natural successor of Abraham Lincoln; and oddly enough declared in favor of "the most efficient means to raise the moral standard of the people."

The Democratic State Convention met at Springfield, April 15, 1868. Hon. A. L. Thornton, of Shelby, presided. The proceedings were not harmonious. The disturbing question was that of paying the national debt in "greenbacks," as proposed by Mr. Pendleton of Ohio. The committee on resolutions brought in majority and minority reports, the former, (which was adopted), made by eight, favoring payment of the 5-20 bonds, the vast bulk of the national debt, in legal tender notes, but where the faith of the government was pledged to pay gold, to so fulfill the obligation; favored the abolition of the national bank system; and instructed the delegates to the national convention to vote as a unit for the nomination of George H. Pendleton as a candidate for president. The minority report, made by five members, insisted upon paying the 5-20 bonds in "the lawful money of the country," gold; and opposed trammeling our delegates to the national convention by instruction in favor of Pendleton. For a candidate for governor, the names of S. A. Buckmaster and John R. Eden were presented. On the first ballot, when it was found that Eden was largely in the lead, the name of Buckmaster was withdrawn and Eden was nominated by acclamation. The remainder of the ticket was made up of William Van Epps of Lee for lieutenant-governor; Gustavus Van Hoorbecke of Clinton, secretary of state; Jesse J. Phillips of Montgomery, treasurer; John R. Shannon of Randolph, auditor; W. W. O'Brien, of Peoria, congressman at large; and for penitentiary commissioners, John W. Connett of Cook, W. W. Garrord of Edgar, Calney Zarley of Will.

The canvass of 1868 was unattended by interesting events, and the election in November resulted in favor of the Republicans by large majorities, that for governor being 44,707.

John McAuley Palmer was born on Eagle Creek, Scott county, Kentucky, September 13th, 1817. During his infancy his father, who had been a soldier in the war of 1812, removed to Christian county in Western Kentucky, where lands were cheap. Here the future governor of Illinois spent his childhood and received such meagre schooling as the new and sparsely settled country afforded, to which he added materially by diligent reading, for which he evinced an early aptitude. The father, an ardent Jackson man, was also noted for his anti-slavery sentiments, which he thoroughly impressed upon his children. In 1831 he emigrated to Illinois and settled in Madison county. Here the labor of improving a farm was pursued for about two years, when the death of the mother broke up the family. About this time Alton College was opened on the "manual labor system," and in the spring of 1834 young Palmer with his elder brother, Elihu, afterward a minister of the gospel and noted for his learning and eccentricities, entered this school and remained 18 months. Next, for over three years, he tried variously coopering, peddling and school teaching.

During the summer of 1838 he formed the acquaintance of Douglas, then making his first canvass for congress, who, young, eloquent and in political accord, won his confidence, fired his ambition, and fixed his purpose. The following winter, while teaching near Canton, he began to devote his spare time to a desultory reading of law, and in spring entered a law office at Carlinville, making his home at his brother Elihu's, stationed at that place in the ministry. On the next meeting of the Supreme Court he was admitted to the bar, Douglas, who took a lively interest in him, being one of his examiners. He was not immediately successful in his profession, and would have located elsewhere than Carlinville, but for the want of means. Thus his early poverty was a blessing in disguise, for to it he now attributes the success of his life. From 1839 on, while he diligently pursued the practice of his profession, he was more or less involved in local politics. In 1843 he became probate judge; in 1847 he was elected to the constitutional convention, where he took a leading part. In 1852 he was elected to the State Senate, and at the special session of February, 1854, true to the anti-slavery sentiments bred in him, took a firm stand in opposition to the repeal of the Missouri compromise on two sets of resolutions then before the legislature; and when the Nebraska question was made a party issue he refused to receive a renomination for senator at the hands of the Democracy, issuing a circular to this effect. Still, as if hesitating to break with his party, a few weeks later he participated in the congressional convention which nominated T. L. Harris against Richard Yates, and which approved unqualifiedly the principles of the Kansas-Nebraska act. But later in the campaign he made the plunge, and running for the senate as an anti-Nebraska democrat, was elected. The following winter he put in nomination for the United States Senate Mr. Trumbull, and was one of the five steadfast men who voted for him until all the whigs came to their support. In 1856 he was made chairman of the Republican State Convention at Bloomington. In 1859 he was defeated for congress. In 1860 he was a republican elector for the State at large. In 1861 he was appointed one of the five delegates (all republicans) sent by Illinois to the peace congress at Washington. In that body he advocated the call of a national convention for an adjustment of the country's difficulties, and that proposition failing, he favored the measures of compromise finally recommended.*

When the civil conflict broke out, he offered his services to his country and was elected colonel of the 14th regiment. Of the engagements in which he participated may be mentioned the capture of Island No. 10; Farmington, where he skillfully extricated his command from a dangerous position; Stone River, where his division for several hours, on the 31st of December, held the advance and stood like a rock, and for his gallantry here he was made Major General of volunteers; Chicamauga, where his and Van Cleve's divisions, for two hours, maintained their position, when, by overpowering numbers, they were cut off. Under Sherman Major General Palmer was assigned to the command of the 14th army corps, and participated in the Atlanta campaign. At Peach Tree Creek his prudence did much to avert disaster. When Gen. McPherson fell, and Gen. Howard, a junior officer, was promoted to the command of the army of the Tennessee, both Generals Hooker and Palmer asked to be relieved.

In February, 1865, Gen. Palmer was assigned to the military administration of Kentucky. This was a delicate post. Kentucky was about half rebel and half union, the latter daily fretted by the loss of their slaves. He, who had been bred to the rules of the common law, he has said, trembled at the contemplation of his extraordinary power over the persons and property of his fellowmen, with which he was vested in the capacity of military Governor. But it is not our province to detail his administration in Kentucky. Suffice it, notwithstanding the many objections urged against him, it is now conceded that he blended a conspicuous respect for municipal law consistent with his functions as a military commander.

The business of Gov. Palmer's life has been the pursuit of the law. Few excel him in an accurate appreciation of the depth and scope of its principles. The great number of his able veto messages abundantly testify not only this but also a rare capacity to point them out. He is a logical and cogent reasoner, and an interesting, forcible and convincing, though not fluent nor ornate, speaker. Without brilliancy, his dealings are rather with facts and ideas, which he marshals in solid phalanx and leads to invincible conclusions. And while he ever betrays the hedgings of legal rules, he is a statesman of a very high order. Physically, he is above the medium hight, of robust frame, ruddy complexion and sanguine-nervous temperament. Nature has endowed him with a

---

* Taken from "Annals of the Army of the Cumberland," a volume of biographical sketches.

large cranial development. He is social in disposition, easy of approach, unostentatious in his habits of life, correct in deportment, democratic in his manners, and as a man of the people, he has a large sympathy for his class. He has been indifferent to the acquisition of wealth.

On the meeting of the legislature, in January, 1869, the first thing to arrest public attention was that portion of Gov. Palmer's inaugural message which took broad State's rights ground. In discussing the rights of railroads, their oppressive charges, and the remedies, he called attention to the proposition in some quarters to enlist the national government in the creation of railroad corporations to construct railways in this and other States and operate them, which he deprecated: "Already the authority of the State is in a measure paralyzed by a growing conviction that all their powers are in some sense derivative and subordinate, and not original and independent;" he asserted that "one of the best established and most distinctly recognized [principles which underlie our system of government, was] that the federal government is one of enumerated powers;" that it was "the clear duty of the national government to decline the exercise of all doubtful powers when the neglect to do so would bring it into fields of legislation already occupied by the States;" and that "a frequent recurrence to the fundamental principles of government [was] essential to civil liberty."

Such old democratic doctrine was distasteful to many republicans, who, with a portion of their press, took ground in opposition to it. The democrats, on the other hand, were heartily pleased with it, and it was moved by them in the house that 35,000 copies of the message be printed, which passed with considerable reluctance. In the senate the republicans moved to cut down this number to 2,000, and here also the democrats became the champions of the republican governor in a debate which followed, characterized by no little acrimony. Indeed, the cordiality in the dominant party, between the legislative and executive departments, was for a time threatened with interruption. Finally the senate concurred with the house, only to reconsider its vote; after the lapse of near two weeks, and the infliction of many speeches, the resolution was agreed to.

The session of 1869, the last under the flexible constitution of 1848, a revision of which had then been authorized by the people, was moved upon by the monopolists, the lobbyists and the "rings" with a thirst for advantages and spoils, unprecedented in the history of legislation in this State. Their action was characterized by an audacity, a prodigality, and an abandon never before exhibited. Their remarkable success in 1867 had but whetted the appetites of the cormorants. Notwithstanding Gov. Palmer, in his message, characterized special legislation as anti-republican and dangerous to the liberties of the people, saying: "Many of the most important functions of government are now claimed and exercised by incorporations by special laws; they take private property and impose and collect taxes; they construct railroads and canals, and, in many instances, by the exercise of their vast powers, control the course of trade, and distract the business of the whole country"—notwithstanding this warning, bills to the number of 2,478 were introduced, covering every conceivable object for corporate purposes, nearly all of which sought some advantage over the general laws of the State or the people. The then leading organ of the dominant party was constrained to say that " no previous legislative body has exhibited such unblushing disregard of all the requirements of common decency as the legislature now in session,"—that it was " reckless beyond precedent."*

But it was early found there was an incumbent of the executive office with both the will and industry to look into their little schemes before they became laws, and with the courage and capacity to expose their many machinations. Perhaps this exercised some restraining influence. In obedience to his determination to carefully overhaul every bill before signing it, and to give him time to do so, the legislature took a recess from March 8th to April 7th. Of the 2,478 bills introduced nearly 1,700 were passed, an immense mass of dry legal verbiage, but none escaped his patient scrutiny—a labor and investigation never before bestowed upon the acts of a legislature. He sifted from the mass a large number which he deemed inimical to the constitution, or to public policy, and at great pains reduced his objections to writing, in terms respectful and indicating the ripe jurist and forcible reasoner. But his vetoes in nearly every important instance were overridden by a determined body, unwilling to brook what they were pleased to characterze an arrogance of both legislative and judicial functions by the executive. The veto under the constitution of 1848 was of little value further than as a short stay of proceedings to induce the legislature to pause and reflect upon their action. Its free use by the executive was not without an interpretation as being only a greater exhibition of insubordination to partisan requirements, after his first avowal of State's rights doctrines. With a short session of three days, the veto messages were disposed of; and after voting each member $40 in addition to the $300 previously voted to each for room rent, fuel and contingencies, over and above his per diem, in utter violation of the constitution, the general assembly of 1869, on the 20th of April, adjourned *sine die*.

Among the acts of general interest passed at this session, was one limiting railroad charges for passenger travel to a maximum rate of 3 cents per mile. The governor fulminated his veto against it, holding that when a charter is once accepted by those to whom it is made, it " in all essential circumstances, takes upon itself the qualities of a contract, and at that instant passes from legislative and becomes subject to judicial control. Such a contract upon well settled principles of constitutional law, cannot be impaired." It was passed over the veto, but has been a dead letter ever since. If law grows out of the necessities of a people, then it is high time that our courts overruled the Dartmouth College case, or revolution will do it for them.

What is known as the " tax grabbing law" to pay railroad subscriptions, passed at this session, is such a reprehensible specimen of legislation as to well merit consideration. It provided that all counties, townships, cities or towns having contracted bonded debts in aid of the construction of railroads through any of them, were entitled to register such bonds with the State Auditor, whereupon it became the duty of the treasurer to set apart to their

*Chicago Tribune.

credits, to be applied toward the payment of their railroad indebtedness, annually, for 10 years, (1) all the taxes for any purpose whatsoever, arising from the property of a railroad so aided and situate within such municipality; (2) so much of the State tax as might be collected upon an increased assessment on all the property of any such municipality over and above the year 1868, excepting in both cases the 2 mill and State school taxes. It was a question whether this was an appropriation of public money, which the Supreme Court had decided to be within the province of the legislature under the power to appropriate money, or whether it was violative of the principle of equality of taxation recognized by the constitution. The governor took the latter view, and in a very able message vetoed the bill; but it was passed over his veto.

The act is very ingeniously drawn with reference to these two views and by its terms, really only diverts the taxes paid upon the property concerned, the same as other property, however the proceeds may return to the corporation or municipality. The late S. K. Casey, senator from Jefferson, championed it, but it is said to have been framed by a Mr. Cassells. It was designed for the benefit of Southern Illinois, which had fallen behind in the race of railroad developement, and met with violent opposition from the north, being denounced as wrong and unjust by every principle of law and honesty. It played an important part in the combinations, rings, and manoeuvering generally, during that remarkable session, and became a law. The bonds registered under the act amount to about $13,000,000, and the tax annually diverted by it amounts to over $60,000, which will probably be largely increased under the revenue act of 1873. This was not the first and only time that a portion of the State tax has been diverted for the benefit of the localities which yield it. In 1867 a law of that kind was passed for the benefit of Mound City, and at this session another to relieve Alexander county for her support of negro paupers.

Lake Front Bill.—Chicago, like a modern Briareus, besides many private measures, now grasped for four parks; parks the north, south, west and east of her; the three first named to be connected by a grand boulevard or avenue, 400 feet wide. These 3 parks were to embrace hundreds of acres of land, much of which would have to be acquired by process of condemnation, and which, unless duly guarded by just and proper legislation, was liable to be converted into a business whereby to dispose of unsaleable lands at high prices, and to acquire the poor man's lot without due compensation, by setting off benefits against damages.

But of these park measures what was known as the Lake Front bill was by far the most important. To raise a park fund it was proposed to confer upon the city council of Chicago power to sell all the right, title, and interest of the State to a strip of canal land, 310 feet wide, lying east of Michigan avenue, and extending from Park Row north to Monroe street, containing 32 acres, land and water; to confirm the Illinois Central railroad in its riparian ownership to, and further for the State to make a grant to it of the submerged lands constituting the bed of Lake Michigan, east of its railroad track, extending north and south nearly two miles in front of the city, and covering an area of 1,050 acres, over

which the navigable waters of the lake rolled to a depth of from
10 to 25 feet. This, of itself was regarded as an imperial grant;
but it was further proposed that the State transfer to the three
railroad companies centering there, her 3 blocks of ground north
of Monroe street and east of Michigan avenue, in consideration
of $800,000, payable to the city of Chicago, for park purposes, in
four equal installments—a price so ridiculously low as to fall short
of its actual market value by $1,800,000. And, as if anticipating
objections from Chicago, which claimed title by dedication, it was
provided that if the city council did not quit claim to the railroad
companies within 4 months, being prior to the maturing of the
second installment, they should be released from further payment
and yet hold the property by fee simple title from the State for
one-fourth the sum offered. These lands, except the bed of the
lake, had been dedicated for public use, but while the State had
parted with her beneficial proprietory title, they were still regarded
as subject to her paramount authority and might control or dispose of them as would best promote the purposes of dedication.*

The bill was passed contrary to the wishes of a large majority
of the people of Chicago and her representatives. The governor
vetoed it on account of the inadequacy of price to be paid for the
3 blocks of ground; of there being no limitation fixed for the com-
mencemet of the outside harbor improvements; of the State having
reserved no right to limit charges for the relief of commerce, and
because the property was not to be subject to taxation. But it
was promptly repassed over the veto. It was one of the measures
in the charmed circle of legislation, ordained to become a law.†
Steps under the law, however, have been arrested by injunction,
issuing from the U. S. Circuit Court at Chicago.

Of the flood of local and private acts pernicious in principle and
contrary to public policy, we can only cite a few from the many
that incurred the governor's veto. A number of localities—
Bloomington, Joliet, Canton, Bond county, &c.—sought franchises
to enable them to employ the taxing power of the State to raise
money to be expended for mere private speculative or fanciful
objects, such as to induce railroad companies to locate their machine shops and erect depots; to start private manufacturing
establishments; build hotels, &c., all supposed to be of general
value to the place securing them, and toward which those most
deeply interested sought to compell all the helpless, voiceless and
reluctant, to contribute alike of their property.

Then there were acts for the incorporation of land companies
(already numerous), whose sole aim was to create huge land monopolies, escape the embarrassments attaching to personal ownership;
the casualities incident to trade and business; distribution after
death; and keep out of market for a long term of years, with the
speculative intent of enhancing its value, property needed for
homes for the people, which in the hands of private parties would
be improved and rendered more valuable to the State.‡ A notable instance was the "Illinois Land Company," which owned some
1,200 acres in East St. Louis, sought to be controlled as above, for

* Gov. Palmer's Message.

† There is a not a very secret scandalous history connected with the passage of this
measure which we do not care to revive here.

‡ Gov. Palmer's Message.

a period of 25 years. But the most presumptuous of these corporations, under a title at the same time the most seductive, not
excepting that of the "Illinois Benevolent Loan Company" for
a pawn-broker's establishment, was that of the "Southern Emigrant Aid Society," a title, as the governor said, which "suggests
ideas of weary strangers, feeble and poor, on the one hand, and of
benevolent men on the other, ministering to their wants, feeding
the hungry and clothing the naked;" but which really established
offices in about 30 counties of this State, (the principle one at
Cairo), to speculate in lands that emigrants would be likely to
need, and receive their money and other valuables on deposit, buy
and sell exchange, and by means of a captivating title, win their
confidence. * Not one provision of this act contemplated the aid
or relief which its title imported.

An important event of this session was the ratification of the
15th amendment to the constitution of the United States, giving
suffrage to the blacks.

Our New Constitution.—The year of grace, 1870, will be distinguished in the annals of Illinois for the peaceful revolution of her
organic law. It is a grand feature in the governments composing
this Great Republic that they frequently undergo most radical
and important transformations without tumult or outbreak from
the populace, showing that their will is the source of power. The
constitution of 1848 had for years been systematically violated in
its plain and positive provisions by nearly every department of
State. The last executive under it, himself records that "The
history of American States presented no example of a government
more defective than that of Illinois." Officers received or took
compensation for their services under authority of laws known to
be inconsistent with the constitution; and what was designed by
its framers to be a most economical government, became, in fact,
extravagantly expensive. The clear limitation upon the powers
of the general assembly was overborne, and legislation was
often hasty, imprudent and depraved until the people felt
that their public and private rights were unsafe; that the officers
charged by the constitution with the enactment, the interpretation, and the enforcement of the laws were alike unworthy of their
full confidence. † The notorious evasions of the plain requirements
of the constitution, and the pernicious practices thus indulged,
tended to sap the integrity of the public service generally, while it
must have also contributed to lessen the respect if it did not beget
the contempt of the people for all law. A popular reverence for
law is the most essential guaranty for the stability of the State, the
peace and good order of society, and the protection to life, liberty
and property of of the citizen.

It was therefore high time to erect new limitations upon the
powers of the several departments, instead of those persistently
disregarded, and viewed as obsolete. Upon the question being
submitted to a vote of the people, at the election of November,
1868, the revision of the old constitution was by them ordered.
The succeeding legislature authorized the election of delegates,

* Gov. Palmer's Veto Message.

† Palmer's Message, 1871.

(apportioned to the districts and corresponding in number to the representatives in the lower house of the general assembly,) who were to meet at Springfield, December 13, 1869, to alter, revise, or amend the constitution. Of the 85 members returned, 44 were set down as republican in politics, and 41 as democratic. But 15 were elected on independent tickets, all in republican districts, of whom 8 were democrats and 7 republicans. Thus neither party had a majority in the convention, and the "independents" held the balance of power, of which they made the most. Its members were composed of learned jurists, experienced statesmen, and profound thinkers, whose work, prepared with much care, has been very generally pronounced the best and wisest in its limitations and restrictions that the union affords. Whether time will approve this high encomium remains to be seen. We can allude to only a few of the prominent features wherein it differs from the old, and which are regarded as salutory reforms.

The change from the fee system to that of fixed salaries, fair and ample in their amounts, will tend more perhaps to eradicate the vice of evading the law and elevating the standard of the public service than anything else. The salary system, in the option of county boards, may also be extended to county officers, and if settlements with these are properly enforced, will both save and increase materially the revenue.—Special legislation has been very greatly circumscribed, and irrevocable, private franchises and immunities are prohibited. This does away with a most fruitful source of corruption in that department of government. It breaks, in a measure, legislative rings and destroys the business of the professional lobbyist, and the result is the halls and corridors of the capitol and hotels are thronged no more by this shrewd, genial and elegantly attired class, ever on the alert and ready with a hint to this member and a whisper to that, and an adroit suggestion to another.—While the number of members of the general assembly has been about double, the steps to be pursued in the enactment of laws are retarded and hedged by wise provisions; the former practices of reading bills by their titles only, and their passage by the bundle, known as the omnibus system, are prevented; and while the per diem compensation of members is allowed to be raised, being now $5, the reprehensible practices of entering into speculative contracts or "commutations" with State officials or others, for stationary, fuel, etc., voted to themselves, which at the last session under the old constitution averaged $500 for each member, and aggregated $54,000, besides their pay of $2 a day, and charges for committee rooms, often neither occupied nor perhaps rented, are all effectually squelched, and instead members are allowed but $50 each.—To the governor, who heretofore as part of the law-making power, was a mere advisory agent and for want of power destitute of influence, has been given a qualified veto for the first time in the history of the State, with good results so far as exercised. Prior to this a bare majority of the legislative department of government was practically the supreme power in the State.—One of the grossest wrongs to individuals heretofore was the taking of private property by municipal and other corporations for public use, as it was called, without compensation, by setting off fancied benefits, no matter how general to the vicinity, against the damages of the owner. This cannot now be done. Neither can a majority (often representing little or no property) of any municipality, now vote to lend its credit or impose a debt upon the property of the minority for the benefit of some corporation or improvement.—The general assembly is prohibited from discharging any county, city or town from its proportionate share of taxes, the commutation of such taxes, or the diverting of them from the treasury, as under the railroad tax-grabbing law of 1869.—The revenue article of the old constitution has been rendered more efficient, and with late legislation will bear more evenly upon the property of the State.—The two-mile tax was abolished.—Minority representation in the legislature, by means of cumulative voting, is a new but promising feature in the organic act, adopted for the first time by any State in the union.—Our judiciary system has been rendered uniform, and greatly modified, whether for good requires to be ascertained. To county courts, as supplemented by a late law, have been given extended civil jurisdiction, and they are authorized to try minor criminal cases with a view of saving to counties large expenditures for boarding prisoners while awaiting the terms of the circuit courts.—But the provision which seeks to control the railroads of the State, prohibiting parallel or competing lines from consolidation, and which declares all railroads public highways, requiring the general assembly to establish reasonable maximum rates of charges, and to prevent unjust discriminations and extortions, is one which, if sustained by the courts, promises to be one of the most important in its beneficial results to the people, as it is one now eliciting the greatest public interest. The question whether a power has grown up in the State greater than the State itself is now in process of solution.

The Great Chicago Fire.—Chicago was first laid off in 1830, at the mouth of the river of that name. Prior to that the point was known as Fort Dearborn, built by the government in 1804. By an unprecedented growth and prosperity, Chicago had by 1871 attained to a city of 300,000 souls. As the radiating centre of more than a dozen trunk lines of railroads, reaching far into the interior, with their innumerable branches and connections, she is enabled to grasp with Briarian hands, as it were, the products of a vast and fertile region; possessed of an extended lake, canal, and river commerce, and a large manufacturing interest, and animated by enterprising and sagacious capitalists, energetic merchants and pushing business men generally, she was truly, not only the chief city of Illinois, but the emporium of the great northwest—the pride of her State and the wonder of the civilized world. While she had miles upon miles of structures of the most combustible nature, being wood, her large business centre was built up of brick, stone and iron blocks, massive in size and of rare architectural beauty; her palatial residences, profusely scattered through many parts of the city, but particularly toward the lake front, were the admiration of every visitor, besides her many well built, superb, and costly church edifices and various elegant public institutions, all these were solid, non-combustible structures, regarded as fire proof. But in the great conflagration, which, like death, knew no distinction, the stately block and most ornate column, as well as the lowliest wooden shanty of the poor, found a common leveler.

It was on the night of October 8th and 9th, 1871, that the ocean of flame burst upon the doomed city. For eighteen consecutive hours, borne by a parched and strong southwesterly gale, the Fire Fiend, gathering strength and volume as he marched, strode through the fated city. The fire broke out in a poor quarter 1½ miles southwest from the business centre, which was closely built up of inferior structures that kindled like tinder and blazed like a bon fire. The flame, fanned by the gale, was so intense that the fire department was powerless before it. At midnight, having devoured 500 buildings, and burnt over an area of 175 acres, reaching the southern limits of the burnt district of the fire of the night proceeding, which was of no inconsiderable magnitude ordinarily, and which it was expected would arrest it, the licking column, casting a shower of kindling brands far in advance, easily leaped the south branch of the river, lighting where several blocks of wooden rookeries, the abodes of squalor and vice, afforded it vivifying food. Sending off flanking columns to the right and left, it pursued a due northeast course before the driving wind toward the court house, the large stone, brick and iron structures in its way, commonly called fire-proof, many of them among Chicago's handsomest blocks, crumbling and melting down by its super-heated breath as completely, if not so speedily, as those of wood. All hope of staying its progress was now abandoned, and the efforts suspended. The court house, from whose basement, (the common jail) 150 prisoners were released to save their lives, was built of large blocks of stone, and though standing isolated in the middle of a square, succumbed, its great bell falling from the dome with a last dying peal. At this time, as if instinct with a deadly strategy, the fire disabled the pumping engines a mile in advance at the waterworks, which cut off the supply of water. Buildings now would suddenly ignite all over, and the danger to human life became exceedingly great.

The left flanking column of flame, gathering volume as it proceeded, swept all that part of the city in the angle made by the south branch and the main river. The right also gathering headway as it went, took a detour almost due east from the south branch toward the lake and northward, making a wide swath and rioting in the destruction of the most superb hotels, splendid business blocks, and elegant dwellings in the city. Here, in the south division, the fairest and most ornate portion of Chicago, and the great centre of her wealth and commerce, 460 acres were swept over by the terrible flames and 3,650 buildings laid in ashes. But aside from the great value and beauty of this portion of the city, less than one-third in territory, or the number of houses, was as yet swept over, or consumed. The three colums of flame, toward noon on the 9th, (Monday) intensified by their union, now vaulted across the river, and, marching in solid phalanx at double-quick, licked up everything in the way; the ocean of flame with a terrible crackling roar as it advanced, in a few hours burnt over an area of 1,470 acres of the 2,533 in the north division, leaving only 500 buildings standing out of the 13,800 which it contained, and rendering homeless 75,000 people.

As a spectacle the conflagration was at the same time the sublimest and most appalling—terrifying to the weak and unnerving the strong. The roaring flame and crackling wood, the crash of falling buildings, the detonations of explosive material in them, and the maddened Babel of human voices, all intermingled, were awful and terrific in the last degree.

The scenes in the streets of the burning city beggar description. All the baser attributes of the human heart found manifestation. Fear, precipitancy, profanity, insults, obscenity, rapacity, theft, robbery, arson and assassination, all wrought to the highest pitch, with intoxication, and amid the noise, confusion and turmoil, found vent and ran riot. Great crowds, fascinated by a mingled feeling of horror and admiration at the grandeur of the terrible spectacle, moved with the dazzling columns of fire as it proceeded. Now and then the crash of a wall near at hand, the report of explosive oils, or the rumor that they were surrounded by the fire, or that a bridge was burnt to cut off their retreat would scatter them in precipitate flight, panic stricken. In many cases, people were driven into the lake for refuge against the scorching flames. Capitalists, rushing to their vaults to save their valuables, were overpowered by the suffocating heat, and never seen again; others, loaded with treasure, were stricken down by assassins and robbed. The speed of the conflagration and its great heat were such that it was impossible to save much property. Besides, owners of vehicles, taking advantage of the occasion, charged enormous prices for taking loads; $10 to $50 was common and $1,000 is recorded. Stores were opened and the crowds invited to help themselves to goods, as they must all go at any rate, while others were entered by hordes of plunderers unasked; and goods piled up in the streets to be carted away, were seized and freely borne off. The torch of the incendiary, for purposes of plundering, was added to the general conflagration. Saloons were thrown open, and under a free invitation, their contents flowed unchecked, maddening the vicious and stimulating to ruffianism. Amidst the turmoil of the crackling and roaring fire, falling walls, dazed animals dashing about, streets gorged by passing vehicles and crowds of people, and the shouting and uproar of men, families became separated, children cried for parents, wives and mothers wailed and became distracted and husbands and fathers, skurrying hither and thither in vain searchings for the lost ones, were frantic with agony and despair. It was a night of unspeakable horrors. Many incidents of tenants occupying rooms in the upper stories of high business blocks wrapt in flames, suddenly appearing at their windows begging for assistance from the frantic crowd below and some of whom found succor and others that perished, are related with thrilling effect in the papers of the time.

The loss of human life, which can never be accurately ascertained, has been estimated at 250. During the first two weeks following, the remains of 107 persons, consisting often of but fragments, or so charred that few could be identified, were collected by the coroner and interred. It is supposed that the intensity of the heat in many cases wholly consumed the bodies, leaving no vestige behind. The whole area burnt over, including streets, was 2,124 acres; number of buildings destroyed, 17,500; sidewalks burnt, 121 miles; total value of property swallowed up by the devouring element, $195,000,000, on which there was an insurance of some $45,000,000, leaving a net loss $150,000,000—these figures being approximate.*

---

* See History of Chicago and the Great Conflagration.

About 98,500 people were bereft, not only of homes, business, and property, but even shelter. These collected at points on the beach of the lake, in the old cemetery south of Lincoln Park, but mostly on the bleak prairie back of the city. Many were blinded from smoke and blistered with heat. Not less than one hundred women were thrown into premature parturion from fright and the excitement caused by the terrible scene. All, the sick and help-less, the young and old, the vile and vicious, the beggar and mil-lionaire, were here promiscuously huddled together. Without suf-ficient clothing in the chill October rain, which set in during the night of Monday; destitute of food since Sunday, and all more or less, exhausted from hunger, the sufferings of the smitten ones was exceedingly great.

And now was manifested on the part of the people of this broad land and the civilized portions of Europe, whither the shock had thrilled, a noble sympathy and practical benevolence, attesting the brotherhood of man. First the people for hundreds of miles in every direction, in prompt response to the click of the telegraph (and but for this modern handmaid to the business of the world, many must have perished), sent in hundreds of car loads of cooked food and provisions of all kinds and raiment of every description, in quantities more than sufficient to relieve the wants of the suf-ferers. Bureaus, to systematically distribute the donations, were organized. Next, and almost simultaneously, followed most liberal contributions of money in large sums by nearly all our great and many small cities and some from Europe, aggregating some $7,000,000. Governor Palmer, deeming it a proper occasion, con-vened the general assembly in extraordinary session on the 4th day after the fire, and that body donated virtually to the stricken city, $2,955,340 from the treasury of the State—finding in the great emergency a way to evade the strict provisions of the new constitution for this purpose by redeeming the canal from the lien of its deepening by Chicago, which, though a valuable improve-ment to that city, is dead and unyielding capital to the State; but no one will blame the legislature for this benevolent act so neces-sary under the circumstances. Six per centum bonds, payable in 10 years, were to be issued for that amount. Not less than one-fifth nor more than one-third of the proceeds were to be used in restoring the bridges and public buildings on the old sites, and the residue in payment of the bonded debt of the city, and to maintain its fire and police departments.

Immediately succeding the fire, stories of incendiarism for pur-poses of plunder became rife; that theft, robberies, and arson were the order in the unburnt portions of the city, and that hordes of "roughs" from other large cities were on the point of invasion. The ignorant, desperate from their losses, were represented as possessed by a mania for further destruction; others in great masses, together with the police, as taking the law into their own hands, shooting down, beating to death, or hanging to lamp-posts, numerous alleged offenders, without close scrutiny as to their guilt or innocence. These stories which were utterly untrue, gained credence in the city at the time and a considerable panic prevailed. Telegrams disseminating them were sent broad cast over the land, and the flying fugitives from the city, whose exodus by the 16th, amounted to 60,000, impressed with these stories, spread reports of seeing blackened corpses of robbers and incendiaries hanging to gibbets. Gen. Anson Stager, a prominent citizen, telegraphed Gov. Palmer on the 10th that great consternation and anxiety existed on account of the presence of "roughs" and thieves, plundering in all directions, and that two incendiaries were shot the night preceding while in the act of firing buildings.

Under the apprehensions prevailing, the police force was largely increased, 1,500 being sworn in on the west side. and 500 on the south. Indeed, on Monday morning, Major Alstruf had tendered the services of a battalion of three militia companies to the superintendent and were accepted. Gov. Palmer, in answer to Gen. Stager's dispatch, proffered a military force to the city, to preserve property and enforce order, which, in the reply by telegraph, was immediately requested by the mayor, to be sent by special train, and later on the same day, 1,000 muskets and amunition was also asked. Adjutant Gen. H. Dilger, at once, by telegraph, ordered to Chicago, the "Bloomington National Guards," "Champaign Cadets," "Sterling City Guards," Rock Fall Zouaves," "Rock Island Light Artillery" with four pieces; and under his immediate charge, the "Springfield Zouaves," "O'Mara Guards," and Capt. Donigan's colored company, 200 men, the latter arriving there early the next day, the 11th, and before evening the other militia companies also arrived, making a military force of 516 men, well armed and equiped to protect the property, maintain order, and enforce the laws in the city. But Gen. Dilger now found the wild rumors of lawlessness to have been greatly exaggerated, and the mayor, professing no knowledge of the dispatches calling for State troops and, at the time, confiding in the strong arm of the military power of the U. S., was ready to issue his proclamation entrusting the peace of the city to Lieut. Gen. Phil. H. Sheridan, of the U. S. army, who was stationed there. The State authority being thus superceded by that of the U. S., Gen. Dilger, with a portion of his force, after some three days time, returned. Some of the police authorities, jealous of the military occupation thus assumed, protested against it for the reason that policemen were acqainted with the people and possessed large discretionary powers in the arrest of parties, the prevention of breaches of the peace, and the commission of crimes; while a soldier was the rigid instrument of orders, regardless of consequences. The city, however, was surrendered to the military, U. S. regulars being ordered thither from Omaha, Forts Leavenworth and Scott, and from Louisville. The police were ordered to act in conjunction with the military, good order was maintained throughout, and, what was perhaps of more importance than all else, confidence was restored.

At the time that the city was thus turned over to military rule, Gen. Sheridan directed a citizen of Chicago, Gen. Frank T. Sherman, to enlist and organize a regiment of infantry for 20 days, to serve as guards in protecting the property of the city. They swore allegiance to the U. S. and obedience to the officers appointed over them; they were to arrest all citizens who, in their judgment, might be suspicious persons, and fire upon, wound or kill any one refusing to obey their commands to halt, after a certain hour in the night. In the regiment was a company of cadets

—students from the University of Chicago, mostly young and non-residents. To this regiment, asserted by high authority to have been illegally called into being, Gen. Thomas W. Grosvenor, a citizen of Chicago, who had earned his title by meretorious conduct in the late war and was maimed for life, became a martyr. About 12 o'clock in the night of the 20th of October, while quietly proceeding to his home, he was ordered by a young cadet to halt and give the countersign or pass-word, and, disregarding the order, was deliberately shot down, expiring in a few hours after.

The Governor, who it seems was not advised until about the 17th of the full extent of the military occupation of Chicago, which he deemed a violation of law, both State and national, had in the meantime, written a letter to the mayor, couched in no ambiguous terms, vigorously protesting against that functionary's virtual abdication of his office and turning the city over to the military control of the U. S. soldiery, asserting the adequacy of the State to furnish all needed protection to the smitten city. The mayor, stung by the lecturing epistle, replied that when the lives and property of the people, the peace and good order of a large city, were in danger, it was not the time to stop and consider questions of policy. But the killing of Grosvenor was a circumstance to awaken reflection upon the anomalous posture of affairs, and 2 days after, at the request of the mayor, the occupation was discontinued.

His excellency, however, did not allow the matter to drop here. He wrote and urged the State's Attorney of Cook county to bring the murderer of Grosvenor before the grand jury, and to advise that body to include in the indictments, besides the party doing the act, R. B. Mason, the mayor, Lieutenant General Sheridan, and Frank T. Sherman, colonel of the 20 day regiment, as being equally guilty. A sharp and not very elegant correspondence followed, and the matter getting into the public press, much criticism was evoked. Later General Sheridan was again appealed to by prominent citizens, to cause 4 companies of U. S. soldiers to be stationed at Chicago for the protection of the immense amount of stores in charge of the Relief fund and Aid Society, and upon his request at Washington they were granted. This still further intensified the matter, and the governor, in a letter to President Grant, protested against this step, asserting the abundant ability of the State to protect every interest of the people dependant upon its internal peace and good order. The letter was referred to Gen. Sheridan with instructions to rescind all orders in conflict with the laws or constitution of this State. Protesting now against an officer of the army passing upon a matter so grave and important, Gov. Palmer brought the whole subject before the legislature and that body, after a thorough investigation by a committee, who brought in majority and minority reports, on the 25th of January, 1872, sustained the former, declaring "as unlawful, and an infraction of the constitution, both of this State and the U. S., the so-called military occupation of Chicago;" but the federal authorities were exonerated from intent to wilfully trespass upon the constitutional rights of this State, or to interfere with its properly constituted authorities during the emergency of the great fire.

CPSIA information can be obtained at www.ICGtesting.com
Printed in the USA
LVOW110840180413

329762LV00005B/445/P

9 781249 023289